THE
SCIENCE OF CORRESPONDENCES
ELUCIDATED.

THE

KEY TO THE HEAVENLY AND TRUE MEANING

~~NEW CHURCH SERVICES~~ *OF THE SCRIPTURES.*

Sixteenth above Q. N. W.
WASHINGTON, D. C.

BY

Rev. EDWARD MADELEY,

EDITED BY HIS SON; REVISED AND GREATLY ENLARGED

BY

B. F. BARRETT.

"For as the heavens are higher than the earth, so are my ways higher than your ways, and my thoughts than your thoughts."—*Isa.* lv. 9.

"For the invisible things of Him from the creation of the world are clearly seen, being understood by the things that are made."—*Rom.* i. 20.

SIXTH AMERICAN EDITION.

GERMANTOWN, PA.:
THE SWEDENBORG PUBLISHING ASSOCIATION.
PHILADELPHIA:
M. S. LANTZ,
No. 20 South Broad Street.

Kessinger Publishing's
Rare Mystical Reprints

THOUSANDS OF SCARCE BOOKS
ON THESE AND OTHER SUBJECTS:

Freemasonry * Akashic * Alchemy * Alternative Health * Ancient Civilizations * Anthroposophy * Astrology * Astronomy * Aura * Bible Study * Cabalah * Cartomancy * Chakras * Clairvoyance * Comparative Religions * Divination * Druids * Eastern Thought * Egyptology * Esoterism * Essenes * Etheric * ESP * Gnosticism * Great White Brotherhood * Hermetics * Kabalah * Karma * Knights Templar * Kundalini * Magic * Meditation * Mediumship * Mesmerism * Metaphysics * Mithraism * Mystery Schools * Mysticism * Mythology * Numerology * Occultism * Palmistry * Pantheism * Parapsychology * Philosophy * Prosperity * Psychokinesis * Psychology * Pyramids * Qabalah * Reincarnation * Rosicrucian * Sacred Geometry * Secret Rituals * Secret Societies * Spiritism * Symbolism * Tarot * Telepathy * Theosophy * Transcendentalism * Upanishads * Vedanta * Wisdom * Yoga * *Plus Much More!*

DOWNLOAD A FREE CATALOG
AND
SEARCH OUR TITLES AT:

www.kessinger.net

CONTENTS.

PART I.
The Science of Correspondences Elucidated.

CHAPTER I.
Importance of the Subject.—Inspiration Defined, and the True Canon of the Word of God Decided 13

CHAPTER II.
Difficulties of the Mere Literal Sense of the Word Stated.—The Literal Sense Proved to be Indefensible and Inexplicable if an Internal Sense be Denied . . . 21

CHAPTER III.
That the Divinity and Sanctity of the Word of God is the Consequence of its Containing an Internal or Spiritual Sense 32

CHAPTER IV.
The Laws of the Science of Correspondences Stated and Confirmed.—The Doctrine of Correspondences well known to the Ancients, and its Corruption the Origin of all Idolatry and Superstition 39

CHAPTER V.
That the Sacred Writers bear the most Ample and Cogent Testimony to the Existence of a Spiritual Sense in the Word of God 54

CHAPTER VI.
The Difference between Correspondence and Metaphor, Fable, etc., stated.—Correspondence defined, with Examples of its Application in expounding the Holy Word 71

CHAPTER VII.
The Science of Correspondences not a Speculative and Visionary Theory, but an Absolute Reality.—Illustrations from Opposites, and various other Subjects.—The Objects for which the Word of God was Revealed only Answered by the Admission of its Internal Sense, which alone Distinguishes it from all other Compositions, and Reconciles its Apparent Contradictions.—Universality of this Divine Science, and the Necessity that Exists for the Word being Written according to it. 85

CHAPTER VIII.
The Difference between the Apparent and Genuine Truths of the Literal Sense of the Holy Word Explained and Illustrated 112

CHAPTER IX.
The Correspondence of War and Implements of War in the Holy Word . . . 124

CHAPTER X.
On the Will and Understanding, as Comprising both the Divine and the Human Mind; on the Marriage of Divine Goodness and Truth therein, and on the Union of Love and Wisdom in the Holy Word, with Illustrations 131

CHAPTER XI.
The Three Degrees of Life, the Trinal Distinction in God, and the Threefold Constitution of the Human Mind and the Holy Word Explained, and their Mutual Correspondence Illustrated 141

viii   *CONTENTS.*

CHAPTER XII.
Colors, Numbers, Weights, Measures, Musical Instruments, etc. 170

CHAPTER XIII.
The Correspondence of Animals, Parts of Animals, and Compound and Monstrous Animals, with Illustrations 190

CHAPTER XIV.
Correspondence of the Vegetable World, with Illustrations 206

CHAPTER XV.
Correspondence of Earths, Minerals, etc., with Illustrations 233

CHAPTER XVI.
Correspondence of the Sun, Moon, and Stars; the Idolatrous Worship of them, and its extensive Prevalence and Influence 239

CHAPTER XVII.
The First Chapters of Genesis, to the 27th Verse of Chapter XI., A Grand Series of Divine Allegories, which can only be Interpreted by the Science of Correspondences 242

CHAPTER XVIII.
History of the Flood, the Ark, and of Noah and his Posterity, an Allegory; or, rather, a Spiritual History clothed in the Divine Language of Correspondences . . 255

CHAPTER XIX.
Sacrificial Worship 266

CHAPTER XX.
The Entire History of the Four Gospels Literally True, but Significative and Representative in every Particular Recorded.—Illustrations from the Lord's Parables and Miracles, His Transfiguration, Life, Ministry, and Crucifixion 279

CHAPTER XXI.
The Book of Revelation Wholly Composed of Divine Symbols or Correspondences . 292
Conclusion 295

PART II.
Additional Illustrations and Confirmations of the Doctrine.

CHAPTER I.
The Key of Knowledge.—Introduction, 303.—Creation of the World, 305.—Contradictory Views of Chronologers Concerning the Age of the World, 307.—Geology in Harmony with Scripture, 308.—The Sun the Instrumental Cause of Creation, 311.—Sir Humphry Davy's View, 313.—Connection between the Creator and His Works, 314.—Plenary Inspiration of the Word of God, 317.—Correspondence, the Sure Rule of Scripture Interpretation 321

CHAPTER II.
The Origin of Correspondence, and why the Scripture is Written in Agreement with it, 325.—Some Proofs Given, 325.—Revelation the Voice of God Speaking to Man's Will and Intellect; therefore of Plenary Inspiration, 332.—Opinions of Ancient and Modern Authors Respecting Correspondence, 337.—The Prayer of Moses, "Lord, I Beseech Thee, Show me thy Glory," Explained, 345.—The Tri-Unity of God, as Consisting of Love, Wisdom, Power, Exhibited in all Creation, 347.—Correspondence of the Three Kingdoms of Nature with the Three Degrees of Life in Man 348

CHAPTER III.
The Lord's Word Magnified above all His Name, 352.—Comparisons Between the Literal and Spiritual Senses of the Word of God; Illustrations of, 353.—The Use of

CONTENTS.

Correspondence in Explaining Difficult Passages of Scripture, 355.—Its Use in Explaining the Miracles and Parables, 357.—Correspondence of the Sun, Moon, and Stars, 360.—The Israelitish Journey from Egypt to Canaan, 366.—Explanation of Various Scripture Phrases, 367.—Ezekiel's Vision of Holy Waters, 369.—Two Miracles Illustrated by the Law of Correspondence, viz., "Death in the Pot," and the Restoration of Sight to the Man Born Blind, by Washing in the Pool of Siloam, 377.—The Tribute-Money found in the Fish's Mouth, 387.—Religion and Science Connected, 391.—Conclusion 396

CHAPTER IV.

A KEY TO THE SPIRITUAL SIGNIFICATION OF NUMBERS.—Introduction, 398.—Numbers 1 to 12, Inclusive—One, 403.—Two, 411.—Three, 419.—Four, 426.—Five, 434.—Six, 445, —Seven, 451.—Eight, 460.—Nine, 466.—Ten, 469.—Eleven, 475.—Twelve, 478.—A Rule for Discovering the Signification of other Numbers 487

CHAPTER V.

A KEY TO THE SPIRITUAL SIGNIFICATION OF WEIGHTS AND MEASURES 490

CHAPTER VI.

PRECIOUS AND COMMON STONES, THEIR MEANING IN SCRIPTURE.—A General Account of the Stones mentioned in the Sacred Scriptures, the Purposes to which they were applied, and their various Significations 503

CHAPTER VII.

Stones used for Altars, Pillars, Witnesses, and Memorials 509

CHAPTER VIII.

Tables of Stones for the Ten Commandments 515

CHAPTER IX.

The Breast-Plate of Aaron, called the Breast-Plate of Judgment, and also Urim and Thummim 529

CHAPTER X.

The Science of Correspondence Applied as a Key to the Spiritual Interpretation of the Principal Symbols in Revelation xxi. Chapter, and its Applicability and Sufficiency Demonstrated 549

CHAPTER XI.

The Word and its Inspiration.—No Written Word before the Fall.—The Ancient Word that became Lost.—Source of the Grecian Mythology.—All Religious Knowledge from Divine Revelation.—The Scriptures a Light to all Nations.—The Medium of Communication between Angels and Men.—Nature of the Word in Heaven.—Illustrating and Confirming the Doctrine of Correspondence.—Distinction between Verbal and Personal Inspiration.—No Written Word on any Earth but ours, and the Reason why 562

CHAPTER XII.

The Doctrine of Correspondence Applied as a Key to the Spiritual and True Meaning of Matthew xvi. 18, 19.—The Rock on which the Church is Built.—The Keys of the Kingdom of Heaven, etc. 590

CHAPTER XIII.

Correspondence Applied to the Interpretation of Isaiah vii. 15.—"Butter and Honey shall he Eat, that he may know to refuse the Evil and choose the Good" . . 595

CHAPTER XIV.

The Correspondence of Salt, 599.—Some Illustrative Examples from the Word, 600.— The Preserving Principle of Salt, and its Correspondence, 601.—Its Fructifying Principle, and Its Correspondence, 602.—Its Conjoining Principle, and its Correspondence 604

CONTENTS.

CHAPTER XV.
Correspondence Applied to the Interpretation of Matthew xxiv. 20: "Pray ye that your flight be not in the Winter, neither on the Sabbath day" 608

CHAPTER XVI.
Correspondence of the Serpent, with Illustrative Examples from Scripture . . . 616

CHAPTER XVII.
Natural and Spiritual Substance and Form.—Truth and Love are Substantial.—The Natural and Spiritual Body.—Objects in the Spiritual World, and the Law of their Existence.—Discrete Degrees, Confirming the Doctrine of Correspondence.—God, the Infinite and self-existing Substance 627

CHAPTER XVIII.
Correspondence of the Human Body and its Parts to Things Spiritual and Divine . 635

CHAPTER XIX.
The True Worship of the Lord Represented by the Offerings of the Wise Men from the East.—The Spiritual meaning of Gold, Frankincense, and Myrrh, as unfolded by Correspondence 642

APPENDIX.

SEC. I.—Dissertation on the Possibility and Necessity of Divine Revelation; on the Canon of Sacred Scripture, and the Genuineness and Authenticity of the Various Books Composing the Word of the New Testament and their Uncorrupted Preservation; with a Brief Analysis of, and a few Remarks on, each Book 651

SEC. II.—The Canon of Scripture 653

SEC. III.—The Books of the Authorized Version of the Bible which are not Plenarily Inspired, 656.—Ezra and Nehemiah, 659.—Ruth, 659.—Esther, 660.—Job, 661.—Proverbs, 662.—Ecclesiastes, 662.—The Song of Solomon 663

SEC. IV.—The Apocrypha 666

SEC. V.—Rabbinical Literature 666

SEC. VI.—The Septuagint, or Greek Version of the Old Testament 667

SEC. VII.—The Versions of the Scriptures used by Emanuel Swedenborg . . . 668

SEC. VIII.—On the Integrity of the Word of God, and its Miraculous Preservation . 670

SEC. IX.—The Epistles of the Apostles 676

SEC. X.—The Jewish Canon of the Old Testament 683

SEC. XI.—The Four Different Styles in which the Word of God is Written . . 685

SEC. XII.—The Ancient Word 686

SEC. XIII.—Why was not the Internal Sense of the Word Revealed before? . . 688

SEC. XIV.—The Authorized English Version of the Bible 688

SEC. XV.—Degrees 690

SEC. XVI.—Druidism 696

SEC. XVII.—The Pythagorean Doctrine of Metempsychosis 702

SEC. XVIII.—The Hieroglyphics, Hieroglyphs, or Sacred Writings and Engravings, and the Representative Images of the Egyptians 704

SEC. XIX.—How was it that the Spiritual Method of Interpretation Practised by the Early Christian Fathers, ceased in the Church, or what were the Causes of its Decline? 720

SEC. XX.—The Document Theory, and the Assyrian Tablets 724

SEC. XXI.—The Three Terms, Correspondences, Representatives, and Significatives . 726

PART I.

THE
SCIENCE OF CORRESPONDENCES
ELUCIDATED.

ABBREVIATIONS.

The following are the abbreviated titles of the works of Swedenborg quoted or referred to in this work.

A. C.	stand for	Arcana Cœlestia.
A. E.	"	Apocalypse Explained.
A. R.	"	Apocalypse Revealed.
T. C. R.	"	True Christian Religion.
C. S. L.	"	Conjugial and Scortatory Love.
H. H.	"	Heaven and Hell.
D. L. W.	"	Divine Love and Wisdom.
D. P.	"	Divine Providence.
S. S.	"	The Sacred Scripture.
D. L.	"	Doctrine of the Lord.
W. H.	"	The White Horse in the Revelation.
H. K.	"	Hieroglyphic Key.
I. S. B.	"	Intercourse between the Soul and the Body.

THE
SCIENCE OF CORRESPONDENCES.

CHAPTER I.

IMPORTANCE OF THE SUBJECT.—INSPIRATION DEFINED, AND THE TRUE CANON OF THE WORD OF GOD DECIDED.

THE subject of this treatise is one of momentous interest to every well-disposed and reflective mind. Accustomed to reverence the Bible[1] as a book containing the revealed will and wisdom of the Supreme Being, written under immediate inspiration, and professing to regard it as the fountain of all spiritual light, and the source of all religious knowledge, we must, if indeed we are humble and teachable, feel greatly rejoiced when we learn that there exists *a certain and universal rule* of interpretation, by which its glorious truths can be disclosed, its heavenly wonders unfolded, its consolatory doctrines displayed, and its sacred precepts made plain. In this state of mind we are prepared rationally to perceive the true nature and character of the Holy Word as "the power and wisdom of God,"—the only authentic source of religious knowledge and spiritual wisdom (John i. 1, 2; Rom. i. 16; 1 Cor. i. 24). We shall be disposed to regard it as a spiritual meat and drink,—"the green pastures and still waters" for the repose and refreshment of the Lord's flock (Ps. xxiii. 2); and as we receive the heavenly nourishment by which our souls live, we shall exclaim, with the prophet Jeremiah, "Thy words were found, and I did eat them; and they were unto me the joy and rejoicing of my heart" (xv. 16).

---

[1] Bible is a word derived from "*biblos*," the Greek name for *papyrus*, the most ancient material out of which its derivative, *paper*, was made. Biblus, the Egyptian plant, gave to the Greeks their name for paper, and this again gave their name to the earliest translation of the Hebrew Scriptures as "*the Book*," and which has been adopted into all languages as the designation of the Sacred Scriptures in a collected form.

The Jews call their Hebrew Bible, "The Book of Holiness," or "The Holy Book."

Incontrovertible reasons might be adduced for the absolute necessity of a direct revelation, and also what are commonly called the presumptive and positive but irresistible evidences, both internal and external, satisfactory as they are, in proof of the genuineness, authenticity, and integrity of those books which form the Word, together with the overwhelming testimonies in favor of their verity derived from the wonderful literal fulfillment of many of the inspired predictions,[2] and from their marvellous effects in advancing human civilization wherever they have been freely circulated; likewise the invincible proofs of the divinity of the Holy Word, as exemplified in the perfect harmony, simplicity, and practical tendency of its doctrines, and their universal adaptation to the exalted purposes proposed; the further corroborative testimony which might be adduced from important philosophical investigations, philological inquiries and responses, scientific scrutiny, and archæological discoveries, together with its miraculous preservation from age to age, amid the fiercest commotions and devastations, and the dismemberment of all the nations that have ever existed on the face of the earth;[3] and the wonderful unity of the whole, though written by the instrumentality of various men, at distant periods,—all of which facts and circumstances strongly argue a divine inspiration and prescience. I pass over these multiplied arguments, satisfactory as they are, and take far higher grounds than these in behalf of the inspiration of the Word, and appeal to the inward consciousness, experience, and reason of all.

To admit that a book is the pure dictate and voice of God, demands that we should require it to be authenticated, as well as discriminated from other productions, not merely by verbal exegesis, critical analysis, and historical researches (however valuable they

---

[2] "A prophecy, literally fulfilled, is a real miracle: one such, fairly produced, must go a great way in convincing all reasonable men."—COLLINS.

[3] "Four thousand years this great volume has withstood not only the iron tooth of time, but all the physical and intellectual strength of man. Pretended friends have corrupted and betrayed it; kings and princes have perseveringly sought to banish it from the world; the civil and military powers of the great empires of the world have been leagued for its destruction; the fires of persecution have been lighted to consume both it and its friends together; and at many seasons, death, in its most horrid forms, has been the almost certain consequence of affording it an asylum from the fury of its enemies. Though it has been ridiculed more bitterly, misrepresented more grossly, opposed more rancorously, and burnt more frequently than any other book, and perhaps than all other books united, it is so far from sinking under the efforts of its enemies, that the probability of its surviving is now much greater than ever. The rain has descended, the floods have come, the storm has arisen and beat upon it; but it fell not: for it was founded upon a rock. Like the burning bush, it has been in flames, yet it is still unconsumed,—a sufficient proof that there is no other revelation from God,—that He who spake from the bush, is the author of the Bible."—PAYSON.

may be in furnishing expositions and confirmations of the letter), but by the highest and most cogent evidence.[4] "I speak as to wise men, judge ye what I say" (1 Cor. x. 15). "Prove all things, hold fast that which is good" (1 Thess. v. 21). Far be it from me, however, to decry or undervalue the use and application of profound philosophical, archæological, and scientific researches, applied to the enodation and illustration of the letter of the Word of God, from which, when directed by sound piety and judgment, there is nothing to fear. On the contrary, honor and gratitude are due to all who, in a right spirit, engage in Biblical criticism. For it is of the utmost consequence that the literal sense of the Word should be as critically correct, and as absolutely definite as possible; because this sense, adapted to all readers, is the only just source and faithful standard of all true doctrine and genuine morality.[5]

A careful examination of the Bible may lead an impartial and reflective mind to see that it consists of two kinds of writings, distinguished by two very different degrees of inspiration:—one primary, plenary, and infallible—the other secondary and partial, which might appropriately be considered as the result of the spiritual illumination of the writer's rational mind. The first, or superior degree of inspiration, is that in which the speakers and writers were inspired as to the very *words* they uttered and recorded. For the time their individuality was suspended. Their mind, reason, and memory were altogether subservient to the prevalent influence of the Spirit of Jehovah, who "spake by them, and his word was in their tongues," which were as "the pen of a ready writer" (2 Sam. xxiii. 2; Ps. xiv. i.). The writers were only seen in their representative characters. Their states were intermittent; at times they were in the Spirit, and had direct intercourse with the spiritual world, and conscious communion with God, while at others they were in their ordinary state of mind.[6]

---

[4] "One is tempted to remark how much we may lose by the cold, dry way in which we are apt to read the sacred history, as mere matter of criticism, historical or moral, contrasted with the high and thrilling views wherewith the ecclesiastical rules of interpretation warrant those who adopt them."—*Tracts of the Times*, lxxxix., p. 101.

[5] On the above important topics much has been ably written by a host of learned, indefatigable, and skilful men—of all ages and countries, whose names and works it is unnecessary to enumerate. Judiciously read, with every allowance for the respective authors' means of information, religious sentiments, and predilections, these works will satisfy every inquiry of the student on the historical, chronological, and philological evidences, both internal and external, or on the unquestionable genuineness and authenticity of the sacred books which compose the Word of God. (*See Appendix, on the Integrity of the Word of God in the Letter.*)

[6] "During the prophetical ecstasy the very actions and words of a prophet are symbolical, as is rightly observed by Irenæus."—LANCASTER, *Perp. Com.*, p. 16. (See Isa. xx. 3; Ez. iv. 1; xxxiv. 33.)

Thus every term, yea, every "jot and tittle" (Matt. v. 18) of such books was dictated or spoken by the Lord himself,—necessarily contains a heavenly, spiritual sense, distinct from but within the literal sense, and consequently both senses are most holy and divine. Now the books of the Bible written according to this peculiar style are the pure and plenary WORD OF GOD. For "inspiration," Swedenborg says, "implies that in all parts of the Word, even the most minute,—as well the historical as other parts,—are contained celestial things, which refer to love or goodness, and spiritual things, which refer to faith or truth, consequently things divine. For what is inspired by the Lord, descends from Him through the angelic heavens, and so through the world of spirits, till it reaches man, before whom it presents itself as the Word in the letter." (A. C. 1837.)

The second or lower degree of inspiration is that which is generally supposed to belong to the entire Bible, in which the writers, for the edification of the Church, were led by the illumination and direction of the Holy Spirit as far as THE SENSE is concerned, without being inspired as to the words they used, or in the descriptions of the events and facts they related.

The views of the New Church, therefore, do not differ from those of other Christian expositors and commentators in regard to the authority which belongs to the latter class of writings, the subsidiary objects for which they were composed, or the mode of interpretation usually adopted (see Appendix, p. 651); but we widely differ from all others as to the character of those books which are affirmed to be plenarily inspired. And the distinction is, that these are maintained to be of immediate divine authority, and thus more sacred—more practical than modern theologians admit. We believe them to be the divine truth itself,—an emanation from the divine goodness itself, —and holy even to the very letter. And further confirmed as it is to us by the most convincing evidence that this very Word of God, thus plenarily inspired, is written according to peculiar laws, which are applicable to no other compositions whatsoever. And moreover, that the books so written are, in the Old Testament—those enumerated by our blessed Lord, in Luke xxiv. 44, with reference to Himself, namely, "THE LAW" (the Pentateuch, or five books) "OF MOSES,"

"Inspired persons remain merely human beings in respect of purposes not immediately connected with their special missions and endowments."—*Kentish's Notes and Comments*, 2d Ed., p. 131.

[7] In the celebrated catechism of Rabbi Abraham Jagel, originally extracted from Maimonides, it is asserted that "Moses acted as the mere amanuensis of God in writing

THE PROPHETS AND THE PSALMS,"[8] and in the New Testament, the FOUR GOSPELS,[9] which relate to the history of our Lord's incarnation, ministry, and glorification, and record his very words; together with the book of REVELATION, which the Apostle John calls "the revelation and testimony of Jesus Christ," and which he says was "signified" to him, or as the original word ἐσήμανεν means, *symbolically shown to him*. These Scriptures, then, are contradistinguished from all human compositions whatsoever; and while the histories recorded are all, in the general sense, literally true,[10] yet the whole is capable of being interpreted by the known, determinable, harmonious, universal, and unerring law on which they rest, and according to which they were written.

That the term Gospel (or "glad tidings," or "news that is well ")[11] is taken to mean the *Four* Gospels, and that *these* were always regarded as, in some sense, more holy than the Epistles, is evident—

both the historical and ceremonial parts of his five books."—*Porta Mosis*, p. 164.

"The entire Old Testament is a connected series of mysteries, relating to Christ, who, though one, is represented by various types and emblems."—*De amor et Cult. in Spir. et Ver.*, p. 31.

[8] The Son of Sirach seems to allude to this threefold division of the Scriptures, in the preface to the book of Ecclesiasticus, written about 130 years before the Christian era, where he mentions "The Law, the prophets, and the other books of our Fathers."—WOLF, Bib. Heb., vol. i., p. 255.

[9] "Tatian, a little after the middle of the second century, composed a Harmony of the Gospels; the first of the kind which had been attempted, which he called *Diatesseron* [of the four], which demonstrates that at that time there were four gospels, and no more, of established authority in the Church. Irenæus, not long after, mentions all the Evangelists by name, arranging them according to the order wherein they wrote, which is the same as that universally given them throughout the Christian world to this day, assigning reasons why the gospels can be neither fewer nor more. Early in the third century, Ammonius also wrote a harmony of the four gospels."—*Campbell's Prelim. Diss. to the Four Gospels*, vol. i., p. 134. See also *Westcott's Canon of the New Test.*, p. 355.

"The gospel writers were four—but the gospel is one" (*Origen, Cont. Marcion*, sec. i., p. 9). "Like that river which went out of Eden to water the garden, it was by the Holy Ghost ' parted, and became into four heads.'"—*Burgon's Sermons*, p. 62. [Cyprian uses the same figure.]

Origen, as quoted by Eusebius, presbyter of Alexandria, also says "The four evangelists alone are received without dispute by the whole Church of God."—*Hist. Eccl.*, lib. vi., cat. 25. Augustine, who flourished A. D. 398, writes that "The four gospels have the highest authority."—*Lardner's Gospel Hist.*, vol. xii., p. 302.

[10] By finding a spiritual sense in the Word of God, Hilary will not allow that historical truth is weakened or betrayed.—" In the beginning of our treatise we warned others against supposing that we detracted from the belief in transactions by teaching that the things themselves contained within them the outgoings of subsequent realities."—*Comm. in Matt. vii.*, i., p. 640.

Cyril of Alexandria also says, "Although the spiritual sense be good and fruitful, yet what is historical should be taken as [true] history."—*Comm. in Isa.*, lib. i., Orat. 4, vol. ii., pp. 113, 114.

"Remember," Tertullian remarks, "that when we admit of spiritual allegories, the true literal sense of the Scripture is not altered."

[11] "The Greek word for *Gospel* means *glad tidings, good or joyful news*. Our English word 'Gospel,' which is compounded of the Saxon word *God*—good, and *spell*—a history, narrative, or message, very accurately expresses the sense of the original Greek."—(See *Junii Etym. Ang.* and Parkhurst.)

first, from the circumstance that oaths from a period antecedent, at least, to the time of Justinian (A. D. 527), have been administered in the four Gospels;[12] secondly, from the ancient form universally prevailing in the Christian Church so early as the third century, of ordaining Bishops to their sacred functions in which *the book of the Four Evangelists* was *held open over the candidate's head;* and, lastly, from the practice of the Church, in which a custom has long existed, and is even now retained, which, if it has any meaning, was designed to mark a *greater* degree of reverence for the *Gospels* in comparison with the Apostolic Epistles; for, the congregation is directed, in the rubric of the Church of England communion service, to *stand* while the holy Gospel is read, but to sit during the reading of the Epistles.[13]

Bishop Tomline thus writes on the inspiration of the entire Bible, in his *Elements of Christian Theology:*—"When it is said that the Sacred Scriptures are divinely inspired, we are not to understand that God suggested every word, or dictated every expression, nor is it to be supposed that they were inspired in every fact which they related, or in every precept which they delivered." "It is sufficient to believe that by the general superintendence of the Holy Spirit, they were directed in the choice of their materials, and prevented from recording any material error."[14]

In what, then, does the difference consist between the view now propounded, and that which was held by this orthodox prelate of the Establishment, whose opinion on this topic has been echoed on all sides, and would, it is presumed, be admitted as a precise exposition of what is generally believed on the subject of inspiration throughout the Christian world? It consists in this: the Bishop's mode of interpretation, like ours, is strictly applicable to the Epistles, and such portions of the Word as are not included by the Lord in the text just noticed; but we believe, from evidence apparently irresistible,

---

[12] Cyril, in his apologetical discourse to Theodosius, describing the Council of Ephesus, says: "The sacred synod being assembled in Mary's Church, had Christ himself for their head; for the Holy Gospel was as a solemn throne, preaching, as it were, to the venerable prelates, 'Judge ye righteous judgment!'"—*Labbe.* Concil. iii., p. 1044. *Cited by Dr. Wordsworth.*

[13] In the Eastern churches, lights were carried before them when they were going to be read.

[14] "How do we get from under that difficulty [viz., that of reconciling purely physical truths and scientific facts with the Bible]? I believe, by simply adopting a doctrine which is laid down in a passage from *Reason and Knowledge,* a book recently issued by Dr. Candlish: 'All that is in Scripture is not revelation. To a large extent the Bible is a record of human affairs—the sayings and doings of men; not a record of divine doctrine or of communications from God.'"—Speech of Duke of Argyle, delivered at a meeting of the National Bible Society of Scotland, held at Glasgow, 1864.

that by far the greater part is of an incomparably more exalted character than such a standard of interpretation is calculated to establish,—for we believe that these latter books contain, in the original at least, truth without the admixture of error, and that they were inspired both as to materials and sense, as to phraseology and words, as to precepts and facts,—every particular expression therein being holy and divine. And that, thus, the oracles of God (Rom. iii. 2; Heb. v. 12; 1 Pet. iv. 11; *lively oracles*, Acts i. 35), like a casket enclosing brilliant pearls and gems, contain a lucid heavenly meaning, distinct from, but within, the letter.

Indeed, to the pious mind, it is a truly lamentable reflection that the inspiration of the Word of God has been reduced to so low a test by modern expositors. Nothing, certainly, can tend more to the support and encouragement of the most rank infidelity. Dr. Palfrey, for instance, late Professor of Biblical Literature in the University of Cambridge, Mass., speaking of the Pentateuch, says that "We are not debarred from supposing that it had its origin in the imperfect wisdom of Moses."—(*Acad. Lect. on the Jewish Scrip. and Antiq.*, vol. i., lect. iv., pp. 85, 86.)

Professor McLellan, in his *Manual of Sacred Interpretation*, designed to aid theological students in Biblical exegesis, among others lays these *maxims* down as a canon of direction for the expositor: "The object of Interpretation is to give the precise thoughts which the sacred writer intended to express. No other meaning is to be sought but that which lies in the words themselves. Scripture is to be interpreted by the same method which we employ in discovering the meaning *of any other book;*" and Dr. Davidson, in his *Sacred Hermeneutics*, speaking of the true principles of interpretation, says that "The grammatical meaning [of the Scriptures] is the same with the historical; and both constitute *all the meaning* intended by the Holy Spirit. When the grammatical or historical meaning of a passage is ascertained, all the theology of the passage is also known" (p. 227).

To the same purport, Dr. Thirlwall, the Bishop of St. David's, in his charge, 1863, affirms that "a great part of the events related in the Old Testament have no more apparent connection with our religion than those of Greece and Rome. . . . The history, so far as it is a narrative of civil and political transactions, has no essential connection with any religious truth, and, if it had been lost, though we should have been left in ignorance of much which we should have desired to know, our treasures of Christian doctrine would have remained whole and unimpaired. The numbers, migrations, wars, battles, conquests, and reverses of Israel have nothing in common with the teachings of Christ, with the way of salvation, with the fruits of the Spirit. They belong to a totally different order of subjects."—P. 123. "Our Church has never attempted to determine the nature of the inspiration of the Holy Scriptures."—*Ib.*, p. 107.

Dr. Orville Dewey, one of the most distinguished theologians of the Unitarian school, writes on this subject as follows:

"If any one thinks it necessary to a reception of the Bible as a revelation from God, that the inspired penmen should have written by immediate dictation; if he thinks that the writers were mere amanuenses, and that word after word was put down by instant suggestion from above; that the very style is divine and not human; that the style, we say, and the matters of style—the figures, the metaphors, the illustrations, came from the Divine mind, and not from human minds; we say, at once and plainly, that we do not regard the Scriptures as setting forth any claims to such supernatural perfection, or accuracy of style. It is not a kind of distinction that would add anything to the authority, much less to the dignity, of a communication from heaven. Nay, it would detract from its power, to deprive it, by any hypothesis, of those touches of nature, of that natural pathos, simplicity, and imagination, and of that solemn grandeur of thought, disregarding style, of which the Bible is full. Enough is it for us, that the matter is divine, the doctrines true, the history authentic, the miracles real, the promises glorious, the threatenings fearful. Enough, that all is gloriously and fearfully true,—true to the Divine will, true to human nature, true to its wants, anxieties, sorrows, sins, and solemn destinies. Enough, that the seal of a Divine and miraculous communication is set upon that Holy Book."—(*Works*, English Ed., p. 465.)

And in a Tract (*Belief and Unbelief*), published in 1839, with the avowed purpose of defending the Bible from the objections of infidelity, he says, "The Scriptures are not the actual communication made to the minds inspired from above. They are not the actual Word of God, but they are the record of the Word of God." "If there ever were productions which show the free and fervent workings of human thought and feeling, they are our sacred records. But the things [in them] which we have to deal with are words; they are not divine symbols of thought." Again, he says, "If we open almost any book, especially any book written in a fervent and popular style, we can perceive, on accurate analysis, that some things were hastily written, some things negligently, some things not in the exact logical order of thought; that some things are beautiful in style, and others inelegant; that some things are clear, and others obscure and hard to be understood." "And do we not," adds the same writer, "find all these things in the Scriptures?"

Speaking of the twenty-fifth and following chapters of Exodus, Andrews Norton, Professor of Sacred History in Harvard University, Mass., says: "Seven chapters are filled with trivial directions [respecting the ark, the tabernacle, and its utensils]. So wholly unconnected are they with any moral or religious sentiment, or any truth, important or unimportant, except the melancholy fact of their having been regarded as a divine communication,—that it requires a strong effort to read through with attention these pretended words of the Infinite Being. The natural tendency of a belief that such words proceeded from Him, whenever such belief prevailed, must have been to draw away the regard of the Jews from all that is worthy of man, and to fix it upon the humblest object of superstition."—*Evidences of the Genuineness of the Gospels*, add. notes, cxxvii.

In these divinely inspired chapters, Swedenborg in his *Arcana Celestia* shows the importance and explains the spiritual meaning of every sentence and every word, as teaching countless lessons of instruction, and as having in each particular an important representative meaning, and a practical application, in which the celestial and spiritual order and realities of heaven and the divine presence and blessing in sacred worship are presented to the contemplation and acceptance of the prepared mind. They describe the very sanctuary in which the Lord can dwell with man, and of which he says: "For the Lord hath chosen Zion; He hath desired it for his habitation. This is my rest forever: here will I dwell, for I have desired it. I will abundantly bless her provision; I will satisfy her poor with bread. I will also clothe her priests with salvation, and her saints shall sing aloud for joy" (Ps. cxxxii. 13–16). And again, "Behold the tabernacle of God is with men, and He will dwell with them, and they shall be his people, and God himself shall be with them, and be their God" (Rev. xxi. 3). And it was with precisely such a precept on the interpretation of these very chapters, that the Apostle Paul thus addresses the Christian Church at Corinth: "Ye are the people of the living God; as God hath said [Ex. xxix. 45; Lev. xxvi. 12], I will dwell in them, and walk in them; and I will be their God, and they shall be my people" (2 Cor. vi. 16).

Surely, *less reverent* ideas of inspiration than these quoted above cannot possibly be held by such as profess to believe in its existence at all. They must appear to every devout mind as little less than a disavowal of inspiration altogether, and instead of a defence, to be a total abandonment of the truth, and a virtual denial of the sanctity and authority of the Word of God.

If we look into the Christian world, we shall find men, distinguished for their learning and piety, as widely at variance in their sentiments and interpretations of the inspired Volume as noonday differs from midnight darkness; supporting tenets of religion irrational in themselves, and diametrically opposed to each other, by the most confident appeals to its sacred pages; disputing with the bitterest acrimony about doctrines that are admitted to be mere implications, and not unfrequently distorting the plainest facts of science, and even accredited events of history, in support of favorite theological opinions. We find men, gifted with most profound powers of investigating the secret laws of nature, who can unfold, amid a blaze of demonstration, the most wonderful phenomena of physical existence, and unravel the perplexing mysteries of creation and mathematical science, but who either profess themselves embarrassed with the conflicting difficulties and obscurities of revelation, or openly avow their conviction that the Bible and nature are at variance with each other. And as facts in nature are constant and undeniable, and as it would be most absurd to suppose that the Divine Being would speak and act inconsistently, so, therefore, they at once conclude that the Bible cannot be divine—cannot have God for its author.[15]

---

[15] Newman lays down the following axiom and conclusions with reference to the Word of God:—

"1. The moral and intellectual powers of man must be acknowledged as having a right and duty to criticise the contents of the Scripture;

"2. When so exerted, they condemn portions of the Scripture as erroneous and immoral:

"3. The assumed infallibility of the entire Scripture is a proved falsity, not merely as to physiology and other scientific matters, but also as to morals."—*Phases of Faith*, p. 115.

The notorious Rev. Chas. Voysey, in his lecture on the Bible, delivered at St. George's Hall, London, 1871, is reported to have said, that "though it contained much that is beautiful and true, yet it makes no claim to a divine origin and authority. In it there are absolute and irreconcilable contradictions and downright falsehoods. Even the religious and moral teaching is not uniform or coherent, but in some places contradictory of itself, and some of it degrading to God. There were moral blemishes in the life and character of Jesus, as reported in the gospels themselves, that He used uncharitable language, gave way to bad temper, and was destitute of natural affection."

"I know of no work on the subject [the plenary inspiration of the Scriptures] that I dare place in the hands of a student of theology. I know of none which, even to a young man of ordinary acuteness, does not suggest greater difficulties than it removes."—*Swainson's Lectures on the Authority of the New Testament*, p. 150.

"The Scriptures are fast becoming, to a great degree, a dead and obsolete letter; and the editors of our religious journals publicly acknowledge the mournful fact. On this subject the *Christian Examiner*, one of the most ably conducted and well-known of religious periodicals, has the following remarks:—'No one who is accustomed to regard with much attention the history and tendency of religious opinions can fail of being convinced that the question concerning the inspiration of the Scriptures is soon to become the most absorbing question of Christian theology. The minds of men are

Bishop Colenso, insisting vehemently on the Bible possessing a human element, and being merely "a human book," containing not only a literal sense, but one that bears no other meaning whatever, except that which lies upon the surface, says: "In this way, I repeat, the Bible becomes to us a human book, in which the thoughts of other hearts are opened to us, of men who lived in the ages long ago, and in circumstances so different from ours." "We must not blindly shut our eyes to the real history of the composition of this book, to the legendary character of its earlier portions, to the manifest contradictions and impossibilities, which rise up at once in every part of the story of the Exodus, if we persist in maintaining that it is a simple record of historical facts. We must regard it, then, as the work of men, of fellow-men like ourselves."—(*Pent. and Book of Joshua*, p. ii., p. 382, §§ 511, 512.)

---

in that position in reference to this subject which cannot long be maintained. They must move one way or the other. They must attain to some sort of consistency, either by believing less or by believing more. The authority of the Scriptures, and especially those of the Old Testament, must either become higher and stronger, *or be reduced almost to nothing*. It is vain to imagine that, with the present secret or open scepticism, or at least vague and unsettled notions, with which they are regarded, even by many who are defenders of a special revelation, they can be read and taught in our churches, schools, and families, as books, *sui generis*, so as to command much of real reverence for themselves.'"—*The Nineteenth Century*, p. 47.

"The general remarks respecting the inspiration of the Old Testament apply also to the New. . . . All the writings in the New Testament as well as the Old contain marks of human origin, of human weakness and imperfection."—*Tracts for the Times*, pp. 4-10.

Sentiments so utterly degrading to Divine Revelation are endorsed by numbers who profess to be the moral and religious teachers of the day. They are views which seem naturally to arise out of a denial of the plenary inspiration of the Word of God. To such conclusions the reasoning of the late Rev. Baden Powell, in his work on inspiration, and of the learned clergymen who were the authors of the *Essays and Reviews* most certainly lead. So again Miss H. Martineau can thus speak of the Holy Gospels: "In general, it is no light work for the sincere and reverent mind to read the Gospel history, so as to come within reach of the actual voice of Jesus, and listen to it among the perplexing echoes of his place and time; to separate it from the Jewish construction of Matthew, the traditional accretions of Mark and Luke, and the Platonising medium of John;—a care and labor which it is profane and presumptuous to omit or make light of."—*Eastern Travels*, vol. iii., p. 175.

To the above, which could be extended almost indefinitely, often written in terms we should be sorry to transfer to our pages, we will add but the following conclusive answer by Swedenborg:—

"The natural man, however, cannot still be persuaded to believe that the Word is Divine Truth itself, in which is Divine Wisdom and Divine Life, inasmuch as he judges of it by its style, in which no such things appear. Nevertheless, the style in which the Word is written, is a truly Divine style, with which no other style, however sublime and excellent it may seem, is at all comparable, for it is as darkness compared to light. The style of the Word is of such a nature as to contain what is holy in every verse, in every word, and in some cases in every letter; and hence the Word conjoins man with the Lord, and opens heaven." "Hence man has life by and through the Word." "Lest therefore mankind should remain any longer in doubt concerning the divinity of the Word, it has pleased the Lord to reveal to me its internal sense, which in its essence is spiritual, and which is to the external sense, which is natural, what the soul is to the body. This internal sense is the spirit which gives life to the letter; wherefore this sense will evince the divinity and sanctity of the Word, and may convince even the natural man, if he is of a disposition to be convinced."—(*S. S.*, 1-4.)

CHAPTER II.

DIFFICULTIES OF THE MERE LITERAL SENSE OF THE WORD STATED.—THE LITERAL SENSE PROVED TO BE INDEFENSIBLE AND INEXPLICABLE IF AN INTERNAL SENSE BE DENIED.

TO multitudes of readers the mere letter of the sacred Scriptures often appears vague and unconnected (Isa. lx. 7-9; Jer. xix. 5; Matt. xxiv. 27-29); hard and unmeaning (Ps. cix. 13; Jer. xlviii. 11-15; Hos. xiii. 6; Mic. i. 16-21; John xxi. 2); to abound with gross absurdities and unintelligible mysteries (Gen. iv. 15; Judg. v. 20; Isa. vii. 20; lx. 16; Ez. xxviii. 13); to contain numerous statements which seem irrational, self-contradictory, or inconsistent with others (Ex. xx. 5, 6; xxiv. 10; Ez. xviii. 20; Isa. xliii. 3; Luke xxii. 43; John i. 18-20); to comprise many which are antagonistic to the modern discoveries in chronology, opposed to the well-known principles of the physical sciences, and discordant with the ascertained facts of profane history (Gen. i., ii.; Joshua x.; Isa. xlv. 7; Matt. xxvii. 9; Rev. xi. 8); to include narratives of violence, treachery, cruelty, uncleanness, and injustice seemingly approved by God, yet diametrically opposed to his infinite and unchangeable attributes and qualities of mercy, purity, faithfulness, and justice (Gen. xxxiv. 15; 1 Sam. xv. 33; Gen. xxvii.; Judges iv., v.); to give commands of an immoral tendency, irreconcilable with spotless perfection (Ex. xxxii. 27; Josh. viii. 21-25; Ps. cxxxvii. 9; Hos. iii. 1-3); and to be occupied with trivial circumstances and with affairs which appear too insignificant, and even revolting, to have ever claimed so much attention from the Lord of the universe (Ez. v. 12; Zech. viii. 5).

How many honest people, "for lack of true knowledge," have in consequence treated the holy verities of divine revelation with the utmost derision, either as myths of barbarous ages, or fragments of falsehoods strangely blended with truth, or as a contemptible tissue of ignorance and imposture; and have not hesitated to revile all religions as systems alike of despotism, superstition, and credulity,—the delusions of priestcraft and the offspring of fanaticism and fervid imaginations. How many virtuous, intelligent, and candid minds are there who are perplexed, and distressed, and alarmed, even at their own thoughts while reading their Bibles!

It is surely time, then, for Christians to inquire what is the real nature of God's Word,—to examine into the origin, sanctity, and authority of that blessed Book on which, as upon an adamantine foundation, all virtue and intelligence infallibly rest, and whence all true religion and spiritual knowledge are derived;—to investigate, earnestly and narrowly, its claims to universal reverence and obedience;—and to vindicate its hallowed doctrines and its divine precepts from all contumely by a rational demonstration of its being what it professes to be,—the very WORD OF GOD. And unless this be done, it needs no prophetic eye to see, no prophetic tongue to foretell, that infidelity and scepticism will soon reign triumphant, that darkness and blindness as to all spiritual knowledge, will soon cover every mind, as is described by the holy prophet Isaiah, where he says, "The Lord hath poured out upon you the spirit of deep sleep, and hath closed your eyes; the prophets and your rulers, the seers hath He covered. And the vision of all is become unto you as a book that is sealed, which men deliver to one that is learned, saying, Read this, I pray thee: and he saith, I cannot; for it is sealed;[16] and the book is delivered to him that is not learned, saying, Read this, I pray thee: and he saith, I am not learned," (xxix. 10-12.) The utter destitution of all true doctrine, and a right interpretation of the Scriptures, is predicted as a consequence of the prevalence of iniquity, in these words, "Behold, the days come, saith the Lord God, that I will send a famine in the land, not a famine of bread, nor a thirst for water, but of hearing the words of the Lord: and they shall wander from sea to sea, and from the north even to the east, they shall run to and fro to seek the word of the Lord, and shall not find it. In that

---

[16] "The Hebrew word for search, signifies to dive into the sublime, profound, mystical, allegorical, and prophetical senses of Holy Scripture. 1 Cor. i. 20—*where is the profound searcher.*"—*Motives to the Study of Bib. Lit.*, p. 18.

"The hidden wisdom of the Scripture is to be considered as treasure hid in the earth, for which men must search with that same zeal and labor with which they penetrate into a mine of gold; for when our Saviour commands us to *search the Scriptures* for their testimony of himself, the language of the precept implies that kind of searching by which gold and silver are discovered under ground. He who doth not search the Word of God in that manner, and with that spirit, for what is to be found underneath it, will never discover its true value."—*W. Jones's Lect. on the Fig. Lang. of Holy Scrip.*, new ed., pp. 20-21.

St. Jerome, *Ep.* 13. *to Paulinus*, says, "All that we read in the sacred books is *pure* and *bright*, even in the *bark;* but it is sweeter in the *pith*. And he that would come at the *kernel*, must first break the *shell*. '*Open mine eyes, that I may see wondrous things out of thy law.*'"

day shall the fair virgins and young men faint for thirst." (Amos viii. 11-13.)

In order to understand the true nature and character of divine revelation, it is essentially requisite that our reasoning faculties should be employed, that our understanding should be elevated, that our hearts should be humbled and that our lives should be purified, for not to the self-conceited, to the worldly "wise and prudent," but unto "babes" only, can genuine wisdom be "revealed." (Matt. xi. 25; Luke x. 21.) We should approach the Word with reverence and with faith. We should "put our shoes from off our feet [that is, cast aside all sensual reasonings and all carnal suggestions], because the place whereon we stand is holy ground." (Ex. iii. 5.)[17] This surely expresses the state of mind which we ought to cherish when we approach the Holy Word in order to profit by its sacred contents, and be prepared to meet its Divine Author there as in the temple of his presence,—a state of profound humility and fervent piety,—accompanied with a desire to learn his will, that we may do his commandments. Without an humble and willing disposition of the soul, and a removal of the veil of unbelief from the mind, the glories of the inner sense cannot be made manifest unto us: "Do not my words," saith the Lord; "do good to him that walketh uprightly?" (Mic. ii. 7); and the apostle Paul testifies that "The natural man receiveth not the things of the Spirit of God; for they are foolishness unto him: neither can he know them, because they are spiritually discerned" (1 Cor. ii. 14). Thus the Psalmist prays, "Lord, open thou mine eyes, that I may behold wondrous things out of thy law" (Ps. cxix. 18). While the Lord Jesus says, "Search the Scriptures; for in them ye think ye have eternal life, and they are they which testify of ME" (John v. 39); and after his glorious resurrection we read in Luke xxiv. 45, that "then opened He the understandings of his disciples, that they might understand the Scriptures." For, as the illustrious Swedenborg observes, "It is universally confessed that the Word is from God, is divinely inspired, and of consequence is holy; but still it has remained a secret to this day in what part of the Word its divinity resides, inasmuch as in the letter it appears like a common writing, composed in a strange style, neither so sublime nor so eloquent as that which distinguishes the best secular compositions. Hence it is that whosoever

---

[17] To loose the sandals, slippers, or shoes from off the feet, as a mark of deference and respect, has prevailed from the earliest ages, as a representative custom, over the East. This is done on entering a mosque, or pagoda, or the presence of any person of distinction.—See *Peacock's Summary View*, page 81.

worships nature instead of God, and in consequence of such worship makes himself and his own *proprium* [or self-hood] the centre and fountain of his thoughts, instead of deriving them out of heaven from the Lord, may easily fall into error concerning the Word, and into contempt for it, and say within himself while he reads it, 'What is the meaning of this passage? What is the meaning of that? Is it possible this should be divine? Is it possible that God, whose wisdom is infinite, should speak in this manner? Where is its sanctity, or whence can it be derived, but from superstition and credulity?'

"But he who reasons thus, does not reflect that Jehovah the Lord, who is God of heaven and earth, spake the Word by Moses and the prophets, and that, consequently, it must be divine truth, inasmuch as what Jehovah the Lord himself speaks can be nothing else; nor does such a one consider that the Lord, who is the same with Jehovah, spake the Word written by the Evangelists, many parts from his own mouth, and the rest from the spirit of his mouth, which is the Holy Spirit. Hence it is, as He himself declares, that in his words there is life, and that He is the light which enlightens, and that He is the truth. (John vi. 63; iv. 10–14; Mark xiii. 31; Jer. ii. 13; Zech. xiii. 1; Rev. vii. 17.)"

The divine and blessed Word of the ever-living God was written for the sake of spiritual usefulness—"to perfect the man of God, that he may be thoroughly furnished unto all good works" (2 Tim. iii. 17); that it may fertilize the human mind, dropping upon it like the gentle "dew" (Deut. xxxii. 2); and descending like refreshing "showers" (Isa. iv. 11), that by its means we may possess "eternal life;" for "by every word proceeding out of the mouth of God doth man live" (Deut. viii. 3; Matt. iv. 5). It was given "for doctrine, for reproof, for correction, and instruction in righteousness" (2 Tim. iii. 16); "to convert the soul, to make wise the simple; to rejoice the heart, to enlighten the eyes" (Ps. xix. 7, 8). For a "defence" against our spiritual enemies (Eph. vi. 17); for our "sanctification" (John xvii. 17); for our "regeneration" (1 Pet. i. 23); and, to comprise all in one word, for our "salvation" (2 Tim. iii. 15). "The words of the Lord are pure words: as silver tried in a furnace of earth, purified seven times" (Ps. xii. 6).[18]

---

[18] "The whole *holy Scripture*, with Christ everywhere understood therein, consists of two parts, letter and spirit; even as man, for whose instruction the same was given, is constructed of two parts, *body* and *soul;* the letter, or *written contents* thereof, being as the *body*, and the *spirit*, or Christ himself, with the *knowledge* or *truth* of Him contained therein, being as the *soul* of these divine books. The latter of which is likewise to be

Now, unless there be a spiritual and heavenly meaning in the divine Word, distinct from, though one with, the letter, how is this spiritual usefulness, so essential to the welfare of the soul, to be promoted in an immense number of passages, such as the following:—where the prophet is almost universally allowed to be speaking of the Lord's advent, and giving the indubitable sign of it, that " a virgin should conceive and bear a son, and shall call his name Immanuel [God with us, see Matt. i. 23]," it is added (Isa. vii. 18):—"And it shall come to pass in that day, that the Lord shall hiss for the fly that is in the uttermost part of the rivers of Egypt, and for the bee that is in the land of Assyria." And in the 20th ver., "In the same day shall the Lord shave with a razor that is hired, *namely*, by them beyond the river, by the king of Assyria, the head and the hair of the feet; and it shall also consume the beard." "And it shall come to pass in that day that a man shall nourish a young cow and two sheep." Also in ver. 23, "And it shall come to pass in that day, *that* every place shall be, where there were a thousand vines at a thousand silverlings, it shall be for briers and thorns." Or this: "In Judah is God known; his name is great in Israel. In Salem also is his tabernacle, and his dwelling-place in Zion. There brake He the arrows of the bow, the shield, and the sword, and the battle. Thou art more glorious and excellent than the mountains of prey. The stout-hearted are spoiled, they have slept their sleep: and none of the men of might have found their hands. At thy rebuke, O God of Jacob, both the chariot and horse are cast into a deep sleep" (Ps. lxxvi. 1–6). Or this: "God came from Teman, and the Holy One from Mount Paran. His glory covered the heavens, and the earth was full of his praise. And his brightness was as the light; He had horns coming out of his hand: and there was the hiding of his power. Before Him went the pestilence, and burning coals went forth at his feet. He stood and measured the earth: He beheld, and drove asunder the nations; and the

---

esteemed so necessary to be understood with the former, that, as *the human body without the soul is dead, so the letter of Scripture, without the spirit, is dead also*. Nay, it is a *killing and condemning word* only to them that have it. As St. Paul expressly says, ' The letter killeth, but the spirit giveth life' (2 Cor. iii. 16)."—*Holloway's Letter and Spirit*, vol. i., int. pp. v., vi.

"The twofold sense of the Word bears a resemblance to body and soul, the literal sense being like the body and the internal sense like the soul; and as the body lives by the soul, so the literal sense lives by the internal; the life of the Lord flowing through the latter into the former, according to the affection of the person who reads it."—(*A. C.* 2311.)

"According to the opinion of the Essenes, the sacred Scriptures, like man, are composed of body and soul; of the outward letter and the inward spirit."—(*Geschicte, Lehren, and Meinangen aller religiosen Secten der Juden*, by *P. Beer Brunn*, 1822, vol. i., p. 68.)

everlasting mountains were scattered, the perpetual hills did bow: his ways are everlasting. I saw the tents of Cushan in affliction: and the curtains of the land of Midian did tremble. Was the Lord displeased against the rivers? was thine anger against the rivers? was thy wrath against the sea, that thou didst ride upon thine horses and thy chariots of salvation? Thy bow was quite naked, according to the oaths of the tribes, even thy word. Thou didst cleave the earth with rivers. The mountains saw thee, and they trembled: the overflowing of the water passed by: the deep uttered his voice, and lifted up his hands on high. The sun and moon stood still in their habitation: at the light of thine arrows they went, and at the shining of thy glittering spear" (Hab. iii. 3-11). Or where the prophet says, "And it shall come to pass in that day, that the light shall not be clear nor dark: but it shall be one day which shall be known to the Lord, not day nor night: but it shall come to pass that at evening-time it shall be light. And it shall be in that day, that living waters shall go out from Jerusalem; half of them toward the former sea, and half of them toward the hinder sea: in summer and in winter shall it be. And this shall be the plague wherewith the Lord will smite all the people that have fought against Jerusalem; their flesh shall consume away while they stand upon their feet, and their eyes shall consume away in their holes, and their tongue shall consume away in their mouth. In that day shall there be upon the bells of the horses, HOLINESS UNTO THE LORD; and the pots in the Lord's house shall be like the bowls before the altar. Yea, every pot in Jerusalem and in Judah shall be holiness unto the LORD of Hosts" (Zech. xiv. 6, 7, 8, 12, 20, 21).

"Without the spiritual (or internal) sense," says Swedenborg, "it is impossible for any one to know why the prophet Jeremiah was commanded to buy himself a girdle, and not to draw it through the waters, but to go to Euphrates, and hide it there in a hole in the rock (Jer. xiii. 1-7); or why Ezekiel the prophet was commanded to make a razor pass upon his head and upon his beard, and afterwards to divide them, and to burn a third part in the midst of the city, and to smite a third part with the sword, and to scatter a third part in the wind, and to bind a little of them in his skirts, and at last to cast them into the midst of the fire (Ezek. v. 1-4); or why Hosea was twice commanded to take to himself a harlot to wife (Hos. i. 2-9; iii. 2, 3); or what is signified by all things appertaining to the tabernacle: as by the ark, the mercy-seat, the cherubim, the candlestick, the altar of incense, the shew-bread on the table, and veils and curtains. Who would know, without the spiritual sense, what is signified by Aaron's holy garments; as by his coat, his cloak, the ephod, the urim and thummim, the mitre, and several things besides? Or, without the spiritual sense, who would know what is signified by all those particulars which were enjoined concerning burnt-offerings, sacrifices, meat-offerings; and also concerning Sabbaths and feasts? The truth is, that nothing was enjoined, be it ever so minute, but what was significative of something appertaining to the Lord, to heaven, and to the Church. From these few instances, then, it may be plainly seen that there is a spiritual sense[19] in all and every part of the Word." (S. S. 16.)

If we turn our attention to the preceptive portions of the Gospels, usually regarded as so plain and practical, we shall be surprised to find how much there is which could not be literally observed without breaking up all kinds of human association, and destroying all capacity for usefulness, affording indisputable evidence that they were only designed to be spiritually understood and obeyed, in which case each expression teems with "life." To instance only two or three passages from the Lord's Sermon on the Mount, as where he says, "And if thy right eye offend thee, pluck it out, and cast it from thee: for it is profitable for thee that one of thy members should perish, and not that thy whole body should be cast into hell. And if thy right hand offend thee, cut it off, and cast it from thee: for it is profitable for thee that one of thy members should perish, and not that thy whole body should be cast into hell." "But I say unto you, that ye resist not evil: but whosoever shall smite thee on thy right cheek, turn to him the other also. And if any man will sue thee at the law, and

---

[19] "The Scriptures resemble man. As a man consists of three parts,—a rational mind, a sensitive soul, and a visible body,—so the Scriptures have a threefold sense, a literal sense, corresponding with the body; a moral sense, analogous to the soul; and a mystical or spiritual sense, analogous to the rational mind."

"The literal sense is perceived by every attentive reader. The moral sense is somewhat more difficult to be discovered. But the mystic [or inmost] sense none can discover with certainty, unless they are wise men, and also taught of God."—(*Origen, De Principiis*, lib. iv., Rom. v., a Levit. opp. tom. ii., p. 209.)

"The literal meaning," says Mr. Isaac Williams, "for the most part, is as the body, the spiritual meaning as the soul; as the soul is united with the body, so must the literal and spiritual meaning be held together; both are necessary for the life of the written Word. And though the latter be considered usually as the latent and interior sense, yet it is often so obvious and Scriptural, that it speaks, as it were, visibly through the letter, *illuminates* it, and gives it its character."—*Williams' Beginning of the Book of Genesis*, pp. 32, 75.

It might be objected against the truth of the science of correspondences that, from the apostolic times to the present, those who have held that there is a spiritual sense in the Word of God have not understood it. But it may be answered, that most of the prophecies were hidden from the prophets (Matt. xiii. 16, 17, 35); and that the disciples did not understand the nature of the Lord's "*Kingdom*," even while they proclaimed that it was "*nigh at hand.*" (Luke xxiv. 21.)

THE MERE LITERAL SENSE INDEFENSIBLE.

take away thy coat, let him have thy cloak also. And whosoever shall compel thee to go a mile, go with him twain. Give to him that asketh thee, and from him that would borrow of thee, turn not thou away" (Matt. v. 29, 30, 39, 40, 41, 42).

Even the preceptive portions of the Holy Word, such as the Lord's Sermon on the Mount, cannot be understood when viewed in their merely literal sense. When viewed, however, as to their spiritual import, they are seen to overflow in every sentence with infinite wisdom, and to teem with divine life.[20]

But these are the solemn declarations of the inspired Word, taken promiscuously from the sacred pages. Who, I ask, can comprehend them? Who can explain their import? Who can see their reference to righteousness, conversion, regeneration, sanctification, and salvation,—to promote which they must unquestionably have been inspired and written,—unless it be admitted that they have an internal and spiritual sense? And if this be admitted, it follows of necessity that a rule exists by which that sense can with certainty be drawn forth; or otherwise the Word would be a mockery of human reason, and a snare to the simple heart, unworthy of infinite intelligence. From the book of Genesis to the book of Revelation, thousands of passages are to be found equally as mysterious and difficult to understand in the mere letter; and their constant occurrence in the Word of God at once proves the necessity of some rational and invariable law to interpret the whole, and the probability of its existence.

---

[20] "The whole law of Moses is like to a living creature, whose body is the literal sense; but the soul, the more inward and hidden meaning, covered under the sense of the letter."—Philo Judæus. Prefixed, by Henry More, as a motto to his *Defence of* "*Conjectura Cabbalistica,*" or "*Threefold Cabbala, and Triple Interpretation of the three first Chapters of Genesis,* ed. 1653. This author's Treatise on Iconisms, is described by Clowes "to be nothing else but an imperfect sketch of the doctrine of correspondence."

CHAPTER III.

That the Divinity and Sanctity of the Word of God is the Consequence of its Containing an Internal or Spiritual Sense.

IN what, let us now ask, does the peculiar divinity and sanctity of the Holy Word consist? By what arguments or reasonings is the indubitable certainty of its truth to be established? and how is it to be distinguished from works of human composition?

These are most vital and momentous inquiries, and cannot be answered without thoughtful reflection and laborious research. In this work I can only profess to offer a few brief and general remarks. Happy shall I be, however, if the reader should be sufficiently interested to follow the principles which are advanced, until it is rationally perceived and acknowledged that the Holy Word, throughout all its inspired pages, teems with the divine "spirit," and is filled with the divine "life" (John vi. 63).[21]

I would begin by observing, then, at once, that the divinity and sanctity of the Word of God consist in its being an inspired revelation of the divine will and wisdom, from the mouth of the Lord himself; and as these are not apparent in the letter, the Word must contain a heavenly, spiritual sense, which is, as it were, its breathing, living soul.

The spirit of the Word is united with the letter, and pervades every sentence and expression, just as the soul is contained in the body; and as the life of the soul, momentarily derived from God, descends and flows into and animates every corporeal organ, so the divine life of the Lord flows into the minds of humble and prepared believers, as in faith and with affection they read the inspired pages. That world

---

[21] The position that the phrase ὁ λόγος τοῦ θεοῦ, is never used of the written Word, or the Revelation of the will of God, contained in the Scriptures, must appear unwarranted to those who impartially and carefully examine the following passages: cxix. Ps., xxx. Prov., 5; vii. Mark, 13; x. John, 35; iv. Heb., 12.—(*Henderson's Div. Inspir.*, 2d ed., n. s., p. 488.)

"The phrase Word of God implies that the [plenarily inspired] Scriptures are God's both in matter and expression."—(*Carson's Theor. of Inspira.*, pp. 25, 42.)

of wonders, the human frame, consists of forms in endless variety, exactly corresponding with principles and faculties of the mind which inhabit it, and as all the parts and portions of the nervous tissues and muscular fibre are harmoniously combined, and the minutest vessel, the smallest artery and vein, the slenderest and most delicate filament, are one and all required to make up the perfection of the whole; and as each receives its vitalized influx for the sake of some specific usefulness, so each part and expression of the Holy Word is the receptacle of an inward spirit, has its peculiar analogy, its appropriate place, and its distinct use; and contributes to the harmony, the completeness, the divine perfection of the whole.

While, therefore, the letter of the Word, especially in the Old Testament, appears to treat much of natural objects and appearances, the inward sense treats only of spiritual, celestial, and divine realities. The very title, "THE WORD OF GOD," implies a revelation of his existence and nature, his boundless love and wisdom, his infinite purposes and thoughts, together with the existence, the capacities, the responsibility, and the destiny of the human soul, and the infallible doctrines and truths, essentially for man in the relation in which he stands to his great Creator; and the knowledge of which, without such supernatural communications, it were impossible to attain (Job xi. 7, 8). And if this be the real character of the Sacred Writings, they must, in consequence, be full of interior truth and goodness as emanations from the divine mind, yet adapted to the comprehension of men on earth. The Apostle Paul, therefore, declares, "All Scripture is given by inspiration of God;"[22] or, as the

---

[22] "The verb '*is*,' which constitutes the whole affirmation, is deficient in the original Greek, and is applied by the English translators as an index to their interpretation of the passage. The sentence undoubtedly requires a verb *somewhere*, but the place of its insertion depends upon the judgment of the translator. In the received version it stands in the first clause:—'All Scripture *is* given by inspiration of God, etc.' Baxter, Grotius, Schleusner, and others, render the passage thus: 'All Scripture given by inspiration of God, is also profitable, etc.' The original, I think, will admit, without violence, of either rendering, though inclined myself to regard the common version as more concordant to the Greek idiom than the other. But even thus translated, the *theopneusty* ascribed to the '*all*,' or every 'Scripture,' does not in itself define the *precise nature* or *degree* of the inspiration affirmed. That portion of the Scripture which is justly denominated the *Word of God* is *essential divinity itself*—a verbal embodiment of the *eternal truth* which forms a constituent part of the Divine nature. While, therefore, we recognize a general *theopneusty*, or *divine breathing*, ascribed by Paul to *all* the books constituting the Old Testament Scriptures, we still regard this as something incomparably lower than that *plenary* divine afflatus under which *the Word*, strictly so called, was written."—*Prof. Bush's Reply to Dr. Woods*, pp. 31, 32.

" Every writing divinely inspired [is] also profitable for instruction, for conviction [of error], for recovery [to that which is right], for training up in righteousness." "The venerable Syriac version, whose antiquity is almost, if not quite, Apostolic, reads 'For

Greek term θεοπνευστος has been aptly and emphatically translated, "God-breathed," or God-inspired, or divinely inspired (2 Tim. iii. 16, 17), that is, full of the Divine Spirit and the Divine life,—"All Scripture divinely inspired of God is profitable for doctrine, for reproof, for correction, for instruction in righteousness, that the man of God may be perfect, thoroughly furnished unto all good works." And the Apostle Peter says, "Knowing this first, that no prophecy of Scripture is [or cometh] of any private interpretation. For the prophecy came not in old time by the will of man; but holy men of God spake as they were moved [φερομενοι, borne away, carried out of themselves] by the Holy Spirit" (2 Pet. i. 21); or, as Dean Alford renders it, "had utterance from God, being moved by the Holy Spirit." Josephus, the Jewish historian, speaking of the plenarily inspired books of the Old Testament, adds, that they were written according to πνευστιά, or the inspiration that comes from God; and Philo, a contemporary Jewish philosopher, calls the Scripture φεοψιστ oracles, that is to say, oracles given under the immediate agency and dictation of God.

The ideas of men and angels naturally embody themselves in suitable sounds and expressions—the tones express the sensibilities of the will, and the words reveal the thoughts of the intellect. In this we are images of God, whose voice has spoken in audible terms from most ancient times, as an intelligible dictate,—who wrote on stone tablets the Decalogue, or "ten words,"—and commanded and inspired seers and prophets what to speak and what to write. What are words but symbols of ideas, between which there is the closest correspondence and the most intimate dependence; and as without man's words

---

every writing which has been written by the Spirit is valuable for instruction,' etc. The Vulgate confirms this interpretation:— 'Omnis, scriptura divinitus inspirata, utilis est ad docendum,' etc."—(*Dr. P. Smith's* "*Testim. to the Messiah*," vol. i., p. 27.)

Dr. A. Clarke translates this passage as follows, and is supported by the best authorities. "The particle και (*and*)," he says, "is omitted by almost all the versions, and by many of the Fathers, and certainly does not agree well with the text." "All Scripture given by inspiration of God, is profitable for doctrine," etc.—(*Comment. in loc.*)

Dr. Wardlaw has rendered it thus: "Every divinely inspired writing is profitable for instruction, conviction, reformation, and education in righteousness." And adds, that "the first thing affirmed in these words is the plenary inspiration of the Old Testament Scriptures."—(*Introd. to Bishop Hall's Contempl.*, pp. xii., xiii.)

Professor Stuart renders the first clause, "Every Scripture inspired of God," or "God inspirited."—(*Canon*, p. 304.)

It has also been translated by others, "All Scripture divinely inspired of God." And, "Every God-breathed writing." "Theopneustos" has been construed by some with an active signification, of which it appears to be susceptible. It is then rendered, "*divinely-breathing;*" and it is understood to express the fact that the inspired Word is full of God; that through it as a medium, God breathes forth, or communicates, in human language, his will and wisdom to mankind.

we cannot comprehend his human and finite ideas, so without God's words we cannot understand his infinite and divine ideas. The very *language*, then, of the Word of God, if indeed He be the Author, must be inspired as well as the *ideas*.

The words of a man contain only his finite thought and intelligence; and by hearing or reading them, and attending to the sense they are designed to convey, we become more or less acquainted with the prevailing sentiments of a finite mind; but the Word of God has an INFINITE BEING for its author, and eternal purposes to serve; for thus saith the Lord, "My thoughts are not your thoughts, neither are your ways my ways. For as the heavens are higher than the earth, so are my ways higher than your ways, and my thoughts than your thoughts" (Isa. lv. 8, 9). Yea, He has moreover solemnly declared, that "HIS NAME is called THE WORD OF GOD" (Rev. xix. 13).[23]

Whatever, then, may be the appearance of the letter, or the surface of the outward covering, the Holy Word must be designed to accommodate and convey to man, as far as possible, in a way precisely adapted to the condition and circumstances of his mind, in all ages, the infinite truth, the perfect intelligence, the unbounded love, and the unchangeable goodness,—or, in other words, the divine will and wisdom—of the Supreme Being, of which it must be the rich depository. Thus, Divine Revelation could never be designed to instruct us in mere human history or physical science, in the laws of astronomy or the facts of geology, in the elementary constitution of the earth or the political events of empires,—for we acquire all this kind of knowledge in an external way, by the exercise of the outward senses, and without the aid of special inspiration: but must have been designed to instruct man in the subjects and objects of genuine religion,—in spiritual and celestial, yea, divine, wisdom,—in the holy operations of repentance and conversion, of charity and faith, of righteousness and truth; thus, in our duty towards God and our duty towards our neighbor, our regeneration and final salvation. These must have been the objects of Divine Revelation,—the only objects worthy of an all-wise and benevolent Deity. Without such an inspired revelation, thus mercifully adapted to his states and necessities, man could never have known anything concerning his soul, or

---

[23] "Among the numerous passages of the New Testament in which the phrase, *the Word of God* occurs, there is not one in which it signifies the Bible, or in which that word could be substituted for it without a manifest absurdity."—*Thirlwall's Charge*, 1863, p. 105.

his eternal life, or even of the existence of God, still less could he have known anything of religion, which is the love of God above all things and his neighbor as himself, and on which revealed commands it is declared by the Lord himself, "hang all the law and the prophets" (Matt. xxii. 37–40); or on which depend all the unspeakable blessings of salvation.

That the Word of God, however, contains faithful historical relations, records which are literally true, prophecies which have been permitted to have a general accomplishment even in the world, and relates true miracles, that an external reverence for its contents, apart from superstition, might be thereby possessed among the most sensual of the human race, is freely and fully accorded. But this, great as are the objects attained, is wholly insufficient to prove that it is a series of books dictated by the immediate inspiration of God.

"Who does not see," says the Rev. S. Noble, in an admirably sustained argument on this subject, "that the difference between compositions that are really the Word of God and the compositions of men must be as great as between the works of God and the works of men? And wherein does the latter difference most remarkably consist? Is it not in the interior organization which the works of God possess, beyond what appears in their outward form? When we look at a picture or a statue, which are among the most exquisite productions of human ingenuity, after we have seen the surface, we have seen the whole: and although there are pieces of curious mechanism, which contain a complication of parts within their outside case, this only carries us one step farther: when we look at any of the parts, we see the whole:—the interior texture of the material of which they are composed not being the work of the human artist, but of the Divine Creator. Whereas, when we look at any of the works of his omnipotent hand, beautiful and exact as they are in their outward form, still, the most beautiful and wonderful parts of them are within. Some of these hidden wonders are discoverable to the diligent inquirer by means of dissections and by the aid of glasses: but when the most ingenious investigator has extended his researches into the interior construction of any natural production to the utmost limits that human means can conduct him, he must, if he is a wise man, be convinced, that what he has thus discovered, is, after all, but general and superficial, compared with the greater wonders which still lie concealed within. The most expert anatomist never, for instance, reached the seat of the soul,—still less the principle of consciousness and life of which the soul itself is merely the organ; all which, and even the material forms which are their first envelopes, still lie beyond the most subtile forms that the gross observation of the senses can discover. The farther, however, the observation of the senses can extend, the greater are the wonders which appear. Just so it is with the Word of God; and so it must be, if it has in reality God for its Author. To suppose the literal sense of the Word of God to be all that it contains, because nothing more is obvious to a superficial inspection, is just as reasonable as to affirm that the human body consists of nothing but skin, because this is all that meets the unassisted eye: but as the researches of anatomists have assured us that within the skin which covers our frame there are innumerable forms of use and beauty, each of which consists again of innumerable vessels and fibres; whilst, after science has carried her discoveries to the utmost, the principle that imparts life to the whole still eludes the search: so the letter of the Holy Word, which may be regarded as *its* skin, includes within it innumerable spiritual truths, adapted in some measure to the apprehension of spiritually-minded men, but more completely to the intellects of purely spiritual beings; whilst the Essential Divine Wisdom, which gives life to the whole, is beyond the comprehension of the highest finite intelligence, and can only be known to its Infinite Original. And such must be the character of the whole of the Word of God, as well of those passages which afford a clear instructive sense in the letter as of those which do not: for the Word of God, to be truly so, must be like itself throughout, and must everywhere be composed upon one uniform principle. Every mind that reflects deeply upon the subject, will, I am persuaded, see, that to deny the Holy Word to possess such contents as we have described, is equivalent to denying it to have God for its Author."—*Plenary Inspiration of the Scriptures Asserted*, &c., pp. 63–8. I take the present opportunity of strongly recommending this able work to the reader."[24]

---

[24] "The spiritual sense of the Psalms," says Bishop Horne, "is and must be peculiar to the Scriptures; because of those persons and transactions only, which are there mentioned and recorded, can it be affirmed for certain that they were designed to be figurative. And should any one attempt to apply the narrative of Alexander's expedition, by Quintus Curtius, or the commentaries of Cæsar, as the New Testament writers have done, and taught us to do to the histories of the Old, he would find himself unable to proceed three steps with consistency and propriety. The argument, therefore, which would infer the absurdity of supposing the Scriptures to have a spiritual sense, from the absurdity of supposing history or poems merely human to have it, is inconclusive; the sacred writings differing, in this respect, from all other writings in the world, as much as the nature of the transactions which they relate, differs from that of all other transactions; and the Author who relates them differs from all other authors."—*Comm. on the Psalms*, pref., p. xvi.

CHAPTER IV.

The Laws of the Science of Correspondences Stated and Confirmed.—The Doctrine of Correspondences well known to the Ancients, and its Corruption the Origin of all Idolatry and Superstition.

"IT is universally confessed," says Swedenborg, "that the Word is from God, is divinely inspired, and of consequence holy; but still it has remained a secret to this day in what part of the Word its divinity resides, inasmuch as in the letter it appears like a common writing, composed in a strange style, neither so sublime, nor so elegant, nor so lucid as that which distinguishes the best secular compositions. Hence it is, that whosoever worships nature instead of God, or in preference to God, and in consequence of such worship makes himself and his own proprium [or selfhood] the centre and fountain of his thoughts, instead of deriving them out of heaven from the Lord, may easily fall into error concerning the Word, or into contempt for it, and say within himself, as he reads it, What is the meaning of this passage? What is the meaning of that? Is it possible this should be divine? Is it possible that God, whose wisdom is infinite, should speak in this manner? Where is its sanctity, or whence can it be derived, but from superstition and credulity? with other suggestions of a similar nature.

"But he who reasons thus does not reflect that Jehovah the Lord, who is God of heaven and earth, spake the Word by Moses and the prophets, and that consequently it must be divine truth, inasmuch as what Jehovah himself speaks can be nothing else; nor does such an one consider that the Lord, who is the same with Jehovah, spake the word written by the Evangelists,—many parts from his own mouth, and the rest from the Spirit of his mouth, which is the Holy Spirit. Hence it is He himself declares, that in his words there is life, and that He is that light which enlightens, and that He is the truth. The natural man, however, cannot still be persuaded to believe that the Word is divine truth itself, in which is divine wisdom and divine life,

...ATED AND CONFIRMED.   39

...y its style, in which no such things

...e in which the Word is written is a divine
...ther style, however sublime and excellent it
...comparable; for it is as darkness compared to
...of the Word is of such a nature as to contain what
...ry verse, in every word, and in some cases in every let-
...nence the Word conjoins man with the Lord, and opens
... There are two things which proceed from the Lord,—divine
...and divine wisdom, or, what is the same thing, divine good and
divine truth: for divine good is of divine love itself, and divine truth
is of the divine wisdom: and the Word in its essence is both of these;
and inasmuch as it conjoins man with the Lord, and opens heaven, as
just observed, therefore the Word fills the man who reads it, under
the Lord's influence and not under the influence of proprium or self,
with the good of love and the truth of wisdom,—his will with the
good of love, and his understanding with the truth of wisdom.

"Hence man has life by and through the Word. Lest, therefore,
mankind should remain any longer in doubt concerning the Divinity
of the Word, the internal sense thereof is revealed, which in its essence
is spiritual, and which is to the external sense, which is natural, what
the soul is to the body. This internal sense is the Spirit which gives
life to the letter; wherefore this sense will evince the divinity and
sanctity of the Word, and may convince even the natural man, if he
is willing to be convinced."—S. S. 1-4; A. E. 1065.

In the New Church, then, and for the benefit of all who are willing
to receive the truth, it has been disclosed,—and the discovery is the
most important that has taken place since the completion of the New
Testament, that the Holy Word is so written, that each expression
corresponds to some distinct spiritual idea, that is, an idea which relates to the Lord, the spiritual world, and the human mind; to goodness, truth, and their activities, or to love, wisdom, and life. Now
these spiritual ideas, together with those of the letter, are shown to
be so wonderfully connected as to form one perfect unbroken chain
of eternal truth from first to last,—one grand series of heavenly particulars, which constitutes the internal and external, or the spiritual
and literal senses of the Word of God. The laws which thus unfold
the true character of the Sacred Oracles are denominated laws of
correspondence. This term is derived from *con*, *re*, and *spondeo*, meaning radically *to answer with*, or *to agree*, denoting, in the sense in which

it is used in the New Church, the reciprocal relation of objects in higher and lower degrees,—a mutual union of the internal with the external,—the harmony of substance and form,—the concord of cause and effect. From this definition it may be perceived that the science of correspondences is not, as some have rashly asserted, a mere clever invention, an arbitrary device, an imaginary theory, a fanciful conceit,—but that it is a systematic, uniform, and certain rule of interpretation, founded upon the nature, qualities, and uses of all terrestrial objects, and all the phenomena of life.[25] These have one and all the most exact correspondence with eternal realities and mental operations, for natural objects and truths are the mirrors in which spiritual subjects and infinite wisdom are reflected.[26] Hence, man has been

[25] The want of a strict rule of interpretation, for which the world was at that time so totally unprepared, is thus acknowledged by Augustine, "where he lays down the principle which guided him in the investigation of historical types." [*Tract for the Times*, lxxxix., p. 38.] "These secrets of Divine Scripture we *trace out as we may, one more or less aptly than another*, but as becomes faithful men, holding thus much for certain; that not without some kind of foreshadowing of future events, were these things done and recorded [in the Word]; and that to Christ only, and his Church, the City of God, are they to be referred in every instance."—*De Civ. Dei*, xvi. 2. By the Science of Correspondences, however, all distrust and uncertainty are removed.

"The severe schooles shall never laugh me out of the philosophy of Hermes, that this visible world is but a picture of the invisible, wherein, as in a pourtrait, things are not truly, but in equivocal shapes, and as they counterfeit some more real substance in that invisible Fabrick."—Sir Thomas Browne. Ob. A.D. 1682.

Milton says,   "What if earth
Be but the shadow of heav'n; and things therein
Each to other like, more than on earth is thought."
   Paradise Lost, book v., lines 574-6.

A similar idea is thus expressed by Barrow: "What we see in *a lower degree somewhere to exist*, doth probably *otherwise exist in a higher degree*."—*Works*, vol. iv., p. 170.

"The Platonists," says Archbishop Leighton. "divide the world into two, the sensible and intellectual world, they imagine the one to be the type of the other, and that sensible and spiritual things are stamped, as it were, with the same stamp. These sentiments are not unlike the notions which the masters of the Cabalistical doctrine among the Jews held concerning God's SEPHIROTH and SEAL, wherewith, according to them, all the worlds, and everything in them, are stamped or sealed; and these are probably near akin to what Lord Bacon calls his '*paralella signicula;*' and *symbolizantes schematizmi*. According to this hypothesis, these parables, which are often taken from *natural things* to illustrate such as are *divine*, will not be *similitudes taken entirely at pleasure*, but are often in a great measure *founded in nature*, and the things themselves."—*Leighton's Works*, vol. iv., p. 156.

[26] "Figures taken from natural things and actions are introduced into the Word of God to express divine things and actions, in such a manner, that, by looking upon one, we may, as it were in a picture, behold the other."—*Honert's Institut. Theolog.*, etc., part 2.

"It is not a little remarkable that, according to Prescott, the Peruvian Mythology, before the conquest, was 'not unlike that of Hindostan.' 'They adopted also a notion,' says he, 'not unlike that professed by some of the schools of ancient philosophy, that everything on earth had its archetype or idea, *its mother*, as they emphatically styled it, which they held sacred, as in some sort its spiritual essence.'"—*Conq. of Peru*, vol. i., p. 37.

"Bacon hath wisely observed, that the works of God minister a singular help and preservative against unbelief and error: our Saviour, as he saith, having laid before us two books or volumes to study; first, the *Scriptures*, revealing the will of God, and then the *creatures*, expressing his power; whereof the *latter is a key unto the former*."—*Bacon's Adv. of Learning*, b. 1. Such was the piety and penetration of this great man.

emphatically called by the ancients a *microcosm*, or little world, and considered as an epitome of the *macrocosm*, or great universe ;[27] and as the lower or natural region of the mind is thus the world in its least effigy, so the superior or spiritual region of the mind is a heaven in *its* least effigy, on which account man may also be called a *microuranos*, or little heaven (T. C. R. 604). And a fragment of the very earliest philosophy which has been handed down to us, attributed to Hermes Trismegistus (the Greek name for Thoth, the personification of Egyptian wisdom), affirms, that "there is nothing in the heavens which is not in the earth in an earthly form; and there is nothing on the earth which is not in the heavens in a heavenly form."[28]

For as the indefinite particulars of which the universe is composed

---

"For it will be found true, that the invisible things of God, that is, the things concerning his Being and his Power, and the economy of his spiritual kingdom, which are the objects of our faith, are *clearly seen from the creation of the world,* and *understood by the things that are made.*"—*Jones's Sermon on the Nat. Evid. of Christianity,* preached 1787.

"There was an opinion [I should rather call it a tradition] among some heathen philosophers that the world is a parable, the literal or bodily part of which is manifest to all men, while the inward meaning is hidden, as the soul in the body, the moral in the fable, or the interpretation in the parable." "We may call the world a fable, or parable; in which there is an outward appearance of visible things, with an inward sense, which is hidden as the soul under the body."—*Sallust Peri Theown.,* cap. 3. *Jones's Lec. on the Fig. Lang. of Scrip.,* p. 70.

[27] Philo says that "man is a little world, and that the world is one great man;" and Origen calls man "*Minorem Mundum,* a Microcosme."—*H. More's Conj. Cab., Defence of,* p. 205.

"Out of all beings known to us, *man* is the most elevated; as in his form, at the same time one and complex, he contains all inferior existences."—*Abbe De Lamennais, Equisse D'une Philosophie,* vol. i., p. 409. See *Morell's Hist. of Mod. Philos.,* 2d ed., vol., ii. p. 297.

"Properly understood, earthly substances are the types, representatives, and shadows of heavenly things."—*Dr. A. Clarke's Commentary,* vol. v., p. 562.

"Davis, in his *History of the Chinese,* tells us that the Chinese physiologists expressly call man a *little universe,* or microcosm; to which they extend the dual principle, as originating the existence, as well as maintaining the order and harmony, of the natural universe."

"The universe is but a great mirror of the mind of man."—*Gilfillan's Lit. Port.,* p. 8.

"Now this earthly world which we do see is an exact picture and pattern of the spiritual, heavenly world which we do not see. As Solomon says in the Proverbs, 'The things which are seen are the doubles of the things which are not seen.'"—*Kingsley's Village Sermons,* p. 187.

[28] "Things invisible to the carnal eye are clearly seen by the enlightened eye of the mind—being understood by the lively and sensible description of them in the things that are made. The material world and its objects are pictures or similitudes, in some view or other, of the actings of God in the spiritual world. Upon this plan the lively oracles of truth appear to have been written."—*Serle's Hor. Solit.,* p. 137.

"The whole of the visible creation is but the outside of a vast magnificent house or temple, whose inside is heaven, or the angelic kingdom; and this again is but the outside of a temple or house still more vast and magnificent, whose inside is Jesus Christ, the only living and eternal Lord our God."—*Clowes' Miscell. Thoughts,* p. 53.

"That the teaching of Nature is symbolical, none, we think, can deny."—*Neale and Webb's Introd. Ess. to Durandus on Symb.,* p. xlv.

"Philosophy, fable, poetry, and the most refined metaphysics, have not been able to form an idea of the universe which surrounds us, without at the same time imagining another universe of which this is the image."—*Richer's La Nouv. Jerus. on Correspon.,* vol. i., 2d part, p. 355.

must have had a divine origin, so they must all bear analogies to each other, and reflect infinite intelligence and goodness: they must, therefore, of necessity be invested with a moral, a spiritual, yea, a divine significance, the visible objects of the outward world exactly corresponding with invisible realities in the world within, and these again to the infinite principles in the divine mind, as their secondary and primary cause of existence and subsistence.[29] All this is in exact

---

[29] Between the work of creation and preservation on the one hand, and that of redemption [and the author might have added also, most truly, that of regeneration] on the other, there seems to be a great analogy; as the sacred writers frequently borrow images from one to explain the other. 'The invisible things of God from the creation of the world are clearly seen.' Things visible do not only prove the *divine power* and *Godhead*,—the existence and glorious perfections of God,—but they also serve as a mirror to represent the invisible things of God. And between these two representatives there is such a correspondence, that an attentive view of things natural and temporal may help us to form better conceptions of things spiritual and eternal. . . . Without this effect, philosophy is but a vain amusement. But when things visible correspond to what is revealed in the Scriptures concerning the invisible things of God, and these correspondences are traced under the guidance of the written Word, these two great books [creation and Revelation] help to explain each other."—*Cosmology: Pub. at Bath*, 1791. Tom. iv., p. 180.

"The world is certainly a great and stately volume of natural things, and may not improperly be styled the hieroglyphics of a better."—*Fruits of Solitude*, p. 3.

"Nature is a book written on both sides, within and without, in which the finger of God is distinctly visible; a species of Holy Writ in a bodily form: a glorious panegyric on God's omnipotence expressed in the most visible symbols."—SCHLEGEL.

In the book of Sohar, a similar sentence occurs: "*Quodcunque in terrâ est, id etiam in Cœlo est, et nulla res tam exigua est in Mundo, quæ non alii simili, quæ in Cœlo est, correspondeat.*"

"All things in nature are prophetic outlines of divine operations, God not merely *speaking* parables, but *doing* them."—TERTULLIAN: *De Resur.*, c. 12.

"Julian, in an oration, expresses himself thus: 'Not view and contemplate the heaven and world with the same eyes that oxen and horses do, but so as from that which is visible to their outward senses, to discern and discover another invisible nature under it."—*Jul. Orat.*, iv., p. 148. *Cited by Cudworth, Intel. Syst.*, vol. ii., p. 260.

"Plato, in his Timæus, calls the world 'a made or created image of the eternal gods.' By which eternal gods he there doubtless meant that 'first,' and 'second,' and 'third,' which, in his second epistle to Dionysius, he makes to be uncreated principles of all things; that is, his trinity, by whose concurrent efficiency and Providence, and according to whose image and likeness, the whole was made, as a grand chain of resulting effects."—See *Cudworth's Intel. Syst.*, vol. ii., p. 367.

"The world may well be called an image; it depending upon that above [as an image in a glass], which is threefold."—*Plotinus, cited by Cudworth*, vol. ii., p. 315.

"Empedocles held, according to the Pythagorean doctrine, that there are two worlds, the one intellectual, the other sensible: the former being the *model* or archetype of the latter." [25 Exod., 40.]—See *Simplici in Physic. Arist.*, also *Plut. de Placitis Phil.*, b. 1, c. 20.

"The symbolic language of the prophets is *almost* a science of itself. None can fully comprehend the depth, sublimity, and force of their writings who are not thoroughly acquainted with the peculiar and appropriate imagery they were accustomed to use."—BISHOP VAN MILDERT.

"The visible world throughout is a pattern of the invisible."—*Jones's Lect. on the Fig. Lang. of Scrip.*, p. 34.

"When the maker of the world becomes an Author, his word must be as perfect as his work."—*Jones's Lectures on the Figurative Lang. of the Holy Scrip.*, p. 1.

"If God made this world the particular kind of world which he is found to have made it, in order that it might in due time preach to mankind about himself, and about his providence:—if He contrived beforehand the germination of seeds, the growth of plants, the analogies of animal life,—all, evidently, in order that they might furnish illustrations of his teaching; and that so

agreement with the teaching of the apostle Paul, when he says, "For the invisible things of Him [God] from the creation of the world are clearly seen [" being considered in his works are distinctly seen."—*Hor. Rom.*, p. 6], being understood by the things that are made, *even* his eternal power and godhead" (Rom. i. 20).

These analogies or correspondences many theologians and philosophers have admitted, from the fact that they can scarcely escape the recognition of the devout and reflective mind. Thus the author of *Tracts for the Times* (lxxxix.), speaking of the mode of interpreting the Sacred Word adopted by the early Fathers of the Christian Church, and the ground and reason of it, makes these important and suggestive remarks: "What if the whole scheme of sensible things be figurative?" "What if these [correspondences in the Jewish tabernacle and ark] are but a slight specimen of one great use which ALMIGHTY GOD would have us to make of the external world, and of its relation to the world spiritual? Certainly the form itself of speaking, with which these symbols are introduced [as made according to heavenly patterns], would seem to imply some such general rule." And again, "'That was the true light.' 'I am the true vine.' 'Who will give you the true riches?' taking for granted, in a manner,

---

great Nature's self might prove one vast parable in his hands;—*why* may not the same God, by his Eternal Spirit, have so overruled the utterance of the human agents whom He employed to write the Bible, that their historical narratives, however little their authors meant or suspected it, should embody the outline of things heavenly; and while they convey a true picture of actual events, should *also*, after a most mysterious fashion, yield in the hands of his own informing Spirit, celestial doctrine also?" "Our purpose has only been to vindicate the profundity, or rather *the fulness* of Holy Writ, and to show that under the obvious and literal meaning of the words there lies concealed a more recondite and a profounder sense—call that sense mystical, or spiritual, or Christian, or what you will. Unerringly to elicit that hidden sense is the sublime privilege of inspired writers, and they do it by allusion, by quotation, by the importation of a short phrase, by the adoption of a single word,—to an extent which no one would suspect who had not carefully studied the subject."—*Burgon's Inspiration and Interpretation*, pp. 168, 174.

"The philosophical ground on which they [the ancient nations] proceeded is this,—that *all matter or universal nature must of necessity be the form and visible idea of the essence or spirit within*. Each object in religion has thus its corresponding sign and character in one of nature; and those of nature in return are held in esteem and reverence from their consecration to the uses of religion. The extent, indeed, to which this system was carried in Egypt has at all times been proverbial. It formed the subject of expressed astonishment and secret admiration to the ancient historians of the world. The mythology of the West was, in fact, almost founded on [or rather identical with] Egyptian worship. We trace up to an Eastern origin the system of Pythagoras; the ethics of Aristotle; and even the philosophy of Plato, so far more spiritual and sublime than either; and have no question, from a comparatively abundant evidence, that the principles which appeared so great and glorious to the Greeks, existed on the Indus and the Nile ages before the first dawn of civilization in the West. The Jews, too, through every period of their varied history, were no less addicted to this fascinating study than the Eastern nations. The fact is of an extreme importance; since, in their possession of the Bible, we behold *the origin* of that philosophy which led them to the adoption of this system of correspondence."—*Tucker's Scrip. Stud., Inner Sense*, pp. 268, 269.

the fact that there was somewhere in the nature of things a true counterpart of these ordinary objects, a substance of which they were but unreal shadows; and only informing us in each case, with authority, what that counterpart and substance was." "This doctrine of correspondence between things seen and unseen, was familiar and very acceptable" [to the Fathers] (p. 165).

To the same purpose, Heylin, in his *Select Discourses*, observes, "There is an analogy betwixt the visible and invisible world, which the Scriptures declare to be the foundation of the Mosaic rites, and from which other religious ceremonies receive their fitness and utility. The terms unclean, defiled, polluted, are applicable to minds as well as bodies, and that with a propriety which is easier felt than explained. The correspondent terms of cleansing, baptizing, purifying with water, or with fire, as the case may require, or the subject can bear,—these, too, have a just and obvious signification in morals as well as naturals: for the systems of both worlds run parallel, so that realities in the superior have their respective shadows in the inferior, and are fitly represented by them" (i. 36 and 38, London, 1749).

That the natural world is full of analogies is universally acknowledged. Thus, Swainson writes:—"It is unnecessary to enforce the axiom long established by sound philosophy, that natural and moral truths are but parts of the great system of nature. Nor need we go over those arguments that have been already so ably and so powerfully urged by others, to show that every thing in this world is evidently intended to be the means of moral and intellectual improvement, to a creature made capable of perceiving in it this use. This perfect analogy between the moral and the natural world, no Christian in these days will even think of questioning, much less of disputing" (192). "Between material and immaterial, there is no other relation than that which is afforded by analogy; without this they would be widely and totally distinct; with this, they are united, and one reciprocally illustrates the other. Analogy, or symbolical representation, is, therefore, the most universal law of nature, because it embraces and extends its influence over the natural, the moral, and the spiritual world: a property which no other law yet discovered is known to possess" (193). "Things which in their essential nature are totally opposite, are found, on closer investigation, to possess mutual relations, and to be governed by the same law. Hence we discover three sorts of analogies pervading the system of nature, in the widest and most exalted application of the term: the first regards the spiritual truths of revelation; the second, those which belong only to the moral system; while the third are drawn from the phenomena of the material world" (201).—*Preliminary Discourse on the Study of Natural History, Cab. Cyclo.*, pp. 283, 290.

Another profound writer thus ably illustrates the subject of analogy in connection with religion. "While analogy," says he, "is the happy instrument of conveying light into subjects in general, it is peculiarly so when employed in elucidating the truths of religion. Here the force of contrast with which it acts is at the maximum. We bring together the things of heaven and the things of earth; and bestow on the most remote and inaccessible objects some portion of that circumstantial particularity which belongs to those present and visible. To behold truths, in themselves so high above our comprehension, in connection with those which are familiarly inculcated on us by experience, must call forth our strongest admiration, and powerfully interest us on both sides, but particularly on that of our religion. Divine wisdom then descends from its ethereal seat, as the accessor of the throne of the Eternal, and communes with us face to face, and hand to hand. We find that the subjects on which the Scripture treats are not chimeras, not creations of the fancy, which have no substantial existence; but things which ARE: things in which we live, and move, and have our being. It no longer appears to us in the light of a scheme, contrived in the bowers of philosophic seclusion, and addressing itself only to the contemplative and impassioned devotee, like the day dreams of the Koran, emerging from the gloom and solitude of the cave of Hara; but it shines forth conspicuously, as an energizing principle, as a knowledge which is power, as a work of the Lord, carried on in the passing scene, with which we cannot help sympathizing without doing violence to all the principles of our nature."—Hampden's *Essay on the Philosophical Evidences of Christianity.*

The Rev. W. Kirby, M.A., in his interesting *Bridgewater Treatise*, thus expresses himself on the same subject:—"Whoever surveys the three kingdoms of nature with any attention, will discover in every department objects that, without any affinity, appear to represent each other. Nor is this resemblance confined to forms; it extends also to character. If we begin at the bottom of the scale and ascend up to man, we shall find two descriptions in almost every class, and even tribe, of animals: one, ferocious in their aspects, often rapid in their motions, predaceous in their habits, preying upon their fellows, and living by rapine and bloodshed; while the other is quiet and harmless, making no attacks, shedding no blood, and subsisting mostly on a vegetable diet. Since God created nothing in vain, we may rest assured that this *system of representation* was established with a particular view. The most common mode of instruction is, placing certain signs or symbols before the eye of the learner, which represent sounds or ideas; and so the Great Instructor of man placed this world before him as an open, though mystical book, in which the different objects and words of a language, from the study of which he might gain wisdom of various kinds, and be instructed in such truths relating to that spiritual world to which his soul belonged, as God saw fit thus to reveal to him. In the first place, by observing that one object in nature represented another, he would be taught that all things are significant, as well as intended to act a certain part in the general drama; and further, as he proceeded to trace the analogies of character in its two great branches just alluded to, he would be led to the knowledge of the doctrine, thus symbolically revealed, that in the invisible world there are two classes of spirits,—one benevolent and beneficent, and the other malevolent and mischievous: characters which, after his fall, he would find even exemplified in individuals of his own species. [This doctrine of analogy] is a very useful and interesting study, and belongs to man as the principal inhabitant of a world stored with symbols, to ascertain what God intended to signify by the objects that He has created and placed before Him, as well as to know their natures and uses. When we recollect what the Apostle tells us (Rom. i. 20), that the 'invisible things of God from the creation of the world are clearly seen;' and that spiritual truths are reflected as by a mirror (1 Cor. xiii. 12), and shown as it were enigmatically, we shall be convinced that, in this view, the study of nature, if properly conducted, may be made of the first importance" (vol. ii., pp. 523–525).

Even Emerson admits that " words are signs of natural facts. The use of natural history," says he, " is to give us aid in supernatural history. The use of the outer creation is to give us language for the being and changes of the inward creation. Every word which is used to express a moral or intellectual fact, if traced to its root, is found to be borrowed from some material appearance.

" *Right* originally means *straight; wrong* means *twisted; spirit* primarily means *wind; transgression,* the *crossing of a line; supercilious,* the *raising of the eye-brow.* We say the heart to express emotion;

the head, to denote thought; and thought and emotion are, in their turn, words borrowed from sensible things, and now appropriated to spiritual nature. Most of the process by which this transformation is made, is hidden from us in the remote time when language was framed, but the same tendency may be daily observed in children. . . . But this origin of all words that convey a spiritual import,—so conspicuous a fact in the history of language,—is our least debt to nature. It is not words only that are emblematic; it is things which are emblematic. Every natural fact is a symbol of some spiritual fact. Every appearance in nature corresponds to some state of the mind, and that state of the mind can only be described by presenting that natural appearance as its picture. An enraged man is a lion, a cunning man is a fox, a firm man is a rock, a learned man is a torch. A lamb is innocence, a snake is subtle spite. . . . Light and darkness are our familiar expressions for knowledge and ignorance; and heat for love. . . . It is easily seen that there is nothing lucky or capricious in these analogies, but that they are constant and pervade nature. These are not the dreams of a few poets, here and there, but man is an analogist, and studies relations in all objects. . . . Because of this radical correspondence between visible things and human thoughts, savages, who have only what is necessary, converse in figures. As we go back in history, language becomes more picturesque, until its infancy, when it is all poetry; or all spiritual facts are represented by natural symbols. The same symbols are found to make the elements of all languages. It has, moreover, been observed, that the idioms of all languages approach each other in passages of the greatest eloquence and power, and as this is the first language, so it is the last. This immediate dependence of language upon nature,—this conversion of an outward phenomena into a type of somewhat in human life,— never loses its power to affect us."—*Essay on Nature*, p. 5.

The author of *Essays and Analogies* perceived, with most reflecting minds, that "Analogy is as universal as the universe itself, and every analogy, like every man, is, or includes, the natural, moral, and spiritual kingdoms" (note, p. 133).

"There is an analogy," writes an elegant author, "between external appearances of nature, as intelligible hieroglyphs, and particular affections [of the soul], strikingly exemplificative of that general harmony which subsists in all the universe. 'Material objects,' as Mr. Gilpin has justly remarked, 'being fixed in their appearances, strike every one in the same manner; whereas ideas, being different in most per-

sons upon the same subjects, will seldom serve by way of illustration.'"
—Buck's *Harmonies of Nature*, vol. ii., pp. 130, 131.

For, as Dr. Young has pertinently observed in his *Night Thoughts*, "the analogy of Nature is Christianity itself in a veil or parable."

Bishop Horne also recognized the same analogies in creation. He says: "The visible works of God are formed to lead us, under the direction of his Word, to a knowledge of those which are invisible; they give us ideas by analogy of 'a new creation,' and are ready to instruct us in the mysteries of faith and the duties of morality."
—*Pref. to Comm. on Psalms*, pp. xxiv., xxv.

In Swedenborg's *Diary*, a posthumous work printed by Dr. Tafel, of Tubingen, is the following interesting statement:

"No one [scarcely] reflects upon those things which exist in visible nature as being the images of celestial and spiritual things; as that a plant or a tree arises from its seed, and grows, and by its root and bark extracts a sap, which is the life of the plant or tree, and which is hence distributed into all its interior or central parts in like manner as spiritual things should relate to celestial things. Moreover, all things, even the minutest in the plant and tree, respect the fruit as their end, that is, the renovation, and hence the perpetuity, of the life of the tree. The same is the case with all fruits, even with those which are enclosed in hard shells, within which are the *nuclei* or fruits. The shells and the various surfaces, one within another, by which the juice [or sap] is conveyed to the interior and inmost principles until the fruit is ripened, represent correspondent things in man when being regenerated, namely, the natural, scientific, rational, and intellectual things; which [latter] are spiritual, and which in this manner, as from a common plane, divided into infinitely various ways, can be conveyed and distributed into all things, even to the most particular, and into the inmost recesses. Hence arises in such things [viz., plants, trees, fruit, etc.] their perpetuities, which in the life of man corresponds to eternity. In like manner all things of the animal kingdom, even the most particular, are constituted; and consequently all parts of the human body, even to the minutest.

"It is also surprising that all things made by man, such as works of art, statues, pictures, and innumerable other things, which on the outside appear beautiful, and are esteemed of great value, are nevertheless interiorly nothing but clay and mud, and devoid of beauty; it is only the external surface which the eye admires. Whereas those things which grow from seeds, begin from an interior principle, and increase and assume an external. Such things are not only beautiful to the sight, but the more interiorly they are examined, the more beautiful they appear. It is the same with the life of man; those things which begin from what is external, thus which proceed from the man himself, may be compared to artificial works, whose external form is esteemed and admired, but whose internals are of no value. Whereas those things which proceed from God Messiah are formed from inmost principles, and may be compared to those things in nature which are beautiful from within. This is what is meant by what God Messiah says in Matthew concerning the lilies of the field, that 'Solomon, in all his glory, was not arrayed like one of these,' while lilies, however, are disregarded" (n. 251).

These eternal laws of correspondence, overlaid, indeed, in successive ages, and among widely different nations, by endless varieties of metaphor, fable, analogy, mythic episodes, legends, and observances, may be said to constitute an "intelligible and truly human," if not divine, "element" of relationship among all peoples and tribes of the globe, and the existence of which is proved by manners, customs, and languages, that nothing else can possibly explain. It appears, from the oldest records, that this science was well known to, and highly appreciated by, the ancients. It was especially cultivated among the Eastern nations of Egypt, Assyria, Chaldea, Syria, Canaan, and Arabia, as the "chief of all the sciences," as the "living science," in comparison with which all other sciences were regarded as dead. The book of Job, one of the most ancient we possess, abounds with correspondences, but they have not that serial connection which distinguishes the fully inspired Word of God. Indeed, all ancient oriental literature affords indisputable evidence to the truth of this science. From it originates the sacred and profane symbols of antiquity. It pervaded every system of theology and morality. As mankind, however, degenerated from purity and intelligence, it was desecrated to vile and superstitious purposes. It finally sank into Grecian fable,—was associated with all that was monstrous, impious, and absurd, and was then for ages lost. From the successive profanation of this sacred science arose the later Egyptian hieroglyphics, the Hindoo, Celtic, Persian, Grecian, Roman, and Scandinavian mysteries and initiatory rites, their oracles and mythologies; Orpheus and the Indian Apollo; the Wadilions of Titan, and the giants invading heaven; the fables of the golden age and the garden of Hesperides; the story of Pandora and her box of evil; the translation of Astrea by the Romans, of

Dhrura among the Hindus, of Buddha among the Ceylonese, and of Xaca among the Calmucks of Siberia; the incarnations of Vishnu in India, and the fables and allegories of so many nations respecting a universal flood. All these are traceable to the prolific source of corruption and confusion. Hence sprang up all idolatry,[30] in which the

---

[30] "There is great reason to believe," says the author of *Tracts for the Times*, lxxxviii., "that the Pagan mysteries took their rise from something more holy than themselves."—P. 9.

"The ancients, it must be confessed, almost always spoke in allegories."—*Voltaire's Phil. Dict.*, art. *Allegory*.

Bishop Warburton affirms that "it was an universal opinion that the heathen mysteries were instituted pure."—*Div. Leg.*, vol. i., p. 172.

"Druidism is thought by many to be derived, though not without perversions and corruptions, from the Patriarchal religion."—*Archæologia*, vol. viii., p. 16.

"It is singular," says Hutchinson, "that the Magi of Matt. ii. 1, is rendered by an Irish version, *Draoithe*, the Druids, or the true wise men. Magi in the east, Druid in the west."—*Hist. Cumb.*, vol. ii., p. 193.

Clement of Alexandria, who was himself supposed to have been initiated into the Heathen mysteries, asserts, that "*the truths taught in them had been stolen by philosophers from Moses and the Prophets.*"—*Strom.*, v., p. 650.

Coronation symbols and ceremonies have the same origin.

On this subject Kirby and Spence make the following admirable observations:—"In no country was [the origination of idolatry] more lamentably striking than in Egypt, whose gods were all selected from the animal and vegetable kingdoms. This species of idolatry doubtless resulted from their having been taught that things in nature were symbols of things above nature and of the attributes and glory of the Godhead. In process of time, while the corruption remained, the knowledge which had been thus abused, was *lost* or dimly seen. The Egyptian priesthood perhaps retained some remains of it; but by them it was made an esoteric doctrine, not to be communicated to the profane vulgar, who were suffered to regard the various objects of their superstitious veneration, not as symbols, but as possessed of an inherent divinity; and probably the mysteries of Isis in Egypt, and of Ceres at Eleusis, were instituted that this esoteric doctrine, which was to be kept secret and sacred from the common people, might not be lost."—*Introduction to Entomology*, vol. iv., p. 403.

Swedenborg, writing on the same subject in the *True Christian Religion*, truly says, "The idolatries of the gentiles of old took their rise from the science of correspondences, because all things that appear on the face of the earth have correspondence, consequently, not only trees and vegetables, but also beasts and birds of every kind, with fishes and all other things. The ancients, who were versed in the science of correspondences, made themselves images which corresponded with heavenly things; and were greatly delighted with them by reason of their signification, and because they could discern in them what related to heaven and the church; they therefore placed those images not only in their temples, but also in their houses, not with any intention to worship them, but to serve as means of recollecting the heavenly things signified by them. Succeeding ages, when the science of correspondences was obliterated, began to adore as holy, and at length to worship as deities, the images and resemblances set up by their forefathers, because they found them in and about their temples."—n. 205.

"Not only the most intelligent among the Egyptians, but all those who were devoted to philosophy among the other barbarous nations, admired the symbolical mode of inspiration." "To the same purport Origen and the other ancient Christian Fathers."—*Clemens Alexandrinus, Strom.*, lib. v., cap. 8, p. 671. *Cited by Mosheim in a Note; see Cudworth's Intel. Syst.*, vol. ii., p. 303.

"Amongst the ancient Etruscans, everything in religion and politics was emblematical. They thought the earth only the representative or mirror of heaven. The year, the gods, everything, in fact, had a triple name: the civil or common, the sacerdotal and the mysterious or occult—a secret which none dare pronounce or utter. This custom is found in the triple name of Rome, of which Pliny speaks; the mysterious name of this mistress of the world was Amor [Love]; its sacerdotal name, Flora or Anthusa; and its civil name, Roma."—*Keene's Bath Journal*.

"The term which answers to the word idolatry is not found in any ancient lan-

corresponding forms in nature and representations in art were deified and worshipped instead of the attributes and perfections of God which

guage. It is an expression of the Greeks, of the later ages, and was not brought into general use until the second century of our era. It verifies 'The adoration or worship of Images.' It is a term of reproach;—an expression of abuse or insult. No people have ever taken upon them the title of 'Idolaters.'"—*L'Abbé Bazin's Philos. of Hist., trans. by Gandell*, 8vo, p. 165.

"The word idol, idolater, idolatry, is found neither in Homer, Hesiod, Herodotus, nor any author of the religion of the gentiles."—*Voltaire's Phil. Dict., art. Idol.*, vol. ii., p. 32.

"As man was made an *Image* of the Deity, so were the *material world* and its parts made copies or *rudiments* of the *immaterial* or heavenly (Col. ii. 8). Whence also the tabernacle afterwards, which was made, as we are told, after the *pattern of heavenly things* (Heb. viii. 5), was called a worldly sanctuary (Heb. ix. 1), as were the services of it *worldly rudiments* (Col. ii. 20), because it was made after the *heavenly pattern* by the medium of the world, which had been originally made after *the same*. For as the Apostle, speaking of created things in general, plainly tells us (Rom. i. 20), '*The* invisible things *of God*, from the creation of the world, are clearly seen [or are suitably perceived or discerned], being understood by the things *that are made*.' As the Psalmist also, speaking of particulars, says, '*The* heavens *declare the* glory of God, *and the* firmament *showeth his* handy-work.' (Ps. xix. 1.) That is, they show, or *figure out*, things that are not in themselves, but far above and beyond themselves, even in *God*, and in the heaven of *holiness*, and in his *divine operations* and *works* on his *intellectual* creatures, *angels*, and *men*. Accordingly, the *world* has been termed by some *God explained*. They should have said God *adumbrated* and typically represented; for such it is: and so to contemplate this *glass* of his creatures and works in this system, is to learn to know *Himself*, and his higher and more glorious operations. The *light, spirit, vapors, rain, fruits, waters, bread, wine*, etc., being not only for our bodily uses here, but also to raise our thoughts to another more excellent *glory, spirit, water, meat, drink*, etc., in heaven."—*Holloway's Letter and Spirit*, pp. 1, 2.

"The first corruptions of mythology originated in the superaddition and admixture of sensual, physical, political, and imaginative allegories and fables."—See *Grote's Hist. of Greece*, vol. i., pp. 11, 12.

"Bishop Warburton is compelled by truth to acknowledge, in book ii., p. 172, 'that the wisest and best men in the Pagan world are unanimous in this, that the mysteries were instituted pure, and proposed the noblest end by the worthiest means.'"—*Taylor's Iamblichus*, note, p. 149.

"St. Austin himself cannot but own that the [Pagan] mysteries were principally instituted by the Ancients for the promotion of virtue and a good life, even where he is accusing paganism in general for its neglect of moral virtue."—*De Civ. Dei*, lib. ii., cap. 6 and 26.

"The mysteries had their common original from those of Isis and Osiris in Egypt." "Everything therein was instituted by the Ancients for instruction and amendment of life. (The most celebrated were the Orphic, the Bacchic, the Eleusinian, the Samothracian, the Cabiri, and the Mithraic.)"—*Arrian Diss.*, lib. iii., cap. 21. *Bishop Warburton's Div. Leg.*, vol. i., book 1, pp. 172, 173, 196, 197.

"Servius, in commenting on the 'Mystica vannus Iacchi' of Virgil, observes that the sacred rites of Bacchus pertained to the purification of souls."—*Taylor's Iamblichus*, note, p. 136.

"Eupolemus, Artaplanus, Melo, and Philo, all agree that the Babylonish traditions of the Egyptian priests of Heliopolis were, as to [many things], derived from Abraham."—*Eusebius*, i. 9, c. 17.

"We say, therefore, that the Pagans in this, their theologizing of physiology, and deifying the things of nature and parts of the world, did accordingly call everything by the name of God, or God by the name of everything."—*Cudworth's Intellect. Syst.*, vol. ii., p. 259.

"Even Serranus can allow that Plato spake many things which he understood not, drawn out of the Phœnician or Syrian theology. These Plato frequently mentions, and calls them ineffable and unintelligible. For as the traditions were of Hebrew extraction, and such as referred to the Jewish mysteries and divine worship, it is no wonder they were unintelligible to the wisest heathen. Therefore Plato calls them *myths*,—fables which in their philosophical notion signify some mysteries handed down from the ancients, the reasons whereof were hidden and unknown, notwithstanding the assistance of allegory or mythology. The learned Julius Scaliger affirms the same."—*Ellis's Knowledge of Div. Things from Revelation, not from Reason or Nature*, pp. 98, 99.

"Idolatry in all its ramifications is but the

they signified.[31] The doctrine of a primeval chaos, the metempsychosis, or the transmigration of souls, together with the poetic legends and fables of antiquity, all had a like origin.

But though the mythological fables of ancient times present a confused admixture of allegorical symbols and arbitrary figures, introduced by the license of poetic imagination, mysteriously and ingeniously combining a crude system of natural and moral philosophy; yet, heterogeneous, uncertain, extravagant, and obscure as they appear, from the vestiges and traces of correspondence which they still retain, the meaning of many of the less corrupted becomes obvious and interesting to those acquainted with this science. [The same deplorable corruptions and perversions of spiritual ideas originated magic, divination, demonology, necromancy, witchcraft, alchemy,

---

corrupt transmission of original pure religion."—*O'Brien's Round Towers of Ireland*, 2d ed., p. 192.

All fabulous animals have a like origin.

"We Christians deride the Egyptians without cause, they having many mysteries in their religion, for as much as they profess, that perishing brute animals are not worshipped by them, but the eternal ideas."—*Orig. Cont. Cels.*, lib. iii., p. 120. Cited by Cudworth, *Intel. Syst.*, vol. ii., p. 277.

"It is more than probable," as the learned Mr. Pemble observed, "that Zoroaster, Hermes, Orpheus, Plato, and others, drew their knowledge, which they had in part of *many high mysteries*, out of a deeper and clearer fountain than the muddy, shallow springs of their own natural reason, though in the passage this water was much soiled by them with the filth of many idle fables and silly conceits."—*Vindiciæ Gratiæ*, p. 48.

"The arcane and recondite theology of the Egyptians was concealed from the vulgar, two manner of ways, by fables of allegories, and by symbols or hieroglyphics. Eusebius informs us that Porphyrius wrote a book 'concerning the allegorical theology both of the Greeks and Egyptians.' Neither can we doubt but that all the devout Pagans acknowledged some living and understanding deities or other; nor easily believe that they ever worshipped any inanimate or senseless bodies, otherwise than as some way referring to the same, or as images and symbols of them."—*Cudworth's Intel. Syst.*, vol. i., pp. 536, 539.

[31] Knowing, as we presume, nothing of the science of correspondence, we yet find a multitude of writers more or less impressed with views closely approximating to the truth, as to the source of all idolatry. Take the following:

"There never was, there never could be, any religion invented by man. Religion must be a subject purely of revelation from God, and as in the first ages [after the fall] we find it spiritual, and conveyed to the mind through the medium of natural things, which were necessarily employed as the instruments and media by which alone a knowledge of spiritual things could by possibility be communicated to the understandings of men. The first corruption that was introduced into religion was a stopping short, a not looking through the thing to that which was signified by it, and paying divine honors to springs and rivers, and trees and rocks [the elements and animals, men and demons], and all the host of heaven, which the Apostle calls the worshipping of the creature rather than the Creator. This may be called philosophical religion, against which the Apostle warns us. 'Beware lest any man spoil you through philosophy and vain deceit.' (Col. ii. 8.) To that succeeded the gross and carnal state, when, because they did not like to retain God in their thoughts, 'He gave them up [by his permissive Providence] to a reprobate mind, to work all manner of uncleanness with greediness.' (Rom. i. 28.) But yet in reality there are not so many different religions, but only a corruption of the one religion, and he who carefully and impartially investigates the heathen mythology, will discover in its doctrines a mystery and a sublimity of theological sentiment which can only be explained by a comparison of the same truths, but unsophisticated, as they are found in the Bible."—*Orange's History and Antiquities of Nottingham.* Col. i., p. 42.

astrology, and charms, with numberless other superstitions which for ages bound, as in adamantine fetters, the free-born mind.]

"The translation of the Word," says a sensible and pious writer, "into a language of such extensive use as the Greek, was fraught with important results. And from this source at least, if not from an earlier acquaintance with the Hebrew original, many of the sages, poets, and philosophers of the heathen world drew some sparks of the light of the heavenly fire which glowed within it. 'Which of your sophists,' says Tertullian, addressing his Pagan contemporaries, 'have not drunk from the fountain of the prophets? It is from these sacred springs that your philosophers have refreshed their thirsty spirits; and if they have found anything in the Holy Scriptures which hit their fancy, or which served their hypothesis, they took and turned it to a compliance with their curiosity, not considering those writings to be sacred and unalterable, nor understanding their true sense.'"—D. H. H. in *Amer. N. J. Mag.*, vol. xxii., p. 431.

To this same effect wrote the apostle Paul to the Romans: "Because that, when they knew God, they glorified *Him* not as God, neither were thankful, but became vain in their imaginations, and their foolish heart was darkened. Professing themselves to be wise, they became fools, and changed the glory of the incorruptible God into an image made like to corruptible man, and to birds, and four-footed beasts, and creeping things. Wherefore God also gave them up to uncleanness, through the lusts of their own hearts, to dishonor their own bodies between themselves: who changed the truth of God into a lie, and served the creature more than the Creator, who is blessed for ever, Amen" (i. 21–25). But in the Lord's good time, and in the multitude of his mercies, the period has happily arrived when this long-lost science, purged and defecated from the corrupting dregs of profanation, and without danger to human welfare, can be restored as a blessing to his Church, a holy medium of communion between himself and angels and men,—a ground and pillar of the truth; nor will it ever again be withdrawn. Thus He has fulfilled his gracious promise: "He hath turned to the people a pure language, that they may all call upon the name of the Lord, to serve Him with one consent" (Zeph. ix. 9); so that men need no longer "walk in darkness," but may "have the light of life."

CHAPTER V.

That the Sacred Writers bear the most Ample and Cogent Testimony to the Existence of a Spiritual Sense in the Word of God.

WE are now permitted to know and make trial of this great exegetical law. Since the first systematic promulgation of the heavenly doctrines of the New Church, in the middle of the last century, which include this rule of interpretation, and as if to confirm their truth and importance, science, in every branch of knowledge, has been permitted to be investigated with an ardor and success heretofore unknown. Ancient treasures of learning and remains of antiquity have by unwearied researches been brought to light, and labors, both mental and physical, have been expended upon them, unexampled in any former age. To open the prison-house of ignorance and superstition, the world has been explored, as it never was before, in search of all kinds of knowledge. A wide field of delightful investigation, perpetually expanding itself, is rendered accessible on every side, in which the prepared mind may disport and expatiate, and, by the sacred and sublime science of correspondence, every ascertained truth, every scientific fact, and every degree of intelligence, may be made subservient to revealed wisdom and goodness, and to the indefinite advancement of mankind in virtue and in truth.

Natural and external objects can only exist as effects from prior causes, which are internal and spiritual, belonging to the spiritual world, though latent or concealed here. These objects receive their appropriate forms from the interior principles of angels, demons, and spirits, and of which they are the constant exponents; and nothing exists *within* their minds but what, by an eternal and unchangeable law of the spiritual world, finds its constant and appropriate corresponding form *without*. This nature and constitution of the spirit-world is one source of the felicity of heaven, where all is beautiful and delightful because what is without exactly corresponds to what is within, and undergoes changes analogous to the changes of state; and the same law also determines the phenomena of hell, where all without, like all within, is doleful and monstrous.

These principles and ideas in regard to the spirit-world lie at the very root of the sciences of correspondences. They illustrate and explain it. For the fixed objects of the natural world receive all their indefinite forms by a like correspondence with the spiritual world; and according to the respective uses to which they are designed respectively to contribute.

Even the representations of the Jewish dispensation were all, originally, "*types and patterns*" of heavenly realities. When the spiritual sight of Moses was opened, he received direct instruction from the Lord out of heaven concerning the tabernacle, the ark of the testimony, and all their contents and furniture; and the Lord said unto him, "According to all that I show thee, after the pattern of the tabernacle, and the pattern of all the instruments thereof, even so shall ye make it" (Ex. xxv. 9). Then follows a particular description, and it is added, "And look that thou make them after the *pattern* which was shown thee in the mount" (ver. 40). The word translated *pattern* means also likeness or similitude (Deut. iv. 16–18).

"Not only all beasts, but also all things which are in the world, correspond, and according to correspondences represent and signify spiritual and celestial things, and in the supreme sense the divine things which are of the Lord. And hence it may be seen of what quality the ancient churches were, which were called representative churches, namely, that in singular their sacred rites were represented the things which are of the Lord and of his kingdom, thus which are of love and faith in Him. And that on such occasions heaven was conjoined with the man of the Church by such things; for internal things were presented to view in heaven. The Word of the Lord was also given for that end, for in it all and singular things, even to the smallest iota, correspond and signify; hence by the Word alone there is connection of heaven with man. That this is the case, is known to no one at this day; wherefore the natural man, when he reads the Word, and inquires where the divine [essence or principle] lies concealed therein, and when he does not find it in the letter, by reason of the vulgar style, begins first to hold it in low estimation, and next to deny that it was dictated by the Divine [Being] Himself, and let down through heaven to man; for he is ignorant that the Word is divine from the spiritual sense, which does not appear in the letter, but still is in the letter; and that that sense is presented to view in heaven, when man reads it reverently, and that the subject treated of in that sense is concerning the Lord and concerning his kingdom.

These divine things are what render the Word divine, and by [or through] which sanctity flows in through heaven from the Lord, even into the literal sense, and into the very letter itself. But so long as man does not know what a spiritual principle is, neither can he know what the spiritual sense is, thus neither what correspondence is. And so long as man loves the world in preference to heaven, and himself in preference to the Lord, he is not willing to know those things, nor to apprehend them; when yet all ancient intelligence was hence derived, and hence also is angelic wisdom. The mystic arcana in the Word, which several divines have vainly busied themselves in exploring, only lie concealed therein."—A. C. 9280.

"Correspondence is the appearance of the internal in the external, and its representative therein."—A. C. 5423.

"The spiritual [thus] acts in the natural, and forms it to a likeness of itself, that it may appear before the eyes, or before the world; that [according to true order] the end may become the cause, and the cause become the effect, and thus that the end, by the cause, in the effect may exhibit itself visible and sensible; this trine is given from creation; the ultimate products which are in our world are various,—as many as are the subjects in the three kingdoms of nature,—the animal, the vegetable, and the mineral; therefore, all products [both in heaven and upon earth] are correspondences. [Thus] correspondence is the manifestation of causes in their effects" (A. E. 1081 *et seq.*). It connects the infinitely varied and perfect works of creative skill and energy in the spiritual world with those of the natural world; the inward mind with outward nature; the innumerable faculties of the soul with the complicated yet harmonious forms of the body; spiritual ideas with natural; revelation with reason; religion with philosophy; God with man; and links the life which now is to the ages of eternity. It is to the Word of God what the laws of physical science are to the phenomena of the universe. Without any acquaintance whatever with scientific researches and deductions, a man may indeed live, and enjoy a considerable share of worldly pleasure; but, destitute of a knowledge of these laws, what can he learn? Will the pebble or the fossil disclose to him its origin? Will light by its coruscations explain to him the mysteries of optical phenomena? Will the planets without the demonstrations of astronomy reveal to him how they obey the electro-magnectic forces, and how their constant equilibrium is preserved? Or will the thunder-cloud and lightning-flash familiarize him with the nature of the imponderable agents—light, heat, and electricity? No. So, neither will the Word of God reveal to man the arcana of spiritual existence and mental activity, the knowledge of which is so essential to his eternal well-being and so earnestly to be desired, without some acquaintance with the divine style in which it is written, and the law by which it may be consistently and with certainty interpreted.

The science of correspondences also includes within it representatives, which have a chief relation to the existence and form of objects in a lower state, which correspond; and significatives, which have more immediate relation to language and words. Thus the various organs of the body are representatives of the diversified faculties of the soul, through which they derive from God their innumerable forms and relations, their harmony, unity, and use, but when they act together they correspond; or as all created objects are representatives of the living heavenly realities of which they are the material forms, so they all correspond in their active uses. And all expressions by which such things are described or spoken of in the Word, all the rituals of worship, and all discourse and actions described there, are significative, as Swedenborg most clearly shows, when he asserts that "between the things which are of the light of heaven, and those which are of the light of the world, there exist correspondences, and the correspondences which exist in those things which are of the light of the world, are representatives" (A. C. 3337). For between the light of heaven and the light of the world, "or between those things which are in the light of heaven and in the light of the world, there is given a correspondence, when the external or natural man makes one with the internal or spiritual man, that is, when the former is subservient to the latter; and in this case, the things which exist in the light of the world are representative of such things as exist in the light of heaven" (A. C. 3223). "For the things which exist by derivation from things spiritual in things natural, are representatives."—A. C. 2987.

Thus, also, we learn that the numberless representatives which the patriarchs, prophets, and apostles saw, and the significatives which they heard in the spiritual world in visions or dreams, or when their spiritual senses of sight and hearing were miraculously opened, and which they were inspired to write and describe in the Word of God, were, in their highest significance, the living images and representative spiritual forms of the wisdom and goodness of the divine mind which gave them birth; and, in a lower sense, of the inward thoughts.

affections, perceptions, ideas, and discourse of the spiritual inhabitants with which they correspond. "Hence then it may appear what correspondence is and whence it is, what representation is, and whence; viz., that correspondence is between those things which appertain to the light of heaven, and those which appertain to the light of the world—that is, between those things which appertain to the internal or spiritual man, and those which appertain to the external or natural man; and that representation is whatever exists in the things appertaining [to an external state and] to the light of the world—that is, whatever exists in the external or natural man, considered in respect to the things appertaining to the light of heaven, that is, appertaining to the internal or spiritual man."—A. C. 3235.

It must, however, be always borne in mind, as Swedenborg asserts from his own conscious experience, that "the representatives and significatives contained in the Word of God [were not originally derived from human intelligence, skill, and observation, however acute and penetrating, for these at most can only confirm their existence and application, but] from the representatives which exist in another life; it was from another life that such representatives came to the men of the Most Ancient Church, who were celestial, and were together with spirits and angels while they lived in the world; these representatives were derived from them to their posterity, and at length to those who knew only that such things were significative, without knowing what they particularly signified; but inasmuch as they had existed from the most ancient times, and were applied in divine worship, they were therefore accounted venerable and holy. Besides representatives there are also correspondences which both in sound and signification differ in the natural world from what they are in the spiritual world; thus, heart denotes the affection of good, eyes understanding, ears obedience, hands power, besides numberless others; these are not so represented in the spiritual world, but they correspond, as natural to spiritual; hence it is, that each particular expression, as to the smallest dot or tittle in the Word, involves things spiritual and celestial; and that the Word is so inspired, that, when it is read by man, [the] spirits and angels [attending upon him] instantly perceive it spiritually, according to representatives and correspondences. But this science, which was so cultivated and esteemed by the ancients after the flood, and by which they were enabled to think with spirits and angels, is at this day totally obliterated, insomuch that scarce any one is willing to believe that such a science exists; and they who believe, consider it merely as somewhat mystical and of no use, and this by reason that man is become altogether worldly and corporeal, so that when mention is made of what is spiritual and celestial, he immediately feels a repugnance, and sometimes disdain, yea, even to loathing; what, then, will he do in another life, which abideth forever, where there is nothing worldly or corporeal, but only what is spiritual and celestial, which constitutes life in heaven."—A. C. 2763.

And again, in another important passage, "The Word was sent down from the Lord to man, and consequently is different in its origin from what it is in its external form. The Word as being divine is not only written for man, but also for the angels attendant on man, so as to serve not only for use to the human race, but also for heaven; and that thus the Word is a medium effecting the union of heaven and earth; this union is by the Church, and indeed by the Word in the Church, which Word, therefore, is of such a nature, and is distinguished from all other writings. Inasmuch as the learned part of the world are ignorant that things divine and celestial lie inwardly concealed, even in the historical parts of the Word, if they were not impressed with a holy veneration for the books of the Word received from their earliest years, they would easily be induced to say in their hearts that the Word is not holy, and that its holiness is only thus derived from the holy impressions received in early life; when yet this is not its true source, but the Word is holy because of its internal sense, which is celestial and divine, and which is effective of the union of heaven with earth—that is, of angelic minds with those of men, and thus of the latter with the Lord."—*Swedenborg.*

It has been said that it is ridiculous to call correspondences a science; but the late Bishop of Durham has said that "the symbolical language of the prophets is almost a science in itself" (*Boyle Lectures*); and Bishop Horne calls it quite a science when he says, "If men, in these days, have not been accustomed to such contemplation, is it not high time they should become so? Can they begin too soon to study and make themselves master of a science which promises to its votaries so much entertainment, as well as improvement; which recommends the Scriptures, to persons of true taste and genius, as books intended equally for our delight and instruction: which demonstrates the ways of celestial wisdom to be ways of pleasantness, and all her paths to be peace."—*Introd. to the Psalms.*

"It is so common," says Professor Bush, "to represent this doctrine of the science of correspondences, and the spiritual sense of the Word, as the *ne plus ultra* of extravagance and absurdity, that the utmost solicitude is warranted as to the full and fair exhibition of the theory in reference to the *fundamental principles* on which it rests. Yet we see the whole matter resolving itself into a *law* as fixed and invariable as the law of creation itself, with which, in fact, it becomes almost identical. The Word of God rises under the process into a new revelation, clothed with a sublimity, sanctity, and divinity of which we had not previously the remotest conception. It stands before us the living Oracles of Truth, which are no longer separate from the very being of its Author. He is himself in his own truth. New treasures of wisdom gleam forth from its pages, and the most barren details of history, the recorded rounds of obsolete rituals, the dryest catalogues of names, the most trivial specifications of dates, places, and enactments, once touched with the mystic wand of the spiritual sense, teem with the riches of angelic conception. The cosmogony of Genesis becomes the birth-register of the new-born soul. The garden of Eden smiles in every renovated mind in *the intelligence* and *affection* emblemed in its trees, and fruits, and flowers. The watering streams are the fructifying knowledges and truths of wisdom, which make increase of the spiritual man. The Tree of Knowledge, the Tree of Life, the wily serpent, are all within us, and within us all. The scenes transacted in the Paradisiac purlieus are more or less the scenes of our own individual experience, and the narrative ceases to be looked upon merely as the chronicle of events that transpired thousands of years before we were born."—*Reply to Dr. Woods*, p. 66.

That the sacred Scriptures have such a spiritual sense within them, distinct from the letter, which is the shell or resting-place thereof, they themselves plainly teach and positively assert. The Lord Jesus himself says, "It is the spirit which quickeneth; the flesh profiteth nothing: the words that I speak unto you, they are spirit, and they are life" (John vi. 63). The enlightened mind will see that the "spirit and life" constitute the inward spiritual sense; and that for this reason the Word is called in the Revelation "THE LAMB'S BOOK OF LIFE" (xx. 12; xxi. 27). In Hosea it is written, "I have spoken by the prophets, and I have multiplied visions, and I have used similitudes," saith Jehovah, "by the ministry of the prophets" (xii. 10). What are similitudes? what are the prophetical words, and the actions of the prophets, I ask, apart from their hidden signification? and, without it, how are they to be understood? David thus prays: "Open thou mine eyes, that I may behold wondrous things out of thy law" (Ps.

cxix. 18). This is surely a prayer to the Lord that He will enlighten the sight of the understanding, and make manifest to human discernment the invisible things of his Word and kingdom. And, again, he affirms: "My tongue is the pen of a ready writer" (Ps. xlv. 1). Who is the ready writer but the Lord himself? The Psalmist was but an instrument in his hand, to record his inspired wisdom and his revealed will. Precisely the same testimony is borne, in a historical form, in some of the last inspired words of David, where it is written: "The Spirit of the Lord spake by me, and his word was in my tongue" (2 Sam. xxiii. 1, 2). And in reference to what he wrote, he further says: "I will open my mouth in a parable; I will utter dark sayings of old" (Ps. lxxviii. 2). And yet, as these *dark sayings* were only a plain and simple narration of the history of the children of Israel, what do we justly conclude, but that the whole is a divine allegory as well as a true history, recorded for our spiritual edification, and to promote our eternal welfare. So also of Cyrus, in his representative character as a type of the Lord in his glorified humanity, and also of each of his faithful followers, it is written: "I will give them the treasures of darkness, and hidden riches of secret places;" and that these expressions have respect to the communications of wisdom and intelligence, in all abundance through the Word, is evident from what follows as the divine end of these marvellous gifts, namely, "That thou mayest know that I, the LORD, who call thee by thy name, am the God of Israel" (Isa. xlv. 3).[32]

---

[32] "Are we concerned with the affairs of David and Israel? Have we anything to do with the ark and the temple? They are no more. Are we to go up to Jerusalem, and to worship in Sion? They are desolated and trodden under foot by the Turks. Are we to sacrifice young bullocks according to the law? The law is abolished, never to be observed again. Do we pray for victory over Moab, Edom, and Philistia; or for deliverance from Babylon? There are no such nations, no such places in the world. What, then, do we mean, when, taking such expressions into our mouths, we utter them in our own persons, as parts of our devotions before God? Assuredly we must mean a spiritual Jerusalem and Sion: a spiritual ark and temple; a spiritual law; spiritual sacrifices; and spiritual victories over spiritual enemies; all described under the old names, which are still retained, though 'old things are passed away, and all things have become new.' (2 Cor. v. 17.)"—*Horne's Commentary on the Psalms*, p. xiii.

"As to symbolism, it is the normal expression of being. There is meaning fulness of grave moment in every organic and inorganic form; yea, our very speech is but a string of metaphors, as if we could not utter thought without the poetry deep in nature oozed out and become evident. Idea itself is carved in pictures—the word meaneth *an image*. And for authority of this, the old law teems with it; it is, in fact, one bold, God-written figure: and the commentator of the new law did no act, or spake no word, without a further intelligence and meaning beyond the mere ordinary reading. If He healed, He spat upon clay; if he preached, He spake from a ship: if He prayed, He went up into a mountain: even out of his garments breathed a virtue, and his words were potent to raise the dead. These material forms, this sound, sight, smell, and taste—these common, unphilosophical, dull

Now turn to the Gospels. It is there written that "Jesus spake unto the multitude in parables; and without a parable spake He not unto them: That it might be fulfilled which was spoken by the prophet, saying, I will open my mouth in parables; I will utter things which have been kept secret from the foundation of the world" (Matt. xiii. 34, 35). Again, the same things are declared in another place: "And with many parables spake He the Word unto them, as they were able to hear it. But without a parable spake He not unto them; and when they were alone, He expounded all things to his disciples" (Mark iv. 33, 34). Now what were these parables and dark sayings, without the spiritual things secretly signified—that is, without their internal and heavenly meaning, pre-eminently called by the Psalmist (Ps. cvii. 43) and by John the Evangelist (Rev. xvii. 9) WISDOM? We are clearly taught that, "from the creation of the world," this divine style of instruction has been adopted in accommodation to the nature and condition of the human race, and as men were able to bear, and prepared to understand, these parabolic mysteries have been expounded. This, again, the Lord intimates, at the end of the Jewish and the establishment of the Christian dispensation, where He says to his disciples: "Blessed are your eyes, for they see; and your ears, for they hear. For verily I say unto you, that many prophets and righteous men have desired to see those things which ye see, and have not seen them; and to hear those things which ye hear, and have not heard them" (Matt. xiii. 16, 17). And the apostle Paul asserts the same doctrine where he writes: "For we know in part, and we prophesy in part; but when that which is perfect is come, then that which was in part shall be done away" (1 Cor. xiii. 9, 10).

This method of imparting spiritual instruction to mankind, under the natural imagery of correspondence, served also to prevent the wicked and unprepared from injuring themselves by perverting the truth, and turning it to vile purposes; therefore, when the disciples inquired of the Lord the reason why He spake to the multitude in parables, He said: "I speak to them in parables, because they, seeing, see not; and hearing, they hear not, neither do they understand; for this people's heart is waxed gross, and their ears are dull of hearing, and their eyes they have closed; lest at any time they should see with their eyes, and hear with their ears, and should understand with their

---

sensible things—in the shallow thinker's estimation, are pregnant with the Eternal's power and will. A great type, a mystic symbol, a prophetic riddle of the Unfathomable Profound, is the whole of Creation."—*Chippendale's Thoughts for the Thoughtful.*

hearts, and should be converted, and I should heal them"[33] (Matt. xiii. 13-15); that is, lest they should believe and acknowledge the Lord, and outwardly receive his truth and goodness, while their hearts were full of hypocrisy and evil; in which case it was foreseen that they would afterwards have awfully profaned his divine gifts, and denied Him, and, returning to their evil ways, their salvation would thus have been rendered impossible.

This parabolic mode of address was thus mercifully overruled, it appears, to protect the mysteries of sacred truth and goodness from profanation and abuse, and to restrain presumptuous men from plunging headlong into the most fatal and irretrievable states of hypocrisy.

It was to represent this accommodation of divine truth to human perception, and to check such deplorable arrogance and wickedness, that "Moses put a vail upon his face" when he descended from the Lord's presence on Mount Sinai (Ex. xxxiv. 33), denoting the obscurity of the letter of the Word, which vails the glory of its hidden wisdom from the unprepared, and attempers it to the prepared, beholder. How beautifully does the apostle Paul elucidate this significant act, and point to a period when the inward glory should be revealed. "Moses," says he, "put a vail over his face, that the children of Israel could not steadfastly look to the end of that which is abolished; but their minds were blinded: for until this day remaineth the same vail untaken away in the reading of the Old Testament; which vail is done away in Christ. But even unto this day, when Moses is read, the vail is upon their heart. Nevertheless when it shall turn to the Lord, the vail shall be taken away" (2 Cor. iii. 12-16).[34]

Again, we read, "Upon all the glory shall be a defence" (Isa. iv. 5). While "the glory" is truly descriptive of the inward spirit of

---

[33] "So that they see not with *their* eyes, nor hear with *their* ears, nor understand with *their* hearts, nor are converted, that I should heal them."—NEWCOME.

See Mark iv. 11, 12. "Since seeing they see, and do not perceive; and hearing they hear, and do not understand; so that they are not converted and their sins forgiven."—KUINOEL.

Luke viii. 10. "Since seeing they do not see; and hearing they do not understand."—DR. L. CARPENTER.

[34] Augustin, in reference to this very passage, observes, that "They who take the writings of Moses according to the literal sense, do not desire to be learned in the kingdom of heaven, neither do they pass over to Christ, that He might remove the vail [which is upon their hearts]:" and comparing believers in the merely verbal sense of the Pentateuch to the unbelieving Jews, says, that when "they read the book of Moses, they have the vail upon their hearts, and as this is not removed, they do not understand the Law."—*Cont. Faust.*, lib. xii., cap. 4.

Boyle also, on the same subject, makes the following interesting remark: "The human understanding, like Moses in the mount, does by an assiduous converse with God acquire a lasting luminousness."—*On the high veneration Man's Intellect owes to God*, p. 92.

the Word, its literal sense must assuredly constitute its protection and "defence."

In the Psalms we read, "Bless the Lord, ye his angels that excel in strength, that do his commandments, hearkening unto the voice of his Word" (ciii. 20). The angels, then, have the Word of God for their instruction and delight; and all we know of angels is most intimately connected with the Word of God; without it, indeed, heaven would no longer be heaven. What follows, but that as there is a literal sense, adapting the divine wisdom to men on earth, so there must be within it a heavenly internal sense, adapting its interior life to the angels in the kingdom of God, and to regenerating men on earth. Thus the Word of God is a medium connecting earth with heaven, angels with men, and both with the Lord.

In the Acts the divine law is called the "lively" or "living oracles" (viii. 8),[35] in exact agreement with the Lord's own declaration, that his words are "spirit and life," and also with the inspired affirmation made to Moses, and cited by our blessed Lord himself: "Man doth not live by bread only, but by every word that proceedeth out of the mouth of God doth man live" (Deut. viii. 3; Matt. iv. 4; Luke iv. 4).[36]

---

[35] "LIVING ORACLES. The word translated *oracles* signifies a *divine revelation, a communication from God himself*, as is here applied to the *Mosaic Law*; to the *Old Testament* in general (Rom. iii. 2; Heb. v. 12); and to *Divine revelation* in general (1 Pet. iv. 11)."—*Dr. A. Clarke's Comm. on Acts* viii.

"In the Phœnician tongue the *Oracle* is called the *Mouth of God*; and to say *we consult the mouth of God*, is the same as to say we consult the oracle."—*Le Clerc. See Cooke's Hesiod, the Theogony*, l. 625.

[36] "Locke, on this text (2 Cor. iii. 6), says, 'In fact, we find Paul truly a minister of the spirit of the law, especially in his Epistle to the Hebrews, where he shows that a spiritual sense ran through the Mosaical institutions and writings.' Now from hence it appears that Locke was of opinion that the law of Moses, besides the literal sense, had a spiritual meaning, which could not be discovered without inspiration."—*Benson on the Epistles*, introd., p. xvii.

"Jerome observes that 'whatsoever is promised to the Israelites carnally, will at one time or other be fulfilled in us spiritually.'"—*In Præf.*, lib. iv., *in Jere.*

"By the divine promise of the Lord, made to the prophet Jeremiah (ch. xxxi. 31, 32), was meant that God, under the Dispensation of *Christianity*, would give his people the spiritual interpretation, understanding, and use of the Law, or Old Testament, with the Types, and Symbols, and Sacraments, by writing, stamping, or impressing them, as it were, upon their spirits; even to serve them as a *divine ladder* whereon to mount up, by contemplation (through faith and the operation of the Holy Spirit), from earth to heaven, and from the *mysteries* in the *Word* to their everlasting *verities* in God Himself."—*Holloway's Letter and Spirit*, vol. i., p. ix.

"Surely, the deliverance of Israel, and their reception of the Divine law at the foot of the mount, were typical of God's mode of dealing with his people under the dispensation of the 'better covenant.' He finds them in a state of carnal bondage under sin and Satan. They groan for deliverance, but have not strength to effect it for themselves. God undertakes for them, not by ordinary means, but extraordinary; not by natural, but by miraculous, which result in the abolishing of death, and bringing life and immortality to light. He appoints them a leader; He gives them, in the page of revelation, the pillar of the cloud by day and the pillar of fire by night. As they follow their leader in the exercise of a simple faith, they

That the apostle Paul most distinctly recognized the same doctrine of an internal sense in the divine Word, is evident from all his writings, as where he asserts that "The letter killeth, but the spirit giveth life" (2 Cor. iii. 6); and this is true not only of the mere observance of the letter of the law of Moses, to the neglect of that spiritual interpretation which Christianity, or the Gospel dispensation, reveals as contained within it, but it also implies, more remotely, that the letter of the Word of God, when separated from the inward spirit which giveth life, by a denial of its existence, is constantly perverted by sensual interpretations and reasonings, which deaden and destroy within us all reverence for its authority and character. So in his Epistle to the

---

experience deliverance; as they look to the pillar of the cloud and the pillar of fire, they are directed. He feeds them with 'bread from heaven,' and makes waters to gush out for them in the desert; He smites the spiritual rock which follows them; He reveals his will to them; He writes it as a law in their hearts; He makes them 'a temple,' 'a tabernacle,' in which He dwells by his Spirit; He 'places his name' among them; He is their God—they are his people."—*Fisk's Pastor's Memorial of Egypt, the Red Sea, the Wilderness, and the Holy Land.*

"As the people of Israel were types, and are generally allowed to be so, of the elect of God in all ages; so the enemies which they were enjoined to root out, seem to symbolize those spiritual foes which the Christian is enjoined to avoid during his warfare upon earth. This idea appears the more probable from the radical import of their names, which correspond very closely with those mentioned by the apostle in 2 Tim. iii. 2, etc. Thus the *Amorites* mean the proud, boasting rebels (Amos ii. 9). The *Canaanites*, the covetous, or worldly trafficking, such as those mentioned in Rom. xviii. 4, 11, etc. The *Hittites*, fierce, terrifying, truce-breakers, etc. The *Perizzites*, persecutors, scatterers, blasphemers, etc. The *Hivites*, mere worldly livers, wild and disorderly persons, pleasure-lovers, etc. The *Girgashites*, filthy wanderers, incontinent, etc. All these seven nations are frequently called by a general name, *Canaanites;* and literally and spiritually the word is true concerning them, that they are greater and mightier than the people of God, impossible to be vanquished by human strength, and reducible only by the LORD God of SABAOTH. And, alas (the Christian while on earth may say), they are yet in the land!"—*Serle's Hor. Solit.*, p. 24.

"It is abundantly evident that besides the literal sense of Scripture, there was a higher sense adopted; for, as to this fact, Eucherius (*Bishop at Lugduni*, A. D. 434) speaks most decidedly in his preface to this book, which sprang out of the mode of interpretation which then prevailed. We should so regard the Scriptures *according to the idea which the Scripture itself gives us.*" "As in man there is a body and a soul, so in Scripture it was believed that there is a literal and an historical sense; but that under this there is a spiritual sense, relating to higher or to spiritual things." "The Scriptures appeared as a veritable oracle, every word being *full of a deep signification.*" "At the time of Christ and his Apostles, this mode of interpreting the Old Testament prevailed not only among the Jews at Alexandria, but also in the schools of Palestine; *and it was adopted in reference to the New Testament.* This mode of interpreting the Old Testament for the uses of Christianity *was prevalent throughout the entire apostolic age and afterwards.*"—*Dr. Lutz's Bib. Hermen.*, 1849, pp. 18, 107. *Extracted from Dr. Tafel's reply to Dr. Mæhler.*

Dr. Conyers Middleton, in his *Defence*, assures us that "The allegorical way of expounding, for which we have the authority of most of the primitive fathers and the best Jewish writers, was so far from giving scandal in former ages of the Church, that, on the contrary, to slight it was looked upon as heretical, and full of dangerous consequences." "*There are none of the heretics who maintain that the Scriptures of the Old Testament ought not to be held mystically, or otherwise than of the identical things mentioned.*"—*Biblioth. Patrum. per Marg.* Paris, 1589, tom i., c. 3, pp. 270, 409.

Clement of Alexandria also tells us that "the whole Scripture is written in the parabolical style" (*Strom.*, lv., tom. ii., p. 568. Ed. by Potter), for which he gives several reasons.

Romans he thus writes, "For he is not a Jew who is one outwardly; neither is that circumcision, which is outward in the flesh: but he is a Jew who is one inwardly; and circumcision is that of the heart, in the spirit, and not in the letter; whose praise is not of men, but of God" (ii. 28, 29). And this explanation is in perfect accordance with the teaching of the Old Testament, where we read of "the circumcision of the heart" (Deut. xxx. 6; Jer. iv. 4).[37]

In the Epistle to the Ephesians, also, the apostle, when he is speaking and exhorting on the important subject of marriage, declares that what Adam says in the second chapter of Genesis respecting the union of man and wife, is "a great mystery; concerning Christ and the Church" (v. 30-32).

The apostle Peter, also, alludes to Noah's ark, and says that it is "The like figure whereunto even baptism doth also now save us" (1 Pet. iii. 20, 21). Thus what is written respecting the ark and the flood, is evidently to be interpreted, and, indeed, can only be intelligibly understood, as a series of divinely-inspired figures and types respecting human redemption and salvation. Not only do the apostles spiritually explain some of the divine allegories of the Old Testament, and the ceremonies of the Jewish dispensation, but in like manner, also, certain narratives which are there recorded, and were historically true.

In his Epistle to the Galatians, the apostle Paul, referring to the Patriarchal history, says: "It is written that Abraham had two sons, the one by a bond-maid, the other by a free-woman. But he who was of the bond-woman was born after the flesh; but he of the free-woman was by promise: Which things are an allegory: for these are the two covenants; [and] as he that was born after the flesh persecuted him that was born after the Spirit, so it is now"(iv. 22-24).[38] In speak-

---

[37] "External circumcision was a symbol of mental and moral purity, and extirpation of evil affections and desires. Hence, in the Old and New Testament, circumcision is applied to the mind."—*Bloomfield's Synopsis*, vol. iv., p. 262.

"Macknight well observes that the Apostle, by distinguishing between 'the spirit and the letter' of the law of Moses (Rom. ii. 29), intimates that the rites enjoined in that law were typical, and had a spiritual or moral meaning; as Moses also expressly declared to the Jews."—*Ib.*, vol. v., p. 404.

[38] In the original, "which things are allegorized," that is, "allegorically applied," "without destroying their historical verity."—See *Bishop Marsh's Lect.*, p. 32. *Kitto's Cyc. Bib. Lit.*, p. 115.

"In allegories framed by man, the groundwork is generally fiction, because of the difficulty of finding one true series of facts which shall exactly represent another. But the great Disposer of events, 'Known unto whom are all his works,' from the beginning to the end of time, was able to effect this; and the Scripture allegories are therefore equally true in the letter and in the spirit of them. The events signifying, no less than those signified, really happened, as they are said to have done. Why the allegories of this most perfect form, with which the book of God abounds, and which are all pregnant with

TESTIMONY OF THE SACRED WRITERS. 67

ing of the children of Israel, their representative journey, and what befell them in the way, as signifying things spiritual, he thus writes to the Corinthians: "Moreover, brethren, I would not that ye should be ignorant, how that all our fathers were under the cloud, and all passed through the sea; and were all baptized unto Moses in the cloud and in the sea; and did all eat the same spiritual meat; and did all drink the same spiritual drink; for they drank of that spiritual Rock which followed them: and that rock was Christ. Now all these things happened unto them for ensamples [τύποι types]: and they are written for our admonition, upon whom the ends of the world are come" (1 Cor. x. 1-4).

In the Epistle to the Hebrews we meet with little else than a spiritual interpretation and application of Jewish history. Their burnt-offerings and sacrifices, their meat-offerings and drink-offerings, their priesthood and rituals of worship, the golden censer and the ark of the covenant, the golden pot that had contained the manna, Aaron's rod which had budded, the table of the covenant, and over it the cherubim of glory overshadowing the mercy-seat, their fasts and festivals, their civil and ecclesiastical government, their battles and journeys, their captivities and deliverances,—in a word, the whole history of the Jews, as recorded in the Word of God, was, as to every particular, representative of spiritual and divine things (Heb. ix., etc).[39]

---

truth of the highest import, should be treated with neglect and contempt, while the imperfect allegories of man's devising are universally sought after and admired, as the most pleasing and efficacious method of conveying instruction, it is not easy to say."—*Horne's Comment. on the Psalms, pref. to new ed.*, p. xvii.

"St. Cyril of Alexandria, in his Commentaries on Isaiah, says, 'The words of the holy prophets always carry a mighty depth, and creep along by *abstruse* and *hidden courses*. Therefore, we are not to suppose that the outward surface of the letter always presents the truth intended; but that the *internal* and *spiritual meaning* of *the letter*, joined *with* and conceived *under* the letter, is rather to be considered. For the style of the holy prophets is everywhere *obscure*, and full of *dark sentences*, as containing the *unfolding* of the *divine mysteries*.'"—*Holloway's Letter and Spirit, etc.*, vol. i., int. liii.

[39] "There is one way, and a very obvious one, in which the consideration of the ritual and history might confirm the early Christians in their mystical explanations of the whole external world. They found some particulars, both ritual and historical, mystically expounded in the New Testament, and plain implications, almost assertions, that the whole was capable of similar exposition: e. g., that 'Moses made *all* things according to the pattern shewed him in the mount,' and that '*all* that befell God's people in the wilderness happened unto them as types of us.' When, therefore, in the natural world they had ascertained a few chief symbols, it was reasonable for them to infer that these, too, were but specimens, single chords of a harmony to be fully made out hereafter; they would feel like learners of a language, who have picked up the meaning as yet but of a few words here and there, but have no doubt whatever that the whole has its meaning: and perhaps they would think that they found warrant for this in such texts as that of St. Paul to the Romans, 'The invisible things of Him from the creation of the world are clearly seen, being understood by the things that are made.' This would seem to lay down the principle or canon of mystical interpretation for the works of Nature, as the other texts just now specified, for the Mosaic ceremonies and the history

And this spiritual interpretation of the Old Testament, the sacred writer distinguishes from the mere letter, by calling it "solid food" (Heb. v. 12–14). And thus warranted by apostolic example, it has been common phraseology, from the earliest period of Christianity, to speak of the sacrifices of the heart, or the hallowing of all the affections (Heb. xiii. 15, 16; Rom. xii. 1); of the altar and the temple of the soul (1 Cor. iii. 16, 17; vi. 19); of "a better country, that is a heavenly," as promised under the type of Canaan (Heb. xi. 16); of a spiritual "bondage" from which the soul must be delivered (Rom. viii. 31);[40] of spiritual enemies from whom we must be protected, and

---

of the Jews."—*Tracts for the Times*, lxxxix., p. 185.

"The mention of the sanctuary and tabernacle, the ark, and certain other particulars, must of course lead reflecting minds, even without further information, to the surmise, that in regard likewise of other points not specified, and in short in its whole range and detail, the Jewish economy was typical of the Christian."—*Ib.*, p. 165.

In a noble passage of Origen in the fifth Homily of Leviticus, cited by the writer of *Tracts for the Times*, lxxxix., on account of the light which it seems to throw on analogy, he says, "The details of the law concerning sacrifices are to be received in a different sense from that which the literal text points out. Else, when they are publicly read in the church, they tend rather to the hindrance and subversion of the Christian faith than to the admonition and edification of men. But if we search and find in what sense these things are said, and mark them, as they ought who think of God, who is the declared Author of these laws, then the hearer will become a Jew indeed, but, 'a Jew inwardly,' according to the distinction of St. Paul in the Epistle to the Romans. Things visible retain with invisible no small affinity; so that the Apostle affirms, 'the invisible things of God, from the foundation of the world;' to be seen, 'being understood by the things which are made.' As therefore a mutual affinity exists between things visible and invisible, earth and heaven, soul and flesh, body and spirit, and of combinations of these is made up this present world; so also Holy Scripture, we may believe, is made up of visible and invisible parts; first, as it were, of a kind of *body*, i.e. of the letter which we see with our eyes; next of a *soul*, i.e., of the sense which is discovered within that letter; thirdly, of a *spirit*, so far as it contains also in itself certain heavenly things; as says the Apostle, 'they serve to the example and shadow of things celestial.'"—Sect. i., t. ii., p. 205. T. T., p. 55.

Scott, in his comment on Exodus xxvi., wherein are described the ark, its shape, materials, and decorations, admits that the whole is representative of spiritual things. He says, "The whole represents the person and doctrine of Christ, his true church, and all heavenly things." And again, in his introductory remarks on Leviticus, the same eminent writer says, "It principally consists of ritual laws, delivered to Moses from above the mercy-seat during the first month after the Tabernacle was erected; though moral precepts are frequently interspersed. In these ceremonies the Gospel was preached to Israel; and the solemn and exact manner, and the many repetitions with which they are enforced, are suited to impress the serious mind with a conviction that something immensely more important and spiritual than the external observances is couched under each of them."

"Jerusalem was but a type of the Christian Church, as the carnal Israel, or the carnal seed and posterity of Abraham, were of true and sincere Christians. And therefore Paul expressly distinguishes between the earthly Jerusalem and the Jerusalem which is above (or from above, *i. e.*, the Christian Church), [which he says is the mother of us all]."—*Dean Sherlock's Sermons*, 1., p. 6.

[40] The seven impious nations, or classes of inhabitants, who possessed the land of Canaan, and who were overthrown, or made subservient, or were extirpated by the descendants of Israel, represented different kinds of idolatry, and various hereditary evil lusts and false persuasions of the natural and sensual mind, which, warring against the powers of heaven in the soul, must be either extirpated or subdued in spiritual combat, before man can be fully regenerated and attain a state of eternal peace.

spiritual dangers from which we hope to escape (1 Tim. vi. 12; 2 Tim. iv. 7); of spiritual trials in the wilderness, which we have to endure (1 Pet. iv. 12); of a spiritual Red Sea and Jordan, over which we must pass; of heaven-descended manna, on which we must feed; of living waters gushing from the Rock of Truth, by which we must be refreshed; and of that delightsome land visibly outstretched before us from Pisgah's mount, which we may inherit as an everlasting possession. A land thus described in the beautiful language of correspondence, in order to represent a heavenly state of mind, or the establishment of heaven in the soul, and also to afford us faint ideas of the surpassing loveliness, the inconceivable grandeur, the beatific glory of the heavenly world; the abundance of its precious blessings, the splendor of its spiritual and diversified scenery, the ineffable delights, the ecstatic virtues and the exalted graces of the ever-blessed inhabitants, of which the outward objects, in all their indefinite variety, are all exact correspondences. "A good land and a large, a land flowing with milk and honey" (Ex. iii. 8). "A land of hills and valleys, and drinketh water of the rain of heaven; a land that the Lord thy God careth for: the eyes of the Lord thy God are always upon it, from the beginning of the year even unto the end of the year" (Deut. xi. 11, 12). "A land of brooks of water, of fountains and depths that spring out of valleys and hills; a land of wheat, and barley, and vines, and fig-trees, and pomegranates; a land of oil olive and honey; a land wherein thou shalt eat bread without scarceness, thou shalt not lack anything in it; a land whose stones are iron, and out of whose hills thou mayest dig brass" (Deut. viii. 7–9). And what does all this justly imply, but that the whole of the eventful history of the Children of Israel, narrated by the plenarily inspired penman, is to be spiritually explained and understood. Thus the Holy Word inculcates its own spirituality, and the writings of the apostles most abundantly confirm the testimony.[41]

In the Greek *Devotions* of Bishop Andrews, translated in *Tracts for the Times*, lxxxviii. (fourth day, p. 48), occurs the following interesting passage, which indicates that the above nations were regarded by that author as figurative of unclean principles in the mind; it occurs in the prayer for grace.

"[Defend me from]
Pride . . . . Amorite.
Envy . . . . Hittite.
Wrath . . . . Perizzite.
Gluttony . . . . Girgashite.
Lechery . . . . Hivite.
The Cares of Life (Covetousness) Canaanite.
Lukewarm Indifference (Sloth) Jebusite.
[Give me]
Humility, pitifulness, patience, sobriety, purity, contentment, ready zeal."

[41] Voltaire, in ignorance of the true interpretation of the Divine Word, sarcastically quotes the passage in Gen. xv. 18, where the Lord said to Abraham, "Unto thy seed I have given this land, from the river of Egypt unto the great river, the river Euphrates:" and says, "The critics ask, how could God

promise the Jews this immense country which they have never possessed? and how could God give to them *forever* that small part of Palestine out of which they have so long been driven?"—*Phil. Dict., art. Abraham*, vol. i., p. 13. Such baseless objections against the Word of God fall to the ground, like as Dagon did before the ark (1 Sam. v.), when the true principles of interpretation are known.

That eminent men have had some idea of the true method of expounding the Word of God, though unacquainted with the direct laws of correspondence, might be confirmed by an abundance of evidence. I quote in proof a passage from Bishop Horne's *Commentary on the Book of Psalms*. The prelate says, "The spiritual sense is, and must be, peculiar to the Scriptures; because of those persons and transactions only, which are there mentioned and recorded, can it be affirmed for certain that they were designed to be figurative. And should any one attempt to apply the narrative of Alexander's expedition by Quintus Curtius, or the Commentaries of Cæsar, as the New Testament writers have done, and taught us to do to the histories of the Old, he would find himself unable to proceed three steps with consistency and propriety." "The argument, therefore, which would infer the absurdity of supposing the Scriptures to have a spiritual sense, from the acknowledged absurdity of supposing histories or poems merely human to have it, is inconclusive: the sacred writings differing in that respect from all other writings in the world, as much as the nature of the transactions they relate differs from all other transactions, and the AUTHOR who relates them differs from all other authors."

Origen says, "They who find fault with the allegorical exposition of the Scripture, and maintain that it has no other sense than that which the text shows, take away the key of knowledge."—*In Matt.*, cap. xxiii.

"In all things," says Augustine, "that He [God] hath spoken unto us (in his written Word), we must seek for the spiritual meaning, to ascertain which your desires in the name of Christ will assist us. By which, as by invisible hands, ye knock at the invisible gate, that invisibly it may open to us, and ye invisibly may enter in, and invisibly be healed."—*Psalm* ciii., *Enarratio*. And again the same writer says, "Barley, as you know, is so formed that you come with difficulty to the nourishing part of it, wrapped up as it is in a covering of chaff, and that chaff stiff and cleaving, so as not to be stripped off without some trouble. Such is the letter of the Old Testament, clothed with the wrappings of carnal sacraments, or tokens; but if you once come to its marrow, it nourishes and satisfies."—*In Joan*, tr. 24, 25. "*What is the chaff to the wheat, saith the Lord.*" (Jer. xxiii. 28.)

Augustine also remarks that "Now no one doubts that both objects become known to us with greater delight by means of similitudes, and things that are sought for with some difficulty are discovered with more pleasure. Magnificently, therefore, and healthfully for us, hath the Holy Spirit so adapted the Sacred Scriptures as to satisfy our hunger by passages more manifest, and by those that are more obscure to prevent fastidiousness."—*De Doct. Chris.*, lib. ii., vol. iii., p. 49.

CHAPTER VI.

The Difference between Correspondence and Metaphor, Fable, etc., stated.—Correspondence defined, with Examples of its Application in expounding the Holy Word.

WE have already seen that the only science by which the Word of God can be spiritually unfolded, and clearly distinguished from all other compositions whatsoever, is the science of correspondences. Let us investigate and illustrate the nature and application of its first principles. The science of correspondences is capable of being established and confirmed by the strictest reasoning and deduction of philosophy. Indeed, the absolute principles of all philosophy must be sought and found within us, and this is true of the philosophy on which correspondence rests; but, as Swedenborg states, "it may also be gathered from analogies, and even from geometry itself" (H. K. 41). This mode of reasoning, however, would lead us into a long train of metaphysical inquiries and researches for which general readers have but little leisure, and still less inclination. In general, we may say of science, that it is a knowledge of the relation which exists between the divine ideas and divine works; between what is infinite and what is finite; between what is spiritual and what is natural; and between what is mental and what is material. While fable has no higher aim than to inculcate moral maxims which have relation only to earthly existence; while figures of speech are but adornments of discourse and ornaments of rhetoric; and while comparison merely likens one natural object in appearance to another for the capricious purpose of illustration; correspondence is the positive affinity or relation which natural objects bear to spiritual realities. It is precisely the relation of the producing cause to its resulting effect; of the inward essence to the manifested form; of the spiritual world to the natural world; of the soul to the body; of the various faculties of the mind and their spiritual uses, to the various organs and viscera of the body and their respective natural uses. Thus, as the whole of the natural world corresponds in all its multitudinous particulars to the spiritual world, and the visible objects in both worlds correspond to the world of mind, —the affections and thoughts of men, spirits, and angels; and these again, in their purest and holiest significance, to the Divine affections and thoughts of God,—just so the literal sense of the Holy Word, which appears to treat of terrestrial objects and affairs, corresponds to its internal sense, which treats only of divine and "heavenly things" (John iii. 12), which are, so to speak, mirrors reflecting the image of the Great First Cause, the Creator and Sustainer of all. The figures of speech, and beauties of diction, in the literal sense, are but "subsidiary ornaments of the casket" which contains purest gems of inestimable price. Such is the nature of that harmonious and indissoluble bond by which all things, spiritual as well as natural, are connected with their Supreme Original, and are preserved by the same law as that by which they were primarily created.

Imagery is usually divided, first, into Tropes or Figures, including Allegory, Metaphor, Metonymy, Parable, Prosopopœia, and Synecdoche; and, secondly, including visible images and similitudes, as the Emblem, the Symbol, and the Type, all of which, however, are allied to, and have their essence or ground in, correspondences and representatives.

Correspondence must not be confounded with metaphorical figures of speech. Hindmarsh strikingly explains the difference between metaphor and the language of correspondence. "A mere figure or metaphor," says he, "is the resemblance in some certain way, which one thing bears to another, not according to the true nature and fitness of things, so much as by the arbitrary choice of a speaker or writer, who is desirous of illustrating his subject, and rendering it familiar to the comprehension. Consequently, there is no necessary union between the subject and the figure, nor is the one an effect of the other, or in any wise dependent on its existence and subsistence, as is the case in all correspondences. An example will illustrate the truth of my observation. Virgil, in his *Æneid*, lib. ii., likens the destruction of Troy, with her lofty spires, to the fall of an aged oak on being hewn down by the woodman's hatchet. This is a simile, or figure, but not a correspondence; for there is no necessary connection between the city of Troy and a mountain oak, nor between her lofty spires and the wide extending branches of a tree. The one is not within the other, as its life and soul; nor can the relationship subsisting between them be considered like that of cause and effect, essence and form, prior and posterior, soul and body, which, nevertheless, is the case with all true correspondences. The difference between a mere figure and a correspondence may again appear from the following consideration. A mere figure or simile is the resemblance which one natural object or circumstance is supposed to bear to another natural object or circumstance; whereas, a correspondence is the actual relation subsisting between a natural object and a spiritual subject, or a natural form and a spiritual essence; that is, between outer and inner, lower and higher, nature and spirit; and not between nature and nature, or spirit and spirit. This distinction should be well attended to. The language of correspondences is the language of God himself, being that in which He always speaks, both in his Word and in his works: but figure and metaphor, together, with the language of fable, are the mere inventions of man, which took their rise when the divine science of correspondences began to be lost in the world."—Preface to Hindmarsh's translation of Swedenborg's *Hieroglyphic Key to Natural and Spiritual Mysteries*, pp. 3–5.

All natural things exist from a spiritual origin, and all things spiritual from a divine origin, or the Lord. The human body, with all its parts and functions, is elaborated from the soul, its faculties and powers, and therefore corresponds to it in every particular of its structure, form, and use. So the whole Universe is not the product of an immediate and direct fiat of Omnipotence, but is the result of a series of spiritual causes and divine ends. Hence all things therein, even to the most minute atoms, are correspondences; the language of which is intelligible to angels, from the realities with which they are surrounded corresponding to their own states of mind, and suggests to the enlightened mind spiritual ideas. Thus correspondence originates in the very nature of angels and of God.

"Heaven, in the Word, in the internal sense, does not signify the heaven or sky which is apparent to the eyes of the body, but the kingdom of the Lord universally and particularly. He who looks at things internal from those that are external, when he views the heavens or sky, does not think at all of the starry heaven, but of the angelic heaven; when he beholds the sun, he does not think of the sun, but of the Lord, as being the sun of heaven; and so when he sees the moon, and the stars also; yea, when he beholds the immensity of the heavens, he does not think of material immensity, but of the immense and infinite power of the Lord; so also in other instances, since there is nothing but what is representative. He likewise regards earthly objects in the same view; thus, when he beholds the first dawn of the morning light, he does not think of the day-dawn, but of the rise of all things from the Lord, and their progression to the full day of wisdom; in like manner, when he looks on gardens, shrubberies, and beds of flowers, his eye is not confined to any particular tree, its blossom, leaf, or fruit, but he is led to a contemplation of the celestial things represented by them, neither does he behold only the flowers, their beauties and elegancies, but is led to regard also the things which they represent in the other life; for there is not a single object existing in the sky or in the earth, which is beautiful and agreeable, but what is in some way representative of the Lord's kingdom. The ground and reason why all things in the heavens or sky, and on the earth, both collectively and individually, are representative, is because they originally existed, and do continually exist, that is, subsist from an influx of the Lord through heaven. The case in this respect is like that of the human body, which exists and subsists by its soul; wherefore all things in the body, both collectively and individually, are representative of its soul: the soul is in the uses and ends regarded, but the body is in the execution of such uses and ends. In like manner all effects whatsoever are representative of the uses which are their causes; and the uses are representative of the ends which are their first principles. They who are in divine ideas never confine their sight to mere external objects, but continually, from them and in them, behold things internal; and internal things are, most essentially, those of the Lord's kingdom; consequently, these are in the veriest end of all. The case is similar in regard to the Word of the Lord: they who are in divine ideas never regard the Word of the Lord from the letter, but consider the letter and the literal sense, as representative and significative of the celestial and spiritual things appertaining to the Church and to the Lord's kingdom. With them the literal sense is only an instrumental medium of leading the thoughts to such objects."—A. C. 1807.

"Everything in the vegetable kingdom which is beautiful and ornamental derives its origin through heaven from the Lord; and that, when the celestial and spiritual things of the Lord flow into nature, such objects of beauty and ornament are actually exhibited, and that thence proceeds the vegetative soul or life. Hence, also, come representatives."—A. C. 1632.

The invisible, or, as many philosophers prefer calling it, the subjective world, acts within or upon the visible or objective world; for everything in the natural universe, as we have shown, continually subsists as an effect terminating in some use by means of influx from what corresponds therewith in the spiritual world as its efficient cause; it is thus the plane or resting-place of something spiritual. All this admits of easy illustration, and may be abundantly confirmed. For instance, there is a constant influent life momentarily derived from the Lord, and descending from the soul into all the particular members, viscera, and forms of structure, however minute, belonging to the body, without which the material organization would soon be deranged, and the elements composing them would speedily fall to pieces, and be dispersed. Thus there is an exact correspondence established by creation between all the various parts and functions of the body, and the manifold principles and faculties of the soul which gave them existing forms and activities in the natural world, and may be said for a time to inhabit them. There is, for example, an exact correspondence between the organ of vision—the eye, its structure, and its use—and the mental eye or the understanding and its powers. The brilliancy and earnest gaze of the eye will often search and reveal the quality of inward thought without the utterance of a word, or where the speech would be ambiguous (1 Sam. xvi. 7; Luke xxii. 61).

Here the tacit operation of the intellect in and through the eye proves that there exists the closest correspondence and connection. Thus, also, what light is to the natural eye, truth is to the understanding; what vision is to the eye, perception is to the soul. And it is common in all languages, for those who know nothing of the divine science of which we are treating, whence such forms of expression were originally derived, to speak of insight, of seeing and not seeing; of seeing in some particular light, or with various degrees of illumination; of blindness, darkness, shade, and brilliancy in reference to intellectual energy and rational discernment.

As a further most striking elucidation, there exists a correspondence between the heart,—a vital organ of the body, its physiological structure and its multifarious uses—and the human will, as a vital organ of the soul, with its complex affections and its complicated spiritual uses, for the will is the more immediate seat of all spiritual life; while the varied forms and functions of the heart as to every particular correspond, again, to the spiritual forms, activities, and offices of love. As the heart is the centre of all motion to the vital fluid in the body, so the will is the centre of circulation to the soul of all inward life. As the heart may be said to reign throughout the bodily organs by its proceeding arteries and veins, and holds them all in harmony, so the will by its ruling desire or love, and its proceeding derivative vessels of affection and thought, rules within and throughout the mind, and holds all mental principles in unity there. There is also a continuous influence flowing from the will into the bodily heart which proves the existence of a correspondence. Excitements of the passions always disturb, more or less, the movements of the heart, and thence influence the whole body; and just so the affections of the mind produce changes in the will, and thence in the life. As the blood is perfected in the heart, and there acquires its heat and vitality, and is rendered fit for its important purposes in sustaining the whole economy of the body, and is thence by the successive expansion and contraction of its muscular walls, impelled in continual and health-restoring streams to the most remote extremities of the human frame, so it is in regard to the will. In that receptacle of life within the mind, the living affections of goodness and truth are formed in the regenerating mind, and there receive heavenly qualities; and thence by action and reaction, streams of divine life can flow perpetually forth to vivify the whole spiritual system. That the will-principle is always signified by the heart in the Word, sometimes in a good sense and sometimes in an opposite sense, must be evident to every intelligent reader of those numerous passages where the heart is mentioned. The Lord, who alone judgeth righteously because He knoweth the secrets of the will, says, "I am He who searcheth the reins [or kidneys] and hearts; and I will give unto every one of you according to your works" (Rev. ii. 23). The Psalmist prays, "Search me and know my heart" (Ps. cxxxix. 23). We read of an "honest heart" and an "evil heart;" a "double heart" and "singleness of heart;" a "fearful heart" and a "strong heart;" of a "hardened heart" and a "liberal heart;" of a "broken heart" and a "glad, joyful heart;" of an "impure heart" and a "clean heart;" a "heart of stone" and a "heart of flesh;" of a "willing heart," of an "understanding heart," a "proud heart" and a "lowly heart,"—expressions which can only relate to various and opposite states of the will, and to the affections and thoughts thence derived.

To refer again to common forms of expression, what is more common than to attribute to an affectionate friend a warm heart, and to give him a cordial salutation. This mode of speaking in the language of correspondence, derived from the spiritual signification of the bodily organs, in reference to faculties and states of the mind, is universal, and has existed in all ages. To a sagacious man is ascribed a sharp nose; to an acute perception, a keen eye. This important doctrine is still further exemplified in the human countenance, in speech, and in gesture. How frequently is it observed, and how easy is it to prove, that the face is the index of the mind; for it changes its features according to the variations of inward feeling; and the speech and gesture, when spontaneous, are always outward indications of mental states; for the mind, except where dissimulation is practised, always flows into and exhibits itself in the lineaments of the countenance, which is pleasing or displeasing, gentle or fierce, tranquil or agitated, bold or timid, as the mind within is more or less influenced by prevailing passions; while speech is the form of active thought, which by correspondence flows into its tones of utterance, which are manifestations of the feelings and gestures which are expressive of the desires and determinations of the will. Swedenborg treats this subject with his usual clearness and felicity of expression, where he writes as follows:—"All things pertaining to man, whether internal or external, correspond to heaven; the universal heaven, being in the sight of the Lord as one man, all things therein, even to the most minute particular, being so arranged as to correspond to whatever belongs to man" (Ps. xlv. 9; Rev. xxi. 9).

"The whole face, where the sensories of the sight, the smell, the hearing, and the taste are situated, corresponds to the affections and thoughts thence derived in general; the eyes correspond to the understanding (Isa. xxxiii. 17, 30); the nostrils to perception (Gen. ii. 7); the ears to hearing and obedience (Matt. xi. 15); and the taste, to the desire of knowing and becoming wise (Ps. cxix. 103); but the forehead corresponds to the good of love, whence all the others are derived, for it constitutes the supreme part of the face; and immediately includes the front and primary part of the brain, whence are the intellectual things of man" (Ezek. ix. 4). From these considerations, it is evident what is signified by the servants of God being *sealed* in their foreheads (Rev. vii. 3), namely, that "it is to be in the good of love to the Lord from the Lord, and thereby to be distinguished and separated from those who are not in that love" (A. E. 427). Thus the invisible mind is visibly and distinctly portrayed and emblemized in the forms and activities of the body, both singly and collectively, because there exists between the soul and its material frame the strictest correspondence.

Now, all that we have thus endeavored to express is called correspondence; for the abstract principles of man's mind contained in his will and understanding and which constitute his inner world or life, being conspicuously represented in the organs of the body, their motive powers, and their active uses which constitute his outer world, there is a mutual correspondence and intercourse between them as between causes and their effects; the soul is exhibited in the body as its true image, and they operate as one.

But what correspondence is, and what influx, shall be illustrated by examples. The variations of the face, which are called the countenance or features, correspond to the affections of the mind, wherefore the face is varied as to its features as the affections of the mind are as to their states: those variations in the face are correspondences, consequently also the face itself, and the action of the mind into it, in order that the correspondences may be exhibited, is called influx. The sight of man's thought, which is called the understanding, corresponds to the sight of the eyes, wherefore also from the light and flame of the eyes appears the quality of the thought from the understanding; the sight of the eye is correspondence, consequently also the eye itself and the action of the understanding into the eye whereby the correspondence is exhibited, is influx. The active thought which is of the understanding corresponds to the speech which is of the mouth; the speech is correspondence as likewise is the mouth and everything belonging to it, and the action of thought into speech, and into the organs of speech, is influx. The perception of the mind corresponds to the smell of the nostrils; the smell and the nostrils are correspondences and the action is influx; hence it is that a man who has interior perception is said to be of an acute nostril, or of quick scent, and the perception of a thing is expressed by scenting or smelling it out. Hearkening, which denotes obedience, corresponds to the hearing of the ears, wherefore both the hearing and the ears are correspondences, and the action of obedience into the hearing, in order that man may raise the ears, or listen and attend, is influx; hence it is that hearkening and hearing are both significative—to hearken and to give ear to any one denoting to obey, and to hearken and hear any one denoting to hear with the ears. The action of the body corresponds to the will; the action of the heart corresponds to the life of the love; and the action of the lungs, which is called respiration, corresponds to the life of the faith; and the whole body as to all its members, viscera, and organs, corresponds to the soul as to all the functions and power of its life. From these few observations it may be seen what is meant by correspondence and by influx, and that whilst the spiritual principle, which is the life of man's will and understanding, flows into the acts which are of his body, and exhibits itself in a natural effigy, there is correspondence; and that thus the spiritual and natural by correspondences act as one, like interior and exterior, or like prior and posterior, or like the efficient cause and the effect, or like the principal cause which is of man's thought and will, and the instrumental cause which is of his speech and action. Such a correspondence of natural things and spiritual exists not only in all and singular the things of man, but also in all and singular the things of the world, and the correspondences are exhibited by the influx[42] of the spiritual world, and all things appertaining to that world, into the natural world, and all things appertaining to it. Thus all the countless organs and forms of the body with their numberless uses typify, signify, or correspond to the endless distinct faculties or powers constituting the soul and mind with their diversified uses. It is on account of this correspondence that the various members and viscera of the human frame with their respective operations and uses are so frequently mentioned in the Holy Word, both in regard to God and the soul of man, in reference to the laws of worship and the precepts of life, and are often applied to inanimate things, where it is evident that mere bodily organs cannot possibly be meant. Such expressions, when predicated of the Lord, not only refer to Him as in Himself an all-glorious and Divine Man, but also signify some distinct qualities of the divine mind, and operations of the divine energy which would otherwise be totally incomprehensible. Of the Lord it is said in Isa. xi. 5, "Righteousness shall be the girdle of his loins, and faithfulness the girdle of his reins." Here the prophet is speaking of the Lord's manifested form, or his glorified Human Nature, as the very divine goodness itself and truth itself, self-derived and sole-subsisting, and from which the church in heaven and on earth is perpetually supplied with all degrees of love and wisdom, and preserved therein. And in Zech. iv. 10, to signify his omnipresence and all-pervading Providence, by virtue of his wisdom and understanding, it is stated that "the eyes of the Lord run to and fro through the whole earth." In the same sense it is written in Psalm xi. 4 that "His eyes behold and his eyelids try the children of men," where the Lord's eyes and his eyelids denote his Divine Providence and omniscience and intelligence, and the mediums by which they operate, namely, the internal and external truths and doctrines of his Word. Elsewhere we have

---

[42] Influx is derived from the Latin word *influo*, to inflow or flow in.

frequent mention made of the arm or hand of the Lord, to signify his divine omnipotence, as in the following passage: "He had horns coming out of his hand, and there was the hiding of his power"[43] (Hab. iii. 4); and speaking of his eternal victories over death and hell, for the accomplishment of human redemption, obtained by the inherent omnipotence of his own Divine Human Nature, it is said in the Psalms that "He hath done marvellous things; his right hand and his holy arm hath gotten Him the victory" (xcviii. 1).

It was from this signification of the hand as denoting power, and of the sense of touch as representing communication, translation, and reception of power and virtue, that the Lord laid his hands upon the sick and they recovered; and that to accomplish special uses in relation to ministerial functions, inaugurations into the priesthood of the Jewish dispensation (Numb. viii. 9-12), and also into the ministry of the Christian church, from its very first commencement (Acts iv. 3; viii. 19; xiii. 3; 1 Tim. v. 22), were effected as divine order requires by the imposition of hands. This act bears the same signification elsewhere in the Word, as in the act of blessing, and on other occasions (Numb. xxvii. 18-23; Matt. xvii. 7; Mark v. 23; Rev. i. 17).

When Moses, Aaron, and the elders of Israel have a representative vision of the Lord to signify that He manifests himself to the perceptions of his true church by means of his Holy Word, it is said that "they saw the God of Israel, and there was under his feet, as it were, a paved work of a sapphire-stone, and as it were the body of heaven in its clearness" (Exod. xxiv. 9-11). We read also of the Lord's heart to denote his divine will, purpose, or love (Isa. lxiii. 4; Matt. xi. 29); of his head, to signify his infinite wisdom and intelligence, by which He governs all worlds; and of the hair of his head, to denote the ultimate energies of his Divine Providence, by which the lowest and vilest of the human family may be saved (Rev. i. 14). To represent the omnipotence of truth from the Lord, in its ultimate or lowest activity, destroying and dissipating all the false persuasions of that self-righteousness which disclaims the need of purity or cir-

---

[43] "The hand is the chief instrument of exerting our strength, and is, therefore, very properly used to denote the power of God."—*Howard's Comp. for the Festivals and Fasts of the Ch. of Eng.*, 1761, p. 129.

"The *arm* and the *hand* are natural terms, when applied to the ability of a man, which express his capacity or readiness of *power*. . . . These are figurative expressions of common acceptation, for the conveyance of these common ideas. Agreeably to these we are to understand the terms when applied by Jehovah to Himself. By his arm, then, we are to understand the *extent* of his power, as his *stretched-out arm*, or infinite might, reaches to all things."—*Serle's Hor. Sol.*, p. 139.

cumcision of heart, we are supplied with the historical relation of Samson, the Nazarite, whose prodigious strength is said to have resided in his hair, slaying the Philistines, emphatically called the uncircumcised (Judges xvi. 17). In the life of real religion, which revealed truth teaches and enjoins, and which is exemplified in the ordinary duties of the Christian life, lies this only real spiritual strength and security. This alone conjoins man to the infinite source of all power. On the preservation of his hair, according to his vows, his strength is said to rest. Shorn of this—disjointed from omnipotence—his vows broken, and he is but weak and defenceless, like any other unregenerate man. In the highest sense Samson was a type of the Lord as the great Redeemer or Deliverer of the human race from death and hell, and his hair will represent the manifestation of the power of truth in the life and conduct of his professing church. That power is feeble or strong to accomplish the divine purposes in proportion as men live in obedience to the truths of his Word. Hence, too, we see the reason why calling the prophet Elisha,[44] who represented the Lord and his Word, " bald head "[45] was blasphemy of the deepest dye, while the spiritual punishment of such impiety which the daring blasphemer thus induces upon himself, though it appears to his disordered imagination as the infliction of divine vengeance, is exactly represented in the destruction of the " forty and two children " by the " two she-bears out of the wood " (2 Kings ii. 23). How interesting and instructive do these narratives become when they are expounded in every divine particular related!

In Ezekiel's prophecy we read, " I, the LORD God, will take away the stony heart out of your flesh, and will give you a heart of flesh " (xxxvi. 26), where a stony heart signifies a hardened will,[46] insensible to good impressions; for flesh, in this and many other passages, signifies goodness, which is the reason why the Lord says He gives us his flesh to eat that we may have eternal life (John vi. 54); and the

---

[44] Elisha means in English the salvation of God.

[45] " Bald-head is an epithet of scorn and contempt still used in the East, and is given to those who are weak or mean, whether they have hair on the head or not. Hence, the epithet has often been applied to Christian missionaries."—*Roberts's Oriental Illust.*, 2d ed., p. 214.

In the spiritual sense, it signifies a destitution of the *ultimates* of religion, and is a term of reproach justly applied to all who make the truth of God and a moral life subservient to selfish purposes, and who abound in self-conceit.

[46] See Dr. Rice's excellent and interesting work, *Illustrations of Physiology*. Boston, U. S., 1851.

" The instruments or organs [of the body] constitute the *media* of communication between the world without and the world within, the *material* creation and the *spiritual*."—*Dr. G. Moore's Power of the Soul over the Body*, 2d ed., p. 35.

heart, being the centre of vitality, corresponds to the inmost and central affections of the will. In the Psalms it is said, "I will bless the LORD, who hath given me counsel; my reins also instruct [correct] me in the night seasons" (xvi. 7), where the reins, or kidneys, of which chastisement is here predicated, signify the things which relate to faith and the intellect, or faculty of receiving them. For, as the reins in the animal economy serve the important office of purifying the vital fluids, so the truths of faith, or truths internally believed, when practically applied in the great work of man's regeneration, search and explore, correct and purify, all things of his mind and life, insomuch that without them the mind and life cannot be examined, corrected, and purified aright. This process of casting out evil affections and unclean thoughts takes place in the night of trial and temptation, and appears as a punishment till the morning of a new state of deliverance and joy arises upon the grateful soul, as it is written: "Behold, thou desirest truth in the inward parts, and in the hidden part thou shalt make me to know wisdom" (Ps. li. 8); and again: "Oh let the wickedness of the wicked come to an end, but establish the just; for the righteous God trieth the hearts and reins" (Ps. vii. 9). The Lord also thus reproves his people by the prophet Jeremiah, for the mere external or lip profession of the truth of religion or of faith, without allowing it to search out and correct the inward evils and impurities of their hearts and thoughts: "Thou art near in their mouth, and far from their reins" (xii. 2).

Again: in the gospel of Matthew we read that the Lord said to his disciples, "Wherefore, if thy hand or foot offend thee [literally, from the Greek, *cause thee to offend*], cut them off and cast them from thee: it is better for thee to enter into life halt or maimed, rather than having two hands or two feet to be cast into everlasting fire. And if thine eye offend thee, pluck it out and cast it from thee: it is better for thee to enter into life with one eye, rather than having two eyes to be cast into hell fire" (xviii. 8, 9). In this extraordinary passage, which the science of correspondences can alone unfold, the hands, as the chief instruments of physical energy and the ultimate of action, denote ability; the feet, as the organs of locomotion and the support for the whole frame, denote the natural or lowest properties of the mind; and the eyes, or organs of vision, signify the intellectual powers. Now we are elsewhere exhorted to have "a single eye and a single heart," and the reason is plain, because, as with the body, if the sight be not directed to the object before the eyes with singleness of energy, two objects appear where there should be only one, and the view is consequently bewildered: so with the mind; if its purpose be not direct and single, it is distracted with the two discordant views of seeking human applause and of trying to appear well with God. And singleness of heart is of necessity connected with singleness of sight, inasmuch as a single and direct view of subjects is the result of singleness of affection, just as surely as a double and indirect view follows from discordant feelings. When, therefore, any evil or false principles in the natural mind are, by the presence of truth, made manifest as the cause of our offending against the holy principles of the Word, we are to renounce them and cast them from us, for how much better is it for us to enter into eternal life "halt or maimed," that is, imperfectly instructed and struggling under the effects of ignorance, rather than, after being well instructed, having the form of godliness, but, as the Apostle says, "denying the power" (2 Tim. iii. 5),—a hand, a foot, an eye devoted to the world and self, while the other is ostensibly in the service of religion. Such double-minded conduct assuredly renders man a miserable hypocrite here, and obnoxious, hereafter, to the self-inflicted punishments of "hell-fire," or the burning torments of evil affections thus rendered more furious for having been smothered in this world.

Again: in Jeremiah it is said, "Behold, their ear is uncircumcised, and they cannot hearken" (vi. 10), to signify that unwillingness to learn and obey the principles of divine truth, which arises from impurity of heart. Hearkening denotes readiness to obey, even in the ordinary language of men; therefore many of the statutes of Israel had especial reference to the ear, and the Lord also frequently and solemnly said at the commencement or conclusion of his divine instructions, "Who hath ears to hear, let him hear" (Matt. xiii. 9); and again, "Let these sayings sink down into your ears" (Luke ix. 44). An unwillingness to be instructed in the divine truth, and a disinclination to obedience, arising from evil lusts cherished in the will, is thus described in the language of correspondence by the prophet: "To whom shall I speak, and give warning, that they may hear? Behold, their ear is uncircumcised, and they cannot hearken; behold, the word of the Lord is unto them a reproach; they have no delight in it" (Jer. vi. 10). "They hearkened not unto me, nor inclined their ear, but hardened their neck: they did worse than their fathers" (Ib., vii. 26). But turn to the Psalms, where the exultation of the heart is described, where divine blessings are received and acknowledged, and where the life and joy which animate the mind, internally and externally, when it becomes receptive of faith and charity, are the subjects treated of, and where every term has its peculiar and distinct meaning, we read, "Let the floods clap their hands; let the hills be joyful together before the Lord" (xcviii. 8, 9); "The mountains skipped like rams, and the little hills like lambs" (cxiv. 6); "The voice of the Lord maketh the cedars to skip like a calf; Lebanon and Sirion like a young unicorn" (xxix. 6). Who can interpret these, and a multitude of similar passages in the Sacred Word, in their merely literal sense? What enlightened mind does not see that the various parts and motions of the human body are in these instances employed as significant figures, because, when viewed in connection with their uses, they precisely correspond with properties and states of the mind? To affirm, as some have done, that these and similar expressions are mere ornamental types and oriental figures, is to regard them as designed only to amuse the imagination, and is almost equivalent to a denial of their inspiration and solemn verity.

CHAPTER VII.

The Science of Correspondences not a Speculative and Visionary Theory, but an Absolute Reality.—Illustrations from Opposites, and various other Subjects.—The Objects for which the Word of God was Revealed only Answered by the Admission of its Internal Sense, which alone Distinguishes it from all other Compositions, and Reconciles its Apparent Contradictions.—Universality of this Divine Science, and the Necessity that Exists for the Word being Written according to it.

THIS doctrine of the structure of the Word of God—this law by which it must of necessity be expounded, in order to yield throughout its sacred pages "instruction and correction in righteousness"—is no speculative or visionary theory, as some have erroneously supposed, but a truly consistent, luminous, and universal method of interpretation. It may be trusted without hesitation, because it is founded on the immutable basis of eternal truth,—on the ever-enduring laws of divine order, on the unalterable relation which all created objects have to their Creator, and which all external objects have to internal realities.

Correspondences are the only forms which can contain the living truths of God and heaven, convey them into the inmost depths of the soul, and impress them permanently there. They are universally understood; they exist alike in all times and under all circumstances; they are more or less enshrined in all languages, and are equally obvious to all. "Whatsoever anywhere appears in the universe," says Swedenborg, "is representative of the Lord's kingdom, insomuch that there is not anything contained in the universal atmospheric region of the stars, or in the earth and its three kingdoms, but what in its manner and measure is representative; for all and singular the things in nature are ultimate images, inasmuch as from the Divine [principle] proceed the celestial things appertaining to good, and from these celestial things the spiritual things appertaining to truth, and from both the former and the latter proceed natural things. Hence it may appear how gross, yea, how terrestrial, and also inverted, human reason is, which ascribes all and singular things to nature separate or exempt from influx prior to itself, or from the efficient cause. . . . Inasmuch, now, as all and singular things subsist from the Divine [principle], that is, continually exist, and all and singular things thence derived must needs be representative of those things whereby they had existence, it follows, that the visible universe is nothing but a theatre representative of the Lord's kingdom, and that this latter is a theatre representative of the Lord Himself."— A. C. 3483.

All terms are of necessity modified by the sense of the connection as well as by the imperfection of languages. The same term is often used in the Holy Word as the translation of two or even more distinct words; and, on the other hand, several words are often used to translate a single expression. A single word in the original may have two or more significations, either to be determined by the context or dependent on the subject treated of and indicated, sometimes, only in the most trifling difference in the form of the word, or in the use of particles and expletives. Many words and their modifications, in the Hebrew, Greek, and Latin, have no corresponding terms or forms of expression in any modern tongue. These niceties in the original sometimes occasion perplexity to the reader of Swedenborg, and give to correspondence the appearance of being an arbitrary and uncertain science, which, of course, cannot be wholly removed without some knowledge of the original languages themselves. Nice distinctions in the original are not always capable of transferrence into other languages.[47]

The ancient Hebrew is not only the oldest, but the most significant language known, and was peculiarly appropriate to the purpose of enshrining the science of correspondences in the earlier ages of the world. The roots of several of the Semitic languages, such as the Arabic, Syriac, Chaldaic, etc., are so closely assimilated to the Hebrew

---

[47] "I find that the same object preaches truths of an opposite nature by the medium of the same symbol. This, however, can create no confusion, because the context will always determine in what light the symbol is to be considered. But if you carefully consider the human world, you will find the same ambiguity in men's actions. For the same outward expression springs frequently from opposite motives."—*Essays on Universal Analogy between the Natural and Spiritual Worlds*, p. 32.

"One and the same natural thing may be a symbol of *contrary* spiritual mysteries."— *H. More's Cab. Def.*, p. 239.

"The same qualities, infinitely good and perfect in God, may become *imperfect and evil* in the creature; because in the creature, being limited and finite, they may be *divided and separated* from one another by the creature itself. There is no evil, no guilt, no deformity, in any creature, but in its *dividing* and *separating* itself from something which God had given to be in union with it."— *Law's Appeal*, pp. 24, 41.

as often to throw considerable light on Hebrew words and phrases, and to confirm their signification.

Correspondences are grounded in use, representatives in rituals of religion and human operations, and significatives in what is uttered or written; the whole, however, having the same ground of meaning, is included in the phrase we have so often used — the science of correspondences. Now, it will be seen at once, that, as all good things are liable to abuse through the perversion of reason, and may be applied to evil as well as good purposes, so the correspondence, the representation or the signification will change, and the object or expression which in a good sense denotes something good or true, or some spiritual blessing, will, when referring to or describing a perverted state, denote something evil or false, or some blessing changed to a curse; for, "If ye will not hear, and if ye will not lay it to heart, to give glory unto my name, saith the Lord of hosts, I will even send a curse upon you, and I will curse your blessings" (Mal. ii. 2).

When this law of correspondence, radiant with celestial lustre, is applied to those Scriptures which constitute the perfect Word of God, they exhibit one harmonious scheme of profound wisdom, reflecting the Divine Mind of its glorious Author, and worthy of his infinite intelligence and goodness; one connected series of beautiful, practical, vital, everlasting truths, suited to the endless progress of the soul in the life of heaven. It is indeed "the key of knowledge" (Luke xi. 52), which can alone unlock the cabinet which contains the priceless gems of truth, glowing with innumerable splendors, derived from the pure and precious wisdom of God, — the doctrines and precepts of eternal life. This mode of interpreting the Holy Oracles is as widely different from what has been called "spiritualizing" as the substance is from its shadow. The mere spiritualizer forces his own imaginary, and often extravagant, meaning on Scriptural terms and phrases to suit some ingenious notion fabricated in the realms of luxuriant fancy; interchanging and commingling the subjective and the objective; capriciously changing the sense, whenever it suits his purpose, and, in his futile attempts to expound the Word of God, profanes the truth instead of unfolding it.[48] He has not been unaptly

---

[48] "To most educated persons in the nineteenth century, these [spiritualistic and arbitrary] applications of Scripture appear foolish. In whatever degree [this mode of interpretation] is practised, it is equally incapable of being reduced to any rule. It is the interpreter's fancy, and is likely to be not less, but more, dangerous and extravagant when it adds the charm of authority from its use in past ages. In it we assume what can never be proved, and an instrument is introduced of such subtlety and pliability as to

represented as on a deep and mighty ocean, without a star to guide, a compass to direct, or a helm to regulate his course. The science of correspondences is the very reverse of all this, for it rests, as we have endeavored to show, on fixed data, on unchanging laws. The same word, or expression, or phrase, in the same connection, always bearing the same spiritual signification, or its opposite, wherever it occurs in the plenarily-inspired books of the Old and New Testaments. Were it otherwise, the meaning would be arbitrary, uncertain, and valueless.

As men, by virtue of their freedom, are capable of perverting the richest blessings into curses, of profaning the holiest truths by falsifying them and connecting them with evils of heart and life, of abusing as well as using God's best gifts, so numerous opposites exist in creation, and conformably therewith there are many expressions and phrases in the Word which are the reverse of each other, as light and darkness, day and night, life and death, heat and cold, summer and winter, clean and unclean animals, useful and noxious vegetation, fruitful and barren trees and land.[49] And we may easily see how such perversion originates and operates in the human mind, for, as unclean and voracious animals may be supported by the same kind of food, or as wholesome and poisonous vegetables may grow in the same soil, receiving the same rays of heat and light from the sun, but

---

make the Scriptures mean anything,—'Gallus in campanili,' as the Waldenses described it; the weathercock on the church-tower, which is turned hither and thither by every wind of doctrine."—*Jowett's Essays and Reviews*, 9th ed., pp. 369-398.

The richest specimen of this fanciful, ingenious, but altogether uncertain method of expounding the Holy Word, I probably ever met with, is an elaborate volume entitled "Moses Unveiled," by William Guild, Minister of the Parish of King Edward, Edinburgh.

"An unlicensed imagination has produced disastrous effects in the interpretation of Scripture."—*Davidson's Hermeneutics*, p. 10.

For absurd specimens of this kind of interpretation, see Bright, Cumming, Walksley, and other commentators' expositions of the Book of Revelation, Bishop Marsh's *Lectures*, p. 369-375, and Dr. A. Clarke's *Letter to a Methodist Preacher*, in which this ingenious trifling with the Holy Word, not to say profanation of its sacred truths, is well exposed.

"That the spiritual interpretation of the Scriptures, like all other good things, is liable to abuse, and that it hath been actually abused, both in ancient and modern ages, cannot be denied." "Men of sense will consider that a principle is not, therefore, to be rejected because it is abused," (*Bishop Hurd's Int. to Proph.*, p. 64,) "since human errors can never invalidate the truths of God."—*Bishop Horne's Pref. to the Psalms*, p. viii., new ed., 1830.

[49] Augustine appears to have had a correct idea on this subject. He says in his *De Doc. Chris.*, iii. 35, t. iii., pars. i., 42 D. "The same thing may sometimes stand for contraries, here in a good sense, there in a positively bad one;" and he instances the leaven of the Pharisees, and the leaven of the parable; the lion, and the serpent.—See *Tracts for the Times*, lxxxix., p. 174.

"Adam, one while, is the spiritual or intellectual man; another while, the earthly and carnal."—*H. More's Philosoph. Writings*, p. 176, London, 1662.

"Cabalistical appellatives stand for bad as well as good meaning."—*Maclean's Hist. of the Celtic Language*, p. 267.

according to their own peculiar nature and quality, so the wicked and the good among men alike receive the divine influences of love and wisdom from God; but as the unclean animals and poisonous vegetables change the respective elements on which they live into their own corresponding natures, so the wicked pervert the heavenly gifts, and change them, so to speak, into their contraries, or the opposite qualities of hell. For the Lord is no respecter of persons: "He maketh his sun to rise on the evil and on the good, and sendeth rain on the just and on the unjust" (Matt. v. 45). When the prophet, therefore, is deploring the perversity of Israel, he says, "Ye have turned judgment into gall, and the fruit of righteousness into hemlock" (Amos vi. 12).

All good natural objects in the universe, and their uses, exist from the Lord; they are the outbirths and infinitely varied forms of his love and wisdom; but all[50] noxious things and uses originate in evil, and are the opposite perverted forms of goodness and truth; hence, according to their peculiar qualities and properties, they are malignant and destructive, filthy and poisonous. All things must have had their origin in the spiritual world by corresponding influx, either through heaven or hell, into what is homogeneous, while their forms and uses derive fixity and existence in the world of nature.[51]

Whatever is accordant with the Divine Will, corresponds to or represents or signifies somewhat relating to heaven, or just order; and whatever is, from any cause, contrary thereto, exists of Divine permission, and corresponds to or represents or signifies somewhat relating to hell, or perverted order. Whatever relates to heaven has relation also to goodness and truth in the human mind and life, and whatever relates to hell has relation to evil and falsity in the mind and life. The Word, in its literal sense, is designed for the use of man while in this world, or in a merely natural state; and man, while in this probationary state of existence, is placed midway between heaven and hell, so as to be the subject of the influence of each alike. Here is the ground of his freedom and his capacity for regeneration; hence arises antagonism in nature and the mind, and hence, too, the opposite meanings of the same term in different parts of Scripture, referring to and adumbrating the antagonistic principles and states

---

[50] See Gen. i. 4; viii. 22; Lev. xi. 47; Ps. cvii. 33-35; Ezek. xliv. 23.

[51] "Such is the analogy between the spiritual and material world, that transactions of the highest importance in the former pass on and express themselves in the latter, so as to become the objects even of sense." —*Heylin, Lect. I.*, p. 36.

of the Church collectively, or the man of the Church individually.[52]

As another illustration, a mountain, as being one of the most elevated portions of the earth's surface, corresponds to an exalted or inmost principle of the mind, thus to some ruling affection of the heart. This may be either good or evil. If good, it is "Mount Zion, the mountain of holiness,"[53] denoting a state of love to the Lord; if evil, it is "the destroying mountain," denoting a state of the love of self. Of the former mountain,—an elevated state of love to God,—we read, "The Lord bless thee, O habitation of justice, and mountain of holiness" (Jer. xxxi. 23). And in predicting the glorious dominion of the love of God in the soul, and the divine blessings thence resulting, the prophet says, "And in this mountain shall the Lord of hosts make unto all people a feast of fat things, a feast of wines on the lees, of fat things full of marrow, of wine on the lees well refined" (Isa. xxv. 6). This signification of the term mountain supplies the reason why, in ancient times, houses of worship were built, worship was celebrated, and sacrifices were offered on hills and mountains; and hence, too, in a corrupt and perverted state of the human mind, whether as the Church collectively or individually, idolatry set up its graven and molten images in thousands of monstrous and bestial forms, and burnt incense to them in the high places and on the hills (2 Kings xvi. 4)—representative of that gross, sensual, and selfish worship which is so utterly opposed to the Divine commandments (Ex. xx. 4), and which springs either from the love of self in all its corrupt, cruel forms, signified by molten images, or is fashioned by the graving-tools of self-intelligence, in all its false and hateful varieties, signified by graven images. Of the latter mountain, a state in which the evil love of self—signified in its opposite sense by a mountain—is permitted to *assume* preëminence, we read, "Behold, I am against thee, O destroying mountain, saith the Lord, which destroyest all the earth: and I will stretch out mine hand upon thee, and roll thee down from the rocks, and will make thee a burnt mountain. And they shall not take of thee a stone for

---

[52] See H. H., n. 113.

[53] Jerome, speaking of Mount Zion, affirms that it is a foolish thing to call an irrational and insensible mountain holy, or to believe it to be so."—*In Jerem.*, xxxi.

"If, as I believe, and endeavor to prove, divine and saving truths of the Word of God are concealed under the forms of the figures, or parables, or proverbs of Nature, can you seriously ask what is the use of universal analogy? It is a key to the Bible and to Nature. If you see no use in the key, you will probably see no use in that which it is to unlock. To be consistent, you should ask what is the use of the Bible."—*Essays on Anal.*, p. 155.

a corner, nor a stone for foundations; but thou shalt be desolate forever, saith the Lord" (Jer. li. 25, 26). In reference to this signification of a mountain, as denoting the love of self and the world, our blessed Lord said to his disciples, "If ye have faith as a grain of mustard-seed, ye shall say unto this mountain, Remove hence to yonder place; and it shall remove" (Matt. xvii. 20). And again, speaking of the blessed ascendency and reign of love and wisdom from the Lord, grounded in humility and the eternal subjection and removal of the proud and lofty principle of self-love opposed thereto, the prophet exclaims, "Who art thou, O great mountain? Before Zerubbabel thou shalt become a plain: and he shall bring forth the headstone thereof with shoutings, crying, Grace, grace, unto it" (Zech. iv. 7).

A hill is a less lofty elevation of the earth's surface than a mountain, and when both are mentioned together, as they often are, then a hill will signify the principle of charity, while a mountain will signify love to the Lord. Thus we read in the prophet that at the day of the Lord's appearing or manifestation for the establishment of his church, "The mountains shall drop down new wine, and the hills shall flow with milk" (Joel iii. 18). Blessings of celestial and spiritual truth, in richest abundance, are here represented as flowing, distilling, dropping, from the sacred and elevated principles of love to the Lord and of charity towards our neighbor; enriching, refreshing, nourishing the soul, and enabling to bring forth and abound in the genuine virtues and graces of a Christian life.

Again, *treasures*, in the Word of God, signify all that on which a man's heart is chiefly placed,—that which, above all other things, he values most. Hence there are treasures of goodness and truth, and, on the contrary, treasures of wickedness and falsity; so we read, "A good man out of the good treasure of his heart bringeth forth good things: and an evil man out of the evil treasure bringeth forth evil things" (Matt. xii. 35). Well, then, may we be exhorted by our blessed Lord to "lay up for ourselves treasures in heaven, where neither moth nor rust doth corrupt, and where thieves do not break through nor steal" (Matt. vi. 20).[54]

As another illustration of what has been advanced, let us refer to the signification of natural light[55] and heat, as corresponding in their

---

[54] "Worldly wealth is but the shadow of that true wealth which only good men are enriched with, and consisteth not in gold and silver, but with treasures of knowledge here, and of eternal happiness hereafter."—*Ross's Musês Interpreter*, p. 292.

[55] "LIGHT is most certainly the universal type of *knowledge* or *demonstration*, whether

existence, their effects, and their uses, to spiritual truth and love. It will then be seen that their negatives, which are the consequences of their absence or privation, viz., darkness and cold, signify ignorance and indifference, and that their perverted opposites are falsity and lust. This will be most easily and amply confirmed, by every intelligent mind, from Scripture testimony, from analogical reasoning, and from scientific facts. Thus all the qualities and predicates which are attributable to light are equally applicable, in an inner sense, to truth in the understanding, and such as are ascribed to fire are equally referable to love in the will. What glory and interest do these correspondences alone throw over a large portion of the Holy Word! Through them you will at once perceive why the historical fact is related of the Egyptians that "they sat three days in darkness that might be felt," while "the children of Israel had light in all their dwellings" (Ex. x. 23); and how this natural event was a just representative of a spiritual truth attested by the experience of men in every age. Egypt was celebrated above other nations, in ancient times, for the cultivation of the sciences; the Egyptians, therefore, in a bad sense, represented mere worldly knowledges and science. The children of Israel represented the members of the Lord's church, drawing their stores of spiritual intelligence from the fountain of light—the Word of God. Now, the visible effects of such states, with each of these classes, are precisely what we find described in the inspired history; the former sit in despair, surrounded by spiritual darkness, the density of which makes it sensible even to sensual discernment; "for if the light that is in thee be darkness, how great is that darkness" (Matt. vi. 23); while the latter have the light of divine truth to bless and irradiate all their dwellings,—all the principles and states of their minds and lives with heavenly perception and intelligence, consolation and peace.

Knowing the correspondence of light, among thousands of beautiful and practical truths, we shall see the reason why it is said of the holy city, New Jerusalem, seen by John, and which signifies the Lord's

---

of *natural*, *moral*, or *spiritual* truth; for if not, what is meant by the light of *nature*, of *reason*, and of *conscience?*"—*Essays on Analogy*, p. 289.

"In thy light [O Lord] shall we see light." (Psalm xxxvi. 9.) Iamblichus, the Platonist, who flourished about the year 340, said that "God had light for a body, and truth for a soul."

"As the sun cannot be known but by his own light, so God cannot be known but with his own light."—*Plotinus*.

"In the ancient writings of the East, where the marriages of the gods and demigods are described, it is always said the ceremony was performed in the presence of the god of fire."—*Roberts's Orient. Illust.*, 2d ed., p. 21.

true church, that "Her light was like a stone most precious, even like a jasper stone, clear as crystal" (Rev. xxi. 11), to represent the purity, the preciousness, the splendor of the heaven-descended doctrines; and why it is said of the Lord that "He covereth himself with light as with a garment" (Psalm civ. 2), to signify the investment of his divine character in the truth of his Word, accommodated to the states of his creatures.

When, again, we are acquainted with the correspondence of fire,[56] as signifying, in a good sense, love—both divine and human—the love the Lord bears to his creatures, and the love they bear to Him and to each other in various degrees of intensity, we shall understand how the Lord defends and protects his own church, and every member of it, by the emanating influences of his infinite love and wisdom, for this is signified where He says, "I, the Lord, will be unto her," that is, his church, "a wall of fire round about" (Zech. ii. 5), an encircling sphere through which no enemy can break. The same things are also denoted in 2 Kings, where we read that the young man who was alarmed for the safety of his master had his spiritual sight opened, and saw a representation of this protecting sphere in the spiritual world surrounding the prophet of God; for "Behold, the mountain was full of horses and chariots of fire, round about Elisha" (vi. 17).

How encouraging is the thought that such, too, are the encircling spheres which comfort and protect the sincere Christian in all states of tribulation, temptation, and trial, in all seasons of affliction, sorrow, and distress. Again, to signify that it is the Lord alone who cleanses the human mind from pollution, and imbues it with his own divine love and wisdom, He says that "*He will baptize*" true believers "*with the Holy Spirit and with fire*" (Luke iii. 16); and to denote spiritual purification and protection, resulting from the inward operations of love and wisdom on the heart and mind, we read, "And it shall come to pass, that he that is left in Zion, and he that remaineth in Jerusalem, shall be called holy, even every one that is written among the living in Jerusalem: when the Lord shall have washed away the filth of the daughters of Zion, and shall have purged the blood of Jerusalem from the midst thereof by the spirit of judgment, and by the spirit of burning. And the Lord will create upon every dwelling-place

---

[56] "It is needless to remark that *desire* is in all languages compared to a fire."—*Bloomfield's Synopsis, Am. S.,* 1 Cor. vii. 9.

"By fire is sometimes signified love. It is this fire which God wishes should always burn upon the altar of our hearts."—*Lauretus, Art. Fire.*

of mount Zion, and upon her assemblies, a cloud and smoke by day, and the shining of a flaming fire by night; for upon all the glory shall be a defence. And there shall be a tabernacle for a shadow in the daytime from the heat, and for a place of refuge, and for a covert from storm and from rain" (Isa. iv. 3-6). Each expression in these glorious declarations would be seen, had we opportunity of unfolding them, to be filled with spirit and life; but from what has been already advanced, the humble and devout Christian will readily perceive the general meaning and application of the entire passage.

When we thus learn the spiritual import of light and fire, we see the reason why in the representative temple at Jerusalem the fire and light were never suffered to "go out" (Lev. vi. 13; xxiv. 2), and why in the representative worship so many offerings to Jehovah were directed to be made by fire; for the light of heavenly truth must irradiate our understandings with undying hope, and the flame of heavenly charity must be kindled on the altar of our hearts and never allowed to be extinguished. Our worship, to be intelligent, sincere, internal, profitable, must spring from enlightened reason and hallowed affection; so will our imperfect services be acceptable to Him who "regardeth not the outward appearance, but looketh on the heart" (1 Sam. xvi. 7). When, again, we admit that the opposites of truth and love are fantasy, or imaginary light, or falsity, and burning concupiscences, or soul-tormenting lusts, how transpicuous numerous passages of the Word of God, otherwise inexplicable, become,—as where the Psalmist says, "I lie among them that are set on fire" (Psalm lvii. 4); and where the prophet says, "Behold, all ye that kindle a fire, that compass yourselves about with sparks: walk in the light of your fire, and in the sparks that ye have kindled. This shall ye have of mine hand; ye shall lie down in sorrow" (Isa. l. 11). Again, we can distinctly and rationally perceive why the children of Israel were forbidden to "light a fire on the sabbath-day" (Ex. xxxv. 3), and what is signified where it is written that "wickedness burneth as the fire" (Isa. ix. 18), and also why evil lusts and their torments in hell are called "unquenchable fire" (Mark ix. 44), "devouring fire," and "everlasting burnings" (Isa. xxxiii. 14). We see also the reason why, under the representative dispensation of the Jews, Nadab and Abihu were slain for offering strange fire unto the Lord (Lev. x. 1, 2), or fire not taken from the golden altar, which had been miraculously kindled, and was never suffered to go out. This criminal presumption was significative of approaching the Lord in sacred worship, not from the holy principle of love and charity, but from the wrathful spirit of unhallowed zeal, or the strange fire of self-love. Thus the sacred Word is no longer a dead letter, but is replete with life.

So, again, to represent the grand idea that God ever was and is, as to his inmost essence, divine love itself, He revealed Himself under the Most Ancient, the Ancient, the Israelitish, and even the Christian dispensation by fire; and as divine love, when acting upon whatever is contrary to itself in men or evil spirits, is felt by them as tormenting and destructive, therefore the Lord is also called "a consuming fire" (Deut. iv. 24).

From this signification of fire many common forms of expression are derived, as that we say of a man, he is inflamed by anger and warmed by love; heated by controversy and cooled by reflection; animated by the glow of philanthropy and torpid as affection grows cold; and these mental changes are often plainly perceived and correspondently indicated in the blushes or paleness of the countenance and the warmth or coldness of the skin. Hence it was, without doubt, that fire, among the Oriental nations, from the most ancient times, was so universally regarded as an emblem of the Lord, who is love itself; and that in a more corrupt age, when the true signification was lost, consecrated fires became the objects of superstitious adoration to the Egyptians, Chaldeans, Assyrians, Persians, and other nations of the East.[57]

Once more (for this portion of our subject is most important to be understood), the element of water may be adduced as another illus-

---

[57] "In the religion of Zoroaster, it was declared a crime, punishable with death, to kindle fire on the altar of any newly erected temple, or to rekindle it on any altar when it had been by accident extinguished, except with fire obtained from some other temple or from the sun."—*Ketto's Pict. Bible*, vol. i., p. 271.

"The ancient Persians consecrated fire as an oblation, the most analogous to the nature of God. Thus, as we find by an inscription on an Egyptian obelisk, the sun was styled the framer or opificer of the world. The representative became the object of worship, and the antitype was forgotten."—*Euseb. de prep. Evang.*, liii., c. 12; *Dr. Leland's Advantage of the Chris. Rev.*, vol. i., p. 229; *Serle's Hist. Solit.*, p. 347.

"Bray says that in the curious and ancient poem Gododin, *the sacred fire*, near the cursus of Stonehenge [on Salisbury plain], is called '*the perpetual fire*,' and remarks in a note that Stonehenge was a temple of the Sun, and fire was invariably used in the worship of its deity."—*Part of Devonshire*, vol. i., p. 137.

"On the religion of the ancient Assyrians, Layard expresses his belief that, originally, it was pure Sabæanism, in which the heavenly bodies were worshipped as mere types of the power and attributes of the Supreme Deity, and there is a strong probability that this form of worship had its origin among the inhabitants of the Assyrian plain. The fire-worship of a later age was a corruption of the purer form of Sabæanism, and there are no traces of it upon the earliest monuments."—*Vaux's Nineveh and Persepolis*, p. 277.

tration of the beauty and consistency of the science of correspondences. This transparent liquid is often mentioned in the Sacred Scriptures to signify, in a good sense, natural truth or doctrine derived from the letter of the Word, and adapted to the external state of all men as to their faith and obedience. Pure water, when applied to wash the feet or the body, cleanses from defilement; so the truth of the literal sense of the Word can purify the mind and life from the stains of sin. "If I wash thee not," said the Lord to the Apostle Peter, "thou hast no part with me" (John xiii. 8).[58] What water is to the weary traveller fainting for thirst in the parched desert, so are the doctrines of the Word to the spirit that desires and seeks for them—cherishing, invigorating, life-giving. Water is essential to the existence, growth, and fruitfulness of all the vegetable tribes; it supplies a refreshing beverage which, serving to modify the solid food for the purposes of digestion, is also indispensable to the support of animal life; so the knowledge of external or doctrinal truth, received by faith in the understanding, and obeyed in simplicity of heart, satisfies spiritual thirst, and is essential to the preservation and renovation of spiritual life in the soul. Thus at the command of Jehovah, Moses struck with his rod the rock in the arid wilderness, and water in abundance streamed forth to supply the fainting congregation of Israel (Ex. xvii. 1–6). So when the soul in a wilderness state is apparently bereft of comfort and ready to sink in despair, lo! faith, in obedience to divine direction, strikes the rock of the Word on which the Lord stands, and the refreshing waters of consolation gush forth in life-restoring streams.

Waters are sometimes spoken of as bubbling fountains, at others as flowing streams; sometimes in large, at others in small quantities; as living and life-giving; as desolating and destructive; as sweet and bitter; as transparent and muddy; as existing at one time in rich abundance, at another as distressingly deficient. When the meaning of water is understood, how full of instruction, how numerous and varied are the lessons of wisdom thus disclosed to our view, and how easy of application by all! In the Book of Genesis we read that "a river went out of Eden, to water the garden" (ii. 10). A garden, or guarded plot of ground, represents the prepared mind, and the various trees, plants and flowers cultivated therein, with their blossoms, fruits and fragrance, will signify all kinds and degrees of intelligence and rational delight. But "the river"—the stream of eternal

---

[58] "To wash the feet is to cleanse our actions."—*Lauretus, Art. Feet.*

truth from the Word of life, that "fountain of living waters,"—must flow through it and upon it, or all man's intelligence and intellectual pleasures are nothing worth, and must wither and perish.

When, therefore, man is described as receptive of natural truth, and obedient thereto, thus, as enjoying the refreshing and perpetual flow of heavenly delights, through the medium of the Word, it is said, "And the Lord shall guide thee continually, and satisfy thy soul in drought, and make fat thy bones: and thou shalt be like a watered garden, whose waters fail not" (Isa. lviii. 11). And again: "Their soul shall be as a watered garden; and they shall not sorrow any more at all" (Jer. xxxi. 12). The plenitude of divine truth, flowing eternally from the Lord by his Word, is hence represented as "a river of unfailing water," and as descending showers—"showers of blessing," refreshing and making fruitful the Lord's church in general, and all the principles of the human mind in particular, like as water irrigates and fertilizes the parched and thirsty soil through which it glides: thus we read in Deuteronomy, "My doctrine shall drop as the rain, my speech shall distil as the dew, or be as the small dew upon the tender herb, and as the showers upon the grass;" and in the Psalms, "Thou visitest the earth, and waterest it: thou greatly enrichest it with the river of God, which is full of water: thou preparest them corn when thou hast so provided it. Thou waterest the ridges thereof abundantly: thou settlest the furrows thereof: thou makest it soft with showers: thou blessest the springing thereof" (lxv. 9).

Such truths or doctrines of the literal sense of the Word as are genuine in their outward form, and lead to the reformation and regulation of the motives, as well as of the life, are denominated "living waters" (John vii. 38), and "waters of life" (Rev. xxii. 1); but when the internal and spiritual truths of the Word revealed through the letter are treated of, the mental fact is represented in that miraculous display of divine power, recorded in John ii., where water was converted into wine. This signification of water, in a good sense, is moreover positively affirmed by the Lord Himself, "For," says He, "as the rain cometh down, and the snow from heaven, and returneth not thither, but watereth the earth, and maketh it bring forth and bud, that it may give seed to the sower, and bread to the eater: so shall my Word be that goeth forth out of my mouth" (Isa. lv. 10, 11); and again He graciously promises, "I," the Lord, "will pour water upon him that is thirsty, and floods upon the dry ground: I will pour my spirit upon thy seed, and my blessing upon thine offspring: and they shall spring up as among the grass, as willows by the watercourses" (xliv. 3, 4). When it is seen that by seas and floods of waters are signified in a heavenly sense the collection of divine truths in the Holy Word and in the human mind, then we shall know why David, in describing the security of the Lord's church in heaven and on earth, was inspired to say, "The earth is the Lord's, and the fulness thereof; the world, and they that dwell therein. For He hath founded it upon the seas, and established it upon the floods" (Ps. xxiv. 1, 2).[59]

On account of the correspondence of water, when applied to purposes of purification, the Jews were commanded to institute various kinds of ablutions or washings; and, for the same reason, the sacred ritual of baptism was instituted, to be a standing and solemn memorial of regeneration, which issues in the purification of the mind and life; for thus is the prophecy accomplished, where it is written, "Then will I sprinkle clean water upon you, and ye shall be clean; from all your filthiness, and from all your idols, will I cleanse you"[60] (Ezek. xxxvi. 25); and, again, in that divine promise that in the fulness of time the truth of the Holy Word should be unfolded for the purposes of spiritual purification, the Lord says, "In that day there shall be a fountain opened to the house of David and to the inhabitants of Jerusalem for sin and for uncleanness" (Zech. xiii. 1). "There is a generation that are pure in their own eyes, and yet is not washed from their filthiness" (Prov. xxx. 12). And so the Apostle

---

[59] "And the Church which He [Christ] has founded, we behold it as sitting upon many waters, upon the great ocean of truth, from whence every stream that has at all or at any time refreshed the earth was originally drawn, and to which it duteously brings its waters again."—*Trench's Hulsean Sects.*, p. 170.

[60] "Ablutions appear to have been amongst the oldest ceremonies practised by different nations, and are still associated with nearly all religions. The Egyptian priests had their diurnal and nocturnal ablutions; the Greeks their sprinklings; the Romans their lustrations and lavations; the Jews their frequent washings and purifications. Whence could this universal practice arise but from a knowledge of the significance of washing?" —See *Dr. I. Townley's Notes to the More Nevo. of Maimonides*, p. 352.

"The Mexicans, whose origin is involved in obscurity, bathe their children the moment they are born, a custom which, notwithstanding its present superstitious associations, seems to have been unquestionably derived from ancient times, when the science of correspondences was well known; for when the midwife immerses them she says, 'Receive the water; for the goddess Chalciuhcueje is the mother.' 'May this water cleanse the spots which thou bearest from the womb of thy mother, purify thy heart, and give thee a good and perfect life.' In another part of the ceremony, she says, 'May the invisible God descend upon this water, and cleanse thee of every sin and impurity, and free thee from evil fortune.' For further particulars of this interesting ceremony, see the *Abbé Clavigero's Hist. of Mex.* The Brahmins of Hindostan also baptize their children, and mark them with red ointment, saying, 'O Lord, we present this child, born of a holy tribe, to thee and thy service.' It is cleansed with water, and anointed with oil."—See *Lord's Banian Rel.*, ch. ix.

Paul, speaking of the purification of the Lord's Church, both generally and individually, from defilement, writes to the Ephesians as follows: "Christ loved the church and gave Himself for it; that He might sanctify and cleanse it with the washing of water by the Word. That He might present it to Himself a glorious church, not having spot, or wrinkle, or any such thing; but that it should be holy and without blemish" (v. 25-27).

From ancient times men plunged themselves into the Ganges, the Indus, the Euphrates, the Nile, and the Jordan, all rivers esteemed sacred, to represent and signify, in a good sense, purification from sin in the streams of divine wisdom, by honest endeavors to apply its sacred truths to the removal of evil from the life, and thus reformation of the character. John the Baptist came as the Lord's forerunner, and, for a similar reason, baptized all who came unto him in the boundary river Jordan, "unto repentance, for the confession and remission of sins," representative of the only effectual means of cleansing the soul from spiritual defilement, through the doctrines of repentance and reformation which are found in the letter or external boundary of the Word, and thus of truly preparing the way of the Lord.

When we thus understand what is signified by water, how full of eternal interest and practical instruction does the Lord's conversation with the Samaritan woman become, as He sat on Jacob's well. That fountain was deep, and represented the Holy Word in its outward letter; but the Lord, sitting upon it, represented the same Word, bearing testimony to Him as the God of Jacob, and filling its internal sense with living water from Himself. "If," said He to the woman, "thou knewest the gift of God, and who it is that saith to thee, Give me to drink,"—for *He* thirsts, and is only satisfied when his creatures freely partake of his blessings,—"thou wouldest have asked of Him, and He would have given thee living water. Whosoever drinketh of this water,"—the mere doctrinal truth of the letter,—will find it fail to satisfy the inmost cravings of the soul, and "shall thirst again; but whosoever drinketh of the water that I shall give him,"—the pure, eternal, life-giving streams of divine truth, revealed to angelic and human perception in the internal or spiritual sense,—"shall never thirst; but"—if he inwardly supplicates it—"the water that I shall give him shall be IN HIM a well [or fountain] of water springing up into everlasting life." It will satisfy every want of the soul; it will be regarded as the best gift of God to his creatures, and become a sacred medium of perpetual communion with Him, and a perennial source of comfort, beatitude, and joy (John iv. 6–30). Though every incident in this beautiful and divine narrative teems with significance, we have only space to indicate the above general ideas.

A defect of water, therefore, will denote a destitution of truth, and a thirst for water an earnest desire to receive it, as in Amos, "Behold, the days come, saith the Lord God, that I will send a famine in the land, not a famine of bread, nor a thirst for water, but of hearing the words of the Lord" (viii. 11). "If any man thirst," saith the Lord, "let him come unto me, and drink. Whosoever drinketh of the water that I shall give him shall never thirst; but the water that I shall give him shall be in him a well [or fountain] of water, springing up into everlasting life" (John vii. 37; iv. 14).

But, in its opposite sense, water, as we have already seen, will signify truth perverted or falsified,—man's self-derived intelligence and "carnal wisdom." This profanation of truth is meant in the internal sense by the miracle of Moses, when "he stretched forth his rod over the waters of Egypt, and they became blood" (Ex. vii. 19); while the contrary was represented by his making the bitter waters of Marah sweet (Ex. xv. 23–25). The substitution of self-dependence for full reliance on the divine aid and Spirit, in the attainment of truth, and of self-intelligence and perverted reason in the place of genuine wisdom, is signified by these words of the prophet: "My people have committed two evils; they have forsaken me, the fountain of living waters, and hewed them out cisterns, broken cisterns, that can hold no water" (Jer. ii. 13). Hence, too, temptations, which are the result of the activity of false principles, in connection with the powers of darkness and evil, threatening to overwhelm and destroy man's soul, are signified by the raging flood, from which, under divine guidance, the ark of salvation can alone deliver him, agreeably to that most gracious promise in Isaiah, "When thou passest through the waters, I will be with thee: and through the rivers, they shall not overflow thee: when thou walkest through the fire, thou shalt not be burned; neither shall the flame kindle upon thee" (xliii. 2); and to signify the direful torment which such as wilfully reject or pervert the truth induce upon their own minds, and which, in appearance, is attributed to the Lord, He is said to "hiss for the fly in the uttermost part of the rivers of Egypt, and for the bee in the land of Assyria" (Isa. vii. 18, 19). So, also, in like states of affliction, the Psalmist complains and says, "The floods of ungodly men made me afraid" (Ps. xviii. 4);

"Deep calleth unto deep at the noise of thy water-spouts: all thy waves and thy billows are gone over me" (xlii. 7); "I sink in deep mire, where there is no standing; I am come into deep waters, where the floods overflow me. . . . Let not the water-flood overflow me, neither let the deep swallow me up" (lxix. 2, 15).

On account of this signification of water, a river, or flowing stream of water, fertilizing the lands through which it rolls, exactly corresponding, in a good sense, to the inflowing of heavenly truths in rich abundance into the mind, renovating all its powers, and causing it to be fruitful in intelligence and good works; but in an opposite sense, it signifies a desolating stream of false persuasions, inducing ignorance and death. Thus, in the promise made to the faithful, it is said, "Thou shalt make them drink of the river of thy pleasures" (Psalm xxxvi. 8); and where the Holy Word, as the fountain of intelligence, is described, it is said, "There is a river, the streams whereof shall make glad the city of God, the holy place of the tabernacles of the Most High" (Psalm xlvi. 4). And again, "For thus saith the Lord, Behold, I will extend peace to her like a river, and the glory of the Gentiles like a flowing stream" (Isa. lxvi. 12). The divine promise of heavenly truths and intelligence in all abundance, to the humble and prepared soul, is also thus expressed, "When the poor and needy seek water, and there is none, and their tongue faileth for thirst, I the Lord will hear them, I the God of Israel will not forsake them. I will open rivers in high places, and fountains in the midst of the valleys: I will make the wilderness a pool of water, and the dry land springs of water" (Isa. xli. 17, 18). But an exuberance of false principles, overflowing and desolating the mind, is signified where a river is spoken of in its opposite sense, as in the Psalms, "If it had not been the Lord who was on our side, now may Israel say, then the waters had overwhelmed us, the stream had gone over our soul: then the proud waters had gone over our soul" (cxxiv. 1, 4, 5). And in Isaiah, "Go, ye swift messengers, to a nation scattered and peeled, to a people terrible from their beginning hitherto: a nation meted out and trodden down, whose land the rivers have spoiled" (xviii. 2). And in the divine expostulation with man, in consequence of his forsaking the Lord's Word as the only fountain of truth, and vainly depending on his own self-derived intelligence, fancying that this is true wisdom, "Hast thou not procured this unto thyself, in that thou hast forsaken the Lord thy God, when He led thee by the way? And now what hast thou to do in the way of Egypt, to drink the waters of Sihor? or what hast thou to do in the way of Assyria, to drink the waters of the river?" (Jer. ii. 17, 18.)

In the sublime prophetic vision of the holy waters proceeding out of the sanctuary, or Word of God, the prophet describes their outgoings as successively reaching to "the ankles," "the knees," and "the loins,"—the waters and their varying depths denoting the truths of the Word accommodated to all states of perception; the natural and sensual state and its perceptions being signified by the ankles, the spiritual-natural state being signified by the knees, the spiritual state being signified by the loins, and the celestial or highest state being signified by waters to swim in, for this intelligence and wisdom is so far above the natural man as to be ineffable. These states of exterior, interior, and inmost perception are necessarily opened as the prophet *measures* a thousand, denoting the quality of reception, that it is full and complete, because applied to the life and conduct. And beyond that highest state to which man or angel can attain, the inmost spirit of these waters, these vital truths, is seen and acknowledged as "a river that cannot be passed over,"—waters which carry health and life whithersoever they come (Ezek. xlvii. 3–9).

Now precisely the same kind of reasoning is applicable, and similar proofs might be adduced, in reference to most other terms and expressions used by the inspired prophets and evangelists.[61] The Word of God, in its internal sense, does not treat, then, of individuals and nations and the annals and statistics of the human race, nor yet of the objects of natural history, nor yet of times and seasons, light and heat, war and peace, cities and countries, birds and beasts, fishes and

---

[61] "By finding a spiritual sense [in the Word of God], Hilary will not allow that historical truth is weakened or destroyed." "In the beginning of our treatise we warned others against supposing that we detracted from the belief in transactions by teaching that the things themselves contained within them the outgoings of subsequent realities."—*Comment. on Matt.* vii., p. 640.

Cyril of Alexandria also held that although the spiritual sense be good and fruitful, yet what is historical should be taken as [true] history."—*Comment. in Esai,* lib. i., orat. 4, vol. ii., pp. 113, 114.

These analogies are so clear and interesting, that you can scarcely open a book on religious subjects where they are not in one way or other introduced; thus, the *Christian Witness* (No. 86, p. 53) writer says: "There are many striking and beautiful analogies between the natural and spiritual worlds. Facts and phenomena in the one are often used in the Scriptures to illustrate the truths of the other. There is a seed-time in the world of mind as well as in the world of matter. The gentle dews distil, and the early and latter rains descend, both in the world of nature and in the world of grace. In the beautiful language of inspiration, the influences of Gospel grace [and truth] are represented as coming down like rain upon the grass, and like showers that water the earth. When these refreshing and fertilizing influences are withdrawn, then comes drought and barrenness both in the natural and in the spiritual world."

reptiles, plants and trees, flowers and fruits, islands and lakes, rivers and seas, wind and floods, rain and dew, hail and snow, and all the objects and phenomena of the natural world; for these, in their merely literal acceptation, are not the subjects of inspiration at all, nor, if they were, could any knowledge respecting them impart righteousness and tranquillity to the soul. But the Word, in its holy internal, treats of the Infinite Jehovah—his wisdom and his will, of spiritual subjects and everlasting realities, of the properties and qualities of the human soul, of repentance and regeneration; for of these all created things are but corresponding types. Nor, again, does the Word of God treat, in its interior and heavenly sense, of the chronology of kingdoms and empires—of the genealogy, nomenclature, and biography of their rulers and history of their people, nor of their religion and laws, their rituals and ceremonies, their customs and manners; for though, in their literal sense, the things recorded in the historical books of the Word were actual occurrences, yet, as such *only* and having no higher reference, how can they contribute to salvation, or be said to have been written by the plenary inspiration of God? But all these worldly facts and occurrences, without exception, represent mental states and spiritual conditions, inward and outward facts and operations of man's experience, and are the images and symbols which adumbrate the objects of an eternal world, and the attributes and perfections of the Godhead. Nor, lastly, was the Word of God inspired to reveal to us the proverbs and sayings, the exhortations and discourse, the promises and threatenings, the counsel and experience of mere men, however wise or distinguished; in its holy internal sense all these forms of address are significative of truths and doctrines appertaining to the Lord, to the soul, and to eternal life.

With these exalted views, the Word of God comes to us invested with ever new and irresistible authority, so far as our will coincides with the Divine will; it interferes not with our freedom, and it commends itself to our highest reason. It is no longer filled with dark, inexplicable mysteries or historic fallacies, or regarded in reference only to by-gone times and people, with some incidental references to morality here and there; but it teems with interest and importance, conveying to us a grand connected series of unchanging rules of life, ever unfolding more clearly to our view, as the clouds of the letter are penetrated, and having in every page and line, in every "jot and tittle" (Matt. v. 18), the most direct relation to our souls and to the great interests of an eternal state.[62] Thus the historical, the prophetical, the doctrinal, the devotional, and the ethical portions of the Word

---

[62] Bishop Warburton says, "the prophetic style seems to be *a speaking hieroglyphic.*"—*Div. Leg.*, b. iv., § 4.

"The Therapeutæ," writes Bruno, "interpreted the Scriptures of the Old Testament allegorically, and being wont to seek the spiritual meaning of the Law, they more readily embraced the Gospel than those who looked no further than the outward letter."—*De Therap.*, p. 193. Pliny says that this sect had been in existence several thousand years.—*Nat. Hist.*, lib. v., cap. xviii. The name means a physician; and Philo says they were so called because they cured men's souls of the diseases which they have contracted by their passions and vices.—*Philo de Vita Contemplativa.* They have been supposed to be the Essenes, an ancient sect of the Jews, or probably a division of that sect, and called Therapeutæ from the strictness of their morals and the purity of their conduct.—See *Jenning's Jewish Antiq.*, p. 320.

In *The New Baptist Magazine* for April, 1827, there is inserted a letter from M. Mayers, at Vienna, giving an account of a most remarkable sect of Jews in Poland, called after their founder, Sabbathia Zewy, Sabbathians, and also Soharites, on account of the veneration in which they hold a cabalistical work, called *Sohar*. On their establishment in Poland, they declared their total rejection of the *Talmud*. They are distinguished for their strict morality and integrity. In the *Confession of Faith* which they have published, among other remarkable things, they assert their belief respecting the Holy Scriptures, as follows:—"We believe that the writings of Moses, the Prophets, and all earlier Teachers, are not to be taken literally, but figuratively; and as containing a secret sense hid under the mere letter. These writings are to be compared to a beautiful woman, who hides her charms under a veil, and expects her admirers to take the trouble of lifting it; which is also the case with the Word of God, being hidden under the veil of a figurative sense, which cannot be lifted even with the highest human ingenuity, and greatest degree of wisdom, without the assistance of Divine grace. In other words, the things spoken of in the Thorah [Word of God], must not be taken literally, according to the mere phraseology, but we must pray for the teaching of the Divine Spirit, to be enabled to discern the kernel which lies hid under the mere shell or husk of the letter. We therefore believe that it is not sufficient merely to read the words of the prophets to know the literal meaning, but that it requires Divine aid in order to understand, in many places, the fundamental of the letter; and thus we find David prays, 'Open thou mine eyes, that I may behold wonderful things out of thy law' (Ps. cxix. 18). If King David had been able to understand the Word of God by his own inquiries, he would not have thus prayed; but his supplication was to comprehend the secret and hidden mysteries of the Thorah. To this effect are also the words of the Sohar: 'Woe to the man who asserts that the Thorah is a mere record of historical facts of ancient times, and contains but a narrative of common things; if this were the case, it might also be composed in the present time. But the narratives and subjects contained in the holy writings are only used as figures for the mysteries deeply hidden under the letter.' And whoever considers the primary sense as the principal object of the Scriptures, is guilty of death, and forfeits all claim to a future state. Therefore says the Psalmist, 'lighten mine eyes' (Ps. xiii. 3); that is to say, that I might discern the secrets hidden under the letter of the law, 'lest I sleep the sleep of death.' In another passage it is remarked by the Sohar, 'If the Thorah were only to be taken in a literal sense, why should David say, "The law of the Lord is perfect, more to be desired than gold, yea, than much fine gold" (Ps. xix.). It is therefore undeniable that great and many mysteries are hidden under the letter of the Thorah, to inquire into which it is the duty of every one who wishes to become orthodox.'"—See also *Crit. Bib.*, vol. iv., p. 257.

This recognition of an inward sense in the Word of the Old Testament, closely assimilates, as far as we are able to judge, to the doctrines of the Therapeutæ or Essenes, at the time of our Lord's incarnation, referred to in the previous note. Though, from the undoubted testimony of ecclesiastical writers of every age, numbers of learned and pious Christians, to which many venerable names of modern times might be added, have held fast the doctrine of an internal sense in the Sacred Scriptures, but they have had, however, no definite ideas of the laws of correspondence, now so miraculously unfolded in the writings of Swedenborg, nor yet of the distinct books in which that sense can alone be sought with success.

"All the expressions in the Word are significative of heavenly things, and all the things are representative thereof, and this even to the least tittle."—A. C. 5147.

of God are alike written according to the invariable science of correspondences. This is the only fixed principle on which it can be expounded and successfully defended from the cavils of infidelity and the inconsistencies of a false faith;—the only rule which, together with the aid of the Spirit, removes all difficulties, reconciles all con-

---

"Believing in the words of my Lord Jesus Christ, I do not think that there is a jot or tittle in the law and the prophets which is devoid of mysteries."—*Origen, Hom.* i. *in Exod.*

"It became us to believe the Sacred Scriptures, not to have one apex or tittle void of the wisdom of God."—*Ib., Hom.* 2, *in Jer., cited in Hanmer's View of Antiquity,* p. 231. See Matt. v. 18; Luke xvi. 17.

"St. Augustine wrote a whole Book under the title of *Letter and Spirit,* in which he has shown that not only the Histories, Precepts, Parables, and Figures of the Old Testament, but those of the New, are to be both interpreted spiritually of the operations of *God in Christ,* and applied also by Faith and the power of the Holy Ghost to our spirits, to make us likewise spiritual; otherwise the whole is but *the letter that killeth,* and not the Spirit that giveth life."—*Halloway's Letter and Spirit,* vol. i., Int., p. xlviii.

"If Scripture has not an undercurrent of meaning, double, triple, quadruple, or even yet more manifold, I confess not only that my work is a mere waste of labor, time, and paper, which would comparatively matter little; but it also follows that all primitive and mediæval Commentators, from the first century till the Reformation, have more or less been deceiving the Church of God,—have been substituting their fancies for his immutable verities,—have adopted the system which is alike the offspring and the parent of error,—that their folios have been a hindrance to the cause of truth, and the labors of their loves an insult to the genuine principles of interpretation. Take for instance the following extracts:

"The Mystical Interpretation of Scripture, as every one will allow, *is the distinguishing mark of difference between ancient and modern Commentators.* To the former it was the very life, marrow, essence, of God's Word; the kernel, of which the literal exposition was the shell; the jewel, to which the outside and verbal signification formed the shrine. By the latter it has almost universally been held in equal contempt and abhorrence. It has been affirmed to be the art of involving everything in uncertainty, to take away all fixedness of meaning, to turn Scripture into a repository of human fancies, to be subversive of all exactitude, and fatal to all truth."

—*Neale's Mystical and Literal Interpretation of the Psalms,* pp. 377, 379.

"What do we mean by a literal interpretation? One in which words have the same sense ascribed to them which they usually bear in daily life. Now this is one-half of the truth needed for a right interpretation of the Scriptures. The Word of God is a revelation to man. To be useful to men it must be definite and intelligible, and in this sense literal. But it is also a revelation from God. Now to be Divine, it must contain higher truths, nobler thoughts, more full and deep conceptions than such as man conveys to his fellow-men. Therefore, in employing human language, it must exalt and expand the meaning of the terms which it employs. It belongs to that kingdom of God which eye hath not seen, neither hath it entered into the heart of man. Hence all its messages bear this same character."—*Birk's First Element of Sacred Prophecy,* p. 250.

"Natural things, persons, motions, and actions, declared or spoken of in Scripture, admit of also many times a mystical, moral, or allegorical sense. I know this spiritual sense is as great a fear to some faint and unbelieving hearts as a spectre. But it is a thing acknowledged by the most wise, most pious, and most rational of the *Jewish* Doctors. I will instance in one who is *ad instar omnium,* Moses Ægyptius, who compares the Divine Oracles 'to *Apples of Gold* in *pictures of silver.*' For that the outward Nitor is very comely, as Silver curiously cut thorough and wrought; but the inward spiritual or mystical sense is the Gold, more precious and more beautiful, that glisters through those cuttings and artificial carvings in the letter."
—*H. More's Def. of the Cabala, Introd.,* p. 107, ed. 1653.

"The ancient interpreters of the Bible were persuaded and firmly believed that it contained, besides the plain and obvious meaning, mysterious and concealed truths; they thought that in a book so holy, and coming from the Fountain of all wisdom, there cannot possibly be a redundant word, or even a superfluous letter, or a grammatical anomaly; and consequently, whenever such do appear, they must have been designedly introduced with a view of indicating some unknown truth."—*Hurwitz* "*Essay on the Uninspired Literature of the Hebrews.*"

tradictions, and, impressing equal value upon what may appear trivial as upon the most important portions of the Word, irradiating the whole with the bright beams of infinite glory. Under this mode of interpretation Scripture truly becomes the interpreter of Scripture, perplexity and doubt are banished, and it is at once demonstrated that the Holy Word is, like its Author, divine—that his spirit fills every "jot and tittle" of it with sublimity, sanctity, and life, and distinguishes it broadly from all human compositions whatsoever.

Mosheim, the ecclesiastical historian, from among "*a prodigious number of interpreters*" of the early ages of Christianity, mentions Pantænus, Clement the Alexandrian, Tatian, Justin Martyr, Theophilus, Bishop of Antioch, Origen, and others, who were illustrious for their piety and learning and love of truth, who "*all* attributed a double sense to the words of Scripture; the one obvious and literal, the other hidden and mysterious, which lay concealed under the veil of the outward letter;" and that "the true meaning of the sacred writers was to be sought in a hidden and mysterious sense arising from the nature of the things themselves."—*Eccl. Hist.*, note 50, cent. II., p. 2, c. iii., 4, 5; cent. III., p. 2, c. iii., 5.

And Bishop Horne, speaking of the same testimony of ancient Christian writers and expositors, distinguished alike for their learning and piety, says, "They are unexceptionable witnesses to us of this matter of fact, that a spiritual mode of interpreting the Scriptures, built upon the practice of the apostles in their writings and preachings, did universally prevail in the church from the beginning."—*Comm. on Psalms*, pref., pp. xi., xii. (new ed. 1836.) Primitive language, in fact, had no other expressions than those which were grounded in a certain intuitive perception of correspondences, and thus, at the same time, God was seen and adored in his glorious workmanship, and man was divinely instructed in the things of eternal life.[63]

---

[63] The author of *Tracts for the Times*, lxxxix., says, "There is no discrepancy between the tone of the Apostles and that of the Church in after days, in respect of their both assuming, clearly and deliberately, a certain correspondence, intended by the Creator, between the material and spiritual worlds" (p. 183). And again, "We need not, perhaps, hesitate to admit in the most unreserved way,—indeed, it might be hard to find any one who has ever denied,—the universal adoption, by the early Christian writers, of the allegorical way of expounding the Old Testament." "Not only in the prophetical writings do they find our Lord and his Gospel everywhere; not only do they trace throughout the Levitical services the example and shadow of the future heavenly things, but they deal also in the same way with the records of history, whether Patriarchal or Jewish" (p. 14).

An old Latin writer, cited and translated by H. B. P. in the *Aurora*, vol. i., p. 74, makes the following interesting observations: "I am of opinion that the first AUTHORS of this [Hieroglyphia] wisdom were not from Egypt; for (if we credit the testimony of Alexan-

When, in consequence of man's fall from this state of intelligence and purity, it became needful to provide him with a WRITTEN record of God's will and wisdom, adapted to raise him from his lapsed condition, and restore him to the paradise of wisdom and happiness, the certainty is, that it would be written in the only universal and unchanging language, the language of correspondence; for, while the arbitrary words of human languages are perpetually changing, both in sound and sense, for want of some unalterable standard, the language of correspondence is as fixed and determined as the universe itself.[64] Had divine truth been revealed to man in mere didactic phraseology or preceptive forms of speech, it would have supplied no positive evidences of religious truth, no fixed basis for internal conviction; nor could it have been translated from one language into another without losing much of its intrinsic clearness and force; nor

der, in his book of Jewish history, as well as of Eupolemus, the author of a book on the Jewish kings) Abraham lived in Heliopolis with the Egyptian priests, and the seeds of sciences scattered by Abraham (some of which he professed to have been handed down to him by Enoch) were not wanting in those symbolical and enigmatical *veils under which* the wisdom of the ancients was concealed. It is added, that this world, crowded with such various objects, and adorned with such beautiful imagery, was presented by God to the view of the first men, *in order that through those outward representations, they might perceive, as it were through a faint cloud, the bright rays of divinity which shone within.* It was not without reason that Epictetus observed that there existed in the minds of men, *symbols of God,* which He impresseth upon us by the surrounding representations of himself; wherefore it may easily be believed, that the various objects which are beheld on the face of the earth, were regarded by Adam, by Enoch, by Noah, and others of the primitive ages, as so many letters illuminated with the divine glory, whereby the Eternal Mind did stamp the impression of his name on man. I am the readier to accede to this opinion from the custom of their posterity, who *so oftentimes concealed the mysteries of religion under symbols and figures that nothing was more common.* And, indeed, the ancient Hebrews so highly valued the figurative mode of speech, that whatever was spoken shrewdly and fraught with wisdom, was called Maschal, an appellation which properly relates to parables and similitudes."—*De Symbolica Ægyptiorum Sapientia.*

[64] "The forms of divine truth in its ultimates, are moulded and fixed in all the objects of the visible world, which is, as it were, the *chase* containing the corrected types of all written language. The *sounds* and the *signs* may be different, according to the states of different nations, but the *substance* they involve is the same in all languages. Plato (in *Cratylo*, pp. 383, 425, ed. Sorrani) has well said that language is of divine imposition; that human reason, from a defect in the knowledge of natures and qualities, which are indicated by names, could not determine the cognomena of things. He maintains that names are the *vehicula* of substances; that a fixed analogy [correspondence] exists between the name and the thing; that language, therefore, is not arbitrary in its origin, but fixed by the laws of analogy; and that God alone, who knows the nature of things, originally imposed names strictly expressive of their qualities. Of the same opinion were the Stoics, substituting only nature for God, as the creating and nominating agent. Zeno, Cleanthes, Chrysippus, labored to prove that *sounds* were originally expressive of the nature of things; and that no word or sound could be without such original. That not only the eye and the ear, but the touch, the taste, and the smell, were concerned in determining them. They who may desire to see a full account of their system and opinions, may consult *Galen de Decret, Hippo, Plato,* lib. ii., *Nigidius Agel,* 10-5, *Laert.* 7-3, *Varro de Ling. Lat.,* and *Dion. Hal. de Comp. Verb.* The profound and eloquent commentary of Hierocles on the verses of Pythagoras, will also furnish argument and illustration in almost every page Vide Glas. Ed. 1756."—R. K. C. *New-churchman,* p. 235. Philadelphia.

could it have been handed down, from age to age, in the pure state in which we possess it. The laws of correspondence are based on the inseparable connection which exists between spiritual causes and natural effects; they preserve and perpetuate all the visible works of creation, and are necessarily interwoven with all human experience, mental and material; the inspired Word, therefore, enshrined in the language of correspondence, has retained, and must retain, its significance and authority, its comprehensiveness and grandeur, through all generations, and in every tongue in which words are appropriated to the objects of the outer world and the operations of its inhabitants.[65] From this divine source man may continually enrich himself with new and unfailing treasures, at the same time that he

---

[65] What an intelligent author affirms of figurative imagery is far more truly and correctly applicable to the science of correspondences. "It is the excellence of this mode of speaking, that it is not confined to the people of any particular nation or language, but applies itself equally to all the nations of the earth, and is universal. It was not intended for the Hebrew or the Egyptian, the Jew or the Greek, but for *man;* and therefore it obtains equally under the Patriarchal, Jewish, and Christian Dispensation; and is of common benefit to all ages and all places. Words are changeable: language has been confounded; and men in different parts of the world are unintelligible to one another as barbarians; but the visible works of nature are not subject to any such confusion; they speak to us now the same as they spoke in the earliest ages, and their language will last as long as the world shall remain, without being corrupted."—*W. Jones, Lects. on the Fig. Lang. of Scrip.*, p. 237.

Paine, in his *Age of Reason*, says, "The idea or belief of a Word of God, existing in print, or in writing, or in speech, is inconsistent with itself, for these reasons among many others: the want of a universal language, the mutability of language, the errors to which translations are subject, the possibility of totally suppressing such a Word, the probability of altering it, or of fabricating the whole and imposing it upon the world."—8vo ed., 1818, part i., p. 51.

These specious objections, to which, in the common mode of explaining the Scriptures, no satisfactory answer ever has or can be given, are dissipated before the great principles of interpreting the oracles of God advocated above, like darkness at the rising of the sun. Not one of them has the shadow of a support on which to rest. Here is the "*universal language*" which Paine thought was wanting.

To my astonishment, just as the above note was being printed (1st ed.), I met with arguments substantially the very same, and calculated to subvert the divinity, sanctity, and authority of the Word of God, advocated in the *Dublin Review*, for October, 1847, one of the most influential organs of the Roman Catholics. The passage occurs in a paper against the indiscriminate reading of the Bible. "It was laid down," says the writer, "that faith was in *living persons;* but the Bible is a mere material book, not possessed of life, incapable of motion, and unable by any power of its own even so much as to propose itself for belief. But it will be answered that, when any one is said to read and believe the Bible, such a person really believes in Christ, whose words and revelation are found in the Bible. Yes: but how do you know that his words are found in the Bible? It is now eighteen hundred years since our Saviour and his apostles were on the earth. If their revelation was committed to a book, as you suppose, how do you know that in the course of time this book has not been falsified? How do you prove the identity of the Bible of the nineteenth century with the Bible of the first?"

To the devout and reflective mind, what a powerful argument should the above extract supply (coming as it does from the representatives of a large proportion of the Christian world) for the absolute necessity of the mode of interpretation now revealed to mankind, unless, indeed, we are prepared to see the foundations of all truth undermined. Let the reader contrast it with the following declarations of the Word itself: John i. 1; Luke iv. 4; Isa. xl. 8; Ps. cxix. 89; ciii. 20; Matt. xxiv. 35; Mark xiii. 31; Micah ii. 7; John vi. 63; xx. 31.

traces in living characters, amid the boundless works of creative energy, the divine love and wisdom of their all-glorious Author. As the objects of the outward universe are thus contemplated, they awaken devotional feelings and kindle heavenliest aspirations, and the divinity of the Word becomes, as it were, identical with the great laws of creation and life; its truth is established beyond all controversy and doubt.[66]

---

[66] The author of *Tracts for the Times*, lxxxix., speaking of the peculiar phraseology of Scripture, says (and his arguments would have been still more weighty and convincing had he been acquainted with the science of correspondences), "Nominalists are ready enough to say, '[that this mode of writing] is the imperfection of language; the Almighty himself, condescending to make use of human words and idioms, could not otherwise convey ideas of the spiritual world than by images and terms taken from objects of sense.' Or again: 'It is the genius of orientalism; if God vouchsafed to address the men of any particular time and country, He would adopt the modes of speech suited to that time and country.' Or, 'The whole is mere poetical ornament, the vehicle of moral or historical truth, framed to be beautified and engaging in its kind, in mere indulgence to the infirmity of human nature.'

"But would it not be enough to say, in answer to all these statements together, that even if granted in fact, they fail as explanations, since the question would immediately occur, who made language, or orientalism, or poetry, what they respectively are? Was it not One who knew beforehand that He should adopt them one day as the channel and conveyance of his truth and his will to mankind? Surely reason and piety teach us that God's providence prepared language in general, and especially the languages of Holy Scripture and the human styles of its several writers, as fit *media* through which his supernatural glories and dealings might be discerned; and if they be so formed as necessarily to give us notions of a certain correspondence between the supernatural and visible, we can hardly help concluding that such notions were intended to be formed by us."

The same writer proceeds thus: "If the whole were mere necessity, arising out of the imperfection of human speech, or if it were oriental boldness of phrase or poetical ornament, the symbols would probably be more varied than we find them to be—the same external object would not so constantly occur to express the same invisible thing, through so large a collection of compositions, so widely differing in style and tone. As to the imperfection of human speech, we all feel every hour how it causes us to modify and alter our images; we take the best symbol which occurs to us at the time, but we use it in a kind of restless, unsatisfied way, like persons aware that it is not simply the best; and by the time we need it again, we have lighted, very likely, on something far truer and more vivid; and thus we go on in conversation or in writing, improving or marring our imagery, as the case may be, but still letting it be felt that it is by no means fixed and unchangeable. Again: as to poetical ornament, variety and versatility of resource, it is obviously a great ingredient of that sort of excellency: to be always resorting to the same similitude or analogy would rather, of course, betray want of skill or power. The third solution, that of orientalism, may seem at first sight to be more satisfactory as to this particular circumstance of the same figure constantly repeated. Granting, however, that the literature of the Eastern nations is, in some respects, like their manners, more fixed and monotonous than ours, and accordingly that it uses to express things out of sight by a certain uniform imagery, suggesting the notion of a settled and understood imagery, yet, in the first place, we know not how far this literature may have been originally modelled in the Hebrew Scriptures, instead of their taking any tone from some previous form of it, the very existence of which, after all, is but conjectured. Next, such a statement would put in a stronger light the fact of that kind of style having been adopted by the Holy Ghost, whereby its symbolical words would seem to be raised to the rank of divine hieroglyphics, so to call them.

"The fixedness, therefore, of the Scriptural imagery does not seem to be sufficiently accounted for by any criticisms of this kind; but it is accounted for if we suppose the material world originally constructed with a view to the sacred analogies which this symbolical alphabet of Scripture (if we may so denominate it) suggests."—Pp. 171-3.

If the Word had been written without a literal sense exactly corresponding to its inward spirit, a medium of conjunction between heaven and earth, angels and men, would have been wanting, and there would have been no ground or basis on which divine truth could have rested, so as to remain fixed with man. Attendant angels can perceive the spiritual sense while man peruses the letter in faith and sincerity, even where he is not acquainted with the internal sense, and he can claim a holy state of adjunction with them; but when the genuine doctrines of the letter and the truths of the internal sense are acknowledged by him, and received in affection, he may then enter into a blessed state of association and conjunction with them.

"The literal sense of the Word is also a defence for the genuine truths concealed in it, lest they should suffer violence; and the defence consists in this, that the literal sense can be turned every way, in all directions, and be explained according to the reader's apprehension without its internal being hurt or violated, for no hurt ensues from the literal sense being understood differently by different people. But the danger is, when the divine truths which are hidden therein are perverted, for it is by this that the Word suffers violence. To prevent which, the literal sense is its defence; and it operates as such a defence with those who are under the influence of religious errors, and yet do not confirm them in their minds; from these the Word suffers no violence. The literal sense, acting as a guard or defence, is signified by the cherubim in the Word, and is also described by them."—D. S. S., n. 97.

Swedenborg elucidates this interesting point most convincingly, where he says, "That the Word without its literal sense would be like a palace without a foundation; that is, like a palace in the air and not on the ground, which could only be the shadow of a palace, and must vanish away; also, that the Word, without its literal sense, would be like a temple in which there are many holy things, and in the midst thereof the holy of holies, without a roof and walls to form the containants thereof; in which case its holy things would be plundered by thieves, or be violated by the beasts of the earth and the

---

"In reading the Bible [or Word of God], you cannot avoid perceiving that all the prophets and all the sacred writers use the figurative language of parable. It is the language of inspiration and the symbolical language of nature." "The operations of the spiritual and moral kingdoms in man are typified, *in toto*, by those of the kingdoms of nature, as it is termed by philosophers."—*Essay on Universal Analogy*, pp. 15, 36, 38.

birds of heaven, and thus be dissipated. In like manner it would be like the tabernacle, in the inmost place whereof was the ark of the covenant, and in the middle part the golden candlestick, the golden altar for incense, and also the table for shew-bread, which were its holy things, without its ultimates, which were the curtains and veils. Yea, the Word without its literal sense would be like the human body without its coverings, which are called skins, and without its supporters, which are called bones, of which, supposing it to be deprived, its inner parts must of necessity be dispersed and perish. It would also be like the heart and lungs in the thorax deprived of their covering which is called the *pleura*, and their supporters which are called the ribs; or like the brain without its coverings which are called the *dura mater* and *pia mater*, and without its common covering, containant and firmament which is called the skull. Such would be the state of the Word without its literal sense; wherefore it is said in Isaiah, that 'the Lord will create upon all the glory a covering'" (iv. 5).—S. S., n. 33.

CHAPTER VIII.

THE DIFFERENCE BETWEEN THE APPARENT AND GENUINE TRUTHS OF THE LITERAL SENSE OF THE HOLY WORD EXPLAINED AND ILLUSTRATED.

IN many parts of the sacred Scriptures,[67] however, particularly in the Gospels, we find true doctrine plainly revealed for the simple in heart,—"the babes in Christ" (1 Cor. iii. 1; 1 Pet. ii. 2); but would we behold the hidden splendors of heaven, which fill the inner courts of the sanctuary, "the everlasting gates must be unfolded,"— we must enter through "the veil," and as we meditate on what we see, we cannot fail to adopt the exclamation of the patriarch, and say, "This is none other than the house of God, and this is the gate of heaven" (Gen. xxvii. 17). Nor let it for one moment be supposed that the internal sense of Scripture invalidates or injures, in the slightest degree, its extrinsic meaning and authority. On the contrary, as the soul animates and confers dignity on the body in which it dwells, so the spiritual sense gives life to and exalts the literal sense, which is acknowledged to be eminently holy in consequence of the heavenly meaning of which it is the repository, and which, far from being disparaged, is preserved by it and for it with the most scrupulous exactness. Of the Word of God in both senses it may be truly said, in the language of the author of the Epistle to the He-

---

[67] "There is a striking passage in Augustine," says the author of *Tracts for the Times*, lxxxix., p. 45, "which collects, as it were, into a point, the confessions on this head of every generation of believers: 'The style itself in which Holy Scripture is framed, how open is it to every one's approach, how impossible to be searched out by any but a very few! What things it contains that are obvious and open, these, like a familiar friend, it speaks simply to the heart, both of unlearned and learned. As to those, on the other hand, which it hides in mysteries, neither does it elevate them by lofty speech, such as might deter from a nearer approach the dull and untaught mind, as a poor man sometimes fears to approach a rich one; but Scripture invites all by a lowly kind of speech, intending not only to feed all with obvious truth, but also to exercise and prove all by that truth which is remote from view; having in its easy parts whatever its hard parts contain. But lest being open to view, they should incur contempt, the same truths again are made desirable by concealment; to meet the desire, they are, as it were, produced anew; and being so renewed, they insinuate themselves with a kind of delight. Thus wholesome correction is provided for corrupt minds, wholesome nourishment for feeble minds, and wholesome enjoyment for great minds. That mind alone is set against this teaching, that, either through error knows not its healing power, or through sickness loathes it as medicine.'"—*Ep*. 137, § 18, t. ii., p. 340.

brews, that it "is quick, and powerful, and sharper than any two-edged sword, piercing even to the dividing asunder of soul and spirit, and of the joints and marrow, and is a discerner of the thoughts and intents of the heart" (iv. 12). The letter is composed so as to engage the attention of children and to arouse the indifference of the most supine. Here the rudimental elements of truth and goodness are offered for acceptance. It calls "sinners to repentance" by exciting their hopes and awakening their fears. External promises are annexed to obedience, threatenings to disobedience. To adapt its inward spirit to the lowest and weakest, appearances of truth, or truths as they present themselves to the natural understandings of men, are often substituted for genuine truths, things relative for things absolute. Without impairing the intrinsic verity, the value, the purity, or the efficacy of the Word, in the least, the most salutary lessons are presented therein, under every possible diversity of form, and so wonderfully and mercifully is the whole accommodated to every character, and brought down to the level of every apprehension, that all minds, both simple and intelligent, the illiterate and the learned, may be gradually led, by means of it, from the slavery of sinful propensities and habits, to the liberty of heaven,—from spiritual darkness to God's marvellous light,—without injury to their freedom. These adaptations of truth to the varieties of human perception may be compared to lenses of various powers—convex for one, concave for another. There are also numerous instances in which genuine doctrine concerning the Lord, and the essentials of salvation, shine clearly and unmistakably, even through the cortex of the letter.[68] These agree in every respect with the deeper truths of the inward spirit, and may always be universally recognized. As the mind receives and obeys, it becomes expanded and elevated, prepared for higher degrees of spiritual light and usefulness. It is like the dawn which precedes the rising of the sun, or the spring which heralds the coming year.

Nor must we omit to notice the fact that all the great doctrines of

---

[68] See Matt. xxii. 37; Isa. xlv. 22; Matt. xix. 17; John xiv. 9, 10; Rev. xxii. 12.

"We have compared the letter of the Word of God to the skin that covers the body, and its hidden contents to the interior organs and members; . . . but to illustrate the present subject, the Holy Word may be compared to a beautiful female clothed in becoming drapery, but whose face and hands remain uncovered: thus, while the greater part of the letter of the Scriptures consists of truths veiled over by natural images, which cannot be deciphered without a key, the things most indispensable to be known are openly displayed."—*Noble's Plen. Insp.*, p. 115.

So Augustine, cited by Bishop Hall, asserts, "There is not so much difficulty in the Scriptures to come to those things which are necessary to salvation."—*Ep.* 3. And in another place, "In those things which are openly laid down in Scripture, are found all those things which contain our *faith* and *rules of life*."—*De Doct. Chris.*, lii., c. 9.

the Christian religion, those which involve the first steps of moral duty and are essential to salvation, must clearly and legibly be drawn from, and supported by, the literal sense of the Word, in which divine truth lies couched in all its fulness and power.[69] It is the "hem" of the Lord's outer garments, whence healing virtue issues forth on every side (Matt. xiv. 36). Just as appearances in the works of God are to be explained by the ascertained deductions of scientific research, so the appearances of truth in the letter of the Word of God must be expounded by the facts of true doctrine in order to harmonize with genuine wisdom.[70]

The fallacies arising from primary impressions on the mind are "truths in the time of ignorance," and have to be removed or dissipated in the progress we make in all kinds of knowledge. Nor, constituted as we are, capable of an everlasting advancement in intelligence, is this any imperfection; on the contrary, it lies, in reality, at the root of all improvement. We are surrounded with fallacies and appearances of truth, natural and mental, which observation, experience, and reflection only can explain and correct. Thus all things appear to originate from mere nature. The sun appears to move daily round the earth, to rise in the east and to set in the west. It appears to us as though we beheld objects out of the

---

[69] See Rom. i. 16; Ps. xxix. 4; Luke iv. 32; Isa. viii. 20.

[70] "The truths of the literal sense of the Word are, in some cases, not naked truths, but only appearances of truths, and are like similitudes and comparisons taken from the objects of nature, and thus accommodated and brought down to the apprehension of simple minds and of children. But whereas they are at the same time correspondences, they are the receptacles and abodes of genuine truth; and they are like containing vessels,—like a crystalline cup containing excellent wine, or a silver dish containing rich meats; or they are like garments clothing the body,—like swaddling-clothes on an infant, or an elegant dress on a beautiful virgin; they are also like the scientifics of the natural man,—which comprehend in them the perceptions and affections of truth of the spiritual man."—*S. S.*, n. 40.

"When the Word of God (which is true) is literally false, it is spiritually true. This spiritual sense is covered by another, in a vast number of places, and uncovered in some,—rarely, indeed, but nevertheless in such a manner that the places where it is concealed are equivocal, and agree with both [senses]; whereas the places where it is disclosed are unequivocal, and agree only with the spiritual sense."—*Paschal's Thoughts*.

"It is the manner of Scripture," says Gregory of Nyssa, "to describe what *appears to be* instead of what really is."—*Ep. de Python*, p. 870. "Or in other words," adds Dr. Davidson, "the diction of the Bible describes circumstances and physical truths *optically*, according to the popular opinions and customary phraseology of men, without strict scientific accuracy."—*Sacred Hermeneutics*, p. 118. "An object seen in two different mediums appears crooked or broken, however straight and entire it may be in itself."—*Addison*.

"Even the most advanced language is not yet, and never will be after all, more than the language of appearances. The visible world, much more than you suppose, is a passing shadow, a scene of illusions and of phantoms. What you call a reality is still in itself but a phenomenon considered in relation to a more exalted reality, and to an ulterior analysis. . . . The expression of appearances, accordingly, provided it be exact, is, among men, philosophically correct, and what it behoved the Scriptures to employ."—*Gaussen's Theopneusty*, pp. 250-1.

eye or at a distance from us. The sky over our heads appears concave, the earth beneath our feet as a plain. These appearances with many others are so described in the letter of the Word; but the genuine truth obtained by scientific investigation and rational analysis, is, we know, the reverse of all this, when we substitute states of life for space and time. To speak according to apparent truths, however, best suits the universal forms of ordinary intercourse, and is sufficient for all the practical purposes of life, because best adapted to the apprehension of all; and when the realities and genuine facts are understood, this mode of speech is attended with no difficulty whatever. To speak according to *appearances* has been well described by Grindon as *the great law of language*, "because all language deals primarily with ultimates and externals," or what is first presented to the outward senses and to the apperceptions of the external mind. Nay, further, the language of appearances is equally well, and in some cases, perhaps, far better and more universally, adapted to the expression and apprehension of truth than the correct theory and nomenclature of science, which are always changing, or the strict language of philosophy, which would be understood by few unaccustomed to abstract inquiries.

Even in religious doctrines many fallacies exist, which experience alone can rectify. For instance, it appears to some, even honest, minds, that faith alone saves man from sin, and to others, that good works alone are the ground of acceptance with God. From the mere appearances of the literal sense of Scripture, many have inferred that God is angry and vindictive and delights in punishing the sinner for his transgressions; that the soul is a mere vapor, and the spiritual world a mysterious void; that the body will rise at some future day from the grave, and the earth will be sublimated into a heaven, and that heaven and its joys are the capricious gifts of God, and will even borrow confirmation of these opinions from the letter of the Word. But all such views are the offspring of appearances mistaken for realities, and of subsequent fallacious reasonings thereon, which can only be corrected and dissipated by a right discrimination between apparent and genuine truths, according to the rule of interpretation here advocated. It is even so with natural knowledge. While one mind will perceive a scientific law in its native lustre, another, without a question of insincerity, will have but an obscure idea of it; a third will regard it as a fallacy of the senses, and a fourth will entirely reject it as absolutely false and untenable. Hence we are supplied with an incontrovertible argument in favor of the necessity of the Word of God, as we find it, being outwardly suited to the early states of all for whom it was designed.

All men are first external and carnal, and by nature inclined only to what is evil; yet they have to be impressed with the indispensable truth of God's existence and government and the hatefulness of sin, before they can trust his guidance, be reclaimed from iniquity, attain newness of heart and life, become spiritually-minded, and have correct ideas of spiritual things. "Howbeit," saith the apostle Paul, "that was not first which is spiritual, but that which is natural; and afterward that which is spiritual" (1 Cor. xv. 46). "But the natural man receiveth not the things of the Spirit of God, for they are foolishness unto him; neither can he know them, because they are spiritually discerned" (1 Cor. ii. 14). A child, for instance, sees any given truth relating to the life and conduct merely in its simple appearance, so that parental affection will assume the form of anger, and parental instruction the form of cruelty; but a young man will perceive the same truth in a less imperfect state of the intellect, and see it in another light; mature age, however, will again strip it of many adventitious coverings; while old age will look at it in a higher degree of light, and see it in a totally different point of view, and will from long experience and observation adopt and enforce only what is genuine.[71] When the deluded sensualist, therefore, approaches the Divine Word, he sees, as he only can see, no further than the mere appearances of the letter. He is warned to escape "the wrath to come." He is threatened, that his natural fears and hopes may be awakened, and that he may be impressed with his awful state by nature and by choice. He looks at the Lord as "an austere man" and a "hard master." He is thus, may be, induced to seek deliv-

---

[71] Take as an illustration the petition in the Lord's Prayer, "Give us this day our daily bread." The child utters it, and is taught from it that all that he enjoys is absolutely given by the Lord. But as childhood passes away, he discovers that his food and clothes are the results of the labor of his parents, and now he prays for life and strength for them. In youth he learns that though they labor, it is "God who gives the increase," and he now prays for the blessing of the Lord on his own works as well as on his parents. When youth passes and manhood dawns, he begins to feel the need of intelligence to guide him aright, and now he thinks of a spiritual bread on which his soul can live, and he prays for light and knowledge instead of the literal food of his childhood. And still on, when intelligence has awakened his understanding, he sees the need of spiritual wisdom, and begins to search for it in the Word of God, to regenerate his heart and life. He still uses the same words, but prays for interior light. And when this is vouchsafed, it teaches him that beyond all this he has another and a higher need—the love of God in his soul—and at the divine footstool of his Father he seeks and asks for this love in the words of his childhood's prayer, "Give us this day our daily bread." —ED.

erance from evil and error, and, in dependence on Him who is "mighty to save," is encouraged to take the first step in the path of repentance. The simple in heart and mind approach the same Word, they read and understand its doctrines, and obey its precepts in simplicity, and partake of its unspeakable consolations, rejoicing as from time to time they see "greater things than these." When the intelligent, who have made some progress and acquired some experience in the regenerate life, read the Word, they can more clearly and rationally see the unfoldings of the internal sense; and, as they advance in goodness, will have still deeper mysteries and more glorious wonders displayed to their delighted view, until "perfect love casteth out fear" (1 John iv. 18), and the light shining brighter and brighter upon them reveals the open day, and enables them to discern truths in that light by which angels see. (Prov. iv. 18.) "For we know in part," says the apostle Paul, "and we prophesy in part. But when that which is perfect is come, then that which is in part shall be done away. When I was a child, I spake as a child, I understood as a child, I thought as a child; but when I became a man, I put away childish things. For now we see through a glass, darkly; but then, face to face: now I know in part; but then shall I know even as also I am known" (1 Cor. xiii. 9-12).[72] So also the Lord himself, who is "the same yesterday, to-day, and forever" (Heb. xiii. 3), is perceived and acknowledged, as to his Divine characteristics, just in proportion as truth is unfolded and purity of heart is attained. He is regarded in man's first efforts as a stern teacher, before He can be seen as the God of all wisdom and whose laws all proceed from his unbounded love; but when man has made advanced progress in the regenerate life, and has become partially acquainted with the influence of love upon his heart, in all its beautiful and tender varieties, then, and not till then, can he see God as He really is, love itself and wisdom itself. And these changes of state are obviously finite, and attach only to the creature, and in respect to God himself are but appearances of truth.[73]

---

[72] "Now, we see by means of a mirror reflecting the images of heavenly and spiritual things, in an enigmatical manner, invisible things being represented by visible; spiritual by natural; eternal by temporal."—*Dr. A. Clarke's Comment.*

[73] "You know," observes Maimonides, "what the wise man says (Prov. xxv. 11): *A word spoken according to his two faces, is as* apples of gold *in* net-work of silver. Therefore, when a word spoken *according to both its faces* (that is, according to its *exterior* and interior signification) is said to be *like apples of gold in net-work of silver*, the meaning is, that the *exterior* sense of such word is good and precious as *silver*, but that the *interior* is yet much more excellent: this being in comparison of the *other*, proportionably as *gold* is to *silver* in value. Nor is this all, but it has yet this farther meaning, viz., that there likewise is something in the *exterior* sense, that naturally leads to a closer inspection and consideration of the interior, without which this would not be observed. Even as

In accommodation to human discernment, the letter of the sacred Word sometimes speaks of the Lord as having his dwelling-place above the outward firmament; as pleased or displeased with every separate action and thought of each single individual; as changing his mind; as capriciously seeming to grant admission into heaven for a reward, and as arbitrarily casting into hell as a punishment to chastise man for transgressions against his precepts; and as attributing to Him evil as well as good,—electing some and rejecting others, as absent at one time and present at another, coming down and going up, seeing and not seeing, knowing and not knowing.[74] In such language of mere appearance is the truth presented to us in the letter of the Word, and thus adapted to the states of the unreflecting and the simple; but those who have advanced in states of intelligence may plainly perceive that the kingdom of heaven is WITHIN (Matt. xii. 28; Mark i. 15; Luke xvii. 20, 21); that God cannot possibly have any favorites, for He is justice itself and is no respecter of persons (2 Sam. xiv. 14; 2 Chron. xix. 7; Acts x. 34; Rom. ii. 11; Eph. vi. 9; Col. iii. 25; 1 Pet. i. 17; James ii. 9); that He imputes evil to no one (2 Cor. v. 19); that He is omniscient and omnipresent; that as sin on man's part abstracts nothing from his infinite perfections, for He is goodness itself (Ps. cxlv. 9), and truth itself (John xiv. 6), and unchangeably the same (Mal. iii. 6), therefore both sin and its torment must originate with man; for as man accepts or abjures the invitations of the Saviour, he secures the things belonging to his eternal peace and joy, or, on the contrary, is the artificer of his own misery, and brings upon himself the condign punishment he suffers. The great and genuine truth, confirmed by wisdom and experience, is, that the mind forms its own heaven or its own hell

---

an apple of gold covered (as aforesaid) *with a silver net-work*, if you stand too far off, or do not look attentively at it, seems to be *all silver*. But when the attention of one who has good eyes, is attracted by the *worth* and *beauty* of the *silver*, to look more nearly at it, he discerns the *golden apple* that lies *veiled within*. So oftentimes [he might have said always] are the words of the prophets. Their *exterior* parts present things many ways useful and excellent, either for direction about morals, or for the outward government of the Church, and other like good purposes and uses; while the interior part, or *spirit* of the same, is of superior excellency, to build up them that believe in the outline mysteries of faith." "This is the exposition of that *Jew*, and is an exposition not unworthy of a *Christian*."—*Cited by Halloway*, "*Letter and Spirit*," pp. 4, 5.

[74] "It is," says Cicero, "the common opinion of all philosophers, of what sect soever, that the Deity can neither be angry nor hurt anybody."—*De Officii*, iii. 27.

An ancient Pagan writer has composed a discourse to show that the Atheist, who denies a God, does Him less dishonor than the man who owns his being, but at the same time believes Him to be cruel, hard to please, and terrible to human nature. "For my own part," says he, "I would rather it should be said of me, that there was never any such man as Plutarch, than that Plutarch was ill-natured, capricious, inhuman."—*Anniv. Calend.*, p. 764.

in time and to all eternity. The sympathies of our nature, our affections, and our thoughts, purified, elevated, and refined by the operations of the Holy Spirit in the work of regeneration, will be forever active in promoting the welfare and ministering to the happiness of others, and in that glorious and ever-enlarging work finds a corresponding reward in the approval of conscience, and in a perpetual increase of wisdom, love, and blessedness; and, on the other hand, if selfishness rule the mind and destroy these sympathies, and corrupt these affections and thoughts, the sensual appetites alone remain, which always minister to disappointment, wretchedness, punishment, and wrath.[75] "Tribulation and anguish upon every soul of man that doeth evil; but glory, honor, and peace to every man that worketh good" (Rom. ii. 9, 10). "Behold," saith the Lord, "for your iniquities have ye sold yourselves" (Isa. l. 1). "They that plow iniquity and sow wickedness, reap the same" (Job iv. 8). And again: "Your iniquities have turned away these [blessings], and your sins have withholden good things from you" (Jer. v. 25). Nor is there, as it at first sight might be supposed, anything derogatory to the character of God, nor the slightest prevarication or perversion of the truth in such forms of expression; for man is born into all kinds and degrees of hereditary tendency toward evils and errors, and it was essential to his freedom and advancement in the life and light of heaven that truths relating to the Divine character and operations should be clothed with appearances in the Word to suit his lowest states of thought and love. On this subject, Swedenborg thus writes: "A further reason why it is permitted to think that Jehovah turns away his face, is angry, punishes, tempts, and even curses and kills, is in order that men might believe that the Lord alone governs and disposes all and everything in the universe, even evil itself, punishment and temptation; and when they have received this most general idea, those who can be further instructed might afterwards learn how, or in what manner, He governs and disposes all things, and that He turns the evil of punishment and the evil of temptation into good" (A. C. 245). Thus in Isa. viii. 17 an apparent truth is

---

[75] "Misery is the *natural* inevitable consequence of men's voluntary corruption of themselves; and they who resolve all the punishment and miseries of another life into a purely positive infliction of God, do think with the vulgar."—*Bishop Brown's Divine Analogy,* p. 339.

"The Jews did not perceive that the attribution of wrath and jealousy to their God could only be a figure of speech; and what is worse, it is difficult to persuade many Christians of the same thing, and solemn inferences from the figurative expressions of the Hebrew literature have been crystallized into Christian doctrine."—*Wilson,* **Essays and Reviews,** 9th ed., p. 171.

presented, calculated to awaken the attention of the most careless reader: "I will wait upon the Lord, that hideth his face from the house of Jacob." It can only be in appearance that the ever-present Jehovah hides his face; just as the natural sun appears to withdraw when hidden by a cloud. The truth is, that just as a cloud rises from the earth and shrouds the sun from view, so do the gross thoughts and persuasions, signified by a cloud, spring from the earthly mind or carnal nature, intercept the mental vision, and prevent the beams of mercy, signified by the Lord's face, from being perceived. As it is declared by the Lord Himself, "Your iniquities have separated between you and your God, and your sins have hid his face from you" (Isa. lix. 2). Here the genuine truth gleams through the letter, and becomes manifest; the cloud is dissipated, and the sun shines in all his effulgence. So also, in Genesis, we read, "God did tempt Abraham" (xxii. 1). This could only be said in appearance, for the Apostle James states the genuine truth where he says, "Let no man say when he is tempted, I am tempted of God; for God cannot be tempted with evil, neither tempteth He any man; but every man is tempted when he is drawn away of his own lust and enticed" (i. 13, 14). Again, it is said, "God is angry with the wicked every day" (Psalm vii. 11). This representation of the Almighty must be an appearance arising from the disposition of the sinner being opposite to the nature of infinite love and zeal, and not from any angry passion burning in the pure bosom of Deity. With the wicked, God appears to be angry "every day," or in every state, because of their wilful opposition to his Word; therefore, we read, "With the merciful thou wilt show thyself merciful, and with the upright man thou wilt show thyself upright. With the pure thou wilt show thyself pure, and with the froward thou wilt show thyself unsavory [or froward]" (2 Sam. xxii. 26, 27; Ps. xviii. 25, 26). The Apostle John, then, affirms the genuine truth, whatever may be the appearance to the contrary, where he says, "God is love" (1 Eph. iv. 8); and we are assured by the Lord Himself that "fury is not in Him" (Isa. xxvii. 4), and that his nature is unchangeable, "the same yesterday, to-day, and forever" (Heb. xiii. 8). It is man that hates his God, and regards his service as that of "a hard master" (Matt. xxv. 24); but God, being immutable love and goodness, can never hate the creatures of his hand. "As I live, saith the Lord God, I have no pleasure in the death of the wicked; but that the wicked turn from his way and live" (Ezek. xxxiii. 11).

Thus, true doctrine makes the literal in harmony with the internal sense, and reconciles every difficulty. In the Psalms we read, "Do not I hate them, O Lord, that hate thee? I hate them with perfect hatred, I count them mine enemies" (cxxxix. 21, 22). How plain it is that these words must have an inward spiritual sense, else they cannot be consistently understood, and would be unworthy a book whose Author is love itself, and who has taught us by precept and example to love even our enemies. Who, then, are our enemies that we have to hate? The Lord tells us, "If any man come to me, and hate not his father, and mother, and wife, and children, and brethren, and sisters, yea, and his own life also, he cannot be my disciple" (Luke xiv. 26). What an extraordinary declaration is this, coupled with the other! What says the Apostle John? "He that hateth his brother is in darkness" (1 Epist. ii. 11). Turn to iii. 15, "Whosoever hateth his brother is a murderer;" and in the 20th verse, "If a man say, I love God, and hateth his brother, he is a liar." What says the divine commandment? "Honor thy father and thy mother: that thy days may be prolonged upon the land which the Lord thy God giveth thee" (Ex. xx. 12). How can all this be reconciled, unless we allow that the Scriptures contain a holy internal sense? In the literal sense of the fourth commandment we are taught the doctrine of external obedience, to honor and obey our natural parents; but in the spiritual and heavenly sense we are commanded to honor and obey our heavenly Father, the Lord Jesus Christ, and our spiritual mother, his Church, "the bride and wife of the Lamb;" or, in another sense, to celebrate his divine goodness or love, and his divine wisdom or truth, by a life of order; then will our days be prolonged, or, according to the spiritual idea, then shall we acquire a fitness for endless life in the heavenly Canaan. In an opposite sense, our own father and mother, and the enemies whom we have to hate with perfect hatred before we can become the Lord's disciples, are the unclean and unholy hereditary principles of evil and falsity in the unregenerate mind; for they are the parents and kindred of its impure gratifications, wherein its degraded life consists. This father and mother, together with all their corrupt offspring, yea, and our own impure life also, we are to hate, to abhor, to cast out, and to destroy their dominion within us, as it is written, "For I am come to set a man at variance against his father, and the daughter against her mother, and the daughter-in-law against her mother-in-law. And a man's foes shall be they of his own household. He that findeth his life shall lose it; and he that loseth his life for my sake shall find it" (Matt. x. 35, 36, 39); and, again, "Happy shall he be that taketh thy little ones," O daughter of Babylon, "and dasheth them against the stones" (Psalm cxxxvii. 9).

In Genesis we read that "it repented the Lord that He had made man on the earth, and it grieved Him at his heart" (vi. 6). Here, again, we have an apparent truth, resulting from man's rebellious disobedience and obstinate impenitence, mentioned in the previous verse, and hence a change is ascribed to the Divine Being; but He declares his own true character where He says, "God is not a man that He should lie, nor the son of man that He should repent" (Num. xxiii. 19). So, again, we read, "the Lord hardened Pharaoh's heart" (Ex. vii. 13). This also is expressed according to the appearance, and in accommodation to the state of the Israelites, who supposed that what the Lord permitted He willed. The genuine truth is asserted in Ex. viii. 15, 32, where it is twice said, "Pharaoh hardened his own heart" (see also 1 Sam. vi. 6). By grief and repentance, when predicated of Jehovah, are signified, in the internal sense, the operations of his divine mercy and wisdom, which are spoken of so as not to transcend finite conceptions, in agreement with the nature of mercy and forgiveness as exercised among men; and for the same reason human properties and characteristics are so often ascribed to the Lord.

On this part of our subject, Swedenborg thus writes: "Whosoever is disposed to confirm false principles by appearances, according to which the Word is written, may do so in innumerable instances. But there is a difference between confirming false principles by passages from the Word, and believing in simplicity what is spoken in the Word. He who confirms false principles, first assumes some principle of his own, from which he is unwilling to depart, and whose authority he is determined at all events to support, for which purpose he collects and accumulates corroborating proofs from every quarter, consequently from the Word, till he is so thoroughly self-persuaded with regard thereto, that he can no longer see the truth. But whosoever in simplicity, or out of a simple heart, believes what is spoken in the Word, does not first assume principles of his own, but thinks what is spoken to be true, because the Lord spake it; and in case he is instructed as to the right understanding thereof, by what is spoken in other parts of the word, he instantly acquiesces, and in his heart rejoices: nay, even supposing a person, through simplicity, to believe that the Lord is wrathful, that He punishes, repents, grieves, etc., whereby he is restrained from evil, and led to do good, such belief is not at all hurtful to him, inasmuch as it leads him to believe also that the Lord sees all things both generally and particularly, and when he is principled in such belief he is afterwards capable of being enlightened in other points of faith, at least in another life, if not before: the case is different with those who are self-persuaded in consequence of preconceived principles, and who are riveted in the belief thereof through the pernicious influence of selfish and worldly love."—A. C., n. 589.

Again, the same author says, " In many passages of the Word we find anger, wrath, and vengeance attributed to God, and it is said that He punishes, casts into hell, tempts, with many other expressions of a like nature. Now, where all this is believed in a child-like simplicity, and made the ground of the fear of God, and of care not to offend Him, no man incurs condemnation by such a simple belief. But where a man confirms himself in such notions, so as to be persuaded that anger, wrath, vengeance, belong to God, and that He punishes mankind, and casts them into hell, under the influence of such anger, wrath, and vengeance, in this case his belief is condemnatory, because he has destroyed genuine truth, which teaches that God is love itself, mercy itself, and goodness itself, and, being these, that He cannot be angry, wrathful, or revengeful. Where such evil passions, then, are attributed in the Word to God, it is owing to appearance only. It is the same in many other instances."— S. S., n. 94.

Truths accommodated to our gross perceptions are, for the most part, apparent truths; but seen in spiritual light, their appearance is changed, a transfiguration, so to speak, takes place; they are invested with new splendors, and are spiritually discerned. Let us " not judge, then, according to the appearance, but judge righteous judgment " (John vii. 24); for, from making no distinction whatever between the apparent and real truths of Scripture, which correspondence thus opens and explains, all the false and heretical doctrines which have agitated and divided the Christian world have sprung. Hence we see the importance of true doctrine to enable us rightly to understand the revealed Word (see, for illustration, Gen. vi. 7; Ex. xxxiii. 12-14; Jer. xviii. 8-10; Hos. xi. 8, 9; Joel ii. 10-12; Jonah ii. 9, 10; Rev. xv. 1-7).

CHAPTER IX.

The Correspondence of War and Implements of War in the Holy Word.

WE frequently read in the Holy Word of cruel wars, and of weapons of war, which, because they all, either in a good or a bad sense, represent states of spiritual warfare, and describe the instrumentalities by which they are carried on, appear in the letter of the Word to be sanctioned and applauded, and are sometimes represented as commanded by Jehovah; as, "The Lord hath sworn that the Lord will have war with Amalek from generation to generation" (Ex. xvii. 16). Nothing can be more abhorrent to the Divine character or revolting to Christian feeling than the ferocious spirit of war; and yet the Lord commanded the children of Israel not only to exterminate the Amalekites, but the inhabitants of Heshbon and Bashan. In Deuteronomy we read how this was done: "And the Lord our God delivered the king before us, and we smote him and his sons and all his people. And we took all his cities at that time, and utterly destroyed the men and the women and the little ones of every city; we left none to remain" (ii. 33, 34; iii. 6). While such revolting cruelty was permitted on account of the degeneracy of mankind, and was even attributed to the Lord, because it was, as in all other similar cases, a lesser evil for a greater good, it must be evident that it was recorded by inspiration for some more hidden meaning than the mere history, though that history be true. Let us call to mind "the foes of our own household" (Matt. x. 36), the adversaries lurking in our own bosoms, the enemies of our eternal peace, and how beautiful is the lesson of instruction with which we are at once supplied! How deeply interesting is the command to destroy, by the power of truth and love, all our bitter antagonists, our selfish passions and unclean persuasions, to let not one remain! Both in the Old and New Testaments armor and instruments of war are continually mentioned in reference solely to their internal significations. Turn to Joel: "Prepare war," saith the Lord; "beat your plowshares into swords, and your pruning-hooks into spears; let the weak say, 'I am strong'" (iii. 10). Now read Isa. ii. 4: "They shall beat their swords into plowshares, and their spears into pruning-hooks; nation shall not lift up sword against nation, neither shall they learn war any more." We have here, in the literal sense of the Word, two divine commands and predictions the very opposite of each other. There is another striking instance in the New Testament of a precisely similar description, amounting to an apparent contradiction. In Luke it is said that "the Lord hath visited us to guide our feet into the way of peace" (i. 79); and we read that the angels sang at his nativity, "Glory to God in the highest, and on earth peace, good-will towards men [or to men of good will]" (ii. 14). But what does our blessed Lord himself say? "Think not that I am come to send peace on earth; I came not to send peace, but a sword" (Matt. x. 34). Equally inexplicable in the letter only are two passages of similar import, which the Lord spake nearly at the same period to his disciples, one of which is recorded in Matt. xxvi. 52: "All they that take the sword shall perish with the sword;" and the other in Luke xxii. 36, where He says, "He that hath no sword, let him sell his garment and buy one." By the mere letter these apparent contradictions never can be harmonized; the spiritual sense can alone reconcile them. Every other mode of interpretation leaves them unexplained mysteries. How interesting and instructive, how plain and simple, how pure and true are all such passages when their hidden meaning is unfolded by the great law of correspondence! As we read them, let us contemplate that triumph over sin and folly, in intention, thought, and deed, which must ever precede a state of internal peace, and which devout and humble faith in the Word of God, our armory and our "quiver," and ready obedience to its commands, always gives; for doing this we have "our feet shod with the preparation of the gospel of peace" (Eph. vi. 15). Let us think, therefore, of our spiritual warfare against evil and hell; "for we wrestle not against flesh and blood, but against principalities and powers, against the rulers of the darkness of this world, against spiritual wickedness in high places" (Eph. vi. 12). Let us think of the panoply of strength requisite to give us victory over all our inward foes and persecutors—"the helmet of salvation," "the breastplate of righteousness," "the shield of faith," "the sword of the Spirit," "the spear" of true doctrine, the sharp-pointed arrows of truth, and "the whole armor of God" (Eph. vi. 10-17); clothed and armed with which we have to wage this inward combat, destroying, by the power of faith and love, all our spiritual enemies, young and old, before we can sit down in tranquillity—before the Lord Jesus Christ can impart to our souls "that peace which the world can neither give nor take away," and all becomes at once luminous, intelligible and practical, and in the inspired language of the Psalmist we are ready to exclaim, "Plead my cause, O Lord, with them that strive with me; fight against them that fight against me. Take hold of shield and buckler, and stand up for my help. Draw out also the spear, and stop the way against them that persecute me: say unto my soul, I am thy salvation" (Ps. xxxv. 2, 3); "Gird thy sword upon thy thigh, O most mighty, with thy glory and thy majesty. Thine arrows are sharp in the heart of the king's enemies" (xlv. 3, 6); "Blessed be the Lord my strength, who teacheth my hands to war and my fingers to fight" (cxliv. 1), and to ascribe from the heart all the power and the glory to Him alone. "Thou, O Lord, hast given me the shield of thy salvation: and thy right hand hath holden me up, and thy gentleness hath made me great. Thou hast enlarged my steps under me, that my feet did not slip. I have pursued mine enemies, and overtaken them: neither did I turn again till they were consumed. I have wounded them that they were not able to rise: they are fallen under my feet. For thou hast girded me with strength unto the battle: thou hast subdued under me those that rose up against me. The Lord liveth; and blessed be my rock; and let the Lord God of my salvation be exalted" (Ps. xviii. 35-39, 46).

Again: treating of the final destruction of all our spiritual enemies, the sacred prophet, addressing his divine deliverer, in whose name and by whose strength the regenerating Christian ever "comes off more than conqueror," says, "Thou [O Lord, by thy Word] art my battle-axe and weapons of war: for with thee will I break in pieces the nations, and with thee will I destroy kingdoms; and with thee will I break in pieces the horse and his rider; with thee also will I break in pieces man and woman; and with thee will I break in pieces old and young; and with thee will I break in pieces the young man and the maid; I will also break in pieces with thee the shepherd and his flock; and with thee will I break in pieces the husbandman and his yoke of oxen; and with thee will I break in pieces captains and rulers" (Jer. li. 20-23). It is in this, the true inward sense of temptation conflict, that the apostle Paul exhorts Timothy to fight the good fight of faith and lay hold on eternal life, and as an encouragement sets before him his own example and experience at the close of his ministry in these touching words: "I am now ready to be offered, and the time of my departure is at hand. I have fought a good fight, I have finished my course, I have kept the faith: henceforth there is laid up for me a crown of righteousness, which the Lord, the righteous judge, will give me at that day; and not me only, but unto all them also that love his appearing" (2 Tim. iv. 6-8).

In connection with this spiritual signification of warfare, and in further illustration of the science of correspondences, let me recall your attention to the battle fought by "the children of Israel with the Amalekites;" and I allude to it thus specifically, because in the internal sense subjects of the most edifying tendency are presented before us, which yet do not appear on the surface of the history. Without some deeper meaning than that of the letter, it is nothing more than the narration of a battle and a victory, a descriptive scene of strife and bloodshed, together with a most remarkable intervention of Divine power. It is thus stated: "Then came Amalek, and fought with Israel in Rephidim. And Moses said unto Joshua, Choose us out men, and go out, fight with Amalek: to-morrow I will stand on the top of the hill with the rod of God in mine hand. So Joshua did as Moses had said to him, and fought with Amalek: and Moses, Aaron and Hur went up to the top of the hill. And it came to pass, when Moses held up his hand, that Israel prevailed: and when he let down his hand, Amalek prevailed. But Moses' hands were heavy; and they took a stone and put it under him, and he sat thereon; and Aaron and Hur stayed up his hands, the one on the one side, and the other on the other side; and his hands were steady until the going down of the sun. And Joshua discomfited Amalek and his people with the edge of the sword" (Ex. xvii. 8-13). In the spiritual import of this sacred history, it treats of a state in man's regeneration, or the gradual process by which he is saved from evil and hell. The hosts of Israel signify, collectively, the Lord's church, and, individually, every sincere member of it, who, in consequence of the indefinite number of affections and thoughts, faculties and powers, constituent of the human mind, and the abundant principles of goodness and truth of which they may be receptive, is called "a host." The armies of Amalek[76] signify those spiritual adversaries which, with deadly animosity, oppose our progress towards the kingdom of God, or in the attainment of a heavenly state of mind and life, represented

---

[76] *Amalek* means, in English, "a striking or smiting people."

by the land of Canaan. These implacable enemies of our salvation include not only "the principalities and powers of darkness," but all those false principles and selfish persuasions springing from the love of evil,—those disorderly tempers and unclean thoughts, those malicious dispositions and cruel lusts,—in which they delight to dwell. The battle, therefore, in every particular recorded, was so described in the Word of God as to represent the spiritual conflict between the powers of heaven and hell which is waged in every bosom in the course of regeneration; the means which can alone be effectually employed for the soul's deliverance, and the certain victory to be obtained through perseverance in the Christian course. The fact of Joshua marshalling Israel's hosts, and, under the direction of Moses, leading them forth to the combat, represented the authority of the truth adapted to the natural man, which arranges all within the mind in due order, under the immediate direction of the truth, adapted to the spiritual man, derived from the spirit of the Holy Word, signified by Moses. The battle was fought in a valley, and a valley means the low state of the natural mind, where opposition to heavenly things is always to be met, and which is called elsewhere "the valley of decision" (Joel iii. 14). The success of the battle is not made to depend either on the personal valor of the combatants or on the military skill of their leaders, but on the singular circumstance of the hands of Moses being "held up" towards heaven or "let down" towards the earth, as he stood or sat on the top of a neighboring hill. The hands always mean ability or power, both of the understanding and the will,—the former being signified by the left hand and the latter by the right; and the hands of Moses signify the power of truth derived from the Word when received in the mind, and also the faculties of apprehending and obeying it. A hill, in contradistinction to a valley, denotes a state of charity or love actuated by lofty or heavenly motives, in opposition to such as are low, carnal, or grovelling. This is the hill of blessing, the source of all spiritual strength, that girds us for the battle. "I will lift up mine eyes to the hills," saith the Psalmist, "from whence cometh my help" (Psalm cxxi. 1). The holding up of the hands of Moses was an impressive figure of the lifting up, by the power of truth, of all the inward faculties of the soul towards the Lord, that they may be constantly renewed and invigorated by the divine energy and life. "Let us lift up our hearts with our hands unto God in the heavens" (Lam. iii. 41). But the letting down of his hands will represent a decline of the mental faculties towards the earthly nature, or towards those objects of self and the world, which are beneath,—thus, the substitution of self-will for the Divine Will, of self-intelligence for the Divine Wisdom, and of self-dependence for the Divine Providence. The heaviness of the hands of Moses denotes man's proneness to rest on his own power, in the hour of danger and temptation; and that even truth, however vivid may be its impression on the memory and intellect, is, in such a season of self-reliance, drawn downwards towards earthly objects and sensual pursuits, and is then powerless against the armies of Amalek, which, notwithstanding its presence, prevails over the hosts of Israel. "Aaron and Hur," therefore, we learn, "took a stone and placed it under Moses, and stayed up both his hands, till the going down of the sun, and Amalek was discomfited." Aaron and Hur, the servants and priests of the Most High God, represent the varied principles of faith, accommodated to the outward and to the inward man,—the truth believed from affection and rationally perceived. These are the ministers of the Lord in the soul,—the only principles that can aid and support the sinking, the desponding mind, in the time of spiritual warfare. They are the reactive agents, in unison with the operations of God, for the promotion of our salvation, essential mediums of spiritual victory in the hour of trial. The stone placed under Moses signifies the truth, which inculcates a life of order in the use of the senses, and is thus a support to the divine law in the Word, which rests thereon, and is, in the letter, often meant by a "stone" or "rock." Such a consistent life is the real prop and support of all inward truth and goodness, and is absolutely essential to preserve them from being wasted. The hands of Moses being firmly sustained till the going down of the sun, signifies that such elevation of man's inward powers and gifts, both of reason and freedom, of thought and will, must be perseveringly maintained, till the state of spiritual conflict here treated of is terminated. Then our enemies being vanquished, we shall build, like the triumphant and grateful Israelites of old, the altar of true spiritual worship in our hearts, inscribing it with the holy name, "JEHOVAH NISSI" (the Lord my banner), in the heartfelt acknowledgment that all power to resist evil and do good comes from the Lord alone, who has solemnly proclaimed that "He will have war with Amalek from generation to generation" (Ex. xvii. 16)."[77]

---

[77] Origen appears to have had a perception that the record of this battle was designed for some spiritual purpose, not apparent in the letter; for, speaking of it, he observes

"I would here pause a little, and ask those who are not willing to understand the relation spiritually, but only according to the letter, whether they can possibly think that the Almighty God could have regarded the hands of Moses in giving the victory either to Israel or to Amalek, as they were raised up or let fall? I would ask such persons whether they think this worthy of having been uttered by the Holy Spirit?"—*In Lib. Reg.*, cap. xx. And Barnabas, in his explanation of the Miracles, says, "The lifting up of the hands of Moses signifies the application of the Law in its highest meaning: but the letting down of his hands signifies a low, an earthly, and a literal exposition."—*De Vita Mosis*.

---

[78] "Are not the two grand vital organs, the *heart* and the *lungs*, truly analogous in many important points to the two vital systems of the soul, viz., the *mind*, or system of thought, and the moral affections of the heart [or will]?"—*Essay on Analogy*, p. 195.

For an argument on the sexual system, which so extensively exists in the animal and vegetable kingdoms, see an interesting and instructive work by L. H. Grindon, entitled *The Sexuality of Nature*. This intelligent writer says, in his general introduction, p. 1, "Nature is a system of nuptials. Everything in creation partakes either of masculine or feminine qualities:—animals and plants, earth, air, water, color, heat, light, music, thought, speech, the sense of the beautiful, the adaptation of the soul for heaven, all exist as the offspring of a kind of marriage. Restricted commonly to the institution of wedlock, as it exists among mankind, the word 'marriage' rightfully holds a meaning far wider. It denotes all unions analogous to the human in the history both of matter and spirit. As universal laws, sex and marriage rank accordingly with the most important and comprehensive subjects on which science and philosophy can employ themselves. Innumerable phenomena, both of matter and mind, are explained by reference to them as a central principle; while in the immensity of their empire, and in splendid uniformity of their vanity, they offer the grandest proof that man is Nature concentrated, and Nature, man diffused. They constitute a bond of affinity, which certifies every part of creation to be of common origin and plan, the manifold expression of one primitive idea."

"Loves and marriages," says Dr. Mason Good, "are common to all nature."

"God is both a man and an immortal maid."—*Orph. Frag.* Which is the same thing as asserting that He is perfect wisdom and perfect goodness.

In the most ancient historical times, "we shall find every nation, notwithstanding the variety of names, acknowledging the same deities and the same system of theology; and, however humble any of the deities may appear in the Pantheon of Greece and Rome, each, who has any claim to antiquity, will be found ultimately, if not immediately, resolvable into one or other of two primeval principles, the great god and goddess of the Gentiles."—*Cory's Mythol. Enq.*, p. 6.

Mythological beings are all divided into masculine and feminine. Davis, in his *History of the Chinese*, tells us that they have among them "fragments of traditionary knowledge ascribing the production of the universe to the coöperation of the active and passive, or male and female, principle. The celestial principle was male, the terrestrial was female; all animate and inanimate nature was also distinguished into masculine and feminine. Nor do they confine this distinction to the animal and vegetable world only, but extend it to every part of nature. Numbers themselves have their genders: a unit and every odd number being male, two and every even number female."

"If reason and truth [that is, the understanding] be the most strong and *male faculty* in human nature, and if sentiment or love [that is, the will principle] be the most beautiful and *female* parts of the same, then it is evident that every man is in himself both *male* and *female*; and so likewise is every woman. The great distinction is, that in woman the feeling heart predominates, so as to give a general characteristic, and in man the rational mind or head predominates in a like degree, so as to form a characteristic. . . . If we extend our views and reflections in like manner to any and all the various systems of the visible creation, whether animate or inanimate, we shall, I believe, find the same truths illustrated continually in *male and female expression*."—*Essays on Analogy*, pp. 227, 239.

"Which two great sexes animate the world."
Milton's Paradise Lost.

In the Hebrew language, most objects that are double by nature or art, as the eyes, the hands, the feet, etc., are expressed by the *dual number*; such terms generally refer to the two essentials of the life and mind in conjunction—the left eye or hand denoting the perception and power of the intellect, and the right eye or hand the perception and power of the will-principle.

CHAPTER X.

ON THE WILL AND UNDERSTANDING, AS COMPRISING BOTH THE DIVINE AND THE HUMAN MIND; ON THE MARRIAGE OF DIVINE GOODNESS AND TRUTH THEREIN, AND ON THE UNION OF LOVE AND WISDOM IN THE HOLY WORD, WITH ILLUSTRATIONS.

THERE are two distinct departments of the human mind which we are taught is a finite resemblance of the Divine Mind. These are the will, or voluntary principle, which is the seat of all the feelings, affections, and desires, and the understanding, or intellectual principle, which is the repository of all the thoughts, ideas, and opinions. The former is internal, the latter external. These two faculties in man are the receptacles of a continuous flow of life from the Lord, and, in their separate and united activities are, in one way or other, constantly referred to in the sacred volume. They partake of a distinction like that of sex, and to which, indeed, the masculine and feminine principles exactly correspond, both in God and man. They are both essential to conscious rational existence, and their union, corresponding harmony, and resulting offspring, are always represented in the Word by the union of male and female, the marriage covenant, and the parental relationship. The diverse constitution of the sexes correspond; a man thinks more from the understanding, a woman thinks more from the heart; the male acts more from the dictates of reason, but a woman acts more from the impulse of affection. Hence they are helps-meet for each other, and, in true heavenly marriage, "are no more two but one flesh."[78] (See p. 130.)

Because man from creation was thus endowed with these two faculties, he is said to have been formed "in the image and likeness of God" and to have had breathed into him "the breath of life" (or, more correctly translated from the Hebrew, "breath of lives"), "and man," it is added, "became a living soul" (Gen. i. 26; ii. 7). For, when he is restored to order by regeneration, man is still an image of God, by virtue of his intellectual gifts and their reception of truth and intelligence from the Lord, through the inspired life of his divine wisdom; and a likeness of God, by virtue of his voluntary powers and their reception of goodness from the Lord, through the inbreathings of the life of divine love. When these principles are received in heart and soul, and reproduced in the conduct and conversation, man then becomes both an image and likeness of God. And as marriage between one man and one woman is, in a good sense, the true type and representative of all kinds of internal union of love and wisdom, charity and faith, in the soul, therefore it is solemnly enjoined, "what God has joined together, let no man put asunder" (Mark x. 9).

There are two essential attributes of divine existence—divine love and divine wisdom. The former is the very divine essence or substance and the latter is the very divine form of God, and neither could have being or existence without the other. Their infinitely perfect union, energy, and operation constitute the *third* essential in the threefold character of the divine nature. With man, who is, as we have already seen, created in the image of God, finite love and finite wisdom are the two corresponding and essential attributes of mind, whose united and inseparable activity, in the outward life and conduct, constitute the *third* essential of human existence. It is to be observed that the whole natural universe, with its indefinite contents, was created from infinite love as the divine end, by means of infinite wisdom as the instrumental cause. The objects of the visible universe are the ultimate or lowest effects of the combined operation of God's love and wisdom, and are the corresponding finited images of all the realities of the spiritual world, which acts in and upon the natural world; while, again, the objects of both worlds are, collectively and singly, images, more or less remote, of the innumerable faculties and principles existing in man, and of the infinite attributes and perfections existing in God. Every man, both in his mind and in the corresponding forms of his body, is, therefore, an image of his great Maker, and also a universe in its least form.

For instance, the two universal elements of primordial creation are light and heat; the two universal attributes of nature are time and space; the two universal characteristics of bodies are substance and form. All these correspond to the two universal faculties of the will and the understanding, and their finite properties of freedom and reason as constituent of mind, and to their two universal, though ever-varying, states of affection and thought; and these, again, are the finite corresponding images and forms of the infinite essentials of Divine goodness and intelligence, which are the activities and outgrowings of the Lord's infinite will and understanding, and of his incommunicable attributes of omnipresence and eternity. In like manner the heart, with its vital motions, corresponds to the will and its activities, and the lungs, with the powers of respiration, correspond to the understanding and its operations, and these are the two universal receptacles of life in the bodily frame. Now, between the primary departments of the mind, their combined activities, and the things which they receive, there is a mutual relationship necessarily established, essential to the existence of each, like that which subsists between the chief organs of the bodily frame, the heart and the lungs. Thus the will and understanding, in agreement with man's freedom and reason, may become receptive of goodness and truth, or their opposites, evil and falsity, which are their respective perversions; and between goodness and truth, and also between evil and falsity, there is a mutual affinity exactly represented by a marriage. Hence, by a marriage, in the Word, is always signified, in a good sense, the internal union of some principle of heavenly love or charity in the will, with a corresponding principle of heavenly wisdom or faith in the understanding; and, in an opposite sense, the infernal union of some principle of evil in the will, with its corresponding principle of falsity in the understanding. And since the Lord's reciprocal conjunction with man is the effect of the previous union of goodness and truth in the soul, so it is often called a marriage covenant, in which the Lord is designated the bridegroom and husband, and the church, the bride and wife (Hos. ii. 16; Rev. xix. 7).

On account of this twofold constitution of the human mind, both in general and in particular, we find that all the bodily organs are likewise double, or arranged in pairs. For the same reasons, binary forms of expression, in several parts of speech, are found so frequently in the sacred Word, which, in appearance, are synonymous, as, search and try, void and empty, wilderness and desert, briers and thorns, rod and staff, babes and sucklings, nations and people, poor and needy, righteousness and faithfulness, thief and robber, sin and iniquity, joy and gladness, mourning and weeping, anger and wrath, justice and judgment; so, also, we find numerous correlatives associated, as, man and woman, husband and wife, father and mother, sons and daughters, brother and companion, kings and priests, bridegroom and bride, ploughmen and vine-dressers, flocks and herds, threshing-floor and wine-press, heart and spirit, flesh and blood, hunger and thirst, eating and drinking, bread and wine, hills and valleys, land and sea, heat and light; or two things are joined together whose properties and uses are susceptible of union, or are mutually dependent, as, sun and moon, fire and flame, gold and silver, brass and iron, wood and stone, Zion and Jerusalem, Judah and Israel; two words are also associated together, as, "take and eat," "strait gate and narrow way," "wide gate and broad way," "spirit and fire," to labor and be heavy-laden, ploughing and feeding cattle, etc.; and sometimes the same term is simply repeated with or without adjuncts. Now, in all these cases, one of the terms (or the parallelism in which it occurs) refers to some principle or characteristic of the will, or to some quality or state of the affections, desires, and actions thence derived; and the other has respect to some principle of the understanding, or to some quality or state of the thoughts and memory, and the words which result therefrom, whether holy or profane. One term has reference to goodness, or some good state of mind, and, in an opposite sense, to evil, or some evil state of mind, as the context will show; and the other term bears the same relation to truth, or, in an opposite sense, to falsity. One will be predicated more or less of some celestial truth, or of some particular love and its delights, or its opposite lust and its pleasures, and the other will be predicated more or less of some spiritual truth, or its opposite falsity, or of some specific thought or idea, either pure or unclean. For in the divine Word there can be nothing useless, nothing superfluous.

These conclusions are confirmed by that wonderful passage, among others, in the prophecy of Jeremiah, where the Lord, by the mouth of the prophet, in treating of the omnipotence of divine truth emanating from Himself in his Word, and active for the redemption and salvation of the human race, says, "Thou art my battle-axe and weapons of war: for with thee will I break in pieces the nations, and with thee will I destroy kingdoms; and with thee will I break in pieces the horse and his rider; and with thee will I break in pieces the chariot and his rider; and with thee also will I break in pieces man and woman; and with thee will I break in pieces old and young; and with thee will I break in pieces the young man and the maid: I will break in pieces with thee the shepherd and his flock; and with thee will I break in pieces the husbandman and his yoke of oxen; and with thee will I break in pieces captains and rulers" (li. 20–23). Here the various particulars described signify the diversified principles constituent of man's will and understanding, affections and thoughts, mind and life, and are associated in pairs. All kinds and degrees of evil in the will, and of falsity in the understanding, must be dispersed, or destroyed, or subdued, by the power of God's Word; and the union of all kinds and degrees of goodness and truth in the heart and mind, the affections and thoughts, the inward motives and the outward conduct, must be established and confirmed by the Lord, in accordance with his love and wisdom, if He is to reign over us. Then, and not till then, is the divine declaration accomplished in Christian experience, "Mercy and truth are met together; righteousness and peace have kissed each other" (Ps. lxxxv. 10).

Again: eating and drinking are bodily acts requisite to the nourishment and support of the natural frame.[79] There are, also, two kinds of food provided for man's support, liquid and solid. These two operations and two sorts of aliment are constantly alluded to in the Word, and signify, in a good sense, the two distinct kinds of spiritual nourishment required and provided for the support of the soul, viz., goodness and virtue of various degrees for the will, denoted by the varieties of solid food, and wisdom and knowledge of various kinds for the understanding, denoted by the varieties of liquid food; and the whole process of digestion is, in every particular, significative of that spiritual process by which the mind inwardly "learns and digests," or receives and appropriates that nourishment which recruits our spiritual strength, and more and more perfects our growth in the regenerate life; or, on the contrary, if the will and understanding be of an infernal quality, then the food which is desired for its sustentation consists of selfish gratifications and erroneous persuasions, which are represented by unclean animals and noxious plants, by mixed bread and adulterated wine, by unwholesome fruit and bitter water, and it is said of them "the whole head is sick and the whole heart faint" (Isa. i. 5).

To eat bread or flesh signifies, in a good sense, to receive from the Lord, to apprehend, and spiritually to incorporate celestial and vital principles of love or goodness in the will and affections; and to drink wine or blood is to imbibe from the same divine source, to comprehend, and spiritually to appropriate heavenly and living principles of wisdom or truth in the understanding and thoughts. Bread, in a

---

[79] "The analogy between body and mind is very general; and the parallel will hold as to their food as well as any other particular."—*Croker's Life of Dr. Johnson, by Boswell*, vol. i., p. 28.

"As the heathen made such a multiplicity of gods out of one and the same person, so likewise did they confound their sexes, making some deities of both sexes. Hence it is that the Greeks used the word Θεος, both for gods and goddesses; and after the same manner was the word *Deus* used by the Romans."—*Dr. Townley's Notes to the More Nevochim of Maimonides*, p. 357.

good sense, always represents divine goodness or love, and wine divine wisdom or truth; for goodness and truth are the spiritual and everlasting substances which nourish the soul unto eternal life, precisely as bread and wine support the natural body; hence we are taught to pray for "our daily bread" (Matt. vi. 11), "the bread of heaven" (Psalm cv. 40), and "to buy wine without money and without price" (Isa. lv. 1),—the "wine that maketh glad the heart of man, and bread which strengtheneth man's heart" (Psalm civ. 15). In the opposite sense we read of "defiled bread" (Ezek. iv. 13), and of "wine which is the poison of dragons" (Deut. xxxii. 33), where it is self-evident that the corruption and profanation of goodness and truth, or, what is the same thing, the vile and impious principles of evil and falsity are described.

How plain, how interesting, and how edifying does even this short exposition make a multitude of otherwise inexplicable passages of the inspired Scriptures! I need only refer to one or two, and even without a verbal explanation you will be surprised and delighted to see how much you may understand respecting them. In John vi. 51 the Lord said to the Jews in the synagogue at Capernaum, "I am the living bread which came down from heaven: if any man eat of this bread he shall live forever: and the bread that I will give is my flesh, which I will give for the life of the world." The Jews, who only understood these words sensually, asked in skeptical derision, "How can this man give us his flesh to eat?" to which the Lord, without further explanation, immediately replied, "Verily, verily, I say unto you, Except ye eat the flesh of the Son of man, and drink his blood, ye have no life in you. Whoso eateth my flesh, and drinketh my blood, hath eternal life; and I will raise him up at the last day. For my flesh is meat indeed, and my blood is drink indeed. He that eateth my flesh and drinketh my blood, dwelleth in me, and I in him" (53-56). Here the Lord's flesh signifies his divine love or goodness, and his blood, called "the blood of the New Testament" or covenant, can signify nothing else than divine wisdom or truth, which is "shed for many, for the remission of sins" (Matt. xxvi. 28). This seems, also, to explain what the Apostle Paul means in 1 Cor. v. 7, where he says, "For even Christ our passover is *sacrificed* for us." The original Greek word, here translated sacrifice, evidently means "slain;" for the passover was not a sacrifice, but was eaten by the people. So, by parity of reasoning, the Lord Jesus Christ was *slain*, or *glorified his humanity*, that all Christian believers, "having their hearts sprinkled from an evil conscience" (Heb. x. 22), by the blood of the new covenant, or the divine truths of the Word of God, might partake of his flesh and blood, his divine goodness and truth, and incorporate these blessed principles into their very nature, or spiritual constitution, as the Lord said (John vi. 57), "As the living Father hath sent me, and I live by the Father, *so he that eateth me, even he shall live by me.*"

It was to represent this internal communication of sacred gifts and virtues by the Lord, and their reception and appropriation on the part of man, that the Holy Supper was instituted as a perpetual memorial representative of the Lord's glorification, and also of man's regeneration, and as a powerful means of advancing it. For Swedenborg distinctly and truly teaches that "the greatest power inheres in correspondences, because in them heaven and the world, the spiritual and the natural, are conjoined, and therefore that the Word is written according to mere [or pure] correspondences; wherefore it is the conjunction of man with heaven, thus with the Lord. The Lord, by this means, is in first principles, and at the same time in lasts, wherefore [church] sacraments [which are the holiest forms of all worship, and a substitute for all the representative ceremonies and rituals of former dispensations of religion] are instituted on the principles of correspondence, in which, accordingly, a divine potency resides" (*Sp. Diary*, pt. vii.). The Lord made his humanity Divine, and perfectly united it to the indwelling Father, by the successive incorporation of infinite principles of goodness and truth; hence He says, "I have meat to eat that ye know not of" (John iv. 32), and this divinely mysterious process of glorification was the exact pattern of man's regeneration, in which work man becomes, in his finite degree, freely and fully receptive of living principles of goodness and truth from the Lord, which induce upon him the divine likeness, conjoin him with the only source of all life, blessedness, and power, and open up to him a state of eternal advancement in wisdom, love, and use.

Again, in Ezekiel we read: "Thus saith the Lord God, Speak unto every feathered fowl, and to every beast of the field, Assemble yourselves and come; gather yourselves on every side to my sacrifice that I do sacrifice for you, even a great sacrifice upon the mountains of Israel, that ye may eat flesh and drink blood. Ye shall eat the flesh of the mighty, and drink the blood of the princes of the earth, of rams, of lambs, and of goats, of bullocks, all of them fatlings of Bashan. And ye shall eat fat till ye be full, and drink blood till ye be drunken, of the sacrifice which I have sacrificed for you. Thus ye shall be filled at my table with horses and chariots, with mighty men, and with all men of war, saith the Lord God" (xxxix. 17–20). And similar descriptions are in the Revelation, where John says, "And I saw an angel standing in the sun; and he cried with a loud voice, saying to all the fowls that fly in the midst of heaven, Come, and gather yourselves together unto the supper of the great God; that ye may eat the flesh of kings, and the flesh of captains, and the flesh of mighty men, and the flesh of horses, and of them that sit on them, and the flesh of all men, both free and bond, both small and great" (xix. 17, 18). Without the inward life and spirit, how can the divinity, the holiness, the reasonableness and practical tendency of these passages be comprehended? But when that sense is perceived and acknowledged, and the signification of eating, drinking, and the elements of food is understood, they are no longer mysterious predictions, but teem with lessons of infinite intelligence, are replete with the unfoldings of unchanging love, radiant with the beams of sacred glory, and are at once seen to be truly worthy of their omniscient Author. In a general sense we are taught by those words that the Lord has provided richest feasts of purest and holiest blessings and satisfactions in his Word and kingdom, for all who are prepared to partake of and appropriate them by faith and love. Every thought capable of elevation into the atmosphere of heaven, signified by the feathered fowls that fly in the midst of the firmament, and every affection inspired with the life of love and charity, signified by the beasts of the field that walk upon the surface of the ground, are freely and earnestly invited and entreated, by the yearnings of infinite love and compassion, to partake of all kinds and degrees of spiritual nourishment and delight prepared for the understanding and the heart, that man may worship the Lord in "the beauty of holiness," and obey his commandments with a cheerful mind, and consequently be replenished, strengthened, and renovated with "feasts of fat things and wines on the lees," the Lord's "sacrifice on the mountains of Israel," "the supper of the great God!"

On account of this signification of two persons or things, when associated in the Word, the Lord sent forth the seventy disciples by "two and two" (Luke x. 1), to preach the glad tidings of redemption and salvation in his name. For the whole essence of the Gospel may be regarded as the love and wisdom of the Lord; nor, unless these divine principles are unitedly received in the will and understanding of man, can the Gospel become to him "the power of God unto salvation" (Rom. i. 16). There must be a reciprocity of action and reaction established between the infinite will and the finite will, and between the infinite understanding and the finite understanding by the process called regeneration, if the human mind is to become a coherent one, and live forever in conjunction with its Maker. Thus both the love and wisdom emanating from the Lord must be received, and, as it were, reflected back again to their divine source. To receive and retain a given truth in the understanding only, is to combine it with erroneous persuasions and with selfish affections in the will, thus to profane and defile it, and destroy its virtue. He who does this induces upon himself a state of hypocrisy with its direful torment. Hence such impure associations are so strictly forbidden in the Word by a variety of laws, made obligatory even in their literal acceptation in the representative economy of the Jews, and the infringement of which subjected aggressors to severest penalties. But in their inward meaning these laws and penalties are filled with instruction of the most solemn import. Without some internal significancy and capacity of application to the human mind, such laws and penalties cannot be seen in rational light to yield any wisdom worthy of the supreme Lawgiver.[80] For this reason, then, it is, that we are forbidden to sow with divers seed, to plow with an ox and an ass together, or to wear garments woven of mingled woollen and linen yarn (Deut. xxii. 9–11);[81] for a truth received in the intellect must be yoked or united

---

[80] One would imagine that no serious person could read the Mosaic law, and believe it to be *inspired of God*, without perceiving that, in every particular, it must have been designed for holier purposes, and to convey a loftier morality, than what appears on the surface of the letter; and that it could be only in its inward and heavenly sense that the Lord Jesus says of it that "*not one tittle thereof should fail*" (Luke xvi. 17).

"Moses," says Origen (*Adv. Cels.*, i. 18), "never wrote anything which had not a twofold meaning. If in this spiritual sense we say that God promulgated the law, then it appears a code worthy the Divine Majesty; but if we rest in the letter, and understand what is written in the law as the Jews and common people do, then *I blush to say that God gave such laws.*" "Nor was this principle, that we must put such a sense upon the words and facts of Scripture as is worthy a divine production, peculiar to Origen only; but it was also adopted by Augustine and many others of the fathers."—*Bretschneider's Apology for the Modern Theology of Protestant Germany, by Evanson*, p. 53.

In reference to the same subject, Origen further says (*in Levit.*, cap. vii., *in Num.*, cap. xvi., xxi., *et in Matt.*, cap. xxiii.) that "he is a high-priest unto God who holds the (spiritual) science of the law, and understands the reasons of every mystery, and who is acquainted with the law both in the spiritual and literal sense;" but that "all those who literally expound the law are vain preachers." For "they truly make the law an Old Testament who understand it in a carnal manner; but to us, who understand and expound it spiritually and in its evangelical sense, it is always New."

[81] Dr. Townley considers that these heterogeneous mixtures, whether of garments, seeds, or animals, were evidently forbidden to prevent idolatry; or according to Thomas Aquinas (*Prim. Sec.*, qu. 102, art. 6), out of hatred to idolatry, because the Egyptians made mixtures of this nature, in seeds, animals, and garments, to represent the different conjunctions of the planets.

to its own proper and corresponding principle of goodness in the heart, if it is to be preserved from profanation, and thus to be successfully employed, not only to promote our usefulness in this world, but our preparation for a heavenly state.

In order to represent to us more significantly the above twofold characteristic of the Lord's divine proceeding, as consisting of infinite love and infinite wisdom in indissoluble union, there are, both in the Old and New Testaments, two terms or names conjoined, as, Lord God, Jehovah God, Jesus Christ, the Lord-God and the Lamb, the Father and the Son, etc., which names are not, as might be supposed from the mere appearance of the letter, appellations referable to some distinct duality and individuality of person in the Godhead, a supposition equivalent to the monstrous and intolerable idea of more gods than one; but they are designed to mark the distinction recognized by human thought in the one true God, between divine love and divine wisdom, or, what is the same thing, between divine goodness and divine truth,—the two essential constituents of Godhead coëxistent in the divine Mind, the ground of infinite perfection, and the abode and source of all the attributes of Deity. Reason testifies that it cannot be otherwise. The terms Lord, or Jehovah, Jesus, and Father, generally signify, in the Holy Word, some quality of the essential divine principle of love or goodness; and the terms God, Christ,[82] and Son, for the most part signify some characteristic of the other divine principle of wisdom or truth, according to the subject or state under consideration. How immeasurably above mere reasoning and views which are dependent on the bodily senses do such enlightened conclusions and instructions as these elevate the soul, freeing it at once from all cavil, doubt, and inconsistency, directing its undivided adoration to the one true and holy God of heaven and earth—the Lord Jesus Christ, in his own glorified Human; and because He is thus infinite love or goodness itself, and infinite wisdom or truth itself, the apostle Paul bears this most explicit testimony respecting Him, that "In Him [the Lord Jesus] dwelleth all the fulness of the Godhead bodily." The Father sends forth the Son, as heat sends forth light; and as heat and light are one in the sun, so love and wisdom —the Father and the Son—are one in the glorious person of the Lord Jesus Christ, the "Sun of righteousness."

---

[82] The Hebrew word *Jesus*, when translated into English, means *deliverer* and *saviour*. The Hebrew word *Messiah* and the Greek word *Christ* mean *anointed*, and hence *king*.

CHAPTER XI.

THE THREE DEGREES OF LIFE, THE TRINAL DISTINCTION IN GOD, AND THE THREEFOLD CONSTITUTION OF THE HUMAN MIND AND THE HOLY WORD EXPLAINED, AND THEIR MUTUAL CORRESPONDENCE ILLUSTRATED.

WE have seen, in the former chapter, that the will and understanding of man are the two primary constituent powers of the human mind. Yet man is not a complete image of his Creator until he brings forth the ends of his will and the causes of his understanding into their proper effects, namely, words and works; these, therefore, form a third essential constituent of his nature. By virtue of possessing and exercising this power, fixity and identity are imparted to all the interior principles of the mind and life. Now, the three corresponding principles of the Divine Mind are, the infinite will of God, comprising divine ends, the infinite understanding of God, comprising divine causes, and the eternal activity of these two principles, in perfect union, comprising all divine effects. In the Sacred Scriptures the all-begetting principle of love, proceeding from the divine will, is designated "the Father;" the all-producing principle of wisdom, proceeding from the divine understanding, or "the Word made flesh," is denominated "the Son;" and the eternal energy and activity of these two principles, now proceeding from the Lord's glorified Human in perfect union, are called "the Holy Spirit."[83] Thus

---

[83] In the ethical philosophy of the ancient Egyptians, the first principle of the mind is said to have been *intellect*, the second *will*, and the third, which was the joint efflux of these, *concord*, or *harmony of action*.—See *Serle's Hor. Sol.*, p. 331.

"Plato had no doubt of a great mystery being concealed in Moses' account of the three men who appeared unto Abraham."—*De Sacrificiis et de Abrahamo*, p. 367, cited in *Morhen's Notes to Cudworth's Int. Sys.*, vol. ii., p. 327.

"The three names of the Deity mentioned in Sacred Writ, I Am (Jehovah), God (Elohim), and Lord (Adonai), are referred by Philo to the three divine natures [or essentials] into which he divides the Deity."—*Ib.*, p. 329.

"The Platonic hypotheses seem to be really nothing else but infinite goodness, infinite wisdom, and infinite active power, not as mere qualities or accidents, but as substantial things, all concurring together to make up one Θεῖον, or Divinity."—*Ib.*, p. 408.

The inscription on the great obelisk of the Major Circus was, "the great God, the Begotten of God, the All-resplendent."

Heraclitus mentions an inscription which was a triad: "First God, then the Logos, and the Spirit with them; but all these united by nature and uniting in unity."

"The esse of an angel is that which is called his soul, his existence is that which is called his body, and the proceeding from both is that which is called the sphere of

divine love from eternity willed, and divine wisdom, as a cause, operated the work of creation, and came forth in time as the wisdom, or

his life. By this trine an angel is an image of God."—*Swedenborg, Athanasian Creed*, 18, p. 43.

"Father, Son, and Holy Ghost are not represented as so many names, but as *one name;* the one divine nature of God being no more divided by these three than by the single name of *Jehovah* thrice repeated in Num. vi. 22-26."—*W. Jones, of Nayland, on the Trinity.*

"The Hebrew letters which compose the tri-syllabic name JEHOVAH, are expressive of *time past, time present,* and *time to come.*"—See *Maimonides Mor. Nev.*

"Of the *infinite self-existent essence* implied by this name it is impossible for us to form a full and adequate idea, because we, and all other creatures, have but a *finite, derivative* essence. . . . The word JAH (as in Psalm lxviii. 4) stands simply for the *divine essence*, or for Him *who* IS, and who necessarily MUST be. . . . The term EHJAH occurs nowhere but in Ex. iii. 14, and means not only Him who necessarily *is*, but who necessarily *will be*. It regards the future eternal, and demonstrates the immutability of the divine existence. The title JEHOVAH, which contains the other two, includes the *past*, the *present*, and the *future* Eternal, that is, according to our conceptions; for all things, and every division of that duration which we understand by time, are present with Him, though successive to us. Thus the inspired Apostle (finding no word in Greek to represent the idea of the Hebrew) uses periphrasis, or comment on the word, and expresses the name JEHOVAH by ' He that *is*, that *was*, and that *is to come*' (Rev. i. 4)."—*Serle's Hor. Sol.*, pp. 1-4.

"JEHOVAH descended to become JESUS for their [his children's] sakes. And JESUS is JEHOVAH, or He could not be 'the same yesterday (i. e., from eternity), *to-day* (i. e., through all time), and *forever* (i. e., to eternity), all which the name JEHOVAH implies."—*Ib.*, p. 7.

"The three grand attributes of God: infinite plenitude of life, infinite knowledge, and infinite power."—*Druidical Triad.*

"Because goodness, wisdom, and power are the three essential divine attributes, therefore the Deity was originally represented by the ancients under three principal forms. The principle of the divine goodness was represented among the Egyptians by the god Osiris, among the Greeks by Jupiter, and among the Persians by Oromazes. The divine wisdom, or second principle, was represented by the goddess Isis in Egypt, by Pallas, or Minerva, in Greece, and by the goddess Mythen in Persia. The third principle the Egyptians called Orus, the Greeks, Apollo or Hercules, and the Persians Mithras. This latter people, who had neither temples nor statues, adopted only three principal divinities. Indeed, Mr. Ramsay is of the opinion that all the gods of the heathen mythology are but different forms of these three, viz., 'one supreme god, the principal of all beings; a goddess, his wife, sister, or daughter; and a middle god, who is his son, his representative or vicegerent.' This, with some qualifications, may very probably be true."—*D. H. H., Am. New Jer. Mag.*, vol. xviii., p. 374.

The oracle cited out of Damascius the philosopher, by Patritius, asserts that throughout the world a triad or trinity shines forth, which resolves itself into a monad, or perfect unity; and also that this doctrine was the fundamental principle of the Orphic philosophy. Voscius observes that this idea held a principal place in the mythology of the ancients.—See *Cudworth's Int. Sys.*, vol. i., p. 492; *Prichard's Anal. of Egyp. Mythol.*, pp. 39, 47.

"First God, then the Word and Spirit, all uniting in One whose power can never end."—*Oracle of Serapis, Suidas;* see *Fontenelle's History of Oracles*, 1750, Eng. ed., p. 9.

The ancient Egyptians believed in the unity of the godhead, and expressed his attributes by triads. According to Pythagoras, the Samian philosopher, the symbol of all things, or fulness, was the Monad, or active principle, or Father; the Duad, or passive principle, or Mother; and the result or operation of both united. It is remarkable that the ancient trinities of the Hindoos, as well as the Egyptians, emblematized the male or paternal principle, the female or maternal principle, and the offspring, and that this is identical with the early Chinese philosophy.

"Among the ancient Chinese characters which have been preserved, we find one like the Greek *delta* (Δ). According to the *Chinese Dictionary, Kang-hi*, this character signifies *union*. According to *Choueouen*, a celebrated work, Δ is *three united in one*. The *Licou chou tsing hoen*, which is a rational and learned explanation of ancient characters, says, 'Δ signifies intimate union, harmony, the chief good of man, of the heaven and of the earth: it is the union of the three.'"—*Dr. A. Clarke's Comm.*, John i.

Numberless pantheistic superstitions, at-

Word incarnate, in the person of Jesus Christ, and accomplished the work of redemption and the glorification of the assumed humanity; and the Holy Spirit is continually striving to go forth in "the spirit and power" of the Word, to effect human regeneration and salvation.

Swedenborg, treating on this momentous subject, clearly and beautifully unfolds it as follows: "In every divine work there is a first, a middle, and a last, and the first passes through the middle to the last, and thereby exists and subsists; hence the last is the basis. The first, also, is in the middle, and, by means of the middle, in the last; and thus the last is the containant. And because the last is the containant and basis, it is also the firmament. The learned reader will be able to comprehend the propriety of calling these three, end, cause, and effect, and also *esse* (to be), *fieri* (to become), and *existere* (to exist). He who comprehends this reasoning will comprehend, also, that every divine work is complete and perfect in the last; and likewise that in the last is contained the whole, because the prior things are contained together in it. From this ground it is, that by the number three, in the Word, in its spiritual sense, is signified what is complete and perfect; and also, the all or whole together. Because this is the signification of that number, therefore it is so frequently applied in the Word, when that signification is intended to be expressed, as in the following places: Isa. xx. 3; 1 Sam. iii. 1–8, xx. 5, 12–42; 1 Kings xvii. 21, xvii. 34; Matt. xiii. 33, xxvi. 34; John xxi. 15–17; Jonah i. 17; John ii. 19; Matt. xxvi. 39–44; Luke xxiv. 21; besides many other passages where the number three is mentioned. It is mentioned where a work finished and perfect is the subject treated of, because such a work is signified by that number." —S. S. 27–29.

And again: "From the Lord proceed these principles, the celestial,

---

surd cosmogonies, and confused notions, etc., were founded on the corruptions of this philosophy as it became more debased and licentious.

"The number *three* was held sacred by the ancients, being thought the most perfect of all numbers, as having regard to the beginning, middle, and end."—*Dr. Thornton's Eclogues of Virgil*, p. 507.

"Three was a sacred and mystical number among the Druids."—*Davis's Mythol. of the British Druids*, p. 79.

"The Hebrews expressly acknowledged the perfecting property of the number *three;* for with them the letter *shin*, ש, which is in itself a trident, denoted the number *three*, or the utmost perfection of everything."—*Tripl.*, vol. i., p. 52.

"The great majority of the Hebrew roots assume tri-literal combinations as the average form, and the same number of letters are, by most philologists, ascribed to the original Greek roots."—*Conybeare's Lect.*, 2d ed., app., pt. 2, p. 301.

"The ancients had a singular predilection for the number *three;* hence they took it as a divisor preferable to the more rational mode of halves. Of this take an instance from Livy: 'Ejusdem rei causa ludi magni voti æris trecentis, triginta, tribus millibus.'"

the spiritual, and the natural, one after another. Whatsoever proceeds from his divine love is called celestial, and is divine good; whatsoever proceeds from his divine wisdom is called spiritual, and is divine truth; the natural partakes of both, and is their complex in ultimates. The divine principle proceeding from the Lord, in its progress to ultimates, descends through three degrees, and is termed celestial, spiritual, and natural. The divine principle which proceeds from the Lord and descends to men, descends through those three degrees, and when it has descended, it contains those three degrees in itself. Such is the nature of every divine principle proceeding from the Lord; wherefore, when it is in its last degree, it is in its fulness. Such is the nature and quality of the Word; in its last [or lowest] sense it is natural, in its interior sense it is spiritual, and in its inmost sense it is celestial; and in each sense it is divine.[84] The distinction between these degrees cannot be known, except by the knowledge of correspondence; for these three degrees are altogether distinct from each other, like end, cause, and effect, or like what is prior, posterior, and postreme, but yet make one by correspondence; for the natural degree or principle corresponds with the spiritual, and also with the celestial."—S. S. 6, 7.

"He who does not know the regulations of divine order with respect to degrees cannot comprehend in what manner the heavens are distinct from each other, nor even what is meant by the internal and external man. Most persons in the world have no other idea of things interior and exterior, or superior and inferior, than as of something continuous, or cohering by continuity, from a purer state to a grosser; whereas things interior and exterior are not continuous with respect

---

[84] "The celestial [or inmost] sense of the Word cannot easily be unfolded, not being so much an object of intellectual thought as of will-affection. The true ground and reason why there is in the Word a sense still more interior, which is called celestial, is, because from the Lord proceed Divine Good and Divine Truth—Divine Good from his Divine Love and Divine Truth from his Divine Wisdom; each is in the Word, for the Word is the divine proceeding. It is on this account that the Word imparts life to those that read it under holy influence. The marriage of the Lord with the church, and consequently a marriage of goodness and truth, is contained in every particular of the Word."—S. S., n. 19.

"What belongs to the spiritual sense of the Word has more particular relation to the church; and what belongs to the celestial sense, to the Lord; the contents, also, of the spiritual sense have relation to Divine Truth, and the contents of the celestial sense to Divine Good."—S. S., n. 80.

"[Even] the literal sense of the Word is threefold, viz., historical, prophetical, and doctrinal, each whereof is such that it may be apprehended even by those who are in externals."—A. C., n. 3432.

"The Word contains in itself all prior principles, even from the first, or all superior principles, even from the supreme; the ultimate being what includes and contains them. This fulness of the Word may be compared with a common vessel of marble, in which are innumerable lesser vessels of crystal, and in these still more innumerable of precious stones, in which and about which are the most exquisite delicacies of heaven, which are for those who from the Lord perform noble uses."—A. E. 1087.

to each other, but discrete. Degrees are of two kinds, there being continuous degrees and degrees not continuous. Continuous degrees are like the degrees of light, decreasing as it recedes from flame, which is its source, till it is lost in obscurity; or like the degrees of visual clearness, decreasing as the light passes from the objects in the light to those in the shade; or like the degrees of the purity of the atmosphere from its base to its summit,—these degrees being determined by the respective distances. But degrees that are not continuous, but discrete,[85] differ from each other like what is prior and what is posterior, like cause and effect, and like that which produces and that which is produced. Whosoever investigates this subject will find that in all the objects of creation, both general and particular, there are such degrees of production and composition, and that from one thing proceeds another, and from that a third, and so on. He that has not acquired a clear apprehension of these degrees cannot be acquainted with the difference between the various heavens, and between the interior and the exterior faculties of man; nor can he be acquainted with the difference between the spiritual world and the natural, nor between the spirit of man and his body; nor, consequently, can he understand what correspondences and representations are, and their origin, nor what is the nature of influx. Sensual men cannot comprehend these distinctions, for they suppose increase and decrease, even with respect to these degrees, to be continuous; on which account they can form no other conception of what is spiritual than as something more purely natural. Thus they stand, as it were,

---

[85] "Discrete is a philosophical term signifying *separate*, and is applied to two or more things that do not run into one another, but, though contiguous, have each their distinct boundary."—*Noble*.

The vast importance of this distinction of degrees will be at once perceived, if we consider that the erroneous assumption that all beings and things have proceeded forth continuously, or by degrees of continuity, from the centre to the circumference of all creation; thus, that the soul and the body, God and man, spirit and matter, are but various gradations, and that God is an all-extended substance, existing throughout space, has given birth, both in ancient and modern times, to every heterogeneous system of pantheism, materialism, and secularism, which infidel philosophy, and an erroneous theosophy, have invented. In order, therefore, further to assist the earnest and intelligent inquirer in his search after truth, and to enable him more clearly to comprehend the great doctrine of triple degrees, which is indispensable to a just view of the divine character and existence, to a correct idea of the nature of the human mind, and to the accurate knowledge of the science of correspondences, and thus to a true interpretation of the Word of God, a few additional extracts are given in the APPENDIX, from the invaluable writings of Swedenborg, who has so amply and so clearly unfolded this grand subject, on which, indeed, the laws of correspondences may be said to rest. A few of the innumerable confirmations, and illustrations from other sources, are also given.

The *Vestiges of Creation*, and the speculations of Darwin and Huxley on progress in development, are framed upon *continuous* degrees; hence their specious errors, their fallacious reasonings, their mistaken arrangements of facts, and their mischievous conclusions, tending to mere materialism and Atheism, and of necessity terminating there

without the gate, far removed from all that constitutes intelligence."—H. H. 38.

"The essential Divine [principle] is in the supreme sense of the Word, because therein is the Lord; the Divine [principle] is also in the internal sense, because therein is the Lord's kingdom in the heavens, hence this sense is called celestial and spiritual; the Divine [principle] is also in the literal sense of the Word, because therein is the Lord's kingdom in the earths, hence this sense is called the external, and likewise the natural sense, for in it are gross appearances more remote from the Divine [principle]; nevertheless all and singular things therein are Divine." "The case, with respect to these three senses, is as it was with the tabernacle: its inmost, or what was within the veil, where the ark was, containing the testimony, was most holy, or the holy of holies; but its internal, or what was immediately without the veil, where was the golden table and candlestick, was holy; the external, also, where the court was, was also holy."—A. C. 3439.

In further elucidation of the subject of degrees, the same enlightened author elsewhere says: "It is discovered by means of the investigation of causes from effects, that degrees are of two kinds, one in which are things prior and posterior, and another in which are things greater and less. The degrees which distinguish things prior and posterior are to be called degrees of altitude, or discrete degrees; but the degrees by which things greater or less are distinguished from each other are to be called degrees of latitude, and also continuous degrees. Degrees of altitude, or discrete degrees, are like the generations and compositions of one thing from another; as, for example, they are like the generation and composition of any nerve from its fibres, or of any fibre from its fibrillæ; or of any piece of wood, stone, or metal, from its parts, and of any part from its particles. But degrees of latitude, or continuous degrees, are like the increments and decrements of the same degree of altitude with respect to breadth, length, height, and depth; and as of large and small masses of wood, stone, or metal."—I. S. B., n. 16.

"The science of geometry teaches that nothing can be complete, or perfect, except it be a trine, or a compound of three; for a geometric line is nothing unless it becomes an area, and an area is nothing unless it becomes a solid; therefore the one must be multiplied into the other in order to give them existence, and in the third they coexist. As it is in this instance, so it is likewise in the case of all and every created thing, they have their limit and termination in a third.

Hence we see why the number THREE in the Word signifies what is complete and perfect."—T. C. R., n. 387.

There are, then, three degrees of life[86] in every man, constituting man in the image, and enabling him to attain the likeness, of his Maker. These degrees are discrete or distinct, and are appropriately represented in the well-known ancient and expressive triad of the *heart*, the *head*, and the *hand*. The first end is of the will or love; the mediate end, or instrumental cause, is of the understanding or wisdom; and the ultimate end, or effect, has respect to use in the life. These degrees, though they are discretely distinct, and exhibit three distinct classes of phenomena, are, under the influence of reason and conscience, unanimous in their activities and conjoined by correspondence. Each of these degrees, however, is capable of endless mutations in itself, which are called continuous degrees. These are the variations of intensity and density, or a greater or less degree of remoteness of state, as progressions from light to shade, from heat to cold, from soft to hard. But discrete degrees are distinct, as the spiritual world is distinct from the natural world, or the soul from the body, or a cause from the effect, or the producer from the thing produced; and it is only between this latter kind of degrees that correspondence exists.

All things, however infinitely varied, manifest in their end and essence the divine love, in their form and cause of existence the divine wisdom, and in their operation and use the divine power, or the united effect and energy of both love and wisdom. In the Lord these three essentials of deity "are distinctly one." That some true idea of this doctrine was explicitly held in the earlier periods of Christianity, we have the most direct testimony in the first epistle of John, where it is written, "There are three that bear record in heaven, the Father, the Word, and the Holy Ghost: and these three are one. And there are three that bear witness in earth, the spirit, and the water, and the blood: and these three agree in one" (v. 7, 8).[87] Now there is nothing that exists throughout the three kingdoms of nature but what, even as to its particulars, bears witness to this trinity

---

[86] "Isis, Osiris, and Horus comprise in thought the whole system of Egyptian mythology, with the exception, perhaps, of Ammon and Kneph, the concealed god and the creating power."—*Bunsen's Egypt's Place in Univ. History*, p. 413.

What Bacon asserts is not a little remarkable, viz., that "in the celestial hierarchy of Dionysius, the senator of Athens, the highest place or degree is given to the angels of love, which are termed *seraphim*; the second to the angels of light, which are termed *cherubim*; and the following place to the angels of power and ministry."

[87] The long, frequent, and learned disputations respecting the authenticity and gen-

in God, and this triple life in the soul as God's image. It is revealed to us that in the spiritual world there are three heavens, which being discretely distinct correspond to each other; and there must likewise be three hells as their opposites.[88]

All outward nature is threefold, and this is derived from correspondence. There is the great universal trine of aeriform fluids, liquids, and solids, or atmospheres, waters, and earths. The imponderable

---

uineness of the seventh verse, in no way affects the present argument. I may here observe, that it is now generally allowed to have been spuriously introduced into the Epistle of John. It exists, however, in one of the Greek MSS. known by the title of "*The Codex Montfortii*," in Trinity College, Dublin, which Martin of Utrecht considered to be as old as the eleventh century, but which Dr. A. Clarke regarded as a production of about the thirteenth. It occurs in the Greek translation of the Acts of the Council of Lateran, held A.D. 1215. It is inserted in the Latin Vulgate, a valuable version made by Jerome in the fourth century; it is cited by Vigilius Tapsensis, a bishop and Latin writer in the latter end of the fifth; and is found in Latin MSS. as early as the ninth or tenth. According to Dr. A. Clarke, some of the Latin writers insert the passage thus: "There are three that bear record in heaven, the Father, the Word, and the Holy Ghost: and these three are one in CHRIST JESUS."

The three degrees of initiation into the ancient mysteries of Egypt, Greece, etc., were, without doubt, derived from the above doctrine of discrete degrees. Among various nations the number three conveys the idea of fulness and perfection.

I take the present opportunity of observing that the signs, symbols, and three degrees of Free-Masonry are a peculiar compound of a few correspondences, adopted from the ancient cavern mysteries, most probably from those of the Sun-worship of Heliopolis, and phrases and figures borrowed from the symbolic sculpture, painting, etc., of more modern times, and incorporated into ceremonies which, on mere assumption, without the slightest evidence, are said to have originated with the building of Solomon's temple.—See the works of Hutchinson, Preston, Capt. G. Smith, Dr. Ashe, Dr. Oliver. etc., on *Free-Masonry*.

The Christian symbols of the middle ages, with the exception of some coincidences, most likely accidental, were not correspondences at all, but only enigmatical comparisons, often very obscure. A large proportion of them were derived from the heathen mythologies. The remainder were founded upon some fanciful associations or resemblances, which particular objects and their habitudes, mystic words and signs, arbitrary marks and combinations, the forms and properties of the vestments, utensils, and instruments connected with religious worship, and the various professions and trades, etc., were supposed to bear to certain moral rules and sentiments, regarded as necessary for the right direction and government of the conduct. This symbolism was further used to designate the presumed or admitted qualities of persons; or was applied to distinguish them from each other. It was also employed as a tropical vehicle of doctrinal mysteries and monastic professions, vows, charms, etc., and for the purposes of secret association and recognition.—See *Glossary of Architecture*, and Professor Pugin's splendid *Glossary of Ecclesiastical Ornament and Costume*.

"All styles of architecture are hieroglyphics upon a large scale: exhibiting to the heedful eye, forms of worship widely differing from each other; and proving, that in almost every religion with which we are acquainted, the form of the temple was the *hierogram* of its god, or of the peculiar opinions of its votaries."—*Bardwell's Temples*, p.55.

"In the most ancient monuments of India and Egypt, as in those of the middle ages, architecture, statuary, and painting are the material expressions of religious thought."—*Portal's Des Couleurs Symboliques*.

The science of correspondences being lost, the abstract ethics of Christianity were thus sought to be extensively imprinted on the memory and conscience. In correspondence there is nothing arbitrary or fanciful. The thing signified must be the proximate cause of that to which it corresponds, and be recognized in its form and use. The former must live, so to speak, within the latter, as the soul lives in the body, or as thought enshrines itself in speech, or as the intellect exists in the eye, or as the affections of the heart animate the countenance; all which act together as cause and effect.

[88] Deut. xxxii. 22; 1 Kings viii. 27; Psalm lxxxvi. 13, cxv. 6, clxxiii. 1; Mark i. 10; Luke xii. 33; Acts ii. 34, vii. 56, 2 Cor. xii. 2; Heb. vii. 26.

agents are three, heat, light, and electricity; and the latter is again a trine, comprising electricity, galvanism, and magnetism. The atmosphere is threefold, consisting of aura, ether, and air. The objects of the world are divided in general into three kingdoms, the animal, the vegetable, and the mineral.[89]

Animals, again, subdivide themselves into three grand orders, beasts or terrestrial animals, birds or aerial animals, and fishes or aquatic animals, in reference to the three elements which they traverse. Again, terrestrial animals are divided into three classes, cattle, wild beasts, and reptiles; aerial animals are distinguished into birds of the air, water-fowl, and land-birds. Clean animals are described in the Mosaic law by three characteristics, as parting the hoof, cloven-footed, and chewing the cud. Clean fishes,[90] with fins and scales, are divided into three kinds, those inhabiting waters or oceans, seas or lakes, and rivers. (Lev. xi. 3, 9.) Aquatic animals are divided into three kinds, animalculæ, amphibiæ, and fishes. Vegetables, or the productions of the earth, are also divided in the Scriptures into three classes, grass, herbage, and trees. If we select a tree as a further illustration, in regard to its general form we have the root, the trunk, and the branches, and in reference to its products we have leaves, blossoms, and fruit. Even the animal kingdom comprehends, as we said, in general, a ternary arrangement of gaseous, liquid, and solid bodies; and the latter, again, into earths, stones, and metals.

All motion has been resolved into a trine. In the mineral kingdom it is the angular, as seen in the crystal; in the animal kingdom it is the circular, as seen in the organization of the body and the circulation of its fluids; and in the mental world it is the spiral, "the type of the spirit itself," ascending in true order, and an eternal system of gyrations, towards perfection.

Throughout animated life, and even among vegetable forms, there are the masculine principle, the feminine principle, and their offspring. The varieties of races among men are threefold—the Caucasian, the Mongolian, and the Ethiopian. The Ethiopian, again, presents three perfectly distinct species, viz., the African, the Malay, and the American.

---

[89] "The members of the animal kingdom are correspondences in the first [or highest] degree, because they live; those of the vegetable kingdom are correspondences in the second [or middle] degree, because they only grow; and those of the mineral kingdom are correspondences in the third [or lowest] degree, because they neither live nor grow."—Swedenborg's H. H., n. 104.

[90] "Among the ancient Romans, it was not lawful to use *fish without scales* in the feasts of the gods; for which Pliny, l. xxxii., c. ii., quotes a law of Numa."—Harris's Nat. Hist. of the Bible, Art. Fish, note.

Like as the mind is discriminated, in general, into three degrees of life, natural, spiritual, and celestial, so the faculty of the understanding, in particular, comprises what is scientific, rational, and intellectual, and the will what is of pleasure, affection, and love. The duties of life are also threefold, civil, moral, and religious. The human body is the outward form of the mind, and, from the constitution of the latter, we should at once conclude that multitudes of trinal forms exist in the former. And so it is. In its general form the body is a trine, composed of the head, the trunk, and the extremities. The senses are threefold, sight, hearing, and feeling; the latter, again, is a trine, including smell, taste, and touch.[91]

Speaking of the interior constitution of the body, its viscera, etc.,

---

[91] Mythology asserts the triple origin of the human race. Cuvier says that "all the races of mankind, however diversified, are included under three primary divisions: 1st, the Fair, or Caucasian varieties [distinguished for intellectual power]; 2d, the Black, or Ethiopian [remarkable for the activity of the will, or the affections or passions]; and 3d, the Yellow, or Mongolian [whose chief characteristics are physical activity]." Pritchard, also, classes the varieties of the human race into *three* sections, arranged according to the prevailing form of the cranium, and differing from Cuvier only in name.—See *Cuvier, Pritchard, Jamesa,* and *Triplicity*. Each of the above races are, in all probability, again divisible into a subordinate trine, as, for instance, the Ethiopian, which Blumenbach divides into, 1, the Armenian; 2, the Negro; and 3, the Malay.

Pythagoras placed all perfection in the number *three*.—(See note, p. 143.) "*Three* was a number in high estimation amongst the Greeks, the Romans, and even amongst all nations, civilized and barbarous."—*Nuttall's Archæol. Dict.* Hence many of their deities were represented with three faces, or three heads. The judges of the dead, the fates, the furies, and the sons of Saturn, among whom the world was divided, were *three*. "The power of almost all the gods is shown by a *threefold emblem*, viz., Jupiter's three-forked thunder, Neptune's trident, Pluto's dog with three heads, because all things are contained in the number three."—*Servius on Virgil's Eighth Eclogue.*

"I know that my brethren [the Jews], generally, object to the idea of the Trinity; but why should we find any difficulty in receiving that which the Scriptures reveal. It is a remarkable fact, that, notwithstanding the objections of my brethren to the Scriptural account of Father, Son, and Holy Spirit, they have some undefined idea of importance attached to the triple number, and they observe many customs with respect to it, without exactly knowing the reasons for such a line of conduct.... Man, in himself, is an image of the triune nature of the Deity, for he is triune in his nature and character, being composed of body, soul, and spirit, and yet he is but one man; and in this way I understand that passage in Gen. i. 27, 'So God created man in his own image, in the image of God created he him.' Signifying hereby a complete oneness or identity by this mysterious and incomprehensible union. And thus we correctly see something of the triune character of the One Divine, omnipotent, incomprehensible Lord God."—*Marcus, Seghle Beenoo, or Skill and Understanding,* pp. 45, 46.

The Pagodas, or Pagan temples of India, consist of three divisions. The first forms the main body, answering to the nave of our cathedrals; the second, the sanctuary, answering to the choir; and the third, the chapel, where the sacred image is kept, answering to the chancel.—See *Bartolomeo, by Johnston,* p. 62.

"I look upon the Bible like the courts of the temple. All is alike sacred; but it is in the inmost recess—the Holy of Holies—that God resides."—*Tucker's Scripture Studies,* Pref., p. vi.

"Do you ask in what the perfection [of mind, or of intelligent creation] consists? I answer, in *knowledge,* in *love,* and in *activity*. That mind, which has a wide range of thought, knows much of God and of his wisdom, and loves what it knows,—which is bound by a strong affection to its Creator and its fellow-beings, and acts as well as loves,—which puts forth all its powers, employs all its knowledge in the service of God, and in blessing his creatures,—that mind is

Swedenborg thus writes: "No series can be complete or effective without involving at least a trine, that is, a first, a middle, and a last. These three must be so ordered that the first term disposes the second, and disposes the ultimate both mediately and immediately. Thus there is a trine that purifies the blood, namely, the spleen, the pancreas, and the liver. A trine that secretes the blood and serum, namely, the pancreas, the omentum, and the liver. A trine that circulates the secretions, namely, the pancreatic, the hepatic, and the cystic ducts. A trine that prepares the chyle, namely, the stomach, the small intestines, and the large intestines. A trine also that secretes and excretes the worthless parts of the serum, namely, the kidneys, the ureters, and the bladder. . . . Nothing can be bounded, completed, or perfect that is not a trine. Sometimes even a quadrine is necessary, or a still more multiple series or sequence, exactly according to the ratio between the first and the last term, that is, to their distance from each other and the nearness or remoteness of their relationship. Meanwhile, whatever be the relation, there must be at least a trine to procure harmony, otherwise no termination or conclusion is possible. To instance only geometry, arithmetic, physics, rationals, and logic. In *geometry*, two linear extensions alone take in nothing and conclude nothing; a third thing is respected as the concluding agent, and therewith as the conclusion, whether in a triangle, a body of trine dimension, an algebraic equation, or any other thing of this class. In *arithmetic*, two numbers form only a ratio, but when a third term is added, or generated by the two first, we have then an analogy, either conterminous, or harmonic, or of

---

a perfect mind; and it is as happy as it is perfect. Its happiness partakes of the purity and sanctity of the divine felicity."—*Channing's Memoirs*, vol. i., p. 275.

Theologians of almost every creed have adopted the number three to denote fulness and perfection. The Chaldeans respected it, as being illustrative of *figure, light,* and *action;* the Egyptians, of *matter, form,* and *motion;* the Persians, of *past, present,* and *future;* Orpheus, of *light, life,* and *wisdom;* the Greeks, of *the god of heaven, the god of the earth,* and *the god of the sea;* the early Cretans, of *life, cause,* and *energy;* and the Hindoos, of *power, understanding,* and *love.*

"The number *three* was held sacred by the ancients, being thought the most perfect of all numbers, as having regard to the beginning, middle, and end."—*Dr. Thornton's Eclogues of Virgil,* p. 507.

"*Three* was a sacred and mystical number amongst the Druids."—*Davis's Mythol. of the British Druids,* p. 79.

"The Hebrews expressly acknowledged the perfecting property of the number *three;* for with them the letter *Shin* (ש), which is in itself a trident, denoted the number *three,* or the utmost perfection of every thing."—*Tripl.,* vol. i., p. 52.

"The ancients had a singular predilection for the number *three,* hence they took it as a divisor preferable to the more natural mode of halves. Of this take an instance from Livy, 'Ejusdem rei causa ludi magni voti aeris trecentis, triginta, tribus millibus (Lib. xxii., c. 10), trecentis, triginta, tribus, triente: praeteria bubus Iovi trecentis. Tum lectisternium per tridium habitem, decemveris sacrorum curantibus.'"—*Pinkerton's Essay on Medals,* vol. i., p. 198.

some other kind. In *physics*, two powers or forces regarded as causes always likewise respect some third, whereby an effect is produced, and in this a fourth, or fifth, and so on. In *rationals*, nothing which deserves to be called a judgment, such as ought to exist in all the conclusions and determinations of the will, can possibly be formed from two reasons,—there must always necessarily be some third. In *logic*, two premises are requisite to constitute a full syllogistic form, or a full argument; more than two in a sorites. What is at last concluded from two becomes the property of the conclusion itself, but this it derives from the premises. So in every science and art, the binary is ever the imperfect; hence some third thing is always involved, either tacitly or openly. This is universally the case in the anatomy of the body, which is the mirror, prototype, and complex of all arts and sciences."—*An. Kingdom*, vol. i., p. 315, n. 229, and note.

And this threefold discrimination, could we extend our inquiries, might be traced, or demonstrated to exist, throughout the indefinite particulars of which the universe is composed. Thus every object of human thought appears under the type of a trinity, emanating from the very fundamental laws of all existence, and constituting all finite forms, more or less remote, of the infinite source of infinite goodness or love, unerring wisdom or truth, and almighty power.

The Divine Word itself is, as we have seen, adapted by a threefold characteristic, both as to its inward sense and outward letter, to communicate nutriment of goodness and truth in endless variety to the three great classes of the human family, both in heaven and upon earth; viz., those who are more distinguished in their mental character for the predominance of affection, those who are preëminent in their intellectual endowments, and such as are remarkable for their simple and child-like obedience; and also to the three discrete degrees of life in every man, as they are successively opened and brought into activity by the influences of heaven. The prohibitory injunctions of the Word enforce a threefold shunning of evils as sins against God, evils of conduct, evils of thought, and evils of will; so the religion which is further taught therein requires three essentials to constitute it genuine in its quality and saving in its efficacy, which, again, exactly correspond to man's threefold capacity of reception. With man, the inmost of all things is love in the will; love clothes itself with wisdom and power in the understanding; and both determine to deeds and words, as the outward form of their existence. In order, therefore, that man may insure his eternal salvation, it is not only necessary for him to receive a principle of love in his heart, and of truth or faith in his intellect, but these principles must become fixed in the soul by being brought forth and made manifest in a holy and righteous life. Hence it is never taught that man will be judged according to his faith or his love, but in accordance with his deeds, for in these only have faith and love any permanent existence within us. (Rev. xxii. 12; Rom. ii. 6.) A man may, indeed, *appear* to possess them, but they are not appropriated—not incorporated into his nature as his own, and in the judgment they are dissipated, agreeably to the Lord's own declaration, where He says "Whosoever hath, to him shall be given; and whosoever hath not, from him shall be taken away even that which he seemeth to have" (Luke viii. 18).

This great doctrine, when applied to the Divine Word, will enable us clearly to understand a large portion of its sacred contents. Wheresoever triplicate expressions occur, they have an almost invariable reference, either in a good or evil sense, to this trine of discrete degrees. Thus, the three essentials requisite to the existence of every solid body, length, breadth, and thickness, precisely correspond to the threefold union of love, truth, and their active powers, which are always requisite to the existence of any spiritual object. Hence, of the Lord's church as being one complete whole, deriving a threefold life of wisdom, love, and use from the Lord, it is said, "the length, and the breadth, and the height" of the Holy City, described as being a cube of three equal dimensions, "were equal" (Rev. xxi. 16). The ark, which, as the apostle Peter says, was a type of baptism (1 Epis., iii. 21) or regeneration, to represent the triple constitution of the human mind as being an image of the Divine Mind, was constructed with lower, second, and third stories (Gen. vi. 16); and the temple at Jerusalem, for a like reason, had an outer court, an inner court or holy place, and the inmost chamber or holy of holies, with appropriate fittings and furniture, and separated from the inner court by a veil, which none but the high-priest lifted and passed, and he only once a year, with ceremonies and incense, was the immediate dwelling-place of the Shekinah, or the Divine presence. From this the Lord's humanity is denominated the temple of his body (John ii. 21). And as the Lord in his divine humanity was the "Word made flesh," so the temple represented in a subordinate sense the Word of God, constituted, as we have shown it to be, of an outer, inner, and inmost sense.[92]

---

[92] The abnegation or renunciation of self, in its threefold form of self-reasoning or prudence, self-intelligence or conceit, and self-righteousness or vainglory, is strikingly

So in the divine parable of the Lord, designed to represent the threefold process of man's regeneration, in which divine truth is first received into the memory and understanding, in the next place is elevated into the affections or will, and then brings forth the fruit of well-doing in the life and conduct; and, further, that this is to be done by man with the same earnestness as though he did it of himself —as though, "working out his salvation with fear and trembling" (Phil. ii. 12), all depended on his own energies; yet with the inmost acknowledgment that all power and glory come from the Lord to whom alone they belong, it is said, "The earth [the human mind, or church] bringeth forth fruit of itself; first the blade, then the ear, after that the full corn in the ear" (Mark iv. 28). The Lord has not only revealed Himself to man as a triune Deity, but his thrice-holy name, JEHOVAH (Isa. vi.), is a trinal compound, expressive of the character of Him "who *is*, who *was*, and who *is to come*" (Rev. i. 8). His infinite operations are threefold. He is the Creator from eternity, the Redeemer in time, and the Regenerator forevermore; and He has assumed a threefold series of double terms, descriptive of the infinity of his divine love, wisdom, and power, where He proclaims himself "the Alpha and Omega; the beginning and the end; the first and the last" (Rev. xxii. 13).

The Lord's glorification of his humanity, as by temptations and victories He removed from Himself all the hereditary tendencies, voluntary and intellectual, which were entailed upon Him by being "made of a woman, made under the law" (Rom. i. 3, viii. 3; Gal. iv. 4; Heb. ii. 9-16), was a threefold, divine process, by which He forever united the indwelling Divinity with his humanity; and this, in every particular, was representative of the threefold work of human regeneration. Both these works are treated of in the Word at the same time and under the same imagery. Thus, "Behold, I cast out devils, and I do cures to-day and to-morrow, and the third day I shall be perfected" (Luke xiii. 32). To cast out devils signifies, in reference to man's regeneration, to expel evil affections and false persuasions from the mind by the power of divine truth; to do cures to-day and to-morrow signifies to liberate man from the infestations of hell,

---

displayed in the prophecy of Hosea, where, after the inspired seer exhorts the backsliding and rebellious Israelites to return unto the Lord, and teaches them how to approach Him acceptably, and plead with Him in prayer, they are instructed further to say. "*Ashur* shall not save us; we will not ride upon *horses*; neither will we say any more to the *work of our hands*, Ye are our gods: for in thee the fatherless findeth mercy" (xiv. 3).

thus the restoration of the whole mind from a state of spiritual disease to a state of spiritual health; and the crowning perfection of this work of the Lord in the soul is described as that of the third day, and signifies an eternal confirmation in goodness and truth, and an everlasting state of conjunction with the Lord himself, as the result and reward of outward conformity to the inward dictates of charity and faith.

That the gradual process by which the Lord obtained victory over hell and made his humanity divine was in all respects similar in kind to that of man's regeneration, He himself testifies where He says, "To him that overcometh will I grant to sit with me in my throne, even as I also overcame, and am set down with my Father in his throne" (Rev. iii. 21); with this amazing difference, however, in degree, that in the Lord the work was infinite, in man it is finite. He was indeed "tempted like as we are tempted" (Heb. ii. 18; iv. 15), but unlike us in this, that no man could convict Him of sin (John viii. 46). He, by his own power, perfectly glorified his human nature (John xiv. 30); and if we perpetually depend upon his restraining and upholding mercy, He will perfect our regeneration by a corresponding process.

The Lord's divine purpose in this threefold work of man's regeneration is to secure the eternal happiness of his creatures by an entire renewal and renovation of the heart, the understanding, and the life, and this change is called in the Scriptures a new creation or new birth; for "except a man be born again he cannot see the kingdom of God"[93] (Matt. iii. 4). It is sometimes described by three terms, which, unless they have a discriminated meaning, bear the appearance of useless repetitions, as in the following text: "Every one," saith the Lord, "that is called by my name, I have created for my glory; I have formed him; yea, I have made him" (Isa. xliii. 7). All such are again described negatively, where it is written that they are "born, not of blood, nor of the will of the flesh, nor of the will of man, but of God" (John i. 13). Again, sincere desires and earnest efforts, first for the descent of principles of heavenly goodness from the Lord into the will, with their reception and appropriation; secondly, that principles of spiritual wisdom may be imparted to the understanding, with their acceptance and adoption; and thirdly, that the conjunction and united operation of such holy desires and

---

[93] Greek, *born from above.*

heavenly thoughts as are thus communicated and excited, may determine to a life of obedience, which, under the united influence of patience, perseverance, and watchfulness, never fails of success, but sooner or later opens up an ever blessed state of conjunction with the Lord and association with the angels of his kingdom, is thus impressively taught by the Lord himself in the language of correspondence, where He says, "Ask, and it shall be given you; seek, and ye shall find; knock, and it shall be opened unto you: for every one that asketh receiveth, and he that seeketh findeth, and to him that knocketh it shall be opened" (Matt. vii. 7, 8). Here to ask and receive has respect to the will or the affections and goodness; to seek and find has reference to the understanding or the thoughts and to truth; and to knock and have opened has relation to the conjunction of goodness in the will with truth in the understanding, and to their activity in the life and conduct, or words and works.

The divine marriage song recorded in Psalm xlv. treats, in the inward sense, of the subjugation of all the enemies of the Lord's church, and the complete and eternal union between Himself and his people, resulting from the outflowings of his infinite mercy and compassion. In a more specific sense it treats of the marriage-union of love and wisdom, or goodness and truth, in every faithful mind, together with the endless and ineffable delights which are the result of the removal of every obstacle to its completion. The threefold duties of the nuptial covenant of the church towards her true Lord and husband, on which, with each member of the church in particular, the union of love and wisdom in the soul and the possession and enjoyment of such beatitudes depend, are thus described: "Hearken, O daughter, and consider, and incline thine ear; forget also thine own people and thy father's house; so shall the king greatly desire thy beauty; for He is thy Lord, and worship thou Him" (10, 11). To hearken to the Lord is, in the spiritual sense, to give attention to divine instruction from the Word; to consider is to digest such counsel in the mind, so as to perceive its reasonableness and truth; and to incline the ear is to obey its injunctions without reserve. Thus we are taught that to learn, to perceive, and to do the truth, or, in other words, to understand it from enlightened thought, to perceive it from heavenly affection, and faithfully to perform the duties which it makes obligatory upon us, are the means of attaining a state of eternal conjunction with the Lord, and as a consequence everlasting blessedness. Then, indeed, may it be truly said that, forgetting our "own people" and our "father's house"—dissolving and disowning all connection with our inherited evil and sin, and relinquishing all association with falsity and folly, the hereditary tendencies, inclinations and persuasions of the natural mind no longer prevent the marriage-union of goodness and truth from being consummated in the soul. When this work is accomplished, then man puts on that spiritual beauty or comeliness of spirit which the King is said "greatly to desire;" and in reference to the full acknowledgment of the Lord as the only true God, in his glorified Humanity, it is added, "for He is thy Lord, and worship thou Him."

The same threefold connection of ideas occurs in other forms of expression of similar import, as where the Lord says, "Take ye heed, watch and pray" (Mark xiii. 33); and again, at the conclusion of the parable of the sower, He added, "He that received seed into the good ground is he that heareth the Word, and understandeth it: who also beareth fruit, and bringeth forth, some an hundred-fold, some sixty, some thirty" (Matt. xiii. 23). The sower is the Lord himself; the good ground is the prepared mind; the seed is the divine truth of the Word; to "hear the Word" is to attend to its divine teaching, to "understand it" is to discern its truths and doctrines, and to "bear fruit" is to regulate accordingly the external mind and outward conduct under the combined influence of internal principles of love and wisdom; in which case man is enabled to effectuate all kinds and degrees of good works by the Lord's presence and power in the soul, the completeness of which is represented by the "hundredfold, the sixty, and the thirty."

The motions and positions of the human body [94] are significant when assumed as representations of conditions and emotions of the mind; but when they agree with the inward thoughts and affections which prompt them, they are then the corresponding images of mental states, either progressive or fixed. Wherever they are associated in a trine, like other triads, they refer to the above degrees of the mind and life. Thus in the Psalms it is written, "Blessed is the man that walketh not in the counsel of the ungodly, nor standeth in the way of sinners, nor sitteth in the seat of the scornful" (i. 1), where walking denotes the activity or progression of thought grounded in intention; standing has relation to the life of intention grounded in the

---

[94] "It may be observed that all verbs of posture or gesture, as to *stand*, to *sit*, to *go*, to *walk*, etc., in good Greek writers, have the signification of *esse*, or *existere*, to be."—*Macknight's Prelim. Essays*, iv., p. 97.

will and its stability; and sitting, which is a position of rest, signifies a conformable and determinate state of the inmost mind and life. Hence it may at once be seen what is distinctly signified by "the counsel of the ungodly," "the way of sinners," and "the seat of the scornful," namely, a confirmed state of error and evil, in thought, intention, and will, thus a confirmed state of hatred against goodness and truth; and that true blessedness consists in nothing less than bringing all the active powers of the understanding, the will, and their united energies, into subordination to the sacred influences of wisdom, superinducing an abhorrence of wickedness and folly, and a supreme love of goodness and truth. Again, when the Lord would teach us how they that wait on Him, by worshipping Him, and by obeying his commands,—thus consecrating their whole souls to his service, should renew their strength,—receive continually from Him fresh accessions of power to elevate the understanding towards heaven and Himself, to enable the affections to make unwearied progress in the paths of goodness, and to give a mighty and unshrinking energy to all the lower faculties of the soul, He says, "They that wait upon the Lord shall renew their strength; they shall mount up with wings as eagles; they shall run, and not be weary; and they shall walk, and not faint" (Isa. xl. 31).

The faithful Christian receives from the Lord three degrees or kinds of goodness, as the precious gifts of his unspeakable love. These are, celestial, spiritual, and natural, and are grounded in love to Him, in charity towards the neighbor, and in the love of moral and civil usefulness and excellence. These degrees are above, or rather within, each other, like causes and their effects, and make one by correspondence. Though by birth every one possesses the capacity of receiving these living and life-giving principles of goodness, still, man must advance in the regenerate life, by successive states of illumination, repentance, and obedience, before he is prepared to receive them. When these principles of heavenly goodness, with the sacred truths which they inspire from the Word, vivify all the affections, thoughts, and activities of the mind and life, then man is replenished and enriched with every possible satisfaction and delight, and is introduced into the encircling spheres of heaven. These spheres, in which the fullest and freest confession is made that such ineffable blessings can come from the Lord alone, are typified by the sweet fragrance of incense and the ascending odors of sacrifices, which God is represented as perceiving, and with which He is said to be well pleased (Gen. viii. 21;

Ex. xxx. 34, 35; Phil. iv. 18). Hence this humble, devout, and truly just acknowledgment is present in all heartfelt supplication for divine mercies, and in Rev. v. 8 is called "the golden vial full of odors, which," it is added, "are the prayers of saints." When, therefore, the Magi, or WISE MEN from the East, led by a star,[95]—instructed

[95] "It is singular," says Hutchinson, "that the Magi of Matt. ii. 1 is rendered by an Irish version, *Drawithe*, the Druids, or the true wise men. Magi in the East, Druid in the West."—*Hist. of Cumberland*, vol. ii., p. 193.

"The Persian Magi, who were best initiated into the Mithraic mysteries, admitted a deity superior to the sun as the true Mithras, but looked upon the sun as the most lively image of this deity, in which it was worshipped by them; as they worshipped the same deity symbolically in fire, as Maximus Tyrius informeth us (*Diss.* 38, p. 371, agreeably to which is that in the Magi oracles, commonly ascribed, says Mosheim, to Zoroaster, sec. 2, v. 29, p. 1179, in Stanley's *History of Philosophy*): 'All things are the offspring of one fire,' that is, 'of one supreme Deity.' ... The Persian Mithras was commonly called threefold or triple. Thus Dionysius (*Epis.* 7 at *Polycarp*, p. 91 to 2 opp.), the Pseudo-Areopagite: 'The Persian Magi to this very day celebrate a festival solemnity in honor of the Triplasian (that is, the threefold or triplicated) Mithras. ... Here is a manifest indication of a trinity in the Persian theology, whose distinctive characters are *goodness, wisdom*, and *power*.' ... And now we have proposed the three principal attributes of the Deity. The first whereof is infinite goodness, with fecundity; the second, infinite knowledge and wisdom; and the last, infinite, active, and perceptive power. From which divine attributes the Pythagoreans and Platonists seemed to have framed their trinity of archical hypostases, such as have the nature of principles in the universe, ... which Pythagoric trinity seems to be intimated by Aristotle in these words: 'As the Pythagoreans also say the universe and all things are determined and contained by three principles.'"—*Cudworth's Int. Sys.*, vol. 1., pp. 317, 47, 48.

Polycarp says: "Amongst the Persians, those who were skilful in the knowledge of the Deity, and religious worshippers of the same, were called Magi."—*De Abst.*, lib. iv., p. 165, cited in *Cudworth's Int. Sys.*, vol. i., p. 470.

Magi. "All the eastern nations, the Persians, the Indians, the Syrians, concealed secret mysteries under hieroglyphical symbols and parables. The *wise men* of all those religions knew the sense and true meaning of them, whilst the vulgar and uninitiated went no further than the outward and visible symbol, and so discerned only the bark by which they were covered."—*Origen, Cont. Cels.*, i. 1, p. 11.

"What the Magi were in Persia, the same were the Druids in Britain. The testimony of Pliny is conclusive on this point: 'Why should I commemorate,' says he, 'these things with regard to an art which has passed over the seas, and reached the bounds of nature? Britain, even at this time, celebrates Druidism with so many wonderful ceremonies, that she seems to have taught it to the Persians, and not the Persians to the Britons' (lib. xxii.). The Druids were the Magi of the Britons, and had a great number of rites in common with the Persians: the term *Magus*, among the ancients, did not signify a magician in the modern sense, but a superintendent of sacred and natural knowledge."—*Borlase's Antiq. of Cornwall*, cxxi., p. 138.

"Among the Persians," writes Porphyry, "those *wise persons* who were employed in worship were called Magi."—*Univ. Hist.*, vol. v., p. 163.

"Magi among the Persians answers to σοφοι, or φιλοσοφοι, among the Greeks; *Sapientes*, among the Latins; *Druids*, among the Gauls; *Gymnosophists*, among the Indians; and *Priests*, among the Egyptians."—*I. S. F., Demonol.*, p. 96.

Moore, in his *History of Ireland*, derives the word *Druid* from *Draoid*, in Irish signifying a cunning or wise man. The "Magicians of Egypt" is rendered in the Irish version, "The Druids of Egypt."

"The science of correspondences and representations was the principal science of those times amongst the Arabians, the Ethiopians, and others in the East. Wherefore, also, in the Word, by Arabia, Ethiopia, and the sons of the East, in the internal sense, are meant they who are in the knowledges of heavenly things. But this science in time perished, inasmuch as when the good of life ceased, it was turned into magic. It was first obliterated amongst the Israelitish nation, and afterwards amongst the rest; and at this day it is obliterated to such a degree, that it is not even known that such a science exists; insomuch that, in the Christian world, if it be said that all and singular things of the

by the light of heavenly knowledge, derived from ancient revelation, of which that star was a true figure,—went to Bethlehem for the purpose of worshipping the new-born Saviour, we read that they brought and opened and presented to Him three kinds of costly gifts, "gold, and frankincense, and myrrh" (Matt. ii. 11).[96] This homage and these gifts represented the adoration and free-will worship which the truly wise and humble Christian presents to the Lord when, so to speak, He is spiritually born and makes Himself divinely manifest in the regenerating soul, prepared to receive Him in sincerity and acknowledge Him in truth. He comes in lowly guise as the Word, or Son of Man, shrouded in the appearances of the literal sense. He discloses Himself to the interior natural affections, in that state represented by Bethlehem.[97] The bright star of heavenly knowledge precedes and betokens His presence. The pure and precious gold, more ductile and less susceptible of corrosion than the other ordinary metals, the odorous and costly frankincense, from the earliest ages dedicated to spontaneous worship, and the fragrant myrrh, used in the process of embalming, and distinguished for its antiseptic and preservative qualities, represent the free-will offerings of the heart and mind from the good principles of holy love and charity, signified by gold (Rev. iii. 18); from a living and enlightened faith in the instructions of the Word, signified by frankincense (Rev. v. 8); and from both love and faith preserved in the adoration of grateful worship and devout external obedience in the life, signified by myrrh (Psalm xlv. 8). The perfumes exhaled from these aromatic gums (Mal. i. 11) denote the acceptableness of such worship, because they correspond to the heavenly spheres emanating from such blessed principles; and which, like the odor of Mary's precious ointment of spikenard, fill

---

Word in the sense of the letter, from correspondences signify celestial things, and that hence is its internal sense, it is not known what this means."—A. C., n. 10252. (The first volume of this great work was published in the year 1749.)

"The orientals were expecting the Lord's advent, from the representatives of worship and of statutes which remained with them; and being acquainted with the knowledges of good and truth, were, on that account, called 'men of the East.' That the Arabians were so called, appears from what is said in Jeremiah concerning Kedar and the kingdoms of Hazar (xlix. 28); and that Job was the greatest of all the men of the East is evident from what is said of him" (i. 3.—A. E., n. 422.)

"Inasmuch as the ancients were in representatives and significatives of the Lord's kingdom, in which kingdom is nothing but celestial and spiritual love, they had also doctrinals, which treated solely concerning love to God and charities towards the neighbor, from which doctrinals they were called wise."—A. C. 3419.

[96] In Arabia there was abundance of gold, frankincense, and myrrh.—Plin. Hist. Nat. 1, vi., c. 28. Gold was the most precious metal then known; and "frankincense," says Beloe, "was of all perfumes the most esteemed by the ancients."—Herod. Thal., cvii., note 125.

[97] Heb. House of bread.

or pervade the whole house or mind where the Lord is present, affecting with inmost joy and gladness all in heaven or on earth who are within their exhilarating influence (John xii. 3). On account of this signification of gold and spices, it is recorded that the Queen of Sheba also presented them to Solomon, when she came from a far Gentile country to hear his wisdom and behold his glory, because, in a good representative character, Solomon was an eminent type of the Lord Himself (1 Kings x. 2).

Sometimes (as above, Psalm i. 1) a trinal connection of ideas occurs in an opposite sense and application, in reference to the perverted will, understanding, and life of the unregenerate man. Thus, three degrees of malignity against our neighbor, and abstractedly from persons, all degrees of opposition to the heavenly principles of charity, or brotherly love, signified, in a good sense, by neighbor, may be described as hatred from corrupt thought, from evil intention, and from a confirmed state of depravity in the will. These three degrees of hatred are said to be followed by three corresponding degrees of chastisement, for, according to the unchangeable law of eternal order, every evil bears its own punishment: "But I say unto you," saith the Lord, "that whosoever is angry with his brother without a cause, shall be in danger of the judgment: and whosoever shall say to his brother, Raca, shall be in danger of the council: but whosoever shall say, Thou fool, shall be in danger of hell fire" (Matt. v. 22).

Again, the threefold effects or states of inward tribulation and distress, arising from the deprivation of truth in each of the three degrees of the mind and life, are described by the three distinct expressions of "lamentation, and mourning, and woe" (Matt. ii. 18), where, if these terms were to be regarded as mere repetitions of the same idea, and of no further use than to increase its intensity, they would be utterly unworthy of a place in a divinely inspired book.

Wherever, therefore, the names of persons and places, nations and countries, occur in the historical portions of the divine Word, they are not mentioned in reference only to individual men or specific nations, or particular localities on the earth, but in respect of their spiritual signification, and hence, also, they are often associated in triple order.[98] Thus, though the three patriarchs, Abraham, Isaac,

---

[98] *Hermes Trismegistus* taught that "the Supreme God—the fountain and original of every thing, the first principle of all things, the spirit which produces all things,—has different names, according to his properties and operations."—See *Ramsay's Theology and Mythology of the Pagans*.

Plato denominated the trinal essentials

and Jacob, were real persons, whose posterity constituted the Jewish church, yet they, as well as all other persons and things spoken of in relation to that people, bore a representative character, varying according to the circumstances predicated, but having constant relation to the church on earth and in heaven, yea, to the Lord Himself. For this reason are these patriarchs so often mentioned in the Word, and even among his most splendid appellations the Lord assumes the significative title of "the God of Abraham, Isaac, and Jacob."[99] In the inmost sense these names relate to the Lord Himself, as to the assumption and glorification of his Humanity, the degrees of life received from Him in the heavens, and his threefold operation for our redemption and salvation: Abraham signifying his supreme or essential divine principle; Isaac, his divine rational principle; and Jacob, the divine natural, or, so to speak, the last and lowest principle of his

---

of Deity, "Ἀγαθος" [the Good], "Λογος" [the Word or Truth], and "Ψυχη" [the Spirit].—*Ib.*

"Names in Scripture are express designations of natures, attributes, qualities, conditions, etc."—*Holloway's Letter and Spirit,* vol. i., p. 285.

Where the name LORD is printed in the authorized version of the Bible in capital letters, the reader should remember that in the original Hebrew it is JEHOVAH; and when the Hebrew word *Adonai* is also translated Lord (as in Ps. cx. 1), it stands in common characters. JEHOVAH ADONAI is frequently translated LORD God (as in Gen. xv. 1).

Jo, Jaw, and Jove were heathen appellations, supposed to have been derived from the sacred trisyllabic name, which has been variously pronounced by different nations.

The original meaning of *Adonai* is a ruler, or disposer, or a basis and support. Our English word *Lord* has a similar signification, having been derived from an old Saxon word, *Laford,* which is by interpretation a *bread giver,* or *sustainer.*

The Hebrew *El* means power, and its plural *Elohim,* all power or omnipotence.

[99] Abram and Abraham mean in English, *a high father,* and *father of a great multitude.* The aspirate, or letter *h,* thus added to the name marks the distinction between the Lord's Human Essence and his Divine Essence; and in reference to man, the state before and the state after regeneration. Isaac means *laughter;* denoting the affection of truth, and its interior delight; and Jacob means a *supplanter,* and *the heel,* which is the lowest part of the body, afterwards changed, by divine authority, to Israel, meaning *a prince of God;* or, *prevailing with God.*

Jerome observes that "the frequent repetition of 'I am the GOD of Abraham, the GOD of Isaac, and the GOD of Jacob,' is not without its meaning."—*Hieron. Com. in Marc.* xii. 26.

"St. Ignatius, in his *Epistle to the Magnesians,* says, 'The most divine prophets lived according to Christ Jesus, that is, they, in their *persons* and *lives,* represented what Christ Jesus was *to be,* and *to do.*' "—*Holloway's Letter and Spirit,* vol. i., Int., p. xxviii.

"That the prophets represented the state of the Church to which they belonged, with respect to doctrine derived from the Word, and with respect to life according to such doctrine, is very evident from what is said of them, as Isa. xx. 2, 3; Ez. xii. 3-7, 11; Hosea i. 2-9, iii. 2, 3; 1 Kings xx. 35-38; Ez. iv. 1-17. In all these, and other passages, they '*bore,*' by representation, 'the iniquities of the house of Israel, and the house of Judah,' and thus pointed them out, but without expiating them; and the very same is taught of the Lord our Saviour, when it is said, 'Surely He hath borne our griefs, and carried our sorrows' (Isa. liii. 1-12), and which prediction is declared in the Gospel to have been accomplished, where it is written, 'When the even was come, they brought unto Jesus many that were possessed with devils; and He cast out the spirits with his word, and healed all that were sick; that it might be fulfilled which was spoken by Esaias the prophet, saying, 'Himself took our infirmities, and bare *our* sicknesses' (Matt. viii. 16, 17), for He endured the assaults of hell, that He might open up a way of salvation to all believers."—*T. C. R.* 251.

divine Humanity. This may be confirmed by the literal meaning of the names, and by reference to the numerous passages of the Word in which they are mentioned. In a respective sense, these three patriarchs signify what is celestial, spiritual, and natural, in regard to man, thus they represent the Lord's church on earth; and, in a particular sense, all those who are receptive of his divine love in their hearts, of his divine wisdom to enlighten their reason, and who permit the united influences of both to descend into and regulate the lowest principles of their minds and lives. These, as to their externals, their internals, and their inmost principles, are the true followers of the Lamb, who is the Lord Jesus Christ in his glorified Humanity, or, in other words, they have attained his likeness. They are grounded in the love of obedience to his truth, in the love of their neighbor, and in the love of Him above all things. It is consequently said of them that they are "with Him, and are the called, and the chosen and faithful" (Rev. xvii. 14). The Lord's covenant, or everlasting state of conjunction with all such faithful believers, and its irreversible confirmation, is therefore signified by the covenant of an oath, which he declared to have "sworn with Abraham, Isaac, and Jacob."

That the angelic heavens in general, as well as the regenerate human mind in particular, together with the infinite and unutterable joys and delights derived immediately from the presence of the Lord, are also represented by those three distinguished personages, is evident from the Lord's words, where He calls heaven "Abraham's bosom" (Luke xvi. 22); and still further where He says that "Many shall come from the east and west, and shall sit down with Abraham, and Isaac, and Jacob, in the kingdom of God" (Matt. viii. 11); and in Luke it is said that "They shall come from the east, and from the west, and from the north, and from the south, and shall sit down in the kingdom of God" (xiii. 28, 29). These divine forms of expression serve to designate and comprehend all the sacred principles of goodness, wisdom, and intelligence, with their perceptions, delights, and joys, which constitute the felicity of the angels, and of consequence universally prevail throughout the three orders of life into which the heavens are arranged. In their inmost sense these patriarchs signify the Lord Himself, from whom alone, as their divine source, all degrees of blessedness and satisfaction proceed. The four cardinal points of the heavens, or the quarters of the world, from whence those are said to come who are prepared to enter into the kingdom of God, signify, in a good sense, the various states of spiritual life. The east, being that portion of the heavens in which the sun appears to rise, signifies the highest degree of celestial love and wisdom, in which the Lord reveals his glorious presence to the inmost perceptions of the soul, and, in its supreme sense, the Lord Jesus Christ, as to the primary operations of his love and wisdom on the mind, for the promotion of man's salvation.[100] Thus in Ezekiel's magnificent vision of the temple in heaven, we read that "the glory of the God of Israel came from the way of the east" (xliii. 2); and hence arose the ancient significative practice of worshipping with the face towards the east, which was even continued under the Christian dispensation.[101] The west, being the extreme point of the heavens over against the east, where the sun appears to set, signifies the inferior state of charity and faith. The south, in which quarter the sun attains his meridian power and splendor, signifies the highest state of intelligence; and the north, which is over against it, a state of obscure knowledge,—a feeble state of heavenly life. In the inward sense of these passages, therefore, we are mercifully taught that all who are in any degree principled in love and wisdom, or charity and faith, will be admitted into the kingdom of God. To sit down there with Abraham, Isaac, and Jacob, denotes a blessed state of confirmation, an eternal conjunction with the Lord, an everlasting association with "the spirits of the just made perfect," an endless condition of rest, and peace, and joy.

To represent the fulness and perfection of such beatitudes as are the invariable results of a righteous life,—and to signify the free access thereto through the pearly gates of spiritual knowledge and obedience adapted to all, and which all are invited to enter,—the Holy City, New Jerusalem, which signifies heaven and the church, is described as having "on the east three gates; on the north three gates; on the south three gates; and on the west three gates. And the gates of it," it is said, "shall not be shut at all by day: for there shall be no night there" (Rev. xxi. 13, 25). In the opposite sense, by the east will be denoted the love of self, which is opposed to the love of God; by the west, the love of the world; by the south, self-derived intelligence; and by the north, a state of falsity and evil (Isa. ii. 6; Ezek. viii. 6; Psalm lxxv. 6; Hos. xi. 10; Jer. i. 14, vi. 1).

---

[100] In Luke i. 78, the Lord Jesus, as the Saviour, is called the "Day-spring," literally, the *rising of the Sun*.—"ORIENS," *Vulgate Version, and Dawson's Lexicon*,—"ORTUS," *Swedenborg*. See Mal. iv. 2.

[101] See *Ambrose, Dionysius Areop., Origen, in lib. Num., hom. 5, Epiphanius Adv. Oss., Prochorous in vit., John, c. 5, Clement Strom.*, vii., p. 523.

It was on account of the above spiritual signification of persons that the Lord, while He sojourned on the earth, selected as his more immediate and constant followers the three disciples, Peter, James, and John. At the time of his transfiguration on Mount Tabor (Matt. xvii. 1–8), in his agonizing visit to the garden of Gethsemane (Matt. xxvi. 37), and when He entered into the house of Jairus, the ruler of the synagogue, to raise his daughter from the dead (Mark v. 37; Luke viii. 51), "He suffered no man to follow Him, save Peter, and James, and John." If we exclude the idea that this selection was grounded in the representative character of those distinguished apostles, no satisfactory reason can possibly be assigned for it, and the evident signification of the act, deduced from its frequent occurrence, is entirely lost. The twelve apostles, like the twelve patriarchs of the preceding dispensation, represented and signified all the heavenly principles constituent of the Lord's church, both universal and particular, and sometimes their contraries, and each apostle in particular represented and signified some specific grace, or its perverted opposite. Thus, Peter is a Greek word for a rock or stone; he was also called Cephas, or Kephas, which is a Syriac word with the same meaning, and Simon, or Simeon, which is a Hebrew word for hearing, and is always first mentioned when the names of the apostles are given. From these particulars it may be gathered that Peter signifies the Lord as to divine truth, and abstractly a principle of faith; faith alone, or separated from the Lord and from charity—which is a perverted faith, when he tempted and denied his Lord and Saviour; but on the contrary, faith springing from love, and conjoining him to the Lord, when he confessed his divinity, and accompanied Him with James and John. Of a perverted and delusive faith, which enlightens the understanding, but leaves the heart unchanged, the Lord spake when He addressed Peter, and said unto him, "Get thee behind me, Satan; for thou art an offence unto me" (Matt. xvi. 23; Mark viii. 23; Luke iv. 8).[102] To a sincere and devout faith in the Lord, and confidence in his Word, "the *keys of the kingdom of heaven*" *are always given* (Matt. xvi. 19); that is, power to open the soul to an influx of the principles and life of heaven. On the confession of this glorious faith in the Lord Jesus Christ, the church is erected as upon a rock, and defies the omnipotent boasts of her angry assailants.

James and John were brothers, the sons of Zebedee. Like Peter,

---

[102] In the original, the word translated *Satan* means *an adversary;* such is the character *of faith alone,* or a mere *persuasive faith.*

who sometimes represents faith alone, and a boasting self-confidence, so these two disciples are at times spoken of in a low sense, as representative of mistaken zeal, and its claims to undue authority; or external charity and good works, with the arrogation of self-merit, proceeding from the promptings of self-love (Matt. xx. 20–28; Luke ix. 53, 54). In a good sense, however, James was a type of the Lord's love, or, abstractly, of the principle of charity, or faith grounded in affection; and John was a type of the Lord's operation, or the works of charity, or faith deriving ardor and activity from the pure love of God, and made manifest in humility, gentleness, benevolence, and all kinds of good and useful deeds and words.[103] The specific signification of the apostle John may be abundantly proved from his personal history, as recorded in the Scriptures. He had the privilege of leaning on the Lord's bosom at the institution of the Holy Supper (John xiii. 23); he was pre-eminently distinguished as "that disciple whom Jesus loved" (John xix. 26; xx. 2; xxi. 7, 20, 24); and to him, more than to others, revelations were vouchsafed respecting the church in heaven and upon earth. These remarkable circumstances and characteristics serve to confirm the signification given as genuine, for all such as manifest their faith and affection by a good life, are truly the beloved of the Lord. James, his brother, therefore, must be a type of spiritual charity, or of faith received in the heart. In the regeneration, this principle supplants and expels all selfish feeling. Faith in the heart and faith in the life, or charity and good works, are brethren; they spring from the same divine origin. The selection, then, of these three apostles by our blessed Lord, on such frequent and memorable occasions, teaches us, in the internal sense, most edifying, invaluable lessons of divine wisdom; for these disciples represented the perfect union of divine love, wisdom, and their resulting life, in the Lord Jesus Christ—thus that He was God in human form. They also represented every regenerating man, and teach us that, unless the essential principles of the regenerate life, represented by Peter, James, and John, are present in the soul, and accompany the divine energies, we can receive no spiritual blessing. Faith must be imparted to the understanding, faith must be implanted in the will, and faith must become active in a good and obedient life; or, in other words, faith, charity, and good works, the three constituents of heaven and religion, must be engrafted in the soul and manifested in the life and conduct,

---

[103] James means in English *a supplanter or maintainer*; John, *the gift of God*, and *merciful or gracious*; and Zebedee, *a dowry*.

or the Lord can do few or none of those mighty works in our behalf, on the accomplishment of which our eternal salvation depends (Matt. xiii. 58; Mark vi. 5). Moreover, to represent to us the energy and zeal of truth, when it proceeds from a principle of celestial charity, and is grounded in goodness of life, James and John were surnamed by the Lord, "*Boanerges, which is, The sons of thunder*" (Mark iii. 17).

I have already remarked, that the human understanding, when individually considered, is found to be discriminated, like the other faculties of the soul, into three degrees of intellectual power and excellence. The lowest of these is the scientific principle, or the power of acquiring and retaining worldly knowledge; the next above is the rational principle, or the power of discernment and discrimination, as between various kinds of truth, and between truth and error; and the highest degree of intellectual power is that which enables man to receive spiritual intelligence, or wisdom and its perceptions.

These three degrees succeed each other, or are successively opened, by an orderly arrangement in the work of regeneration; for man is first natural, then he becomes rational, and afterwards spiritual. Without this trinal intellectual capacity, man could not be elevated above the science of the world. Hence, speaking of the church and of each regenerating member, in order to portray the threefold blessings which would attend such a union and subordination of the intellectual faculties as would prepare man to receive the light of heaven, to irradiate the whole mind, the Lord says by the mouth of his prophet, " In that day there shall be a highway out of Egypt to Assyria, and the Assyrian shall come into Egypt, and the Egyptian into Assyria, and the Egyptians shall serve with the Assyrians. In that day shall Israel be third with Egypt and with Assyria, even a blessing in the midst of the land; whom the Lord of hosts shall bless, saying, Blessed be Egypt my people, and Assyria the work of my hands, and Israel mine inheritance" (Isa. xix. 23–25). By Egypt, that land of mysterious wisdom, where knowledge was so extensively cultivated that it was frequented by the sages of all nations for the acquisition of science, is signified the scientific principle itself, together with all external or natural truths.[104] Egypt has either a good or a

---

[104] " Herodotus describes the inhabitants of the cultivated portions of Egypt as the best informed, or most learned, of mankind. In one of his last works Theophrastus used the same expression."—*Bunsen's Egypt's Place in Univ. Hist.*, pp. 1, 2.

" Assyria is that false state of seeming happiness, and power of wickedness, which is called the kingdom of darkness. And this is the most noble object of fortitude, to destroy the power of this kingdom within ourselves."—*More's Dep. of Cabala*, p. 168.

bad signification in the Word, as such knowledge is said to have been applied to useful ends, or perverted to idolatrous and magical purposes. Assyria, from its relative position to Egypt, and from the tendency of its inhabitants to metaphysical speculation, denotes the rational principle, the reasonings of which are either true or false, as the reason is enlightened from heaven, or draws its subtle conclusions from the fallacies of the world and the senses; for the reason is an intermediate and conjunctive principle between what is natural and spiritual, and, according to man's state, partakes of the quality of both. By Israel in the midst is signified the spiritual principle, or the internal of the understanding, gifted with genuine intelligence and wisdom; and in an opposite sense, the profanation of the intellectual faculties, and the truths they receive, to the vile objects of self-derived prudence, commingling them with the deceitful and lurid glimmerings of self-love. In the passage I have quoted these terms are all used in a good sense, and by a highway, which serves to connect distant countries and places, is signified the orderly arrangement and subordination which unites by correspondence every degree of intellectual excellence. Thus the mind is gradually prepared for the reception of those celestial and spiritual influences which illustrate and govern the perceptions, reasonings, and thoughts, and make man the work and inheritance of Jehovah Zebaoth,—the Lord of Hosts.

In an opposite sense, by Egypt is signified sensual knowledge, and by Assyria carnal reasoning. These give birth to false principles in extremes, which, like flies, spring from the river's corrupting filth, and become a tormenting plague; and also to false reasonings thence derived, which, like bees, when spoken of in a bad sense, suck their stores, indeed, from rich and favorite flowers, and find sensual pleasure therein, denoted by their honey-stores, but carry with them venom and a sting. When these principles are permitted to insinuate themselves into the church or the human mind, they bring with them certain desolation and inevitable misery. They are the result of the falsification and profanation of truth and knowledge in the soul, and the abuse or perversion of the intellectual and rational faculties. Hence, to describe such an awful state, and the complete and grievous desolation which necessarily succeeds, the Lord says, "It shall come to pass in that day, that the LORD shall hiss for the fly that is in the

---

In the history of the descendants of the patriarchs, that of Egypt is always more or less closely interwoven. Pharaoh was the common name of the kings of Egypt up to the final destruction of the monarchy by Alexander the Great.

uttermost part of the rivers of Egypt, and for the bee that *is* in the land of Assyria. And they shall come, and shall rest all of them in the desolate valleys, and in the holes of the rocks and upon all thorns, and upon all bushes" (Isa. vii. 18, 19).[105]

The vast importance of this distinction of degrees will be at once perceived, if we consider that the erroneous assumption that all beings and things have proceeded forth continuously, or by degrees of continuity, from the centre to the circumference of all creation; thus, that the soul and the body, God and man, spirit and matter, are but various gradations, and that God is an all-extended substance existing throughout space, has given birth, both in ancient and modern times, to every heterogeneous system of pantheism, materialism, and secularism which infidel philosophy and an erroneous theology have invented. In order, therefore, further to assist the earnest and intelligent inquirer in his research after truth, and to enable him more clearly to comprehend this great doctrine of triple degrees, which is indispensable to a just view of the Divine character and existence, to a correct idea of the nature of the human mind, and to an accurate knowledge of the science of correspondences, and thus to a true interpretation of the Word of God, a few additional extracts are given in the APPENDIX, from the invaluable writings of Swedenborg, who has so amply and so clearly unfolded this grand subject, on which, indeed, the laws of correspondence may be said to rest, and also a few of the innumerable confirmations and illustrations from other sources.

---

[105] See *Schelegel, Phil. of Hist.*, vol. i., and APPENDIX, "on the Hieroglyphics of Egypt."

"Every one may see that the historical relations of the patriarchs are such that they may indeed be serviceable in regard to the ecclesiastical history of that time, but that they are very little serviceable in regard to spiritual life, which nevertheless is the end which the Word was intended to promote. Add to this, that in some places we meet with nothing but mere names, as of the posterity of Esau (Gen. xxxvi.), and so in other chapters, in which, so far as regards the mere historical relations, there is so little of anything divine, that it can in nowise be said that it is the Word of the Lord, divinely inspired as to every particular expression, and even as to every dot and tittle, that is, that it was sent down from the Lord through heaven to man, by whom those relations were written; for what was sent down from the Lord must need be divine in all and singular things, thus not as to historicals, as being the transactions of men, but only by virtue of those things which lie deeply hid and concealed therein, all and singular of which treat of the Lord and of his kingdom; the historicals of the Word are in this particular distinguished above all other historicals in the universe, that they involve in them such hidden contents. If the Word was the Word merely as to historicals, that is, as to the external or literal sense, then all the historicals which are therein would be holy; and what is more, several persons who are spoken of therein would be esteemed as saints, and it would come to pass, as in the case with many, that they would be worshipped as gods, because they are treated of in the most holy of all writings; when, nevertheless, all these were men, and some of them were little solicitous about divine worship, and had nothing about them above the common lot of men. Hence, then, it may plainly appear, that the external or literal sense is the Word only by virtue of the internal or spiritual sense, which is in it, and from which it is."—*A. C.* 3228, 3229.

CHAPTER XII.

Colors, Numbers, Weights, Measures, Musical Instruments, etc.

"THE Bible," or Word of God, in the just and forcible language of Professor Bush, "rises under the application of a *law* as fixed and invariable as the *law* of creation itself, with which, in fact, it becomes almost identical, into a new revelation, clothed with a sublimity, sanctity, and divinity of which we had not previously the remotest conception. It stands before us the living Oracle of Truth, which we no longer separate from the very being of its Author. He is Himself in his own truth. New treasures of wisdom gleam forth from its pages, and the most barren details of history, the recorded rounds of obsolete rituals,[106] the driest catalogues of names, the most

---

[106] "Heraldry is, in fact, the last remnant of the ancient symbolism, and a legitimate branch of Christian art; the griffins and unicorns, fesses and chevrons, the very mictures or cloins, are all symbolical,—each has its mystic meaning, singly and in combination, and thus every genuine old coat-of-arms preaches a lesson of chivalric honor and Christian principle to those that inherit it —truths little suspected nowadays in our heralds' offices."—*Lord Lindsay, on Christian Art*, ii., p. 49.

The rich color of gold is that of heat, the color of silver is that of light; the former is applied to the splendor of the sun, the latter to the light reflected by the moon. Polished brass resembles gold, and polished iron resembles silver.—See Isa.

"Celestial rosy red, love's proper hue."
Milton's Paradise Lost.

Yellow was in high esteem among the ancient Indians; red, among the Egyptians; purple, among the Syrians and Romans; and white, among the Jews.

"Colors had the same signification amongst all the people of high antiquity. This conformity indicates a common origin, which attaches itself to the cradle of the human race, and finds its greatest energy, or active life, in the religion of Persia. The dualism of light and darkness offers, indeed, the two types of the colors, which became the symbols of the two principles, the benevolent and malevolent. The ancients only admitted two primitive colors, *white and black*, from which all others were derived; in like manner, the divinities of paganism were the emanations from the good and the evil principles.

"The language of colors, which is intimately connected with religion, passed from India, China, Egypt, and Greece to Rome; it was again revived in the middle ages; and the painted windows of the Gothic cathedrals find their explication in the books of the Zend, the Vedas, and the paintings in Egyptian temples.

"The identity of the symbols supposes the identity of the primitive creeds. In proportion as a religion is removed from its principle, it degrades and materializes itself; it forgets the signification of colors, and this mysterious language reappears with the restoration of religious truth.

"In mythology, Iris was the messenger of the gods and of good tidings, and the colors of the girdle of Iris, the rainbow, are the symbols of regeneration, which is the covenant or conjunction between God and man. In Egypt, the robe of Isis sparkles with all colors, and with all the hues which shine in nature. Osiris, the all-powerful god, gives light to Isis, who modifies it, and transmits

trivial specifications of dates, places, and enactments, once touched with the mystic wand of the spiritual sense, teem with the riches of angelic conceptions. The cosmogony of Genesis becomes the birth-register of the new-born soul. The garden of Eden smiles in every renovated mind in the *intelligence* and *affection* emblemed in its trees and fruits and flowers. The watering streams are the fructifying knowledges and truths of wisdom which make increase of the spiritual man. The Tree of Knowledge, the Tree of Life, the wily serpent, are all within us and within us all. The scenes transacted in the paradisiac purlieus are more or less the scenes of our own individual experience, and the narrative ceases to be looked upon merely as the chronicle of events that transpired thousands of years before we were born."—*Reply to Dr. Woods*, p. 66.

The prismatic rays of the sun are clearly divisible into a trine, for there are the calorific rays, the colorific, and the chemical, having relation to love, wisdom, and use. Colors, as well as all other phenomena and appearances of nature mentioned in the Word, are representative, and allusions to them are very frequent. They derive their innumerable tints and hues from the refractions and reflections of the rays of heat and light from the sun, in various degrees of intensity, combined more or less with darkness, or blackness, and shade. A beam of light refracted and reflected by a prism on a dark screen, or by drops of water descending from a dark cloud, at a known angle, will exhibit an appearance of seven distinct hues, as in the rainbow. There are, however, but two fundamental elements of color,—red, which is derived from the flaming light proceeding from the heat, and white from light. All colors are modifications of these

---

it by reflection to men. Isis is the earth, and her symbolic robe was the hieroglyphic of the material and of the spiritual worlds.

"The painted windows of Christian churches, like the paintings of Egypt, have a double signification, apparent and hidden: the one is for the multitude, and the other is addressed to mystic creeds.

"Symbolic science, banished from the church, takes refuge in the court; disdained by painting, we find it again in heraldry. The origin of armorial bearings is lost in antiquity, and appears to have originated with the first elements of writing: the Egyptian hieroglyphics, like the Aztec paintings, indicated the signification of a subject by speaking emblems or arms. It is sufficient to consider the Mexican pictures, and the explanation of them which has been preserved, to banish all doubt on this subject."—See *Recueil de Thevenot*.

"The selam, or nosegay of the Arabs, appears to have borrowed its emblems from the language of colors; the Koran gives the mystic reason of it. 'The colors,' says Mahomet, 'which the earth displays to our eyes, are manifest signs for those who think.'—*Koran*, chap. xvi. This remarkable passage explains the chequered robe which Isis, or Nature, wore, conceived as a vast hieroglyphic. The colors which appear on the earth, correspond to the colors which the seer beholds in the world of spirits, where everything is spiritual and, consequently, significative. Such is, at least, the origin of the symbolical meaning of colors in the books of the prophets and the Apocalypse."—*Portal's des Couleurs Symboliques*.

with obscurity or blackness.[107] Colors, then, represent the modifications of the intermingling rays of spiritual heat and light by those principles and things which have respect to the natural mind. They denote the varied qualities of the respective principles treated of, both as to the intellect and the will, the thoughts and the affections. The irradiations of wisdom and truth in the dark clouds and appearances of the literal sense of the Word are the reflections of heaven's own splendors,—adaptations of the beams proceeding from the Sun of Righteousness to the ever-changing states of the human mind in the process of regeneration. In the time of trial and temptation they are "the bow round the Almighty's throne" (Rev. iv. 3), and the "bow in the cloud" (Gen. ix. 13),—a token of God's eternal covenant with his faithful children, a memorial in the clouds of ignorance and error, in the mere appearances of truth, and in the dense vapors which sorrow and suffering cast over the natural mind, of his unchanging

---

[107] The three primitive colors, derived from the light and heat of the sun, are red, blue, and yellow. From them, and their intermingling and diversified shades, are produced the beautiful, brilliant, and ever-changing colors we behold, whether in the indefinitely varied and harmonious hues of the three kingdoms of nature, and in the clouds of the atmosphere, or as exhibited in the splendid tints of the rainbow.

THE TRINITY OF LIGHT.—In light we have a most remarkable illustration of the doctrine of the Holy Trinity, which is an article of faith with many, of doubt with some, and of disbelief with others; but if we can prove by ocular demonstration that there exists in nature a trinity in unity and an unity in trinity quite as marvellous, it ought to confirm the faithful, convince the doubtful, and overthrow the sophistry of the unbeliever. An investigation into the laws and properties of light will enable us to do so. Light is easily separated into its component colors, by transmitting it through a glass prism, where it is resolved into red, orange, yellow, green, blue, indigo, and violet, which constitute, when combined, white or ordinary light. This band of colors is called the prismatic spectrum. Now it will be perceived that red, yellow, and blue are its primary or essential colors, the others being merely produced by the admixture or overlapping of two adjoining primary colors: thus, orange is found between the red and yellow, green between the yellow and blue; so that, in fact, we have only the three primary colors to deal with, each of which has its peculiar properties and attributes distinct from the others: thus, the red is the calorific or heating principle; the yellow is the luminous or light-giving principle; while it is in the blue ray that the power of actinism, or chemical action, is found. Now it is this trinity of red, yellow, and blue which constitutes, when combined, the unity of ordinary or white light. When separated, this unity of light is divided into the trinity of colors. Although one and the same, neither can exist without the other: *the three are one, the one is three.* Thus we have a unity in trinity, and a trinity in unity, exemplified in light itself; and "God is light." Plants will live and grow luxuriantly under the influence of the red and yellow rays; but, however promising the appearance, the blossom dies, and no fruit can be produced without the enlivening power of the blue rays. When this invisible action is wanting, the trinity in unity is incomplete; life is unproductive until the three, united in one, bring all things to perfection. Thus each member of the trinity in unity of light has its especial duty to perform, and is in constant operation, visibly or invisibly, although only one power. Even far beyond the visible violet ray of the prismatic spectrum the spirit of actinism prevails; its chemical influence can be proved to extend beyond the limits of our vision. Thus there is in light an invisible agency always in action; and the more the subject is investigated, the more striking is the illustration between the Holy Spirit of God made manifest, and the wonderful properties of light which have been gradually unfolded by the researches of man.—*From Temple Bar, for January.*

loving-kindness and faithfulness, bringing hope and consolation to the human heart. Colors, in general, signify truths derived from goodness, and their various modifications; or, on the contrary, different fallacious appearances of evil and error, in the constantly varying states of mental perception both as it respects the intellect and the will.[108] They consequently denote the *quality* or *state* of which they are predicated. So far as they partake of red, they denote the quality of a thing or state, as to good, or love, or to its opposite, the obscurity of evil, and have an immediate reference to the will; and so far as they partake of white, they signify truth in its purity, and its purifying influences, resplendent from good; and, in the opposite sense, truth without goodness, or faith alone, and have more immediate relation to the understanding. (See Isa. i. 18.) But it will be at once seen that all shades of black, on which the variegations of obscurity depend, denote qualities originating in evil and falsity. Hence heaven is represented as an eternal state of day,—for "there is no night

---

[108] "Colors have an influence on the passions, and they, as well as their harmonies, have relation to moral and spiritual affections."—*St. Pierre's Stud. of Nat.*, p. 176.

Swedenborg illustrates this recondite subject as follows: "In order to the existence of color, there must be some substance darkish and brightish, or black and white, on which, when the rays from the sun fall, there exist, according to the various tempering of the darkish and brightish, or black and white, from the modification of the influent rays of light, colors, some of which take more or less from the darkish and black property, some more or less from the brightish or white, and hence arises their diversity. A resemblance of this exists in spiritual things. There the darkish property is the intellectual proprium of man, or the false; and the black property is the will proprium, or evil, which absorbs and extinguishes the rays of light; but the brightish and white property is the truth and good which man thinks he does of himself, which reflects and throws back from itself the rays of light. The rays of light which fall on and modify these are from the Lord, as from the sun of wisdom and intelligence, for such are the rays of spiritual light, and they are from no other source."—*A. C.* 1042-3.

"Black and white being variously tempered by the rays of light, are changed into beautiful colors, as into blue, yellow, purple, and the like, by which, according to their arrangement, as in flowers, divers forms of beauty and agreeableness are exhibited, whilst the black and white, as to their root and ground, still remain."—*A. C.* 731.

"Between the tropics, where there is scarcely any horizontal refraction, the solar light, as viewed in the heavens, displays in a serene morning *five* primordial colors. In the horizon, where the sun is just going to exhibit his disc, a dazzling white is visible; a pure white at an elevation of forty-five degrees; a fire color in the zenith; a pure blue forty-five degrees below toward the west; and in the very west *the dark veil of light* still lingering in the horizon. You there see those five colors, with their intermediate shades generating each other. Each of those colors seems to be only a strong tint of that which precedes it, and a faint tint of that which follows, though the whole together appear to be only modulations of a progression of which *white* is the first term, *red* the middle, and *black* the last."—*St. Pierre's Stud. of Nat.*, ii., pp. 108-112.

"Inasmuch as red signifies the quality of a thing as to good, therefore, also, names, and things which are named from the same expression in the original tongue, signify the good in which they originate. Thus red, in the original tongue, is called Adam, whence is derived the name Adam, and also the name Edom; and hence, also, man is called Adam, and the ground Adama, and the ruby Odam; thus these names and these things are from red. . . . That Edom was so called from red, see Gen. xxv. 30. . . . That the ruby or carbuncle is also so called from red, see Ex. xxviii. 17; xxxix. 10; Ez. xxviii. 13."—*A. E.* 364.

there" (Rev. xxi. 25),—proceeding from celestial fire or love, which vivifies the inmost of the soul; while its inhabitants are described as "clothed in white" (Rev. vii. 9). But, on the other hand, hell is described as an everlasting state of darkness and sorrow and terror, proceeding from infernal fire, or that unchanging state of malice and hatred which torments.

On this ground of the representative meaning of colors, they are often mentioned in the Word, in both senses, and are sometimes arranged in a trine. Three of the most splendid and expensive colors were commanded by the Lord to be used in the construction and embellishment of the Tabernacle,—"Blue, and purple, and scarlet" (Ex. xxv. 4, 5; xxvi. 1, etc.). These three colors serve most accurately to discriminate the threefold quality of the sincere worshipper, whose mind is represented by the Tabernacle and its beautiful furniture. Blue is descriptive of the quality of celestial light or truth, and its splendor as seen in the firmament of the intellect; purple, the quality and brilliancy of celestial heat or love in the affections of the will; and scarlet denotes the quality and warmth of enlightened faith and mutual charity reflected in the outward life. The brilliant colors of the costly gems set in the breastplate of Aaron (Ex. xxviii. 30), and of the precious stones which formed the foundations of the Holy City (Rev. xxi. 19, 20), signify the indefinitely varied modifications and qualities of heavenly wisdom and intelligence, beaming forth from the Word of God, translucent and shining with the celestial and spiritual resplendencies of heaven, signified by the precious gems. These bright and priceless truths of the Holy Word are the source of all just judgment, and are, also, the firm and glorious foundations on which the church is erected.[109]

---

[109] The twelve stones in the urim and thummim are representative of all the varieties of divine truth in the Holy Word, which shine with such beauty and glory in the minds of the faithful,—brilliant, transparent, sparkling, glowing with inward radiant principles of love, charity, goodness, and benevolence, of which they are but the outward forms. They were ordered by express Divine command to be arranged in trines, and worn on the breast, or over the heart, of the high-priest when he entered the tabernacle. They were worn upon the heart to signify that the corresponding principles must be regarded with inmost affection. They were divided into four orders of trines, distinctly significative of the twofold constitution of the internal and external man; each trine having especial relation to the three degrees of the mind and the life, and the signification of each stone being determined by its color and its place. This may be seen more clearly from the following arrangement (see Gen. xxix., xxx., xxxv.):

1st row. Sardius, Topaz, Carbuncle, { signifying and representing the three degrees of celestial goodness in the internal will, with their purity and burning brilliancy.
Reuben, Simeon, Levi,

2d row. Emerald, Sapphire, Diamond, { signifying and representing the three degrees of celestial wisdom in the internal understanding, with their transparent and sparkling lustre.
Judah, Dan, Naphtali.

The literal sense, in many historical particulars, especially in figures or numbers, weights and measures, has been made to give way for the spiritual sense, or has been arranged without any other definite idea than what seems the purpose of the inner life, or Divine mind. This will fully account for the apparent breaks, inconsistencies, and contradictions which learned commentators have professed to discover in the historical narratives,—such as the number of the Israelites who left Egypt, the time of their sojourn there, the arts and sciences among them, and many incidents in the wilderness,—all of which are of little or no importance when we consider the divine and internal object which the Lord had in view by the inspiration of his Word.

Of the Lord, it is intimated by the prophet that He alone is all-wise, all-good, and all-powerful, but that man is "*less than nothing, and vanity.*" And, in a lofty and sublime strain of inspiration, asks, "Who hath measured the waters in the hollow of his hand, and meted out heaven with a span, and comprehended the dust of the earth in a measure, and weighed the mountains in scales, and the hills in a balance"? (Isa. xl. 12, 17). Nor is this said merely in oriental phrase, of that divine and overruling intelligence and goodness which have so mysteriously and with only perfect order arranged the atoms and directed the combinations of those elemental substances of which the material globe is composed. Far higher was the design, which was to call forth our unquestioned faith and gratitude for eternal mercies, for the overrulement of every moment and event, by the secret operation of his ever-present and ever-wakeful providence, to advance our preparation for happiness and heaven. To this end the Lord, in the wonderful process of regeneration, Himself arranges and subordinates, in true order, the affections and thoughts, and the goodness and truth which they receive, so as to constitute the heavens of the internal mind as his own peculiar dwelling-place, and also the earth of the external mind as his glorious footstool. The mountains are the exalted principles of love to the Lord; the hills are the less elevated principles of charity towards the neighbor; the waters are the

---

3d row.	Ligure, Gad,	Agate, Asher,	Amethyst, Issachar,	signifying and representing the three degrees of spiritual love or charity which are active in the external will, but modified in brilliancy.
4th row.	Beryl, Zebulon,	Onyx, Joseph,	Jasper, Benjamin,	signifying and representing the three degrees of faith or knowledge in the external understanding, less transparent and more opaque than the three degrees of internal wisdom.

Similar things are signified in the order of the stones in the foundations of the New Jerusalem.—See Rev. xxi.

divine truths of his Word, which, by the activity of his power and love, He makes the instrument of his will in the accomplishment of his work. This just and accurate equilibrium, subordination, and complete arrangement of all things in relation to the order of man's regeneration and salvation, are signified by his being represented as measuring the waters in the hollow of his hand, meting out heaven with a span, comprehending the dust of the earth in a measure, weighing the mountains in scales, and the hills in a balance; for to Him, and to Him *alone*, the exact measure and degree, the quantitative and qualitative analysis of every state of his regenerate children is distinctly known, both in time and in eternity. "O the depth of the riches both of the wisdom and knowledge of God! How unsearchable are his judgments, and his ways past finding out" (Rom. xi. 33).

Numbers,[110] weights, and measures have their spiritual signification

---

[110] "There are simple numbers which are significative above all others, and from which the greater numbers derive their significations, viz., the numbers, two, three, five, and seven. The number two signifies union, and is predicated of good; the number three signifies what is full, and is predicated of truths; the number five signifies what is holy: from the number two arise 4, 8, 16, 100, 800, 1600, 4000, 8000, 16,000, which numbers have the same signification as two has, because they arise from the simple number multiplied into itself, and by multiplication with ten: from the number three arise 6, 12, 24, 72, 144, 1440, 144,000, which numbers also have the same signification as the number three has, because they arise from this simple number by multiplication; from the number five arise 10, 50, 100, 1000, 10,000, 100,000, which numbers have the same signification as the number five has, because they arise thence by multiplication; from the number seven arise 14, 70, 700, 7000, 70,000, which also, as arising thence, have a similar signification. Inasmuch as the number three signifies what is full, and what is full denotes all, hence the number twelve derives its signification of all things and all persons; the reason of its being predicated of truths derived from good is, because it arises out of three multiplied into four, and the number three is predicated of truths, and four of good, as was said above."—*A. E.* 430.

"By every number in the Word is signified somewhat of thing or state, and the quality thereof is determined by the numbers which are affixed. The greater and compound numbers signify the same with the lesser and simple from which they arise by multiplication."—*A. E.* 847, 506.

"Philo observes that the number *four* contains the most perfect proportions in musical symphonies, viz.: *Diatessaron, diapente, diapason*, and *disdiapason*. For the proportion of *diatessaron* is as four to three; of *diapente*, as three to two; of *diapason*, as two to one, or four to two; of *disdiapason*, as four to one."—*H. More's Def. of Cabala*, p. 153.

"All numbers are contained in *four*, virtually; by all numbers is meant *ten;* for when we come to *ten* we go back again."—*Ib.*, p. 153.

"In the constant recurrence of the number seven in connection with the rites of these Indians, they offered a curious parallelism with the Hindus. In all that relates to Agni, the specific impersonation of fire, the mystical number *seven* is always used. In offering an oblation by fire, the Hindu priest uttered this prayer: 'Fire! seven are thy fuels; seven thy tongues; seven thy holy sages; seven thy beloved abodes; seven ways do seven sacrifices worship thee; thy sources are seven; may this oblation be efficacious!'" —*Colman's Hind. Myth.*, p. 116; *Squiers*, p. 117.

"Our word seven," says A., in a paper on the Sabbath, "carries the mind back to the origin of the human language. Eliding the *en*, which is merely a termination, we have *sev*, as the body of the word. Now, according to the recognized laws of philology, *sev* may exist in different dialects or languages in different forms. *Sev*, for instance, may become *seb*, the root of the German or Teutonic *sieb(en)*, seven. It is easy to see how the *b* may soften into *p*. Then we have *sep*, the

in the Word of God. This is the reason why they are so often employed, and why such frequent and solemn mention is made of numbering, telling, counting, weighing, and measuring. Unless such a spiritual signification be annexed to these terms, numerous passages will, in the literal sense, be obscure and unintelligible. They are

---

root of the Latin *septem* (seven). In the Celtic *sah* we have the Sanscrit *sap* (the Hebrew *Sabbath*), with a slight vowel change, and the Greek ἑπ (*hep*), with a change in the aspirate. Here then we find the word *sep*, or *seven*, diffused over the entire circle of ancient and modern civilization. Over the same circle, let it be added, the seven-day worship is diffused. Obviously, the one is bound up with the other."—*Sabbath Leisure*, p. 3.

"Of the seven chief luminaries of the heavens (visible to the unassisted eye), the moon is not only the nearest, but the most closely connected with the earth, round which it revolves in a period of about eight and twenty days. In so revolving, the moon undergoes four marked changes. There is, first, from the new moon to the half moon; secondly, from the half moon to the full moon; thirdly, from the full moon to the half moon; and, fourthly, from the half moon to the new moon. The entire revolution is thus divided into four distinct parts. But the fourth of twenty-eight is seven, and so we come again upon the number seven as a fixed, and not a fixed only, but a sacred number. Hence an influence to strengthen the reverence for the number seven, which arose from the number of (what were considered to be) the celestial rulers. But the four phases of the moon suggested similar divisions of time. Lunar weeks ensued, and from lunar weeks came lunar years. Again seven is consecrated as a sacred number."— *Ib.*, p. 3.

"The ecclesiastical year of the Hebrews is a lunar year; it is laid out, so to say, in sevens. The seven became in Israel a sacred multiple—seven days; seven weeks; seven times seven weeks, or the year; seven years, or the Sabbatical year; seven times seven years, or the year of jubilee. Every stage was marked and celebrated with worship. The septennial year, in all its parts and numbers, was a year of worship. The entire year of worship finished every fifty years, but finished only to begin again, with all its astronomical divisions, its religious rites, and its social observances. But Israel was the [representative] channel for conveying God's best blessing to the world. It is, therefore, to the Divine Providence that this cycle of worship is to be traced [it is the language of correspondences, grounded in appearances, significative of realities]; and it is this Heavenly Father that ought to receive our thankful acknowledgments."—*Ib.*, pp. 3, 4.

Twelve is a compound number, being the product of three multiplied by four. By three is signified, as we have seen, *all*, or that which is full and complete, applied to truths and doctrines; and by four is signified conjunction, as applied to all principles of goodness, internal and external. Hence the number twelve signifies the whole complex of the doctrines of truth and goodness, or of faith and charity united,—the reception of all of which constitutes the Church. It was to represent this that the twelve patriarchs and twelve tribes of Israel constituted the Jewish Church; and that at the commencement of the Christian Church twelve apostles were selected as the Lord's immediate disciples; while the city New Jerusalem, the church to be established in the days of the Lord's second advent, is represented as having *twelve* foundations and *twelve* gates.

"If we consider that the waters of the deluge were *forty* days and *forty* nights coming on the earth; that for *forty* years the Israelites did penance in the wilderness; that *forty* stripes were the appointed punishment of malefactors; that *forty* days were allowed the Ninevites to repent; that Moses, Elijah, and [our blessed Lord] Jesus Christ fasted each *forty* days and *forty* nights, we must admire the uniformity of the divine economy, and believe that the period was not *without reason* so singularly distinguished."—*Bishop Dehon's Sermons*, vol. i., p. 366.

"Forty was a round number, and is still employed as such in the East, to express an indefinite quantity."—*Von Bohlen's Intro. to Gen.*, vol. i., p. 82.

"According to the ingenious remark of St. Jerome, the number forty [in the Word] seems to be consecrated to tribulation; the Hebrew people sojourned in Egypt ten times forty years; Moses, Elias, and the Lord Jesus Christ fasted forty days; the Hebrew people remained forty years in the desert; the prophet Ezekiel lay for forty days on his right side."—*Cahen*, iv., p. 158; note on Num. xxiii. 1.

used in all their relations, whether simple or compound, to express the various qualities of things in a combined form, and the various states of the church and her members, either in a genuine or in an opposite sense. The relations which number and order bear to the things and objects of the natural world are of precisely the same nature as are the relations and arrangements as to the quality of the things of the spiritual world and the human mind. We have already seen that the number three signifies fulness or perfection, and denotes a complete state, comprising the discrete degrees of life from beginning to end. It is generally predicated of truth, or of its opposite, falsity,—of what is sacred, or what is polluted. Thus, in addition to the instances already given, the divine command to "keep a feast unto the Lord three times in the year" (Ex. xxiii. 14–17), signifies fulness and perpetuity of the worship of the Lord from a cheerful and grateful heart. These three festivals of unleavened bread, or the passover; of the first-fruits of the harvest, or the feast of weeks; and of the ingathering, or feast of tabernacles, were designed to represent man's complete spiritual deliverance from the thraldom of falsity, and his purification by successive trials and victories,—the insemination of truth in a tender state of heavenly affection, and the implantation of goodness in the will. Multiples of the same number have, for the most part, a similar signification with the simple number, but one that is more complex and extensive. Thus, the number six, like three, denotes what is full and complete; but in a greater or fuller degree, all states of labor preceding a full state of heavenly rest. Sometimes both simple and compound numbers are mentioned in a subordinate relation to other numbers, and then the signification is somewhat varied: thus, nine in relation to ten, and ninety-nine in relation to one hundred, denote fulness of a former state, previous to entering upon a new one. The number seven, again, refers in general to what is holy and inviolable, and, in an opposite sense, to what is profane: thus, a hallowed and enduring state of rest and peace, after the labors and conflicts of temptation, was represented by the Sabbath, which, under the Jewish dispensation, succeeded six days of toil, and was kept inviolate.

But these states of returning trial and rest not only involved subjects of a particular kind, but those of general and universal order; hence, the Jews were commanded not only to keep the seventh day holy, but the seventh year was commanded to be a sabbath of rest; and the end of seven times seven years, or seven sabbaths of years, a jubilee was to be proclaimed by sound of trumpets, slaves were manumitted or set at liberty, alienated property was restored to the original possessor or his descendants, and the uncultivated ground yielded a miraculous increase, equivalent to three harvests (Lev. xxv.). "Seven times a day do I praise thee," said the Psalmist (cxix. 164), to signify that the sweet incense of praise, to be acceptable to the Lord, must perpetually arise from a holy, undivided heart. To teach us that Christian forgiveness towards an offending brother must be full, plenary, and holy, we are divinely enjoined to forgive him "not seven times, but seventy times seven" (Matt. xviii. 21, 22); and to denote a holy state of complete purification, out of Mary Magdalene "was cast seven devils" (Mark xvi. 9.) In this pure and holy state of mind and life signified by the number seven we have conjunction with divine omnipotence, and thence we are supplied, through the Word, with superhuman strength against our spiritual adversaries. To represent this to the very life, we read that, at the siege of Jericho, seven priests were commanded to bear seven trumpets of rams' horns, and the ark of God, and, followed by all the people, were to make a circuit around the walls of the city on seven successive days; but on the seventh day they were to compass the city seven times. Then the walls thereof fell, and the city and its inhabitants were destroyed (Josh. vi.).

Grievous temptations, and their duration,—or full states of trial and suffering,—are usually signified by the number forty, which is a compound of four multiplied by ten, denoting fulness and conjunction; for, by the endurance of temptations, goodness and truth are conjoined in the soul. The same is signified by twice forty, or eighty, and, in a greater degree, by four hundred, which is a compound of forty multiplied by ten. Thus, to represent the trials and temptations which the Christian will experience in the course of his regeneration, the children of Israel were miraculously led forty years through the wilderness (Deut. viii. 4). Similar states of afflicting trial were signified by the solemn fast of Moses on Mount Sinai for forty days and forty nights (Deut ix. 9; x. 10); by the forty days of suffering endured by Elijah; by the forty days in which the prophet Ezekiel was commanded to bear, representatively, the iniquities of the house of Israel (Ezek. iv. 6); and, lastly, by the forty days in which the Lord endured his grievous temptations in the wilderness (Matt. iv. 2). The strength of "fourscore years" is, therefore, described as being "labor and sorrow" (Ps. xc. 10); and the children of Israel are, from this signification, said to have been afflicted in Egypt "four hundred years" (Gen. xv. 13; Acts vii. 6).

Weights and measures are employed in the Word of God to signify quantity and quality as to the subjects of which they are predicated, or to denote the estimation in which they are held. In general, weight has relation to good[111] and its quality, and, in an opposite sense, to evil,—thus to states of things in reference to the will; and measure has relation to truth and its quality, and, in an opposite sense, to falsity,—thus to states of things in reference to the understanding. This brief signification of weights and measures, and their application, will at once enable us to perceive some of the deepest lessons of divine wisdom contained in the Word.

By weights and measures are signified, in reference to the soul, rules and explorations, and just judgment as to the quality and character of the mind and life. Thus in Leviticus, among other divine laws, we are supplied, in the spiritual sense of the Word, with a divine rule for self-examination, which, if any one conscientiously applies to the inward states of his soul, will bring down the strictest justice and judgment into all his words and works. Nothing is so common as for men to deceive themselves in regard to this important duty. It is seldom performed as it ought to be, and is often substituted by vain and powerless acknowledgments of sinfulness, uttered, perhaps, in words of Holy Writ, but unfelt, as not being the result of practical acquaintance with the inward states of the heart. If sins are to be remitted, however, they must be put away by repentance; and how can they be removed unless they are seen? We are too frequently self-satisfied with the delusive and dangerous notion that we are no worse than others, while the evils within us are only concealed by a fair exterior,—honest before men, but unjust in the sight of God,—outwardly "whited sepulchres, but inwardly filled with dead men's bones and all uncleanness" (Matt. xxiii. 27). How important, therefore, when considered in its eternal meaning, is the divine law of mental introspection to which we have alluded, and in which the Lord solemnly warns and exhorts us as follows: "Ye shall do no unrighteousness in judgment, in mete-yard, in weight, or in measure. Just balances, just weights, a just ephah, and a just hin shall ye have" (xix. 35, 36). Instructing us that if, without self-deception, we would

---

[111] "In Egypt, the vessel of clay weighed upon the balance of the judgment of souls represents the deceased's *state of good*, of love, and of piety; as is proved by the inscription of the manuscript of *Tentamoun*."—Portal. See *Brit. Mag.*, vol. xxi., p. 520. See APPENDIX, *Egyptian Hieroglyphics*.

attain the just measure or quality of an angel, and the standard weight of the balance of the sanctuary, we must not only examine the quality of our words and deeds, but of our desires and thoughts, our persuasions and intentions, our motives and ends of life. The exploration of the church in general, so as to ascertain the quantity and quality of truth and goodness therein, and thence to examine the inward states of the worshippers, and the intrinsic value of their worship, in order that revelation might be made, is also described as follows: "I lifted up mine eyes again, and looked, and behold a man with a measuring line in his hand. Then said I, Whither goest thou? And he said unto me, To measure Jerusalem, to see what is the breadth thereof, and what is the length thereof" (Zech. ii. 1, 2). And the same things are signified by these words in the Revelation, "And there was given unto me a reed like unto a rod: and the angel stood, saying, Rise, and measure the temple of God, and the altar, and them that worship therein" (xi. 1). This measuring-line and reed serve likewise to point out our own individual duties, and the means of performing them, whether they are moral or religious. By those heart-searching truths of the Holy Word, which exhibit to us our inward character, we can try our thoughts, explore our motives, and analyze our affections, and thus discover with certainty the external character of our words and works. When, therefore, the church was brought to its consummation or end, by the profanation of all the heavenly principles of goodness and truth; all the holy things of the Word, signified by the consecrated vessels of the Temple, being applied to evil purposes, Belshazzar is described at his impious feast polluting the golden vessels, and then, it is said, there "came forth fingers of a man's hand, and wrote upon the plaister of the wall of the king's palace," to represent the divine exploration and judgment, as revealed in the very letter of God's Word; while, to signify that the external church was totally destroyed, because that within it all truth and goodness had been profaned and adulterated, and its quality in the divine sight was only that of falsity and evil, in all the various degrees of the minds of its professors, "this was the writing that was written, MENE, MENE, TEKEL, UPHARSIN" (Dan. v. 25–27), numbered, weighed, divided. *Numbered* as to truth, which was found to be awfully corrupted; *weighed* as to goodness, which was discovered to be hypocritical and defiled; *divided* or disjoined from the Lord and heaven, because faith and charity were separated, and about to perish, in which case the church must cease to exist on earth. And such must be the awful and miserable doom which, after death, will most assuredly be pronounced upon all spiritual idolaters who, from the inward love of evil, had profaned the holy truths of religion, and had impiously applied them to their own sensual and selfish purposes, and had likewise defiled and perverted every principle of goodness, love, and charity,—those golden vessels of the Lord's sanctuary,—by hypocrisy, deceit, ambition, and pride.

Mention is often made in the Word of musical instruments, in consequence of their correspondence, which depends upon the difference in their sounds.[112] These are of two kinds, namely, stringed instruments, the solid parts of which are composed of soft wood, as the harp, psaltery, lyre, etc., and wind instruments made of metals, as the trumpet, cymbal, etc.; of animals' horns, as the horn, and of hollow wood and reeds, as the pipe; together with those in which the sound is produced by vibratory members being stretched over hollow cylinders or circles, as the tabret, the drum, and the timbrel. In stringed instruments the sounds are produced by discrete or perfectly distinct movements, and are more particularly predicated of the understanding, or, rather, of the distinct degrees of spiritual affection, and such discrete sounds excite within us the affections of truth; but wind or breathing instruments, being capable of a continuous pro-

---

[112] That various passions, emotions, and affections are more or less excited into activity, by different and corresponding sounds, is the experience of all. Dean Sherlock has advanced an idea in accordance with this view:

"A diversity of sounds," he says, "is fitted by nature to express and to excite very different passions. Love, joy, admiration, desire, fear, sorrow, indignation, give some distinguishing notes and accents to the very voice. And such different notes will also as forcibly imprint such passions on our mind as they naturally represent, and that many times, whether we will or no; which is a great secret in nature, and shows an unaccountable sympathy between sounds and passions."—i., p. 351.

Sound is internal to language, just as affection is internal to thought. Hence tone, which originates in them the affections of the will, alters the sense of words. How different, again, are masculine tones from feminine tones; the former indicate the harshness of the intellect, for which man is peculiarly distinguished,—the latter, the softness of affection, which is characteristic of woman.

"The Almighty has adapted many substances to the production of pleasing sounds; the air which ever surrounds us is capable of conveying those sounds, inspired, indeed, in power, but unaltered in quality; while to man is given a set of faculties in nothing more delightfully exercised than in their reception and appreciation, together with the power, by skilfully arranging and combining them, to produce an endless and charming variety of melody and harmony. Man's heart is strung with sympathetic cords, which vibrate in unison with the several combinations of musical sounds; nor is the effect thus produced accidental or anomalous, the same feelings are always excited by the same combinations. Chromatic music, or a succession of semitones, soothes and relaxes the spirit; a succession of chords, as in martial music, rouses the soul even to active exertion; plaintive and melancholy feelings are awakened by the minor mode; the major mode and the diatonic scale, the simplest arrangements of musical sounds, assume an endless variety of expression, and, like the natural modulation of the human voice, excite various emotions, but most usually inspire joy and gladness."—*Review, Public Opinion.*

longation of sound, have a more specific reference to the will, or, rather, to the various degrees of celestial affection, such continuous sounds being those which more particularly excite within us the affections of goodness and charity. Perfect harmony depends upon the skilful union of both these kinds of instruments, and their association with the human voice, and is representative of the harmonic union of the will, understanding, and life,—of spiritual and celestial affections, when receptive of goodness and truth, together with the inward exultation, delight, and desires thence resulting. And with these, for the same reason, because representative of inward states of delight and joy, singing and dancing are frequently united. Thus, in Psalm cl. we read, "Praise ye the Lord. Praise God in his sanctuary: praise Him in the firmament of his power. Praise Him for his mighty acts: praise Him according to his excellent greatness. Praise Him with the sound of the trumpet: praise Him with the psaltery and harp. Praise Him with the timbrel and pipe: praise Him with stringed instruments and organs. Praise Him upon the loud cymbals: praise Him upon the high sounding cymbals. Let every thing that hath breath praise the Lord. Praise ye the Lord." In this divine Psalm we are exhorted, in the spiritual sense, to render praise to the Lord, not only with the holy thoughts of the understanding, but with all the pure and fervent affections of the will united in one harmonious concord. We are to praise Him with all our powers for his wonderful works of creation, redemption, regeneration, and salvation, and for the glorious attributes by which they were and still are accomplished. To praise Him with wind instruments is to celebrate Him from the inmost or celestial affections of love and goodness in the heart; and to praise Him with stringed instruments and cymbals, is to exalt Him from spiritual affections of wisdom and truth in the understanding, thus to delight in the Lord, and to worship and serve Him from the harmonious agreement and concord of the whole mind. For let man, as to the complex faculties of his intellect and reason, be contemplated as like a stringed instrument, as the psaltery, and, as to his voluntary principles, like a wind instrument, as the organ, every note, by virtue of his hereditary tendencies to evil and error, may be said, before regeneration, to be deranged and discordant. What, then, is the process of regeneration but the attuning of all the affections and thoughts, words and works, so that every string and pipe gives forth its appropriate sound, and combines with all the rest in perfect unity, uttering in harmonious notes and melodious tones songs of adoration, gratitude, and praise, and giving suitable expression to the inmost delights of the soul.

Sometimes stringed instruments or wind instruments are spoken of by themselves, as when deliverance or redemption by the power of divine truth is treated of, where we read, "The Lord was ready to save me: therefore we will sing my songs to the stringed instruments all the days of our life, in the house of the Lord" (Isa. xxxviii. 20). That to sing to the Lord denotes to praise and glorify Him is self-evident; and to do this with a timbrel, as Miriam did, after the wonderful passage and deliverance from the Red Sea (Ex. xv. 20), signifies to perform this great duty of thanksgiving to the Lord for his abounding mercies, from an inward ground of heartfelt confidence and gratitude.[113]

On account of this signification of musical instruments, and their distinction into two classes, several Psalms, which have relation to the spiritual affections of wisdom or truth, were directed to be sung in the representative worship of the Jewish Temple, accompanied by neginoth or gittith, which were stringed instruments (Ps. iv., liv.); while others, which have more immediate reference to the celestial affections of love or goodness, and faith thence derived, were required to be sung upon nehiloth, or upon wind instruments (Ps. v., viii.; Hab. iii. 19).[114] Sometimes instruments of music are spoken of in an

---

[113] See for illustrations: Lam. v. 14, 15; 1 Cor. xiv. 15; Eph. v. 19; Ps. xxx. 11, xxxiii. 1-5, lxviii. 25, lxxxi. 1-4, lxxxvii. 7, cxliv. 9, cxlix. 1-4; Isa. xxxi. 3, 4, li. 3, 11; 2 Sam. xxi. 11; Luke vii. 32, xv. 25; Matt. xi. 17.

[114] *Neginoth*, Heb., literally pulsations, from a verb which signifies to strike the strings of a musical instrument, either with the fingers, or with a plectrum,—a quill, or bow.

Nehiloth, or more correctly, *Nechiloth*, or *Hannechiloth*, is derived from a root which signifies to bore or perforate, doubtless signifying wind instruments of some kind, all of which are formed of hollow tubes.—See *Clowe's Translations of the Psalms*, pp. 24, 27.

Neginoth, Hasheminith, a harp with eight strings. Haggittith, the harp of Gath.

Shigonoth, a concert of various stringed instruments.

Shoshannino, a six-stringed instrument.

Shushan-eduth, a six-stringed lute.

Some psalms are directed to be sung by virgins, with the responses of a youth; others by alternate choruses; others by voices and instruments of the treble pitch; and others were to be accompanied with timbrel, harp, psaltery, cymbals, and trumpets.

All have their peculiar and spiritual significance.—See Ps. lxviii. 25, lvii. 8, xlix. 4, lxxi. 22, cl. 3, lxxxi. 2, 3; Ez. xxxiii. 3; Rev. i. 10, xiv. 2, xviii. 18; Num. x. 2.

Musical tones and instruments are often referred to by Swedenborg, as presenting different correspondences, according to their distinct correspondences.—See *A. C.* 8337.

Berlioz, in his work *On the Orchestra*, says that "the quality of the tone of the trumpet is noble and brilliant; it suits warlike ideas, as also songs of triumph. It lends itself to the expression of all energetic, lofty, and grand sentiments."

"The fable of Orpheus, who is said to have charmed all creation, monsters, rocks and trees, heaven and hell, was most probably at first a simple allegory, denoting and describing the orderly effects of instruction in wisdom and philosophy, in morality and civil discipline, and among all degrees of man, barbarous and civilized. That when prompted by love, it is all-powerful, and introduces harmony and concord into all the affairs of the world, mental and material." —See *Lempriere's Clas. Dict.*, and *Bacon's Wisdom of the Ancients*, Art. ORPHEUS.

opposite sense, to denote the sinful delight which the unregenerate take in what is evil and false. Such insane pleasures, originating in self-homage, together with its enchanting persuasions, are signified by the worship of Nebuchadnezzar's golden image, which was accompanied with all kinds of music (Dan. iii.). And it is to such evil and impure pleasures, especially when they arise from the profanation of what is good and true, that the Lord alludes, where He says, "Take thou away from me the noise of thy songs; for I will not hear the melody of thy viols. Woe to them that are at ease in Zion, and trust in the mountain of Samaria. That chant to the sound of the viol, and invent to themselves instruments of music, like David" (Amos v. 23; vi. 1, 5). And, again, speaking of the self-intelligent, who despise the instructions of the Divine Word, it is said, "The harp, and the viol, the tabret, and pipe, and wine, are in their [polluted] feasts; but they regard not the work of the Lord, neither consider the operation of his hands" (Isa. v. 12).

The harp is a well known stringed instrument, often mentioned in the Word, and signifies, in the internal sense, the voice of praise from spiritual truth, and thence confession, from sincere joy of heart, that all deliverance from sin is effected by the power of divine truth proceeding from divine mercy. Hence, in praising and blessing God for victorious deliverance from all spiritual enemies and troubles, and the consequent elevation of the mind, together with the gladness and comfort of soul thence derived, the inspired penman writes: "I will also praise thee with the psaltery, *even* thy TRUTH, O my God; unto thee will I sing with the harp, O thou Holy One of Israel" (Ps. lxxi. 22). This is the reason why angels are represented as having "the harps of God" (Rev. v. 8); for thus all confess Him with one accord, and from inmost delight. To represent the soul-enchanting harmony of such acknowledgment and its attendant joys among the inhabitants of heaven, the apostle says, "I heard a voice from heaven, as the voice of many waters, and as the voice of a great thunder: and I heard the voice of harpers harping with their harps" (Rev. xiv. 2). With this signification of the harp before us, how beautiful and instructive is the account we have of Saul and David, where we read, that in consequence of obstinate disobedience "the Spirit of the Lord departed from Saul," and an evil spirit was permitted to trouble him; but he commanded his servants to provide him a man who could play skilfully upon the harp. And David was brought before him, "And it came to pass," it is said, that "when the evil spirit from

God was upon Saul, that David took a harp, and played with his hand; so Saul was refreshed and was well, and the evil spirit departed from him" (1 Sam. xvi. 14-23). The sphere of such confession, arising from the harp of truth being melodiously attuned to our states by the Lord's presence and providence, is truly angelic, and full of power. Evil spirits, who can live and rejoice only in scenes of jarring discord, are expelled from communion with the soul, turbulent passions are calmed, reason resumes the sceptre, polluted affections and thoughts are driven away, despair and grief are dissipated,—so that the blessed angels can draw near to minister to man's consolation and joy, and restore him, if he will, to innocence, intelligence, and felicity.

On this subject Swedenborg's remarks are numerous, interesting, and most edifying. Thus, in one place, he says, " Formerly, in divine worship, several kinds of musical instruments were applied, but with much distinction; in general, by the wind instruments were expressed the affections of good, and by the stringed instruments the affections of truth, and this from the correspondence of everything sonorous with the affections. It is a known thing that by some kinds of musical instruments are expressed natural affections of one quality, by some natural affections of another quality, and, when suitable harmony conspires, that they actually call forth those affections. They who are skilled in music are aware of this, and also act accordingly in applying the several instruments to the purpose intended. This circumstance has its ground in the very nature of sounds, and of their agreement with the affections. Man learnt this, at first, not from science and art, but from the hearing and its exquisite sense. Hence it is plain that it does not originate in the natural world, but in the spiritual, and in this case is derived from the correspondence of things which flow from order in the natural world with things in the spiritual world. Harmonious sound and its varieties in the natural world correspond to states of joy and gladness in the spiritual, and states of joy and gladness in the spiritual world exist from affections, which, in that world, are the affections of good and truth; hence, now it may be manifest that musical instruments correspond to the delights and pleasantnesses of spiritual and celestial affections, and that some instruments correspond to the latter affections, some to the former."—A. C. 8337.

"As things celestial are the holy things of love, and the good things thence derived, so things spiritual are the truths and good things of faith; for it is the part of faith to understand not only what is true, but also what is good, the knowledges of faith implying both; but to be such as faith teacheth, is the part of the celestial [principle]. Inasmuch as faith implieth the knowledge both of goodness and truth, they are signified by two instruments, the harp and the organ. The harp is a stringed instrument, as every one knows, and therefore signifies spiritual truth; but the organ is between a stringed instrument and a wind instrument, and therefore signifies spiritual good.

"In the Word mention is made of various instruments, and each has its particular signification, as will be shown, by the divine mercy of the Lord, in its proper place. At present we shall only adduce some passages from David in relation thereto, as, for instance, 'I will offer in the *tent* of Jehovah sacrifices of *shouting*, I will *sing* and *play* to Jehovah' (Psalm xxvii. 6). Where by tent is expressed what is celestial, and by shouting, singing, and playing, what is spiritual. Again, '*Sing* to Jehovah, ye just, for his praise is comely for the upright; confess to Jehovah on the *harp*, *play* unto Him on the *psaltery*, an instrument of ten strings; *sing* unto Him a new song, *play* skilfully with a *loud noise*, because the Word of Jehovah is right, and all his work is in truth' (Ps. xxxiii. 1–4), signifying the truths of faith, whereof such things are predicated. Things spiritual, or truths and the good things of faith, were celebrated by the harp and psaltery, by singing and the like; whereas things holy, or the celestial things of faith, were celebrated by wind instruments, as trumpets and the like; hence so many instruments were used about the Temple, and it was ordained so frequently that this or that should be celebrated with particular instruments, and this was the reason why instruments were applied and understood to signify the things themselves which were celebrated by them, as in the cases now before us. Again, 'I will confess unto thee with the instrument of *psaltery*, thy truth, O my God; unto thee will I *play* with the *harp*, O thou Holy One of Israel; my lips shall *sing* when I *play* unto thee, and my soul which thou hast redeemed' (Ps. lxxi. 22, 23). Where, in like manner, the truths of faith are signified. Again, 'Answer to Jehovah in confession, *play* on the *harp* to our God' (Ps. cxlvii. 7). In which passage confession has respect to the celestial things of faith, and therefore mention is made of Jehovah; whereas, to play on the harp has respect to the spiritual things of faith, and therefore mention is made of God. Again, 'Let them praise the name of Jehovah in the dance, let them *play* unto Him with the *timbrel* and *harp*' (Ps cxlix. 3). The timbrel signifies good, and the harp truth, which they praise. Again, 'Praise God with the sound of the *trumpet;* praise Him on the *psaltery* and *harp;* praise Him with the *timbrel* and pipe; praise Him on *stringed instruments* and *organs;* praise Him on the *cymbals* of hearing; praise Him on the *cymbals* of shouting' (Ps. cl. 3–5),—signifying the good things and truths of faith, which were the ground of praise. Nor let any one suppose that so many different instruments would have been here mentioned, unless they had had such spiritual signification. Again, 'Send out thy light and thy truth, let them lead me; let them bring me unto the mountain of thy holiness, and to thy habitations, and I will go unto the altar of God, unto the God of the gladness of my rejoicing, and I will confess to thee on the *harp,* O God, my God' (Ps. xliii. 3, 4),—signifying the knowledges of goodness and truth. So in Isaiah, 'Take a *harp,* go about the city, make sweet *melody, sing* many songs, that thou mayest be remembered' (xxiii. 16),—signifying the things respecting faith, and the knowledges thereof. The same is expressed still more plainly in the Revelation: 'The four animals and the four and twenty elders fell down before the Lamb, having every one of them *harps,* and golden vials full of odors, which are the prayers of the saints' (v. 8). Where it must be evident to every one that the animals and elders had not harps, but that by harps are signified the truths of faith, as by golden vials full of odors are signified the good things of faith. In David they are called praises and confessions, which were made by instruments (Ps. xlii. 5; lxix. 31); and in another place, in John, 'I heard a voice from heaven, as the voice of many waters; and I heard the voice of *harpers harping* with their *harps;* and they *sung* a new *song'* (Rev. xiv. 2). And in another place, 'I saw them that had gotten the victory stand near the sea of glass, having the *harps* of God' (Rev. xv. 2). It is worthy to be remarked, that angels and spirits, according to their differences with respect to goodness and truth, distinguish tones, and this not only in the case of singing and of instruments, but also in the words of speech, and admit only such tones as are in concord, so that there is an agreement of tones, consequently of instruments, with the nature and essence of goodness and truth."—A. C. 419, 420.

The Egyptian priests appear to have been their musicians. Their flute was only a cow's horn, with three or four perforations in it, afterwards imitated in metal, and even still called horns. Their harp or lyre had only three strings. The Grecian and Jewish harp or lyre had seven, eight, and ten strings, probably somewhat like a modern guitar or lute, and was small, being held in the hand. The Jewish trumpets were rams' horns, but afterwards were also made of silver and other metals, and were both straight and bent. Their flute was the same as the Egyptian. Their organ was an arrangement of pipes, similar to what are called Pandæan, or shepherd's pipes; and perforated pipes, or flutes, sometimes made of reeds, and were both single and double. The sackbut or psaltery was, in all probability, a triangular instrument, furnished with ten strings, and struck by a rod, or by a plectrum. Their other musical instruments were those of percussion, as the timbrel or tabret, a kind of tambourine; the triangle, or triangular rods, in pairs, both plain and charged with rings. The citherns of the ancients were made of bronze or brass, and were furnished with bars and rings. However simple these ancient instruments were, they bear precisely the same signification as the more complicated and complete of modern times, for all kinds are equally divisible into the three classes just mentioned. Such music as the Jews had at their command, singing and even dancing, appears to have been interwoven into all their religious festivals and ceremonies of worship, and this could only have been from their correspondence.

Both cheerful and mournful singing and dancing are often spoken of in the Word, to denote and express inward joy, and its corresponding delight, in the external mind; for "joy of heart finds utterance in singing, because when the heart is full of joy, and thence the thoughts also, it then pours itself forth in singing" (Ap. Ex. 326). This gladness and joy are not derived to man from the natural world, or from mere scientific skill, but from the spiritual world, by perception or intuition; the external sounds and their harmonious or melodious combinations being the corresponding base on which they rest, and by means of which the affections are brought forth. Choirs for conducting the praises of congregations in public worship, therefore, ought to be pious and intelligent persons, who, themselves, inwardly feel and respond to the appropriate tunes and melodies which they introduce; and then the congregations will be greatly aided in their united responses of satisfaction and delight. Like the true poet, the master of music also owes his peculiar skill to an inferior kind of inspiration or spiritual intuition. The prophets frequently accompanied their plenarily-inspired songs and predictions with the melody of musical instruments.

CHAPTER XIII.

The Correspondence of Animals, Parts of Animals, and Compound and Monstrous Animals, with Illustrations.

ALL kinds of animals have their peculiar correspondences, in agreement with their forms, characteristics, and uses; for they all derive their existence from spiritual causes, and, by virtue of their instinct, are in momentary connection with the spiritual world. In the Word of God the beasts of the earth—the tame and useful as well as the wild and ferocious, the clean and the unclean—correspond, in general, to various good or evil affections, according to their orders and qualities, and the subject of which they are predicated. The birds, or winged tribes of animals, distinguished by their astonishing quickness of sight,—both clean and unclean,—agreeably to their respective genera and characters, and the subject treated of, correspond to the various kinds and degrees of thought, reason, intelligence, and the power of understanding, and are predicated both of what is holy and what is profane. For these faculties and their attainments impart to man intellectual acuteness and penetration, enabling him to fly, as it were, with wings, and disport himself in the atmosphere of knowledge. The fishes and the reptiles, according to their respective forms and habitudes, correspond to those low external principles of man's earthly nature, which, before the mind is regenerated, flit and grovel among sensual objects and selfish pursuits.

In the very characteristics of many animals, to say nothing of their forms and uses, which are both good and evil, there is a striking correspondence which is almost universally admitted. Thus, how frequently are corresponding qualities of the mind associated with various animals, or parts of animals. In the ferocity of the tiger, the cunning of the fox, the strength of the lion, the subtlety of the serpent, the filthiness of the swine, the innocence of the lamb, the cruelty of the wolf, the voracity of the vulture, the nocturnal propensities and powers of the owl and the bat, the soaring power of the eagle, the rapid flight of the swallow, the affection of the turtle for its mate, the virulent poison of the asp, the deadly sting of the scorpion, the destructive propensities of the caterpillar, the treachery of the spider, the instructive prudence and industry of the bee, etc., we may at once recognize the general correspondence of those animals.[115] Who, if he reflects on the subject, may not perceive that the croaking of the frog represents mere atheistical reasonings against the truth and authority of God's Word? This was the reason why among the plagues of Egypt one was of frogs, which came up and covered the land (Ex. viii.); and why "the spirits of devils, working miracles, and going forth into the whole world," are described as "three unclean

---

[115] The names of most of the animals in Hebrew, and probably all, were the roots known, are expressive of some of their leading qualities or characteristics, and the sound is derived from their cries.

"Clean and unclean beasts are introduced by the sacred writers to signify the pure and impure affections of the people; agreeably with the natural propensities of the animals mentioned. See Ez. viii. 10; Rev. xviii. 2."—*Bellamy*, Lev. xix. 31, note.

The word translated *cockatrice* has been variously rendered basilisk, asp, viper, hydra, etc. One of the most venomous kinds of oviparous serpents appears to be meant. It was thought by Dr. Blaney to have received its Hebrew appellation by an onomatopœia, from its *hissing*.

"It is well known that the names affixed to the different animals in Scripture always express [in the original language] some prominent feature and essential characteristic of the creature to which they are applied (*Dr. A. Clarke*). It is an interesting fact, also, that nearly all the animals among the Hindoos have names given to them which either allude to their shape or their habits."—*Roberts's Oriental Illustr.*, 2d ed., p. 5.

"Certain it is that man combines in himself the passions of all animals, and that which predominates, whether from nature or habit, becomes displayed in his physiognomy by something like the features of the animal which is its characteristic. In a mixed assembly, a physiognomist may fancy that he traces the natures of the most artful and cruel animals. Animals differ from man in this respect, inasmuch as each species may be said to possess only one kind of expression."—*St. Pierre's Harmonies of Nature*, vol. ii, p. 4.

Among the Hindoos, an artful, treacherous man is called a *jackal*, an animal in habits and propensities akin to the fox, and is supposed to be often meant in the Word by the original term translated *fox*. See Roberts's *Oriental Illus.*, p. 172, and *Harris's Nat. Hist. of the Bible*, Art. Fox.

"The Bible, throughout, contains figurative representations of the passions and affections in man, by the application of the propensities and affections of animals. It is a way of carrying information most powerfully illustrative."—*Bellamy*, Gen. iii., note 5.

"The pursuers of vain knowledge are like owls,—sharp-sighted in vanity, and blind at the approach of true light."—*Bias*.

"Agens of Athens, according to Andronion, was of the *serpent breed*, i. e., *circumspect*, or *prudent*, and the first king of the country (Herod., l. viii., c. 41), and Diodorus says that this was a circumstance deemed by the Athenians inexplicable; that some had mentioned concerning Cecrops, that he underwent a metamorphosis, *that he was changed from a serpent into a man*. That is, from being a sensualist, like a beast, he became virtuous. Such was the application of the propensities of animals to signify the like propensities in man."—*Ib.*, Lev. xix. 31, note. See also APPENDIX, *Metempsychosis*.

"Men, left to the corruptions of their own hearts, are (as the Psalmist says), 'even as beasts before God.' . . . There was a *moral*, as well as a spiritual, doctrine implied in the prohibition of certain animals under the law. God's people were not to resemble in their manner the predominant evil tempers of many beasts, who, for those evil tempers, were marked out as vile and unclean. The fierceness of some, the gluttony of others, and the filthy, base, or savage dispositions of the rest, were to be held in greater abhorrence than their mere flesh, which, entering the mouth as such, 'could never defile the man;' and men, living under dominion of those depravities, are, therefore, more impure in the sight of God than those beasts which are possessed of them possibly can be, in the sense of the law."—*Serle's Hor. Sol.*, pp. 246, 247, and note.

spirits like frogs, [proceeding] out of the mouth of the dragon, and out of the mouth of the beast, and out of the mouth of the false prophet" (Rev. xvi. 13, 14). Or, again, who cannot recognize a horse, as descriptive of ability and power? Or, again, who does not see that the eggs of that malignant reptile called a cockatrice, basilisk, or asp, are corresponding forms of the germs of evil originating in falsity, thus of sensual affections in the heart, which, if eaten, or inwardly appropriated, cause death; or if crushed, or made externally manifest, bring forth the poisonous viper? Or, that the spider which spins its gossamer web with which it fabricates its filmy covering and snare from its own bowels, and stealthily watches to seize the unwary victim entangled in its meshes, is a true correspondent of those cunning arguments and contrivances, grounded in treacherous falsehood, which derive their flimsy substance, and weave a mysterious and deceitful texture, from man's own self-intelligence, prompted by the artful persuasions of hell, and with which weak minds are successfully deluded and snared? Hence we read in the prophet this description of so depraved a state of the church and the mind: "None calleth for justice, nor *any* pleadeth for truth: they trust in vanity, and speak lies; they conceive mischief, and bring forth iniquity. They hatch cockatrice' eggs, and weave the spider's web; he that eateth of them dieth, and that which is crushed breaketh out into a viper." And to denote the frailty, deceitfulness, and unworthiness of such false assumptions, it is added: "Their webs shall not become garments, neither shall they cover themselves with their works: their works are works of iniquity, and the act of violence is in their hands" (Isa. lix. 4-7). And Job, speaking of the weakness and instability of self-righteousness, says, "The hypocrite's hope shall perish: whose hope shall be cut off, and whose trust shall be a spider's web. He shall lean upon his house, but it shall not endure" (viii. 14, 15). A single touch of truth dissolves the elaborate but flimsy fabric which man contrives for the odious purpose of concealing his own deformities and corruptions, and ensnaring the innocent, and where he reposes in fatal security; but he will perish in the ruins of the deceitful habitation he has constructed.

So, again, in a good sense, a lion[116] at one time signifies the omnipotence of truth in defending the Lord's church, where the motive is good, as where it is written, "Who shall rouse him up?" (Gen. xlix. 9);

---

[116] In the Egyptian hieroglyphics, and the ' is evidently the symbol of power; sometimes sculptures of Nineveh and Persepolis, a lion lions are represented as winged and horned,

and on this account the Lord Himself was pleased to assume the name of "the Lion of the tribe of Judah" (Rev. v. 5). But at another time, a lion is spoken of in an opposite or bad sense, to signify the power of infernal falsity, actuated by a bad motive, which desolates and tears and destroys goodness and truth in man, as in the Psalms: "Save me from the lion's mouth" (xxii. 21). Among other spiritual blessings, therefore, promised to the members of the Lord's true church, it is said, "No lion shall be there, nor any ravenous beast go up thereon; it shall not be found there" (Isa. xxxv. 9).

As a further illustration of this part of our subject, we will consider the signification of the horse. This noble and powerful animal, so graceful in symmetry, so swift in motion, and so eminently serviceable to man, is very frequently spoken of in the Word. When the subject treats of man in the process of regeneration, or is predicated of heaven and the Lord, the horse corresponds to the affection or desire of understanding truth for the sake of eternal use, or the faculty of making progress in spiritual knowledge rationally understood; and, in an opposite sense, when the subject treats of the unregenerate, or is predicated of hell, the horse corresponds to the desire of acquiring knowledge for the sake of self,—the love of self-derived intelligence, under whose perverted and perverting influence vain and conflicting reasonings against truth, and in confirmation of falsity, appear to be the result of intellectual inquiry. Every just description that could be given in regard to the form, the physiology, the instinct, and the various qualities and habitudes of the horse, serves to demonstrate the correctness of this signification. The strength of the horse denotes intellectual power; his fleetness, quickness of intellectual discernment; his form, intellectual beauty; his sagacity, intellectual perception; his snorting, intellectual reasonings; his aptitude for the battle, and his fierceness in the encounter, intellectual skill and contention; his hoofs are mentioned to denote the lowest scientific principles or ultimate of the intellect; the color will denote the various qualities of the understanding; and when yoked to the chariot or wagon, they will represent the power of the understanding associated with varieties of doctrines. In the book of Job (xxxix. 25), therefore, speech and understanding are attributed to the horse, and, in the language of correspondence, a person distinguished for his intellectual endowments, whether he employs them in favor of truth and doctrine derived from the Word of God, or in confirmation of false principles derived from the infernal world and from his own self-intelligence, and,—abstractedly from persons,—the faculty itself, is denominated "a horseman."

If this spiritual signification be applied to the horse wherever it is described or spoken of in the sacred books of the Word, from Genesis to the book of Revelation, we shall always have a consistent, intelligible, and truly edifying sense. For instance, in consequence of man's proneness, by reason of his fallen nature, to depend upon his own prudence and cunning, in preference to the Divine Providence, he is disposed to multiply and trust the vain reasonings and pretexts of a perverted intellect, rather than place confidence in the Divine wisdom and direction from above, that in the spiritual sense of the Word he is forbidden by the Lord "to multiply horses" (Deut. xvii. 16). The divine declaration, "A horse is a vain thing[117] for safety: neither shall

---

[117] *Heb.*, "a lie." The Hebrew word for horse signifies also *to explain*. According to some writers, the horse, among the animal hieroglyphics of Pythagoras, appeared to mean, in one sense, *literary fame*.

"The signification of a horse, as denoting the intellectual principle, was derived from the ancient church to the wise round about, even into Greece; hence it was, that in describing the sun by which is signified love, they placed therein the god of their wisdom and intelligence, and attributed to him a chariot and four fiery horses; and in describing the god of the sea, inasmuch as by sea was signified sciences in general, they also allotted horses to him; hence, too, when they described the birth of the sciences from the intellectual principle, they feigned a flying horse, which with his hoof burst open a fountain, where were virgins who were the sciences; nor was anything else signified by the Trojan horse, but an artful contrivance of the understanding to destroy walls; at this day, indeed, when the intellectual principle is described, agreeably to the custom received from the ancients, it is usually described by a flying horse, or Pegasus, and erudition by a fountain; but it is known scarcely to any one that horse, in a mystical sense, signifies the understanding, and that a fountain signifies truth; still less is it known that these significations were derived from the ancient Church to the Gentiles."—*A. C.* 2762. See also 7729.

The horse, among the Hindoos, was anciently offered in sacrifice. Max Müller says that "there is an entire hymn addressed to the sun as a horse."

"According to Plato, 'the horse signified, in a good sense, reason and opinion, coursing about through natural things,' and 'in a bad sense, a confused fantasy.'"—See *Symb. Comm. of Brixianus*, No. 13. A.D. 1591.

"Bishops on the day of their consecration have been wont to ride on horses covered with white robes, to represent that which we read in the Apocalypse, 'The armies which are in heaven follow Him riding on white horses' (xix. 14). The armies which are in heaven are good and just men and prelates, who, as these heavenly riders do daily follow God in all good works; who, for this reason, are said to be in heaven, because they love and seek after heavenly things above; whence the apostle saith, 'Our conversation is in heaven' (Phil. iii. 20). These armies, that is, good and just prelates, follow Jesus whensoever they vanquish vices in themselves by discipline, in their neighbors by admonition."—*Durandus on Symbolism*, tr. by *Neale and Webb*, p. 177.

"On the 5th December, being Friday, the son of the Sultan of Morocco rode a white horse. When he came in sight, there was a general exclamation from those on the roofs, 'A white horse!' They all turned round and smiled, and beckoned to each other, and general joy seemed to be diffused. The Sultan rides a white horse. The color of the horse denotes the humor of the Prince; white being, of course, that of joy and gladness, and the other shades accordingly. Muley Ismael distinguished thus: When he rode a red horse he had a lancet or sabre; when he rode a black one, a musket and gunpowder. In the *Arabian Nights* there is something like this; in commenting on which, Mr. Lane mentions, and I can also confirm, that the Turks signify anger against any class of their tributaries by issuing the Harutch papers of a red color, and adds: 'To exhibit the striking and dramatic spectacle described by our

he deliver any by his great strength" (Psalm xxxiii. 17), is a most striking form of instruction, in order to impress upon us the utter vanity of mere human reasonings and their inability to effect our deliverance from sin and to obtain the gifts of eternal salvation; the worthlessness of self-dependence, the deceitfulness of self-intelligence; that mere intellectual excellence and confidence are hollow and dangerous, mere intellectual attainment and power, weakness itself; that faith alone, or truth alone, is spurious and impotent, neither conjoining man with God or his neighbor, nor insuring for him any heavenly inheritance. Again, to represent the contrariety which must always exist between trust in God and mere intellectual confidence,—to teach us that, as the Lord's delight is inseparable from his infinite goodness, so He can take no pleasure in man's understanding, however clear, vigorous, and well stored with knowledge, unless it be conjoined with purity of heart and life,—it is said, "The Lord delighteth not in the strength of the horse" (Psalm cxlvii. 10). To express a sincere and humble conviction of the insufficiency, the impotence, and the folly of men placing their dependence for salvation on the selfish reasonings of faith alone, they are exhorted to turn to the Lord, to confess their iniquities, and say unto Him, "Asshur shall not save us; we will not ride upon horses: neither will we say any more to the work of our hands, Ye are our gods: for in thee the fatherless findeth mercy" (Hos. xiv. 3). And in another remarkable passage, "Some trust in chariots, and some in horses: but we will remember the name of the Lord our God. They are brought down and fallen: but we are risen and stand upright" (Psalm xx. 7, 8). In reference to a fallen and degraded state of the church, where her members would become blind as to a right discernment and use of truth, and to signify the opposition with which self-reliance on intellectual power must always be met, before it is finally removed; to rebuke that self-conceit which ever accompanies mere intellectual skill, and to represent the direful condition into which those who cherish such principles will plunge themselves, together with the miserable punishment which

---

author, may, I conceive, be more effective than any words could be.' In this way the black flag of the pirate has been selected, and the red flag of the rover. Next to the flag, the war horse is the shield for this blazon.... The Sultan wore a green bernous, with the hood up. A man on each side fanned him. This hooded people had thrown back the capes of their salams, and the folds of haik from off their heads, so that the aspect of the crowd was suddenly changed, and the universal white was considerably mingled with red and blue. I was much gratified at seeing, even from a distance, the chief of this singular empire, the manner of his march, and the greeting of his people."—*Urquhart's Pillars of Hercules.*

they bring upon their souls, but which appears to their perverted imaginations as the wrathful inflictions of a divine vengeance, it is prophetically said, "The stout-hearted are spoiled, they have slept their sleep: and none of the men of might have found their hands. At thy rebuke, O God of Jacob, both the chariot and horse are cast into a dead sleep" (Psalm lxxvi. 5, 6). "In that day, saith the Lord, I will smite every horse with astonishment, and his rider with madness: and I will open mine eyes upon the house of Judah, and will smite every horse of the people with blindness" (Zech. xii. 4). "Woe to them that go down to Egypt for help; and stay on horses, and trust in chariots because they are many; and in horsemen because they are very strong; but they look not unto the Holy One of Israel, neither seek the Lord!" (Isa. xxxi. 1.)

In Isa. v. 28, the divine judgments threatened against rebellious Israel, and to be accomplished by the agency of the heathen nations, are thus described: "Whose arrows are sharp, and all their bows bent, their horses' hoofs shall be counted like flint, and their wheels like a whirlwind." Where by arrows, or darts and bows, are signified false doctrines, from which combat is waged; by horses are signified things intellectual, in this case perverted; and by their hoofs are denoted falsity in the ultimates of an evil life. And also Ezek. xxvi. 10, 11, where the inspired prophet is speaking of the devastation of Tyre, or the destruction of those who depend for salvation on truth or faith alone, signified by Tyre in a perverted sense, and says, "By reason of the abundance of the horses of the king of Babylon, their dust shall cover thee: thy walls shall shake at the noise of the horsemen, and of the wheels, and of the chariots, when he shall enter into thy gates, as men enter into a city wherein is made a breach. With the hoofs of his horses shall he tread down all thy streets: he shall slay thy people by the sword, and thy strong garrisons shall go down to the ground." Unless spiritual subjects are included in these words, what can they mean? Without an interior sense, would they be anything but expressions of sound, when yet every expression in the Word has weight because from God.—See A. C. 7729; also Micah iv. 13.

In Rev. ix. 17, we have a symbolical description of formidable Euphratean horses, seen in vision by the apostle, in the spiritual world. And from the signification given to horses, we may plainly see that they are spoken of in a perverted sense; that they denote some distinctive religious doctrines, and the pernicious influence of those false reasonings which spring from evil in the heart, by which they are maintained. In this wonderful vision these defiled and mischievous reasonings are here disclosed. Those who cherish them suppose themselves intelligent above others. It is, therefore, the doctrine of faith alone, and momentaneous salvation thence derived, which is here abstractedly but accurately described. The understandings and interior reasonings of such as admit this false and fatal notion are called horses, but monstrous in their forms and destructive in their nature. They are represented as having heads like lions, to denote their ruling fantasies and love of dominion, substituted for genuine wisdom and humility. Out of their mouths are said to issue fire and smoke and brimstone, to signify that their inward sensual thoughts, from whence their words proceed, are nothing but the concealed love of self and the world, signified by fire; the inflated pride of self-conceit, signified by smoke; and the lusts and concupiscences of the merely carnal mind, signified by brimstone. They are said to have tails like serpents, having as their extremities serpents' heads, to describe and represent the crafty fallacies of their reasonings, and to denote their cunning power to persuade and captivate others; and the artifice by which they make the literal sense of the Word appear to confirm their opinions. And it is added, as the resulting effect, that by such perverted reasonings "they do hurt;" that is, they injure goodness and truth in the minds of the well-disposed, and dissipate the importance of obedience, and the necessity of good works, as essential to human salvation.

For a confirmation of this brief and imperfect exposition of what is regarded as a most difficult passage, we have only to turn to Ezek. xxxviii. 22; Psalm xi. 6; Isa. xxxiv. 8–10; Rev. xiv. 9, 10; Deut. xxix. 21–23, and many other places where these representative images are used, and bear a precisely similar signification.

But in a good sense, from the sagacity, beauty, strength, fleetness, and utility of the horse, we may trace out its direct correspondence, and plainly perceive that it signifies the faculties of the intellect in subordination to goodness of heart and life,—the affection of spiritual intelligence, a living desire to receive, to comprehend, and to use the wisdom of God. In this sense the horse is frequently mentioned in association with other animals, and is described by appropriate phrases and epithets. Thus, when He who is the sole fountain of wisdom and intelligence revealed Himself, by a representative of this kind, to the apostle John, "He sat," it is said, "on a white horse;" and his name was called "the Word of God;" and because the angels of heaven receive all their intelligence and illumination from the Lord by means of his Word, therefore it is said that "The armies which were in heaven followed Him upon white horses, clothed in fine linen, white and clean" (Rev. xix. 11, 13, 14). Again, in the holy feast which the Lord provides at his sacred table, the guests are to be "filled with horses and chariots, with mighty men, and with all men of war" (Ezek. xxxix. 20), by which is signified, that when man is prepared to approach the Divine Word, in full reliance on the Lord's mercy, he shall be replenished with all degrees of spiritual intelligence,— enabled to appropriate all needful kinds of heavenly truth and doctrine, and is thence supplied with the requisite strength to vanquish his spiritual foes. In order to represent the union of the love of God in the heart with the attainments of wisdom from his Word in the understanding, as the essential mediums of introducing the soul into a glorious state of heavenly delight and peace, "a chariot of fire, and horses of fire," were seen in the spiritual world by Elisha, at the translation of the prophet Elijah, and, in grief on account of the loss of his master, he exclaimed, "The chariot of Israel, and the horsemen thereof" (2 Kings ii. 11, 12; xiii. 14). Elijah, and afterwards Elisha, were so called, because they represented the internal and external quality of the Word.[118] For such, indeed, are its outward character and inward power, when its burning and shining truths and doctrines of life are received in genuine affection, and obeyed from a sincere faith. They elevate man's soul into heaven, and introduce him into consociation with angels. They surround him with the sphere of divine protection in every time of danger and distress. And could we see, with the organs of spiritual vision, of which the organs of natural sight are the true corresponding forms, like the young man who was alarmed for the safety of his master, Elisha, in the midst of infuriate enemies, we should behold, with the clearness and distinctness of spiritual discernment, the mountain on which he stands "full of horses and chariots of fire round about" him (2 Kings vi. 17). Such are "the horses and chariots of salvation" (Hab. iii. 8) which wait to convey every faithful Christian along the paths of righteousness to his eternal home in the kingdom of God. And to teach us, still further, that the powers of the understanding were designed to be diligently cultivated in all kinds of science and knowledge, and that, in subordination to divine wisdom, they are to be consecrated to the

---

[118] Hence their names, Elijah, *a strong Lord*; and Elisha, *God that saves*.

Lord's service, it is said, "In that day [of the Lord], shall there be upon the bells of the horses, HOLINESS UNTO THE LORD" (Zech. xiv. 20).

In the book of Revelation, which is wholly composed of symbolic writing, arranged by plenary inspiration, even as to every expression, according to the science of correspondences, and which treats only of divine and spiritual subjects, we read that the apostle John was favored with a most magnificent vision, recorded in the 5th and 6th chapters, in which he "saw in the right hand of Him that sat on the throne, a book, written within and on the back side, and sealed with seven seals." He wept that no one was found worthy to open it, but was comforted with the assurance that "the Lion of the tribe of Judah" had "prevailed to open the book, and to loose the seven seals thereof." By this was signified that the Lord Jesus Christ, who is omnipotent and omniscient (Matt. xxviii. 18; John ii. 24, 25), knows and perceives the secrets of every heart, and that to Him judgment belongs, because He alone, as the very divine truth or Word, can reveal the inmost states of the life of all men, both in heaven and upon earth. The opening of the seals, therefore, was designed to signify the revelation that was about to be made of the interior character of all those who approach the Word of God, as to their reception and appropriation, or rejection and profanation of its sacred truths, and the charity and faith which they inspire, together with the quality of their understandings and intelligence. When the first seal was opened, there issued out of the book a white horse; on the opening of the second seal, there proceeded from it a red horse; on the opening of the third seal, there went forth a black horse; and on the opening of the fourth seal, there came out a pale horse. Each horse had its appropriate rider, each of whom was differently equipped, and to each of them a particular divine commission was intrusted. Every single expression in these chapters, like the rest of the inspired Word, has its peculiar significance and application. I can only direct the reader's attention, at this time, to the meaning of the horses.

We have already made some remarks on the signification of colors, as denoting the qualities of those subjects or things treated of; for colors are occasioned by the modifications of heat and light, and the reflection and refraction of their rays by the objects on which they fall, or in which they are received. The colored horses which proceeded out of the book as its seals were successively broken, signify and represent various qualities of the understanding, and the whole is a revelation of the inward states of all who approach the Volume of eternal truth with a desire to know its sacred contents.

The WHITE HORSE and his rider signify the understanding of those who are illustrated by genuine truths, whose translucent purity is denoted by white. These are receptive of a heavenly principle of charity from the Lord, as well as a holy principle of faith. By the power of truth, when thus united to goodness of heart and purity of life, all kinds of evil and falsity are overcome and dissipated. Man goes forth, with the " crown and bow," in the Lord's name, " conquering and to conquer."

The RED HORSE and his rider signify the understanding of those who, while they receive the truth, disregard the goodness of the Word and reject the charity which it inculcates; who, for selfish purposes, occasion contentions and dissensions among men, on the doctrinal tenets and outward forms of religion. In all such, every evil passion and propensity prevails, and they deprive the truth of the Word of its vitality and power. They do violence to love and mercy, and destroy all peace from the earth. That a red color denotes quality as to good or its opposite evil, has been already shown. Hence, to signify the adulteration of all principles of goodness and charity in the perverted church, she is represented as " a harlot " who had forsaken her rightful husband, " arrayed in purple and scarlet, and sitting upon a scarlet-colored beast, full of names of blasphemy " (Rev. xvii. 3, 4). And to denote the extreme perversion and corruption of all truth with such as violate its sanctions by rejecting the sacred principles of charity, even the Lord's vesture is described as being " dipped in blood " (Rev. xix. 13).

By the BLACK HORSE and his rider are signified the understanding of those who wilfully oppose the influence of divine truth,—who falsify and darken its holy counsels by vain and impious reasonings, and induce upon themselves the gloom of eternal ignorance, but who, though they hold all divine instruction concerning what is good and true in lightest estimation, indicated by the balances of justice, and the proclamation of " a measure of wheat for a penny, and three measures of barley for a penny," are yet not permitted to infringe or injure its inward sanctity,—" to hurt either the oil or the wine." The color black denotes the quality of such a state, for we have seen that it signifies the darkness and obscurity of falsity and evil.

By the PALE HORSE, and its rider, *Death*, are manifestly signified all who approach the Holy Word, but without understanding anything of its transcendent glories, because they are in confirmed states of evil, both of heart and life. Though they have a name to live, they are dead (Rev. iii. 1). They hear and learn the truth, and profess to love it, but utterly destroy its life in themselves, and endeavor to deprive all around them of its health-restoring energy and consoling influence. For paleness is the color of a corpse, and denotes the absence of all spiritual life. To describe the miserable result of such direful profanation, and the hopeless end of such insane conduct, it is said that "hell followed;" for persistence in so dreadful a course conjoins man, here and hereafter, with infernal spirits, hastens the judgment by speedily and certainly filling up the measure of his iniquities, and plunges him, from his own free choice, into a state of spiritual death. Similar things are also signified by the chariots and colored horses which the prophet Zechariah saw in vision and described (Zech. i. 8; vi. 1-8).

Now this signification of a horse, as denoting the intellectual faculty, and the result of its active energies and its powers of memory and reasoning, might be extensively illustrated and confirmed from the Grecian mythology.

"The signification of the horse," says Swedenborg, "as expressive of understanding, was derived from the ancient churches to the wise men round about. How much the ancients excelled the moderns in intelligence may be manifest from this consideration, that the former knew to what things in heaven several things in the world corresponded, and hence what they signified; and this was not only known to those who were of the church, but also to those who were out of the church, as to the inhabitants of Greece, the most ancient of whom described things by significatives, which at this day are called fabulous, because they are altogether unknown; that the ancient Sophi were in the knowledge of such things is evident. Hence it was, that, when they would describe the sun, in which they placed their god of wisdom and intelligence, they attributed to it a chariot and four horses of fire; and when they would describe the god of the sea [Neptune, to whom more power was ascribed than to any other god except Jupiter], since by the sea was signified sciences derived from understanding, they also attributed horses to him; and when they would describe the origin of intelligence and wisdom, or the rise of the sciences from understanding, they also feigned a winged horse, which they called Pegasus, whose hoof broke open a fountain, at which sat nine virgins called the sciences, and this upon a hill." [The nine liberal arts were called muses, either from the similarity of their intellectual origin, or because men, by inquiring of them, learned the things of which they before were ignorant.] For from the ancient churches they received the knowledge that the horse signifies the intellectual principle of understanding; his wings, the spiritual principle of spiritual truth; the hoof, what is scientific derived from understanding, or truth in the ultimate sense, where is the origin of intelligence; virgins, the sciences; a hill, unanimity, and, in the spiritual sense, charity; and a fountain, doctrine from which sciences are derived; and so in all other cases. [Minerva, the goddess of wisdom, is figured on some medals as drawn in a chariot by four horses. Mars, the god of war, is frequently described as rushing forth in a chariot drawn by furious war-horses; and Oceanus, also, who presided over rivers and fountains, was drawn by fabulous sea-horses supplied with wings]. Nor is there anything else signified by the Trojan horse than an artificial contrivance devised by their understanding for the purpose of destroying the walls. Even at this day, when understanding is described after the manner received from those ancients, it is usual to figure it by a flying horse, or Pegasus; so, likewise, doctrine is described by a fountain, and the sciences by virgins; but scarcely any one knows that the horse, in the mystic sense, signifies the understanding; still less, that those significatives were derived to the gentiles from the ancient representative churches.[119]—W. H. 4; A. C. 7729.

---

[119] "The sun signifies the Lord as to his divine love. But when the science of correspondences became corrupted and obliterated, the worship of the sun as an idol became almost universal. Many remnants of sun worship may be traced in the names of places, in many customs which we know to have existed, and in many which are still observed. We have Sunday, as the vulgar name of the first day of the week. From this arose the custom of making bonfires on the first night of May (*Morris's Ireland*, pp. 20, 23), and the aborigines of Ireland call the previous eve, 'La Bealtine,' or the 'day of Belen's fire.' The word *Beltein* is also a name given to a fair held in Peebles, in Scotland, at the beginning of May, and is said to signify 'the feast of the sun,' which was once observed at that season."—*Lawson's Dis.*, p. 277.

"It is to be noted that the scientifics of the ancients were altogether other than the scientifics at this day; they treated concerning the correspondences of things in the natural world with things in the spiritual world. The scientifics, which at this day are called philosophics, such as are those of Aristotle and the like, were unknown to them: this is also evident from the books of the earlier writers, several of which are written in such terms as signified, represented, and corresponded to interior things. That this was the case may be manifest from the following considerations, amongst others which might be mentioned, viz., that they assigned to Helicon a place on a mountain, and by it they meant heaven; that they assigned to Parnassus a place beneath on a hill, and by it they meant scientifics; that they asserted that a flying horse, which they called Pegasus, did there break open a fountain with his hoof; that they called the sciences virgins, and so forth; for they knew from correspondences and representatives, that a mountain denoted heaven, that a hill denoted that heaven which is beneath, or which is with man, that a horse denoted the intellectual principle, that the wings with which he flew were spiritual things, that a hoof was the natural principle, that

The Hindoos attribute seven horses to the sun. The Oriental nations, who worshipped the sun, not only represented him as riding along the sky in a chariot drawn by the fleetest and most beautiful horses, to communicate his light and warmth to the world; but, when all idea of correspondence was lost, they consecrated to the sun the finest steeds and chariots, and, as the sun arose, rode to the eastern gates of their cities to pay their homage. The Jews at one time became infected with this species of idolatry; for we read that Josiah "took away the horses that the kings of Judah [his predecessors] had given [or consecrated] to the sun, at the entering in of the house of the Lord [or the court of the temple towards the east], and burned

---

a fountain was intelligence, and that the three virgins, who were called Charites, were the affections of good, and that the virgins, who were named the virgins of Helicon and Parnassus, were the affections of truth. In like manner they assigned to the sun horses, whose meat they called ambrosia, and drink nectar; for they knew that the sun signified celestial love, horses the intellectual things which are thence derived, and that meats signify celestial things, and drinks spiritual. By derivation from the ancients also, it is still a custom that kings, at their coronation, should sit upon a silver throne, should be clad in a purple robe, be anointed with oil, should wear on their heads a crown, and carry in their hands a sceptre, a sword and keys, should ride in royal pomp on a white horse, under whose feet should be hoofs of silver, and should be waited on at table by the most respectable personages of the kingdom, besides other ceremonies; for they knew that a king represented the divine truth which is from the divine good, and hence they knew what is signified by a silver throne, a purple robe, anointing oil, a crown, a sceptre, a sword, keys, a white horse, hoofs of silver, and being waited upon by the most respectable personages. Who at this day is in possession of this knowledge, and where are the scientifics which teach it? The above ceremonies are called emblematical, from an entire ignorance of everything relating to correspondence and representation. From these considerations it is manifest of what quality the scientifics of the ancients were, and that those scientifics led them into knowledge concerning things spiritual and celestial, the very existence of which also at this day is scarcely known. The scientifics which succeeded in place of the above, and which are properly called philosophies, rather draw the mind away from the knowledge of spiritual and celestial things, because they may be applied also to confirm falsities, and likewise cast the mind into darkness when truths are confirmed by them, inasmuch as several of them are bare expressions, whereby confirmations are effected, which are apprehended by few, and concerning which even those few are not agreed. Hence it may appear evident how far mankind have receded from the erudition of the ancients, which led to wisdom. The gentiles derived the above scientifics from the ancient Church, the external worship of which consisted in representatives and significatives, and the internal in those things which were represented and signified."—*A. C.* n. 4966.

"Royalty and government were, from the earliest times, distinguished by symbolical insignia."—*Jones's Lect. on Fig. Lang. of Scripture*, p. 260.

"In their representative processions, the Chinese still carry, at the end of long silver rods, figures in silver of strange animals, hands, scales, fishes, and other mysterious things."—*Bernier: Pinkerton's Coll.*, vol. viii., p. 201.

"Symbols [in the Sacred Scriptures] are often borrowed from the lower parts of creation, such as animals, mountains, seas, rivers, and the like. And the signification of them is founded (according to the notions which the ancients had of their natures, magnitudes, uses, etc.) upon the principle of affinity and similitude."—*Bictero's Signs of the Times*, App., p. 219.

Swedenborg has expounded the entire Book of the Revelation, sentence by sentence, in two admirable works, entitled, *Apocalypse Revealed*, two vols., and *Apocalypse Explained*, a posthumous publication in six volumes.

In a Brahmanic legend, a fish is represented as instructing Manu in his first incarnation in all kinds of knowledge.

the chariots of the sun with fire" (2 Kings xxiii. 11). Nor is this recorded in the Word merely for the sake of the history, but in order to teach us that all spiritual idolatry must be renounced and forsaken, that the soul may become the chosen temple of Jehovah's presence and blessing, and that man may "worship Him," as the Sun of Righteousness, "in spirit and in truth."

The signification of other animals might be as distinctly proved as that we have been considering. Let it be admitted, then, that there is a correspondence between animals and the principles constituent of the mind, both in this world and in another, and we shall at once perceive the reason why animals were seen in the spiritual world in the visions of the prophets and apostles, many of which were unlike any existing in this world, and why the prevailing dispositions of the mind are, in the Word, called doves and owls, lambs and wolves, sheep and dogs, etc. We shall then read a lesson of holiest wisdom in the divine promise that believers should "take up serpents" (Mark xvi. 18), and "tread upon serpents" (Luke x. 19). We shall see how, in the regeneration, the varied affections and desires of the mind, with their delights, spiritual and natural, rational and sensual, are brought under the benign, the peaceful, the harmonious influences of the Lord and heaven, in which "The wolf shall dwell with the lamb, and the leopard shall lie down with the kid; and the calf and the young lion and the fatling together; and a little child shall lead them. And the cow and the bear shall feed; their young ones shall lie down together: and the lion shall eat straw like the ox. And the sucking child shall play on the hole of the asp, and the weaned child shall put his hand on the cockatrice' den." "The wolf and the lamb shall lie down together: and dust shall be the serpent's meat" (Isa. xi. 6–8; lxv. 25); also why it is promised that "a man shall nourish a young cow and two sheep" (Isa. vii. 21); and why, again, they are pronounced blessed "who sow beside all waters, and send forth thither the feet of the ox and the ass" (Isa. xxxii. 20). You will at once understand, too, that the covenant which God is said to make with beasts and birds and creeping things of the earth, means his eternal covenant with man's immortal soul, or with all the affections and thoughts and faculties of both the internal and external mind, represented by the various orders of animals. Read the following inspired passage with this exalted view, and without further explanation you will find it filled with beauty, sublimity, wisdom, and life, worthy of Him who is its Divine Author. "In that day, I, Jehovah, will make a covenant for them [my people] with the beasts of the field, and with the fowls of heaven, and with the creeping things of the ground: and I will betroth thee unto me in righteousness, and in judgment, and in loving kindness, and in mercies. I will even betroth thee unto me in faithfulness, and thou shalt know the Lord" (Hos. ii. 18-20).

When the affections of the heart rise towards the Lord, and manifest themselves in the exalted love of the neighbor, and when the thoughts of the understanding find their true and permanent abode in the same elevated and heavenly principles, they derive their internal character and quality from the Lord, and are said to be known to Him,—that is, acknowledged as proceeding from Him; then, in the language of correspondence, He is represented as saying, "Every beast of the forest is mine, and the cattle upon a thousand hills. I know all the fowls upon the mountains and the wild beasts of the field are mine" (Ps. l. 10, 11).

CHAPTER XIV.

Correspondence of the Vegetable World, with Illustrations.

THE objects and productions of the vegetable kingdom of nature, of which growth, but neither sensation nor locomotion, is predicable, are, equally with those of the animal kingdom, used in the Word of God as the appropriate representative forms and correspondences of holy and spiritual subjects and objects, or their opposites.[120] Thus, shrubs and flowers, herbs and trees in general, "from the cedar-tree in Lebanon, even unto the hyssop that springeth out of the wall" (1 Kings iv. 33); "from the rose of Sharon to the lily of the valley" (Cant. iii. 1); all "trees pleasant to the sight and good for food" (Gen. ii. 9); "thorns, also, and thistles" (Gen. iii. 19); nettles and brambles (Isa. xxxiv. 13); wormwood and hemlock, correspond to or represent the countless things of intelligence, observance, and knowledge both true and false, wholesome and pernicious, and to

---

[120] Jupiter's statue was made of oak; and Tacitus affirms that in Germany the images of the gods consisted of rude trunks of *unpolished oak.*—*Potter's Antiq.*, vol. i., p. 191. Isa. xl. 20.

Robust is from the Latin word, *robur*, strength, and which is the name for an oak. The Hebrew word for oak also denotes strength.

In the age when the science of correspondences and all true religion became corrupted into idolatry, "trees were the original temples of the gods; they were also the symbols or images of them; and their several attributes were expressed by several trees, which were perpetually appropriated to their respective deities, and called by their names: and therefore addressed and appealed to, as if they had themselves the attributes and powers of their prototypes, to hear the covenants made in their presence, and punish the violators of them."—*Dr. Gloster Ridley's Notes on Melampus*, p. 259. London, 1781.

It must not be overlooked that plants and vegetables, including those of even the most noxious kinds, like the doctrines and truths adapted to the various natural and sensual principles of the mind to which they correspond, are capable of being overruled for use and service to man, as well as being capable of abuse. Such is especially the case with all plants possessing medicinal qualities. A justly celebrated author remarks, that "If a stranger had visited a wandering tribe before one property of herbalism was known to them; if he had told the savages that the herbs which every day they trampled under foot were endowed with the most potent virtues,—that one would restore to health a brother on the verge of death, that another would paralyze to idiocy their wisest sage, that a third would strike lifeless to the dust their most stalwart champion; that tears and laughter, vigor and disease, madness and reason, wakefulness and sleep, existence and dissolution were coiled up in those unregarded leaves,—would they not have held him a sorcerer and a liar? To half the virtues of the vegetable world mankind are yet in the darkness of the savages I have supposed. There are faculties within us with which certain herbs have an affinity, and over which they have power. The Moly of the ancients was not all a fable."—*Bulwer's Zanoni*, vol. iii.

innumerable kinds and degrees of doctrine and persuasion which may be implanted, germinate, and fructify within the mind, together with the thoughts, perceptions, and affections which belong thereto. They are, so to speak, the outward emblems, the diversified forms, and natural types of existences in the spiritual world and the world of mind. This may, in a great measure, be confirmed from the physiology, colors, properties, qualities, and uses of flowers, plants, and trees; their respective productions, and the different localities where they are found.

Trees, as a whole, or in their complex, denote such principles as pertain to the entire mind and life, and also such as are thence derived, of a lower degree, or having a less degree of spiritual life, than those signified by animals. Gardens, vineyards, olive-yards, forests, groves, and meadows, denote various degrees and states of intelligence and wisdom, doctrine and knowledge. This is indicated by the very names of the trees in the representative garden of Eden, for one is called "the tree of life," and the other "the tree of *knowledge* of good and evil" (Gen. ii. 9); hence, also, we read of "trees of righteousness" (Isa. lxi. 3), and "trees of the Lord" (Ps. civ. 16).

The roots of plants and trees, hidden beneath the ground, will signify the faculties of exploring the Word, and of acquiring thence, and retaining in the outward memory, whatever knowledge is congenial to the mind, and desired for its support, and also the principle of charity as the base of genuine wisdom; or, in a contrary sense, of perverting knowledge to selfish purposes, and making it the ground of fanaticism and folly. We therefore see what is meant where the Lord, speaking by the mouth of his prophet, describes man delivered from his spiritual enemies, under the expressive name of Amorites, and says, "Yet destroyed I the Amorite before them, whose height *was* like the height of the cedars, and he *was* strong as the oaks; yet I destroyed his fruit from above, and his roots from beneath" (Amos ii. 9); and where the seed having no root,—that is, no ground in charity,—withers away (Mark iv. 6). The stem and the branches denote the truths or false principles themselves, combined or separate, and in the act of being confirmed (Ps. lxxx. 11). The leaves, which are either perennial or evergreen, are, as it were, the organs of respiration to the vegetative soul, and denote internal or external knowledge and doctrine; thus also faith, which, when alone, is described as a tree with leaves only, and is therefore condemned (Matt. xxi. 19). The fruits which are the ultimate effects, and the very purpose of the vital faculty, containing the seeds, in which are the primary germs of a new generation, signify all kinds and degrees of good and useful works, made manifest in a righteous life, and their corresponding rational delights, or of evil works, rendered obvious in a corrupt life, and their corresponding sensual pleasures,—heavenly works, produced from the pure and exalted love of God and man, or infernal works, fabricated from impure motives, prompted by the love of self and the world. In these works are either the elemental germs of a glorious progression in the rich blessings of charity and faith, extending even into eternal ages, or, on the contrary, of the multiplication of evil and folly, and their attendant and endless miseries (Jer. xv. 16). Thus the Lord, speaking of false prophets and of false persuasions and doctrines, says, "Ye shall know them by their fruits. Do men gather grapes of thorns, or figs of thistles? Even so every good tree bringeth forth good fruit; but a corrupt tree bringeth forth evil fruit. A good tree cannot bring forth evil fruit, neither can a corrupt tree bring forth good fruit. Every tree that bringeth not forth good fruit is hewn down, and cast into the fire. Wherefore, by their fruits ye shall know them" (Matt. vii. 16–20). And again: "Either make the tree good, and his fruit good; or else make the tree corrupt, and his fruit corrupt: for the tree is known by his fruit" (Matt. xii. 33).

Flowers of multifarious form and brilliancy of hue signify, in a good sense, intellectual perceptions and their indefinite delights; while their variations, in quality and degree, are denoted by their configurations, colors, odors, and other properties.[121]

---

[121] The poetic language of flowers is but an imaginary symbolism, which may be regarded as an outbirth of their correspondence, and indicates its loss. Thus, Dr. Standenmaier observes. "On the earth, too, in infinite numbers, shine forth the flowers, the gracious children of the Spring, decked out in all the brilliancy of colors, while they shed their soft balmy breath, like incense, through the air; and these lovely children, O youth, have they never addressed thee in a soft tender voice? Oh! assuredly, God hath given them a language to address us, and the language of flowers was ever, for reflective minds, a beautiful tongue. But this mysterious sense, which everywhere pervades and manifests itself through all creation, what is it else but a sense of the eternal and the divine? All flowers,—those luminous stars sown in the grass,—are, like the stars above them, letters for the great name of the Eternal, which mortals cannot utter or pronounce. Each manifests to thee his omnipotence, wisdom, goodness, and love; each is a gentle revelation of the Deity. And as thou, O youth, hast a divine principle, canst recognize, seek, revere, and love the God who hath given it thee; so have these flowers, in particular, much to say to thee. Contemplate their innocent nature, their still existence, their calm workings according to eternal laws, and consider, moreover, how lovingly they turn to the sun, how humbly they bow before him to imbibe strength and vigor and life from his rays, and to borrow all their lustre from the splendor of his beams. *The great Sun, Divine Love,* hath given them to us to excite corresponding love in our breasts, as they themselves, in love and joy, turn to the sun, the source

Among the ornamental and useful trees of paradise were those "*pleasant to the sight*," signifying the perceptions of such truths as were designed to afford inmost gratification to the understanding and reason; and esculent trees, or trees bearing delicious and nourishing fruit, called "*trees good for food*" (Gen. ii. 9), to signify the perceptions of goodness intended more immediately to invigorate and delight the affections and dispositions of the will. How vividly and how beautifully does Swedenborg illustrate the true nature of the divinely inspired writings from the correspondences of the vegetable world, in the following brief but interesting passage:

"The Word is like a garden which may be called a heavenly paradise, containing delicacies and delights of every kind, delicacies of fruits and delights of flowers, in the midst of which are trees of life, and beside them fountains of living water, and forest trees round about the garden. Whoever is principled in divine truths, by virtue of doctrine, is in the midst of the garden, among the trees of life, and in the actual enjoyment of its delicacies and delights. When a man is not principled in truths by virtue of doctrine, but only from the literal sense, he abides in the boundaries of the garden, and sees nothing but forest scenery; but when a man is in the doctrine of a false religion, and has confirmed its falsities in his mind, he is not even in the forest, but in a sandy plain without, where there is not even grass." "The man who leads himself, judges of that paradise, which is the Word, from its circumference, where are the trees of the forest; but the man whom the Lord leads, judges of it from the midst thereof, where are the trees of life. The man whom the Lord leads is also actually in that midst, and looks upward to the Lord; but the man who leads himself sits down in the circumference, and looks outward to the world."—T. C. R. 259; A. E. 1072.

There are those vegetables, also, mentioned in the Word, whose specific signification depends upon their productions. Such are the

---

of light" [and heat].—*Symbolical Language of Flowers: Dublin Review*, 1842.

"Each plant [in a good sense] is the image of a divine thought, which presents itself to our eyes under a material image, corresponding to its moral [or spiritual] sense."—*M. de Courcelles: Traité des Symboles*, p. 16.

It was doubtless from the remains of the science of correspondences that the ancient Phœnicians and Celtic Druids held the oak and oak-groves in such veneration. Some writers derive the word Druid from the Greek word δρυς, an oak; but it is most probably derived from a more ancient source. In their own language, the word *Druidh* means *wise men*; others derive it from *Derwydd*, or *Dar wydd*, the British term, from *Derw*, or rather *Dar*, the male oak. But it is as possible that the oak received its peculiar name from the sacred admiration with which it was regarded. Bardd, translated Bard, literally signifies one that illustrates, master of wisdom.—*William Owen*.

medicinal plants, as the aloe and the balm of Gilead; the vestuary, as the cotton-tree and flax, etc. Now, if we attentively survey the characteristics and uses which thus distinguish the genera, and even species, of herbs and trees, they will materially assist us in perceiving and confirming the signification of each. Nothing, for instance, can more fitly represent a weak condition of faith, when grounded in the mere appearances of the letter of the Holy Word, and, in an opposite sense, of mere faith alone, destitute of all vital influence and power, than the elastic but feeble reed, on the river's bank, shaken by every wind. Yet such is the fulness of divine mercy, that we are assured by the Lord that He will not "break the bruised reed" (Isa. xlii. 3; Matt. xii. 20); "He will strengthen the weak hands, and confirm the feeble knees" (Isa. xxxv. 3). In the opposite sense, by a bruised reed is signified an external, irresolute faith,—faith separate from charity, and its weak and miserable delusions, on which no one can rely without danger. "Behold," says the prophet, "thou trustest upon the staff of this bruised reed, even upon Egypt, on which if a man lean, it will go into his hand and pierce it" (2 Kings xviii. 21; Isa. xxxvi. 6). But a firm and true faith, rooted and grounded in love, and the perceptions thence derived, will be signified by the nobler, stronger, and more durable productions of the vegetable tribes. Thus, where faith derived from charity, in the internal man, becomes operative in the external, and is intellectually and rationally confirmed by scientific knowledge into conscientious conviction, it is signified by the gnarled but majestic oak, whose branches form an umbrageous retreat, and whose roots strike deep into the solid earth. Such faith, perception, and conscience, however powerful, are comparatively of a low order; they are represented, therefore, by a tree, which, though distinguished for its strength and vitality, yet produces no fruit suitable for human food. Such was the signification of an oak, when Joshua renewed the covenant between the Lord and Israel: "He took a great stone, and set it up under an oak" (Josh. xxiv. 26), to represent the steadfastness of that covenant on the part of God, and the fidelity with which it ought to be observed on the part of man. Such was also the signification of the oak groves of Mamre, where Abraham, Isaac, and Jacob sojourned (Gen. xxxv. 27); and on this signification is grounded the reason why the angel who appeared unto Gideon in the world of spirits was seen sitting under the shade of an oak (Judg. vi. 11). In a bad sense, however, an oak signifies the sensual confidence and presumptuous boastings of the natural mind, under the influence of which man idolizes and worships his own intellect as real power. In the expressive language of the prophet, "He heweth down and taketh the oak, which he strengtheneth for himself among the trees of the forest: he maketh a god and worshippeth it; he maketh it a graven image, and falleth down thereto, and prayeth unto it, and saith, Deliver me, for thou art my god" (Isa. xliv. 14–17). And, further, to denote that such vanity will in the end expose its deluded victims to derision, and in the hour of trial will wither forever away, it is said, "They shall be ashamed of the oaks which ye have desired, and ye shall be confounded for the gardens that ye have chosen. For ye shall be as an oak whose leaf fadeth" (Isa. i. 29, 30).

When the church is spoken of in the Word, as to the reception of goodness and truth of a celestial quality or degree, mention is always made of the olive-tree. This goodly tree, with its outspreading branches, which flourishes only in warm and sunny situations, which with its products constituted some of the riches of Judea, and from whose fruit a fragrant and valuable oil is extracted, signifies the celestial principles of love to God and charity towards all men, derived from God's infinite love towards his creatures.[122] In reference to such a characteristic, it is said, "The Lord called thy name, A green olive-tree, fair, and of goodly fruit" (Jer. xi. 16). In the prophetic visions of Zechariah, he saw in the spiritual world two olive-trees by the golden candlesticks, one upon the right side of the bowl, and the other upon the left side thereof, which were representative of these celestial principles, and of which the angel said, "These are the two anointed ones,[123] that stand by the Lord of the whole earth" (Zech. iv. 3, 14). The same principles were also signified by the two witnesses seen in vision by the apostle John, of which he says, "These are the two olive-trees, and the two candlesticks standing before the God of the earth" (Rev. xi. 4). On account of this signification of the olive, the oil was, by divine command, the principal ingredient employed for the purpose of anointing priests and kings, when conse-

---

[122] The olive-tree, from the effect of its oil in suppling, relaxing, and preventing and mitigating pain, seems to have been adopted from the earliest period as an emblem of the benignity of the divine nature, whence olive branches became the emblems of peace to various and distant nations.—See *Carpenter's Scripture Natural History*, p. 418.

Peace and reconciliation, the offspring of love, have from most ancient times been symbolized by an olive-branch. From the Greek word for olive was derived the Greek word for mercy.—See *Harris's Natural History of the Bible*, English edition, p. 285.

[123] Heb., *sons of oil.*

crated to their holy and responsible offices, and also for the anointing of the sacred vessels of the tabernacle and temple. In the Mosaic ritual the people were commanded to present it to Jehovah in several of the free-will offerings of their representative worship; and it was used, by divine direction, for supplying the golden lamps in which the lights were to be kept burning continually before the Lord (Lev. xxiv. 2–4); teaching us that when the true worship of the Lord is celebrated in the inner temple of the soul, the oil of divine love is always given to cause the lamps of truth and doctrine to burn before the Lord in a constantly-ascending flame of love to God and benevolence to man, made visibly manifest in a charitable and useful life. So, when the Psalmist speaks of his growth in the celestial life of love and charity, which blesses, imbues, and sanctifies the inmost of the soul, and expresses his gratitude to the Lord for this precious gift of his love, he says, "I am like a green olive-tree in the house of God" (Psalm lii. 8); and, again, "Thou anointest my head with oil" (Psalm xxiii. 5).

When the true signification of oil is known, the miraculous increase of the widow's oil by Elisha the prophet, recorded in 2 Kings iv., may be seen, in every particular of the inspired history, to be an exact representation of the influx of divine love into the affections, for the support of spiritual life, in all seasons of temptation, peril, and distress; for it is the life of heaven in the soul, which induces unwavering confidence, brings sweetest satisfaction, vivifies all the principles of the mind, and saves from spiritual death. It was from this signification of oil, as denoting the heavenly principles of love and charity, that under the Jewish representative economy, priests, prophets, and kings were consecrated to their respective offices and functions by being anointed with a holy ointment,[124] made by divine direction according to the skilful art of the apothecary (Ex. xxx. 25), and of which olive oil was the chief ingredient, to denote that in the administration of all the ecclesiastical and civil affairs of the kingdom, and in the exercise of the authority and talents and ministry intrusted to their charge, they were to be inwardly imbued with the holy affections of love and charity, and that all the governing principles of the mind and life were to be consecrated by the unction of

---

[124] The Hebrew word, Messiah, and the corresponding Greek word, Christ, literally mean "anointed."
Similar things are signified, if all such passages are interpreted in their individual sense, in which priests and kings signify and represent the governing principles of mind and life.

these precious principles. Hence we read, "Behold, how good and how pleasant it is for brethren to dwell together in unity! It is like the precious ointment upon the head, that ran down upon the beard, even Aaron's beard; that went down to the skirts of his garments" (Ps. cxxxiii. 1, 2). The Lord's love for man, and man's love of the Lord and of his neighbor, are "the oil of gladness" (Ps. xlv. 7), and "the oil of joy" (Isa. lxi. 3).

Again, in the beautiful and impressive parable of the ten virgins with their lamps (Matt. xxv. 1–13), designed by our blessed Lord and Saviour to set before us the efforts and qualifications necessary to obtain a blessed and everlasting state of conjunction with Him, and of association with the angels of his kingdom, we are told that the lamps of the five foolish virgins were extinguished for want of oil in their vessels, to teach us the all-important lesson, that however brilliantly the flame of truth may appear to shine upon us for a season, irradiating all around with its brightness, yet, unless it be constantly supplied with the pure oil of celestial love, it will soon go out, and leave us shrouded in thickest darkness; and that unless we obtain this sacred principle from its own source,—the abiding love of the Lord Jesus Christ in our souls,—and earnestly labor to make it our own by works of penitence, obedience, and charity, the door of the nuptial chamber will be eternally closed against us. Our protestations and importunities will be unavailing, and the awful sentence will go forth against us, "Verily, I say unto you, I know you not." On the other hand, if in our vessels with our lamps we are abundantly supplied from the Lord with his precious oil,—if the affections of our hearts are receptive of the celestial gifts of love and charity,—then will the light of heavenly truth burn more and more brilliantly upon our path; and when in the midnight conflict of temptation we hear the sudden and startling cry, "Behold the bridegroom cometh, go ye out to meet him," we shall be prepared to obey the summons, to arise and trim our lamps, and to enter with our Lord into the secure and blissful marriage chamber of heaven.

When the church, or a man of the church, as to goodness and truth of a spiritual character or degree, is spoken of, it is signified by a vine, which is the noblest plant of the creeping kind, celebrated for its tendency to extend its roots and branches without limit, for its rich clusters of fruit, and for the wines which are obtained therefrom, and "make glad the heart of man" (Psalm civ. 15). And in reference to the establishment of the church by the Lord, and the derivation of all its constituent principles from Him, both in general and in particular, He says, "I am the true vine" (John xv. 1); and the Psalmist, evidently speaking of the Israelitish church, says, "Thou hast brought a vine out of Egypt: thou hast cast out the heathen and planted it. Thou preparedst room before it, and didst cause it to take deep root, and it filled the land. The hills were covered with the shadow of it, and the boughs thereof were like the goodly cedars. She sent out her boughs unto the sea, and her branches unto the river" (Psalm lxxx. 8–11). To represent a state of apostasy of this church, or of any of her members, and the sad and destructive results which, though they spring from the ascendancy of false and evil persuasions and lusts, appear to be the consequences of Divine displeasure, it is added, "Why hast thou then broken down her hedges, so that all they which pass by the way do pluck her? The boar out of the wood doth waste it, and the wild beast of the field doth devour it" (12, 13). He then supplicates the Lord's mercy for its restoration in these words, "Return, we beseech thee, O God of hosts: look down from heaven, and behold, and visit this vine; and the vineyard which thy right hand hath planted, and the branch which thou madest strong for thyself" (14, 15).

Similar things are described in the prophecy of Isaiah, where the church in general, and every member thereof in particular, is treated of under the type of a vineyard, which, though gifted with every blessing, and protected from all enemies, so as to afford it the most ample opportunity of yielding richest fruits, in correspondence with the divine care bestowed upon it, yet it only brought forth the bitter clusters of the wild grape. "Now I will sing to my well-beloved [saith the Lord], a song of my beloved touching his vineyard. My well-beloved hath a vineyard in a very fruitful hill; and he fenced it, and gathered out the stones thereof, and planted it with the choicest vine, and built a tower in the midst of it, and also made a wine-press therein: and he looked that it should bring forth grapes, and it brought forth wild grapes. And now, O inhabitants of Jerusalem, and men of Judah, judge, I pray you, betwixt me and my vineyard. What could have been done more to my vineyard, that I have not done in it? wherefore, when I looked that it should bring forth grapes, brought it forth wild grapes? And now go to; I will tell you what I will do to my vineyard: I will take away the hedge thereof, and it shall be eaten up; and break down the wall thereof, and it shall be trodden down: and I will lay it waste: it shall not be pruned, nor digged; but there shall come up briers and thorns: I will also command the clouds that they rain no rain upon it. For the vineyard of the Lord of hosts is the house of Israel, and the men of Judah his pleasant plant: and He looked for judgment, but behold oppression; for righteousness, but behold a cry" (Isa. v. 1–7).

When the elemental principles of the church, both in general and in particular, are described in regard to natural goodness and truth with their delights, or their opposites, then we have mention made of fig-trees, fig-leaves, and figs. The correspondence of these fruit-trees may be confirmed from the circumstances that they flourish in barren and stony situations, where little else would grow, and do not properly blossom, but shoot out their fruit even before the leaves appear. Thus, when the prophet is speaking of the defect of that natural usefulness which precedes the attainment of spiritual knowledge,—the good fruits of external faith and charity, thus of the want of mutual affection and simple obedience in the church and in man,—he says, "There shall be no figs on the fig-tree, and the leaf shall fade" (Jer. viii. 13). And when, again, a flourishing state of the church is spoken of, or man in a state of regeneration, when the fruits of a good life by keeping the divine commandments are abundant, then it is said, "The fig-tree yields its strength" (Joel ii. 22).

Fruits correspond to works, either good or evil, according to their kind, and agreeably to the subject of which they are predicated; and leaves to knowledges and truths thence derived, either genuine or falsified. The sweet fruit of the fig-tree signifies natural goodness, or goodness in an external form, such as is manifested in an outwardly moral life. But the works of morality may be done from vile and impure, as well as from righteous and pure, motives, from hypocrisy as well as from sincerity. This important distinction which obtains among the members of the professing church, and between the principles constituent of the natural mind, as to the inward quality of a moral life, is thus described in a vision of the prophet Jeremiah: "The Lord showed me, and, behold, two baskets of figs were set before the temple of the Lord. One basket had very good figs, even like the figs that are first ripe; and the other basket had very naughty figs, which could not be eaten, they were so bad. Then said the Lord unto me, What seest thou, Jeremiah? And I said, Figs; the good figs very good; and the bad, very bad, that cannot be eaten, they are so bad" (xxiv. 1–3). When the outward works of the church or of man are corrupt,—prompted by utter selfishness, defiled by loathsome covetousness,—they are "like vile figs that cannot be eaten." And when, by transgression, man lost, or still loses, his innocence and integrity, he is represented in the Word as vainly attempting to screen his nakedness and guilt by sewing "fig-leaves" together,—as endeavoring to hide his inward depravity by the hypocritical veil of a mere external conformity to the outward decencies of life,—framing doctrines from the letter of the Word to excuse his unclean lusts, and to cover the pride of self-love. On account of this signification of the fig-tree and its fruit, and in order to represent to us that the Lord knows by his truth and constantly explores the real state of the church, and the interior quality of all her members, He was pleased to perform, when He sojourned on earth, a striking miracle on a barren fig-tree, which was a type of the church at its end, and which, exhibiting an exuberance of leaves, ought also to have borne a proportionate abundance of fruit. The Lord hungered,[125] to denote his

---

[125] Origen says that "in the righteous, Jesus is always hungry, being desirous to eat the fruit of the Holy Spirit in them."—*In Matt., Trac.* xxx.

"There is a wonderful significance in the simple image running through the whole of Scripture, according to which men are compared to trees, and their work to fruit; the fruit being the organic product and evidence of the inner life, not something arbitrarily attached or fastened on from without."—*Trench's Notes on the Parables*, p. 348. (See Ps. i. 3; Jer. xvii. 8; John xv. 2, 4, 5; Rom. vii. 4.)

That is, the time of gathering ripe figs, or the time of fig-harvest, was not yet arrived, so that the tree, bearing an abundance of leaves, ought also to have borne fruit. In the original there is no expression answering to the word *yet*; or, probably, like the fig-tree cumbering the ground (Luke xiii. 6-9), the tree here spoken of might have been always barren, and would have so continued.

"How barren a tree is he who lives, and spreads, and cumbers the ground, yet leaves not one seed, not one good work to generate after him. I know all men cannot leave alike, yet all may leave something, answering their proportion, their kinds."—*Owen Feltham.*

No little discussion and diversity of opinion among commentators on this subject. In notes on Matthew, *Crit. Bib.*, the writer offers the following paraphrase to meet the difficulty. "If perhaps (εἰ ἄρα) he might find some figs on it (for it was not yet the usual season for figs to be fit for gathering on fig-trees in general), but he found leaves only." From Norden's *Travels in Egypt*, the writer concludes, with Calmet's editor, that it was the *Sycamore fig-tree*, which is always green, grows by the wayside, and bears fruit *several times in the year*, so that no time, without a near examination, could any one tell if it bore fruit (Mark xvi. 3, 4).

"Remember, O Christian, that thy sinful nature can afford no hope, nor the shadow of a hope; not a desire, nor even a wish to desire the least good thing that relates to [the Lord] Jesus Christ. These are exotics on earth, and must be transplanted from heaven. No fruit or flower of grace can spring from thy carnal nature; nothing naturally flourishes there but the baleful weeds of self-will, of unbelief, and pride.' Thy soul, by natural pollution, is become a dark, a waste, a thorny wilderness; and none but Christ, the husbandman of the Church, can convert it into a garden. But the divine Redeemer has once made this wilderness 'to blossom as the rose;' will He not keep as well as water it every moment? will not He reduce the beasts of the forest, with every noxious and creeping thing? Take courage, then, believing soul. Thy heavenly Father 'despiseth not the day of small things.' Thy faith, though now perhaps minute as 'the smallest of all seeds,' is, notwithstanding, precious, and shall one day rise in such luxuriousness that 'all the fowls of the air shall nest in the branches of it;' the holiest grace, and most happy desires shall wing their way to their heart, and shall rest with delight in the soul."—*Serle's Hor. Sol.*, p. 8.

It is truly painful to find a distinguished theologian deliberately affirming that this sacred parable, and "the one of the thistle

divine and ceaseless desire that man should receive his life and spirit, and bring forth the blessed fruits of repentance, reformation, and regeneration (Matt. xxv. 31-46). It is said, therefore, that He saw it afar off,—far distant from Himself and heaven, bearing nothing but leaves,—nothing but truths and doctrines which were falsified,—mere outward conformity,—the acknowledgment of the lips, while the heart was far from Him. "But the time of figs was not yet,"—glorious and continual opportunities of producing richest fruits had passed by unimproved. The sun had shone and the dews had fallen upon it in vain. Its doom was therefore pronounced, "No man eat fruit of thee hereafter forever." The axe was "laid to its root" (Matt. iii. 10). Judgment was executed, and "the fig-tree was immediately dried up from the roots" (Mark xi. 12-20).

When those principles in the natural mind, which, by the reception of what is evil and false, do injury to charity and faith, or, on the contrary, may, in the regenerating process, be deprived of their hurtful qualities, and made subservient to good purposes, are spoken of in the Word under corresponding imagery drawn from the vegetable kingdom, they are described by prickly, stinging, and noxious plants, shrubs, and trees, as thorns and thistles, nettles and briers, etc. Such natural principles as are denoted by thorns and briers, when they are made subordinate to use, serve for protection and defence to interior principles. Hence we read of the householder who planted a vineyard, of which it is said, he "hedged it round about" (Matt. xxi. 33). When the desecrated church is treated of, or when the human mind is described as no longer cultivating and cherishing therein the heavenly plants of paradise, but as giving birth and permanent existence to such natural principles as are injurious to goodness and truth, producing disorder and desolation, among other divine judgments it is declared that "Thorns shall come up in her palaces, nettles and brambles in the fortresses thereof" (Isa. xxxiv. 13). But when a luxuriant state of the Lord's church or of the human mind is the subject of prediction or promise, in which the plants of heavenly extraction and spiritual growth, that bring delight to the soul, are by regeneration substituted for the wild, hurtful, and disorderly productions of an unregenerate state, then we read, "The wilderness and the solitary place shall be glad for them; and the desert shall rejoice

---

and cedar (2 Kings xiv. 9) are two *fables;*" and that "in neither case is it God that is speaking, nor yet messengers of his delivering his counsel, but men, and from an *earthly standing point,* not a divine."—*Trench's Notes on the Parables,* note, p. 2, 5th ed.

and blossom as the rose. It shall blossom abundantly, and rejoice even with joy and singing: the glory of Lebanon shall be given unto it, the excellency of Carmel and Sharon. They shall see the glory of the Lord, and the excellency of our God" (Isa. xxxv. 1, 2).

Having thus explained the spiritual signification of the olive-tree, the vine, the fig-tree, and the bramble, we shall be prepared to understand the truly wonderful and divinely-inspired parable of the trees going forth to choose a king over them, in which these particular trees are mentioned.

The children of Israel, we read, did evil in the sight of the Lord. They built altars and reared groves, and consecrated them to the infamous worship of Baal. They were, in consequence, given up to the power of their inveterate enemies, were compelled to dwell in dens and mountains, and were greatly impoverished. Then they cried unto the Lord in their distress, and He sent an angel, who commissioned Gideon to become their deliverer. After obtaining a signal victory over the hosts of Midian, the Israelites desired that he would become their ruler; but he refused, saying, "I will not rule over you, neither shall my son rule over you: the Lord shall rule over you." After his death, however, the children of Israel returned to their idolatry. They remembered not the Lord their God, but made Abimelech[126] their king. On this, Jotham, the youngest son of Gideon (all his brethren having been perfidiously put to death, and he having with difficulty escaped), ascended to the summit of Mount Gerizim, and receiving by divine inspiration a message from God, he spake to the men of Shechem the following parable:

"The trees went forth on a time to anoint a king over them; and they said unto the olive-tree, Reign thou over us. But the olive-tree said unto them, Should I leave my fatness, wherewith by me they honor God and man, and go to be promoted over the trees? And the trees said to the fig-tree, Come thou, and reign over us. But the fig-tree said unto them, Should I forsake my sweetness, and my good fruit, and go to be promoted over the trees? Then said the trees unto the vine, Come thou, and reign over us. And the vine said unto them, Should I leave my wine, which cheereth God and man, and go to be promoted over the trees? Then said all the trees unto the bramble, Come thou, and reign over us. And the bramble said unto the trees, If in truth ye anoint me king over you, then come and put your trust

---

[126] *Abimelech* means in English, *Father and King*.

in my shadow: and if not, let fire come out of the bramble, and devour the cedars of Lebanon" (Judges ix. 8-15).

Jotham proceeded to apply the words of this parable to what Israel had done, in that they had chosen Abimelech, a low-born, haughty, and cruel man, to be their king, in preference to the lawful heir, whom he had treacherously destroyed, and predicted that the fire of civil discord would be kindled among them, and terminate, as a consequence, in their mutual destruction.

Although this inspired parable, in its proximate sense, was strikingly applicable to the historical circumstances in which the kingdom of Israel was then placed, it is perpetuated in the Word of God, not simply to convey admonition to nations and their rulers, but because, in its holy internal sense, it has reference to something that transpires in the minds and experience of all men. In the idolatrous worship of the rebellious Israelites, and the punishment of slavery and oppression to which they were subjected by the implacable Midianites, which, as a corresponding result of their impious conduct, they brought upon themselves, we see striking representative figures of the awful departure of men from the pure worship of the true God, to the worship of self, and, as a consequence, the awful and distressing captivity of the soul to sensual passions and cruel propensities, which ever seek to exalt themselves above the love and service of God, and to which they are obnoxious. From such appalling states of spiritual bondage and tyranny nothing can deliver us but a humble acknowledgment of our transgressions. This brings to our aid Divine interposition. When mercies are apparently withdrawn, and past deliverances are forgotten or feebly remembered, how prone are we to turn again to our evil ways, and resume our evil habits, to forget our gracious Deliverer, and to enthrone within us, as the chief ruler of our desires and thoughts,—our father and king,—the low-born, ambitious, sordid, and ferocious love of self, signified by Abimelech. Thus we stand in need of the constant correction and admonition contained in the parable of the trees.

The bramble, as a hurtful shrub, signifies those individuals who, like Abimelech, are influenced only by low, selfish, domineering desires and worldly motives; and, in the abstract, such desires and motives themselves, together with the states of mind and life in which they are cherished. Gideon, on a previous occasion, had said, "The LORD shall rule over you;" but the people were not willing to be led and governed by Him. Therefore, in seeking for a supreme ruler, they are represented as applying first to the olive-tree, significative of internal celestial goodness derived from love; secondly, to the fig-tree, significative of external celestial goodness grounded in obedience; thirdly, to the vine, significative of spiritual goodness proceeding from a sincere affection of truth, all originating in the Lord; and the refusal of these trees implies that the people were become so selfish and wicked that they would not submit to the Lord, nor to any heavenly influence of goodness or truth proceeding from Him. Lastly, they apply to the bramble, significative of spurious goodness springing from hypocrisy, under which is the infernal love of dominion, signified by the expressions attributed to this tree, "Put your trust in my shadow," and which, notwithstanding appearances to the contrary, they desired should reign over them. For, in such a sensual, carnal state, here represented by Israel, a state from which peace and concord are absent, the olive-tree of celestial love and charity is neither desired to reign, nor could reign, without "leaving its fatness wherewith God and man are honored." Nor could the fig-tree of natural goodness and truth be promoted, where mutual good-will and social kindness are banished, without "forsaking its sweetness and good fruit" of genuine piety and morality. Nor yet could the vine of sacred wisdom assume dominion without "leaving its" delicious "wine which cheereth God and man,"—well-pleasing to the Divine giver, and a source of delightful refreshment to the humble receiver. So the trees are described as applying to the bramble,—the evil which springs from falsity and hypocrisy,—as their true king. This they regard as their only good. The bramble willingly accepts the sovereignty, and they fancy themselves secure. This willingness on the part of the bramble forcibly indicates its suitableness to the disposition of those over whom it is elected to reign; but, mark the awful conclusion. When truth is separated from its life, when the outward profession of godliness is but the hypocritical covering of inward lusts, knowledge confers the power of doing evil instead of good; and, unless prevented by timely and heart-felt repentance, the burning fire of concupiscence breaks forth to the destruction of conscience, and the annihilation of all tranquillity and joy. Even the glorious cedars of Lebanon,—those truths revealed from heaven, which may be perceived and confirmed by the lofty powers of the reason,—bend before its desolating progress, and it rages in its unquenched and tormenting fierceness forever (Isa. lxvi. 24; Mark ix. 43-48).

In the sermon on the mount, our blessed Lord and Saviour instructs us, from the objects of the vegetable world, how we are to distinguish between good and evil intentions. We are to know them by the fruits which they bring forth, or the effects they have upon our tempers and conduct. "Do men," says He, "gather grapes of thorns, or figs of thistles? Even so every good tree bringeth forth good fruit; but a corrupt tree bringeth forth corrupt fruit. Every tree that bringeth not forth good fruit is hewn down and cast into the fire. Wherefore by their fruits ye shall know them" (Matt. vii. 16–20). In order to repress an overweening and injurious anxiety for the morrow, to withdraw us from all trust in our own vain prudence, to excite within us an implicit dependence on the care and protection of Him without whose superintending Providence nothing could exist, and to teach us, finally, that truth or faith alone, however glittering and gaudy, is insufficient for our salvation, He directs our attention to the verdure and beauty of the grass and the flowers which enamel the fields, but may be, notwithstanding, cast into the oven. In seasons of trial and temptation, the truths of heaven appear to be withdrawn, as the flowers fade during the inclemency of winter. But on the return of another spring and summer, the sun arises in its strength and they are renewed, and appear again in all their brilliancy, glory, and fragrance, to adorn, to delight, and to refresh the mind. "Consider," says He, "the lilies of the field, how they grow; they toil not, neither do they spin: and yet I say unto you, that even Solomon in all his glory was not arrayed like one of these. Wherefore, if God so clothe the grass of the field, which to-day is, and to-morrow is cast into the oven, shall He not much more clothe you, O ye of little faith? Therefore take no thought, saying, What shall we eat? or, What shall we drink? or, Wherewithal shall we be clothed? (for after all these things do the Gentiles seek): for your heavenly Father knoweth that ye have need of all these things. But seek ye first the kingdom of God and his righteousness; and all these things shall be added unto you" (Matt. vi. 28–33).

In regard to such evil and false principles as are implanted by birth in the natural mind, He affirms in another place, "Every plant which my heavenly Father hath not planted, shall be rooted up"[127] (Matt.

---

[127] "*Every plant, etc.* Every doctrine which, like the vain traditions of the elders, is not founded on the Word of God, but a human invention, shall be eradicated and destroyed."—*Hewlett's Comm.*

"Tares and weeds are false principles: not every kind of sin, but wrong and perverse teaching. 'Such spurious seeds,' remarks St. Basil, 'are produced not by any change in the seed corn, but subsist by an origin of their own, having an appropriate kind. Yea and they fulfil the image of those who adul

xv. 13). And John the Baptist, speaking from an inspired dictate of the power of divine truth, which is revealed to man in order to extirpate such false and evil principles from the mind, declares, "And now also the axe is laid unto the root of the tree: therefore every tree which bringeth not forth good fruit, is hewn down and cast into the fire" (Matt. iii. 10). The Lord also teaches us, in the parable of the tares[128] and the wheat (Matt. xiii. 25–36), the just distinction which obtains between genuine and spurious faith and charity; such good fruits as originate from the Lord Himself and from the activities of his Holy Spirit, or such false doctrines as are the productions of self-intelligence, and such spurious practices as originate in self-righteousness, the fruits of mere external zeal and formal morality, which claim as a merit the applause of men, instead of the praise of God. In the parable of the sower, the Lord again teaches that if the seed, which is the Word of God, or the divine truths of heaven revealed therein, fall "among thorns," which fitly represent the sordid cares and sensual pleasures of this world, it is said that "the thorns spring up with it and choke it." "But that on the good ground," He says, "are they who, in an honest and good heart, having heard the Word, keep it, and bring forth fruit with patience" (Luke viii. 7, 14, 15). Again, our Lord compares Himself, in the process by which He was glorified, to "a corn of wheat falling into the ground," and afterwards "bringing forth much fruit" (John xii. 24). The same figure is a striking representative of man's regeneration, by the inward reception of truth and goodness, and of his spiritual growth and fruitfulness.

The return of vegetation in the season of spring is so true an emblem of the process of regeneration by which man obtains newness of life, and also of the resurrection of the soul into a new state of

---

terate the doctrines of the Lord, and in no genuine way become disciples of his Word, but rather are corrupted by the teachings of the evil one, yet mingle themselves with the healthful body of the Church.'"—*Hexaëm*, v. 5, p. 41, B.

"By the tares of the world, or conventional maxims, the seeds of Christian Truth are being daily choked and destroyed."—*R. Montgomery Martin's Analysis of the Bible*, pref., p. 11.

[128] The Greek word translated *tares*, nowhere else occurs. It is thought to mean the *lolium temulentum*, a bastard or degenerate wheat, which, when mingled with good wheat and made into bread, produces vertigo; whence the additional name, *temulentum*. It is very difficult to distinguish it from pure wheat until the harvest is at hand, when the grain becomes nearly black.

"This morning I plucked a globe of the dandelion,—the seed vessel,—and was struck, as never before, with the silent, gentle manner in which Nature sows her seed; and I asked if this is not the way in which the spiritual seed, *truth*, is to be sown. I saw, too, how Nature sows her seed broadcast; how the gossamer wing of the dandelion seed scatters it far and wide; how it falls as by accident, and sends up the plant where no one suspects. So we must send truth abroad, not forcing it on here and there a mind, not watching its progress anxiously, but trusting that it will light on a kindly soil, and yield its fruit. So Nature teaches."—*Dr. Channing's Memoirs*, vol. iii., pp. 477, 478.

existence in the spiritual world, that few can mistake it. Under this symbol, the apostle Paul speaks of a resurrection from spiritual death, and also of the resurrection to spiritual life at the death of the body, calling them fools who did not perceive so plain an analogy. "Thou fool," says he, "that which thou sowest is not quickened, except it die: and that which thou sowest, thou sowest not that body that shall be, but bare grain, it may chance of wheat, or of some other grain. So also," adds he, "is the resurrection of the dead" (1 Cor. xv. 36, 37, 42). For it is the vital germ, within the body or substance of the seed, which brings forth and vegetates,—the outward coverings when separated from the living germ are decomposed, and either absorbed or dissipated; and just so it is with the natural body, when the living, sentient spirit is by death separated therefrom. And lest the gross-minded Corinthians, to whom he was addressing this letter, should mistakenly suppose, that, instead of speaking to them on the subjects of regeneration and resurrection to eternal life, he was advocating the Jewish notion of the resurrection of the material body, he emphatically adds, "There is a natural body, and there is a spiritual body. Now this I say, brethren, that flesh and blood cannot inherit the kingdom of God: neither doth corruption inherit incorruption. So when this corruptible shall have put on incorruption, and this mortal shall have put on immortality, then shall be brought to pass the saying that is written, Death is swallowed up in victory" (verses 44, 50, 54). The Lord also says that such as hear his word and believe it, are raised from the grave; they pass from death unto life (John v. 24, 25). And in his first general Epistle, the apostle John writes, "We know that we have passed [already passed] from death unto life, because we love the brethren. He that loveth not his brother abideth in death" (iii. 14).

The trees signify the church and her members as to the reception of the knowledges, doctrines, and truths of the Word, the good affections thereto belonging, and the works which proceed therefrom; and in an opposite sense, the perversion of all truth from the implantation of false principles in the mind, together with the evil affections thereto belonging, and the vile works which are thereby produced, as is evident from a great variety of passages in the Word of God. Thus, "Blessed is the man whose delight is in the law of the Lord; in his law doth he meditate day and night. And he shall be like a tree planted by the rivers of water, that bringeth forth his fruit in his season; his leaf also shall not wither, and whatsoever he doeth shall prosper. The ungodly are not so, but are like the chaff which the wind driveth away" (Psalm i. 2-4). And again we read, "Thus saith the Lord: Cursed be the man that trusteth in man, and maketh flesh his arm, and whose heart departeth from the Lord. For he shall be like the heath in the desert, and shall not see when good cometh; but shall inhabit the parched places in the wilderness, in a salt land and not inhabited. Blessed is the man that trusteth in the Lord, and whose hope the Lord is. For he shall be as a tree planted by the waters, and that spreadeth out her roots by the river, and shall not see when heat cometh, but her leaf shall be green; and shall not be careful in the year of drought, neither shall cease from yielding fruit" (Jer. xvii. 5-8). And in order to teach us that He will humble the proud and exalt the lowly,—that He will cause the verdure of mere intellectual attainments and the hope of external profession to wither forever away,—that the mind which is destitute of intelligence, as the tree of the arid desert is of moisture, but which sincerely desires it, He will make to flourish by the rivers of living waters, the Lord says, "All the trees of the field shall know that I the Lord have brought down the high tree, have exalted the low tree, have dried up the green tree, and have made the dry tree to flourish: I the Lord have spoken and have done it" (Ezek. xvii. 24). Professing members of the church, who fail to bring forth the fruits of usefulness in the life, are further described as " trees cumbering the ground " (Luke xiii. 7).

The hyssop, bitter to the taste, and flourishing on walls, is spoken of in the Word to signify external truth and its corresponding goodness, or the genuine doctrines of the letter of the Word, and a life of charity in agreement therewith; for such doctrines inculcate the bitterness of self-denial, and thus are mediums of spiritual purification. Hence this herb[129] was commanded to be used in the Levitical ceremonials for the cleansing of leprosy, and in composing the waters of purification. In this sense, too, the Psalmist, from the depths of contrition, implored the divine mercy in these memorable words, " Purge me with hyssop, and I shall be clean: wash me, and I shall be whiter than snow" (Psalm li. 7). But the lofty, majestic, and evergreen cedar, which Solomon contrasted with the lowly hyssop, abounding in the forests of Lebanon, and yielding an aromatic and valuable wood, which, in consequence of its durableness, was regarded as incorruptible, signifies, in a good sense, the internal or spiritual truth

---

[129] In Hebrew, this herb is called by a word which denotes its detersive and cleansing qualities.

of the Word of God rationally perceived, and its appropriate goodness,—a rational knowledge of things spiritual, and inward perceptions thereof, applied to exalted and enduring goodness of heart and life. Hence cedar-wood was so extensively used in the construction of the representative temple, and the Psalmist says, "The righteous shall grow like a cedar in Lebanon" (Psalm xcii. 12). "The trees of the Lord are full of sap: the cedars of Lebanon, which He hath planted" (Psalm civ. 16). He calls upon "fruitful trees and all cedars, to praise the name of the Lord" (Psalm cxlviii. 9, 13). And the unwilling prophet pronounced Israel's goodly tabernacles as "cedar-trees beside the waters" (Num. xxiv. 6). So, again, "the tree of life," which signifies, in a supreme sense, the Lord Himself, as to his divine love, whence proceeds the eternal wisdom of his Word, and, in a subordinate sense, man's inmost love and life derived from Him, and directed towards Him, is described as bearing twelve manner of fruits,—producing, by the Lord's presence and influence in the affections and thoughts, all kinds and degrees of good works,—works of use and charity, freely done by man, apparently as of himself, but in reality from the operations of the Lord in him and by him. And it is further said of this "tree of life" that "the leaves"—all external knowledges and doctrines—"are given for the healing of the nations," that is, were designed to restore men from the enervating maladies of sin to states of spiritual health and vigor, and thus lead them to a cheerful and conscientious observance of all the outward duties of moral and civil life (Rev. xxii. 2; Ezek. xlvii. 12).

The palm is sometimes called the date-tree. It is evergreen, always flourishing and fruitful, and is celebrated for the three hundred and sixty uses to which the lofty trunks, the aspiring branches, the umbrageous leaves, and the pleasant and nourishing fruit, are said to be applicable. It grows by springs of sweet water, and its Hebrew appellation, in its radical meaning, expresses its uprightness and stature, —it never naturally grows crooked. It was one of the constantly-recurring ornaments of the carved work of Solomon's temple, and pilasters were made in the beautiful form of its trunk. Branches of palm were carried anciently before conquerors, in their triumphant processions, as signals of victory. Hence they were borne and cast before the Lord, on his entrance into Jerusalem, with cries of hosanna (John xii. 13), representative of his triumphant entrance as the Redeemer into his church, and each individual composing it; and were seen by John in the hands of angels (Rev. vii. 9), as denoting victory and confession. For palms signify, in the Word, wisdom and intelligence from the Lord, in acts and use, producing all kinds and degrees of spiritual goodness; thus perfect uprightness from the love of goodness, leading to the confession that all victory over spiritual enemies is from faith in conjunction with divine power, and so to the renunciation of self-merit. The Israelites, in their journey from Egypt, pitched their first camp at a resting-place where they found twelve fountains of water and threescore and ten palm-trees; so the regenerating Christian, in his progress through the wilderness of temptation, finds divine consolation, refreshment, and rest at Elim, a state of instruction and affection, in which the truths of faith in all abundance, and the good affections thence resulting, in all fulness, are found for the support and encouragement of the fainting soul. "The righteous shall flourish like the palm" (Ps. xcii. 12). But when the palm is mentioned in an opposite sense, it denotes self-derived intelligence, self-worship, and a vain and spurious morality. The idols, therefore, spoken of in Jer. x. 5, are described as being "upright as the palm-tree;" for in such a state of mental perversion and pride there is no confession of divine aid, and it is said they "speak not," and are powerless to do any good; "they must needs be borne, because they cannot go."

When the Lord predicts the establishment of a new Dispensation of goodness and truth in the minds of men, and describes the resulting changes which would ensue,—the streams of spiritual and natural knowledge and intelligence which He would cause to flow from Himself, through his Word, to banish ignorance,—to illustrate and enrich the external mind, together with the abundant glories and manifold privileges with which the members of the church would in consequence be blessed and adorned, and the rational and ever-new truths and delights with which they would be amply supplied in the process of regeneration, He says, in the language of correspondence, by the mouth of the inspired prophet, "I will open rivers in high places, and fountains in the midst of the valleys: I will make the wilderness a pool of water, and the dry land springs of water. I will plant in the wilderness the cedar of Shittah, and the myrtle and the olive-tree; I will set in the desert the fir-tree, and the pine, and the box-tree together"[130] (Isa. xli. 18, 19; and, again, Isa. xxxv. 1, 2, 7).

---

[130] See Rev. J. H. Smithson's valuable *Translation of Isaiah*, pp. 365, 419.

The cedar denotes rational truth of a superior order; the myrtle, rational truth of an inferior order; the oil-tree, the perception of goods and thence of truth: the fir-tree, natural truth of a superior order; the pine, natural truth of an inferior order; and the

These trees are evergreens of the lowest order, and include all kinds; they manifestly denote the *most external* of those divine gifts with which the soul is enriched in the progress of its great change from a desert to a fruitful field, and in which flourishing state it blossoms in loveliness and fertility, and is said to "rejoice and blossom like the rose." But in regard to the spiritual blessings and celestial delicacies of love and wisdom in the internal faculties of the soul, and their perpetual increase, together with the safety and rest obtained by the faithful members of so glorious a dispensation, trees bearing relishing, nourishing, gladdening fruit, are introduced, as in the following passage (Deut. viii. 7–9), to the words in it. While of the perpetuity and security of such a state it is written, "They shall sit every man under his vine, and under his fig-tree; and none shall make him afraid" (Micah iv. 4). "Blessed," therefore, "is the man that trusteth in the LORD, and whose hope the LORD is. For he shall be as a tree planted by the waters, and that spreadeth out her roots by the river, and shall not see when heat cometh, but her leaf shall be green; and shall not be careful in the year of drought, neither shall cease from yielding fruit" (Jer. xvii. 7, 8).

Again, the same wonderful and momentous subject of the regeneration of man, with the gradual process by which it is effected, is thus spoken of by another prophet: "I," Jehovah, "will be as the dew unto Israel: he shall grow as the lily, and cast forth his roots as Lebanon. His branches shall spread, and his beauty shall be as the olive-tree, and his smell as Lebanon. They that dwell under his shadow shall return; they shall revive as the corn, and grow as the vine: the scent thereof shall be as the wine of Lebanon" (Hos. xiv. 5–7). Here the commencement of regeneration is described, in which the divine influences descend into the soul as the gentle dew is deposited on the tender herb (Deut. xxxii. 2). By this the principles within the mind are renovated and vivified. To grow, or rather blossom, as the lily signifies,—to become receptive of truths of heaven appropriate to such a state in the understanding, to perceive their beauty, and that they were designed to encourage us in states of trial, to give us victory in every conflict of temptation, and to enable us with joyful hearts to bring forth the fruits of piety and holiness in the life.[131] To cast forth roots as Lebanon, signifies not only to acquire

---

box, the understanding of good and truth in the natural principle.—*A. E.* 730. Grass denotes science from a spiritual origin, by which spiritual truth is confirmed.—*A. E.* 627.

[131] "The lotus is a water-lily, whose broad leaf, in the greatest inundations of the Nile, rises with the flood, and is never over

but to retain such truths, so that they will be allowed to extend their influence downwards into the lowest or natural and sensual principles of the mind, where they become fixed and confirmed elements of spiritual life. By the branches spreading in the open atmosphere is signified a succeeding state, in which truths and knowledges are extended towards heaven,—are multipled, arranged, and invigorated, because they are all regarded as having relation to the fruits of love and charity, of which, when they are brought forth, or made manifest in the attractive excellences of a good life, it is said, the beauty shall be as the olive-tree. By the scent being as Lebanon is signified, that thus the highest state of intelligence from rational perception is attained, and man becomes, in his finite degree, fully receptive of celestial truth and love from the Lord; "a fragrant tree of his right hand planting" (Isa. lx. 21),—"a tree of righteousness," laden with the rich fruits of wisdom, virtue, intelligence, obedience, and use, prepared to be transplanted to the paradise of God. Hence it is added, "they that dwell under his shadow shall return; they shall revive as the corn, and grow as the vine: the scent thereof shall be as the wine of Lebanon."

It is from this correspondence of the vegetable world to the church, the man of the church, and the interior principles of the human mind, both in respect to good and evil, truth and falsity, that trees are said to know (Ezek. xvii. 24); to clap their hands (Isa. lv. 12); to sing and rejoice (Ps. xcvi. 12); to praise the Lord (Ps. cxlviii. 9); to envy (Ezek. xxxi. 5); to be withered (Joel i. 12); to be cumberers of the ground (Luke xiii. 7); to be burnt up (Joel i. 19).[132]

Again, the Lord's feet signify his divine natural principle, and, in consequence thereof, the literal sense of his most Holy Word, and also his church on earth. For the feet are those parts of the body which are in immediate contact with the ground, and on which the body rests as upon a base; and the literal sense is that containant on which the divine will and wisdom rest, and are revealed to the church.

---

whelmed."—*Bryant;* see *Bib. Researches,* vol. i., p. 269.

"The white majestic flowers were formerly woven into the crowns of conquerors."—*Beaut. of Nat. and Art Disp.,* vol. xii., p. 141.

[132] "Spirit of Grace! my heart renew,
  Each faithful Christian cries;
And where the weeds of error grew,
  Let plants of truth arise.

"My soul, a howling wilderness,
  Shall then such beauties wear,
That heaven with rapture shall confess
  Thy workmanship is there."—*Serle.*

The fruit of trees, whether proper for the use of man and animals or not, and whether they are berries, nuts, or pulpy fruit, will always serve to assist us in ascertaining the specific signification of the tree which produced it, and to confirm the genuineness of the meaning.

Hence, when the prophet Isaiah predicts the future glorious state of the Lord's kingdom on earth, when the exalted doctrines and truths of the Word, represented by the noblest productions of the vegetable kingdom, would be discovered, and his people would plainly perceive that the outward letter and the church by whom it is received, were the very hold, or resting-place, or sanctuary of the Lord with man, He says, "The glory of Lebanon shall come unto thee, the fir-tree, the pine-tree, and the box together, to beautify the place of my sanctuary; and I will make the place of my feet glorious" (lx. 13); or, as Bishop Lowth more emphatically translates the latter clause, "that I may glorify the place whereon I rest my feet."

To denote, further, that all these faculties and blessings are derived —every moment of existence—from the Lord alone, through his blood, and are the gifts of divine love, which is ever active for their preservation and cultivation, He says, "I am the true vine, and my Father is the husbandman. Every branch in me that beareth not fruit He taketh away: and every branch that beareth fruit, he purgeth it, that it may bring forth more fruit." "Abide in me, and I in you. As the branch cannot bear fruit of itself, except it abide in the vine; no more can ye, except ye abide in me. I am the vine, ye are the branches: he that abideth in me, and I in him, the same bringeth forth much fruit: for without me ye can do nothing" (John xv. 1–5). How full of consolation and instruction are these divine expressions when rightly understood!

That trees, in the Word, signify man, and, abstractedly, principles of the human mind, both good and bad, is still further evident from what the Lord says by the prophet Ezekiel, when predicting the judgment which they induce upon themselves who profanely associate the doctrines and truths of the Holy Word with their own sensual lusts and false persuasions, and that they would perish by the love of evil. "Son of man, set thy face toward the south, and drop *thy word* toward the south, and prophesy against the forest of the south field; and say to the forest of the south, Hear the word of the LORD; Thus saith the Lord GOD; Behold, I will kindle a fire in thee, and it shall devour every green tree in thee, and every dry tree: the flaming flame shall not be quenched, and all faces from the south to the north shall be burned therein. And all flesh shall see that I the LORD have kindled it: it shall not be quenched. Then said I, Ah, Lord GOD! they say of me, Doth he not speak parables?" (Ezek. xx. 46–49.) And also what the Lord says by the same prophet where he is treating of the destruction of a perverted church generally and individually, by skeptical reasoning, and the establishment of a New Church among the Gentiles, and describes the process of vivification, or regeneration, in each individual member, He says, "And all the trees of the field," etc. (Ezek. xvii. 24).

In further proof, let me direct your attention to the signification of wood, which in general corresponds to natural goodness. Wood is obtained from a tree which bore some kind of appropriate fruit, in agreement with its peculiar nature; from most kinds an oil may be expressed; it may be enkindled, and serve the purpose of affording genial warmth to the body; it was anciently employed in the construction of temples, called houses of God, and in the formation of various musical instruments employed in the celebrations of worship; it is also extensively used in the construction of habitations, and the fabrication of innumerable articles of convenience and use; and from all these characteristics, and many others founded in its uses, its physiological structure, and even its chemical composition, it may be most satisfactorily proved that various kinds of wood, especially such as are precious and durable, correspond to various principles of goodness or charity, natural, rational, spiritual, or celestial, or their intermediates, appertaining both to the internal and the external mind and life. But in the opposite sense, wood which has no intrinsic value, the fruit of the tree whence it is hewn being described as evil, or in itself abounding with such qualities as are hurtful or destructive, or where it is perverted to a wicked purpose, corresponds to what is evil, in some of the above degrees, and has relation to the lusts of the unregenerate man and his wicked doings. In the former, or good sense, therefore, cedar-wood, as signifying works of charity performed from rational intelligence and goodness, is spoken of so frequently in reference to the Temple at Jerusalem, and in the Mosaic ritual is directed to be applied in the purification of the leper, when the plague of leprosy was healed (Lev. xiv. 4). It is this principle of goodness in the will and life which builds up the Lord's dwelling-place in the soul, and without which it is impossible that man can be renewed and cleansed after he has been smitten by the direful "plague of his own heart;" for he has profaned to evil purposes the holy things of God's Word, and such are given up to their uncleanness who "change the truth of God into a lie" (Rom. i. 25). This profanation of truth is always signified by the plague of leprosy; and because the Jews, being in possession of the Word of God, were more than other nations addicted to this evil, therefore that plague was more prevalent among them than among other nations. And hence the Lord Jesus not only cleansed the lepers who were brought or who came to Him, approaching Him as goodness itself, but commanded his disciples also to cleanse them. "Now are ye clean," says He on another occasion, "through the Word which I have spoken unto you" (John xv. 3); "Sanctify them through thy truth: thy Word is truth" (John xvii. 17).

It was because wood, in a good sense, and in the lowest degree, corresponds to natural goodness, or charity, that the bitter waters of Marah, in the wilderness, were miraculously made sweet by Moses casting therein a tree, according to the express command of Jehovah (Ex. xv. 25). In the bitterness of those waters we may see a just representation of that state of spiritual trial, induced by murmuring and disobedience, in which the knowledges of divine truth, however desirable, are attended with bitter and perplexing thoughts, and afford no satisfaction to the thirsty mind, because they are separated from the heavenly principle of love or goodness. In this case, the Lord shows us a tree of healing virtue, which, if cast into the waters, will instantly deprive them of their bitterness; and what is this, but a heavenly principle of charity in the heart, brought out or made manifest in a good life and conduct! In the opposite sense, wood denotes the evil lusts of self and the world, for these are the opposites of charity or goodness; as the woods, for instance, of which idols were made (Isa. xlv. 20), or which were used for funeral piles (Isa. xxx. 33). Wood has also the same contrary signification when those are treated of who attribute goodness to themselves, instead of to Him from whom alone it proceeds, thus who suppose that their works of goodness and charity are meritorious. These are said to have forsaken the worship of the Lord, and are called worshippers of idols made of wood, the works of their own hands (Jer. i. 16). In the same sense it is thus spoken of in the prophecy of Habakkuk, "The stone shall cry out of the wall, and the beam out of the timber [or wood] shall answer it" (ii. 11); "Woe unto him that saith to the wood, Awake; to the dumb stone, Arise, it shall teach!" (ii. 19.) Here the prophet is denouncing self-righteousness and self-conceit, and warning those who are destitute of genuine truth and goodness, against all such delusive dependence. Evil lusts, signified by wood, are represented as answering to sensual suggestions,—as echoing and confirming all false principles in the understanding,—as assenting to the vain imaginations which they excite, and as instigating their possessors to seek instruction for evil purposes, thus to forsake the eternal truth, the Rock of Ages, and to throw their confidence upon their own idle speculations and pretended merits; but a woe is pronounced upon all such as thus "say to the wood, Awake; to the dumb stone, Arise, it shall teach;" who thus set up the idols of their own unclean hearts in the place of God and of his Word, for "they sacrifice unto devils, not to God. Of the rock that begat them they are unmindful, and have forgotten God that formed them" (Deut. xxxii. 17, 18).

"All goods which exist in act are called uses, and all evils which exist in act are also called uses, but the latter are called evil uses, and the former good uses. Now, as all goods are from the Lord, and all evils from hell, it follows that no other than good uses were created by the Lord, but that evil uses originated from hell. By uses, we mean all things that appear on earth, as animals of all kinds and vegetables of all kinds; of both the latter and the former, those which furnish use to man are from the Lord, and those which do hurt to man are from hell." "The things that do hurt to man are called uses, because they are of use to the wicked to do evil, and because they contribute to absorb malignities, and thus also as remedies. Use is applied in both senses, like love; for we speak of good love and evil love, and love calls all that use which is done by itself." " Evil uses on earth mean all noxious things in both the animal and vegetable kingdoms, and also in the mineral kingdom." "Such in the animal kingdom are poisonous serpents, scorpions, crocodiles, dragons, owls, mice, locusts, frogs, spiders, noxious worms and insects, also flies, moths, lice, mites, and injurious animalcules; in a word, those that consume grasses, leaves, fruit, seeds, meat and drink, and are noxious to beasts and men. In the vegetable kingdom they are all malignant, virulent, and poisonous herbs, as hemlock and aconite, and pulse and shrubs of the same kind; in the mineral kingdom, all poisonous earths. These few particulars, adduced for the sake of science, are sufficient to show what is meant by evil uses on earth." "Nothing whatever exists in the natural world that does not derive its cause and origin from the spiritual world, and that good is from the Lord, and the evil from the devil, that is, from hell. By the spiritual world is meant both heaven and hell." "Now, it is influx from hell which operates those things that are evil uses, in places where those things are which correspond." "Such, likewise, are the appearances in the spiritual world, which are all correspondences; for the interiors of the mind of the inhabitants of both heaven and hell are, by such effigies, presented actually before their uses."—See D. L. W., pp. 336–347; also Ap. Ex. 109; H. & H. 103–190.

CHAPTER XV.

Correspondence of Earths, Minerals, etc., with Illustrations.

THE inorganic substances of the mineral kingdom, of which growth, motion, and sensation are not predicable, are likewise spoken of in the Word of God, to represent and signify, in a good sense, the principles of love and wisdom, and, in a negative sense, those of evil and error, in the very externals, or least sensitive principles, of the mind and life,—to such spiritual things as are manifest even to sensual discernment, and form the lowest and firmest basis of a heavenly and eternal state; or, on the contrary, to such infernal things as, confirmed by corporeal affection and sensual reasoning, extinguish all heavenly truth.

Of these correspondences several striking examples have already been given, from which it may be clearly inferred that the precious metals and stones, according to their indefinite varieties, colors, principles, and uses, correspond to those infinitely various kinds of goodness and truth which serve to enrich, adorn, and give stability to the extreme principles of the mind and life. But in their opposite sense, metals and stones signify evil and erroneous principles and persuasions in their external forms. That such is their signification, might be abundantly proved from the Word, as when the Lord is describing by the mouth of his prophet a grossly corrupt state of the church and the mind, together with the direful punishment which it necessarily induces, and which is called God's anger, and appears to be the infliction of his vengeance (for the wrath or fury of God, is, as we have previously shown, only an appearance of truth), He says, "Because ye are all become dross, behold, therefore, I will gather you into the midst of Jerusalem. As they gather silver, and brass, and iron, and lead, and tin, into the midst of the furnace, to blow the fire upon it, to melt it; so will I gather you in mine anger and in my fury, and I will leave you there and melt you" (Ezek. xxii. 19, 20). But when He speaks of an exalted state of his church and of the mind, together with the glories and blessings which belong thereto,

He says, "For brass I will bring gold, and for iron I will bring silver, and for wood brass, and for stones iron" (Isa. lx. 17). We have before observed, that the precious stones which adorned the breast-plate of the high-priest, and those which are the foundations of the New Jerusalem, signify all kinds and degrees of divine wisdom and knowledge in the Word translucent and resplendent from pure goodness, from which intelligence and just judgment are derived, and on which the church in heaven and on earth is founded. The Lord Himself, as to his divine Word or truth, and its eternal durability, as derived from this divine love, is also called "a rock," on which his church is said to be erected. In a perverted church He is represented as a stone which the builders—the teachers of a false religion—have rejected; but in the true church He is acknowledged as the "head-stone of the corner" (Ps. cxviii. 22; Matt. xxi. 42),—the "living stone, disallowed indeed of men" (1 Pet. ii. 4),—"the tried stone, the precious corner-stone, the sure foundation" (Isa. xxviii. 16), on which all faith and hope and love must rest. That stone is called the corner-stone, or chief corner-stone, which is placed in the extreme angles of a foundation, conjoining and holding together two walls of the pile, meeting from different quarters. So also in the beautiful and instructive parable of the wise and foolish builders, in which is portrayed the characters of such as erect their spiritual habitations on the immovable rock of the Word of God, or divine truth, by hearing and doing the Lord's will; in which case they are conjoined to Him in an everlasting covenant; and, on the contrary, to such as build their spiritual houses on the delusive sand of human imagination, faith alone, and mere external profession, in which case their minds, disjoined from the eternal source of life, are brought to irretrievable ruin, and the knowledge they have acquired is dissipated. "Whosoever heareth these sayings of mine," saith the Lord, "and doeth them, I will liken him unto a wise man, who built his house upon a rock: and the rain descended, and the floods came, and the winds blew, and beat upon that house; and it fell not: for it was founded upon a rock. And every one that heareth these sayings of mine, and doeth them not, shall be likened unto a foolish man, who built his house upon the sand: and the rain descended, and the floods came, and the winds blew, and beat upon that house; and it fell: and great was the fall thereof" (Matt. vii. 24-27). Here, the solid rock manifestly signifies divine truths, which, when received into the mind from affection, combined with goodness of heart, and brought down into the conduct, cohere together in unbroken unity, and man erecting thereon his spiritual house, is enabled successfully to resist every storm of temptation, for he is conjoined to the Rock of Ages, even the Lord Jesus Christ. But by sand is as plainly meant truths devoid of coherence, because received into the understanding separated from love and its life,—mere outward profession of faith, without spiritual affection; then truths of the holiest quality are but speculative knowledges in the memory and natural understanding, which, losing their cohesion and firmness, and deprived of all connection with their divine source, are profaned to evil purposes, and deprived of all that strength and consistency needful for man's support in times of spiritual trial and opposition. A dependence on these brings eternal ruin to the soul.

On account of this spiritual signification of stones, as denoting sacred truths of an external character, and their qualities of firmness and durability, pillars of stones, and heaps of stone, were, in ancient times, set up as witnesses of covenants, boundaries of land, and testimonials of affection, and were not unfrequently consecrated, as things connected with holy worship, by pouring oil upon the top of them (Gen. xxviii. 18; xxxv. 14). And of the temple of Solomon we read that it was completed of stones ready prepared, "so that there was neither hammer, axe, nor any tool of iron heard in the house while it was in building" (1 Kings vi. 7). An altar to Jehovah was, on the same account, commanded to be erected of unhewn stones, or stones unpolluted by the workman's tool (Ex. xx. 25), to represent to us that worship can only be acceptable to God when it is the dictate of pure truth drawn from the Holy Word, unperverted and undefiled by the vain imaginations of self-intelligence.

In consequence of the science of correspondences being well known in ancient times, "historians distinguished the periods, from the first age of the world to the last, into the golden, silver, copper, and iron ages, to which also they added an age of clay. The golden age they called those times when innocence and integrity prevailed, and when every one did what is good from what is good, and what is just from what is just; the silver age they called those times when there was no longer any innocence, but still a species of integrity which did not consist in their doing what is good from what is good, but in their doing what is true from what is true; but the copper and iron ages they called those which were still inferior. The reason why they gave such appellations to those times was not from comparison, but from correspondence; for the ancients knew that silver corresponds to truth, and gold to good, and this from communication with spirits and angels." "But who at this present day knows that the ages were called golden and silver by the ancients from correspondence? yea, who at this day knows anything about correspondence? And yet he that does not know this, and especially he that makes his chief gratification and wisdom to consist in disputing whether it be so or not, cannot even attain to the least knowledge concerning the innumerable things which are correspondences."—A. C. 5658.

There are various kinds of gold mentioned in the Word, or gold from various localities, as Uphaz, Ophir, Sheba, Havilah, and Tarshish, and they correspond to various kinds and degrees of love and goodness appertaining to the Lord, his Word, his kingdom, and our neighbor, according to the signification of the place mentioned, and the subject treated of. Thus gold from Uphaz signifies the precious principle of celestial goodness, and the wisdom thence derived, or the most exalted love of God, with its rich blessings, and the meaning of the word Uphaz expresses its fineness or purity (Jer. x. 9; Dan. x. 5). Gold from Ophir signifies spiritual goodness, or the love of the neighbor, derived from the love of God; and the name Ophir means *making fruitful* (Isa. xiii. 12; Ps. xlv. 9). Gold from Sheba signifies the love of truth, derived from the Holy Word, and its application to good and useful purposes in life. Sheba means compassing about; and gold from Havilah and Tarshish denotes the lowest order of love and goodness exemplified in the love of external or scientific knowledge, and in promoting what is profitable and benevolent in moral and civil life (Gen. ii. 11, 12; Isa. lx. 9). Havilah means speaking or declaring, and Tarshish contemplation or examination. From these examples it may be seen how the meaning of Hebrew words often assist the true signification of the things predicated, and how varieties of the same object, both in a good and a bad sense, are to be interpreted. The love of goodness of any degree, when tried and purified by the process of temptation, is called "gold tried in the fire;" that is, unalloyed or genuine (Rev. iii. 18). In an opposite sense, gold signifies the carnal and perverted and inordinate love of self and worldly pleasure of various kinds; it is then described as used in the construction of idols, and its tendency to profanation; it is said, in strains of lamentation, "How is the gold become dim! how is the most fine gold changed! The precious sons of Zion, comparable to fine gold, how are they esteemed as earthen pitchers, the work of the hands of the potter" (Lam. iv. 1, 2).

Again, what natural substances can more fitly represent the carnal concupiscences of the natural man, their inflammatory tendency, the direful falsehood, which, like thick smoke, arises therefrom, darkening the very day, and the excruciating torment occasioned by their activity, both in this world and that which is to come, than the bituminous minerals of sulphur and pitch? Hence they are mentioned in the Word in this sense; as where the Lord by the inspired prophet is describing the judgment which a perverted church brings down upon itself, or a state of mind confirmed by the love and practice of evil and falsehood, in selfish lusts and fantasies, and the direful results, he says, "It is the day of the Lord's vengeance, and the year of recompenses for the controversy of Zion. And the streams thereof shall be turned into pitch, and the dust thereof into brimstone, and the land thereof shall become burning pitch. It shall not be quenched night nor day; the smoke thereof shall go up forever" (Isa. xxxiv. 8–10). Hell itself and its ceaseless punishments, with the burning, soul-tormenting lusts of self and the world,—the ever-active agents of all distress and misery, both as they exist in the spiritual world and in the disorderly minds of men on earth,—are called "a lake of fire burning with brimstone" or sulphur (Rev. xix. 20; xxi. 8). And the Psalmist, speaking of the dreadful anguish which such evil concupiscences and their fantasies certainly induce upon men when they are indulged and confirmed, says, "Upon the wicked He shall rain snares, fire and brimstone, and a horrible tempest: this shall be the portion of their cup" (Psalm xi. 6).[133]

Again, salt, we know, is a compound, in certain given proportions,

---

[133] "I am at a loss to conceive the reason why they are to be considered grievously in error who suppose our Saviour to be threatening the wicked, not with corporeal and sensible fire, but with mental pains and tortures. This was formerly the opinion of grave and eminent men among the Christian fathers, of whom Dion. Petarius makes mention in his *Dogmat. Theolog.*, tom. iii., p. 103. And not a few of the moderns also, who are wholly removed from all suspicion of pernicious errors, firmly maintain the same doctrine. As our Saviour frequently compares the joys of heaven to a feast, I do not see why it is to be considered dangerous to the divine truth to suppose that He also spoke figuratively of the punishments of hell, and in order to demonstrate more vividly and clearly the dreadful sufferings which the wicked will have to undergo, borrowed an image from the most exquisite torments inflicted upon human malefactors. For my own part, I conceive no greater injury is done to the Christian religion by supposing the fire with which the rich glutton is tormented, to be figurative, than by regarding the feast, at which Lazarus is said to be present along with Abraham, as an image and emblem of supreme felicity."—*Dr. J. L. Mosheim's Note to Cudworth's Int. Sys.*, vol. iii., p. 367.

"If I understand your letter, your imagination is haunted with the idea of *literal flames*, and hell is created, not as including all moral evils, but as a great fire. The spiritual interpretation of Scripture has so far made its way among all classes of Christians in this part of the country (U. S. A.), that I do not know an individual who believes in the literal fire as the punishment of the condemned."—*Dr. Channing's Letter to a Friend*, dated Boston, Nov. 1841; *Memoirs*, p. 468.

of an acid and an alkali which have an affinity for each other. In a good sense salt corresponds to the affection of combining truth with goodness, faith with charity, knowledge with practice. This desire, when incorporated in the mind and diffused through the life, preserves them from the corruption of sin. The prophet Elijah, therefore, under a representative dispensation, when miracles were permitted, is said to have cast salt into the spring of the waters of Jericho, because the waters were unwholesome and the ground was unfruitful, saying, "Thus saith the Lord, I have healed these waters; there shall not be from thence any more death or barren land" (2 Kings ii. 21), to teach us most significantly that the waters—the doctrines of eternal truth—can impart no permanently renovating virtues to refresh the soul, and render man fruitful in good works, unless man coöperates with the divine Bestower, by uniting therewith the interior spiritual affections and holy desires which embody themselves in goodness of life, and impart a heavenly quality to every word and action.

On account of this signification of salt in a good sense, it was an indispensable law to Israel, that with all the offerings presented to Jehovah, salt should be offered (Lev. ii. 13); and the spiritual ground of this law is recognized in the Gospel, where, in manifest reference to the heavenly union of truth and affection in the mind, signified by salt, we are thus divinely instructed and exhorted by our blessed Lord, "Every one shall be salted with fire, and every sacrifice shall be salted with salt. Salt is good: but if the salt have lost his saltness, wherewith will ye season it? Have salt in yourselves, and have peace one with another" (Mark ix. 49, 56). But, in the opposite sense, salt denotes an unholy commixture of truth with evil, which is profanation, and the awful effect of this deplorable state is condemnation. Thus, Lot's wife became a pillar of salt, because she looked behind her and separated knowledge from duty (Gen. xix. 26); hence we have the solemn warning, "Remember Lot's wife" (Luke xvii. 32). We read also of certain cities which were given up to salt, or devoted to desolation; and to the same purport it is said, in reference to the want of this conjoining affection, "[The Lord] turneth a fruitful land into barrenness (or salt), for the wickedness of them that dwell therein" (Psalm cvii. 34).[134]

---

[134] "Salt, in the original Hebrew, is expressed by a term denoting incorruptibility and perpetuity."—*A. C.* 2455.

"Most of the Asiatic nations have affixed to salt a certain sacred property."—*Forster's Pinkerton's Coll.*, vol. ix., p. 281.

The Orientals express a vacant countenance by saying, "*there is no salt in it.*"

CHAPTER XVI.

CORRESPONDENCE OF THE SUN, MOON, AND STARS; THE IDOLATROUS WORSHIP OF THEM, AND ITS EXTENSIVE PREVALENCE AND INFLUENCE.

THOSE sublime objects of creative energy in the material universe, the sun, the moon, and the stars, are constantly employed in the Word of God to signify the grand universals of life and salvation. For instance, the sun, in relation to the regenerate man, corresponds to the Lord Himself, "the Sun of righteousness," and thus also to the love of God and our neighbor, for this love is derived from his essential life, and is spoken of as the fountain of every celestial beatitude; as in Malachi, "Unto you that fear my name shall the Sun of righteousness arise with healing in his wings" (iv. 2). But in relation to the unregenerate man, the sun corresponds to the evil love of self and the world, which, "when it is up," or risen, that is, permitted to be active, and increases concupiscence, instead of ministering blessings, is described as "scorching" the good seed of truth, so that under the baneful influence it "withers away" (Matt. xiii. 6), and as causing the heaven-descended manna to vanish (Ex. xvi. 21). The sun is spoken of in the same sense in the Psalms, where it is said, "The Lord is thy keeper: the Lord is thy shade upon thy right hand. The sun shall not smite thee by day" (cxxi. 5, 6); signifying that the Lord can alone protect us from the destructive influence of self-love and its burning passions.[135]

---

[135] "The worship of the sun, by the Egyptians, by the Phœnicians, and Philistines, was the worship of one invisible God, symbolized by the visible source of created light and life." They afterwards worshipped Baal, or Seth, as the sun-god. "Thus symbols became idols."—*Bunsen's Keys of St. Peter*, pp. 38, 39.

"The Egyptians represented the Supreme Being and his divine attributes—his immensity and omnipotence, his fecundity and infinite perfection—under the symbol of the sun; and they represented Nature, or matter, which is altogether dependent on that Supreme Being, and diversified every moment, under the image of the moon, who borrows her light from the sun, and is perpetually changing her appearance. This mode of representation was undoubtedly the primary cause of idolatry and superstition; men growing by degrees forgetful of the Supreme Being, and confining their attention to that glorious luminary, the sun, as the immediate cause of what they beheld, instead of considering it as the material representative of its spiritual source, the invisible Producer of all visible objects."—*Nat. Del.*, vol. i., p. 792.

A very remarkable book was published in Dublin, in 1862, entitled *Primeval Symbols, or*

The sun, as the centre of attraction to the planetary worlds and the proximate source of heat, light, life, and fruitfulness to this natural world, is the representative emblem of the Lord Himself as to his divine love; for this principle is the centre of all vitality in the church and the mind. In the winter season all creation mourns, as it were, the sun's apparent absence; many animals become torpid, and the vegetable kingdom withers apparently; but on the return of spring, and the more direct rays of the sun, the kingdoms of nature are all warmed into new life, and renewed into activity by his vivifying and genial influences, and universal nature rejoices at the sun's apparent approach. In all this we may trace and confirm the beautiful correspondence of the sun. The moon, dependent upon the earth, but shining with a borrowed lustre derived from the sun, and whose reflected glories dissipate the darkness of so many of our nights, is, in a good sense, a striking figure of a true faith in the Lord and his Word; for faith derives all its effulgence and life from love, and dissipates all the doubt and darkness which so often prevail in the night of trial and temptation. Hence, in the sublime promise of a perpetual state of that heavenly joy and delight which flow from the love of God, and faith in his Word, the Evangelical Prophet exclaims in rapture, "Thy sun shall no more go down, neither shall thy moon withdraw itself" (Isa. lx. 20). It is from the principles and perceptions of the same love and faith that we are led with heartfelt sincerity to worship and serve the Lord, as being goodness itself, and truth itself; and to ascribe to the outflowing energies of his Holy Spirit all works of benevolence and use, by whatever agents they are made manifest. Then, in the language of correspondence, we are said to "Praise Him for the precious fruits brought forth by the sun, and for the precious things put forth by the moon" (Deut. xxxiii. 44).

The stars which bespangle the skies with their innumerable coruscations, and emit rays of light into the atmosphere, are emblematical,

---

the Analogy of Creation and New Creation, by W. Featherstone H, Barrister-at-law, in which it is attempted to be shown that the seven days of creation have the most wonderful and striking analogy to the Lord Jesus Christ and his work of redemption, and to the several stages in which man follows Him in the regeneration, "or new creation." One cannot perceive that the writer has ever read the works of Swedenborg; yet, amid great confusion and uncertainty, and without any guide to direct him, he has yet hit upon many ideas which are true and confirmatory of the truth of the science of correspondences, and which are valuable as proceeding from an independent mind. For instance, in his introduction, he says: "How all our knowledge arises from the study of the works and the Word of the Great Creator, and consists in the perception of the various relations (taking the Word in its widest signification) which his works bear to Himself; and these works are full of analogies within analogies, or, in the language of the Son of Israel, 'all the things are made double one against another.'"—p. 3.

in a good sense, of the knowledges of goodness and truth, which irradiate the mental firmament with rays of spiritual intelligence. When, therefore, a desecrated and benighted state of the church is treated of, the sun is represented as darkened and "shrouded in sackcloth of hair," to denote the utter extinction of love and charity; the moon is spoken of as "turned to blood," to signify that all genuine faith is darkened and corrupted; and the stars are said to "fall from heaven, even as a fig-tree casteth her untimely figs, when she is shaken of a mighty wind," to represent the awful apostasy from truth, when the revealed knowledges of heavenly things are hurled to the earth, and made subservient to the vilest purposes (Joel ii. 10; Matt. xxiv. 29; Acts ii. 20; Rev. vi. 12, 13). On the other hand, when the strength and glory of the church are treated of, she is represented as a wonder seen in heaven, "a woman clothed with the sun" (Rev. xii. 1),—encircled by a protecting sphere of divine love; as having "the moon under her feet,"—supported by a pure, holy, and firm faith; and upon her head "a diadem of twelve stars,"—crowned with the inextinguishable splendors of spiritual knowledge or intelligence.

The communications of divine truths from the Lord were made, in ancient times, not only by inspired speeches, but also by the perceptions which were excited into activity by visions or dreams. These were all representatives, from which the prophets taught the people the divine will and promises, and recorded them as the very Word of God. Joseph was favored with a prophetic dream of this kind, when he saw the sun, the moon, and the eleven stars, in appearance make obeisance before him. This can only, in the mere letter, apply to the single historical fact of Joseph, his brethren, and his parents in Egypt; but, in the internal or spiritual sense, by Joseph is signified the Lord Jesus Christ, and also, in regard to man, he signifies divine truth from the Lord in heaven and the church, or in the spiritual man; but the sun and the moon signify here natural goodness and truth, or goodness and truth in the natural mind; father and brethren signify and include the Jewish religion; while the eleven stars signify all the knowledges thereof. Bowing, or obeisance, denotes adoration, accompanied with the acknowledgment that all the rites and ceremonies of that religion had, in their internal character, a special relation to the Lord Jesus Christ in his divinely glorified humanity,—our heavenly Joseph, the source of all goodness and truth and knowledge. It is He who sustains his church in Egypt, and supplies abundance of corn in states of spiritual famine; but claims to be acknowledged as Lord of all.

CHAPTER XVII.

THE FIRST CHAPTERS OF GENESIS, TO THE 27TH VERSE OF CHAPTER XI., A GRAND SERIES OF DIVINE ALLEGORIES, WHICH CAN ONLY BE INTERPRETED BY THE SCIENCE OF CORRESPONDENCES.

THE first chapters of Genesis, to the history of Abram,[136] are a series of pure divine allegories, which can only be explained by the science of correspondences, according to which they are written as to the most minute particulars.[137] The progress of natural science compels those who admit them as a revelation from heaven, to regard them as divine allegories, in which spiritual subjects are presented to our view under the form of historical facts. For instance, the account of the creation in the first chapters of Genesis, cannot have been designed to be a literal history of the formation of the universe; for, if thus considered, it is full of insurmountable perplexity and inconsistency, and opposed to the numerous and incontrovertible facts which researches in geology, astronomy, and archæology have brought to light.[138] But if we contemplate it as a plenarily inspired description

---

[136] No authentic history exists in the world older than that of the patriarch Abraham.

[137] In Swedenborg's *Arcana Cœlestia*, every sentence in the books of Genesis and Exodus is explained according to the science of correspondences, and proved to have reference to the Lord, the human mind, and the spiritual world.

[138] The literal interpretation of the first chapters of Genesis has involved both ancient and modern commentators in insurmountable difficulties; and the truly wonderful discoveries of astronomy and geology completely disprove it.

Celsus, one of the earliest opposers of the Gospel, derides the Mosaic history of creation as an incredible philosophical tale; he treats with levity the history of Adam's formation, of Eve being made from his rib; of the commands that were given them, and of the serpent's cunning, in being able to evade the effect of those commands. Origen, in answer to him, says that he does not treat the subject with candor, but hides what he ought to have made known, viz., that all this was to be understood in *a figurative sense*, not giving the reader the words, which would have convinced him that they were spoken *allegorically.—Cont. Cel.*, l. iv., p. 186, 189.

"A few years ago an approximation to a correct calculation of the lapse of time in the formation of a part of the earth's surface was made by Sir Charles Lyell, after a visit to the Valley of the Mississippi, in the United States. That accomplished geologist described the bed of mud and sand deposited by the river Mississippi, which extended on the delta of the river, over an area of about 13,600 square statute miles, to the depth of at least 528 feet, or the tenth of a mile, and which in the upper part of the bed included an area of at least 13,600 statute miles, to a depth of 264 feet. Observations had been made on the average width, depth, and velocity of the stream, and experiments on the proportion of sediment carried down by the river proved that every year 3,702,758,400 cubic feet of solid matter were brought down,

242

EXPLAINS THE FIRST CHAPTERS OF GENESIS. 243

of the most ancient church, and the gradual process of man's regeneration, till, by the creation of new heavens and a new earth, from

---

by the river. After a careful investigation of details, Sir Charles Lyell and his friends demonstrated that a period of at least 100,500 years had elapsed in the formation of the alluvial deposit of the Mississippi."—*Lyell's Second Visit to the U. S.*, vol. ii., p. 250.

The Baobab-tree of Senegal (*Adansonia digitata*), measured by Adamson, is supposed to have attained the age of 5150 years. De Candolle considered it probable that the celebrated *Pascodium* of Chapultepec, in Mexico (*Cupresses dislicha*, Linn.), may be still more aged.—See *Lyell's Princ. of Geol.*, vol. iii., b. 4, c. 8, p. 128.

See Baden Powell, Dr. Nichol's *Architecture of the Heavens*, Dr. Hitchcock's *Religion of Geology*, Dr. Mantell's *Geology*, Bunsen's *Egypt*, Layard's *Nineveh*, and *Essays and Reviews*.

Philo calls it a manifest proof of ignorance to suppose that God really was engaged six days in the production of things."—*Vid. Sixt. Senens. Bib.*, 1, v., p. 338.

Among the innumerable and inexplicable difficulties of the merely literal sense is this: light is said to have existed, together with morning and evening, day and night, and all kinds of vegetation to have been created, three days before the sun was formed.—See Gen. i. 1-14.

"Bodinus has declared that 'the unskilful insisting of our divines upon the literal sense of Moses [in the first chapters of Genesis] had held many hundred thousands of atheists.'"—*Dr. H. More's Cab.*, p. 225.

"There is no way of preserving the true [literal] sense of the first *three* chapters of Genesis, without attributing to God things unworthy of Him, and for which [or the interpretation thereof] one *must* have recourse to allegory."—*Augustine, de Gen. cont. Manichæos.*

"The literal interpretation of the first chapters of Genesis has been a perpetual source of doubts and difficulties to the best commentators, and of raillery and ridicule to the enemies of revealed religion in all ages."—*Dr. C. Middleton's Essay on the Allegorical and Literal Interpretation of the Creation and Fall of Man.*

"The literal acceptation of the Mosaic history of the creation and fall of man, by its seeming inconsistency with the character of divine wisdom and goodness, induced certain heretics of the primitive Church to assert the existence of two Gods, or independent principles—the one evil, the other good. While the same method of interpreting induced other simple Christians also, as Origen tells us, who honored the Creator, and thought nothing superior to Him, to ascribe such things to Him as they would not believe of the most cruel and unjust men. . . . And, in truth, there is not any part of the Holy Scriptures that has so much exercised the wit and invention of commentators as this very history of the creation, by the difficulty of reconciling it with the allowed attributes of the Creator."—*Ib.*

"To what man of sense, I beg of you, could one make believe that the first, the second, and the third *day* of creation, in which, notwithstanding an evening and a morning are named, could have existed without sun, without moon, without stars? that during the first day there was not even a sky! Who shall be found so idiotic as to admit that God delivered himself up, like a man, to agriculture, by planting trees in the garden of Eden, situate towards the east; that one of these trees was that of life, and that another could give the science of good and evil? No one, I think, can hesitate to regard these things as *figures*, beneath which mysteries are hidden."—*Origen: Huet, Origeniana*, p. 167.

"All human calculations are futile in geological and ethnological inquiries. Epochs of vast duration are fully established by the nature of the organic remains of plants and animals that characterize the different formations; while the very intervals which separate these formations are evidences of other periods hardly less astonishing. In fact, geological epochs present some analogy to astronomical distances: the latter have been computed, the former are beyond calculation; and the mind is almost as incapable of realizing one as the other. It cannot grapple with numbers which approximate to infinitude. It is stated by Prof. Nichol, of Edinburgh, that 'light travels at the rate of 192,000 miles in a second of time; and that it performs its journey from the sun to the earth, a distance of 95,000,000 of miles, in about eight minutes. And yet, by Rosse's great telescope, we are informed that there are stars and systems so distant, that the ray of light which impinges on the eye of the observer, and enables him to detect it, issued from that orb 60,000 years back.'"—*Westminster Rev.*, 1846.

"The best scholars of the day, in common with Bochart, regard the so-called *ancestors* of Abraham as geographical names of nations, countries, tribes, or cities, and not as individuals."—*Nott and Glyddon's Types of Mankind*, pp. 112, 469, 549.

the natural degree he advances to the celestial, then we shall behold it full of the most beautiful instruction, and teeming with spiritual life. By days are denoted states of mind,—days of labor, states of trial and temptation, in appearance attributed to the Lord, because without his divine presence and assistance man could not become regenerate; and the day of rest, or Sabbath, a state of victory, and consequently of sacred rest and eternal peace. By the evening and the morning are signified advancements from one holy state to another. By the greater luminaries are signified the principles of love and faith, and their establishment within the soul in order to rule the day and the night, or to regulate and control the varied states of the heart and life. By the inanimate objects which were educed, or created, are meant the orderly arrangement of such things as are corporeal and natural; by the vegetables, such as have relation in general to the understanding and intelligence; and by the animals, such as have reference to the will and the affections. To create and form these, signifies thus to regenerate the whole man,—to "make all things new," to restore the soul; and the work is, lastly, pronounced very good.[139]

Baron Bunsen " relegates with firmness the long lives of the first patriarchs to the domain of *legend*, or of *symbolical cycle*." He reasonably "conceives that the historical portion [of Genesis] begins with Abraham."—*Bunsen's Bib. Res; Dr. R. Williams, Essays and Reviews*, 9th ed., p. 57.

Honert, in his *Institutiones Theol. Typ., Emblemat. et Prophet.*, etc., published 1739, maintains that " the creation of heaven and earth were prefigurative of the dispensation of the gospel;" and *God's resting on the seventh day*, "a type of (what the end of that dispensation is) our cessation from all grief, and enjoyment of all felicity in the kingdom of heaven;" and this, he says, "more particularly appears from 2 Cor. iv. 6; Gal. vi. 15; Isa. lxiii. 17."—See *Historia Literaria*, vol. i., p. 327.

From the irreconcilable contradictions disclosed by geological discovery, the whole narration of the six days' creation cannot now be regarded by any completely informed person as historical. The evidence in support of this conclusion is briefly discussed in my work, *On the Connection of Natural and Divine Truth*, 1838; in my article, CREATION, in *Kitto's Cyclop. of Bib. Lit.*

[139] "The Avesta and the Vedas refer, like the book of Genesis, to the first preaching [or teaching] of Monotheism, and of divine worship among mankind; not to the creation, but to the renewing, *bárá*, of heaven and earth, and to the renewing of man in the image of God."—*Bunsen's Keys of St. Peter*, p. 58.

"'God said,' at the creation, 'Let there be light, and there was light.' This, as related in the book of Genesis, is a [representative] pattern of the 'new creation in Christ Jesus,' and is so applied by the Apostle Paul. 'God, who commanded the light to shine out of darkness, hath shined in our hearts to give the light of the knowledge of the glory of God in the face of Jesus Christ' (2 Cor. iv. 6)."—*Bloomfield's Sermons*, p. 355.

"The [account of] creation, which is related in the book of Genesis, is a pattern of the new creation in Christ Jesus; and is so applied by the apostle: '*God who commanded the light to shine out of darkness, hath shined in our hearts to give the light of the knowledge of the glory of God in the face of Jesus Christ.*' Till this light shines in the heart of man, he is in the same state as the unformed world was when *darkness lay upon the face of the deep;* and when the new creation takes place, he rises in baptism or regeneration, of which baptism is the representative figure, as the new earth did from the waters, by the *spirit of God moving upon them*."—*Jones's Fig. Lang. of Scrip.*, p. 35.

"Neither in the written Word, nor in the organic creation of God, is there a single part unmeaning; a single part superfluous; a single part without its use and object, its bearing upon some distant relation, its importance in the general harmony; not one jot, not one tittle, not one letter. . . . No instructed Christian can read the first chapters of Genesis without feeling assured that under those simple statements lie prophecies and mysteries of the Christian Church."—*Dr. Sewell's Letter on the Inspiration of Holy Scripture*, pp. 83, 101.

"St. Cyril of Alexandria wrote two treatises on the books of Genesis and Leviticus, in which he says: 'When the Word of God, delivered by Moses and the prophets, is laid before men, it is presented to them with its peculiar covering upon it. For, as Christ had the array of his flesh, so the Word has the veil of the letter: the letter being apparently seen, as the flesh of Christ was; while the spiritual sense lying concealed within, as did his Divinity in his Humanity, is not perceptible to the outward sense. . . . For these things [of the law], according to the outward letter, may be *seen* or *heard*, as might the body of Christ, by the worthy and unworthy, indifferently; but blessed are they that *see*, and *hear*, and *perceive* the life-giving spirit concealed within.'"—*Holloway's Letter and Spirit*, Int., vol. i., p. lii.

"The first chapters of Genesis (at whatever period they were composed) were regarded by all the learned Jews as an allegory, and even as a fable not a little dangerous, since that book was forbidden to be read by any before they had attained the age of twenty-one. The Jews knew no more about original sin than they did about the Chinese ceremonies; and although divines generally discover in the Scriptures everything they wish to find there, either *totidem verbis*, or *totidem literis*, we may safely affirm that no reasonable divine will ever discover in it this surprsiing and overwhelming mystery."—*Phil. Dict.*

From ascertained facts, well known and undisputed among scientific men, in Ethnology, Astronomy, Geology, Chronology, and Archæology, it must be evident to all rational minds that the first eleven chapters of Genesis, to the history of Abraham, are wholly symbolic and unhistorical. Dr. Lepsius (*Chron. der Ægypten*, p. 176) dates the age of Menes, the first Egyptian king, 3893 B. C., or 5755 years to the present time [written in 1862]; and yet in that remote time Egypt was already possessed of her arts, institutions, and hieroglyphic language. The researches of the learned Chevalier Bunsen furnish nearly the same conclusions. Of the great antiquity of the human species, there can be no question. Dr. Prichard gives it as his matured opinion, in the last page of his fifth and last volume of *The Researches*, that "the human race has been chiliads of centuries upon the earth." Proofs of the vast antiquity of the earth and of man's long sojourn upon it multiply every day. "These views," observes Sir Charles Lyell, "have been adopted by all geologists, whether their minds have been formed by the literature of France or of Italy, of Scandinavia or England; all have arrived at the same conclusions respecting the great antiquity of the globe, and that, too, in opposition to their earliest prepossessions, and to the popular belief of their age."—See also *Nott and Glyddon's Types of Mankind*, pp. 319, 326.

It is not a little remarkable, and has not escaped the notice of many commentators, that the names of all the ten patriarchs, from Adam to Noah, descriptive spiritually of successive states of delusion in the Church, and the means of man's future deliverance from hell by the works of redemption and glorification, form a complete sentence, thus:—

Adam,	man,	earthy.	
Seth,	appointed,	set.	
Enos,	miserable, (and)	fallen man,	desperation.
Cainan,	lamenting,		possession.
Mahalaleel,	the God of glory,	praising God,	God's illumination.
Jared,	shall descend,	coming down,	ruling.
Enoch,	to instruct,	taught,	dedicated.
Methuselah,	his death sends,		the spoil of his death.
Lamech,	to the afflicted,	poor,	humbled, smitten.
Noah,	consolation,	ceasing,	rest.

The ages ascribed to the above patriarchs are sufficient to prove that they were representative characters only, and not real individuals.

"*Giants in the earth in those days.*" A strong or mighty man, or one of valor and bravery, is called Gibbor; and in the spiritual sense is one who is governed by fantasy, and distinguished by profanation and self-love. Those who are represented as having attained uncommon stature are always described as men of violence, the enemies of the Lord and his people; as, Goliath of Gath, Og, king of Bashan; Saul, king of Israel, and the sons of Anak and the Nephilim. They are described, therefore, as springing from the commerce of "the sons of God and the daughters of men," for no other terms could so well describe these holy truths of revelation when prostituted to selfish lusts and worldly ends. The magnitude of their bodies is, in all cases, but the outward form of their souls puffed up and expanded, or spread out by false suggestions and evil emotions, the awful and gigantic result of their profanation, and fantasy, and self-persuasion.

"In the writings of Moses, chiefly in the beginning of Genesis, there occur documents of much higher antiquity than Moses' own writings."—*Dr. J. Heringa's Notes to Dr. G. F. Seiler's Biblical Hermeneutics, translated by the Rev. D. W. Wright*, ed. 1835, p. 93.

"That the book of Genesis was, in part, composed or compiled from previously existing documents, or from true traditionary accounts existing in the Church at the time of its composition by Moses, is a point which is now very generally admitted among those who are conversant with Biblical criticism. This was also the opinion of Vitringa, Le Cene, Calmet, and Astruc."—See the *Introd. of Horne, Eichorn, Jahn, and Bertholdt, Dr. I. P. Smith's Cong. Lect.*, p. 207, and *Stuart on the O. T. Canon*, p. 51; *Dr. Henderson on Divine Inspiration*, p. 312, and Note T, p. 488.

"The first two chapters of Genesis, as indeed the whole of the first eight [or rather eleven], are now generally admitted by scholars to be made up of fragments [or are remains] of earlier books or earlier revelations, the exact meaning of which the writers of the Pentateuch seem hardly to have appreciated when they transcribed them into the form in which they are now found. The history of the Jews and the Jewish religion commences with the call of Abraham."—See *Fergusson's T. and P. Worship*, pp. 6, 7.

[When the above was written (1862), comparatively little was known of those extraordinary evidences of the antiquity of man on this globe which have been found in the lacustrine cities of Switzerland, the shell middens of the Baltic shores, or the paleolithic and neolithic or flint ages. For years the discoveries were regarded by many with suspicion,—as either accidental in their nature, or as the results of deception; and though of late years the evidences on this subject have been greatly extended, and their field widened, the health of the author was so far affected that he took little notice of them, and probably had forgotten this note. Modern discoveries leave no doubt that man was coeval with the extinct mammoth, whose remains are found mingled with the flint weapons of these early denizens of this world. It was usual for those who accepted the ordinary Biblical chronology of Usher, to regard the whole of the astronomical calculations of Egypt, Assyria, and China as forgeries, and their lists of monarchs as mythic and unreliable. It is certain, however, now, that even these ages, though they carry us back so far, are but modern as compared with the paleolithic age,—though we are dealing not with the *creation* of man, but only with evidences which he has left of his being. Time past has been divided, for the sake of reference, into three ages: 1, the flint age; 2, the bronze age; 3, the iron age. The latter is identified with real history, and the change from the 2d to the 3d appears to be the boundary between real and mythic history. But of the 1st era, which has been subdivided into the paleolithic and neolithic ages, no remains in literature are extant; it is doubtful whether there was any method in use for the transmission of thought except by word of mouth, though evidences of ornamentation and drawing have been found on some of the flints. If we refer to Gen. iv. 22, we read, "And Zillah, she also bare Tubal-Cain, an instructor of every artificer in brass and iron." It is certain that the metal called brass is of modern invention, or possibly copper may be meant. But the mention of iron, to the exclusion of flint and bronze, clearly shows that the passage is not *historical*. According to the Bible chronology, this birth took place about 3875 years B. C., or 5754 years ago, at which time it is extremely doubtful whether the working of iron was known. But even granting that it was, there still remain beyond, far beyond, the bronze, the neolithic, and the paleolithic ages; and these, as we have seen, carry us back to ages of which man has left behind him proofs of his existence scattered over the whole globe. These remains, however, are all in the superficial strata, and in fact yield no data from which we can calculate the antiquity of man. This field of investigation, however, is one upon which scientists have barely entered.—ED.]

"Many of the proper names occurring in the tenth chapter of Genesis remain unchanged, as the appellations of races and kingdoms. Others are found in the plural or dual number, proving that they bear a personal and national reference; and a third class have that peculiar termination which, in Hebrew, signifies a sept, or tribe."—*Dr. Eadie's Early Oriental Hist., Enc. Met.*, 1852, p. 2.

"Dr. M. will have it that the Mosaic account of the fall is an allegory. *I agree it is so.*"—*Bishop Warburton's Letters to Bishop Hurd.*

"I take the whole of this narrative to be allegorical."—*Reutish's Notes and Comments*, 1848, p. 2.

See also APPENDIX on the various styles in which the Word is written.

Again, it is seen by this science that the garden of Eden[140] (Gen. ii. 15), with its beautiful scenery and delightful fruits, corresponds to the mind of man, which Adam[141] is therefore commanded "to dress

---

[140] *Eden* means, in English, "delight."—See Isa. li. 3; Ezek. xxiii. 13; xxxi. 9.

"It is observable that *Aden*, in the Eastern dialect, is precisely the same word with Eden, which we apply to the garden of Paradise. It has two senses, according to a slight difference in its pronunciation: its first meaning is *a settled abode;* its second, *delight, softness,* or *tranquillity*. The word *Eden* had probably one of these senses in the sacred text, though we use it as a proper name."—*Sir W. Jones's Works*, vol. iv., p. 528.

"Know," says Rabbi Simon Bar Abraham, cited by Hutchinson (*Hebrew Writings*, p. 21, *from Buxtorf*), "that in the trees, fountains, and other things of the garden of Eden, were the figures of most curious things by which the first Adam [or Church] saw and understood *spiritual* things; even as God hath given to us the forms and figures of the tabernacle, of the sanctuary, and of all its furniture, the candlestick, the table, and the altars for types of *intellectual* [subjects, or] things, and that we might from them understand heavenly truths. In the trees, likewise, and fountains or rivers of the garden, he prefigured admirable mysteries."—*Theoph. Text of Prof. Antiq.*, p. 137.

Dr. Adam Clarke, from his extensive and learned researches, thus enumerates the opinions of interpreters on the locality of Paradise. "It would astonish an ordinary reader, who should be obliged to consult different commentators and critics *on the situation of the terrestrial Paradise*, to see the vast variety of opinions by which they are divided. Some place it in the third heaven, others in the fourth; some within the orbit of the moon, others in the moon itself; some in the middle regions of the air, or beyond the earth's attraction; some on the earth, others under the earth, and others within the earth; some have fixed it at the north pole, others at the south; some in Tartary, some in China; some on the borders of the Ganges, some in the island of Ceylon; some in Armenia, others in Africa, under the equator; some in Mesopotamia, others in Syria, Persia, Arabia, Babylon, Assyria, and in Palestine; some have condescended to place it in *Europe*, and others have contended it either exists not, or is invisible, or is *merely of a spiritual nature, and that the whole account is to be spiritually* understood!"—*Comment. in loci*. Another writer affirms that the site of Eden is now at the bottom of one of the great oceans.

"If thou wilt keep thy habitation and preserve thy dwelling-place in Paradise, in the garden of God, thou must dress it and keep it. 'Keep thy heart with all diligence' (Prov. iv. 23)."—*W. Sherwin, a writer of the seventeenth century.*

"The geography of the rivers in Paradise is *inexplicable*, though it assumes the tone of explanation."—*F. W. Newman's Phases of Faith*, p. 110.

"Many learned and laborious treatises have been published on the site of Paradise, or the garden of Eden; some affirming it to be above the moon, others above the air; some that it is the whole world, others only a part of the north, or under the arctic pole; some thinking that it was nowhere, while others supposed it to be somewhere in the West Indies. Rudbeck, a Swede, asserts that Sweden was the real Paradise. The learned Bishop Huet gives a map of Paradise, and says it is situated upon the canal formed by the Tigris and Euphrates, near Aracca; another writer in the place possessed by the Caspian Sea. Mahomet assured his followers that Paradise was seated in heaven, and that Adam was cast out from thence when he transgressed." Humboldt (see *Cosmos*, Bohn, vol. i., p. 364-5) brings up the rear with telling us that every nation has a Paradise somewhere on the other side of the mountains." —*Bohn's Hudibras*, vol. i., p. 11.

The Greeks had their garden of Alcinous; the Romans, their garden of Flora; in Africa, they had the garden of the Hesperides; and in the East, those of Adonis.—See, also, *Gardens of Epicurus, Sir W. Temple*. See *Spence's Polymetis*, cited in *Letters on Mythology*, p. 126.

[141] *Adam* means "man," and is a generic term for the whole human race (Gen. v. 2). Adam was the name given to the most ancient Church on this earth, significative of its true quality.

"Adam," according to the apostle Paul, was the "figure of Him that was to come." —Rom. v. 14.

"The Adam and Eve of sacred writ some (among whom I think is Dr. Warburton) have supposed to have been allegorical or hieroglyphic persons of Egyptian origin. According to this opinion they were the names of two hieroglyphic figures respecting the early state of mankind."—*Dr. Darwin's Bot. Gard.: Art., Portland Vase.*

"The Mosaic history of Paradise and of Adam and Eve has been thought by some to

and to keep." The rivers signify the inflowing of divine wisdom and truths, which promote the refreshment, growth, and fruitfulness of all the powers and principles, virtues and graces of the mind. "The tree of life in the midst," signifies the Lord Himself, and his Word, and thence celestial joy, together with an inmost perception and acknowledgment that all life, all good, all knowledge, and all delight, are derived from Him, for He alone is life itself, and the source of all life. "The tree of knowledge of good and evil"[142] signifies the

---

be a sacred allegory, designed to teach obedience to divine commands, and to account for the origin of evil; as otherwise knowledge could not be said to grow upon one tree, and life upon another, or a serpent to converse. The tree of the knowledge of good and evil, and the tree of life, must have been emblematical or allegorical."—*Dr. Darwin's Temple of Nature.*

"Adam and Eve are only put as representatives, male and female, of the entire human species all over the globe."—*O'Brien's Round Towers of Ireland*, 2d ed., p. 231.

"Adam, according to the Cabalists, was not *one man*, but the whole human race."—*Baruch*, liv. 3, partie. ch. x.

Vitringa, in his dissertation, "De Arbore Prudentiæ in Paradiso, ejusque mysterio," contends that the tree of the knowledge of good and evil signifies prudence, and that the history is an allegory.

"The first Adam, the original type of humanity, separated from God, and acted during the ages of unresisted evil as the god of this world, striving after an independent and extra divine existence. The second Adam, on the other hand, the type of the new creation, exhibited the return of man to a perfect union with the divine nature."—*Morell's Sketch of Schelling's Phil. of Rev., Hist. of Mod. Phil.*, vol. ii., pp. 152, 153.

"Paul calls Adam τοπος τοῦ μελλοντος, *i. e.* a type of Christ," Rom. v. 14. Comp. 1 Cor. xv. 45–47.—*Stuart's Com. on the Heb.*, p. 125.

"In human beings, the mind occupies the rank of the man and the sensations that of the woman."—*Philo Judæus: Works*, vol. i., p. 49.

"Adam [man] is here (Gen. i. 27) collective, as the pronouns and verbs following show, but never a proper name; and it is first so employed in Tob. viii. 8. With the article, *âdâm* signifies the human race."—*Von Bohlen*, Int., p. 17.

[142] "The first religious ordinance which was conveyed to man, was under the combined symbol of the trees of life and knowledge; and, given to man in that state of innocence and purity, was evidently designed as the mode and form in which the Deity would ever communicate with his race. As men grew and multiplied on the earth, the symbolic principle thus given to them would gain a corresponding strength and influence. Thus every idea of worship would naturally possess an emblematic character. It would be inseparable from religion, in the minds of the true believers."—*Tucker's Scrip. Stud.*, pp. 270, 271.

Origen says, "What rational man will believe that God, like a husbandman, planted a garden, and in it a real tree of life to be tasted? or, that the knowledge of good and evil was to be obtained by eating the fruit of another tree? And as to God walking in the garden, and Adam hiding himself from him among the trees, no man can doubt but that these things are to be understood figuratively and not literally, to signify certain mysteries, or recondite senses."—*Philoc.*, c. i., p. 12.

Augustin, in the preface to his twelve books on the first three chapters of Genesis, says, "No Christian will say that they are not to be understood figuratively, when he recollects that the apostle declares how all these things happened to them in a figure."

Heylin well observes, that, "In forming our notion concerning the fall of man from the account given in Scripture, we must make due allowance for the imperfection of human language, which cannot express spiritual things otherwise than by figures founded in that analogy which subsists between the visible and the invisible world." "The sacred [writer] was obliged to represent intellectual things by sensible images, which he uses, if I may so speak, as a kind of hieroglyphics. Such in particular is the *tree of knowledge*, which appears to have been a well-chosen symbol, and well understood by the Jews, because a tree or plant is still frequently used by the Jewish writers, to signify some principal part of knowledge implanted in the mind. Hence our Lord himself, after reprobating some false doctrines

mere pleasure of knowledge for selfish purposes and for selfish considerations, together with the fallacious and sinful persuasion that life, goodness, knowledge, and pleasure are self-derived; of the fruit of which man is solemnly warned "not to eat, lest he die."[143] Thus a tendency towards God and goodness, and a contrary tendency towards self and self-dependence, are denoted by these two remarkable trees. By the serpent tempting and seducing the woman, is signified the sensual nature and principle of the mind, which is ever prompting man to throw off all allegiance to God, all reverence for his Word, all reliance on the Divine Providence, and to depend upon his own miserable prudence and self-will, thus to regard himself as the source of his life and the fountain of all that is worth calling good. When thus the sanctity of goodness and truth was voluntarily profaned, man lost his innocence, integrity, and tranquillity, and was self-expelled from Eden; and instead of the glorious trees of paradise, his mind produced nothing but "thorns and thistles," and with a wrathful spirit, he became a tiller of the ground. Hence originated all evil; and it is still the same serpentine principle that lurks in every bosom, and tempts man to every act of disobedience against the divine commandments,—to substitute fallacious appearances for realities, and, given up to their uncleanness, through the lusts of their own hearts, to "change the truth of God into a lie" (Rom. i. 25). Where-

---

of the Pharisees, adds, 'Every plant which my Father hath not planted, shall be rooted up,' i.e., 'Every doctrine which is not of divine institution shall be eradicated.' When, therefore, we read that the first man was placed in a fruitful garden, we must infer that his mind, too, had its paradise suited to its capacities, and abounding with its various objects of knowledge."—*Disc. on Original Sin.*

The tree is neither called an apple-tree, nor by the name of any other natural fruit tree, but "*the tree of the knowledge of good and evil;*" bearing, therefore, mental or spiritual fruit.

"The fruit of a material tree could not, by any virtue inherent in it, convey '*the knowledge of good and evil*' or cause that, by eating it, a man should '*live for ever.*'"—*Bp. Horne's Sermons*, p. 24.

"'T is but one and the same soul in man entertaining a dialogue with herself, that is set out [in Gen. ii.] by these parts: the serpent, Adam, and the woman."—*More's Cab. Def.*, p. 228.

"An idea of lost integrity seems to have pervaded the whole Pagan world, and to have mingled itself with the religious belief of all nations." "The ancient Celtic Druids believed in the defection of the human soul from a state of rectitude;" and it is asserted to be the invariable belief of the Brahmins, that man is a fallen creature. The arguments in both these cases are principally derived from the severe penitential discipline to which they submitted, with a view of ultimately regaining their lost perfection. The Hindoos have an entire Purana on this very subject.—See *Bridge's Test. of Prof. Antiq.*, p. 144; *Faber's Hor. Mos.*, vol. i., pp. 65-71; and *Horne's Introd. to the Crit. Study of the S. S.*, 8th ed., vol. i., pp. 145, 146, where authorities are cited.

[143] Heb., "Dying thou shalt die."

M. Diderot, one of the class of unbelievers, taking the gross, literal interpretation for granted as being the true one, ridicules the whole history thus: "The God of the Christians, for an apple, punished all the human race, and killed his own Son. This only proves that God is a Father who makes a great deal to do about his apples, and cares very little about his children."—*Thoughts on Religion*, p. 9.

fore the apostle wrote to the Corinthians, "I am jealous over you with godly jealousy: I fear, lest by any means, as the serpent beguiled Eve through his subtilty, so your minds should be corrupted from the simplicity that is in Christ" (2 Cor. xi. 3).

That the serpent, in all its varieties, is a true type of the sensual principle of the human mind, under its various phases, might be proved from the most abundant evidence.[144] Distinguished for its

---

[144] "The slyest and subtilest of all the animal figurations, the *serpent*, is the *inordinate desire of pleasure*."—*Dr. H. More's Moral Cab.*, p. 70.

Philo, who explained the allegories of the Mosaic law agreeably to the ancient belief of the Hebrews, in a treatise on the formation of the world according to the account of Moses, says, "These are not fabulous tales, such as the poets make use of, but they are figurative descriptions, leading us to allegorical and recondite senses, to which, if any one rationally attends, he will see that the *serpent* is used for the emblem of *sensual pleasure*; he lays his whole stress upon his belly,—he carries poison in his tongue . . . . which qualities are purely descriptive of the sensual [or voluptuous] man."—*De Opific. Mundi, Secund Moys. Op.* (T. 1., p. 38: ed. Lond.) The learned Rabbi Maimonides, in his *Mor. Nov.*, says that "The serpent has relation to the mind of man; and that in the account that is given of the creation, the ancient Rabbies, from the time of Moses, held that these things, reduced to an historical form in the first chapters of Genesis, were not to be literally understood; but that this was the method by which, in ancient times, they instructed the people" (ch. xxix., pp. 265, 272). Clemens Alexandrinus, who lived in the second century, was of the same opinion.

"The allegorical meaning of the first chapters of Genesis is also fully illustrated by St. Paul (2 Cor. xi. 3). 'I fear, lest as the serpent beguiled Eve, through his subtilty, so your minds should be corrupted from the simplicity that is in Christ.' Thus does Paul give the true meaning of the allegory; signifying, in plain language, that the first people were beguiled, or seduced from their native simplicity, not by a beast, called a serpent, but by giving way to their sensual passions. For as this was the case with the Corinthians, the apostle's comparison would not have been at all applicable, unless he had understood the serpent to be the symbol of *the sensual principle of man*, as the most ancient Jews did before him."—*Bellamy on Genesis*, p. 15.

"In the above passage Paul seems to unfold the true meaning and hidden sense of the Mosaic parable . . . and, in applying it to the case of the Corinthians, the apostle's simile would not be pertinent, unless we take the serpent, as many of the learned have done, to be the symbol of lust and sensual pleasure."—*Dr. C. Middleton's Essays, etc.*

"In the mythology of most ancient nations there are traces which attest that the idea of the serpent, as the *evil principle*, prevailed from the most remote antiquity. The serpent is represented as the cause of the first transgression, and fall of man; and Arimanes, assuming the form of a serpent, seeks in vain to overcome his antagonist, Orosmandes, who represents the good principle of the ancient Persians. It is believed that the ancient Greeks made choice of the allegory of the great serpent killed by the arrows of Apollo, to represent the pestilential vapors emanating from the marshy slime which covered the earth after the deluge, or after annual inundations, and which could only be dissipated by the rays of the sun; afterwards, this Python became the attribute of Apollo and his priestesses at Delphi, and it subsequently served for the emblem of Foretelling and Divination. Analogous circumstances probably gave rise to the fable of the Lernæan hydra, exterminated by the labors of Hercules and his companion Iolas. Among the ancient Egyptians, the serpent was the symbol of fertility. They represented under the form of a serpent, enclosed by a circle, or entwined round a globe, the Cneph of their cosmogony, who is the same as Ammon, or the Agathodemon, the spirit or soul of creation—the principle of all that lives, who governs and enlightens the world. The priests of that people kept in the temples living serpents; and when dead, interred them in those sanctuaries of superstition. As an emblem of prudence and circumspection, the serpent was a constant attribute of Æsculapius, and the same veneration was paid to those reptiles as to the father or the god of medicine and magic. The Ophites were Christian sectaries, who, towards the second century of our era, established a worship which was particularly distinguished from that of the Gnostics in this,—that they adored

subtlety and watchfulness, its incapability of locomotion, except by writhing upon its belly, its peculiar power of fascination by which it

a living serpent; conforming themselves to the ancient traditions of their race, they regarded that animal as the image of wisdom, and of the sensual emotions which it awakens. The monuments of the Mexicans, of the Japanese, and of many other nations who owe the foundation of their civilization to the ancient inhabitants of Asia, attest that the serpent played also a part, more or less important, in their religious mysteries; but time, and the relations which exist between those nations and Europeans, have partly abolished these usages; and at this day it is only among negro tribes, and on the west coast of Africa, that the serpent figures among divinities of the first rank."—*Schlegel's Essay on the Physiognomy of Serpents*, cited *N. C. Advocate*, vol. ii., p. 175.

"The whole of the conversation between Eve and the Nachash may be allegorical,—a hieroglyphical description of that which took place [in the mind]. There is nothing new in this mode of interpretation; it has been adopted by several learned commentators.—(See *Abarbanel; Pol. Synop. Critic.*) Such an interpretation of the passage is in unison with the apostle's allusion to Eve's transgression: 'I fear lest by any means as the serpent [is represented to have] beguiled Eve through his subtilty, so your MINDS should be corrupted from the simplicity that is in Christ'" (2 Cor. xi. 3).—*Dr. Lamb's Heb. Hiero.*, pp. 105, 106.

"This [spiritual] mode of interpretation," says the learned Dr. C. Middleton, "is embraced by several of the ancients, particularly St. Augustine, who tells us that the same thing is acted over again in every one of us as often as we fall into sin, that was represented by the serpent, the woman, and the man, for there is first, says he, a suggestion or insinuation, either by a thought, or the senses of the body, by which if our inclination is not prevailed with to sin, then is the subtilty of the serpent baffled and vanquished; but if it is prevailed with, then we yield, as it were, to the persuasions of the woman; and when our reason has thus consented to execute what our lust had moved, then is man effectually driven out and expelled from all possessions of happiness as from Paradise."—*Dr. Gene's Cont. Manich.*, l. ii., c. 12; *Ib.*, c. 3.—*Letter to Waterland.*

"This kind of symbolical representation of the serpent," says Bellamy, "did not consist in the unmeaning worship of the image, but was introduced to represent the sensual passions and affections, also the principle of circumspection, or prudence of the sensual principle in man; for which qualities, the serpent was then, and is now, allowed, by the best writers on those subjects, to be more famous than any other animal" (Lev. xxx. 31, note, p. 333).

"The serpent with the power of speech is the impulse of desire."—*Teller.*

"In a Tamul verse, the serpent is called a 'creature of deep searchings and great mystery.' Thus it is a proverb among the Hindoos of this day, when a man acts with such cunning as to elude the observation of others, '*Pàmbu pambin kāl areyum*,' that is, 'the serpent knows its own feet;' meaning no other is acquainted with its ways. A wicked man is called 'the seed of the serpent,' and he who is rapid in the accomplishment of his vile purposes, is called '*the serpent-eyed one.*'"—*Robert's Oriental Illustrations*, 2d ed., p. 8.

In some of its numerous forms the serpent was associated by the Egyptians, Phœnicians, etc., with all their rituals of religion; and in ages of darkness and corruption, serpent worship prevailed over nearly the whole world, and was introduced into all the ancient mysteries. It is also worthy of remark, that the leading ideas of that direct prophecy of the Lord's advent, as the bruiser of the serpent's head, are to be found among the traditions of both oriental and occidental nations, the Indians, the Greeks, and the Goths of Scandinavia. In India, sculptured figures are found in the temples, which represent the incarnation of one of their personifications of the triad of deity. Kreeshna is depicted with one foot on a serpent's head. Another figure is encompassed with the folds of that reptile, which is in the act of biting his heel.—(See *Maurice's Hist. of Hind.*, plates, vol. 2, p. 290.) In the same mythology, an emblematic compound of a man and an eagle, is represented as placed at the portals of a garden, to prevent the intrusion of serpents. He is said to have destroyed them all except one, which he slung round his neck as a trophy.—(See *Moor's Hind. Panth.*, p. 336.) The Scandinavian Thor is said to have bruised the head of the great serpent, and it is predicted that he shall, in another encounter with the monster, overcome and slay him.—(*Edda*, fab. 32.) The true correspondence of the serpent in Paradise, once well understood, was intermingled with the numerous legends of the Greeks. Thus, the garden of Hesperides, with its tree bearing golden fruit, was said to be guarded by a serpent. Hercules slew this serpent and bore

seeks its prey, its poison-fang, and its voracious appetite, no other animal is so complete a representative of the sensual principle of man's mind and life. "A wicked and adulterous generation" the Lord calls "a generation of vipers" (Matt. iii. 7; xii. 34); and they are also described in Deuteronomy, where it is said, "Their wine is the wine of dragons, and the cruel venom of asps" (xxxiii. 33). This principle, like the serpent in a bad sense, is distinguished for its wily prudence, its fascinating influence, and its deadly venom; in its sensuous reasonings it always cleaves to the ground, and is ravenous after all kinds of carnal pleasure. And when man listens to the serpent's voice, he eats of the forbidden fruit, and forfeits his purity and peace.

From this interpretation of the serpent, we may see the reason why the Lord Jesus Christ,—the Messiah,—in the earliest prophecy of the Word respecting Him, is represented under the figure of "the seed of the woman" that should "bruise the serpent's head." For He came and assumed human nature with all its hereditary infirmities, being born of a woman, that He might subdue the sensual principle, and thus destroying in his Humanity what the apostle calls "the works of the devil, that He might give authority to all that believe

---

away the precious fruit in triumph, and is therefore represented in the constellation as trampling on the serpent's head.

"We have the assurance of Bishop Horsley, that the Church of England does not demand the literal understanding of the document contained in the second (from verse 8) and third chapters of Genesis as a point of faith, or regard a different interpretation as affecting the orthodoxy of the interpreter;" "and indeed no unprejudiced man can pretend to doubt, that if, in any other work of Eastern origin, he met with trees of life and knowledge, talking and conversable snakes, he would want no other proofs that it was an allegory he was reading, and intended to be understood as such."—*Coleridge's Aids to Reflection*, p. 250.

"The legitimate or illegitimate alternative of human activity, represented in the first pages of the Bible by *the tree of the knowledge* [or distinction] *of good and evil* (Gen. ii. 17), is expressed in a general manner in these words of Jesus: '*A good man, out of the good treasure of his heart, bringeth forth good things; and an evil man, out of the evil treasure, bringeth forth evil things*' (Matt. xii. 35; Luke vi. 45). On the allegory of the forbidden fruit, see Book II. ch. xx., note 7; p. 66, note 18." The note referred to is as follows: "*The fall*, related in Gen. iii. 1-6, brings into action, under the veil of an allegory, the three fundamental passions, the sources of all sin,—the passion of independence, the desire to act without control,—'*Yea, hath God said, ye shall not eat of every tree of the garden?*'—the passion of pride, the desire of becoming greater,—'*Ye shall be as gods, knowing good and evil*'—and the passion of sensuality, the 'fleshly lusts that war against the soul,—'*The tree appeared good for food, and pleasant to the eyes.*' He who does not recognize moral evil in this picture, is but ill acquainted with the world and with his own heart. IT IS NO LONGER DOUBTED that this narrative is allegorical; and we go still further, it was fitting that it should be so; an exact analysis of the passions was impossible in the new-born experience of the first ages. . . . In order to relate *the origin of evil*, it was necessary to present the fact in an emblematic picture."—*Christianity: its perfect adaptation to the Mental, Moral, and Spiritual Nature of Man*, by A. Coquerel, translated by the Rev. D. Davidson, M. A., with a Preface written expressly for the English edition by the author. This work has been received in England with signal approbation.

on Him to do likewise" (1 John iii. 8). The same was signified by the serpent of brass [145] which Moses, by divine direction, set upon a pole, that the people, when grievously bitten by the poisonous fiery serpents of the wilderness, might look thereunto and be healed (Num. xxi. 8, 9). In a good sense, by brass, or, as it should be rendered, copper, is signified natural goodness, flowing from the rational discernment of the truth; as by gold is signified goodness of a celestial quality, flowing from the inmost perceptions of love and faith. Hence, in describing a highly advanced state of the human mind and the church, the prophet says, "For brass I will bring gold" (Isa. lx. 17). It was from this signification of brass, that it was required to be presented to the Lord in the free-will offerings for the tabernacle, and that the altar of burnt-offering was made of this metal (Ex. xxv. 3; xxxix. 39). The serpent of brass, therefore, pointed out that sin of the Israelites which was the immediate cause of their distress, and directed their attention to the only certain means of restoration. They had loathed the bread of heaven, and desired the means of indulging their gross sensual appetites. This sensualism was represented by the venomous serpents which bit them. But Moses made a serpent of brass, and elevated it on a pole. The Holy Word, as the great prophet of God, instructs us that we can only escape the deadly fangs of sensuality by subjugating the natural mind, becoming circumspect in all our conduct, and receiving from the Lord new external as well as internal principles of goodness, which will sanctify our lowest desires, and exalt them into connection with Himself. The Lord, in this respect, is our Divine exemplar. He bruised, in his Human Nature, the serpent's head. By his inherent omnipotence He subdued all things to Himself. He glorified his Humanity, and united it forever to Himself; thus He became the very divine good even to the last and lowest principles of rational and sensual life. He alone is omnipresent, infinitely circumspect, and provident over all, so that to Him, under the deadly plague of sin, are we to look for deliverance with faithful and obedient hearts; that, like as He conquered the serpent and glorified his Humanity, so we may experience, through the influence of his Spirit, a full renewal of our carnal minds, that

---

[145] Speaking of brass, Harris says that it "is a mixed metal, for the making of which we are indebted to the German metallurgists of the thirteenth century. That the ancients knew not the art of making it is almost certain. None of their writings even hint at the process. There can be no doubt that *copper* is the original metal intended by the Hebrew word translated brass, and which literally means, to scrutinize."—*Nat. Hist. of the Bible*, Eng. ed., p. 55.

they may no longer be at enmity with Him. He therefore says, "As Moses lifted up the serpent in the wilderness, even so must the Son of Man be lifted up, that whosoever believeth in Him should not perish, but have eternal life" (John iii. 14, 15).

When, however, the true signification was lost, the Israelites, prone to adopt the idolatry of the nations around them, worshipped the serpent of brass as a god, and burnt incense to it, and its meaning then became reversed; wherefore, Hezekiah, the good king of Israel, broke it in pieces (2 Kings xviii. 4). To instruct us that, if we pervert these holy truths by inwardly cherishing sensual affections, and substitute for real goodness the specious appearance of an empty morality, we shall be tempted to look to it in the dangerous spirit of vainglory, and even to rely upon it for acceptance with God. Under this superstitious pretext of holiness we shall become worshippers of ourselves, and make our lusts our lawgiver. In this sad state, like the wise and good king of Israel, we must break our idol in pieces, whatsoever false semblance it may assume. We must renounce the infatuated delusions of self-righteousness, to which such worship gives birth; and in the spirit of true repentance and humility we must conform, from inward motives as well as in outward life, to the instructions of true wisdom. For outward conformity to truth, without inward goodness, is corrupt, empty "as the sounding brass;" and, instead of being available to promote our advancement in the regenerate life, will only bring us into states of eternal condemnation.[146]

---

[146] "In the account of man's fall, it will be observed that there is no mention of the interference of an evil spirit. And in the whole course of the sacred history there is not one text from which we can rightly infer that there is an order of beings, such as are generally represented by the fallen angels, or that sin existed before Eve's transgression. ... How incredible it is, that an order of angels, who enjoyed much nearer communion with God [than man], and far excelled him in every intellectual faculty, should be the authors of sin. ... The two passages (2 Pet. ii. 4-6, and Jude 5-7), which may be thought by some to establish the received opinions, evidently allude to the same event, 'the great apostasy of Cain.' ... And no argument can be drawn from these passages, unsupported by collateral evidence, in favor of the generally received opinions. There is a perfect silence in Scripture respecting any fallen angels, or the existence of sin prior to Adam's transgression; our Lord in his discourses never uses an expression which implies such a notion; nor is mention made by Him of any separate class of beings like the fallen angels. ... By the devil and his angels (Matt. xxv. 41) is meant the whole body of wicked souls. ... This question may be asked: If such be the case, how came the opinion so general respecting fallen angels, and whence was it derived? There can be no doubt respecting the source whence it was obtained. The first notion of the existence of a fallen angel is found in the Zendavesta. The Ahriman of Zoroaster is the original model of Satan. The later Jews became conversant with the Persian mythology, and introduced this, with various other notions, into their writings; and it seems to have been adopted by the early Christians without any inquiry into the Scriptural authority upon which it rested. Our immortal countryman, Milton, by clothing this fiction of the Persian mythology in all the beauty and attraction of poetry, has so recommended it to our imagination, that we almost receive it as of divine authority; and we feel a reluctance to be convinced that all his splendid fabric is based on falsehood." *Dr. Lamb's Heb. Hierog.*, p. 112 *et seq.*

CHAPTER XVIII.

History of the Flood, the Ark, and of Noah and his Posterity, an Allegory; or, rather, a Spiritual History clothed in the Divine Language of Correspondences.

THE references made to Noah and the flood in the Bible are very few, viz.: Isa. liv. 9; Ezek. xiv. 20; Matt. xxiv. 38; Luke xvii. 27; 1 Pet. iii. 20; 2 Pet. ii. 5; iii. 6; Heb. xi. 7. They give no indication whatever, when properly translated and rightly understood, of having respect to any physical event.

The history of a universal flood as recorded in the sixth, seventh, and eighth chapters of the book of Genesis, is not an inspired account of a flood of literal waters sweeping over the whole earth, but of a devastating inundation of false persuasions and evil lusts, superinduced by licentious conduct and carnal security, over the whole church collectively and the mind individually, which, sweeping away all the landmarks of goodness and truth, accomplished a judgment upon a perverted generation. "The flood came and took them all away" (Matt. xxiv. 39), and thus inaugurated a new epoch in human history. A new dispensation or religion was mercifully established, signified by the ark in which righteous Noah, his family, and all kinds of living creatures were preserved from destruction. Hence the apostle Peter writes concerning the ark, and speaks of it as the means of salvation, saying, "The like figure whereunto *even* baptism doth also now save us (not the putting away of the filth of the flesh, but the answer of a good conscience toward God), by the resurrection of Jesus Christ" (1 Pet. iii. 21).

Now, the flood is represented, according to most chronologists, as having taken place about four thousand two hundred years ago; yet there are trees believed to have been in existence at least five thousand years, and recent researches have brought Egyptian monuments to light considered to be above six thousand years old. But, I would ask, if this history were to be understood in its merely literal sense, of what real use is it to the immortal soul? How does it advance our progress in the divine life? How does it prepare us, as all revelation professes to do, for the kingdom of heaven? It must refer to a far more terrible judgment than that which includes only the destruction of the bodily life, even of the mass of mankind then inhabiting the earth. It describes, in natural and figurative language, a flood which now and in all ages ruins and sweeps away the immortal soul, and teaches us that an ark of eternal salvation is always provided for the humble, penitent, and faithful believer, in which he may be prepared for an eternal state of blessed association with angels and conjunction with the Lord.

The purpose of the ark is described to have been the preservation of every living thing of all flesh; and for this end he was to take into the ark, firstly, his own family, consisting of eight persons, together with seven pairs of all clean animals, and pairs of everything that creepeth upon the earth; and, secondly, he was commanded to take into the ark "of all food that was eaten" a sufficiency for at least a year and ten days. Now, the ark, being described as three hundred cubits of eighteen inches long, fifty cubits broad, and thirty cubits high, could not have been of larger capacity than the Great Eastern steamship. Sir Isaac Newton and Bishop Wilkins make the tonnage of the ark less than that vessel; but Dr. Arbuthnot, by increasing the cubit to twenty-two inches, makes the dimensions larger. But we may judge how insufficient such a vessel would be from the fact which Dr. Pye Smith admits, "that of existing mammalia (or animals which suckle their young), more than a thousand species are known; of birds, fully five thousand; of reptiles, very few of which can live in water, two thousand; of insects, using the word in the popular sense, the number of species is immense, to say one hundred thousand would be moderate; each has its appropriate habitation and food, and these are necessary to its life; and the larger number could not live in water. Also the innumerable millions upon millions of animalcules must be provided for, for they have all their appropriate and diversified [food], places, and circumstances of existence."— *Relation between the Holy Scriptures and Geological Science*, page 135.

Nor do these numbers form the only difficulty; for, as the same writer observes, "All land animals have their geographical regions, to which their constitutional natures are congenial, and many could not live in any other situation. We cannot represent to ourselves the idea of their being brought into one small spot, from the polar regions, the torrid zone, and all the other climates of Africa, Europe,

America, Australia, and the thousands of islands, millions of which live only on animal food, and the disposal of them, without bringing up the idea of miracles more stupendous than any which are recorded in Scripture, and, may we not add, utterly incredible." On the other hand, the Doctor gravely concludes that the flood was only partial, and not, as literally described, universal, and that the ark only contained the animals of the district.

"The language employed [however] in Gen. vii. derives its force," says Dr. W. T. Hamilton, most truly, "as expressive of complete universality, not merely or mainly from the meaning of the several individual terms, but from the structure of the whole. The complete covering of the entire earth's surface is asserted, and the submergence of the loftiest mountain summits, not merely on the earth, or the land, but under the *whole heaven*, is affirmed. Further still, the destruction of animal life, human and brute, is declared to have been complete; and then, as if to make assurance doubly sure, the saved are enumerated, Noah and those with him in the ark, and these are declared to have been the only living creatures preserved from destruction: 'And Noah only remained alive, and they that were with him in the ark.' This closing declaration applies to the human race, and to all creatures in which was the breath of life, not merely in any one land, or province, but *under the whole heaven*."

"The animal distribution," again writes Milner, "from one common centre, the mountains of Ararat, to repopulate the world, it is impossible to reconcile with zoological facts, without supposing a series of the most astounding and useless miracles, concerning which a total silence is preserved in the Scripture narrative. We know that the kangaroos and emus of New Holland, the llamas of Peru, the sloths, armadilloes, and ant-eaters of Paraguay, to mention no other instances, never could have accomplished the passage from the places of their location to any central part of the old world and back again, from the scene where the ark of Noah was set afloat, by natural means. Neither can the polar bear, the hippopotamus, the ostrich, and the eider fowl, the reindeer and the giraffe, to refer to no more examples, exist together in a state of nature requiring a great diversity of climates; and supposing them aggregated by the Divine Power, and sustained in a common temperature, the difficulty of conceiving a building capable of accommodating a tenth of the single pairs of all the species is prodigious. The difficulty increases when we consider the vast number of fresh-water fish and reptiles of the rivers to be provided for [to all of which, as well as those fitted to live in the salt-water, the brackish water produced by the rain would be fatal]. To supernatural agency, indeed, all things are [supposed to be] possible; but when nothing is said of its action in the record (not even the slightest hint of a miracle),—when the object imagined to have been effected by it must have been, to a great extent, useless,—and when the congregation of the animals is represented as in the main the work of Noah" [we may well imagine that some other explanation of the catastrophe is required, and must be found].

The evidence as to the actual occurrence of the Noachic deluge, whether universal or partial, adduced by various learned writers and commentators, is the ancient and wide-spread traditions of floods, which are said to have taken place among all nations, and from the most remote periods; including those of the Grecian and Roman mythology. Dr. Pye Smith, Dr. Redford, Harcourt, and Kitto enumerate the Chaldeans, Phœnicians, Assyrians, Medians, Persians, Druids, Greeks, Romans, Africans, Scythians, Celtic tribes, Goths, Hindoos, Chinese, Burmese, Mexicans, Peruvians, Araucania Indians of South America, Aztecs, Miztics, and Apotecs, North Americans, Tahitians, Sandwich Islanders, Western Caledonians, and the Crees, or Arctic Indians; and assert that all preserve in their mythologies or histories the principal facts recorded by Moses. But much that has been written by ancient historians, and interpreted by modern writers on this subject, is fanciful, uncertain, and most fallacious. The allegories of ancient mythology have also been greatly perverted and much misunderstood. Hence have arisen the confused and contradictory opinions attributed to them. The source of all heathen worship, and, we may add, of all heathen mythology, indeed, was the corruption of the truths of revealed religion; so all the above nations derived their views, originally, from a more ancient Word than we now possess, altogether written according to the science of Correspondences, and of which, in all probability the first eleven chapters of Genesis formed a part.[147] From a profound ignorance of this science, modern writers have either wilfully overlooked or totally misapprehended the myths and analogies of the ancient world. The description of the Deluge in Genesis is altogether a divinely-inspired parable, a spiritual or mental history, arranged in the form of a narrative, and filled with

---

[147] See the interesting accounts of the Chaldean account of the creation and deluge, discovered and read by Mr. George Smith, of the British Museum, the originals of which were presented to that museum.

holy instruction and heavenly lessons of wisdom. Over the inner glory is thrown this outward covering, which has protected it from fearful abuse, and prevented awful profanation. Many have been the absurd theories proposed to account for the waters of the Deluge. Dr. Burnett supposed that the surface of the earth was smooth and dry; that the outer crust or shell cracked and broke, causing the water to spread over it, and elevating the mountains and hills from the plain. Whistar considered that a comet was brought into collision with the world, which broke open the fountains of the great deep, and that the waters were dried up by a miraculous wind. Others have imagined that a comet both brought the water with its tail and dried it up again after the flood. Kircher supposed that the air was converted, for the time, into water, without reflecting upon the necessity of air to support life, and that if the whole atmosphere were compressed into water, it would only stand thirty-two feet above the surface,—not sufficient to cover a single hill deserving the name. The leading commentators are satisfied, however, with the absurd assertion that there was a miraculous creation of water sufficient for the purpose, and a dissipation or annihilation of it at the end of the flood. Again, the heaviest fall of rain known has been stated at about seven inches in forty-eight hours, occasioning most devastating floods; but the waters of the Deluge must have risen at the incredible rate of six hundred and fifty feet every twenty-four hours, for forty days and nights in succession. Indeed, the vast rate at which it must have fallen may be best imagined when we consider that it is calculated the amount required to cover the mountains would be forty times that of all the oceans on the face of the earth. Such an accumulation of water would present serious astronomical objections. Both the bulk and diameter of the earth would be so increased as to seriously interfere with the diurnal and orbital motions of the earth, and these alterations must have had a disturbing influence upon the whole solar system. Indeed, Dr. Pye Smith says that it could not have taken place without its effects being felt throughout the entire stellar universe. While, on the other hand, geologists affirm, with one consent, that the surface of the earth nowhere exhibits the traces of a universal flood, which they agree to regard as a physical impossibility.

Think of the vast capacity of the ark, even though it were only that of the Great Eastern; yet it had but one small window in the upper story, affording a most imperfect light, and all the rest must have been involved for more than a year in entire darkness. Glass, even, is a modern discovery. True, some enlightened writers affirm that the ark was illuminated by the reflection of large and most brilliant gems or by phosphorescent substances. Reason revolts at the idea. Again, the ark had also but one door on the vast sides. The accumulation of refuse must have been enormous, and nothing is said of ventilation. How could this be literally understood? We might ask where, after such a surging flood, was the olive branch to be found? And from whence did Noah obtain the vines he planted? Other difficulties and inconsistencies are to be found in the narrative itself. Noah, for instance, was commanded to admit pairs of animals into the ark, and then to take of *clean beasts*, of which no mention is elsewhere made till the laws of Moses were compiled, by sevens. Some explain the number to mean seven pairs, and others seven animals. It is, however, asserted that after Noah and his family had gone into the ark, the beasts, birds, and creeping things went in unto Noah "two and two of all flesh, wherein is the breath of life. And they that went in, went in male and female of all flesh, as God had commanded him: and the Lord shut him in."

That Noah was not a real, but a representative character, like Adam, Enoch, Methuselah, and others, seems plain from the length of time which he is said to have lived, nine hundred and fifty years; and from his name, which means rest, or consolation. The destruction or end of one church, which was overwhelmed by evil lusts and false persuasions, and the commencement of another in which righteousness and truth might dwell, was indeed to all a source of divine comfort. That Noah, the ark, and the flood were altogether typical of this great regenerating change, is also evident from what the apostle Peter says of them in the third chapter of his first Epistle, second verse, as "being the like figure whereunto even baptism doth also now save us (not the putting away of the filth of the flesh, but the answer of a good conscience toward God), by the resurrection of Jesus Christ." For what does the sacrament of baptism mean but to present to us a sign of purification from all sinfulness by divine truth, and thus salvation from "the floods of ungodliness" and iniquity? Hereby is attained a state of spiritual rest from temptation, affliction, and sorrow, and of divine consolation and peace, when the ark rests safely on the mountains of Ararat,—the mountains of love and light, as the name imports.

We seem forced, then, from these and a multitude of other considerations, to regard the entire narrative of the Deluge as a parable or allegory, and all the traditions referring to it as of the same character; with this exception, that the parable of the Bible is divinely inspired in its spiritual sense and import, is holy and true, and practically good in every particular, while the pagan traditions are but human corruptions of the remains of revealed religion existing among them. Noah and his sons were adored as deities, and even the ark is said to have been worshipped as a goddess under various names. The whole parable, then, instead of being a description of a literal flood of water, is an inspired account of the moral condition of the human race at that time, when they had become completely wicked, or had filled up the measure of their iniquities. The judgments and providences of God, temptations, heresies, profaneness, and persecution, the prevalence of error, trouble, and even wars, disease, and death, are all likened, both in divine and ancient writings, to irresistible and destructive floods. Especially is the end of one church or dispensation of religion and the commencement of another represented in divine language by a flood, and called also the end of the world. Thus the end of the Adamic dispensation is represented by Noah's flood; the end of the Jewish dispensation is foretold by Daniel as a flood; and the end of the first Christian dispensation is predicted by the Lord Himself as like Noah's flood. The very form of the ark, in general so like the temple at Jerusalem, composed of three stories, shows that it was designed to represent the mind of man, with its three degrees; and the beasts, birds, and creeping things denote the affections, the thoughts, and the lowest principles of the life. By a flood is signified an inundation of evil and falsity, sin and folly; and it is in the ark of salvation, provided for us in the divine Word, that we can alone find safety, as it is narrated they of old did, from the overwhelming torrents. The animals entered by pairs and by sevens, for truth must always be united to its true partner, goodness, in order to be fruitful; and the holy quality of all regenerate principles is presented to us in the septuple of the clean animals. This flood extinguished the life of God within the soul of the ungodly, together with all the heavenly principles of love and charity, signified by its overwhelming all flesh, and covering the hills and mountains.

That the ark was, in all its measurements and arrangements, a divine figure of the human mind in the process of being regenerated or redeemed from the destructive elements of evil and falsity, thus preserved from the powers of hell and death, is not only evident from its general form, but from all the other particulars named. The three stories, or mansions, or rooms, signify the three degrees of truth in the mind and all its faculties. The window in the uppermost story of the ark means intellectual light, received by the church and by every man, from Above, or from the Lord. The door in the side, or way of access into the church, and that which admits into the mind spiritual life, signifies the outward doctrine of sacred charity, to which we hearken, and by which we are admitted to the protection, peace, and blessedness which are promised: thus internal and externl instruction. Hence all this is said to be done to establish a covenant between God and man.

Nor is it to be passed over, as of trifling significance, that the same waters which destroyed the ungodly, preserved Noah and all within the ark from the same destruction. The forty days denote, as they always do in the Word, all the states of grievous temptation through which every one is led in the regenerate life. Hence, to signify similar things, Moses was in the mount forty days and forty nights; the children of Israel sojourned forty years in the wilderness; the prophet Elijah journeyed forty days and forty nights from the wilderness to Horeb, the Mount of God, on the strength of his miraculous food; the prophet Ezekiel was commanded to bear, representatively, the iniquity of Judah forty days; and, finally, the Lord Jesus was led into the wilderness, where for forty days He bore grievous temptations.

And the ark is said finally to have rested on the mountains of Ararat, which implies an elevated state of light and love. Various states of fluctuation and change in the regeneration are also signified by sending forth first a raven and then a dove to see if the waters were abated. And complete regeneration and liberty are denoted by going forth and building an altar to sacrifice to the Lord.

The literal sense is clearly untenable, and the narration could never have been intended to be understood in any other than a spiritual sense. By this interpretation, the sacred oracles are preserved from the cavils and ridicule to which they have been subjected; science is not defied, but vindicated; and reason is not discarded, but honored. The history is so wonderfully arranged, as to every particular, that an examination of it by the inquiring and reflecting mind will issue in regarding the whole narrative as a holy and divinely-inspired revelation of Him who knoweth the secrets of every heart,—a symbolic mental history couched, for wisest reasons, in the language of similitude and correspondence, and thus most worthy of God to give and of man to receive. Every sentence of it, when properly understood, is filled with a heavenly meaning, and every word teems with light and life.

So, also, the subsequent history of the Tower of Babel,[148] and the confusion of tongues said to have been consequent on its unhallowed erection, is a series of corresponding images, arranged in the factitious form of a narrative, to signify and represent the further departure of mankind from the simplicity of truth and the true worship of God. "The people of the earth," it is said, "journeyed from the east" (Gen. xi. 2), that is, they departed from a holy state of charity and love, denoted by the east,—thus from the Lord. Their worship became more profane and their conduct more corrupt, and they are represented, therefore, as building for themselves habitations there, endeavoring to find rest and security in the degraded plain or valley of Shinar.[149] In that low state, bricks, or false principles framed from their impure imaginations, originating in and confirmed by the burning lusts of self-love and the love of the world, were substituted for the stones of truth, and the pure doctrines thence derived; and the slime, or pitch, or bitumen of unclean concupiscence was supplied in the place of mortar,—the conjoining principles of affection and mutual love springing from goodness. The sad result was the origination and multiplication of heresies, idolatries, and countless false sentiments in religion,—the increase and strengthening of numberless evil lusts, and the substitution of doctrines of faith for the life of charity, thus originating all kinds of doubt, denial, and mental confusion, ending in spiritual destruction. Thus men brought upon themselves the direful judgment and punishment signified by the "fire and brimstone" rained upon them apparently from God out of heaven, denoting a state of self-inflicted torment, directly opposed to the divine will and wisdom.

According to this view of the nature and character of the Word, we may see how wicked men and nations, and even apparently evil actions, were capable of representing what is holy, good, and true.

---

[148] *Babel* means, in English, "perplexity," "confusion."

[149] *Shinar*, in English, means, "the watching of one sleeping," or "the charge of the city."

"Contemplation of the divine essence is the noblest exercise of man; it is the only means of attaining to the highest truth and virtue, and therein to behold God is the consummation of our happiness here. The confusion of tongues at the building of the tower of Babel should teach us this lesson. The heaven those vain builders sought to reach, signifies, symbolically, the mind, where dwell divine powers. Their futile attempt represents the presumption of those who place sense above intelligence, who think that they can storm the intelligible by the sensible."—*Vaughan's Hours with the Mystics*, vol. i., p. 73. *Therapeutæ.*

Both the unjust judge and the unfaithful steward represented, in the internal sense, the Lord's divine operations for man's welfare, and what we are required spiritually to do, in order to secure his divine blessing and protection. The descendants of Israel, though as a people they were a vile, obstinate, sensual, and rebellious race from the beginning,[150] were yet made subservient to the divine purposes, in representing a true spiritual church, without being one themselves; and though they "made the Word of God of none effect by their traditions" (Matt. xv. 6), yet they became the depositaries of that Volume of eternal life, in which the particulars of their own history were recorded for the use of all future ages, as the shadows of the kingdom of God both in heaven and on earth.[151] Wicked kings, as Saul and Ahab, by virtue of their regal authority, and impious priests, as the sons of Eli, by virtue of their sacerdotal character, were, under that representative dispensation, and in a good sense, types of the Lord, and are called "the Lord's anointed." Concerning David, Israel's king, it is thus written in a prediction of the advent of the Saviour, whom he represented, "David, my servant, shall be king over them, and they shall have one Shepherd, and they shall dwell in the land; *even* they and their children, and their children's children forever: and my servant David *shall* be their prince forever" (Ezek. xxxvii. 24, 25). And, again: "The children of Israel shall return, and seek the Lord their God, and David their king" (Hos. iii. 5). Thus, in a good sense, of David, notwithstanding his enormous crimes, it is written, not of his personal, but of his representative character, that "he was a man after God's own heart" (Acts xiii. 22); for in all the particulars of his remarkable history he was the chosen representative of the Lord, and his whole life was representative of the progress of every regenerating mind.[152]

---

[150] Ex. xxxii. 9; Deut. ix. 6-13; 2 Kings xxi. 15; John viii. 44; Acts vii. 51.

[151] "'We find St. Paul (says Locke) truly a minister of the spirit of the laws; especially in the Epistle to the Hebrews, where he shows that a spiritual *sense* runs *throughout* the Mosaic institution and writings.' He shows us that the letter is only as the veil which concealed the brightness of the face of Moses; that the history of Abraham and his two sons is an allegory; and that Melchisedec represented the Lord; he shows us, in a word, that '*the* WHOLE *dispensation was so conducted as to be the figure and the shadow of a spiritual system.*'"—*Dr. Blair.*

[152] David is a type of our Lord, and through Him of the Church, which is his body, and through that again of each individual Christian, as being a member of that body; and therefore the Psalms generally are adopted by the whole Church in her assemblies, and by separate believers in their closets, with equal propriety, as the language of their devotions; they are an inspired Liturgy, provided for all ages and all lands."—*Tracts for the Times,* lxxxix., p. 129. David means, in English, "beloved, dear."

"Nothing has done more hurt among *Christians* than taking the Psalms, or hymns of David, the *Beloved,* literally, as if they related only to temporary transactions or deliverances wrought for the Jews." "None but the real *David* was a man after God's own heart."—*Bp. Horne's Abstract of Hutchinson's Works*, p. 383.

"The book [of the Psalms] contains *subjects far more sublime, spiritual, and interesting* than merely the history of David and the affairs of his kingdom. We cannot for a moment suppose that the trials and triumphs, the joys and sorrows, the afflictions and victories of the son of Jesse, are the subjects which the God of heaven has appointed to promote devotion in all his temples; or that the opposition and persecution which David met with at the hands of Saul, on his way to the throne; or the sorrows which Absalom occasioned afterwards; or the victories which David obtained over Moab, Edom, and Philistia, are to form the songs of Sion in all ages. Nay, it would be absurd to think that the affairs of any one man, however eminent, should be ordained of God as the subject-matter of the prayers and praises of all the redeemed in all lands [for ever]. The book of Psalms doubtless sets forth the Lord Jesus Christ and the affairs of his kingdom of grace. Its main design is to set forth the Saviour of the world, and to direct our eyes and hearts to the true David, king of Sion, the God of Israel. In this bright mirror we behold the glory of his person, kingdom, and priesthood; we here see his humiliation, conflicts, and sorrows. The oppositions, persecutions, and contempt which he endured, and the glorious victories which he obtained, are here set before us. It is a clear and perfect mirror wherein the Church may view herself in all the different states, circumstances, and conditions she passes through on her journey heavenward. Here we behold the Church of Christ in prosperity and adversity, in light and darkness, in joys and sorrows, in trials and in triumphs by turns. At one time we see her declining, sinking in sin, and carried into captivity; then reviving again, and returning with singing unto Sion. At times we see her struggling with temptations, afflictions, and trouble; at other times rising above oppressions, and triumphing in her God. To-day in sorrow, weeping in the dust; to-morrow happy, and singing on the mount of joy. The book of Psalms furnisheth us with a full view of the Lamb's wife through all the heavenly road, and with all she meets with during her pilgrimage through the wilderness, till she arrives at the mount of God in the Holy Land. Here her beauty, riches, honors, her conquest, joy, and safety are all correctly described. The books of Scripture have a *double sense*, the literal and the spiritual; this cannot be said of any other book in the world; human writings have only a natural, but the Bible has a spiritual sense also, which proves it to be the book of God. At times we, through blindness, can discern only the natural; and here we should check vain conjectures. At other times, the spiritual almost appears; and sometimes both are discerned with equal clearness. Upon this plan we are to interpret the Psalms as having a double meaning. Also, the Psalms applied to Israel are, in the higher sense, to be understood of the *spiritual Israel*. We are, in a far higher sense than they, delivered from bondage and slavery; we go through the sea, and travel in the wilderness. We have, spiritually, God's pillar, tabernacle, and mount; we have bread from heaven, water from the rock, and prospect of a land of rest. We have enemies, difficulties, and dangers; captivities and deliverances. In like manner are we to understand the figures borrowed from the natural world. We read here of creation; heaven, earth, and sea; of sun, moon, and stars; of air, thunder, dew, and rain; of light and darkness, summer and winter. All such things are figures of higher things in the new creation, the world of grace. In short, whatever be the figures used in the Psalms, whether David, Israel, the ceremonial law, or anything in creation, or in the history of man, they are shadows of far higher and better things in Christ's kingdom."—*See Bishop Horne on the Psalms, condensed from Jones's Scripture Directory*, ed. 1815, pp. 73-78.

That the book of Psalms, and the Prophets, throughout the inspired pages, contain an internal and spiritual sense, they themselves testify. David, "the oldest Psalmist of Israel" (2 Sam. xxiii. 1), affirms that "his tongue was the pen of a ready writer" (Ps. xlv. 1); and at the period of his bodily decease, claims the spirit of inspiration for his sacred songs, when he said, "The spirit of the Lord spake by me, and his word was upon my tongue" (2 Sam. xxiii. 2). "I, Jehovah, have spoken by the prophets, and I have multiplied visions, and used similitudes by the ministry of the prophets" (Hosea xii. 10). We have only to turn to the New Testament, and in the Gospels, the Acts of the Apostles, the Epistles, and in the Book of Revelation we shall find the most ample evidence of this internal meaning, especially in its application to the Lord Jesus Christ, and as, in that sense, being fulfilled not only in Him, but also in the constant experience of every Christian believer.—See Acts iv. 25; Heb. ii. 6; Acts ii. 25, 30; Rom. xv. 9; x. 18; Matt. xxvii. 43; Heb. x. 5; John xiii. 18; Rom. viii. 36; Heb. i. 8; Eph. iv. 7, 8; Rom. xi. 9, 10; Acts i. 20; Matt. xiii. 34; iv. 6, 7; Heb. iii., iv.; Matt. xxii. 44; Rom. xv. 11; Luke xx. 17; Acts iv. 11; 1 Pet. ii. 7.

CHAPTER XIX.

Sacrificial Worship.

NO other worship but what was internal, such as prevails in heaven, existed in the earliest ages among those of the most ancient church,[153] signified by Adam; but when that church declined from its pristine integrity, purity, and spirituality, men had no longer an intuitive perception of correspondences, as heretofore, and then they began to collect and cultivate them as a science. Then, also, external worship, representative and significative of internal, was first instituted, and stated forms were established.

According to correspondences, the firstlings of the flock signify worship from inmost spiritual affection. Thus, the offering of "Abel, a keeper of sheep," which signifies worship from love, was said to be more acceptable to Jehovah than the offering of "Cain, a tiller of the ground," which signifies worship from faith without inward love. Abel's offering was first-fruits; not so that of Cain (Gen. iv.). The worship of the ancient church, signified by Noah, was purely representative. With the members of that dispensation, all external objects and operations whatever symbolized the glorious realities of heaven, representing truths with their perceptions, and affections with their delights, together with all the activities of the mind into which they flowed. Their external worship, therefore, was a precise type of their internal character, and was represented by Noah's sacrifice, of which we read that "He builded an altar unto the Lord; and took of every clean beast, and of every clean fowl, and offered burnt-

---

[153] "The man of the most ancient church performed no other worship but what was internal, such as prevails in heaven, for with them heaven communicated with man, so that they made one; that communication was perception; thus being angelic men, they were also internal men; they were sensible indeed of the external things relating to the body and the world, but they cared not for them; in every particular object of sense they perceived somewhat divine and celestial; as for example, when they saw any high mountain, they did not perceive any idea of a mountain, but of height, and by virtue of height they perceived heaven and the Lord; hence it came to pass that the Lord was said to dwell on the highest, and He himself was called The Highest and most exalted, and afterwards the worship of the Lord was solemnized on mountains; the case was similar in other instances."—*A. C.*, n. 920.

offerings on the altar. And the Lord smelled a sweet savor" (Gen. viii. 19, 20). Here the clean beasts denote the different degrees of charity, and the various affections of goodness in the heart, both with angels and men: and the clean fowls signify the true principles of faith in the understanding; each particular kind of animal corresponding to some specific heavenly virtue or grace in the mind.

In succeeding ages, sacrificial worship became established, and to slay and offer the sacrifice signified wholly to consecrate to the Lord the thing denoted thereby; thus indicating the change effected in man by regeneration, when his natural mind or unregenerate life is, as it were, slain, that he may receive the Lord's life, and be wholly devoted to his service. Fire, we have seen, signifies, in a good sense, heavenly love. To offer animals by fire was a representative act, signifying worship grounded in charity and obedience, from a sincere and thankful heart, which the Lord is said "to smell as a sweet savor;" signifying that such worship is accepted, and causes a sensible perception of his sacred presence to be experienced, which diffuses angelic joy over the whole mind.[154] "Sacrifices were the chief representatives of worship in the Hebrew church, and afterwards in the Jewish. Their sacrifices were made either from the herd or from the flock, consequently they consisted of animals of various kinds, which were clean, as of oxen, cows, he-goats, sheep, rams, she-goats, kids, and lambs, and moreover of turtles and young pigeons. All these signified internal things of worship, that is, things celestial and spiritual, the animals taken from the herd denoting celestial-natural things, and those from the flock denoting celestial-rational things; and as both things natural and things rational are of various kinds, being more or less interior, therefore so many genera and species of those animals were made use of in the sacrifices; which may appear, also, from this consideration, that it was prescribed in the burnt-offerings, and also in the sacrifices of divers kinds, as in the daily sacrifices, in those of the Sabbaths and feasts, in the voluntary, eucharistic, and votive sacrifices, in those that were expiatory of guilt and of sin, and also in those that were purificatory and cleansing, and likewise in the sacrifices of inauguration, what animals should be offered. The animals, also, were expressly named, and also their number, in every kind of sacrifice, which would never have been done unless each had had some peculiar signification, as manifestly appears from those pas-

---

[154] "Spencer traces the origin of sacrifices to the invention of heathen nations."—*Greenfield's Connex.*, p. 481, note 66.

sages where sacrifices are treated of, as Ex. xxix.; Lev. i., iii., iv., ix., xvi., xxiii.; Num. vii., viii., xv., xxix. . . . As to what concerns sacrifices in general, they were commanded indeed by Moses to the children of Israel; but the most ancient church, which was before the flood, were altogether unacquainted with sacrifices, nor did it ever enter into their minds to worship the Lord by the slaying of animals. The ancient church, which was after the flood, was likewise unacquainted with sacrifices; it was, indeed, principled in representatives, but sacrifices were first instituted in the succeeding church, which was called the Hebrew church, and thence this mode of worship was propagated among the Gentiles, and descended to Abraham, Isaac, and Jacob, and their posterity."—A. C., n. 2180.

No portions of the Old Testament have been less understood or more misapprehended, for want of the science of correspondences, than the rituals and sacrifices of the Mosaic economy. A general impression has indeed prevailed throughout the Christian church, that the sacrifices had some indistinct reference to the Lord Jesus Christ, and the great work of redemption which He accomplished; but the views held have been so external, so inconsistent, so limited in their application, and so unsatisfactory, as to have left this important subject involved in the most perplexing difficulties. The Jewish dispensation was only the representative of a true spiritual church. Hence the laws and ordinances, rites and ceremonials, of the Israelites were denominated, in the apostolic age, "figures of the time then present" (Heb. ix. 9); "the example and shadow of heavenly things" (viii. 5);[155] also, "patterns of things in the heavens" (ix. 23); and "shadows of good things to come" (Col. ii. 17; Heb. x. 1). This view is a key to their history, as recorded in the volume of inspiration.[156]

The Jews were chosen, agreeably to their own earnest desire (for it could not have been otherwise), to represent in outward form a spiritual church, or the inward life of true religion. They were of so external, so obdurate a character, as to be incapable of being led ex-

---

[155] Macknight translates this passage more emphatically thus: "Priests who serve with the representative and shadow of heavenly things."

[156] "To see clearly that the Old Testament is figurative, and that by temporal blessings the prophets understood other blessings, it is only necessary to observe, in the first place, that it would be unworthy of God to call men only to the enjoyment of temporal felicities; secondly, that the language of the prophets plainly set forth the promise of temporal blessings, and that, nevertheless, they say that their language is obscure, that their meaning is not that which they openly express, and that *it will not be understood till the end of time*. Finally, it must be remarked, that their language is contradictory, and destroys itself, if one should think that they meant by the words *law* and *sacrifice* no other than the law and sacrifices of Moses."—*Pascal's Thoughts*, tr. by D. H. H., Int. Rep., 1847, p. 192.

cept by the hope of earthly rewards and the fear of temporal punishments. The prophet declares that they "perverted the words of the living God," and looked upon their representative service as burdensome and grievous (Jer. xxiii. 33-40); "Wherefore," says the Lord, "I gave them also statutes that were not good, and judgments whereby they should not live" (Ezek. xx. 25). This was eminently the case with the burnt-offerings and sacrifices, which they regarded, not as means of attaining purity and holiness, but as piacular substitutes for obedience. The sacrifices of the Jews were permitted, not commanded, by the Lord, because of the hardness of their hearts, and their proneness to the most cruel rites; such as divorce for trivial offences against a husband's will, and the law of retaliation (Matt. v. 38, 39). "Thus saith the Lord of Hosts, the God of Israel; put your burnt-offerings to your sacrifices, and eat flesh. For I spake not unto your fathers, nor commanded them in the day that I brought them out of the land of Egypt, concerning burnt-offerings or sacrifices: but this thing commanded I them, saying, Obey my voice, and I will be your God, and ye shall be my people" (Jer. vii. 21-23). But the permission of sacrifices was so overruled by an inspired series of restrictive laws as to make them exactly representative, in every particular, of the voluntary sacrifices of the heart, the mind, and the life. Other most important reasons may be adduced for their permission. The worship of the Jews was to be directed to one supreme and only God, free from idolatrous rites, because it was figurative of the angelic worship which exists in heaven, and hence, as we have seen, it is called "the patterns of things in the heavens,"—"figures of the true" (Heb. ix. 23, 24).

During its continuance they were required to fulfil every iota of the divine law, and therefore to render their representations complete; and, that the Word might be written, they had to offer burnt-offerings and sacrifices, and sin- and trespass-offerings. It is never once intimated in the law that even sin- and trespass-offerings were designed and accepted as expiations of moral turpitude, for such presumptuous or wilful sinfulness was chiefly punished with death (Num. xv. 30), but as propitiatory sacrifices, in humble acknowledgment of sins of ignorance and ceremonial uncleanness and neglect; and without which, so degenerate had the human race become, the Lord could not, previous to his incarnation, have had a dwelling-place with his creatures.

"The church which was instituted among the posterity of Jacob was not essentially a church, but only the representative of a church. In representations, the person is not reflected upon, but only the thing which is represented; wherefore divine, celestial, and spiritual things were represented, not only by persons, but by things inanimate, as by Aaron's garments, by the ark, the altar, the oxen and sheep which were sacrificed, by the candlestick with the lights, by the bread of arrangement on the golden table, by the anointing oil, the frankincense, and other similar things. Hence it was that kings, both bad and good alike, represented the Lord's regal principle; and the high-priests, both bad and good alike, when they discharged their office in an external form according to the statutes and commandments, represented the things appertaining to the Lord's Divine priesthood. To the intent, therefore, that the representative of a church might exist among them, such statutes and laws were given them by manifest revelation as were altogether representative; wherefore, so long as they were principled therein, and observed them strictly, so long were they capable of representing; but when they turned aside from them to the statutes and laws of other nations, and especially to the worship of another god, they deprived themselves of the faculty of representing; in consequence whereof they were driven by external means, which were captivities, overthrows, threats, and miracles, to laws and statutes truly representative, but not by internal means, like those who have internal worship in the external."—A. C. 4281.

When the Jews fell into the destructive notion that their sacrifices and offerings were vicarious equivalents for wilful iniquity, and that by their means moral guilt, equally with ceremonial impurity, and transgression, and sins of ignorance, was pardoned in the divine sight, the Lord thus tenderly expostulates with them, and exhorts them to worship Him from the heart, to hearken to his voice, and to keep his commandments: "Hear, O my people, and I will speak: O Israel, and I will testify against thee: I am God, even thy God. I will not reprove thee for thy sacrifices or thy burnt-offerings, to have been continually before me. I will take no bullock out of thy house, nor he-goats out of thy folds. For every beast of the forest is mine, and the cattle upon a thousand hills. I know all the fowls of the mountains: and the wild beasts of the field are mine. If I were hungry, I would not tell thee: for the world is mine, and the fulness thereof. Will I eat the flesh of bulls, or drink the blood of goats? Offer unto God thanksgiving; and pay thy vows unto the Most High" (Psalm l. 7-14). And, again, "To what purpose is the multitude of your sacrifices unto me? saith the Lord: I am full of the burnt-offerings of rams and the fat of fed beasts; and I delight not in the blood of bullocks, or of lambs, or of he-goats. When ye appear before me, who hath required this at your hand, to tread my courts?[157] Wash you, make you clean; put away the evil of your doings from before mine eyes; cease to do evil; learn to do well; seek judgment, relieve the oppressed, judge the fatherless, plead for the widow. Come now, and let us reason together, saith the Lord: though your sins be as scarlet, they shall be as white as snow; though they be red like crimson, they shall be as wool. If ye be willing and obedient, ye shall eat the good of the land: but if ye refuse and rebel, ye shall be devoured with the sword: for the mouth of the Lord hath spoken it" (Isa. i. 11, 12, 16–20). Moreover, the Lord further declares, "I spake not unto your fathers, nor commanded them, in the day that I brought them out of the land of Egypt, concerning burnt-offerings or sacrifices: but this thing commanded I them, saying, Obey my voice, and I will be your God, and ye shall be my people: and walk ye in all the ways that I have commanded you, that it may be well unto you" (Jer. vii. 22, 23). That obedience was what the Lord commanded and desired, of which sacrifices were in reality representative emblems, is constantly affirmed. In the Proverbs it is written, "To do justice and judgment is more acceptable to the Lord than sacrifices" (xxi. 3). The prophet Samuel reproved Saul for his disobedience in these memorable words: "Hath the Lord as great delight in burnt-offerings and sacrifices, as in obeying the voice of the Lord? Behold, to obey is better than sacrifice, and to hearken than the fat of rams. For rebellion is as the sin of witchcraft, and stubbornness is as iniquity and idolatry" (1 Sam. xv. 22, 23). Hence the important question of the prophet, "Wherewith shall I come before the Lord, and bow myself before the high God? shall I come before Him with burnt-offerings, with calves of a year old? will the Lord be pleased with thousands of rams, or with ten thousands of rivers of oil? He hath showed thee, O man, what is good; and what doth the Lord require of thee, but to do justly, and to love mercy, and to walk humbly with thy God" (Micah vi. 6–8).

The Psalmist, also, in his prayer to God for the remission of sin, says, "O Lord, open thou my lips; and my mouth shall show forth

---

[157] "None of those who offered animals in sacrifice before the law, did it by divine precept."—(*Answers to the Orthodox.*) "Most of the ancient Fathers came to the same conclusion."—*Outram's Dissert. on Sacrifice*, p. 14.

thy praise. For thou desirest not sacrifice; else would I give it: thou delightest not in burnt-offering. The sacrifices of God are a broken spirit: a broken and a contrite heart, O God, thou wilt not despise" (li. 15-17). When one of the scribes asked the Lord, "Which was the first commandment of all?" He answered him, "The first of all the commandments is, Hear, O Israel; the Lord our God is one Lord: and thou shalt love the Lord thy God with all thy heart, and with all thy soul, and with all thy mind, and with all thy strength: this is the first commandment. And the second is like, namely this, Thou shalt love thy neighbor as thyself. There is none other commandment greater than these. And the scribe said unto Him, Well, Master, thou hast said the truth: for there is one God; and there is none other but He: and to love Him with all the heart, and with all the understanding, and with all the soul, and with all the strength, is more than all whole burnt-offerings and sacrifices. And when Jesus saw that he answered discreetly, He said unto him, Thou art not far from the kingdom of God" (Mark xii. 28-34). In an exhortation to repentance, the prophet Hosea says, "For I desired mercy, and not sacrifice; and the knowledge of God more than burnt-offerings" (vi. 6); and the Lord, in his rebuke of the Pharisees, said, "Go ye, and learn what that meaneth, I will have mercy, and not sacrifice" (Matt. ix. 13); and, again, "Woe unto you, scribes and Pharisees, hypocrites! for ye pay tithe of mint and anise and cummin, and have omitted the weightier matters of the law, judgment, mercy, and faith: these ought ye to have done, and not to leave the other undone" (Matt. xxiii. 23). Thus sacrifices were never required, nor ever accepted as substitutes for the sinner's disobedience. This David acknowledged, and therefore said to the Lord, "Sacrifice and offering thou didst not desire; mine ears hast thou opened: burnt-offering and sin-offering hast thou not required. Then said I, Lo, I come: in the volume of the book it is written of me, I delight to do thy will, O my God: yea, thy law is within my heart" (Psalm xl. 6-8). This inspired prayer is applied by the writer of the Epistle to the Hebrews to the Lord Himself, and to the works of the glorification of his Humanity and the redemption of the human race, which He mercifully came to accomplish. "For the law," says he, "having a shadow of good things to come, and not the very image of the things, can never with those sacrifices which they offered year by year continually make the comers thereunto perfect. For it is not possible that the blood of bulls and of goats should take away sins. Wherefore when He cometh into the world, He saith, Sacrifice and offering thou wouldest not, but a body hast thou prepared me: in burnt-offerings and sacrifices for sin thou hast had no pleasure. Then said I, Lo, I come (in the volume of the book it is written of me) to do thy will, O God. Above when He said, Sacrifice and offering and burnt-offerings and offering for sin thou wouldest not, neither hadst pleasure therein; which are offered by the law; then said He, Lo, I come to do thy will, O God. He taketh away the first, that He may establish the second" (x. 1, 4-9).

While the doctrine of obedience to the divine commandments, as essential to salvation, like all other doctrines of genuine religion, is thus drawn from the literal sense of the Scriptures, and confirmed thereby, it must not be forgotten that every passage cited from the Word of God has besides, and within the literal sense, a spiritual signification. Sacrifices and offerings are here chiefly mentioned in their opposite, or bad sense, as denoting external profession of worship without internal life,—the impious and vain-glorious offerings of self-righteousness, intelligence, and merit; the corrupt sacrifices of self-will and self-prudence, instead of the humble, teachable, meek, trustful, and sanctified affections of the regenerate mind.

The animals belonging to the flock and herd, and the various viands, which were thus voluntarily offered to the Lord in the Jewish sacrifices and oblations, were not arbitrarily selected, but were exact representative types and figures of such things as are good and true, and of the various thoughts and desires of the mind, which, in the regeneration, become receptive of goodness and truth. Each offering, and every circumstance connected with the offering, had its distinct spiritual signification.[158] The sacrifices and offerings as a whole repre-

---

[158] "The Jews (see *Hist. Crit. du V. T.*, liv. iii., cap. vii.), of which number St. Barnabas was himself originally one, and to whom he wrote, had of a long time been wholly addicted to the mystic and spiritual method of interpreting the law, and taught men to search out a spiritual meaning for almost all the ritual commands and ceremonies of it. This is plain from the account which Aristeas has left us of the rules which Eleazar, the high-priest, to whom Ptolemy sent for a copy of the Mosaical law, gave him for the understanding of it, when it being objected to him, that the legislator seemed to have been too curious in little matters, such as the prohibition of meats and drinks, and the like; he showed him at large that there was a further hidden design in it than what at first sight appeared, and that these outward ordinances were but as so many cautions to them against such vices as were principally meant to be forbidden by them. And then he goes on to explain this part of the law, according to the manner that Barnabas has done in [his] epistle. (*Apud Euseb. Praeparat. Evangel.*, lib. viii., cap. ix.) But this is not all: Eusebius (*Praepar. Evang.*, lib. viii., cap. x.) gives us yet another instance to confirm this to us, viz., of Aristobulus, who lived at the same time, and delivered the like spiritual meaning of the law that Eleazar had done before. And that this was still continued among the Hellenistical Jews, is evident by the account that is left us by one of them.

sented the entire process of the Lord's glorification from first to last, and, consequently, of man's regeneration. Now, man is regenerated by "ceasing to do evil, and learning to do well" (Isa. i. 16, 17); and to do these great works, he must freely receive of the wisdom and love, the strength and life of the Lord, and thus be conjoined to Him. Holy worship is the grand preparative for this conjunction. With intense, yea, infinite desire, the Lord desires spiritually to eat the passover with us (Luke xxii. 15). He knocks and calls that we may open the inner door of our minds, when, by the influence of his Spirit —the spirit of his love and wisdom—He "will come in to us, and will sup with us" (Rev. iii. 20). He hungers that we may receive and love his goodness. He thirsts that we may accept and believe his truth. He, from the most ardent desire for the salvation and happiness of his creatures, deigns to impart the divine principles of his own life to every prepared and willing soul, that men may be eternally conjoined with Him in heart, and mind, and life. Hence, the sacrifices and offerings of the Jews are denominated "a covenant" (Psalm l. 5), and even called the meat and bread of God (Lev. xxi. 6); and the altar is designated his table (Ezek. xli. 22). Nothing can be presented as grateful to the Lord but what is derived from Him, thus what is pure and perfect, what is clean and sound. The inward gifts and outward graces of the regenerate mind are the only offerings truly acceptable in the divine sight. In their sacrifices and burnt-offerings, their meat-offerings and drink-offerings, the Jews were on this account forbidden to present what was imperfect or polluted

---

who was contemporary with St. Barnabas, and than whom none has been more famous for this way of writing: I mean Philo (*Apud Euseb. Hist. Eccl.*, lib. ii., cap. xvii.) in his description of the Therapeutæ. They interpret the Holy Scriptures, viz., of the Old Testament, allegorically. For you must know, continues he, that they liken the law to an animal, the words of which make up the body, but the hidden sense, which lies under them, and is not seen, that they think to be the soul of it."—*Archbishop Wake's Preface to the Epistle of Barnabas*, secs. 24-30.

Origen says, "Unless they [the Levitical laws and ceremonies] be all taken in another sense than the literal, when they are recited in the church, as we have frequently declared, they are a greater stumbling-block, and tend more to the subversion of the Christian religion, than to its advancement and edification."—*In Levit.*, cap. vii. And again, "The laws of the sacrifices, which are given in the book of the Law, are to be fulfilled according to their spiritual meaning; for no man, having a right or sound reason, can admit that rams, and goats, and calves are fit offerings for an immortal and incorporeal God."—*In Levit.*, cap. iii.

The Rev. W. Greswell, in his work on *The Correspondency of the Mosaic Ritual and Christian Religion*, thus writes: "The whole body of the law of Moses was animated by a spirit which identified it with the gospel of Jesus Christ. *Every part* of its multiform and complicated ritual, when distinctly examined, and rightly understood, will be found to possess a *figurative or typical sense and import, and to teach some gospel truth.*"—Pref., p. viii. "We are taught to believe that all the sacrifices mentioned in the Old Testament, and not merely the sin and trespass offerings of the laws, *were of a typical import*, i. e. were intended *to prefigure something under the Christian dispensation that is of a corresponding nature.*"—p. 59.

(Deut. xv. 21), for worship defiled by self-righteousness and self-derived intelligence is profane and condemnatory; therefore, when the prophet is describing such a corrupt state of the church, in general and in particular, he says, "Ye offer polluted bread upon mine altar; and ye say, Wherein have we polluted thee? In that ye say, The table of the Lord is contemptible. And if ye offer the blind for sacrifice, is it not evil? and if ye offer the lame and sick, is it not evil?" (Mal. i. 7, 8.)[159]

Various degrees of goodness, innocence, and charity—natural, spiritual, and celestial—and the purified affections in which they actively dwell, and the states which they induce upon the mind, are signified, in a good sense, by domesticated animals and their young,—the flock and the herd, the lamb, the calf, and the kid, the ram, the ox,[160] and the he-goat. Different kinds of truth, wisdom, and intelligence, received in affection, together with the holy thoughts and sentiments to which they give birth, were signified by the clean birds, as the young pigeon and the turtle-dove. Thus all kinds of spiritual nourishment for the support of the will and the understanding, the affections and the thoughts, were signified by the meat-offerings and drink-offerings,—the cakes, the corn, the flour, the oil, the wine, the choicest viands, both liquid and solid, which were presented to the Lord; for the inward gifts which sustain the soul, and which were thus represented, appertain to the Lord Himself, from whom they flow into his kingdom in heaven and on earth, as the food of angels, the support of all spiritual life.

In the same sense, burnt-offerings and sacrifices signified in general adoration from a grateful heart, free-will "sacrifices of righteousness and thanksgiving" (Psalm iv. 5; cvii. 22),—rendering to Him "the calves of our lips" (Hos. xiv. 2),—the inward acknowledgment that all our blessings of love and wisdom, charity and faith, are derived from Him alone,—the consecration of all our faculties, spiritual and natural, intellectual and voluntary, our affections and thoughts, our words and deeds, to his service. Worship from love and charity was represented, in a good sense, by burnt-offerings and meat-offerings; worship from wisdom and faith was signified by sacrifices and drink-offerings. In reference to this spiritual signification and application

---

[159] "As things which were imperfect, unclean, ill-favored, ill-colored, etc., were emblems of vice [or various vices] and depravity, they are represented as odious [to God]: whilst things, clean, odorous, bright [and perfect], were emblems of virtue [or various virtues], and are represented as acceptable [to God]."—*Hutchinson's Use of Reason Recovered*, p. 285.

[160] "The Hebrew word translated *ox*, means the male or horned cattle of the beeve kind, at full age, when fit for the plough. Younger ones are called bullocks."—See *Harris's Nat. Hist. of the Bible*, Eng. ed., p. 298.

of the sacrificial worship of the Jews, the apostle Paul thus writes to the Romans, "I beseech you, therefore, brethren, by the mercies of God, that ye present your bodies a living sacrifice, holy, acceptable unto God, which is your reasonable service"[161] (Rom. xii. 1). And in the Epistle to the Hebrews we read, "To do good and communicate, forget not: for with such sacrifices God is well pleased" (xiii. 16). Nor without much self-denial, the mortification of the natural mind, the subjugation of the fleshly lusts, is that state of mind attained, in which such living, holy, and acceptable worship can be performed, or those precious gifts received which can be suitably presented. "I will not," said David, "offer burnt-offerings unto the Lord my God of that which doth cost me nothing" (2 Sam. xxiv. 24).

We have said that the Jews fell into the fatal delusion that their sacrifices were piacular. Nor has this great error been confined to Judaism. It has been interwoven, in all its deformity, into the Christian religion, and the sacrifice of the Lord, or the glorification of his Humanity, which consisted in the hallowing and consecrating to infinite purposes the entire Humanity which He assumed in the world, with all its faculties and powers, has been extensively and most mistakenly regarded as a vicarious sacrifice for even the wilful transgressions of the human race, and represented as offered by the second person in the Trinity to the first person, as a distinct Being, or God, to appease his wrath, and propitiate his favor; and, moreover, that his suffering and death on the cross being a vicarious substitute for the punishment of sinners, the infinite merits of his spotless righteousness are imputed to all that believe in Him. How full of mystery, perplexity and inconsistency is this fatal notion! It substitutes the innocent for the guilty, although guilt and innocence cannot be transferred without the violation of all justice. Unless there be more than one God, it represents the Lord Jesus Christ as the pacifier and the pacified, the priest and the victim, the identical God, whose vengeance was appeased and whose justice was satisfied, by his own sufferings, while it confounds all rational and Scriptural difference between the infinite and the finite by imputing the incommunicable merits of the Creator to the finite creature. How broadly does this system contrast with the simple, glorious, and obvious doctrines of

---

[161] "The terms here used are sacrificial, and forcibly intimate that, as under the Old Testament dispensation the burnt-offerings were wholly the Lord's property, so Christians are required to give up themselves entirely to the service of God."— *Horæ Romanæ*, note, p. 67.

"Sacrifices were a symbolical address to God, intended to express before Him the devotions, affections, dispositions, and desires of the heart, by significative and emblematical actions."— *Scrip. Doct. of the Atonement Examined*. By J. Taylor, 1751.

the New Testament! The atonement or at-one-ment is there described as a work of reconciliation,—as effecting an important and essential spiritual change in man, his motives, his thoughts, and his words and works thence proceeding, but without implying any change whatever in the immutable Godhead. The apostle Paul, therefore, in writing to the Romans, says, "We joy in God through our Lord Jesus Christ, by whom we [not God, WE] have now received the atonement" (v. 11). The Greek word [Καταλλαγήν] translated here atonement, means reconciliation, and with its modifications is so translated wherever else it occurs in the New Testament.

The Lord "bore our sins and carried our sorrows" (Isa. liii. 3) by taking upon Himself our depraved nature, with all its hereditary defilements, and, by removing these evils from his Humanity, He "consecrated it for evermore" (Heb. vii. 28), and thereby received power from the indwelling Divinity to remove, likewise, the evils of all those who look unto Him and put their trust in Him. For now "He is able to save to the uttermost them that come unto God [the indwelling Divinity] by Him [the glorified Humanity]" (Heb. vii. 25). "For in that He Himself hath suffered being tempted, He is able to succor them that are tempted" (Heb. ii. 18). Hence we further read, that "When the even was come, they brought unto Him many that were possessed with devils: and He cast out the spirits with his word, and healed all that were sick: that it might be fulfilled which was spoken by Esaias the prophet, saying, Himself took our infirmities, and bore our sicknesses" (Matt. viii. 16, 17).

"To bear our sins," then, was to sustain temptation; and to put them away, signifies not only that He conquered all evil tendencies, and removed them from his Humanity, but also, that in the hour of severest spiritual trial and conflict He is both able and willing to stretch forth his gracious hand to save all from the inherent corruptions of their nature, as well as their actual sins,—thus to deliver from the bondage of sin, the fears of eternal death, and from the miseries of hell, all who acknowledge their transgressions, believe in Him, and keep his commandments. By the power and efficacy of divine truth, as "the Word made flesh," which is so often called "the blood of Christ," and "the blood of the New Covenant [or Testament], shed for the remission of sins" (Matt. xxvi. 28), man is cleansed from the impurities of his life and heart just in proportion as, by obedience thereto, he puts his evil away, and, by divine assistance, manfully endures the temptations and trials by which the work is accomplished; and of this process the grievous temptations which the Lord endured in the glorification of his Humanity were representative. Thus the apostle Paul writes to the Romans, "Therefore we are buried with Him by baptism unto death: that like as Christ [the Lord's Humanity] was raised up from the dead by the glory of the Father [or the indwelling Divinity], even so we also should walk in newness of life. For if we have been planted together in the likeness of his death, we shall be also in the likeness of his resurrection: knowing this, that our old man is crucified with Him, that the body of sin might be destroyed, that henceforth we should not serve sin. For he that is dead is freed from sin. Now if we be dead with Christ, we believe that we shall also live with Him. . . . For in that He died, He died unto sin once: but in that He liveth, He liveth unto God. Likewise reckon ye also yourselves to be dead indeed unto sin, but alive unto God through Jesus Christ our Lord" (Rom. vi. 4-11).

The Lord Jesus Christ, then, offered a perfect sacrifice of obedience to his own divine law; "He consecrated a new and living way for us through the veil, that is to say, his flesh" (Heb. x. 20); He became our example (1 Pet. ii. 21). We are exhorted continually to approach Him without fear, to follow Him, to be like Him, who was made "perfect through sufferings" (Heb. ii. 10), and "learned obedience by the things which He suffered; and being made perfect, He became the author of eternal salvation unto all them that obey Him" (Heb. v. 8, 9).

Like as the Lord gained a complete victory over hell, and accomplished his work of glorification by laying down his life and taking it again (John x. 18), so man, in humble and full dependence upon Him, must work out his own salvation (Phil. ii. 12); and the lifegiving blood of the New Covenant will supply every obedient believer with the means of victory over death and hell (Rev. xii. 11). We are, consequently, "to follow the Lord in the regeneration" (Matt. xix. 28), not by the observance of Jewish sacrifices, nor yet by looking upon the Lord as a piacular victim, who suffered death in our stead, but by obedience to the Divine will and wisdom, thus by shunning the evil which that wisdom condemns, and doing the good which that will approves; by a life of heavenly "charity or love out of a pure heart, and of a good conscience, and of faith unfeigned" (1 Tim. i. 5).

Such is the true, spiritual, and only acceptable worship of which the sacrifices of Abraham and the patriarchs, the ceremonial worship of the Israelites, and the life and ministry of our divine Redeemer were eminently representative.

CHAPTER XX.

THE ENTIRE HISTORY OF THE FOUR GOSPELS LITERALLY TRUE, BUT SIGNIFICATIVE AND REPRESENTATIVE IN EVERY PARTICULAR RECORDED.—ILLUSTRATIONS FROM THE LORD'S PARABLES AND MIRACLES, HIS TRANSFIGURATION, LIFE, MINISTRY, AND CRUCIFIXION.

IN the parabolic instruction of our Lord and Saviour, Jesus Christ, in the miracles which He wrought, and in the whole progress of his life and ministry on earth, as recorded in the four Gospels,[162] we have the most incontestable evidence, and the most positive assurances, that the entire literal sense was designed to convey a more interior signification. Hence He made a most remarkable distinction between understanding his *speech*, and hearing, or hearkening to his words; between what He *said* and what He *spake* (John viii. 43; xii. 49). The apparently irrelevant and ambiguous answers which the Lord so often gave to the queries of those by whom He was surrounded, are of themselves sufficient to prove that the meaning of all He said and did, could not be discovered in the letter, or from the outward form of the event. When He washed his disciples' feet, an act which represented the purification of the externals of the mind and life, in which work we are privileged to help each other, the Lord did not explain the symbols He presented before them, but said to Peter, "What I do thou knowest not now, but thou shalt know hereafter;" and, again, "I have given you an example, that ye should do as I have done to you" (John xiii. 4–17). When He reproved the disciples for ambition and the love of dominion, external pretensions to holiness, and vainglory, He set before them a little child,—whose engaging qualities of simplicity, innocence, honesty of purpose, humility of mind, and docility, correspond to the Christian character,—and he required them to imitate its artless conduct, to adopt its unpretending simplicity, and to practise its filial obedience. When the woman of Samaria was asked for water, the Lord directed her attention to Himself as the fountain of "living water," "the Word

---

[162] For the reasons why there were *four* Gospels, see *Noble's Plenary Inspiration of the Scriptures Asserted*, etc., pp. 580–583.

made flesh," the well-spring of eternal truth, of which, "Whosoever drinketh," He added, "shall never thirst" (John iv. 6-15). When He crossed the Lake of Tiberias with his disciples, and they had forgotten to provide themselves with bread, He said unto them, "Take heed and beware of the leaven of the Pharisees and of the Sadducees" (Matt. xvi. 6); and because they interpreted what He said unto them as if it had relation to their neglect, He added, "How is it that ye do not understand that I spake it not to you concerning bread, that ye should beware of the leaven of the Pharisees and of the Sadducees? Then understood they how that He bade them not beware of the leaven of bread, but of the doctrine of the Pharisees and of the Sadducees" (11, 12). When the Jews required from Him a sign from heaven, in attestation of his authority, He "answered and said unto them, Destroy this temple, and in three days I will raise it up" (John ii. 19). They immediately referred what He had said to the erection of their temple, and deridingly replied, "Forty and six years was this temple in building, and wilt thou rear it up in three days?" No explanation was then given, but it is added that "He spake of the temple of his body. When therefore He was risen from the dead, his disciples remembered that He had said this unto them; and they believed the scripture, and the word which Jesus had said" (20-22).

Many other similar instances might be adduced, but these are sufficient to prove most unquestionably that all which the Lord said, and what is said of Him, was significative, and that all his divine works were representative.

If we read carefully the beautiful parables of our Saviour, we shall find them teeming with spiritual instruction, of which very little appears on the surface or in the letter. In them the Lord spake by pure correspondences, and each single expression is full of "spirit and life." Take, for example, the seven parables recorded in the thirteenth chapter of Matthew. Of these, a learned, pious and intelligent writer has made the following truly interesting remarks:

"The several parables contained in this chapter stand in a connected order as to their internal sense, and thus follow each other in a regular series expressive of the whole process of regeneration, commencing with the first reception of heavenly truth from the Word, and advancing through all gradations of its growth to the full maturity of heavenly love and life. Accordingly, the first parable of the sower describes the first insemination of truth, which is the first step towards the regenerate life. The second parable of the tares of the field describes the manifestation of evils and falses in consequence of such insemination, which is a second step, and an effect of the first. The third parable of the grain of mustard-seed describes the small increment of heavenly life, whilst man supposes that he doeth good from himself alone, and not from the Lord, which is a third state in the regeneration. The fourth parable of the leaven, etc., describes the temptations consequent on the reception of heavenly truth and good, which is a fourth state. The fifth parable of treasure hid in a field, describes the further effect of the reception of heavenly truth and good, in leading man to renounce his proprium or his own proper life, that he may appropriate the life of heaven, which is signified by selling all that he hath and buying the field, and which is a fifth state. The sixth parable of the merchant-man seeking beautiful pearls, describes the effect of heavenly truth in leading man to the acknowledgment of the Lord, as the alone source of all good and truth, and the consequent renunciation of self-love and its guidance, which is a sixth state. The seventh parable of a net cast into the sea, describes the last effect of the reception of heavenly truth and good, in accomplishing a full and final separation between goods and evils, and between truths and falses, so that goods and truths are brought into conjunction with heaven, whilst evils and falses are cast down into hell; and this is the seventh and last state of the regenerate life."[163]

The miracles of our Lord were not only works of mercy actually done on behalf of a few individuals, or wrought in testimony of his exclusive divinity and sovereignty, but were, in every particular, representative and significative of what He is still doing, and will be forever doing, to promote the salvation of his creatures. Just as diseases, for instance, disorganize, afflict, and destroy the powers of the body, so sin and folly, the offspring of evil, disturb the order of life and destroy the spiritual faculties of the soul, rendering it incapable of receiving the vital influences of heaven, except in a perverted degree. Hence, He opened the eyes of the blind, to denote that the truth of his Word can unclose the darkened understanding and dissipate the mists of spiritual ignorance. He healed the sick, to signify that He only can restore the diseased and feeble mind to spiritual health and strength. He cleansed the lepers, to signify that He alone can deliver man from those filthy and contagious states of evil in

---

[163] *Gospel according to Matthew, translated from the original Greek, and illustrated with Extracts from the writings of Swedenborg, by the Rev. J. Clowes, M. A.* See Notes to chap. xiii. "It is my persuasion that the [seven] parables in this chapter are not to be considered disjointedly, but to be taken together as a connected series."—*Alexander Knox's Remains*, vol. i., p. 408.

"Doubtless these seven [parables] have a certain unity, succeeding one another in natural order, and having a completeness in themselves."--*Trench's Notes on the Parables*, p. 142.

which he profanes the divine truth. He opened deaf ears, and commanded the dumb to speak, and caused the lame to walk, in order to exhibit the process of those inward operations of his mercy by which men are prepared to listen to the instructions of true wisdom, are disposed to offer thanksgiving to Him in the grateful acknowledgment that He is the only giver of "every good and perfect gift," and are enabled to walk in the way of the divine commandments. He raised the dead, to prove that He alone possesses the ability to awaken man from the lethargy and corruption of spiritual death, and to give immortal life to the soul, once "dead in trespasses and sins" (Eph. ii. 1), for "to be carnally-minded is death, but to be spiritually-minded is life and peace. Because the carnal mind is enmity against God" (Rom. iii. 6, 7). He cast out devils, to show that by faith and love, derived from Him as their divine source, man may reject from his natural mind those unclean lusts and affections, and those false and foul persuasions, thence derived, which, before the work of regeneration is begun, obsess his spirit.[164] He walked on the tempestuous sea,

---

[164] The following extracts, from various authors, will serve to show that a very general perception of the truth, on this important subject, has existed in the Christian Church.

"There is a remarkable fragment of Origen produced by the martyr Pamphilus, which represents him as speaking of the evangelical narrative generally: 'Though these things have a spiritual meaning, yet the truth of the history being *first established*, the spiritual sense is to be taken as something over and above. For what if our Lord, in a spiritual sense, be always curing the blind, when He casts his light on minds blinded with ignorance; yet He did not the less at that time heal one corporally blind. And He is ever raising the dead; yet He did then really perform wonders of that kind also, as when He raised Jairus's daughter, and the widow's son, and Lazarus. And though at all times, when awakened by his disciples, He quiets the storms and whirlwinds of his church; yet it is unquestionable that those things also, which are related in the history, really took place on that occasion.'"—*Apol. pro. Orig.*, p. 36; *D. ad. Celc. Orig. Ed. Bened.*, t. iv., cited in *Tracts for the Times*, lxxxix., p. 58.

"The works which Jesus then did, were the symbols of those things which He by his power is always doing."—*Origen in Matt.*, cap. xv. "Whatsoever Jesus did in the flesh was, as to every particular, a similitude and type of what He will do hereafter."—*In Isa.*, cap. vi. "The true miracles of Christ, and the healing of the sick, are of a spiritual kind."—*In Matt.*, cap. xxv. He explains the miracles of healing allegorically; for instance, the lunatic in Matt. xiv. " is a spiritually diseased man, who at one time is virtuous, but more frequently assailed by the epilepsy of sinful passions."—T. xiii., s. 4.

"To the same purpose Athanasius, with respect to our manner of thinking and speaking of things divine and the mysteries of the gospel, with great truth and elegance expresseth himself thus: 'These things are expressed indeed after the manner of men, or in human language; but they are conceived in a godlike or heavenly manner.'"—*Things Divine and Supernatural conceived by Analogy with things Natural and Human, by the author of "The Procedure, Extent, and Limits of the Human Understanding,"* p. 87. London: 1733.

"Although the works of Jesus were done at this time, we should consider well what their signification is in relation to future times; ... for the then present acts of the Lord declare the form of the future."—*Hilary, in Matt.*, cap. x., s. 5, et cap. xxi.

"The cures which Jesus wrought upon the blind were indeed great, but, unless He daily do as mighty works to us, they are not great."—*John of Jerusalem, Homil.* xxx.

"If there had been nothing more than a temporal use to be gained by [the miraculous cure of the sick], then did He [the Lord] noth-

and rebuked the winds and waves, not only to prove that He was the God of nature, in human form, but to signify that his omnipotent power alone can subdue and control the raging influence of hell, and that He is ever in the act of assuaging the troubles, and dissipating the doubts and fears, of his faithful followers. He miraculously increased a small quantity of food, and supplied the wants of multitudes, to signify his ability and willingness to impart in rich abundance, to all who truly come unto Him, the elements which are needed for the support of spiritual life and energy in the soul.

"Divine miracles," says Swedenborg, "differ from magical miracles, as heaven from hell. Divine miracles proceed from divine truth,

---

ing of great importance to those who were healed by Him."—*Irenæus*, lib. v., cap. xii., s. 6. "The different kinds of sickness and disease existing at that time among the people whom the Saviour cured, relate to the spiritual infirmities of human souls."—*In Matt.*, cap. xvii.

"He is at this day performing those still greater cures, on account of which He condescended to exhibit those lesser miracles" (*Augustine in Serm.* 88); and that "our Lord intended that those cures which He performed bodily should also be understood spiritually."—*In Serm.* 98, s. 3.

"When He [the Lord Jesus] healed the sick, gave sight to the blind, and enabled the lame to walk, He not only proved his authority, but suggested the inference that He had come to restore our corrupted nature to its original purity, to enlighten the ignorant, as all men were, and to enable us to stand in the path of life."—*Hind's History of Christianity*, vol. i., p. 95.

"The miracles of our Lord on the bodies of men . . . appear . . . not merely as indications of a divine power, which had authority to command, but also as themselves the vehicles of spiritual instruction. . . . Our Lord himself, in his cures, did sometimes studiously connect the external malady with the diseases of the soul; or we may say, seemed earnestly to endeavor to turn the thoughts of the bystanders from the bodily disease to the sins that occasioned it, and were connected with it; as by using the words, 'Thy sins be forgiven thee,' instead of merely dispelling the disease. . . . And of course, a good man would not limit the instructions, thus conveyed, to those particular instances themselves; but would consider them rather as intimations of a great system, and of an extensive correspondence in the evils of the body and soul, which we know not how to limit, any more than we can limit the divine order and arrangement of all things. . . . From all this analogy, the thought will occur to one, whether every bodily distemper may not be but the analogy or figure of some corresponding malady of the soul, not of course existing in the same person, as they are often most free from any such connection; but implying some resemblance in the diseases and distempers which prevail in the two worlds of matter and spirit. . . . Nothing [again] is more frequent than the words of hearing and of seeing, and of deafness and blindness, as applied to the soul. Our Lord himself repeatedly uses this figurative language; and on one remarkable occasion connects the lesson of spiritual blindness with that of the bodily eye, and draws the attention from one to the other; for on healing the man that was blind from his birth, He declared of the Pharisees, 'I am come, that they who see not may see, and that they who see may be made blind.'"—*Thoughts on the Study of the Holy Gospels, etc., by the Rev. Isaac Williams, B.D., late Fellow of Trinity College, Oxford,* pp. 247–253.

"Oh, Jesus! once tossed on the breast of the billow,
Aroused by the shriek of despair from thy pillow,
Now seated in glory, the mariner cherish,
Who cries in his danger, 'Help, Lord,' or we perish."
And, oh, when the whirlwind of passion is raging,
When hell in our hearts his wild warfare is waging,
Arise in thy strength thy redeemed to cherish,
Rebuke the destroyer—'Help, Lord,' or we perish." *Bishop Heber.*

and go forward according to order; the effects, in ultimates, are miracles, when it pleases the Lord that they should be presented in that form. Hence it is that all divine miracles represent states of the Lord's kingdom in the heavens, and of the Lord's kingdom in the earths, or of the church; this is the internal form of divine miracles. Such is the case with all the miracles in Egypt, and also with the rest that are mentioned in the Word. All the miracles, also, which the Lord Himself wrought when He was in the world, signified the approaching state of the church, as the opening the eyes of the blind, etc., signifying that such as are represented by the blind, etc., would receive the Gospel, and be spiritually healed, and this by the coming of the Lord into the world. Such are divine miracles in their internal form. Magical miracles appear like divine miracles, because they flow from order, and order appears like in the ultimates where miracles are presented. [But] although in the external form [magical miracles] appear like divine miracles, they nevertheless have in them a contrary end, viz., of destroying those things which are of the church; whereas, divine miracles have inwardly in them the end of building up those things which are of the church."—A. C., n. 7337.

"The miracles which the Lord performed when He sojourned on the earth were actual facts, as well as representative works. Their performance was not, as many suppose, effected by the exercise of arbitrary power in opposition to the laws of creative order, but dispensing with those mediums, or the setting aside of those intermediate modes of operation by which the great Creator brings forth all effects in the order of nature,—thus the activities of the spiritual world, whose creations are instantaneous, and not progressive, being brought near the natural world, and acting more directly upon matter, control or suspend all mediums, and produce a spontaneous and instantaneous effect both on organized forms and natural substances. Hence, at the Lord's presence infernal spirits were compelled to retire, inveterate diseases were healed, new arrangements of internal and external structure were supplied, withered limbs were restored, health was infused into the disordered frame, the very dead were raised to life, water was turned into wine, bread was multiplied by a word, the raging sea was calmed. It was an extraordinary descent of spiritual force into nature, or into the things of the natural world, which thus effected all known miracles. They were no direct breach of divine order, but rather a manifestation of that superior order which prevails in the spiritual world, and which, when permitted to enter into the natural world, supersedes or extinguishes for the moment, and within the space allotted for its action, the common order of nature, just as a vivid concentrated sunbeam, or a flash of lightning from heaven, supersedes and extinguishes all minor earthly flames."—*Hindmarsh's Essay on the Lord's Resurrection*, page 70.

Nor should it be forgotten that these mighty works cannot be done in man, and for him, without his own free and hearty coöperation with the Lord Jesus Christ, his God and Saviour, from whom all power is derived. Wherefore He says, "Behold, I give you power to tread on serpents and scorpions,"—that is, power to subdue all the false and deadly persuasions of sensuality,—"and over all the power of the enemy, and nothing shall by any means hurt you" (Luke x. 19).

The works of the Saviour were likewise representative, as must be evident from his own divine declaration, where He says, "Verily, verily, I say unto you, He that believeth on me, the works that I do shall he do also; and greater works than these shall he do; because I go unto my Father" (John xiv. 12), where we are taught that these mighty works are to be wrought in us by the combined activities of love and wisdom, signified in the spiritual sense by the Father and the Son; that they are to be done by the united operation of the human will with the Divine will; and that they are as much greater than those which had reference to the renovation and preservation of the body as the soul is superior to its earthly tabernacle.

As an example of the manner in which the Lord's miracles are to be explained and understood, we will briefly instance the deeply interesting one, literally performed at the marriage in Cana of Galilee, and recorded in the first twelve verses of John ii. Cana was a city of the Gentile nations, which signifies, in the spiritual sense, the state of those who acknowledge their destitution of divine truth, and who, in consequence of their ignorance of the Word of God, are preserved from the dreadful evils of profanation, which had consummated a previous dispensation. It was to enlighten and instruct such humble minds, that the Lord condescended to sojourn in the flesh; and, to represent his divine purposes and operations more vividly, He made the first wondrous display of his mercy on the delightful occasion of a nuptial ceremony in Galilee of the Gentiles. A marriage, we have seen, signifies the union of love and wisdom in the will and understanding; hence, also, conjunction with the Lord, for without such a union of the constituent principles of the church, and of every individual, no such conjunction can be experienced. When the sincere desire for it exists, however, the Lord is said to be called or invited to the feast. He is present, as to his divine love, denoted by his name, Jesus; for it is from the infinite ardor of his love that He wills to "save his people from their sins" (Matt. i. 21). He is present together with the inward good affection, denoted by the Mother of

Jesus,[165] which prompts the perception of that holy principle, and with his disciples, significative of all the divine truths and doctrines derived from Him through his Word, and needful to supply the fulness of instruction. The third day denotes a complete state of preparation. The feast commenced, but it was suggested by Mary, who represented heavenly affection, that they had no wine. External truth, signified by the water, with its cleansing and refreshing qualities, existed in abundance; but interior truth, signified by wine, which exhilarates the inmost principles of the soul, was wanting.[166] When the Lord was thus applied to, He apparently gave a discouraging answer, but in reality teaches that internal truth, however desired, cannot be given till the hour or state arrives in which man is duly prepared for it, and which is induced by a willing and simple obedience to the truths already acquired. The servants are therefore directed to do whatsoever the Lord saith. The six water-pots of stone, "set after the manner of the purifying of the Jews, containing two or three firkins apiece," signify the divine Word itself, and the purifying tendency of its doctrines; and their numbers and measures denote fulness, adapted to every state of the church and the mind. To be filled to the brim signifies, that as the Word is obeyed, it is seen to be replenished,—to overflow with an infinite abundance of truths.

To select one more illustration of the internal sense of the Gospels, let us refer to the narrative of the Lord's transfiguration on the mount, related by three of the Evangelists (Matt. xvii.; Mark ix.; Luke ix.). This wonderful event was designed in general to teach that the whole Word bears unbroken witness to the great truth that the divine love, wisdom and power are the indwelling attributes of the Lord Jesus Christ. Three of the disciples, Peter, James and John, were present. I may observe that the Lord was so seen by these disciples, when, being withdrawn from the body, their spiritual sight was opened. Though it is described, like the ancient prophetic visions, as if it had happened in the natural world, it was in reality a transaction which took place in the spiritual world. We have before observed, that by the three disciples, Peter, James and John,

---

[165] See Luke viii. 21; John ix. 27.

[166] "Wine, in many passages, is put by us for the Holy Scriptures, which contain *within them* the purest force of heavenly wisdom, by which the understandings of men are warmed, and their affections inebriated. While Christ wrought in Cana of Galilee they wanted wine, and wine is produced for them; that is, the shadows (of the letter) are removed, and the truth is presented to view. The good wine is the Old Testament, but this (good wine) does not appear, unless in the letter it be spiritually understood."—*Augustine App. in Serm.* xc.

"By wine, the spiritual intelligence of the divine law is denoted. Whence the Lord at the marriage in Cana turned the water into wine."—*Durandus on Symbolism*, p. 153.

are signified the three essentials of all religion, viz., faith, charity or love, and good works or the fruits of charity. None but those in whom these ennobling principles are found united and active can spiritually discern the Lord's glory in his Word. It is said that after six days the Lord took them up into a high mountain apart. After six days signifies a state of rest, peace and joy, denoted also by the Sabbath,—a holy and heavenly state which can only be attained by passing through the previous states of labor and trial, and by enduring the severe conflicts of temptation, signified by the six days in which man has to do "all his work." By a high mountain, called by an apostle "the holy mount" (2 Pet. i. 18), is signified a state of inmost affection; denoting, when predicated of the Lord, his divine love for his creatures, and when predicated of them, their love towards Him. High signifies what is exalted and interior; and apart denotes the separation which obtains, in this exalted state, between what is earthly and heavenly. By the Lord being transfigured[167] is not meant that there ever was, or can be, any change in Him; but He so represented Himself in the presence of his disciples to denote that the effulgence of his inmost Divinity can only be revealed to those who are prepared to ascend the mount of love. There they can see and commune with their God and Saviour. From that lofty elevation, losing sight of his sufferings and sorrows,—his states of humiliation and temptation,—He is beheld in all the splendors of his glorified Humanity. Nor is the glory which is thus manifested, any extraneous appearance assumed in a moment, and for temporary purposes, but it is an inward emanation, perpetually flowing from the inherent essentials of his own divine nature. The Lord's face, which was refulgent as the sun, signified his infinite goodness and mercy, beaming with splendors from his divinely glorified Person. His garments, which appeared white as the light, signified those sacred and eternal truths in all their radiant purity, with which He clothes or invests Himself as with raiment (Psalm civ. 2). By Moses and Elias are not only signified the great lawgiver and the prophet, but the Word itself, which they were instrumental in recording; Moses denoting the historical portions, and Elias the prophetical. Their conversation with the Lord was unquestionable evidence that the whole Word treats concerning Himself and his divine operations. Through the same holy medium, man also may, as it were, hold converse with his God. By Peter saying, "Lord, it is good for us to be here: if thou

---

[167] Lit., "He transfigured himself."

wilt, let us make here three tabernacles; one for thee, and one for Moses, and one for Elias," is denoted the blissful perceptions given to a true faith, that the highest privilege of the Christian is to hold intercourse with the Lord through his Word, thus to open the mind towards Him, that dwelling with us and in us He may continually replenish all the faculties of the soul with his divine gifts. The cloud into which the disciples entered, and with which they were overshadowed, represented the literal sense of the Word, which, veiling its inward truths, accommodates them to the state of the beholder, and becomes a "light or bright cloud," when these truths are seen to shine through it. A voice out of the cloud is the response or confirmation of divine truth, as heard in the pure doctrines of religion, and taught even in the letter of the Word. These doctrines instruct us that the Lord glorified his maternal or material Humanity, and made it divine according to his own infinite will and good pleasure; that all the fulness of the divinity dwells in the glorified Humanity, the "beloved Son;" and that having learned this all-important, all-glorious truth, we must ever harken to the still small voice,—the dictates of a genuine conscience formed by the plastic and vital operation of truth. By the disciples hearing the voice, falling on their faces, and being sore afraid, is signified a disposition to obedience, adoration from the deepest humiliation of heart, and thence inward reverence for the Lord and dread of evil. Jesus touching them signifies divine communication of new strength and life from Himself. His saying, "Arise, and be not afraid," signifies the consequent elevation of state, from which all fear is banished, because the Lord is seen as "mighty to save," and as saving to the uttermost all who come unto Him. And, lastly, by the disciples "lifting up their eyes and seeing no man save Jesus only," is meant, that in this exalted state of the understanding, and so far as finite power can discern the infinite, the Lord Jesus Christ is perceived in all his grandeur and glory, and acknowledged from the heart to be the only God of angels and men,—the Creator, Redeemer and Saviour of his creatures, the All in all of the church in heaven and on earth, "the Alpha and the Omega, the beginning and the ending, who is, and who was, and who is to come, the Almighty" (Rev. i. 8).

The Lord's birth into the world,[168] his baptism, temptations and

---

[168] From the earliest ages of Christianity, this glorious vision has been regarded as containing an inward signification, and even some perception of its spiritual import may be traced in various authors; thus John of Jerusalem writes, "He who follows the letter of the Scripture, and remains exclusively in the valley, cannot see Jesus clothed in

THE GOSPEL HISTORY ALL SIGNIFICATIVE.

ministry, his crucifixion, resurrection and ascension, were, as to every historical circumstance recorded in the holy Gospels, not only true as to the literal facts (see *ante*), but also significative of his approach to the church in general, and to every prepared mind in particular, and of his reception, acknowledgment and glorification in the regenerating mind; and thus, by consequence, they are made to represent all the various steps and degrees in the spiritual pathway through which we must walk to obtain an everlasting state of conjunction with Him, and the blessings of his salvation.[169] The temptations in the wilderness, or the grievous assaults and suggestions of the infernal

---

white raiment; but he who follows the Word of God up the mountain, that is, he who ascends the sublime sense of the law, to him Jesus is transfigured. So long as we follow the obscurity of the letter, Moses and Elias do not talk with Jesus; but if we understand it spiritually, then straightway Moses and Elias, that is the law and the prophets, come and converse with the Gospel."—(*Homil.*, xxxii.) So again Origen writes, "Unless thou ascend the mountain of God, and there meet with Moses; unless thou ascend the lofty sense of the law; unless thou reach the height of spiritual intelligence, thy mouth is not opened by God. If thou abide in the low plain of the letter, and do no more than make Jewish narratives of historical texts, thou hast not met Moses on the mount of God, neither hath God opened thy mouth, nor taught thee what thou oughtest to say."—[*In Ex.*, cap. iv.] In another place, speaking of the same subject, he observes, "Moses and Elias appeared in glory when they talked with Jesus, and in this fact the law and the prophets are shown to agree with the Gospels, and to be resplendent with the same glory, when spiritually understood."—(*In Epist. ad Rom.*, cap. i.) He also says, "Christ is transfigured, when He is discerned theologically in the Spirit, according to his high dignity; and not according to the simple notions of the illiterate multitude. The shining raiment means his discourses, and the evangelical and apostolic writings. Whosoever discerns Christ in this way, also beholds Moses and Elias, who, by synecdoche, are put for all the prophets."—*Comment. in Matt.*, t. xii., f. 37.

[169] "Did we really lay it to heart, as we read verse after verse of the GOSPELS,—did we in earnest put our minds to the thought,—that this Jesus of Nazareth, the Son of Mary, is indeed the Most High God, Creator and Possessor of heaven and earth, and of all things visible and invisible; did we realize our conviction of this truth in connection with each and all of his actions and discourses, and of the scenes and circumstances in which we find him engaged, we should, of course, feel on all these subjects that which considerate persons feel in regard of all God's words and works, viz., that the least of them is far too deep for us; the most trivial of his commandments is exceeding broad; the slightest, to our conception, of his acts must have eternal and infinite associations and consequences. The words, then, and doings of our Blessed Saviour, being as they are the words and doings of God, it cannot be but they must mean far more than meets the ear or the eye; they cannot but be fully charged with heavenly and mysterious meaning, whether we are, as yet, competent to discern some part of that meaning or no; and to look at them in that light may be called Mysticism; but is it any more than the natural and necessary result of *considerate* faith in his divine nature?"—*Tracts for the Times*, lxxxix., p. 119.

"On the whole, there seems no want of Scriptural authority for the allegory as applied by the Fathers to the New Testament, considered both in what it includes and in what it omits. Most modern interpreters even, and almost all devotional writers, recognize it in principle, some perhaps more or less unconsciously; but the great difference between them and the ancients seems to lie rather in this—that the ancients fear not to carry it out, in every part of the Gospels, and as far as it will go in every case, whereas we, in modern times, each draw his own arbitrary line, according to our own taste, or our notions of what is useful or convincing, or out of deference to the judgments we expect from others."—*Tracts for the Times*, lxxxix., p. 133.

Neither the Acts of the Apostles nor the Epistles are treated in this way by any of the Fathers as having a parabolical sense or spiritual meaning, except where citations are made from what the Lord said in the Gospels, or what Moses and the prophets had written, or where some evident allu-

powers, signified by the devil and satan, were endured by our blessed Lord in their utmost intensity, while He was clothed with an infirm Human, which, with all the hereditary proclivities and corruptions of our degenerate nature, He had assumed for our redemption, or deliverance from hell. They are very briefly portrayed by the pen of inspiration (Matt. iv.; Luke iv.), and can only be rationally understood from a knowledge of the inward sense, in which they describe the states of direful temptation and inconceivable anguish that He passed through, as He subjugated the infernal hosts in that wonderful process by which He delivered man from their influence, and made his Humanity Divine. In a subordinate sense, as the Lord was "tempted in all points like as we are" (Heb. iv. 15), the inspired account of his temptations must of necessity be significative of the discouragements, trials, temptations and sufferings with which every Christian is exercised in a finite degree, as he faithfully follows the Lord in that purifying process of regeneration, whereby man is eternally saved from death and hell. When He presents Himself to our minds, and we are unprepared for his glorious presence, because we are unwilling to cast out the subtle and impure affections and thoughts which fill our unregenerate bosoms, it is then said that "there is no room for Him in the inn" (Luke ii. 7); and, again, in tenderest accents we hear Him bewailing our condition in language of love and pity, saying, "The foxes have holes, and the birds of the air have nests, but the Son of Man hath not where to lay his head" (Matt. viii. 20; Luke ix. 58); for, alas! human cunning is preferred to divine wisdom, self-dependence to Divine Providence, and the heart is filled with unclean and selfish desires, and the understanding is overwhelmed with worldly solicitude, and no preparation can be made for the reception of Him who, as the Son of Man, presents Himself before us in his own blessed Word. "He cometh to his own, and his own receive Him not" (John i. 11). In their perversity of soul they say, "We will not have this man [the eternal Truth] to reign over us" (Luke xix. 14); we acknowledge no sovereign as ruling over us but "the prince of this world" (Luke xix. 14); "We have no king but Cæsar" (John xix. 15). The circumstances attending our Lord's crucifixion were significative of a depraved state of the church and the human mind. Swedenborg places this subject in a powerful light. He says:

---

sions are made to what is there recorded; or in explanation of visions, as Paul's conversion and Peter's vision, and the signification of a few proper names, under which they thought some mysteries might be concealed.

"That the Lord Himself, as the chief Prophet, represented the state of the church in its relation to the Word, appears from the circumstances attending his passion; as, that He was betrayed by Judas; that He was taken and condemned by the chief priests and elders; that they buffeted Him; that they struck Him on the head with a reed; that they put a crown of thorns on his head; that they divided his garments, and cast lots for his vesture; that they crucified Him; that they gave Him vinegar to drink; that they pierced his side; that He was buried, and rose again on the third day. His being betrayed by Judas, signified that He was betrayed by the Jewish nation, who at that time were the depositaries of the Word; for Judas represented that nation. His being taken and condemned by the chief priests and elders, signified that He was taken and condemned by the whole Jewish church. Their scourging Him, spitting in his face, buffeting Him, and striking Him on the head with a reed, signified that they treated in a similar manner the Word, with respect to its divine truths, all which relate to the Lord. Their putting a crown of thorns on his head, signified that they had falsified and adulterated those truths. Their dividing his garments and casting lots for his vesture, signified that they had divided and dispersed all the truths of the Word, but not its spiritual sense, which his vesture or inner garment represented. Their crucifying Him, signified that they had destroyed and profaned the whole world. Their giving Him vinegar to drink, signified that all was falsified and false, and therefore He did not drink it, but said, 'It is finished.' Their piercing his side, signified that they had entirely extinguished every truth and every good of the Word. His being buried, signified the rejection of the residue of the Humanity taken from the mother; and his rising again on the third day, signified his glorification. Where these circumstances are predicted in the Prophets and the Psalms, their signification is similar."[170]

---

[170] D. L., n. 16.

John of Jerusalem observes, "Do not suppose that it was only in former times Christ was betrayed by the priests, condemned by them, and delivered over to be crucified, but even now He is betrayed and condemned to death; for Christ is the Word of Truth, and they who falsely interpret the Word of Truth, betray Him to be mocked and crucified."—*In Matt.*, cap. xx.

The apostles also make a practical application of the Lord's crucifixion.—See Rom. vi. 6; Gal. ii. 20, v. 24, vi. 14; Heb. vi. 4-6.

Cunning is preferred to divine wisdom, and self-dependence to the Divine Providence; and the heart is filled with unclean, selfish desires, and the understanding is overwhelmed with worldly solicitude, and no preparation can be made for the reception of Him who, as the Son of Man, presents Himself before us in his own blessed words, "He cometh to his own, and his own receive Him not" (John i. 11). In their perversity of soul they say, "We will not have this man [the eternal Truth] to reign."

CHAPTER XXI.

THE BOOK OF REVELATION WHOLLY COMPOSED OF DIVINE SYMBOLS OR CORRESPONDENCES.

THE Apocalypse, or Book of the Revelation, is the last of the inspired Word, and is wholly composed of divine symbols.[171] Like the books of Daniel, Ezekiel, etc., it has been looked upon as awfully mysterious, and is commonly and variously interpreted as having reference only to historical events relating chiefly to the political changes which either have taken place, or may hereafter take place, in the outward forms of the church and among the several empires and kingdoms of the world. Many of the predictions scattered throughout the prophetical portions of the Word have indeed been permitted to have some visible and very general accomplishment in historical facts, for important reasons already adduced; and, also, because of the close connection which exists between natural and spiritual events.

Such were the predictions of the Lord's first coming, the overthrow of Babylon, Nineveh, Tyre, etc., the destruction of Jerusalem, the dispersion of the Jews, the establishment of the Christian church, and many others. By this means, a devout reverence for the sacred Word, as a revelation from God, has been preserved among the human race amid ages of darkness and desolation; and although the Apocalypse could not hitherto be expounded in its internal sense, because the key to its interpretation had not yet been given, still the reading and study of it must have been attended with permanent and incalculable advantages. It completed the canon of the plenarily-inspired Word. It has excited, in every age, an earnest desire, and an ardent expectation, that the time would come when its hidden wonders and wisdom would be discovered to the faithful.

The all-important doctrines of the sole and exclusive divinity of the Lord Jesus Christ,—of keeping the divine precepts as the ap-

---

[171] "The inspired title of this last book of the New Testament conveys, most pointedly, the idea of instruction supernaturally communicated."—*Dr. Henderson's Inspiration*, p. 339.

pointed means of salvation,—of the resurrection from the dead, and of states of eternal life or eternal death as awaiting every one in the spiritual world,—of the blessedness and realities of heaven, and the disorders and miseries of hell,—all these, and numerous other subjects of Christian life and doctrine, are unequivocally recorded in the very letter of the Apocalypse. "Blessed," therefore, as it is written in the introduction, "Blessed is he that readeth, and they that hear the words of this prophecy, and keep those things which are written therein" (i. 3); while we are admonished, at the conclusion, neither to add thereto nor to diminish therefrom (xxii. 18, 19).

This truly wonderful book is composed, then, as to every single expression, agreeably to the science of correspondences; and now the arcana of its internal signification are unfolded (of which many striking examples have been given in these pages), it is seen to be a living spring of divine wisdom, to treat of the states of the Christian church at the period of its final consummation, and of the Lord's Second Advent, not in person, but "in the clouds of heaven" (Rev. i. 7), in "the power and great glory" of his Word, to establish a new and everlasting dispensation of love and wisdom in the hearts and minds of men, called the New Jerusalem. In the last two chapters, this New Church, both as to her establishment, internal quality and external form, is treated of under the sublime and magnificent description of "a new heaven and a new earth," which it is promised should "descend from God out of heaven," as "the holy city, New Jerusalem," having precious stones for her foundation, golden streets, walls of jasper, gates of pearl; whose length, breadth and height are equal; as having a river of the water of life, and the tree of life; and as being "the bride and wife of the LAMB."[172]

The bright and morning Star of Truth, then, has arisen upon a benighted world. The Sun of Righteousness is dissipating "the face of the covering cast over all people, and the veil spread over all na-

---

[172] For an exposition of the book of Revelation, see Swedenborg's *Apocalypse Explained*, 6 vols., 8vo, and *Apocalypse Revealed*, 2 vols., 8vo. See also *A Review of the Principles of Apocalyptical Interpretation*, 2 vols., 8vo, by the Rev. Augustus Clissold, M.A., formerly of Ex. Col., Oxford; containing an examination of the opinions of Protestant expositors. The object of the learned and intelligent author in this work is "to show that the systems of interpretation which have been prevalent have entirely failed; and that the only resource for the church is in the spiritual [system], as explained by Swedenborg." And by the same, *An Exposition of the Apocalypse*, 4 vols., 8vo.

"In all Scripture there is a spiritual sense, a spiritual *Cabala*, which, as it tends directly to holiness, so it is best and truest understood by the sons of the Spirit, who love God and therefore know Him. Everything is best known by its own similitudes and analogies."—*Jeremy Taylor's Sermons*.

tions" (Isa. xxv. 7); men need no longer "walk in darkness," amid the uncertain glimmerings of imagination and corrupt traditions, nor sit in "the gloom and shadow of death." The laws by which the life-giving pages of the Word of God may be distinguished from human compositions, and consistently and with certainty expounded, are now revealed from heaven, and unfolded to human perception. The key is supplied to unlock this glorious cabinet of jewels, and the good and wise may enrich themselves with eternal treasures.[173] The "wells of salvation" are opened, and "living waters" can flow forth in health-restoring streams, to refresh and bless every prepared mind. But, in the language of the prophet, lo! a divine voice is heard to utter, "None of the wicked shall understand, but the wise shall understand" (Dan. xiii. 9, 10).

---

[173] The truth of the science of correspondences, as well as its importance in the interpretation of Holy Scripture, may be seen exemplified in Part II. of this work, Chap. X., p. 549, where it is rigidly applied, as a method of interpretation, to the principal symbols in Rev. XXI. chapter.

CONCLUSION.

TO conclude: The Word of God is, in its literal sense, by virtue of its inward life and spirit, in "its fulness, its sanctity, and its power." Its literal sense was represented by the emblematic cherubim, said to have been placed at the entrance of the garden of Eden, with a flaming sword to prevent the intrusion of the unworthy and profane within its hallowed enclosure; but its spiritual sense is the tree of life in the midst, bearing all kinds of delicious fruits, to which the faithful are declared to have "a right," or power to appropriate them, and whose "leaves," or eternal doctrines and truths of piety, charity, and usefulness, are designed "for the healing of the nations" (Gen. iii. 24; Rev. xxii. 2). The interior truths and doctrines of the spiritual sense are "the upper springs," and the exterior knowledges and doctrines of the literal sense are "the nether springs,"—the blessings of a "south land,"—the gifts of our heavenly Father to every faithful Christian who, in the divine strength, overcomes his spiritual enemies (Joshua xv. 19). Instruction from the letter of the Word is "the former or early rain" at seed-time, while "the latter rain," which ripens and matures the harvest, denotes instruction from the spiritual sense (Joel ii. 23). And, again, speaking of the Lord, and of the descent of the divine blessings and influences of his Holy Word, internal and external, to refresh and renovate the soul, the Psalmist says, "He shall come down like rain upon the mown grass, as showers that water the earth" (Psalm lxxii. 6).

The Word externally is the wondrous bush which Moses saw, burning and shining with inward fire, yet unconsumed (Ex. iii. 2-4; Deut. xxxiii. 16). It was also signified by the breastplate of Aaron, set exteriorly with twelve precious stones, but from which issued the Urim and Thummim, the light and flame of justice and judgment (Ex. xxviii. 30). The literal sense is the dark vapor obscuring the glorious sky, its inward sense is the resplendent bow rich with every heavenly hue of comfort and happiness (Gen. ix. 13). The Holy Word is signified by the marvellous ladder seen in vision by the patriarch; by means of it man holds consociation with angels and communion with God. Its foot, or literal sense, in accommodation to our low estate, rests upon the earth; but its summit, or inmost sense, reaches the heavens. The divine glory is above it, and as we read and meditate on its holy pages in faith and love, angels ascend and descend upon its sacred steps (Gen. xxviii. 12, 13; John i. 51;[174] Rev. xiv. 6). Its literal sense is "a field which the Lord hath blessed;" its spiritual sense is the concealed treasure which enriches the happy possessor more and more, even into the countless ages of eternity. Its literal sense was signified by the Lord's outer garments, which the soldiers parted among them, for it is capable of being wrested to confirm the most opposite doctrines; but its glorious spiritual sense was represented by the Lord's "vesture," or inner garment, "woven without seam from the top to the bottom" (John xix. 23; Psalm lxxii. 17, 18). Its literal sense is the cloud that accommodates the rays of the sun to every beholder, but a knowledge and perception of its inward sense presents the sun in all its ineffable splendor, and is the Lord's advent to the soul "in power and great glory" (Mark xiii. 26; Luke xxi. 27; Matt. xxiv. 30). The tables, or literal sense, are, under divine direction, the workmanship of Moses; but the writing, or spiritual sense, is the writing of God (Ex. xxxiv. 1). Like the heaven-descended manna, the Word is thus adapted to every state, " He that gathereth much hath nothing over, and he that gathereth little hath no lack. Every man may gather according to his eating." The Lord is here and elsewhere in the Gospels called the Son of Man, in relation to his word of divine truth. He was "the Word made flesh" (John i. 14; Ex. xvi. 18). This view of the Word of God gives "a fulness" to it which produces a constantly-increasing conviction of its "sanctity," and stamps it with the impress of "divinity." It reveals it as "a mine in which we may continually dig, and still find beds of inexhaustible spiritual wealth to reward our unwearied re-

[174] The sublime and beautiful vision of the Cherubim, seen by the prophet Ezekiel and described in the first chapter of his prophecy, is, in every particular, descriptive of the Word of God, both as to its hidden contents and outward form, its inmost essence and outward influences. Swedenborg thus briefly and beautifully opens the internal sense and meaning of the entire chapter. "The divine external sphere of the Word is described, verse 4. Is represented as a man, verse 5. Its conjunction with spiritual and celestial things, verse 6. The natural sense of the Word, its quality, verse 7. The spiritual and celestial sense of the Word conjoined with the natural, its quality, verses 8, 9. Divine love of goodness and truth, celestial, spiritual, and natural, therein distinct and united, verses 10, 11. That they regard one end, verse 12. The sphere of the Word is from the Divine Good and the Divine Truth of the Lord, from which the Word lives, verses 13, 14. The doctrine of goodness and truth in the Word and from it, verses 15-21. The Divine Essence of the Lord above it and in it, verses 22, 23; and from it, verses 24, 25. That the Lord is above the heavens, verse 26. And that He is Divine Love and Divine Wisdom itself, verses 27, 28."—S. S. 97.

search;" for "the deeper it is worked, the richer and more abundant the precious ore becomes."[175] The truths which are thus unfolded are perpetually opening anew, and are ever increasing in brilliancy and beauty and expanding in glory and authority before the inward vision in proportion to the soul's progress in the Christian life (Prov. iv. 18; John xvi. 18; 2 Peter iii. 13); for to this mighty end was it given, to aid our advancement in goodness and truth, not only on earth, but in the never-ending ages of eternity;[176] or, to adopt the

---

[175] Dr. Henderson.

[176] It was a "general custom among the Fathers to suppose that Scripture contains latent mysterious meanings beyond the letter, the apprehension of which is disclosed to a faithful life.

"Now this mode of interpretation is so general in the Ancient [Christian] Church, that something of the kind may be considered as the characteristic difference between the interpretation of catholic Christians and those of heretical teachers; that the latter lower and bring down the senses of Scripture as if they were mere human words, while the former consider the words of Divine Truth to contain greater meanings than we can fathom, and therefore amplify and extend their signification as if they were advancing onward into deeper and higher meanings, till lost in ever increasing and at length infinite light and greatness, beyond what the limited view of man is capable of pursuing.

"Nor does it appear at all unreasonable beforehand—before considering it as a matter of fact, that this should be the case: I mean that the Divine Word should be in its secret range thus vast and comprehensive, as the shadow of the heavens in still and deep waters.

"But it might be said that this mode of interpretation has arisen from the nature of the Hebrew language, in which each word contains many deep and ulterior meanings, which may be considered as types of each other. But this observation will, in fact, lead us to the same conclusion of its Divine character: it is, indeed, only going further into the subject—sending us back one step more in tracing the chain which reaches from God's throne. For if the sacred language which the Almighty has chosen in order to reveal Himself to mankind is of this typical nature, it proves that such is the language of God; that in numerous analogies and resemblances, differing in time, importance, and extent, but with one drift and scope, He is used to speak to us, blending figure with word spoken. But when we come to the matter of fact, as proved by the Scriptures themselves, the principle itself must be allowed as right, whatever limitations men may prescribe to the application or use of it. It is very evident how much our blessed Lord has Himself pointed out to us these deep and latent meanings, where we could not otherwise have ventured to suppose them to exist; as, for instance, in the sign of the prophet Jonah and the lifting up of the serpent in the wilderness. And in almost all his references to the Old Testament, our Lord has led us to seek for mines of secret information disclosed to the eye of faith, beyond the letter. And it is to be observed that Scripture has not generally pointed out to us those instances in which allegorical interpretation is most obvious and important, but often those in which it is less so; as if, thereby, it rather suggested to us a general law than afforded any direction respecting its limit and extent. If from our Lord's own example we pass to the writings of St. Paul, it is needless to mention the numerous striking instances in which he has unfolded to us the spiritual and high senses of the Old Testament. And passing from Apostles to Apostolical writers, we find the same system acknowledged, as if it were incidentally, but almost universally.

"With regard, therefore, to this system of interpretation, we have in many instances Divine authority for it; and beyond where we have this authority, it might be thought that we have no sanction for such applications and explanations; in which case it would be similar to the moral principles or doctrines that are deduced from Holy Scripture, which may be said to flow more or less clearly from the Word itself, and to be supported by analogy, natural consequence, or agreement with other passages; and these to be decided by the judgment of individuals, and that natural weight of authority which we allow to be due to the opinions of great and good men. But further than this, as with regard to moral principles of doctrine, so also with respect to such particular interpretations, it is perhaps the case

language of a truly great and good man, "It has God for its author, salvation for its end, and truth without any mixture of error for its matter."

But, you are ready to ask, is this wonderful science of correspondences, that so miraculously unfolds the sacred pages, difficult to acquire? I answer, No. Even children may be readily taught to understand much concerning it.[177] It is, in fact, the earliest language of nature, and the language from which true poetry and eloquence derive all their charms. It is the most impressive and delightful form of instruction, and supplies the most healthful and elevating exercise to the imagination and reason. All other kinds of knowledge are handmaids in its service, and tributary to its confirmation. While the internal meaning is hidden from those who are unprepared

---

(as it has been well observed), that for some of them there may be such a concurrent testimony in early and distinct churches as to amount to a catholic consent, which consent would, of course, have the same kind of sacred authority as would attend a similar agreement with respect to doctrine.

"Sufficient for our purpose it is that such a method of considering Holy Writ is catholic, not to say Apostolical and Divine."—*Tracts for the Times, on Reserve*, pp. 21-25.

I subjoin the following remarkable passage from *The Gospel Treasury Opened*, in several sermons preached at Kensington and elsewhere, by John Everard, D.D. It is extracted from one of four sermons on Joshua xv. 16, 17. London, 2d edition, 1679.

"If the literal Scriptures were the Word of God, why doth the Holy Ghost so often say, 'he that hath ears to hear, let him hear'? And why doth the prophet Isaiah say, that 'hearing they may hear and not understand, and seeing they may see and not perceive? Make the heart of this people fat, their ears dull, and their eyes heavy, lest they should see with their eyes, and hear with their ears, and understand with their hearts, and be converted, and I should heal them.' This is spoken not in regard of those that are ignorant, but of those that are very knowing, and yet their knowledge and gifts and precise holiness, according to the letter, is but a stumbling-block and an occasion of their falling into death and destruction; and thus to know all things is but to be ignorant of all things.

"Beloved, the Word of God is subtile, pure, high, holy, heavenly, powerful, quickening, spiritualizing; but the letter is not only dead in these regards, but killing and destructive in that sense formerly expressed. If you live and die with this Word, it will do you no good; I mean the letter of the Word, and the grammatical, external sense, which these men call the Word of God. Yet I tell ye all this is nothing, though you have it exactly by heart; yet this can be of no service to God nor profit to you; this is but bodily labor and bodily exercise, which profiteth nothing; this is but the flesh, this is but man's teaching; the spirit of it, the Word of God, you never yet found. But yet let us not say, if the spirit be all, what do we want with the letter? let us then cast it away. No, no; by no means. The letter is of use to regulate the flesh, and to prescribe and direct the outward man in bodily exercises: but I say it teaches not, nor feeds not the inward man and the heart. That must be that bread which the Father giveth, which comes down from heaven. 'Tis neither Moses, nor the knowledge of the whole law, nor of all the Scriptures can give us that bread; as Christ saith, John vi. 32, 33, 'Verily, verily, Moses gave them not that bread from heaven, but my Father giveth you the bread from heaven; for the bread of God is He which cometh down from heaven and giveth life to the world.'

"And yet this is that I advise still: be sure to maintain the letter undefiled, untouched, uncorrupted. Let his tongue cleave to and forever rot in his mouth, that goes about to abrogate the letter; for without the letter you cannot have the spirit."

"Sensual man requires sensible objects as symbols of spiritual things."—*Vandervelde*.

[177] See *Reed's Sunday Lessons on Correspondences for Children*.

for more than the sum of the letter, and from the unhallowed gaze of the worldly prudent, to babes it is promised that wisdom shall be revealed (Matt. xi. 25), and to the pure in heart, that they shall see God (Matt. v. 8). "The secret of the Lord is with them that fear Him" (Ps. xxv. 14). "I understand more than the ancients, because I keep thy precepts" (Ps. cxix. 100).

Let us bring, therefore, to the study of this heavenly doctrine, pure desires, serious thoughts, enlightened reason, an humble and sincere faith, an ardent love, a teachable disposition, a pious and useful life; for "if any man will do his will, he shall know of the doctrine whether it be of God" (John vii. 17). To this must be added an intimate acquaintance with the literal sense of the Word, a knowledge of the mental faculties, a devout habit of reflection on the divine operations as exemplified in the world of nature, and on the forms, qualities, and uses of the objects with which we are constantly surrounded, and its general principles become easy of attainment, and every step we take is attended with accessions of intelligence and delight. Even a small degree of information on this momentous science is an inexpressible blessing. The longer and closer it is studied, the dearer it becomes to its possessor, because it leads him to love the sacred Word of God with increased fervor, to trust revealed truth with a firmer and daily-increasing confidence, and to recognize it as the divinely-appointed means of filling the humble and faithful soul to all eternity, with wisdom, love, peace, and unutterable joy. It is endless in its onward and upward progression, because the things of the natural world, which as outward effects correspond to the objects of the spiritual world, as their inward causes, exist in indefinite variety; for, "all the powers and activities of nature, all its laws, its substances, its forms and changes, are at once the effect and the mirror of spiritual energies;" and because, further, man is not only, as we have already said, a world in its least form, having within him the various principles to which all things in the created universe correspond; but, by regeneration, he becomes a heaven in its least form, possessing ever-growing faculties of eternal life, corresponding with all the glorious realities of the heavenly world above. Of such the Lord speaks when He says, "The kingdom of God is within you" (Luke xvii. 21).

The practical influence of this great doctrine of the Sacred Scriptures on the heart, the mind and the life, is invaluable. It brings from the clouds of heaven "*showers of blessing*" (Ez. xxxiv. 26). Its cordial reception, and the inwrought persuasion of its truth, cannot fail to assist in purifying the heart and renovating the character. It is the loftiest and most authoritative standard of righteousness and truth. It is an unerring criterion for the detection of evil and error. It tears away the flimsy veil of indifference or conceit. It searches out our most secret transgressions. It is "the key of [saving] knowledge" (Luke xi. 52). To you it may be given to know, by its means, "the mysteries of the kingdom of heaven" (Matt. xiii. 11).

"Ho, every one that thirsteth, come ye to the waters; and he that hath no money, come ye, buy, and eat; yea, come buy wine and milk without money and without price. For as the rain cometh down, and the snow from heaven, and returneth not thither, but watereth the earth, and maketh it bring forth and bud, that it may give seed to the sower, and bread to the eater: so shall my word be that goeth forth out of my mouth: it shall not return unto me void, but it shall accomplish that which I please, and it shall prosper in the thing whereto I sent it" (Isa. lv. 1, 10-13).[178]

---

[178] "The Word of the Lord is compared to rain and snow coming down from heaven, because by rain is signified spiritual truth, which is appropriated to man, and by snow natural truth, which is as snow whilst only in the memory, but becomes spiritual by love, as snow becomes rain-water by warmth."—See *A. E.* 644; *Clowes's Misc. Thoughts, etc.*, p. 150.

PART II.

CONTAINING

ADDITIONAL ILLUSTRATIONS AND CONFIRMATIONS
OF THE DOCTRINE OF CORRESPONDENCE.

BY

DIFFERENT AUTHORS.

ADDITIONAL ILLUSTRATIONS AND CONFIRMATIONS OF THE DOCTRINE OF CORRESPONDENCE.

THE KEY OF KNOWLEDGE:
BY THE USE OF WHICH THE HOLY SCRIPTURES ARE OPENED AND THEIR HEAVENLY MEANING REVEALED.*

By Rev. THOMAS GOYDER.

Woe unto you, lawyers! for ye have taken away the Key of Knowledge.—LUKE xi. 52.

CHAPTER I.

INTRODUCTION—CREATION OF THE WORLD—CONTRADICTORY VIEWS OF CHRONOLOGERS CONCERNING THE AGE OF THE WORLD—GEOLOGY IN HARMONY WITH SCRIPTURE—THE SUN THE INSTRUMENTAL CAUSE OF CREATION—SIR HUMPHRY DAVY'S VIEW—CONNECTION BETWEEN THE CREATOR AND HIS WORKS—PLENARY INSPIRATION OF THE WORD OF GOD—CORRESPONDENCE, THE SURE RULE OF SCRIPTURE INTERPRETATION.

Introduction.

THE Bible is universally admitted by the Christian world to be a Divine Revelation from God to man, and considered the standard and test of all religious truth. No Christian can be indifferent to its precepts or regardless of its reproofs. It is believed to contain the very riches of heaven, which, if received in the human understanding and life, will make man mentally rich, wise and happy. Any work which opens up its sacred contents, or reveals some uniform method of interpretation whereby its heavenly and true meaning may with certainty be obtained, must be considered a desideratum

---

* First published in London, June, 1838.

of the highest value, and would tend much to the throwing down of the boasted strongholds of infidelity, as well as to the furtherance of the interests of vital Christianity.

The Christian religion undoubtedly surpasses all other systems of Theology in the known world. It is purely of a spiritual cast, relating to the mind of man, and to all those varied changes and progressions of his will and understanding in love and wisdom, which successively follow in the course of his progress in the Divine life. These states or changes are, in general, treated of in Scripture in a variety of pleasing ways, in the parables, miracles and narratives; and are also more particularly shadowed forth in the literal history of the Israelitish journey from Egypt to Canaan. It is, therefore, hoped that the following pages may be found useful in assisting the pious Christian in his spiritual contemplations, so that while his eyes are opened to a clear perception of Divine Truth, in his bosom may be enkindled a more ardent and pure love to Him who is the Author and Giver of every real blessing.

No contemplative man who carefully studies the harmonies of nature, can fail of knowing that every object in the created universe is an effect springing from a prior cause; and that such cause must owe its birth to some end which the Creator had in view in the wonderful productions of his plastic hand. The end, which is the good intended by the Creator to the forms He proposes to bring into existence, is the Divine Love; the cause is the Divine Wisdom which the love of Deity uses as a means to accomplish the designs purposed; and the effects are the results of the Divine Operative Energy in all the outward forms of which the created universe is composed. There is a real connection between the end and its cause, and also between the cause and its effect. No effect can possibly exist independent of its cause, neither can there be any cause in which the end is not inwardly concealed.

Here, then, we learn a most cheering truth: that creation is safe while Wisdom, the Divine cause of its existence, remains, and that it must continue everlastingly fresh and imperishable while the Love of God, as the end, shall fill it with life and vigor. When God's *love* shall be no more, his *wisdom* as the first-begotten will die, the Divine *Spirit* will cease to operate, and then the heavens and the earth shall perish. Outward creation can no more exist independent of the perpetual operation of God therein, than can the organized body of man without the soul or spirit. "God is love," and as that love, He is the

Father of all. God is wisdom, the "True Light" which, as the first emanating sphere of the Divine love, is in Scripture called "the only-begotten Son." From the union of these two proceeds the Divine operative energy or Spirit, which, in giving existence to heaven and earth, imparts life to the wide creation. The true law by which all human and angelic existences are sustained, is, as expressed by the only Wisdom, or "Word incarnate," "I in them, and thou in me, that they may be made perfect in One." (John xvii. 23.)

Creation of the World.

In laying before the reader the system which, in all cases, will give a faithful and correct interpretation of Holy Scripture, we propose to commence with the creation of the world, and to show that this great work, in its beginning, progression and completion, shadowed forth the love, wisdom and power of the Creator; and that all the objects in Nature are so formed, as to be either remotely or proximately connected with God, the supreme First Cause. This connection necessarily renders the Lord's presence in the created universe, full, perfect and complete; and hence arise the attributes ascribed to the Divine Being, of omnipresence, omniscience and omnipotence. By love, as the end or intention of creation, God is present in all; by wisdom, He knoweth all; and by his operative influence, He is powerful in all. Without his goodness, wisdom and power, nothing could exist. God is, undoubtedly, the ALL in all.

If, then, God be present in his works as their actual existence evidently proves, it follows that there must be some close resemblance, affinity and correspondence between Him and them, and that a Divine influx of life, flowing momentarily from Him into them, supports and sustains the whole. This affinity not only exists between God and his works generally, but there is also a correspondence between all parts of his works from the highest to the lowest. All creation is one grand chain harmoniously fitted and linked together by the wisdom of Him who cannot err. Who, then, can apprehend danger, while reason, enlightened by revelation, declares the first link of that chain to be in the hand of God?

Assuming, for the present, this theory to be correct, we must see that a right understanding of this corresponding connection is essentially necessary to a just knowledge of the works of God; and that which opens to the mind true views of his works, must correctly explain the wonders of HIS WORD.

With respect to the creation of the world, we may truly say, it is so vast and profound a subject that the mind seems lost in wonder, and trembles at the thought of entering upon an inquiry into that which, by an almost impenetrable veil of mystery, seems to be hid from human ken. We cannot suppose that man, whose faculties and intellectual powers are finite, and consequently limited, can, however ardent he may be in search of truth, arrive at a full and perfect knowledge of all the minutiæ, those singulars and particulars which enter into and make up the fulness of creation's mighty work: a kind of general knowledge concerning it, is all we can expect.

In looking at creation as a whole, we behold beauty, regularity, and order; we see how each part performs its appointed use, and that the whole, by the action of its several parts, is maintained entire, free from any appearance of dissolution, and exhibiting to the beholder not the slightest symptoms of decay. The same sun which "in the beginning" warmed and enlightened our earth, shines still upon it with unabated vigor and power; the moon which then shone with its borrowed light, still rides majestically in the blue-arched sky; the rain still descends to water our thirsty plains, to fertilize our fields, to make the earth yield her increase, for the purpose of affording to man in all generations, "seed to the sower and bread to the eater." Heaven's breezes still continue to kiss the mountains, and to impart health, vigor and prolification to animal and vegetable life. Every animal is furnished with an organized body exactly adapted to the element in which it lives. In fact, all creation seems to be constantly singing one universal song of praise, that "God is good to all, and his tender mercies are over all his works."

These phenomena, with ten thousand others that might be named if necessary, but which the reader is left to supply for himself, are among the strongest evidences of contrivance and design. These again lead unquestionably to the acknowledgment of a Designer whom we call the Great First Cause, the omnipresent, omniscient, and immutable God.

No wise man can find the least difficulty in attributing the creation of the material world to an Almighty Hand—to that hand which received (if we may so speak) its impetus from the purest love, and was directed by infinite wisdom; and as we must consider the Divine Being to be a God of the most perfect order, it follows that creation, springing from Him, must be viewed as an orderly, progressive and gradual work. We have no hesitation in saying, that if creation shall ever admit of a rational and satisfactory explanation, it must be in agreement with the strictest principles of true philosophical and scientific knowledge.

Although upon the creation of the world much has been written by divines, philosophers and poets, yet but little that has yet appeared, has been satisfactory. The subject, strictly speaking, is not theological, but purely one of philosophical and scientific research. It is now pretty generally acknowledged by the most able and learned divines, that the first chapters of Genesis are an allegory, and that they contain not *literal* history, but spiritual and divine subjects reduced to a historical form. Literal history, in which, nevertheless, are contained spiritual truths relating to the church of God, heaven and the soul of man, commences at the twelfth chapter of Genesis, with the call of Abraham. It was not only the opinion of many of the ancient fathers of the church, that the first chapters of Genesis were written in an allegorical style, but that the whole Word of God, comprehending the Law, the Prophets, the Psalms, the Gospels and Apocalypse, were so written as to contain within the literal and historical sense, those divine and spiritual subjects which relate to the church of the Lord, and to the progressive states of affection, thought and life of man; and that they were to be interpreted, not after a carnal, but after a spiritual manner. This view of these ancient fathers has been kept alive in the church by the ablest and best theological writers in every age down to the present. This we shall prove by a few extracts from their writings as we proceed.

Contradictory Views of Chronologers.

In Genesis i. 1, we read, "In the beginning God created the heaven and the earth." From this passage, viewing it in the most literal sense possible, we learn not *when* God created the world, but that He did create it in the *beginning*. From what particular date we are to reckon the *beginning* of its existence, or what is its real age, the Word of God gives no information whatever, and science will never be able to discover. The putting of dates to the Bible in respect to the era of creation, reckoning from the year one, and thus making the present age of our globe about six thousand years, is altogether gratuitous and arbitrary: it endeavors unwisely to mix religious with physical truth, and by mingling together what should be kept separate, the mind becomes bewildered in its contemplation of both. By giving to the world an arbitrary age of about six thousand years, many have supposed the science of Geology to be opposed to Revelation, and that it altogether contradicts the Mosaic account of creation. If it were not that many pious and intelligent Christians have felt their minds disturbed at this supposition, we should have passed it by unnoticed, smiling at the weakness that could generate the idea.

Chronologers enumerate 132 contrary opinions concerning the age of the world (a proof this, that they know nothing about it), but in all these, there are none who reckon more than 7,000, or less than 3,700 years from the creation to the birth of Christ, making a difference in these calculations of no less a period than 3,300 years. The general opinion, however, fixes the birth of Christ in the four thousandth year of the world, and reckoning nearly 2,000 from that event, makes its present age about 6,000 years; but the reasons on which these opinions are founded, are exceedingly various, all arbitrary, and grounded in conjecture.

The calculation of the age of the world made by the Hindoos in their religious belief, is ponderous when compared with this. Their religion teaches them to recognize the existence of one supreme invisible Creator, the Ruler of the universe, whom they call BRAHMA. They likewise acknowledge two other deities, one of whom is VISHNU, the Preserver, and the other SIVA, the Destroyer. The deity *Vishnu*, as preserver, is declared to have made many appearances in the world, and the great ends of Providence are said to have been accomplished by the incarnations of this deity. According to this religion, there have been nine incarnations of Vishnu, and one more yet to come, all of which make up the period of 4,320,000 years, making a difference between their age of the world and ours of only 4,314,000 years. Allowing the Hindoo theology with its idle ceremonies to be false and fabulous, yet these superstitious people have, perhaps, as much ground for their long date as we have for our short one. Revelation is silent about the age of the world; and when that is silent, it is a mark of wisdom in us to be silent too, and not aim to be wise above what is written. These statements, differing widely as they do, prove the fact, that any attempt to fix the era of creation originates in folly and conjecture.

Geology in Harmony with Scripture.

Professor Sedgwick, in his "Discourse on the Studies of the University" (p. 149), tells us, the geologist proves by incontrovertible evidence of physical phenomena, that "there were former conditions of our planet separated from each other by vast intervals of time, during which man and the other creatures of his own date had not been called into being. Periods such as these belong not, therefore, to the moral history of our race; and come neither within the letter nor the spirit of Revelation. Between the first creation of the earth and that day in which it pleased God to place man upon it, who shall dare to define the interval? On this question Scripture is silent; but that silence destroys not the meaning of those physical monuments of his power that God has put before our eyes, giving us at the same time faculties whereby we may interpret them and comprehend their meaning." This extract contains so much of truth that it cannot, we think, be disproved.

But some may ask: Is geology, then, to be allowed to contradict the Mosaic account of creation, and to disprove the date revealed to Moses? We answer, that geology can neither contradict nor disprove what the Scripture never states. The most literal account of creation given by Moses is, "In the beginning God created the heaven and the earth;" this is all, without fixing any time. Geology does not contradict this, but maintains it, and by laborious and praiseworthy examinations of physical phenomena, proves the existence of a Divine Architect, and ascribes to Him the work "in the *beginning*." Revelation gives no date: WE have made this, and having so done, we find fault with geology because it has sought out and exposed our errors. The poet Cowper was deceived in this; for he, supposing that God had revealed to Moses creation's date, aims a blow at Geology. In his poem entitled "The Task," he says—

> "Some drill and bore
> The solid earth, and from the strata there
> Extract a register, by which we learn
> That He who made it, and reveal'd its date
> To Moses, was mistaken in its age."

Here the worthy poet was certainly mistaken in his conclusions; for *where* in Revelation do we find the date revealed to Moses? Nothing of the kind is given in any part of the sacred Volume. He was, in this instance, led astray by his muse—the license of poets is proverbial; but still truth is not to be sacrificed at the shrine of poetical license. The laborious and incontrovertible proofs of the earth's great antiquity given by the science of geology, are not to be swept away by a single dash of a poet's pen.

From our divinity authors, nothing has yet appeared on the creation that is worth notice. They simply state that God created the world out of *nothing*: but, unfortunately for them, of this creation out of nothing the Scriptures never speak. They offer no remarks tending rationally to illustrate the orderly progression of creation's work. Bishop Hall, in commenting on Gen. i. 1,—"In the beginning God created the heaven and the earth,"—says: "In the beginning of time, God—the Father, Son and Holy Ghost—made, of nothing, the whole great and goodly frame of the world, both the heaven and the earth, and the other elements, with all the furniture and inhabitants of them all." Certainly the good bishop, in this comment, has not overloaded our minds with information, with subjects too high for us. Had he said nothing, we should have been quite as wise.

To form just views of the creation of this world, it is essentially expedient to keep the mind fixed upon one supreme Being, without whose love, wisdom, and power, nothing could be or exist. We must also view the Almighty as a single Divine Being, as a God of the most perfect order, producing every thing progressively, according to the laws of Divine Wisdom. God, in his providence, to encourage us in the pursuit of truth, has not, in so many words, revealed in the Book of inspiration *how* the world was created; but in placing us upon the globe on which we live, and surrounding us with all the beauties and wonders of creation, He has richly endowed us with reason, with capacious powers and faculties of mind, by the exercise of which (the great book of creation being always present) we may, by patient study and careful examination, tracing up ultimate effects through a long chain of instrumental causes, finally arrive at some degree of knowledge as to the origin and progressive work of creation; so that we may be able to prove to demonstration that, "In the beginning God created the heaven and the earth." By attributing to the Almighty the glory of this mighty work, we can take up the language of the Psalmist and say: "He hath laid the foundations of the earth, that it shall not be removed for ever" (Ps. civ. 5). "The heavens declare the glory of God, and the firmament showeth his handy work" (Ps. xix. 1).

If in this investigation we exercise our *reason*, God's best and noblest gift (for without it even immortality would be a blank), we shall be able to see clearly where the worldling but gropes in the dark. Our reason must be sacrificed to God, that is, not destroyed, but *dedicated* and *consecrated* to his service, which is the meaning of "to sacrifice." If this be done faithfully, we shall walk in the true light—we shall enjoy a morning without clouds, and our sun shall never go down.

The Sun the Instrumental Cause of Creation.

Reason teaches that the globe upon which we live is entirely dependent for all its nourishment and support upon the central sun in the system. If the sun were removed, our globe would instantly cease to be, animal and vegetable life would perish, and all would be reduced to a nonenity. The earth would be deprived of all heat and light, it would instantly lose its motion,[1] and destruction would follow; for it only lives while it moves. In the bounded space of this universe large bodies revolve, which, performing their circuits round the sun as a common centre, grow to their respective ages. The sun, like an anxious parent, regards these revolving globes no otherwise than as his own offspring which have attained to a considerable maturity; for he continually consults their general and particular interests; and although they are distant, he never fails to exercise over them his care and parental protection, since by his rays he is, as it were, present in his provisions for them; he cherishes them with the warmth issuing from his immense bosom; he adorns their bodies and members every year with a most beautiful clothing; he nourishes

---

[1] In a work entitled "The Sacred History of the World," by Sharon Turner, among many excellent things are some most extraordinary and unphilosophical statements. In vol. i., pp. 8, 9, the author says: "It was nearly 6,000 years ago, according to the chronology of the Hebrew Scripture, that it pleased the Almighty to determine on the creation of the earth which we inhabit. The sacred history of the world is built on the grand truth expressed in the first verse of the Pentateuch -- In the beginning God (Elohim) created the heavens and the earth." It is a pity this writer did not produce chapter and verse for this "nearly 6,000 years ago." And with respect to the phrase, "In the beginning," no one can successfully contend that the word "beginning" means 6,000 years ago. Again this author says, "Our earthly day is that space of time in which our globe turns once completely round. This action of time, which we subdivide into twenty-four parts or hours, does *not* depend upon the sun, nor arise from it. As it is only an entire rotation of the earth, it could occur as well *without* a solar orb as with one. The annual circuit or year, which is the completed orbit of the earth round this luminary, could not take place without a sun; but a day requires the existence and revolving motion of the earth alone." Vol. i., p. 18. To talk of days without a sun is surely not that kind of philosophy which will gain many advocates in the nineteenth century. But we ask, What is the cause of the earth's rotation? To this our author replies and says, " Physics have not discovered, nor can rational conjecture assign any reason for the diurnal rotation of the earth, except the commanding will and exerted power of the Creator." P. 19. To this it is replied, that all life and motion are (primarily) of the will and power of the Creator; but nevertheless it is submitted to the Christian philosopher, that the rotatory motion of the sun is the instrumental cause of the earth's motion, and that if it were possible to stop the former, the latter would instantly cease.

their inhabitants with a perpetual supply of food; he promotes the life of all things, and enlightens them with his luminous radiance. Since the sun thus executes all the functions of parental duty, it follows from the connection and tenor of causes, that if we are desirous to unfold the history of the earth from her earliest infancy, and to examine her from her origin, we must have recourse to the sun himself; for every effect is a continuity of causes from the first cause; and the cause by which anything subsists is continued to the cause by which it exists; subsistence being a kind of perpetual existence.

From the above train of reasoning, we now come at this conclusion: that as the earth receives all its nourishment from the sun as a parent, and requires his perpetual presence to keep it in being, it is manifest that it must have burst forth from him as from a fruitful womb; and that the sun, being a created instrument in the hand of the Divine Creator, is therefore to be regarded as the instrumental cause, origin and parent of this our world.

We must, then, view the sun as the instrumental cause of the creation of this world. Here the materialist stops his inquiry, attributing everything to what he calls Nature, and worships this as God. But Christians must make no halting in their way; they must carefully trace effects up to their cause. The sun could no more create itself than could the earth. We must ascertain the origin of the natural sun; and to do this, we must look through it to the spiritual world of causes, and finally to the Lord himself as the Fountain of life and being. In this stage of the inquiry, Revelation alone can afford us the required assistance.

In the Sacred Scripture, God himself is called a *Sun*, and the Sun of righteousness—a Sun which never goes down or becomes dim, but is truly "an everlasting light" (Isa. lx. 19). It is a truth that Jehovah God is the great First Cause and common Centre of all things. His love is the fount of life, and his wisdom, as the first emanating sphere or brightness of that love, may be considered as the Divine Sun of the eternal world, whose creative rays of heat and light, or love and wisdom in union, fill the heavens with glory, and the angels with joy and gladness. Now to connect the created universe with God as the First Cause (for without this connection creation would expire), we must view the sun of this natural world as a created receptacle, formed by the Divine Wisdom, and adapted to receive and concentrate the creative rays of the Sun of righteousness. By this concentration, is produced an intensity of heat, which may be termed a body of PURE FIRE, or the sun of our solar system. This reception and concentration of the creative rays of the Divine Sun, produces the rotatory motion of the natural sun upon its own axis, by which light and heat are widely dispensed around. This, again, gives all the motion to the planetary orbs in our system, producing the changes and vicissitudes in the diurnal motion of morning, meridian, evening and night, as well as those of the annual motion round the sun, of the four seasons, spring, summer, autumn and winter.

Thus we may see that the sun of our world derives its heat and light from being perpetually operated upon by the Sun of the eternal world; and that if the connection subsisting between them were to be broken or interrupted, the sun would instantly lose all its vigorous principles of heat and light, and the consequence would be, the total destruction of that planetary system of which the sun is the centre. We may safely subscribe to the statement already made, that, however long the chain of causes and effects may be, the first link of that chain is in the hand of God. Stability, firmness and duration are given to everything, because God is the ALL in all. There is, then, no doubt but that this our globe is an outbirth or offspring of the sun, and that it performed thousands of revolutions round its parent before it became fit for the habitation of animals and lastly of man.

Sir Humphry Davy's View.

Sir Humphry Davy, a philosopher to whom the world is greatly indebted, says:

"The globe in the first state in which the imagination can venture to consider it, appears to have been a fluid mass, with an immense atmosphere revolving in space round the sun. By its cooling, a portion of its atmosphere was probably condensed into water, which occupied a part of its surface. In this state, no forms of life such as now belong to our world, could have inhabited it. The crystalline rocks, called by geologists primary rocks, and which contain no vestiges of a former order of things, were the result of the first consolidation on its surface. Upon the further cooling, the water which more or less had covered it, contracted, depositions took place; shell-fish and coral insects were created, and began their labors; islands appeared in the midst of the ocean, raised from the deep by the productive energies of millions of zoophytes. These islands became covered with vegetables fitted to bear a high temperature. The submarine rocks of these new formations of land became covered with aquatic vegetables, on which various species of shell-fish and common fishes found their nourishment. As the temperature of the globe became lower, species of the oviparous reptiles appear to have been created to inhabit it; and the turtle, crocodile, and various gigantic animals seem to have haunted the bays and waters of the primitive lands.

"But in this state of things, there appears to have been no order of events similar to the present. Immense volcanic explosions seem to have taken place, accompanied by elevations and depressions of the earth's surface, producing mountains, hills and valleys, and causing new and extensive depositions from the primitive ocean. The remains of living beings, plants, fishes, birds and reptiles, are found in the strata of rocks which are the monumental evidences of these changes. When these revolutions became less frequent, and the globe became still more cooled, and inequalities of temperature were established by means of the mountain chains, more perfect animals became its inhabitants, some of which have now become extinct. Five successive races of plants and four of animals, appear to have been created and swept away by the physical revolutions of the globe, before the system of things became so permanent as to fit the world for man. In none of these formations, whether called secondary, tertiary or diluvial, have the fossil remains of man or any of his works been discovered. At last man was created; and since that period there has been little alteration in the physical circumstances of our globe."[2]

Connection between the Creator and his Works.

In the orderly progression of creation, everything appears to bear the impress of a Divine hand. Every stage in creation's work seems to lead on to the end in view—the creation of man, the image and likeness of his Maker, who by the gift of reason could contemplate the living scene of beauties around him, could examine the qualities and properties of the physical phenomena which met his wondering eyes; and, looking through these, could open his grateful heart, and send forth his breath of praise to Him who is the Author and Supporter of the whole. He could observe that the Divine love and wisdom, which dispensed life and blessing around, radiate eternally from the Divine presence. Feeling an increase of pleasure in such elevated contemplations, he might take up the language of the

---

[2] See a work entitled, "Consolations in Travel, or, The Last Days of a Philosopher," pages 124-127.

psalmist and say, "As the hart panteth after the water brooks, so panteth my soul after thee, O God. My soul thirsteth for God, for the living God." (Ps. xlii. 1, 2.)

No person can contemplate creation, with all its wonders and beauties, without acknowledging that the power, wisdom and goodness of God are eminently displayed therein. What power short of omnipotent, could fill the blue ethereal space with myriads of suns, stars and planets, appearing more brilliant than polished spheres of gold and silver? What wisdom, not perfect and infinite, could arrange these at immense distances from each other, could order and direct their respective courses, and yet so adapt them by a corresponding connection, as to form one grand whole; all the parts of which are in rapid motion, yet calm, regular and harmonious; invariably keeping the paths prescribed to them :—these planetary orbs, again, being worlds peopled with myriads of intelligent beings formed for endless progression in perfection and felicity? Who can think of these things, and not acknowledge that infinite wisdom is displayed therein? And who can doubt of God's goodness in creation, when he sees that every living thing is gifted with an organic structure, exactly adapted to the situation in which it lives, to the means of obtaining food, to the method of defending itself from danger, and to the enjoyment of its existence? The wants of animal life are abundantly supplied to the numerous families of living creatures, and with as much regularity and certainty as if God had but one to attend to. These things can speak no other language than that of inspiration, which, with a power no rational mind can or would wish to disprove, proclaims that "God is good to all, and his tender mercies are over all his works!" That man must be more than blind, who, if he reflect on creation at all, cannot discover the power, wisdom, and goodness of God displayed therein.

Viewing creation's mighty work in this way, we at once discover an indissoluble connection existing between the Creator and the created; the latter requiring the perpetual presence and operation of the former to perpetuate its existence. Creation is not only an outbirth from Deity, but it at the same time exhibits, in all its multifarious forms, a faithful image of Him, the connection being so strong and certain between God and his works, that all outward objects, as effects, are to be viewed as so many types, representations and symbolic emblems, which constantly exhibit and shadow forth the attributes, the goodness, the perfections and wisdom of the great First

Cause. There is, throughout all nature, a close connection between the essence of a thing and its form; the essence being the spirit, soul or life, and the form the external manifestation; hence the forms of things exhibit to the intellectual eye of man the true quality of the essences which respectively gave them birth; and to produce precision and exactness, both of distinction and description, names were also anciently given to mark and express the respective qualities of the things named.

If, then, the life or operative Spirit of God must constantly flow into all creation, that it may be kept in existence, in activity and growth, by which it can alone perform the uses it was evidently designed; it follows, that, as it is animated by the Spirit of God, and upheld by his power, it must reflect back an image of Him, and show forth in all its successive productions, the universality of his power and goodness. The created universe may very properly be termed a living temple, in which the living God delights to dwell, filling every part thereof with the breath of life; while each object, in the enjoyment of individual existence, seems to sing for joy, and bask in the sunshine of pleasure. It is certain that we "cannot go where universal love smiles not around!"

If the view we have thus taken of creation be correct, (of which a rational doubt can hardly be supposed)—if the goodness, wisdom and power of God are felt and seen in his works—if the whole, as a type, reflects a faint image of the Divine perfections; and if all outward objects are corresponding emblems of the affections, thoughts and powers of the human mind, thereby connecting the material world with man, and by and through man with the Creator, then we must clearly observe an unbroken connection, a relationship and correspondence between all creation and the omnipotent One who produced and still supports the whole. This view will lead us to a right understanding of the reasoning of St. Paul, who, in addressing the Romans, says: "The invisible things of Him from the creation of the world are clearly seen, being understood by the things that are made, even his eternal power and Godhead; so that they are without excuse." (Rom. i. 20.) The *invisible* things of God are certainly the operations of his creative power and goodness. These are as the essences which give birth and being to all external forms, while the forms in their order, quality and appearance, make the invisible essences to be intellectually seen and understood. If those properties which relate to the eternal power and Godhead are to be understood by the things that are made, then it follows that creation is a representative image of the Divine Being, and that his unity, goodness, power and wisdom are exhibited in all its parts.

As Nature is the orderly production of God, and as a connection exists between the Lord and his works, so it is reasonable to conclude that a similar law of corresponding relationship must be observed between Him and his Word of Revelation. The wisdom of God must be contained in those sacred writings which are emphatically denominated the WORD, and as such, must treat primarily of the spiritual creation of man; that is, of the renovation of his mind, by which he is prepared for an eternal state of existence, and not merely of the outward things of nature, only so far as they are mentioned as corresponding emblems to represent those affections, thoughts and states of life, with their successive variations and changes which take place in man, while in him the regenerating process is going on.

Plenary Inspiration of the Word of God.

The Bible is generally acknowledged by Christians to be the Word of God; but this acknowledgment is grounded more in authority than in any internal conviction of the fact. What appears to be wanting is proof; but how is this to be given? Not by an appeal to the opinions of those who lived in ancient times—not by producing a long list of venerable names of men who lived in the days of other years, with their sentiments attached; for such a list could prove nothing but the opinions of those whose names it contained. If the Bible be the Word of God, it must contain within itself the certain evidences of that fact; and that it does contain these, we hope clearly to demonstrate by many examples. Any book acknowledged to be the Word of God, must be written by his immediate dictation; for what is the dictation of any being, but his word, will and command? And as every human writing contains, upon the subject treated of, the mind and spirit of the writer, so those Scriptures which bear the high title of the "Word of God," must contain the Divine mind, spirit and will. They must have been dictated by the Spirit of God to the persons who were appointed to write them, and of course written by a plenary inspiration. The subjects, therefore, of such a written Word must be lofty, such as are worthy a Divine Being, and adapted to guide man in all his journey through the vicissitudes of this transitory scene of things, and to bring him in safety to the haven of his appointed rest.

The Word of God, like his works in outward creation, must be one perfect harmonious whole; a regularly connected chain of end, cause and effect must be observed to pervade each. As creation was produced by regular laws according to the Divine will and pleasure, in which God himself is constantly present to sustain and uphold, preventing thereby any of its parts from dilapidation or disuse; so his Word, which is a revelation of his will to his sentient creatures, must also be produced in a similar regular order, and must contain, within its literal sense, the stores of Divine wisdom, goodness and power, in which the Lord himself is so essentially present by his Spirit, that not "one jot or tittle" of the Divine law can ever fail. It is hence certain that those Scriptures which are the WORD, are of plenary inspiration, because written by Divine dictation throughout: if not so written, they are not the Word of God.

St. Paul, in his epistle to Timothy, says: "All Scripture is given by inspiration of God, and is profitable for doctrine, for reproof, for correction, for instruction in righteousness: that the man of God may be perfect, throughly furnished unto all good works." (2 Tim. iii. 16, 17.) These expressions clearly state that the whole of the perfectly inspired Scripture, is given to insure the growth and perfection of the human character—to enlighten the understanding and purify the will; thus, by making man wiser and better, to fit him for the enjoyment of angelic perfection. The Greek *single word* here rendered by five, "given by inspiration of God," is, respecting the plenary inspiration of Scripture, exceedingly strong and expressive. The word is Θεοπνευστος (*Theopneustos*); and being compounded of Θεος, God, and πνεω, to breathe, literally means *God-breathed*. "All Scripture God-breathed," is therefore profitable for doctrine, reproof and correction.[3] The phrase "all Scripture," comprehends all those books called the Law and the Prophets, including the Psalms. These are also styled the Law and the Testimony, to which the Lord alluded when, after his resurrection, He said to his disciples: "All things must be fulfilled which are written in the law of Moses, and in the Prophets, and in the Psalms concerning me." (Luke xxiv. 44.)

Among ten thousand privileges enjoyed in the true spiritual church

---

[3] The original of this verse does not state that ALL Scripture is given by inspiration; for every writing is scripture. Some writings, that are even bound up with our common Bibles, are not admitted to be canonical, because not given by inspiration; and yet they have had, and still continue to have, their use in the church. What the verse expressly states is, that "all Scripture God-breathed," or "given by inspiration," is profitable, etc.

of Christ, is *one* which may truly be termed the introductory means of obtaining all the rest; without which, a correct knowledge of the Word of God throughout cannot be fully obtained. Nothing surely can contribute more to the furtherance of the interests of vital religion, or to the wide extension of theological truth, than to point out a method by which the Word of God can be faithfully and harmoniously interpreted—by which the sacred cabinet can be unlocked and its heavenly treasures explored. It is surely reasonable to suppose that, as there is a certain orderly and progressive method to be carefully pursued in obtaining correct scientific and philosophical knowledge, and that any deviation from the general rule must involve us in doubt and error; so there must be one general and uniform system to be pursued in the search of spiritual or religious truth, a deviation from which must equally involve us in ignorance, doubt and error.

When we take a view of the present state of the Christian world, and observe that doctrines as opposite to each other as light and darkness are taught as Christian verities—that all are pronounced to be truly Christian, though widely different and opposite; we must think that something is wrong somewhere, or opposite views could not be taught as springing from one and the same source. This fact is before the eyes of every one who reflects at all, and if there be any truth to be drawn from it, it is this: that all our errors arise from not "knowing the Scriptures nor the power of God."

One system says, with the lips of its professors, that there is but one God; that in the Godhead, nevertheless, are three Persons of one substance, each of whom is distinctly and by himself God and Lord; but that in some mysterious way or other these three are but one God. This explanation, if it must be so called, is generally guarded from any further inquiry, by "ask not how this can be;" be silent and have faith! The same system, in its further mysterious teaching, says that God is "without body, parts, or passions;" and if we ask, How can a being without either body, parts, or passions, be three persons of one substance? we are answered, and told that it is a very great mystery, impious to inquire into, and that the human understanding ought to be bound under obedience to faith. Thus the truth, the grand truth of the Divine Unity, is, by unmeaning creeds, hid from our eyes, and the human race left to wander in the mysterious labyrinths of universal doubt.

Another system, peculiar to itself, teaches that God has elected a certain number of the human race to heaven and happiness, without any foresight of faith, good works, or any conditions performed by the creature; and designedly consigned the rest to everlasting wrath and perdition for their sins. This appears to be the very dregs of heathen fatalism and necessity, which the reformer of Geneva gathered together and tried to refine into the constituent principles of Christianity, but which he made worse in the process. This gloomy theory is most decidedly opposed by the Arminian scheme, which says of it, that it is altogether false and anti-Christian, and in opposition to it, maintains that God wills, and has provided means for, the happiness of all; that by these He has made salvation attainable by all; thus that man and not God is the author of all his misery.

Another system teaches that *faith alone*, without works, is all that is necessary to salvation; while another, opposed to this, says, that faith without works, or a holy life, is dead and of no use, and that charity, holiness and purity are essential to the attainment of life everlasting.

Another system denies the divinity of the Christian Redeemer, and teaches that Jesus Christ is nothing more than a human creature, in all respects like unto other men, fallible and peccable, and therefore not an object of religious worship. This system is, by the Trinitarian scheme, loaded with all kinds of obloquy, and called the half-way house to infidelity. It may be such half-way house leading to infidelity—perhaps it is: but if it be, popular Trinitarianism will, in this respect, always be found to be its next-door neighbor.

We might still go on describing the great differences in the doctrines now taught, each of which claims for itself the character of orthodoxy—all are right and true, though different and opposite, while the advocates of each system respectively, say, "The temple of the Lord are we." Our object, however, is not to dwell upon these differences, but to point out that RULE or heavenly SCIENCE, by which the Word of God throughout can with certainty and correctness be explained. Nothing more strikingly shows the total absence of such rule or method than the vastly different and opposite doctrines which are now zealously taught. Amidst all this mental confusion—these "wars and rumors of wars"—it must be acknowledged that a sure rule of Scripture interpretation, would indeed be a light in the hands of private Christians, as well as a help to those whose business it is, on the Sabbath, to dispense the Word of Life to their fellow men.

Correspondence, the sure Rule of Scripture Interpretation.

The Rule, then, which is here recommended as the only sure one by which the sacred records of Divine Truth can be elucidated, is that immutable relationship or correspondence existing between all the objects of the world of nature, whether animal, vegetable or mineral, and the affections, thoughts, and intellectual properties of man, as the world of mind. This *Rule*, which is named the Science of Correspondences, from the universality and certainty of its application when faithfully studied and correctly applied, will be found to be, as expressed in the title-page of this work, "The key of knowledge" to the Holy Scriptures, by the use of which a true system of Theology will be restored, and the Word of God with clearness and certainty explained. This science grows out of and is exhibited in universal creation. It can therefore never err in itself, because it is the order of the Creator, and exhibited throughout his works. A man, it is true, may commit some errors in explaining it, but these are to be attributed to the explainer and not to the science; for that, in itself, is infallible and certain.

Correspondence, then, may be termed a universal language, in which the Divine Being speaks to his creatures, both in his works and in his Word. The first voice which is heard, or the first truth made apparent in universal creation, is, that there is a God, and that there is *but* One, who, from the harmony, regularity and beauty of his works, is infinite in wisdom and goodness. To this voice or truth, human reason at once assents without the least difficulty or hesitation. As it is in the works of God, so is it in his Word; for Revelation throughout, invariably points to one God, in essence and *Person* ONE, who is at once the Creator, Redeemer, and Saviour; God manifest in the flesh, whom the apostle styles the "True God and Eternal Life." If Revelation be deprived of this self-evident truth—the perfect unity of God, as a single Divine Being—no clear light can enter the mind upon any theological subject whatever. All the bright truths of the Word will become obscured—the selfhood and self-derived intelligence of man will come in between him and the Sun of righteousness—to him the Divine Luminary will become eclipsed, and, in respect to religious truth, nothing but darkness and gross darkness can cover his moral land.

In stating, first, what the science of Correspondence is, we cannot, perhaps, define it better than by saying that it treats of the relationship which exists between the essence of a thing and its form or outward appearance, and that the form points out the nature and quality of the essence within. Correspondence, according to its etymology—it being compounded of two Latin words, *con*, with, and *respondere*, to answer,[4] to answer with or together, to fit, to suit, or match; thus denoting the reciprocal relation of one thing to another—is a science which treats of the harmony, agreement and concord existing between cause and effect, essence and form, spirit and matter, soul and body, heaven and earth. We may here observe, that correspondence can only be applied to those things which proceed from God in the orderly course of creation; it cannot be mixed up with, or applied to, any object or thing manufactured or made by man.

By this universal science, all outward nature (including the vast varieties of its objects), is seen as a whole to be a representative image of man, while the objects thereof correspond to his various affections and thoughts, both good and bad. Man again is seen to be created, as the Scriptures declare him to be, in the image and likeness of God; all the powers and principles of his mental constitution when in order, shadow forth, by the law of correspondence, the infinite perfections of his adorable Creator. Thus, a regular chain of connection is established between the Lord and his works—God is the supporter of the whole, the *All* in all.

Correspondence was a subject familiar to the men of the most ancient times, who esteemed it the science of sciences, and cultivated it so universally that all their books were written in agreement with it. The hieroglyphics of the Egyptians, and the fabulous stories of antiquity, were founded upon it. All the ancient churches were representative; their ceremonies, and even their statutes, which were rules for the institution of their worship, shadowed forth, by correspondence, the spiritual things of worship and of heaven; in like manner, everything in the Israelitish church, the burnt offerings, sacrifices, meat offerings and drink offerings, with all the particulars belonging to each, were of this spiritually representative character; they were all types and shadows of good things to come.

The science of faithfully representing, by outward objects, the spiritual states and conditions of the mind and life, was not only known, but also cultivated in many kingdoms of Asia, particularly in

---

[4] Some have thought that correspondence might be more properly derived from *cor*, the heart, and *respondens*, answering: but as the signification is the same either way, it is of little consequence. Derive it which way you please, the meaning is still the same.

the land of Canaan, Egypt, Assyria, Chaldea, Syria, Arabia, in Tyre, Sidon, and Nineveh; from thence it was conveyed into Greece, where, as appears from the works of the most ancient Grecian writers, it was changed into fable.

All things that appear on the face of the earth, being objects which compose the *macrocosm* or great world, are corresponding emblems of all the various affections, thoughts, intellectual faculties and powers of man, whom the ancients called the *microcosm* or little world; consequently, not only trees and vegetables, but also beasts, birds, fishes of every kind, with all other animals, down to the worm and creeping things of the ground. These are all mentioned in Scripture in reference to the mental properties of man. Hence the Lord says by the prophet, " In that day will I make a covenant for them with the beasts of the field, and with the fowls of heaven, and with the creeping things of the ground." (Hosea ii. 18.) This covenant is certainly not made with unthinking animals, but with reflecting man, who is here described as to his affections and thoughts, from the highest to the lowest, by beasts, birds and creeping things.

In agreement with the universal principles of correspondence, the ancients, who were versed therein, made themselves images to represent things celestial, and were, no doubt, greatly delighted therewith. By reason of their spiritual signification, they could, and did, discern in them what related to heaven and the church. Hence they placed those images both in their temples and houses, not with any intention to worship them, but to serve as means of recollecting the celestial things signified by them. In Egypt and in other places, they made images of calves, oxen, serpents, and also of children, old men and virgins. Why they did this, correspondence alone can show. Calves and oxen signify the affections and powers of the natural mind; serpents, the prudence and cunning of the sensual man; children, innocence and charity; old men, wisdom; and virgins, the affections of truth. Succeeding ages, when the knowledge of correspondence became obliterated, because they found these pictures and images set up by their forefathers in and about their temples, began to worship them as deities; and from this, idolatrous worship took its rise. The ancients performed their worship in gardens and groves, and also on mountains and hills; by the language of correspondence, gardens and groves signify wisdom and intelligence, and every particular tree something relating thereto: a mountain denotes the highest principle of celestial love to the Lord; and hills, brotherly love and charity. It is from this their spiritual signification, that we read in Scripture, "The mountains and the hills shall break forth before you into singing, and all the trees of the field shall clap their hands." (Isaiah lv. 12.) This true science not only lucidly explains all Scripture, but also the manners and customs of those who lived in the primitive times; and if ever the ancient Grecian fables, or the Egyptian hieroglyphics, shall be truly deciphered, it must be by this means. No other method will ever correctly unfold their meaning.

CHAPTER II.

THE ORIGIN OF CORRESPONDENCE, AND WHY THE SCRIPTURE IS WRITTEN IN AGREEMENT WITH IT—SOME PROOFS GIVEN—REVELATION THE VOICE OF GOD SPEAKING TO MAN'S WILL AND INTELLECT; THEREFORE OF PLENARY INSPIRATION—OPINIONS OF ANCIENT AND MODERN AUTHORS RESPECTING CORRESPONDENCE—THE PRAYER OF MOSES, "LORD, I BESEECH THEE, SHOW ME THY GLORY," EXPLAINED—THE TRI-UNITY OF GOD, AS CONSISTING OF LOVE, WISDOM, POWER, EXHIBITED IN ALL CREATION—CORRESPONDENCE OF THE THREE KINGDOMS OF NATURE WITH THE THREE DEGREES OF LIFE IN MAN.

The Origin of Correspondence.

TO point out the origin of correspondence, and why the Word of God is written according to it, we must endeavor to show the orderly descent of Divine Truth from its beginning in the bosom of Deity, to its being embodied in the natural language of men on earth. This is, indeed, no very easy task; but still some knowledge, however faint we may deem it, can be obtained by those who thirst for the truth that they may be freed from error and doubt. To obtain information upon this lofty and momentous subject, we must make a direct appeal to the Word itself; for that alone is the centre and source of knowledge. David says, "Forever, O Lord, thy Word is settled in heaven." (Ps. cxix. 89.) Now of this Word, which he here describes as being forever settled in heaven, he says in the 105th verse of the same psalm, "It is a lamp unto my feet, and a light unto my path." This language evidently declares that the Word of God has its beginnings in heaven, where it is in everlasting brightness, and from thence descending to the earth, becomes to the human race the lamp to their feet, and the light to guide them in their religious path or walk.

Some Proofs Given.

This descent of the Divine Truth from heaven to earth, so that it may be to man his true and steady light to guide him in all his ways, is beautifully described in Psalm xviii. 9, where we read: "He (the Lord) bowed the heavens also, and came down, and darkness was under his feet." To bow the heavens and come down, is a Scripture phrase signifying the Lord's presence, not only in the heavens, his more exalted dwelling-place, but in the earth, and in all parts of his wide and living creation.—"He bowed the heavens *also*, and came down."

The mind of man when venturing to contemplate the Majesty of heaven, can readily conceive Him to be a Being whose essence is love, unbounded and pure, and that the proximate *sphere* thereof, being the brightness by which love is made known, is the most pure and perfect wisdom. Love and wisdom, then, are the essential properties which constitute, if we may so speak, "our Father in the heavens." These two dwell in everlasting union; they cannot be separated in act, however man, through his prejudice and foolishness, may separate them in thought, and suppose them to be two distinct entities. *Love*, as the source of creation, is the essence of wisdom, the source and root of all being; and as such, in Scripture, is called FATHER; Divine Wisdom, as being the first and only sphere of Love, is the form of such Love, and is called SON, and the *first* and ONLY-BEGOTTEN. As love dwells within wisdom, and cannot be separated from it, so Divine Revelation, inasmuch as it is God's own Word declaring the truth, teaches that the Father is in the Son—that the Son came forth from the bosom of the Father, and that the Father and the Lord Jesus Christ as the Truth, are ONE. "I and the Father are one." (John x. 30.)

The first emanating sphere of the Divine Majesty is termed the Wisdom of God, and an everlasting light. This is the only Truth! it is the Word that was in the beginning with God, and *was* God, of which Jesus Christ was the manifested form.[5] This is agreeable to the Divine declaration, "the Word was made flesh." (John i. 14.) This sphere of Divine Truth in the heavens, where the psalmist says it is forever settled, must exist in its highest degree of celestial brightness, and partaking of all the qualities of angelic purity and wisdom, must faithfully describe them and bring them forth: but in its further descent through the heavens to men on earth, that is, in bowing the heavens and coming down, it is received in a lower degree of finite existence, and entering the minds of those persons, who were the prepared instruments to embody the Word of God in human language, must partake of those affections, thoughts and properties peculiar to

---

[5] Inasmuch as Jesus is the Truth itself, therefore Pilate's question. "What is truth?" as put to the Lord, received a distinct answer when Jesus came forth, wearing the crown of thorns and purple robe, and said, in reference to himself. "Behold the Man!"—See John xix. 5.

man while existing in a world of nature. As such, the language of the *written* Word must be made up of those things which appear in this world; all of which, by an immutable law of correspondence, are used to express the qualities and properties of mind, whether they be good or bad, true or false. While, then, it is a truth that the Word or Wisdom of God is in all the heavens—forever settled there, and from whence angelic perfection is derived; it is equally true that the same Word "bowed the heavens and came down," and thus became to man on earth his lamp of safety, his everlasting light, his sure and certain guide. Man, in reference to his existence in this world, is indeed made a little lower than the angels: but because the truth of God meets him here, supplying all his wants and leading him to the heaven of angels, he is therefore crowned with glory and honor.

Divine Truth, in bowing the heavens and coming down, is presented to men on earth, accommodated to their wants, to their states of affection and thought. It is therefore clothed in the garments of human language, and, in its literal sense, the Divine brightness within is clothed or covered; thus it is the WORD in its most external form, in which the light or brightness of its internal spirit terminates in the shade or cloud of the letter. In Scripture, heaven is called the Lord's throne, but the earth, his footstool. The idea presented to the mind by the throne of God, is that of Divine justice and judgment dwelling together, from whence every one is to receive the just reward of his doings; for it is an unquestionable law of Divine order, both in nature and in grace, that "whatsoever a man sows, that shall he also reap." In heaven, where the throne of God is, Truth is in its glory, in its brightness: but on the earth, which is the Lord's footstool, it is clothed in human language, and its *literal sense*, though a guard and defence to the glory within, is, when compared to its internal contents, as darkness to light. Hence it said, that in bowing the heavens and coming down, "*darkness* was under his feet." The Word of God is not *darkness* to the Christian: all its literal truths are to him the clouds of heaven, in which the spiritual man can always discern the presence of the Lord coming with power and glory. But to the wicked, to those who are in states of opposition, who love darkness rather than light because their deeds are evil, to such the Word in its literal form is darkness; for they can discern nothing of that light which shines through the letter from the Divine brightness within. Yet notwithstanding their blindness and opposition, their contempt of all sacred things, the Lord's presence in his Word is pre-eminently full and complete; the Spirit of God pervades the whole, and his life sustains every jot and tittle.

This universal presence of the Lord in his Word, which gives life and spirit to the whole, is finely described by the psalmist in these words, "He rode upon a cherub and did fly; yea, he did fly upon the wings of the wind. He made darkness his secret place; his pavilion round about him were dark waters and thick clouds of the skies." (Ps. xviii. 10, 11.) These expressions, the dark waters and thick clouds which form the Divine pavilion, are expressive of those appearances of truth in the literal sense, by which the Divine brightness is as it were obscured by those perversions of the natural and carnal mind, which are here called *dark waters* and *thick clouds*. The truth of these remarks is experienced in every-day life and abundantly borne out by the madness of those atheistical comments upon Scripture, which are daily issuing from the school of materialism and infidelity. They are made by persons whose only object is to throw obloquy and contempt upon a Book, the contents of which they do not understand. They act as if they had neither eyes to see its glory, nor hearts to feel its power. They would fain have us believe that the Bible is a worthless and even immoral book, invented in the dark ages by ignorance and priestcraft. But to these gratuitous and unproved charges, we reply that the sight of the owl is not sufficiently strong to enable it to look upon the sun in its brightness. Surely these dark waters and thick clouds which rise up from their perverted minds, obscure the genuine light of truth. They follow their own *will-with-a-wisp*, and are led into innumerable doubts and errors, because they have no wish to know the Scriptures nor the power of God.

The Divine brightness within the letter of the Word, when fully received, accomplishes in man full and perfect regeneration. It is therefore said that "At the brightness that was before him, his thick clouds passed, hailstones and coals of fire." (Ps. xviii. 12.) It will be seen at once that these thick clouds, hailstones and coals of fire cannot stand before the Divine brightness—they passed away! These words show the order which the divine truth, as the brightness of Jehovah, pursues in freeing man from all falsity and evil and saving the soul alive. This brightness is the spiritual truth of God infilled with the warmth of celestial love. Wherever this goes forth, into whatever mind it enters, the first things to be dispersed are the thick clouds, then the hailstones, and lastly the coals of fire. The thick clouds are here put to denote those false and perverted notions which rise up as mists from the carnal mind, and which obscure the light of heaven; but these will certainly pass away when the man, with a true energy of soul, begins to contemplate the truth of heaven. The spiritual brightness of Revelation will penetrate his thick clouds, and open to his mind a new and glorious scene. This brightness will also cause the hailstones to pass away. Hailstones, literally, are frozen drops of rain congealed into hard lumps, in consequence of the absence of heat. They descend to the earth in a destructive, not in a productive capacity. As hailstones they are of no use whatever in fertilizing the land; before they can be rendered beneficial to the soil they must, by the application of heat, be turned into a liquid; then, and not till then, are they made useful.

So in a spiritual sense, all those doctrines of religion which are professed by the lips, which exist in the understanding as so many cold and frozen speculations, but which regard not the life, are not animated by the fire of heaven, and in which the celestial warmth of love and devotion is not—these are the hailstones which, in religion, are destructive and worthless. But no sooner does the Divine brightness appear than the hailstones pass away. When the warmth of love and purity of life is found to mingle with the doctrines we profess—when every doctrine is seen to regard the life, and that the life of religion is to do good, then our hailstones pass away; our frozen drops of speculation are melted and changed to the fertilizing waters of life. Then, too, though last, yet greatest in importance, will the *coals of fire* pass away. These are the true emblems of all those lusts, concupiscences, and depraved desires which, if suffered to remain in the natural mind, will, like coals of unhallowed fire, burn up and destroy every vestige of the heavenly state in the soul of man. But these, at the Divine brightness, will retire, and leave the man in full possession of light and peace and every joy.

In further explanation of the nature of correspondence as well as of its use as a key to unlock the sacred cabinet of Divine Revelation, we may observe that in this material world the forms of things only meet our corporeal vision. By our bodily sight we can look upon and examine minutely the form, construction, and organization of all bodies, whether mineral, vegetable or animal; but the essence or spirit which gave them birth and keeps them in existence, this we cannot see; it is no object of bodily sight, but of mental vision— of deep intellectual reflection and thought; hence it belongs more especially to the soul or mind. All outward forms are coverings of the secret operations and wonders of the Creator, and are expressive of the qualities of the spirit or life within.

As it is with the material world and its objects, so is it with the world of mind and its intellectual objects and affections. The ancients, who were in the habit of calling man a *microcosm* or little world, were accustomed to delineate his mental condition by the outward appearances in the *macrocosm* or great world of nature. Thus they described a good and wise man by the appearance of the earth dressed in beauty, fertility and fruitfulness—by gardens, groves and paradises; while evil and ignorant men they compared to rude and barren deserts, to wildernesses and solitary places, where nothing but sterility appeared, or where thorns and noxious weeds grew. They saw, almost at a glance, the relationship or correspondence between *barren earth* and the *barren mind*, and they described the latter by such appropriate terms as expressed correctly the appearance of the former. This method of speaking they derived from the ancient church in the time of Noah, whose members were grounded in the knowledge of correspondence; a science according to the principles of which the Word of God is written, and by which it can alone be correctly explained.

The language of Scripture, when speaking of the descent of Divine love and wisdom from God into the human mind, by which, when affectionately received, the life of man is made heavenly and fruitful, is: "The wilderness and solitary place shall be glad for them; and the desert shall rejoice and blossom as the rose. It shall blossom abundantly, and rejoice with joy and singing: the glory of Lebanon shall be given unto it, the excellency of Carmel and Sharon; they shall see the glory of the Lord, and the excellency of our God." (Isa. xxxv. 1, 2.) Here the wilderness and solitary place are said to rejoice with joy and singing, because they see the glory of Jehovah and the excellency of God. This, in the language of correspondence, is a beautiful description of the altered condition of man upon his warm reception of the Divine influences. The once barren soul then begins to bear fruit, the fruits of a pure enlightened wisdom. It is thus that the desert rejoices and blossoms as the rose.

In man there are three degrees of knowledge, the one, as it were, within the other; namely, religious, philosophical and scientific. Religious truth is the first and highest in order; it is a sacred statement of positive facts, and consists of an interior acknowledgment of God, the ardent worship of Him, and the reduction of all truth to practical life: this is the kernel, spirit or essence which gives vigor and animation to the other two. Philosophical knowledge is only religious truth perceived in the rational mind, and there clearly and intellectually discerned. Scientific truth is but the same Divine original brought down to the lowest region of the understanding, and there carefully wrought out by experimental proof. Each recognizes the other as a part of the harmonious whole, and they act unitedly together. True science leads us to philosophy, philosophy to religion, and religion to God. True and undefiled religion is nothing more nor less than a man bringing to his Maker the fruits of his heart. If religion declares a fact, philosophy makes it to be intellectually discerned, and science experimentally proves it.

Thus religion, philosophy and science mutually strengthen each other. The life from God the Creator descends first into the human mind; from thence it passes to fill all creation with those living forms which, in the world of nature, truly represent and shadow forth all those qualities of affection and thought belonging to man, the world of mind; and returning through him to the great Giver of all good, not void, but scented by his breath of praise, holds all things in one beautiful and unbroken chain of connection; from whence arises the science of correspondence, or the relationship existing between essence and form, spirit and matter.

As it is with the material and moral worlds, so it is with the Word of Revelation; for as this opens to our view the eternal world, it cannot be the production of man; but is, as the Apostle expresses it, "God-breathed," or "given by inspiration of God." In consequence of its plenary inspiration, it is the light of the world, and the sacred glory of the Israel of God. Now "upon all the glory there is a covering and a defence." Its literal and mere historical records form its covering, which acts as a protection to that spirit and life within, which make up its interior brightness, its real imperishable glory. Many read the sacred volume in the same spirit and temper of mind as they read other books; the consequence is that they see nothing but the mere history of past events, in which they do not observe themselves to be personally interested. They abide in the letter which, without the spirit, killeth. Were they to contemplate its spiritual sense, they would find themselves minutely described as to all their states of affection, thought and action; thus as to their growth in love and wisdom, or their decline into evil and error. In this study every good man would find that it is indeed "the Spirit that quickens," and makes him alive to his everlasting interests. Too many, however, act like the idle gazers in the world, who content themselves with looking upon the forms of things; they never examine the beauty of their interior organization, much less contemplate the Essence or Spirit whence they spring. Their hearts deceive them, and their heads, directed by prejudice, lead them astray.

God speaking to Man's Will and Intellect.

In carrying correspondence out to its legitimate use in unfolding the great truths of Revelation, the first thing to be acknowledged is, that the Word of God is the medium through which the Lord speaks to every man. It is the voice of God speaking most powerfully to the will and intellect—to the heart and understanding. Man is therefore addressed as the microcosm or little world, and all objects in the great world of nature are mentioned in Scripture, in reference to the varied affections, thoughts, perceptions and powers of mind which collectively make up the perfection of man as the moral world.

We read in Scripture, "the mountains skipped like rams, and the little hills like lambs."[6] (Ps. cxiv. 4.) Mountains and hills are called upon to praise the Lord, as well as "fruitful trees, beasts, cattle and creeping things." (Ps. cxlviii.) In reading such passages as these, many pass them over with a simple acknowledgment of their being highly figurative, and in this way leave us quite as much in the dark as if nothing had been written: but the rule of interpretation for which we are contending, makes them as clear as daylight. Man is the world in miniature, and as such, he has his mountains, hills, seas, lakes, rivers, beasts, birds, cattle and creeping things. A mountain, in nature, is the most elevated portion of the earth; and what is highest in the material world, corresponds to what is supreme in the mental. Thus in man the most elevated affection, whether it be good or bad, is his mountain. Love to God is the supreme or highest affection of the soul. The affections of brotherly love and charity, whence spring joy, peace and union, are his hills. The pleasure arising from these, with the true delight they bring to the mind when in lively exercise, are here described by the mountains and hills skipping like rams and lambs.

The mountains are called upon to praise the Lord, to instruct us

---

[6] Sons of the flock.

that the supreme affections of the soul, signified by mountains, should breathe a constant song of adoration to Him who is the Author and Giver of all good. Not only these supreme affections, but all the lower ones; all our perceptions and thoughts from the highest to the lowest, should render the meed of praise: thus not only mountains and hills, but fruitful trees, beasts, cattle and creeping things. By this spiritual signification of a mountain, as denoting the supreme love of the soul, all passages in Scripture where this term occurs, are of easy interpretation. If the supreme love be fixed on the Lord, such love is truly celestial, and in Scripture is called the mountain of the Lord, the Mount Zion, beautiful for situation, the joy of the whole earth, and the mountain that brings peace to the people. By this rule of interpretation we see, almost instantly, the meaning of these words: —"Touch the mountains and they shall smoke!" (Ps. cxliv. 5.) The Lord's touch is the Divine communication and presence; the mountains, the supreme affections; while the phrase "they shall smoke," denotes that the effect of such communication will certainly follow; namely, the evils of self-love and the falsities thence arising as smoke, will be destroyed.

It is to man, with respect to all his affections and thoughts from the highest to the lowest, that the Word makes a constant and powerful appeal, and with the knowledge of correspondence before us, we discover the meaning of this passage: "Thus saith the Lord God to the mountains and to the hills, to the rivers and to the valleys; behold I, even I will bring a sword upon you, and I will destroy your high places." (Ezek. vi. 3.) Here the supreme affections signified by mountains, are evil, and all in subordination take their quality from the supreme. Hence it is said I will bring a sword upon you and destroy your high places. With this key of interpretation we see the reason why Jesus went up into a mountain to pray. He did so to instruct us that all true prayer springs from the highest or supreme affection. We see also why the Lord's transfiguration was made before Peter, James and John; and why it took place upon a *mountain* apart, with many other interesting particulars. The Lord, who is the Judge of all hearts, can alone know the actual quality of our supreme affections. He it is who examines and estimates these, and this is described in Isaiah, by Jehovah "weighing the mountains in scales, and the hills in a balance" (xl. 12).

If the supreme affection should be evil instead of good; placed upon self instead of upon the Lord, it is still denoted by a mountain;

but it is then called a destroying mountain. "Behold I am against thee, O destroying mountain, saith the Lord." (Jer. li. 25.) This also shows the meaning of the Lord's words in the Gospel, where speaking of this evil mountain of self-love, He says: "If ye have faith as a grain of mustard seed, ye shall say unto this *mountain*, Remove hence to yonder place, and it shall remove; and nothing shall be impossible to you." (Matt. xvii. 20.) The science of correspondence shows also, that all beasts, birds of wing, creeping things of the ground, together with all the subjects of the vegetable and mineral kingdoms, are mentioned in Scripture in reference to man as the little world, and that they denote his affections and thoughts from the highest to the lowest. All the clean, gentle and useful animals signifying the heavenly and pure affections; while the fierce, treacherous and cruel denote the impure, defiled and hurtful. It is in agreement with this instructive law of correspondence, that the Lord, in sending forth his disciples to preach the Gospel of his kingdom, said: "Behold I send you forth as sheep in the midst of wolves; be ye therefore wise as serpents and harmless as doves." (Matt. x. 16.)

Man being the object of Divine care, is constantly attended by the great Shepherd of Israel, and Revelation as constantly makes its appeals to him. Before the work of regeneration is commenced in him, he is called earth without form, and void, while darkness is upon the face of the deep. In this state he is, prophetically, thus described. "I beheld the earth, and lo! it was without form and void: and the heavens, and they had no light. I beheld the mountains, and lo! they trembled, and all the hills moved lightly. I beheld, and lo! there was no man, and all the birds of the heavens were fled." (Jer. iv. 23–25.) Here the *earth*, by correspondence, is the external mind; without form and void, shows that there was no heavenly beauty therein, but that it was void of all good, and a spiritual blank as it respects wisdom or truth. The heavens having no light, shows that there were no spiritual truths to enlighten the internal mind; the consequence was that the mountains and hills trembled and moved lightly—no fixed stability in the affections; there was no man; for a *man*, truly and spiritually such, is a regenerate person, an image and likeness of God; and hence all the birds of the heavens were fled, which teaches that there were no celestial thoughts occupying his soul. In this state of mental darkness and desolation, man is thus addressed: "O earth, earth, earth, hear the Word of the Lord." (Jer. xxii. 29.) That the clods of the ground are not called upon to hear the Word of God, is at once apparent to every one. But after the process of regeneration is passed through, and man comes into a happy celestial state, how different is the description, how changed is the scene! then the language of Scripture is, "Sing, O heavens; and be joyful, O earth; break forth into singing, O mountains; for the Lord hath comforted his people, and will have mercy upon his afflicted." (Isa. xlix. 13.)

In the Psalms it is written, "How sweet are thy words unto my taste! yea, sweeter than honey to my mouth" (cxix. 3). The Word of Revelation must indeed contain something wonderful and vast, of great moment to our present and future peace, if all its words are sweet to our taste, and sweeter than honey to our mouth. What makes them thus sweet to our taste, and like honey to our lips? Surely not the mere words, not the literal sense of the Divine records; for this sense seems to treat of little else but the troubles of the Jews; of their bondage and deliverance, of their wars with the idolatrous nations, of their repeated promises of obedience, and of their constant breach of those promises; of their backslidings, wanderings and deviations from the laws of truth and rectitude; of their religious rites and ceremonies; of their burnt-offerings and sacrifices. These, literally, do not concern us in any other way than as matters of history. We are not personally affected by them. We gain nothing by the obedience of the Jews to their ceremonial laws; neither can we lose anything by their neglect.

The great truth remains to be again and again enforced, which is, that the righteousness of Christians must exceed that of the Scribes and Pharisees, or else they will likewise perish in the way. What was the righteousness of the Jewish Scribes and Pharisees, but a rigid and slavish exactness in the performance of ceremonies, in which the heart felt no warmth of love, and by which the life was not improved? It is a known thing that they neglected the weightier matters of the law, justice, judgment and mercy. Every man will see that his righteousness must exceed this, or he can have no claim to be a disciple of Christ. Without this, his religion is destitute of spirituality; the fire of love glows not in his bosom, nor does the light of wisdom irradiate his path.

The words of Divine Truth, to be sweet to a man's taste, must contain something of spirituality in them; they must describe the heavenly state with its happiness and purity, together with the order pursued in the formation of it in the soul of man, without which there can be neither true enjoyment nor solid peace. The best commentators upon Scripture, both among the ancients and moderns, have maintained that there is some spiritual instruction contained in the sacred text, which is guarded by the literal covering from the rude gaze of every licentious eye, as well as from the unhallowed sphere of each polluted mind. Those who would find these treasures of wisdom must lose their sins—their inward pollutions of life and practice; for it is a law of Divine Truth, that holy things are not to be given to dogs, nor pearls to be cast to swine. (Matt. vii. 6.)

The spiritual things of God and heaven, together with the states and intellectual properties of mind, are in Scripture throughout represented and shadowed forth by all the objects in nature, these being mentioned therein to denote such affections, thoughts, and states of life. If this view were seen and attended to in our private meditations, there would be little difficulty in obtaining a correct interpretation of the Word of God. A few examples by way of illustration will prove this assertion, and show how sweet the Lord's words are to our taste.

In reading Scripture to advantage, we should believe that the great world of nature with all its parts and objects, both animate and inanimate, are mentioned therein in reference to man as the world of mind; and that they are all outward emblems which shadow forth his various mental properties. Thus where the Scriptures speak of gardens, groves, fertile fields, rich fruits, and paradises watered by gentle rains, or through which flowing streams wind their course, as is stated of the garden of Eden, through which a river flowed, parting into four heads that it might water the whole, such descriptions are written for the purpose of showing that man, the moral world, is represented in a high state of spiritual regeneration; when his cultivated mind produces the rich fruits of love and charity, when his state of wisdom is bright and cheering, and when his mind blooms with every virtue and mental excellence. On the other hand, when in Scripture we read of barrenness, of sandy deserts, of parched-up herbage, dry places, wildernesses, the growing of thorns, thistles, briers and the like; all these are so many descriptions of man in a mentally rude and unregenerate condition, in which the heart or will, being evil, is the bad ground, producing nothing in outward life but falsities and injurious thoughts, which are denoted by thorns, thistles and worthless weeds. There is no passage of Scripture, when viewed in this light, but what is of easy interpretation.

Opinions of Ancient and Modern Authors.

Profound commentators were perfectly aware that Scripture was not to be confined to a mere literal explanation, but that it was to be expounded after a spiritual manner; they saw a glory within the letter—a light that could not be hid. Origen, one of the most celebrated writers in the third century, says: "Unless thou ascend the mountain of God, and there meet with Moses; unless thou ascend the lofty sense of the law; unless thou reach the height of spiritual intelligence, thy mouth is not opened by God. If thou abide in the low plain of the letter, and do no more than make Jewish narratives of the historical text, thou hast not met Moses on the mount of God, neither hath God opened thy mouth, nor taught thee what thou oughtest to say." The same author, speaking of the transfiguration of the Lord upon the mount, observes, "Moses and Elias appeared in glory when they talked with Jesus, and in this fact the Law and the Prophets are shown to agree with the Gospels, and to be resplendent with the same glory, when spiritually understood." Another ancient writer, John of Jerusalem, says, "Do not suppose that it was only in former times Christ was betrayed by the priests, condemned by them, and by them delivered over to be crucified; but even now He is betrayed and condemned to death; for Christ is the Word of Truth, and they who falsely interpret the Word of Truth betray Him to be mocked and crucified."

This, then, was the mode of spiritual interpretation pursued by these two primitive fathers, and a similar one was adopted by Clemens of Alexandria, Jerome, St. Augustin, Ignatius, Theophilus of Antioch, Chrysostom, and many others.

If we turn our thoughts to the theological writers of modern times, we find amongst the most profound of them the same doctrine recognized, namely, that there is a spiritual sense contained within the letter of the sacred text. The Rev. John Parkhurst, who was the author of a Hebrew Lexicon, and must have been acquainted with every word in the Hebrew Bible, as well as have possessed a critical knowledge of that language, makes a long comment on Gen. ii. 8, "And the Lord God planted a garden eastward in Eden." Upon these words he says: "Surely not for the purposes of a mere Mahometan paradise, but as a school of religious instruction to our first parents. Many arguments might be adduced in confirmation of this truth. Such a method of teaching, by the emblems of paradise, was suited to the nature of man, who is capable of information concerning spiritual things, by analogy, from outward and sensible objects. It was also agreeable to the ensuing dispensations of God who, in that religion which commenced on the fall and was in substance re-instituted by Moses, did instruct the people in spiritual truths, or the good things to come, by sensible and visible objects, rites and ceremonies; by the cherubim, by sacrifices, by the distinction of clean and unclean animals, by abstinence from blood, by the institution of priests, altars, burnt-offerings, drink-offerings, holy washings, etc.

"And even under the Christian state, much of our religious knowledge is communicated to us partly by the Scriptures referring us for ideas of spiritual and heavenly things to the visible works of God's creation, to the emblems of Paradise, and to the types of the patriarchal and Mosaic dispensations; partly by the ordinance of the Sabbath-day; and partly by the two sacraments of Baptism and the Lord's Supper, which are outward and visible signs of inward and spiritual benefits. It is further manifest that *two* of the trees of Paradise, that of life and that of the knowledge of good and evil, were of a typical or emblematic nature; the one, the sacrament of life (Gen. ii. 9; iii. 22); the other, of death. (Gen. ii. 17; iii. 17–19.) And so after the fall, the rough leaves of the fig-tree were used by our first parents as a symbol of contrition. And since in that sacred garden was also every tree that was pleasant to the sight or good for food, surely of the soul of man as well as of his body, it may safely be inferred, that the whole[7] garden was so contrived by infinite Wisdom, as to represent and inculcate on the minds of our first parents a plan or system of religious truths revealed to them by their Creator; especially since the paradisiacal emblems of trees, plants, waters, and the like, are frequently applied by the succeeding inspired writers to represent spiritual objects, and convey spiritual lessons; and that with a simplicity and beauty not to be paralleled from any human writer."[8]

[7] "Know," says Rabbi Simon Bar Abraham —cited by Mr. Hutchinson, *Hebrew Writings*, p. 21, from Buxtorf's *Arc. Fœd.* 83—"Know that in the trees, fountains, and other things of the garden of Eden, were the figures of the most curious things by which the first Adam saw and understood *spiritual things;* even as God hath given to us the forms or figures of the tabernacle, of the sanctuary, and of all its furniture, the candlestick, the table, and the altars, for types of *intellectual things*, and that we might from them understand heavenly truths. But no doubt those particulars were more plain and clear to Adam in the garden of Eden wherein he dwelt; as he also was more holy, being a creature formed by the hand of God himself, and an angel of God. In the trees likewise, and fountains or rivers of the garden, he prefigured admirable mysteries."

[8] See Parkhurst's Hebrew Lexicon, under ב

In this extract the intelligent writer speaks of man being instructed in spiritual truths by "sensible and visible objects." This is indisputable evidence that he considered a spiritual sense to be contained within the letter; and if we were to withdraw our minds but a little from these merely sensible objects, we should discover a lesson of the purest wisdom taught us in these emblems of Paradise and its joys.

In showing what these spiritual things are, which are represented by outward objects, we observe, first, that the word Adam signifies mankind in general, both male and female. This is evident from Gen. v. 1, 2—"This is the book of the generations of Adam. In the day that God created man, in the likeness of God made He him; male and female created He them, and blessed them, and called THEIR NAME Adam,[9] in the day when they were created." The most ancient church and people named Adam or Man, were in a high state of wisdom and intelligence, which state was denoted by the garden in which they dwelt. Man is not the creator of his own state of wisdom and intelligence, but it is the Lord's work in him, and is effected while he submits to the Divine control. Hence it is said that "the Lord God planted the garden eastward in Eden; and there He put the man whom He had formed." (Gen. ii. 8.) But when, through inclining to sensual pursuits, these people lost that high state of spiritual intelligence, they lost their garden. This was represented by the expulsion from Paradise, and their being sent forth to till the ground.

If the garden of Eden, with all its joys, was a true emblem of the high state of mental cultivation in which the most ancient people dwelt, what shall we say of its two distinguished trees? the tree of life in the midst of the garden, and the tree of knowledge of good and evil, of which latter they were not to touch or eat? The Tree of Life! what an important name is this! a tree which, to man, imparts life! is not this a true emblem of the Lord himself? He is the sacred Tree of Life, who is still in the midst of man's spiritual garden, and whence all his joys and pleasures spring. What, then, are the fruits of this tree, but all the love, purity, goodness, wisdom and knowledge which yield spiritual nourishment to the wide creation? To eat of this tree is to derive, from the Lord alone, all that

---

[9] Sir William Jones intimates that Adam may be derived from *Adim*, a Sanscrit word, signifying the *first*. The Persians, too, whom he concludes to be of the same stock with the Hindoos, denominate the first man Adamah. It is, however, quite certain that Adam, in the oriental languages, means man, generally, or mankind.

we stand in need of for our growth in the Divine life, to feel a confidence and settled tranquillity under Divine Providence, and to have no anxious cares about the morrow; but to eat our daily bread with thankfulness and joy. Let every one eat of the fruits of this tree; he will find them to be like the Lord's words, sweet to his taste and as honey in the mouth. What, again, is that river which went forth to water the garden, but a true emblem of the great abundance of Divine Truth, which, like a sacred stream, forever flows through the spiritually cultivated soul, to enrich and water the mental garden—to increase the wisdom and beauty of the mind?

But what shall we say of the other tree, the tree of knowledge of good and evil? To eat of this tree we must turn away from the Tree of Life. It is, therefore, an emblem of man's *own self*, to which he turns when he supposes himself to be the author and producer of all that he enjoys. He then attributes all to himself, and nothing to the Lord. He inclines to sensual things; in Scripture language, he listens to the seductive reasonings of the serpent, and admits a spurious knowledge into his mind, a kind of profane mixture of good and evil. If we turn from the Lord as the Tree of Life, and pluck and eat of the forbidden fruit, the celestial state will decay in us; we shall lose the garden, be deprived of Eden and its joys, and like Adam be sent forth to till the ground—to cultivate low, sensual and earthly desires.

Many very curious and even fanciful theories have been entertained respecting the locality of the garden of Eden, and much of the midnight oil has been consumed in endeavoring to furnish an account of the precise spot of ground where this garden flourished. "Paradise has, by some romantic writers, been fixed in Hindostan, in that spot called by the Orientals the Paradisiacal regions of Hindostan. Josephus seems to countenance this opinion, since he describes the Ganges as one of the four rivers which watered it. But Becanus contends that the site of Paradise was the more northern region, watered by the Acesines, and that the forbidden fruit was that of the *Ficus Indica*, or Indian fig-tree. Hence this fig was called by the Mohammedans, Adam's fig. The island of Ceylon, situated near the equinoctial, has been declared to be Paradise, from a famous mountain called Pico d'Adama, the name being taken from the supposed print of Adam's foot, still visible. Others, again, declare that Paradise was not situated in any region of the present earth, but fix it in some happy ethereal sublunary region, and declare that at the fall

Adam was precipitated upon Ceylon, where, according to Herbelot, his sepulchre at this day remains, guarded by lions." (*Herbelot, Biblioth. Orient*, p. 52. *Edit. Maestricht*, 1776.) Tertullian places Paradise beyond the equinoctial, in the southern hemisphere, amidst regions of eternal verdure, serenity and beauty, in some happy and secluded spot now immersed in the ocean; and thinks that the flaming sword which turned every way to guard the Tree of Life, was the torrid zone, or burning girdle which surrounds the globe. All these theories respecting the locality of Paradise, more curious than profitable, will vanish like mists before the rising sun of Revelation, which teaches that the garden of Eden denotes that celestial state of wisdom and intelligence in which the people of the most ancient church called man or Adam, lived.

When we reflect on the important lessons of true wisdom taught us in the words of Revelation, and when these are relished by our affections so as to produce real delight; when the lips express pleasure by the acknowledgment of the Lord, and of those doctrines which lead to life and peace, then may each one exclaim in the language of David, "How sweet are thy words unto my taste; yea, sweeter than honey to my mouth." (Ps. cxix. 103.)

Again, Mr. Parkhurst, in his remarks on the word Testimony, says: "The various types and appointments of the law are called by this name, as witnessing somewhat *beyond* themselves, namely *spiritual things*, or the good things to come. Thus the cherubim with the ark are called the testimony. (Ex. xvi. 34.) So the two tables of stone are called the testimony, or the tables of the testimony, because they were to be a perpetual witness or testimony of what the Israelites were to do and forbear. And thus the whole tabernacle is called the tabernacle of testimony, as attesting or bearing witness to *spiritual truths*, or the good things to come, and to the duty of men in dependence on them."[10] (Ex. xxxviii. 21.)

These extracts are sufficient to prove that this writer considered all the rituals of the Jewish church to be emblematical, and that all the visible things in nature are types of spiritual things. Although he does not give any certain rule by which these symbols are to be explained, yet the fact of his belief in an inward spiritual sense is fully expressed. The rule, infallible and true, will be found in the law of correspondence. Thus according to this law, the ark, as containing the Decalogue, signifies the Lord with respect to the Divine Truth

---

[10] See Hebrew Lexicon, under עד

which, when received, gives a true testimony of the interior states of all, according to each one's reception thereof, with its reduction to practical life.

Bishop Lowth, in his translation of Isaiah, frequently speaks of a spiritual or allegorical sense in the Scriptures. The following is this prelate's version of chap. xxvii. 1.

> "In that day shall Jehovah punish with his sword—
> His well-tempered, and great, and strong sword—
> Leviathan the rigid serpent,
> And Leviathan the winding serpent:
> And shall slay the monster, that is in the sea."

Upon this verse his lordship observes: "The animals here mentioned seem to be the crocodile, rigid by the stiffness of the backbone, so that he cannot readily turn himself when he pursues his prey; hence the easiest way of escaping from him is by making frequent and short turnings: the serpent or dragon, flexible and winding, which coils himself up in a circular form: the sea monster or whale. These are used allegorically, without doubt, for great potentates, enemies and persecutors of the people of God: but to specify the particular persons or *states* designated by the prophet under these images, is a matter of great difficulty." Now this difficulty, by the law of correspondence, is entirely removed; for it shows that the sword of Jehovah is the Divine Truth proceeding from his love, which wages a righteous war against all that is false and merely sensual in the understanding, as denoted by the Leviathan, serpent and monster of the sea. The truth proceeding from Divine Love is called "the rod of Jehovah's mouth" (Isa. xi. 4), and also "the sword with two edges proceeding out of the mouth of the Son of Man." (Rev. i. 6.)

Bishop Horne also, in his commentaries on the Psalms, frequently alludes to this allegorical or spiritual sense. In his commentary on Psalm viii. he says: "Nor is it a speculation unpleasing or unprofitable, to consider that He who rules over the material world, is Lord also of the intellectual or spiritual creation represented thereby." In the preface to his commentaries, he observes: "The visible works of God are formed to lead us, under the direction of his Word, to a knowledge of those which are invisible: they give us ideas by analogy, of a new creation rising gradually, like the old one, out of darkness and deformity, until at length it arrives at the perfection of glory and beauty. The sun, that fountain of life and heart of the world, that bright leader of the armies of heaven, enthroned in glorious majesty; the moon shining with a lustre borrowed from his beams; the stars glittering by night in the clear firmament; the air giving breath to all things that live and move; the interchanges of light and darkness; the course of the year, and the sweet vicissitudes of seasons; the rain and the dew descending from above, and the fruitfulness of the earth caused by them; the bow bent by the hands of the Most High, which compasseth the heaven about with a glorious circle; the awful voice of thunder, and the piercing power of lightning; the instincts of animals, and the qualities of vegetables and minerals; the great and wide sea, with its unnumbered inhabitants; all these are ready to instruct us in the mysteries of faith and the duties of morality:—

> 'They speak their Maker as they can,
> But want and ask the tongue of man.'"—*Parnell.*

The excellent Mr. Pascal, as cited by Horne, says: "Under the Jewish economy truth appeared but in a figure: in heaven it is open, and without a veil; in the church militant it is so veiled as to be yet discerned by its correspondence to the figure. As the figure was first built upon the truth, so the truth is now distinguishable by the figure." I would suggest an alteration in this last clause, and say—As the figure was first produced by the Truth, so the truth is now seen by the figure.

The mode of representing qualities of mind by the objects of nature, is recognized in a little work published by the Society for promoting Christian Knowledge, entitled, "The Book of Nature; or, the true sense of things explained and made easy to the capacities of children." The work contains a number of questions put to children, with their answers. The following are selected:—

Q. What are wicked men, who hurt and cheat others?

A. They are wolves and foxes, and blood-thirsty men.

Q. What are ill-natured people, who trouble their neighbors, and rail at them?

A. They are dogs who bark at everybody.

Q. But what are good and peaceable people?

A. They are harmless sheep; and little children, under the grace of God, are innocent lambs.

Q. But what are liars?

A. They are snakes and vipers, with double tongues, and poison under their lips (page 2).

In the same work, after describing the difference between the life of the eel that grovels in the mud, with that of the lark which "mounts towards heaven, and delights itself with sweet music," the child is thus questioned:—

Q. How do the lives of worldly men differ from the lives of Christians?

A. As the life of the eel differs from the life of the lark.

The Rev. William Jones who held the perpetual curacy of Nayland, has also given his testimony to the great utility of correspondence or analogy in the interpretation of Scripture. He says: "The world cannot show us a more exalted character than that of a truly religious philosopher, who delights to turn all things to the glory of God; who, in the objects of his sight, derives improvement to his mind, and in the glass of things temporal, sees the image of things spiritual."[11]

In one of the volumes of Dr. Lardner's Cyclopædia, entitled, "A Preliminary Discourse on the Study of Natural History, by William Swainson, Esq.," there is a whole chapter "On the importance of Analogy," in which it is said that it is, in all subjects, the life and soul of illustration (197). "Such are the general effects and advantages produced by analogy in the elucidation of truth. Things which in their essential nature are totally opposite, are found, on closer investigation, to possess mutual relations, and to be governed by the same law. Hence we discover three sorts of analogies pervading the system of nature, in the widest and most exalted application of the term: the first regards the spiritual truths of Revelation; the second, those which belong only to the moral system; while the third are drawn from the phenomena of the material world" (201). The following section (202) cited from another author,[12] contains some valuable remarks: "The facts of nature and the doctrines of Scripture are generally analogous to each other. Divine Wisdom thus descends from its ethereal seat, as the accessor of the throne of the Eternal, and communicates with us face to face and hand to hand."

> "What, if earth
> Be but the shadow of heaven, and things therein
> Each to other like, more than on earth is thought?"

Extracts from very many other authors might be produced to show in what high estimation the science of correspondence, called by most of them analogy, was held as a safe and sacred rule of Scripture

---

[11] The *Fairchild Discourse* for 1784. [12] Hampden, "Essay on the Phil. Evid. of Christianity."

interpretation. In addition to those already named, we have the concurrence of Bishop Butler, Bishop Warburton, Dean Sherlock, Dr. Jortin, Soame Jenyns, with a long list of other venerable names, celebrated alike for piety and profound thinking. But after all these high authorities, the great point is for each one to see the truth for himself. If we are to arrive at a rational knowledge of the subjects of Revelation, we must, in our own minds, see and know them; for, as Mr. Locke justly observes, "we may as rationally hope to see with other men's eyes, as to know by other men's understanding."[13]

Holy Scripture becomes a delightful book of heavenly instruction when its sacred contents are brought to view by this master Key of Divine knowledge, the science of correspondence. It is then that the man, in his studies, enjoys "the feast of reason and the flow of soul," and perhaps no violence will be done to truth, if we assert that the sweetest moments of human life are those which glide away in contemplating the Sacred Word. Here in sweet retirement from the busy scenes of worldly pursuits, we may—within the sphere of the Divine presence, when the mind is in states of calm tranquillity, and as it were in company with angels—eat of living bread, and partake of that hidden manna which is in the midst of the Paradise of God.

The Prayer of Moses Explained.

Moses, in the ardor of his soul, prayed to God and said: "I beseech thee show me thy glory!" This prayer was graciously answered and granted; for the Lord said in reply, "I will make all my goodness pass before thee, and I will proclaim the name of Jehovah before thee." (Ex. xxxiii. 18, 19.) Now although the goodness and the glory of God are always passing before the eyes of human beings, although they are ever present with us, and vividly apparent both in his works and Word, yet none but those who pray this prayer will ever behold them in their real connection. It is the true prayer of the soul and not merely that of the lips, that can bring down to human perception both the glory and goodness of God. It is only under the cheering influence of this prayer that we can hope to see the truth, and feel the goodness of our beneficent Creator.

In order to see how the Divine glory and goodness are made to pass before us, and how these proclaim to the wondering world the name of Jehovah, we must mentally view the God of heaven and earth as

---

[13] "Essay on the Human Understanding," § 23.

a single Divine Being. This must be the starting-point of all true theology: if this be denied or explained away by a corrupt and vain philosophy, we shall not behold a single ray of the Divine glory, nor shall we have a true perception of either God's goodness or his power.

Every rational man will acknowledge that the glory of God is seen in the works of creation. "The heavens declare the glory of God, and the firmament showeth his handy work." (Ps. xix. 1.) But this glory to the reflecting of our race, is seen as strikingly portrayed in all the varied objects of this our world—from man, the highest created intelligence, down to the smallest pebbles upon the sea-shore—as it is in those brighter shining objects, the sun, the moon, and the star-bespangled sky!" All proclaim the Divine presence; in each we cannot fail to discern " the finger of God."

To show how this goodness and glory are ever present, and passing before our eyes, we must view creation itself as a proceeding or going forth from God. The Divine Operative Energy, or Holy Spirit of God, produces in creation an innumerable number of forms receptive of life, all of which are filled and animated by the life going forth from Him who is the life in all. This is the Scriptural view of creation, and the only rational one that can be offered: " By the Word of the Lord were the heavens made, and all the host of them by the breath [spirit] of his mouth." (Ps. xxxiii. 6.) There must, then, be an internal harmony, a relationship or correspondence between all parts of creation, while the whole, as being the work of God, must proclaim his name, or his quality which is signified by his name; and thus, as a magnificent mirror, must show forth his unity, his love, wisdom, power, goodness and glory! Thus all creation is a representative image of the perfections of Him who first produced and still sustains the whole.

When the human mind ventures to contemplate the Divine Majesty, it can conceive no otherwise than that LOVE, WISDOM and POWER are the three constituent principles which make up and form (so to speak) the very essence and being of Deity. These three form the fulness and perfection of the Divine One. To these, Scripture awards appropriate names as expressive of the Divine qualities. Thus Love, being the origin and parent of all existence, is called Father; Wisdom, which is the form of love and the first and only proximate sphere thereof, is named the Son, and the only-begotten; while the Divine Power, consisting in the perfect union of love and wisdom going forth in creative energy and life-imparting influence, is the Holy Spirit, the breath of Jehovah's mouth, giving life and being to creation's wide domain. Those who think that the names Father, Son and Spirit imply distinct personal entities, deceive themselves by vain carnal reasonings. While they thus think, they can never understand the Scriptures nor the power of God. They can know nothing of the Lord's teaching; for He speaks of the Father as being in the Son; and when He breathed upon his disciples, He said, "receive ye the Holy Ghost," thus designating his living breath or influence, the Divine Spirit or Power they ought to receive. These three, Love, Wisdom, Power, named Father, Son, Spirit, are the sacred trine which form the fulness of the Godhead; and because these centre and meet in the Lord Jesus Christ, the manifested God, it is declared that "in Him dwelleth all the fulness of the Godhead bodily." (Col. ii. 9.) "Of his fulness (then) have all we received, and grace for grace." (John i. 10.) These three Divine Essentials which form the perfection of one God, make up the Divine Tri-unity or Trinity.

The Tri-unity of God exhibited in Creation.

Now it is easy to see that all creation, by the infallible law of correspondence, exhibits, as in a mighty mirror, the Love, Wisdom and Power of Deity; and thus that the Divine Glory is constantly present, passing before our eyes and proclaiming the name of Jehovah,—his quality, providence and care. A little reflection will prove this fact.

The sun in nature, the first and brightest object which meets our eyes, may be considered as the instrumental cause, in the Divine hand, of the creation of all those worlds which revolve within our system, and is therefore a bright representative image of the Divine Sun of righteousness. The constituent principles of the sun are heat, light and proceeding influence. The proceeding rays, in their going forth, impart life and vigor to all in the system. The sun is one body of pure fire; the Lord, as the Divine Sun, is one form of pure Love. Fire, then, in Scripture, corresponds to love. Strange fire, which may be deemed unhallowed, is an evil or impure love which ought not to mingle with our spiritual devotions; hence we find that the offering of strange fire upon the altar in the Jewish representative worship was the cause of the death of Aaron's two sons, Nadab and Abihu. (Lev. x. 1.)

The light of the sun corresponds to the Wisdom of God, which is a Divine Light; so that, in Scripture, light, brightness, effulgence, whiteness and purity are terms expressive of Truth, this being as much a light to the soul as solar light is to the body.

The proceeding rays of the sun which give vigor to the whole system by which the solar power and influence are felt in the material world, thereby refreshing, renewing, rendering it prolific and dressing it up in the richest beauty, so that food and clothing are provided for all that live; these correspond to the power, Spirit or influence of Jehovah, which goes forth for the spiritual refreshment and renovation of the mental system of man, the moral world.

We must surely acknowledge that the essence of God is Love, his form, Wisdom, and his influence, Life; so to show this by correspondence, the essence of the sun is fire, its form light, its proceeding rays, refreshment and life. We may observe this corresponding relationship throughout all creation; by this we may distinctly know how the eternal power and Godhead are seen in the things that are made.

The globe on which we live is called terraqueous, because composed of earth and water. But earth and water, separately considered, will not sustain animal life; and in this case the world would have been a useless thing. In God, Love and Wisdom are united; and from this union proceeds his Spirit, influence or power. In the sun of nature, heat and light are united; whence proceed the rays of invigorating life to vivify the earth, making it both "a bright and a breathing world." So (as is the case in creation) by the proper union of earth and water, under the influence of the sun's heat and light, and these again being filled by Jehovah's creative power, the world is made to teem with plenty, and to produce a rich abundance for the support of animal life.

In Scripture, then, the earth, by correspondence, is an emblem of the mind or heart, which is the ground into which the spiritual seeds of Divine knowledge are sown. Water signifies truth as to its cleansing and nutritious properties; while the fruits of the earth, with all their varieties, denote all the works of charity and love, which appear in the general conduct and outward life. It is by these that the mental plain is richly adorned with fruits of love and flowers of wisdom.

Correspondence of the Three Kingdoms of Nature.

Again, the world is divided into three portions called kingdoms, namely, the animal, vegetable and mineral. Neither of these could exist separately or alone; they must all be united and form a one. The mineral is the lowest in order, and the foundation of the other two. Without this there could be no vegetable, and without the vegetable, the animal could not exist. It may, perhaps, be said that the mineral could exist without, and independent of the other two; but in reply it is urged that, in this case, it would be quite useless; and it surely would be no mark of wisdom to suppose that God ever created a useless thing. The animal kingdom, because it possesses the greatest portion of life, is the highest in order; the vegetable is the next, and the mineral the lowest.

In Scripture, then, according to the law of correspondence, all the objects of the animal kingdom, as beasts, birds and creeping things, are mentioned in reference to the affections in man, both good and bad; the good are denoted by the clean, gentle and useful animals, and the bad by the wild, ferocious and cruel. With this view we at once discover the reason why the disciples are called sheep and lambs, and the Lord himself the Lamb without spot;—why He is also called a Shepherd who leads his flock into green pastures beside the still waters, and why those who follow the Divine guidance are said to "grow as calves of the stall." We also learn why none but clean animals were to be offered in sacrifice, instructing us by this ritual, that no unclean or polluted affection was to intrude in the solemnities of worship. We see, too, why the wicked are described by bears, wolves, foxes, dogs, and the like, and why in spiritual things the obtuseness of their intellectual faculties arising from the impurity of their affections, is described in Scripture by owls, bats and birds of night.

The objects of the vegetable kingdom, as trees, plants and shrubs of all kinds, are mentioned in reference to the growing thoughts and perceptions of the mind, with all their vast varieties, both true and false. Thus an evil heart produces, spiritually, a barren intellect; the former is aptly shadowed forth by dry and worthless ground, the latter by thorns and thistles, the legitimate but wretched productions of a barren soil. On the other hand, a purified heart produces a luminous intellect; the former is represented by the richly cultivated and fertile ground, and the latter by luxuriant fruit-bearing trees, by the useful plants and odoriferous flowers. Here again we see the reason why the Scriptures so frequently speak of gardens, groves and paradises; of cultivated fields waving with corn "ripe already to the harvest;" of all kinds of luxuriance, beauty and fertility; and why they as frequently speak of deserts, stony places and barren land, with their worthless productions. The one is descriptive of man in a state of spiritual cultivation, and the other of his mentally barren condition, his misery and desolation.

While, then, these spiritual conditions of mind as to affection and thought, are described by the objects of the animal and vegetable kingdoms, those of the mineral shadow forth the outward actions of the life, as being fixed and rendered permanent. The good are denoted by gold, silver and precious stones; the indifferent and bad by the baser minerals, as tin, lead, common pebbles and the dust of the balance. Here we may see the meaning of the passage, "I will turn my hand upon thee, and purely purge away thy dross, and take away all thy tin" (Isa. i. 25); also of these words, "For brass I will bring gold, and for iron I will bring silver, and for wood brass, and for stones iron." (Isa. lx. 17.)

The Creator, in his wisdom, has made all things to speak of his goodness and to declare his power. All creation, by the law of correspondence, shadows forth the glory of Jehovah, exhibiting beauty and symmetry in the perfection of his works. In the bright light of Revelation, the wisdom of Jehovah shines pre-eminently grand; and to behold this, to have a clear perception of those glories which beam therefrom, is a privilege so exalted that with it nothing can be compared. Man, whom the Scripture declares to have been created in the image and likeness of God, does, both by his bodily and mental constitution, shadow forth the glory and beauty of Jehovah.

In God we discern, because revealed in his Word, three essential properties which make up the fulness of Godhead—Love, Wisdom, and proceeding Life. In created man, as the image and likeness, this trine or three-fold order exists both in soul and body. The soul of man consists of two faculties, will and understanding—the former receptive of love from God, and therefore the seat of his affections and passions; the latter receptive of wisdom, and thus the seat of all his thoughts and intellectual powers. The union of these two produces his spirit of operative power, which is shown forth in all his words, actions and general life. In the organized body, which is the instrument in and by which the soul, as the living man, shows forth intelligence and power, we observe the same harmonious order. The two principal organs of the body, as a whole, and upon which the activity of all others depend, are the heart and lungs; the one purifies and sends forth living blood for the renovation and health of the system, and the other inhales and breathes the vital air. These two, again, acting unitedly in a healthy state, produce the third principle or effect, which is exhibited in all the pleasures and phenomena of life. The heart, therefore, is mentioned in Scripture to signify something relating to love, desire or affection both good and bad, pure and impure, and the organs of respiration, or soul, spirit and breath, something relating to truth, wisdom or knowledge. This tri-une order which originates in God, is exhibited in all creation; and hence arises that law of mutual relationship or correspondence between the whole. Thus pure Christianity, which diffuses love, wisdom, health and life throughout the whole spiritual creation, may properly be termed the heart and lungs of the world.

In the globe upon which we live, the same order is apparent: it consists of hard substances, as rocks and metals; of soft, as vegetable earth; and of fluids, as waters: so the human body is made up of its bones, corresponding to rocks; its flesh, to vegetable earth; and the blood, as the circulating fluid, answering to the waters which circulate through the earth for the refreshment of all its parts. In the material world, nothing is more unsightly than bare rocks without any vegetable production of grass, flowers or fruits; in respect to man, nothing is more frightful than a mere skeleton without any flesh, sinews and skin; and in religion, nothing presents so barren a view as faith alone, without any of the fruits of holiness, purity and life. This state, in Scripture, is represented by the dry bones, to which the voice of Revelation speaks and says: "O ye dry bones, hear the Word of the Lord." (Ezek. xxxvii. 4.)

Now all this perfect order, both in the material and moral worlds, shows the infinite wisdom of the great Designer who, by an immutable law of creation, has done all things well; so that the goodness, wisdom and beauty of Jehovah are everywhere seen both in his works and Word. Who, then, can behold these things unmoved? Who can restrain the fulness of his heart from bursting forth in the language of David and saying: "Oh that men would praise the Lord for his goodness, and for his wonderful works to the children of men!" (Ps. cvii. 8.)

CHAPTER III.

THE LORD'S WORD MAGNIFIED ABOVE ALL HIS NAME—COMPARISONS BETWEEN THE LITERAL AND SPIRITUAL SENSES OF THE WORD OF GOD; ILLUSTRATIONS OF—THE USE OF CORRESPONDENCE IN EXPLAINING DIFFICULT PASSAGES OF SCRIPTURE—ITS USE IN EXPLAINING THE MIRACLES AND PARABLES—CORRESPONDENCE OF THE SUN, MOON AND STARS—THE ISRAELITISH JOURNEY FROM EGYPT TO CANAAN—EXPLANATION OF VARIOUS SCRIPTURE PHRASES—EZEKIEL'S VISION OF HOLY WATERS—TWO MIRACLES ILLUSTRATED BY THE LAW OF CORRESPONDENCE, VIZ.: "DEATH IN THE POT," AND THE RESTORATION OF SIGHT TO THE MAN BORN BLIND, BY WASHING IN THE POOL OF SILOAM—THE TRIBUTE MONEY FOUND IN THE FISH'S MOUTH—RELIGION AND SCIENCE CONNECTED—CONCLUSION.

THE Psalmist in addressing the Divine Being, says: "Thou hast magnified thy Word above all thy name" (cxxxviii. 2). Now the Lord's Word is truly magnified, because it treats of infinitely higher subjects than what appears to the natural sight in the sense of the letter. In its literal form and clothing it may appear to the superficial reader to be loose and disconnected; in this appearance it is compared to sand: but the spiritual truths which are stored up within, are called "treasures hid in the sand." (Deut. xxxiii. 19.) With respect to the truth it contains generally and as a whole, which forms the base or foundation upon which every Christian rests his hope, it is called a rock; but in allusion to its spiritual truth with the delights thereof, as applicable to all the states of human life, it is the *honey* within the rock. To every true Christian who contemplates the Word with a holy reverence, the Lord gives "to suck honey out of the rock, and oil out of the flinty rock." (Deut. xxxii. 13.) The Word with respect to its beauty and fertility, even in the letter, is compared to and called a Paradise; and inasmuch as it is God-breathed, a Divine and not a human production, it is the Paradise of God: but with respect to the celestial nature of its interior contents, it is the hidden manna within the Paradise, of which every one who really desires may eat and live forever.

The Literal and Spiritual Senses Compared.

The Word in reference to its literal construction, appears, especially to the careless reader, not only to contain various doctrines, but even such as appear to be opposed to each other; in this sense it is represented by Joseph's coat of many colors: but as to its interior spirit and life, which is one uniform whole, it is the living Joseph himself, who, as the representative of the Lord, though despised and hated by his externally-minded brethren, goes before to provide food for them, and to save nations from famine and death.

The Word, again, as to its letter, appears to be so constructed as to be capable of division and sub-division, and is represented by those outer garments of the Lord which, at his crucifixion and rejection, the soldiers who denote those who contend for the letter but not for the spirit of Revelation, divided amongst them; while the fact of each man looking at, and contending for, the superiority of his own part, without any reference to the others, appears to be the origin of all those opposing sectarian doctrines, whose advocates wrangle and fight about comparative trifles; thus straining out gnats and swallowing camels; while the inward spirit of its contents is alike unknown to and disregarded by all. But the spiritual sense of Revelation, which is one unbroken and uninterrupted system of Divine instruction relating to all the affections, thoughts and states of human life, and to their progressions into higher degrees of perfection, is represented by the Lord's inner garment, the vest without seam woven from the top throughout. This vest, because it was without seam, the soldiers agreed not to rend, but to cast lots for it whose it should be. This fact instructs us that the Divine Providence is ever watchful over the Word of Revelation; that its inward life may not be injured, but that it may be kept whole and entire, they cast lots for it whose it should be. The lot, which excludes all human interference in spiritual matters, has undoubtedly fallen, not upon those who deny but upon those who admit a Divine spirituality to be contained in the Word throughout, and that it is unbroken, that is, without seam. It has fallen upon that church and dispensation of spiritual truth which, in Rev. xxi., is designated the Holy City New Jerusalem which descended from God out of heaven. Here the sacred vest is preserved whole and entire, which will be the means of again bringing together all the Lord's outer garments, or those literal truths which, in connection with the spirit of Revelation, are harmonious and beautiful;

and which, by the law of correspondence, are the legitimate coverings of the Lord as the Word.

Admitting the spirituality of the Word, and applying this immutable law of correspondence as the only true Key of knowledge in the illustration of its contents, how easy are all its truths unfolded, and how grandly do they rise up before us, displaying, in one rich and lovely scene, the providence and wisdom of God. Is the Divine Truth generally, in its literal form, called a rock? a foundation upon which to build our hopes and expectations? then do we see the important instruction figured forth by Moses striking the rock in the wilderness, and the waters gushing out to supply the thirst of the people. To strike is to have communication with; the rock is the Word as a whole; hence the act of striking the rock teaches us to communicate with the Word of God, and that from such striking or communication, an abundance of truths, as the waters of life, will quickly flow for the cleansing of all interior impurities, as well as for the nutritious improvement and health of the soul. This is purely an apostolic interpretation, founded upon that immutable law according to which all Scripture is written, and by which alone it can be explained.

The apostle Paul, speaking of the various things which happened to the Israelites, says: "Now all these things happened unto them for ensamples; and they are written for our admonition, upon whom the ends of the world are come" (1 Cor. x. 11); and speaking of the water from the rock, he says, they "did all drink the same spiritual drink, for they drank of that spiritual Rock that followed them, and that Rock was Christ" (ver. 4). Christ, then, is the Rock, because He is the Word—the living Truth which follows us in our journey to the heavenly Canaan. We drink of that spiritual Rock, for from "his fulness have all we received and grace for grace." (John i. 16.)

When it is clearly seen that all existences in nature are types and emblems shadowing forth the realities of heaven, and that Scripture mentions these in reference to spiritual realities, so that by visible things the invisible are brought forth, then, indeed, it will be clearly seen that the Lord has magnified his Word. With this knowledge the Book of God becomes unsealed, and its sacred contents presented to view. Now Scripture declares man to have been created in the image and likeness of God. No one can doubt the truth of this statement; if so created, he must, in his very constitution, shadow forth the perfections of his Creator. There is, therefore, a mutual relationship between all his mental powers and bodily organs; and in Scripture the latter are put to signify the former.

The soul, or living man, receives immediately all his powers from the Lord, while the body receives, mediately, its strength and power of action from the soul. That which gives to the organic structure both its form and power is the immortal man or soul; and this again receives all his power from the Lord. Hence in Scripture, the bodily organs are mentioned to signify the powers, principles and faculties of the mind. This, when seen and acknowledged, will explain all those parts of the Word where the bodily organs are mentioned. Thus by the head, the supreme part, is signified wisdom and intelligence; by the eye, the understanding; the ear denotes obedience; the nostrils, the grateful perception of what is good and true; the lips, tongue, and organs of speech generally, the acknowledgment and confession of the Lord; the arms and hands, the powers of the mind; and the legs and feet, the external life and general conduct. Again, most of the bodily organs run in pairs; and where this is not outwardly observable, it is so by a more minute inspection. The reason of this is that there is a close correspondence between the two essential properties of Deity, which are love and wisdom, and the forms receptive of these in man.

For the reception of Divine Love and Wisdom, the two mental faculties of will and understanding were created, the corresponding bodily organs of which are: in the head, the two hemispheres of the brain, called the cerebellum and cerebrum; and in the body, the heart and lungs. In respect to the organs being in pairs, we may mention the eyes, ears, nostrils, cheeks, lips, shoulders, arms, hands, legs, and feet. All the organs on the right side of the body possess a greater degree of power than those on the left, and in Scripture are mentioned in reference to the *will*, and to somewhat of power as to good or evil, while those on the left are named in reference to the understanding, bearing some relation either to truth or falsity. This knowledge will explain all those passages of Scripture where the bodily organs are named.

Correspondence explains difficult Passages of Scripture.

The Lord says: "When thou doest alms, let not thy left hand know what thy right hand doeth." (Matt. vi. 3.) Literally neither the left hand nor the right hand can know anything about alms-giving. To do alms from the right hand is to exercise power in their distribution from the love of good, and from a pure motive: but to impart that motive to the left hand first, or before the deed is done, is to give alms from truth, in order that they may appear in the light and be known abroad; thus the alms are not done in secret, but for the sake of appearing, and for some selfish gratification. In this case there may be a worldly reward, but none from our Father in the heavens. The deed has been done from a sinister motive, from the left hand; it is utterly barren of all true religion, all spiritual reward.

Again, the Lord says: "If thy right eye offend thee, pluck it out and cast it from thee;" and "if thy right hand offend thee, cut it off and cast it from thee." (Matt. v. 29, 30.) Here by the eye is meant the understanding, and by the right eye a knowledge of truth from interior goodness. But as the offence of the right eye is described, it is the understanding of truth perverted by evils of life, whence come offence, spiritual crime and death. To pluck this out, is to cease from such state of perversion, while to cast it from you is to utterly hate and abhor it. Similar observations will apply to the right hand, only with this difference, that the *hand* is an emblem of power, and the right hand power from goodness of heart: but the offending right hand is the power derived from evil and its degrading pursuits; this, too, must be cut off and cast away, be utterly abhorred and hated, or heaven with its glories can neither be entered nor seen.

Another important lesson is taught us in the fact of the Lord sending out his apostles and disciples by two and two, and giving them power over unclean spirits. (Mark vi. 7.) This was done to teach us that the two faculties of will and intellect must be engaged unitedly in the work—that the love and practice of truth, with the knowledge of it, must go together. When these two are united, a power is given over all the unclean affections and perverted principles of the mind; so that true religion grows in the soul, and heaven is formed within; hence we read that the disciples who were thus sent out by two and two, returned and said: "Lord, even the devils are subject unto us through thy name." (Luke x. 17.) When the will and intellect are united so as to progress in the regeneration together, everything then prayed for and desired is, that spiritual improvement may increase, which will explain these words of the Lord: "Again I say unto you, that if two of you shall agree on earth as touching anything that they shall ask, it shall be done for them of my Father which is in heaven." (Matt. xviii. 19.)

The Lord condescended to wash his disciples' feet, and said: "If I, your Lord and Master, wash your feet, ye ought also to wash one another's feet." Here by a knowledge of the spiritual signification of the feet, this passage opens in all its value and importance. The feet denote the external life and general conduct in the world. To wash is to cleanse and purify. All purification of soul, is effected by the truths of Revelation; for these are the cleansing waters which are from the Lord, and applied by Him. Without this *outward* purification, there can be no evidence of an *inward;* for the language of the Lord is: "If I wash thee not, thou hast no part with me." If we feel the necessity of this spiritual cleansing, we shall, like Peter, address the Saviour and say: "Lord, not my feet only, but also my hands and my head:" not only that part of my life which is outward and external, as being connected with the world, but also the powers of my soul, with all that is high, supreme and inmost. We ought, then, if we call Jesus Christ, Master and Lord, to wash each other's feet; that is, in the true spirit of Christianity, to assist in cleansing and regulating each other's outward life and conduct, that so the purity within may be exhibited by the cleanness without.

We have already shown that the human body, as a whole, as well as all its parts, members and organs, are mentioned in Scripture in reference to the soul, and to its various faculties, principles and powers. If this be a truth, of which, judging from the examples already given, there can hardly remain a rational doubt, we have only, under Divine guidance, to follow on with the same chain of reasoning, in order to be convinced that the Word of God is truly wonderful, and that it is to every spiritual traveller to Zion, his faithful and steady conductor —his pillar of cloud by day; his pillar of fire by night.

Explains the Miracles and Parables.

We read in Scripture of the poor, the maimed, the halt, the lame, blind and diseased; of the deaf and dumb, of the captives and the dead. Now the coming of the Lord was effectually to release the human race from these maladies and diseases. He came to set the captives free, to give sight to the blind, to preach the glories of his kingdom to the poor, to restore health to the diseased, to unstop the ears of the deaf, to make the lame man leap as the hart, and the tongue of the dumb to sing; He came to quicken the dead to life by proclaiming the acceptable year of the Lord. If we suppose that these diseases, maladies and imperfections are to be confined to those of the body, we not only deceive ourselves, but we reduce the Word of God to a dead letter; and if the miracles wrought by Jesus Christ are to be confined merely to the restoration to health of a few sick people, and to the raising of some three or four individuals from the dead, then the miracles become deprived of their vast importance, spirituality and use. The miracles of Jesus Christ were not done merely to show his power in the days of his flesh, and then to cease; but they were especially done to set forth his eternal power and Godhead, by showing, spiritually, that He is performing like miracles for the benefit of the human race in every age and generation of the world.

The law of correspondence can alone open these subjects in their true import, and prove beyond all doubt that the testimonies of the Lord are wonderful. By this law all diseases, maladies and imperfections of body, are named in reference to perversions and imperfections of mind; while the curing of these denotes the restoration of the soul to spiritual health and soundness. Thus by the poor are meant, not those who have little or no worldly wealth, but those who are *poor in spirit,* who have not the truth of heaven, but who ardently desire it. It is to these (whether rich or poor in a worldly sense) that the Gospel is preached, and these are they whom the Lord fills with good things. The rich are those who are in raptures with their own self-derived knowledge, whose worldly, carnal wisdom leads them to despise being led by the truths of Revelation. These are the rich in their own estimation, who because they receive not wisdom from God, are described as those whom the Lord sends empty away.

This view will open to us a most important truth, that we are not to make a spiritual estimation of man, either from his worldly wealth or worldly poverty. It will show clearly what cannot be rationally denied, that the lords and nobles of the land, if lovers and seekers of what is good and true, may be among that class of persons whom the Scriptures call poor; while the daily laborer, priding himself in his own spurious knowledge and vanity, while at the same time he is neglecting the spiritual duties of religion, may be among those whom the Scripture designates the rich. This will fully explain the Lord's words, "Blessed be ye poor; for yours is the kingdom of God." (Luke vi. 20.) And again, "It is easier for a camel to go through the eye of a needle, than for a rich man to enter into the kingdom of God." (Matt. xix. 24.)

The lame, halt, diseased and maimed, signify those whose inward evils of life ruin their spiritual constitution, so that they can make no progress nor walk in the Divine life; they stumble in the way and halt in their purposes. By the Lord healing these maladies, we are instructed that when the truth is received and applied to the life, their inward pollutions are removed, and restoration to spiritual health is effected. Then, too, the tongue, as the organ of speech, by which is denoted acknowledgment and confession of the Lord, and which before was dumb or silent in the praise of God, becomes loosed, and breaks forth in songs of praise. It is then that the man comes into a luminous and happy frame of mind; he has changed his own filthy robes—his false and insane persuasions, for the white and shining garments of heaven—the pure truths of Revelation; he is then found "sitting at the feet of Jesus, clothed, and in his right mind." (Luke viii. 35.) This renovation of state is effected when Messiah's kingdom rules in the mind of man; for "then shall the lame man leap as a hart, and the tongue of the dumb shall sing." (Isa. xxxv. 6.) The former wilderness state of his understanding shall pass away, together with the dry, arid condition of his will, while the truths of Revelation, as the waters of life, shall break out as streams in the desert.

It is in consequence of the spiritual signification of the maimed, lame and blind, as denoting evils and ignorance of spirit, that in the Jewish church, the rituals of which were all representations of good things to come, no person was allowed to minister at the altar, or perform the ceremonies of worship, who had any blemish of body, such as being diseased, lame, deformed or blind. (Lev. xxi. 16–24.) This Divine law was written to instruct us that the pure worship of God cannot proceed from spiritual ignorance and deformity of mind.

The blind and deaf are the objects of the Lord's mercy. He came to open the blind eyes, and to unstop the ears of the deaf. Here, again, the true law of Scripture interpretation affords the means of acquiring a correct explanation. By the eye is meant the understanding, and by the ear, hearkening and obedience of life. The blind eye is the intellect wrapt in spiritual ignorance; the deaf ear, carelessness of, and contempt for, all heavenly instruction, whence arise disobedience and a life of carnality and false pleasure. But when the eye becomes enlightened by the truths of heaven, and the ear lends a willing obedience to the voice of God, then the maladies are removed, and the things of God and heaven are seen and heard.

Those whose affections are bound down to the perishable things of the world, who are by false, atheistical, or other persuasions, led astray from the pure path of life; these are bound in the hard fetters of a mentally slavish bondage, and are called prisoners and captives: they are, as the Scripture expresses it, led captive by the devil at his will. Now nothing can set them free from this captivity, but the truth as it is in Jesus; and if the truth shall set them free, they shall be free indeed. Hence one of the grand objects of the Lord's coming, was to give "liberty to the captives."

Those, again, in whom the life of heaven has become extinct, who have no spiritual affection for purity and wisdom, these are called *dead*. They are dead to all the living joys of heaven, and grovel in the uncleanness of sensuality. But even these, at the voice of the Lord, or when truth finds its way into their hearts, and is therein received and loved, shall rise up from their deathly condition—from that state of death in trespasses and sins, and spring upwards to that of life, righteousness and peace. These restorations are the real effects of the reign of Christ in his church, and they are even now in this day taking place; which will explain clearly this saying of our Lord: "Verily, verily, I say unto you, the hour is coming, and *now is*, when the dead shall hear the voice of the Son of God: and they that hear shall live." (John v. 25.) It is to these spiritual evidences of the reign of Christ that the Lord alludes, when, in answer to John's disciples who asked Him the question, "Art thou He that should come, or do we look for another?" He replied: "Go and show John again those things which ye do hear and see; the blind receive their sight, and the lame walk; the lepers are cleansed, and the deaf hear; the dead are raised up, and the poor have the Gospel preached to them; and blessed is he whosoever shall not be offended in me." (Matt. xi. 5, 6.)

These, then, are the grand subjects taught in the Book of Life. The truths of Revelation are the sacred testimonies of God. They clearly describe all the varieties of human affection and thought, as well as every man's growth in wisdom, righteousness and peace. Surely, then, we must acknowledge with David, that the testimonies of the Lord are wonderful.

Correspondence of the Sun, Moon and Stars.

The wonders of the Book of God will further appear, as we contemplate the vast scene around us, and view the grand theatre of creation as reflecting by its objects the goodness, wisdom and power of the Creator. The Scriptures call upon us to contemplate these things, and as such they must be designed to teach us the spiritual matters of eternity. The prophet invites us to reflection, and says: "Lift up your eyes on high, and behold who hath created these things." (Isa. xl. 26.) All created things speak, in their uses, the power of the Creator, and declare his wonders to the people. If we lift up our eyes on high, we observe the sun, moon and stars as the brightest objects in nature. Now these are frequently mentioned in Scripture; and this is the reason why we are called upon to lift up our eyes on high, that we may contemplate their relative uses, and draw forth the spiritual lessons they teach.

The sun shines by its own light, and borrows nothing from any other created object; it is, therefore, in nature, the bright emblem of the Lord of heaven, as the never varying and everlasting Sun of righteousness, who borrows nothing from any other being, but constantly dispenses his Divine heat and light—his love and wisdom—for the life and health of that creation He himself has produced.

The moon has no light in itself, but reflects only that which she has borrowed from the sun. The moon, in Scripture, is therefore put to signify the Church of God, which has no light or truth of her own, but reflects only that wisdom she has borrowed or received from her Lord.

The stars, from their distance and the small portions of light they transmit to us, are emblems of all those principles of knowledge with which the mind is gifted, and by which it expands to higher degrees of perception.

The essential property of the Divine Being is LOVE. "God is love." This is represented by the heat of the sun, and his Wisdom by its light. Thus God is the fountain of all being. In reference to man, the sun is mentioned in Scripture to signify *love* received from, and directed to, the Lord; the moon, his pure faith which forms the church in him; and the stars are all the varieties of knowledge which beautify and ornament his mind. This will at once explain all those Scriptures where the sun, moon and stars are mentioned. All things of love, faith and knowledge are to be ascribed to the Lord, and dedicated to his praise; for man has nothing of his own. Hence the language of David, "Praise him sun and moon; praise him all ye stars of light!" All men are created with the two faculties of will and understanding; the former is the known receptacle of love from God, which will explain this passage: "In them hath He set a tabernacle for the sun." (Ps. xix. 4.)

How do the Scriptures describe the end and desolation of the church, when by corruption and false doctrine the love of self supplants the love of God? when ignorance supplies the place of a pure enlightened faith, and when all the vast varieties of spiritual knowledge perish and decay? They describe this state in their own language of correspondence. The Lord, speaking of this spiritual desolation, says: "Immediately after the tribulation of those days, shall the sun be darkened and the moon shall not give her light, and the stars shall fall from heaven, and the powers of the heavens shall be shaken." (Matt. xxiv. 29.) When in the church there is no celestial love to the Lord, the sun is darkened; when there is no pure faith in Him as the One Lord of heaven, the moon gives no light; and when all spiritual knowledges fail, the stars fall from heaven; and then it is that the powers of the heavens—the internals of the church and of man—become shaken to their very centre.

The facts in nature and in religion are, by correspondence, so true to each other, that it is next to impossible to mistake their meaning. In nature, if the sun were to be darkened, the moon could give no light; for she has none to give but what she borrows from the sun. So in the church, if there be no love, there can be no faith; and where both love and faith are absent, there can be no heavenly knowledges. When the church is in a high state of glory, how different is then the description. John the Revelator in describing it, says: "And there appeared a great wonder in heaven; a woman clothed with the *sun*, and the *moon* under her feet, and upon her head a crown of twelve *stars*." (Rev. xii. 1.) The woman denotes the church, as to the affectionate reception of all that comes from the Lord, and which constitutes her unfading glory. She is imbued with celestial love—clothed with the sun: she is grounded in a pure enlightened faith in the one Lord God the Saviour—the moon under her feet: she is possessed of a rich fulness of knowledge including all varieties, which are the twelve stars upon her head, and which form her everlasting crown and diadem. Surely these descriptions are grand, beautiful and correct! Our affections are touched by them; our reason assents to their truth, and both united urge the lips of every true Christian to speak the language of David, and say: "The testimonies of the Lord are wonderful, therefore doth my soul keep them." (Ps. cxix. 129.)

By the science of correspondence, this true key of knowledge, every part of Divine Revelation, to those who love the truth for its own sake, is rendered plain and easy to be understood; but to the evil, the careless and vicious, this science can offer no charms, for it enters too minutely into the secret recesses of the heart; and while it lays bare the polluting degradation of all sinful lusts, it unravels the mysterious web of falsity and deceit, showing that "the secret of the Lord is (*only*) with those who fear Him." (Ps. xxv. 14.) True repentance is the first duty of man; and he who refuses to perform this first work, cannot expect to be made acquainted with the secrets of the Most High. Let us apply this key to some further illustrations.

The prophet Zechariah states, that " this shall be the plague wherewith the Lord shall smite all the people that have fought against Jerusalem; their flesh shall consume away while they stand upon their feet, and their eyes shall consume away in their holes, and their tongue shall consume away in their mouth." (Zech. xiv. 12.) Jerusalem, the city of Palestine where stood the temple in which worship was celebrated to Jehovah as the true God, is everywhere mentioned in Scripture to signify the church of the Lord, in which the love of God in true devotional worship is felt, and his truth seen. The church emphatically denoted by Jerusalem, is the city of God and the tabernacle of the Most High. There still flows the river—an abundance of divine truth which makes glad the city. There God himself is still in the midst of her, and she can never be moved. To fight against this city, is to oppose, both in thought and practice, the love, purity, wisdom and truth which form the true church both in the world and in the human soul. From this madness of opposition to all that is pure, holy and true, what can be expected to arise but a plague? what but a plague and pestilence more dreadful in its effects than any that can happen to the body? It is a plague that reaches the soul—the real and conscious man; and which describes the miserable state of mental desolation by the outward appearance of the body. The condition of those who fight against Jerusalem is, as to their spiritual existence, truly wretched; and is here represented by the consuming away of the flesh, of the eyes in their holes, and of the tongue in their mouth.

The true spiritual church of God, the holy city Jerusalem, is filled with the highest, richest blessings of which the human mind can be receptive. It infuses love, charity and benevolence into the human will; it enlightens the understanding with truths of the highest order, makes life a blessing, and throws a sacred charm throughout all creation. Here, in the Holy City, we are taught that God is our common

Father, that we are all brethren, and that every true delight follows the pursuit of virtue. Here, again, the understanding is enlightened with truths that raise us up above the clods of the earth; we are taught that God is immutable and good; that man is free; that the soul, the real man, is immortal; and here resistless demonstration shows that there is another and a better world. Those whose affections are fixed upon the Lord, are described in the Word of God, not with their flesh consumed away, with their eyes wasted in their sockets, and their tongues consumed in their mouths; but as altogether comely, fair and beautiful, as fat and flourishing, with their eyes opened, keen, penetrating and uplifted; and with their tongues employed in tasting of the bread of life, and loosened to speak of and sing the praises of the Most High. Now the description of those who fight against Jerusalem is the very reverse of this; their flesh, eyes and tongue consume away. When the spiritual sense of these words is seen, how clear, but how truly distressing will the description appear. Here three distinct terms are used, the flesh, the eyes and the tongue; these, belonging to such as fight against Jerusalem, wither away, so that nothing is left but a skeleton of dry bones.

The flesh of the human body, in comparison with the bones, possesses the greater portion of life, and in Scripture is mentioned to signify all that belongs to the superior faculty of the mind, the will. The flesh of the unregenerate man denotes all that kind of spurious goodness which is not derived from the Lord, but drawn from his own impure desires, and which can yield no spiritual consolation to the soul, but is consumed as soon as brought forth. The prophet Isaiah thus describes how unsatisfying this is, and of such a man he says: "He shall snatch on the right hand and be hungry, and shall eat on the left hand and not be satisfied; they shall eat, every man, the flesh of his own arm" (ix. 20). The prophet Jeremiah also, speaking of the unregenerate, says: "Cursed is the man that trusteth in man, and maketh *flesh* his arm" (xvii. 5). All the good that cometh down from God out of heaven, is the bread of life, and this the Lord calls his flesh: "The bread that I will give is my flesh, which I will give for the life of the world." (John vi. 51.) Of this flesh, or Divine goodness, man should eat, or receive into his affections, that so his soul may be nourished to eternal life. The Lord's words are important: "Except ye eat the flesh of the Son of Man, and drink his blood, ye have no life in you" (John vi. 53); that is, unless the Lord's love be received in the will, and his spiritual truth, denoted by his blood, in the understanding, there can be no angelic life—no heaven within.

Those who fight against Jerusalem, whose impurity of life offers a determined opposition to all that is celestially good and pure, can have no heavenly beauty or comeliness; all that is good in them decays under the plague and pestilence of selfish desires; all the goodness of heaven in them withers away—their flesh consumes while they stand upon their feet; they have a name by which they live and are dead.

Another most awful state of their spiritual degradation is further described by "their eyes shall consume away in their holes." If ever there was a true description given of the wicked man, this is one; but though true, it is awfully distressing. By the eye is meant the understanding; that being as much the eye of the soul, as the organ of vision is of the body. The bright eye is the understanding enlightened; the blind eye, the understanding closed against the reception of the truths of Revelation; and the consumed eye, the understanding perished and lost. Where there is no love for the things of heaven, there can be no true knowledge of them, because the man takes no delight in them. In respect to heavenly things, when the will is depraved the understanding is dark; this life persisted in, is fighting against Jerusalem. This must produce the decay of all spiritual knowledge,—the perishing of the intellect. Where there is no good, there can be no apprehension of truth; where there is no flesh, the eyes will consume away in their holes. This will be followed by the last sad state of degradation—"their tongue shall consume away in their mouth."

The tongue to the human body performs a double office, that of *taste* and *speech*. With respect to the former, it denotes the relish, appetite and desire for all that is good and pure; and with respect to the latter, confession and acknowledgment of the Lord: but when this is consumed away, we are instructed that there is then no relish for anything of a heavenly kind, no acknowledgment or confession of the Lord. The man is spiritually ruined. There is nothing good in him—his flesh is consumed; no understanding of truth—his eyes are consumed; no relish for the food of heaven, no acknowledgment of the Lord—his tongue is consumed away in his mouth. He is spiritually nothing but a skeleton of dry bones without any sinews, flesh or skin.

The Journey from Egypt to Canaan explained.

The science of correspondence, this master-key to correct theological knowledge, renders the Scriptures valuable beyond conception; for by exhibiting them in their true light, it shows their contents to be applicable to all the varied states of human life, both as to affection and thought. They are then discovered to be a present and constant Revelation, displaying at one view the religious states of all men, as well the evil as the good. They are seen to contain accurate descriptions of those trials, temptations and conflicts through which all must pass in their march from the earthly to the heavenly state.

With this view, the journeyings of the Israelites from Egypt to Canaan become exceedingly important; for in this case the names of the places mentioned in their journey from Egypt whence they made their exodus, together with their wanderings and encampments in the wilderness, their murmurings and promises of fidelity, their victories and defeats, with every other circumstance connected therewith, until their final possession of the land, are all representations of the corresponding progressive states of temptation, doubt and mental wanderings through which the sincere Christian passes in his spiritual journey from a state of earthly-mindedness, denoted by Egypt as the land of bondage, to that of celestial peace and rest enjoyed after the conflict has subsided, and which is shadowed forth by the land of Canaan flowing with milk and honey. To give a minute description of all these, comes not within the intention of this work; it would require a separate volume to do it justice.

Suffice it to say, that the land of Canaan, including all the boundaries of Israel's dominions, represents the church which is the Lord's kingdom in the world; every place having its spiritual signification corresponding to its situation with respect to its distance from, or proximity to, Jerusalem as the capital of the land. Now the extension of the land of Canaan, by which is meant the church, was from the river of Egypt even to the river Euphrates of Assyria. This appears from the covenant made with Abram, where it is said, "Unto thy seed have I given this land, from the river of Egypt, unto the great river, the river Euphrates." (Gen. xv. 18.) Hence it is said that Solomon "reigned over all kingdoms from the river [Euphrates] unto the land of the Philistines, and unto the border of Egypt." (1 Kings iv. 21.) All those places which are not included within the dominions of Israel denote those states of mind in which the careless and unthinking dwell, regardless of those spiritual truths of Revelation which bring life and immortality to light, which yield purity and wisdom to the mind.

Those who are carnally minded, lovers to distraction of the false pleasures of sense, to the total exclusion of the spiritual pleasures of truth, are, in Scripture language, on the outside of the boundaries of Israel; they are dwellers in Egypt, the land of bondage, and like the captive Israelites their sensual condition compels them to hard drudgery in mortar and in brick; they are required to complete the tale of bricks while they are refused straw. As the Israelites were infested and tasked by the Egyptians, so these are enslaved by evils and falsities of every kind. In this state they are made to produce *bricks*, or arguments that are fictitious and false, while they are themselves compelled to search for the *straw*, the lowest principles of scientific knowledge, in order to complete their work. But even here the Divine Truth reaches them, and speaks in the same language as that which Moses addressed to Pharaoh, and says: "Let my people go that they may serve me." But the ruling principle in that mind which bends to sinful habits, is too apt to return an answer, and in pride or contempt for all that is spiritual, say, as Pharaoh said to Moses, "Who is the Lord that I should obey his voice to let Israel go? I know not the Lord, neither will I let Israel go." (Ex. v. 2.) Out of this ignorant Egyptian bondage man, however, must come, or he shall never possess true liberty, or enjoy the sweets of the heavenly life. He cannot taste the milk and honey of Canaan without leaving the land of Egypt.

Various Scripture Phrases explained.

A knowledge of correspondence proves the Word of God to be a most precious treasure to the Christian mind: its truths become enchanting, and the soul is filled with ecstatic delight. Not a word can be found therein that is not filled with the richest wisdom. However apparently trifling some narratives may appear in the letter, yet when correspondence, this true key of knowledge, is applied, their spiritual sense becomes instantly developed, the scene brightens before us, our personal interest is discovered, and our animated affections urge the lips to say, as Jacob did when he awoke from his dream: "Surely the Lord is in this place, and I knew it not." (Gen. xxviii. 16.) Believe it, kind reader, to be a great truth, that the Holy Word can only become valuable to you, as its sacred narratives are seen to be descriptive of your own spiritual states of affection, thought and life.

We read in Scripture of walking, running, standing and sitting; of going up and down; backward and forward: all these expressions, which literally seem to apply only to the body and to its rest and varied activities, are significative of mental operations, and describe both the rest of the mind and its progressive changes of state. Thus as walking and running in reference to the body, are the successive changes of its place; so in respect to the mind, they denote its spiritual progressions or changes of state. Walking, as being a slower change of place than that of running, if said to be upward or forward, is the progression of the understanding into higher degrees of intelligence and wisdom; but if downward or backward, it is then a receding from truth, followed by a successive entrance into obscurity and ignorance; the lowest degree of which is designated "outer darkness;" while running refers to the more rapid progressions of the will, if upward or forward, into higher states of good; if downward or backward, to lower desires of evil. The good are therefore said to go upward and forward; the evil downward and backward. We are hence taught, "They that wait upon the Lord shall renew their strength; they shall mount up with wings as eagles; they shall run and not be weary; they shall walk and not faint." (Isa. xl. 31.) Here we find that they who wait on the Lord renew their strength by running and walking, to instruct us that there can be no weariness of will or fainting of the understanding, when love prompts quickly to action, and wisdom points the way.

With this interpretation we see the lesson taught us in the fact of the two apostles running together to the Lord's sepulchre, and why it is said that the "other disciple (John) did outrun Peter and came first to the sepulchre." (John xx. 4.) John, the beloved disciple, in his representative character, denotes ardent love; Peter, faith or truth. The will or love is quick and ardent to attain its object; the understanding comparatively slow in its minute inquiries into and deductions of faith. John came up first to the sepulchre, but went in last: Peter came up last, but entered first. This instructs us again, that although the will, in its ardency, arrives early at the end of its desires, yet it is the understanding that first explores the truth, and imparts the knowledge gained to the anxious will. Thus, again, to *sit* before the Lord, is to will and act from Him, consequently to be at peace: to *stand* before Him, is to look to Him and comprehend his Divine will, whence comes a cheerful obedience to Divine precepts, which in Scripture is called walking with God.

In the Word of Life, the expressions "to go in," and "to go out," frequently occur; the former denoting a penetration of the mind into the interior recesses of Love and Wisdom; the latter a going forth, or out, of the energies of the mind into the external and common duties of life. In both these conditions those who enter into the church and place themselves under the Lord's government, are said to be saved; they find true enjoyment in everything, and hence it is written, "they shall go in and out and find pasture." (John x. 9.)

Ezekiel's Vision of Holy Waters.

The Scriptures open with amazing beauty to the thoughtful Christian; but to the mere worldling and sensualist they offer no charms. This will be made apparent by an explanation of the following remarkable vision: "Afterward he brought me again unto the door of the house; and, behold, waters issued out from under the threshold of the house eastward: for the forefront of the house stood toward the east, and the waters came down from under the right side of the house, at the south side of the altar. Then brought he me out of the way of the gate northward, and led me about the way without unto the outer gate by the way that looketh eastward; and, behold, there ran out waters on the right side. And when the man that had the line in his hand went forth eastward, he measured a thousand cubits, and he brought me through the waters; the waters were to the *ankles*. Again he measured a thousand, and brought me through the waters; the waters were to the *knees*. Again he measured a thousand, and brought me through; the waters were to the *loins*. Afterward he measured a thousand, and it was a river that I could not pass over; for the waters were risen, waters to swim in, a river that could not be passed over." (Ezek. xlvii. 1–5.)

In this chapter we have an account of what is generally termed Ezekiel's *vision of holy waters*. It is certainly one of the most singular, interesting and instructive of any contained in this whole prophecy. No one can read it with any degree of thoughtful attention, especially if he attach inspiration and sanctity to the Scriptures, without being convinced that some *spiritual* and heavenly instruction, relative to the *spirit* or *mind* of man must be contained in the literal expressions. If it were not so, of what earthly or heavenly use would it be to know that upon the first measuring, the waters rose to the *ankles*, upon the second to the *knees*, upon the third to the *loins*, and that upon the fourth they so miraculously increased as to become an immense impassable RIVER? We may indeed suppose it to be singularly mysterious and miraculous, and look at it with the gaze of empty wonder. But the mind penetrating no deeper than the shell of knowledge, and resting, though not satisfied, in the mere literal expressions, we shall lose all its internal value and brightness, and be altogether unaffected with its mighty power and truth. Never will the Christian world have any real knowledge of the truths of Revelation, until they begin, with a true energy of mind, to think deep. They must leave off the folly of applying them to "the deeds of days of other years," and apply them to their own present *states* of mind, of affection, thought and life. Then, and then only, will they be able to see the beauties of Revelation's page; then will they joyously extract its honey sweets, then will they draw forth its *spiritual truths* —those living waters from the eternal Fountain of salvation. It is impossible that this vision can be at all interesting to merely worldly-minded men, to those who have no taste or relish for the mental delights of a pure religion; to those whose God is their belly, and their *heaven* the mammon of this world. We can but regret the existence of such states; for surely a few moments of human life cannot be better spent than in the contemplation of those things which connect us with God and heaven, and with the vast concerns of an eternal scene.

The first thing which presents itself for our meditation, is the true and indeed the only signification of the Temple or *House of God*, whence these *waters* which were *measured* and which increased in depth and magnitude at each measuring, issued. In the first verse, the waters are described as issuing out from under the threshold of the house *eastward*, and that they came down from under, from the right side of the house, at the *south* side of the altar. The prophet then states that the man who had the *line* in his hand to measure the depth of the waters, brought him out of the way of the gate *northward*, and led him to the gate that looked toward the *east*, where the waters ran out on the *right side*. Here, on the *right side*, the measuring of the waters took place. At each measuring of a thousand cubits the waters increased. At the first measuring, they were to the *ankles*; on the second, to the *knees*; on the third, to the *loins*; and on the fourth, they were a river that could not be passed over. The instruction contained in this singular prophecy will open to our minds in all its beauty and magnificence, if we carefully and minutely observe the *order* which is here laid down, and by which the prophet was brought to behold the miraculous increase of these waters. But if we are careless in our meditations; if we ramble over the Word of God in the same way that we would over some light and trifling fairy tale; in this case it is impossible that the truths should appear to us; and although the truth in itself is clear and bright, and must forever remain so, yet through our folly the truth in us becomes *dim* and obscure; yea, the light within becomes darkness.

Now the order to which our attention is to be drawn, is that which refers to the *east, south* and *north* quarters, as connected with the prophecy. The waters are said to issue from under the threshold of the house EASTWARD, and to come down from the right side of the house, at the SOUTH of the altar; while the prophet, in order effectually to behold these wonders, was brought out of the way of the gate NORTHWARD! Keeping, then, in mind the order here named, as to the east, south and north quarters, which shall be explained as we proceed, we now return to inquire first into the true signification of the temple, or house of God, whence these waters flowed.

Who, in reading the Holy Scripture, does not at once perceive that by the *temple*, or *house of God*, so frequently mentioned therein, is meant the *church* of the Lord, both militant on earth and triumphant in the heavens. The true church of God is emphatically styled his house, because therein all the solemnities of a pure spiritual worship are celebrated. Here, persons of kindred minds, whose bosoms glow with love to God and each other; whose understandings are enlightened with Truth Divine, and to whom heaven is opened, while each mind is receptive of its blessings,—here in states of charity and peace, retired from the busy bustling scenes of worldly life, they offer up their united, their mingled breath of praise to Him whose love sustains them, whose providence provides, and whose power protects. Each one, in the delightful and free exercise of an unconstrained worship, would be filled with the marrow and fatness of the Lord's house, and would drink of the streams of his pleasures; and each from the *heart*, as from a consecrated altar, would offer up the warm, the sincere aspirations of the soul. It is into this *spiritual* but no less real house of God whence sweetest perfumes rise, that the love and wisdom of God descend to enrich the worshippers, and the house is filled with his glory. Whether we speak of the church generally, as being composed of the myriads of happy beings who worship in sincerity and truth, or speak of it in its application to each person individually, it is still the same thing; for the mind of every man individually, whose worship is sincere and true, who offers to the Father of his being, his best and supreme affections, as the *first* fruits of his moral land, is, in its least form, the church, the temple, and house of the Lord. It is *here*, at the rational faculty of the soul, whence all knowledge enters from the Lord, and issues therefrom—it is here as from the *door* of the mind, the *threshold* of the house, whence these sacred waters flow. In their progress they impart life and health and blessing to every principle, faculty and power of the whole man—from the secret springs of his existence, his hidden motives and thoughts, to the very circumference of his being, terminating in his most trifling act. For it is a pleasing truth, as stated in the eighth verse, that these waters issuing out toward the *east* country, go *down* into the desert, and go into the sea; and it shall come to pass that everything shall live, whithersoever the *waters* shall come.

Who cannot see that this is a clear and certain description of the complete renovation of the whole man by the flow of these waters? from the inmost of his being; from his supreme *love*, whence the waters rise as from the *east* country, and from thence passing into the desert, they fertilize the moral plain, renewing the will and all its affections, as the *ground* in which the seeds of immortal truth are sown; thus making the mind that was once a *desert* in respect to everything heavenly and divine, to rejoice and be glad for them, and to bud and blossom as the rose. These waters passing from the desert, "go into the *sea*," as into the outward boundaries of our existence, imparting a spiritual quality and truth to every kind of external knowledge and science of which the mind is possessed, rendering all these serviceable to the interests of a pure religion, and to the promotion of our eternal interests. Everything must live where these waters come.

There can be no difficulty in ascertaining the true meaning of *waters*, *rivers* and *fountains*, so frequently mentioned in Scripture. These are called the waters of life, and the pure river that flows in the city of our God. What are those things which can renovate the mind of man, satisfy his intellectual thirst, and thus bring life and immortality to light, but the pure, the bright and unspotted *truths* and doctrines of Revelation, which eternally flow from the Lord of life? These spiritual truths, these Divine realities and blessings, which water our mental plain every moment, are what are meant by waters, rivers and fountains, so frequently spoken of in the Word of God; these are signified by the waters coming from the east country, and issuing thence from the *threshold* of the house.

With this knowledge before us of the signification of *waters*, with what beauty and rational conviction do those passages of Scripture where these terms occur, appear to our minds: "Ho! every one that thirsteth, come ye to the *waters*," is the language of the Lord by the prophet Isaiah, lv. 1. Here to *thirst*, is ardently to *desire* the truth for its own sake, the object being to obtain knowledge, that the life of heaven may grow within. Whosoever does thus *desire* or *thirst* may come and *drink* of the water of life freely. "*Come*," is the Divine parental invitation—"Come and *buy*"—that is, "Come and *procure* for yourselves from the everlasting Fountain of salvation, those waters or truths, which will nourish the soul unto eternal life." We can give nothing to the Divine Being as an equivalent for these blessings; all that is asked is, reception, gratitude and thankfulness of heart. Hence the language of this invitation is, "Come ye to the waters; buy wine and milk without money and without price!" Can we refuse this pathetic, this most merciful invitation? Can we still bend our minds down to the sensual corruptions of the world, while this invitation sounds in our ears? and can we still, serpent like, crawl upon the belly and eat dust all the days of our life? Surely it cannot be so with us; the voice of our heavenly Father must reach our hearts, and inspire us with better things, where He says, in the verse following this invitation: "Wherefore do ye spend money for that which is not *bread?* and your labor for that which satisfieth not? hearken diligently unto me, and eat ye that which is good, and let your soul delight itself in fatness." (Isa. lv. 2.) To the same purpose is the language of the great Saviour—the good Shepherd of the flock. He says: "If any man *thirst*, let him come to me and drink. He that believeth on me, as the Scripture hath said, out of his belly shall flow rivers of living water." (John vii. 37, 38.) "And the *water* that I shall give him, shall be in him a fountain of water springing up into everlasting life."

Now with respect to these waters, they are said to come from the *east*—to enter at the fore-front of the house toward the *east*—to flow or come down from the right side of the house at the *south* of the altar; and that the prophet was brought out of the way of the gate *northward*, to behold the measuring and increase of the waters.

It must be at once apparent to every reflecting mind, that as the *waters* denote the truths of Revelation, and the *house* the *church* of the Lord and *mind* of man, so the *east*, whence these waters issued, the *south* of the altar to which they flowed, and the *north* from whence the prophet was brought to behold the measuring of the waters, and the phenomena of their increase, must have reference to some certain *states* and condition of mind in which alone this miracle could be seen. It is to be lamented that men, generally speaking, can be but rarely persuaded to think spiritually upon the Scriptures; it is too much trouble; they unthinkingly imagine that heavenly things are very remote, at a great distance off; that it is quite time enough yet to think of them, and that they shall have more time in a few years to devote to them; never thinking for a moment that the same procrastinating principle which urges the delay *now*, will do the same *then*—it is the thief of time—the *canker worm* that destroys in us the golden fruits of true religion, and turns our brightest expectations to rottenness and dust.

It is thus that we fritter away the *spring, summer* and *autumn* of human life, to die in lamentation in the *winter;* we come to the end before sound reflection begins, and thus, like children in their sports, we have played with our *pebbles* and lost our *treasure*. Even those who make profession of religion, can hardly be brought to endure the trouble of thinking for themselves—of inward meditation on the great doctrines of Christianity! They seem to prefer a mysterious faith in incomprehensible theories, to the sound deductions of enlightened reason and truth. But unless we exercise our *reason* under the influence of Revelation, we must be content with the *shadow* instead of the *substance* of the Word of God. If we exercise *reason* under the influence of Revelation, we obey the command of God, where He says: " Come now and let us reason together;" this reasoning will open the further wonders of this vision. In the Scriptures we frequently read of the *four* quarters, the *east, west, north* and *south;* they are always mentioned to denote states of the mind and life; and if, according to the rule laid down by the apostle, we were to attend to the operations of nature, the invisible things of God and heaven might be clearly seen, because they would be understood by the things that are made.

In nature, the *east* is the quarter where the sun rises with its heat and light to bless, to enlighten and warm the earth; the *south* is where the light is in its greatest splendor and brightness; the *west* is where the sun sets, when we feel a diminution of its rays; while the *north* is the quarter where the light terminates in obscurity and shade. In a religious sense the *Lord* himself is the *east*, whose countenance as the sun shining in its strength, is everlastingly rising upon the families of mankind. The *heat* of this sun is his changeless *love*, the light is his eternal wisdom. All who are principled in an ardent state of *love* to Him, are called sons of the light, children of the day-spring from on high, and *wise* men of the *east*. To these the *star* in the east will appear; the bright morning star, or knowledge from love, will never fail to go before them to guide their steps and lead them to the Lord God the Saviour; it will stand over where the Lord is. These are the wise men who, opening their treasures, will present to the Lord gifts, gold, frankincense and myrrh—all the celestial, spiritual and natural goodness which they have derived from Him, and which they cheerfully offer, and dedicate to his service.

In nature, all light comes from the sun; in religion, all spiritual truth, which is heavenly light, comes direct from the Lord, as the Sun of righteousness. Hence these *waters*, by which are meant the truths of Revelation, flowing onward to bless the house of God, are said to come from the EAST. These coming from the east are said to flow to the SOUTH of the altar, because, as in nature, the south is the quarter in which light is in its power and splendor, so the *south*, in a religious sense, is that advanced state of the understanding in which the divine truth is seen in its spiritual power and brightness; the altar denoting worship in connection with such elevation of mind.

All who are sincere in their religious professions and devotions, whatever be their mental condition respectively, are accepted by the Lord, whether they be principled in a most ardent love to the Lord denoted by the *east*, or in a *love* less ardent denoted by the *west*, where the sun begins to fade from our sight: whether they are in states of high intellectual brightness signified by the *south*, or in those of comparative obscurity and shade represented by the *north;* still, whatever their condition may be, they are filled with that fulness of joy which their states respectively are capable of receiving. Each in the language of Revelation has his measure filled, the good measure, pressed down and shaken together and running over. Thus the Lord gathers together his elect from the four winds, from the *east*, the *west*, the *north* and the *south*, to sit down in the tranquil abodes of his kingdom.

We can have no knowledge of the real quality or spiritual sense of Divine Truth in its glory, nor see how it operates within by its nutritious powers, and how it applies to all the successive states in the regenerate life, unless we are brought out of our mental obscurity.

As we can have no knowledge of the beauties of any science without penetrating into its secrets, so neither can we have any view of the *depth* of these living waters, while we dwell upon the surface of mere literal truth. We must come out of darkness before the light can be seen; and this will explain to us the reason why the prophet was brought out of the way of the gate NORTHWARD, in order to behold the waters at the SOUTH of the altar. In Ezek. xlvi. 9, speaking of worshipping in the temple, it is said, " he that entereth in by the way of the *north* gate to worship, shall go out by the way of the *south* gate;" and some may be so extremely literal in their views, as to suppose that this can only allude to some custom of the Jews of going in at one gate and out at the other: but something of a higher import than this is meant; for this, literally, to us is of no value at all. It teaches that the man who enters in at the *north* gate, who commences his worship and religious life in the mere *shade* and ignorance of truth, will, if he be faithful in his worship, increase in spiritual intelligence and wisdom as he journeys in his onward and upward road; he will go on journeying like the patriarch towards the *south*; his intelligence and wisdom will increase within; what was at first dark and obscure will become bright and shining; and though he came in at the *north*, he will go out by the way of the *south*. This man will not stand still in the Divine life; truth and wisdom will increase in him. He will not return by the way of the gate whereby he came in.

Now it is at the *south* of the altar where these waters are measured to ascertain their depth; and upon the *first* measuring they were *shallow*, merely to the *ankles*. To *measure*, literally, is to ascertain quantity, or length and breadth of the thing measured; but spiritually, to *measure*, as used in Scripture, is to *explore*—to *meditate* and investigate the qualities or states of life. Hence, in Rev. xi. 1, it is said, " Rise, and measure the temple of God, and the altar, and them that worship therein;" denoting exploration into the quality of *faith* and *life*, as well as the states of those who worship. Here, however, the waters of the sanctuary are measured—the truths of Revelation, these living waters of life, are explored as to their true depth, their quality, sanctity and divinity. Upon the first measuring, they were only to the *ankles;* they are seen at first but as shallow waters, relating only to the external life and outward actions, as being denoted by the *feet* and *ankles*, the lowest parts of the body; but upon the second measuring, the waters are discovered to be deeper; they come up to the *knees*, showing that they contain higher degrees of knowledge than those which apply to the merely outward life, and that they enter into our motives and intentions. Upon the third measuring, the waters still increase—they are now to the *loins;* showing that the intelligence of the spiritual man is still deeper, and that it relates to the conjunction of all that is divinely good and true in the soul, which is shown by the waters rising to the LOINS, or middle of the body. But the fourth measuring—this perfect exploration, shows the true quality and divinity of these living waters: they are waters to swim in, the river is impassable; teaching us by this last exploration, that the truths of Revelation are infinite, and that they unfold all the celestial states of life and thought, both of *angels* and men. Surely, then, the truths of Revelation may justly be called the waters of life: they contain all the *law* and will of God to man. Knowing their value and worth, may we not take up the language of the Psalmist, and say: "O how I love thy law; it is my meditation all the day"? The Lord has certainly magnified his *Word* above all his name.

Surely, then, the Word of God is spirit and life throughout, and ought to be interpreted after a spiritual manner. The ministers of Christ, as masters in Israel, whose duty it is to dispense religious instruction to the people, should reflect upon the great responsibility of their sacred calling. They should be active and diligent in their heavenly work—they should penetrate the interior recesses of Wisdom's page, and thus be like "the scribe instructed unto the kingdom of heaven, who bringeth out of his treasure things new and old." (Matt. xiii. 52.) They should not be like the Jewish lawyers, the expounders of the Divine law, who made everything subservient to their selfish and worldly-mindedness. Their love of the world made religion to consist in ceremonies and traditions; they devoured widows' houses while they, for a pretence, made long prayers; they lost all relish for spiritual things, and with it the true key of Scripture interpretation, which led the Lord of heaven to say to them: "Woe unto you, lawyers! for ye have taken away the key of knowledge." (Luke xi. 52.)

Nature and Design of Miracles.

By the law of correspondence, the Book of Life, which without it is sealed with seven seals, becomes opened, and the secrets of the Lord are revealed to those who fear Him. By this, the true spiritual nature and design of all the miracles and parables recorded in Scripture are of easy solution. We will select two by way of proof; one from the Old Testament, the other from the New.

Respecting the first miracle, we read that the prophet Elisha, upon his return to Gilgal, found that there was a dearth in the land. While the sons of the prophets were sitting before him, he said unto his servant, "set on the great pot, and seethe pottage for the sons of the prophets. And one went out into the field to gather herbs, and found a wild vine, and gathered thereof wild gourds his lap full, and came and shred them into the pot of pottage: for they knew them not. So they poured out for the men to eat. And it came to pass as they were eating of the pottage, that they cried out and said, O thou man of God, there is death in the pot! and they could not eat. But he said, Then bring meal; and he cast it into the pot; and he said, Pour out for the people, that they may eat. And there was no harm in the pot." (2 Kings iv. 38-41.)

This miracle consists in changing the deleterious quality of the food, and thus making it harmless, by throwing in meal or fine flour; and there will be but little difficulty in drawing out the spiritual instruction, if we transfer our thoughts from the food which nourishes the animal life, to that which is necessary to the sustenance of the soul of man. In Scripture the food which, literally, is applicable to the body, is mentioned spiritually to represent that which when taken into the system, nourishes mental existence, and promotes growth in the Divine life. All the good that cometh down from God out of heaven, is, in the language of Scripture, expressed by *food* generally. It is called the bread of life, the bread of God, the body and flesh of the Lord, marrow and fatness, and the meat which perisheth not; while Divine Truth, ever descending from the same source for our growth in wisdom, is called by the names of various liquids corresponding exactly to our mode and manner of receiving it. Thus it is called the water of life, as also milk, wine and strong drink. Truth in the Christian's first reception thereof, is applied to the regulation of the outward life and conduct. In this reception it is the purifying or cleansing waters; but when received in a higher ground, so as to afford the first degree of internal nourishment, it is called milk, as being adapted to the first, or infant state of the Christian life. When received in a still higher degree, so as to be rationally perceived, giving vigor to the understanding and opening every power thereof to the clear knowledge of spiritual truth, thus forming the kingdom of heaven in the soul, it is then called wine; but when received in the highest degree of ardent intense affection, it is called strong drink, and wine on the lees. (Isa. xxv. 6.) It is thus named from the fact, that the truth so received, imparts exhilarating pleasure, strength and power to the natural mind.

In regard to this miracle, we learn first, that there was a dearth in the land. This, in a natural point of view, is a defect or scarcity of food. At such times hunger and distress prevail, the inhabitants become emaciated, and many die of actual starvation. Transfer, then, this condition as applicable to the bodily life, to that of the soul—the immortal man, and this dearth will then be seen to denote a defect in the reception of heavenly food in the *land* or church. With regard to the food itself, there is no defect or dearth; for the Lord has bountifully supplied it; our table is still spread—our cup runneth over. Whether we acknowledge it or not, it is nevertheless certain that the Divine goodness and mercy have followed us all the days of our lives. But there is a dearth, or defect in our reception of these: this is the dearth of which the Scriptures spiritually speak, and of which they so often lament. The Lord says by the prophet: "Behold the days come, saith the Lord God, that I will send a famine in the land; not a famine of bread nor a thirst for water, but of HEARING the words of the Lord." (Amos viii. 11.) Here there is no defect or scarcity of bread and water—of the good and truth of heaven; but there is in the reception of these a dearth or famine, consisting in not hearing the words of the Lord. There is no thirst after the truth—no hearing, or real obedience of life. That this is the true meaning of a famine is plain from this passage in the Psalms, where speaking of the really good, it is said: "They shall not be ashamed in the evil time; and in the days of famine they shall be satisfied" (xxxvii. 19). May we not say, in reference to every spiritual Christian who desires most ardently the bread and water of life—the good and truth of heaven, that, while the worldling makes a total rejection of, and pays a disregard to, the very food of heaven, he enjoys his rich feast? is satisfied with the fatness of the Lord's house, and drinks of the streams of his pleasure? I do not believe that a single individual can be found, who is thus spiritually minded, that would relinquish his heavenly food, together with the true pleasure it yields, for all that the world could give him in exchange.

The dearth was said to be in Gilgal. This place was within the boundaries of Canaan, and stood between Jericho and the banks of the Jordan. It was the place where the Israelites made their first encampment after crossing the river. Now, inasmuch as the whole of Canaan is representative of the Lord's church or kingdom, Gilgal, being on the border of the land, denotes the external of the church, and, as it were, the commencement of it in man. Here, at Gilgal, the mess of pottage was prepared; and here, in reference to state, or the beginning of the spiritual life, man receives his first instruction—his first food—his mess of pottage. The doctrine of natural truth, such as is apparent in the literal sense of the Word, serves to introduce the mind into higher degrees of purity and wisdom. This first knowledge is here represented by Gilgal, the place at which the Israelites first encamped, and through which they passed to the interior of the land. All knowledge, whether religious, philosophical or scientific, is progressive; it is gained, not all at once, but by "line upon line, precept upon precept, here a little and there a little." (Isa. xxviii. 10.) We commence, as it were, in the outer border of Wisdom's land, in the mere rudiments of natural truth; and by passing through these, we come into possession of those higher degrees of intelligence, which open to the soul a view of the interior riches of Revelation, and which are only found in the centre of the land. But what if at this Gilgal, at the very threshold of the church, where we receive our first instruction in doctrine and life, where is prepared our first meal; what, if it should be discovered here, that the food prepared for our repast, instead of being nutritiously good, is injurious and unwholesome? that upon tasting thereof, its quality be found detrimental to the spiritual life, as well as destructive to our growth in true religion? What if this discovery should lead to the exclamation which was made by the sons of the prophets while they were eating, "O thou man of God, there is death in the pot"? In this case, nothing can be done to render the food eatable, but by throwing in meal or fine flour. After this had been done, it is said, "there was no harm in the pot."

To see clearly the spiritual instruction contained in this extraordinary miracle, we should know what it was that caused this death; what is meant by the pot itself, and what by the food it contained. The cause of this death we learn from verse 39; for, after the prophet had commanded his servant to seethe pottage for the sons of the prophets, it is said that one went out into the field and gathered wild gourds from a wild vine, and came and shred them into the pot of pottage; for they knew them not; that is, they knew not their quality. These wild gourds, then, gathered from a wild, and not from the true Vine, were the real cause of there being *death in the pot.*

The general doctrine of the church, which declares the existence of a God, and that a life according to his commandments is essential to future peace, is here denoted by the pot or vessel, and all the singulars and particulars of faith, life and practice, when mingled together, become the spiritual food of man, and is here signified by the pottage prepared in the vessel. The prophet Elisha gave no command to gather wild gourds from a spurious or wild vine; this was done in ignorance; they knew them not. Christ, as the Lord God the Saviour, is the true vine, and all the doctrines, truths and purities of life, which originate in and spring from Him, are the wholesome fruits from the Living Vine; these become the proper food of man: they contain, not death in the pot, but life and everlasting peace.

The Word of God as the great containing vessel, has within itself everything essentially necessary to promote the growth of heavenly love and wisdom in the soul of man. All that is spiritually good and true, delightful to the eyes and good for food, are contained in this grand vessel, the Word of Revelation; we have no need to go *out*, and gather spurious food from some foreign source—the wild gourds from a wild vine, to mingle with the food of heaven; or, to collect the false persuasions, doctrines and wild human inventions, to mix with the interior truths of Revelation; for if this be done, the effect will be unavoidable; death will be introduced into the pot, and the food rendered unclean. If Divine instruction, as food, is to be dispensed to the people, it must be prepared within the sacred vessel, and extracted solely therefrom.

The pure doctrines of heaven as contained in the Word of Truth, teach that there is one true and everlasting God, the only Source of life, the Author and Giver of all the blessings enjoyed both by angels and men. This is the first great truth of all pure religion; it is the keystone of Christianity, the strength and support of all our hopes. These doctrines teach also that God is strictly One in essence and person—a single Divine Being, and that He is the Lord God the Saviour, in whom all fulness dwells, His essential Love is called Father; his Wisdom or Truth, the Son; and his Operative Influence, the Holy Spirit—one God, in whom all fulness dwells, whence issue those everlasting blessings to his creation, which fill heaven with wonder and the earth with praise. These doctrines again teach that

God is good to all, that He is immutable and impartial, that his wisdom is infinite—his love unbounded and free. He has created all, redeemed all, He loves all, and with parental tenderness calls all to accept of life and salvation. If any man perish, it is not because God has left him, or abandoned him to his fate without help and without pity; his own iniquity separates him from God, and his sins hide from his view the clemency which everlastingly beams from his Father's face. If he perish, it is because he loves evil and not good; he prefers darkness to light, and the sordid gratifications of sense to the refined pleasures of heaven. If, through folly, or a corrupt system of teaching, which always suits a mind inclined to depravity, he should endeavor to charge his misery upon the Divine Being, the voice of Truth will stifle his complaint. Did he never read or hear these words?—"As I live, saith the Lord God, I have no pleasure in the death of the wicked; but that the wicked turn from his way and live: turn ye, turn ye from your evil way; for why will ye die, O house of Israel?" (Ezek. xxxiii. 11.) We are also taught that man is an immortal being, and that bodily death is the appointed gate of life, through which the man is ushered into a real world, where life is continued amidst eternally increasing joys. At this important period, man experiences a resurrection either to joy or shame, according to his past life.

These doctrines, and many others equally valuable, are taught in the Word of Inspiration: they make up the proper religious food of the human race; with this should every one be fed at Gilgal, or upon his first entrance into the church. But, instead of this being the case, we have quite another theory. One God is indeed acknowledged with the lips, but this is completely neutralized by the unmeaning creed that follows. It is taught, as though it were all Gospel, that there are three Divine persons in God, each of whom is by himself distinctly God and Lord; but this nevertheless is declared to be an incomprehensible mystery. It certainly is a mystery, and never can be understood because it is an untruth. Falsehood is wofully mysterious; truth is simple and clear. To this fundamental error is added, the doctrines of absolute predestination to death of the many, partial election of the few to life and peace; faith alone justifying, the appeasing of wrath in one Divine Person by the sufferings and death of another, heaven purchased for the elect, while the non-elect are brought into being that they may endure eternal pain for the glory of God!

Of these pernicious theories the Scriptures know nothing. Do you ask, reader, how we then came by them? The answer is ready: they are the wild gourds gathered from without—from the wild vine; they have been ignorantly shred into the mess of pottage, spoiled the wholesomeness of the food, and introduced *death into the pot* instead of life. To destroy their sad effects, Elisha threw in the meal or fine flour, to teach us that when the pure truth of goodness, signified by the fine flour, is thrown in, all that is false and injurious is then dissipated, and the food becomes harmless.

A Further Test of the Value of Correspondence.

The other miracle which we shall select from the Gospels, in further corroboration of the value of that mode of Scripture interpretation for which we contend, is that of restoring sight to the man born blind. This miracle is recorded in the ninth chapter of John, and certainly the means used in the restoration of sight are both singular and remarkable. It is said that Jesus "spat on the ground, and made clay of the spittle, and He anointed the eyes of the blind man with the clay, and said unto him, Go, wash in the pool of Siloam (which is, by interpretation, sent). He went his way, therefore, and washed, and came seeing." (John ix. 6, 7.)

The infidel who, in theology, displays more of sarcastic wit than of sound sense, would be led to smile at this miracle, and perhaps to call it a silly narrative. He might say, if Jesus Christ possessed all power in heaven and earth, why not speak the word at once, and thus give sight to the blind, without this process of anointing the eyes with clay, and commanding the man to go and wash in a pool? To such persons we would say, that in matters of spiritual religion (and there is no other religion), they "do err, not knowing the Scriptures nor the power of God." (Matt. xxii. 29.) The miracle is not recorded, merely to show the power of the Lord in restoring natural sight to one individual: but it is beautifully descriptive of the process by which the Lord restores all men who are obedient to his commands, to that spiritual sight which gives a clear perception of the vast realities of eternity. To have a right knowledge of this miracle, every part must be carefully noticed. We should know what is spiritually meant by being born blind, what by the clay, the pool of Siloam, and washing therein.

In a spiritual sense every man is born blind, that is, destitute of knowledge and science. He comes into the world feeble and altogether helpless; more imperfect and ignorant than any of the animal creation; but however paradoxical it may seem, this apparent imperfection of man at his birth, is his true perfection. It is impossible to look upon man and contemplate his astonishing energies of mind, without being struck with the fact, that there is some power inherent in his constitution which is not to be discovered even in the most sagacious animals. These come into their existence with full possession of all the science and knowledge necessary to their life, above which they never do or can rise. This, their perfection, in reference to man, is their imperfection. Man, on the contrary, is born without any science or knowledge whatever; in utter ignorance, without any connate or innate ideas, and thus *blind:* but this imperfection at his birth, in reference to animals, is his great perfection; for in early life we find the mind, as a celestial sprout, beginning to put itself forth; it is indeed at first but tender and weak, and, as it were, folded up like an unopened bud; but it soon begins by little and little to open. This expansion exhibits one beauty after another in succession—the powers of mind become progressively developed, so that the arcana of nature are explored with wonder and delight. The mind of man, which in infancy appeared like a closed germ or bud, presently becomes an opening blossom, exhibiting all that mental richness, beauty and strength which we observe in the mature age of a wise, good and intelligent man.

The human subject, though born blind, *i.e.* without any science or knowledge, soon outstrips the perfection peculiar to animals. Their highest excellence soon becomes his footstool; for the inferior animals stop where man begins. The powers of the human mind are truly astonishing; but at this we shall not be surprised when we reflect that Revelation has assured us that man is an image and likeness of his Maker. How soon do we find an intelligent man who but a few years previous was blind as it respects all science and knowledge, become quite familiar and conversant with the wonders of nature! He presses nature close; while she, in return for his industry, rewards his diligence by telling him all her secrets. To this first kind of knowledge the animals never arrive; but even here man makes no stand. He rises above the world in which he dwells, and soars with wonderful facility to other worlds in the universe; he calculates the magnitude of the sun, moon and stars; describes the relative distances of the planets, with their size and density—the time of their respective revolutions round the sun; foretells eclipses and the return of comets; shows the velocity with which light travels; the peculiar formation and constitution of different bodies which receive and reflect solar light, so as to produce the phenomena of colors in rich and beautiful variety. But even here man stops not. This image and likeness of God, thirsts after his great prototype, and ascends, by his powers of mind, to the very throne of the Almighty, and with awe and reverence contemplates his Creator, the Author of his life—the Giver of all his blessings.

In respect to celestial knowledge, man, in the infancy of his intellectual being, is blind; and Jesus (or the Divine Truth in which love is present) in passing by, recognizes the state. Now the first thing necessary to open the understanding, the eye of the soul, to a sight of Divine realities, is to unite the external truths of Revelation with moral goodness and pliability of heart. The truths of the literal sense of the Word, when mingled with that moral goodness peculiar to a well-disposed mind, will greatly assist, when reduced to practical life, in opening the blind eyes to a perception of heavenly realities. This union of the outward truth with its corresponding goodness of life, is described in the miracle by the *clay* with which the Lord anointed the eyes of the blind man; and if, after this process, we obey the Divine command, and go and wash in the pool of Siloam, which is, by interpretation, SENT; there can be no doubt but that we shall joyfully return in the full possession of sight.

The pool of Siloam is still with us, and its cleansing virtues, its miraculous properties, are as fresh, as vigorous, and as young as ever. The Word of Divine Revelation, which contains the waters of life, at once nutritious and cleansing, is the pool of Siloam, and the sent of God. To go and wash in this pool, denotes the willingness with which we apply all its truths to the purification of the understanding, that so we may feel their cleansing virtue within, and see clearly the way to life, to happiness and heaven. If any man wishes to be relieved from mental blindness, and hides the things of God and heaven from his view, the only cure for this malady is to unite the most simple truths of Revelation with natural goodness of heart, and then to live as these truths direct: he will then be found acting in obedience to the Divine command. His eyes have been anointed with the clay; he has gone to the pool of Siloam; he has washed there, and has returned SEEING!

The great value of correspondence in leading to a correct interpretation of Scripture, will be further manifest by showing that true religion will always be found in perfect harmony with every true discovery that has been or ever shall be made, either in philosophy or science. There is not the least discrepancy between the true doctrines of religion and those of science. If both are true, they are perfectly harmonious; for truth in all cases is immutable and certain. If there should be discord or opposition between them, there is something wrong somewhere; either the doctrines of religion, by a false interpretation, are made untrue; or if not, the science is untrue, and will not admit of experimental proof; for if both are true, they must harmonize and mutually support each other.

The doctrines of true religion have nothing to fear, but everything to hope for and expect from the march of science. The morning light of science is hailed as a real blessing! It is viewed as one of the most powerful auxiliaries to religion; and one that will assist in scattering to the moles and to the bats those false doctrines with which the church has been too long pestered. In what is called the dark ages of bigotry and ignorance (which always go together), the religious world opposed most decidedly every new discovery of scientific truth, if such discovered the established creeds to be false. A holy war was raised against the new-born discovery; and the cry of "the church in danger," was sufficient to excite popular clamor. The truth is that the church was in no danger, but the creeds were. It is a poor church that is endangered by the march of science; it is of but little consequence whether such a church live or die.

The advocates of Christianity will do more real good in proving its truth by fair indisputable and rational argument, than they ever have done or can do by making laws for its defence, and punishing those who attempt to sap or destroy the sacred edifice. To inflict punishment for supposed offences committed against religion, is to say, in other words, that religion itself is defective and weak; that it has no means of proving the force of its own doctrines, and that therefore it is expedient to call in the aid of human laws for its defence. The Christian religion wants nothing of this kind. All human laws are so many pests and hindrances to its prosperity and growth. Christianity, like the glorious orb of day, shines not with any borrowed lustre; its light is in itself, and its truths for the general good are scattered far and wide. It travels in its own strength, shedding around, in its progress, those benign influences which will enlighten, warm and bless all who come within their sphere. Its line is gone out through all the earth; and the time will—must come—when there shall be neither speech nor language where the voice of Christianity is not heard.

Every religion must ultimately stand by its own native power, or fall by its own weakness. If *true*, its roots will strike deeper and wider in the minds of men, as their understandings advance in knowledge and wisdom; if *false*, no human laws can possibly prevent its overthrow and desolation. The Christian Revelation as contained in the Bible, is a most powerful and solemn appeal to our reason, and can offer no violence to it in any way whatever; and it may safely be depended on as a truth, that any religion which requires us, in the great business of faith or life, to lay aside our reason and take up with a belief in unintelligible mysteries, is false and spurious. Such a system of theology stoops to this mean artifice in order the more effectually to perpetuate its unworthy existence.

Signification of the Tribute-Money found in the Fish's Mouth.

Religion and science act together something like cause and effect; what the former states, the latter proves. Religious truth is as the Lord and Master, while all the sciences are servants. Every science, like the fish mentioned in the Gospel, has within itself its own tribute-money, and whenever it is demanded, will cheerfully render it up to promote the spiritual interests of the church of God. When Christ asked Peter, "What thinkest thou, Simon? of whom do the kings of the earth take custom or tribute? of their own children or of strangers?" Peter replied, "of strangers:" "then," saith the Lord, "are the children free. Notwithstanding, lest we should offend them, go thou to the sea, and cast a hook, and take of the fish that first cometh up; and when thou hast opened his mouth, thou shalt find a piece of money: that take and give unto them for me and thee." (Matt. xvii. 25-27.)

Nothing but the immutable law of correspondence can unfold the religious instruction contained in this singular miracle. It was a practice with the Israelites, as appears from the historical parts of the Word, to take custom or tribute from strangers who were not of their church. Those who are the true members of the Lord's body or church, are the spiritual and heavenly minded; they are the *free*, and the children of the kingdom; while the *strangers* signify those who are merely naturally-minded and worldly. In respect to man, individually, we know that the higher affections and thoughts of the mind, which connect him with God and heaven, are called spiritual; and the lower, which connect him with the world, are called natural. The spiritual mind is the Lord and Master, the natural is a servant and tributary. In every well-regulated mind, the supreme affections and thoughts provide comforts and pleasures for the lower, while these in return pay the tribute, are obedient to, and serve the higher. To instruct us, then, in this universal law, it was provided and effected that neither the Lord nor Peter should pay the tribute, but a *fish*, by which is signified the living scientific knowledge in the external or natural mind.

To show what it is that willingly serves the interests of true religion by providing the tribute-money, Peter was commanded to go to the sea, to cast a hook, to take the fish that first cometh up; and that he would find, upon opening his mouth, a piece of money, with which he was to pay the tribute. If the Lord's words are spirit and life (and no Christian can doubt it), we ought to receive them as such, and look at them as sacred vessels containing the wisdom of the Most High. Those who skim lightly over the pages of sacred writ, may probably be surprised at the tribute-money being found in the fish's mouth, not reflecting that it is always found there. It was there at " the beginning, is now, and ever shall be, world without end."

In respect to this tribute, Peter was the apostle who was to procure it. He received the Divine command, " Go *thou* to the sea and cast a hook." Peter was the apostle who was first called, he was a fisherman, and by following the Lord he was to be made a fisher of men. This apostle, in his representative character, denotes all those who are grounded in a settled faith or confidence in all the Lord's promises. They are not doubters of, but believers in, the truths of Revelation. This principle of faith in the Lord, in his divinity and power, is called the rock upon which the Lord would build his church. Spiritual faith in the Lord, in his providence and care, in the universality of his love, in his compassion and unchanging goodness, united with obedience of life, opens heaven to the soul. Hence to Peter as the representative of this living faith, the keys of the kingdom of heaven were given. The power of this faith, signified by the keys, when rightly exercised both in thought and life, opens, as a key does a door, the heavenly state in the soul, and introduces the man into the full enjoyment of angelic bliss. Whatsoever this faith binds on earth, by showing its entire opposition to the angelic state, is bound in heaven, that is, comes not into spiritual liberty and peace. Whatsoever this faith shall loose on earth, by showing its conformity with the heavenly life, shall be loosed in heaven—shall come into the full liberty and exercise of the Divine life. This spiritual faith represented by Peter, brings man into perfect liberty of mind. Those who are principled therein, are, in matters of religion, free; for the blessings of those truths which bring life and immortality to light, they are not tributary to any earthly power. In these things they owe no allegiance but to the Lord alone: Peter, therefore, could not pay the tribute without violating the Divine arrangement of spiritual truth. If tribute be required, the command is still in force, "Go to the sea and cast a hook."

In a former part of this work we showed that the several portions of the world of nature, such as mountains, hills, rivers, seas, and the like, are, in Scripture, mentioned in reference to man as the world of mind. By the sea, according to correspondence, is meant divine truth in its extremes or terminations, and which is properly termed natural truth; for as the sea is the boundary of the land, so natural truth is the extreme boundary of human knowledge. In this mighty deep are contained all the principles of scientific truth, which are, by the same law of correspondence, the fishes of the sea, and by which man keeps his connection with the world and its objects. In Scripture, not only the sun, moon and stars, the beasts of the earth, creeping things and flying fowl, with storms, vapors and clouds, but even the *fishes* of the sea are called upon to praise the Lord. I heard, says John the Revelator, every creature that was in the sea, praising the Lord, and saying, "Blessing, and honor, and glory, and power, be unto Him that sitteth upon the throne, and unto the Lamb for ever and ever." (Rev. v. 13.) Now all these do constantly praise the Lord; for every true science within the wide range of human knowledge, will be found to contain its meed of praise, and by paying the tribute, to own religion as its master and lord.

We may, perhaps, think that there can be not the slightest connection between science and religion—that these subjects are perfectly distinct, having no mutual relationship whatever: but this arises from our ignorance—from our unwillingness to obey the Divine command given to Peter; "Go to the sea and cast a hook,"—go and investigate the interior principles of science, and every one of them will be found to contain within itself the tribute which it owes to spiritual religion, and which it cheerfully renders up. The Lord said to Peter, "take up the fish that first cometh up, and thou shalt find a piece of money." —that is, not any particular fish, but any one, the first that comes up; to instruct us that every science, no matter what, contains its own tribute, which it pays at the shrine of religion. Every fish when its mouth is opened, or when the interior principles of science are explored by Peter, or by those grounded in a pure faith, will be found to contain the tribute-money. When this is discovered and demanded for the interests of true religion, it is instantly yielded up.

All the SCIENCES which describe the wisdom of God, as made apparent in the harmonies of nature, and in all her wonder-working combinations, progressions and changes, are, in Scripture language, signified by the FISHES of the sea. These sciences, when internally explored, will be found to contain infallible proofs of the existence of a Supreme Being, pointing, at the same time, to the spirituality and superiority of religion, which they constantly serve, and to which they are tributaries. What is this but proving the truth of what John the Revelator asserts, that he heard the fishes of the sea giving praise to God and saying, "Blessing, and honor, and glory, and power, be unto Him that sitteth upon the throne, and unto the Lamb for ever and ever"? The science of Astronomy, Chemistry, Geology, Phrenology, Optics, Botany, and every true science, acknowledges true religion as Lord and Master, and pays the tribute. Let us examine two or three of these spiritual fishes of the sea with respect to the testimony they give of religion.

Religion teaches the worship of one God, who, as the central Sun of righteousness, diffuses his love and wisdom without partiality to all his creation, and that He is good, universally good to all, inasmuch as "He maketh his sun to rise on the evil and on the good." (Matt. v. 45.) Astronomy teaches that there is one sun in the centre of its system, diffusing light and heat, without partiality, to all the planets revolving round, for their nourishment and support. Here astronomy, like the fish, yields up the tribute-money, serving obediently the interests of religion, by showing how the "invisible things of God are seen by the things that are made."

Religion teaches that the mind of man, in the process of regeneration by which alone he is purified and made fit for heaven, passes successive changes of state, by which means, as to affection and thought, a separation is made of what is earthly and gross, from that which is heavenly. This change or purification is effected by the operation of the love of God in man's will and intellect, which *love* in the corresponding language of Scripture, is called *fire*. The science of chemistry, which has been properly termed "Fire Science," because the action of fire or heat enters into all the parts of chemical study, treats on a small scale of the changes effected by heat in natural bodies, and of the general laws relating to the composition and decomposition of substances. It is in allusion to the Lord of heaven being the only Regenerator of the minds of men, that He is said to "sit as a refiner and purifier of silver: and He shall purify the sons of Levi, and purge them as gold and silver, that they may offer unto the Lord an offering in righteousness." (Mal. iii. 3.) This passage describes, spiritually, the Lord's constant presence with man, together with his watchful care over him, while passing through his regenerating process. When the Lord's image is reflected from the person in whom the process is going on, the work is accomplished—the heavenly state is gained. Here the Lord's care is said to be like that of a purifier of silver. Science illustrates this spiritual truth; for I am informed that the refiner of silver sits with his eye steadily fixed upon the furnace to prevent injury being done to the metal by exceeding the proper time of refining. The refiner knows when the purifying time is completed by seeing his own image reflected from the silver.

Connection of Religion and Science.

Religion teaches that the Scriptures speak of man as a LITTLE WORLD; and that he has a vast variety of affections, desires, thoughts, and principles of action; some high, lofty, elevated and aspiring, which relate to his religious life; others of a lower order, which regard his moral life; and a third class the lowest, which relate to his civil or worldly life; that human nature in its progress to spiritual perfection, like the globe in its revolutions passes through successive changes of state as to affection and thought; thus that man, as to his mental constitution, contains within himself the evidences of these changes, and that he has impressed on the mind the remnants or remains of a primitive condition, corresponding to the early formations of the crystalline rocks, depositions and fossil remains, which indicate a primitive order of the globe. Scripture speaks of man as being, by the Almighty, both "fearfully and wonderfully made." This statement is proved not only by his astonishing mental capabilities, but also by the marvelous construction of his organic frame. All the astonishing wonders in man's creation are declared to be the work of an Almighty Creator, who in the beginning made heaven and earth and all that is in them, who in due time created man in his image and likeness, to have the full dominion over the beasts, birds and creeping things. Geology is a science which undertakes to explain the internal and external structure of the earth; and from the laborious investigations of those master minds in science, we may hope to gain some rational theory respecting its formation. This science proves, and we think satisfactorily, the great antiquity of the earth, and so far is it from opposing religion, that it pays to it a tribute. It traces, by rigid examinations of the earth's rocks, strata, fossil remains and depositions, all creation up to the great First Cause, who in the *beginning* was its Former and Maker, and to whom all praise is due.[14] It does not, it is true, give us any date as to time, when the beginning was. This is omitted for the best of reasons, because Revelation makes no statement of time, therefore geology can prove none. Go on, then, Geology, thou industrious little fish! swim about in the mighty deep you inhabit, and bring us more knowledge still about the world in which we dwell. Religion calls upon you to do this, that you may pay your tribute at her sacred shine.

Religion teaches that man is a spiritual and an immortal being; that at the dissolution of his material body he will experience a resurrection to another world, either of bliss or degradation according to the quality of that life, as to evil or good, which he has formed for himself in this. Hence the Scriptures speak of two kinds of resurrection; the one to life, the other to condemnation. The true Christian, at his resurrection, enters a world perfect and real, where evils and sorrows are forever shut out, and where health is everlasting, and the mirth of the high spirit hath undying life. The ground of man's immortality is in the rich gift which he has received from his Maker, of the two faculties of will and understanding. Into these the Divine life of love and that of wisdom flow. They are called in Genesis the breath of *lives* (plural) which God breathed into his nostrils, by which man became a living soul. This is the ground of our immortality, and it explains these words of the Lord to his disciples, "Because I live, ye shall live also." (John xiv. 19.) Man, therefore, is so constructed that, by his mental powers and bodily organization, he can hold commerce with two worlds. By his powers of mind, he holds connection with the spiritual or heavenly world, and by means of his organized body, with the world of matter. There must then be, as already stated, a close corresponding connection between the mental powers and all parts of that organic structure of body, by which they are developed and exhibited in nature; each mental power having,

---

[14] Modern Geology in this respect is very different from some of the ancient theories; for while this science traces all creation up to one Almighty God, most of the ancients, instead of teaching the world to be derived from a wise and powerful Being, taught that the material world gave birth to their deities.

in the material body, its own organ, by which it is brought forth and known as a real existence. PHRENOLOGY is a science which, though young and, like all new theories, has at present to struggle with principalities and powers, and with deep-rooted prejudices in high places—is nevertheless one that promises fair to yield vast pleasures to the reflecting mind. It has, by the most patient examinations of the human brain, of its form, organization and development, proved it to be the material instrument by which man carries on a constant intercourse with the external world—that it is an aggregate of parts, and that each has its own proper function which consists in manifesting outwardly some distinct power of mind. These parts, which are called organs, are about thirty-five in number, and are divided into two classes or orders—the first called FEELINGS, or Affective Faculties, and belong to the will; the second, INTELLECTUAL, or Perceptive Faculties, and belong to the understanding.

Whatever, then, may be urged against this new science, and however it may be checked in its infancy or impeded in its growth to manhood; however numerous its imperfections in some points may now be; yet, inasmuch as it is founded upon a just philosophy of mind, there can be no doubt of its truth in the main. It will certainly be found to be a living fish, and if its mouth be opened, or its internal principles examined by Peter, or by those capable of doing it, the tribute-money will be found therein; for it proves the existence of a Supreme Being, all-wise and good; and has placed in the highest part of man's intellectual being, what is called the organ of veneration, which, being seated in the centre of the moral sentiments, when enlightened and influenced by the intellectual, will be exercised rationally in the worship and praise of God.

RELIGION teaches that Divine truth, as light from the Sun of righteousness, comes directly from its source in God, and enters the mind of man, by whom it becomes refracted and applied to his own state and wants; but through whom it can never pass to another person with the same degree of illumination. The presence of this intellectual light is instantly recognized by the formation of conscience, and in the power of distinguishing right from wrong.

The science of OPTICS, among a vast variety of other curious things, teaches that the rays of solar light are emitted from the sun in direct or straight lines, but that every ray becomes bent or refracted as it passes through any transparent object to illuminate another; thus receiving variation and change in passing through one to the other, and not imparting the same degree of brightness, or correctness of light, to the second object as to the first. The presence of this light is instantly recognized by its revealing the form and color of objects.

Religion teaches that every man grows in purity, wisdom and happiness, in the same proportion as his mind is unvaryingly turned to the Lord as the true and everlasting Sun of righteousness, so as to live and flourish under his influence; and it also teaches that man, by his creation, is gifted with the power thus to turn.

BOTANY treats of the internal and external structure, of the functions, of the organs, and of the similitudes and dissimilitudes of the almost infinite multitude of the objects in the vegetable kingdom; and shows that solar light and heat are essential to the life and growth of all her forms; that vegetables have a tendency in themselves to turn to the sun, that they may thereby grow and produce their fruits; and that if by any foreign force they are deprived of this their inherent tendency, they soon wither and die. Learn then, reader, an instructive lesson from these words of the Saviour: "Consider the lilies of the field, how they grow; they toil not, neither do they spin." (Matt. vi. 28.) How do the lilies grow? By the tendency they have to turn to the sun, and to receive the fulness of his rays. Man, spiritually, grows in the same way; were he constantly to turn to the Sun of righteousness, he would grow in virtue, wisdom and true religion, and that, too, without any labor—without toiling or spinning.

Religion teaches that each person, upon receiving love and wisdom from God, applies them to his own purposes, and produces those fruits of life according with the actual state or condition of his own mind; and as there are no two modes of reception exactly alike, there can be no two states alike; hence human characters vary in degree of conduct and knowledge, showing the truth of Scripture, that every one is rewarded according to his works. These differences are not in the Divine Love and Wisdom, but are modifications thereof in the recipient subject. Science teaches that the rays of the sun, acting uniformly upon all vegetables, expand and open up their interior qualities, causing each to produce its like; thus presenting an endless variety in their species and qualities. There is no gathering grapes of thorns or figs of thistles.

In Scripture, man is frequently compared to trees of various kinds, and the Lord is called "the true Vine," while those who are his real disciples are the branches which abide in Him and bear fruit. David says: "The trees of the Lord are full of sap, the cedars of Lebanon which He hath planted." (Ps. civ. 16.) Man is evidently here the subject treated of, and the Divine life of united love and wisdom, when received, becomes the vital fluid to the soul of man. It rises up, and, circulating throughout the whole mental frame, produces that beauty and richness of mind, that knowledge, intelligence and purity of action, which, in the language of correspondence, are the leaves, blossoms and fruits of the mental tree. Botany, in this case, pays its tribute, by showing that the sap, as the vegetable fluid, is composed of the nourishment extracted from the earth, by the roots of trees and plants; which, rising up, circulates through the trunk and every limb and fibre of the plant, producing thereby its leaves, blossoms and fruits.

We might successfully go through all the sciences, and prove that every fish has within itself its own tribute-money, and that all of them are now willingly paying, at the shrine of Religion, their tribute and praise. It is certain that Religion claims Science as her handmaid. Those doctrines of theology that are sterling and sound, will always find science ready to prove and establish their truth. As it has been correctly observed that "an undevout astronomer is mad," so a man of scientific research, without religion, is mad too.

It has been said, that "the proper study of mankind is man;" and surely he only can be said properly to know himself, who sees every thing around him in connection with his eternal destination. It is to be deeply lamented that the gratification of the bodily senses should occupy so fully our anxiety and care, should consume so much of our time, while those spiritual things which relate to the wisdom of life, and to all the solid pleasures of human existence, are comparatively neglected, as though they were deemed secondary or of minor importance. The time will certainly come to every man, when he will regret the moments he has suffered to pass away unimproved; when hours, weeks and years that have been consumed in spiritual idleness, will stand before him like so many ghastly skeletons, upbraiding him for not covering them with *sinews, flesh* and *skin*, that so the living breath of God might have produced them as so many angelic forms.

How different is the life of the good man—the sincere Christian, whose early days have been spent under the cheering beams of the Sun of righteousness; whose succeeding ones have been surrounded with pleasures, and whose end is peace, because his heaven is sure. This is the man who enjoys his feast with a true relish; who experiences a calm even amidst the storms of life, and whose every hour improves the prospect of eternity.

Conclusion.

To bring the main points of this essay into a short compass, we shall conclude by observing, that The Lord God of Heaven, the everlasting Sun of righteousness, is a SINGLE DIVINE BEING,[15] the alone Source of life, the one Creator and Upholder of all things. All created existences came forth from his love by his wisdom. The proximate sphere of his glory is the bright SUN of all the heavens, and the everlasting light of creation. The going forth of these Divine creative rays formed the *sun* in nature to be their receptacle, and to become the instrumental cause of producing those worlds which revolve in our system; making these again to be the abodes of rational and intelligent beings, formed to make endless progressions in love and wisdom; and to pass through natural life to the attainment of that which is spiritual, everlasting and pure. The sphere of Divine Truth thus descending with life and vigor, produced all creation as a mighty mirror in which the love, wisdom, goodness, providence and presence of God are clearly reflected and seen. This truth at last, by Divine arrangement, flowed into the previously prepared minds of those appointed to embody it in natural language, and by maintaining a strict relationship between spiritual states of mind and the objects of nature, a close correspondence between them is observed throughout the inspired language of Revelation, so that the Divine Truth thus embodied, partaking, in its descent from God to man, of all the states of affection and thought both of angelic and human life, becomes the " Lamp unto our feet," and emphatically " the Word of God." It is the true light of every man's little world, full of spirituality and life, and is as the " finger of God," to point to the regions of immortality and peace.

---

[15] Plutarch, in his Dissertation on the word EI, engraved on the temple of Apollo, makes the following remarks: " εἶ, (says he) THOU ART; as if it were εἶ ἕν, Thou art One. I mean not in the aggregate sense, as we say, one army, or one body of men composed of many individuals; but that which exists distinctly must necessarily be one; and the very idea of being implies individuality. One is that which is a simple being, free from mixture and composition. To be one, therefore, in this sense, is consistent only with a nature entire in its first principle, and incapable of alteration and decay." Again, Plutarch, when arguing against the Stoics, who supposed if there were a plurality of worlds, that many Jupiters or gods would be necessary to govern them, says: " Where is the necessity of supposing many Jupiters for this plurality of worlds? Is not One Excellent Being, endued with reason and intelligence, such as He is whom we acknowledge to be the Father and Lord of all things, sufficient to direct and rule these worlds? If there were more supreme agents, their decrees would be vain, and contradictory to each other."

Now as the Word of God is written in agreement with the science of correspondence, it follows that nothing but this science can correctly explain its sacred contents. He, therefore, who desires to be further acquainted with these matters, is requested to read the Theological Writings of Emanuel Swedenborg. They will afford him information of the most instructive and delightful kind.

Reader! I must now bid you farewell! Sufficient has been said, it is hoped, to excite in your mind a veneration for those Divine Oracles of Truth which shadow forth, by the luxuriant appearances in nature, that everlasting land of promise, where an exuberance of celestial felicity must ever reside, and where forever flow the luscious streams of milk and honey.

A KEY TO THE SPIRITUAL SIGNIFICATION OF NUMBERS.*

CHAPTER IV.

INTRODUCTION—NUMBERS 1 TO 12, INCLUSIVE—ONE—TWO—THREE—FOUR—FIVE—SIX—SEVEN—EIGHT—NINE—TEN—ELEVEN—TWELVE—A RULE FOR DISCOVERING THE SIGNIFICATION OF OTHER NUMBERS.

Introduction.

THE most ancient men who were of a celestial character and had communication with angels, derived from them the spiritual signification of numbers, both simple and compound; and were in the habit of describing spiritual and moral subjects by the mere arrangement of them in a longer or a shorter series. This knowledge, together with the science of correspondences in general which teaches the relation subsisting between things natural and things spiritual, constituted the wisdom of the sages of antiquity, and was transmitted by them to their posterity as the basis of all their ecclesiastical computations and historical descriptions. But in process of time the signification of compound numbers was first lost, and at length even that of the simple numbers; so that in the present day few suspect that anything more is implied by the various numbers contained in the Sacred Scriptures, than what they purport to be according to the common natural idea attached to them.

The Word of the Lord, however, being altogether spiritual in its origin, and written in strict conformity to the above-mentioned science, treats of heavenly and divine things under natural images; and consequently, when it introduces numbers as well as names, it is for the sole purpose of expressing the qualities of things, and the various states of the church, either in a genuine or in an opposite sense. Hence the several stages of man's regeneration are described, in the

---

* From a work by Robert Hindmarsh, first published in Manchester, England, in 1820.

first chapter of Genesis, by the *first, second, third, fourth, fifth* and *sixth* days of creation, terminating in the *seventh* day or sabbath of rest, when, the power of evil being subdued, man enters into a state of heavenly tranquillity and peace.

In commemoration of this latter state, and to keep it perpetually in view as the end to be obtained after the labors of repentance, reformation and regeneration, the *seventh* day was appointed to be kept holy, and is generally used to denote all states of sanctity in the church. In the supreme sense the number *seven*, and the *seventh* day, denotes the glorification of the Lord's Humanity, or its full and perfect union with his Divinity. In the same sense the number *three* denotes his resurrection, because on the *third* day after his crucifixion He rose from the dead. It also on many occasions denotes a complete state from beginning to end. The number *eight* signifies the beginning or commencement of a new state, on which account circumcision was appointed to be performed on the *eighth* day. The number *ten* signifies remains, and therefore *tithes* were instituted in the Jewish church, and given to the priests as an acknowledgment that every mercy and blessing was derived solely from the Lord. So again the number *twelve* denotes all the truths and goods of the church: hence the Jewish or Israelitish people were arranged into *twelve* tribes; and hence the Lord chose *twelve* apostles who were his more immediate followers; and hence also the city New Jerusalem is described as having *twelve* gates, and at the gates *twelve* angels, and the wall of the city as having *twelve* foundations.

That numbers signify the qualities of things, is further evident from Apoc. xiii. 18, where it is written, "Here is wisdom: Let him that hath understanding count the *number of the beast:* for it is the *number of a man;* and his number is *six hundred threescore and six.*" Man, in respect to his *affections*, good or evil, is in the Word frequently compared to a *beast:* hence the members of the church in general are called *sheep*, or a *flock of sheep;* and their teachers are called *shepherds*. Again, so far as they are receptive of divine truths, and acquire therefrom states of *intelligence* and *wisdom*, they are also properly denominated *men*. Now as numbers are expressive of qualities, it is plain that by *counting* the number of the beast, is signified to *investigate, scrutinize, examine* and *ascertain* the quality of the doctrine or faith alluded to. It follows, therefore, that the *number of the beast*, or the *number of a man*, denotes the quality of the church described in the above chapter, particularly as to its affection for truth, or as to the doctrine and faith which it professes. And this quality is represented by the number 666, to signify that every truth and every good of the Word has been falsified, perverted and destroyed.

This number, 666, is the sum or result of 6×100 *plus* 6×10 *plus* 6; and it denotes the character or quality of faith separate from charity or a good life, as comprehending all falsities and evils in one complex, or the falsification of every divine truth of the Word, and the profanation of what is most holy. The number 6 from which the number of the beast arises by triplication, signifies the same as 3×2, also the same as 12, of which it is the half, viz., all the truths and goods of the church; and in an opposite sense, in reference to the beast, all falsities and evils collectively. The triplication of this number extends its signification, involving not only a state of profanation, but also the full consummation or end of the church whose leading doctrines are here characterized in symbolic language.— A. R. 610. Ap. Ex. 847. A. C. 4495, 10217.

Other numbers in like manner have their peculiar significations, without a knowledge of which it is impossible to form a correct judgment of the many extraordinary things contained in the Word: and even the plainest historical descriptions, which to the generality of readers appear to have no other sense than what is usually understood by the terms employed, have yet a latent internal signification, which can only be unfolded by the science of correspondences and of numbers.

To elucidate, therefore, the elements of this science, more particularly in respect to *numbers*, and to enable the reader in some measure to comprehend that wisdom which distinguishes the Divine Records from every human production, we shall give briefly the spiritual signification of the numbers 1 to 12 inclusive, together with a rule for discovering the signification of any other number as far as 1,000,000, or even 100,000,000, mentioned in Dan. vii. 10.

Examples showing the application of the different numbers, and in confirmation of the various significations belonging to those of each class, simple and compound, will then be given from the Word both of the Old and the New Testament. From all which will be seen the great importance of the science of numbers in deciphering the language of Holy Writ; a science, indeed, little known at the present day, having been lost to the world for many ages, but which, nevertheless, in conjunction with that of correspondences in general, is the only true key to the internal, genuine and spiritual sense of Divine Revelation. The authorities from the different works of EMANUEL SWEDENBORG, who is to be considered as the reviver of this science, will also be given in their proper places, for the satisfaction of the reader.

It may be observed as a general rule, that, when numbers are *doubled* or *multiplied*, they involve the same signification as the simple or radical numbers, from which they arise, but more fully; and that numbers *divided* involve the same also as their integral numbers, but not in so full a degree.—A. C. 3239, 3960, 5291, 5335, 5708, 10255.

The *multiplication* likewise of any number signifying *a few*, and of *fractional numbers*, as $\frac{1}{2}$, $\frac{1}{4}$, $\frac{1}{10}$, etc., diminishes their value, and causes them to signify still less than the whole numbers, of which they are parts, until their power is nearly extinguished. Hence their signification becomes so reduced that the expressions necessarily denote an end or last term; as for example, the end of a church, or of any particular state belonging to the church, when that is the subject more immediately under consideration.—A. C. 813.

It may be proper further to observe, that in cases where mention is made, in the Word, of *numbering, telling,* or *counting,* yet without specifying any particular number, by such expression is signified *knowing* or *ascertaining the quality* of the persons, things or subjects treated of; also *arranging* and *disposing into order* according to their respective qualities. Thus Jehovah is said "to *tell the number* of the stars, and to call them by their names," Ps. cxlvii. 4; "to *muster* the host of the battle," Isa. xiii. 4; and "to *bring out* the host of heaven *by number*," Isa. xl. 26; by which is spiritually understood, that the Lord alone arranges and disposes into order the things signified by the host of heaven and by the stars, viz., the truths and goods of faith and love. The seed of Abram is said to be *innumerable*, "as the dust of the earth, and as the stars of heaven," Gen. xiii. 16; xv. 5; not because his descendants were, or were to be, more numerous than other nations, (Deut. vii. 7,) but on account of the spiritual things represented and signified by them, viz., the truths and goods of heaven and the church, which are innumerable.

In like manner, and with reference to the same spiritual blessings, Jehovah promises by the prophet "to multiply the seed of David as the host of heaven, which cannot be *numbered*, and as the sand of the sea, which cannot be *measured*," Jer. xxxiii. 22. And in another place, "The *number* of the children of Israel shall be as the sand of the sea, which cannot be *measured* nor *numbered*," Hos. i. 10. The same is also understood by the words of Balaam, when he took up his *parable*, and said, "Who can *count* the dust of Jacob, and the *number* of the fourth part of Israel?" Num. xxiii. 10; where it is plain that *counting* or *numbering*, inasmuch as the passage forms a part of a *parable*, is not to be taken literally but spiritually. Again, mention is made of "*telling* or *counting* the towers of Zion," Ps. xlviii. 12; Isa. xxxiii. 18; of "*numbering* the houses of Jerusalem," Isa. xxii. 10; of "*taking the sum* of the children of Israel, after their *number*," Ex. xxx. 12; Num. i. 2; of "passing flocks under the hands of him that *telleth* them," Jer. xxxiii. 13; and of "*numbering* our days," Ps. xc. 12; where by *counting, telling* and *numbering*, is signified *examining, considering* and *marking the quality* of truths and goods in the church, and in our own minds; also *arranging* and *disposing into order*, by divine assistance, the various states of life as we enter upon them. In like manner Job says, that "his steps are *numbered* or *counted*," Chap. xiv. 16; xxxi. 4. And our Lord in the Gospel assures us, that "the very hairs of our head are all *numbered*," Matt. x. 30. In an opposite sense, to *number* is to *wind up*, to *finish* and *condemn*: thus it is written of Belshazzar and his kingdom, "*Mene, mene, tekel, upharsin;* thou art *numbered, numbered, weighed*, and *divided*, that is, *finished* and *condemned*," Dan. v. 25 to 28. And again, "Therefore will I *number* you to the *sword*, and ye shall all bow down to the *slaughter*," Isa. lxv. 12. In the same sense the Lord is said to have been "*numbered* with the transgressors," Isa. liii. 12. David also was condemned for "*numbering* the people of Israel and Judah;" and in consequence thereof "a pestilence was sent among them, which carried off seventy thousand men," 2 Sam. xxiv. 1 to 15. The reason why so severe a punishment followed the act of *numbering* the people was, not because there was any evil or crime in the thing itself, abstractly considered, but because it represented and spiritually implied the presumption of man's will and his own self-derived intelligence, in attempting to arrange and dispose into order the things of heaven and the church, together with the destruction inevitably attending the same; when yet the Lord alone is possessed of such power, and He alone claims the prerogative of exercising it according to the dictates of his own divine wisdom.—A. C. 10217, 10218. A. R. 364. Ap. Ex. 453.

As in the explanation to be given in the following pages, of the spiritual signification of certain numbers, mention will frequently be made of *remains*, and also of *fulness*, or a *full state*—terms well understood by those who are already acquainted with the doctrines of the New Jerusalem, but perhaps obscure and unintelligible to others—it may be expedient to state the sense intended to be conveyed by each expression.

By *remains* are meant all states of the affection of good and truth, with which man is gifted by the Lord, from infancy to the end of life; thus all states of innocence, charity, mercy and faith, whereby the evils of human nature may be counteracted, softened and subdued, in order that the principles of a new and heavenly life may be implanted and established within him. It is by *remains* that man has communication with heaven; that he is capable of overcoming in spiritual temptations, and entering into actual conjunction with the Lord; that he is afterwards preserved from falling into evil; and that after death he is rendered blessed and happy forever in heaven.

By *fulness*, or a *full state*, is signified an entire period from beginning to end; thus when man is fully prepared to receive the influx of innocence from the Lord, or when the truths of faith are in conjunction with the good of charity. The state is therefore said to be *full*, when spiritual good has received its quality from truth, and consequently when man, being regenerated, regards truth from a principle of good, and no longer regards good from a principle of truth, as he did before regeneration, or during the process of its accomplishment. *Fulness of state* or *fulness of time*, is also an expression used to denote the consummation or end of the church, when there is no longer to be found in it either faith or charity, in the true sense of those words. It is in reference to such a state of the church, that the Lord is said to come in the *fulness of times*, in order to establish a new church in the room of the former.

Having made these preliminary observations, we now proceed to explain the numbers from *one* to *twelve* inclusive; adding also a rule for determining the signification of numbers above twelve.

One.

Oneness or *unity* is constituted of several various things so arranged as to be in concord or harmony with each other; which concord or harmony of several things arises from their all having respect to *one* origin, that is, to *one* Lord who is the life of all. Hence heaven, though consisting of innumerable societies, is nevertheless *one*; and man, though consisting of a great variety of powers, faculties, members and organs, is yet *one*. There is no such thing as *one absolutely*, or *one simply*, but *one harmonically*, consisting of many various things collected together into *one form*, and tending to *one end* or *use*, and on that account called *one*.—A. C. 457, 1285, 3035, 3241, 3986, 4149, 5962, 7836, 8003, 9828. H. & H. 56, 405.

In the Divine Unity itself there are infinite things appertaining to divine love and divine wisdom, which, though distinct, or capable of distinct contemplation, are yet perfectly and pre-eminently *one*.—D. L. 14, 17 to 22.

We are therefore instructed by the Sacred Scriptures, that God, the creator and preserver of heaven and earth, is *One* in essence and in person: and though He is designated by many names and characters, especially by the terms Father, Son and Holy Spirit, yet these are not to be regarded as evidences of a plurality of divine persons, but solely as characteristic denominations of the three great essentials belonging to the Divine Being. For as the human soul, body and operation are three essential constituents of *one* man, so in like manner, but infinitely above the comparison, the Father, Son and Holy Spirit are three essentials of *one* God, who is no other than our Lord and Saviour Jesus Christ.—A. C. 14, 15, 2149, 3704, 10816. H. & H. 2 to 6. D. L. 45, 46, 60. T. C. R. 2, 3, 164 to 170.

One has various significations, according to the subject treated of, and in each case includes many particulars. Sometimes it more immediately refers to the divine good, as in Matt. xix. 17; xxiii. 9; sometimes to the divine truth, as in Matt. xiii. 45, 46; xxiii. 8; Luke xv. 8; John viii. 18; and at other times to both in union or conjunction, as in Gen. ii. 24; Matt. xix. 5; John x. 30.—A. C. 3241, 3986, 4149.

Like other numbers, *one* also is capable of an opposite signification; and hence *one talent* denotes faith in a state of separation from charity, or the knowledge of good and truth committed to the memory only, and not to the life, as in Matt. xxv. 14 to 30; Luke xix. 20.—Ap. Ex. 193, 675.

The Lord calls himself the *First* and the Last, to signify that He is the *One* Only God of heaven and earth, the sole fountain of love, wisdom and life, from whom are derived all things in heaven and the church, from *first* principles to ultimate or last effects.—A. R. 29, 38. Ap. Ex. 41, 56.

One, understood as the half of two, denotes some degree of conjunction.—A. C. 9530.

One is predicated of good, and indicates what is perfect.—Ap. Ex. 374.

The *first-begotten* or *primary* essential of the church, in appearance, or as to time, is truth or faith; but in reality, or as to essence and value, is good or charity.—C. L. 126. A. C. 2435, 3325, 4925, 9223, 9224.

The Lord is called the *first-begotten*, because from Him are derived love and faith in the church.—A. C. 352.

He is also called the *first-begotten from the dead*, because He is, even as to his Humanity, the very or essential truth united with the divine good, from whom all men, in themselves dead, continually derive their life.—A. R. 17. Ap. Ex. 28.

The *first-begotten* of Egypt represented faith separate from charity.—A. C. 1063.

The *first-begotten* among clean beasts and the *first-fruits* of the earth were dedicated to Jehovah, to denote that all things of good and truth, with every spiritual and natural blessing, are derived from Him alone.—A. C. 9223.

The *first* day and the *eighth* day, as well as the *seventh*, are called a sabbath, Lev. xxiii. 39, because they denote the beginning of a new state, in which the conjunction of good and truth takes place.—A. C. 9296.

EXAMPLES.

(1.) Gen. xxxviii. 27 to 30. "And it came to pass in the time of her travail, that, behold, twins were in her womb. And it came to pass when she travailed, that the one put out his hand; and the midwife took and bound upon his hand a scarlet thread, saying, This came out *first*. And it came to pass as he drew back his hand, that, behold, his brother came out; and she said, How hast thou broken forth? this breach be upon thee: therefore his name was called Pharez. And afterwards came out his brother, that had the scarlet thread upon his hand; and his name was called Zarah."——The subject treated of in this passage, in the spiritual sense, is that of *primogeniture*, or priority in the church; it having been a disputed point from the most ancient times, whether the good which is of charity or the truth which is of faith, is the *first-begotten*. For as good, when man is re-born, does not evidently appear, but is concealed in his interiors, and only manifests itself in a certain affection unnoticed by the external or natural man, until regeneration is completed; while truth, which enters by the senses and lodges in the memory, plainly discovers itself; therefore many have adopted the erroneous supposition that truth is the *first-begotten*, or most essential principle of the church; and indeed so essential, that, under the name of faith it is capable of effecting salvation without the good which is of charity: when nevertheless the Word in its genuine sense teaches that good is actually the *first-begotten*, and truth only apparently such. This is described by the various circumstances attending the birth of the twins Zarah and Pharez. The first who put out his hand on which the midwife bound the scarlet thread, represented spiritual good or charity; and therefore the *primogeniture, priority, or superiority*, was actually his, because he first opened the womb; which was confirmed by the midwife's binding a scarlet thread on his hand, and saying, *This came out first*. The scarlet-colored thread also signifies spiritual good, and the hand denotes the power thereof; which being first manifested, is therefore actually entitled to the right of *primogeniture;* see Ex. xiii. 2, 12; but being afterwards drawn back or concealed, it leaves to spiritual truth or faith the apparent right of superiority. The birth of Pharez, brother of the former, is called by the midwife a *breach*, because she supposed him to be the same child, on whose hand she had tied the scarlet thread, and it appeared to her that he had broken or torn it asunder; by which circumstance also is spiritually signified, that truth represented by Pharez, is at first apparently separate from good, though in reality it is not; for this child had not broken the thread, having never worn it, and consequently having never been entitled to the right of *primogeniture*, except in the estimation of the midwife, who represented the natural mind on its first reception of divine truth. By the complete birth afterwards of Zarah, with the scarlet thread on his hand, is represented and signified that good is at length acknowledged to be actually the *first-begotten* in the church, because Zarah who represented good or charity, first opened the womb by putting forth his hand, though he afterwards drew it back, and thereby permitted his brother to take the birthright or precedence, at least for a season. In like manner, during the first stages of regeneration, man is apparently under the influence and dominion of truth or faith; but when his regeneration is effected, he is then manifestly under the influence and dominion of good or charity. The same things are represented by Esau and Jacob struggling together in the womb of Rebekah, and by Jacob's taking hold on Esau's heel at the time of their birth, Gen. xxv. 22 to 26: also by Jacob's laying his right hand upon the head of Ephraim the younger son of Joseph, and his left hand upon the head of Manasseh the elder son, when he blessed them both, Gen. xlviii. 13 to 20.—See A. C. 4916 to 4930.

(2.) Deut. vi. 4. "Hear, O Israel, Jehovah our God is *One* Jehovah."——The divine love and the divine wisdom, or the divine good and the divine truth, which are denoted by the two terms *Jehovah* and *God*, are here expressly said to be *one*.—See A. C. 2921. T. C. R. 6, 37 to 47.

(3.) Ps. xxvii. 4. "*One* thing have I desired of Jehovah, that will I seek after, that I may dwell in the house of Jehovah all the days of my life, to behold the beauty of Jehovah, and to inquire in his temple."——The *one* thing to be desired is here described as involving at least *three* things, viz., dwelling in the house of Jehovah, beholding his beauty, and inquiring in his temple; that is, abiding in the good of love to the Lord, and in the delight of learning and perceiving the truths appertaining to that good. But as they all tend to *one* end or use, which is conjunction with the Lord and final happiness, they may in this sense be regarded as *one*.—See Ap. Ex. 799. A. C. 414, 3384.

(4.) Zech. xiv. 9. "In that day Jehovah shall be *one*, and his name *one*."——Here the divine essence called Jehovah, and the divine form which is his name, are both declared to be *one*. The first is the pure Divinity, the second is the Divine Humanity; which, though in some respects distinguishable as two before the Lord's incarnation, by reason of his then manifesting himself in the person of an angel, who was also at times called Jehovah, as in Gen. xix. 24; Ex. xxiii. 20 to 23, are now perfectly *one*, in consequence of his glorification, or union of the human essence with the Divine.—See A. C. 6000.

(5.) Matt. vi. 33. "Seek ye *first* the kingdom of God, and his righteousness, and all these things shall be added unto you."——The kingdom of God is the Lord himself, and his church: his righteousness (or justice) denotes good proceeding from Him: and to seek this *first*, is to desire with the chief affections of the heart to perform useful service to mankind, from pure, disinterested love to the Lord and to our neighbor. When the Lord, and the good proceeding from Him, are thus made the objects of a man's affections and life, then all other things, whether spiritual or natural, that are conducive to his eternal welfare and happiness, will be added unto him.—See Ap. Ex. 1193. A. C. 5449, 9184. H. & H. 64.

(6.) Matt. xix. 5. "For this cause shall a man leave father and mother, and cleave to his wife: and they twain shall be *one* flesh."
——The *union* or *conjunction* of two minds is here called *one* flesh; from which it plainly appears that *oneness* or *unity* is not to be regarded as *one* thing simply, but as arising from two or more in a state of harmony and concord.—See A. C. 10169. Ap. Ex. 725. H. & H. 372. C. L. 215.

(7.) Matt. xix. 17. "There is none good but *one*, that is God."
——The divine unity is here clearly set forth, particularly in reference to the attribute of goodness or love.—See A. C. 10154, 10336, 10619. Ap. Ex. 254.

(8.) Matt. xxiii. 8, 9. "Be not ye called Rabbi: for *one* is your Master, even Christ, and all ye are brethren. And call no man your Father upon the earth: for *one* is your Father who is in heaven."——The terms Rabbi, Master, and Christ, have respect to divine wisdom or divine truth, while the term Father is intended to distinguish divine love or divine good, each belonging to one and the same God, and each expressive of his divine unity.—See A. C. 3703. Ap. Ex. 746.

(9.) Matt. xxv. 14, 15. "The kingdom of heaven is as a man travelling into a far country, who called his own servants, and delivered unto them his goods. And unto one he gave five talents, to another two, and to another *one*, to every man according to his several ability; and straightway took his journey. Then he that had received the five talents, went and traded with the same, and made them other five talents. And likewise he that had received two, he also gained other two. But he that had received *one*, went and digged in the earth and hid his lord's money."——The man travelling into a far country is the Lord, who on his departure from the world, and his apparent absence or distance after that time, is described as taking a long journey. The talents given to the different servants denote all the knowledges of truth and good derived from the Word, together with the faculty of perceiving and understanding their nature and use. To trade with the talents is to acquire intelligence, wisdom and true spiritual life by means of those knowledges. They who, from *some* or a *few* knowledges acquire *much* intelligence and wisdom, are represented by the servant who increased his *five* talents to *ten*; the number *five* denoting little or few, and the number *ten* much. And they who are continually endeavoring to form in themselves the *conjunction* of good and truth, or of charity and faith, are represented by the servant who of *two* talents made *other two*; the number *two* denoting a state of spiritual conjunction, and *other two*, making together *four*, the same thing in greater fulness and perfection. But they who receive the knowledges of truth and good in the *memory only*, and make not the proper use of them, by acquiring through their means states of intelligence, wisdom and spiritual life, are represented by the servant who received *one* talent, and who went and digged in the earth and hid his lord's money; the earth here denoting the memory of the natural man, and digging and hiding money therein the unjust application of his faculties to those external pursuits which are grounded in self-love and the love of the world.—See Ap. Ex. 193, 675. A. C. 2967, 5291.

(10.) Mark x. 21. "Jesus beholding him, loved him, and said unto him: *One* thing thou lackest: go thy way, sell whatsoever thou hast, and give to the poor; and thou shalt have treasure in heaven; and come, take up the cross and follow me."——The *one* thing here spoken of as lacking, consisted in the following particulars, viz., 1. That he had not withdrawn his heart from the love of riches: 2. That he had not endured temptations, and so resisted or fought against the concupiscences of evil: and 3. That he did not as yet acknowledge the Lord as God incarnate. The Lord therefore exhorted him to sell what he had and give to the poor, that is, to remove from his mind the inordinate love of riches, to renounce his proprium, together with the false traditions of the Jewish church, and at the same time to do the works of charity; also to take up his cross, that is, to resist the evil propensities of his nature by enduring temptations; and lastly to follow the Lord, that is, to acknowledge and worship Him as the only God of heaven and earth.—See D. Life, 66. Ap. Ex. 122, 893, 934.

(11.) Luke x. 41, 42. "Jesus answered and said unto her, Martha, Martha, thou art careful and troubled about many things. But *one* thing is needful: and Mary hath chosen that good part, which shall not be taken away from her."——The *one* thing needful is love to the Lord, which involves every other good. It was this love, accompanied with close attention to the words of Jesus, for which Mary was distinguished, (see ver. 39,) and which is called that *good* part, which shall not be taken away from her.

(12.) John viii. 17, 18. "It is written in your law, that the testimony of two men is true. I am [*one*] that bear witness of myself, and the Father that sent me beareth witness of me."——In this passage *one* (though not literally expressed in the original) is yet understood, and predicated of divine truth, which being the same thing as spiritual light, and Jesus being himself that light or truth, it is therefore said that He bears witness of himself; for light is its own evidence. And as divine good is inseparable from divine truth, being within it as its very life, it is also said that the Father, by which expression is meant divine good or divine love, beareth witness of Jesus: "for," says He, "I am *not alone*, but I and the Father that sent me," ver. 16. And again "He that sent me is with me: the Father hath not left me *alone*," ver. 29. It is observable that, though Jesus, in the above passage, makes a comparison between the testimony of two men, and that of himself and the Father, yet He does not give us to understand that the Father and He are two different and distinct persons, like two men, but states, first, that He himself is *one* that bears witness, and then (not that the Father is *another* that bears witness also, as might perhaps be expected by those who regard the Father and Son as two distinct persons, but simply) that the Father who sent Him likewise bears witness of Him; by which is meant, as already explained, the united testimony of divine good and divine truth to the high character which our Lord had just before given of himself. Nothing is more common in the Word, than for two or more distinct individuals to represent the different essentials, attributes and offices belonging to the one God; as for example, Abraham, Isaac, Jacob, Moses, Aaron, Joshua, Samuel, David, Solomon, etc.: yet who would, on that account, infer that there are as many divine persons in the Godhead *represented*, as there were individual men, patriarchs, prophets, priests, and kings, *representing?* Surely no one can thus mistake the Sacred Writings. The testimony of two men, therefore, which is cited by our Lord in the way of comparison with the testimony of himself and the Father, or what is the same thing, with the testimony of his own divine truth and divine good, ought never to be regarded as any proof of there being two Divine Persons in the Godhead, more especially as He is careful in the comparison to omit all mention of any other Divine Person but *himself alone*, who is expressly called the Everlasting Father, as well as the Son, in Isa. ix. 6.—See A. C. 3704, 9503. Ap. Ex. 635.

(13.) John x. 30. "I and my Father are *one*."——Jesus, who speaks, is the Humanity; his Father is the Divinity; and these are said to be *one*, comparatively as the body and soul of a man are one; that is, one in life, one in action, consequently one in essence and one in person. The same may be said of divine wisdom and divine love, or divine truth and divine good: though they are distinguishable the one from the other, and capable of being separately contemplated, yet in operation, end, and use, they are perfectly *one.*—See A. C. 3704, 9315, 9818, 10053, 10125, 10579. A. R. 21. D. Love, 14 to 16. C. L. 82, 118. D. Wis. 1.

(14.) John xvii. 11, 21, 22. "Holy Father, keep through thine own name those whom thou hast given me, that they may be *one*, as we are. . . . That they all may be *one*, as thou, Father, art in me, and I in thee; that they also may be *one* in us: that the world may believe, that thou hast sent me. And the glory which thou gavest me, I have given them; that they may be *one*, even as we are *one*."
——Two kinds of *union* or *oneness* are here spoken of; that subsisting between the Father and the Son, and that between the Lord and man. The former is, in the strictest sense of the word, what it imports to be, a *union* of the Divine and Human essence in one person or form. The latter may properly be termed *conjunction*, because it is a relation opened and afterwards subsisting between the Creator and the creature, or between what is infinite and what is finite, which can never be identified as absolutely *one:* whereas in the former case the union is most perfect, there being nothing of the Divinity but what is at the same time Human, and nothing of the Humanity but what is at the same time Divine, each infinite, and both *one.*—See A. C. 1013, 2034, 2803, 10067.

Two.

The number *two* belongs to the celestial class of expressions, being predicated of goods or evils, and denotes all good or evil in the complex.—A. C. 10624. Ap. Ex. 430. A. R. 322.

It also signifies union, conjunction, or the heavenly marriage of good and truth, or of charity and faith.—A. C. 5194, 5291, 5893, 8423. Ap. Ex. 430. A. R. 322.

Conjunction in general, proved from all parts of the human frame. —C. L. 316.

All and singular things in conjunction, consequently what is full. —A. C. 9037, 9166, 9529.

What is perfect.—A. C. 9861.

What is successive, or another in succession.—A. C. 5623.

All things as to good.—A. R. 322.

Good and truth from the Lord, also from self.—A. C. 9942.

The same in relation to *three*, as *six* are to *seven*, viz., labor, combat, and dispersion of what is evil and false; sometimes also what is profane.—A. C. 720, 900. But when contrasted with three or seven as a holy number, it denotes what is relatively profane.—Ib. 720.

Duplication, or a number *doubled*, has the same signification as the simple number from which it arises.—A. C. 5291. It also denotes extension, communication, and influx.—A. C. 9622. Likewise much. —A. R. 762. Two and two or pairs.—A. C. 747.

EXAMPLES.

(1.) Gen. vii. 2. "Of every clean beast thou shalt take to thee by sevens, the male and his female: and of beasts that are not clean by *twos*, the male and his female."——By every clean beast are signified the affections of good in man: and their being taken into the ark by sevens, denotes a state of holiness, such being the signification of the number *seven*. The male and his female denote the conjunction of truths with goods. By the unclean beasts are signified evil affections: and their going by *pairs* or by *twos* into the ark, denotes a state of relative profanation: for the number *two*, when the subject treated of is the state before regeneration, bears the same relation to three, as six days of labor do to the seventh of rest, and consequently signifies a state respectively unholy or profane. The male and female of unclean beasts denote the conjunction of falsities with evils.—See A. C. 713 to 721.

(2.) Ex. xxxiv. 1. "And Jehovah said unto Moses, Hew thee *two* tables of stone like unto the first; and I will write upon these tables the words that were in the first tables, which thou brakest." ——The reason why the ten commandments were written on *two* tables was, because the number *two* denotes conjunction in general, and the *two* tables of the law denoted conjunction with the Lord. Hence they are called *tables of the covenant* between the Lord and man, Deut. ix. 9; hence also the ark, into which the tables were put, is called the *ark of the covenant*, Josh. iii. 11.—See T. C. R. 285, 287.

(3.) 2 Kings ii. 23, 24. "And he went up from thence to Bethel: and as he was going up by the way, there came forth little children out of the city and mocked him, and said unto him, Go up, thou bald-head, go up, thou bald-head. And he turned back and looked on them, and cursed them in the name of Jehovah: and there came forth *two* she-bears out of the wood, and tare forty and two children of them."——The reason why the children were cursed by Elisha, and afterwards torn in pieces by *two* she-bears merely on account of their calling him bald-head, cannot be understood without first knowing what Elisha represented, and what is signified by baldness, and what by bears. That it could not be the wish of Elisha that such an immoderate punishment should be inflicted on a number of little children for so trifling a cause as that of calling him bald-head, must be plain to every intelligent reader; for who that has the least spark of humanity in his breast, could be so cruel and unjust? The conduct of the children in taunting and reproaching the prophet, was indeed a crime, but surely not of so atrocious a character as to require the punishment of death, and in a manner the most revolting to our feelings. But the church being at that time a representative church, it was permitted by the Divine Providence that such an event should take place, for the purpose of holding up to view the dangerous consequences of vilifying, reprobating or despising the Lord and his Word. For Elisha as a prophet represented the Lord as to the Word, and consequently the Word itself. By calling him bald-head, was signified to deprive the Word of its natural or literal sense, as they do who reject it as a thing of no account, who also despise its plain style, and think, if it contain divine truth, that it might have been expressed in more elegant and intelligible language. By bears out of the wood was signified the power of the Word arising out of its literal sense; also they who exercise such power, whether they be good or evil, especially such as separate the external from its internal sense: the bears are said to be she-bears, because the female among animals denotes affection; hence the she-bear denotes the affection of natural truth, as well as its power. And by the forty-two children or boys who were torn by the bears, were signified all who blaspheme or despise the Word on account of its natural sense being such as it is, together with the punishment which they unavoidably bring upon themselves in another life. The reason why *two* bears were concerned in the destruction of the children was, because that number involves a full state either of good or evil according to the nature of the subject, in the present case a full state of evil, or what is the same thing, the conjunction of evil and falsehood, and the full punishment thereof.—See Ap. Ex. 781, 1086. A. C. 3301. A. R. 47, 575.

(4.) Isa. xvii. 6. "Yet gleaning grapes shall be left in it, as the shaking of an olive-tree, *two* three berries in the top of the uppermost bough, four five in the outmost fruitful branches thereof, saith Jehovah the God of Israel."——The prophet here treats of the vastation of the church, and speaks of the few remaining who are in good and truth. A comparison is made with the shaking of an olive-tree, because by an olive-tree is signified the church in respect to the good of love, and by its branches the truths thence derived. *Two* three signify a few who are in good and thence in truths; *two* denote good, and three truths. Four five signify a few who are in good; four good, and five a few. The olive-tree is described as being fruitful, to denote those in the church who are in the good of life. Such being the signification of the different numbers here mentioned, they are therefore said to be *two three*, and *four five*, not *two or three*, and *four or five*.—See Ap. Ex. 532. A. C. 649.

(5.) Amos iv. 8. "So *two* three cities wandered unto one city, to drink water; but they were not satisfied."——The subject treated of in this passage is the defect of genuine truth at the end of the church, when they who desire to obtain it from spiritual affection, cannot discover it in the various systems of doctrine, which are then generally taught. *Two* three cities denote all who are in the affection or love of truth from good: a city is the truth of doctrine: to drink water, is to learn truths; to wander from one city to another, is to make inquiry concerning the different doctrines: and to receive no satisfaction, is to be unable to discover genuine truth in any of them.—See Ap. Ex. 532.

(6.) Zech. iv. 2, 3, 11, 12, 14. "And the angel said unto me, What seest thou? And I said, I have looked, and behold, a candlestick all of gold, with a bowl upon the top of it, and his seven lamps thereon, and seven pipes to the seven lamps, which were upon the top thereof: and *two* olive-trees by it, one upon the right side of the bowl, and the other upon the left side thereof. Then I said unto him, What are these *two* olive-trees upon the right side of the candlestick, and upon the left side thereof? And I again said unto him, What be these *two* olive-branches which through the *two* golden pipes empty the golden oil out of themselves? Then said he, These are the *two* anointed ones that stand by the Lord of the whole earth."——The golden candlestick, with the seven lamps, etc., denotes the New Church, which will be in illustration by virtue of truth derived from the good of love. The *two* olive-trees, the *two* olive-branches, and the *two* golden pipes, denote the good of love to the Lord and of charity to the neighbor, together with the truths derived therefrom; the olive-tree on the right being love to the Lord; and that on the left, charity to the neighbor: and as these are wholly derived from the Lord, who is the only God of the church, they are therefore described as " the *two* anointed ones that stand by or before the Lord of the whole earth."—See A. R. 43. Ap. Ex. 375, 638. A. C. 9780.

(7.) Matt. ii. 16. " Then Herod, when he saw that he was mocked of the wise-men, was exceeding wroth, and sent forth, and slew all the children that were in Bethlehem, and in all the coasts thereof, from *two* years old and under, according to the time which he had diligently inquired of the wise-men."——According to the natural sense of the historical transaction related in this chapter, it appears that wise-men from the east came to Jerusalem about the time of the birth of our Lord, inquiring, " Where is he that is born King of the Jews? For we have seen his star in the east, and are come to worship him." Herod, the reigning king, being informed of this circumstance, and entertaining no other idea of a King than that of an earthly prince or ruler, feared lest himself and his family might be superseded in the government of Judea by the newly-born child. To make sure, therefore, of his destruction, he issued an order that all the children under his jurisdiction of *two* years old and under, should be immediately put to death. But the design of Herod being previously known to Infinite Wisdom, the new-born King of the Jews was by divine appointment removed to the land of Egypt, where he continued till the death of the tyrant. Thus the jealousy and cruelty of Herod on the one part, and the divine providence and protection on the other, are fully exemplified in the facts historically described. But if the same transactions and circumstances be viewed according to their spiritual purport, it will then be seen that when the Lord came into the world, all spiritual truth, all innocence, charity and heavenly affection, represented by the children, were extinguished and destroyed in the church, as well as in the world at large; for this is what was spiritually signified by Herod's destroying the children of *two* years old and under. And as, notwithstanding all the efforts of Herod, or the powers of darkness represented by him, the young child Jesus was still, by the divine interposition, miraculously preserved, so we are instructed by this example of a wise and merciful Providence, that a new church on earth was to be established by the Lord, now incarnate, who is himself the sole Fountain of all spiritual truth, innocence, charity and heavenly affection. Hence it is written in the prophecy of Jeremiah, in reference to this very event: "Thus saith Jehovah, A voice was heard in Ramah, lamentation and bitter weeping; Rachel weeping for her children, refused to be comforted for her children, because they were not. Thus saith Jehovah, *Refrain thy voice from weeping*, and *thine eyes from tears:* for thy work shall be rewarded, saith Jehovah, and *they shall come again* from the land of the enemy. And *there is hope in thine end*, saith Jehovah, that *thy children shall come again to their own border.*" Jer. xxxi. 15 to 17. By Rachel was represented the spiritual internal church, and by her children truths derived from a spiritual origin. By her weeping, and refusing to be comforted for her children, because they were not, is signified that no spiritual truth was left remaining. By the exhortation to refrain from weeping, and from tears, and the promise that her work should be rewarded, is signified that there would be no more grief on that account, because the Lord was born, from whom would be derived a new church, which would be in truths from spiritual affection: her work or labor alludes to the combat of the Lord against the infernal powers, and his victory over them, for the purpose of establishing his church: and her reward is heavenly happiness. By the children coming again from the land of the enemy to their own border, and by hope in the end, is signified the establishment of a new church in the room of that which had perished: to come again from the land of the enemy, is to be led out of an infernal state: hope in the end, denotes the commencement of a new church at the expiration of the old: and the return of the children to their own border, is the reception of spiritual truths by those who shall become members of that new church.—From this view of the subject, it appears that the number *two* is predicated of the conjunction of truth with good, or of faith with charity; and that *two years* and *under*, being the age of the children destroyed, imply a want of conjunction in those things which are constituent of a church, and their consequent extinction in the human mind.—See Ap. Ex. 695. T. C. R. 205.

(8.) Matt. x. 9, 10. "Provide neither gold, nor silver, nor brass in your purses; nor scrip for your journey, neither *two* coats, neither shoes, nor yet staves: for the workman is worthy of his meat."——When the Lord sent forth his twelve disciples to preach the kingdom of God, He gave them this command, thereby instructing them that they ought not to possess or cherish any good and truth derived from themselves, but solely that which is derived from the Lord. By gold, silver, brass in the purse, and a scrip, are signified various kinds of good and truth derived from self, and not from the Lord.

By *two* coats, *two* pair of shoes, and *two* staves, are signified truths of different orders, internal and external, and their powers both from the Lord and from self; which mixture of things from the Lord and of things from man, being a species of *profanation*, and destructive of spiritual life, was therefore prohibited by him. But the disciples were allowed to take *one* coat, *one* pair of shoes, and *one* staff, as appears from Mark vi. 8, 9; Luke ix. 3; by which was signified, that all must be derived from the Lord alone, who would bestow every necessary blessing upon them gratuitously.—See A. C. 4677, 9942. Ap. Ex. 242.

(9.) Matt. xviii. 19, 20. "I say unto you, that if *two* of you shall agree on earth, as touching any thing that they shall ask, it shall be done for them of my Father who is in heaven. For where *two* or three are gathered together in my name, there am I in the midst of them."——In this passage *two* is predicated of good, and *three* of truth, not in relation to *two* or *three* persons only, but abstractly and universally: hence by the *two* first mentioned are denoted all who are in good, and by the *two* or *three* afterwards mentioned, all who are in truth derived from good. By *two* or *three* being gathered together is signified the conjunction of good and truth, or of charity and faith, in one mind: and as all good and truth are derived from the Lord, and may be considered as manifestations of his presence, it is therefore said of these *two* principles of the heavenly life, that the Lord is "in the midst of them."—See Ap. Ex. 411, 532.

(10.) Luke x. 35. "And on the morrow, when he departed, he took out *two* pence, and gave them to the host, and said unto him: Take care of him; and whatsoever thou spendest more, when I come again, I will repay thee."——The whole parable of the man who fell among thieves, is a description, first, of those who profess to be of the church, like the priest and Levite, and yet neglect to perform works of charity; and, secondly, of those who make no such profession, like the Samaritan, and yet love the truth, and are desirous of helping and benefiting their neighbor to the utmost of their ability. The man who had been stripped and wounded and nearly killed by thieves, represents all such as had been deprived of truths and infested with false doctrines by the different teachers in the Jewish or perverted church, so that their spiritual life was nearly extinguished. By the Samaritan's binding up his wounds, pouring in oil and wine, setting him on his own beast, bringing him to an inn, and taking care of him, is signified an endeavor on the part of those who are in states of charity to their neighbor, to relieve him in every possible way, by kindness, instruction, or otherwise. And by his giving *two* pence to the master of the inn, on his departure, and recommending him to his care, as to one better instructed, and more able to supply his wants, than himself, are signified all things belonging to charity in general, which are in the power of those represented by the Samaritan. From this brief explanation of the above parable, it appears that the number *two* is predicated of the good of love and charity; and that *two* pence, being a sum of small value, and characteristic of the *scanty knowledge* of the gentiles, further imply that such charity was exercised according to the best of their judgment, knowledge or understanding.—See Ap. Ex. 375, 376, 444. A. C. 9057.

(11.) Luke xxi. 1 to 4. "And he looked up, and saw the rich men casting their gifts into the treasury. And he also saw a certain poor widow casting in thither *two* mites. And he said, Of a truth I say unto you, that this poor widow hath cast in *more than they all*. For all these have of their abundance cast in unto the offerings of God: but she of her penury hath cast in *all the living that she had*."———In this passage the *two* mites evidently denote all things of charity and faith in conjunction, and consequently in their fulness: for it is said of the poor widow, who made an offering of them, that she gave *more* than all the rich men had given, even *all the living that she had*.—See T. C. R. 459.

(12.) Apoc. xi. 3, 4. "And I will give power unto my *two* witnesses, and they shall prophesy a thousand *two* hundred and threescore days, clothed in sackcloth. These are the *two* olive-trees and the *two* candlesticks standing before the God of the earth."———The *two* witnesses here spoken of are the *two* essentials of the New Church; the first of which is, that the Lord is the God of heaven and earth, and that his Humanity is Divine; the second is, that conjunction with the Lord is effected by a life according to the precepts of the decalogue: and these *two* witnesses are said to be clothed in sackcloth, because heretofore these *two* great essentials of love and wisdom, good and truth, charity and faith, have not been received and acknowledged in the church. The same are also described as *two* olive-trees and *two* candlesticks standing before the God of the earth; the *two* olive-trees being love and wisdom, and the *two* candlesticks being charity and faith, both derived from the Lord. The reason why the *two* witnesses are called *two* olive-trees and *two* candlesticks, which yet are *four* in number, is because *two*, as well as *four*, signify conjunction, and hence one thing in the church. This conjunction of good and truth into one is called the heavenly marriage, which constitutes the very essence, life and perfection both of heaven and the church. —See A. R. 490 to 493. Ap. Ex. 375, 635 to 639. A. C. 9780.

Three.

The number *three* belongs to the spiritual class of expressions, being predicated of truths or falsities, and denotes all truth or falsity in the complex.—A. C. 10624. A. R. 315, 348, 400. Ap. Ex. 194, 430, 532.

It also signifies fulness in regard to any subject.—A. C. 10127. Ap. Ex. 430.

An entire period from first to last, consequently what is continuous or successive.—A. C. 2788, 5122, 5144. Ap. Ex. 532.

What is full and complete from beginning to end.—A. C. 4010, 5122, 4495. T. C. R. 210, 211, 387. A. R. 505. Ap. Ex. 430, 532.

What is perfect—because in all nature and in man himself there prevails a successive order, as end, cause and effect.—A. C. 9864, 9825. D. L. W. 296, 297.

What is holy and inviolable, like the number *seven*. A. C. 482.—But is frequently predicated of things not holy.—A. R. 505.

The resurrection of the Lord.—A. C. 901.

A full state of the church from beginning to end, also the last state.—A. C. 1825.

A new state after the end.—A. C. 5123.

The last and at the same time the first, or the end and at the same time the beginning.—A. C. 4901.

A *third* part, in like manner as the number *three*, denotes all, especially in reference to truth.—A. R. 322, 400, 541. Sometimes what is not yet full and complete.—A. C. 2788, 5159.

The *third* day, like the *seventh*, involves what is holy, and this by reason of the resurrection of the Lord on the *third* day: it denotes also the coming of the Lord into the world, and to glory, likewise every coming of the Lord to man.—A. C. 720, 728, 901, 2788.

Triangular forms represent things true and right, as *four-square* forms represent things good and just, and *round* forms, things good in general, especially of the external man, or in the lowest degree. —A. C. 8458, 9717, 9861. A. R. 905.

EXAMPLES.

(1.) Gen. xviii. 6. "And Abraham hastened into the tent unto Sarah, and said: Make ready quickly *three* measures of fine meal, knead it, and make cakes upon the hearth."——By the *three* men or *three* angels, who came unto Abraham, were represented the three essentials belonging to the Lord, viz., the Essential Divine, the Divine Human and the Holy Proceeding. By making ready *three* measures of fine meal, is signified preparation for conjunction: fine meal signifies the celestial and spiritual principles of love: and *three* measures thereof denote not only a full state, but also what is holy.—See A. C. 2170 to 2177.

(2.) Ex. xix. 11, 12. "And Jehovah said unto Moses, Go unto the people, and sanctify them to-day and to-morrow, and let them wash their clothes, and be ready against the *third* day; for the *third* day Jehovah will come down in the sight of all the people, upon mount Sinai."——The descent of Jehovah in an external appearance before the eyes of the Israelites, signified the coming of the Lord, and illumination of the understanding by an influx of divine wisdom from Him: hence by their sanctifying themselves, washing their clothes, and making ready against the *third* day, is evidently denoted a full state of preparation to receive Him. With the Israelites who only *represented* a church, and were not a *real* church, this preparation consisted in putting on an extraordinary appearance of sanctity and purity in externals, while their internals were closed against the influences of heaven. But with a member of the real church, it is effected by deep repentance and humiliation both of heart and life.—See A. C. 8788 to 8793.

(3.) Ex. xxiii. 14, 17; Deut. xvi. 16. "*Three* times thou shalt keep a feast unto me in the year. *Three* times in the year all thy males shall appear before the Lord Jehovah."——Feasts in ancient times were instituted in commemoration of man's deliverance from his spiritual enemies, and his consequent regeneration, which was effected by the coming of the Lord into the world. They therefore signified worship from a cheerful and grateful heart. In the Israelitish church they were appointed to be held *three* times in a year, to denote the *continual* and *perpetual* worship of the Lord; a year being expressive of an entire period, and the number *three* signifying what is full or complete from beginning to end, thus full and perfect deliverance from a state of damnation, and at the same time purification from falsities, the implantation of truth and good, and finally regeneration. The first feast, which was the feast of unleavened bread, called also the feast of the passover, signified purification from falsities: the second, which was the feast of harvest or of the first-fruits of labor, called also the feast of weeks, signified the implantation of truth in good: and the third, which was the feast of ingathering, called also the feast of tabernacles, signified the implantation of good itself, when man no longer acts from a dictate of truth, but from the pure affection and delight of love, that is, of charity. This latter is the new heavenly life communicated by the Lord to man through the previous process of regeneration. By every male appearing *three* times in the year before the Lord Jehovah, is signified the continual presence of the Lord with man in the truths of faith: and this presence of the Lord is effected, in proportion as man lives according to the precepts of divine truth, under the influence of love, charity and the good of innocence, these constituting the habitation of the Lord in the human mind.—See A. C. 7093, 9286 to 9297.

(4.) Hosea vi. 2. "After two days will He revive us, in the *third* day He will raise us up, and we shall live in his sight."——The *third* day, in allusion to the coming of the Lord and his resurrection from the dead, denotes an entire period from beginning to end, also the communication of spiritual life to man by regeneration, and at the same time a state of holiness, while the two preceding days denote a previous state of impurity.—See A. C. 720, 2788, 4495, 5890. Ap. Ex. 532.

(5.) Amos i. 3, 6, 9, 11, 13. "Thus saith Jehovah, For *three* transgressions, and for four, I will not turn away the punishment thereof."——By *three* and *four* transgressions are not meant so many in number, according to the natural or obvious signification of the terms, but by *three* is meant every transgression of the divine law from a principle of *falsity*, and by *four* every transgression from a principle of *evil*. The number *three*, in a good sense, is predicated of *truth*, and in an opposite sense, of what is *false*, in each case involving an idea of what is full and complete. In like manner the number *four* is predicated either of what is *good* or of what is *evil*, and at the same time involves the conjunction of good with truth, or of evil with falsity.—See Ap. Ex. 532.

(6.) Zech. xiii. 8, 9. "And it shall come to pass that in all the land, saith Jehovah, two parts therein shall be cut off and die, but the *third* shall be left therein. And I will bring the *third* part through the fire, and will refine them as silver is refined, and will try them as gold is tried."———By all the land, or the whole earth, is meant the whole church: by two parts therein being cut off, is meant that all good would perish: by a *third* part being left, is meant that something of truth would remain, but scarce any thing of a genuine character: and by bringing a *third* part through the fire, refining and trying them as silver and gold, is meant purification from falsities and evils, for the purpose of implanting in their stead genuine good and truth. *Two* parts are predicated of good, and a *third* part of truth.—See Ap. Ex. 242, 532.

(7.) Matt. xiii. 33. "The kingdom of heaven is like unto leaven, which a woman took and hid in *three* measures of meal, till the whole was leavened."———By the woman here mentioned is signified the church as to its affection or love of divine truth, whether existing in a society or in an individual. By leaven is meant the false principle opposing the truth, (called also by our Lord the leaven of the Pharisees, and of the Sadducees, Matt. xvi. 6, 11, 12,) which produces a kind of spiritual fermentation in the mind, and is permitted to take place for the sake of man's purification. Of this nature are temptations, without which man's regeneration cannot be advanced: it is therefore said that the kingdom of heaven is like unto such leaven. By the *three* measures of meal are meant all the principles of truth and good hitherto received by man from the Lord: and by the woman's hiding the leaven therein, until the whole was leavened, is signified that man's whole spiritual life is affected, renovated and purified, by means of the various temptations through which he passes.—See A. C. 7906. Ap. Ex. 532.

(8.) Matt. xvi. 21. "From that time forth began Jesus to show unto his disciples how that He must go unto Jerusalem, and suffer many things of the elders and chief priests and scribes, and be killed, and be raised again the *third* day."———The *third* day, especially in reference to the Lord, signifies what is full and complete: hence his resurrection on the *third* day denotes the perfect glorification of his Humanity, or its full union with his Divinity, all that is written of Him in Moses, the Prophets, and the Psalms, having been accomplished in and by Him.—See A. C. 2788, 4495.

(9.) Luke xiii. 7. "Then said He unto the dresser of his vineyard, Behold, these *three* years I come seeking fruit on this fig-tree, and find none: cut it down, why cumbereth it the ground?"———By the fig-tree is here meant the Jewish church, which was a church only in externals, and therefore, properly speaking, the mere representative of a church. By its bearing no fruit, is signified that they were destitute even of natural good, or good in the lowest degree, from a spiritual origin. By seeking fruit on that tree for *three* years, and finding none, is signified that the Jewish people were, from first to last, or from the very beginning of their history to the end, a depraved and rebellious race, without either internal or external good, and having nothing of the character of a true church among them: on which account it is said of the tree, "Cut it down, why cumbereth it the ground?" That the Jewish nation would also continue in this unfruitful state, even after their dispersion and intermixture among Christians, from whom they might receive much useful instruction concerning the Lord as the true Messiah, and concerning his spiritual kingdom, is foreseen and plainly described in the following verses, where the vine-dresser says: "Lord, let it alone this year also, till I shall dig about it, and dung it: and if it bear fruit, ——; and if not, then after that thou shalt cut it down." The English translators have inserted the word *well* after fruit, in order to complete the literal sense: but in the original the passage is left in suspense, or in the form of an ellipsis, without any term expressive of a favorable result; which very circumstance, in the internal sense, tacitly announces a prediction, that the Jewish nation, under the symbolical character of a fig-tree, would never produce fruit, that is, would never become a true church, notwithstanding the opportunities afforded them of hearing the gospel from Christians, in addition to their possessing the law of Moses and the prophets. The same is signified by the Lord's words to the fig-tree, when He found nothing thereon, but leaves only: "Let no fruit grow on thee *henceforward forever.*" Matt. xxi. 19; Mark xi. 13, 14.—See Ap. Ex. 403.

(10.) Apoc. xii. 4. "And his tail drew the *third* part of the stars of heaven, and did cast them to the earth."——By the tail of the dragon is signified the falsification and adulteration of the truths of the Word, by those who reason in favor of a trinity of persons in the Godhead, and who teach that faith separate from charity is sufficient for salvation. By the stars of heaven are meant the spiritual knowledges of good and truth derived from the Word. By drawing the *third* part of the stars of heaven, and casting them to the earth, is signified the perversion, extinction, and destruction of all those spiritual knowledges or heavenly truths.—See A. R. 541. Ap. Ex. 718 to 720.

(11.) Apoc. xvi. 13. "And I saw *three* unclean spirits, like frogs, come out of the mouth of the dragon, and out of the mouth of the beast, and out of the mouth of the false prophet."——By the dragon is signified the doctrine of three divine persons and of justification by faith alone, together with all such persons in the church, particularly in the Protestant or Reformed church, as acknowledge this doctrine and live accordingly, that is, in evil. By the beast, which in this case is the beast rising up out of the sea (chap. xiii. 1) are signified the men of the external church, or the laity, who confirm themselves in the same acknowledgment and faith. And by the false prophet, or beast rising up out of the earth (chap. xiii. 11), are signified the men of the internal church, or the clergy, who teach and maintain the doctrines above alluded to. The mouth of the dragon, beast and false prophet, evidently denotes their doctrine, preaching and discourse. By unclean spirits are signified lusts, or impure desires, in this case the lusts of falsifying truths; and by frogs, to which they are compared, are meant reasonings from such lusts. The number *three* denotes all, likewise altogether and merely; thus when applied to unclean spirits resembling frogs, it denotes *mere* reasoning from an evil and disorderly state of mind.—See A. R. 701, 702. Ap. Ex. 998 to 100.

(12.) Apoc. xxi. 13. The wall of the holy city, New Jerusalem, had " on the east *three* gates, on the north *three* gates, on the south *three* gates, and on the west *three* gates."——By the New Jerusalem as a city, is meant the New Church as to doctrine. By the wall thereof is meant the Word in its literal sense, from which doctrine is derived: for as a wall is a defence to a city and its inhabitants, so the literal sense of the Word is a defence to its spiritual or internal sense. By the gates of the city is meant introduction into the New Church by means of the knowledges of truth and good derived from the Word. And by there being *three* gates on each quarter of the city, is signified that a full and free entrance is granted to all who are in a higher or lower degree of love and wisdom from the Lord: for by the east is signified the love and affection of good in a superior degree, and by the west the same in an inferior degree; by the south is signified wisdom and the affection of truth in a superior degree, and by the north the same in an inferior degree. The whole number of gates is said to be *twelve*, because, like the number *three*, they are predicated of truths from good, and involve what is full, complete and universal.—See A. R. 899 to 901.

Besides the preceding examples, many others are to be found in the Word wherein the number *three* is particularly conspicuous, and claims an interpretation far beyond that of the literal and obvious meaning usually attached to it. Among them are the following, where it is written, That the Israelites should go *three* days' journey into the wilderness, and sacrifice to their God, Ex. iii. 18. That there was a thick darkness in all the land of Egypt for *three* days, so that they did not see one another for *three* days, Ex. x. 22, 23. That the fruit of the trees planted in the land of Canaan should be accounted as uncircumcised for *three* years, Lev. xix. 23. That the *third* year was to be the year of tithing, Deut. xxvi. 12. That Joshua commanded the people to prepare themselves for passing over Jordan within *three* days, Josh. i. 11. That Jehovah called Samuel *three* times; that Samuel ran to Eli *three* times; and that Eli perceived the *third* time, that Jehovah had called Samuel, 1 Sam. iii. 1 to 8. That *three* things were proposed to David, that he might choose one of them, viz., seven years of famine, *three* months' flight before his enemies, or *three* days' pestilence in the land, 2 Sam. xxiv. 12, 13, That Elijah stretched himself upon the widow's child *three* times. 1 Kings xvii. 21. That Elijah ordered water to be poured on the burnt sacrifice, and on the wood, *three* times, 1 Kings xviii. 33. That Isaiah walked naked and barefoot *three* years for a sign and wonder, Isa. xx. 3. That Ezekiel was commanded to take a razor, to pass it over his head and his beard, to weigh and divide the hair, and to burn a *third* part with fire, to smite a *third* part with a knife, and to scatter a *third* part in the wind, as a sign of judgments about to fall on Jerusalem, Ezek. v. 1, 2, 12. That Daniel, having the windows of his chamber open towards Jerusalem, kneeled upon his knees *three* times a day, and prayed, Dan. vi. 10. That Daniel mourned *three* full weeks, Dan. x. 2, 3. That Jonah was in the belly of the fish *three* days and *three* nights, as an emblem of the Son of Man being *three* days and *three* nights in the heart of the earth, Jonah i. 17, Matt. xii. 40. That the man, who planted a vineyard, and let it out to husbandmen, sent servants to them *three* times, and afterwards his son, Luke xx. 9 to 13. That Peter denied the Lord *three* times, Matt. xxvi. 34, 69 to 75. That the Lord distinguished the times of his life into *three*, saying, Go and tell that fox, Behold, I cast out devils, and I do cures *to-day* and *to-morrow*, and the *third* day I shall be perfected: nevertheless I must walk *to-day* and *to-morrow*, and *the day following*, Luke xiii. 32, 33. That the Lord *three* times said to Peter, Lovest thou me? and that Peter was grieved thereat the *third* time, John

xxi. 15 to 17. That the marriage in Cana of Galilee was on the *third* day, John ii. 1. That the Lord said to the Jews, Destroy this temple, and in *three* days I will raise it up. But he spake of the temple of his body, John ii. 19 to 21. That he prayed in Gethsemane *three* times, Matt. xxvi. 36 to 44. That he was crucified the *third* hour, Mark xv. 25. That there was darkness over the whole land for *three* hours, from the sixth hour until the ninth hour, Mark xv. 33. That the superscription on the cross was written in *three* languages, in Hebrew, in Greek, and in Latin, John xix. 20. That the Lord rose from the dead on the *third* day after his crucifixion, being the first day of the week, Matt. xxviii. 1 to 7.

Four.

The number *four* belongs to the celestial class of expressions, being predicated of goods or evils, and denotes all good or evil in the complex.—A. C. 10624. Ap. Ex. 430.

It also signifies conjunction to the full, in like manner as the number *two*.—A. C. 8877, 9103, 9864.

All good, also the conjunction of good and truth.—A. R. 322, 348.

Union, as consisting of pairs, in like manner as the number *two*, when it regards marriage.—A. C. 1686, 8872, 9601.

Things conjoined, like good and truth.—A. C. 6157.

When considered in relation to *five*, by which are signified remains, then the number *four* denotes goods and truths not yet become remains, that is, not yet appropriated by man.—A. C. 6157.

A *fourth* part, as well as the number *four*, denotes all good.—A. R. 322.

Anything *quadrated*, or *four-square*, denotes what is just, or what bears an equal respect to the different states of good and truth. In general, *round* forms represent things good; *four-square* forms, things just, that is, things good in the external man; and *linear* or *triangular* forms, things true and right, also in the external man.—A. C. 8458, 9717, 9861. A. R. 905.

The *four* quarters or corners of the world, called the east, the south, the west, and the north; the *four* winds; the *four* seasons of the year, called spring, summer, autumn, and winter; and the *four* times of the day, called morning, mid-day, evening, and night; signify all states of good and truth; the east, spring and morning, denoting good in its rising, also superior or interior degrees of love from the

Lord; the south, summer and mid-day, denoting truth in its light, also superior or interior degrees of wisdom and intelligence; the west, autumn and evening, denoting good in its decline, also inferior or exterior degrees of love; and the north, winter and night, denoting truth in obscurity, also inferior or exterior degrees of wisdom and intelligence; and frequently the total privation of them, which is ignorance, error and folly.—A. C. 3708, 9642, 9648. H. & H. 141 to 153. D. Love, 121. A. R. 342, 343.

EXAMPLES.

(1.) Gen. xiv. 8, 9. "And there went out the king of Sodom, and the king of Gomorrah, and the king of Admah, and the king of Zeboiim, and the king of Bela, (the same is Zoar,) and they joined battle with them in the vale of Siddim; with Chedorlaomer the king of Elam, and with Tidal king of nations, and Amraphel king of Shinar, and Arioch king of Ellasar: *four* kings with five."——By the five kings first mentioned are signified evils and falsities in general, together with the lusts and persuasions thence arising: and by the *four* kings, against whom they fought, are meant truths and goods in the external man, which before regeneration are only apparent truths and goods. The number *four*, as applied to these last kings, denotes union or conjunction, in like manner as the number *two*: while the number *five*, as applied to the former kings, denotes disunion. The whole history of Abraham being a description of the process of man's regeneration, and of the Lord's glorification while on earth, the particulars contained in this chapter concerning the battle of the *four* kings against *five*, the victory of the former over the latter, their capture of Lot, and his recovery by Abram, are to be understood, spiritually, as follows. The five kings, as already observed, denote evils and falsities belonging to the natural or external man, who is represented by Lot dwelling in Sodom: the *four* kings are apparent truths and goods, by means of which gross evils and falsities are overcome or removed in the first stage of man's regeneration, and by which also the Lord in his childhood conducted the early process of his glorification. But Abram, who is the interior rational man, being informed that Lot is captured by the *four* kings, that is, perceiving that the external man is as yet under the influence and dominion of such truths and goods as are merely apparent and not genuine, hastens to the relief of his brother Lot, in other words, purifies the external man, dissipates not only the evils and falsities therein, but also the mere appearances of truth and good, and introduces in their stead the celestial and spiritual things of love and faith, so that the external and the internal are conjoined, and in the case of the Lord, united as one.—See A. C. 1681 to 1719.

(2.) Ex. xx. 5. "I am Jehovah thy God, a jealous God, visiting the iniquity of the fathers upon the sons, upon the thirds and upon the *fourths*, to them that hate me; and showing mercy unto thousands, to them that love me and keep my commandments."——By visiting the iniquity of the fathers upon the sons, is not meant that the children shall suffer the punishment due to the crimes of the parents; for this is expressly contrary to the divine law, Deut. xxiv. 16; but that evil is transmitted hereditarily from one generation to another, and that without repentance it successively increases. In the true spiritual sense, the term *thirds*, usually but not necessarily understood of children of the *third* generation, denotes falsities in a state of fulness from beginning to end, consequently in a long continued series: and the term *fourths*, usually but not necessarily understood of children of the *fourth* generation, denotes falsities conjoined with evils in a long series. Hence by visiting the iniquity of the fathers upon the sons, upon the *thirds* and *fourths*, is signified the prolification of the false principle from evil, and that continually. This is said to be the case with those who hate Jehovah, that is, who wholly deny the divinity of the Lord and give themselves up to an evil life: whereas of those who love Jehovah, or who worship the Lord, and live in conformity to his commandments, it is said that He showeth mercy unto thousands, in other words, that He perpetually communicates to them, by an influx of good and truth from himself, the blessings of heaven and eternal life—See A. C. 8875 to 8881.

(3.) Ex. xxvii. 1, 2, 4. "And thou shalt make an altar of shittim-wood, five cubits long, and five cubits broad: the altar shall be *four-square*, and the height thereof shall be three cubits. And thou shalt make the horns of it upon the *four* corners thereof: his horns shall be of the same: and thou shalt overlay it with brass. And thou shalt make for it a grate of net-work of brass: and upon the net shalt thou make *four* brazen rings in the *four* corners thereof."——By the altar was represented the Lord as to divine love, also worship directed to Him from pure love: by shittim-wood, of which it was to be made, is signified the good of merit and justice of the Lord; for wood in general signifies good, and shittim-wood, being an excellent kind of cedar, signifies spiritual good; and in reference to the Lord, his merit and justice. The length and breadth of the altar being the same, denotes equality with respect to good and truth, and consequently the marriage or conjunction of both. Thus it was ordered to be *four-square*, because this kind of dimension signifies what is just in the Lord, and in the worship directed to Him: and the worship is said to be just, when the good and truth contained in it are from the Lord and not from man. The height thereof also was to be three cubits, to denote that the degrees of good must be full and complete: for height has respect to the degrees of good, and three cubits to their fulness. By the horns upon the *four* corners of the altar is signified the power of truth derived from good in every way: horns denote power, *four* denote conjunction, and corners denote firmness and strength; hence by horns on the *four* corners is signified power in every way and direction. By the *four* brazen rings on the *four* corners of the net-work of brass, is signified the sphere of good, by which conjunction is effected: the net-work denotes the extreme or outermost principles of life corresponding to the interior: the rings denote the sphere of divine good; their number *four*, conjunction; and their quality brass, natural good, or good in the external. From all which and other particulars, when spiritually understood, it plainly appears that the altar of burnt-offering with its various appendages, was built for the purpose of representing, in visible forms, the true worship of the Lord, which is that of the heart, the understanding and the life.—See A. C. 9714 to 9729.

(4.) Ex. xxviii. 16. "*Four-square* it shall be, being doubled; a span shall be the length thereof, and a span shall be the breadth thereof."——By the breast-plate of judgment is signified the divine truth shining forth from the divine good in an external or visible form. It was called the breast-plate of *judgment*, because thereby responses were given from heaven, and divine truth was revealed. By its form being *four-square*, when doubled, is signified what is just and perfect; the term *four-square* denoting what is just, as being derived from the Lord who is the Fountain of justice; and the term *doubled*, like the number *two*, implying perfection, conjunction and fulness. There were in the breast-plate *four* rows of precious stones, *two* on the right side and *two* on the left: those on the right represented things celestial, and those on the left things spiritual; while their inclosure in one *square* represented the perfect conjunction of good and truth, as proceeding from the Lord, both generally and particularly.—See A. C. 9857 to 9874.

(5.) Ezek. xxxvii. 9. "Thus saith the Lord Jehovah, Come from the *four* winds, O breath, and breathe upon these slain, that they may live."——By wind or breath in the Sacred Scriptures, is signified the influx of divine truth from the Lord through the angelic heaven, whereby new life is inspired into man by regeneration: hence by the *four* winds, in allusion to the *four* quarters of the spiritual world, are signified all the goods of love and all the truths of faith in conjunction; the eastern and southern quarters denoting good and truth in the highest or most perfect state; and the western and northern quarters, good and truth in a lower and more obscure state. The same is signified by the *four* winds in Matt. xxiv. 31; also by the *four* winds blowing from the *four* corners of the earth in Apoc. vii. 1; and in various other passages.—See Ap. Ex. 417, 418, 665. A. R. 342, 343.

(6.) Dan. vii. 2, 3. "Daniel spake, and said, I saw in my vision by night, and behold, the *four* winds of the heaven strove upon the great sea. And *four* great beasts came up from the sea, diverse one from another."——By the *four* winds are here signified falsities conjoined with evils; by winds falsities from evils, and by *four* their conjunction. The subject treated of in this passage being different from that in the prophet Ezekiel above adduced, the signification of the *four* winds accordingly changes to an opposite sense, as is usual in the Word: and instead of denoting an influx from heaven for the regeneration of man, they here announce an influx from hell generating evils and falsities of every description. It therefore follows that *four* great beasts immediately came up from the sea, by which are signified all kinds of evil and false principles in conjunction, originating in the love of dominion, and after successive accumulations at length destroying the whole church. On this account the *fourth* or last beast is described as being "dreadful and terrible, exceedingly strong, devouring the whole earth, treading it down, and breaking it in pieces," ver. 7, 23.—See Ap. Ex. 418, 556, 650.

(7.) Zech. i. 18 to 21. "Then I lifted up mine eyes, and saw, and behold, *four* horns. And I said unto the angel that talked with me, What are these? And he answered me, These are the horns which have scattered Judah, Israel and Jerusalem. And Jehovah showed me *four* smiths. Then said I, What come these to do? And he spake, saying, These are the horns which have scattered Judah, so that no man did lift up his head: but these are come to fray them, to cast out the horns of the gentiles, which lift up their horn over the land of Judah to scatter it."——In this passage the vastation of the church is described, and then its restoration. By Judah, Israel and Jerusalem, is signified the church, and its doctrine. The *four* horns which scattered them, signify the falsities of evil which have vastated the church: horns denote power; and the number *four* shows that the effect was complete, by reason of the conjunction of evils and falsities. The *four* smiths have the same signification as the iron on which they work, namely, truth in the ultimates, which is powerful and strong, consequently the same as a horn of iron. It is therefore said of them, "These are come to cast out the horns of the gentiles, which lift up their horn over the land of Judah to scatter it:" the horns of the gentiles are the falsities of evil, which have vastated and destroyed the church. As the *four* horns which scattered Judah, Israel and Jerusalem, do, on the one part, signify the power of false principles when in conjunction with evil; so the *four* smiths do, on the other part, signify the power of truth when in conjunction with good; and it is by this power that the church is restored.—See Ap. Ex. 316.

(8.) Zech. vi. 1 to 5. "And I turned and lifted up mine eyes and looked, and behold, there came *four* chariots out from between two mountains, and the mountains were mountains of brass. In the first chariot were red horses, and in the second chariot black horses, and in the third chariot white horses, and in the fourth chariot grizzled robust horses. Then I answered and said unto the angel that talked with me, What are these, my lord? And the angel answered and said unto me, These are the *four* spirits of the heavens, which go forth from standing before the Lord of all the earth."——The subject treated of in this passage is the propagation of the church among those who as yet are not in the light of divine truth, because they are not yet in possession of the Word. *Four* chariots are first seen to come out from between two mountains, by which are signified the doctrinals of good: chariots denote doctrinals; and their number being *four*, denotes the conjunction of good and truth therein: a mountain denotes love, consequently two mountains denote the two kinds of love, which constitute the essentials of the church, viz., love to the Lord and love to our neighbor, these being the true principles of all union and conjunction; and the mountains are said to be of brass, because brass denotes external or natural good, which is first manifested at the commencement of a church. By the red, black, white and grizzled robust horses, are understood the various qualities of the understanding of divine good and truth at the beginning and in the future progress of the church: by the red horses the quality of the understanding with respect to good, and by the white horses the quality of the understanding with respect to truth, both in the beginning of the church: by the white horses are denoted the quality of the understanding as to truth, and by the grizzled horses the same as to truth and good united, both in the succeeding states of the church: and by their being called also robust or strong horses is denoted the quality of the understanding with respect to its power of resisting falsities and evils. These horses and chariots are called the *four* spirits (or *four* winds) of the heavens, to denote the influx of divine good and divine truth into the church, in all its fulness and power of conjunction: and they are said to go forth from standing before the Lord of the whole earth, to denote that such influx proceeds solely from the Lord, who is the God of the church. In the succeeding verses, it is stated that the black horses went forth into the north country, and that the white followed after them, in consequence of which the spirit of Jehovah was quieted; by which is signified, that the understanding of divine truth was at first obscure, but afterwards more clear and perfect, with those who had heretofore been in ignorance, and thus conjunction was effected between the Lord and his church. The north country denotes a state of ignorance and obscurity. By the grizzled horses going forth towards the south country, and the robust horses walking to and fro through the earth, is signified that they who from the good of life are in the affection or desire of knowing the truths of the church, at length come into genuine spiritual light, and have the power of resisting evils and falsities, and thereby become the true church of the Lord. The south country denotes a state of intelligence, or the clear perception of divine truth.—See A. C. 3708. Ap. Ex. 355, 364, 418.

(9.) Matt. xiv. 25. "And in the *fourth* watch of the night Jesus went unto them, walking on the sea."——By the sea are here signified the ultimate or lowest principles of heaven and the church. By the Lord's walking upon the sea, is signified his presence in those principles, and an influx of life from Him into such as are still in externals, enabling them to keep in subjection the disorderly and turbulent affections of the natural man. But as it too often happens that man's faith in the Lord is weak and wavering, therefore this state of mind is also represented in the succeeding verses by Peter's beginning to sink through fear, while he was walking on the water to go to Jesus, who, on his crying out for help, immediately stretched out his hand and saved him. By the *fourth* watch in which this transaction occurred, is signified the first state of the church, when good begins to act by truth: for the *fourth* watch, being the last watch of the night, and ushering in the dawning of the day or morning, involves the end of a preceding state, and the commencement of a new one, when good is in conjunction with truth, thus when the Lord makes his advent to man.—See Ap. Ex. 514.

(10.) John iv. 35. "Say not ye, There are yet *four* months, and then cometh harvest? Behold, I say unto you, Lift up your eyes, and look on the fields; for they are white already to harvest."—— By the harvest are signified all things conducive to man's spiritual nourishment, namely, truths of doctrine and goods of life, the full implantation of which in him, together with their approaching conjunction by regeneration, is denoted by *four* months yet to come. The fields which signify the church, are said to be white to harvest when the truths of faith derived from charity are pure and genuine, or when the understanding and affections are under the influence of heavenly light and heat.—See Ap. Ex. 911.

(11.) Apoc. iv. 6. "And in the midst of the throne, and round about the throne, were *four* beasts full of eyes before and behind." ——By the throne is meant the universal heaven in which the Lord is present by his Word. By the *four* beasts which were seen in the midst of the throne, and round about the throne, is signified the Word with respect to first and last principles, or with respect to divine love and divine wisdom in union. They are said to be full of eyes before and behind, to denote not only the divine wisdom contained both internally and externally in the Word, but also the divine care, circumspection and providence, lest the interior heavens should be approached in any other spirit than that of the good of love and charity. These *four* beasts are the same as the *four* animals, living creatures, or cherubim, mentioned in the first and tenth chapters of Ezekiel, having the faces of a lion, a calf, a man, and an eagle; by each of which is signified something properly characteristic of the Word; as for example, by the lion is meant the divine truth of the Word in respect to its power; by the ox or calf, the same as to affection; by the man, the same as to wisdom; and by the eagle, the same again as to knowledges whereby the understanding is formed. —See A. R. 239 to 246. Ap. Ex. 277 to 281.

(12.) Apoc. xxi. 16. "And the city lieth *four-square*, and the length is as large as the breadth."——By the city New Jerusalem is signified the New Church in regard to its doctrine. By its being *four-square*, is signified what is just, having an equal respect to the different degrees of good and truth, in like manner as the *four* sides of a *square* bear reference to the *four* quarters of the heavens. And hence it is said that the length, by which is meant the good, is equal to the breadth, by which is meant the truth; thus that good and truth in the New Church constitute one, like essence and its form. In general it may be observed, that *quadrangular* forms signify what is just and good, and *triangular* forms what is right and true, each in the external or lowest degree.—See A. R. 905, 906.

Five.

When the number *five* has relation to such numbers as signify much, it then denotes a little or a few.—A. C. 649, 798, 5291. Ap. Ex. 548.

It also signifies disunion, because a little.—A. C. 1686.

Any thing small, or a short time.—A. R. 427.

Likewise much, as well as a little, and something, according to the nature of the subject treated of.—A. C. 5291: fully illustrated, 5708, 5956. Ap. Ex. 430.

The same as 10, 100, and 1000, viz., much, all, what is full, and in the supreme sense, in reference to the Lord, what is infinite.—A. C. 9716.

Remains, but not in so full a degree as the number *ten* implies.—A. C. 5291, 5894.

What is equal of good and truth.—A. C. 9716.

As much as is sufficient or necessary.—A. C. 9689.

All the remainder.—A. R. 738.

When contrasted with four, denotes disunion.—A. C. 1686.

All of one part, when *ten* denotes all of good and truth.—A. C. 9604, 9665.

When *ten* signifies all, then the half of that number, or *five*, signifies some; when *ten* signifies fulness, then *five* signifies as much as is sufficient, or what is correspondent; and when *ten* signifies much, then *five* signifies something.—A. C. 10255.

A *fifth* part, in like manner as the number *five*, signifies remains, etc.—A. C. 6156.

To *quintate* signifies the same as to *decimate*, that is, to make remains, or to collect goods and truths, also to preserve.—A. C. 5291.

EXAMPLES.

(1.) Gen. xlv. 22. "To all of them he gave each man changes of raiment: but to Benjamin he gave three hundred pieces of silver, and *five* changes of raiment."——Benjamin, as the medium of reconciliation or conjunction between Joseph and his ten brethren, represents that new principle of divine truth from the Lord, which equally partakes of internal good, represented by Joseph, and of natural or external truths, represented by the other ten sons of Jacob: for the design of regeneration being to unite the internal and the external of man, that process is described in this chapter; and Benjamin represents the medium or point of conjunction between those two states or degrees of life. By the changes of raiment given to each man, is signified that new truths were communicated to the natural principle on this occasion: for raiment denotes truths, and a change of them new truths, or such as are more holy than the former, in consequence of their conjunction with good. And by Benjamin's receiving a greater portion than the rest, viz., three hundred pieces of silver, and *five* changes of raiment, is signified, that the medium itself of conjunction, as being nearer the source of internal good represented by Joseph, is more fully receptive of truth from such good; and as having also an immediate influence or power over truths in the natural principle, represented by his ten brethren, is gifted at the same time with an abundance of truth from that principle now in a state of regeneration. Three hundred pieces of silver denote fulness of truth derived from good: for the number three hundred, like three, from which it arises by multiplication with a hundred, denotes fulness, and a hundred much. *Five* changes of raiment also denote much, or an abundance of truths from the natural or external principle.—See A. C. 5822, 5954 to 5956.

(2.) Ex. xxii. 1. "If a man shall steal an ox or a sheep, and kill it, or sell it; he shall restore *five* oxen for an ox, and four sheep for a sheep."——By an ox is signified the affection of good in the exterior man, or exterior good; and by a sheep, the affection of good in the interior man, or interior good. By stealing them is signified to deprive another of such goods; by killing them is signified to extinguish them; and by selling them is signified to alienate them, so that they are no longer in one's possession. The correspondent punishment and restitution for the commission of such evils, are signified by the law which enjoins that *five* oxen shall be restored for an ox, and four sheep for a sheep. Punishment to a great degree, and at the same time amendment with respect to exterior good, are signified by the restoration of *five* oxen, the number *five* here denoting much, or to a great degree, or what is sufficient: and punishment to the full, and at the same time amendment with respect to interior good, are signified by the restoration of four sheep, the number *four* here denoting to the full. The reason why interior good is to be restored *to the full*, that is, this good constitutes the spiritual life of man; and unless spiritual life be restored to the full, exterior good which constitutes the natural life, cannot be restored; for this latter life is restored by the former, just as the external man is regenerated by the internal. But exterior good, or good in the natural principle, cannot be restored *to the full*, because the stroke or wound inflicted upon it by evil of life, remains as a perpetual scar: nevertheless it may be restored *to a great degree*, or to a degree *sufficient* to make it harmonize with interior good in the spiritual principle. That these circumstances belonging to man's spiritual life might be expressed in language consistent with the rest of divine revelation, that is to say, by correspondences, it was therefore laid down as a law in the Jewish representative church, that *five* oxen should be restored as the penalty for one ox, and *four* sheep as the penalty for one sheep, that should be either stolen, killed, or sold. On any other ground of interpretation than the spiritual one here given, what reason can be assigned why *five* oxen, and only *four* sheep, should be restored? especially when it is considered, that the value of a single ox far exceeds that of a sheep, and consequently that the penalty of *five* oxen must press much more heavily on the ability of the criminal to make restitution, than the penalty of *four* sheep, though the guilt in each case is the same? This difficulty or apparent inequality in the divine law, which arises from the letter only when separated from its spiritual sense, is however not merely removed by a knowledge of the science of correspondences, and of the spiritual signification of numbers, according to which this and every other part of the Word is written, but is absolutely converted into a beauty; because the whole passage is now seen to be a manifest proof of the divine goodness, wisdom and justice, and no longer detains the mind with images drawn in shadow, but displays to an enlightened understanding all the brilliancy and perfection of truth.—See A. C. 9098 to 9103. Ap. Ex. 548.

(3.) Lev. xxvi. 8. "And *five* of you shall chase a hundred, and a hundred of you shall put ten thousand to flight."——When the number *five* is contrasted with a higher number, it then denotes something small, or a few, or indeed all of one part; while the greater number denotes much, or all of the other part. So in the present passage by *five* is meant a small portion of spiritual good and truth received from the Lord, in comparison with the great multitude of evils and falsities in man by nature, signified by a *hundred* of the enemy, which small portion is nevertheless made available to the removal of those evils and falsities during the process of regeneration. The same explanation will apply to a *hundred*, when contrasted with *ten thousand*.—See A. R. 427. Ap. Ex. 548.

(4.) Isa. xix. 18. "In that day shall *five* cities in the land of Egypt speak the language of Canaan, and swear to Jehovah of hosts: each one shall be called the city of the sun."——By this passage is signified, that at the coming of the Lord into the world, many of the gentiles who, in consequence of their ignorance of the Word, were but natural men, would, on hearing the gospel preached to them, become spiritual men, embrace the genuine doctrine of the church, and worship the Lord from a principle of pure love and charity. The period alluded to by the words, "in that day," is the coming of the Lord, when the state of those who are in natural or external scientifics, will be changed by their reception of the divine truths of the Word. *Five* cities in the land of Egypt, speaking the language of Canaan, denote the genuine truths of the doctrine of the church communicated to, and received by them in abundance: *five* denotes many, or in abundance: cities denote the truths of doctrine: the language or lip of Canaan denotes the genuine doctrinals of the church: to swear to Jehovah, is to make confession of the Lord: each one being called the city of the sun, signifies that the doctrine, even in its external form, will be that of love and charity from a spiritual origin, and will shine with heavenly light, as with the radiance of the sun. The translators of the English Bible appear to have mistaken the sense of the last clause in the verse, and have rendered it thus: "One shall be called the *city of destruction*." But the context, as well as the original expression (*ir hacheres*), which is literally *the city of the sun*, plainly implies something good, not evil—a blessing, and not a curse—as the result of the Lord's advent, and the establishment of a new church among the gentiles.—See Ap. Ex. 223, 391, 548, 654.

(5.) Matt. xxv. 1, 2. "Then shall the kingdom of heaven be likened unto ten virgins, who took their lamps, and went forth to meet the bridegroom. And *five* of them were wise, and *five* were foolish."——-By the kingdom of heaven is signified the church: the same also is signified by a virgin in respect to the affection or love of divine truth. Ten virgins, therefore, signify all who are of the church, and who have an affection for the truth, either internal or external, either for the sake of truth, or for the sake of some worldly and natural advantage. By the *five* wise virgins are meant all of the former description, and by the *five* foolish virgins all of the latter: for as the number of each class cannot be supposed to be determined by the precise number expressed, it is plain that by *five* are meant some, or some part of the whole, and indeed all of a similar character, whether it be that of wisdom or of folly. By their lamps are signified the knowledges of truth and good from the Word, also the truths of doctrine and of faith. By oil is signified the good of love and charity: and by the bridegroom is understood the Lord. All the virgins had lamps, by which is understood, that all were in the possession of knowledges from the Word. But some of them had no oil in their vessels with their lamps; that is to say, they were destitute of the good of love in their hearts, though possessed of light in their understanding: hence the latter are called foolish virgins, while the former are called wise. From this parable therefore it is evident, that the number *ten* signifies all the professing members of the church in general, and that the number *five* signifies some, or a certain part of them.—See Ap. Ex. 252, 548, 675.

(6.) Matt. xxv. 14, 15. "The kingdom of heaven is as a man travelling into a far country, who called his own servants and delivered unto them his goods. And unto one he gave *five* talents, to another two, and to another one, to every man according to his several ability, and straightway took his journey."——By the man travelling into a far country is meant the Lord, who, since his personal departure from the world, appears to be absent, or is generally thought to be so; though in reality He is equally present with men, as He was when in the flesh; nay, more so, for being now in a body altogether Divine, and bearing no relation whatever to either time or space, He is omnipresent. By his servants are signified all mankind, but especially those who belong to the church. By delivering unto them his goods, is signified that He communicates to all, though in different degrees, according to their capacity of reception, the knowledges of good and truth, which constitute the wealth of heaven; to those who are of the church in a direct manner by his Word, and to others, viz., to gentiles who are out of the church, in an indirect manner by those laws of religion which they regard as divine. By the servant who received *five* talents, are signified all those who have admitted *some* goods and truths from the Lord into their minds, and who thus have received *some* though comparatively but *a few* remains. Of this servant it is said in the succeeding part of the parable, that by trading he gained other *five* talents, so that they became *ten*; by which is signified, that by diligence, and a proper use of the *few* knowledges at first received, he at length acquired *much* wisdom : for as the number *five* denotes somewhat, or a few, so the number *ten* denotes much, or all; each number being predicated of remains, which consist of the various knowledges of truth and good, together with affections for the same, received from the Lord and treasured up in the mind from infancy. By the servant who received *two* talents, are signified all such as in advanced or mature age have adjoined charity to faith; the number *two* here, as in other parts of the Word, denoting conjunction. By the servant, who received only *one* talent, are signified all those who admitted into their minds faith separate from charity. These are said to hide their lord's money in the earth, when their knowledge of heavenly things is confined to the memory, without application to the life, and when at the same time they give themselves up to earthly and sensual pleasures. From the preceding explanation it may be seen, that the number of talents given to the different servants by their lord, as *five*, *two*, and *one*, have reference not merely to the original gift, but likewise to the use afterwards made of the gift by the receivers. To the servant who is said to have received only *one* talent, by which is understood *faith alone*, the offer of charity in conjunction with faith is ever made by his lord, as well as to him who is said to have received *two* talents: but in the one case faith or mere knowledge is received, and charity rejected, while in the other case both faith and charity are received and conjoined by actual life. And hence by the application of different numbers to the talents received by different persons, according to their true spiritual signification, we are enabled to discover what is the kind of life, which will hereafter meet with the divine approbation, and what that, which will inevitably prove our ruin.—See A. C. 2967, 5291. Ap. Ex. 193, 675.

(7.) Mark vi. 38 to 44. "He saith unto them, How many loaves have ye? go and see. And when they knew, they say, *Five*, and two fishes. And He commanded them to make all sit down by companies upon the green grass. And they sat down in ranks by hundreds and by *fifties*. And when He had taken the *five* loaves and the two fishes, He looked up to heaven, and blessed, and brake the loaves, and gave them to his disciples to set before them; and the two fishes divided He among them all. And they did all eat, and were filled. And they took up twelve baskets full of the fragments, and of the fishes. And they that did eat of the loaves, were about *five thousand* men."—— By the Lord's feeding the multitude with *five* loaves and two fishes, is signified the communication of good and truth to the members of his church, according to their capacity of reception, which as yet was but little. Loaves denote goods; and their number being *five*, denotes that as yet they were but few, because the church was then only in its commencement among men of an external character. Fishes denote natural truths, or those truths which the natural man is first receptive of; and their number being *two*, denotes that still there was a principle of good in conjunction with the truth received by the people. By their sitting down on the green grass in ranks of hundreds and fifties, is signified the disposition or arrangement of all things in the newly-formed church according to divine order: green grass denotes the first or lowest state of spiritual life in man: and ranks of hundreds and fifties denote orderly arrangement according to the various states of reception. By their eating, and being filled, is understood spiritual nourishment or instruction as they could bear it. By twelve baskets full of fragments and of fishes remaining, are signified the knowledges of good and truth proceeding from the Lord in all abundance and fulness, consequently full instruction and full blessing. The number of men, who did eat being *five thousand*, denotes all of the church who are in truths derived from good: men denote those who are in truths; and women and children, mentioned by the Evangelist Matthew (xiv. 21), denote those who are in goods. This miracle was wrought by the Lord in a similar manner to that of the production of manna in the wilderness, namely, by the extraordinary and sudden conversion of spiritual food into natural food, the multitude who were present not being at all aware of the circumstance during the time of their repast, but astonished beyond measure when they came to reflect upon it afterwards. By miracles of this description the Lord has made it fully manifest that He is both the Creator and Preserver of man.—See A. C. 5291. Ap. Ex. 430, 548, 617.

(8.) Luke xii. 6. "Are not *five* sparrows sold for two farthings, and not one of them is forgotten before God?"——*Five* sparrows here evidently denote what is of little value or estimation in comparison with man. Birds in general denote things intellectual, or things relating to the understanding in man, such as thoughts, ideas, reasonings, principles, intentions, truths, or falsities, according to the nature of the subject treated of. Birds of a higher order, as eagles, represent thoughts formed on rational principles, and consequently of an interior quality; but birds of an inferior order, such as sparrows, etc., represent thoughts of a trifling and external character, or such as occupy the lower region of the mind. Hence the Lord, when speaking of his divine providence over every thing relating to man, assures his disciples, that the *least* as well as the *greatest* things in and about Him are under his immediate notice and regard. This is expressed as usual by such objects in nature as correspond to, and are significative of, those things in man which are of the lowest consideration, namely, sparrows, which are said not to be forgotten by God, and in ver. 7, the very hairs of the head, which are said to be all numbered. —See A. C. 5096, 5149. A. R. 757, 837. Ap. Ex. 453, 548. T. C. R. 42.

(9.) Luke xii. 52. " From henceforth there shall be *five* in one house divided, three against two and two against three."——The signification of the number *five* varies according to its relation to other numbers: thus when it is preceded or followed by ten, twenty, or higher numbers, it signifies some, a few, or a little; but when preceded or followed by lower numbers, as two and three, it then signifies all or many. In the present passage, by *five* in one house are meant all or many in the church at large, or all or many things in one individual mind. By their being divided, three against two and two against three, is signified that truths will be opposed to evils, and evils to truths; also that falsities will be opposed to goods, and goods to falsities: for such is the double signification of the numbers three and two, three being predicated either of truths or falsities, and two either of goods or evils. This opposition, which is expressive of a state of temptation into which the members of the church are permitted to fall when the Lord comes to establish his church among men, is the means whereby the process of regeneration is effected; for hereby man is led to see and acknowledge the impurities and corruptions of his nature, and seeing them, to renounce, resist and overcome them by the aid of divine truth and good received from the Lord. It is in reference to this state of trial and spiritual temptation, that the Lord says in ver. 51, "Suppose ye that I am come to give peace on earth? I tell you, Nay; but rather *division*." And in another place, "Think not that I am come to send peace on earth: I came not to send peace, but a *sword*," Matt. x. 34; that is, not a false peace, or heedless and fatal security, but the power of divine truth, whereby all spiritual enemies may be subdued, and true heavenly peace established in the mind, agreeably to these his divine words, "Peace I leave with you, my peace I give unto you; not as the world giveth, give I unto you," John xiv. 27; thus proving himself to be what the prophet of old declared He would be, "the Prince of peace," Isa. ix. 6.—See A. C. 4843, 5023, 5291. Ap. Ex. 504, 532, 548, 724.

(10.) Luke xiv. 16 to 20. "A certain man made a great supper, and bade many. And they all with one consent began to make excuse. The first said unto him, I have bought a piece of ground, and I must needs go and see it: I pray thee have me excused. And another said, I have bought *five* yoke of oxen, and I go to prove them: I pray thee have me excused. And another said, I have married a wife, and therefore I cannot come."——By the great supper to which many were invited, is signified heaven and the church, where spiritual nourishment or instruction is communicated by the Lord to man. It is called a supper or evening repast, in reference to the end of a former church and the commencement of a new one. The persons invited were the Jews, who yet excused themselves from attending the supper, urging reasons which were all grounded in the love of external, worldly and corporeal things, separate from those of an internal and heavenly nature. By the first stating that he had bought a piece of ground and must needs go and see it, is signified that he had procured to himself such religious principles as were congenial with his love, and that his attention and thoughts would henceforth be directed to them in preference to any other: a piece of ground or a field, being that which is fitted to receive seeds, denotes in the genuine sense a state of spiritual good in the mind qualifying it for the reception of heavenly truths; but in the opposite sense, a state of evil in the mind which will admit only of falsities or gross errors: and the desire of going to see it, implies that the powers of the understanding would be willingly employed in confirmation of the same. By the second excusing himself on the ground of his having bought *five* yoke of oxen, which he was desirous of proving, is signified that all his natural affections, lusts and pleasures arising from his intercourse with the world, were too dear and captivating to be renounced, and therefore he was still disposed to indulge them: oxen denote natural affections, either good or evil, but in the present case evil affections or lusts which withdraw the mind from heaven; and *five* yoke of oxen denote all such affections and lusts: to prove them, is to live in the indulgence of them. By the answer which the third made to the invitation, viz., that he had married a wife and therefore could not come, is signified that evils and falsities arising from self-love and the love of the world, were so united or conjoined in him, as in a kind of infernal marriage, and had likewise gained such an ascendancy over him, that all his affections were already engaged, and consequently that he had no desire to change his life: marriage in a good sense denotes the conjunction of goods and truths, but in an opposite sense, as here, the conjunction of evils and falsities.—See A. C. 5291. Ap. Ex. 252, 548, 1162. H. & H. 377.

(11.) Luke xvi. 27, 28. "The rich man in hell said unto Abraham, I pray thee, father, that thou wouldst send Lazarus to my father's house; for I have *five* brethren; that he may testify unto them, lest they also come into this place of torment."——By the rich man are meant the Jews, who are said to be rich, because they were in possession of the Word, or the divine truths of revelation which constitute the riches of heaven: by Lazarus are meant the gentiles, who are said to be poor because they were then destitute of the Word: and by Abraham in whose bosom Lazarus was seen, is signified the Lord. Hence by the *five* brethren of the rich man are signified all of a similar quality and description with himself. The torment which he experienced in hell, did not consist in any pain or punishment inflicted upon him by natural fire, as is generally supposed; for a spirit cannot possibly be injured or tormented by such fire. Neither did his prayer to Abraham spring from any love or kindness to his brethren, who were still in the body; for an infernal spirit is not susceptible of affection or tenderness to either friend or foe. But by the pain or torment of which he complained, is signified the restraint he was under, and the pungent distress he experienced, in no longer having the opportunity of perverting the divine truths of the Word, and consequently of doing mischief to others thereby; it being the chief delight of every infernal spirit to infest the good, and if possible to destroy them without mercy; which delight, on being prohibited from rushing into action, is converted into wretchedness and unspeakable misery. The ardent desire on the part of the rich man to pervert the Word and to destroy souls, together with the punishment attending it, is thus expressed in ver. 24: "Father Abraham, have mercy on me, and send Lazarus that he may dip the tip of his finger in water, and cool my tongue; for I am tormented in this flame." By the water into which he wished Lazarus to dip the tip of his finger, is signified the divine truth of the Word: and by his tongue which was heated and tormented by flame, is signified his ardent desire and lust of perverting such truth, with the punishment annexed to it. To cool the tongue, is to assuage the thirst or desire of perverting truth by indulging the inclination: but as he was denied this gratification, he therefore complained that he was tormented by the flame, that is, by the lust within him, which is described as a burning flame. And the only reason why he expressed a desire that his *five* brethren might not come into a similar state of torment with himself, was, that, if he could not by his own malicious exertions accomplish the above purpose, he hoped that all others who were in spirit like himself, might, while they had the opportunity, still continue to act as he had done, that is, pervert the divine truths of the Word with a view to the destruction and final ruin of the innocent.—See A. R. 282, 725. Ap. Ex. 455, 548.

(12.) Apoc. ix. 5. "And to them it was given that they should not kill them, but that they should be tormented *five* months."—— By the locusts which came forth out of the smoke, that ascended from the bottomless pit, mentioned in the preceding verses, are signified the ultimate or sensual principles in man, which receive the influx of infernal falsities. By their being commanded not to hurt the grass of the earth, nor any green thing, nor any tree, but only those men who have not the seal of God in their foreheads, is signified the divine providence of the Lord in preserving the literal or external sense of the Word from being openly denied, and thereby destroyed, at the end of the church, though the true sense of it is perverted by those who are not in truths derived from good: the grass of the earth is scientific truth grounded in the literal sense of the Word: the green thing is the good of faith, or the life thereof: trees are the knowledges or perceptions of truth and good: and the men, who have not the seal of God in their foreheads, are those who are not in truths derived from good. By their not being permitted to kill such men, but only to torment them *five* months, is signified that the faculty or capacity of understanding what is true and of choosing what is good, is not absolutely taken away from them, but only a state of stupefaction or insensibility to truth is induced upon them for a short time, that is, so long as they suffer themselves to be seduced by fallacious reasonings: to kill men, is to deprive them of the faculty or capacity of understanding, perceiving and choosing what is true and good; for man is man by virtue of such faculty, which always remains with him, though the actual understanding of truth and perception of good may be suspended, and for a time extinguished: to torment them *five* months, is to induce a degree of stupor and insensibility as to the understanding of truth for a short time, or so long as they are in the state above described; for a month, like all other times, is expressive of state, and the number *five* denotes something, a little, a short time, and consequently so long as the state alluded to continues.—See A. R. 424 to 427. Ap. Ex. 543 to 548.

Six.

The number *six* belongs to the spiritual class of expressions, being predicated of truths or falsities, and denotes all truth or falsity in the complex.—A. C. 10624. A. R. 322. Ap. Ex. 194, 430, 532.

It also signifies all things of truth from good.—A. C. 9555.

All things of faith and charity, or of truth and good, like the number *twelve*.—A. C. 3960, 7973. A. R. 245.

All states of labor, combat and temptation before rest and peace arising from the conjunction of good and truth.—A. C. 737, 1903, 4178, 8494, 8975, 10360.

Man's proprium.—A. R. 519.

First states of instruction and regeneration, when man is in combat, and is led by truth to good.—A. C. 9272, 10667, 10729.

All states of labor, combat and temptation preceding full regeneration.—A. C. 6 to 13, 737, 900, illustrated.

The dispersion of what is false in temptations, also the holy principle of faith which is implied in temptations.—A. C. 737.

Preparation for celestial marriage.—A. C. 10637.

Reception of truth before conjunction with good.—A. C. 8506.

The end of a preceding state.—A. C. 8421.

What is complete from the beginning to the end.—A. R. 489.

The end of the former church, and commencement of the new.—A. C. 9741.

When the number *six* has relation to *twelve*, or to *three*, being considered as the half of one, and double the other, it then signifies the holy principle of faith; because *twelve* signifies all things belonging

446 A KEY TO NUMBERS.

to faith, and *three* signifies what is holy.—A. C. 737, 3239, 3960, 8148.

When considered as compounded of *three* multiplied by *two*, it then signifies all things relating to truth and good; for the number *three* signifies fulness, or the all of truth, and the number *two* signifies the marriage or conjunction of truth with good.—A. R. 245, 610.

The *sixth* part, *sixth* day, and *sixth* hour, have the same signification as the number *six* itself, viz., what is full, complete and perfect from beginning to end.—A. R. 610. A. C. 8421.

EXAMPLES.

(1.) Gen. i. 31. "And God saw every thing that He had made, and behold, it was very good. And the evening and the morning were the *sixth* day."——By the *six* days of creation are meant all states of labor, combat and temptation during the process of man's regeneration, until, by repeated advances from lower to higher degrees of the spiritual life called evening and morning, he enters into a state of heavenly rest and peace, signified by the seventh day. And as this cannot be effected by any power belonging to man, but only by a divine agency operating through the medium of truth received into the understanding and affections, it is therefore said that God created, that is regenerated man, and then ceased from all his labor. Thus the *sixth* day denotes the completion or end of the states above described, whereby man first becomes an image, and afterwards a likeness of the Lord. The former states or stages are declared to be *good*, but this last *very good*, by reason of the end which is now attained, namely, the conjunction of good and truth, or the heavenly marriage.—See A. C. 6 to 13, 60 to 63.

(2.) Ex. xvi. 26. "*Six* days ye shall gather it (manna); but on the seventh day, which is the sabbath, in it there shall be none."——By manna is signified the good which is acquired by means of truth, or by living according to the dictates of truth. By the Israelites gathering manna *six* days, but not on the seventh, is signified that such good may, according to divine order, be acquired in states of labor, combat and temptation, or before the actual conjunction of truth with good takes place, but not afterwards: *six* days denote states of labor, combat and temptation, during which truth leads or introduces to good: the seventh day denotes the conjunction of good and truth, consequently a state of rest and tranquillity when man is led by the Lord without labor and combat, because he is led from affection and delight, and because his labor or earnest endeavor to procure good is superseded by the actual possession of it. The state of man before regeneration and his state after it, are widely different the one from the other; in the former he acts from truth, and thereby acquires good; in the latter he acts from good, and thence perceives truth. When arrived at this latter state, it would be disorderly in him to return to the former: on which account the Lord says in the Gospel, "In that day, he who shall be on the house-top, (in the principle of good,) and his vessels (or truths) in the house, let him not come down to take them away: and he that is in the field, (in the good acquired by truth,) let him likewise not return back. Remember Lot's wife," Luke xvii. 31, 32.—See A. C. 8462 to 8510.

(3.) Ex. xx. 9 to 11. "*Six* days shalt thou labor, and do all thy work. But the seventh day is the sabbath of Jehovah thy God: in it thou shalt not do any work, thou, nor thy son, nor thy daughter, thy man-servant, nor thy maid-servant, nor thy cattle, nor thy stranger that is within thy gates. For in *six* days Jehovah made heaven and earth, the sea, and all that in them is, and rested the seventh day: wherefore Jehovah blessed the sabbath-day, and hallowed it."
——By the *six* days of labor are signified the various states of combat, which precede and prepare for the celestial marriage, or the conjunction of good and truth in man. The seventh day denotes that holy marriage or conjunction, with all the felicities arising from it, and in the supreme sense the union of the Lord's Divinity and his Divine Humanity. By the son, daughter, man-servant, maid-servant, cattle and stranger ceasing from labor, is signified that all things belonging to the internal and external man ought to partake of that rest and peace which is represented and typified by the seventh day. And by the heaven, the earth, the sea and all that is in them, which Jehovah made, are signified in general those internal and external principles of spiritual and celestial life, which man receives by regeneration from the Lord.—See A. C. 8888 to 8895.

(4.) Ex. xxi. 2. "If thou buy a Hebrew servant, *six* years he shall serve; and in the seventh he shall go out free for nothing."
——By a Hebrew servant are signified all those members of the church who are in the truths of doctrine, but not in the good of life corresponding with such truths, and abstractly the truths themselves: hence to buy a Hebrew servant, is to procure those truths. They are called servants, because the truth which they profess is itself a

servant in respect to good, being subservient thereto: and they are called Hebrews, because a Hebrew signifies one who belongs to the church, and who therefore can perform service or use in the church. By his serving *six* years is signified that such persons undergo a state of labor and some degree of combat, during which the truth of faith is confirmed in them by the Lord: *six* years denote labor and combat, the result of which is confirmation in the truth. By his going out free for nothing in the seventh year, is signified a state of confirmed truth without any labor of his own. The seventh year in general bears the same signification as the seventh day or sabbath, namely, the conjunction of good and truth, or the celestial marriage, thus a state of peace and freedom, which succeeds a state of servitude: but in the present case, as the subject treats of those external men in the church who are in truth and not in the corresponding good of life, the seventh day merely denotes the confirmation of truth with them, which is effected by the Lord gratuitously, that is, without any labor of their own.—See A. C. 8974 to 8976.

(5.) Lev. xxv. 3, 4. "*Six* years thou shalt sow thy field, and *six* years thou shalt prune thy vineyard, and gather in the fruit thereof. But in the seventh year shall be a sabbath of rest unto the land, a sabbath for Jehovah: thou shalt neither sow thy field, nor prune thy vineyard."——The two states of the regenerate life are here alluded to; the first being a state of instruction in the truths and goods of faith, and appropriation of the same, signified by sowing the field, and pruning the vineyard for *six* years, and gathering in the fruit thereof; the second being a state of rest, tranquillity and peace signified by the seventh year, when all labor should cease.—See A. C. 9272 to 9274.

(6.) Num. xxxv. 14, 15. "Ye shall give three cities on this side Jordan, and three cities shall ye give in the land of Canaan, which shall be cities of refuge. These *six* cities shall be a refuge, both for the children of Israel, and for the stranger, and for the sojourner among them; that every one who killeth any person unawares, may flee thither."——By those persons who killed another without design, or, as it is usually expressed, by accident, were represented all those in the church, who by their false reasonings and persuasions on the subject of faith do a serious injury to another, and even extinguish his spiritual life, yet without any such intention or purpose, as is the case with some zealous but well-meaning and conscientious professors. Such man-slayers were exempt from punishment, on betaking themselves to one of the cities of refuge which were expressly appointed for their benefit; by which circumstance was signified that, whatever errors of judgment may mislead a man, yet if he act uprightly, sincerely and conscientiously, bearing no malice or enmity against his neighbor, a merciful providence is made in his behalf, by protecting him from the punishment that would otherwise have fallen upon him. *Six* cities of refuge were appointed, three on the one side, and three on the other side of Jordan, because the number *six*, like the number *three*, denotes what is holy, and at the same time what is full and complete. See A. C. 9011. A. R. 610.

(7.) Isa. vi. 2. " Above it stood the seraphim; each one had *six* wings; with twain he covered his face, and with twain he covered his feet, and with twain he did fly."——By the seraphim is signified the Word, properly doctrine from the Word, also the divine providence of the Lord in guarding and defending the superior or interior heavens from being approached in any other spirit than that of love and charity. By wings, in like manner as by arms or hands, is signified the power of divine truth; also circumspection, presence and defence: and by there being *six* in number to each seraph is signified the fulness and perfection of such power, which is the same thing as the divine omnipotence and omnipresence. By the twain with which he covered his face, is signified the protection of the interior things of the Word, of heaven, and the church, from violation and profanation: by the twain with which he covered his feet, is signified the protection also of the exterior things belonging to the same: and by the twain with which he did fly, is signified the power of instruction, communication and perception of the divine things contained in the Word. The cherubim seen by the prophet Ezekiel have a similar signification; and of them it is said that " their wings touched each other, and covered their bodies on this side and on that side; that the noise of their wings was like the noise of great waters, as the voice of the Almighty when he speaketh ; and that the likeness of the hands of a man was under their wings," Ezek. i. 23, 24; iii. 13; x. 5, 8, 21—See A. R. 245. Ap. Ex. 282 to 285. A. C. 8764.

(8.) Ezek. ix. 2. "And behold, *six* men came from the way of the higher gate, which lieth toward the north, and every man with a slaughter-weapon in his hand."——By a man with a slaughter-weapon coming from the gate towards the north, is signified the false principle derived from evil entering into the church, and vastating or destroying it. The same is also understood by *six* men; but this number is added, to show that the destruction is total and complete.—See A. R. 440. A. C. 737, 2242.

(9.) Ezek. xxxix. 2. "And I will turn thee back, and leave but the *sixth* part of thee."——By Gog, the chief prince of Meshech and Tubal, of whom these words are spoken, is signified external worship separate from what is internal; or the perverted church, which places all worship in the observance of its external rites and ceremonies, without any regard to a life of charity. By *sextating*, or leaving but a *sixth* part of Gog, is signified the total destruction of every truth derived from good in such a church: the *sixth* part denotes the same as the number *six* itself, being predicated of truths, and in the opposite sense, of falsities.—See A. R. 610, 859. A. C. 737, 1151.

(10.) Ezek. xlv. 13. "This is the oblation that ye shall offer, the *sixth* part of an ephah of an homer of wheat; and ye shall give the *sixth* part of an ephah of an homer of barley."——The ephah, the homer and the omer, being dry measures, have in the Word the same signification as the things contained in them, and are predicated of good; while the hin, the cor and the bath, being measures for liquids, are in general predicated of truth. The oblation to be offered was ordered to be the *sixth* part of an ephah of wheat and barley, to denote that the worship of the Lord must be wholly and entirely directed to Him from those pure affections of the heart which are represented in the Word by wheat and barley.—See A. R. 610. A. C. 8468, 8540, 10262.

(11.) Mark xv. 33. "And when the *sixth* hour was come, there was darkness over the whole land until the ninth hour."——By the darkness which overspread the whole earth at the time of the Lord's crucifixion, for three hours, viz., from the *sixth* unto the ninth hour, was signified and represented the total defect of love and faith throughout the church, or the actual presence of evils and falsities of the grossest description. The sun denotes love, and the light thereof faith or truth, which being totally extinguished by the rejection and crucifixion of the Lord who is himself the "sun of righteousness," and the "true light which enlighteneth every man that cometh into the world," gross darkness or mere falsities necessarily succeeded. This darkness is described by the Evangelists as continuing for three hours, that is, from the *sixth* to the ninth hour, in order to show that the prevalence of false principles derived from evil was total and universal; for such is the spiritual purport of the numbers *three*, *six*, and *nine*.—See A. C. 1839. Ap. Ex. 526.

(12.) John ii. 6. "And there were set there *six* water-pots of stone, after the manner of the purifying of the Jews, containing two or three firkins apiece."——By the marriage in Cana of Galilee, to which both Jesus and his disciples were called, is signified the establishment of a new church among the gentiles. By the water which was converted into wine, is signified the truth of the external or literal sense of the Word, such as it was with the Jews, opened and explained according to the internal and spiritual sense, such as it was to be among Christians. By the *six* water-pots of stone, which were placed there, after the manner of the purifying of the Jews, are signified all those things in the Word, and in the Jewish worship, which were representative and significative of divine spiritual things in the Lord and from the Lord. The water-pots are said to be of stone, because a stone signifies truth in the natural principle: and their number was *six*, because *six* denotes all, and is predicated of truths. The external purification or washing of the Jews also represented and signified the internal purification of the heart, whereby regeneration is advanced, and the church established.—See Ap. Ex. 376. A. R. 610.

Seven.

The number *seven* and all *septenary* numbers in general refer to what is holy, but in an opposite sense to what is profane.—A. R. 10. A. C. 5265.

It signifies what is holy and inviolable, like the number *three*.—A. C. 395, 433, 482, 813. Ap. Ex. 430.

What is most holy, as being of the Lord alone; in the supreme sense the essential divine principle, and in a representative sense the celestial principle of love. It always adds a degree of holiness to the subject treated of, which holiness is from the celestial principle, or charity.—A. C. 716, 717, 5265.

Fulness in regard to what is holy.—A. C. 10127.

A state of peace and rest.—A. C. 85, 87, 395.

The union or conjunction of good and truth, after six days of labor.—A. C. 10360.

An entire period from beginning to end, thus a full state.—A. C. 5265, 6508, 9228, 10127.

All things, and all persons, and hence what is full and perfect.—A. R. 10, 65. Ap. Ex. 257.

The last state of regeneration, when man is in good, and at the same time in peace, and in heaven with the Lord.—A. C. 10367, 10668.

The coming of the Lord, the end of a former state, and the beginning of a new state with those who are about to be regenerated.—A. C. 728, 9296.

The celestial marriage, or state of heavenly peace.—A. C. 8976.

The celestial man, the celestial church, the celestial kingdom, and the Lord himself.—A. C. 433, 1988.

The kingdom of the Lord in heaven and on earth.—A. C. 85.

Seven days, or a *week*, whether of days, months, or years, denote an entire period, great or small, from beginning to end, including every state of reformation, regeneration and temptation, both in general and in particular.—A. C. 2044, 3845.

In the opposite sense *seven* denotes what is profane.—A. C. 433, 5268.

The *seventh* day, or *sabbath* of rest, signifies the union of the Divinity called the Father, with the Divine Humanity called the Son, thus the Divine Humanity itself, in which that union has taken place.—A. C. 851, 10360.

Also the conjunction of the Lord with heaven, with the church, with an angel of heaven, and with a man of the church.—A. C. 10360. Also the conjunction of good and truth.—A. C. 8504, 8507-9, or the state when man is in good.—A. C. 9274. See also as to opposite states of mind, A. R. 672, 676. The *seventh* month, what is holy.—A. C. 852.

The *seventh* or *sabbatic* year, also the year of *jubilee*, after a period of *seven times seven* years, represented the marriage of good and truth in the inmost heaven, and a state of celestial peace and tranquillity. —A. C. 8802, 9974.

Seven-fold denotes what is holy and inviolable.—A. C. 395, 433.

EXAMPLES.

(1.) Gen. ii. 2. "And on the *seventh* day God ended his work which He had made: and He rested on the *seventh* day from all his work which He had made."——By the six days of labor in which God is said to work, are signified all preceding states of regeneration, when man is chiefly led by truth to good: and hence by the *seventh* day is denoted the end of those states of truth, and the commencement of a new state, which is a state of good, when there is no longer any labor or combat, but rest and peace. And as the process of regeneration from first to last is conducted by the Lord alone, therefore it is said that God *rested* on the *seventh* day from all his work.—See A. C. 84 to 88.

(2.) Gen. xli. 1 to 7. "And it came to pass at the end of two full years, that Pharaoh dreamed, and behold, he stood by the river. And behold, there came up out of the river *seven* well-favored kine, and fat-fleshed; and they fed in a meadow. And behold, *seven* other kine came up after them out of the river, ill-favored and lean-fleshed; and they stood by the other kine, upon the brink of the river. And the ill-favored and lean-fleshed kine did eat up the *seven* well-favored and fat kine. So Pharaoh awoke. And he slept, and dreamed the second time: and behold, *seven* ears of corn came up upon one stalk, fat and good. And behold, *seven* thin ears, and blasted with the east-wind, sprung up after them. And the *seven* thin ears devoured the *seven* fat and full ears: and Pharaoh awoke, and behold, it was a dream."——The two dreams here related, the one concerning the *seven* kine, and the other concerning the *seven* ears of corn, refer to the regeneration of the interior and the exterior of the natural principle. By the *seven* well-favored and fat-fleshed kine, which fed in a meadow, are signified the truths of the interior natural principle, which have respect to faith and charity, and multiply in man through the medium of scientifics. The kine or cows denote those truths: they are said to be well-favored, or beautiful in aspect, because spiritual beauty is derived from the affection of the truth of faith: they are also said to be fat-fleshed, because fat is predicated of the good of love and charity, and flesh of the will-principle vivified by the Lord: and they are further described as feeding in a meadow, or rather in the sedge or long and large grass at the side of the river, to denote instruction in scientifics. By the *seven* other kine, ill-favored and lean-fleshed, which ate up the *seven* well-favored and fat-fleshed kine, are signified the falsities of the natural principle, which are opposed to faith and charity, and apparently exterminate the truths at the commencement of regeneration, though in reality these latter are not exterminated, but stored up in the interior, to be there filled with good, and afterwards brought forth in the external. The reason why there were *seven* well-favored and *seven* ill-favored kine, is, that in the former case the number *seven* signifies what is holy, and adds sanctity to the subject treated of; but in the latter case it signifies what is unholy and profane, being taken in the opposite sense, as is usual in many parts of the Word. So again, in the second dream, by the *seven* ears of corn on one stalk, fat and good, are signified the scientifics of the exterior natural principle, which are of use, as being subservient to faith and charity. They are said to be fat, because of their fitness to receive the good of faith; and good, because of their fitness to receive the things of charity. And by the *seven* thin ears, blasted with the east-wind, which devoured the *seven* fat and good ears, are signified the scientifics which are of no use, because they are filled with lusts, and apparently exterminate the good scientifics, in the same manner as falsities apparently exterminate truths. The ears are said to be thin, because they are of no spiritual use or advantage; and blasted with the east-wind, because the fire of lusts in the end consumes them. Both the fat ears and the thin ears were in number *seven*, as were the fat and lean kine, to denote in the one case what is holy, and in the other case what is unholy and profane.—See A. C. 5193 to 5219, 5265 to 5270.

(3.) Ex. xxxiv. 18. "The feast of unleavened bread shalt thou keep: *seven* days shalt thou eat unleavened bread."——By the feast of unleavened bread is signified worship and thanksgiving to the Lord for deliverance from evil, and from the falsities of evil. The feast itself denoted the commemoration of that event, and especially the glorification of the Lord's Humanity: and unleavened bread denotes good purified from evils and falsities. By eating thereof *seven* days is signified the reception and appropriation of divine good and truth, in a state of sanctity from beginning to end.—See A. C. 9287 to 9289, 10655, 10656.

(4.) Ps. cxix. 164. "*Seven* times a day do I praise thee, because of thy righteous judgments."——*Seven* times a day denotes always, or perpetually, also with the whole heart.—See Ap. Ex. 257. A. C. 395, 9228.

(5.) Isa. xxx. 26. "The light of the moon shall be as the light of the sun, and the light of the sun shall be *seven-fold*, as the light of *seven* days, in the day that Jehovah bindeth up the breach of his people, and healeth the stroke of their wound."——By the light of the moon is signified a state of intelligence and wisdom arising from faith in the Lord, in the spiritual kingdom; and by the light of the sun is signified a state of wisdom and intelligence arising from love to the Lord in the celestial kingdom: for by the moon is denoted faith, and by the sun love. By the light of the former becoming as the light of the latter, and by the latter being *seven-fold* as the light of *seven* days, is signified that the splendor of divine truth among the angels of the inferior heavens will, after the coming of the Lord, be similar to that which before existed in the superior heavens, and the splendor of divine truth in these will be abundantly increased, and in the highest possible degree of purity and perfection. *Seven* and *seven-fold* denote what is holy, pure, full and perfect. The breach of the people denotes falsities of doctrine in the church, and the stroke of their wound denotes evil of life. To bind up and to heal these, is to produce reformation both of doctrine and of life by means of divine truth. The day in which this was to be effected, denotes the coming of the Lord into the world for the redemption and salvation of mankind.—See Ap. Ex. 257, 401, 962. A. C. 719, 9228.

(6.) Dan. ix. 25. "Know therefore and understand, that from the going forth of the commandment to restore and to build Jerusalem, unto the Messiah the Prince, shall be *seven* weeks."——From the going forth of the commandment, denotes from the period when the Word of the Old Testament was completed: unto the Messiah the Prince, is until the coming of the Lord: and *seven weeks* denote a full and entire period from beginning to end, the completion of which is called the fulness of times.—See Ap. Ex. 684. A. C. 6508, 9228.

(7.) Matt. xii. 43 to 45. "When the unclean spirit is gone out of a man, he walketh through dry places, seeking rest, and findeth none. Then he saith, I will return into my house from whence I came out; and when he is come, he findeth it empty, swept and garnished. Then goeth he, and taketh with himself *seven* other spirits more wicked than himself, and they enter in and dwell there: and the last state of that man is worse than the first."——The conversion of man is here described by the unclean spirit going out of him. Dry places, or places without water, denote where there are no truths. His relapse into evils of life, and in consequence thereof a state of profanation, are signified by the return of the unclean spirit, together with *seven* others more wicked than himself. The house empty, swept and garnished, is the mind deprived of truths and goods, and therefore full of falsities and evils, which are spiritual uncleanness. Hence it is plain that the number *seven*, when applied in an opposite sense, that is, in relation to evils and falsities, signifies a full state of spiritual depravity, or the destruction of all good and truth.—See Ap. Ex. 257, 1160. A. C. 3142, 4744, 9228.

(8.) Matt. xv. 34 to 37. "Jesus saith unto them, How many loaves have ye? And they said, *Seven*, and a few little fishes. And

He commanded the multitude to sit down on the ground. And He took the *seven* loaves and the fishes, and gave thanks, and brake them, and gave to his disciples, and the disciples to the multitude. And they did all eat and were filled: and they took up of the broken meat that was left, *seven* baskets full."——By the Lord's feeding the multitude with *seven* loaves and a few little fishes, is signified instruction relative to things good and true, and at the same time reception on the part of the people. The loaves denote good, and were *seven* in number to denote fulness, as well as a state of sanctity: the fishes denote truth, and are said to be few and small, because the people as yet were ignorant of those divine truths, which distinguish between the Christian and the Jewish dispensation. The surplus of broken meat consisting of *seven* baskets full, confirms the signification of the number *seven*, as implying fulness and abundance.—See Ap. Ex. 257.

(9.) Matt. xviii. 21, 22. "Then came Peter to Him, and said, Lord, how oft shall my brother sin against me, and I forgive him? till *seven* times? Jesus saith unto him, I say not unto thee, Until *seven* times; but until *seventy times seven*."——The number *seven* first mentioned signifies much, or many times; but when increased to *seventy times seven*, it denotes perpetually, or without end. And such is the nature of Christian charity, that it requires man to be constantly in the spirit of love, always disposed to forgive injuries, and to do good to others.—See A. C. 433. Ap. Ex. 527, 820.

(10.) Apoc. i. 4. "John to the *seven* churches, which are in Asia: Grace be unto you, and peace, from Him who is, and who was, and who is to come; and from the *seven* spirits which are before his throne."——By the *seven* churches in Asia are not meant *seven* churches, but all who are of the church throughout the Christian world, where the Word is received, and the Lord thereby known. And again by the *seven* spirits before his throne are meant all who are in divine truth, and abstractly divine truth itself; the number *seven* here, as in other places, denoting all things and all persons, and consequently what is full and perfect, at the same time that it involves a state of sanctity.—See A. R. 10, 14.

(11.) Apoc. i. 20. "The mystery of the *seven* stars, which thou sawest in my right hand, and the *seven* candlesticks. The *seven* stars are the angels of the *seven* churches; and the *seven* candlesticks, which thou sawest, are the *seven* churches."——By the *seven* stars is signified the New Church in the heavens, which is also called the

New Heaven: for as the Word is in the heavens as well as on the earth, and the church is such by virtue of the Word and the knowledges of good and truth thence derived, hence the universal church in the heavens is described by *seven* stars, each society therein shining as a star, by reason of the light which it receives from the Lord through the medium of his Word. The heavenly societies, as well as the individuals thereof, are also called angels. By the *seven* candlesticks is signified the New Church on earth, which is the New Jerusalem descending from the Lord out of the New Heaven. The candlesticks, stars and churches are said to be *seven*, not in reference to their number, but to the things signified by that number, which are all the states of good, truth and holiness communicated by the Lord to the church, which in itself is one, both in the spiritual and in the natural world.—See A. R. 64 to 66.

(12.) Apoc. v. i. "And I saw in the right hand of Him that sat on the throne, a book written within and on the backside, sealed with *seven* seals."——By the book written within and on the backside, is signified the Word as to its particular and general contents, or as to its internal and external sense. By its being sealed with *seven* seals is signified that its contents were altogether hidden from the understanding or perception of men, until revealed by the Lord, who as to his Divinity is described by Him that sat on the throne, and as to his Humanity by the Lion of the tribe of Judah, and by the Lamb. —See A. R. 256, 257.

(13.) Apoc. xii. 3. "And there appeared another wonder in heaven, and behold, a great red dragon having *seven* heads and ten horns, and *seven* crowns upon his heads."——By the great red dragon are signified all those in the Protestant or Reformed churches, who make three persons of God, and two of the Lord, and who separate charity from faith, supposing that this latter, and not the former, has a saving power. The professors of this faith generally address the Father as one God, for the sake of the Son as another God, praying that He would send the Holy Spirit, as a third God, to sanctify and regenerate them; thus forming in their imaginations three distinct Gods, though with their lips they make confession of only one God. The same professors, in their doctrine concerning the Lord, separate his Humanity from his Divinity, and thereby make two persons of Him, one of which they consider as having existed from eternity, and therefore in several respects equal to the divine person of the Father, while the other is regarded by them as little, if at all, different from the person of another man. It is further insisted upon by the professors of this doctrine, that faith in the merits of the Saviour, without any regard to charity or a good life, is all that is necessary to secure man's salvation.* Thus in every part of their doctrine they are opposed to the New Church, which teaches that there is only one God in one divine person, in whom is a trinity of essentials, like soul, body and operation in man; and that our Lord and Saviour Jesus Christ is that God; and further, that if man would be saved, charity and faith must be united in him as one, and together bring forth the fruits of a good and useful life, yet under the continual acknowledgment that all the good he does and all the truth he thinks, are derived solely from the Lord. But, as before observed, the dragon denotes all those who hold to a trinity of divine persons, and justification by faith alone both in doctrine and in life. By his having *seven* heads is signified a state of spiritual insanity arising from a false interpretation and profane application of the truths of the Word. In a genuine sense the head denotes wisdom and intelligence, because it is the seat thereof: but in an opposite sense it denotes folly and insanity. The number *seven* in a good sense, is predicated of things holy; but in an opposite sense, of things profane; and also signifies what is full, total and complete. By the ten horns of the dragon is signified much power: the horns of an animal, like the arms or hands of a man, denote power; and the number ten signifies much; implying that the false doctrine above described was universally prevalent in the Reformed or Protestant churches—which was actually the case at the consummation of the Age, or end of the first Christian church (1757). By the *seven* crowns or diadems upon his heads, is also signified the falsification and profanation of all the truths of the Word: for the precious stones in a crown or diadem, denote the truths of the Word, particularly in its literal sense; but in the present case, the same truths perverted and destroyed.—See A. R. 537 to 540.

(14.) Apoc. xvii. 3. "I saw a woman sitting upon a scarlet-colored beast, full of names of blasphemy, having *seven* heads and ten

---

* This was the generally accepted doctrine at the time Swedenborg lived and wrote; but it is not the prevailing belief among Protestant Christians of to-day. The teachings of the New Church and the influx from out the new heaven of angels, have greatly modified the beliefs of Christians on this as on many other subjects. And every year the essential importance of charity or righteousness of life is more and more insisted on in nearly all Protestant churches. This is one of the signs of the New Age on which the world has entered.—AM. EDITOR.

horns."—By a woman is meant the church, but in the present case the Roman Catholic religious persuasion, founded upon a false, perverted and profane interpretation of the Word. By the beast is signified the Word which, in reference to its power of communicating life to man, is elsewhere described by four animals or living creatures, as in Ezek. i. 5 to 25; x. 1 to 22; and by four beasts in the midst of the throne of heaven, and round about the throne, full of eyes before and behind, Apoc. vi. 6. But when the Word is falsified and profaned, as it is by the Roman Catholic hierarchy, it is then represented by a scarlet-colored beast, full of names of blasphemy. The scarlet color denotes truth from a celestial origin, but in the opposite sense the same truth falsified and perverted: and to be full of names of blasphemy, is to be altogether adulterated and profaned. By the *seven* heads is signified a state of spiritual insanity, arising from a perverted and profane interpretation of the Word; and by the ten horns is denoted much power, and the prevalence of the abuses and delusions practised by the church of Rome. The number *seven* is predicated of things holy or profane, according to the nature of the subject treated of; and also signifies what is full, total and complete. It is therefore equally applied to the dragon in chap. xii., and to the scarlet-colored beast in this chapter, to denote the total perversion of divine truth, and the profanation of things holy, both by Protestants and by Roman Catholics.—See A. R. 723, 724, 737.*

---

* In the preface to the Penny "Peep" Catalogue of the Art Treasures Exhibition (of which nearly one hundred thousand copies have been sold) are the following remarkable passages:—"Looking at the *early* pictures, then, in a spirit of calm and loving inquiry, we may learn much from them. . . . . Certain colors had certain *meanings*. White was the *emblem* of purity; *blue*, of Divine Truth; *red*, of Divine Love. Hence we find these colors worn by the Saviour and the Virgin Mary."

Here, then, is a principle enunciated to at least 100,000 people who perhaps never heard such words before. Again, the following has been printed and sold in the various stationers' shops.

"THE NUMBER 'SEVEN.'—The following interesting and singular compilation of the application of the number 'Seven' throughout the Word, will excite in the mind a desire to peruse the Sacred Scriptures, and to study their interior or deeper meaning:—

"In six days creation was perfected, the 7th was consecrated to rest. On the 7th of the 7th month a holy observance was ordained to the children of Israel, who fasted 7 days and remained 7 days in tents; the 7th year was directed to be a sabbath of rest for all things; and at the end of 7 times 7 years commenced the grand jubilee; every 7th year the land lay fallow; every 7th year there was a general release from all debts, and all bondsmen were set free. From this law may have originated the custom of our binding young men to 7 years' apprenticeship, and of punishing incorrigible offenders by transportation for 7, twice 7, or three times 7 years. Every 7th year the law was directed to be read to the people. Jacob served 7 years for the possession of Rachel, and also another 7 years. Noah had 7 days' warning of the flood, and was commanded to take the fowls of the air into the ark by sevens and the clean beasts by sevens: the ark touched the ground on the 7th month; and in 7 days a dove was sent, and again in 7 days after. The 7 years of plenty and the 7 years of famine were foretold in Pharaoh's dream, by the 7 fat and 7 lean beasts, and the

Eight.

The number *eight* belongs to the celestial class of expressions, being predicated of goods or evils, and denotes all good or evil in the complex.—A. C. 10624. Ap. Ex. 430. A. R. 739.

In general, it bears the same signification as the numbers *two* and *four*, from which it arises by multiplication.—Ap. Ex. 430. A. C. 9659.

It denotes conjunction to the full, also fulness itself, and what is

---

7 ears of full and the 7 ears of blasted corn. The young animals were to remain with the dams 7 days, and at the close of the 7th to be taken away. By the old law, man was commanded to forgive his offending brother 7 times; but the meekness of the last revealed religion extended his humility and forbearance to 70 times 7. 'If Cain shall be avenged 7 fold, truly Lamech 70 times 7.' In the destruction of Jericho, 7 priests bore 7 trumpets 7 days. On the 7th they surrounded the walls 7 times, and after the 7th time the walls fell. Balaam prepared 7 bullocks and 7 rams for a sacrifice. 7 of Saul's sons were hanged to stay a famine. Laban pursued Jacob 7 days' journey. Job's friends sat with him 7 days and 7 nights, and offered 7 bullocks and 7 rams as an atonement for their wickedness. David, in bringing up the ark, offered 7 bullocks and 7 rams. Elijah sent his servant 7 times to look for the cloud. Hezekiah, in cleansing the temple, offered 7 bullocks and 7 rams and 7 he-goats for a sin-offering. The children of Israel, when Hezekiah took away the strange altars, kept the feast of unleavened bread 7 days, and again other 7 days. King Ahasuerus had 7 chamberlains, a 7 days' feast, sent for the queen on the 7th day; queen Esther had 7 maids to attend her; in the 7th year of his reign Esther is taken to him. The wise king Solomon was 7 years building the temple, at the dedication of which he feasted 7 days. In the tabernacle there were 7 lamps: 7 days were appointed for an atonement upon the altar, and the priest's son was ordained to wear his father's garments 7 days. The children of Israel ate unleavened bread 7 days. The Feast of Tabernacles was 7 days. Abraham gave 7 ewe lambs to Abimelech as a memorial for a well. Joseph mourned 7 days for Jacob. Jesse caused 7 of his sons to pass before Samuel, but David was anointed king. The Rabbins say God employed the power of answering this number to perfect the greatness of Samuel, his name answering the value of the letters in the Hebrew word which signify 7; whence Hannah, his mother, in her thanks, says that 'the barren had brought forth 7.' In Scripture are enumerated 7 resurrections,—the widow's son by Elijah, the Shunamite's son by Elisha, the soldier who touched the bones of the prophet, the daughter of the ruler of the Synagogue, the widow's son of Nain, Lazarus, and our blessed Lord. Out of Mary Magdalene were cast 7 devils. The Apostles chose 7 deacons. Enoch, who was translated, was the 7th after Adam, and Jesus Christ the 77th in a direct line. Our Saviour spoke 7 times from the cross, on which he remained 7 hours; he appeared 7 times; after 7 times 7 days sent the Holy Ghost. In the Lord's Prayer are 7 petitions, contained in 7 times 7 words, omitting those of mere grammatical connection. Within this number are connected all the mysteries of the Apocalypse revealed to the 7 churches of Asia; there appeared 7 golden candlesticks, and 7 stars in the hand of him that was in the midst; 7 lamps being the 7 spirits of God; the book with 7 seals; the lamb with 7 horns and 7 eyes; 7 angels with 7 seals; 7 kings; 7 thunders; 7 thousand men slain; the dragon with 7 heads and 7 crowns; the beast with 7 heads; 7 angels bring 7 plagues, and 7 phials of wrath. The vision of Daniel was 70 weeks. Nebuchadnezzar ate the grass of the field 7 years. The elders of Israel were 70. Christ sent out 70 disciples."

It is evident from the above quotations, which are all from the Scriptures, that the number SEVEN has a meaning beyond the merely numerical idea which is of the utmost importance to the right understanding of God's Word. The doctrine of correspondences shows us, both in a good and in a bad sense, what this meaning is. For it is obvious that *seven*, when predicated of the Dragon and his *seven* heads and *seven* crowns, has a different, yea, an opposite signification to that when predicated of the Lamb with *seven* horns and *seven* eyes.—*London Intel. Repository* for Aug. 1858.

entire, in every mode or respect, and at the same time the commencement of a new state.—A. C. 9659.

The beginning of a following or new state, when man lives from good or charity, and no longer from truth or faith as before.—A. C. 9227.

It therefore has reference to purification, which ought to be always going on as from a new beginning; hence the rite of circumcision on the *eighth* day.—A. C. 2044.

Something distinct from what preceded.—A. C. 2866.

The beginning of a second state in regeneration, when the life is formed from, and the man is led by, good.—A. C. 9227, 9296.

Every beginning, or every new state, with its continuation.—A. C. 2044, 2633.

Something different from what has preceded.—A. C. 2866.

The *eighth* day is also called a sabbath, Lev. xxiii. 39, because it denotes the beginning of a new state, in which the conjunction of good and truth takes place.—A. C. 9296.

EXAMPLES.

(1.) Gen. xvii. 12. "And he that is *eight* days old shall be circumcised among you, every man-child in your generations."——As a week, consisting of seven days, signifies an entire period of state as well as of time, being predicated of reformation, regeneration, temptation, etc., and this in reference alike to an individual man, and to the church in general; so the *eighth* day, being the first day of a following week, signifies every beginning or commencement of a new state. On this account, in the Israelitish representative church, males of *eight* days old were ordered to be circumcised, in token of man's future purification from the unclean lusts originating in self-love and the love of the world. The reason also why the command extended to males only, was, because a male, as distinguished from a female, signifies the truth of faith; and no one can be purified from the unclean loves above-mentioned, unless he be in possession of truth, at least in some degree. It is by virtue of truth that man knows what is pure and what impure, what is holy and what profane; and without such knowledge as a medium whereby celestial love from the Lord may commence its operations on the external man, his purification and regeneration cannot be effected.—See A. C. 2044 to 2046.

(2.) Ex. xxvi. 25; xxxvi. 30. "And they shall be *eight* boards, and their sockets of silver, sixteen sockets: two sockets under one board, and two sockets under another."——By the tabernacle was represented heaven in general; by the ark, containing the testimony, the inmost or third heaven; by the habitation, containing the table for the show-bread, and the candlestick, the middle or second heaven; and by the court about the tabernacle, the lowest or first heaven. Among the various things appointed to be in that part of the tabernacle called the habitation, were *eight* boards or planks on the western side, each having two sockets or bases of silver, making sixteen in the whole, by which is signified every mode of support from good, and by truth grounded in good. The boards or planks signify good yielding support; for wood in general denotes good: their number *eight* bears the same signification in this place as the numbers *two* and *four*, from which it arises by multiplication, and denotes what is full and perfect in every respect, as also the conjunction of good with truth: their sockets or bases signify support: the silver of which they consisted, denotes truth derived from good: the number *sixteen* denotes the same as *eight*, viz., what is full and complete: and the number *two* denotes conjunction.—See A. C. 9659 to 9661.

(3.) Lev. xiv. 10. "And on the *eighth* day he shall take two he-lambs without blemish, and one ewe-lamb of the first year without blemish, and three tenth-deals of fine flour for a meat-offering, mingled with oil, and one log of oil."——The *eighth* day here denotes the beginning of a new state with him who had been a leper, and who had passed through a process of purification for seven preceding days. The lambs without blemish which were then to be offered, together with the fine flour mingled with oil, signify innocence and good, in conjunction with genuine truth. The previous state is that in which man, while regenerating, is led by truth to good; the latter state, which is also called a full state, is that in which, being regenerated, he regards truth from good. Similar things are understood, in Lev. xv. 29, by the seven days' purification of a woman, and by her bringing an offering of two turtles, or two young pigeons, on the *eighth* day.—See A. C. 2906, 7839.

(4.) Lev. xxiii. 39. "Also in the fifteenth day of the seventh month, when ye have gathered in the fruit of the land, ye shall keep a feast unto Jehovah seven days: on the first day shall be a sabbath, and on the *eighth* day shall be a sabbath."——Three annual feasts were instituted among the Israelites, to denote the deliverance from hell and introduction into heaven, of all those of the human race who are willing to receive new life from the Lord, and thus take the benefit of his advent into the world. The first feast called the feast of unleavened bread, and also the feast of the passover signifies purification from falsities, and deliverance from the power of spiritual enemies: the second, called the feast of harvest, and also the feast of weeks, signifies the implantation of truth in good: the third, called the feast of in-gathering, and also the feast of tabernacles, signifies the implantation of good, which is full deliverance from hell, and introduction into heaven. By the fifteenth day of the seventh month is signified the end of a former state, and the beginning of a new one; the *fifteenth* day having the same respect to *fourteen* preceding days, as *eight* days have to *seven*. By the *first* day being a sabbath, and the *eighth* day a sabbath, is signified the conjunction of truth with good, and reciprocally the conjunction of good with truth; which conjunction, when it first takes place, is also the beginning of a new state. Hence it appears that the *first*, the *eighth*, and the *fifteenth* days, in the passage above quoted, have similar significations.—See A. C. 9286, 9296. A. R. 585.

(5.) Lev. xxv. 22. "And ye shall sow the *eighth* year, and eat yet of old fruit until the ninth year: until her fruits come in ye shall eat of the old store."——By sowing in the *eighth* year is signified instruction, and the reception of truth in a new state: and by eating of old fruit until the ninth year, is signified the appropriation of external good and truth until more interior truth be received, and conjoined with a corresponding good. To sow signifies both to teach and to learn the truths and goods of faith: the *eighth* year denotes the commencement of a new state: old fruit denotes external goods and truths, these being first acquired, and afterwards those which are internal: the ninth year denotes full reception, and also conjunction. —See A. C. 9272, 9274.

(6.) Num. vi. 10. "And on the *eighth* day he shall bring two turtles or two young pigeons to the priest, to the door of the tabernacle of the congregation."——Here again the *eighth* day signifies the commencement of a new state: and by the two turtles, and two young pigeons, are signified innocence and charity, also the truths and goods of faith in conjunction.—See A. C. 870, 10210.

(7.) Ezek. xl. 9. "Then measured he the porch of the gate *eight* cubits, and the posts thereof two cubits, and the porch of the gate was inward."——By the various parts in and about the new temple described by Ezekiel, and their dimensions and numbers, are signified the various kinds and qualities of good and truth, internal and external. The porch leading inward, denotes introduction by truth to good: its dimensions, *eight* cubits, denotes that such introduction is ample, full and complete for those who have commenced the work of regeneration; and the posts, being two cubits, denote the goods and truths of the natural principle in a state of conjunction, whereby also man is introduced into the interior things of the church and heaven.—See A. C. 7847, 9659.

(8.) Ezek. xl. 31. "And the arches thereof were toward the outer court, and palm-trees were upon the posts thereof; and the going up to it had *eight* steps."——By the arches or upper parts of the porches, are signified external goods; by the palm-trees, interior truths; and by the *eight* steps of the ascent, full introduction to spiritual good.—See A. C. 7847, 9296, 9659.

(9.) Ezek. xl. 41. "Four tables were on this side, and four tables on that side, by the side of the gate; *eight* tables, whereupon they slew their sacrifices."——By tables are signified the same as by the things placed upon them: hence by the *eight* tables on which they sacrificed their sacrifices, four on this side and four on that, is signified worship in general from every affection of good and truth; the number *eight* denoting fulness, conjunction and newness of life.—See A. C. 9296, 9659.

(10.) Micah v. 5. "And this shall be the peace: when the Assyrian shall come into our land, and when he shall tread in our palaces, then shall we raise against him seven shepherds, and *eight* principal men."——The Assyrian here denotes reasonings concerning the goods and truths of the church from self-derived intelligence: and full deliverance from them is signified by seven shepherds and *eight* principal men being raised against him. Seven shepherds, abstractly from persons, denote the celestial things of the internal man; and *eight* principal men are the primary truths of good. The number *eight*, especially when preceded by *seven*, signifies what is full, perfect and complete. Hence it is, that the effect produced either in the church or in an individual of the church, on the removal of false reasonings and disputations, is said to be peace.—See A. C. 1186, 1572, 9659.

(11.) Luke ix. 28, 29. "And it came to pass about an *eight* days after these sayings, He took Peter, and John, and James, and went up into a mountain to pray. And as He prayed, the fashion of his countenance was altered, and his raiment was white and glistering." ——The transfiguration of the Lord upon a mountain was an exhibition of the glory both of his divine Person and of his Word. And the reason why of all his disciples He took only Peter, James and John, was, that they represented faith, charity, and the works of charity; and that no others but such as are principled therein, can possibly discern either the divinity of the Lord's Humanity, or the divinity, sanctity and interior glory of his Word. This manifestation of his glory is said by the Evangelist Luke to have been about *eight* days after a discourse with his disciples, related in the preceding verses, and by Matthew and Mark after *six* days. By both numbers are signified nearly the same things in effect; for *six days* denote the first stage of regeneration, when man is led by truth to good through many trials, temptations and spiritual labors; after which he enters upon a new state, which is that of his actual regeneration, being then in the possession and enjoyment of heavenly good. The same is also signified by the words, *about an eight days after;* the number *eight* denoting a new state of the spiritual life, in which the conjunction of good and truth takes place, and is manifested in the external by works of charity, piety, and general usefulness.—See Ap. Ex. 64, 821, 1070.

(12.) Apoc. xvii. 11. "And the beast that was, and is not, even he is the *eighth*, and is of the seven, and goeth into perdition."—— By the beast is signified the Word, as already explained in the 14th example under the number SEVEN; of which it is said, that it was, and is not, meaning that it was once received in the Romish church, and read by the people, but afterwards taken away from them, and not read. By its being called the *eighth*, that is, the *eighth* mountain and the *eighth* king, is signified that it is essential divine good, and at the same time essential divine truth: for by the seven mountains are signified the divine goods of the Word, and by the seven kings its divine truths; and that these might be all comprehended in one general view, it is therefore said that the beast which was, and is not, is itself the *eighth*, and of the seven. The number *eight* signifies good; and the number *seven* is predicated of what is holy. By the beast going into perdition is signified, that the Word is rejected and made of none effect, by being taken from the laity who are thereby prevented from seeing the profanations, adulterations and gross abuses practised by the Romish clergy, lest they should altogether recede from the papal yoke and dominion.—See Ap. Ex. 1054, 1067. A. R. 733, 737.

Nine.

The number *nine* belongs to the spiritual class of expressions, and, like the numbers *three* and *six*, is predicated of truths or falsities.—Ap. Ex. 194, 430, 532. A. R. 322. A. C. 10624.

It signifies what is full and complete.—A. C. 2788. Ap. Ex. 194 Also conjunction.—A. C. 2075, 2269.

When the number *nine* bears the same relation to *ten* as *ninety-nine* to *a hundred*, by which latter number is signified conjunction by remains, it then denotes a state just preceding conjunction.—A. C. 1988, 2106.

For the opposite signification—want of conjunction on account of the defect of faith and charity—see A. C. 2075.

The *ninth* hour, day, week, month, year, or age, signifies a full and complete state, thus the end of a former state, and the beginning of a new one.—A. C. 2788. Ap. Ex. 194.

EXAMPLES.

(1.) Gen. xvii. 1. "And when Abram was ninety years old and *nine*, Jehovah appeared to Abram, and said unto him, I am the God Shaddai; walk before me, and be thou perfect."——By Abram was represented the Lord while in the world, and by the different years of his age are denoted the different states and degrees of conjunction between his human and his divine essence. The number *one hundred* signifies the same in the Word as the number *ten*, being compounded of *ten* multiplied by *ten*; and by *ten* are signified remains, which in the case of the Lord are divine goods, whereby conjunction was effected. Hence by *ninety and nine* years, not quite reaching to a *hundred*, also by *nine* years, being short of *ten*, is signified the state just preceding or entering upon full conjunction. The same is signified by *ninety and nine* years in ver. 24. To the above may be added the reason why Jehovah here calls himself the God *Shaddai*, though this was originally the name of the false god worshipped by Abram when he lived in a land of idolatry: it was because Abram was still inclined to worship the god of his fathers, having been educated and to a certain degree confirmed in such worship; and because the Lord does not suddenly break, but gradually bends, those principles of religion which a man has imbibed from infancy, and conscientiously believes to be true. See Josh. xxiv. 2, 14, 15. Jehovah therefore announces himself to Abram by a name which he had hitherto esteemed most sacred: for as yet he was not acquainted with the name Jehovah, as appears from Ex. vi. 3; "I appeared unto Abraham, unto Isaac, and unto Jacob, in the god *Shaddai;* but by my name *Jehovah* was I not known to them." The name Jehovah, though revealed to Abram, was yet lost by his posterity in Egypt; for when Moses saw the angel of Jehovah in the bush, he inquired his name, and being told, he communicated it to the Israelites, who ever after retained it, but esteemed it too holy to be pronounced by them. See Ex. iii. 13 to 15. The word *Shaddai,* translated by some *Almighty,* or *All-sufficient,* and by others a *Thunderer,* properly signifies a *Vastator,* and hence also a *Tempter,* and after temptation a *Benefactor.* It is adopted as one of the names of Jehovah in various parts of the Word, as in Gen. xxviii. 3; xliii. 14; xlix. 25. Ezek. i. 24; x. 5. Joel i. 15; and is often found in the book of Job.—See A. C. 1988 to 1992, 2106.

(2.) Lev. xxiii. 32. "It shall be unto you a sabbath of rest, and ye shall afflict your souls in the *ninth* day of the month at even: from even unto even shall ye celebrate your sabbath."——By the affliction here spoken of is signified the humiliation of the external man in the presence of the internal, which is effected by self-compulsion in a state of temptation, until the worship of the Lord becomes an act of freedom and delight. By doing this on the *ninth* day of the seventh month, previous to the tenth day, which was to be a day of atonement, and a sabbath of rest, is signified that it would be productive of conjunction between the internal and the external man. The *ninth* day, as well as the number *nine* itself, here signifies such conjunction.—See A. C. 1947, 2075.

(3.) Lev. xxv. 22. "And ye shall sow the eighth year, and eat yet of old fruit, until the *ninth* year; until her fruits come in, ye shall eat of the old store."——By sowing is signified teaching and learning the truth of faith, and by the fruit or produce of the land is signified the good which is acquired by means of truth. The seed is the truth of the Word, and the land or field is the church, or an individual mind, which receives the truth. By the *ninth* year is signified the conjunction of truth with good. A further explanation of this verse is given in the fifth example under the number EIGHT.— See A. C. 9272, 9274.

(4.) 2 Kings xxv. 1 to 3. "And it came to pass in the *ninth* year of his reign, in the tenth month, in the tenth day of the month, that Nebuchadnezzar king of Babylon came, he and all his host, against

468   A KEY TO NUMBERS.

Jerusalem, and pitched against it, and they built forts against it round about. And the city was besieged unto the eleventh year of king Zedekiah. And on the *ninth* day of the month the famine prevailed in the city, and there was no bread for the people of the land."
——As many expressions in the Word have an opposite signification, according to the nature of the subject treated of, so in this place the numbers *nine*, ten, etc., are to be understood as implying that there was a defect of those spiritual principles at other times signified by them. Thus the number *nine*, which in its genuine sense denotes a state of conjunction, or a state immediately preceding conjunction, in the present passage signifies that there was no conjunction, in consequence of there being neither faith nor charity with those who then constituted the church. This is understood by the famine which prevailed in the city, and by the want of bread for the people of the land.—See A. C. 2075.

(5.) Matt. xx. 3 to 5. "And he went out about the third hour, and saw others standing idle in the market-place; and he said unto them, Go ye also into the vineyard, and whatsoever is right, I will give you. And they went their way. Again, he went out about the sixth and *ninth* hour, and did likewise."——By the third, sixth, *ninth*, and eleventh hours mentioned in this parable, are signified the various states of life of those who die in old age, in manhood, in youth, and in childhood, and who have all procured to themselves a degree of spiritual life. To labor in the vineyard, is to procure the knowledges of truth and good from the Word, and to apply them to uses of life. The third, sixth, and *ninth* hours alike signify a full state, or what is complete even to the end, being such as takes place with old men, young men, and those entering upon mature age: but the eleventh hour denotes a state not yet full, but capable of reception and of being perfected hereafter, being such as belongs to well-disposed boys and young people. The design of the parable is to show, that all men have a capacity for the reception of spiritual life from the Lord, and that each one will be rewarded hereafter according to the degree of his reception, and the use which he is qualified to perform in the Lord's kingdom.—See Ap. Ex. 194. A. C. 2788.

(6.) Matt. xxvii. 45. "Now from the sixth hour there was darkness over all the land unto the *ninth* hour."——By the darkness, which was over all the land from the sixth to the *ninth* hour, that is, for the space of three hours, at the time of the Lord's crucifixion, was represented and signified the universal prevalence of falsities derived from evil in the Jewish church. The sun signifies love to the Lord, and the light thereof faith in Him, the total absence of which is described by darkness. The *ninth* hour, the sixth hour, and three hours, signify what is full, total and universal.—See A. C. 1839, 2788. Ap. Ex. 526.

Ten.

The number *ten* in general signifies remains, which are all states of the affection of good and truth, with which man is gifted by the Lord, from the first stage of infancy to the end of his life; these being treasured up from time to time in his interiors for future use.— A. C. 576, 1906, 2141, 2284, 5291, 5894, 6156.

It also signifies all things, and all persons.—A. C. 4638, 9416, 10221. D. Life, 61. A. R. 101, 515. Ap. Ex. 124, 675.

All who are in the church, as well those who are in good and truth, as those who are in evil and falsity.—A. C. 4638.

What is full and complete.—A. C. 1988, 3107, 3176.

Much, or many, also some.—A. C. 4077, 5291. A. R. 101, 515. Ap. Ex. 124, 675.

As much as is sufficient for use.—A. C. 9757, 8468. Also with respect to other numbers.—Ap. Ex. 124.

The same as 100, and 1000, viz., much, all, what is full, and in the supreme sense, in reference to the Lord, what is infinite.—A. C. 9716. Ap. Ex. 548.

A *tenth* part, *tithes*, or *tenths*, signify the same as *ten*, but in a less degree, a sufficiency, viz., remains, or all states of love and charity, also of innocence and peace.—A. C. 576, 1738, 5291, 8468, 8540.

One *tenth*, or one *tenth-deal*, signifies celestial good, or good of the highest degree, represented by a lamb, with which it was to be offered. Num. xv. 1, 5; xxviii. 13, 21, 29; xxix. 4, 10, 15.—A. C. 2180, 2276.

An age in the Word is *ten* years.—A. C. 433.

Two *tenths*, or two *tenth-deals*, signify spiritual good, or good of the middle degree, represented by a ram. Num. xv. 6; xxviii. 12, 20, 28; xxix. 3, 9, 14.—A. C. 2180, 2276, 2280.

Three *tenths*, or three *tenth-deals*, signify natural good, or good of the lowest degree, represented by a bullock. Num. xv. 9; xxviii. 12, 20, 28; xxix. 3, 9, 14.—A. C. 2180, 2276.

In cases where the number *ten* signifies much, the *tenth* part denotes little or a few.—A. C. 8468.

When *ten* is used in connection with five.—Ap. Ex. 600.

EXAMPLES.

(1.) Gen. xiv. 20. "Blessed be the most high God, who hath delivered thine enemies into thy hand. And he gave him *tithes* of all."——The various states of the Lord while in the world, especially in his infancy or childhood, are described in this chapter. His internal man which was Jehovah, is understood by the Most High God, Possessor of heaven and earth; his interior man, as to spiritual things, by Abram the Hebrew; and his external man by Lot. When the interior man was purified by the internal man, or Jehovah, then both together were to be regarded as Jehovah, because the internal and the interior were united as one, each nevertheless retaining its proper distinction: and when, lastly, the external man was also purified, or in perfect union with the internal and the interior man, then all together constituted a Divine Man, that is, Jehovah in the Humanity. This was his full glorification, on the completion of which He rose from the dead, and ascended into heaven. But during this process many things were transacted, and many states passed through, which are all described in the history of Abraham, Isaac and Jacob. By Melchizedek, king of Salem, are represented the celestial things of the Lord's interior man, whereby this latter was purified; on which account he was called the priest of the Most High God, ver. 18. By his blessing Abram, and also the Most High God, is signified that the Lord's interior man was in the enjoyment of all celestial and spiritual things from his internal man which was Jehovah, consequently in a state of conjunction or union therewith. By Abram's giving Melchizedek *tithes* of all, is signified that the Lord acquired to himself, that is, to his Humanity, all the celestial things of love called remains, by his continual combats with, and victories over, the powers of hell, represented by the king of Sodom and the other kings his associates whom Abram had overthrown.—See A. C. 1702, 1707, 1725 to 1738.

(2.) Gen. xviii. 32. "And he said, Oh let not the Lord be angry, and I will speak yet but this once: Peradventure *ten* shall be found there. And he said, I will not destroy it for *ten's* sake."——By Abraham's pleading in behalf of the inhabitants of Sodom, that they might be preserved from destruction on condition that a certain number of righteous men should be found among them, is signified the Lord's mercy towards the human race, and his intercession for them while in his state of humiliation in the world, when He prayed to the Father as to another Being distinct from himself. And by

Jehovah's saying to Abraham, I will not destroy the city for *ten's* sake, is signified, that every man in whom the remains of good and truth shall be found, without being choked or destroyed, will be saved. *Ten* denotes remains, or those states of good and truth which man has received from the Lord, and whereby his salvation is effected. —See A. C. 2282 to 2285.

(3.) Gen. xxxi. 7. "And your father hath deceived me, and changed my wages *ten* times: but God suffered him not to hurt me."
——By changing the wages *ten* times, or in *ten* manners, is signified a great change of state, during the process of the Lord's glorification, which is here described in the internal sense, particularly as to the good represented by Laban: the number *ten* denotes much. That this change of state, however, did no real injury to Jacob; in other words, that it did not prevent the continual influx of the Divinity into the Humanity represented by Jacob, but was rather made to contribute to the perfect union of both, is signified by the last clause of the verse, "But God suffered him not to hurt me."—See A. C. 4077, 4078, 4179.

(4.) Ex. xxvi. 1. "Moreover, thou shalt make the tabernacle (habitation) with *ten* curtains of fine twined linen, and blue, and purple, and scarlet: with cherubim of cunning work shalt thou make them."——By the tabernacle properly so called, with the things in it and about it, were represented the three heavens, the inmost, the middle, and the lowest; also the three degrees of life in man: by the ark particularly, which contained the testimony, was represented the inmost or third heaven; by the habitation where the table for the show-bread and the candlestick were, the middle or second heaven; and by the court, the lowest or first heaven. The *ten* curtains of the habitation signified all the interior truths of faith, which constitute the second or middle heaven, or what amounts to the same, all the interior truths appertaining to the new intellectual principle of the regenerate man. Their number, *ten*, signifies all: their substance being of fine twined linen, and blue, and purple, and scarlet, signifies their celestial origin and quality, together with the good thence derived: and the cherubim of cunning work denote the divine providence and care of the Lord, in the protection of heaven from the assaults of infernal spirits.—See A. C. 9593 to 9597.

(5.) Lev. xxvi. 26. "And when I have broken the staff of your bread, *ten* women shall bake your bread in one oven, and they shall deliver you your bread again by weight: and ye shall eat, and not be satisfied."——By breaking the staff of bread is signified to deprive man of spiritual food or spiritual nutrition: bread denotes everything that nourishes the spirit or soul, especially the good of love. By *ten* women baking bread in one oven, is signified that in all things relative to the church in man there would be scarce anything of good and truth; in other words, that there would be a general defect in the reception of good and truth: women denote the affection of truth, which is constituent of the church in man; the number *ten* denotes all; bread denotes good and truth which nourish the soul; and the oven where that spiritual food is prepared, denotes the human mind. By delivering bread by weight is signified the scarcity and want of such things as are conducive to spiritual nourishment: wherefore it follows, " Ye shall eat, and not be satisfied."—See Ap. Ex. 555, 675. A. R. 101.

(6.) Deut. iv. 13. "And He declared unto you his covenant, which He commanded you to perform, even *ten* commandments, and He wrote them upon two tables of stone."——The *ten* commandments, or, as it is expressed in the original, the *ten* words, which were given by Jehovah to Moses, as the first-fruits of the Word, signify all divine truths, because they contain the whole law in a compendious form.—See A. R. 101. Ap. Ex. 675.

(7.) Dan. i. 20. "And in all matters of wisdom and understanding that the king inquired of them, (Daniel, Hananiah, Mishael, and Azariah,) he found them *ten* times better than all the magicians and astrologers that were in all his realm."——By magicians and probably astrologers or diviners, in ancient times, were meant persons who cultivated the science of spiritual things, and their analogies or harmonies with natural things. But after those very remote times alluded to, the same terms were applied to those who perverted such knowledge, and made it subservient to worldly and interested ends. Daniel and his companions, who were of the tribe of Judah then in a state of captivity, represented what remained of the church, with whom the knowledge of spiritual things was still preserved; and therefore they were said to be *ten* times more excellent in all matters of wisdom and understanding, whereof the king inquired of them, than all the magicians and astrologers that were in all his realm. Here the number *ten* evidently signifies much, being the same sense which it bears in many other parts of the Word.—See A. R. 101, 515. Ap. Ex. 124, 675. A. C. 5223.

(8.) Dan. vii. 7. "After this I saw in the night-visions, and behold, a fourth beast, dreadful and terrible, and strong exceedingly: and it had great iron teeth: it devoured and brake in pieces, and stamped the residue with the feet of it, and it was diverse from all the beasts that were before it, and it had *ten* horns."——By the four beasts which Daniel saw come up out of the sea, are described the successive states of the church from its commencement to its end, when every good and truth of the Word were destroyed. The first state of the church is described by the first beast, which was a lion with eagle's wings: the second state is described by a bear, which signifies that the Word was indeed read, but not understood: the third state is described by a leopard, which denotes the falsification of the truths of the Word: and the fourth or last state is described by the fourth beast dreadful and terrible and exceedingly strong, which signifies the total destruction of all truth and good in the church. Its *ten* horns signify falsities of every kind, and their universal prevalence: horns denote falsities, and the number *ten* much and all.—See A. R. 101, 574. Ap. Ex. 316, 556, 675. A. C. 2832.

(9.) Zech. viii. 23. "Thus saith Jehovah of hosts, In those days it shall come to pass, that *ten* men shall take hold out of all languages of the nations, even shall take hold of the skirt of him that is a Jew, saying, We will go with you; for we have heard that God is with you."——By this prophecy is not meant, as generally supposed, the restoration of the Jews, and their introduction into the land of Canaan, with a number of others from every nation who may wish to accompany them, but the convocation and accession of the gentiles to the true Christian church. By the Jews here mentioned are signified all who acknowledge the Lord and love Him. By *ten* men out of every language of the nations taking hold of his skirt, is signified that all of every religious denomination, who have a desire of knowing and understanding truth from the Lord, will endeavor to obtain information and instruction from those who are able to give it, especially from the Word itself. *Ten* men denote all: all languages of the nations denote every religious denomination: to take hold of the skirt of him that is a Jew, is to embrace the truth proceeding from the Lord, particularly the literal or external sense of his Word: and the desire which is expressed of going with the Jew because God is with him, implies an affection or love of the truth for its own sake, with an intention of living in obedience to it.—See A. R. 101. Ap. Ex. 433, 455, 675. A. C. 3881.

(10.) Luke xv. 8. "What woman having *ten* pieces of silver, if she lose one piece, doth not light a candle, and sweep the house, and seek diligently till she find it?"——By the woman here alluded to, is signified the church as to the affection of truth, or what is the same thing, the affection of truth itself in the church, or in the member of the church. By her having *ten* pieces of money, and afterwards losing one piece, is signified the possession of an abundance of truths from the Word at one time, or in one state, and the loss or apparent extinction of some of them at another time, or in another state. A piece of money denotes truth, or the knowledge of truth; and the number *ten* denotes an abundance, much, or all: to lose one, is to neglect some truth or precept of the Word, which might have been profitable had it been duly attended to. By her lighting a candle, sweeping the house, and seeking diligently till she find it, are signified self-examination from affection, purification from evils, and close attention to the particular as well as general state of the whole mind, with a view to discover and bring into actual use and life the truth, which had been suffered to remain inactive, or which had been apparently extinguished. To light a candle, is to produce the light of truth from the love thereof, for the purpose of self-examination: to sweep the house, is to examine fully the state of the mind, also to prepare it for the reception of good, by the removal of evils: to seek diligently till the piece of money be found, is to continue the examination until the truth be restored.—See Ap. Ex. 675.

(11.) Luke xix. 13. "And he called his *ten* servants, and delivered them *ten* pounds, and said unto them, Occupy till I come."—— By the nobleman going into a far country is signified the Lord taking his departure from the world, and then appearing to men to be absent. By receiving for himself a kingdom, is signified that with respect to his Humanity He became the God of heaven and the church, which constitute his spiritual kingdom. By his returning is signified the communication of divine good and truth, from his Humanity when glorified, to those on earth who are willing to acknowledge and worship Him as their God. By his *ten* servants are signified in general all who are in the world, and especially all who belong to the church: and by the *ten* pounds which He gave them to negotiate with, are signified all the knowledges of truth and good from the Word, together with the faculty of perceiving or understanding them, whereby intelligence and heavenly wisdom may be obtained. —See Ap. Ex. 223, 675. A. R. 101.

(12.) Apoc. xi. 13. "And the same hour there was a great earthquake, and the *tenth* part of the city fell, and in the earthquake were slain of men seven thousand: and the remnant were affrighted and gave glory to the God of heaven."——By a great earthquake is signified a remarkable change of state with those in the spiritual world who had been of the church, but were in falsities of doctrine and in evils of life. By the *tenth* part of the city falling, is signified that all such were entirely separated from heaven and cast into hell: the *tenth* part denotes the same as *ten*, viz., all: and a city denotes doctrine, in the present case false doctrine, together with those who embrace and confirm it. By seven thousand being slain is signified the destruction of all who profess the false doctrine of justification by faith alone, and who on that account do not bring forth the fruits of charity in their life. By the remnant being affrighted, and giving glory to the God of heaven, is signified that they who in some degree adjoined to faith the good works of charity, when they saw the destruction of the former, being in great concern for their spiritual life, were separated from them, and acknowledged the Lord as the only God of heaven and earth.—See A. R. 515 to 517. Ap. Ex. 673 to 678.

Eleven.

The number *eleven*, when it has relation to *ten*, signifies all things even to redundance or superfluity: for as *ten* denotes all, so *eleven*, as being more than *ten*, denotes what is redundant or superabundant.— A. C. 9616.

When it has relation to *twelve* which signifies all things in fulness, it then denotes a state not yet full, as to the reception of truths and goods, but capable of becoming so, as in the case of well-disposed boys and children.—Ap. Ex. 194.

The *eleventh* hour, day, week, month or year, signifies the same as *eleven* hours, days, etc., viz., all even to redundancy, when the subject treated of points out an excess above *ten*; and nearly all, or an approach to fulness, when the subject treated of is a state somewhat below the full complement denoted by *twelve*.—Ap. Ex. 194. A. C. 2075.

A state not yet full, yet a state of reception, such as appertains to well disposed children and young persons.—Ap. Ex. 194.

EXAMPLES.

(1.) Gen. xxxvii. 9. "And Joseph dreamed yet another dream, and told it his brethren, and said: Behold, I have dreamed a dream more, and behold, the sun, and the moon, and the *eleven* stars, made obeisance to me."——By Joseph who dreamed this prophetic dream, is here represented in the supreme sense the Lord himself, and in a respective sense the divine truth proceeding from Him, especially that divine truth which teaches the Divinity of his Humanity. By his brethren are here represented those of the church who are in faith separate from charity, and who refuse to acknowledge the Divine Humanity of the Lord. By the sun and moon in this passage, are signified natural good and natural truth, because predicated of Jacob and Leah, by whom such good and such truth are represented in the Word. On other occasions the sun denotes celestial good, and the moon spiritual good or truth, and in the supreme sense both signify the Lord,—the sun as to divine good, and the moon as to divine truth. By stars are signified the knowledges of good and truth: and as the knowledge or doctrine of the Divinity of the Lord's Humanity is the chief knowledge or doctrine in the church, and this was represented by Joseph, it follows, that the *eleven* stars, which, with the sun and moon, were seen to make obeisance to Joseph, denote all the other knowledges of good and truth, which are subordinate to the primary and most essential knowledge concerning the Divine Humanity of the Lord.—See A. C. 4687, 4693 to 4698.

(2.) Ex. xxvi. 7. "And thou shalt make curtains of goats' hair to be a covering upon the tabernacle: *eleven* curtains shalt thou make."——By the curtains of goats' hair intended for a covering upon that part of the tabernacle called the habitation, are signified the exterior truths of faith derived from external celestial good, which is the good of mutual love: for by the curtains of fine twined linen, and blue, and purple, and scarlet, are signified the interior truths of faith, as already explained in the fourth example under number TEN. The curtains of goats' hair were *eleven* in number, to denote all even to redundance and superfluity: for as *ten* signifies all, so *eleven* signifies all that is sufficient, and moreover a superfluity; which is further denoted by doubling the last curtain, and causing it to hang over the back and sides of the habitation, as stated in ver. 9, 12, 13, of this chapter.—See A. C. 9615, 9616.

(3.) Ex. xxxvi. 14. "And he made curtains of goats' hair for the tent over the tabernacle (habitation): *eleven* curtains he made them."——By the *eleven* curtains of goats' hair are here also signified the same things as in the preceding example, viz., all the exterior truths of faith from a celestial origin, even to redundance or superfluity.—See A. C. 9615, 9616, 10750.

(4.) 2 Kings xxv. 2. "And the city was besieged unto the *eleventh* year of king Zedekiah."——By the city being besieged unto the *eleventh* year when the famine prevailed, and there was no bread, is signified that there was no longer conjunction by the things relating to faith and charity. The number *eleven*, when preceded by the numbers *nine* and *ten*, each in reference to the siege of the city, as in ver. 1, denotes a complete state of desolation as to the things of the church. Famine in the city, and want of bread for the people of the land, as expressed in ver. 3, signify that there was nothing of faith and nothing of charity remaining.—See A. C. 2075.

(5.) Matt. xx. 6. "And about the *eleventh* hour he went out, and found others standing idle; and he saith unto them, Why stand ye here all the day idle?"——By the *eleventh* hour, when some laborers were hired to work in the vineyard, is signified a state of life not yet full with respect to the reception of truths and goods, but yet capable of full reception by further instruction: for the twelfth hour to which all labored, signifies truths and goods in their fulness. The state of well-disposed boys and children who die before they come to years of maturity, and who are instructed and perfected after death, is here described by the laborers engaged at the *eleventh* hour: while the states of old men, young men, and those entering upon maturity, are described by the hiring of other laborers at the third, sixth, and ninth hours; all of whom are said to receive a like reward, by which is signified, that all are accepted by the Lord according to their several degrees of regeneration.—See example five, under number NINE. Ap. Ex. 194.

(6.) Matt. xxviii. 16. "Then the *eleven* disciples went away into Galilee, into a mountain, where Jesus had appointed them."——By the *twelve* disciples, whom the Lord chose for his more immediate followers, in like manner as by the *twelve* tribes of the children of Israel, were represented all the truths and goods of the church. The same were also represented by the *eleven*, after the defection of Judas who betrayed the Lord, yet with a difference in respect to fulness and perfection. And again the same were represented, in a different respect, by the *ten* disciples who were assembled together on the day of the Lord's resurrection, and on whom the Lord breathed the Holy Spirit, at the same time giving them power to remit or to retain sins; for on that occasion both Judas and Thomas were absent: see John xx. 19 to 24. The number of disciples being reduced from *twelve* to *eleven*, by the apostacy of Judas, they still represented all the truths and goods of the succeeding Christian church, but not in so full a degree: and probably this very circumstance may have been permitted to take place, and to be recorded in the Word, not only as representative of the infidelity of the Jewish church, but also as prophetic of the obscure and imperfect reception of divine truth, which would distinguish the professors of Christianity in every age of the church, until the commencement of the New Jerusalem. For as it was foreseen that the Christian church would come to its consummation or end in consequence of not fully acknowledging the Lord, so the number *eleven* being expressive of all the truths and goods belonging to the church, is used by the Evangelists to denote at the same time their obscure and imperfect reception: whereas in the Apocalypse, a book peculiarly descriptive of the end of the former church, and the commencement of a new one under the name of the New Jerusalem, the number *twelve* uniformly marks the full reception of divine truth by those who shall become members of this last and truly Christian church. Hence in the 7th chapter we read of the number of those who were sealed being *twelve thousand* of each tribe of the children of Israel, making a total of *twelve times twelve thousand*, or *a hundred and forty-four thousand*, besides "a great multitude which no man could number, of all nations, and kindreds, and people, and tongues:" and in the 21st chapter we further read of the city, New Jerusalem, "having a wall great and high, with *twelve* gates, and at the gates *twelve* angels, and names written thereon, which are the names of the *twelve* tribes of the children of Israel:" and again of "the *twelve* foundations of the wall, in which were the names of the *twelve* apostles of the Lamb:" also of the dimensions of the city, which were "*twelve* thousand furlongs in length, breadth, and height, the wall being a hundred and forty-four (*twelve* times *twelve*) cubits, according to the measure of a man, that is, of an angel."

Twelve.

The number *twelve* belongs to the spiritual class of expressions, being predicated of truths or of falsities, and denotes all truths or all falsities in the complex.—A. C. 10217, 10264. Ap. Ex. 253.

It is a most holy number, because it signifies all the holy things of faith.—A. C. 648.

A universal number, comprehending all things of the church, and of the Lord's kingdom in general and in particular.—A. C. 3268, 3863.

It signifies all things of faith derived from charity.—A. C. 1667, 1988, 2089, 3268, 4603. A. R. 348.

All things of love and thence of faith in one complex.—A. C. 575, 577, 1667, 3239, 7973.

All truths and goods in one complex, which proceed from the Lord and constitute heaven.—A. C. 6335, 6640, 9603.

All things of the doctrine of truth and good, or of faith and love.—A. C. 3858.

The most common or cardinal things of the church, by which man is initiated into spiritual and celestial things, and thus regenerated.—A. C. 3913. A. R. 916.

The common things of the church, consequently of faith and love, or of truth and good; and in an opposite sense, the common things of no faith and no love, or all things of what is false and evil.—A. C. 3926.

All things of the church, likewise all persons, who are in good and truth from the Lord, and who acknowledge Him as the God of heaven and earth.—A. R. 348. Ap. Ex. 340. L. J. 39. A. C. 3129, 3354, 3858, 6397.

In the opposite sense it denotes principles opposite to those of faith and love, viz., the general principles of falsity and evil.—A. C. 3926.

Being compounded of three multiplied by four, it derives its signification from both of those numbers: hence, as three signifies all in respect to truth, and four all in respect to good, the number *twelve* denotes all truths derived from good, or all truths and goods in the church.—T. C. R. 217. A. R. 348, 915. Ap. Ex. 340. A. C. 3913, 9873.

The *twelfth* hour, etc., signifies the same as *twelve* hours, etc., viz., a full, complete and perfect state.—Ap. Ex. 194. A. C. 6000.

The half, and all the multiples of *twelve*, have a like signification as the simple number.—A. C. 7973.

EXAMPLES.

(1.) Gen. xiv. 4. "*Twelve* years they served Chedorlaomer, and in the thirteenth year they rebelled."——The subject treated of in this chapter is the state of the Lord's Humanity while in his infancy, and his entrance into temptations as soon as He arrived at maturity, which with Him was at or about *twelve* years of age, being much earlier than with other men. The four kings denote apparent goods and truths; and the five kings, against whom they fought, denote evils and falsities derived hereditarily from the mother, but which did not manifestly show themselves until the time arrived when the Lord might, according to divine order, sustain temptations, and thus fight against and overcome those hereditary propensities. Hence it is said that the five kings served Chedorlaomer *twelve* years, and that in the thirteenth year they rebelled; by which is signified that hereditary evils and falsities were kept in a state of subjection so as not to appear during the Lord's infancy and childhood, by such goods and truths as appertained to his external man, and which in themselves were apparent goods and truths, and not genuine or divine. By their rebelling in the thirteenth year, is signified that his first temptation in childhood commenced; his victory over which by apparent goods and truths, and at length his purification from even these latter, is described in the succeeding parts of the same chapter.—See A. C. 1660 to 1668.

(2.) Gen. xvii. 20. "As for Ishmael, I have heard thee: behold, I have blessed him, and will make him fruitful, and will multiply him exceedingly: *twelve* princes shall he beget, and I will make him a great nation."——By Ishmael were represented such in the church as become rational or spiritual men, by the reception of truth from the Lord; of whom it is said that they shall be blessed, made fruitful, and be multiplied exceedingly. By the *twelve* princes which he shall beget, are signified the primary precepts of charity and faith: the number *twelve* signifies all things of faith; and the term *princes* is predicated of charity, and the primary things thereof, which are the precepts of divine truth.—See A. C. 2087 to 2090.

(3.) Gen. xlix. 28. "All these are the *twelve* tribes of Israel: and this is it that their father spake unto them, and blessed them; every one according to his blessing he blessed them."——By the *twelve* tribes of Israel are signified all the truths and goods of the church in the aggregate. The blessing pronounced upon each denotes the happiness which every one will experience, who enters into either of the spiritual states represented by the *twelve* tribes.—See A. C. 6445 to 6448.

(4.) Ex. xxviii. 21. "And the stones shall be with the names of the children of Israel, *twelve*, according to their names; like the engravings of a signet, every one with his name shall they be according to the *twelve* tribes."——By the precious stones are signified the goods and truths of the church; and by their number being *twelve*, according to the names of the *twelve* tribes of Israel, are signified all such goods and truths in the complex, each stone and each name denoting some specific good and truth, and the whole being arranged in their order according to the form of heaven.—See A. C. 9875 to 9878.

(5.) 1 Kings x. 20. "And *twelve* lions stood there on the one side and on the other upon the six steps: there was not the like made in any kingdom."——By Solomon's throne was represented the divine truth derived from the divine good; and by the *twelve* lions upon the six steps, on the one side and on the other, were represented all the truths of heaven and the church in their power, whereby man is enabled to fight and overcome in spiritual temptation: lions denote truths in power, and the number *twelve* all.—See Ap. Ex. 253, 430. A. C. 5313, 6367.

(6.) 1 Kings xix. 19. "So he departed thence, and found Elisha, the son of Shaphat, who was ploughing with *twelve* yoke of oxen before him, and he with the *twelfth*: and Elijah passed by him, and cast his mantle upon him."——By Elijah, and afterwards by Elisha, was represented the Lord as to the Word, in which are all truths derived from good. When the time, therefore, came for transferring that representation from the one to the other, which was announced by Elijah's casting his mantle upon Elisha, the latter was found ploughing with *twelve* yoke of oxen before him, and he with the *twelfth*, by which is signified the formation of the church by the divine truths of the Word. The act of ploughing, spiritually understood, denotes the preparation of the mind by good for the reception of truths; the oxen also employed in ploughing, denote goods in the natural or external man; and the number *twelve*, as in other cases, signifies all. —See Ap. Ex. 430. A. C. 5895.

(7.) Ezek. xliii. 16. "And the altar shall be *twelve* cubits long, *twelve* broad, square in the four squares thereof."——The altar was a representative of worship; and it is described as *twelve* cubits long and *twelve* broad, to denote that the worship of the Lord should be according to all the principles of good, and all the principles of truth; the length of the altar being predicated of good, and its breadth of truth, in the same manner as the length and breadth of the New Jerusalem are. Thus the dimensions of the altar which is said to be square in the four squares thereof, denote what is just, having an equal respect to the four quarters of the world, or to every degree of good and truth in the church.—See A. R. 905 to 907.

(8.) Matt. xiv. 20, 21. "And they did all eat and were filled: and they took up of the fragments that remained, *twelve* baskets full.

And they that had eaten were about five thousand men, besides women and children."——Every particular contained in the description of the miracle recorded in this chapter, has a spiritual signification. The five thousand men, besides women and children, who were fed by the Lord, signify all in the church who are in truths derived from good; the men those who are in truths, the women those who are in good affections, and the children those who are in innocence. The bread and the fishes signify the goods and truths of the natural man: the multitude eating of these, denotes the spiritual nourishment received by the members of the church from the Lord: and the *twelve* baskets of fragments that remained, signify the consequent knowledges of truth and good in all abundance. See a further explanation of this miracle in the seventh example under number FIVE.—See Ap. Ex. 430, 548.

(9.) Matt. xix. 28. "And Jesus said unto them, Verily I say unto you, that ye who have followed me in the regeneration, when the Son of Man shall sit in the throne of his glory, ye also shall sit upon *twelve* thrones, judging the *twelve* tribes of Israel."——By the *twelve* disciples of the Lord sitting upon *twelve* thrones, judging the *twelve* tribes of Israel, is not meant that the disciples will hereafter sit in judgment on mankind; for they, as well as every other created being, are utterly incompetent to such a work; but that the Lord alone, as the Son of Man, or the Word, will judge the human race from and according to the truths and goods of the church, or according to the truths derived from good, which were represented by the *twelve* apostles, as well as by the *twelve* tribes of Israel; the number *twelve* here, as in other places, denoting all such truths and goods proceeding from the Lord.—See A. R. 798. Ap. Ex. 333, 430, 431. A. C. 5313, 6397.

(10.) Matt. xxvi. 53. "Thinkest thou that I cannot now pray to my Father, and He shall presently give me more than *twelve* legions of angels?"——By *twelve* legions of angels is signified the universal heaven, or all the angels thereof: hence by more than these, is evidently signified the divine omnipotence.—See Ap. Ex. 430.

(11.) Luke ii. 42. "And when he was *twelve* years old, they went up to Jerusalem, after the custom of the feast."——As the number *twelve* signifies all things, and is predicated of truths derived from good which constitute the church, therefore the Lord, when He was *twelve* years of age, left his nominal father Joseph and his mother Mary, and after three days was found in the temple, sitting in the midst of the doctors, both hearing them and asking them questions; by which circumstance is signified the initiation and introduction of his Humanity into all things relating to heaven and the church: wherefore He said to Joseph and Mary, after they had found Him, " Wist ye not that I must be about my Father's business?" ver. 49.—See Ap. Ex. 430.

(12.) Luke viii. 43, 44. "And a woman having an issue of blood *twelve* years, who had spent all her living upon physicians, neither could be healed of any, came behind Him and touched the border of his garment: and immediately her issue of blood stanched."——By the woman here mentioned is signified the church as to the affection of truth, or what is the same thing, the affection of truth itself. By her having an issue of blood *twelve* years, is signified that the church, though in the desire and love of truth, was not as yet in the possession of it, but on the contrary surrounded with false principles, and at the same time in a state of spiritual uncleanness. The number of years, *twelve*, during which she was so afflicted, denotes what is full or total. Her application to other physicians, which proved to be vain and without success, signifies that purification and regeneration cannot be effected by any other power than that of the Lord and his Word. By her coming behind Jesus and touching the border of his garment, and her issue of blood being immediately stanched, is signified that on her approaching the Lord through the medium of his Word, even in the literal sense, a healing virtue was communicated to her, and the power of divine truth was manifested in the removal of falsities and evils, or in the purification of her spirit from the defilements of sin. This first act of the divine power of the Lord seems to refer more immediately to the suppression of evil in the external, while the understanding is as yet but faintly enlightened, and capable of discerning the great truths of the Word only in an obscure degree; which state of the spiritual life is represented by the woman's coming *behind* Jesus, and touching the *border* of his garment: for to approach the Lord *from behind*, and not to have a *direct view of his countenance*, is the same thing as to discern his Humanity not yet fully glorified, without an internal acknowledgment of his supreme and exclusive Divinity; and to touch the *border* or *extremity* of his garment, is the same thing as to embrace the Word in its *literal* or *external* sense, without being as yet fully enlightened to perceive its genuine internal sense. That the further process of purification and regeneration might, however, be distinctly represented in the case of this woman, it is stated in the 47th and 48th verses, that a second act of divine power of the Lord took place upon her, when she came into his *direct presence*, and fell down *before Him*, declaring unto Him before all the people her faith in his divine omnipotence, and consequently in his supreme Divinity: for to come into his *direct presence*, to view his *divine countenance*, and then to fall down in self-abasement *before Him*, implies a more full and more interior acknowledgment of his divine person and character, and at the same time a more profound and enlightened perception of the internal sense of his Word, than she had before exhibited; her conduct on this occasion in some respects resembling that of the apostle John, in Apoc. i. 10 to 17, when he first heard the voice of the Son of Man *behind* him; and afterwards, being turned to *see* the voice that spake unto him, he beheld the person of his Lord in all his divine majesty and glory. In this latter case the Lord said to John, "Fear not; I am the First and the Last:" and in the former case He addressed the woman in this consolatory language, "Daughter, be of good comfort; thy faith hath made thee whole; go in peace." It further appears that the whole case of this woman is representative of the conversion of the gentiles to the Christian religion, and their gradual but willing reception of the divine truth of the Word, first in its literal sense, and afterwards in its genuine internal sense; in other words, of their acknowledgment of the Lord, first as the Son of God, (for the most part attended with an idea of another divine person superior to Him, and a third equal or inferior to Him,) and lastly, in agreement with the Prophets and the Lord's own words in the Gospel, as the supreme God, or everlasting Father himself in a Divine Human Form.—See Ap. Ex. 79, 195. A. C. 10130.

(13.) John xi. 9. "Jesus answered, Are there not *twelve* hours in the day? If any man walk in the day he stumbleth not, because he seeth the light of this world."——As the number *twelve* signifies goods and truths in their fulness, so *twelve* hours of the day denote all states of spiritual light or intelligence derived from them: hence to walk in the day without stumbling, is to live conscientiously according to the dictates of divine truth.—See Ap. Ex. 194, 430. A. C. 6000.

(14.) Apoc. xii. 1. "And there appeared a great wonder in heaven, a woman clothed with the sun, and the moon under her feet, and upon her head a crown of *twelve* stars."——By a great wonder (or rather sign) seen in heaven, is signified a revelation or manifest testification concerning the New Church, the difficult reception of its doctrine, and the persecution or assaults which it will have to sustain. By the woman clothed with the sun, and having the moon under her feet, is signified the New Church of the Lord, first in the heavens, and therefore called the New Heaven, afterwards on the earth, and therefore called the New Jerusalem. She is said to be clothed or surrounded with the sun, because the church represented by her, especially among the angels of heaven, is in love to the Lord and in charity towards the neighbor, which state of spiritual affection produces around them a heavenly sphere of light and love resembling a sun. The moon also is said to be under her feet, to denote a future state of intelligence and faith with those who shall become members of the New Church on earth: for as the sun which is the chief luminary in heaven, signifies love, so the moon which is subordinate to it and derives all its light from it, signifies intelligence and faith, particularly in the natural or external man. By a crown of *twelve* stars upon her head is signified the wisdom and intelligence of the New Church, acquired by the knowledges of divine good and divine truth from the Word: a crown upon the head denotes wisdom and intelligence; stars denote the knowledge of good and truth from the Word; and the number *twelve* denotes all.—See A. R. 532. Ap. Ex. 705 to 709.

(15.) Apoc. xxi. 12 to 14. " And it had a wall great and high, and had *twelve* gates, and at the gates *twelve* angels, and names written thereon, which are the names of the *twelve* tribes of the children of Israel. On the east, three gates; on the north, three gates; on the south, three gates; and on the west, three gates. And the wall of the city had *twelve* foundations, and in them the names of the *twelve* apostles of the lamb."——By a wall great and high is signified the Word in its literal sense, from which the doctrine of the New Church is derived, and by which it is confirmed and defended: the term *great* being predicated of good, and the term *high* of truth. By the *twelve* gates are signified all the knowledges of truth and good by which man is introduced into the church; the three gates on the east being for those who are in a greater or superior degree of love and the affection of good; the three gates on the west, for those who are in a less or inferior degree of the same; the three gates on the south, for those who are in a greater or superior degree of wisdom and the affection of truth; and the three gates on the north, for those who are in a less or inferior degree of the same. By the wall having *twelve* foundations, is signified that the Word in its literal sense contains all things appertaining to the doctrine of the New Church; the foundations thereof denoting its doctrinals, and the number *twelve* all. By the names of the *twelve* apostles of the Lamb which were written in the *twelve* foundations, are signified all things appertaining to the doctrine of the New Jerusalem from the Word concerning the Lord, and concerning a life according to his commandments; the Lamb denoting the Lord as to his Divine Humanity, and his *twelve* apostles all things relating to his church.—See A. R. 898 to 903. Ap. Ex. 430.

(16.) Apoc. xxii. 2. "In the midst of the street of it, and of either side of the river, was there the tree of life, which bare *twelve* manner of fruits and yielded her fruit every month: and the leaves of the tree were for the healing of the nations."——By the street of the city is signified the truth of doctrine in the New Church: and by the midst thereof is signified the inmost principle of the truth of doctrine, and whatever is thence derived. By the river and its sides is signified divine truth in great abundance, producing intelligence and wisdom in every degree. By the tree of life, which bare *twelve* kinds of fruits, is signified the Lord as to his divine love, from whom are derived all the goods of love and charity, called good works, which man performs apparently as of himself: fruits denote the good things of love and charity manifested in acts of useful service to mankind; and *twelve* denotes all. By the tree yielding its fruit every month is signified, that the Lord produces the goods of love in man according to every state of truth in him: a month, as being determined by the moon which signifies faith in the understanding, denotes the various states of truth derived from good, and entering into conjunction with it. By the leaves of the tree which were for the healing of the nations, are signified rational truths calculated to amend the life of those who are in evils and thence in falsities: nations in a good sense denote those who are in goods and thence in truths, but in an opposite sense, as in this place, those who are in evils and thence in falsities.—See A. R. 933 to 936. Ap. Ex. 430.

In addition to these examples of the spiritual signification of the number *twelve*, many others are to be found in the Word of similar import; as, That Moses built an altar under the hill, and *twelve* pillars according to the *twelve* tribes of Israel, Ex. xxiv. 4. That *twelve* cakes of fine flour, called the show-bread, were set in two rows upon a table before Jehovah, Lev. xxiv. 5, 6. That the princes of Israel were *twelve*, Num. i. 44. That those *twelve* princes brought to the dedication of the altar *twelve* chargers of silver, *twelve* silver bowls, *twelve* spoons of gold, *twelve* bullocks, *twelve* rams, *twelve* lambs, and *twelve* kids, Num. vii. 84, 87. That *twelve* thousand of the children of Israel, a thousand from each tribe, were sent out to war against the Midianites, Num. xxxi. 4 to 7. That *twelve* men were sent out to search the land of Canaan, Deut. i. 22 to 24. That *twelve* men took *twelve* stones out of the midst of Jordan, and laid them down at the place where they lodged, as a memorial that the waters of Jordan were cut off: and that *twelve* stones were also placed in the midst of Jordan, in the place where the feet of the priests stood, who bare the ark of the covenant, Josh. iv. 1 to 9, 20. That the molten sea, which Solomon made, stood upon *twelve* oxen, 1 Kings vii. 25. That Elijah took *twelve* stones, and built an altar in the name of Jehovah, 1 Kings xviii. 31, 32. That *twelve* thousand of each of the tribes of Israel were sealed, Apoc. vii. 5 to 8. And that the foundations of the wall of the city New Jerusalem were garnished with *twelve* kinds of precious stones, Apoc. xxi. 19, 20.

A Rule for discovering the Signification of every other Number.

From the explanation of the preceding numbers may be discovered the signification of all others not distinctly specified; as for example, the signification of 83, the age of Aaron, when he and Moses spake unto Pharaoh, and demanded the release of the children of Israel, Ex. vii. 7. This number being compounded of 80 and 3, we first look for the signification of 80, and find that it denotes the same as 40, viz., temptations; also the same as 8 and 10, viz., a new state, arising from the insinuation or gradual introduction of remains into the human mind. We next proceed to the number 3, and find that it denotes fulness, more particularly in respect to truth, and consequently to the doctrine of divine truth in the church. Then combining these various significations, it is discovered that 83, the age of Aaron, involves the state or quality of the doctrine of the church at that time represented by him; which state or quality was, that it taught the necessity of resisting or shunning evils as sins, and thus of undergoing temptations, in order that man may be introduced into a new state of spiritual life, and that the affections of good and truth which he has received from the Lord, may be brought into full operation and effect.—See A. C. 7284, 7285.

Again, we read in Dan. xii. 11, that "from the time the daily sacrifice shall be taken away, and the abomination that maketh desolate set up, there shall be 1290 days." Now, in order to ascertain the signification of 1290 days in this passage, we have only, *first*, to observe the general nature of the subject treated of, which is evidently the perverted state of the church: *secondly*, to mark the spiritual signification attached to each of the component numbers, but taken in an opposite sense, which may be known by referring to their proper places in this work; and, *thirdly*, to combine the distinct significations into one general sense. Thus the number 1290 consists of 1000, 200, and 90, added together; and each of these again is the product of factors less than twelve. We find, then, that 1000 denotes what is full and complete; 200, conjunction, being predicated particularly of evils; and 90, a full state of falsities; which significations united produce the idea intended to be conveyed concerning the perverted and desolate state of the church in the latter times, when the daily sacrifice would be taken away, and the abomination that maketh desolate would be set up; in other words, when the true worship of the Lord would perish, and evils and falsities would abound.

So again, if we would discover the true signification of the number 1335, in the verse immediately following that above cited, we must proceed in a similar way to reduce it to its component numbers, and unite their distinct significations into one sense; still observing the general tenor and spirit of the passage, as the rule to govern us in deciding whether the particular numbers are to be taken in a good sense, or in an opposite sense. Now 1335 consists of 1000, 300, 30, and 5, added together; and the number 1000, as before, signifies what is full and complete; 300, the holy principle of remains; 30, some degree of combat against evils, also fulness of remains, a principle of holiness from the Lord, and the beginning of a new state; and 5, as much as is sufficient for spiritual use. Collating these distinct significations together, the result is, that the number 1335 points out that blessed state and period, when, after the destruction and desolation of the former church, a New Church shall be established by the Lord, in which righteousness, holiness and purity of life shall distinguish its members, according to their several degrees of regeneration. It is therefore written in the verse alluded to, "Blessed is he that waiteth, and cometh to the *thousand three hundred and five and thirty* days." Dan. xii. 12.

In like manner the signification of the following numbers, with

A GENERAL RULE.

every other contained in the Word, may in some degree be ascertained by reducing them to the *simple, primitive,* or *radical* numbers, from which they arise either by *multiplication* or *addition*, or by *both together*, viz.:

        745—Jer. lii. 30.
        832—Jer. lii. 29.
      1365—Num. iii. 50.
      1400—1 Kings x. 26.
      1775—Ex. xxxviii. 25, 28.
      2300—Dan. viii. 14.
      2400—Ex. xxxviii. 29.
      4500—Ezek. xlviii. 16, 30, 33, 34.
      4600—Jer. lii. 30.
      8580—Num. iv. 48.
    16,750—Num. xxxi. 52.
    22,000—Num. iii. 39.
    22,273—Num. iii. 43.
    25,000—Ezek. xlviii. 8, 9, 10, 13, 15, 20, 21.
    50,070—1 Sam. vi. 19.
    70,000—2 Sam. xxiv. 15.
  120,000—Judges viii. 10.
  180,000—1 Kings xii. 21.
  337,500—Num. xxxi. 43.
  601,730—Num. xxvi. 51.
  603,550—Ex. xxxviii. 26.   Num. i. 46.
1,000,000—Dan. vii. 10.
100,000,000—Dan. vii. 10.

A KEY TO THE SPIRITUAL SIGNIFICATION

OF

WEIGHTS AND MEASURES.*

CHAPTER V.

AS mention is frequently made in the Word, not only of *numbers*, but also of *weights* and *measures*; and these latter as well as the former, have in all cases an internal or spiritual signification, without a knowledge of which it is impossible to form a just or adequate conception of the sanctity of the various subjects treated of where they occur; it is desirable that, to the preceding KEY to the Spiritual Signification of Numbers, should be added a smaller one to that of Weights and Measures, which being of a similar quality and construction, will, it is hoped, equally serve to introduce the student into the temple of wisdom, and on some occasions procure admission for him even when the larger Key has failed to insure it.

Tables of Scripture Weights and Measures.

I. *Weights of the Balance.*

A shekel in weight, 137 grains, value in money 1s. 3d.

A shekel of the sanctuary (supposed by some, but perhaps without sufficient reason, to be double the weight and value of a common shekel) 274 grains, value 2s. 6d.

A gerah or obolus, the twentieth part of a shekel, value 1½d.

A maneh, 50 sacred shekels, 2 lb. 3 oz. 6 pwt. 10.286 gr., value in silver £3 2s. 6d.; in gold £75.

A talent, 3000 sacred shekels, 113 lb. 10 oz. 1 pwt. 10.286 gr., value in silver £187 10s.; in gold £2250.

A mule's burden, two hundred weight.

II. *Measures of Capacity of Things that are Dry.*

A cab, 2.8333 pints.

A chomer, the tenth part of an ephah, 5.1 pints.

A seah, one peck, one pint.

---

* By Robert Hindmarsh. First published in Manchester, England, in 1820.

An ephah or bath, the tenth part of a homer, three pecks, three pints.
A lethec or half-homer, five ephahs, near three bushels.
A homer, ten ephahs, near six bushels.
A choenix, a quart.

III. Measures of Liquids.

A caph, .625 pint.
A log, .833 pint.
A cab, 3.333 pints.
A hin, one gallon, two pints.
A bath, the tenth part of a cor or homer, seven gallons and a half.
A firkin, four gallons and a half.
A coron chomer, seventy-five gallons, five pints.

IV. Measures of Application.

A hair's-breadth, the forty-eighth part of an inch.
A finger, .912 inch.
A hand's-breadth, 3.648 inches.
A span, 10.944 inches.
A foot, twelve inches.
A cubit, one foot 9.888 inches.
A holy cubit, three feet, or a yard.
The king's cubit, a foot and nine inches.
A reed, six cubits and a hand's-breadth, or ten feet 11.328 inches.
A pace, five feet, and probably in some cases only a step, or two feet and a half.
A furlong, or the eighth part of a mile.
A mile, a thousand paces, one mile four hundred and three paces one foot.
A sabbath day's journey, seven hundred and twenty-nine paces three feet.*

Note.—The quantities, supposed to be contained in the preceding weights and measures, are by no means accurately ascertained; some making them to be considerably more, and some less, than what are here stated. We have chiefly followed the calculation given in the Tables annexed to a small English Bible, printed at Edinburgh in the year 1748, by Adrain Watkins, printer to His Majesty. It is, however, of little consequence, whether they be correct in this particular or not; since the spiritual signification belonging to the different names both of the Jewish weights and measures, is not in the least affected by our ignorance of the exact quantities they represented, as compared with the weights and measures now in use.—Gold and silver by weight served in ancient times for money instead of stamped coin.

In general it may be observed, that *weights* signify the states of a thing as to *good*, and *measures* the states of a thing as to *truth*: for gravity in the natural world corresponds to good in the spiritual

---

* A few corrections in the above tables as originally published by the author, have been made, generally on the authority of Dr. Arbuthnot.—EDITOR.

world, and extension corresponds to truth. The reason of this is, that in heaven where correspondences originate, there is neither gravity nor extension, there being no space there such as belongs to nature; and yet there is an appearance both of gravity and of extension, because there is an appearance of space, which appearance is for the sake of distinguishing in a visible and sensible manner the different qualities and states of things in the spiritual world. In an opposite sense, *weights* are predicated of *evil*, and *measures* of *falsity*. Whence it follows that things good and true tend upwards, that is, to heaven and the Lord, who is called the Most High, because He is the inmost of all; but things evil and false tend downwards, that is, to hell, which is said to be in the depths below, because it is in the outermost or extreme principles of life.—A. C. 3104, 3405, 4482, 5658.

Again, *weights* represent the quantity of good in the church, or in an individual of the church; and *measures* represent the *quality* thereof, which is determined by the truth with which it is conjoined. —A. C. 8533, 9603. Hence to *weigh* or *measure* any thing, when spiritually understood, is to explore and ascertain its quantity and quality as to good and truth.—Ap. Ex. 629. A. R. 313, 486.

A *balance*, or *pair of scales*, signifies the estimation of a thing as to truth and good.—A. R. 313. Ap. Ex. 373.

Measures of different capacities signify the states of things as to truth, and also as to good, the one following as a consequence of the other.—A. C. 8533, 9603.

Measures of dry things serving for food, such as an *ephah*, an *omer*, a *homer*, etc., with which wheat, barley, and flour were measured, signify goods; and measures of liquids serving for drink, such as a *bath*, a *hin*, a *cor*, etc., signify truths.—A. C. 8540.

In like manner measures of application, such as *hand-breadths*, *spans*, *feet*, *cubits*, *reeds*, *paces*, *furlongs*, *miles*, etc., have a similar signification; the length of an object having more immediate reference to good, and its breadth to truth.—A. R. 485, 904 to 910. Ap. Ex. 627. A. C. 9603.

To this account of the signification of weights and measures, which affords a general view of their application and use in the Sacred Scriptures, it will be sufficient to add such of the particular weights and measures as are of the most frequent occurrence; by the help of which, and the examples that follow, it is presumed the reader will be enabled to discern many traits of divine wisdom displayed in the language of revelation, which entirely escape the notice of those who are unacquainted with its spiritual sense.

WEIGHTS.

A *shekel*, from its being the usual unit of value among the Jews, signifies the price or estimation of a thing according to quantity; the price of what is holy; the estimation of good and truth; also truth itself derived from good: for being a weight both of silver and of gold, it is used to denote the value of both.—A. C. 2959, 3104, 10221, 10222.

A *shekel of the sanctuary*, or a *shekel of holiness*, is so called, because it refers to truth and good from the Lord, which constitute the essential principle of sanctity in the church.—A. C. 2959, 3104, 10221, 10222.

A *shekel* of twenty *gerahs* signifies the estimation of the good of remains.—A. C. 2959, 10222.

Half a shekel signifies as much as is sufficient for use. And as a whole *shekel* consisted of twenty *gerahs*, the *half-shekel*, of ten *gerahs*, sometimes denotes all, because the number ten bears the same signification, and further implies remains, which are the truths and goods treasured up in the interiors of man by the Lord.—A. C. 3104, 10221.

A *gerah* or *obolus* involves the same signification, but not in so full a degree, as the *shekel*, of which it is the twentieth part, viz., truth from good.—A. C. 2959, 10221.

A *pound* or a *talent* as money, signifies the knowledges of truth and good from the Word.—Ap. Ex. 193, 675. A. C. 7770. Also the faculty of liberty and rationality, together with prudence, circumspection, judgment, etc.—D. P. 210. Goods and truths from the Lord; the truths of faith; also remains.—A. C. 5291.

A *talent of pure gold* denotes celestial good, from which, as from one single fountain, flow all spiritual things.—A. C. 9574.

A *talent*, as a weight either of silver or gold, signifies truth and good in great purity; and in an opposite sense, falsity and evil of a most malignant quality.—A. R. 714. Ap. Ex. 1026.

Lead, as a weight, signifies either good or evil in the exterior natural man: for as *lead* among the metals named in the Word, is of the most ignoble and inferior order, so it is used to denote, in a good sense, the lowest or most external natural good, and in an opposite sense the lowest or grossest kind of evil. Hence, a *stone of lead*, a *weight of lead*, or a *talent of lead*, signifies evil, and the false principle derived from evil.—A. C. 8298, 8540.

A *stone*, when considered as a weight, and in a sense opposite to its genuine meaning, signifies the false principle from evil: for such is the nature of evil that it tends downwards, and causes the false principle with which it is conjoined, to descend like a heavy substance in the natural world, to the deep below in the spiritual world, that is, to hell.—A. C. 8279. But falsity or error, if it be not derived from evil, has no such tendency of itself: and hence many who are in falsities as to doctrine, and yet in good as to life, are capable of being elevated, after instruction, into heaven.—A. C. 8298.

MEASURES.

An *omer*, being the tenth part of an *ephah*, signifies as much of good as is sufficient for use; for an *omer*, as well as an *ephah*, signifies good; and as ten signifies fulness, so a tenth part denotes a sufficiency, also a little or few.—A. C. 8468, 8533, 8540, 10136, 10262.

An *ephah*, being a measure of wheat, barley, and fine flour, and the tenth part of a *homer*, is predicated of good, and denotes the quantity thereof, that is, the quantity of reception, whether it be much or little.—A. C. 8468, 8540, 10136, 10262. The *ephah* was usually divided into ten parts, by which number was signified much, all, and fulness. But in Ezek. xlv. 13, and xlvi. 14, the *ephah* is divided into six parts, by reason of the subject there treated of being the new temple, or spiritual kingdom of the Lord, in which the numbers 12, 6, and 3, are chiefly in use.—A. C. 10262.

A *homer* containing ten *ephahs*, signifies fulness; and being a measure of wheat and barley, is therefore predicated of good.—A. C. 8468, 8540, 10262. Ten *homers*, Num. xi. 32, signify too much, or superfluity.—A. C. 8469.

A *chœnix*, being a measure of wheat and barley among the Greeks, signifies the quality and degree of the estimation of good and truth from the Word.—A. R. 314. Ap. Ex. 374.

A *hin*, being a measure of wine and oil, is predicated of truth, and denotes the quantity thereof, also the quantity or degree of conjunction.—A. C. 8540, 10136, 10262. The *hin* was divided into four parts, to denote conjunction; for such is the signification of the number four. The same is also signified by the oil, which was measured in the *hin*, and mixed with the fine flour in the meat-offerings; the flour denoting reception, and the oil conjunction.—A. C. 10262.

A *cor*, being a measure of liquids, and containing ten *baths*, is predicated of truth in a state of fulness, and denotes the quantity thereof. —A. C. 10262.

A *bath*, being a measure of liquids, is predicated of truth, and denotes the quantity thereof as being small or few.—A. C. 8468, 8540, 10262.

Reeds, cubits, furlongs, and other measures of application, signify the states and qualities of things either with respect to good or truth, or the conjunction of both; also the faculty, power and manner of exploring and discerning those states.—A. R. 485, 904. Ap. Ex. 627. A. C. 9603.

EXAMPLES.

(1.) Ex. xvi. 16. "This is the thing which Jehovah hath commanded; Gather of it (manna) every man according to his eating: an *omer* for every man, according to the number of your persons, take ye every man for them which are in his tents."——By gathering manna, every man according to his eating, is signified reception and appropriation of the good of truth, according to the faculty or capacity of each individual: manna denotes the good of truth, or that good which results from a knowledge of, and obedience to, the divine laws. By the quantity gathered, viz., an *omer* for every man, according to the number of persons in the tents, is signified as much as is sufficient to supply the spiritual necessity of each, and promote the general good of society: an *omer*, which was the tenth part of an *ephah*, denotes as much as is sufficient for use.—See A. C. 8467 to 8470.

(2.) Ex. xxix. 40. "And with the one lamb thou shalt offer a tenth-deal of flour mingled with the fourth part of a *hin* of beaten oil; and the fourth part of a *hin* of wine for a drink-offering."—— The sacrifice of a lamb in the morning represented the removal of evils by the good of innocency from the Lord, and the implantation of good and truth in the internal man: the sacrifice of a lamb in the evening represented the same in the external man. A tenth-deal of flour mixed with beaten oil, signified spiritual good from a celestial origin, as much as is necessary for conjunction: a tenth-deal, or tenth of an *ephah*, denotes the quantity of good, or what is sufficient for use; flour denotes truth from celestial good, which is the same as spiritual good; oil denotes celestial good; and the fourth part of a *hin* denotes what is sufficient for conjunction. So in like manner the fourth part of a *hin* of wine for a drink-offering signifies as much of spiritual truth as is sufficient for conjunction: wine denotes spiritual truth; a *hin*, the quantity of truth; and the fourth part, like the number four, conjunction.—See A. C. 10134 to 10139.

(3.) Ex. xxx. 12, 13. "When thou takest the sum of the children of Israel, after their number; then shall they give every man a ransom for his soul unto Jehovah, when thou numberest them; that there be no plague amongst them when thou numberest them. This they shall give, every one that passeth among them that are numbered: *half a shekel* after the *shekel* of the sanctuary, (a *shekel* is twenty *gerahs*,) a *half-shekel* shall be the offering to Jehovah."—— By taking the sum of the children of Israel, or numbering them, is signified the orderly arrangement and disposition of all things relating to the church. By every man giving a ransom for his soul unto Jehovah, is signified purification or deliverance from evil by the truth of faith, and by an acknowledgment that all truths and goods are from the Lord. By *half a shekel*, after the *shekel* of the sanctuary, are signified all things of truth from good; the reason of which signification is, that, as the *shekel* consisted of twenty *gerahs*, so the *half-shekel* consisted of ten, and the number ten denotes all, likewise remains, which are the truths and goods received by man, and treasured up in his interiors by the Lord. The *shekel* itself denotes truth from good, and, considered as a weight, the quantity of each. It is called the *shekel of the sanctuary* or *of holiness*, because truth and good are holy, being derived from the Lord who alone is holy. The offering of *half a shekel*, therefore, to Jehovah, denotes that all things of the church are from Him.—See A. C. 2959, 10216 to 10223.

(4.) Lev. xix. 35, 36. "Ye shall do no unrighteousness in judgment, in *mete-yard*, in *weight*, or in *measure*. Just *balances*, just *weights*, a just *ephah*, and a just *hin* shall ye have."——By the weights and measures here named, as well as by those mentioned in Ezek. xlv. 10 to 14, are signified rules of exploration and just judgment as to the state and quality of good and truth in the church.— See Ap. Ex. 373, 629. A. R. 313, 486, 487. A. C. 8540.

(5.) Isa. v. 9, 10. "Of a truth many houses shall be desolate, even great and fair, without inhabitant. Yea, ten *acres* of vineyard shall yield one *bath*, and the seed of a *homer* shall yield an *ephah*." ——The subject here treated of is the vastation or desolation of the church. By many houses great and fair becoming desolate and without inhabitant, is signified that with the members of the church the affection of good and the intelligence of truth would perish: great is predicated of good and the affection of good; and fair or beautiful is predicated of truth and the intelligence of truth. By ten *acres* of vineyard yielding only one *bath*, and the seed of a *homer* yielding only an *ephah*, is signified that there would be scarce any remains either of spiritual or of celestial things, which consist in faith and charity: ten *acres* denote fulness and much, the same being also signified by a *homer*; but a *bath* and an *ephah*, each being the tenth part of a *homer*, denote fewness and little; for according to the rule previously laid down, p. 469, when the number ten signifies much, a tenth part denotes little or few. See A. C. 576, 8468. Ap. Ex. 675.

(6.) Isa. xl. 12. "Who hath *measured* the waters in the hollow of his hand, and *meted* out heaven with the *span*, and comprehended the dust of the earth in a *measure*, and *weighed* the mountains in *scales*, and the hills in a *balance?*"——The just arrangement and estimation of all things in heaven and the church, according to the quality of good and truth therein, is here described by *measuring*, *spanning*, and *weighing* in a *balance*. By the waters are signified truths; by the heavens, interior or spiritual truths and goods; by the dust of the earth, exterior or natural truths and goods, belonging to heaven and the church; by mountains, the goods of love; by hills, the goods of charity; and by *measuring* and *weighing* them is meant the just appreciation and arrangement thereof by the Lord, according to their respective qualities.—See Ap. Ex. 373, 629. A. R. 486. A. C. 3104, 9603.

(7.) Ezek. xl. 2, 3, 5. "In the visions of God Jehovah brought me into the land of Israel, and set me upon a very high mountain, by which was as the frame of a city on the south. And He brought me thither, and behold, there was a man whose appearance was like the appearance of brass, with a *line* of flax in his hand, and a *measuring-reed*; and he stood in the gate. And behold, a wall on the outside of the house round about, and in the man's hand a *measuring-reed* of six *cubits* long, by the *cubit*, and a *hand-breadth*; so he *measured* the breadth of the building one *reed*, and the height one *reed*."——In this and the three following chapters is contained a description of the new temple seen by Ezekiel in spiritual vision, with the dimensions of its various parts, as of the wall, the gate, the porch, the threshold, the posts, the doors, the steps, the windows, the chambers, the court, the altar, etc., which are marked by the numbers of *reeds, cubits* and *hand-breadths*. By the building, house and temple, is signified the church; by the gate and entrance, introductory truth; by the interior of the temple, the things relating to the internal of the church; and by the porch and court, the things relating to its external. The length, the breadth, and height of the various parts, denote the good and truth of the church, with the degrees of each: length being predicated of good, breadth of truth, and height of their degrees. That such is the spiritual signification of the dimensions of the house and temple, is plain from chap. xliii. 10, 11, where the prophet is ordered to "show the house to the house of Israel, that they may be ashamed of their iniquities, and that they may *measure* the pattern, and *keep* the whole form thereof, and all the ordinances thereof, and *do them*."—See Ap. Ex. 629. A. C. 9604.

(8.) Ezek. xlvii. 3 to 5. "And when the man that had the *line* in his hand went forth eastward, he *measured* a thousand *cubits*, and he brought me through the waters; the waters were to the ankles. Again he *measured* a thousand, and brought me through the waters; the waters were to the knees: again he *measured* a thousand, and brought me through; the waters were to the loins. Afterward he *measured* a thousand, and it was a river that I could not pass over: for the waters were risen, waters to swim in, a river that could not be passed over."——A description is here given of the manner in which intelligence, with the members of the church, increases by the reception of divine truth proceeding from the Lord, signified by the waters issuing out from under the threshold of the house towards the east, and coming down from the right side of the house, at the south side of the altar, as mentioned in ver. 1. By the east is signified love to the Lord, because the east in heaven is where the Lord appears as a sun; and the right side from thence, which is called the south, is where divine truth is received in its greatest light, on which account the waters are said to come on the south side of the altar. By the waters which reached to the ankles, is signified intelligence such as is possessed by the sensual and natural man; for the ankles in the human body denote the sensual and natural principle. By the waters which reached to the knees, is signified intelligence such as is possessed by the spiritual-natural principle. By the waters which reached to the loins, is signified intelligence such as is possessed by the spiritual man; for the loins denote the marriage of truth and good, which constitutes the spiritual principle. By the waters which could not be passed over, is signified the intelligence of the celestial man, properly called wisdom, which being ineffable and far above the comprehension of the natural man, is therefore compared to a river that could not be passed over, whose waters also were waters to swim in. The *measuring* with a *line* from place to place a thousand *cubits*, signifies exploration and designation of the different qualities of divine truth in heaven and in the church, according to its various reception by angels and men.—See Ap. Ex. 629.

(9.) Hosea iii. 2. "So I bought her (the adulteress) for fifteen pieces of silver, and for a *homer* of barley and a *half-homer* of barley."

——By the woman an adulteress is here meant the house of Israel who, by their vain traditions and corrupt doctrines, had falsified every truth and adulterated every good contained in the Word. By her being bought for fifteen pieces of silver, and for a *homer* and *half-homer* of barley, is signified that the Israelitish church possessed so little of truth and of good, that its estimation, even taken at the full, was of little or no intrinsic value: the fifteen pieces of silver are predicated of truth, and denote the deficiency thereof both of quantity and quality: the same is also signified by the *homer* and *half-homer* of barley, which are predicated of good.—See Ap. Ex. 374. A. R. 315. A. C. 8468.

(10.) Zech. ii. 1, 2. "I lifted up mine eyes again, and looked, and behold, a man with a *measuring-line* in his hand. Then said I, Whither goest thou? And he said unto me, To *measure* Jerusalem, to see what is the breadth thereof, and what is the length thereof."

——Jerusalem here signifies the new church of the Lord; and by *measuring* it, to see its breadth and length, is signified to explore and hence to ascertain the quality and quantity of truth and good appertaining to its doctrine: to *measure* with a *measuring-line*, is to explore and discover the quality and quantity: its breadth denotes the truth of doctrine; and its length the good of love.—See Ap. Ex. 629. A. C. 9603.

(11.) Zech. v. 5 to 8. "Then the angel that talked with me went forth and said unto me, Lift up now thine eyes, and see what is this that goeth forth. And I said, What is it? And he said, This is an *ephah* that goeth forth. He said moreover, This is their resemblance through all the earth. And behold, there was lifted up a *talent of lead:* and this is a woman that sitteth in the midst of the *ephah*. And he said, This is wickedness; and he cast it into the midst of the *ephah*, and he cast the *weight of lead* upon the mouth thereof."——In this passage is described the profanation which took place in the church, of which the prophet speaks. By the *ephah* is signified good; by the woman evil, or wickedness, as expressly stated in the words of the text; and by the *weight, talent,* or *stone of lead* upon the mouth of the *ephah,* is signified the false principle derived from evil, which closes up and infests the good, and thus by a kind of mixture with good produces a state of profanation.—See A. C. 8540.

(12.) Dan. v. 25 to 29. "And this is the writing that was written, *Mene mene, tekel upharsin.* This is the interpretation of the thing; *Mene,* God hath *numbered* thy kingdom, and finished it. *Tekel,* thou art *weighed* in the *balances,* and art found wanting. *Peres,* thy kingdom is divided, and given to the Medes and Persians."——The subject here treated of, in the spiritual sense, is the consummation or end of the church, and the profanation of the holy things of the Word, represented by the vessels of gold and silver, out of which the king of Babylon, his princes, and wives and concubines drank, in praise of false gods. By the writing on the wall is signified that the church was entirely destroyed. By *mene mene,* or *numbered numbered,* is signified an exploration of the quality of the church both as to truth and good, more particularly as to truth. By *tekel,* or thou art *weighed in the balances,* is signified the estimation of the quality of good, which was found and adjudged to be adulterated and profaned. By *peres* is signified dissipation, extermination, and separation from every good and truth of the church: literally, *upharsin* signifies *and they divide;* the letter *u,* as a conjunction prefixed to the word, denoting *and;* and *pharsin,* a variation of the word *peres,* or *paras,* being the participle of the present tense, plural number, denoting *they divide* or *are dividing,* implying that innumerable evil and false principles concurred in dissipating and destroying every thing good and true belonging to the church.—See A. C. 3104, 9093, 10217. A. R. 313, 316. Ap. Ex. 373, 453.

(13.) Apoc. xi. 1. "And there was given me a *reed* like unto a *rod:* and the angel stood, saying, Rise, and *measure* the temple of God, and the altar, and them that worship therein."——By a *reed* like unto a *rod* or *staff,* is here signified the power of exploring and discerning the quality of the church and its worship; which power or capacity being exercised by man apparently of himself, yet under an acknowledgment that it is in reality from the Lord, is therefore first compared to a *reed* in reference to the weakness or inability of man, and afterwards to a *rod* or *staff* in reference to the power of divine truth from the Lord. By rising and *measuring* the temple of God, and the altar, and them that worship therein, is signified seeing, knowing, and examining the state of the church in heaven in respect to the truth of doctrine, the good of love, and worship thence derived: to *measure* is to know and examine the quality of a thing; the temple of God is predicated of the truth of doctrine; the altar, of the good of love: and they that worship therein, when considered abstractly from persons, of worship itself.—See A. R. 485, 486. Ap. Ex. 627 to 629.

(14.) Apoc. xxi. 15 to 17. "And he that talked with me had a golden *reed* to *measure* the city, and the gates thereof and the wall thereof. And the city lieth four-square, and the length is as large as the breadth: and he *measured* the city with the *reed*, twelve thousand *furlongs:* the length and the breadth and the height of it are equal. And he *measured* the wall thereof, a hundred and forty and four *cubits*, according to the *measure* of a man, that is, of an angel."—— Here again a *reed* signifies the power or faculty of understanding and knowing: and as this power is derived from the good of love, and given by the Lord to those who are in such good, which is signified by gold, therefore the *reed* is described as a *golden reed*. By *measuring* the city, the gates and the wall of the city, which is the holy Jerusalem, is signified the application of the above faculty in examining and investigating, with a view to understand and know the quality and character of the New Church as to its doctrine, its introductory truths, and the literal sense of the Word, from which its doctrine is derived; the city denotes the New Church, as to doctrine; the gates, introductory truths, or the knowledges of truth and good; and the wall, the Word in its literal sense, serving as a defence and security against all spiritual enemies. By the city being four-square, or so situated as to front all the four quarters, is signified an equal or just respect to good and truth, and all the states of life thence derived. The same is signified by the length being equal to the breadth, 12000 *furlongs;* the length or longitude from east to west being predicated of good, and the breadth or latitude from south to north being predicated of truth; while the height or altitude denotes the degrees of both in their various relations and proportions: 12000 *furlongs* denote all the goods and truths belonging to the church. The dimensions of the wall, 144 *cubits*, show the quality of the Word in its literal sense, as containing all the goods and truths of heaven and the church: *cubits*, like other *measures*, denote the quality of a thing;

and the number 144, like the number 12000, and 12, from which both arise, denotes all. The *measure* is said to be the *measure* of a man, that is, of an angel, because the church on earth consisting of men, and the church in heaven consisting of angels, are regarded by the Lord as one church, being formed of the same principles of divine love and divine wisdom, though received in different degrees by each respectively. By a man is signified intelligence and wisdom derived from the Word, whether it be in an individual or in a society; and by an angel is signified divine truth, also a heavenly society, and an individual of such a society, receptive of divine truth from the Lord, who is the sole fountain thereof. Thus it appears that the dimensions of the New Jerusalem are not to be regarded as the dimensions of a great city, according to the natural idea suggested by the terms used, but that they are to be wholly referred to the spiritual things of heaven and the church, particularly to the doctrine of divine truth and good derived from the Word, and now revealed by the Lord through the instrumentality of a chosen servant.—See A. R. 904 to 910. Ap. Ex. 629. A. C. 9603.

Conclusion.

From the preceding view, limited and imperfect as it is, of the spiritual signification of *numbers, weights* and *measures* in the Word throughout, it is evident that without a knowledge of this most ancient science, according to which the things relating to heaven and the church are constantly described, the true and genuine sense of divine revelation must in a great measure remain buried in obscurity. Many passages indeed are to be found, especially in the historical parts both of the Old and the New Testament, in which the necessity of having recourse to a spiritual sense distinct from that of the letter, is not so obvious as it is in some which have been brought forward in this small treatise. Yet when we consider that the Word was dictated by Jehovah himself, that it descended through all the heavens to man, and consequently that in its origin it is holy and divine; then it must be acknowledged that it contains an internal as well as an external sense, and that the former pervades every part of the latter. If so, it follows that *numbers, weights* and *measures,* as expressed in the literal sense, must in all cases form the basis of another more interior sense, which may be regarded as wine in comparison with water, John ii. 7 to 10; as a soul in comparison with its body of flesh, John vi. 63; or as heaven itself in comparison with the earth, Isa. lv. 9.

PRECIOUS AND COMMON STONES,

AND

THEIR MEANING IN SCRIPTURE.*

CHAPTER VI.

A GENERAL ACCOUNT OF THE STONES MENTIONED IN THE SACRED SCRIPTURES, THE PURPOSES TO WHICH THEY WERE APPLIED, AND THEIR VARIOUS SIGNIFICATIONS.

IN the Sacred Scriptures mention is frequently made of rocks and stones, rough or unwrought stones, wrought or hewn stones, artificial stones or bricks, corner-stones, mill-stones, chalk-stones, and also of precious stones, gems, and pearls; by which are spiritually understood either genuine truths, apparent truths, or perverted truths, which latter are more properly called falsities. And it is from the use or application of the expressions, that we learn to know when to refer them to one signification and when to another. For it is to be well observed, not only with respect to stones, but to many other substances in nature, that the same term carries with it, on different occasions, very different meanings; and that, in some cases, it bears a sense directly the reverse of what it elsewhere conveys, which is always determined by the nature of the subject treated of. For example; when the Lord himself is called a Rock, as in Ps. xviii. 2, 31, 46; or a Stone, as in Matt. xxi. 42; Ps. cxviii. 22; Isa. viii. 14; it is plain, that the term is to be understood in its genuine sense, as significative of divine truth. But when, on the other hand, mention is made of the Rock of the perverted Church, as in Deut. xxxii. 31, 32; the dumb stone, as in Hab. ii. 19; or of committing adultery with stones, as in Jer. iii. 19; or of taking up stones to stone Jesus, as in John x. 31; it is equally plain, that the term, in such cases, denotes false principles of doctrine and of life, which are entirely opposed to the divine truth of the Word.

---

* By Robert Hindmarsh. First published in London, 1851.

Among the various purposes to which stones, both common and precious, are assigned in the Sacred Scriptures, in consequence of the signification which they obtained in the earliest ages of the world, the following are particularly distinguishable, viz. :—

1. Stones for altars, pillars, witnesses and memorials.
2. Tables of Stone for the Ten Commandments.
3. Stones for temples and other buildings.
4. Stones for idols, etc.
5. Precious stones for the breast-plate of Aaron, and for the foundations of the New Jerusalem.

Hence we read in different parts of the Word,—

1. Of the Stone of Israel. Gen. xlix. 24.
2. Of the Rock of Israel. 2 Sam. xxiii. 3.
3. Of the Rock of salvation. Deut. xxxii. 15; 2 Sam. xxii. 47; Ps. xviii. 2, 31, 46.
4. Of a stone rejected by the builders, which yet became the head-stone of the corner, on which whosoever falleth, shall be broken; but on whomsoever it shall fall, it will grind him to powder. Ps. cxviii. 22; Matt. xxi. 42, 44; Mark xii. 10, 11; Luke xx. 17, 18.
5. Of a stone of stumbling, and a rock of offence, over which both the houses of Israel and the inhabitants of Jerusalem shall stumble, and fall, and be broken. Isa. viii. 14, 15.
6. Of a stone cut out of a mountain without hands, which smote the image of Nebuchadnezzar, and brake it in pieces, and which afterwards became a great mountain (or rock), and filled the whole earth. Dan. ii. 34, 35, 45.
7. Of a stone with seven eyes, said to be the eyes of Jehovah, which run to and fro through the whole earth. Zech. iii. 9; iv. 10.
8. Of the head-stone of the temple, which shall be brought forth with shoutings, while the cry of grace, grace, is raised unto it. Zech. iv. 7.
9. Of great stones, costly stones, and hewed stones, for the foundation of the house or temple of Jehovah, and for other parts of the building. 1 Kings v. 17, 18; vi. 7, 36; Hag. ii. 15, 18; Matt. xxiv. 1, 2; Mark xiii. 2; Luke xxi. 5, 6.
10. Of the same for Solomon's house, and for the house of Pharaoh's daughter. 1 Kings vii. 8–12.
11. Of the stones of Zion, in which her children take delight. Ps. cii. 14.
12. Of the two tables of testimony, tables of stone, on which the

commandments were first written with the finger of God, and afterwards broken by Moses. Ex. xxiv. 12; xxxi. 18; xxxii. 15, 16, 19; Deut. iv. 13; v. 22; ix. 9-17.

13. Of the two tables of stone, which were renewed by Moses. Ex. xxxiv. 1, 4, 27-29; Deut. x. 1-5; 1 Kings viii. 9.

14. Of altars of stone, and rocks, for the worship of Jehovah. Ex. xx. 24, 25; Deut. xxvii. 5, 6; Josh. viii. 30, 31; Judg. vi. 20, 21; xiii. 19, 20; 1 Kings xviii. 31, 32, 38.

15. Of the stones of the altar becoming as chalk-stones. Isa. xxvii. 9.

16. Of stones and heaps of stones for pillows, pillars, memorials and witnesses. Gen. xxviii. 18, 22; xxxi. 45-48, 52; xxxv. 14, 20; Ex. xxiv. 4; Josh. iv. 1-9, 20-24; vii. 26; viii. 29; xxii. 10-34; xxiv. 26, 27; 1 Sam. vii. 12; 2 Sam. xviii. 18.

17. Of stones for land-marks. Deut. xix. 14; xxvii. 17.

18. Of twelve stones, which the Israelites took out of the midst of Jordan, when they passed over it, for a memorial. Josh. iv. 2-8, 20-24.

19. Of other twelve stones, which Joshua set up in the midst of Jordan, where the feet of the priests stood, who bare the ark of the covenant. Josh. iv. 9.

20. Of great stones plastered with plaster, on which the words of the law were to be written. Deut. xxvii. 2-4.

21. Of Moses sitting upon a stone, with his hands lifted up, while the Israelites and the Amalekites were engaged in battle. Ex. xvii. 12.

22. Of Moses being put into a clift of the rock, and covered with the hand of Jehovah, while his glory passed by. Ex. xxxiii. 21, 22.

23. Of Moses smiting the rock, on which Jehovah stood, with his rod, so that water came out of it in abundance. Ex. xvii. 6; Num. xx. 10, 11; Ps. lxxviii. 15, 16, 20; cv. 41; cxiv. 8; Isa. xlviii. 21.

24. Of speaking to the rock, that it may give forth water. Num. xx. 8.

25. Of sucking honey out of the rock, and oil out of the flinty rock. Deut. xxxii. 13.

26. Of great stones for covering the mouth of wells. Gen. xxix. 2, 3, 8, 10.

27. Of brick, instead of stone, for building the city and the towers of Babel. Gen. xi. 3.

28. Of altars of brick. Isa. lxv. 3.

29. Of the stones of the sanctuary. Lam. iv. 1.

30. Of stones of fire. Ezek. xxviii. 14, 16.

31. Of stones of emptiness. Isa. xxxiv. 11.

32. Of gravel-stones. Lam. iii. 16.

33. Of smooth stones of the stream. Isa. lvii. 6.

34. Of stones for bread. Matt. iv. 3; vi. 9; Luke iv. 3; xi. 11.

35. Of the dumb stone. Hab. ii. 19.

36. Of the stone crying out of the wall, and the beam out of the timber answering it. Hab. ii. 11.

37. Of committing adultery with stones, and with stocks. Jer. iii. 9.

38. Of a stony heart. Ezek. xi. 19; xxxvi. 26.

39. Of seed falling on stony places. Matt. xiii. 5, 20; Mark iv. 5, 16; Luke viii. 6, 13.

40. Of raising up children to Abraham out of stones. Matt. iii. 9; Luke iii. 8.

41. Of the stones being ready to cry out, in case the disciples of Jesus had been silent on the occasion of his entry into Jerusalem. Luke xix. 40.

42. Of building the church upon a rock. Matt. xvi. 18.

43. Of a stone laid in Zion, a tried stone, a precious corner-stone, a sure foundation. Isa. xxviii. 16.

44. Of a white stone, and in the stone a new name written, which no man knoweth, save he that receiveth it. Apoc. ii. 17.

45. Of five smooth stones, which David took out of a brook, and with one of which he smote Goliath the Philistine in his forehead, and then slew him. 1 Sam. xvii. 40, 49, 50.

46. Of sharp stones for circumcision. Ex. iv. 25.

47. Of hail-stones, great stones cast down from heaven. Ex. ix. 23, etc.; Josh. x. 11; Ezek. xiii. 11, 13; Ps. xviii. 12, 13; Apoc. xvi. 21.

48. Of mill-stones. Deut. xxiv. 6; Isa. xlvii. 2; Jer. xxv. 10; Matt. xviii. 6; Luke xvii. 2; Apoc. xviii. 21, 22.

49. Of stoning men with stones. Ex. xvii. 4; Lev. xxiv. 10–16; Num. xiv. 10; xv. 32–36; Deut. xiii. 10; xvii. 5; xxi. 18–21; Josh. vii. 25; 1 Sam. xxx. 6; 1 Kings xii. 18; xxi. 10, 13–15; Ezek. xvi. 40; xxiii. 47; Matt. xxi. 35; xxiii. 37; Mark xii. 4; Luke xiii. 34; xx. 6; John viii. 5–7; x. 31–33.

50. Of dashing the foot against a stone. Ps. xci. 12; Matt. iv. 6; Luke iv. 11.

51. Of dashing the little ones of the daughter of Babylon against the stones. Ps. cxxxvii. 9.

52. Of judges being overthrown in stony places. Ps. cxli. 6.

53. Of sons being as plants, and daughters as corner-stones. Ps. cxliv. 12.

54. Of the rock, the holes of the rocks, the caves of the earth, the clefts of the rocks, and the tops of the ragged rocks, into which the wicked shall go, for fear of Jehovah. Isa. ii. 10, 19, 21.

55. Of the wicked calling upon the mountains and rocks to fall on them, and hide them from the divine presence. Apoc. vi. 16.

56. Of slaying men on rocks and stones. Judg. vii. 25; ix. 5, 18.

57. Of taking up stones to cast at Jesus. John viii. 59; x. 31–33; xi. 8.

58. Of gathering stones out of a vineyard. Isa. v. 2.

59. Of building a house upon a rock. Matt. vii. 24, 25; Luke vi. 48.

60. Of Jehovah as a rock. Deut. xxxii. 4, 15, 18, 30, 31; 1 Sam. ii. 2; 2 Sam. xxii. 2, 32, 47; Ps. xviii. 2, 31, 46; xxxi. 2, 3; xl. 2; xlii. 9; lxi. 2; lxii. 2, 6, 7; lxxviii. 35; lxxxix. 26; xcii. 15; xciv. 22; xcv. 1: Isa. xxxii. 2.

61. Of false gods as a rock. Deut. xxxii. 31, 37.

62. Of images or idols of stone. Lev. xxvi. 1; Deut. iv. 28; xxviii. 64; xxix. 17; Judg. xvii. 3, 4; xviii. 14–21, 30, 31; 2 Kings xvii. 41; xviii. 4; xix. 18; xxiii. 14, 24; Ps. lxxviii. 58; xcvii. 7; cvi. 36, 37; Isa. x. 19; xxi. 9; xliv. 9, 10, 15, 17; xlv. 17, 20; xlvi. 1; xlviii. 5; Dan. v. 4, 23; Micah i. 7; Nahum ii. 14; Hab. ii. 18; Apoc. ix. 20; xiii. 14, 15; xiv. 9, 11; xv. 2; xix. 20; xx. 4.

63. Of the body of Jesus being laid in a new tomb hewn out of the rock, and a great stone rolled to the door of the sepulchre, and sealed. Matt. xxvii. 60, 66; xxviii. 2; Mark xv. 46; xvi. 3, 4; Luke xxiii. 53; xxiv. 2; John xix. 41, 42; xx. 1, etc.

64. Of an angel rolling back the stone from the door of the sepulchre, and sitting upon it. Matt. xxviii. 2; Mark xvi. 3, 4.

65. Of a paved work of sapphire-stone under the feet of the God of Israel, resembling the body of heaven for clearness. Ex. xxiv. 10; Ezek. i. 26; x. i.

66. Of the appearance of the wheels, seen by Ezekiel, like unto the color of a beryl-stone. Ezek. i. 16; x. 9.

67. Of two onyx-stones on the shoulders of the ephod, having the

names of the children of Israel engraven on them. Ex. xxv. 7; xxviii. 9-12; xxxv. 9, 27; xxxix. 6, 7.

68. Of the precious stones called Urim and Thummim, for the breast-plate of Aaron. Ex. xxv. 7; xxviii. 17-21; xxxv. 9, 27; xxxix. 8-14.

69. Of precious stones presented by the queen of Sheba to Solomon. 1 Kings x. 10.

70. Of precious stones brought to Solomon from Ophir, in the navy of Hiram, king of Tyre. 1 Kings x. 11.

71. Of precious stones for the foundations, the windows, the gates, and the borders of the church to be established among the Gentiles. Isa. liv. 11, 12.

72. Of precious stones for the clothing of the king of Tyrus. Ezek. xxviii. 12-16.

73. Of precious stones for the adorning of the whore of Babylon. Apoc. xvii. 4; xviii. 16.

74. Of precious stones for the wall and foundations of the New Jerusalem. Apoc. xxi. 18-20.

In all the cases above enumerated stones denote, as before observed, truths, either genuine, or apparent, or perverted; which will sufficiently appear from the observations now following on some of the passages already referred to.

CHAPTER VII.

Stones used for Altars, Pillars, Witnesses, and Memorials.

Stones for Altars.

(1.) Ex. xx. 24, 25. An altar of earth thou shalt make unto me, and shalt sacrifice thereon thy burnt-offerings, and thy peace-offerings, thy sheep, and thine oxen. And if thou wilt make me an *altar of stone*, thou shalt not build it of hewn stone: for if thou lift up thy tool upon it, thou hast polluted it.

(2.) Deut. xxvii. 5, 6. And there shalt thou build an *altar* unto Jehovah thy God, an *altar of stone*. Thou shalt not lift up any iron tool upon them. Thou shalt build the *altar* of Jehovah thy God of *whole stones*: and thou shalt offer burnt-offerings thereon unto Jehovah thy God.

(3.) Josh. viii. 30, 31. Then Joshua built an *altar* unto Jehovah the God of Israel in mount Ebal, as Moses the servant of Jehovah commanded the children of Israel, as it is written in the book of the law of Moses, an *altar of whole stones*, over which no man hath lift up any iron.

(4.) 1 Kings xviii. 31, 32. Elijah took *twelve stones*, according to the number of the tribes of the sons of Jacob: and with the stones he built an *altar* in the name of Jehovah.

As the essential part of worship consists in two things, namely, good and truth, or charity and faith, therefore, in reference to these mention is made of an *altar of earth* and an *altar of stone*. Worship from a principle of good, or of charity, was represented by the offerings and sacrifices made upon *altars of earth;* but worship from the love of truth or from faith, was represented by the offerings and sacrifices made upon *altars of stone*. The former is the worship of a man already regenerated, or of one who is in charity, and at the same time in faith derived from it: the latter is the worship of him who is undergoing the process of regeneration, and who by faith is led to charity, or by the precepts of truth into the life of good.

The reason why the altar was not to be built of hewn stones, but of unwrought or whole stones, was, that the labor of man in hewing and preparing them according to his own skill and judgment, denoted self-derived intelligence, which, so far as it contains anything of merely human life or human merit, is in itself evil, and therefore cannot enter into, or mingle itself with, the pure worship of the Lord without contaminating, defiling, and in a great degree profaning it. All worship, to be truly acceptable, must be derived from the Lord alone by his Word; the truths of which, being in themselves divine, if received by man in sincerity of heart and integrity of life, will bear above him the consideration of selfish and temporal interests, to the contemplation and love of those which are heavenly and eternal.

(5.) Judges vi. 20, 21. The angel of God said unto Gideon, Take the flesh and the unleavened cakes, and lay them upon this *rock*. And he did so. Then the angel of Jehovah put forth the end of the staff that was in his hand, and touched the flesh and the unleavened cakes: and there rose up fire out of the *rock*, and consumed the flesh and the unleavened cakes.

(6.) Judges xiii. 19, 20. Manoah took a kid, with a meat-offering, and offered it upon a *rock* unto Jehovah. And it came to pass, when the flame went up toward heaven from off the altar, that the angel of Jehovah ascended in the flame of the *altar*.

In both of these instances a natural rock is used as an altar to Jehovah. The rock denotes divine truth, and the fire issuing out of it is divine love: These two concurring in the worship there represented, cause it to become acceptable in the sight of heaven; which is still further confirmed by the circumstance of the angel of Jehovah ascending in the flame of the altar.

(7.) Isa. xxvii. 9. When Jacob shall make the *stones of the altar* as *chalk-stones* that are beaten asunder, the groves and images shall not stand up.

Jacob here is the church diverging from what is spiritual into things natural; and the worship of such a church is described by his making all the stones of the altar as mere chalk-stones beaten asunder, and thus liable to be dispersed by every wind. The stones of the altar are divine truths, from and according to which worship ought to be performed: and these are said to become as chalk-stones deprived of their former consistency and durability, when they are perverted, that is, when they are separated from charity, which gives them the power of cohesion, and when consequently they are dissipated, and are no longer to be found in the church in their purity and integrity. It is therefore written, that, whensoever this shall take place, the groves and images, representative of divine truths, shall no longer stand up.

In the best times of the most ancient and the ancient church, which existed long before the Israelitish people were formed into the representative of a church, groves, gardens and mountains were the places of their worship. Adam, or the most ancient church, worshipped Jehovah in a *garden* which is called the *garden of Eden*, Gen. ii. 8. Noah, or the ancient church, which succeeded the most ancient, after the ark had rested on the *mountains of Ararat*, built an altar to Jehovah, and offered burnt-offerings, on the altar, Gen. viii. 4, 20. Abraham also pitched his tent on a *mountain*, and built thereon an altar unto Jehovah, Gen. xii. 8. He likewise " planted a *grove* in Beer-sheba, and called there on the name of Jehovah, the everlasting God," Gen. xxi. 33. Every tree in those ancient gardens and groves denoted some distinct perception or knowledge of divine truth, and thus reminded the worshippers of the various divine attributes and perfections, which from time to time they assembled together to acknowledge and commemorate. For the same reason they also set up images, statues and pillars in and near their groves: and this they did, not in the way of idolatrous superstition, but from an enlightened view of the works of nature and of art, knowing that every object which presented itself before their external senses, was representative of something heavenly and divine. Hence the sun, the moon, the starry firmament, mountains, hills, valleys, plains, fields, gardens, groves, woods, trees, rivers, fountains, seas, clouds, rocks and stones, beasts, birds and fishes, in endless variety, all contributed in turn to excite ideas and affections strictly analogous to these different objects, but yet totally distinct from them, just as spiritual things are totally distinct from natural things.

But when, in consequence of a long and universal degeneracy among the men of ancient times, their posterity had altogether lost sight of the things signified by the natural objects above named; and when, instead of leading the mind to devout meditation, those objects became the occasion of an external, criminal adoration, without any reference to what was internal, spiritual and divine, which is the characteristic of mere idolatry; then the people of Israel were raised up, and separated from the other nations, as well for the purpose of checking the superstition which everywhere prevailed, as for the formation of a kind of nucleus for the future improvement and happiness of mankind, by becoming the depository of a new revelation from heaven. Then also for the first time it became a divine law, that no images, statues, groves or high places should be suffered to remain, but that they should be universally broken to pieces, cut down, burnt and destroyed. Among the rest, it is remarkable that the brazen serpent which was set up by Moses at the express command of Jehovah, Num. xxi. 8, and which like other images had become the occasion of idolatry, was also, under the divine approbation, broken in pieces by the good king Hezekiah. See 2 Kings xviii. 3, 4.

It has been already observed, concerning the people of ancient times, that, during the state of their integrity, images, statues and groves were in constant use, not as objects of idolatrous veneration, but as mediums serving to introduce to their contemplation things holy, spiritual and divine, and thereby more readily to excite their devotion: which ancient state of society is frequently referred to in both the historical and the prophetical books of the Sacred Writings. The images or statues which were set up within their groves, reminded them of the more interior spiritual things taught by the church: whereas those which were placed on the outside, whether contiguous to them or more distant from them, represented such things as were relatively more exterior and natural. Properly speaking, the groves mentioned in the passage above quoted from Isaiah, involving all that was contained within them, denote worship from spiritual truths; and the images which according to the original were *solar images*, or *solar pillars*, either as bearing the image of the sun or as being exposed to its heat, denote worship from natural truths. It is by reason of this signification of the terms, retained from time immemorial, that the prophet uses such language in describing what will be the situation of the church, when man by his natural and depraved appetites, supported by his fallacious and perverse reasonings, shall utterly depart from the true worship of the Lord, namely, that it will then be divested of all genuine spiritual truths, and at the same time of all genuine natural truths; these being understood by the groves and images which shall no longer stand up, or have an existence in the church.

Stones for Pillars, Witnesses and Memorials.

(1.) Gen. xxviii. 18, 22. Jacob rose up early in the morning, and took the *stone* that he had put for his pillows, and set it up for a *pillar*, and poured oil upon the top of it. And he said, This *stone*, which I have set for a *pillar*, shall be God's house.

(2.) Gen. xxxi. 45-52. And Jacob took a *stone*, and set it up for a *pillar*. And Jacob said unto his brethren, Gather *stones*; and they took *stones* and made a *heap*: and they did eat there upon the *heap*. And Laban said, This *heap* is a *witness* between me and thee this day. Behold this *heap*, and behold this *pillar*, which I have cast betwixt me and thee. This *heap* be *witness* and this *pillar* be *witness* that I will not pass over this *heap* to thee, and that thou shalt not pass over this *heap* and this *pillar* unto me for harm.

(3.) Gen. xxxv. 14. And Jacob set up a *pillar* in the place where God talked with him, even a *pillar of stone*.

(4.) Gen. xxxv. 19, 20. Rachel died, and was buried in the way to Ephrath which is Bethlehem. And Jacob set a *pillar* upon her grave: that is the *pillar* of Rachel's grave unto this day.

(5.) Ex. xxiv. 4. And Moses wrote all the words of Jehovah, and rose up early in the morning, and built an altar under the hill, and *twelve pillars*, according to the twelve tribes of Israel.

(6.) Josh. iv. 1-9, 20. And it came to pass when all the people were clean passed over Jordan, that Jehovah spake unto Joshua, saying, Take you twelve men out of the people, out of every tribe a man, and command you them, saying, Take you hence out of the midst of Jordan, out of the place where the priests' feet stood firm, *twelve stones*, and ye shall carry them over with you, and leave them in the lodging-place where you shall lodge this night. Then Joshua called the twelve men, whom he had prepared of the children of Israel, out of every tribe a man. And Joshua said unto them, Pass over before the ark of Jehovah your God into the midst of Jordan, and take ye up every man of you a *stone* upon his shoulder, according to the number of the tribes of the children of Israel: that this may be a *sign* among you, that when your children ask their fathers in time to come, saying, What mean you by these stones? then ye shall answer them, That the waters of Jordan were cut off before the ark of the covenant of Jehovah, when it passed over Jordan, the waters of Jordan were cut off: and these *stones* shall be for a *memorial* unto the children of Israel for ever. And the children of Israel did so as Joshua commanded, and took up *twelve stones* out of the midst of Jordan, as Jehovah spake unto Joshua, according to the number of the tribes of the children of Israel, and carried them over with them unto the place where they lodged, and laid them down there. And Joshua set up *twelve stones* in the midst of Jordan, in the place where the feet of the priests who bare the ark of the covenant stood; and they are there unto this day. And those *twelve stones* which they took out of Jordan, did Joshua pitch in Gilgal.

(7.) Josh. viii. 28, 29. And Joshua burnt Ai, and made it an heap for ever, even a desolation unto this day. And the king of Ai he hanged on a tree until even-tide: and as soon as the sun was down, Joshua commanded that they should take his carcase down from the tree, and cast it at the entering of the gate of the city, and raise thereon a great *heap of stones* that remaineth unto this day.

(8.) Josh. xxiv. 26, 27. And Joshua wrote these words in the book of the law of God, and took a great *stone*, and set it up there under an oak, that was by the sanctuary of Jehovah. And Joshua said unto all the people, Behold, this *stone* shall be a *witness* unto us; for it hath heard all the words of Jehovah which He spake unto us: it shall be therefore a *witness* unto you, lest ye deny your God.

(9.) 1 Sam. vii. 12. Samuel took a *stone*, and set it between Mizpeh and Shen, and called the name of it *Eben-ezer*, saying, Hitherto hath Jehovah helped us.

From the preceding passages it is plain, that heaps of stones were collected, great stones set up, and pillars erected, not only for the purpose of marking the boundaries between the possessions of one man and those of another, but also as monuments or memorials to testify and evidence, in a way that could not be denied, the truth of certain historical facts, as well as the solemn engagements which had been entered into by individuals, or by a whole people, both with their neighbor and with their God. To the above ancient practice may also be traced the origin of the law of nations. And hence may be seen at least one reason why stones in the Sacred Scriptures are used to signify truths.

CHAPTER VIII.

Tables of Stones for the Ten Commandments.

The Two Tables in General.

(1.) Ex. xxiv. 12. And Jehovah said unto Moses, Come up to me into the mount, and be there: and I will give thee *tables of stone* and a law and commandments which I have written.

(2.) Ex. xxxi. 18. And He gave unto Moses, when He had made an end of communing with him upon mount Sinai, *two tables of testimony, tables of stone*, written with the finger of God.

(3.) Ex. xxxii. 15, 16, 19. And Moses turned, and went down from the mount, and the *two tables of the testimony* were in his hand: and the *tables* were written on both their sides; on the one side and on the other were they written. And the *tables* were the work of God, and the *writing* was the writing of God graven upon the *tables*. And it came to pass as soon as he came nigh unto the camp, that he saw the calf, and the dancing;—(*for in the absence of Moses, Aaron and the people had made a golden calf, and were dancing before it:*)—and Moses' anger waxed hot, and he cast the *tables* out of his hands, and brake them beneath the mount.

(4.) Ex. xxxiv. 1, 4, 28. And Jehovah said unto Moses, Hew thee *two tables of stone* like unto the first: and I will write upon *these tables* the words that were in the *first tables*, which thou brakest. And he hewed *two tables of stone* like unto the first; and Moses rose up early in the morning, and went up unto mount Sinai, as Jehovah had commanded him, and took in his hand the *two tables of stone*. And He (Jehovah) wrote upon the *tables* the words of the covenant, the *ten commandments*.

Similar things are repeated in Deut. iv. 13; ix. 9–17; x. 1–5.

The ten commandments inscribed upon two tables of stone, as is well known, were the first-fruits of the Word, and contain an epitome of the whole duty of man. They are called the *ten words*, because the number *ten* signifies and involves all; and *words* or *commandments* denote truths which have respect to doctrine, and goods which have respect to life. The reason why they were written upon *tables of stone* was, because, as we have already seen, stone signifies truth, properly external truth such as constitutes the literal sense of the Word. These tables were *two* in number, to represent thereby the conjunction of the Lord with the church, and by the church with the human race. Hence they are called the *tables of the covenant*, Deut. ix. 9, 11, 15; and the words inscribed upon them are called the *words of the covenant*, Ex. xxxiv. 27, 28: for a covenant implies the agreement or conjunction of two. On this account the tables, though perfectly distinct, were yet so adjusted to each other, that being placed together, and by application conjoined into one, the writing was continued in straight lines from one table to the other, in all respects as if they were only one table. And it is probable, as well from the circumstance of Moses carrying both the tables in his hands, as from their being laid together in the ark, that their dimensions and bulk must have been very moderate, perhaps considerably less than what have been usually assigned them.

It appears from Ex. xxxii. 15, that "the tables were written on *both their sides;* on the *one side* and on the *other* were they written:" from which passage it might with some plausibility be inferred, that the writing was upon *each side or surface of each stone*, that is, upon both their *fronts* and *backs*. If this conjecture be admitted, then the dimensions of the two tables may have been proportionably diminished: while the writing upon the fronts and backs might still denote the *internal* and the *external* sense of the Word, as in Ezek. ii. 9, 10; and Apoc. v. 1. But as it is more probable that the *two sides*, or rather, in strict conformity with the original, the *two transits*, had respect merely to the two distinct tables which were placed one against the other, the expression seems plainly to imply that both in writing and in reading each of the commandments, a *transition* was made from one table to the other, in the manner already described.

The common opinion is, that so many entire precepts were written upon one table, and so many upon another, as exhibited in almost all Christian churches: which idea has been thought to receive confirmation from its being usually said, that one table is for the Lord, and the other for man. This latter sentiment is indeed true in one respect, that is, representatively, as arising from the *number* of the tables spiritually considered, as well as from the *twofold* duty which man is bound to perform, viz., *first* to the Lord, and *secondly* to his neighbor. And hence we may also see the reason why the Lord in the Gospel comprises the whole of the decalogue in *two* commandments only, saying, that love to the Lord constitutes the *first*, and love to our neighbor the *second*, Matt. xxii. 37–39: when nevertheless it is most evident that his words are not to be taken *literally, strictly,* or *formally,* because the second commandment as written upon the tables, equally with the first, respects our duty to our God, and not so much our duty to our neighbor. Whenever, therefore, mention is made in a general way, that one table belongs to the Lord and the other to man, this language is to be understood *spiritually,* as we shall now explain, and not in such a sense as to imply either that a certain number of the precepts was written upon one table, and a certain number on the other, or that one part only of the divine law is for man, because written on one of the tables as his part of the covenant, and the remainder for the Lord to perform on his part, because written on the other.

The spiritual interpretation alluded to, which has no respect to *number* as such, but to the *thing signified* by number, is to the following effect: Every precept contains a duty for man to perform, and in each he is required to act *apparently by his own power:* yet, as *in reality* he is *of himself* utterly incapable either of shunning evil or of doing good, it therefore becomes necessary that the Lord should *accompany him,* and be perpetually *present with him,* to give him both the inclination and the ability to observe every one, or any one, of his divine laws. In other words, man's part in the covenant consists in his shunning the evil that is forbidden, and in doing the good that is enjoined, *apparently of himself,* yet *in reality from the Lord:* and the Lord's part in the same covenant consists in his actually *supplying man* with all the *purity of motive,* all the *integrity of purpose,* and all the *power of action,* necessary for the occasion; the result of which will be, that, while man thus obeys the divine command, he will yet at the same time ascribe all the merit to the Lord alone. And hence the true reason may be seen, why the words and matter of each commandment were continued from one table to the other, as already described, and not written in the way commonly supposed, with a certain number of commandments on one table and a certain number on the other. By each commandment being inscribed on both tables, the true idea of a covenant or of spiritual conjunction with the Lord, is more fully set forth than it could be by any other means: and we are thereby clearly instructed that while the Lord is in man, man ought also at the same time to be in the Lord. This agrees with his own words in the Gospel: "He that abideth *in me* and *I in him,* the same bringeth forth much fruit: for *without me ye can do nothing,*" John xv. 5.

That the view which we have here taken of the ten commandments written on two tables of stone, yet in such a manner as to exhibit the true conjunction of the Lord and man, is a just one, may be further confirmed by other examples to be found in the Word. When Abram was desirous of some sign to assure him that he and his posterity should inherit the promised land, he was ordered to take a heifer of three years old, and a she-goat of three years old, and a ram of three years old; and he *divided these in the midst*, and laid each piece *one against the other*, Gen. xv. 8–10. This division of each animal into *two parts* or *pieces*, and the position of these *one over against the other*, represented the same thing as the division of the laws into *two tables*, and the *application of both together*, viz., the *conjunction* of the Lord and man: and therefore it is written immediately afterwards in ver. 18, that "in the same day Jehovah made a *covenant with Abram*."

We find also, that in ancient times it was usual even for transgressors and idolators to divide the animals which they offered in sacrifice to their false gods, and to pass between the pieces, as in Jer. xxxiv. 18: whereby was represented the *conjunction* of hell with man, or, what is the same thing, the *conjunction* of evil and of falsity in the human mind.

In general, by the various sacrifices whereof *part* was burnt upon the altar and *part* was given to the people to eat: also by the blood, *half* of which was sprinkled upon the altar and *half* upon the people, Ex. xxiv. 6, 8, was represented the *conjunction* of the Lord and man by means of divine good and divine truth. The same is likewise denoted by the bread which Jesus *brake*, or *divided*, when He fed the multitude, and when He instituted the holy supper. From all which we learn that the great object continually held up to view, both in the writings of Moses called the law, and of the Evangelists called the gospel, is the conjunction of the Lord with man, and thereby is eternal salvation.

The first Pair of Tables which were broken by Moses, and represented the Ancient Word, with Remarks on some of the Apocryphal books, the Fables of the Ancients, and other ancient Writings.

Of the first pair of tables it is said that they were the *work of God*, and that the writing was the *writing of God* graven upon the tables, being *written with the finger of God*. But of the second pair of tables which were like unto the first, we read that *Moses hewed* and prepared them for the writing; and that afterwards *Jehovah himself wrote* on the tables the words that were in the first tables. With a view to explain these extraordinary circumstances, the following observations are submitted:

The two tables containing the divine law in a concise and comprehensive form, and being a kind of first-fruits or harbinger of the succeeding revelation, represented the whole Word. But the first pair in particular, which were broken at the foot of the mountain, represented the Ancient Word, or that code of divine revelation which existed prior to the Word given by Moses and the prophets. This Ancient Word being no longer accommodated to the degenerate state of man, was therefore by the divine providence of the Lord, removed in order to make way for the Word which we now have, as better suited to the temper and genius of the Israelitish people, and indeed of mankind in general.*

That such an Ancient Word did really exist prior to our Word, is evident from this circumstance, that it is expressly quoted by Moses in Num. xxi. 14, 15, who transcribes a passage from one of the historical or rather prophetical books belonging to it, called the *book of the Wars of Jehovah;* alluding in the first place to the wars of the Israelites with their different enemies, and in the next place to the future acts of Jehovah in the Humanity, when He accomplished the great work of redemption by fighting against and overcoming all the powers of hell. Moses in the same chapter, ver. 27–30, gives another quotation from another book of the Ancient Word called *Proverbs*, or rather *Enunciations*, as it appears to have consisted of prophetic declarations. Joshua likewise, when he bade the sun and moon stand still, refers to a third book of the Ancient Word, saying, "Is not this written in the *book of Jasher?*" (i. e. the *book of Rectitude* or *Equity?*) chap. x. 12, 13; again alluding to the wars of the Israelites, and to the victories over man's spiritual enemies, which the Lord obtained while in the flesh. The same book is appealed to as a book of high authority, by the author of the book of Samuel,

---

* As a proof that the event here spoken of was of the *Divine Providence*, it may be sufficient to remark, that, when Moses in great anger and indignation cast the tables to the ground, and brake them in pieces, although he had just before received them in the most solemn manner, and as a most sacred deposit from the hands of Jehovah, still no expression of divine disapprobation is to be found on account of the apparently rash conduct of Moses, but only on account of the wickedness of the people. On the contrary, his intercession in behalf of Aaron and of the people was accepted by Jehovah; and this without any previous atonement being required of him for the purgation of himself.

on the occasion of David's lamentation over Saul and Jonathan: see 2 Sam. i. 17, 18.

But besides the evidence arising from these references and direct quotations from different books of the Ancient Word, other proofs are to be found in our Word, that there existed a church prior to the Israelitish church, and consequently a revelation prior to that received by Moses, or even by Abraham. Balaam, an inhabitant of Syria, and a prophet belonging to a very different people from the Israelites, yet prophesied from the mouth of Jehovah the true God, Num. xxii. 8-18: and in chap. xxiii. and xxiv. throughout, on his surveying the dwellings of Israel in tents and tabernacles, according to their tribes, the spirit of God came upon him, and he openly announced the future greatness of that people, and foretold the coming of the Lord into the world.

It appears also from Gen. xiv. 18-20 that Melchizedek, who was priest of the most high God as well as king of Salem, brought forth bread and wine to Abram and blessed him: whereupon Abram gave him tithes of all, as an acknowledgment that Melchizedek represented some higher or more interior principle of celestial life than Abraham at that time did. This circumstance clearly proves that a church existed prior to that instituted among the posterity of Abraham; that in it the offices of priesthood and royalty were exercised by one and the same person, who thus represented the union of divine good and divine truth in the person of the Lord;* that the symbols of that church, bread and wine, were similar to those appointed in the Christian Church by our Lord himself; and therefore that there must have been in those early ages of the world a revelation or Sacred Scripture suited to the then existing states of mankind, which in process of time has given place to the Word written by Moses, the prophets and the Evangelists.

Moses himself who broke the two former tables and hewed out new ones, also represented the Word, or the divine law in general, especially the legal and historical part of it: and as the new Word was in the external sense to treat much of the Israelitish people, it

---

* This is what is meant in Ps. cx. 4, by the Lord's being a priest forever *after the order of Melchizedek*: for Melchizedek *as a priest* represented the divine good, and *as a king* the divine truth. In the Israelitish church this representation was usually effected by *two distinct persons*, the priest and the king: but in times antecedent to the Jewish theocracy, that is to say, in the ancient church, which existed before and at the time of Abraham, the representation frequently centred in *one person*, who was both priest and king. Such was Melchizedek when, after the battle of the kings, he administered sacramental bread and wine to Abram, blessed him, and received from him tithes of all his acquisitions, Gen. xiv. 18-20.

therefore became necessary to change the *external language* or *expression* of the Word, while its *internal sense* and *divinity* still remained the same. This change of a former external sense of the Word, for a new external sense better adapted to the state of the Jewish nation, by describing their history, manners and institutions, is clearly pointed out, not only by the fact of Moses breaking the first tables, and afterwards hewing out fresh ones, but also by the occasion which impelled him to do it, namely, the total departure of the Israelites, with Aaron at their head, from the worship of Jehovah to the worship of the golden calf, in the formation of which they had all unanimously concurred. And it appears at the same time no less evident, that the same divinity, the same sanctity, and the same internal sense, which had inspired the former Word, are still preserved and continued in that which we now possess. The same *words*, i. e. the same great *truths*, which were inscribed on the former tables, were equally written by the same divine hand on the new tables.

The Apocryphal books which are frequently annexed to the Old Testament, and reputed by Christians of doubtful authority, are not to be considered as forming any part of the Ancient Word here spoken of. Some of them are supposed to have been written in the way of mere allegory. For example, Grotius states his opinion concerning the book of *Judith* to be that it is entirely a parabolic fiction, written in the time of Antiochus Epiphanes, when he came into Judea to raise a persecution against the Jewish church; and that the design of it was to confirm the Jews under that persecution in the hope that God would send them a deliverance. He attempts also an explanation, saying, "that by *Judith* is meant Judea; by *Bethulia* the temple, or house of God; and by the *sword* which went out from thence, the prayers of the saints; That *Nebuchodonosor* denotes the devil; and the kingdom of *Assyria* the devil's kingdom, pride: That by *Holofernes* is meant the instrument or agent of the devil in that persecution, Antiochus Epiphanes who made himself master of Judea, that fair *widow*, so called, because destitute of relief: That *Eliakim** signifies God, who would arise in her defence, and at length cut off that instrument of the devil, who would have corrupted her."

Grotius and others also think, that the book, called *Baruch*, in the Apocrypha, is a mere fiction, or allegorical relation, written by some

---

* Jerom, in his Latin version of *Judith*, promiscuously uses the terms *Eliakim*, and *Jehoiakim*, or *Joakim*; *El* being the name of God in the one case, as *Jehoia* or *Joa* is taken for the name of *Jehovah* in the other.

Hellenistic Jew, and containing nothing of a real history. See *Prideaux's Connection*, vol. i., p. 52.

The same observations will in a great measure apply to many other writings which have been brought down to our times, particularly those of the ancient mythologists, of which the celebrated Lord Bacon says, "It may pass for a further indication of a concealed and secret meaning, that some of these fables are so absurd and idle in their narration, as to proclaim an allegory even afar off. A fable that carries probability with it, may be supposed invented for pleasure or in imitation of history: but what could never be conceived or related in this way, must surely have a different use. For example; what a monstrous fiction is this, That *Jupiter* should take *Metis* to wife; and as soon as he found her pregnant, eat her up; whereby he also conceived, and out of his head brought forth *Pallas* armed! Certainly no mortal could, but for the sake of the moral it couches, invent such an absurd dream as this, so much out of the road of thought."

He further observes, "The argument of most weight with me is: That many of these fables appear not to have been invented by the persons who relate and divulge them, whether Homer, Hesiod, or others; for if I were assured they first flowed from those later times and authors, I should never expect anything singularly great and noble from such an origin. But whoever attentively considers the things, will find that these fables are delivered down by those writers, not as matters then first invented, but as received and embraced in earlier ages. And this principally raises my esteem of those fables: which I receive, not as the product of the age, or invention of the poets, but as sacred relics, gentle whispers, and the breath of better times, that, from the traditions of more ancient nations, came at length into the flutes and trumpets of the Greeks."

The explanations of these things, which have been attempted by learned men of the present age, by no means reach that sublimity of conception, or that superlative degree of wisdom, which there is reason to believe distinguished the sages of ancient times. And yet they are sufficient to produce a conviction in the mind, that whenever our ancestors of most remote antiquity would describe the operations of either spiritual, moral, civil or physical causes, they did it in such terms and under such forms and emblems as we find more or less characterize all their writings. Mr. William Jones, in his *Figurative Language of Holy Scripture*, (p. 318,) states what he supposes to have been signified by the idols of the ancients, the heavenly constellations, etc., etc.

"All *idols* (says he) were originally emblematical figures, expressive of the lights of heaven, and the powers of nature. *Apollo* was the sun; *Diana* was the moon; both represented with *arrows*, because both shot forth rays of light.

"The *forms of worship* were symbolical. They *danced in circles*, to show the revolutions of the heavenly bodies.

"In the *constellations*,—the *Bears* possess the arctic or northern regions. The *Ram, Bull,* and *Lion,* all sacred to the solar light and fire, are accommodated to the degrees of the sun's power, as it increases in the summer months. The *Crab,* which walks sideways and backwards, is placed where the sun moves paralled to the equator, and begins in that sign to recede towards the south. The *Scales* are placed at the autumnal equinox, where the light and darkness are equally balanced. The *Capricorn,* or wild *Mountain-Goat,* is placed at the tropical point, from whence the sun begins to climb upward towards the north. The *ear of corn* in the hand of *Virgo* marks the season of the harvest. The precession of the equinoctial points has now removed the figures and the stars they belong to out of their proper places; but such was their meaning when they were in them.

"*Royalty* and *government* were formerly distinguished by symbolical insignia. A *kingdom* was supposed to be attended with *power* and *glory.* The glory was signified by a crown with points resembling rays of light, and adorned with *orbs* as the heaven is studded with stars. Sometimes it was signified by *horns,* which are a natural crown to animals, as we see in the figure of Alexander upon some ancient coins. The power of *empire* was denoted by a *rod* or *sceptre.* A rod was given to Moses for the exercise of a miraculous power; whence was derived the *magical wand* of enchanters: and he is figured with *horns,* to denote the glory which attended him, when he came down from the presence of God. In *Homer's Iliad,* the priest of *Apollo* is distinguished by a *sceptre* in his hand and a *crown* on his head, to show that he derived his power from the Deity whom he represented. So long as *monarchy* prevailed, the sceptre of kings was a *single rod:* but when *Brutus* first formed a republic at Rome, he changed the regal sceptre into a *bundle of rods,* or *fagot of sticks,* with *an axe* in the middle, to signify in this case that the power was not derived from heaven, but from the multitude of the people, who were accordingly flattered from that time forward with *Majesty.*

"*Time* was represented with *wings at his feet*, a *razor* or a *scythe* in his right hand, a *lock of hair* on his forehead, and his head *bald behind*; *Justice*, with her *sword* and *scales*; *Fortune*, with her feet upon a *rolling sphere* and her *eyes hoodwinked*; *Vengeance*, with her *whip*; *Pleasure*, with her *enchanted cup*; *Hope*, with her *anchor*; *Death*, with his *dart* and *hour-glass*; and many others of the same class, all representing in *visible forms* the ideas contemplated by the mind.

"*Pythagoras* points out, by the letter Y, the road of life branching out into two ways, the one of *virtue*, the other of *vice*. He advises *not to keep animals with crooked claws*; i. e. not to make companions of persons who are fierce and cruel:—*not to stop upon a journey to cut wood*; i. e. not to turn aside to things foreign to the main purpose of life:—*Never to make a libation to the Gods from a vine which has not been pruned*; i. e. not to offer worship but from the fruits of a severe and well-ordered life:—*Not to wipe away sweat with a sword*; i. e. not to take away by force and violence what another has earned by his labor. It was customary with the ancients to use a flat instrument, like the blade of a knife, to wipe away sweat from the skin, and to clear it of the water after the use of the bath. Another saying of Pythagoras was, that it is a foolish action *to read a poem to a beast*; i. e. to communicate what is excellent to a stupid, ignorant person: which is similar to that prohibition in the Gospel, *not to give a holy thing to a dog, nor to cast pearls before swine*."

In addition to the observations above made concerning the writings of antiquity, it may be remarked, that the Apostle Peter in his second Epistle, (chap. ii.,) and Jude in his General Epistle, both appear to have copied from one and the same ancient book which was extant in their day, but is since lost to the world. How otherwise can it be accounted for, that the very same *ideas*, the very same kind of *language*, and the very same *order of delivery*, which we find in the one writer, are so punctually followed by the other? Let the reader only compare the passages here referred to, and he will find no room for a doubt on the subject.

Peter, 2d Epistle.	Jude, General Epistle.
Compare chap. ii., ver. 1, with	Ver. 4.
4	6.
6	7.
10	8.
11	9.
12	10.

Peter, 2d Epistle.	Jude, General Epistle.
Compare chap. ii., ver. 13 to 15, with	Ver. 11, 12.
17	12, 13.
18, 19	16.
chap. iii., ver. 2	17.
3	18.

Peter goes on in the succeeding verses of chap. iii. to speak of the former heavens and former earth; of the heavens and earth which then were; of these latter being reserved for destruction by fire as the former had been by water; and lastly of new heavens and a new earth, wherein should dwell righteousness: all which particulars were no doubt transcribed by him from some ancient writing, not perhaps of absolutely divine authority, like the genuine books of the Ancient Word, but the production of some enlightened man who treated of the succession of different churches in the style and manner of the literal sense of our Word. Jude also, in his Epistle, ver. 14, 15, makes express mention of a prophetical book written by Enoch, the seventh from Adam, and quotes from it a passage which foretells the coming of the Lord to execute judgment upon the wicked. And it is not improbable but several of the references made by the Evangelists to the sayings of prophets not to be found in the Old Testament, may have been intended as appeals to, or citations from, that Ancient Word which, as already observed, was represented by the two tables of stone broken by Moses at the foot of Mount Sinai. Or possibly they may have been contained in some other prophetic books, or written sayings now lost, of which mention is so frequently made in the books of Kings and Chronicles; such as the book of the Chronicles of King David; the book of the Acts of Solomon; the book of Samuel the Seer; the book of Nathan the prophet; the book of Gad the seer; the Prophecy of Ahijah the Shilonite; the Visions of Iddo the seer; the book of Shemaiah the prophet; the book of Jehu, the son of Hanani; the Writing of Elijah the prophet; and the written Sayings of the Seers. See 1 Kings xi. 41; 1 Chron. xxvii. 24; xxix. 29; 2 Chron. ix. 29; xii. 15; xiii. 22; xx. 34; xxi. 12; xxxiii. 19.

The second Pair of Tables, which were substituted for the former, and represented the Word given by Moses and the Prophets.

The two tables which were substituted in the place of the former, represented the Word given by Moses and the Prophets, or that which we now possess. For as the prior revelation was written in a style and manner similar indeed in some respects to our Word,* yet by correspondences more remote, and more difficult of solution than those contained in the history of the Israelitish people; and as in consequence of this circumstance, and at the same time of the gross degeneracy of mankind in general, as before observed, it became necessary to give them a new Word better adapted to instruct, reclaim and amend them, than the former was; on these accounts Moses was commanded to hew or prepare two fresh tables of stone, and to take them up into the mountain to Jehovah, that He might write upon them according to the former writing: whereas the first tables, together with the writing upon them, are said to have been wholly the work of God. By Moses being ordered to prepare the new tables, is therefore meant that he was to be engaged in writing the literal and historical sense of the new Word, which should treat of the Jewish or Israelitish people, over whom he was constituted the head; and by Jehovah's writing upon those tables, is understood that nevertheless that history should be dictated by divine inspiration, and contain within its bosom an internal, heavenly, and even a divine sense.

The distinction which is made between the *tables themselves* and the *writing* upon them, is intended to point out the distinction between the *literal sense* of the Word and its *spiritual sense:* the former being like a ground, plane or table on which the latter is inscribed, and from which it cannot properly be separated because it is everywhere within it.

The Word being thus distinguishable into an internal and external sense, it appears to be not inconsistent with divine order, or the immutable nature of divine truth, that its external should be changed according to the circumstances of mankind, its internal remaining ever the same. But in what manner or respect this change of the external actually took place, which was chiefly on account of the Israelitish people, cannot be better described than in the words of Swedenborg, who in his *Arcana Cœlestia*, n. 10,603, says:

"For the sake of that nation altars, burnt-offerings, sacrifices, meat-offerings and libations were commanded, and on this account, both in the historical and prophetical Word, those things are mentioned as the most holy things of worship, when yet they were allowed,

---

* This appears from the great resemblance between the passage quoted from the Ancient Word in Num. xxi. 27-30 and that in Jer. xlviii. 45, 46.

because they were first instituted by Eber, and were altogether unknown in the ancient representative Church. For the sake of that nation also it came to pass that divine worship was performed in Jerusalem alone, and that on this account that city was esteemed holy, and was also called holy, both in the historical and prophetical Word. The reason was, that that nation was in heart idolatrous; and therefore, unless they had all met together at that city on each festival, every one in his own place would have worshipped some god of the gentiles, or a graven and molten image. For the sake of that nation, also, it was forbidden to celebrate holy worship on mountains and in groves, as the ancients did; the reason of which prohibition was, lest they should set idols there, and should worship the very trees. For the sake of that nation also it was permitted to marry several wives, which was a thing altogether unknown in ancient times; and likewise to put away their wives for various causes: hence laws were enacted concerning such marriages and divorces, which otherwise would not have entered the external of the Word; on which account this external is called by the Lord the external of Moses, and is said to be granted for the hardness of their hearts, Matt. xix. 8. For the sake of that nation mention is so often made of Jacob, and likewise of the twelve sons of Israel as being the only elect and heirs, as in Apoc. vii. 4–8, and in other places, although they were such as they are described in the song of Moses, Deut. xxxii. 15–43, and also in the prophets throughout, and by the Lord himself: not to mention other things which form the external of the Word for the sake of that nation. This external is what is signified by the two tables hewed by Moses. That still in that external there is a divine internal not changed, is signified by Jehovah writing on these tables the same words which were on the former tables."

The first tables, then, are said to have been the *work of God*, and the writing upon them the *writing of God*, because the Ancient Word represented by those tables, was dictated by God both as to its *exterior* and its *interior* contents, without any respect to mere *historical facts*, except only apparently or factitiously in the letter, after the manner of the first ten chapters of Genesis. And the second tables are said to be the *work of Moses*, and the writing upon them to be the *writing of Jehovah*, because a great part of the new Word is indeed as to its *external* or *historical sense* written by the pen of Moses, and treats of the people of Israel over whom he presided;

while its *internal* and *divine sense* is solely from the Lord, and treats of Him and his kingdom alone.

Thus we see that though the wickedness of the Israelites, in departing from the worship of Jehovah to that of a golden calf, was the immediate occasion of the first tables being broken, still new tables were substituted in their place, whose contents were equally holy and divine with the former. And that we may never lose sight of the real Author of the Word, especially as to its spiritual, celestial and divine senses, but may perpetually venerate the whole of its contents as the true medium of conjunction between heaven and earth, as the best gift of the Creator to the creature, and as the very habitation of the Lord with the human race, we are most solemnly assured that every word of the Sacred Writing was impressed upon the tables by Jehovah himself. Deut. x. 2, 4.

We learn, therefore, from a due consideration of the circumstances recorded, particularly in relation to our Word or Sacred Scripture, represented by the two tables of stone last given, that its *interior contents* are derived solely from the Lord; and that its *exterior contents*, though written by the hand of Moses and the Prophets, and though adapted to the state of the Israelites whose history was thus made the vehicle of divine wisdom to mankind, when every former dispensation was found unavailable to their reformation and regeneration, were yet suggested and indited by the same merciful Lord who in all ages of the world has never ceased to bless his creatures with a revelation of himself, and of those divine laws, the observance of which can alone prepare man for a happy immortality in the life to come.

CHAPTER IX.

THE BREAST-PLATE OF AARON, CALLED THE BREAST-PLATE OF JUDGMENT, AND ALSO URIM AND THUMMIM.

The Substance and Form of the Breast-Plate, and Arrangement of the twelve precious Stones.

(1.) Ex. xxviii. 15–21. Thou shalt make the *breast-plate* of judgment with cunning work, after the work of the ephod thou shalt make it; of gold, and of blue, and of purple, and of scarlet, and of fine twined linen shalt thou make it. Four-square it shall be, being doubled; a span shall be the length thereof, and a span shall be the breadth thereof. And thou shalt set in it *settings of stones*, even *four rows of stones:* the first row shall be a sardius, (a ruby,) a topaz, and a carbuncle: this shall be the first row. And the second row shall be an emerald, (a chrysoprasus,) a sapphire, and a diamond. And the third row a ligure, (a cyanus,) an agate, and an amethyst. And the fourth row a beryl, (a Tarshish,) and an onyx, and a jasper: they shall be set in gold in their inclosings. And the *stones* shall be with the names of the children of Israel, *twelve*, according to their names; like the engravings of a signet, every one with his name shall they be according to the twelve TRIBES.

In Ex. xxxix. 8–14, nearly the same words as the preceding are repeated in this chapter; but with this difference, that the former appear in the shape of a command, the latter as the command executed.

As the breast-plate of Aaron formed one of the most magnificent appendages to his sacerdotal dress, and at the same time, from the varied brilliancy and translucency of the precious stones, called Urim and Thummim, which were set upon it, was appointed to be the medium whereby responses from heaven were obtained in the Jewish church, it is interesting to examine its construction, and to inquire in what manner the extraordinary effects ascribed to it were produced.

It has been doubted by some whether the breast-plate formed one square, or two squares in one, making an oblong square, because it is described as being *four-square doubled:* and it has likewise been supposed that the four rows of precious stones, which were set in it, were to be reckoned from right to left in such a manner, that the three stones of each row should be placed laterally, or even with each other. Accordingly some engravings have represented the plate on Aaron's breast, and the rows of stones set upon it, in the way and position just described. But on a more careful examination of the passage above quoted, it will be found that the whole breast-plate was a perfect square, being a span in length and a span in breadth: yet it was a square of a double or twofold character, because it was divided into *right* and *left*, to represent a *celestial* and a *spiritual* principle: and these again were subdivided, to denote the *internal* and the *external* of each: the whole forming four rows in a vertical or upright position, with three stones in each row, and thereby representing and signifying the conjunction of all the truths of heaven with the good from which they are derived, and at the same time their high perfection. (*See Plate.*)

The breast-plate itself was made of gold, of blue, and of purple, and of scarlet, and of fine twined linen: its form being that of a square when doubled; it had two rings at the upper ends, and two at the middle of the sides, whereby it was fastened to the ephod: and each of the precious stones, twelve in number, was set in a socket of gold, and had the name of one of the twelve tribes of Israel engraved upon it. Which particular name was inscribed on one stone, and which on another, does not appear from the description given in the Word: and it would be very difficult if not impossible for us at the present day to determine this point, since the order of the names in other parts of the Word varies on different occasions, each name at one time denoting more or less of the good and the true properly signified by it, according to the nature of the subject treated of, the arrangement in each case adopted, and the relation of the one to the other and to the whole. For examples of this variety in the order of the nomination of the tribes, the reader may consult the following passages:

1. For the order of their birth, Gen. xxix. 32–35; xxx. 6–24; xxxv. 18.

2. For the order in which they are named, before Jacob came to his father Isaac to Mamre, Gen. xxxv. 23–26.

3. For the order when they came into Egypt, Gen. xlvi. 8–19.

4. For the order when they were blessed by their father Jacob, then Israel, Gen. xlix. 3–27.

REPRESENTATION OF THE BREAST-PLATE

With its Precious Stones, their Colors, and Signification.

CELESTIAL.		SPIRITUAL.	
FIRST ROW.	SECOND ROW.	THIRD ROW.	FOURTH ROW.
RED.	REDDISH BLUE.	WHITISH BLUE.	BLUISH WHITE.
Ruby.	Chrysoprasus.	Cyanus.	Tarshish.
1.	4.	7.	10.
Topaz.	Sapphire.	Agate.	Onyx.
2.	5.	8.	11.
Carbuncle.	Diamond.	Amethyst.	Jasper.
3.	6.	9.	12.
Celestial Good.	Celestial Truth.	Spiritual Good.	Spiritual Truth.

First Row, Downwards, Red .... *Celestial love of Good.*

Second Row .... Reddish Blue .... *Celestial Love of Truth.*

Third Row .... Whitish Blue .... *Spiritual Love of Good.*

Fourth Row .... Bluish White .... *Spiritual Love of Truth.*

5. For the order when the heads of the different tribes are named, for the purpose of numbering their armies, Num. i. 5-15.

6. For the order when all the males capable of war, from twenty years old and upward, were numbered, Num. i. 20-43.

7. For the order when they pitched their tents around the tabernacle of the congregation, Num. ii. 1 to end.

8. For the order when the princes of the tribes made their offerings, Num. vii. 12-78.

9. For the order when they marched, the ark of the covenant going before them, Num. x. 14-28, 33.

10. For the order when the heads of the tribes were sent to spy out the land of Canaan, Num. xiii. 4-15.

11. For the order when they were numbered, Num. xxvi. 5-62.

12. For the order when the princes were appointed to divide the land by inheritance, Num. xxxiv. 13-29.

13. For the order when they stood upon mount Gerizim to bless the people, and upon mount Ebal to curse, Deut. xxvii. 12, 13.

14. For the order when they were blessed by Moses, Deut. xxxiii. 6-24.

15. For the order when the lands were divided by lot among them, Josh. xiii.-xix.

16. For the order when certain cities were given by lot to the Levites, Josh. xxi. 4-7.

17. For the order when the cities so given to the Levites are mentioned by name, Josh. xxi. 9-39.

18. For the order when the new or holy land shall be divided by lot according to the tribes of Israel, Ezek. xlviii. 2-8, 23-28.

19. For the order when the gates of the new or holy city are described, Ezek. xlviii. 31-34.

20. For the order when twelve thousand of each tribe are sealed, Apoc. vii. 5-8.

With respect to the names appropriated to each stone, it is probable that some one of the preceding orders of nomination was observed, though not particularly stated in the letter of the Word. The order of their birth is generally supposed to have been the order adopted for the breast-plate, probably because that was the order observed on the two onyx-stones placed on the shoulders of the ephod, as in Ex. xxviii. 10. But this being matter of conjecture only, some incline to that arrangement of the tribes, which represented the celestial order subsisting among the angelic societies in heaven, because in their judgment it is the most perfect. Such appears to have been the order of their encampment, as given in Num. ii. 3–21,* when they were arranged according to the four quarters, the standard of the camp of Judah at the head of three tribes being in the east, that of Reuben at the head of three other tribes in the south, that of Ephraim in like manner in the west, and that of Dan in the north, with the camp of the Levites and the tabernacle of the congregation in the midst. For Judah was the first of the tribes, and bore the highest signification; while Dan was the last, and denoted what was lowest in heaven and the church.† Similar was the order when they marched, the ark of the covenant going before them, Num. x. 14–28, 33. And probably they were in the same position in relation to the four quarters, as that above described, when Balaam beheld them at a distance, and exclaimed, "*How goodly* are thy tents, O Jacob, and thy tabernacles, O Israel!" Num. xxiv. 5.

But as it is possible that some other order than that of encampment may have been required for the breast-plate, which however is not expressed, we shall venture to offer a conjecture on the reason of its being withheld.‡ May it not have been, because the names as seen upon the breast-plate in the spiritual world, were not always determined to any one arrangement, but at times shifted from one stone, or from one order of stones, to another, according to the ever-changing circumstances of the church, or of the people who represented the church, either generally or specifically? And as this variety of state was perpetual, and could not have been so well suggested or designated by any *fixed order* of naming the tribes, may it not have been on this account that the literal sense or the literal record, is silent on the point in question? And yet we are authorized to believe that the names were actually engraven either over, under, or upon the stones in some determinate order, which must therefore have been permanent in the natural world, though variable in the spiritual world. The inconvenience or difficulty which may be supposed to arise from the disagreement here alluded to between what may be

---

* See A. C., n. 3862, 1603, 6335, 9642. Ap. Ex., n. 431.

† See A. C., n. 10,335.

‡ An intelligent member of the New Church (J. A. T.) makes the following remark on this subject: "There seems to be a mysterious reason why this particular order should have been concealed, and that so carefully even in history; for it must have been known to the priests, and even to Josephus, who yet does not mention it in his *Antiquities of the Jews*. Probably it was to prevent an imitation of the *Urim* and *Thummim*, and a magical application of it in obtaining responses, which some cabalistic books have taught with respect to the letter of the Word."

called the *real fact* and the *spiritual use* to be drawn from the whole description of Urim and Thummim, is entirely obviated by *suppressing* in the letter all mention of the order of naming the tribes, or the particular application of the names to their respective stones on the breast-plate: which is a peculiarity not exclusively confined to the present case, but may be observed in various other instances to be met with in the Sacred Scriptures both of the Old and the New Testament.*

They who are desirous of further information as to facts which really did take place, but which yet were not deemed proper to be admitted as *part of the Divine Word*, and therefore frequently referred to the books of the Chronicles of the kings of Judah and Israel, (which do not appear to be those books usually called Chronicles, but some others not now extant,) or to some other history collateral with but distinct from the Sacred Volume: see 1 Kings xi. 41; xiv. 19, 29, etc., and pp. 524 and 525 of this work. Compare also 2 Sam. xxiv. 9, which is a part of the *real Word*, with 1 Chron. xxi. 5; xxvii. 24, which is no part of the Word, but merely a *collateral* or *supplementary history;* and the variation of the *Divine record* from what may probably have been the *literal fact* will immediately appear. Again, compare 2 Kings xxiii. 29, 30, with 2 Chron. xxxv. 20–27; and it will be further seen, that several particulars relative to the good king Josiah, which are recorded as facts in the last-mentioned history, are entirely suppressed in the book of Kings, which is a part of the *Divine Word*.

Similar variations are observable in other historical transactions related in the divine books, when compared with those given in the book of Chronicles: as for example, speaking of the first of David's heroes, it is said in the first book of Chronicles, that "Jashoboam an Hachmonite, the chief of the captains, lifted up his spear against *three hundred*, who were slain by him at one time," chap. xi. 11: but in the second book of Samuel the exploits of the same mighty man

---

* In proof of this, it may be sufficient to remark, that wherever a distinction is observable between the *fact* and the *history*, the *real transaction* and the *record of that transaction*, in all such cases the *latter* and not the *former*, i. e. the *record* and not the *fact*, is to be considered as the proper *basis of revelation*, the true *expression of divine wisdom*, in short, the *Holy Word itself*. For of the vast abundance of facts that really and literally took place among the people of Israel, from their *exodus* out of Egypt to their full establishment in the land of Canaan, *a certain number only* were selected by the Divine Wisdom to constitute the sacred history: and even of these some were modified or varied, some amplified or abridged, in such a way that nothing should appear in the literal record, but what was, is, and ever will be descriptive (by correspondences) of the real states of man's spiritual life.

are thus described: "The Tachmonite, that sat in the seat, (or, as it might have been rendered, Joshab-bashebeth the Tachmonite,) chief among the captains, the same was Adino the Eznite, he lifted up his spear against *eight hundred*, whom he slew at one time," chap. xxiii. 8. Here the Divine record makes the number of the slain to be eight hundred, while the collateral history gives only three hundred.

In the New Testament likewise, we find a striking variation in the account given by Matthew, from that in the Acts of the Apostles, concerning the death of Judas. Matt. xxvii. 3–5, states that, after Judas had betrayed Jesus, he repented, returned the thirty pieces of silver, the price of blood, and went and hanged himself. Whereas in the Acts of the Apostles, i. 18, it is expressly said, that he "purchased a field with the reward of iniquity; and falling headlong, he burst asunder in the midst, and all his bowels gushed out." And it is added, (ver. 19,) that this "was known unto all the dwellers at Jerusalem; insomuch as that field is called in their proper tongue *Aceldama*, that is to say, *The field of blood.*" The reader will here observe, that the Evangelist writes by *Divine inspiration*, and that the Acts of the Apostles is to be regarded only as a *collateral history*. That the Word should have been so written, as to comprise in its bosom nothing but the divine truths of heaven, while in its external form it selects just so much (and no more) of the Israelitish history, as was found necessary to embody those truths; and that at the same time the Church should be able to reap from the whole the spiritual benefit intended, is, to the pious and enlightened mind, matter of astonishment, as well as of eternal gratitude.

Since, therefore, the precise arrangement of the names of the twelve tribes, or the distinct appropriation of them to the particular stones of the breast-plate, cannot now be ascertained, and for the reasons above stated need not, it is sufficient for us to know that the stones themselves, together with the names inscribed upon them, represented all the goods and truths of heaven and the church; that those on the right side (of the high-priest) represented the celestial love of good and the celestial love of truth, or in other words, love to the Lord and mutual love; that those on the left represented the spiritual love of good, and the spiritual love of truth, or in other words, charity towards the neighbor and faith from that charity; while the three stones in each row denoted the perfection and fulness of each kind of love, from its beginning to its end. This signification arises as well from the *colors* of the stones, as from their *number*, which was in each row *three*.

We will therefore now consider the rows in their order; and from the color, transparency and brilliancy of each, endeavor to point out their true signification.*

The first Row, consisting of a Ruby, a Topaz, and a Carbuncle.

There are two fundamental colors, from which all the rest by combination with each other and with certain degrees of shade or colorless media, are derived. These two fundamental colors are *red* and *white;* of each of which there are several varieties. The *red*, being a peculiar display of the *primary* or most essential quality of *fire*, is considered in the Sacred Scriptures as expressive of the *good of love* with which it corresponds: and the *white*, being a peculiar display of the *secondary* property of *fire*, in the same Writings denotes the *truth of wisdom* with which it also corresponds. Now as the modifications and variegations of natural light with shade produce colors of every description, so the modifications and variegations of spiritual light or truth with ignorance, produce all the varieties of intelligence and wisdom. And hence the precious stones in the breast-plate of Aaron become representative either of higher or of lower degrees of wisdom, (which is always to be understood as inseparable from its love,) according to their brilliancy and transparency, and at the same time according to the kind of light which predominates in them, whether it be red or white. If the red predominate, it is a mark of celestial or most interior affection: but if the white have the ascendancy, then the affection and consequent perception denoted, are of a spiritual or more exterior character.

Under this view of the subject we see the reason why the first row or order, consisting of a ruby, a topaz, and a carbuncle, denotes the celestial love of good, together with its wisdom, namely, because the

---

* The same writer referred to in a former note (J. A. T.) again remarks on the tints or colors of the stones as follows: " I think Mr. Hindmarsh is correct, viz., 1st order, *Red;* 2d, *Reddish Blue;* 3d, *Whitish Blue;* 4th, *Bluish White*. Yet I much doubt if any of the stones, which we denominate by those names, will apply. The stones in the breast-plate, I judge, must have been all transparent; and yet our *lazure*, or *lapis lazuli*, and *onyx* and *jasper*, are opaque, and our *agate* but semi-transparent. The *diamond* is classed among the *reddish*-blue, which does not agree; neither the *amethyst* among the *whitish*-blue. Our *topaz* is yellow, and not *red*. In short, I do not find that there is any one of the stones known by the names which we apply to them. Possibly it is necessary only to know generally the colors or tints of the orders, in application to the correspondence."

red or flame-colored light predominates and sparkles in each of those stones. The prophet Ezekiel, alluding more particularly to the stones of this order and to their signification as here given, calls them *stones of fire*, when he addressed the fallen king of Tyrus in these remarkable words: "Thus saith the Lord God, Thou sealest up the sum full of wisdom, and perfect in beauty. Thou hast been in Eden the garden of God; every precious stone was thy covering; thou wast upon the holy mountain of God; thou hast walked up and down in the midst of the *stones of fire*. Thou wast perfect in thy ways from the day that thou wast created, till iniquity was found in thee. Thou hast sinned; therefore I will cast thee as profane out of the mountain of God; and I will destroy thee, O covering cherub, from the midst of the *stones of fire*," Ezek. xxviii. 12 to 16.

The *ruby* is a much-admired gem, of a deep red color, with an admixture of purple. In its most perfect and best colored state, it is of exquisite beauty and extreme value. It is often found perfectly pure and free from blemishes and foulness, but much more frequently debased in its value by them, especially in the larger specimens. It is of very great hardness, equal to that of the sapphire and second only to the diamond. It is various in size, but less subject to variations in its shape than most of the other gems, being always of a pebble-like figure, often roundish, sometimes oblong, larger at one end than the other, in some sort resembling a pear, and usually flatted on one side. In general it is naturally so bright and pure on the surface, as to need no polishing; and when its figure will admit of its being set without cutting, it is often worn in its rough state, and with no other than its native polish. Our jewellers are very nice, though not perfectly determinate, in their distinctions of this gem, knowing it in its different degrees of color under three different names. The first is simply the *ruby*, the name given it in its deepest colored and most perfect state. The second is the *spinel* ruby; under this name they comprehend those rubies which are of a somewhat less bright color than the ruby simply so called. The third is the *balass* ruby; under which name they express a pale yet a very bright ruby, with a less admixture of the purple tinge than in the deeper colored ones, and of less value. The true ruby comes from the East Indies; and the principal mines of it are in the kingdom of Pegu and the island of Ceylon.

In our common English version of the Bible, instead of the *ruby*, the translators have named the *sardius*. But the sardius, being a kind of cornelian verging most frequently to a flesh-color, though sometimes to a blood-red, is neither so valuable nor of so deep a hue as the ruby; and therefore does not so properly answer to the Hebrew word *odem*, as the ruby does. Some authors call the stone here meant a *pyropus*, from the resemblance which its color bears to *fire* or to *flame*.

The modern *topaz* appears to be a different gem from that of the ancients: and indeed the same may be said of several, if not all, of the other precious stones. That which now bears the name of a topaz may be described as follows: When perfect and free from blemishes, it is considered a very beautiful and valuable gem: it is, however, rarely to be found in this state. It is of a roundish or oblong figure in its native or rough state, usually flatted on one side, and generally of a bright and naturally polished surface, tolerably transparent. They are always of a fine yellow color; but they have this, like the other gems, in several different degrees. The finest of all are of a true and perfect gold-color, and hence sometimes called *chrysolites*; but there are some much deeper, and others extremely pale, so as to appear scarcely tinged with yellow. The original topaz emulates the ruby in hardness and the diamond in lustre. The most valuable kinds are said to be found in the East Indies; but they are rarely of any great size. The topazes of Peru come next after these in beauty and in value. Those of Europe are principally found in Silesia and Bohemia, but generally with cracks and flaws.

The Hebrew term, *pitdah*, rendered *topaz* here and in the English Bible, is, however, by Jerome, Rabbi David, and others, called the *emerald*, which is a precious stone of a green color, and very different from either of the modern or the ancient topaz. This latter, from its being classed with the ruby and the carbuncle, in all probability exhibited a beautiful flame-colored appearance which in some specimens might also have been enriched with a fine golden tint. To this may be added the circumstance of its being a production of Ethiopia, and not of the places referred to by our modern jewellers. Job, in his estimate of the value of true wisdom, sets it far above *rubies*, above the *topaz of Ethiopia*, and above the purest *gold*, chap. xxviii. 18, 19; which is an association that seems to justify our conclusion, that the ruby and the topaz bore an affinity with each other, and jointly with pure gold yielded a most exalted signification.

The *carbuncle* is a very elegant gem, of a deep red color, with an admixture of scarlet. Its name in the original implies brightness and splendor as of lightning. This gem was known formerly by the name of *anthrax*. It is said to glitter in the night, and to sparkle much more than the ruby. It is usually found pure and faultless, and is of the same degree of hardness as the sapphire. It is naturally of an angular figure; its usual size is near a quarter of an inch in length, and two-thirds of that in diameter in its thickest part. When held up against the sun, it loses its deep tinge, and becomes exactly of the color of burning charcoal; whence the propriety of the name which the ancients gave it. It is found in the East Indies, and there but very rarely.

The second Row, consisting of a Chrysoprasus, a Sapphire, and a Diamond.

This order or row of precious stones denotes the celestial love of truth, together with its wisdom, and answers to the external of the celestial kingdom, as the first row does to its internal. The stones of the former row derived their signification from their redness; but the stones of this row derive it from their blueness which partakes of a reddish tinge: for it is to be noted that there is a blue derived from and tinged with red, and likewise a blue derived from and tinged with white. The blue from red, which prevails in the stones of this row, denotes the celestial love of truth; but the blue from white, which prevails in the stones of the next or third row, denotes the spiritual love of good. The affections of the human mind here represented by colors, though not easily discriminated by one who reflects but little upon them, are yet to be considered as distinct from each other, as the stones of the two rows when compared together. In each case the stones appear brilliant and resplendent; but the one kind shows an affinity with red light, and the other an affinity with white light. So likewise of the affections above mentioned, the one has more immediate reference to the good of love, and the other to the truth of wisdom.

The *chrysoprasus* is described by some as of a pale green color, with an admixture of yellow; and the name itself seems to imply as much, being compounded of the Greek word *chrusos*, gold, and *prason*, a leek. In Hebrew the term is, נפך, *nophek*, which is rendered differently by different translators. Jerome makes it the *carbuncle*; the Septuagint calls it *anthrax*; Onkelos and the English translators, the *emerald*; and others suppose it to be the *ruby*. Then comes Rabbi David, who in his book of *Roots* pronounces it a *black precious stone.* See Le Dieu *in loc.* and Leigh's *Critica Sacra*, 3d edit., 1650. But it is well known, that the gems or precious stones of the ancients differed in many respects from those which bear the same names among the moderns; and therefore nothing can be positively concluded against the *nophek* of the Scriptures, now called the *chrysoprasus*, being of a cerulean or blue color with a distant tinge of red.

The *sapphire* is a pellucid gem, which in its finest state is extremely beautiful and valuable, being nearly equal to the diamond in lustre, hardness, and price. Its proper color is a pure blue; in the finest specimens it is of the deepest azure; in others it varies into paleness in shades of all degrees between that and a pure crystal brightness and water without the least tinge of color, but with a lustre much superior to the crystal. It is distinguished into four sorts, viz., the blue sapphire, the white sapphire, the water sapphire, and the milk sapphire. The gem known to us by this name is very different from the sapphire of the ancients, which is said to have been of a deep blue, veined with white, and spotted with small gold-colored spangles, in the form of stars, etc. Moses describes the appearance of heaven under the feet of the God of Israel, to be like a paved work of a *sapphire-stone*, Ex. xxiv. 10. And the prophet Ezekiel says, that the throne which was in the firmament over the heads of the cherubim, had the appearance of a *sapphire-stone*, Ezek. i. 26; x. 1. The ancients had an extraordinary esteem for this stone; and those who wore it about their persons, considered it as a passport to good fortune and happiness. The finest sapphires are brought from Pegu in the East Indies, where they are found in the pebble form, of all the shades of blue. The occidental are from Silesia, Bohemia, and other parts of Europe: but though these are often very beautiful stones, they are greatly inferior both in lustre and hardness to the oriental.

The *diamond* is a clear, bright stone, perfectly translucent, which, though naturally colorless like the purest water, is eminently distinguished from all others of the colorless kind by the lustre of its reflections. It derives its name in the original language from its extreme hardness, as it exceeds all the other precious stones in that quality, and can only be cut and ground by its own substance. It is found sometimes in an angular, and sometimes in a pebble-like form: but each kind, when polished, has the same qualities in proportion to its perfection and purity. In its native state it is sometimes bright as if polished by art; but more frequently its surface is obscured with foulnesses of various kinds; and sometimes it is, as the diamond-cutters call it, veiny, that is, it has certain points inconceivably hard on its surface. Like all other transparent minerals, the diamond is liable to be tinged by metalline particles, and is sometimes found with a cast of red, sometimes blue, sometimes green, and not unfrequently yellow. That with a cerulean tinge, delicately announcing its distant affinity with red, appears to have been the diamond that occupied the third place of the second row of precious stones in the breast-plate of judgment. The places whence we obtain the diamond, are the East Indies, particularly the island of Borneo, Visapour, Golconda, and Bengal; also the Brazils in the West Indies.

The third Row, consisting of a Cyanus, an Agate, and an Amethyst.

This row is the first or inmost of the spiritual class, and therefore denotes the spiritual love of good: for the two preceding rows represented the internal and the external of the celestial class. By the spiritual love of good is meant charity; and by the spiritual love of truth is meant faith derived from charity. The stones of this row were of a cerulean or blue color on a white ground; consequently they were of a distinct order from the stones of the second row, which were likewise cerulean, but on a most delicate red ground.

The *cyanus*—called by Jerome, Josephus, and the English translators, the *ligure;* by others the *lazule*, or *lapis lazuli;* and by Kimchi mistaken for the *topaz*—is a beautiful gem, of a fine blue color, and is found sometimes variegated with spots or clouds of white, and with veins of a shining gold color. But most probably the stone in its pure state is that which is meant in the Sacred Scripture by the *cyanus*.

The *agate*, or *achates*, is a valuable gem, variegated with veins and clouds: some having a white ground, some a reddish, some a yellowish, and some again a greenish ground. Cups and vessels are frequently made of agate, which is found in Sicily, Phrygia, and India. The precise color of the stone known among the ancient Jews by the name *shebo*, which our English translators have rendered the *agate*, and the German Jews call the *topaz*, cannot be now ascertained. But from its classification with the other stones of this row, which are known to be cerulean, there is sufficient reason to conclude that this stone also was of the same color, and like them on a white ground, but varying a little from them either in depth of tint or degree of shade.

The *amethyst* is so called, because in ancient times, when the various *charms* of superstition were more in vogue than at the present day, it was supposed to be a preservative against drunkenness, or excess in wine; the term in Greek implying as much. But the name in Hebrew, *achlamah*, is derived from a word which signifies, 1, to dream; 2, to recover from sickness, to grow fat, etc. Aben Ezra says that the stone was so called, because it had the power of causing the person who carried it about with him, to dream. Not to dwell, however, on these and such like fancies, it is sufficient for our present purpose to know, that the gem usually called the amethyst, is of various tints, as purple, violet, blue, etc., and that it is sometimes found nearly colorless, approaching to the purity of the diamond. That which is of a fine cerulean color, with a whitish tinge, appears to be the amethyst of the Sacred Scripture, and the last stone in the third row. They are found in India, Arabia, Armenia, Ethiopia, Cyprus, Germany, Bohemia, and other places: but those from the East are the hardest; and if without spots, they are of the greatest value. They are of various sizes and shapes, from the bigness of a small pea to an inch and a half in diameter.

The fourth Row, consisting of a Tarshish, an Onyx, and a Jasper.

This last row of stones, and second of the spiritual class, denotes the spiritual love of truth, which is the same thing as the good of faith; the third row as described above, denoting the good of charity. The color of each of the stones of this order approaches to white derived from blue, or to a white with a cerulean tint.

The *tarshish*, called also by the English translators the *beryl*, and by some the *turquoise*, the *thalassius*, and the *aqua-marina*, is of a sea-blue color, in some fine specimens approaching to white. Some of these stones are a mixture of green and blue resembling sea-water. According to Pliny, there are some which may be called *chrysoberyls*, on account of their golden or yellow color. These stones are very different from each other with respect to hardness. The oriental are the hardest, and bear the finest polish; and consequently are more beautiful, and of higher value than the occidental. The former kind are found in the East Indies, on the borders of the Euphrates, and at the foot of Mount Taurus. The occidental ones come from Bohemia, Germany, Sicily, the Isle of Elba, etc. And it is affirmed that some of them have been found on the sea-shore.

Tarshish was also the name of a maritime city, mentioned in various parts of the Sacred Scriptures, as in 1 Kings x. 22; xxii. 48; Ps. xlviii. 7; lxxii. 10; Ezek. xxxii. 12, 25; and is supposed to be the same as *Tarsus*, the birthplace of the apostle Paul. As it appears to have been distinguished for its commerce and wealth, the name of the city was probably given to the precious stone, as well on account of the resemblance of its color to the sea-water off the coast, as because it was usually brought in the ships of *Tarshish* from one country to another.

The *onyx* is a much-admired gem, having variously colored zones, but none of them red. In some specimens the zones are beautifully punctuated. In general the onyx resembles the color of a man's nail, being whitish on a cerulean ground.

The *jasper* is a stone of great variety of colors, often of a beautiful green, and sometimes with spots resembling those of a panther; hence called by some of the rabbies the *panther-stone*. Jerome identifies it with the beryl. But the true jasper of the ancients, or that which is mentioned in the Sacred Scriptures, (Apoc. xxi. 11; Ezek. xxviii. 13,) was neither green nor spotted, but a clear, white, pellucid and brilliant stone, in some degree resembling the crystal for purity and whiteness, yet still discovering its relation to the family of azures, by the distant but easily perceptible tinge of blue, which suffuses all its substance.

The Manner of obtaining Responses from Heaven in ancient Times, by Means of the twelve precious Stones called Urim and Thummim.

Having seen what was signified by the twelve precious stones in the breast-plate of Aaron, we now come to explain the manner in which responses were given from heaven by their means. We have already stated, and here repeat, that all the diversity of colors in the stones was produced by the modifications and variegations of two fundamental colors proper to light: these are *red* and *white*, each in a state of brilliancy and splendor illustrative of their true origin which is *fire*, and indeed the *fire of the sun*. From these, through the different degrees of *shade*, arise all the varieties of color, according to the qualities which different bodies possess of receiving, absorbing, compounding, dividing, reflecting or refracting the incident rays of light. Some bodies also have the property of perverting the rays of light in such a manner, as to extinguish their lustre, and to exhibit either a *dead white*, or a *carbonic red*, or a variety resulting from the union of these two colors with a *gloomy black*.

These observations equally apply to the rays of spiritual light, which consist of divine truth proceeding from the divine good of the Lord, and illuminating human as well as angelic minds, in the way of *mediate* as well as *immediate* influx, according to all the diversities of intelligence and wisdom in each. For every color in the spiritual world is a correspondent expression of some distinct perception of divine truth: and hence it is, that, according to the appearance of colors in that world, their vivid brightness or their fading hue, the various states of wisdom among the inhabitants, which are no other than so many continual revelations from the Lord, are visibly represented. But this was particularly the case when occasions offered during the theocracy established among the Jewish and Israelitish people, for consulting and interrogating the Divine Being by means of Urim and Thummim.

By *Urim* in the Hebrew language is signified shining fire, or fire which gives forth light: and by *Thummim* is signified integrity or perfection, which, in reference to the precious stones, must denote their resplendency, brilliancy, and extreme beauty. These were set in the breast-plate which was then called the *breast-plate of judgment*, the *judgment of the children of Israel*, and also the *judgment of Urim*, because thereby responses were given, and divine truths revealed from heaven. The communication thus opened between heaven and the people of Israel through the medium of the high-priest, was at first adopted in conjunction with that direct intercourse with Jehovah which Moses enjoyed during his life; but after the death of Aaron and of Moses, it was established as the usual and regular channel of making known to Jehovah the requests of the people, and of obtaining from Him, in reply, such answers as the Divine Wisdom might dictate.

The manner in which responses were given by means of Urim and Thummim, is not agreed upon by the different writers on the subject. Josephus in his *Antiquities* says that the twelve precious stones cast forth a more than ordinary lustre, when the Israelites were to obtain a victory over their enemies, and that by the appearance or non-appearance of this sign, they judged of the state of their affairs; the lustre and brilliancy of the stones foretelling good success, as their appearing dark and cloudy portended nothing but evil. Others are of opinion that the names of the twelve tribes which were engraven on the stones, as also the names of Abraham, Isaac, and Jacob, together with the words שִׁבְטֵי יְשֻׁרוּן, *shibtey Jeshurun*, i. e. *the tribes of Jeshurun*, or *of Israel*, added to complete the twenty-two letters of the Hebrew alphabet, were the instruments through which God delivered these oracles. It is therefore supposed that as many of the letters as were requisite to answer the proposed question, raised themselves up above the rest: as for instance, when the Israelites asked the Lord, saying, "Who shall go up for us against the Canaanites first to fight against them?" Judg. i. 1; it was answered by the oracle, "Judah shall go up: behold, I have delivered the land into his hand," ver. 2. The word יהודה, *Judah*, engraven on one of the stones, was raised, and cast forth a great lustre; after which the four letters יעלה, *shall go up*, raised themselves on the other stones. But as there is no sufficient authority for this opinion, and as moreover the raised letters in this instance do not give the *whole* of the answer which was delivered, it is not at all probable that responses were given in this way.

The true mode of proceeding and of obtaining answers from heaven on these occasions, appears to have been as follows: The high-priest, (or in his absence, the seer, the prophet, the judge, or the king, whoever it might be that was authorized to put on the ephod, with or without the other appendages of the priesthood,) standing before the ark of the covenant, whether it was in the tabernacle or out of it, and being clothed in all the garments of the sacred office; the mitre on his head, with the golden plate, the holy crown, in its front; the ephod, the robe, the embroidered coat, and the curious girdle, upon his body; together with the breast-plate of judgment, having twelve precious stones set in gold, and names engraven thereon of the twelve tribes of the children of Israel, upon his heart; a solemn appeal was made to Jehovah; He was literally questioned and interrogated as to the success of undertakings which were meditated; and He was required to make known his will by Urim and Thummim, that is to say, by the sparkling resplendency and vibrations of light from one stone to the other, and at the same time by an audible voice from heaven, or else by a tacit perception corresponding with the splendor of the stones, which might determine the revelation thus communicated to the eye, the ear, and the understanding of the petitioner. Hence, when the question was put by man, the angels who were present, united in the prayer which with them was entirely of a spiritual character, though with the people of Israel it was merely natural;

and as all prayer when genuine, has the power of opening heaven, and thereby of ascending to the Lord himself, a response was immediately given by Divine influx, which became perceptible first to the angels, and afterwards to man through their medium, and the medium of light vibrating in the precious stones. As soon as the angels perceived the Divine will by the resplendent colors presented before their eyes in the spiritual world, (it being one of the prerogatives of their high wisdom to be able to interpret those appearances with the utmost accuracy,) they instantly either infused a suggestion, or gave forth an audible sound expressive of the answer so received by them; and this voice, which appeared to proceed from off the mercy-seat that was upon the ark of the testimony, from between the two cherubim, (Ex. xxv. 22; Num. vii. 89,) was distinctly heard by the priest, the seer, or the prophet, and perhaps by several of the people also who were present, the ears of their spirits being then opened for the express purpose, while the precious stones on the breast-plate were miraculously seen to glitter by the rapid vibrations of light, which were in unison and correspondence with the light or wisdom of heaven.

If the question or interrogation put to Jehovah, spiritually considered, had for its end or object the love and worship of Him alone, in opposition to all other gods and in defiance of all enemies; or if it contemplated the practice and felicity of mutual love, in confirmation or in proof of their love to God; in such cases the vibrations of light most probably commenced either in the first, or in the second row of precious stones, and in imitation of the influx of love into every faculty of the human mind, first successively and then simultaneously pervaded, irradiated, and finally spread a blaze of glory over every part of the breast-plate. And this was an affirmative sign, rendered still more certain and indubitable by the audible voice accompanying it, directing the course they were to take, and thus enjoining them to persevere in that line of duty, which the Divine Wisdom, through the medium of the Word already given, had laid down for their use.

Again, if the question put were in relation to any of the various points of charity and true faith, as weapons of spiritual warfare; or to speak more literally, if they inquired of Jehovah whether they should proceed against such and such an enemy or not, and whether the event would be successful or unsuccessful; in this case, if they had been previously obedient to the divine commands in other respects, the vibrations of light commenced either in the third, or in the fourth row of stones; and, by pervading and illuminating the whole, gave a positive token of the Divine approbation, which was further confirmed by the audible voice of an angel.

But, on the other hand, if at any time the people of Israel had rebelled, either by relapsing into idolatry, or by other acts of disobedience, and inquiry were made of Jehovah how they were to conduct themselves on any particular emergency, and in the event of their attacking or being attacked by an enemy, whether success would attend them or not; in this case the lustre of the stones was diminished, the vibrations of the light (if any appeared) were irregular, its brilliancy less vivid than usual, and the response given both to the eye and to the ear of the inquirer was of that negative kind, which sufficiently announced the Divine disapprobation, and the consequent failure of the projected enterprise. On some occasions no answer whatever was returned: and therefore it is written, that " when Saul inquired of Jehovah, Jehovah *answered him not*, neither by dreams, nor by Urim, nor by prophets." 1 Sam. xxviii. 6.

General directions for obtaining a response, in regard to Joshua, the successor of Moses, may be seen in Num. xxvii. 18-23.

For affirmative and other responses, and for cases wherein Jehovah refused to give an answer, when inquired of, see Judges xx. 18-28; 1 Sam. x. 22; xiv. 37; xxiii. 2-12; xxviii. 6; xxx. 8; 2 Sam. ii. 1; v. 19, 23, 24; 2 Kings iii. 11-19.

Such appears to have been the manner of obtaining responses from heaven among the people of Israel, by means of Urim and Thummim, whenever they were anxious to know the Divine will, or the result of any meditated undertaking. And though to many in the present day it wears the complexion of fable and incredible mystery, yet it ought to be remembered that in the times when it was practised, almost all the nations of the earth were in the habit of consulting, through the medium of their priests, the demons whom they both feared and worshipped: and it cannot be questioned but they also, on innumerable occasions, received from them such answers, wrapt up in artful ambiguity, as still left a conviction in the minds of the inquirers that they were possessed of superhuman wisdom. Of this kind was the famous oracle of Apollo at Delphos, among the heathen Greeks, which, however, with the rest of a similar description, was silenced by the coming of the Lord into the world; at which time the demons or spirits, who acted as familiars to the

Pythons and Pythonesses, were removed from their direct association with mankind, and cast into hell.

The Manner of obtaining Responses from Heaven at the Present Day, by Means of the literal Sense of the Word.

Extraordinary and wonderful as the preceding account of the manner of obtaining responses from heaven may appear at the present day, it is not more so than the revelation of divine truth in the literal sense of the Word, and particularly the discovery now made of its genuine internal sense by means of the science of correspondences. For as the precious stones in the breast-plate of judgment represented all the truths of heaven, so in like manner they represented all the truths of the Word, but in their literal or external form, and consequently in their effect; while the different colors arising from the modifications of natural light, denoted the variegations of wisdom and intelligence which may be considered as spiritual light, both in angels and in men. And as the brilliancy and vibrations of the light in the stones, together with the audible voice from off the mercy-seat, presented both to the eye and to the ear of the person inquiring the desired answer; so the same but a more blessed effect is in our times produced by the extraordinary light of divine truth from the internal sense of the Word, which is spiritually seen to irradiate and as it were to vibrate through every part of its literal sense, while, instead of any external voice being heard, the best affections of the heart are excited, and the Divine will is clearly understood.

In this way we perceive the present use and perpetual application of that part of the Word, which describes the miraculous intercourse between Jehovah and the people of Israel, by means of the breast-plate of Urim and Thummim. This intercourse may still be maintained, though not precisely in the same external manner as with the Israelites of old: and yet there is reason to believe that the same internal modifications and variegations of heavenly light which appeared in former times, do now also actually take place in the human mind, on every occasion of consulting the Word purely for the sake of spiritual information and instruction. Thus a person sincerely desirous of knowing the Divine will in relation to any matter either of doctrine or of life, has only to approach the Lord in his Word under a deep sense of his own unworthiness, and an interior acknowledgment that every good gift descends from above. Let him then interrogate the Lord, or inquire of Him, by reading some portion of the Sacred Scriptures for the express purpose of knowing and doing his will; taking care that no improper prejudice or bias of the mind, induced either by education or habits of vice, be suffered to interpose its influence. It is more than probable that the person so reading the Word, or so inquiring of the Lord, will receive an answer most suitable to his state; the pure and radiant light of heaven will appear before his eyes; that is to say, his understanding will be enlightened to discern all necessary truth; the flame of divine love also will be kindled in his bosom; his affections will be still further purified; and he will be supplied with new power to bring his whole life by degrees into complete subjection to the laws of divine order. This conclusion is justified and confirmed by the words of our Lord, " If any man will *do his will*, he shall *know of the doctrine*, whether it be of God," John vii. 17.

CHAPTER X.

THE SCIENCE OF CORRESPONDENCE APPLIED AS A KEY TO THE SPIRITUAL INTERPRETATION OF THE PRINCIPAL SYMBOLS IN REVELATION XXI. CHAPTER, AND ITS APPLICABILITY AND SUFFICIENCY DEMONSTRATED*—"A NEW HEAVEN AND A NEW EARTH"—"THE HOLY CITY, NEW JERUSALEM"—"THE BRIDE, THE LAMB'S WIFE"—"HAVING THE GLORY OF GOD"—MEASURED WITH "A GOLDEN REED"—"THE CITY WAS PURE GOLD"—"THE CITY LIETH FOUR SQUARE"—ITS FOUNDATIONS, WALLS, AND GATES—"THE TEMPLE OF IT"—"THE LAMB IS THE LIGHT THEREOF"—"THERE SHALL BE NO NIGHT THERE"—SOVEREIGNTY OF ITS CITIZENS—QUALIFICATIONS FOR CITIZENSHIP.*

"*A New Heaven and a New Earth.*"

IN the first verse of this chapter, the seer tells us that he saw "a new heaven and a new earth"—the former heaven and earth having passed away. This was seen in a realm within or above nature, and with the seer's spiritual eyes, which were then opened, thus enabling him to behold things in the upper realms; for this vision, he tells us, was vouchsafed him when he "was in the spirit."

The natural heaven and earth, as embracing all material things, denote (because they correspond to) all the spiritual things of God's kingdom in both worlds. The vision of "a new heaven and a new earth," therefore, was a prophetic intimation (under the law of correspondence) of a new order of things to be some day established in both worlds, the spiritual and the natural; or a new angelic Heaven in the superior and a new Christian Church in the inferior realm.

And straightway an angel came to John and talked with him, saying, "Come hither; I will show thee the Bride, the Lamb's wife." Thereupon the angel, he says, "carried me away in the spirit to a great and high mountain, and showed me that great city, the holy Jerusalem, descending out of heaven from God."

Observe the correspondences here. Natural elevation corresponds to spiritual elevation, or exaltation of state. The seer was lifted by Divine influence into a superior spiritual condition, which is what his

---

* By B. F. Barrett. From "The Swedenborg Library," Vol. VII., pp. 236-256.

being carried in spirit to the summit of a high mountain corresponds to; and in that exalted state there is revealed to him, pictorially (under the same great law—correspondence), the Church of the Future —its principles, its spirit, its doctrines and its life. These were to be altogether new. As He that sat upon the throne said: "Behold I make all things new." This Church in respect to its doctrine was seen as a city; for a city corresponds to a church as to doctrine.

"The Holy City, New Jerusalem."

Jerusalem was regarded by devout Jews as the city of the living God. They thought of it and called it the Holy City. It was identified in their minds with all that they held most sacred—with their religion, their worship, their church. Their temple and altar were there. Those who dwelt outside of it went there with their tithes and offerings several times a year. There they held their great national festivals; and, with music, song and dance, gave expression to their intensest national as well as their deepest religious feelings. It was to them *the* place of worship. They never imagined that God *could* be truly worshipped anywhere else. Therefore they called it "the city of God"—"the holiest dwelling-place of the Most High." In their minds it was associated with all that belonged to religion and worship, just as Rome (though far more intimately) is at this day associated in the minds of pious Catholics with their religion, or as Babylon is associated in the minds of Protestant Christians with Roman Catholicism.

If the Church of the Future, then, in respect to its doctrine and worship, were to have been pictorially represented as a city eighteen hundred years ago, what city but Jerusalem should we expect would have been chosen? But it was not the *Old* Jerusalem that John saw; for it was not the old but a *new* system of religious doctrine which was thereby represented. Therefore the city that he beheld was called the *New* Jerusalem. And because the doctrines of the church thereby typified, were to be no cunning device of man's wit or wisdom, but doctrines revealed from heaven by the Lord himself; because they were to be doctrines disclosed or *brought down* to man's understanding from out that high and heavenly meaning of the Scripture which the angels perceive, therefore the New Jerusalem was seen "*coming down from God out of heaven.*"

The New Jerusalem, then, is the type of a new spiritual city—the city of the living God—to be established and built up in human hearts and human society, but of materials which come down from God out of heaven. In other words, the type of a new and glorious Church on earth, and one that will be in sweet accord with the heaven of angels; of a church based not on the vain imaginings of men, but on the precious and enduring truths of God's Word; of a church inspired by the purity, reflecting the glory, filled with the light and liberty and love of God. This is what was symbolized and foreshadowed by the city that John beheld in vision. Or as Swedenborg says, "a NEW CHURCH to be established by the Lord at the end of the former church, which will be associated with the new heaven in divine truths as to doctrine and as to life."

For, consider what is predicated of this city—what it is called and how it is described. It is called

"*The Bride, the Lamb's Wife.*"

And it is so called because of the correspondence and spiritual meaning of marriage. What are the constituents of every regenerate soul, or of every true church whether in the larger or smaller form? Obviously, the truths of wisdom and the goods of love: heavenly laws in the head, and heavenly feelings in the heart. These are the essential things of every true church, as of every true man. And these come down from God out of heaven; nor can they come from elsewhere. What is said, therefore, of this city's descent from God, accords with the idea that a new Church on earth is what was symbolized by it.

But the angel called that city "the Bride, the Lamb's wife." Natural marriage corresponds to spiritual marriage. And spiritual marriage is the union of true and faithful souls with the Lord. Such souls, loving Him supremely, and seeking above all else to know and do his will, hold a relation to Him which corresponds to the relation of a faithful wife to her husband. They are internally and spiritually married to Him. Therefore, in the symbolic language of Scripture, such souls (in the aggregate) are called his bride or wife: and He is called their husband. (Isa. liv. 5; lxii. 5; Jer. xxxi. 32.) Accordingly, in view of that purified state of the church in the then distant future, or of that multitude of souls which would be prepared to receive love and wisdom from the Lord, and thereby to become truly wedded to Him, John says he "heard as it were the voice of a great multitude, and as the voice of many waters, and as the voice of mighty thunderings, saying, Alleluia: for the Lord God omnipotent reigneth. Let us be glad and rejoice, and give honor to Him; for the marriage of the Lamb is come, and his wife hath made herself ready. And to her was granted that she should be arrayed in fine linen, clean and white; for the fine linen is the righteousness of saints." (Rev. xix. 6–8.) If the righteousness of saints is the fine linen in which the Lamb's wife is arrayed, then the saints themselves, or the Lord's true church must be that wife.

The circumstance, therefore, of the angel's calling the New Jerusalem " the Bride, the Lamb's wife," is conclusive of the fact that it typified and foreshadowed a new state of the church on earth;—a state when human hearts would enter into a more intimate and blissful marriage union with the Lord.

"Having the Glory of God."

This also is predicated of the New Jerusalem. And the "glory of God" must be a spiritual or divine glory. And what can that be?

What is a man's true glory? Not his physical strength nor personal comeliness; not his worldly possessions however great; not his social or official position however exalted; not his stores of knowledge however vast,—for these may be unwisely and selfishly used. But a capacious and richly-stored mind, and a heart emptied of selfishness and filled with the love of serving and blessing others—this is a man's true glory. In a word, it is unselfish love guided in its activities by the highest wisdom. And if this be the true glory of a man, then must wisdom and love constitute the chief glory of God. The wisdom of his Word is but an emanation from his love, and given for the enlightenment, exaltation and blessedness of mankind.

Human souls, then—or a church illumined by the wisdom and inspired by the love which is the very essence of heaven, and with which the spiritual sense of the Word is all aglow—may be truly said to have "the glory of God."

"By these words," says Swedenborg, "is described the understanding of the Word with those who are in the doctrine of the New Jerusalem, and in a life according to it [i. e., a life of unselfish love]. With such the Word shines, as it were, when it is read; it shines from the Lord by means of the spiritual sense, because the Lord is the Word, and the spiritual sense is in the light of heaven which proceeds from Him as a sun." "By the glory of God is meant the Word in its divine light." (A. R. n. 897.)

Accordingly it is added, that the light of this city "was like unto a stone most precious, even like a jasper stone clear as crystal." A jasper stone corresponds to and therefore signifies "the divine truth of the Word in its literal sense translucent from the divine truth in the spiritual sense."

Measured with "a Golden Reed."

The angel who showed John the New Jerusalem, "had a golden reed to measure the city, and the gates thereof and the wall thereof." If a new Church is typified by this city, a *golden reed* must typify something whereby this Church may be measured. And what is that? How do we measure human beings? Not with any material standard of measurement—for the real man is not material. We measure *men* by taking the dimensions of their souls, not of their bodies. They are great in the heavenly sense, according as they are wise and good, or according to the strength and purity of their love. Love, then,—love akin to God's own—is the standard of measurement to be applied when human souls are to be measured. And this love is what gold corresponds to.

A golden reed, therefore, typifies the ability derived from the good of heavenly love, to measure the character of an individual, a community or church. What truer standard than this can be conceived of, whereby to measure beings created to be images and likenesses of Him who is Love itself. Or by what other standard of measurement shall we judge the *doctrines* of any church? For a doctrine is true or false, according to its degree of conformity with this standard; that is, according as its tendency is to develop and strengthen this love, or to hinder its development. This, then, is the true test to be applied to every church, and to all its doctrines and inculcations.

And this agrees with what we find in a subsequent verse, where mention is made of the *wall* of this city. The wall encompasses the city; and its extent, therefore, shows its size. And the wall of the New Jerusalem is said to be "according to the measure of a man, that is, of the angel." Unselfish love is the distinguishing characteristic of every inhabitant of the celestial realms. The angels are all of them forms of love. Love of the Lord and the neighbor is their ruling principle. And as every true and regenerate man is an angel, viewed as to his immortal part, therefore the measure of a true man is the measure of an angel. And as the church consists of regenerate men, its measure also must be that of the angel.

"*The City was Pure Gold.*"

It is further said that "the city was pure gold, like unto clear glass." Gold, being the most precious of minerals, ought to typify something very precious in the soul of man. It ought to represent the noblest element of humanity—the essential constituent of heaven and the church. And what is that? Not *faith*, as the old theologies have taught, but *love*. Love is the crowning attribute of Deity. "God is love." And the more unselfish men become—the more thoroughly imbued and dominated by love of the neighbor, and of all that is just, sincere, true and good for its own sake,—the more they become like God. Accordingly the apostle again says: "And he that dwelleth in love, dwelleth in God and God in him."

Now since *pure gold* corresponds to the good of unselfish love, and this love is the essential thing in the church typified by the New Jerusalem, as it is, indeed, the essential thing in the kingdom of heaven—as this is the very substance and marrow of all its teachings and the end to which all its doctrines point, therefore this city was shown to John as of "pure gold."

"All the particulars of the doctrine of the New Jerusalem," says Swedenborg, "relate to love to the Lord and the neighbor. Love to the Lord consists in trusting in Him and doing his commandments; and to do his commandments constitutes love toward the neighbor, because to do his commandments is to be useful to our neighbor." (A. R. n. 903.)

As genuine love, or the disinterested love of use, is what pure gold corresponds to, so clear glass is the correspondent and symbol of the transparent truth of the spiritual sense of the Word. And because love to the Lord and the neighbor—love enlightened and guided by heavenly truth, is to form the animating principle, yea, the very life and soul of the church signified by the New Jerusalem—because this is to pervade all its doctrines, inspire all its activities, shape all its ends, determine all its doings—therefore the city is described as "pure gold like unto clear glass."

"*The City lieth Four Square.*"

It is further said that "the city lieth four square; and its length is as large as its breadth. And he measured the city with the reed, twelve thousand furlongs."

The *form* and *dimensions* of this city are symbolic, like everything else predicated of it. The quadrangle or square is the type or correspondent of strict and impartial justice, which is another distinguishing characteristic of this church—justice toward all men and in all the relations of life. And to represent its catholicity and universality, the city is further described as *cubical;* for "the length and the breadth and the *height* of it are equal"—a type of the fact, that this church will embrace all *kinds* and *degrees* of good and truth, from the lowest natural or scientific to the highest spiritual and celestial. It will recognize the connection and oneness, yea, the divineness, of all kinds of truth, and show science to be, not the adversary but the sincere friend and faithful handmaid of religion; and that God's Word and works are never in conflict, but in complete and cordial agreement.

Its Foundations, Walls and Gates.

The foundations and walls of the city are described as of "precious stones." Stones are the symbols or correspondents of those low but unyielding forms of truth which belong to the literal sense of the Word. On these the church rests as a city on its foundations: for all the doctrines of the New Jerusalem are drawn from and confirmed by the truths of the literal sense. These, too, are its protection—its walls as well as its foundations.

"Since the holy city, New Jerusalem," says Swedenborg, "means the Lord's New Church as to doctrine, its wall means nothing else but the Word in its literal sense, from which doctrine is derived; for that sense defends the spiritual which lies concealed within it, as a wall defends a city and its inhabitants; and the literal sense is the foundation, containant and support of the spiritual sense." (A. R. n. 898.)

The stones with which the foundations of the wall of the city were garnished, are said to be *all precious,* because the truths of the Word which they typify are full of the Lord's own spirit and life; and this is what makes them precious.

And the twelve gates of the city are the symbols or correspondents of all the knowledges of good and truth by which we are introduced into the church, or into a true church state—as people may be introduced into a natural city through gates. And it is said that "every particular gate was of *one* pearl," because there is one precious kind of knowledge which, in spiritual things, pervades all others and conjoins them into one; and that is the knowledge and acknowledgment of the Lord.

"That the Lord is the very gate through which men are to enter into the church and thence into heaven, He himself teaches in John x. 9; and that the knowledge and acknowledgment of Him is the pearl of great price, is meant by his own words in Matthew: 'The kingdom of heaven is like unto a merchantman seeking goodly pearls; who, when he had found *one pearl of great price*, went and sold all that he had and bought it,' xii. 45, 46. The one pearl of great price is the knowledge and acknowledgment of the Lord." (A. R. 916.)

"*The Temple of It.*"

In the 22d verse, the seer says: "And I saw no temple therein; for the Lord God Almighty and the Lamb are the temple of it,"—a declaration conclusive of the fact, that no natural but a spiritual city is here referred to,—a vast multitude of enlightened and sincere worshipers of the Lord Jesus Christ; for it is only of such kind of city that *He* is the temple.

A temple, being a place for external and formal worship, corresponds to a state of internal and real worship. This, therefore, is what it typifies and denotes. And in every state of true worship, the Lord himself is the All-in-all; for all the thoughts, desires and feelings whereby He is truly worshiped, are from Him. Therefore a temple or place of worship becomes the representative of the Lord himself. He is the Living Temple. And men, too, become living temples so far as their hearts come to be the abode of his blessed Spirit. Hence the apostle says to the Corinthian brethren: "Know ye not that ye are the temple of God, and that the spirit of God dwelleth in you?" (See also 1 Cor. iii. 16.) Now the Lord Jesus Christ, in whom "dwelleth all the fulness of the Godhead bodily," is the supreme and only Object of worship in the church signified by the New Jerusalem. He and He alone, therefore, is the true and living Temple in this church. "A temple signifies the church as to worship; and in its highest sense, it signifies the Lord himself as to his Divine Humanity, who is the Object to be worshiped. And since all of the church is from the Lord, therefore it is said, 'for its temple is the Lord God Almighty and the Lamb,' by which is meant the Lord in his Divine Humanity." (A. R. 918.)

"*The Lamb is the Light thereof.*"

Look, again, at the manner in which this city is lighted. Not by any artificial means, nor by the luminaries of the natural world.

"The city had no need of the sun, neither of the moon to shine in it; for the glory of God did lighten it, and the Lamb is the light thereof."

There is but One who can say, "I am the light of the world." He is the same who declares Himself to be "THE TRUTH." He is "the Word," which, though coeval and identical with God, "became flesh and dwelt among men." The Lord Jesus Christ is "the true light which enlighteneth every man that cometh into the world." And what is the glory of God but the refulgence of the Divine Love —the light of spiritual truth which radiates from the ever-living Word, whose glory is especially revealed in its internal sense? This is the light of the spiritual world—the light by which angels see. It is this which illumines all minds on earth and in heaven. Truth emanating from Love and accommodated to human needs;—truth from the Word made flesh, penetrating the dark corners of the earth and enlightening the nations;—truth chasing away the shadows of ignorance and superstition and doubt and fear, showing mankind the heavenly paths, and guiding them upward to the celestial summits— this is "the glory of God." And this it is which is to lighten the church signified by the New Jerusalem. "For the glory of God did lighten it, and the Lamb is the light thereof." And because spiritual salvation comes from walking in the light of spiritual truth, that is, from *living* as the truth requires, therefore it is immediately added: "And the nations of them that are saved shall walk in the light of it."

With this agrees the prediction of the prophet Isaiah concerning the future state of the church: "And they shall call thee the city of the Lord, the Zion of the Holy One of Israel. . . The Lord shall be unto thee an everlasting light, and thy God thy glory. Thy sun shall no more go down, neither shall thy moon withdraw itself; for the Lord shall be thine everlasting light, and the days of thy mourning shall be ended." (Isa. lx. 14, 19, 20.)

"*There shall be no Night there.*"

It is further said of the New Jerusalem: "And there shall be no night there; and they need no candle, neither light of the sun, for the Lord God giveth them light." Let the Key again be applied here, and note the meaning thereby elicited.

There are natural day and night, and spiritual day and night; day and night in the natural realm, and day and night in the soul;

and they correspond one to the other. When the face of the earth is turned toward the sun, it is day-time in the world; and when man's heart or will (his spiritual face) is turned toward the Lord, it is day-time in the soul. But when the earth is turned away from the sun, it is night in the world; and when the heart is turned away from the Lord, it is night in the soul. The correspondence is exact and perfect.

Truth and love are the spiritual correspondents of light and warmth. And these emanate from the Lord as natural light and heat from the natural sun; for He, indeed, is the Sun of the spiritual world. When these are absent from men's souls, or when the church on earth, under the blinding influence of the loves of self and the world, invents and confirms itself in various falsities which shut out the sunshine of heaven and obscure the glory of the Lord, then it is night with the church. It is precisely such a night as this—a state of spiritual darkness—that the prophet Micah refers to, where, speaking of the teachers who cause God's people to err, he says: "Therefore night shall be unto you, and ye shall not have a vision; and it shall be dark unto you, that ye shall not divine; and the sun shall go down over the prophets, and the day shall be dark over them." (iii. 6.)

It is to such a night—such spiritual darkness induced by false persuasions originating in evil loves—that the Lord refers when He speaks of that "outer darkness" into which the wicked are cast: Also when He says: "If, therefore, the light that is in thee be darkness, how great is that darkness!" But in the minds of those who acknowledge the Lord and humbly seek to do his will, there is no such darkness; "no night there." Therefore it is said there shall be no night in the New Jerusalem. There cannot be, since its light is the same as that by which the angels see—the light of the spiritual sense of the Word—a light "like unto a stone most precious, even like a jasper stone clear as crystal."

They who are in this light have no need of human creeds; no need of dogmas or "plans" or "schemes" of men's contriving; no need of the dim, sickly, flickering light of self-derived intelligence,— which is what a candle corresponds to. Nor do they need the more glaring but not less false and seductive light which springs from the selfish love of glory, and is what is here meant by the "light of the sun."

The sun in a good sense corresponds to the Lord; and its light corresponds to the truth which proceeds from Him. But this is sometimes used in Scripture in an opposite sense, and denotes the love of self, the nature of which is the opposite of the Lord's love. When used in this sense, the sun's light signifies the glory of the love of self; for this is what its light then corresponds to. Animated by the fire of self-love, men may sometimes ascend temporarily into the light of exalted wisdom. They may see many truths, and teach them from a selfish love of glory. The light into which such persons elevate themselves, is not the genuine light of the Sun of heaven, but the false and seductive light which originates in pride or the selfish love of fame.

But the dwellers in the New Jerusalem are in the love of *use*, not the love of self. They take delight in the performance of good uses from love to the Lord and the neighbor. And their love of use becoming strengthened by exercise, opens their minds more and more to the understanding and reception of spiritual truth—the light by which the angels see. It is plain, therefore, why it is said, "there shall be no night there." And because they do not regard their wisdom as their own or self-derived, and are not ambitious of the glory of *discovering* truth, but humbly look to the Lord in the revelations He has been pleased to make, and reverently acknowledge Him in the truth they understand and in the love they feel, therefore it is added: "and they need no candle, neither light of the sun; for the Lord God giveth them light."

Sovereignty of its Citizens.

It is further said of the dwellers in this city, that "they shall reign forever and ever." To *reign* is predicated of those who exercise sovereign authority. But there is a natural and a spiritual sovereignty, corresponding like body and soul. In the New Jerusalem all are to be crowned kings and queens; all are to sit upon thrones; for all are to *reign* spiritually. But to reign in this sense is not to exercise sovereignty over any outward kingdom, but over that empire within which is each one's own by divine right—the empire of the soul. Rightly to rule here—wisely to regulate and control all the passions, appetites, thoughts and feelings, and to thoroughly subject the inclinations of the natural man to the laws of the heavenly life —this is to reign in the highest and best sense. This is to be spiritually crowned, and to reign with Him who is " King of kings and

Lord of lords." And in the sight of angels this is far nobler than to sit upon any terrestrial throne.

Those who thus reign over the empire within, will never desire to lord it over others, but only to do good *and serve* from neighborly love. They will seek to govern their feelings and conduct according to the laws of heavenly charity. This is what the angels do. Therefore *they* are said to sit upon thrones and to reign. And because the members of the church signified by the New Jerusalem will all be internally associated with the angels and forever conjoined to the Lord, therefore it is said that "they shall reign forever and ever."

Qualifications for Citizenship.

What, now, are the qualifications for admission into this city? Precisely those which fit one for membership in the kingdom of heaven; and which, therefore, constitute him a member of that true church on earth, which is one with the church in heaven. And it is only the faithful *doers* of the truth, who have their hearts cleansed of selfishness and sin, and are thus fitted for admission into heaven. As the Lord himself has declared: "Not every one that saith unto me, Lord, Lord, shall enter into the kingdom of heaven, but he that *doeth* the will of my Father which is in heaven." And as none can enter heaven without keeping the Commandments, or without shunning all known evil as sin, neither can they enter the true and living church on earth in any other way. Accordingly the terms of admission into the New Jerusalem are thus clearly stated: "Blessed are they that *do his commandments*, that they may have right to the tree of life, and may enter in through the gates into the city." And again: "There shall in nowise enter into it anything that defileth, neither whatsoever worketh abomination or maketh a lie; but they that are written in the Lamb's book of life."

Yes: none but the faithful *doers* of the truth can really enter or have an abiding place in the New Jerusalem; for none others come into that state of union with the Lord and fellowship with the angels, which is the true church state. But all who acknowledge the Lord and humbly strive to obey his precepts, by whatever names they are known on earth, are known and acknowledged in the realms above as belonging to the true and living church. They have "entered in through the gates into the city."

Such, briefly, is the meaning of the New Jerusalem, and of the principal symbols employed in its description, as unfolded by the rule or law of correspondence. As to its reasonableness and consistency, as well as its agreement with other parts of Scripture and the indications of God's purposes in the past history and present condition of the church, the reader will form his own conclusion. But he should not forget or overlook the general state of Apocalyptic interpretation, and the darkness, confusion and contradiction which have hitherto prevailed among learned commentators, with regard to the meaning and purpose of this book. If he wishes to pursue the inquiry, and to learn the signification of the numerous other symbols mentioned in the Revelation, and the true meaning of this wonderful book, we refer him to Swedenborg's extended explanation of it in his "Apocalypse Revealed."

CHAPTER XI.

THE WORD AND ITS INSPIRATION—NO WRITTEN WORD BEFORE THE FALL—THE ANCIENT WORD THAT BECAME LOST—SOURCE OF THE GRECIAN MYTHOLOGY—ALL RELIGIOUS KNOWLEDGE FROM DIVINE REVELATION—THE SCRIPTURES A LIGHT TO ALL NATIONS—THE MEDIUM OF COMMUNICATION BETWEEN ANGELS AND MEN—NATURE OF THE WORD IN HEAVEN—ILLUSTRATING AND CONFIRMING THE DOCTRINE OF CORRESPONDENCE—DISTINCTION BETWEEN VERBAL AND PERSONAL INSPIRATION—NO WRITTEN WORD ON ANY EARTH BUT OURS, AND THE REASON WHY.*

The Word and its Inspiration.

OF all the services which Swedenborg, under the guidance of Divine Providence, has performed to the world, perhaps the greatest is that of throwing a new light on the Sacred Volume, whereby it becomes to us, as it were, a new Book. And this light was greatly needed. There is no subject, perhaps, of a theological nature, about which there is more doubt and discussion at the present day, than in regard to the true character and meaning of the volume called the Holy Scriptures. Some calling themselves Christians, doubt and even deny the Divine authority of a large portion of it, regarding the Old Testament, for instance, as an obsolete code of laws intended only for a by-gone age and nation; while the greater part, perhaps, of the Christian world, though looking upon it as, in a general sense, the Word of God, yet either openly question, or else entertain only vague ideas concerning, its Plenary Inspiration.

In the midst of this obscurity, the Sun of Righteousness has risen on the world, "with healing in his wings:" "the people that walked in darkness have seen a great light; they that dwell in the land of the shadow of death, upon them hath the light shined." (Isaiah ix. 2.) The Lord who was "the Word made flesh," and who is the Word in its spirit and life, has come a second time into the world, and revealed Himself anew to men, by the opening of the internal sense of that

---

* By Rev. O. Prescott Hiller. First published in the London *Intellectual Repository*, from June to December 1864.

Word wherein He dwells. Through his illuminated messenger He has now made known the precise nature of the inspiration of the Sacred Volume, and has shown that that Divine Word is the Lord's very presence amongst men, giving light not only to the Christian, but also to the Gentile world; and still more, that it illumines the heavens as well as the earth, and that it is read by angels, as indeed that Word itself declares—"For ever, O Lord, thy Word is settled in heaven." (Ps. cxix. 89.)

Our purpose in the present Essay is to enlarge upon these points; to show from statements and explanations in the writings of Swedenborg, the true nature of the Divine Word, the precise character and manner of its inspiration, its influence on the world, and the high use it performs as a connecting medium between earth and heaven.

The most effective way, perhaps, of presenting the subject in a clear light will be to treat it historically. In the Most Ancient Church, which existed before man's decline and fall, there was no outward or written Word; none such was needed. The influx of light from heaven into the interiors of men's minds was in that age a sufficient guide. This was because their minds, being in an unperverted state, were turned towards heaven, and consequently could receive the inflowing light and love in their true order, and thus be illumined by the one and warmed by the other. But after the Fall, man could no longer be thus led; for the human mind being then in a perverted state, and turned away from heaven, the truth flowing in became changed into falsity, and the good into evil. This was an effect of the great law, that a disordered mind perverts what flows into it,—that the recipient form modifies the influx, and assimilates it to its own nature. The operation of this law may be plainly seen in the outward universe; for instance, the heat and light of the sun flow into all vegetables alike, and the common earth gives them all nourishment; yet from the same materials, so to speak, the different plants manufacture different and sometimes totally opposite productions. Out of the same nourishment the rose brings forth its charms, and the brier its ugliness; the vine its grapes, and the hemlock its poison. This is because each plant, according to its interior structure and nature, modifies the inflowing light, heat and sap, and turns them to its own uses. Just so is it with the inner world of man's mind. The light and heat of the heavenly Sun are ever pouring truth and love and life alike into every mind; but these are received, rejected or modified according to the conformation, structure and order of the mind into which they fall. A bad man's mind, being in a perverted and corrupt state, changes the inflowing warmth of love into the fire of evil passions, and turns the light, intended for his guidance to heaven, into an instrument for carrying out his own evil designs; thus he turns good into evil, truth into falsity. In such case, it is plainly impossible to instruct man from within, because the heavenly influx is perverted as fast as it comes. The only way he can be taught, is from without, by oral or written instruction,—especially by a written Word, for that lies before his eyes in its integrity, whatever be his own character or views, and still speaks to him as a calm and truthful monitor, pointing out to him the right path, if only he have the will to listen to its teachings.

Now, by the Fall man came into the perverted and disordered state of mind above described, and hence the need of an outward written Revelation. And ever since that time, the human mind has been, in a greater or less degree, in the same perverted state, and hence the continued need of instruction from without. It is from ignorance of this great law that many opponents of the Bible, at the present day, protest against being taught by a Book, by a written Revelation, and maintain that the inner revelation from God into every man's mind is a sufficient guide. Did they understand the law before mentioned, namely, that the recipient subject modifies the influx according to its own nature, and were they at the same time acquainted with the truth, that every man's mental nature and constitution at the present day, is hereditarily disordered and perverted, they would then discern the true ground of the need of a written Revelation, and they would no longer oppose it, but would cling to it as the only means of salvation, the only sure guide to heaven and happiness.

We are instructed in the writings of the New Church, that before the promulgation of the Word which we now possess, there was another which Swedenborg terms the "Ancient Word." This Ancient Word, in fact, is referred to, and even quoted, in two places in our present Scriptures. For instance, in the Book of Numbers (xxi. 14, 15) we find these words—" Wherefore it is said in the Book of the Wars of Jehovah, What He did in the Red Sea, and in the brooks of Arnon, and at the stream of the brooks that goeth down to the dwelling of Ar, and lieth upon the border of Moab." Now, there is no such book, we know, as the " Wars of Jehovah" in our present Bible. Again, in the same chapter (verses 27 to 30) we find another quotation from that Ancient Word, thus—"Wherefore they that speak in proverbs say, Come into Heshbon; let the city of Sihon be built and prepared; for there is a fire gone out of Heshbon, a flame from the city of Sihon; it hath consumed Ar of Moab, and the lords of the high places of Arnon. Woe to thee, O Moab! thou art undone, O people of Chemosh; he hath given his sons that escaped, and his daughters, into captivity unto Sihon king of the Amorites. We have shot at them; Heshbon is perished even unto Dibon, and we have laid them waste even unto Nophah, which reaches unto Medeba." On this quotation Swedenborg remarks—

"The title—'They that speak in proverbs,' would be more properly expressed by 'The Enunciators,' and their compositions should be termed—'Prophetical Enunciations,' as is evident from the signification of the Hebrew word *moshalim*, which not only means *proverbs*, but also *prophetical enunciations;* for the passages quoted by Moses are not proverbs, but prophecies. . . . These 'Enunciations' (he adds) constituted the prophetical part of that Ancient Word, and the 'Wars of Jehovah,' the historical part."

By the "Wars of Jehovah," mentioned in that Word, are prophetically described the Lord's combats with the hells, and his victories over them; the same combats are also meant and described in many passages of the historical part of our Word, as in the wars of Joshua with the inhabitants of the land of Canaan, and in the wars of the Judges and of the kings of Israel. Besides the above quotations, mention is also made of a prophetical book of the Ancient Word called the *Book of Jasher*, or the Book of the Upright. It is mentioned both by David and by Joshua; by David in the following passage—"David lamented over Saul and over Jonathan; also he bade them teach the children of Judah the bow; behold it is written in the *Book of Jasher.*" (2 Sam. i. 17, 18.) It is mentioned by Joshua in this passage—"Joshua said, Sun, stand thou still upon Gibeon; and thou, Moon, in the valley of Ajalon; is not this written in the *Book of Jasher?*" (Josh. x. 12, 13.) In addition to these extracts and references, Swedenborg affirms that from that Ancient Word Moses copied the first chapters of Genesis, which treat of the creation of the garden of Eden, of Adam and Eve, and their sons and posterity till the flood, and also concerning Noah and his sons. D. S. S. 103.

The reason, he says, why, under Divine Providence, that Ancient Word became lost to the world, was because it was of too interior a character to be understood after men had declined into an external and sensual state.

"Since that Word was full of such correspondences as were only remotely significant of celestial and spiritual things, in consequence of which it began to be generally falsified, then, by the Divine providence of the Lord, in process of time it was removed, and at last was lost; and another Word was given, written by correspondences less remote, which was the Word published by the prophets among the children of Israel."*

We can easily conceive this to be the fact, when we observe how entirely that portion of our present Word which was copied from the ancient one, namely, the narrative in the first chapters of Genesis, has been misunderstood, both in the Jewish and in the Christian church. That narrative, as Swedenborg in his *Arcana Cœlestia* shows, is a pure allegory, describing, under the figure of a natural creation, the rise and establishment of the first or Most Ancient Church; next, under the picture of a garden, the wisdom and happiness of the men of that church; and lastly, under the representation of the temptation by a serpent, and the destruction by a flood, the decline, fall, and final consummation of that Church. Yet this allegorical account, the Jews and even the Christians have taken for a narrative of literal facts; thus both obscuring their own minds, and at the same time casting a shade of mystery and inconsistency on the Divine Word. And yet, to minds in any degree of interior discernment, how evidently is it an allegory! The very names of the trees mentioned—the "tree of life," and the "tree of the knowledge of good and evil"—are enough to make it plain that no natural trees were meant; and how could a literal serpent be supposed to think and speak in the manner represented? and how could an ark of the size there described be imagined capable of holding all the animals in the world? These, and many other considerations, would seem sufficient to have shown that at least some interior meaning was intended to be conveyed, quite different from the sense of the letter. But the truth is that men have lost not only all knowledge of the science of correspondences, according to which that allegory was written, but also all perception of interior things, as a consequence of having no love for them; and hence the gross error into which they have fallen of taking this account in its literal acceptation, and thus of entirely misunderstanding and falsifying it. From this single instance we may see the truth of Swedenborg's statement as to the reason why, under Divine Providence, the Ancient Word was withdrawn.

* See the *Doctrine of the Sacred Scripture*, n. 102.

Many important inferences, however, are deducible from the fact of the former existence of that Ancient Word. Our knowledge of that fact, for instance, throws great light on the origin of the mythology as well as the wisdom of the ancient Greeks and Romans, and also on the source of the religions of the oriental nations. In regard to the Grecian mythology, Swedenborg states it to have been derived from the science of correspondences, according to which the Ancient Word was written,—which science, in ancient times, was spread over all the countries of the south-west of Asia, and also over Egypt.

"I have been informed," says he, "that the men of the Most Ancient Church were of so heavenly a genius that they conversed with angels, and that they had the power of holding such converse by means of correspondences; hence, the state of their wisdom became such that, in viewing any of the objects of this world, they thought of them not only naturally, but also spiritually, thus in conjunction with the angels of heaven. I have been further informed that *Enoch*, who is mentioned in Genesis v. 21, 24, together with his associates, collected correspondences from the lips of the celestial men, and transmitted the science of them to posterity; in consequence of which, the science of correspondences was not only known in many kingdoms of Asia, but also much cultivated, particularly in the land of Canaan, Egypt, Assyria, Chaldea, Syria, and Arabia, and in Tyre, Sidon, and Nineveh, and that thence it was conveyed into Greece, where it was changed into fable, as is evident from the works of the oldest writers of that country."—D. S. S. 21.

"How much the ancients," he remarks, "excelled the moderns in intelligence, is manifest from this, that they knew to what things in heaven many things in the world corresponded, and hence what they signified; and this was known not only to those who were of the church, but also to those who were out of the church,—as, for instance, to the inhabitants of Greece, the most ancient of whom describe things by significatives which at this day are called fabulous simply because they are altogether unknown. That the ancient sophi possessed the knowledge of such things is evident from this, that they described the origin of intelligence and wisdom by a winged horse which they called Pegasus, and his breaking open with his hoof a fountain at which were nine virgins, and this upon a hill; for they knew that by a horse was signified the intellectual principle, by the wings the spiritual, by hoofs truth in the lowest degree, which is the basis of intelligence, by virgins the sciences, by hill unanimity, and in the spiritual sense, charity; and so on. But such things at this day are among those that are lost."—A. C. 7729.

Here, then, is the source of that Grecian mythology which has been a matter of such mystery to modern scholars. So also in regard to the wisdom of the ancient Greek philosophers, so often referred to by the opponents of the sufficiency of the "light of nature." We now learn that that wisdom was not derived merely from human reasonings, as commonly supposed, but was derived from that Ancient Word before mentioned,—thus from Revelation.

"It is believed in the world," says Swedenborg, "that man from the light of nature, thus without Revelation, can know many things relating to religion,—as that there is a God, that He is to be worshiped, and also that man is to live after death, with many other truths that depend on these, and that this knowledge is from his own intelligence. But I have been instructed from much experience, that man of himself and without Revelation, knows nothing at all concerning divine things; for man is born into the evils of self-love and the love of the world, which are such as to shut out influx from heaven, and open influx from hell, and which thus make man blind, and disposed to deny the existence of the Divine Being, of heaven and hell, and of the life after death. This is very manifest from the learned of the world, who by means of science have perfected the light of nature to a higher degree than others. That these, oftener than others, deny a Divine Being, and acknowledge only nature, is well known; and also that when they speak from their hearts and not from mere doctrine, they are inclined to deny the life after death, also heaven and hell, and consequently all things which pertain to faith, which they call merely restraints upon the vulgar. Hence it is evident what is the quality of nature without Revelation. Neither do writers on Natural Theology draw their ideas from themselves; but they merely confirm by rational arguments the things which they have learned from the church which possesses the Word.

"There are two considerations, however," he continues, "which put the mind in doubt on this subject; first, that the ancients who were Gentiles, were nevertheless acquainted with the existence of a Divine Being, and knew that worship was due to Him, and also that man's soul was immortal; and secondly, that these things are known, also, to many nations at this day with whom there is no Revelation. In regard to the ancients, it is to be observed that they did not know these things from the light of their own nature, but from Revelation which flowed down to them from the Ancient Church; for the church of the Lord had existed from the most ancient times in the land of Canaan, and thence such things as pertained to Divine worship passed to the surrounding nations, and also to the neighboring Greeks, and from these to the Italians or Romans. From this source both the latter and the former had knowledge respecting the Supreme Deity, and concerning the immortality of the soul, on which subjects their learned men wrote. The ancient philosophers, as Aristotle, Cicero, Seneca, and others, who have written concerning God and the immortality of the soul, did not derive these things originally from their own understandings, but from tradition, and from those who received that knowledge from the Ancient Word. From that Ancient Word, and also from the Israelitish Word, religion emanated from the Indies and their islands, and through Egypt and Ethiopia into the kingdoms of Africa, and from the maritime parts of Asia into Greece, and thence into Italy. But as the Word could not be written otherwise than by representatives, which are such things in the world as correspond to heavenly things, and thence signify them, therefore the religious ideas of the Gentile nations were changed into idolatries, and in Greece into fables, and the Divine properties and attributes into as many Gods, over whom they had one Supreme Deity, whom they called *Jove*, perhaps from *Jehovah*. It is known, also, that they had knowledge concerning paradise, the deluge, the sacred fire, and the four ages, from the golden to the iron age.*

"In regard to the Gentile nations of the present day, who are also acquainted with the existence of a Divine Being, and of a life after death, they have not derived this knowledge from the light of nature, but from the religion handed down to them from ancient times; and this was founded on such knowledge as had emanated in various ways from the church where there was a Revelation; and this was of the Divine Providence of the Lord."—A. C. 8944; T. C. R. 273-5.

Here we have very important information; we learn that all the religious light of the ancient world, equally as of the modern, was derived from Divine Revelation. Thus the wisdom of Socrates so often adduced as an argument in favor of the light of nature, was not—so far as related to the being of a God and the immortality of the soul—drawn from his own meditations solely, but was based on knowledges handed down by tradition, and derived originally from a written Word.

No. II.

In like manner the religions of the modern Orientals—the Hindoos, Chinese, Japanese—so far as those religions contain any truth, are traceable to the same source. It was from the Ancient Word, and afterwards from that of Moses, that religion emanated into the Indies and neighboring islands, and also into Africa. And there are some striking facts which might be adduced in confirmation of this

---

* From this statement it appears how the tradition of a *flood* came to exist among the Greeks and other ancient nations, namely, that it was derived from the narrative in the Ancient Word. In this view the existence of such tradition is not, as has been commonly held, a proof that a literal flood had once existed upon the earth, but only that a *Scripture account* of a flood had been widely circulated among men, which account, however, as we now know, is to be regarded as purely allegorical, and as describing a moral, not a material, inundation.—See *Josephus against Apion*, n. 22, where he shows how many ideas the Grecian philosophers and other writers had derived from the Jews.

statement. Among the Buddhists, for instance, in Thibet, China and Japan, there are found, it is said, the commandments of the Decalogue, almost word for word as they stand in our Bible:—"Thou shalt not kill; thou shalt not steal; thou shalt not commit adultery," etc. The peculiar form in which these commandments are laid down shows plainly the source whence they were originally derived. The truth of this view is confirmed by Swedenborg in the following passage:—

"No one has religion from himself, but through another, who, either himself, or by transmission from others, knew from the Word that there is a God, a life after death, a heaven and a hell, and that God is to be worshiped in order that man may be blessed. The Lord provides that in every religion there should be precepts such as are in the Decalogue: as that God is to be worshiped, his name not to be profaned, a solemn day to be kept, parents to be honored; that one must not kill, nor commit adultery, nor steal, nor testify falsely. The nation which regards these precepts as divine, and lives according to them from religion, is saved; and most of the nations, remote from the Christian world, look upon these laws, not merely as civil ordinances, but as divine, and esteem them holy."—*Divine Providence*, n. 254.

It may be added, that the Mahometan religion, which prevails over so large a part of the Eastern world, though based professedly on the Koran, yet derives what truth it possesses indirectly from the Divine Word; for the moral teachings of the Koran are drawn in great part from the Word both of the Old and New Testament. On this point Swedenborg remarks:

"The Mahometan religion was raised up by the divine providence of the Lord, for the purpose of destroying the idolatries of many nations. Before the existence of that religion, the worship of idols prevailed throughout the world. The reason of such a general prevalence of idolatry was this:—The churches before the coming of the Lord were all representative churches; such, for instance, was the Israelitish church; there the tabernacle, the garments of Aaron, the sacrifices, everything in the temple at Jerusalem, as also their statutes, were all representative. Among the ancients existed the Science of Correspondences, which is also that of representatives. This was the science of sciences, and was especially cultivated in Egypt,— hence their hieroglyphics. From this science they knew what was signified by animals of every kind; also what by trees of every kind; what by mountains, hills, rivers, fountains; and also what by the sun, moon, and stars. And as all their worship was representative, consisting of mere correspondences, therefore they celebrated worship on mountains and hills, and also in groves and gardens; hence, also, they consecrated fountains, and in their adorations of God, turned their faces to the rising sun. Moreover, they sculptured horses, oxen, calves, lambs, and also birds, fishes, and serpents, and these they placed in their houses and elsewhere, in a certain order, according to the spiritual things which they represented, or, what is the same, to which they corresponded. Similar images they placed also in their temples, in order to call to their remembrance the holy things which they signified.* In process of time, when the knowledge of the science of correspondences had perished, their posterity began to worship those sculptures as holy in themselves, not knowing that the ancients, their ancestors, saw nothing holy in the images themselves but only by means of them called to mind the holy things which they represented. From this source, now, arose the idolatries which filled the whole world, as well as Asia and its islands, as Africa and Europe. To the end that these idolatries might be extirpated, it was brought about by the Lord's divine providence, that a new religion, accommodated to the genius of the Orientals, should be raised up, in which there should be something from both Testaments of the Word, and which should teach that the Lord came into the world, and that He was the greatest prophet, the wisest of all, and the Son of God. This was done by means of Mahomet, from whom that religion is called the Mahometan. This religion was raised up through the Lord's providence, and accommodated, as remarked, to the genius of the Orientals, to the end that it might destroy the idolatries of so many nations, and give them some knowledge concerning the Lord, before they came into the spiritual world; which religion would not have been received by so many kingdoms, and thus could not have extirpated their idolatries, unless it had been accommodated in a measure to their ideas and character."—*Divine Providence*, n. 255.

From the above statements, then, we learn that the ancients, the

---

* In this statement of Swedenborg, we have a complete explanation of the strange idolatries of the Egyptian and other ancient nations. We can now understand how the former came to worship calves, serpents and other animals, viz., through finding in their houses and temples the forms of those animals, placed there by their forefathers, who were acquainted with the science of correspondences. For a *calf* corresponds to the *affection of knowing;* a *serpent* to the sensual principle, hence to *circumspection*, which explains what is meant by the wisdom (or rather prudence) of the serpent. From the same source, also, is derived an explanation of the existence of strange compound forms of animals, as the sphynx of Egypt, and the winged bull of Nineveh. The science of correspondences will enable us to interpret these. The sphinx is compounded of a woman's face and a lion's form; a woman is the emblem of affection and love, and a lion of the power of truth; hence the two united represent probably the union of goodness and truth. The winged bull of Nineveh—found by Mr. Layard, and now placed in the British Museum—is compounded of the head of a man with the form of a bull, and winged. Man represents wisdom, a bull natural affection, and wings spiritual truth. Hence the whole figure is a representation of wisdom sustained by spiritual truths, and completed by natural affections,—thus the three principles of the mind in their order, the celestial, the spiritual, and the natural. By the same key, doubtless (the science of correspondences), may all or most of the symbolic hieroglyphics be interpreted; the Rosetta stone is a key merely to the phonetic or alphabetic hieroglyphics, which are wholly a distinct and inferior class.

moderns, the Pagans, the Mahometans, all nations and peoples, indeed, throughout the world, are indebted for their religious knowledge more or less directly to the written Word. Thus the fountain of all religious light is Divine Revelation. In what has been said, this may be seen from a historical point of view; but there is a spiritual point of view from which it appears still more strikingly; for the whole Gentile world is at this moment influenced by the existence of the written Word in Christendom, even though the fact of its existence may be quite unknown to them. This truth, as Swedenborg presents it, is very curious and interesting, and something entirely new. The following is the view he presents of it:—

"There cannot be conjunction with heaven, unless there be somewhere on the earth a church which is in possession of the Word, and which has thus a knowledge of the Lord; because the Lord is the God of heaven and earth, and without the Lord there is no salvation. It is sufficient that there be a church which is in possession of the Word, even though it consists of comparatively few; for still, by means of the Word so possessed, the Lord is present throughout the whole world, since by that means heaven is in conjunction with mankind. In what manner the presence and conjunction of the Lord and heaven are effected in all countries by means of the Word, shall be shown. The whole heaven in the Lord's sight, is as *one man;* such also is the church. In this *man* the church where the Word is read and where the Lord is thereby known, is as the *heart and lungs.* Now, as from these two fountains of life in the human body all the other organs, members and viscera subsist and live, so also all those in every part of the earth who have any religion, who worship one God, and live good lives, and thus make a part of this (collective) *man,* subsist and live from the conjunction of the Lord with heaven and the church by means of the Word. For the Word in the church, even though that church consist of but few respectively, is yet life to the rest from the Lord through heaven,—just as the members and viscera of the whole body receive life through the heart and lungs. The communication also is similar. For this reason the Christians among whom the Word is read, constitute the breast, as it were, of the before-mentioned *man.* They are also in the centre of all; around them (spiritually viewed) are the Roman Catholics; around these are the Mahometans who acknowledge the Lord as the greatest prophet, and as the Son of God; after these are the Africans; and the furthest circumference is constituted by the nations and peoples of Asia and the Indies. In the centre where the Christians are, the light is brightest; for light in the heavens is divine truth proceeding from the Lord as a Sun there; and since the Word is divine truth, the greatest light is with those who are in possession of the Word; light thence, as from a centre, diffuses itself through all the surrounding parts, even to the extremities; and hence the illumination of the nations and peoples out of the church by means of the Word. This may be illustrated by comparison with the heat and light proceeding from the natural sun, which cause vegetation in trees and shrubs, even such as are not exposed to their direct influence, but are planted in shady places, which, nevertheless, do not fail to grow if the sun be only risen above the horizon."—D. S. S. 104–109.

This is a striking and beautiful passage, containing truth as important and interesting as it is novel. And how does it enhance the value of the Holy Word, to know that our possession and pious perusal of it is, unconsciously to us, influencing the most distant nations by spiritual communication! We are apt, with our merely natural ideas, to think that the only means of communication between ourselves and the Indies or Africans, is by crossing vast continents and seas. We forget that there is a world of mind in which there is no space, but in which all are allied by a spiritual connection, which, though unseen and unknown to us, is yet plainly seen by the Omniscient Ruler of the universe. Our author proceeds:—

"It may thus be plainly seen that the Word which is read in the Protestant Church, enlightens all nations and peoples by spiritual communication. Hence it is provided by the Lord that there should always be a church on the earth in which the Word is read, and where consequently the Lord is known. When, therefore, the Word was well-nigh cast aside by the Romish Church, then, by the Lord's divine providence, the Reformation was brought about and the Word was again received. So, likewise, when the Word was entirely falsified and adulterated by the Jewish nation, and thus rendered in a manner null, it pleased the Lord himself to descend from heaven and come into the world to fulfil the Word, and thus renew and restore it, and again give light to the inhabitants of the earth, according to these words of the Lord—'The people that sat in darkness saw a great light; to them that sat in the region and shadow of death, hath light sprung up.' (Matt. iv. 16.) And it having been foretold that at the end of the present church, also, darkness would arise in consequence of its members not knowing and acknowledging the Lord as the God of heaven and earth, and separating faith from charity, therefore, lest the genuine understanding of the Word, and consequently the church, should perish, it has pleased the Lord now to reveal the spiritual sense of the Word, and to show that the Word in that sense, and from that in the natural sense, treats of the Lord and the church, and of them alone, with many other discoveries, by which the light of truth, which was well-nigh extinguished, might be restored."—D. S. S. 110–112.

Having thus far shown that the written Word, even though possessed by comparatively few, yet is and has in all time been a light to all nations, it is now to be shown that the Word is also the great medium of communication with heaven, and that without such a medium men would be in mental darkness, and would at length perish. On this point Swedenborg thus speaks:—

"Since man has broken his connection with heaven by turning his interiors away from heaven, and turning them to the world and himself by means of his love of self and love of the world, and thus withdrawing himself so as no longer to serve heaven as a basis and foundation, therefore a medium was promised by the Lord, which might be to heaven in the place of a basis and foundation, and also a medium for the conjunction of heaven with man. That medium is the Word. Unless such a Word had been given on this earth, the man of this earth would have been separated from heaven; and if separated from heaven, he would no longer have been rational, for the human rational exists from the influx of the light of heaven. I have been informed from heaven that the Most Ancient people had immediate revelation, since their interiors were turned to heaven; and that hence there was at that time conjunction of heaven with the human race. But after their times there was not such immediate revelation, but mediate by correspondences; for all their divine worship consisted of correspondences, whence the churches of that time were called representative churches. For they at that time knew what correspondence was, and what representation was, and that all things on earth correspond to spiritual things which are in heaven and in the church; wherefore the natural things which were the externals of their worship, served them as mediums for thinking spiritually, thus with the angels. After the science of correspondences and representatives was obliterated, then the Word was written, in which all the words and senses of the words are correspondences: thus they contain a spiritual or internal sense in which the angels are. Wherefore, when man reads the Word and perceives it according to the sense of the letter, the angels perceive it according to the internal or spiritual sense. In this way it is, that after man removed himself from heaven and broke the bond of connection, there was provided by the Lord a medium for the conjunction of man with heaven, namely, the Word. In what manner heaven is conjoined with man by means of the Word, may be seen from the following example:—In Isaiah it is written—' In that day there shall be a highway from Egypt to Assyria, and the Assyrian shall come into Egypt, and the Egyptian into Assyria, and the Egyptians shall serve with the Assyrians: in that day Israel shall be a third to Egypt and Assyria, a blessing in the midst of the land' (xix. 23, 24). How man thinks, and on the other hand how the angels think, when these words are read, will appear by comparing the sense of the letter with the internal sense. From the literal sense, man thinks that the Egyptians and Assyrians are to be converted to God, and accepted, and that they are to make one with the Israelitish nation; but from the internal sense angels think of the man of the spiritual church, who is there described; whose spiritual principle is represented by Israel, his natural principle by the Egyptian, and his rational principle by the Assyrian. [A highway from Egypt to Assyria signifies an orderly communication and connection between the natural and rational principles of the mind; and Israel 'a blessing in the midst of the land,' signifies that the spiritual principle within will be a source of blessing and peace to the whole mind.] Here the natural and spiritual senses still make one, because they correspond: wherefore when the angels thus speak spiritually, and man thinks naturally, they are conjoined almost like soul and body. The internal sense of the Word, indeed, is its soul, and the letter its body. Such is the Word throughout; hence it is evident, that it is the medium of conjoining man with heaven."—H. H. 306–309.

In confirmation of the truth that the Word is a medium of communication with heaven, Swedenborg adduces his own experience:—

"That the spiritual angels are in the spiritual sense of the Word, and the celestial angels in its celestial sense, has been proved to me by much experience. While I was reading the Word in its literal sense, it was given me to perceive that communication was opened with the heavens, sometimes with one society, sometimes with another. What I understood according to the natural sense, the spiritual angels understood according to the spiritual sense, and the celestial angels according to the celestial sense, and this in an instant. As this communication has been perceived by me many thousand times, I have not the least doubt remaining as to its reality. There are spirits, also, below the heavens who abuse this communication; for they read over particular passages in the literal sense of the Word, and immediately observe and note the society with which communication is effected. From these circumstances it has been given me to know by sensible experience, that the Word in its literal sense is a divine medium of conjunction with the Lord and with heaven."—D. S. S. 64.

He adds, in another place:—

"While I read through the Word, from the first chapter of Isaiah even to the last of Malachi, and the Psalms of David, and kept the thought on the spiritual sense, it was given me clearly to perceive that every verse communicated with some society of heaven, and thus the whole Word with the universal heaven."—T. C. R. 292.

In the following statement, there is presented a striking and beautiful instance of the spiritual effect produced, not only by reading, but also by singing the Word in a church on earth:—

"There were certain African spirits from Abyssinia with me, whose ears on a certain occasion were opened, that they might hear singing in a church in the world from the Psalms of David. By this they were affected with such delight that they joined in the singing. Presently, however, their ears were closed, so that they could not hear anything thence; but they were then affected with a still greater degree of delight, because it was spiritual, and they were at the same time filled with intelligence, for that Psalm treated of the Lord and of redemption. The cause of this increase of delight was, that there was then granted them a communication with that society in heaven which *was in conjunction with those* who were singing that Psalm in the world."—*Sacred Scripture*, n. 108.

Does not this interesting circumstance teach us the importance of chanting the Word in our public worship? Hymns of human composition, may also, no doubt, be properly and profitably used; but we should never omit the other. And how much it will add to the elevation of our spirits on such occasions, to reflect that while chanting a Psalm, or indeed any part of the Divine Word, we are for the time in spiritual consociation with the angels of heaven! In our private singing or reading of the Word, also, it will tend greatly to increase our interest in the sacred duty, to reflect that every verse we read aloud communicates with some angelic society; and that if we are reading in a reverential frame of mind, our spirits are thereby brought into consociation with its blessed inhabitants.

"The Word in the letter," says Swedenborg, "is like a cabinet, in which lie in order precious stones, pearls, and diadems; and when man accounts the Word holy, and reads it for the sake of uses of life, the thoughts of his mind are comparatively like one who holds such a cabinet in his hand, and sends it up to heaven; and in its ascent it is opened, and the precious things therein come to the angels, who are inwardly delighted with seeing and examining them." —*True Christian Religion*, 238.

It is a curious and interesting fact, that, as stated by our author, the angels are more particularly affected when the Word is read by children.

"It may seem a paradox," says he, "but nevertheless it is most true, that the angels have a clearer and fuller understanding of the internal sense of the Word when it is read by little boys and girls, than when it is read by grown up persons who are not in a state of faith grounded in charity. The reason is, because little children are in a state of mutual love and innocence, and consequently the receptive vessels of their minds are extremely tender and almost of a celestial nature, so as to be pure faculties of reception, which therefore are capable of being disposed by the Lord for the purpose, although this does not come to the children's perception, except by a certain sensation of delight, suitable to their state and genius."—*Arcana Cœlestia*, n. 1776.

We may now see the reason why the Word, especially of the Old Testament, is so full of stories, as the account of the Garden of Eden, the story of Joseph, the history of Samson, and numerous others. It is for the sake of children in particular, that the Word is thus written. Were it a book merely of profound philosophy and theology—as some would wish it to be—is it not evident that none but philosophers and theologians would read it? Children and simple people would be driven from its pages; and thus not only would these lose the delight and benefit derived from its literal sense, and still more from the interior communication thereby opened with heaven, but the angels, also, would be deprived of a portion of their delight, which, as just shown, they receive from the reading of the Word by children and simple good people. And yet, underneath these simple stories is a mine of truth infinite in depth, capable of instructing not only philosophers and theologians, but even the angels of heaven, for ever. So wonderfully constituted is the Divine Word!

No. III.

But now the question may be asked, Are angels entirely dependent on man for the reading of the Word? Do they not possess it themselves in the heavens? Swedenborg answers this question. Certainly they do possess the Word, and read it just as men do. But their Word differs from ours: they have it not there in the literal sense, but in the spiritual sense; the internal sense of our Word, or that which is within the letter, is what constitutes the Word as it appears in heaven.

"The Word in heaven is written in a spiritual style, which differs entirely from a natural style. A spiritual style consists of mere letters, each involving some particular sense; and there are marks above the letters which exalt the sense. As their writing is of such a nature, there are not any names of persons and places in their Word as in ours; but instead of names are the things which they signify. Thus, instead of Moses, is mentioned the historical word; instead of Elias, the prophetical word; instead of Abraham, Isaac, and Jacob, the Lord with respect to his divine-celestial, his divine-spiritual, and his divine-natural principles; instead of Aaron, the priestly office; instead of David, the kingly office, each in relation to the Lord; instead of the names of the twelve sons of Jacob, or the tribes of Israel, and instead of the names of the Lord's twelve disciples, various things respecting heaven and the church; instead of Zion and Jerusalem, the church as to doctrine derived from the Word; instead of the land of Canaan, the church itself; instead of the places and cities in that land, both on this side and beyond Jordan, various things relating to the church and to doctrine. So also with numbers. These do not occur in the copies of the Word written in heaven; but instead of them, the things to which the numbers correspond. It may hence be seen that the Word in heaven corresponds to our Word, and that consequently they are one, for correspondence makes things one."

He adds:—

"What is wonderful, the Word in heaven is so written that the simple understand it in simplicity, and the wise in wisdom; for, as above observed, there are various points and marks over the letters, which exalt the sense, but to which the simple do not attend, nor do they understand their meaning; whereas the wise take note of them, every one in proportion to his wisdom, even to its highest degree. A copy of the Word, written by angels inspired by the Lord, is kept in every considerable society in its sacred repository, in order to preserve it from alteration in any of its points or marks. In the sacred repository where the copy of the Word is kept, the light is bright and flaming, exceeding every degree of light that shines in the other parts of heaven. The reason is, that the Lord is in the Word."—D. S. S. 71–73.

Having thus presented from the writings of Swedenborg, many new and elevating views of the Divine Word, I wish now to set forth in a clear light the nature of its inspiration,—a subject which has been much discussed, but which is not in general clearly understood. In the first place, let us define the word *inspiration*. Inspiration, proper or plenary, means *being filled with the Divine*. When we say, then, that the Word is inspired, we mean that it is filled with Divinity, so as to be purely Divine; and since whatever is Divine is infinite, therefore the Holy Word contains infinite truth,—truth inexhaustible by men or angels. This is taught by Swedenborg in the following passage:—

"It is a divine truth that there are indefinite things in each expression of the Word, which appears to man so simple and rude; yea, that there is contained therein more than the universal heaven; and that its arcana may be presented by the Lord before the angels, with perpetual variety, to eternity."—A. C. 1936.

"The world, even the learned part of it, has heretofore imagined that the historicals of the Word are merely historicals, and infold nothing deeper. And although they have said that every iota is divinely inspired, still by this they meant nothing more than that such historicals were made known by revelation, and that certain tenets may be deduced from them applicable to the doctrine of faith, and profitable to those who teach and to those who are taught; as also that, in consequence of being divinely inspired, those narratives have a divine force on men's minds, and are effective of good above all other histories. But historicals, considered in themselves, effect little toward man's amendment, and nothing towards eternal life, for in the other life they are sunk in oblivion. Of what use, for instance, could it be to know concerning Hagar, a maid-servant, that she was given to Abram by Sarai? or to know the history of Ishmael, or even that of Abram? Nothing is necessary for souls in order to their entering into heaven and enjoying bliss, that is, eternal life, but what has reference to the Lord and is from the Lord. These are the things, to communicate which the Word was given, and which are contained in its interiors. Inspiration implies that in all parts of the Word, even the most minute, are contained celestial things which have reference to love or goodness, and spiritual things, which have reference to faith or truth, consequently things divine. For what is inspired by the Lord, descends from Him through the angelic heaven, and so through the world of spirits, till it reaches man, before whom it presents itself such as the Word is in its letter."—A. C. 1886-7.

This being the character of the Divine Word, namely, that besides the literal sense, it contains an internal sense which is exhaustless in depth and wisdom, it will be at once evident that man had nothing to do with its composition, for in its interiors it is infinitely above man's range of thought. Had it passed through [or proceeded from] any human mind, it would be merely finite and human, not infinite and Divine. The persons, therefore, who were employed as instruments for writing the Divine Word, as Moses, David, and the rest, did not, as some have supposed, first receive the truth into their minds, and then express it in their own way—not at all; that would have destroyed its plenary inspiration altogether: the weak and finite medium could not but have perverted, or at least modified, what it received, so that what was written would not have been a Divine but a human composition. The writers of the Scripture were in truth mere penmen,—they wrote simply by dictation; oftentimes, doubtless, having little or no understanding of what they were writing. They heard a voice, and wrote down what the voice uttered. Thus it was not properly the *men* that were inspired, but the *writing*. That this was the case is thus plainly taught by Swedenborg:—

"I have been informed how the Lord spoke with the prophets by whom the Word was written. He did not speak with them, as with the ancients, by an influx into their interiors, but by spirits who were sent to them, whom the Lord filled with his aspect, and thus inspired words which they dictated to the prophets; so that it was *not influx but dictation*. And since the *words* came forth immediately from the Lord, therefore, *each of them was filled with the Divine*, and contains in it an internal sense which is such that the angels of heaven perceive them in a celestial and spiritual sense, when men perceive them in a natural sense. Thus the Lord by the Word has conjoined the world to heaven."—H. H. 254.

Again, he says:—

"In regard to the prophets, by whom the Word was written, they wrote as the spirit from the Divine dictated; for *the very words which they wrote were uttered in their ears*."—A. C. 7055.

He also states who it was that uttered the voice which they heard:—

"There were angels who were sent to men, and who also spake by the prophets; but what they spake was not *from* the angels but *by* them. For the state of the angels at that time was such that they knew no otherwise than that they were Jehovah,—that is, the Lord; nevertheless, when they had done speaking they presently returned into their former state. This was the case with the angels who spake the Word of the Lord, as has been given me to know by much experience. This is the reason that the angels were sometimes called Jehovah, as was evidently the case with the angel who appeared to Moses in the bush, of whom it is thus written:—'And the *angel* of *Jehovah* appeared to him in a flame of fire out of the midst of the bush. And when *Jehovah* saw that he turned aside to see, *God* called to him out of the midst of the bush.—*God* said to Moses, I Am that I Am.' Ex. iii. 2, 4, 14. From which words it is evident that it was an angel that appeared to Moses as a flame in the bush, and that he spake as Jehovah, because the Lord as Jehovah spake *by* him. For in order that man may be spoken to by vocal expressions, which are articulate sounds in the ultimates of nature, the Lord makes use of the ministry of angels by filling them with the Divine, and by laying asleep what is of their own proprium, so that they know no otherwise than that they are Jehovah; thus the Divine of Jehovah which is in the Supreme, descends into the lowest principles of nature in which man is."—A. C. 1925.

From this passage we learn with distinctness the nature of the inspiration of the Divine Word, and the manner in which the Word was written. We see that it did not come from any man's mind, nor even from any angel's mind, but directly from the Divine, angels and men being made use of merely as instruments—the former to speak it, and the latter to write it down. Nay, in regard to the

Decalogue or Ten Commandments which were the germ, and which contain, as it were, the very essence of the Word, not even the ministry of either men or angels was used; but, as declared, they were written on tables of stone by the very finger of God himself.*

We thus perceive that the Word of the Lord is purely divine, and that man had nothing to do with its composition, but acted merely as its scribe or penman. This must have been the case even in regard to those narratives of facts in which the writer himself was concerned. That part of the Divine word, for instance, which describes the deliverance of the Israelites from Egypt, their journey through the desert, and the attendant circumstances, though written by Moses, yet was not composed out of Moses' own mind and memory, as an ordinary historian would narrate facts which he had witnessed. For had this been the case, it would have been not the Word of God but the word of man; for though the subject of the narrative may have been a history of God's doings, yet that would not have made it the Word of God, but it would still have been a mere *human narrative* of God's doings, and thus the word of man, with all the imperfections to which every human composition is liable. Nor would it have contained any internal or angelic sense; nor, consequently, would it have been able to effect communication with heaven, which, as before shown, the Divine Word does. Consequently the case must have been, that in writing those naratives Moses' own memory was for the time quiescent; he was not allowed to use it, but wrote by simple dictation.

To be satisfied that this must have been the case, we have only to read what is stated by Swedenborg in regard to the wondrous sublimity and beauty of the internal sense of those narratives:—

"The Word of the Lord," says he, "when read by a man who loves it and who lives in charity, is displayed by the Lord to the angels with such beauty and pleasantness, accompanied also with representatives, that every particular is perceived as if it had life. That the Word of the Lord is thus displayed to good spirits and angels, it has been granted me both to see and hear. A certain spirit came to me not long after his decease, as I concluded from the circumstance that as yet he did not know that he was in the other life, imagining that he still lived in the world. It was perceived that he was devoted to studious pursuits, concerning which I conversed with him. But suddenly he was taken up on high, which surprised me, and led me to suspect that he was of an aspiring temper, for such

---

* Ex. xxxi. 18.

are wont to be carried up on high. Presently, however, I perceived that he was taken up amongst those angelic spirits who are just at the entrance into heaven. From this situation he discoursed with me, saying that he saw things of such sublimity as no human imagination could conceive. I was reading at the time the first chapter of Deuteronomy concerning the Jewish people, and concerning the spies who were sent to explore the land of Canaan. As I read, he said that he perceived none of the things contained in the literal sense, but only those in the spiritual sense, and that they were wonderful beyond description. Certain spirits who were with me at the time, and who before could not believe that the Word of the Lord was of such a nature, began now to repent of their incredulity, and said, in that state, that they believed, because they heard the other spirit say that he heard and saw that the Word was so full of wonders. But other spirits still persisted in their unbelief, saying that it was not so, but that it was all mere fancy; wherefore these were suddenly taken up also, and from their elevation discoursed with me, confessing that it was very far from fancy, for that they really perceived it to be so, and this with a more exquisite perception than that of any of the senses which they had in the life of the body. Presently others also were taken up into the same heaven, and amongst them one with whom I had been acquainted in the world, who bore the same testimony, saying that he was too much astonished at the glory of the Word in its internal sense to be able to describe it. Being melted with compassion at man's unbelief, he added, that it was wonderful that they could remain so totally ignorant of the internal things of the Word."—A. C. 1769.

Now, the wonderful things here referred to are contained in the interiors of a chapter which in the letter seems a very ordinary narrative from the lips of Moses, in which he is recapitulating to the Israelites a portion of the adventures which they had passed through. In the literal sense, it is a mere recounting of certain external circumstances and facts recalled by the leader to the minds of his followers, and such as we should certainly have presumed Moses spoke from his own memory. And yet we learn that this simple narrative contains such a wonderful internal sense as to move and delight spirits and angels, and to bring magnificent scenes before their view. Is not this sufficient to satisfy us that no part of that narrative, not even the most insignificant, which passes under the name of the Mosaic record, was composed in Moses' own mind at all, but was written entirely by dictation from the Divine?—for how else could it contain an internal sense far above the comprehension of Moses himself, or of any man? Thus is the whole Word truly a dictation from God, and it is this which gives it its inspiration, that is, its divinity.

No. IV.

But we have now to make clear the distinction that exists between verbal and personal inspiration,—between the plenary inspiration, or full Divinity that belongs to a writing dictated from God, and that partial inspiration, or, as it should more properly be termed, *illumination*, which has occasionally been bestowed upon men. This distinction, which is most important, has in general been overlooked, or rather not understood, by commentators on Scripture. They have spoken of the inspired *writers*, rather than of the inspired *writings*; they speak of Moses, David and Isaiah as men whose minds were in a certain manner acted upon by the spirit of God, and yet who retained their own proper characters, and who wrote from their own thoughts. Now, this we have shown to be an error. The persons who were made use of as instruments for uttering and writing down the Divine Word, and whose names are attached to the various books of Scripture, were, as we have shown, mere penmen, writing by simple dictation,—merely putting down what they heard a voice utter. So far as the mere writing was concerned, a child could have done it as well as they. The reason that men were selected—men, too, of power and character—was because most of them, as Isaiah and Jeremiah as well as the Evangelists, had to be preachers and apostles as well as penmen, and were compelled to utter the Divine testimony in the midst of a wicked and violent people. Yet it is to be understood that the state of their own minds and individual characters was entirely distinguished from the nature of the message which they were sent to utter and to write down. In proof of this, men were sometimes selected whose personal characters were not good, who were wilful and disobedient. Look at the case of the prophet Jonah, for instance. No one could call him a "holy prophet," in view of his personal character; yet what he was commissioned to write is as fully and truly the Word of God as any other part of the Sacred Writings, and has its Divine and internal sense. From this single case, it may be perceived how entirely the inspiration of the prophecy or writing is to be distinguished from the character of the man who was its writer.

With the writers of the Divine Word, then, there was not, properly speaking, any *personal* inspiration at all. And this fact, as before shown, is the very thing that makes the Word Divine, namely, that it passed through no human mind, but merely was uttered by a human tongue, or written down by a human hand, in obedience to an audible dictation. This is expressly declared in these words uttered by David in his character as the "Sweet Psalmist of Israel:"—"The Spirit of the Lord," says he, "spake *by* me, and His Word was in my *tongue*," 2 Sam. xxiii. 1, 2,—in his *tongue*, be it observed, not in his *mind*. But personal inspiration, or *illumination* as it should rather be termed, is an enlightenment of the man's own faculties. It is a greater thing for the writer, but infinitely less for the writing; for it causes what he utters to be still the word of man, not the Word of God; and between these there is an infinite distance, as between what is human and what is Divine. What is uttered or written from mere personal inspiration or illumination contains no internal sense capable of being opened to spirits and angels; hence it is not a medium of connection with heaven as the Divine Word is. It may be truth, even truth without error; but still it is finite truth, not infinite. All that it contains appears on the face of it; it may teach lofty wisdom, yet still finite and human. Whereas the Divine Word, that which comes by dictation directly from the Lord, is in every sentence infinite and inexhaustible, capable of being opened more and more, and of sending forth deeper and deeper truth for ever. Hence, not a jot or tittle, as is declared, of the Divine Word can fail or pass away; for it is eternal as the God from whom it comes.

It may here be remarked, that what Swedenborg claims for himself is not inspiration, but *illumination* :—a peculiar illumination and illustration of his own rational faculties, giving him an interior discernment and perception of spiritual truth, and particularly of the internal or spiritual sense of the Divine Word. This mental illumination, however, was a distinct thing from the opening of his spiritual sight, by which he was enabled to look into the spiritual world. Both of these gifts were necessary to the accomplishment of his mission, which was both to lay open and expound the internal sense of the Word, and at the same time to make known to man the nature and condition of the world of spirits, heaven, and hell. This being the character of Swedenborg's writings,—human, rational expositions of the Scriptures, and explanatory accounts of the state of man after death,—though containing essential and most interior truth, they are still human writings, because they proceeded from or through a human mind. They therefore have no resemblance to, and bear no comparison with, the Holy Word which, having passed through no human mind, but being given by direct dictation from the Lord, is purely Divine and infinite, not only in the matter, but in the manner, and in every word and letter.

Among the writings contained in the Book which we call "The Bible," there are examples of both kinds of inspiration, the verbal and the personal, or, as they should rather be termed, of plenary inspiration and of mental illumination. The book of Proverbs, for instance, belongs to the latter class; the Psalms to the former. And the difference may be at once perceived from the style alone. In reading the Proverbs of Solomon, you perceive yourself to be perusing a book of profound practical wisdom, the composition of a mind enlightened and elevated to a high degree; but when you understand the meaning of the literal sense before you, you know all that is there. The sense is plain, because the writing is human; it is from a mind like our own, only more profoundly enlightened. The water is clear, because comparatively shallow. But in reading the Psalms, you feel yourself sailing over an ocean; your eye may penetrate a little way beneath the surface, but you do not see to the bottom,— you cannot, for it is fathomless; the waters seem less transparent on account of their very depth. Every part of the Proverbs can be understood by any person of ordinary mind; but much of the Psalms is, in the letter alone, nearly or quite unintelligible.

A similar distinction may be observed in the New Testament between the style of the Epistles and that of the Gospels. The Epistles are simple and intelligible, though containing deep truth and great knowledge of the human heart, abounding in excellent practical lessons, and sometimes glowing with apostolic fervor,—as is the case, for instance, with the famous chapter on charity, in the Epistle to the Corinthians. (1 Cor. xiii.) Still you feel them to be human compositions, expressed in ordinary language, such as is common between man and man. (And it is, no doubt, in consequence of this greater plainness, that the Epistles are the favorite resort of preachers at the present day.) But open the Gospels, and at once you find yourself in another region of thought and feeling altogether. The lofty, solemn style at once impresses the reader with a perception of their superhuman character. "And the high priest answered and said, I adjure thee by the living God, that thou tell us whether thou be the Christ, the Son of God. Jesus saith unto him, Thou hast said; nevertheless, I say unto you, Hereafter ye shall see the Son of Man sitting on the right hand of power, and coming in the clouds of heaven." (Matt. xxvi. 63, 64.) On reading such words as these, you feel yourself in a Divine presence; there cannot be familiarity here; this is not the style and language of man;—you are again sailing over an ocean; you are gazing into the blue depths of heaven!

That the Gospels were not written by the Evangelists from their own mind or memory, a very little reflection will show. Those books, be it observed, are not mere statements of historical facts, such as might have been seen and remembered; but they contain, also, long discourses, such as the Sermon on the Mount, in Matthew, and detailed conversations, such as occurred between the Lord and the Jews, as recorded in John. Now these, it will be at once seen, could never have been remembered with any accuracy, as any one may satisfy himself by trying to recollect the language of a discourse which he may have heard but a week or a month ago. And this will be the more evident when we consider that the Gospels were not written till some thirty years after the Lord's crucifixion (the Gospel of John not till sixty years after). How could the writers have possibly remembered the Lord's exact words after that length of time? And no one will for a moment suppose, that these unlettered fishermen ever thought of such a thing as *taking notes* of these discourses and conversations, after the custom of modern times. Moreover, two out of the four Evangelists, namely, Mark and Luke, were not of the number of the twelve Apostles, and themselves probably never saw or heard the Lord at all. It is evident, therefore, that if the Gospels are accurate and reliable statements of what the Lord did, and especially of what He said, they could never have been drawn from the writers' own minds or memories, but must have been written by instruction from above, that is, by inspiration. But this could not have been mere personal inspiration or illumination; for this being merely an enlightenment of man's own faculties, cannot introduce anything into the memory, but merely illustrates what is already there. The Gospels, then, must have been written by plenary inspiration, that is, by *dictation*, in which process the very words are uttered in the writer's ears, and he acts merely as a penman. All parts of the Scripture that have an internal sense must be of this character; and the Gospels have such an internal sense, and thus, like the books of Moses, effect communication with heaven.

In our English Bible the important distinction which exists between those books which are plenarily inspired, and thus have an internal sense, and those which have no such sense, does not appear in the arrangement; they are mingled promiscuously together. Not so with the Hebrew Bible; this distinction is there carefully observed. The books that are not plenarily inspired are thrown together into an Appendix at the end, and are entitled *Hagiographa*. This distinction must have been of Divine appointment and providence; for the Jews, who knew nothing of an internal sense in any of the books, could not have made this distinction themselves. It is to be observed, moreover, that from some cause they have classed two of the plenarily inspired books with the Hagiographa, namely, the Psalms and the Prophecy of Daniel; but they have been careful to admit none of the uninspired books into the higher division. When, however, the first Greek translation was made, commonly called the Septuagint (which was done at Alexandria, in Egypt, about two centuries before the Christian era), the distinction between the two classes of writings was not preserved, as it ought to have been; but they were mingled together,—reference being had, in their arrangement, merely to chronological order. Thus, for instance, the Book of Ruth, which is one of the Hagiographa, was thrown in next after Judges, because the facts mentioned in Ruth belong to that period in the Jewish history. So, also, the Proverbs of Solomon were arranged next after the Psalms of his father David; and so on. Thus the infinitely more important distinction of character and class was sacrificed to the comparatively trifling matter of chronological order. And in this arrangement our English translators have followed, not the Hebrew original, as they should have done, but the Septuagint translation.

The books which, as Swedenborg shows, have an internal sense, and which, therefore, properly constitute the Divine Word, are the following:—the five books of Moses, Joshua, Judges, the two books of Samuel, the two books of Kings, the Psalms of David, the Prophets Isaiah, Jeremiah, Lamentations, Ezekiel, Daniel, Hosea, Joel, Amos, Obadiah, Jonah, Micah, Nahum, Habakkuk, Zephaniah, Haggai, Zechariah, Malachi; and in the New Testament, the four gospels, Matthew, Mark, Luke and John, and the Apocalypse. (A. C. 10,325.) The books which constitute the Hagiographa, and have not an internal sense, are the following:—Ruth, first and second Chronicles, Ezra, Nehemiah, Esther, Job, Proverbs, Ecclesiastes, and Song of Solomon; of a similar character, in the New Testament, are the book of Acts, and the Epistles.

It is an interesting fact that, as stated by Swedenborg, our own earth is the only one in which there is a written Word,—the truths of revelation being made known in all other earths by word of mouth, through spirits and angels. On this earth, too, and on no other, the Lord was pleased to be born, that is, Jehovah was made man. The reason, however, for our being thus distinguished is not of a character to elevate but rather to lower us in our own estimation. It is because the people of this earth are the lowest or most external of all. Swedenborg shows that all the earths or worlds in the universe compose one grand system, the inhabitants of each earth having relation to some part or principle in man,—the whole being derived from Him who is essential man, God himself. The part which our earth corresponds to, is the external or sensual principle, which is the ultimate principle of humanity. On this account it was that the Divine chose to assume an external or ultimate human principle on this earth, rather than on any other. And for the same reason the Word was written here, that is, Divine Truth which in itself is mental and spiritual, was here expressed in a visible material form, namely, by characters or letters written or printed on material substances. Such a thing exists in no other earth. Nevertheless, through the Word thus written here, the great truth which it records of the Divine Incarnation, is made known to the spirits and angels who come into heaven from all other earths. On these interesting points Swedenborg thus speaks:—

"In every other earth, Truth Divine is manifested by word of mouth through spirits and angels, but this is done within families; for the human race, in most earths, dwell apart in families. Wherefore, Divine Truth, thus revealed by spirits and angels, is not conveyed far beyond families, and unless a new revelation constantly succeeds, it is either perverted or perishes. It is otherwise on our earth, where Truth Divine, which is the Word, remains in its integrity for ever.

"The principal reason why it pleased the Lord to be born and assume humanity on our earth, and not on another, was for the sake of the Word,—that this might be written on our earth, and when written, be published through the whole world, and, once published, might be preserved to all posterity; and thus it might be manifested that God was made man, even to all in the other life. That the principal reason was for the sake of the Word, is because the Word is Divine Truth itself, which teaches man that there is a God,—that there is a life after death,—that there is a heaven,—that there is a hell; and, moreover, teaches how man ought to live and to believe in order that he may come into heaven, and so be happy to eternity. All these things without revelation—thus, in this earth, without the Word—would have been altogether unknown; yet man is so created that he can never die.

"That the Word could be written on our earth, is because the art of writing has existed here from the most ancient times,—first, on the rind or bark of trees, next on skins or parchment, afterwards on paper, and lastly by types, as in printing. This was provided by the Lord for the sake of the Word. That the Word, also, might be published through the whole earth, is because a communication of all nations is here given, both by land and water, to all parts of the globe; hence, the Word, once written, could be passed from one nation to another, and be everywhere taught. Such communication was also provided by the Lord for the sake of the Word. That the Word once written could be preserved to all posterity, thus to thousands and thousands of years; and that it has been so preserved, is a known thing. That thus it might be manifested that God has been made Man; for this is the first and most essential thing, on account of which the Word was given. For no one can believe in a God and love a God whom he cannot comprehend under some appearance; wherefore, they who acknowledge only what is incomprehensible, sink in thought into nature, and thus believe in no God. Wherefore it pleased the Lord to be born here, and to make this manifest by the Word, so that it might be known not only on this globe, but also that, through that Word, it might be made manifest to all in the universe who come into heaven from any earth whatsoever; for in heaven there is inter-communication of all knowledges.

"It is to be known that the Word in our earth is the medium of union between the world and heaven; for which end there is a correspondence of all things in the letter of the Word with Divine things in heaven. The Word, also, in its supreme and inmost sense treats solely of the Lord, of his kingdom in the heavens and in the earths, and of love and faith from and in Him, and, consequently, of life from and in Him. Such things are represented to the angels in heaven *from whatsoever earth they come*, when the Word of our earth is read and preached. It is to be known that the Lord acknowledges and receives all, from whatsoever earth they are, who acknowledge and worship God under a human form, since God under a human form is the Lord. And as the Lord appears to the inhabitants of these earths under an angelic form which is the human form, therefore, when spirits and angels from these earths hear from the spirits and angels of our earth that God actually is Man, they receive that Word, acknowledge it, and rejoice that it is so.

"To the reasons which have been adduced why the Lord was born on this earth, and not on another, this may be added,—that the inhabitants, spirits, and angels of our earth have reference in the Grand Man, to the external and corporeal sense; and the external and corporeal sense is the ultimate, in which the interiors of life close, and in which they rest as on their common basis. The case is similar with Truth Divine in the letter which is called the Word, and which, for this reason, also, was given in this earth and not in another. And whereas the Lord is the Word, and its first and last, therefore, that all things might exist according to order, He was pleased to be born on this earth, and be made the Word, according to these words in John—'In the beginning was the Word, and the Word was with God, and the Word was God; and the Word was made flesh, and dwelt amongst us.'"—A. C. 9350–60.

CHAPTER XII.

The Doctrine of Correspondence Applied as a Key to the Spiritual and True Meaning of Matthew xvi. 18, 19—The Rock on which the Church is Built—The Keys of the Kingdom of Heaven, etc.*

THE Lord said to Peter, after he had confessed that He was "the Christ, the Son of the living God,"—"Blessed art thou, Simon Bar-jona; for flesh and blood hath not revealed it unto thee, but my Father which is in heaven. And I say also unto thee, that thou art Peter, and upon this rock I will build my church, and the gates of hell shall not prevail against it; and I will give unto thee the keys of the kingdom of heaven, and whatsoever thou shalt bind on earth shall be bound in heaven, and whatsoever thou shalt loose on earth shall be loosed in heaven." (Matt. xvi. 18, 19.)

The true doctrine of this passage is of immense importance, since it determines the validity or the futility of the claims assumed by the Roman Catholic Church to supremacy and infallibility, as being founded upon the rock against which the gates of hell shall never prevail; and also as possessing the keys of the kingdom of heaven, and consequently the power of opening and shutting heaven, or of exercising dominion over the invisible world. It must be admitted by all that the proper understanding of the Word is of the greatest importance, since the Word is divine truth which cannot enter into the mind as a living principle but in proportion as it is understood; no more than light can enter into the eye except the eye be opened to receive it. Hence the Lord "opened the understandings of his disciples, that they might understand the Scriptures." It is also well known that if a principle be assumed as true when it is not true, that principle will vitiate and falsify an entire system. Nothing, therefore, can be more important to the human mind and to the church than the right understanding of revealed truth. All the errors, per-

---

* From the *Intellectual Repository* for Jan., 1848, pp. 366–370.

versions and falsifications of the Pharisees and the Sadducees arose from their not "*knowing* (or *understanding*) *the Scriptures and the power of God.*" (Matt. xxii. 29.) The divine truth understood and applied to the life is the "power of God." Now, from a false interpretation of the passage in question, a direfully false principle has arisen, which has perverted and destroyed nearly every vestige of Christianity among those where this principle operates.

All these things were said of Peter on account of the confession he made that Jesus was "*the Christ, the Son of the living God;*" upon which the Lord pronounced him blessed, with the surname Bar-jona, or "son of a dove," in order to teach us that the primary, fundamental, and blessed principle of the church, is the acknowledgment of Jesus Christ as "*the Son of the living God.*" This confession and this faith is indeed the rock and foundation of the church, and the source of all blessing to man. For Jesus Christ, as the "Son of the living God," is not a mere man, however highly gifted with wisdom, benevolence, and power; nor is He the supposed second person in the Trinity,—but God Himself "manifest in the flesh,"—or, as the prophet says,—"THE MIGHTY GOD, THE EVERLASTING FATHER, THE PRINCE OF PEACE." This confession, therefore, of Peter, involves the great fundamental doctrine upon which the church must be built; for it acknowledges the Lord in his "glorious Body," or in his Divine Humanity, as the embodiment of all "the fulness of the Godhead." This acknowledgment and faith, as the rock upon which the church is built, is thus denoted by Peter, when pronounced "blessed," and called "Simon Bar-jona," or son of a dove; because Simon, as signifying, in Syriac, *hearing and obedience*, denotes faith in the heart or will, and not merely in the intellect; and faith, as a living principle in the heart and life, is the source from the Lord of all blessing and happiness to man and to the church. *Jona*, or the dove, is an emblem of that harmlessness, innocence, gentleness, meekness, purity and love which constitute the life of a genuine faith,—or of that faith which, as the apostle says, "worketh by love."

Thus the Christian Church is built upon this faith in the Lord Jesus Christ, as "its Author and Finisher," as the sole Object to Whom it should be directed, and from Whom it must derive all its saving efficacy and blessedness. Against the church founded upon this rock of a genuine faith, verily, "the gates of hell shall never prevail!" A rock, when mentioned in Scripture, is an emblem of the Lord as to Divine Truth. Hence the Lord is called a "*Rock*"—

(Psalm xviii. 2, 31)—the "*Rock of Salvation*"—(Deut. xxxii. 15)—and the apostle says, "they drank of that *spiritual Rock* which followed them, and that *Rock* was Christ." (1 Cor. x. 4.) The Rock, therefore, upon which the church is founded, is the divine truth coming from Him who is the Truth itself (John xiv. 6); and the man who hears the Lord's sayings and doeth them, builds his house upon a *Rock*. (Matt. vii. 24.) Because "to hear the Lord's sayings and do them," is to acknowledge Him as the great Object of faith and love,—as the Author and Finisher of our faith,—and to live according to his divine precepts. Hence the man's house, or the church in him, is built upon a Rock; and "however the rains may descend and the floods come, and the winds blow and beat against that house," it will not fall; thus "the gates of hell shall not prevail against it," because it is founded upon a rock.

"The keys of the kingdom of heaven" are given to this faith. For *keys* denote the power of opening and shutting; thus the Lord "has the *keys* of hell and of death;" because "He alone openeth and no man shutteth, and shutteth and no man openeth." (Rev. iii. 7.) Here it is divinely and expressly declared, that the Lord alone hath the keys, or the power to open and to shut, and that *no man* hath that power. How false and profane, therefore, it is to suppose that *any man*, or any *multitude of men*, whether they call themselves a church, a council or a synod, can open and shut heaven or hell, or that they can have any power over the invisible world. This power, therefore, belongs exclusively to the Lord Jesus Christ; nor can it, because it is infinite, be possibly transferred or given to any man. But the faith described above, inasmuch as it is from the Lord, and is, properly regarded, the Lord himself in his disciples and in his Church, therefore the keys are said to be given to Peter in order to teach us that the Lord, through a genuine faith founded upon Himself as the Rock, can close the gates of hell and open the portals of heaven to his Church; and that whatsoever that faith "shall bind upon earth, shall be bound in heaven, and whatsoever it shall loose upon earth, shall be loosed in heaven." Thus the *keys* or this power were not given to Peter *as a man*, but to the *living faith* which Peter then represented. For Peter was evidently a type, sometimes of a *living faith*, and sometimes of a *faith perverted and destroyed*, as in this very chapter (verses 22, 23), where he opposes the Lord on account of what He said respecting his temptations and sufferings, when the Lord calls him Satan, saying: "Get thee behind me, Satan, thou art an offence unto me; for thou savorest not the things that be of God, but those that be of men."

Now every one can see that Peter as "*Simon Bar-jona,*" and Peter as "*Satan*" and an "*offence*" to the Lord, are two very different characters, although comprised in the same man. Those, therefore, who take Peter as the founder of their church, and as having transferred the keys to his supposed successors, must beware lest by so doing they appear as "*Satan*" and as an "*offence*" in the Lord's sight, because "they savor (or seek after) not the things which be of God, but those which be of men." Peter, also, when he thrice denied the Lord, was evidently a type of the faith of the church utterly falsified, perverted and destroyed;—of that faith, and of that church connected therewith, which claims universal power over the minds and bodies of men, and over the invisible world; which withholds the Word of God from the people; which divides the bread from the wine in the sacrament of the Holy Supper; which forbids marriage to the priesthood, although the apostle declares, "*that a bishop should be the husband of one wife*" (1 Tim. iii. 2, 12; Titus i. 6), and that "to forbid to marry is a *doctrine of devils*" (1 Tim. iii. 1–3); and which opens the door to innumerable other abominations, the offspring of the teaching and doctrines of a perverse, falsified, anti-Christian faith,—a faith which *thrice* or utterly denies the Lord, and which entirely perverts and destroys every vestige of genuine Christianity.

The Lord says of those whose province and duty it was in the Jewish Church to teach the people, and likewise of those who occupy the same province in the Christian Church—"Woe unto you lawyers! for ye have taken away the key of knowledge; ye entered not in yourselves, and them that were entering in, ye hindered." (Luke xi. 52.) The *key of knowledge* is evidently the power of unlocking or of interpreting the Scriptures, that we may come to a knowledge of the truth. This key of knowledge is therefore the genuine doctrine by which the truths of the Word are interpreted and explained. Now, if this key had been applied to the interpretation of the passage quoted at the beginning of this article, no such state of things as the history of the church records, could have been witnessed. It would have been seen that every man becomes a member of the church in proportion as a living faith through hearing the Lord's words and doing them, is planted in his mind; upon which faith, as upon a rock, the church is built; and when this is the case with the members of the church in the aggregate, the Lord's kingdom is established.

The necessity of a key to the proper interpretation of Scripture is abundantly obvious. This necessity has been at all times seen and felt; and in the early period of the Christian church they endeavored to apply a key to the interpretation of this as well as of other passages of the Word. But the true key is the doctrine of correspondence between things spiritual and natural,—between the spirit and the letter. This key plainly teaches us what is meant by Peter, by Simon Bar-jona, by the rock, by the building of the church upon the rock, and by the gates of hell, etc. There is probably no passage in which the declaration of the apostle, "that the letter killeth, but the spirit giveth life," has been more fully verified than in this. For a merely literal interpretation has killed or destroyed nearly every principle of an enlightened and living faith in the Lord.

But to show that, as stated, in the earlier ages the most intelligent fathers interpreted the passage as denoting the church built upon an enlightened and living faith in the Lord, we will adduce what Chrysostom says in his 14th Homily on the passage, viz:—"On the rock, that is, on the faith which he confessed." Again, in his 163d Homily, he says—"The Lord does not say that he founds his Church upon Peter, for it is not founded upon any man, but upon the faith." And Augustin, in Tract X. on the first Epistle of John, says, "What is meant when the Lord says, Upon this rock I will build my Church? He means, upon this faith,—upon that which Peter declared when he said, Thou art the Christ, the Son of the living God." Thus the primitive writers plainly show to us, that they understood the passage as relating to the church founded upon the rock of a living faith in the Lord Himself. MINUS.

CHAPTER XIII.

CORRESPONDENCE APPLIED TO THE INTERPRETATION OF ISAIAH VII. 15.—"BUTTER AND HONEY SHALL HE EAT, THAT HE MAY KNOW TO REFUSE THE EVIL AND CHOOSE THE GOOD."*

THE entire prophecy of which these words form a part, relates to the Lord when He came into the world, and which was then especially fulfilled by Him. Commentators of every age have been not a little perplexed as to the meaning of this prophecy. The relation between eating butter and honey, and refusing evil and choosing good, is the difficulty which they could not surmount. It would be curious to examine what the most learned commentators down to Hitzig and Ewald have written upon this passage, in order to make some sense which the natural mind could comprehend and approve. But as this examination would not be profitable, we shall refrain.

That one of the divine names of the Lord in his Humanity is IMMANUEL or GOD-WITH-US, is, from this prophecy, abundantly evident, especially as it is quoted and confirmed by Matthew i. 23. That the Lord in his Humanity is GOD-WITH-US, is the divine basis of Christianity. Upon this great truth, this precious corner-stone, rests the entire structure of the Christian religion. "God manifest in the flesh,"—"God in Christ," are declarations of the Apostle which are equivalent to the appellation IMMANUEL. And when we further see it declared that "in Him dwelleth all the fulness of the Godhead bodily," we need no further proof that it was Jehovah God Himself, as declared by Zacharias, who visited and redeemed His people. (Luke i. 68.)

The great error of the old theology destroys the truth that Immanuel is Jehovah in the Humanity, or that God is manifest in the flesh. Instead of which, as the sole foundation of Christianity, it assumes the incarnation of a supposed second person in the Trinity, or a Son of God born from eternity; and by substituting this unscriptural and irrational idea in the place of *Immanuel*, or God Himself,

---

* From the *Intellectual Repository*, for Feb., 1848.

as becoming incarnate for the redemption of mankind, the entire foundation of the church is erroneous, and every doctrine is, in consequence, darkened with error. Build upon a false principle, and every thing you erect will partake of the falsity. Hence the great importance of a true foundation.

The Lord, as to the human nature He assumed from the virgin Mary, was laden with our infirmities, was in the "likeness of sinful flesh," and "was a man of sorrows and acquainted with grief." But He "sanctified Himself for our sakes, and became perfect through suffering;" that is, He glorified his Humanity. Now the first thing required in the divine process of glorification, as also in the process of regeneration, is the *knowledge of evil*, that we may cease to do it, and as a consequence, learn to choose and to do good. The entire process of regeneration consists in *refusing evil and choosing good as a principle of life*. And as the regeneration of man is an image of the Lord's glorification, it may also be said that his glorification also consisted in knowing and refusing evil and in choosing good. Not that evil, in the sense of sin, ever adhered to Him "who was without sin," but only as infirmity, and as hereditary tendency to evil. To supplant and utterly to reject these hereditary tendencies, is to *refuse the evil*, and, as a consequence, *to choose what is good*. But how the eating of butter and honey is connected with this process, remains to be seen.

And here we cannot be sufficiently thankful to the Father of mercies for the discovery, in these latter days, of the spiritual sense of the Holy Word; for it is from this sense alone that we can, in a satisfactory manner, see the relation between eating butter and honey and refusing evil and choosing good.

It must be evident, even to the natural mind when once awakened to perception and thought concerning the nature of God's Word, that *butter* and *honey* in this passage and elsewhere in the Scriptures, are used in a symbolic or emblematic sense. Thus, when we so often read of "a land flowing with milk and honey," we never think that this is to be taken in a merely literal sense. We well know that there is something implied in the description, and that *milk* and *honey* denote something spiritual and heavenly. Now to *eat butter*, when mentioned in the Word, signifies to appropriate heavenly good from the Lord in the internal or spiritual mind; and to eat *honey* signifies to delight in that good in our external or natural man; for the sweetness of honey corresponds to delight, especially in our external man, where all delights and pleasures are sensibly enjoyed. It is a perception and taste of heavenly good from the Lord, which enables us to know and to perceive how noxious and deadly evil is, and which consequently leads us to refuse it, and to choose what is good. We may know what *evil* is from a perception of what is *good*, and we may see what is *false* from a knowledge of what is *true*; but not contrariwise. Moreover, evil can only be cast out by the power of truth from good. It is in vain to try to extirpate an affection or a motive but from a contrary principle and impulse. True it is, that evil must first be cast out before good can be received and enjoyed, but the rejection can only be effected by the power of good from the Lord. "We must first taste and see that the Lord is good" (Psalm xxxiv. 8), before we can know truly what evil is, and refuse and reject it. Now when this important fact in spiritual development, or in the regenerate life, is expressed in the language of correspondence, it falls into the terms:—"Butter and honey shall he eat, that he may know to refuse the evil and choose the good."

Abraham brought *butter* and *milk*, and set them before the angels who appeared to him in Mamre (Gen. xviii.), to denote the means by which communication and conjunction are effected with the Lord. These means are celestial and spiritual good, to which *butter* and *milk* correspond, and which must be eaten, that is, appropriated by faith and love, as the great principles of life, before we can become spiritual and be saved. The wicked, it is said, "shall not see the rivers, the floods, the brooks of *honey* and *butter*" (Job xx. 17); where it is evident, that *butter* and *honey* are correspondent emblems of something spiritual and heavenly which the wicked cannot see. Again, "butter and honey shall every one eat that is left in the land" (Isaiah vii. 22), plainly denoting that those who are in the church as its real, spiritual members, shall feed on spiritual and heavenly things, which are the pure affections of good from the Lord, and their correspondent delight and happiness in the natural man denoted by the sweetness of honey.

That *honey* corresponds to the delight of heavenly good as experienced in the natural mind, may be easily seen when the passages in the Word where honey is mentioned are properly considered. In 1 Samuel xiv. 27, we read that "Jonathan put forth the end of his rod, and dipped it in a honey-comb, and put his hand to his mouth, *and his eyes were enlightened;*" and again in verse 29—"See, I pray you, how *mine eyes have been enlightened*, because I tasted a little of this honey." Here the tasting of honey and the enlightening of the eyes seem to be placed in a natural connection as cause and effect, but no such connection can be seen between them. When, however, it is seen that delight which is the activity of affection, opens the understanding and causes it to see and to relish truths, then the eyes (or the understanding) are enlightened by the light of truth. For the understanding receives but little light on any subject in which the will is not interested; but so soon as the affections become delighted with the subject on which the mind meditates, the understanding,— the eyes—become enlightened. (See H. H. 603.) Again, the "honey in the carcass of the lion which Samson took and ate" (Judges xiv. 9), denotes the sweetness, serenity and happiness of mind which ensues when evil (the lion) or rather the falsity of evil, is slain;—that is, when by acts of self-denial and combat,—"fighting the good fight," as the apostle says,—the evils to which we are prone have been overcome and removed; hence arise all sweetness and happiness to the soul.

We learn from this brief exposition of the prophecy, how exceedingly precious the knowledge of the internal sense of Scripture is, and how, by the science of correspondences, that sense may be interpreted and understood. It is in this way that the Word shows its "spirit and its life," and how every verse is full of efficacy in its application to our states. For, if we desire to become regenerate and fitted for heaven, we must daily endeavor, through divine mercy, to live in the fulfilment of this prophecy, and spiritually to eat butter and honey, that we may know to refuse evil and choose good.

FIDELIS.

CHAPTER XIV.

The Correspondence of Salt—Some Illustrative Examples from the Word—The Preserving Principle of Salt, and its Correspondence—Its Fructifying Principle, and its Correspondence—Its Conjoining Principle, and its Correspondence.*

The Correspondence of Salt.

THERE is great reason for believing that the correspondence of the objects in the material world, is to be seen both in the quality of their substance and their respective uses. Salt is a substance which enters very largely into the composition of this terrestrial globe. The *sea* affords such large quantities of *common* salt (about one-thirtieth part of its own weight) that all mankind might be thence supplied with sufficient for their use. *Mines* of salt have long been known in England, Spain, Italy, Germany, Hungary, Poland, and other countries of Europe. In different parts of the world there are also huge *mountains* of salt. Of this kind there are two near Astracan in Russia; several in the kingdoms of Tunis and Algiers in Africa, several in Asia and America; and the whole island of Ormus in the Persian Gulf, consists almost entirely of fossil salt. Salt in a *chemical* sense, also, either as crystallizable acids, alkalies, and earths, or as combinations of acids with alkalies, earths, or metallic oxides, enters very largely into the composition of all things in the mineral, vegetable, and animal kingdom.

All things which exist in the material world, exist also in their correspondences in man's microcosm; and as salt enters so largely into all things of outward nature, its correspondence must form some important ingredient in the human mind. In the writings of the illustrious Swedenborg, we are taught that salt corresponds to desire, and that the term salt when it occurs in the Word (and it occurs there frequently) has in every instance this signification. As before observed there are many different kinds of salt: not only are there the varieties of common salt, but also the numerous crystallizable

---

* From the *Intellectual Repository* for Jan., 1842.

acids and alkalies, sulphates, sulphites, nitrates, nitrites, muriates, and phosphates. So also, there are various kinds of desires in the human mind: thus there are the desires of the natural mind—corporeal desires, sensual desires: then again there are the desires of the spiritual mind—desires for spiritual good and spiritual truth; and there are also the desires of the celestial mind—desires for celestial good and celestial truth; and of each of these desires there is a great variety. All desires may, however, be considered under two great divisions; desires for good and truth, and desires for evil and falsity. Thus Solomon says: "The desire of the righteous is only good; the soul of the wicked desires evil." So the term salt in some passages of the Word signifies good desires, and in other passages, evil desires.

Some Illustrative Examples from the Word.

In Lev. chap. 2, ver. 13, we read, "Every offering of thy cake shall be salted with salt; neither shalt thou make to cease the salt of the covenant of thy God upon thy meat-offering. Upon all thy offerings thou shalt offer salt;" and in Leviticus we read that the incense should be salted. These divine words teach us that in all our acts of worship, the good which is in us must continually desire truth—the truth which is in us must continually desire good: the heavenly marriage, the covenant, is the union of good and truth, and the desire of this conjunction is "the salt of the covenant of thy God;" and the man who obeys these divine commands can adopt the words of the Psalmist, "I have *longed* for thy salvation," and of Isaiah, "The *desire* of my soul is to thy name and to the remembrance of Thee." "As a new-born babe he desires the sincere milk of the Word that he may grow thereby." The Lord Jesus says, "Every one shall be salted with fire, and every sacrifice shall be salted with salt. Salt is good, but if the salt have lost its saltness, wherewith will you season it." To be "salted with fire," denotes the desire of good for truth, for desire is the very fire of love. And "salt that has lost its saltness," signifies a negation of all desire of good and of truth.

A man whose mind is enlightened by truth, but who, at the same time, does not seek after purity of affection and of life, has salt; he has desires, but they are not genuine—they are mere lust, and he is "good for nothing." Thus there are many passages in the holy Scriptures in which the term salt bears an evil signification. As in Jeremiah, "Cursed be the man who maketh flesh his arm; he shall not see when good cometh, but shall dwell in parched places in a salt land;" he whose trust is in his self-derived intelligence, and whose delight is in evil loves, dwells in a "salt land;" all good and all truth in him is destroyed by his filthy desires. So also in Zephaniah, "It shall be as Gomorrah, a place left to the nettle, and a pit of salt and a waste to eternity." "The nettle," denotes the ardor and the burning of the life of a man who is in the love of self, and "a pit of salt," denotes the same burning love desiring what is false. Such a man is a Sodom, "as Gomorrah;" for these cities represent the evil, direful, fiery, filthy affections, burning with desires of self-love. In Genesis we read of Lot's wife being turned into a pillar of salt; and this teaches us that when truth in the mind (signified by Lot's wife) no longer looks to good (denoted by Lot), but turns to the love of self —to Sodom; then the mind becomes "a pillar of salt,"—all spiritual life is destroyed. With this view of the subject, how solemn is the Lord's exhortation, "Remember Lot's wife!"

These explanations of the sacred text are gathered from the works of Swedenborg. As, however, in the New Church we are not allowed to follow blindly the teachings of any man, but are permitted to obtain for ourselves a rational perception of the meaning of the sacred page, in order that, having learned the truth we may live it, we shall consider some of the peculiar properties of salt; by this means we may see for ourselves, that salt corresponds to *desire*.

The Preserving Principle of Salt, and its Correspondence.

It has the peculiar property of preserving substances from putrefaction, and is, for this very purpose, extensively used in articles of food. It is also well known that the economy of the human body requires that we should take salt with our food. If the most healthy person were to abstain for any length of time from taking his accustomed portion of salt, his body would become diseased; health and strength would give way to disease and languor, followed with death as a certain result. The same observation is true in reference to cattle. Graziers know that by liberally scattering salt with their feed, they are using one of the most effective means for preserving them from many fatal diseases: and in those parts of the world where cattle are not under the direction of man, Providence has placed within them a strong instinct to seek a supply of salt. In America, sheep and cattle resort in herds innumerable to the different clay salt pits, and that with the greatest eagerness: and in Africa large herds of cattle travel to great distances, at stated seasons, to enjoy the marine plants which are saturated with salt. By this provision their health is preserved.

As it is in the animal economy, so also it is in the mental constitution: if the good we have received does not desire truth,—if the mental food we have received be not mixed with salt, then good corrupts, decays, perishes; so also if the truths we have taken do not desire good, then truth perishes. How forcibly is this exhibited in the state of the former church! In consequence of separating faith from charity, of teaching that faith alone is saving, of losing all affection for good, of having no salt in itself, the church of a hundred years ago had become corrupt, a loathsome corpse, a putrid carcass, about which the birds of desolation gathered together: its truths had become falsities, and all charity had been destroyed. And from this we may learn of what will most assuredly be our condition, if, as individuals, we have not salt within ourselves. If we do not cherish a desire for good, if our faith be without charity, if our knowledge be not attended with a life in accordance with the divine commands, if our profession of religion be without the possession of piety and virtue, then, though our knowledge should appear to us as splendid, glittering from the light of our own intelligence, it is in reality but the cold light of the glowworm, the phosphoric lumen of a decayed fish shining in the dark. Notwithstanding our abundance of knowledges, our souls are in a state of decay, having no health or soundness. Without this spiritual preservative, even our knowledges of truth will be taken away from us; they will wither like flowers cut off from their root; they will sink from our mental hemisphere like fallen stars. Our " knowledge will vanish away," and there will be nothing left in our minds but such errors as will unite with the evils of our hearts. But if we have salt in ourselves, then this holy desire will preserve us in spiritual health and vigor; and of our own souls it may be said, " Now *abideth* faith, hope, and charity." The salt of holy desire will give fixity to everything within us that is good and true, and preserve them for ever.

Its Fructifying Principle, and its Correspondence.

It is well known by farmers and graziers that cattle fatten upon feed in which there is an abundance of salt. Cows give a greater quantity of milk, causing the fluids to become more readily converted into chyle, and giving an increased energy to those juices secreted by the digestive organs. To the fructifying principle of salt is also attributed the superior quality of the Merino wool; and the wool of flocks in our own country, fed within a few miles of the sea-coast, or with plenty of salt, possesses a longer staple and a more pliant texture. Another proof of the fructifying properties of salt is seen in the extraordinary fertility of the cultivated land of China, its fruitfulness arising from the constant practice of the Chinese applying salt as manure,—a practice which is coming into general use in our own country. So also the spiritual salt has a fructifying principle: by it a man becomes a living man, fruitful in good works. Truth is seed; good is ground. Truths merely from thought will lie alone and rot. We may have knowledge in abundance, but if we have not a holy desire of good, our souls will be evil and barren: whereas if good salt be plentifully cast upon the ground—if we desire to do the truth, then these knowledges will take root, spring up luxuriantly, and bring forth an abundant harvest.

The fructifying principle of mental salt is plainly taught us in many passages of the holy Word. We select one from 2 Kings, chap. 2, verse 19 to 21: "The men of Jericho said to Elisha, Behold, the situation of the city is good; but the waters are evil and the ground barren. And he said unto them, Bring a new cruse and put salt therein; and they brought it to him, and he went forth to the spring of the waters, and cast the salt in there, and said, Thus saith the Lord, I have healed these waters; there shall not be from thence any more death or barren land." The prophet Elisha represents the Lord in reference to the Word. Jericho, being near to Jordan, which was the boundary of the land of Canaan, represents the boundary of the human mind,—the external, the natural man. Water denotes truth; earth represents good; a new cruse, or vessel, the knowledges of good and truth; and salt a love of good,—a desire to live the truth. From this short explanation we may see that spiritual salt has a fructifying principle. Our first knowledges of good and truth are received into our external mind,—our natural principle. These knowledges, acquired in the first stages of regeneration, as also the good acts which we at that time perform, are not in reality good or true; they are lifeless and barren; merely natural; they arise from our own love of self. "These waters of Jericho are bitter;" neither is there in us any living spiritual good productive of living faith—of genuine charity; but "the land is barren." If any reader of this work should be mourning this his unproductive and evil state, saying to himself, "the waters are bitter and the land is barren,"—" O, wretched man that I am; who shall deliver me from the body of death?" let him go to the prophet Elisha—the Word of God—the Lord Jesus Christ, and supplicate counsel of Him. Listen to his words: "Bring a new cruse, and put salt therein;" "Have salt in yourselves;" "Cast forth the salt at the spring, the going forth of the waters;" then you shall be saved from this bitterness and barrenness. Exercise a *desire* to live the truth you have received in your external mind; then you will drink of the waters of Jericho—the literal truths of the Word, and become fruitful in works really good. By means of this spiritual salt your works will be acts of true living charity; your knowledges of truth will be saving, and you will bring forth fruit to perfection.

Its Conjoining Principle, and its Correspondence.

It is by virtue of this its uniting property, that the uses we have referred to are effected. Salt conjoins all things. In the arts and manufactures it is extensively employed as a uniting medium, connecting bodies which otherwise could never be joined together.

Thousands of men in this town [Birmingham], employed in making silver-plated articles of jewelry, and in what is here called the gilt toy trade, are in the daily practice of using salt for the purpose of uniting metals. A lump of copper has to be plated with silver. By covering the copper with a medium, a salt, a flux of borax, it will, when placed in a suitable degree of heat, readily take the silver; salt being the conjoining medium. In this instance, as also in a thousand other cases, we may see how the *science of correspondence* is adapted to raise the mind's contemplation from natural and worldly objects to things spiritual and heavenly. Every thing in our daily occupation, in our recreations, imparts a blessing when it is made useful; and every thing around us can be made to aid us in working out our salvation, if God be in our thoughts,—if we are spiritually-minded.

The science of correspondence teaches us that copper represents natural good—that good which is obtained through our connections in civil society, such as obedience to parents and masters, attendance to the external ceremonies of religion,—all that is commonly termed morality. Silver represents spiritual truth—truth obtained not through the external mind, but from within—from God,—truth that is living, saving. The Lord in his merciful providence has so ordered outward circumstances, that every one of us has more or less of this natural goodness—this copper, which is the foundation upon which the holy influences of heaven can operate: but this natural good—this copper, if it be not united with spiritual truth, can never prepare us for heaven. How can our minds be made spiritual? What means are to be used in order that they may be covered over with spiritual good and truth—the gold and silver of heaven? The answer is: Let the copper—natural good—be coated with a flux of salt—holy desire; then the two principles will readily unite; then we shall be adorned with silver—decorated with the beautiful ornaments of spiritual truth and good; with bracelets on our hands, that is, the power derived from divine truth; a chain of gold on our necks—the conjunction of all things in our internal and external minds; ear-rings in our ears—practical obedience to the laws of heaven; and a beautiful crown upon our heads—wisdom from the Lord ruling and blessing our whole soul.

Take another instance of the conjoining property of salt. In the manufacture of soap, the two principal ingredients employed are fat or oil, and water. Now oil and water of themselves cannot be made to unite; it is impossible. Introduce a salt—potash, and they will mix with the greatest readiness, and form soap, an article so essential to cleanliness and comfort. In this case as in the former, salt is the conjoining medium. Fat and oil correspond to good, and water to truth. And as oil and water cannot be united without a medium (salt), so also good and truth cannot form a one, so as to be the means of purifying our hearts, unless they be united with a heavenly salt—a holy desire. We may have what the world calls goodness; we may have truths in abundance; but unless we have this spiritual desire—this desire for good and truth, and thus unite truth in the understanding with good in the will, we shall remain unwashed and unprepared for heaven: while on the other hand, if good and truth be united by the salt of desire, then we shall stand at last with those who have washed their robes—who have purified their hearts.

Again; the salt of holy desire not only conjoins the principles of good and truth in the minds of individuals, but it is also *the grand connecting medium by which Christians are united in church-fellowship*. Without this salt we may assemble together in the same place, join externally in the same prayers and praises, hear the same sermons, be called by the same name, profess the same faith, and still be internally disunited. We may profess to believe that the Lord Jesus Christ is the only God of heaven and earth, see the errors of the former Church, and be able to vindicate the doctrines of the New Dispensation; but if we have no *desire* to live the life of truth—to put on the beautiful garments of Jerusalem, by uniting the acknowledgment of truth in the mind with the love of God and our neighbor in the heart, how can we be truly members of the New Jerusalem?

A mere profession of truth will never unite a man with his brother: there must be the *desire* of truth for the sake of use; especially should this affection be in activity when assembled in holy worship. The Word of the Lord is imperative,—" Every oblation of thy meat-offering shalt thou season with salt; neither shalt thou suffer the salt of the covenant of thy God to be lacking from thy meat-offering. With all thy offerings thou shalt offer salt." And if we obey this command, there will then be no separations, no divisions, no contention, no ill-feeling, no party-spirit, no jealousy; but the "brethren will dwell together in unity:" having "salt in ourselves," we shall be at peace one with another.

Again. *The existence of this spiritual salt in our minds, will give efficiency to all our aims at usefulness.* Certain metals,—copper, zinc, for instance, and leather, placed in water, will produce a galvanic effect; but it will be very feeble. Dissolve a salt in the water; introduce nitric acid, or the acetous acid, and the effect will be powerful. So is it in spiritual things. If we have salt in ourselves, although our numbers may be few and our means limited, we shall produce the best of results. Our works will be labors of charity, deeds of love, and we shall operate powerfully on all "whose hearts God hath stirred up." Again: *By this holy medium all the inhabitants of all the heavens form a one;* the inhabitants of heaven are all closely united together. What is it that conjoins them? It is the salt of pure desire. One heart, one soul pervades all the angelic host. There no one lives to himself; there separate interests are unknown; but each believes and acts upon the principle that 'it is more blessed to give than to receive.' Thus desire, like salt, has a conjoining principle.

Renders Food Savory.

Salt excites the appetite by making food savory. If food be eaten without salt, without a relish or an appetite for it, it does not so fully give its nutritious properties, or incorporate with the body. The same is true spiritually. If the good and truth of the holy Word be received without relish or savor—without the salt of desire, it cannot be incorporated with the life; because nothing can live in a man but what he loves—nothing but what he receives with affection, with spiritual relish and savor.

Thus it is evident that salt corresponds to desire. By desire the truth and good in our minds are preserved from corruption; we are fruitful in every good work; the heavenly marriage of good and truth is celebrated; and we are adorned with the rings, the jewels, the beautiful crown of wisdom, love and use. We enjoy the pleasant sight of brethren dwelling together in unity; we extend the sphere of the New Jerusalem; the truths of the holy Word become incorporated in our life; we are refined from all unholy loves; we are saved from lukewarmness, and burn with holy heavenly love. "Have salt in yourselves."

CHAPTER XV.

CORRESPONDENCE APPLIED TO THE INTERPRETATION OF MATT. XXIV. 20: "PRAY YE THAT YOUR FLIGHT BE NOT IN THE WINTER, NEITHER ON THE SABBATH DAY."*

IN this chapter the Lord foretells the entire destruction of the church He came to establish. As the Jewish church had come to its consummation, so that the Lord as the Son of Man,—as the Divine Truth itself from which the church exists,—"had not where to lay his head;" so, at consummation of the Christian church, the Son of Man, when He should come, "would not find faith upon the earth." (Luke xviii. 8.) Many suppose that these predictions of the Lord have reference only to the literal destruction of Jerusalem by the armies of Titus; but although there are some things in the letter which appear coincident with that destruction, yet there are very many, as all commentators have acknowledged, which cannot be construed into a reference to that event; and therefore it has been admitted by many that the entire series of divine predictions contained in this chapter, have relation to the decline, fall and consummation of the first Christian church which the Lord established; after which He would come again to establish a New Church, signified by the New Jerusalem in the Revelation, in which He, in his Divine Humanity, would be acknowledged as all in all.

A church does not arrive at its consummation until "not one stone in the buildings of the temple is left standing upon another," or until there is an utter desolation of those divine principles of love and faith which constitute the church. The temple about which the disciples inquired, represents the Lord in his Humanity. This is abundantly evident from what the Lord said of the temple in John ii. 21, where it is expressly declared that *He spake of the temple of his body.* There being "not one stone left upon another which should not be thrown down," denotes the utter destruction of all faith in the Lord's Humanity as being Divine,—in which all the fulness of the God-

---
* From the *Intellectual Repository,* for January, 1849.

head dwells bodily,—who hath ascended far above all heavens that He might fill all things;—who hath all power in heaven and on earth,—who hath the keys of hell and of death,—who openeth and no man shutteth, and shutteth and no man openeth, and who alone giveth the blessings and felicities of eternal life. (Rev. ii. 7, 11, 17, 28.)

The slightest elevation of thought as to the object and tendency of revealed truth, might teach us that the events of mere history relating only to the affairs of this life, are, as primary objects, far beneath the dignity of revealed wisdom which can only contemplate eternal objects and ends, and not those which are temporal, except so far as they can be made conducive to the attainment of heavenly and eternal ends, or to the salvation of mankind. The Word of the Lord relates primarily to his kingdom; and as "his kingdom is not of this world," so it may be said in like manner, that his Word is not of this world; hence it does not relate, in its primary or spiritual sense, to the revolutions of earthly polities, or the subversion of earthly governments, or the destruction of earthly cities; although these events may serve, according to the laws of correspondence between things natural and spiritual, as the visible types of the destruction of churches, and of those judgments in the spiritual world by which that destruction is accomplished. Thus by the destruction of Jerusalem, and the abrogation of the Jewish system of worship and the dispersion of the Jews, the total destruction of the Jewish dispensation was effected, and thereby was likewise represented, in the divine predictions of the Lord in Matt. xxiv., the entire consummation of the first Christian church.

Although, as stated above, some things in the destruction of Jerusalem by the armies of Titus appear to coincide with the Lord's predictions, there are, nevertheless, many particulars in the divine record which do not coincide, and which have constrained all commentators to admit that these divine predictions have an *ulterior object* not yet accomplished. This *ulterior object* can only be understood by a knowledge of the spiritual sense of the Word, which in these latter days has been mercifully vouchsafed to the church, and by which we can clearly see the object, scope and end of the Lord's predictions. Thus the true nature of these predictions being only understood from the spiritual sense, we may readily see how immensely important a knowledge of the spiritual sense is; inasmuch as little or no practical profit can arise unless we understand the Scriptures, and see their application to our own states as well as to the states of the church in general. For the Word of God is infinite and universal, comprising all states of the church in the aggregate, and all states of the human mind in particular. Thus the utter desolation of the church in the unregenerate mind, especially at the time of death and judgment, which we know is one of the immediate consequences of death, is especially described in these predictions of the Lord. The inestimable value of the spiritual sense of the Word is especially seen in the fact, that it brings every prophecy as well as every precept home to the heart and life of the individual, so that he there sees the history either of his *regenerate* or of his *unregenerate* state; his *regenerate* state being portrayed in those prophecies which describe the church in states of faithfulness and obedience, and in consequent glory and happiness; and his *unregenerate* state depicted in those prophecies which describe the church in ruin and desolation. Thus the Word spiritually understood, is a constant source of life and light to the mind,—"a fountain of living waters."

When, therefore, the Lord, in the series of prophecies relating to the fall and consummation of the church, says, "*Pray ye that your flight be not in the winter, neither on the Sabbath day,*" we may be certain that there is some important instruction conveyed, which it is of the utmost consequence to know. The merely literal sense of the passage, that the disciples were to pray that when the siege took place it might not be in the winter, must appear to the devout and reflecting mind too insignificant an exposition to be worthy of Divine Wisdom, which ever contemplates eternal ends. There is a winter of the soul as well as of the body; and the *ulterior* or rather the *primary object* of which commentators speak, as being involved in these predictions, is to warn us against taking our departure from this life in the *winter of the soul,*—in that state in which all the affections of the heart are cold and dead to everything spiritual and heavenly,—when the chill of spiritual death has benumbed and frozen every emotion of love and charity in the soul (Matt. xxiv. 12)—when a cold-hearted selfishness has taken possession of the mind, and congealed and contracted all its sensibilities for good, and all its disinterested love of truth. This indeed is a *dreadful winter*, and we should earnestly pray that our flight,—our departure out of this world into the eternal world, may not be in this wintry state. Thus it is that the Lord's words are of universal application. All his disciples, all the members of his church, have now and at all times most earnestly to pray that death and judgment may not overtake them in this winter state.

As to our departure out of this world, it is obvious that we have no control over the time when it is to take place; whether it be in *summer* or in *winter* is not of our appointment. But we have, through Divine Mercy and Power, a control over our states, so that by earnest prayer, self-denial, and sincere repentance, we can cultivate the states represented by the beautiful spring, the glowing summer, and the fruitful autumn, and avoid the cold, dismal, death-like states of winter. We all, indeed, have to pass through these winter states during the process of regeneration, when states of coldness as to things spiritual and heavenly will come upon us; when temptations and trials will assail us; when "we should hasten our escape from the windy storm and tempest." (Ps. lv. 8.) As the people of Israel had to pass through the desert before they could arrive at the "land flowing with milk and honey,"—as the Lord himself had to be tempted of the devil, and to be assailed by wild beasts in the desert (Mark i. 13) before "He could enter into his glory," so we all have to pass through a desert, and a state of winter which is analogous to a desert, before we can receive the "crown of life." But to fall in the desert, or to remain in that spiritual state denoted by *winter*, is to incur spiritual death, and to take up our abode in the "land of darkness, of trouble, and of anguish, whence come the young and the old lion, the viper, and the fiery flying serpent;" (Isaiah xxx. 6,)— where evils and falsities of every kind prevail. How different is this land from that whose skies are never darkened, whose clouds drop fatness, whose hills are covered with flocks, whose plains are adorned with golden harvests, and where each can sit under his vine and fig-tree, and none shall make him afraid!

Nature is a theatre representative of the Lord's kingdom in the spiritual world. "The invisible things of God (says the Apostle) from the creation of the world are clearly seen, being understood by the things that are made." Not only are the things of heaven represented to us, but the sad states and dismal objects of hell are also portrayed to our senses in the world of nature. The wolf and the lamb, the owl and the dove, the nettle and the rose, winter and summer, night and day, are not correlatives, but opposites, which read us valuable lessons when seen in the light of correspondence, and especially when understood as mentioned in the Scriptures. Nature has yet to be studied and viewed from a higher point than our sciences have hitherto contemplated. We are still grovelling in the dust as to the high uses which the study of nature should aim to realize and accomplish.

Night is to day what winter is to the year. The four states of the day denoted by morning, noon, evening, and night, are analogous to the four seasons of the year—spring, summer, autumn, and winter. Spring is the morning of the year, summer its noon, autumn its evening, and winter its night. But in heaven it is declared that there is "no night" (Rev. xxi. 25); there, says Milton, is—

>―――"Grateful twilight;
> Night doth not there assume a darker veil."

And we may rest assured that, as there is "no night in heaven," so there is no winter. These are representative of mental states of darkness, cold and barrenness, which are opposed to the light, the warmth, and the fruitfulness of heavenly states, and therefore can have no place in heaven.

The *spring* of the year is emblematic of that state in which, under the Lord's guidance, man enters upon the childhood of his second birth; hence the spring of the day is called the "*womb* of the morning" (Psalm cx. 3), to denote the nascent states of regeneration in the new birth, when "the day of the Lord's power" is acknowledged, and "the beauties of holiness" begin to appear. In this state, the germs of heavenly intelligence and wisdom begin to grow and expand. The "first-fruits, being *green ears* of corn dried by the fire" (Lev. ii. 14), and the firstlings of the flock, were to be offered to the Lord in worship as emblems of this *spring* state of heavenly innocence and good in the human soul.

The *summer* is representative of that state when the affection of truth glows with ardor, and when everything intellectual is, in consequence, more fully developed and expanded;—when faith is not only enlightened by truth, but actuated by love. This spiritual summer is splendid and glorious in proportion as the "sun of righteousness" rises to a higher and higher altitude in the mind. When the prophet says, "*The harvest is past and the summer is ended and we are not saved*" (Jer. viii. 20), the true meaning can only be seen from the spiritual sense. For our salvation is irrespective of earthly summers and harvests, but by no means of spiritual harvests and summers. For the harvest and summer denote the means of love and truth in all fulness, provided by Him who, in his Divine Humanity, is the "Lord of the harvest" by which man can be saved,—by which he can "reap life everlasting." This harvest and the light and warmth of this summer are abundantly provided for us in the Holy Word, and in the church—especially in the Lord's New Church; and if we refuse to become laborers in this harvest, it must needs pass away, or rather we shall pass away from it, and shall not be saved. This is the ground of the prophet's lamentation.

The *autumn* is an emblem of that state when the fruits of heavenly wisdom and love come to maturity and perfection, and are seen in the conduct and the life. The feast of harvest represented, in the Jewish dispensation, this joyful and happy state of the regenerate mind and of the church.

But the *winter* corresponds to the unregenerate and sinful state of man, and also to states of temptation through which, as we have seen, man must pass in order to be prepared for heaven. Hence, as in nature the winter is made subservient to a fuller and more vigorous development and manifestation of vegetable and animal life in the spring, summer and autumn; so the winter, in a spiritual sense, is made subservient to a more vigorous growth in the spring, summer and autumn states of the soul, of the fruits of righteousness and of the blessings of salvation; and also as a means by which the enjoyment of those states can be enhanced. And inasmuch as these alternations and vicissitudes denoted by the four times of the day and the four seasons of the year, are as necessary for the growth and maturity of all spiritual states of goodness and truth as for the growth and perfection of all things in nature, it is therefore said that "*while the earth remaineth*" or (more literally translated) "*during all the days of the earth, seed-time and harvest, and cold and heat, and summer and winter, and day and night, shall not cease*" (Gen. viii. 22), to denote that in the process of regeneration these alternations and vicissitudes of states are indispensable to the growth of things spiritual and heavenly in the mind.

As the human mind is spiritual in its constitution, it often thinks from laws operative in the spiritual world, and consequently expresses its perceptions and feelings in the language of correspondences between things natural and spiritual. Thus it is common to talk of a *benighted* mind, to denote ignorance; of a *cold* heart, to signify the lack of *warm* friendship and love. But the Word of God uniformly speaks to us according to these emblems and correspondences; and we cannot come to the true meaning of the Word until we thus *spiritually discern*, as the Apostle says (1 Cor. ii. 14), what is revealed to us.

This, then, is the reason why the Lord commands us "to pray that our flight be not in the winter." When the Lord was betrayed, and when He was brought to his final temptations, it *was winter* (John xviii. 18), to denote the entire consummation of the church, when nothing but self-love prevailed, signified by the "*fire of coals*" at which the servants and officers were standing; and at which also Peter was "warming himself" when he denied the Lord. For all denial of the Lord comes from those impure affections which arise from the *coal fire* of inordinate self-love; whereas all acknowledgment and love of the Lord come from the heavenly warmth of the "*sun of righteousness*," as a living principle in the soul.

The *Sabbath day*, on which also our flight should not take place, is extremely important to be known. We are aware of the merely literal idea which commentators in general attach to this injunction of the Lord, namely, that as the Sabbath was so holy in the Jewish church, they should pray that their flight from the siege of Jerusalem might not be on that day, lest they should be guilty of breaking the holy laws of the Sabbath. Such commentators, however, do not remember that the Lord himself, as the Lord of the Sabbath, abrogated those ritual laws, in consequence of which He was so often accused by the Pharisees. No; such comments as these can never bring out the "spirit and life" of the Word. This injunction is as applicable to us as to those to whom it was first addressed. The Word, like its Divine Author, is "the same yesterday, to-day, and for ever," and never loses its especial application to every individual member of the church. Besides, the Lord's injunction in the text was given to his disciples—to Christians, and not to the Jews—and therefore it could not be in the Jewish sense of the Sabbath that it should be understood.

The SABBATH DAY was the most holy institution of the Jewish church. Its observance was guarded by the strictest laws, the violation of which was followed by the severest penalties. The Sabbath was thus considered to be most holy on account of its high representative character. It signified the union of the Divine and Human natures in the Lord; hence it denoted, in the supreme sense, his glorification, and also his work of redemption when accomplished, —when, after his temptations and labors, He entered into his Sabbath of rest; it also signified the regeneration of man, and his consequent salvation, when he enters into his heavenly state of rest and peace which is involved in the term *Sabbath*. This institution, therefore, was most holy in its representative character, because it denoted the consummation of all the divine purposes of redemption and salvation.

But a merely external representative state of holiness, such as then existed among the Jews, when there was no *internal* vital principles of holiness in the heart and life,—when only the *out*side of the cup and the platter was clean, but the *in*side full of extortion and excess,—when the " whited sepulchre appeared beautiful *without*, but *within* was full of dead men's bones and all uncleanness;" (Matt. xxiii. 27)—such a state of merely external holiness, especially when connected with the mention of winter, is here meant by the *Sabbath day*. Such was the state of the Scribes and Pharisees, who were extremely punctilious and sanctimonious in observing all the ritual laws of the Sabbath, but who, in the sight of Him who knoweth what is in man, were " hypocrites, and a generation of vipers."

Such also is the state of all professing Christians who assume a semblance or " form of godliness, but who have none of the life and power thereof," or who, like the church of Sardis, " have a name to live," but who, in the Lord's sight, are spiritually dead. This is indeed a state even more dreadful than the *winter* state already described, since it is connected with hypocrisy and profanation.

Let us, then, earnestly pray that our " flight be not in the winter, neither on the Sabbath day"—that death, when it comes, may not find us taking our departure out of this world in these unregenerate and sinful states, so contrary to the holiness and happiness of heaven. SCRUTATOR.

CHAPTER XVI.

Correspondence of the Serpent, with Illustrative Examples from Scripture.*

AS all things in creation which are according to order, are so many types of the infinite things in God, and as man is created to be the direct finite image and likeness of his Maker, it follows that all created objects are in a certain relation to man, and that they directly correspond to the various faculties, powers, principles, and states of his soul and body. Hence it is that all things in the animal, vegetable and mineral kingdoms bear a direct relation to the innumerable things in the human system, and that if this relation were understood, which it can be by the Science of Correspondences, there would, in the language of the poet, be

> "Tongues in trees, books in the running brooks,
> Sermons in stones, and good in everything."

The knowledge of this relation and correspondence which natural things bear to man, and to the various states, both good and evil, of his internal and external mind, or of the spiritual, rational and sensual degrees of his system, is of the utmost importance to man, if he desire to advance in genuine intelligence and wisdom. This importance becomes much greater, when we consider that this relation of correspondence between external objects or things natural and internal objects or things moral, spiritual and divine, is the very language through which the Lord addresses man, and conveys to his mind all spiritual light, and all the treasures of revealed wisdom and knowledge in his Holy Word.

Of all objects in the animal kingdom the reptile tribe is the lowest, of which serpents of various kinds and species are the most conspicuous. Of all the degrees of man's life the *sensual* and the *corporeal* are the lowest; because they are nearest to the earth, and are actuated by merely earthly appetites, influences and causes. These lowest degrees in man's nature partake the least of what is truly *human* in

---

* From the *Intellectual Repository* for January, 1843.

man; and the serpent, their correspondent emblem, is of all animals the most remote from the human form. As the serpent crawls upon the earth, so the sensual principle in man is the nearest akin to earth, which, if not elevated by the rational and spiritual principles of his nature, may be said to crawl upon the earth in like manner. As sensual things have a tendency to fascinate and charm the mind, because sensual delights are more vividly experienced than any others, so certain kinds of serpents, especially the more malignant, are said by naturalists to fascinate and charm their prey before they devour it. In short, the points of emblematic correspondence between the sensual principle in man and the serpent, would become more obvious, the more we become acquainted with the characteristics of the two objects compared together. But we will first describe, from Swedenborg, what the sensual principle is, and also what its nature is if man be not elevated above it by regeneration.

"The sensual principle is the last and lowest sphere of the life of the human mind, adhering to and cohering with the five bodily senses. He is called a sensual man whose judgment on all occasions is determined by the senses of the body, who believes only what he can see with his eyes and touch with his hands, allowing such things to be something real, and rejecting all others. The interiors of his mind which see by the light of heaven, are closed, so that he has no discernment of any truth relating to heaven or the church. Such a person thinks in extremes, that is, his thought is confined to the last and lowest sphere of things; for he does not think interiorly from any spiritual light, but rests in gross natural light only: hence it is that he is inwardly opposed to the things of heaven and the church, although he can outwardly speak in their favor, and that with a degree of zeal proportioned to the hope of obtaining authority and opulence by their means. Men of learning and erudition who have confirmed themselves deeply in falsities, especially those who have confirmed themselves against the truths of the Word, are more sensual than the rest of mankind. Sensual men reason with shrewdness and dexterity, because their thoughts are so near their speech as to be almost in it, being, as it were, in their lips; and because they make all intelligence to consist in speaking merely from the memory: they are also expert in confirming falsities, and after confirmation believe them to be true; and yet their reasonings and confirmations are grounded in the fallacies of the senses, by which the vulgar are ensnared and persuaded. Sensual men are cunning and malicious above all others. The covetous, the adulterous and the deceitful are particularly sensual, though they may appear men of talent in the eyes of the world. The interiors of their minds are foul and filthy in consequence of their communication with the hells; and in the

Word they are said to be dead. All who inhabit the hells are sensual, and the more so as they are more deeply immersed. The sphere of infernal spirits conjoins itself with the sensual principle of man in the back; and in the light of heaven the hinder part of their heads appears hollow. They who reasoned merely from sensual things, were by the ancients called serpents of the tree of knowledge. Sensual things ought to possess the last place and not the first, and with every wise and intelligent man it is so, and they are kept in subjection to interior things; whereas with an unwise man they have the first place, and bear rule. Where sensual things are in the lowest place, a passage is opened by them to the understanding, and truths are eliminated by the mode of extraction. Such sensual things border most closely on the world; they admit whatsoever flows from the world, and as it were sift it. Man by means of sensual things communicates with the world, and by means of rational things with heaven. Sensual things form a basis which is subservient to the interiors of the mind, some sensual things being subservient to the intellectual part and some to the voluntary part. Where the thought is not elevated above sensual things, man attains but to small degrees of wisdom; but where it is, he enters into a clearer light (*lumen.*), and at length into heavenly light (*lux.*), and then he has perception of those things which flow from heaven. Natural science is the ultimate of the understanding, and sensual delight the ultimate of the will."—T. C. R. 565.

Serpents are of many kinds and species, but they may be divided into two general classes,—venomous, and non-venomous; the former are for the most part viviparous, and the latter oviparous. Those which are not venomous correspond to the sensual principle when in order,—when all its states are subordinate to the higher rational and spiritual principles of the mind. But the venomous kinds of serpents correspond to the sensual principle when in disorder, and consequently rebellious against the higher rational and spiritual powers of our being.

The serpent in the garden of Eden plays a most active part, since the fall of man is attributed to its subtlety and seductive power. This shows us how important it is that we should correctly understand what the serpent means, in order that we may see the nature of that temptation which caused the fall of man, and which still causes the children of men to cherish evil and to commit sin. For the same cause which originated evil, still carries on the dreadful work in all the children of Adam, who do not resist the voice and subtleties of the serpent. No person at the present time can possibly be so childish in his sentiments and ideas as to suppose that this is a literal history

The science of correspondences by which the spiritual sense of the Word is opened, and the light thence arising, can alone explain to us the nature of the fall, and show us the mystery connected with the origin of evil. The serpent in Eden, and also in every other portion of the Word, signifies the sensual principle of our nature, which, in the perfect constitution of our being, is as necessary as a foundation is to a house. Hence the serpent is necessary to the perfection of Eden, and consequently the divine approbation of good was pronounced upon every *creeping thing*, as well as upon every other thing which the Lord God had made. (Gen. i. 15.) This shows us that the serpent was not, as is commonly supposed, an evil spirit that had intruded into the happy abode; but that man, being placed by his Creator in perfect equilibrium between heaven and the world, or between the heavenly things of his spiritual mind and the worldly things of his natural mind, was in the enjoyment of the most perfect spiritual and natural liberty, so that he could turn himself either to the Lord as " the tree of life," and thus live under the guidance and influence of his spiritual mind, or, as the apostle says, " *have his conversation in heaven;*" or, he could turn himself to his natural mind, and thus live in the exercise of merely natural and selfish affections, which is " to eat of the tree of the knowledge of good and evil," or to live a merely natural and sensual life, and consequently to be banished from the garden of heavenly intelligence and wisdom.

Now, the *sensual principle*, as being the nearest to the world and to all external things, has in itself a tendency downwards, or outwards, and is strongly disposed to judge of things according to their outward appearances, and to prefer worldly appearances to heavenly realities, and to lead man to prefer earthly good to heavenly good; that is, to prefer the good of his body and of his merely natural mind and state, to the good of his soul and of his spiritual mind and state. And as this is the case with the sensual principle in every man, the serpent, its direct corresponding emblem in the world of nature, is represented in the Word of God as tempting man to disobey his Maker. This temptation is directed to the delights of the natural mind and the body, all of which relate to the world and to man's life in the world; and when these delights are preferred to the delights of the spiritual mind, self-love arises as a governing principle, and banishes the love of God above all things as the ruling end and motive in the constitution of man; and the love of the world and of worldly things, supplants the love of heaven and of heavenly things; and man, instead of becoming "spiritually minded, which is life and peace," becomes sensually and carnally minded, which is enmity against God, and spiritual death.

The serpent is said in the history of the temptation, to be "more subtle than any beast of the field which the Lord God had made" (Gen. iii. 1), to indicate that the *sensual principle* which, if not elevated and guided by heavenly influences from the Lord in the rational and spiritual degrees of man's life, thinks and reasons solely from merely outward appearances and fallacies, and would fain persuade us that there is nothing real, nothing worthy of our supreme affection and attachment, but that which the eye can see, the ear can hear, and the tongue can taste; and as there is much plausibility in such reasoning from external fallacies and impressions, the serpent is said, in the sacred text, to be "more subtle" than any other animal.

When this subtle reasoning of our sensual principle begins to operate, its first effect is to engender doubt concerning the spiritual state of man and the truth of God's Word. This doubting state is signified and also portrayed in the words of the Serpent:—"Yea, hath God said, ye shall not eat of every tree of the garden?" This doubt leads to the fatal denial that all our life flows momentarily into our souls from God, and confirms the fallacious and false impression that all our life is, in reality, according to the appearance, self-derived, and that we exist independently of God, the only fountain of life, and thus that man in reality is a god, since the peculiar prerogative and characteristic of God is to have life in himself, self-derived and independent. Hence the Serpent says, "In the day ye eat thereof, ye shall be as *gods*, knowing good and evil." For the greatest of all outward appearances is this: that our life is self-derived, and that we possess it independently of God; to believe which, and to confirm it from subtle reasoning according to sensual appearances, is to separate ourselves at once from God, and from all heavenly wisdom,—to be banished from the garden of Eden. This subtlety of the serpent, the emblem of that *supposed* wisdom which arises from the fallacious reasonings of the sensual mind, is called by the apostle, "earthly, sensual and devilish." (James iii. 15.)

Now, that very moment in which man listened to the suggestions of the serpent, or of his *sensual principle*, and gave them the preference over the heavenly perceptions of his spiritual mind from the Lord, EVIL was originated and commenced its deadly work; and the human mind gradually fell into a merely natural, sensual and carnal state, until at length, "from the head to the foot there was no soundness in it, but wounds, and bruises, and putrefying sores." All this deadly mischief was brought upon man, or rather he brought it upon himself, by first listening to the suggestions of his sensual nature; and by continuing to do so, notwithstanding the divine warnings and instructions to repent and desist. At that awful period, when the serpent had caused such dreadful havoc and misery as to leave no soundness whatever in the natural mind of man, the great Redeemer came, according to prophecy, and by his redeeming labors, and by the glorification of his Humanity, "*bruised the serpent's head;*" that is, destroyed the ascendancy of the sensual principle in human nature, and abundantly supplied the divine means from his glorified Humanity, to keep it for ever in subjection in all those who faithfully "follow Him in the regeneration."

It is well known from the writings of Swedenborg, that preservation is continual creation, and that subsistence is continual existence; and it will also be found to be a truth, that the continuation of evil in the world is its continual origination; for it is continued in the same way in which it was first originated, namely, by listening to and following out the suggestions of the serpent, or of our sensual nature, in preference to the heavenly perceptions from the Lord, of heavenly truth and order in our spiritual mind. Hence the origin of evil, and consequently of hell also, is not an impenetrable mystery in the theology of the New Church, which, however, could not have been penetrated and explained, unless the correspondence of the *serpent* had been opened. For it is evident that when those who had suffered themselves to be seduced by the serpent, or who had allowed their higher rational and spiritual powers to be lulled asleep by the beguiling and fascinating influence of sensual things and worldly delights, —when such persons had departed from the world, they could not enter into that pure, holy and celestial sphere of love and wisdom called heaven, because their states of life would be in opposition to that holy and heavenly sphere;—for as the sensual and "carnal mind is enmity against God," they consequently remained beneath heaven, and formed that miserable state of existence in the spiritual world, which is called hell. Hence the origin of hell and of infernal spirits from the human race. When man's natural mind became corrupt, both hereditarily and actually, by the ascendancy of the sensual principle, the equilibrium was no longer between the world and heaven, or between man's natural state and his spiritual state, as heretofore, but between heaven and hell; and angels, on the one hand, dwell with man in the heavenly affections of his spiritual mind—" He gives his angels charge over us to keep us in all our ways;" and, on the other, unclean and evil spirits from hell dwell with him in the corrupt dispositions of his natural mind, as is evident from the evil spirits mentioned in the gospel, whom the Lord cast out.

Man's essential freedom arises from this equilibrium in which he is now placed between heaven and hell, so that he can, by this wonderful provision of divine mercy, eat of the "tree of life," and live for ever; or he can eat of the "tree of the knowledge of good and evil," and spiritually die to the life and happiness of heaven;—he can choose either life or death, the blessing or the curse, which are set before him.

Throughout the Scriptures the *serpent*, wherever mentioned, signifies the sensual principle of our nature; a striking instance to prove this is the next passage in the Word, in which a serpent is named as in Gen. xlix. 17. "Dan shall be a *serpent* in the way, an *adder* in the path, that biteth the horses' heels, so that the rider shall fall backwards." Here the *serpent* also signifies those who reason concerning truths and spiritual things from the fallacies of the senses; the *heels* of the horse also signify the lowest sensual things of the understanding, which the serpent is said to bite when they are injured and perverted by false reasonings; and when this is the case, the rider, or man in his rational capacity, "falls backwards," that is, becomes merely external and worldly. Hence among such persons who suffer themselves to be seduced by sensual things, and who trust to the fallacies and blandishments of the senses and their delights as the only things worthy of their pursuit and attachment, the Lord is said "to send *serpents* and *cockatrices* which shall bite them." (Jer. viii. 17.) Moses' rod was changed into a serpent before Pharaoh and his servants, in order to show the sensual state to which the church among them had become reduced, owing to their perversions and falsifications of divine truth, denoted by the rod of Moses; for it is the seductive power of the serpent or the abuse of our sensual principle which changes, in the strong language of the apostle, "the truth of God into a lie." (Rom. i. 25.) The people of Israel were bitten and destroyed by *fiery serpents* in the wilderness, in order to exhibit to us by the most striking types (for the apostle says that they were types—1 Cor. x. 9) the deadly evils of our sensual nature, when not controlled and governed by spiritual influences from the Lord. And Moses was commanded to lift up a *brazen serpent*, in order that all who beheld it might be cured of the plague. That the brazen serpent represented the Lord, is plain from his own divine declaration: "As Moses lifted up the serpent in the wilderness, even so must the Son of Man be lifted up, that all who believe in Him may not perish, but have eternal life." (John iii. 14, 15.)

To the unenlightened natural mind it may appear very strange that the Lord should be represented by so hideous a creature as a serpent; but the opening of the spiritual sense of the Word has explained to us how this is to be understood. The Lord, by redemption and the glorification of his Humanity, most mercifully accommodated his divine and saving influences to every state of degradation into which man had fallen; the lowest state of sensual evil was represented by the *fiery serpents*, and their deadly effects upon the body. Now, the accommodation and application of redeeming and saving influences from the Lord to this dreadful state of fallen man, are represented by the "*brazen serpent lifted up in the wilderness.*" For we know that the Lord has all the infinite degrees of divine life in his Humanity, which constitute the finite degrees of our humanity; and that He has consequently a divine Rational, a divine Natural, and a divine Sensual principle; for as these are the principal constituents of human nature, and as it would be impossible for us to be men without them, so the Lord, in like manner, would not be a DIVINE and PERFECT MAN without them.

In order, therefore, to save us from the deep-rooted evils of our sensual nature, the Lord as our divine Savior is represented as "*a brazen serpent*," to denote that from the divine sensual principle of his Humanity, He accommodates his saving influences to the depraved sensual nature of fallen man. In this manner it is that the Lord "*can save to the uttermost*," as the apostle says, "all who come unto God by Him," that is, all who come unto the Divine Nature or Godhead which dwells, according to the same apostle, in all fulness in the Lord Jesus Christ. It might also be asked why the serpent was made of brass in preference to any other metal. Why was it not made of gold, or silver, or iron? This question, also, can only be answered from a knowledge of the Science of Correspondences according to which the Word is written. For *brass* signifies goodness from the Lord in the sensual degree of man's life; hence the Lord, as seen in vision by John, "*was, as to his feet, like unto fine brass*" (Rev. i. 15), because the feet, as being the lowest part of the body, represent the lowest part of the mind, which is the sensual; but gold and silver would signify goodness of a higher order, belonging to the celestial and spiritual degrees of the mind; and consequently, if the serpent had been made of any other metal, the Lord would not have been represented in a manner accommodated to the sensual state of man, and the healing and saving effects would not have followed.

The poison of the serpent which is also mentioned in the Scriptures, signifies the deceit and cunning of the perverse sensual principle in man. Thus of the wicked it is said, "Their poison is like the poison of a serpent; they are like the deaf adder that stoppeth her ear." (Ps. lviii. 4.) The adder is said "to be deaf" when it remains insensible to music, or to the voice of the charmer; for in eastern countries it is still customary to charm serpents by music; and when the effects which the charmer wishes to produce for the amusement of the spectators, do not follow, the serpent is said to be deaf. This figure is mentioned to teach us, that when man is sensually-minded he is deaf and insensible to all the charms of spiritual truth and goodness. This charming by the voice and by music reminds us of the Lord's words, "we have piped unto you, and ye have not danced," etc., which denote that, notwithstanding the charming efforts of divine love to awaken in the minds of men the spiritual affections of truth and their consequent delights signified by *dancing*, the human mind still remained deaf and insensible to the heavenly charms.

It is also said of the carnally-minded and wicked, "Though they be hid from my sight at the bottom of the sea, thence will I command the *serpent*, and he shall bite them." (Amos ix. 3.) The *bottom of the sea* denotes the lowest sensual things, in which the wicked are said to be hid; and the *serpent biting them* represents the dreadful evils which will eventually and for ever torment those who remain in such a state. As the Jewish church, when the Lord came into the world, was reduced to a merely sensual state, and the serpent then had dreadfully reared its head, soon however to be bruised by the great Redeemer, the Lord so often called the Pharisees a "*generation of vipers*," because the viper was correspondent to their sensual and malignant state. The Lord enjoined his disciples "to be as wise [or prudent] as serpents and as harmless as doves," because the sensual mind is extremely prudent and circumspect as to everything worldly, which relates to the comfort and happiness of man's life in the world; and the Lord requires his disciples to be equally prudent and circumspect in relation to the spiritual life and happiness of their souls; thus, when the prudence and circumspection of the *external man* is under the guidance and influence of heavenly principles in the *internal man*, the "harmlessness of the dove" is then combined with the "prudence of the serpent," and man is truly wise.

The Lord gives his disciples "*power to tread upon serpents*" (Luke x. 18); and He also gives them "*power to take up serpents*" (Mark xvi. 18). In the former case, *serpents* signify the perverse sensual things in man, and also evil and unclean spirits who, as we have seen above, are in the closest connection with the unclean and wicked things of our sensual nature; to *tread upon them*, is to subdue and reject them by the divine power which the Lord continually gives us for this purpose: and in the latter case, *to take up serpents*, signifies to elevate and purify the things of our sensual nature, which is effected by faith in the Lord and a life of love according to his precepts. Hence, " to take up serpents," spiritually understood, is one of the true signs of a living faith in the Lord. The Lord then " enters into a covenant with the *creeping things of the ground*" (Hosea ii. 18), and purifies and blesses all our external appetites and desires, so that, " whether we eat or drink, or whatsoever we do, we do all to the glory of God " (1 Cor. x. 31).

Ancient mythology also confirms the truth that the serpent is the correspondent emblem of the sensual principle in man. The giants who waged war against the gods, were represented as having, among other hideous features, *their legs and feet like serpents*. Python,* the huge serpent which Apollo, the god of light and truth, slew with arrows, was evidently a mythological emblem of the perverse sensual principle of human nature; and the hydra with many monstrous heads, which Hercules destroyed, had a similar signification. The fury, Envy, was seen by Minerva in her miserable house in hell, eating the *flesh of vipers*,—

"Videt intus edentem
Vipereas Carnes, vitiorum alimenta suorum
Invidiam," etc.

to denote, that this malignant passion is nourished by the corruptions of our sensual nature.

Seeing, then, what the *sensual principle* is, how much we ought to

---

* Those are called Pythons, says E. S., who speak falsities from deceit or purpose, and who utter them in a tone of voice that seems to proceed from spiritual affection. (See T. C. R. 324.)

watch and pray against the perverse influence and operation of sensual fallacies, appetites and pleasures! He who professes the doctrines of the New Church, and does not at the same time, by daily taking up his cross, subdue his natural cupidities and appetites, and keep them under the controlling influence of a religious and spiritual principle, is one of the greatest enemies to the holy cause he professes to advocate. If he does not in time take heed to his ways, and sincerely repent by changing his course of life, from having had so clear a knowledge of the truth, his states will be filled up with a greater measure of wickedness and condemnation, than the states of others not blessed with so clear a discernment of divine truths and eternal realities; for "the servant that knew his Lord's will, and prepared not himself, neither did according to his will, shall be beaten with many stripes." (Luke xii. 47.) MINUS.

CHAPTER XVII.

Natural and Spiritual Substance and Form—Truth and Love are Substantial—The Natural and Spiritual Body—Objects in the Spiritual World, and the Law of their Existence—Discrete Degrees, Confirming the Doctrine of Correspondence—God, the Infinite and self-existing Substance.*

CREATION is an outbirth of the Creator, and in all its parts which are according to divine order, is illustrative of his infinite Love, Wisdom and Power. The old hypothesis, "that all things were created out of nothing," is now for the most part exploded as a groundless fancy, irrational and absurd. Those who still cling to this old fancy, prove that they have not attained to a knowledge of what is truly philosophical and spiritual. This idea of a creation out of nothing, if such an idea can be possible, is supposed to have some ground to stand upon in an assertion of the apostle: "The things which are seen were not made of things which do appear." (Heb. xi. 3.) These words, however, by no means teach that the things which are seen were created out of nothing, but that they were created out of things which do not appear to the bodily sight; and the things which do not thus appear, are the things which exist in the spiritual world, and which are *substantial*, and the proximate cause of the creation and existence of things in the natural world, which are *material*.

Without a knowledge of the spiritual world, and of its relation to the natural; and likewise without some discernment of the nature of the substances and objects which exist in that world, and also of the laws by which they are governed, it is impossible to have proper ideas concerning the creation of all things by God. The natural universe is as a theatre representative of the spiritual and heavenly things which exist in the spiritual universe, and especially in the Lord's kingdom; and the things which exist in this latter are representative of the infinite things of Love, Wisdom and Power which exist in the

---

* From the *Intellectual Repository* for Dec., 1844.

Lord Himself. Thus "the invisible things of God from the creation of the world are clearly seen, being understood by the things that are made, even his eternal power and Godhead." (Rom. i. 20.) The WORD by which all things were made, is the DIVINE TRUTH acting as one with the DIVINE LOVE or GOODNESS. Truth is not a mere conception of the mind in conformity with the true nature of things; still less, is it a mere *fiat* or declaration of the mouth, but it is *the very essential substance of all things*. When therefore the Lord said, "I AM THE TRUTH," He declared that Truth is a substance and a form, which in its divine origin, or in the Lord, is the divine and infinite substance and form, from which all other substances and forms, both in the spiritual and natural worlds, are only derivations and formations.—A. C. 7270.

In the spiritual world these substances and forms constituting the infinite variety of objects and scenery there beheld, are called spiritual and substantial; and because they exist from the Sun of the spiritual world as their proximate origin, they are of a different nature, and are governed by laws essentially different from those by which objects in the natural world are governed; because these latter objects are from the sun of nature as their proximate origin, and hence they have a nature, and are governed by laws peculiar to themselves. To think, therefore, of the substances and forms of the spiritual world with the same ideas as we think of the substances and forms of the natural world, is to think erroneously; hence the cause why people in general, when they hear of a spiritual world filled with objects in varieties infinitely greater than can be seen upon earth, recoil at the idea, and treat it with ridicule, because they can only think of them in the same manner as they think of material objects. And, indeed, before they are instructed how the case is, they must needs be excused.

Let us take the spiritual body and the natural body of man as a basis of our contemplation and reasoning on this subject. These two forms of man, the one spiritual and the other natural, exist simultaneously,—the one is the form of his mind, by which he is an inhabitant of the spiritual world; and the other is his bodily material organization, by which he is an inhabitant of the natural world. That these two forms of man exist simultaneously, is plainly declared by the apostle Paul, when he says, "there is a natural body, and there is a spiritual body;" the apostle speaks in the present tense,—"there is,"—in order to show that these two forms exist simultaneously. And such is the uniform testimony of Swedenborg. This spiritual form is the seat of all man's mental life, but the natural form is the seat of all his bodily life. Man does not enter consciously into the possession and enjoyment of his spiritual form or body, until he has left the natural body by death; no more than the chrysalis, so long as it is in the pupa-state, is in the conscious enjoyment of the power which it has, by virtue of its golden wings, of rising, when it becomes an *imago* or perfect butterfly, from the ground, and winging its flight in the aërial regions, skimming over the flowery meads, and feeding on ambrosia and nectar. Before it can do this, the pupa-state which bound it to the earth must be put off. So long as man is in a material body, he is comparatively in this pupa-state, bound by the laws of space and of time, shackled as to his mental powers, earthbound as to many of his conceptions and ideas, and gross as to his affections and pursuits. The laws of creation and of order require him to pass through this state, which, although indispensable, is not intended to last long; because, as the apostle says in the same chapter, "that which is natural is first, and afterwards that which is spiritual." In this state we are trained and prepared for the heavenly world; and thrice happy are they who suffer themselves to be duly prepared, that is, to be regenerated.

It is of the utmost importance that we should have correct ideas of the nature of spiritual substances and forms, since otherwise there can be no genuine intelligence and philosophy concerning anything above the mere senses. Now, the spiritual body, or the spiritual form of man which is the seat of all his mental life and activity, is evidently subject to a different order, and to different laws from those which exist in the natural world, and to which the natural body is subject. When speaking of mind we use terms taken from natural objects; and we say that the mind is great or little, enlarged or contracted, high or low, acute or obtuse, etc.; but we never think that these properties literally belong to the mind, except only in a remote and figurative sense. Hence we think of mental states and activities independently of the laws of nature; and we form, in some measure, spiritual ideas of mind and its phenomena.

By the term *spiritual*, we mean what is separate from the laws and conditions of nature, and what is peculiar to the laws and conditions of the spiritual world. The spirit or mind of man, when in perfect freedom of thought, thinks already to a certain extent in agreement with the laws of that world which it is destined to inhabit forever. It thinks of departed friends as being exempt from the laws of matter and of space, and as existing in a state and world in which other laws are applicable and operative; it also thinks of them as being in the human form, infinitely more lovely and perfect than when upon earth. When, however, these things are brought in Swedenborg's "*Heaven and Hell*" as facts and truths directly under the mind's eye, and especially if they are urged upon the attention by various arguments, they are in general denied, and considered to be merely imaginary. This arises from the fallacy of the senses, which would fain persuade us that there are no other substances and forms, and consequently no other objects, than those which we behold in external nature around us. We are liable to be led by these fallacies and their false persuasions, (unless the mind is grounded in genuine doctrine and philosophy,) in proportion as our selfish principle is excited, which in controversy is unhappily too often the case. One great means of being elevated above the fallacies of the senses and their false persuasions, is to cherish a disinterested love,—a love void of selfish regard for the object of investigation and discussion.

The doctrine of *Discrete Degrees*—a doctrine which belongs in a peculiar sense to New Church philosophy—teaches us that spiritual substances and forms, although existing in material substances and forms as the cause of their existence and preservation, may be separated from them and continue their existence in a more perfect state, in a world more fully accommodated to their nature and activity. But merely natural forms when separated from their spiritual forms, can no longer exist, but are dissolved into earthly elements and enter into new combinations, serving as new forms for the activities in nature of spiritual substances, and for the reception of the influx of life from God. This is evident from the case of the natural body which dies and is dissolved when the spiritual form or body leaves it at death.

Nature plainly shows us that there are forms within forms, as in the wonderful transformations of insects; and also that an interior form can live in a higher state of perfection than the exterior which is dissolved when the interior quits it. Thus when the *imago* emerges from the *pupa*, as in the case of the common butterfly which sports over our fields, the latter is abandoned and the former needs it no longer. And this is not only the case in many provinces of the animal kingdom, but it is more general in the vegetable kingdom. Every fruit has its husk, its shell, or its rind, and every seed has its capsule. Nor does the fruit or the seed properly put forth its own use, or manifest its proper vegetative life until the husk, the shell and the capsule are removed. These latter are necessary for the formation of the butterfly, and for the maturing of the fruit and seed, just as the material body is necessary for the substantiation, formation and regeneration of the spirit; nor can this latter properly put forth its spiritual and heavenly life in all its beauty, loveliness, wisdom and bliss, until the former is laid down by death.

Thus even in nature we are instructed that there are forms within forms, and that the interior forms may continue to exist in a more perfect state when the exterior are put off and dissolved. But all these facts, evident to our observation, are intended to instruct us, or to illustrate the case when we are instructed, that in man there is a spiritual substance and form which continues to exist after the death of the material body. Man, however, is the sole subject which continues to exist in the spiritual world after the death of the external form, because he possesses rational and spiritual forms for the reception of spiritual and rational life from God, which no animal possesses; he is thereby immortal. The doctrine of Discrete Degrees shows the laws by which interior or spiritual forms and exterior or natural forms are connected together, not by continuity, but by correspondence and influx. (See D. L. W., Part iii.)

It was a maxim of ancient wisdom ascribed to Hermes Trismegistus, that "all things in the spiritual world exist also in the natural world in a natural form; and that all things in the natural world exist also in the spiritual world in a spiritual form." These spiritual forms, says Swedenborg, are, as to their appearance, similar to natural forms, but in every other respect, both as to their origin and the laws by which they are governed, entirely dissimilar. They exist also in the spiritual world in infinitely greater variety than in the natural. The law of their existence is, that they should be the correspondents and exponents of the internal or mental states of the inhabitants whom they surround; so that in those objects as in living emblems, the real states of the spiritual inhabitants may be seen. The frogs, together with the other plagues of Egypt, were correspondences to the infernal states of a degraded church, and striking exponents of the evil lusts which actuated its perverted members. Loathsome objects and horrible scenes are beheld as surrounding the wicked in those nether regions of the spiritual world called hell; and we are instructed that the same history is still and forever applicable to a fallen and perverted church, and to every member who remains unregenerate and wicked. Whereas, the sheep and lambs lying down in green pastures, and feeding beside the still waters (Ps. xxiii.), are objects which correspond to a heavenly state, and are exponents of the peace and happiness of the faithful who live in the acknowledgment that the Lord is their shepherd. It is plainly evident from the prophets, especially from Ezekiel, Zechariah, and John (in the Revelation), that nearly all the scenery and objects which they beheld and describe, were not in the natural but in the spiritual world; for they expressly state that they were " in the spirit," and that they described the things which in that state " they heard and saw."

Now, there are two universal principles or conditions which characterize nature, and consequently all things in nature. These are *space* and *time;* the former is *extended*, and consequently *measurable;* the latter is *successive*, that is, existing from moment to moment, and consequently *determinable*. But space and time as conditions of nature, have no existence in the spiritual world, any more than inches or feet are predicable of mind; and if certain phrases, such as *deep* thoughts, *high* ideas, etc., are frequently predicated of mind, yet no one ever thinks of taking them in their literal sense, but merely as expressions which emphatically and accurately convey the meaning intended [because of the correspondence between natural and spiritual height and depth, of which every one has a perception].

But although *space* and *time* and their conditions have no existence in the spiritual world, yet as objects there for the most part resemble objects in this world as to appearance, it follows that spiritual objects likewise *appear to exist* as in space and time. The laws of their proximity and remoteness are not those of mensuration, but those of mental affinity and repugnance. Similitude of affection causes their attraction and proximity, and dissimilitude causes repulsion and distance, corresponding to the laws of attraction and repulsion in nature. Objects in this world proceed from their beginnings, either as seeds or eggs, according to the laws of succession in nature. They successively grow, arrive at maturity, decay, and perish. But this law of succession is peculiar to natural objects only, and does not obtain in respect to spiritual objects, which do not gradually grow from seeds or eggs, but exist instantaneously according to the changes of state in the minds of the inhabitants. Nor does this appear more strange to them than the succession of growth to maturity in terrestrial objects does to us, because they think not *from objects* but *from states* of mind; whereas we think from objects and not from states. Objects in nature are at the same time the *subjects* of our thoughts; whereas with them objects are only the external representatives and exponents of their thoughts; and states of mind are the *subjects* in and from which they think. (See A. E., Vol. vi., pp. 396, 397.) To understand this rightly, will enable us to see the difference between natural and spiritual objects, the laws by which they are respectively governed, and also the relation which they respectively sustain to the inhabitants of both worlds.

But if spiritual substances and forms are totally exempt from the laws and conditions of space, time and matter, and if to think of them from those laws is to think materially and erroneously, how much more is this the case in respect to divine substances and forms, which are infinitely exempt from the laws of matter, time and space! That God is the infinite and self-existing substance and form, from which all finite substances and forms both spiritual and natural are derivations and formations, is the primary and fundamental truth upon which all human and angelic intelligence must be based. Admit this, and you begin to emerge from the darkness of materialism, atheism, naturalism, into the light of genuine intelligence. When the apostle called God a SUBSTANCE, υποςασις* (Heb. i. 3), he did not mean to instruct us that God is such as material substances are, but that there are other substances besides those in nature, which are infinitely exempt from the laws of matter, space and time. And when the Athanasian Creed, employing in Greek the same term as the apostle, calls God a *substance*—"being of one substance with the Father"— it did not mean to inculcate the gross idea that the *substance* there meant is similar to natural substance; consequently, both the apostle Paul and the Athanasian creed teach, not only that there are spiritual substances, but also a divine substance.

Now, it is impossible to think of a substance without a form, since the former cannot exist without the latter; hence God as a substance must be in a form which is infinite and divine. The apostle accordingly says that God has a form: "Jesus Christ *being in the form of God*, thought it not robbery to be equal with God." (Phil. ii. 6.) Here it is plainly asserted that the human form in which Jesus appeared, especially after his resurrection when He was fully glorified, is THE FORM OF GOD; this divine form is also called by the apostle the Lord's "*glorious body*," and he states that "in Him all the fulness of the Godhead dwelleth BODILY." Hence it is that "*He is equal*

---

* The literal meaning of the term υποςασις is substance, and is so rendered in Heb. xi. 1; and ought to have been so translated in the above passage.

with God," that is, God Himself brought forth to the intellectual view of angels and men in a Divine Human Form, or as a Divine Man, all good, all wise, and everywhere present. The "form of a servant," which, as the apostle says, "He also took upon Himself, in which He made Himself of no reputation, and in which He humbled Himself and became obedient unto death, even the death of the cross" (Phil. ii. 7), was the humanity taken from the mother, which was in the "likeness of sinful flesh." (Rom. viii. 3.) Hence the apostle teaches that the Lord had the form of God and the form of a servant,—both were human; but the form of a servant was the merely human form taken from the mother, which He entirely put off, and the other the Divine Human Form taken from the Father or the essential Divinity, with which form "He ascended far above all heavens that He might fill all things" (Eph. iv. 10), and in which He is the only Object of worship to angels in heaven, because in that form "He is over all, God blessed forever;" and the Lord's divine will can only be done upon earth as it is done in heaven, and his true Church be established, in proportion as He is thus acknowledged and worshiped. APEX.

CHAPTER XVIII.

Correspondence of the Human Body and its Parts to Things Spiritual and Divine.*

THE human body, so fearfully and wonderfully formed, is an epitome of Divine Order, showing how the Deity operates by his life-giving influx, and in what manner *uses* of every kind are performed. The body, viewed physiologically as to its organs, functions and uses, is a type of all the divine operations, and also of the divine economy in the universe. As a *microcosm* or little world, the body is the image of the *macrocosm* or great world. Whatever principles of science have ever been discovered in mechanics, chemistry, hydraulics, hydrostatics, botany, electricity, etc., are perfectly imaged in the human frame by its functions and uses. Thus the body is the temple of all the sciences, both physical and philosophical.†

But this image can be rationally seen only by analogy and correspondence. Thus in the human system there is a perfect image of domestic order,—the *economy* of the body is the type of the *household* in which we should live. How one principle is *subordinated* to another, and how all are *coördinated* together, is perfectly exemplified in man's corporeal system. For without subordination and coördination there can be no order, and without order nothing can subsist in its proper state so as to perform its destined use. Again, in the human system there is a perfect exhibition of civil order and of political government. The *body* politic is conceived of as being in the human form, according to which the mind not only derives its metaphors of language, but its principles of thought. But lastly, the church and kingdom of God are thought of in accordance with the human form; the principles which govern this form also govern the mind when properly thinking about heaven and the church. Hence it is, that heaven is called "Christ's mystical body," and the faithful are said to be members of that body. (1 Cor. vi. 15; Eph. v. 30.)

---

* From the *Intellectual Repository* for January, 1851.
† See Swedenborg's Animal Kingdom, 317.

Now, from what has been said, it will follow that physiology is a most important science, not only to the medical practitioner, but to the general reader, since it forms, more directly than any other science, the basis of theology. It supplies a ground of thought respecting God, his kingdom, and the human soul, more solid and firm than any other kind of knowledge. Even the divine Word itself, the only source of all revealed knowledge respecting divine and spiritual realities, is likened by Swedenborg to a man; and the prophets, especially Elijah and John the Baptist, represented even as to their dress, the Word of God. From the importance, then, of physiology as a science, forming the basis of thought and reflection on subjects relating to the human soul, to God, and universally to things spiritual, celestial, and divine, every individual who desires to be gifted with any degree of spiritual and rational intelligence, should cultivate a knowledge of anatomy and physiology as the principal means of access to the great world of interior realities, or of genuine intelligence and wisdom. This will become more evident when we consider that the body and its parts often occur in the Scriptures, and that it is impossible to understand their true meaning without a spiritual discernment, or a spiritual perception of their correspondence to what is heavenly and divine. This will abundantly appear as we proceed.

The head and its coverings, the hair, the scalp and the skull frequently occur in Scripture, and in most cases in so striking a manner as at once to evince that something ulterior or spiritual is implied. One of the most universal metaphors of language is the *head*, as denoting the chief, primary, essential and governing principle in relation to the subject of which it is predicated. As being the central seat of the powers both of the will and understanding,—as denoting the mind in its first principles, the head is at once an obvious figure of the governing principle of the soul. From the head everything in the body is animated with life. Here it is that all motion, the first indication of life as well as its first correspondent, exists, and from which, with a velocity greater than that of electricity, it is communicated to the entire system. Here likewise dwell all the organs of sense, and here all sensation is experienced. The head being the *top* of the body, we find that in all those passages in the Word where in the common version we meet with the term *top*, in Hebrew it is *head*. Thus, "the tower, whose top (*head*) may reach unto heaven." (Gen. xi. 4.) "The top (*head*) of the ladder reached to heaven." (xxviii. 12.) "Jacob poured oil on the top (*head*) of the stone," etc. This is its common metaphorical meaning, because all correspondences have relation to the human form, and in most cases in Hebrew, designations of objects are taken from parts of the body. Thus we read of "trees clapping their hands." (Isaiah lv. 13.) This is adduced in order to show that everything when viewed from heaven, has relation to the human form, or to what is opposite thereto, and monstrous.

The correspondence of the *head* as the governing principle of the life, will now be obvious and the numerous allusions in the Word to the *head* will be seen in their true and edifying meaning. Hence the Lord is said to be "the lifter up of mine *head*" (Ps. iii. 3), to denote that during the process of regeneration He elevates the governing principle of our life to the love of Himself above all things, by which elevation our head is truly "*lifted up above our enemies*" (Ps. xxvii. 6), the evils to which we are prone. He also "anoints our *head* with oil" (Ps. xxiii. 5), to denote that He flows with his divine love—*oil*—into the inmost or supreme principles of our life, and thus governs and blesses all things in the mind of man. Of what use would it be to anoint the *head* with oil, unless it had this spiritual signification? Hence it is that to *anoint the head* is one of the divine precepts of the Gospel—(Matt. vi. 17)—to open the heart to the reception of the Lord's love. Our iniquities are said to go over *our heads* (Ps. xxxviii. 4) when, during temptations, we feel the sinfulness of our depraved nature, and dread lest it should become the *governing principle* of our life. In this case we feel that "*the whole head is sick*" (Isaiah i. 5), which signifies that even the governing principles of our life are nothing but evil, and that from the Lord alone can we be healed and restored to spiritual health. The mischief or evil of the wicked is said to return upon his own *head* (Ps. vii. 16), to signify, that according to the law of action and reaction, which is as prevalent in spiritual things as in natural, the evil intended always comes back again with sevenfold vengeance upon him who intends it; for all intentions and designs originate in the governing love, or the *head*; here also is the seat of all our *motives*, or of every thing which *moves* us to think, feel and act.

The *hair* which covers the head, and which is found more or less over the whole body, denotes, in relation to the principles of our life, what is most external and ultimate. As in nature or the great world around us all active principles and forces from the sun terminate in inactivity, inertia and fixedness, so in like manner in the little world of man, the body, all the active principles and forces of life from the head, terminate in the bones, cartilages, nails and hairs which are the ultimates where things settle down in comparative inertia and fixedness, deprived of nearly all sensation and life. Now the *hair*, and especially the *hair* of the head, is often mentioned in Scripture in a manner which it is impossible to understand but by means of the spiritual signification, discovered to our perceptions by the science of correspondences. In confirmation of this statement we will adduce out of many passages only a few.

What, for instance, is meant by the Lord's declaration in the prophet, that "*instead of well-set hair there shall be baldness*"? (Isaiah iii. 24). Again, what is signified when it is said that the "*Lord shall shave the head and the hair of the feet*"? (Isaiah vii. 20). And also, what is involved in the divine command to Jerusalem—"*Cut off thine hair, O Jerusalem, and cast it away*"? (Jer. vii. 29). Every man who believes the Word to be divine, can see that something important is involved in these statements; but he cannot have a clear perception of the divine teaching, unless he knows from correspondence the spiritual signification of the *hair*.

Of all the institutions among the Jews, that of the *Nazariteship* was probably the most remarkable: see Numbers vi., where the laws to be observed by the Nazarites are stated. One of these laws commands that the Nazarite, during his vow of separation, or of his especial consecration to God, "should suffer no razor to come upon his head; and that he should let the locks of the hair of his head grow" (verse 5). There were, it appears, two kinds of Nazarites: one like Samson and John the Baptist, who were Nazarites from their infancy; and another kind who voluntarily took upon themselves the vow of the Nazariteship for a season only, after which they returned to their usual avocations, and to their ordinary mode of living. But the distinguishing characteristic of the Nazarite was his *hair:* and in respect to Samson this was especially the case, for it is expressly stated that his wonderful strength consisted in his hair; and that when his locks were shorn, his strength failed him (Judges xvi. 17, 19). Now, no merely rational investigation could ever discover the reason why the strength of Samson consisted chiefly in *his hair*. No rationale of this circumstance can be discovered *à posteriori* by our ordinary modes of thinking and of rational investigation. Hence it is that mere rationalists, or those who reason from merely external grounds of thought, and from skeptical and negative principles, consider the history of Samson to be a mere fable from beginning to end; and so reject the Scriptures. This is the case with many at the present time in the Protestant universities and colleges of Germany, and also with some in this country. But it should be borne in mind that there is a *true* rationalism as well as a *false*, and that the *true* consists in reasoning from more elevated or more interior principles of thought, and thus in "judging not according to the appearance, but judging righteous judgment." But when the doctrine of correspondences and representatives is understood, new fields of thought, especially in relation to the Word of God, are opened to the mind; and what before might appear fabulous, or as the apostle says, *foolishness* to the natural man, assumes now a different aspect, and becomes the "wisdom of God unto salvation." Hence it is that the discovery of the true nature of God's Word, and of its spiritual sense by the science of correspondences, is not only indispensable to its right interpretation, but absolutely requisite to rescue the Scriptures themselves from rejection by the increasing powers of infidelity.

We learn from science that no power can be exercised but by ultimate principles. Thus, none of the internal physical powers of the body in the brain and in the heart, can be exercised but by the arms, hands and feet which are its ultimates. None of the mental powers of the will and the intellect can be realized but by the mouth, and in general by the muscular energies of the body which are ultimates. The same may be said of the steam-engine: none of its wonderful powers can be realized in useful effects, but by suitable machinery consisting of levers and wheels which form its ultimates. All powers, therefore, are exercised in ultimates. Now as the *hair* is the extreme ultimate of man, we may see, from the doctrine of representatives and correspondences according to which the Word of God is written, how it was that the great power of Samson resided in his *hair;* and as all the types and representatives in their supreme sense relate to the Lord, hence Samson was a type of the Lord in the flesh as our Redeemer, that is, clothed with the ultimates of humanity in which He subjugated the hells and accomplished the work of universal redemption. The power of Samson, therefore, represented the Lord's omnipotence when He descended into ultimates, or when the "Word became flesh." And generally He represented the power which every man by regeneration receives from the Lord, who alludes to this power when He says, "If ye have faith as a grain of mustard-seed, ye shall say unto this mountain, Remove hence to yonder place, and it shall remove; and nothing shall be impossible unto you" (Matt. xvii. 20). Hence the very important truth appears that unless we now, while in ultimates, endeavor to remove and reject, through the Lord's mercy and power, evil as the governing principle of our lives, we cannot possibly remove it after death when we leave the world of ultimates, any more than a man can walk without feet, which are his ultimates, or than a locomotive can speed its way without wheels, which are in a like manner its ultimates.

This, then, was the reason why the strength of Samson resided in his *hair*; and why the Nazarite was not allowed, during his Nazariteship, to cut his hair. For hereby was represented the power of celestial good in ultimates: hence we may see the reason why Jesus was called a Nazarene, and why He dwelt in Nazareth (Matt. ii. 23); and also why, when the Lord acknowledged himself to be Jesus of Nazareth, the officers who came to take Him *went backward and fell to the ground* (John xviii. 6), to denote the divine power which came from Him as the Divine Nazarite so remarkably represented by Samson who was a Nazarite from his infancy.

We may now see the signification of "*well-set hair*" in the passage quoted above. This finish and adornment to the body is a type of the orderly arrangement of all principles in ultimates; that is, in our sensual and corporeal affections and appetites. When these are *well-set*, that is, when they are subordinated and arranged under higher principles of spiritual and heavenly order, the Lord can flow in and bless with his divine operation and presence, every state of our lives from inmost to outermost principles. We may also see the reason why Jerusalem is commanded in the passage quoted above, "to cut off her *hair* and cast it away," to signify the cleansing of our sensual and corporeal states, that new ultimates may be formed denoted by the new growth of the hair. It is also evident why the Lord is said, in reference to the king of Assyria, to shave "the head and the hair of the feet," and to "consume the beard" (Isaiah vii. 20); which implies that all who from sensual fallacies as to the ultimate principles of thought, have cherished skepticism and infidelity against Divine Truth, will, at the time of judgment, be rejected. Hence we may also see why *baldness* was considered a reproach in the representative church. (See Lev. xxi. 5; Isaiah iii. 24, xv. 2; Ezekiel vii. 18.) For this imperfection signifies the destitution of truth in ultimates, which is the case with those who are confirmed in false doctrines, and also with those who, from inordinate worldly love and selfishness, are unconcerned about the knowledge of divine truth, except they can turn it to account in promoting some selfish advantage in the way of honor and gain.

As the case of Absalom and his wonderful hair is very peculiar, involving mysteries of wisdom which should be known in order that the Word may be rationally and spiritually discerned, and thus vindicated from the insults and assaults of infidelity, we shall resume the subject together with the correspondence of the skull in another paper. SCRUTATOR.

CHAPTER XIX.

THE TRUE WORSHIP OF THE LORD REPRESENTED BY THE OFFERINGS OF THE WISE MEN FROM THE EAST.—THE SPIRITUAL MEANING OF GOLD, FRANKINCENSE AND MYRRH, AS UNFOLDED BY CORRESPONDENCE.*

NOTHING is more precious to us than time, and the opportunities it every moment presents of working out our salvation by the subjection of every purpose, thought, imagination and act of our *external* to some divine and spiritual principle from the WORD OF GOD in our *internal man*. Thus "to seek first the kingdom of God and his righteousness" is our great and blessed duty, as well as the great safeguard against evil of every kind. The performance of this duty, through faith in the Lord, and the love and practice of his holy precepts, brings with it the blessed assurance that whensoever the Son of Man cometh to summon us hence, He will find us ready, "with our loins girded and our lamps burning."

Our months and days here are most precious because in time, during our probation in the world, we form the plane and the basis of our spiritual and eternal states. We are now in the ultimate plane of creation; and as regeneration can only be commenced in ultimates, "now is the accepted time, now is the day of salvation"; the more we cultivate our privileges here, the more extended, deep and solid will become the plane or base upon which our mansion of bliss hereafter can be erected. This plane or base can be cultivated to an indefinite extent; every moment may add something to its extension and culture. Our natural state may be compared to a vast wilderness, like the uncultivated plains of Australia or America, which in their natural state grow nothing useful for man;† but which are susceptible of cultivation to an indefinite extent, and of producing fruits in every variety for the good of mankind. Thus, whilst we are here, the

---

* From the *Intellectual Repository* for January, 1851.

† See Major Mitchell's account of Australia, in which he says, "that after travelling many miles in every direction, although there was much vegetation and many wild animals, yet they could find nothing truly useful for man." It would hence appear that everything truly useful for man is the result of culture, or of our coöperation with the Lord's Providence.

cultivation of our natural state can be enlarged, and the portions already brought under spiritual culture may be still improved as to quality and capacity for the production of the more exalted fruits of righteousness and of happiness. But when we leave this world, the ultimate of creation, we cannot extend and perfect the base upon which our mansion in heaven is constructed.

Now, all this spiritual culture of our natural state is denoted by the true worship of the Lord. Hence it was that the Latins used a term to denote *worship* which signified *culture*, namely *cultus*. Thus Cicero says—" Religio Deorum *cultu pio* continetur." But the true worship of the Lord is involved in the offerings which the wise men brought unto Him at his nativity,—an event which we have recently commemorated. These offerings were *Gold, Frankincense* and *Myrrh;* and the men who brought them were guided to Bethlehem by a star, which went before them.

All these particulars respecting the Lord's nativity are recorded, not merely as historical events, but for our instruction in righteousness, " that the man of God may be perfect, thoroughly furnished unto all good works." The *Magi*, or the wise men who came from the east, were in possession of knowledges from ancient revelations and traditions, that the Lord would come into the world to accomplish the redemption of mankind by subjugating the hells, glorifying his Humanity, and establishing a new dispensation of his mercy and goodness, or a New Church upon earth. There had always been from the first prophecy that was delivered, " that the seed of the woman should bruise the serpent's head," an anticipation in the minds of the pious of this great event; and when the "*desire of all nations*" was about to come, this hopeful anticipation was exceedingly active. The star which guided the wise men was the emblem of the knowledge they possessed respecting the Lord's Advent; and in reference to us of the New Testament Dispensation, and especially of the New Jerusalem Church, this star of spiritual knowledge should shine more brightly to our minds than it did to the wise men of old. This knowledge should bring us to the Lord at the commemoration of his nativity, and induce us to bring spiritually, in genuine worship, our offerings of Gold, Frankincense and Myrrh.

The Lord's nativity in itself is to be infinitely distinguished from the nativity of every other man. And unless this infinite distinction is in some measure seen, it is impossible to form a true idea of his Humanity, and of his being one with the Father even as the soul is one with the body. The reason why the Christian world in general thinks of the Lord's human nature as similar to the human nature of another man, and why they separate his Divine nature from his Human, is owing to the fact of their not having true ideas concerning his conception and nativity. If they would but think, as the Word plainly teaches, that his Father was the Divine Being Himself, of whom He was conceived, and that, of consequence, his soul was infinitely distinct from the soul of all other men who are conceived of merely human fathers, they would begin at the right point, to contemplate the true nature of the Lord's Humanity, and would see, as the apostle declares, that "in Him dwelleth all the fulness of the Godhead bodily," and that, consequently, his human nature must needs be divine, and not merely human; since no merely human nature, however exalted, could possibly contain all the fulness of the Godhead.

But as everything good and true, everything innocent, holy and happy must be born in us, if we are to become the subjects of regeneration, and thus prepared to enter into heaven; therefore the Lord's nativity, or his being born into the world, represents the birth of everything spiritual and heavenly from Him into our individual world, that is, into our natural man. "Christ in us," says the apostle, "is the hope of glory;" therefore the Lord, as to his divine love and wisdom, must be born in us, as the only hope of attaining to our glorious destiny in heaven. When, therefore, we commemorate the Lord's Nativity, we should remember that the most profitable way of contemplating this subject is, that the Lord as to all the principles of his kingdom (see Luke xvii. 21), must be born within us and that this birth is effected by the acknowledgment of Him in his Divine Humanity.

The Lord was thus born into the world to become our Redeemer and Saviour, in order that his redeeming and saving love and truth might be born in us individually. This blessed spiritual nativity, or this re-birth of man, is accomplished by virtue of the genuine principles of a living, holy worship. This worship is denoted by the offerings of the wise men; and we become truly wise in proportion as we offer up this holy worship to the Lord.

Gold, as the emblem of the first principles of a living worship, signifies the worship of the Lord from pure love or goodness. This is the first essential of all worship and of all genuine religion; and *gold* so frequently mentioned in Scripture, is the proper correspondent emblem of this love or goodness. Hence it was that this precious metal was so universally employed in the structure of the tabernacle and the sanctuary. The ark was overlaid with gold, the altar of incense in like manner, and nearly all the utensils of the sanctuary were either made of gold, or overlaid with it, in order to teach us, by the most striking symbols, that all worship should be performed from the principle of pure love. Hence it is that the Lord says to us, "I counsel thee to buy of me gold tried in the fire, that thou mayst be rich" (Rev. iii. 18), in order to teach us that He in his Divine Humanity, is the only Source whence all genuine love or pure goodness can be received.

But what is genuine love, and what is the relation of pure goodness to genuine love? There are various kinds of love and goodness, and it is of infinite moment to know what is genuine and what is spurious. As it is of importance to know whether gold is genuine, alloyed or spurious, possessing nothing but the color, or the external appearance; so it is of infinitely greater importance to know whether the love and goodness which actuate our life are of a genuine, or of a spurious character, since our happiness or misery in eternity will depend upon our life's love, or on our governing affection. There is natural good, moral good, and spiritual good. Natural good has relation solely to our natural life, its wants and supplies; and its source is the love of self and of the world. This is necessary for our natural state and our self-preservation, but it is not signified by the *gold* mentioned in the Word. No genuine worship springs from this love, and from the consequent goodness predicated of it; for all goodness is predicated of what a man loves, and consequently so long as a man is actuated by principles originating solely in what is selfish and worldly, he can offer to the Lord no *gold* of genuine love and goodness.

Moral good is of a higher order than merely natural and sensual good; because it springs from principles founded in man's rational nature and in his relations to society, and especially to the community in which he lives. These principles relate to what is equitable, just, honorable and becoming in decorum and manners. By this good a man rises above the animal, and above the selfishness of his own nature, and approaches nearer to the dignity of a real and true man. But from this moral good, so far as it originates in selfish and worldly considerations, which have relation to our merely natural life, no spiritual and genuine worship can be offered to the Lord. It is not the pure gold that He can accept; it may appear on its surface like gold, but the substance within is spurious and base, because, being derived from motives originating in the external man only, its quality is merely selfish and worldly. This good may make a man a good citizen of the world, and an orderly and even a virtuous member of society; but it cannot make him a citizen of heaven, nor prepare him to dwell with angels. An atheist may from these principles be an irreproachably moral man; but as his morality can only originate in what is merely natural, it is evident that he cannot thereby rise into a spiritual and heavenly state. Thus no pure *gold* of genuine worship can be offered to the Lord from this source only.

But when a man's moral principles are taken from the Word of God, his morality will have a spiritual and divine principle within it, and he will become not only a good citizen of the world, but a citizen of heaven at the same time; his "citizenship will," as the apostle says, "be in heaven." Hence he can bring his offering of *gold* in the worship of the Lord; his heart will be influenced by that love and goodness from which all true worship springs. The highest order of good that we can receive from the Lord is called *celestial*; this good is received from Him when everything in our internal and our external man is brought under the influence of love to Him above all things; when He is the beginning and the end of all our motives, affections and doings; when we love to live in dependence on Him alone, are resigned to his will, and acknowledge Him as the God of our sorrows as well as of our joys, directing all things, whether in states of prosperity or adversity, for our eternal good. The purest *gold* that we can offer to the Lord in worship, is from these principles, and it is called *celestial good*. Hence it was the first which the wise men, when they had opened their treasures, offered to the Lord.

Frankincense, as being grateful in its odor, was largely employed in the representative worship of the Jews, and generally throughout the ancient world, among the Asiatics, Greeks and Romans. The use of incense, therefore, in worship, was a rite derived from very ancient times. The true signification of this rite, as of every other, can only be known from the correspondence which, when explained, is easily understood. *Frankincense*, as being delightfully fragrant, corresponds to the gratefulness and blessedness of the spiritual life, as formed by the divine truths of God's Holy Word. All worship offered to the Lord from the spiritual affection of truth is grateful to Him; hence we so often read that the odor of incense was grateful to the Lord. Hence also it was that there was an altar of incense. The prayers of the saints are expressly called *incense* (Rev. v. 8), which is a proof that the offering of *incense* corresponds to the worship of the Lord from a spiritual affection of divine truth, that is, an affection irrespective of anything selfish and worldly, whether it be honor or gain. This second offering, therefore, of the wise men, denotes the worship of the Lord from a spiritual ground, or from the pure affection of truth; whereas, the offering of gold denotes the worship of the Lord from pure affection of goodness springing from a pure and exalted love of the Lord. We, therefore, bring an offering of *frankincense* unto the Lord, when we consecrate to Him all the intellectual and moving principles of the mind,—when our thoughts, our imaginations, our plans and projects, in short, when everything which constitutes our intellectual and mental life is brought under the divine influence of love to our neighbor. In this case the *incense* of our worship is grateful and acceptable to the Lord.

Gold and *Frankincense*, therefore, denote the interior and the inmost principles of all holy worship, without which the Lord cannot be approached in love and faith, however He may be approached with the lips and with outward professions of love and worship. He who does not spiritually bring with him this *gold* and *frankincense* when he worships the Lord, cannot worship Him in spirit and in truth, because he has not, through faith and love, the internal vital principles from which all true and acceptable worship springs.

But as an internal principle, our worship is not complete unless our external man as to his appetites and desires, is also consecrated to the Lord. *Myrrh*, therefore, in the order of principles, signifies the establishment of what is good and true from the Lord in our sensual and most external principles of life. Hence it was that Myrrh, as an odoriferous plant, was extensively employed in the service of the sanctuary in making the holy anointing oil. (Ex. xxx.) *Myrrh* also was used as an ingredient in the embalming of bodies; it was thus employed to embalm the Lord's body (John xix. 39, 40), to denote, by the law of correspondence, the preservation of divine and spiritual life in our lowest sensual principles,—in our appetites and sensations, so that whether we eat or whether we drink, we may do all, as the apostle says, "to the glory of God."

Let us, then, bring unto the Lord, when we engage in prayer in our closets, in our family circles, in the public worship of Him, and in all the duties and acts of life, the offerings thus spiritually understood and applied, of gold, frankincense and myrrh. FIDELUS.

APPENDIX.

I. DISSERTATION ON THE POSSIBILITY AND NECESSITY OF DIVINE REVELATION; ON THE CANON OF SACRED SCRIPTURE, AND THE GENUINENESS AND AUTHENTICITY OF THE VARIOUS BOOKS COMPOSING THE WORD OF THE NEW TESTAMENT AND THEIR UNCORRUPTED PRESERVATION; WITH A BRIEF ANALYSIS OF, AND A FEW REMARKS ON, EACH BOOK.

Which are the plenarily inspired books of the Word?

"The books of the Word are all those which have the internal sense; but those books which have not the internal sense are not the Word. The books of the Word in the Old Testament are the five books of Moses, the book of Joshua, the book of Judges, the two books of Samuel, the two books of Kings, the Psalms of David, the prophets Isaiah, Jeremiah, Lamentations, Ezekiel, Daniel, Hosea, Joel, Amos, Obadiah, Jonah, Micah, Nahum, Habakkuk, Zephaniah, Haggai, Zechariah, Malachi. In the New Testament, the four evangelists, Matthew, Mark, Luke, and John, and the Revelation. The rest have not the internal sense."—*Swedenborg, W. H.* 16; *A. C.* 10325.

"In the Gospels are the words of the Lord himself, all which contain in them a spiritual sense, whereby immediate communication is given with heaven; but in the writings of the Apostles there is no such sense, notwithstanding they are books of much use to the church."—*Swedenborg, A. C.* 815.

"In order to constitute a genuine book of the Word, it is necessary that it treat in an internal sense of the Lord Jesus Christ alone and his kingdom. See Luke xxiv. 27, 44; John v. 39, etc., etc."—*Swedenborg, A. C.* 3540.

"In the New Testament the character of essential sanctity or divinity pertains to the four Gospels and the Apocalypse, but not to the Acts of the Apostles and the Epistles. The former, like the Word of the Old Testament, were dictated by the inspiring power which took possession of the writers for that time only. The Acts and the Epistles, on the other hand, were written under that general but more lax kind of inspiration which was inseparable from the persons of the writers, and which may, therefore, be properly termed personal, while the other is denominated plenary, implying the dictation of the very words and phrases employed, all of which contain a higher internal sense, couched under the sense of the letter, and to be interpreted on the principle of correspondence."—*Statement of Reasons for embracing the Doctrines and Disclosures of Swedenborg, by G. Bush, late Professor of Hebrew in the New York City University,* p. 117.

In reference to the above books of the Bible, as constituting the pure Word of God, and the true mode of interpreting them, the late Rev. John Clowes, rector of St. John's church, Manchester, in the preface to his *Translation of the Gospel of Matthew,* thus writes:

"The books [of the Word above enumerated], according to this view of their distinguished characteristics, present us with the following curious and interesting facts:

"1. That more than twenty different writers, living in ages and places remote and distant from each other, are found to agree in expressing themselves in conformity to certain given laws and rules of speaking and writing, which it was absolutely impossible they could learn from each other.

"2. That those laws and rules never entered into the thought or imagination of any writer, either ancient or modern, until he discovered them from the compositions of the above writers.

"3. That those laws and rules involve in them points of most singular wisdom and edification, at once worthy of God to impart, and of the utmost importance to man to comprehend and obey.

"4. That unless those laws and rules be applied to the interpretation of the writings which are constructed in agreement with them, it is absolutely impossible for any one to discover the various sublime and instructive truths contained in those writings.

"5. But that if those laws and rules be applied, out of a real sincere desire to understand the will of the Most High, they are as a golden key to unlock the immense stores of heavenly wisdom, mercy and truth treasured up in His Holy Word."—3d ed., pp. xiii., xiv.

It is also worthy of profound consideration that all the passages of the Old Testament cited or alluded to in the four Gospels and the Revelation, are from the above plenarily inspired books *only*, and include nearly the whole of them, evincing the supreme authority to be attached to them by Christian believers.

Philo, who was contemporary with the apostles, and who quotes from or refers to all the books of the Word which are plenarily inspired, except the Lamentations and Daniel, makes no mention whatever of Ruth, Chronicles, Nehemiah, Esther, Ecclesiastes, or the Song of Solomon.—See *Henderson and Stuart*.

"Tatian, who wrote about the middle of the second century, composed a digest of the evangelical history, which was called τοτεσσαρων, that is, *the Gospel of the four*, or μονοτεσσαρων, that is, *one narrative composed out of the four*. Tatian is the most ancient harmonist on record; for if Theophilus, bishop of Antioch, had before written on that subject (as Jerome insinuates), his work is long since lost."—*Horne's Introd.*, vol. ii., pt. 1, p. 349, 8th ed.

"The four Gospels are *alone* received without dispute by the whole church of God under heaven."—*Origen*, as quoted by *Euseb.*, Hist. Eccl., liv. vi., ch. 25.

"The authenticity of the book of the Revelation was not denied during the two first centuries of the Christian era, and the respectable names of Hermas, Polycarp, and Justin Martyr may be adduced in its favor."—Pref. to the *Rev., Greek Test. for the London University*, p. 542.

"The sense of the inspiration of the evangelists—of some providential guidance by which they were led to select each fact in their history and each word in their narrative—is not more complete in Origen [than in Heracleon's commentaries]. The first commentary on the New Testament [or Gospels] exhibits the application of the same laws to its interpretation as were employed in the Old Testament. The slightest variation of language was held to be significant. Numbers were supposed to conceal a hidden truth. The whole record was found to be pregnant with spiritual meaning, conveyed by the teaching of events in themselves real and instructive. It appears also that differences between the Gospels were felt, and an attempt made to reconcile them."—*Westcott's Canon of the New Test.*, p. 335.

II. THE CANON OF SCRIPTURE.

The classical meaning of the original Greek word κανων, is *a straight stick or rod, staff, measuring rod or pole, beam of a balance*, etc. Hence tropically, *rule, norma;* thence, *law, prescription, fundamental, a guiding principle.* Among some of the Greek grammarians it was employed to denote a list or collection of Greek authors, who would serve as *models*, or examples for other writers. Among the Christian Fathers it obtained an enlarged, and occasionally a technical sense. It was sometimes used to designate a list of the clergy, or of others belonging to a church; a list of Psalms and Hymns appropriate for public worship; and even a list of furniture belonging to a church, etc. Very naturally it came to be employed, about the third century, to designate *a list of the Scriptural books* which were *publicly read in the churches.* See *Davidson's Ed. of Stuart on the Old Test. Canon*, p. 22 et seq.

Dr. Milner asserts that "the Canon of Scripture was fixed at the end of the fourth century."—*End of Controv.*, letter xi.

"It is one of the dictates of Pope Gregory VII. that 'no book or chapter is to be regarded as canonical without the Pope's authority.' (See *Earl. Baron. Annal. Eccl.*, xi., p. 632, ad. A. D. 1076.) Pighius says, 'The church [of Rome] can give canonical authority to books which have no such authority from themselves or their author.' (See his *Hierarch.*, iii. 3.) Stapleton asserts the same. (*Relect. Contr.* 5 qu. 2, art. 4. Cont. 5, lib. 9, c. 14.) He says that 'the Shepherd of Hermas and apostolical constitutions may be added to the Canon, if the church of Rome pleases.' And the Roman professor Perrone thus writes in his *Theological Lectures* (ii., pp. 1051, 1052. Ed. Paris, 1842), 'The Roman church being the mother and mistress of churches, had power to constitute the true Canon of Scripture.'"—*Wordsworth's Canon of the Scriptures*, note, p. 14.

Well may Newman ask, "On what ground do we receive the *Canon* [of the New Testament], but on the authority of the church of the *fourth* and *fifth* centuries. The church at that era *decided* that certain books were of authority."—*Essay on Development*, p. 142.

The absolute want of an authorized and determinate Canon of the Word of God, and a true and certain method of interpretation is powerfully illustrated by the extremes of that pernicious system of mythical exposition in which learned men, such as Bauer, Weisse, George, Strauss, and the Hegelian philosophers of Germany have so eagerly and freely speculated; from the awful and absurd rationalistic, materialistic, and pantheistic mode of interpretation adopted by Weescheider, Bretschneider, etc.; from the idealism of Kant, Fichte, and others; and from the numerous and mournful varieties resulting from all these neological systems. The delusive mode of interpretation adopted in *Essays and Reviews*, written by seven learned clergymen of the Established Church, is but an English outbirth from the same misleading source. It is, therefore, most refreshing to extract from the *Eclectic Review*, for the months of Sept. and Nov., 1825, the following able remarks:—

"The very fact that the classification of the Jews, in the time of Josephus, was supposed to need a revision, would of itself seem to indicate that this classification was not the original one,—was not the one which was current in the time of our Lord, and which we may presume to have been of prophetic origin, and virtually, therefore, divine and authoritative; and so far, therefore, confirms, or seems to confirm, the opinion as to the possible difference between the Old Testament of Josephus, and the Old Testament of our Lord. The changing also of the designation of the division known in our Lord's time as 'the Psalms' (an appropriate designation if it contained the Psalms only), into that of 'the writings,' upon the addition to it of writings that were not Psalms, and when, therefore, the appropriateness of the designation no longer existed, would seem also to confirm our yet further opinion, that the third of the three divisions of our Lord's time included only the Psalms. With regard to the insertion in this division of the book of Daniel, see Stuart, p. 263; and for an admirable defence of its veracity and inspiration, see *Walton's Genuineness of the Book of Daniel.*"—*The Law, the Prophets, and the Psalms; their Divine Inspiration*, by J. Collyer Knight, note, p. 58.

"The very import of the term canonical is a disputed point. Whether the declaration that 'All Scripture is given by inspiration of God,' can be safely extended to all the books included in the Jewish canon,— whether the whole of the Chetubim or Hagiographa, though of undoubted genuineness and authenticity as historical documents, can be considered as indited by the Holy Ghost, and as forming part of the rule of faith,—is by no means so clear as to warrant our demanding an unqualified assent and agreement on this point from all Christian men. Many pious persons have doubted whether the book of Esther, in which the name of Jehovah does not once occur, can be regarded as an inspired composition; and others have had difficulties in admitting the inspiration of Solomon's Song. Were we to take the word canonical as synonymous with inspired, such persons might conscientiously object to giving away those books as canonical Scriptures, and might plead for a canon more literally conformable to our Lord's three-fold classification of 'the Law, the Prophets, and the Psalms.' In their view, the books of Chronicles and the first book of Maccabees would rank in the same class of writings; and although they could not object to their circulation on the same grounds as apply to the positively exceptionable parts of the Apocrypha, such as Tobit, Baruch, and the spurious additions to the book of Daniel, still they would not be able to recognize them as given by inspiration of God."—*Ecl. Rev.*, 1825, pp. 192, 193.

"To the books of Moses, called by preëminence the Law, and the writings of the Prophets, including both Daniel and David in that number, the character of Revelation in the *highest sense* attaches; and we think exclusively."—*Ib.*, p. 388.

"With regard, however, to the books included in the Protestant canon, to which we have referred as possibly uninspired,—the books of Solomon and of Ezra [including Nehemiah], Esther, and the Chronicles,—we would ask: Do they in fact form any part of the Rule of Faith? Do they reveal a single doctrine? Do they contain a single prediction? Do they bear any prophetic witness to the Messiah? Does any one article of faith rest for its support on any passage in these books? Or are their value, their genuine excellence and authority, in the slightest degree invalidated by the doubt whether they are inspired? Does uncertainty on this point shake any portion of the Rule of Faith? Is there the slightest reason for apprehending that a man would less firmly hold the Divine authority of the Word of God,—less firmly believe in any one Christian doctrine, because, on the grounds above specified, he had doubts as to the inspiration (and canonicity in *this* sense) of either the book of Esther or the Chronicles? . . . But we may safely leave these questions to be determined by the good sense of our readers."—*Ib.*, p. 392.

The Rev. S. Noble, in an able critical examination of the papers in the *Eclectic Review*, from which the above passages are quoted, and which forms an article "*On the New-Church Canon of Scripture, as far as regards the Old Testament*," which was inserted in the *Intellectual Repository*, etc., new series, vol. ii., p. 364-379, says: "In one word: he [the reviewer] advocates, with trifling exceptions, in regard to the Old Testament, the pure New-Church Canon of Scripture: and the chief of these exceptions instead of tending to invalidate that Canon, strongly tends to confirm it. . . . Whenever, therefore, in future, the New Church is attacked with the charge of taking away from the Scriptures, she may interpose as a shield, in addition to the evidence collected in *the Plenary Inspiration*, the extensively respected authority of the *Eclectic Review*."

Well may the Rev. R. Hindmarsh ask: "By what rule of evidence is a man to form his judgment of a divine writing? Has he any other to appeal to than the uncertain and fluctuating decisions of the Romish church? What foundation has he for his belief in the sanctity and divinity of any particular books, except the opinions of fallible men, sitting to debate the question among themselves, and deciding by a majority of votes at one time that such and such a book is divine, and at another time that the very same book is destitute of that character; thus extending or diminishing the number of inspired writings not by a reference to any internal evidence, like that of the spiritual sense contained within them, nor to the words of the Lord in Luke xxiv. 44, which form the rule of judgment in this case, but by the caprice of the moment, or the influence of a prevailing party in the church? Even in the Established Church of this country, are not the Apocryphal books, at least seven of them, recommended and read in the national churches equally with those which are acknowledged to be canonical?*

"And with respect to the New Testament in particular, what reason is assigned by the Church of England, for admitting the Letters or Epistles of the different Apostles among the books of divine inspiration? None whatever, except that of general custom, which in itself is no reason at all.

"The truth appears to be, that neither the Romish nor Protestant churches have to this day clearly understood what it is that constitutes a divine book: they have not sufficiently considered the purport of our Lord's words to his disciples, when He told them, that 'all the Scriptures were written concerning Himself;' and that the books which He acknowledged as the Scriptures of divine truth, to be fulfilled in his own person, were those comprehended under the titles of 'the Law of Moses, the Prophets, and the Psalms:' see Luke xxiv. 27, 44. Thus our Lord has Himself laid down the rule by which we are to judge of those books and writings which alone deserve to be honored by the church as divine, viz., that in their inmost sense they treat solely of Him. Now, in many parts of the books of Moses, the Prophets, and the Psalms, no allusion whatever is made, in the literal sense of the expressions used, either to the Lord incarnate, or to his sufferings, death, and resurrection; and yet He came into the world to fulfil in his own person the whole and every particular part of the Sacred Scriptures, as it is written, 'The

---

* These books are, Tobit, Judith, the Book of Wisdom, Ecclesiasticus, Baruch, History of Susannah, and the History of Bel and the Dragon.

Word, which in the beginning was with God, and was God, was made flesh, and dwelt among us.' (John i. 1, 14.) And, again, 'All things must be fulfilled which were written in the law of Moses, and in the Prophets, and in the Psalms, concerning me.' (Luke xxiv. 44.) There must, therefore, be an internal spiritual sense belonging to the Word, not apparent in the latter; and without a doubt the Lord must have opened the understanding of his disciples to discern that sense, according to their measure, when, 'beginning at Moses, and all the Prophets, He expounded unto them in all the Scriptures the things concerning Himself.' (Luke xxiv. 27.)

"The same rule which so well applies to the Old Testament may also be applied to the New; and by it we are enabled to distinguish those books which are absolutely Divine to the very letter, in consequence of being dictated by God Himself, from those which, though excellent in their kind, are yet only the productions of good and pious men. Of the former description are the four Gospels and the Apocalypse; of the latter, are the Acts of the Apostles, and the Letters which they wrote to the different churches, to encourage and confirm them in the cause of Christianity." — *Hindmarsh's Vindication of the Character and Writings of Swedenborg, against the Slanders and Misrepresentations of Pike, of Derby.* 8vo edit., pp. 67, 68. See also *Noble's "Plenary Inspiration of the Scriptures,"* Appendix ii.

"The only writings of the Old Testament that can with certainty be proved to have been recognized by our Lord as Scripture, are 'The Law, the Prophets, and the Psalms' (or according to the briefer and more usual formula, as in Matt. vii. 12; xi. 13; xxii. 40, etc., 'The Law and the Prophets'). See Acts ii. 30.

"The other books of our fathers, or the other books mentioned by Siraclides, and 'the other writings' referred to by Philo (who flourished about A. D. 40); or 'the non-prophetical books' (by them so spoken of, therefore, as if they were distinct from and belonged to neither of the three divisions into which the Scriptures proper were divided), may have been added, indeed, as a sort of appendage, and probably were; just as the Jews of Alexandria added to their Greek version of the Hebrew Scriptures the writings of the Greek Apocrypha, and just as the Church of England to this day appends to its printed Bibles books which it believes to be uninspired. But, though added, there is no ground whatever for supposing that they formed part of Scripture proper, or were collected or appended as divinely inspired, or were regarded as such until the time of Josephus, *i. e.*, until after the destruction of Jerusalem." — *The Law, the Prophets, and the Psalms,* by J. Collyer Knight, 1866, p. 42.

III. THE BOOKS OF THE AUTHORIZED VERSION OF THE BIBLE WHICH ARE NOT PLENARILY INSPIRED.

In what estimation, then, are we to hold those books of the Bible which are not the plenarily inspired WORD OF GOD? This is an important inquiry, a brief answer to which I will attempt, because most unjust objections have been preferred against the New Church on this point, as though we depreciated these writings, when, in reality, we hold them in as much veneration as other Christian denominations do, differing with them, however, in this, that we look upon those books which bear undeniable evidence of having been written by plenary inspiration, according to the science of correspondences and representatives, with more reverence and as of weight-

not an honest and trustworthy narrative, and must be used with great caution as an authority, where anything is involved which affects Levitical influence.'"—*Newman's Hist. of the Heb. Monarchy*, etc., Lond., 1847, p. 146. See also *Parker's Translation of De Wette's Introduction to the Canon of Scripture*.

EZRA AND NEHEMIAH.

Calmet asserts that the books of Ezra and Nehemiah were not included in the earliest canon.—(See *Dict.*, art. SCRIPTURE.)

These books were anciently reckoned one, and were called the first and second books of Ezra, and in the Thirty-nine Articles of the Church of England, the first and second books of Esdras. This division is recognized by both the Greek and Latin churches. A third book is regarded by Protestants as interpolated, and a fourth as a forgery.

These books contain a narrative of events from the return of the Jews from Babylonish exile, extending over a period of 130 years, beginning with the edict of Cyrus, B. C. 536. They are valuable for the elucidation of Jewish history, as containing registers of the returning exiles, the account of the rebuilding and completion of the second temple at Jerusalem (B. C. 515), and as evidences of the literal accomplishment of several prophecies contained in Haggai and Zechariah. The second book is attributed by most writers to Nehemiah, who was cup-bearer to Artaxerxes Longimanus, king of Persia,—not the Nehemiah who returned from captivity with Zerubbabel. By the universal consent of antiquity, Ezra first collected the books of the Old Testament, arranged them in order, and wrote them out in the Chaldee character,—the Jews having lost the use of the ancient Hebrew language during their seventy years' sojourn in Babylon. On this account, and apparently for no other reason whatever, these writings bear his name. There is no direct quotation from, or obvious reference to, these books throughout the New Testament.

Calmet affirms in his *Dict.*, art. Scrip., that the books of Esther and Nehemiah were not included in the sacred canon by Ezra. And the learned Stackhouse, who followed the opinion of Dean Prideaux, further excludes the two books of Chronicles, none of which appear to have been added till the time of Simon the Just. It was 160 years after the death of Ezra to the appointment of Simon to the office of High Priest, who was the son of Onias, the previous High Priest, and the successor of Simon. It was the opinion of the ancient Rabbins, of the Chaldee Paraphrast St. Jerome, and some others, that Ezra and Malachi were the same individual, the former being his proper name, and the latter the name of his office, as it means *angel*, or *messenger*.—(See Haggai i. 13; Mal. iii. 1.)

"The book of Nehemiah was originally united with that of Ezra, as forming together with it one work, to which the name of the latter was given; and it appears that Ezra was regarded as in some sense the author of both. Each of these two books, moreover, appear to be a compilation inartificially put together, so as to occasion historical and chronological difficulties. Only a portion of each can be referred to the individual whose name it bears."—*Ibid.*, p. 22.)

RUTH.

This little book relates the interesting history of Ruth, a native of Moab, but a proselyte to Israel, and of her kinsman Boaz, whose son Obed was the grandfather of David. It evinces the presence of the Divine Providence with those who are faithful to the Lord's precepts and resigned to his dispensations, and illustrates the manner in which apparent evil is always overruled, in their experience, for positive good. A principal object of the unknown author was, however, to record a link in the genealogy of David, and his descent from Judah during ten generations, but the book has no evidence whatever of being divinely inspired. The history is generally considered as belonging to the same period as that of the book of Judges, and is placed by Bishop Tomline about 1250 B. C., but the chronology is very uncertain. It has been attributed by some to Ezra the Scribe, by others to Hezekiah. The Talmudists reckon it as a book of the Hagriographa; there is no reference to it in the New Testament.

ESTHER.

The female whose history is related in this book was a Jewish captive, named Esther, or Edessa, or Hadassa, who appears to have been promoted to the throne of Persia. The events recorded are supposed to come in between the 6th and 7th chapters of Ezra, and to extend over a period not exceeding twenty years. Of king Ahasuerus nothing appears to be known in history. Archbishop Usher supposed that he was Darius Hytaspes; Scaliger and others contended that he was Xerxes; Josephus and Dean Prideaux considered that he was Artaxerxes Longimanus, and the name is always so translated in the Septuagint version; others have asserted, however, that he was Cyaxeres, and others again affirm that Cambyses is meant. It is not known with the least certainty who was the author. Some have attributed it to Mordecai, her uncle (ix. 20); others have contended that it was composed by Joachim, the High Priest; and others, again, have ascribed it to Ezra. The Talmudists regarded it as a production of the joint labors of the Great Synagogue which succeeded Ezra.—(See *Gray and Percy's Key*, p. 119.)

Some commentators have been of opinion that it was translated from the Persian chronicles. (*Kotting. Thesau. Philol.*, lib. ii., cat. i., p. 488. *Aben. Ez. Com. in Proem. Selden in Theol.*, lib. iii., exercit. 5, p. 486. *Gray and Percy's Key*, p. 122.) The authenticity of the entire production has been widely questioned, and the chronology is most uncertain. There is no reference to it in the New Testament. It contains no prophecy, no allusion to the doctrines of religion, and is in no way distinguished from ordinary history. It affords not the slightest indication of being inspired, even in the lowest sense; indeed, the name of God, or Lord, or any other appellation by which the God of Israel was known, never once occurs in it.

The Greek and Romish versions reckon six chapters and ten verses more than the authorized English translation, which are not extant in Hebrew, and are supposed to have been forged by some Hellenistic Jew. It was not regarded as canonical by Melito; Athanasius rejected it altogether; and Gregory Nazienzen (A. D. 370) had such grave doubts respecting it, that he omitted it altogether from his canon. (See J. Collyer Knight, on *The Law, the Prophets, and the Psalms*, p. 50.) Calmet asserts that it was not inserted in the earliest canon. (See *Stuart's canon*.) Luther expressed a wish that it might be expunged from the Protestant canon. (*Conv. Serm.*, p. 494, and *Lib. Arbit.*, tom. iii., p. 82.) Gilfillan calls it "a fine romantic fragment of Jewish history." "That the book of Esther is, for the most part, a translated extract from the Book of the Chronicles of the Kings of Media and Persia," is a point which Dr. Henderson remarks, "is now very generally admitted among those who are conversant with Biblical criticism"

(*Insp.*, p. 322); but De Wette affirms that "it violates all historical probability, and contains the most striking difficulties, and many errors in regard to Persian manners." (§ 198, a.) Dr. Davidson, in his Introductory Essay to *Stuart's Canon*, observes that "the books of Esther, Ecclesiastes, and Solomon's Song, present perplexing anomalies, which have never been cleared away." (P. xv.)

JOB.

This book appears to be a very ancient dramatic composition, of wonderful power and great poetic beauty, designed to personify integrity towards God.

Dr. C. Middleton says: "The book of Job, according to the most probable opinion, is nothing else but a kind of fable, or poetic drama, designed to inculcate the certainty of a Divine Providence; the duty of patience in afflictions, and of submission to the will of God under all his dispensations, how severe or afflicting soever they may happen to be. This was the sense of the most ancient and learned Jews, who had no clear account or probable tradition concerning either Job himself, or the author of the book, which some ascribe to Moses; some to David; some to Isaiah, or one of the later prophets; while others suppose it to have been written after the Babylonish captivity: yet all of them seem to think that Job himself, if such a person ever really existed, must have lived in the times of the Patriarchs. But, be that as it will, it is evident that every part of the book breathes a dramatic and fabulous air: *the council of angels convoked by God; the appearance of Satan among them; his debate with God, and commission from Him; the several speeches of Job and his friends; the conclusion of the whole by the appearance of God himself in a whirlwind;* and all this, as the critics observe, delivered in verse, make it highly probable, or certain rather, that it was intended, as I have said, for an instructive or *moral drama*. Yet we find it referred to by Ezekiel and St. James, in the same manner as if it were a real history; because its moral or doctrinal part could not fail to have the same effect in one way as in the other." (*Essay*, etc.)

From the mention of Job in Ezek. xiv. 14, and James v. 11, most Christian commentators have regarded Job as a real person. From its Aramæan and Arabic diction it is supposed to have been written either by an Aramæan or an Arabian, and though containing no allusion whatever to Jewish history, it has been quoted by almost every uninspired Hebrew writer from the age of Moses to that of Malachi. It contains very important instructions, and transmits to us the earliest records of the patriarchal doctrines of religion. It is said by Horne to approximate in its form to the Mekana, or philosophical discourses of the Arabian poets. "*Who wrote it? When was it written? When annexed to the Canon?*" says Stuart, "are questions about which there has been, and will be, endless dispute." The book is mentioned by neither Philo nor Josephus.

"This book," says the Rev. S. Noble, "makes nearer approaches to the character of an inspired composition [than any of those we have considered], having been written in very ancient times, by a highly illuminated person, deeply grounded in the wisdom of those times, and in the science of correspondences, which formed a great part of that wisdom: whence the book is composed in a style approaching to that of the Word itself, being written by correspondences, and thence containing an internal sense, though not exactly of the same kind, nor arranged in the same perfect order and unbroken series, as is the internal sense of the Sacred Books themselves." —*Int. Rep.*, New Series, Vol. ii., p. 378.

"The book of Job is, by learned theologians, said not to be a Hebrew production. Job lived in the land of Luz—Aramen—of which Edom was a district, and Arabia our modern designation. Job was not a Hebrew of the Hebrews, but an *Arabian ;* and, according to Hales, his probable epoch was about 2337 B. C., that is, from 600 to 800 years before Moses."—*Gliddon's Ancient Egypt*, p. 12.

The Hindoos have a beautiful drama, similarly constructed to the book of Job, which gives an account of "a perfect man," called Ara-Chaudram, and who is represented as the sovereign of a large kingdom. For a detail of the leading facts, and a comparison of them with those which occur in Job, see *Roberts's Oriental Illust.*, 2d ed., pp. 245-254.

"Our opinion on the book of Job agrees with those who consider it a parable to explain the different opinions on Divine Providence. Some of our rabbis expressed themselves in the Talmud by the words 'Job never really existed, but is only a fable;' others, who maintained his real existence, did not all agree as to the time and the place where he lived, so that some of them thought him to have been a contemporary of the patriarchs; others place him coeval with Moses; others, again, fix his period in the reign of David; and, last of all, some class him among those who returned from Babylon; which differences only strengthen the opinion that he never existed."—*Moreh Nebuchim*, part 3, ch. 22, trans. M. B. H., *Heb. Review*, vol. ii., 1835, p. 184.

PROVERBS.

This book contains a collection of concise and sententious maxims for the regulation of the life, designed to admonish the young and to urge them to the diligent study of true wisdom. "We are not," says Bishop Hopkins, "generally to expect connection either of sense or sentences in this book of Proverbs."

Many of them have evidently descended from very ancient times, and some are founded on correspondence. This collection of Proverbs has usually been ascribed to Solomon, though doubts have been entertained whether he really was the compiler of the whole. It also includes the Proverbs said to have been transcribed or copied out by the scribes of Hezekiah, king of Judah, whom he employed to restore the services and writings of the Jewish dispensation (Prov. xxv. 1); the instructions delivered by Agur to his pupils Ithiel and Ucal (Prov. xxx. 1); and the precepts of King Lemuel by his mother (xxxi. 1). There is no trace of plenary inspiration in them; and "with regard to the interpretation of them," says Nicholls, "it is important to remark that some of them, though expressed without limitation, are yet not to be understood as universally true."—*Help to Reading the Bible*, pp. 264, 265.

"The book of Proverbs never once appeals to the Pentateuch, and owing to this and other discrepancies from the book of the law, was only adopted into the canon after strong opposition."—*Tract. Schabb.*, ch. ii., fo. 30; see also *Von Bohlen, Int. to Gen.*

ECCLESIASTES.

This book, like the former, is traditionally attributed to Solomon. In Hebrew it received its name from the initial words—"The words of the preacher." Its object seems to have been to demonstrate the eternal duration of the soul, the vanity of all earthly conditions and pleasures, and the inestimable advantages of religion; "that skepticism never satisfies and quiets the mind, and the deliverance from it is the greatest of all good, as well as the highest duty" (see *Stuart*).

"As it stands in our Vulgate," says a

modern writer, "it certainly bears but few marks of inspiration, and, indeed, we cannot but feel that it needed none to its production. Valuable and interesting in its own way, especially from its age and authorship, and more particularly from the impressive and edifying nature of its last chapter, commentators have rather looked upon it as the moralizing of a Jewish Dr. Johnson, founded entirely on worldly experience—the 'night thoughts' of the wise king, when the world went wrong with him—than one of superhuman authority, justifying the faith and hopes of the Christian reader." It contains no prophecy, and is not referred to in the New Testament. "The claims of Solomon to be the author of Ecclesiastes have not passed entirely without dispute." In prop. iv., p. 348, of his *Demonstratio Evangelica*, Huet refutes the opinions of Grotius, who ascribes the work to Zerubbabel; of the Talmudists, who considered Hezekiah to be the author; and of Kimchi, who ascribes it to Isaiah. Huet decides with St. Jerome and Leusden in favor of Solomon. Jahn says that "it is impossible to say who was the author." Zirkel, in his *Critical Examination* (pub. 1792), considers it to have been written by some of the *later Hebrew writers*, between the years 380 and 130 B. C., or long after the time of the latest inspired Hebrew prophet. The Jena Reviewers ascribe it to a Jew of Alexandria, about 240 B. C. As to this book, it is full of ancient wisdom, and Desvœux thinks it is designed "to prove the immortality of the soul, or rather the necessity of another state after this life, from such arguments as may be afforded by reason and experience" (*Philosop. and Crit. Essays on Eccl.; Maltby's Sermons*, notes, vol. ii., p. 493; *Dr. A. Clarke's Comment.*). Jahn asserts that "the contents are not adapted to the multitude;" and that "the intention of the writer was to repress the restless and eager efforts of men, which hurry them on in heaping up wealth, in securing pleasures, and in acquiring honors; and at the same time to instruct them not to increase the troubles of life by denying themselves the enjoyment of harmless, though uncertain and fleeting pleasures."—*Introd.*, pp. 215, 217.

Stuart writes that "the philosophic doubts and puzzles of Ecclesiastes, and the manner of discussing them, have no parallel either in Proverbs, or in any other part of the Hebrew Scriptures. They remind one of many things discussed by Socrates in the Dialogues of Plato."—*Crit. Hist. and Defence of the O. T. Canon*, Dr. Davidson's Eng. ed., p. 129.

"In *Vayyikra Rabba* (§ 28, p. 161, c. 2) it is said, 'Our wise men were desirous to keep back or conceal the book of Coheleth, because they found in it words which might lead to heresy.' The *Talmud* speaks of some 'who found contradictions in it.' I have seen some among the Jews, who maintained that the book teaches the doctrines of Epicurus."—*Ib.*, p. 337.

If it were the production of Solomon, it must, it is said by some, have been composed in his old age, when he had recovered from the partial apostacy into which he had allowed himself to be most unhappily betrayed by his idolatrous wives. In this case it may have been the result of serious reflection, and it is hoped of deep repentance.

THE SONG OF SOLOMON.

This book, otherwise entitled "A Song of Songs," is supposed by many commentators to have been written by Solomon, or some contemporary, as an Epithalamium, on the occasion of his marriage with an Ethiopian, and gentile daughter of Pharaoh Shishak, or Shishank, King of Egypt, under whose influence he established in Israel an infamous idolatry. It contains many correspondences, and many beautiful metaphors,—but exhibits no connected series, like the pure inspired Word of God. It contains no prediction, is never quoted in Scripture, and is only received as tradition. It serves, however, the important purpose of supplying illustration and confirmation as to the meaning of many Hebrew words, and some ancient correspondences. A writer in the *Crit. Bib.* observes respecting this book, that "it is a mere human composition; that there is not the least intimation in it of a pretension or claim to inspiration; no 'THUS SAITH THE LORD;' that it does not once mention the name of God; and that we have no quotation from it in the New Testament;" and is disposed to ascribe it to some unknown contemporary writer; that "while it may still be suited to the tastes and habits of oriental nations, with us, in the occidental world, it is better, for many reasons, to abstain from the use of it;" and that "it has had its day." (Vol. iv., p. 557).

Dr. Adam Clarke says, "there have been some doubts concerning the author of this book. . . . . Strictly speaking, the Book of Canticles is neither an Ode, an Idyll, a Pastoral, or an Epithalamium; it is rather a composition *sui generis*, and seems to partake more of the nature of what we call a MASK, than anything else,—an entertainment for the guests who attended the marriage ceremony, with a *dramatic cast* throughout the whole, though the *persons* who speak and act are not formally introduced. . . . . The *name of God* is not found in it; nor is it quoted in the New Testament. . . . . Is it not a very *solemn* and indeed *awful thing* to say, 'This is the *voice of Christ to His Church*,' 'This is the *voice of the Church of Christ*,' etc., etc., when there is no *proof* from God, nor from any other portion of his Word, that these things are so? . . . . The principal part of the commentators on this book, especially those who have made it their *separate* study, have in general taken it for granted that this mode of interpretation is incontrovertible; and have proceeded to *spiritualize* every *figure* and every *verse*, as if they had a divine warrant for all they have said. Their conduct is dangerous; and the result of their well-intentioned labors has been of very little service to the cause of *Christianity* in general, or to the interests of true *morality* in particular. . . . . The conviction on my mind, and the conclusion to which I have conscientiously arrived, are the result of frequent examination, of careful reading, and close thinking, at intervals, for nearly *fifty* years; and however I may be blamed by some, and pitied by others, I must say it as fearlessly as I do conscientiously, that in this inimitably fine Hebrew ode I see nothing of *Christ* and his *Church*, and nothing that appears to have been intended to be thus understood; and nothing, applied in this way, that, *per se*, can promote the interests of true Godliness, or cause the simple and sincere to 'know Christ after the flesh.' Here I conscientiously stand; may God help me."—See *Commentary Introduction to the Canticles*, 1844, vol. iii., pp. 2563 et seq.

Wharton refused to admit its divine authority. Origen, in his preface to the commentary on this book, holds it to be an epithalamium, or marriage song, as Ewald supposed in the form of a drama. Bishop *Lowth* calls it "a nuptial dialogue." This idea has been, in modern times, improved by *Lowth*, Bossuet, Michaelis, and other commentators. Bossuet, a critic of profound learning, calls it also a pastoral eclogue, consisting of seven acts, each act filling a day, concluding with the Sabbath, describing, as Eichhorn, Jahn, etc., conclude, "the chaste mutual love of two young persons antecedent to marriage," "having no natural historical foundation." Many commentators, with the Targum, Cocceius, Luther, and St. Bernard, have looked upon this book as either figurative or allegorical, or as an elegant fable. Dr. Pye Smith, however, who, with Eichhorn, Bauer, Jahn, etc., entirely rejects the allegorical meaning, seems inclined to exclude the book from the canon. He considers it to have been written, not by Solomon, but by a far happier person among his contemporaries, yet unknown to posterity. And that, although the mystical sense may **not have been designed by the author, or authors, yet by those who introduced the book into the canon, it was the** *only one* that was regarded.—See *Dr. W. Wright's note to Seiler*, pp. 243–246.

Rosenmüller, with Jarchi, regarded it as "a dramatico-allegorical poem." Theodorus of Mopsuesta, in the 4th or 5th century, held that it was aphrodistic, or libidinous, and, with Josephus, rejected it from the sacred books.—*Caucissius*, vol. i., p. 577. "Had it been a prophetical book," he says, "there would have been some mention in it of the name of God." "The public reading of it was never allowed by the Jews." Le Clerc calls it "a pastoral eclogue." The time of its authorship is also greatly disputed. Its canonicity has been questioned in all subsequent ages.

On its structure there has been a great diversity of opinions. Horne considers that the most probable which refers it to the idyls of the Arabian poets. Stuart thinks that Solomon is the subject of the book, but that there is great difficulty in regard to Solomon being the proper author.—See *Old Testament Canon*, Dr. Davidson's ed., pt. iii., p. 354.

"If the books of Proverbs and Solomon's Song can be proved to be inspired, it is not, we apprehend, on the ground of either external or internal evidence, but on that of the inspired character attaching to their royal author. That God was the author of his wisdom we know, as the Holy Spirit is the author of all true wisdom, the inspirer of 'all good counsels,' as well as of 'all holy desires and good works.' But whether he was 'moved by the Holy Ghost' in penning these compositions, or rather in speaking the proverbs ascribed to him, is not so certain as to rank among articles of faith. There appears to us far stronger grounds for believing that 'Ezra, the priest and scribe,' acted and spake under the guidance of inspiration; but it is observable that he is never spoken of as a prophet, nor does he lay claim to that character. Even, however, admitting both Solomon and Ezra to have been inspired men, it would be very difficult, we conceive, to prove that this character attached to the anonymous authors of the book of Esther and the book of Chronicles. We must, therefore, still contend that these books, though very properly included in the canon as both '*authentic and true*,' are possibly not inspired; and that the question whether they are so or not comes within the proper range of human wisdom."—*Eclectic Review*, Nov., 1825.

"Of the books of the Proverbs, Ecclesiastes, and the Song of Solomon, Rabbi Nathan observes that in former times it was said of these books that they were apocryphal."—*Michaelis, Introd.*, vol. i., p. 71.

Of Esther, Ecclesiastes, and the Song of Songs, Dr. Davidson says, "they present perplexing anomalies which have never been cleared away. Manfully," he adds, "has he [Moses Stuart] endeavored to solve them. But that he has been successful will scarcely be maintained by such as are fully aware of those anomalies in all their extent and magnitude."—*Introd. Essay to Stuart's Cr. Hist. and Def. of the Old Test. Canon*, p. xv.

It has been justly remarked that "Nehemiah, Proverbs, Ecclesiastes, and the Song of Songs speak exclusively of their human authors."

IV. THE APOCRYPHA.

The Apocrypha includes a number of books, generally placed between the Old and New Testaments, none of which were ever received by the Jews as of divine origin. They are not inserted in Melito's Catalogue in the second century, nor does Origen, in the third century, or Epiphanius, in the fourth, acknowledge their authenticity. Of these books, however, the Romish council of Trent, held in the 16th century, decreed that the two books of Esdras, Tobit, Judith, Wisdom, Ecclesiasticus, Baruch, the two books of Maccabees, with which are mixed up, or to which are appended, additions to the books of Esther and Daniel, the Song of the Three Children, the Story of Bel and the Dragon, the History of Susannah, and the Epistle of Jeremiah, should thenceforward be held as canonical or divinely inspired.

"The books not admitted into the canon of Scripture were called 'Apocryphal,' a word derived from the Greek, which means *to hide*, because of their not being submitted to public inspection as the inspired books were; or, according to others, because they were not admitted into the ark, the place where the canonical books were deposited."—*Burnett's Exposition of the XXXIX. Art. of the Ch. of England, revised by Page*, p. 89.

V. RABBINICAL LITERATURE.

The Chaldee paraphrases are translations of the Old Testament, made directly from the Hebrew text into the dialect of the Chaldean language, anciently spoken throughout Assyria, Babylonia, Mesopotamia, Syria, and Palestine; and were made, after the Babylonish captivity, for the use of those who had forgotten, or were ignorant of, the Hebrew. They were called TARGUMS, from a word which means *to explain, to expound*, or *to interpret*. Eight of these have descended to our times, but the last, or the two books of Chronicles, was not known till 1680. The important use of these Targums has been to vindicate the genuineness of the Hebrew text.

The Jews were persuaded that the Oral or Traditionary Law, which originated in the interpretation of the Scriptures by the Scribes, was a code of divine origin, as well as the plenarily inspired Law of Moses. Hence arose numberless Rabbinical glosses and opinions, which became, in process of time, uncertain, obscure, contradictory, and perplexed. These traditions, as they were rightly called (Matt. xv. 2-6; Mark vii. 3-9), were believed to have been delivered by Moses, and transmitted, in unbroken succession, through Aaron, Eleazar, Joshua, and the prophets, to the members of the Greek Sanhedrim, and thence to Simeon, Gamaliel, and ultimately to Rabbi Jehuda, surnamed Hakkadosh (*i. e.*, the holy), president of the Sanhedrim (as they continued to call a council of a remnant of the people, who remained some time in Galilee, about the middle of the second century of the Christian era), who, after the labor of forty years, collected them in six books, because they were too burdensome to the memory, and called them the MISHNA, or repetition of the Oral Law. Eighteen out of the sixty-two treatises into which that work was divided, were translated into English, in 1843, by the Revs. Mr. de Sola and Dr. Raphall, Rabbins of

THE TALMUD AND SEPTUAGINT.

great learning and influence, "at the request of the Uphardim Synagogue," and called by them "*God's Explanation of the Written Law.*" This work became the study of all the learned Jews, who employed their skill and ingenuity in making comments upon it. These comments are collected together, and called the GEMARA, which means *perfection*, and were regarded as the complement, because by them the Mishna is fully explained, and the whole of the traditionary doctrines and precepts of the Jewish law and religion completed. Thus the Mishna is the text, and the Gemara is the comment or note upon the text, and both together make what the Jews call the Talmud, which means *doctrine, disciple*, and includes the civil and canonical law of the Jewish people, together with numberless profane statements and absurd fables. That made in Judea is called the Jerusalem Talmud, and that made in Babylon is called the Babylonish Talmud; the former was completed about the third century of the Christian era, and the latter in the beginning of the sixth.

After the destruction of Jerusalem, and the consequent dispersion of the Jews, various schools were opened, in which the Scriptures were diligently taught. One of the most distinguished of these academies was that of Tiberias, in Palestine, which Jerome mentions as existing in the fifth century. The doctors of this school, early in the fourth or fifth century, agreed to revise the sacred text, and issue an accurate edition of it; for which purpose they collected all the scattered critical and grammatical observations they could obtain, which appeared likely to contribute towards fixing both the reading and interpretation, into one book, which they called MASORAH, that is, tradition, because it consisted of remarks received from others. The *true reading* is, therefore, the subject of the Masorah, as the *true interpretation* is that of the Mishna and Gemara. The Masoretic notes and criticisms have been called "the Hedge of the Law," and relate to books, verses, words, vowel points, and accents. The inventors of this system of marking Hebrew were called *Masorites* or *Massorets*. They counted, with the greatest reverence, the number of each of the words and letters occurring in the Hebrew Bible, and marked the number of the verses of each book and section, and noticed the middle verse, clause, and letter. They marked what they considered imperfect verses, the words they believed to have been changed, and the letters which they deemed superfluous, all repetitions, and different renderings, and the various meanings of the same word. They noted down what letters were pronounced, what were inverted, and such as hang perpendicularly. This work has been regarded as a monument of stupendous labor and unwearied assiduity, united with the greatest veneration, and has been of incalculable service in preserving the accuracy and integrity of the original text of the Old Testament Scriptures.—(See *Prideaux's Connection; Bishop Tomline's Int. to the Study of the Bible*, p. 169; *Horne's (Hartwell) Introd. to a Crit. Study of the Sacred Scrip.*, vol. ii., pp. 37, 417; *Motives to the Study of Bib. Lit.*; and *Kitto's Cyc. of Bib. Lit.*)

VI. THE SEPTUAGINT, OR GREEK VERSION OF THE OLD TESTAMENT.

This translation of the Old Testament into Greek, is the oldest version in existence, except the Chaldee and Samaritan. It was made at Alexandria, and is often called the Alexandrian Version. After the Babylonish captivity, the tribe of Judah alone returned to their native land, accompanied, however, by a number of mixed Jews, who were allowed to settle in Galilee. Many Jews were dispersed abroad, and had settled in the

Grecian empire. It is supposed that at their request Ptolemy Philadelphus, King of Egypt, applied to Eleazar for a copy of the Scriptures in the Greek language; and that the High Priest at Jerusalem appointed seventy men, learned in the ancient Hebrew and Chaldee, to accomplish this important work. It was completed about 280 years before the Christian era. It was approved by the Sanhedrim, or great judicial council of the Jews, consisting of seventy men. From one or other of these circumstances, or from both, it was called *the Septuagint*, or Version of the Seventy. It was deservedly held in great estimation, and was universally used by the Hellenistic Jews, or those who spoke the Greek language, and publicly kept and used in their synagogues. This version is of inestimable value in the criticism and interpretation of the Hebrew text, determining the meaning of numerous words and phrases, throwing light upon many laws and customs, and explaining more precisely many historical facts: for it was made at a period when the Hebrew language, having suffered much decay, was no longer vernacular in Palestine, and had ceased to be understood by the Jews of the dispersion. Most of the quotations in the New Testament are made from it. It was held in high estimation, and was of immense importance, in the first ages of Christianity, and for five centuries was used and read in public worship. Some authors have asserted, but without direct authority, that there was a Greek version of the Scriptures in use 356 years B. C., but that the translation procured by Ptolemy Philadelphus was the more correct and perfect.—See *Dr. A. Clarke's Success. of Sacred Literature*, vol. i., p. 32; *Dean Prideaux's Connection*, vol. iii., p. 43, ed. 1725; *Nolan's Integrity of the Greek Vulgate; Grimfield's Apology; Kitto's Cyc. Bib. Lit.; Bishop Tomline's Introduction*, etc.

VII. THE VERSIONS OF THE SCRIPTURES USED BY EMANUEL SWEDENBORG.

Augustus Nordenskjöld, in his "Remarks on the different editions of the Bible made use of by Emanuel Swedenborg," inserted in the *New Jerusalem Magazine*, for the year 1790, p. 87, says that "he [E. S.] possessed four editions of the Holy Bible in Hebrew:"

"I. That by *T. Pagnini* [*à Benedicto Aria*] *Montano*, fo. 1657, in which he made no remarks in the margin, as I was informed by the person who bought it at the sale.

"II. *Biblica Hebraica punctata, cum Novo Testamento Græco*, 8vo, of the edition of Manasse Ben Israël, Amsterdam, 1639. This was also without remarks.

"III. *Reineccii Biblic. Hebr.*, Lipsiæ, 1739, 4to. This I have happily found; it is filled with remarks, and with the Latin translation of several Hebrew words, as also some observations on the internal sense. The book is much used. It is added to the collection of manuscripts.

"IV. *Biblia Hebraica Secundum Edit. Belgicam Edvardi Von der Hooght, una cum Versione Latina Sebastiani Schmidii, Lipsiæ*, 1740, 4to. There is no remark in the margin, but a great number of lines and asterisks, at the most remarkable places of the Latin version, the original text not being in any manner touched; because, according to the expression of Swedenborg, 'The word is perfect, such as we have it.'

"Of the New Testament in Greek he had none besides that mentioned, No. II., and which is a fresh edition of that by Elzevir in 1624, made by Janson, and the edition of Leusden, Amsterdam, 1741, with the Latin version. It is probable he has followed this edition in translating the *Apocalypse*.

"Of the Latin versions of the Bible, he made use chiefly of that of *Schmidius*,

Lipsiæ, 1740, after the time that he began the *Arcana Cœlestia*, because he found this to be more literal and exact than all the others. Nevertheless, in all his quotations, and above all in the *Arcana Cœlestia*, he has more exactly expressed the sense according to the original language. He has never followed the version of *Arius Montanus*, either of the Old or New Testaments, as I have carefully examined and found to be the case. But he had four copies of the Latin translation of Castelliano, apparently for the purity of the language, which he was very studiously applying himself to, before he learned Hebrew in 1745. In his quotations of the New Testament he only made use of *Schmidt's* translation, 1st ed., which he sometimes has left, the better to express the sense of the Greek.

"From this it appears that he always had the originals in hand. But with respect to the author's translations of Genesis, Exodus, and the Apocalypse, they are directly translated from the originals."

"Sebastian Schmidt was professor of Oriental languages at Strasburgh. Of his version, which is placed opposite the Hebrew text, and was published after the author's decease, there have been several editions. It is *strictly literal;* and is chiefly useful to students in the Hebrew language."—*Horne's Introd.*, vol. ii., part 2, pp. 7, 65. My own edition is that of 1740. To the work are prefixed:—1. A preface, by J. C. Clodius, vindicating the edition of Von der Hooght against some critical censures; 2. Von der Hooght's preface, with the testimonies of some eminent scholars in favor of his edition; and, 3. The testimony and judgment of the Theological Faculty of Strasburgh in favor of Sebastian Schmidt's Latin Translation. (E. M.)

"The design of Sebastian Chahlon, or Castalio, was to render the Old and New Testaments in elegant Latin, like that of the ancient classic authors."—*Ib.*, p. 64.

"The translation of Pagninus [Sanctus, an Italian Dominican] was revised by Benedict Arias Montanus, who has erroneously been considered as a new translator of the Bible in the Latin language. His chief aim was to translate the Hebrew words by the same number of Latin ones; so that he has accommodated his whole translation to the most scrupulous rules of grammar, without any regard to the elegance of his Latinity. Montanus' edition, therefore, may be considered rather as a grammatical commentary than a true version, and as being adapted to instruct young beginners in the Hebrew, than to be read separately; being printed interlinearly, with the Latin word placed exactly over the Hebrew, it saves the student the trouble of frequently referring to his lexicon. In the New Testament, Montanus changed only a few words in the Vulgate version, where he found it to differ from the Greek. This revision has been very frequently printed in various sizes."—*Ib.*, p. 63. (My own edition is that of 1657, fo., "Impensis Christiani Kirchneii. Teppis Johannis Wittigan, Lipsiæ." At the beginning of the Old Testament is a MS. note which states that this translation "was generally admired both by Jews and others acquainted with the Hebrew, for its exactness and fidelity. He is blamed by some, and particularly by Father Simon, for being too literal. Huetius, nevertheless, proposes him as a model for all translators of the Sacred Text, whether of the Old or the New Testament, for the same plan is seen in both. Luther spoke of him and his translations in the highest terms of applause. He died in 1536, aged 70 years."—E. M.)

VIII. ON THE INTEGRITY OF THE WORD OF GOD, AND ITS MIRACULOUS PRESERVATION.

Dr. Moses Stuart observes: "In the Hebrew MSS. that have been examined, some 800,000 various readings actually occur as to the Hebrew consonants. How many as to the vowel-points and accents no man knows. But at the same time, it is equally true, that all these taken together, do not change or materially affect any important point of doctrine, precept, or even history. A great proportion, indeed the mass of variations in Hebrew MSS., when minutely scanned, amount to nothing more than the difference in spelling a multitude of English words [as *honour, honor*].

"Indeed, one may travel through the immense desert (so I can hardly help naming it) of Kennicott and De Rossi, and (if I may venture to speak in homely phrase) not find game enough to be worth the hunting. So completely is this chase given up by recent critics on the Hebrew Scriptures, that a reference to either of these famous collators of MSS., who once created a great sensation among philologers, is rarely to be found."—*On the Old Testament Canon*, p. 169.

"When the very erudite and truly pious Professor Bengel, of Tubingen, published his New Testament, with all the various readings which he had been able to discover, many minds were filled with anxiety, thinking that an entirely new Testament would be the result in the end, if all the various readings were hunted up. They thought it would be better to leave things as they were. But mark: although 40,000 various readings were discovered in the ancient MSS., the New Testament was hardly at all altered thereby."—*Oldhausen, The Genuineness of the N. T. Writings.—Clarke's For. Theol. Lib.*, p. vii.

"Upon the whole we may remark that the number and antiquity of the MSS. which contain the whole or different parts of the New Testament, the variety of ancient versions, and the multitude of quotations from these sacred books in the early Christian writers from the second century downwards, constitute a body of evidence in favor of the genuineness and authenticity of the Christian Scriptures far beyond that of any other book of equal antiquity."—*Imp. Vers. New Test.*, introd., p. xxiii.

The whole subject of various readings, and their probable causes, has been fully and critically discussed in Bishop Marsh's excellent lectures and his translation of *Professor Michaelis' Introduction*.

"These various readings, though very numerous, do not in any degree affect the general credit and integrity of the text, the general uniformity of which, in so many copies, scattered through almost all countries in the known world, and in so great a variety of languages, is *truly astonishing*, and demonstrates both the *veneration* in which the Scriptures were held and the *great care* which was taken in transcribing them. Of the 150,000 various readings which have been discovered by the sagacity and diligence of collators, not one tenth nor one hundredth part make any perceptible, or, at least, any material, variation in the sense. This will appear credible if we consider that every, the minutest deviation, from the received text, has been carefully noted, so that the insertion or omission of an article, the substitution of a word for its equivalent, the transposition of a word or two in a sentence, and even variations in orthography have been added to the catalogue of various readings."—*Conybeare's Theol. Lect.*, pp. 191, 192.

The number of these variations is

greatly reduced, when we include only those books of the Word which are plenarily inspired.

The labors of the critics in confirming the wonderful accuracy of the Word of God in the letter are thus summed up by Professor Gaussen: "As respects the Old Testament, the indefatigable investigations of the four folios of Father Houbigant, the thirty years' labor of John Henry Michaelis, above all, the great *Critical Bible*, and the ten years' study of the famous Kennicott (who consulted five hundred and eighty-one Hebrew manuscripts); and, in fine, Professor Rossi's collection of six hundred and eighty manuscripts. As respects the New Testament, the no less gigantic investigations of Mill, Benzel, Wetstein, and Griesbach (who consulted three hundred and thirty-five manuscripts for the Gospels alone); the latest researches of Nolan, Matthæi, Lawrence, and Hug; above all, those of Scholz, with his six hundred and seventy-four manuscripts for the Gospels and ninety-three for the Apocalypse (without reckoning his four hundred and fifty-six manuscripts for the Acts and Epistles and his fifty-three Lectionariæ). All these vast labors have so convincingly established the astonishing preservation of that text, copied, nevertheless, so many thousand times (in Hebrew during thirty-three centuries and in Greek during eighteen hundred years), that the hopes of the enemies of religion, in this quarter, have been subverted, and, as Michaelis has said, 'They have ceased henceforth to look for anything from those critical researches, which they at first so warmly recommended, because they expected discoveries from them, which have never been made'" (tom. ii., p. 266).

The learned rationalist Eichhorn himself also owns that the different readings of the Hebrew manuscripts by Kennicott, hardly offer sufficient interest to compensate for the trouble they cost! (*Einleitung*, 2 th. s. 700.) But these very misreckonings, and the absence of these discoveries, have proved a precious discovery for the church of God. She expected as much; but she is delighted to owe it to the labors of her very adversaries. "In truth," says a learned man of our day, "but for those precious negative conclusions which men have come to, the direct result obtained from the consumption of so many men's lives in these immense researches, may seem to amount to nothing; and, one may say, that in order to come to it, time, talent, and learning have all been foolishly thrown away." (*Wiseman's Disc. on the Relations*, etc., ii. Disc. 10.) But, as we have said, this result is immense in virtue of its nothingness, and all powerful in virtue of its insignificance. "When one thinks that the Bible has been copied during thirty centuries, as no book of man has ever been, or ever will be; that it was subjected to all the catastrophes and all the captivities of Israel; that it was transported seventy years to Babylon; that it has seen itself so often persecuted, or forgotten, or interdicted, or burnt, from the days of the Philistines to those of the Selucidæ;—when one thinks that, since the time of [the first advent of our Lord and Saviour] Jesus Christ, it has had to traverse the first three centuries of imperial persecution, when persons found in possession of the Holy Books were thrown to the wild beasts; next, the seventh, eighth, and ninth centuries, when false books, false legends, and false decretals, were everywhere multiplied; the tenth century, when so few could read, even among princes; the twelfth, thirteenth, and fourteenth centuries, when the use of the Scriptures in the vulgar tongue was punished with death, and when the books of the ancient fathers were mutilated, when so many ancient traditions were garbled and falsified, even to the very acts of the emperors, and to those of the councils;—then we can perceive how necessary it was that the Providence of God should always have put forth its mighty power, in order that, on the one hand, the church of the Jews should give us in its integrity that Word which records its revolts, which predicts its ruin, which describes Jesus Christ; and on the other, that the Christian churches (the most powerful of which, and the Roman sect in particular, interdicted the people from reading the sacred books, and substituted in so many ways the traditions of the middle ages for the Word of God), should nevertheless transmit to us, in all their purity, those Scriptures which condemn all their traditions, their images, their dead languages, their absolution, their celibacy; which say that Rome would be the seat of a terrible apostasy, where 'the man of sin would be seen sitting as God in the temple of God, waging war on the saints, forbidding to marry, and to use meats which God had created;' which say of images, 'Thou shalt not bow down to them,'—of unknown tongues, 'Thou shalt not use them,'—of the cup, 'Drink ye all of it,'—of the Virgin 'Woman, what have I to do with thee?'—and of marriage, 'It is honorable in all.'"—(*Theophrastus*, 12mo, pp. 168-170.)

Now, although the libraries in which ancient copies of the sacred books may be found have been called upon to give their testimony; although the elucidations given by the Fathers of all ages, have been studied; although the Arabic, Syriac, Latin, Armenian, and Ethiopian versions have been collated; although all the manuscripts, of all countries and ages, have been collected and examined a thousand times over, by countless critics, who have eagerly sought out some new text, as the recompense and the glory of their wearisome watchings; although learned men, not content with the libraries of the West, have visited those of Russia, and carried their researches into the monasteries of Mont Athos, Turkish Asia, and Egypt, there to look for new instruments of the sacred text;—"nothing can be discovered," says a learned person already quoted, "not even a single reading, that could throw doubt on any one of the passages before considered as certain. All the *variantes* almost without exception, leave untouched the essential ideas of each phrase, and bear only on points of secondary importance;" such as the insertion or the omission of an article, or a conjunction, the position of an adjective before or after its substantive, the greater or less exactness of a grammatical construction.

And would we be less rigorous in our demands with respect to the Old Testament?—the famous Indian manuscript, recently deposited in the Cambridge library, will furnish an example.

"It is thirty-three years since the pious and learned Claudius Buchanan, while visiting, on the Indian Peninsula, the Black Jews of Malabar (who are supposed to be the remains of the first dispersion under Nebuchadnezzar), saw in their possession an immense roll, composed of thirty-seven skins, tinged with red, forty-eight feet long, twenty-two inches wide, and which, in its originally perfect state, must have had ninety English feet of development. The Holy Scriptures had been traced on it by different hands. There remained one hundred and seventeen columns of beautiful writing; and there was wanting only Leviticus and part of Deuteronomy. Buchanan succeeded in having this ancient and precious monument, which served for the worship of the synagogue, committed to his care, and he afterwards deposited it in the Cambridge Library. The impossibility of supposing that this roll had been taken from a copy brought by European Jews, was perceived from certain evident marks. Now, Mr. Yeates, lately submitted it to the most attentive examination, and took the trouble to collate it, word by word, letter by letter, with a Hebrew edition of Van der Hooght. He has published the results of his researches. And what have they been? Why, this: That there do not exist, between the Text of India and that of the West, above forty small differences, not one of which is of sufficient importance to lead to even a slight change in the meaning and interpretation of our ancient text; and that these are but the additions or retrenchments of an ר or a ד,—letters, the presence or absence of which, cannot alter the import of the word"—(See *Christian Observer*, vol. xii., p. 170; *Horne's Introd. and App.*, p. 95, ed. 1818; *Examen d'un Exemplaire Indien du Pentateuque*, p. 8).—*Ib.*, pp. 171, 172.

"So much for the Old Testament. But let it not be thought that the Providence that watched over that sacred Book, and which committed it to the care of the Jews (Rom. iii. 1, 2), has done less for the protection of the oracles of the New Testament, committed by it to the new people of God. It has not left to the latter less cogent motives to gratitude and feelings of security" (*Ib.*, p. 174). In the four Gospels and the Apocalypse scarcely any "corrections exist that have been introduced by the new readings of Griesbach and Scholz, as the result of their immense researches, which have any weight at all. [In the entire Testament very few], and in most intances these consist but in the difference of a single word, and sometimes even of a single letter" (*Ib.*, p. 190). "While the Comedies of Terence alone have presented thirty thousand different readings, yet these are only six in number, and they have been copied a thousand times less often than the New Testament" (*Ib.*, p. 196).—See *Wiseman's Disc.*, vol. ii., p. 189.

On this subject it may be as well to quote five of the heads treated of by the celebrated Michaelis. They are as follows:—

"I. By the laws of criticism we are able to distinguish, in most cases, the true reading from the false.

"II. It is not denied that some few of the various readings affect doctrines as well as words, and, without caution, might produce error; but these are so few that the generality of divines would be unable to recollect a single instance, and these few are so easily distinguished by critical rules that not one has been selected by the reformers of the present age as a basis of a new doctrine.

"III. On the other hand, the discovery of the various readings has removed many objections which had been made to the New Testament.

"V. The most important readings, which make an alteration in the sense, relate in general to subjects that have no connection with articles of faith.

"VI. By far the greatest number relate to trifles, and make no alteration in the sense."—*Int. Rep.*, I., N. S., p. 491.

Notwithstanding all this care, as the transcribers were not inspired, "it will be asked," says Waterman, "have no errors crept into the writings thus delivered to us? Are there no various readings? Have no words been added or omitted? Are no sentences obscure? Have no transcribers of the original manuscript made mistakes? Undoubtedly, in all these respects, the answer must be given in the affirmative. Some mistakes have been made by transcribers. Some sentences are obscure. Some words have probably been added or omitted. There are many various readings. Errors have crept in."—*Bible the Word of God*, Lect. 8, p. 222.

The above concessions, therefore, be it remembered, apply to very few passages, and often to unimportant particulars. The integrity of the Hebrew text of the Old Testament, as it exists in the version of Von der Hooght, is admitted to be most miraculously preserved; while, with the exception of a few trifling differences, the Greek edition of the New Testament by Griesbach, and that published by Taylor for the students of the University of London, are deserving of the greatest confidence, in which the various readings are all mentioned at the foot of the page.

It may be observed, as most remarkable, that no doctrine of faith or precept of life is dependent on any doubtful passage; and no errors in the lapse of ages, and by the errors of transcribers, exist, which in the slightest degree invalidate the inspiration or impair the authority of the Word of God, as a plenarily inspired work.

This important subject is ably discussed in a series of papers on *The Integrity of the Word of God in the Letter*, in the *Intellectual Repository*, vol. vi. and vol. i., N. S., where it is shown, "I. That Dr. Bentley's assertion, that 'the real text of the sacred writers does not now lie in any single manuscript or edition, but is dispersed through them all,' is highly reasonable; and that such dispersion is equivalent to preservation, and affords the means, at the Lord's time, of restoration. II. That whether our present Hebrew manuscripts and printed copies of the Word are authentic or not; whether they all agree, or contain many variations; we have received them all, bad, good, and indifferent, from the Jews: that Christians have had no other concern in the matter, than that of faithfully copying, and, of late, collecting together, the variety of materials which the Jews had provided to their hands; and further, that the Jews do not possess any more correct copies than those known to Christians. III. That it is unquestionably true, as advanced by E. Swedenborg, 'that the Jewish nation has been preserved for the sake of the Word;' but 'that this has been done, not because, without them, the text of the Old Testament would have been corrupted by Christians, but because, without them, it would, in its original language, have perished altogether;' it being a certain fact, that, during hundreds of years, the Hebrew Scriptures were never read, nor a word of the Hebrew language understood, by a single Christian. IV. That when E. S. observes, 'that the Word has been preserved, especially the Word of the Old Testament, as to every iota and apex, from the time in which it was written, and this by the labors of the Masorites;' it is advanced by him, not as an assertion of his own, but as the common opinion of the learned of his time, and not from his communication with the spiritual world, from which source he did not derive a knowledge of natural facts, but only of spiritual; wherefore, we are as much at liberty to exercise a rational judgment upon it, as if it still lay only in the writings of the critics, and had never been noticed by him at all: also, 'that when the nature of the Masorah is examined, we must conclude, that when E. S. speaks of the integrity of the Sacred Text through the labors of the Masorites, he can only mean, that they have been instrumental to that object,—not that they have secured it from all [blemish and] defect in the individual copies, and that, with respect to their numbering of the verses, words, and letters, if we take this for an infallible guide, we must imagine the Sacred Volume to be corrupt to a degree far beyond anything that was ever pretended. V. That the fact is, as might hence naturally be expected, that the best Masoretic text, as now existing, does actually contain some indubitable errors, which are proved to be such, by other copies, by ancient versions, by evident reason, and by the spiritual sense;" and that this view of the subject is sanctioned and recognized by E. S. himself; of which instances are given. Very large portions of the Word of the Old Testament are, without doubt, correctly given in his works. To conclude this section, we will remark, that the extreme caution which the Jews have always observed in the transcription of the Holy Writings, especially of the Pentateuch, is not the least remarkable feature in the character of that remarkable people. The manuscript rolls in their synagogues were preserved with uncommon care, in an ark or coffer, and, when the roll containing the law was exposed to the gaze of the congregation, it formed a spectacle of unusual solemnity.

The Rabbinical rules relating to the preparation and transcription of the SEPHER-TORAH, *i. e.*, Book of the Law, for the use of Synagogues, are no less than eighty-eight. They are excessively strict; and these the greatest desire to secure textual accuracy. These copies are directed to be made by sacred scribes alone, called *Sephorim*, who are set apart for this especial purpose. The transcriber must, at the commencement of his task, be in the full enjoyment of health, and, from time to time, must leave off before lassitude supervenes. He must prepare himself for his work by submitting to a prescribed course of medicine, and by observing certain peculiar ceremonials. The Synagogue roll must be copied from ancient and approved manuscripts. It must be written with pure black ink, prepared from materials and with ceremonies according to an ancient Rabbinical receipt. The skins upon which the law is to be transcribed, must be those of a clean animal, carefully prepared for that express purpose, by an appointed individual. The sheets or skins are to be fastened together with strings made of the sinews of a clean animal. Each skin must contain a prescribed number of columns, of a limited length and breadth; each column must contain a regular number of lines and words; and all, except five, must begin with the same letter. The pens must be made of the quills of a clean bird, and the "Tetragrammeton," or ineffable name of Jehovah, must be written with a new pen, devoted to that exclusive purpose; before writing it the scribe must bathe his whole person, and in writing the sacred names of God, he is required to solemnize his mind, by devotion and reverence; and, previously to writing some of them, he must wash his pen. He must not write a single word from memory. He must attentively look upon each individual word in his exemplar, and orally pronounce it, before writing it down. The copy must be examined within thirty days after its completion. Some authors say that the mistake of a single letter, even an imperfectly formed letter, much more a superfluous one, vitiates the entire codex; others state that it is permitted to correct three errors in any one sheet, but if more are found, the copy is condemned as profane, or unfit for religious purposes, and, as the case may be, is either cut to pieces with solemn curses, or preserved for private use.

In such a way did Divine Providence, acting through an almost superstitious reverence for the very words of Holy Writ (for it was little more than superstition with the Jews), secure the authenticity of the text, and guard the canon pure against all corruption.—See also *Professor Gaussen's Theopneustos; Scott Porter's Principle of Textual Criticism*, book ii., caps i., ii.; *Bishop Marsh's Lectures on Criticism*, p. 65; *Hartwell Horne's Introduction to the Holy Scriptures*, etc.

"How trifling soever this scrupulous exactness may appear, yet it suggests to us one observation,—that the Jews were religiously careful to preserve the literal sense of Scripture; and, consequently, notwithstanding their enmity and obstinate aversion to Christianity, they are not to be charged with the additional crime of having corrupted the Bible."—*Chappelou, cited by Gill, pref. to Disc. on Heb. Lang.*

IX. THE EPISTLES OF THE APOSTLES.

Dr. Whitby, quoted with great approbation by Dr. A. Clarke, thus writes respecting the inspiration of the apostles: and if what is advanced be confined, as it ought most assuredly to be, to their Acts and apostolic Epistles, we are perfectly agreed, differing with him, however, *toto cælo*, that the same opinions are applicable to the Gospels and the book of Revelation; for these, as we have already proved, were penned under the highest degree of inspiration, and, containing a heavenly meaning within the letter, are divinely true in every particular.

"I contend only," says he, "for such an inspiration, or divine assistance of the sacred writers of the New Testament, as will assure us of the truth of what they wrote, whether by inspiration of *suggestion* or *direction* only; but not for such an inspiration as implies that even their words were dictated, or their phrases suggested to them by the Holy Ghost. This, in some matters of great moment, might be so, St. Paul declaring that they '*spake the things which were given them of God, in the words which the Holy Ghost teacheth,*' 1 Cor. ii. 13, if that relate not to what the Holy Ghost had taught them out of the Old Testament. But that it was not always so is evident, both from the consideration that they were hagiographers, who are supposed to be left to the use of their own words, and from the *variety* of the *style* in which they write, and from their solecisms, which are sometimes visible in their compositions; and more especially from their own words, which manifestly show that, in some cases, they had no such suggestion from the Holy Ghost, as doth imply that He had dictated those words unto them. For instance, when St. Paul declares his will or purpose to do what he was hindered by the providence of God from doing, as when he says to the Romans, '*When I go into Spain I will come to you,*' chap. xv. 24; '*I will come by you into Spain,*' v. 28. For though he might, after his enlargement, go into the West, where St. Clement (Ep. ad Cor. § 6) says he preached, and even into *Spain*, as *Cyril* (Catechis. 17, p. 204, c.), *Epiphanius* (Hær. 27, p. 107, c.), and *Theodoret* (in 2 Tim. iv. 17, and Præfat. in Psalm cxvi.), say he did; yet it is certain he did not designedly go to *Rome*, in order to an intended journey into *Spain*; and when he says to the *Corinthians*, '*I will come to you when I pass through Macedonia,*' 1 Cor. xvi. 5, and yet confesses in his second *epistle*, 2 Cor. i. 15, 16, 17, that he did not perform that journey; for it is not to be thought the Holy Ghost should incite him to promise, or even to purpose, what he knew he would not perform. This also we learn from all those places in which they do express their ignorance or doubtfulness of that which they are speaking of; as when *St. Paul* says, '*I know not whether I baptized any other,*' 1 Cor. i. 16. And again, '*Perhaps I will abide, yea, and winter with you,*' 1 Cor. xvi. 6. And when *St. Peter* saith, '*By Sylvanus, a faithful brother as I sup-*

pose, have *I written to you*,' 1 Pet. v. 12. For these words plainly show that in all these things they had no inspiration or divine assistance. This, lastly, may be gathered from all those places in which they only do express their hope, and that conditionally, of doing this or that, as in these words, '*I hope to see you in my journey*,' Rom. xv. 24. '*I will come to you quickly, if the Lord will*,' 1 Cor. iv. 19. '*I hope to stay some time with you, if the Lord permit*,' 1 Cor. xvi. 7. '*I hope in the Lord Jesus to send Timothy shortly unto you [so soon as I shall see how it will go with me]*,' Phil. ii. 19, 23. '*And I trust that I myself also shall come quickly*,' v. 24. '*These things I write, hoping to come to thee quickly, but if I should tarry that thou mayest know how to behave thyself in the church of God*' (1 Tim. iii. 14, 15). '*I hope by your prayers to be given to you*' (Philim. 22). '*This will we do, if the Lord permit*' (Heb. vi. 3). '*I hope to come to you*' (2 Ep. John v. 12; 3 Ep. v. 14). For, *spes est incertæ rei nomen*, the word hope implies an uncertainty; whereas the Holy Spirit cannot be uncertain of anything, nor can we think He would inspire men to speak so uncertainly. And there can be no necessity, or even use, of a divine assistance to enable a man to express his *hopes*, seeing all men do, by natural reflection, know them."—*Dr. A. Clarke's Commentary. Introduction to New Testament*, p. v.

To this very conclusive reasoning of Dr. Whitby, on the character of the Apostolic Epistles, from a consideration of their internal evidence, very much more to the same purport might be added. I will instance only a few examples, in which the vast difference between plenary inspiration and what the Doctor would probably call inspired direction, will be most evident to every reflecting mind. "*Brethren, I speak after the manner of men*" (Gal. iv. 13; Rom. vi. 9). "*I thank God that I baptized none of you but Crispus and Gaius; lest any should say that I had baptized in my own name*" (1 Cor. i. 14, 15). "*Who then is Paul, and who is Apollos, but ministers by whom ye believed, even as the Lord gave to every man*" (1 Cor. iii. 5). "*I speak this by permission, and not of commandment*" (1 Cor. vii. 6). "*To the rest speak I, not the Lord.*" "*I give my judgment as one that hath obtained mercy of the Lord to be faithful.*" "*I think also that I have the Spirit of God*" (1 Cor. vii. 12, 25, 40). "*I speak not by commandment; but by occasion of the forwardness of others.*" (2 Cor. viii. 8.) "*When Peter was come to Antioch I withstood him to the face, because he was to be blamed*" (Gal. ii. 11). "*The cloak that I left at Troas with Carpus, when thou comest, bring with thee, and the books, but especially the parchments*" (2 Tim. iv. 13). Language like this never could fall from the lips of a plenarily inspired writer. "*That which I speak, I speak it not after the Lord, but as it were foolishly, in this confidence of boasting*" (2 Cor. xi. 17).

The author of *Tracts for the Times*, lxxxvii., pertinently observes, that "[there are] strong indications which all must have noticed throughout St. Paul's Epistles, that he discloses and withholds Christian knowledge and mysteries, according to the meetness of those to whom he was writing to receive them."—P. 11.

Hence, the Apostle Paul, speaking of the peculiar adaptation of his religious instructions to the varied characters and circumstances of those whom he addressed, says in 1 Cor. ix. 20–22, "*Unto the Jews I became as a Jew, that I might gain upon the Jews; to them that are under the law, as under the law, that I might gain them that are under the law; to them that are without law, as without law, (being not without law to God, but under the law to Christ,) that I might gain them that are without law. To the weak became*

I as weak, that I might gain the weak: I am made all things to all men, that I might by all means save some, and this I do for the Gospel's sake." Thus teaching us, that his preaching and writings are to be regarded as accommodations of the Gospel to the particular states and circumstances of both Jews and Gentiles.

Dr. Beyer, Professor of Greek to the Consistory of Gottenburg, having asked Swedenborg the reason why, in explaining the spiritual sense of the Word in his Arcana Cœlestia, he never quoted from the Apostolic Epistles, he replied from Amsterdam, as follows, under date of April 15, 1766:

"With regard to the writings of St. Paul, and the other Apostles, I have not given them a place in my Arcana Cœlestia, because they are dogmatic [or doctrinal] writings merely, and not written in the style of the Word, as are those of the Prophets, of David, of the Evangelists, and the Revelation of St. John. The style of the Word consists, throughout, in correspondences, and thence effects an immediate communication with heaven (see *Doctrine of the New Jerusalem concerning the Sacred Scripture*, n. 113); but the style of these dogmatic writings is quite different, having indeed a communication with heaven, but only mediately or indirectly. The reason why the Apostles wrote in this style was, that the New Christian Church was then to begin through them; consequently, the same style as is used in *the Word* would not have been proper for such doctrinal tenets, which required plain and simple language, suited to the capacities of all readers.

"Nevertheless, the writings of the Apostles are very good books for the church, inasmuch as they insist on the doctrine of charity and faith thence derived, as strongly as the Lord himself has done in the Gospels, and in the Revelation of St. John, as will appear evidently to any one who studies these writings with attention."—*New Jerusalem Magazine*, 1790, p. 140.

"The letters he [the Apostle Paul] wrote, were intended for those who were already Christians, whose religious nature was already awakened, who had already enjoyed, in this awakening, the revelations of Christianity. His writings, therefore, were designed, not so much to be a revelation of truth, as a further explication of it. Based upon a revelation already made, they were adapted simply to bring the ideas involved into a more explicit and somewhat reflective form, and thus to furnish us with an inspired authority for the value of *systematic theology* in the Church."—*Morell's Philosophy of Religion*, p. 140.

Dr. Orville Dewey, writing on the original use of the Epistles, observes, that "they were particularly called forth by the exigencies, the difficulties, the trials, of the primitive Christians. . . . They took their form from circumstances; and with those circumstances we have, and can have, but a partial acquaintance. . . . Such, for instance, are the answers to questions, the solution of difficulties, the settlement of disputes, which have long since passed away. Such, too, is what relates to the use of prophetical and miraculous powers, to meats offered to idols, etc. These things do not *now* concern us; because we have no miraculous powers, and there are no idols to solicit our offerings. Paul adapted his religious instructions to the men whom he addressed,—to their peculiar character, circumstances, difficulties, and speculations."—*Works*, p. 808.

"Thus the form and character of St. Paul's Epistles are evidently derived from circumstances of his early life, his country, his family, his occupation," etc.—*Dr. W. T. Powell's Discourses* (xv.), pub. by Dr. T. Palgny, 1776.

The following excellent remarks of the late Bishop of Durham, Dr. Maltby, on the writings of the Apostle Paul, express, with a critical authority which must command the respect of all intelligent Christians, the estimate in which we hold these compositions. I quote from a Sermon preached before the University of Cambridge, March 31, 1805, from 2 Peter iii. 15, 16. "*Even as our beloved brother Paul also according to the wisdom given unto him hath written unto you; as also in all his epistles, speaking in them of these things: in which are some things hard to be understood, which they that are unlearned and unstable wrest, as they do also the other Scriptures, unto their own destruction.*"

"Most epistolary writings are obscure, unless we be perfectly acquainted with the situation of the parties, the design with which they wrote, and the circumstances to which they allude. It is indeed of considerable use in the interpretation of a letter, or series of letters, when the chain of correspondence is preserved entire, and when the occasion which called forth the answer is preserved together with the reply. It is well known that many of St. Paul's epistles were addressed to persons who had solicited his advice upon peculiar, and sometimes local and temporary, emergencies. It is equally well known that not one of the letters addressed to him are extant, nor is there any other method of ascertaining the occasions upon which he wrote, than what is supplied by the letters themselves. Many of the epistles turn principally upon controverted points; upon questions, which, from changes in the external condition of the Christian world, have ceased to be agitated; and which, to us (who are not, like the contemporaries of St. Paul, proselytes from Judaism or heathenism) seem to be of little or no moment. Such, for instance, are the disputes, of which we have so many traces in these epistles, concerning the efficacy and duration of the Mosaic economy; the admission of Gentiles into the church of Christ; the necessity of combining the Jewish ritual with the Christian faith; and upon many subordinate points, relative to the ceremonies and superstitions both of Jews and heathens.—Moreover, as the Apostle wrote upon some topics, which, however clear at the time, are since become obscure; so does he, upon one occasion,* at least, studiously and even avowedly hold back a part of his meaning; and upon others,† he refers his readers to those oral communications, which had been previously made to them, and of which no distinct vestiges are preserved to us in Holy Writ. We may indeed venture to suppose, that the epistles which he wrote to one set of converts, were not always, even in his own days, intelligible to another.

"It appears, then, that these parts of the Sacred Volume from various causes are, in point of fact, obscure: and that, according to the more obvious import of St. Peter's words, in the version adopted by our church, the Apostle acknowledged their difficulty, in the very age when the circumstances alluded to were recent; and when the language in which they were written, was the native tongue of many, and well understood by all, to whom they were addressed. Yet to these epistles, which above all other parts of the New Testament, have unavoidably and invincibly become obscure in their phraseology, in their allusions, and in the peculiar direction of the reasoning which they contain, to these epistles, which have so long exercised the talents, and so often baffled the exertions of the most diligent, the most judicious, and the most learned expositors; I say, to these very epistles,

---

* 2 Thess. ii. 5, 6.
† 1 Cor. xi. 2; 2 Cor. xiii. 2; Gal. iv. 13; 1 Thess. iii. 4; 2 Tim. ii. 2; iii. 14.

the attention of men, altogether illiterate, or very scantily furnished with literature, has been chiefly devoted. Guided, not by the original language of Scripture, but by translations; not by the practices or notions of the Apostolic times, but of our own; not by careful, sober, and unprejudiced comparison of argumentative and critical expositions, but by their own zeal; they have drawn from them conclusions unwarranted by the general tenor of the Holy Writings, contrary in many instances to our clearest perceptions of the Divine Attributes, and upon some occasions revolting to common sense, common justice, and common humanity:—to common sense, when they indiscriminately reject and deride the usefulness of learning; to common justice, when they assert that the Deity, without any regard to human actions, has selected some of his creatures for final salvation, and others for final perdition; to common humanity, when they maintain that all who are not the preachers and believers of what they call vital Christianity, are graceless, helpless, hopeless outcasts from the favor of their Creator, their Redeemer, and their Sanctifier.

"The habit of depreciating good works; the disposition to depend upon faith alone; the opinion that grace communicated to the elect supersedes the necessity of their endeavors to be virtuous; the merciless exclusion of all other Christian individuals from the possibility of acceptance with God; these surely are peculiarities which neither reason nor revelation would permit us to consider as favorable to the innocence, or the spiritual improvement, or the future happiness, of their advocates."—*Maltby's Sermons*, 1819, vol. i., pp. 412-433.

"In the Epistles there is perceptible a well marked *personal* element,—the writer speaking here and there solely in his own name, and from his own feelings, quite independently of the Spirit (Tertullian, Jerome)."—*Warrington's Inspiration of Scripture*, p. 36.

Dr. Arnold, "when admitted by Archbishop Howley to priest's orders, proposed doubts, not merely on the authorship, but the canonicity of the Epistle to the Hebrews."—*Dr. Stanley's Letter to the Bishop of London on Subscription*, p. 27.

"On the Epistle to the Hebrews, the greatest diversity of opinion prevails among critics as to its claims to canonical authority and Pauline origin. Some denying both of these, and some admitting the former whilst they repudiate the latter. . . . On no subject, perhaps, in the department of the higher criticism of the New Testament, have opinions been more divided, and more keenly discussed, than on this. Of those who have rejected the claims of the Apostle Paul to the authorship of this Epistle, some have advocated those of Barnabas, others those of Luke, others those of Clement of Rome, others those of Silas, others those of Apollos, others those of some unknown Christian of Alexandria, and others those of some 'Apostolic man,' whose name is no less unknown. . . . That which ascribes this production to Apollos, was first suggested by Luther, and it has been in more recent times adopted by Heumann, Bertholdt, De Wette, Bleek, and apparently also by Tholuck."—See *Kitto's Cyclop. of Bib. Lit.*—art.

"The notion of God appeased by a sacrifice, and remitting, in consideration of it, his wrath against those who had offended him,—this notion of God, which science repels, was equally repelled, in spite of all that his nation, time, and training had in them to favor it, by the profound religious sense of Paul. In none of his Epistles, is the reconciling work of Christ really presented under this aspect. One great epistle there is, which does present it under this aspect, the Epistle to the

Hebrews If other proof were wanting, this alone would make it impossible that the Epistle to the Hebrews should be Paul's; and indeed, of all the epistles which bear his name, it is the only one which may not, in spite of the hesitation caused by some difficulties, be finally attributed to him.

"The tradition which ascribes to Apollos the Epistle to the Hebrews, derives corroboration from the one account of him which we have, that 'he was an eloquent man, and mighty in the Scriptures.' The Epistle to the Hebrews is just such a performance as might naturally have come from 'an eloquent man, and mighty in the Scriptures,' and in whom the intelligence, and the power of combining, type-establishing, and expounding, somewhat dominated the religious perceptions."—*Matthew Arnold's St. Paul and Protestantism, Cornhill Mag.*, 1869, p. 616.

Dr. Arnold asserts that "the Apostle Paul expected that the world would come to an end in the generation then existing. . . . Shall we say, then," he adds, "that St. Paul entertained and expressed a belief, which the event did not verify? We may safely say so, safely and reverently, in this instance; for here he was most certainly speaking as a man, and not by revelation, as it has been providentially ordered that our Lord's express words on this point have been recorded."—[Matt. xxiv. 36.] See Epistles to the Thessalonians.—*Sermons on the Christian Life*, etc., p. 489.

Kitto says "that the Pauline Epistles offered great difficulties, was already felt in the earliest times." And further: "All the [general] Epistles of the Apostle Paul, except the one to the Romans, were called forth by circumstances and peculiar occasions in the affairs of the communities to which they were addressed." And he adds, that "not all Paul's Epistles were preserved; it is at least evident from 1 Cor. v. 9, that a letter to the Corinthians has been lost; and from Col. iv. 16, it has been concluded that another letter to the community of Laodicea has likewise been lost."—*Cyc. Bib. Lit.*, art. *Epistles*.

Archdeacon Paley has shown that "six of the subscriptions of Paul's Epistles are false or impossible; that is, they are either absolutely contradicted by the contents of the epistle, or are difficult to be reconciled with them; viz., 1 Cor.; Gal.; 1 Thess.; 2 Thess., 1 Tim., and Titus. I do not," he concludes, "attribute any authority to these [or the other five] subscriptions. I believe them to have been conjectures founded sometimes upon loose traditions, but more generally upon a consideration of some particular text, without sufficiently comparing it with other parts of the Epistle, with different Epistles, or with history. . . . They are to be considered as only ancient *scholia*."—*Hor. Pauli.*, pp. 87, 88.

In his *Christian Theology and Modern Skepticism*, 1872, the Duke of Somerset, speaking of the Pauline Epistles, says, "they present to us a most interesting phase in the progress of religious thought, they assist to elucidate an important movement in the history of Christianity; but when we are solemnly asked to call these Epistles the Word of God, a feeling of religious reverence forces us to withhold our assent."

"That Jerome considered Paul's epistles as of merely human origin, appears from his accusing Paul of solecisms and errors of grammar, alleging, that he spoke truly of himself when he said he was rude of speech; of course no good man would thus speak of books which he believed to be written by divine inspiration."—*Int. Rep.*, vol. v., p. 104.

Paul was brought up at Tarsus, amongst heathens. He quotes part of a verse from the Phœnomena of Aratus (a poet of Cilicia, the native country of Paul, lived 300 B. C.), against the Epicurean philosophers at Athens. "For we his children are" (Acts xvii. 28), originally spoken of the heathen deity Jupiter, and dexterously applies it to the true God. In 1 Cor. xv. 33, he quotes a senary iambic which is supposed to be taken from Menander's lost comedy of Thais, rendered "Evil communications corrupt good manners." And in his Epistle to Titus, Bishop of Crete (Tit. i. 12), he makes an extract from Epimenides, a Cretan poet, whom he styles a prophet, and whose writings, by the ancient heathens, were regarded as oracles. The general import of the passage is, that "The Cretans were a false people; and united in their character the ferocity of the wild beast, with the luxury of the domesticated one." No one can regard this as of plenary inspiration. See *Porson's Works; Allex's Judgt.*, p. 288; *Hartwell Horne's Introd.*, vol. ii., pt. I, p. 347; vol. i., p. 172.

"The Epistle to the Hebrews, so different in its conception of faith, and in its Alexandrine rhythm, from the doctrine and language of St. Paul's known epistles, has its degree of discrepance explained by ascribing it to some companion of the Apostle; and minute reasons are found for fixing with probability on Apollos."—*Dr. R. Williams, Essays and Reviews*, 9th ed., p. 84.

"The second of the Petruic Epistles, having alike external and internal evidence against its genuineness, is necessarily surrendered as a whole. . . . . The second chapter may not improbably be a quotation; but its quoter, and the author of the rest of the Epistle, need not, therefore, have been St. Peter."—*Ib.*, p. 85.

In conclusion, much doubt and controversy have always existed in the Christian church respecting the authenticity and genuineness of the Apostolic writings, as will be seen by the following sketch.

Eichhorn, in the 7th vol. of his *Kritische Schriften*, affirms that the Epistles to Timothy and Titus were not written by Paul, and that the superscription and introduction are erroneous.

Bauer has attacked the genuineness of the three pastoral epistles; and Schleiermacher that of the 1st Ep. to Timothy.—*Kitto's Cyc. Bib. Lit.*, art. EPISTLES.

Jerome doubted whether the Epistle to Philemon was Paul's. Eusebius says that "the Epistle to the Hebrews was not received by all."—*Lardner's Gospel Hist.*, vol. v., p. 24. Origen affirms that "no man can tell who was the author of it." Erasmus questioned its author and authority. "Hypollitus writes that this Epistle is not Paul's."—*Ib.*, vol. iii., p. 393. "Irenæus doubted its genuineness."—*Ib.*, vol. v., p. 88. It was not received by the Latin churches till the time of Jerome. Tertullian ascribes it to Barnabas; others have attributed it to Timothy, to Alexander, to Apollos (*Monthly Mag.*, Mar., 1815), and by tradition only is it attributed to Paul. Several of the Fathers, and many learned moderns, agree in rejecting its Pauline origin. And F. W. Newman says, "That this Epistle is not from the hand of Paul, had very long seemed to me an obvious certainty,—as long as I had any delicate feeling of Greek style." —*Phases of Faith*, p. 100. Erasmus affirms that the Epistle of James does not savor of an Apostolic gravity. Cajetan doubted of the author, and insists upon its being of less authority. Luther stigmatized it as "*Epistola Straminea*,"— an Epistle of straw,—or worthless; because it corrected the mistakes of Jewish Christians on the doctrine of justification by faith alone, and enforces good works and moral duties as essential to salvation. Perceiving, afterwards, that this extreme censure, in support of a fond opinion, gave offence, he is said to have retracted it.—See *Wetstein's New Test.*, vol. ii., p. 658; *Blackwall's Sacred Classics*, vol. i., p. 301. Erasmus doubted the genuineness of the 2d Epistle of Peter; Eusebius marked it as being, according to some, of doubtful authority. Both Eusebius and Erasmus affirm that the 2d and 3d Epistles of John were not written by that Apostle, but by some other writer, probably of the same name. Cajetan also doubted of the authorship.—See *Bishop Hall's Peace of Rome*, b. i., p. 31. A very sufficient reason for their early disputed authority, was the fact that they were private Epistles, and did not, in all probability, become public till long after the Apostle's decease; neither the 2d or the 3d John are to be found in the Peschito Syriac version.—See *Greek Testament of the London Univ.* Cajeta doubted the authority of Jude. Michaelis agrees with several writers in the early ages of Christianity, in rejecting it as spurious, because the apocryphal books of Enoch and of the Ascension of Moses, were supposed to be quoted in it.—See *Dr. A. Clarke, Hartwell Horne, Townsend* and *Dr. Benson*.

"St. Paul writes like a Christian teacher, exhibiting all the emotions and vicissitudes of human feeling, speaking, indeed, with authority, but hesitating in different cases, and more than once correcting himself,—corrected, too, by the course of events in his expectation of the coming of Christ."—*Jewell, Regius Prof. of Greek in the Univ. of Oxford, Essays and Reviews*, pp. 345, 346.

X. THE JEWISH CANON OF THE OLD TESTAMENT.

"It is well known that the Jews divide the sacred books of the Hebrew Bible into three classes, the Law, the Prophets, and the Holy Writings, called in the Hebrew Chetubim, Cetubim, or Kethubim,* and in the Greek, Hagiographa, that is, Holy Writings."—See *Bishop Mark's Comparative View*, p. 384. This triple division is regarded as of the highest antiquity. The Son of Sirach is thought to allude to it in his preface to the book of Ecclesiasticus, written and published about a hundred and thirty years before the Christian era (*Wolf. Bib. Heb.*, vol. i., p. 255), where he mentions "the Law, the Prophets, and the other books of the Fathers," called also "other books of his country," and "the remaining books." This threefold division of the writings comprehended in the Jewish canon, is still retained, though some books included by Josephus in the second class are now found in the third. The Jewish classification is known to have varied at different periods, but no record has enabled any one to ascertain either the causes of such alterations, or the times when they were made. In the Hagiographa, called by Josephus, "Hymns to God, and Documents or Maxims of Life for the use of Men" (*Cont. App.*, lib. i., sec. viii., tom. ii., p. 441; *Jennings' Ant.*, p. 593), are placed, not only the Proverbs, Job, Song of Songs, Ruth, Ecclesiastes, Esther, Ezra, Nehemiah, and Chronicles, but also, the Psalms, the Lamentations, and Daniel. (*Allen's Mod. Jud.*, pp. 3, 4.) The Law and the Prophets were regarded as written by the highest degree of inspiration, called *the Holy Spirit*, and, with the exception of the Psalms, Daniel, and the Lamentations, the Hagiographa was considered as "written by men who had no public mission as prophets," and as composed

---

* The name Chetubim, or Kethubim, is first met with in Epiphanius, for there was no strictly technical name belonging to it before the Christian era; but it was variously called, and most generally, by the name of writings.

under an inferior degree of inspiration.

On this subject Kitto observes: "The Rabbinical writers maintain that the authors of the Cetubim enjoyed only *the lowest degree* of inspiration, as they received no immediate communication from the Deity, like that made to Moses, to whom God spake face to face; and that they did not receive their knowledge through the medium of visions and dreams, as was the case with the prophets of the second class; but still they felt the Divine spirit resting on them, and inspiring them with suggestions. This is the view maintained by Abarbanel, Kimchi, Maimonides and Elias Levita."— *Bib. Cyc.*, art. HAGIOGRAPHA.

Abarbanel maintains, however, that Daniel's spirit was that of true prophecy. Jacchiades, another Rabbi, states, that Daniel attained to the *highest pitch* of prophecy, and the Talmud ranks him with Zechariah and Malachi. (*Allen's Mod. Jud.*, p. 4–6.) In Dan. i. 4, he is described as a man "skilful in all wisdom. Daniel was received as genuine from the earliest times, as appears from the books of Maccabees, and according to Josephus, who bestows upon it more commendation than upon any other book of the Old Testament. (*Stuart, Antiq.*, lib. x.) It was exhibited to Alexander, within 200 years after the prophet's decease (*Ant.* xx. 4; xi. 8); and together with the other Scriptures, was translated by the LXX. many years before Antiochus Epiphanes; but what is of more authority than all, is, that Daniel is expressly called a prophet by our Lord, in Matt. xxiv. 15; Mark xiii. 14."—(See *Lardner's Works*, 8vo, vol. ii., p. 201, and *Wintle's Prelim. Dis. to Daniel.*)

"The Jews," says Prideaux, "place the prophecies of Daniel only among the Hagiographa: and they serve the Psalms of David after the same rate. The reason which they give for it in respect of both, is, that they lived not the prophetic manner of life, but the courtly; David in his own palace, as king of Israel, and Daniel in the palace of the king of Babylon, as one of the chief counsellors and ministers in the government of that empire."—*Comment.*, 8vo, vol. i., p. 206. Moreover, the Psalms were not completed till the Babylonish captivity, and were not all written by David.—(See Ps. cxxxvii.)

Walton suspects that the book of Daniel was not publicly read by the Jews, lest it should give offence to the princes to whom they were subject, since it contains in the letter such manifest predictions of the change and ruin of the greatest kingdoms under which they lived; so, many suspect the Apocalypse, or book of Revelation, was not immediately published or received in the Christian church on this account, because many calamities to the Roman empire were supposed to be predicted in the literal sense. And that if there be any just ground of conclusion that the book of Daniel was not translated by the LXX., it was omitted lest it should offend Ptolemy, and was afterwards translated into Greek by some other hand, and included in the Hagiographa.—*Proleg.* ix., sec. 51.

Theodoret and Jerome blame the Jews for placing the Lamentations and Daniel in the lowest division of the Scriptures, most evidently dividing them into two classes, distinguished by a superior and inferior degree of inspiration. Josephus includes the Lamentations with Jeremiah, as properly forming one book. The Psalms are not only mentioned by our Lord, in Luke xxiv. 44, but are evidently separated from the class of books with which they have so long been associated, and, besides this, are constantly cited in the Gospels, as containing divine predictions, etc. That the Psalms are strictly prophetical of the Messiah, of whom David, the inspired writer of the greater portion of them, was an eminent type, all must allow. But on account of their poetical form, and their use in worship, as also that some of them appeared to have been written so late as the Babylonish captivity, the Jews inserted the whole book in the Hagiographa. The last reason has been thought by some sufficient to account for Daniel being included in the same division. The Law of Moses, then, the Prophets, and the Psalms, which our Lord affirms (Luke xxiv. 44) treat especially of Himself, and which he thus stamps, as it were, with his own divine signet, will include all those books, and those only, which Swedenborg enumerates, as truly constituting the Word of the Old Testament.—See also, *Noble's Plenary Inspiration*, Appendix ii.; "*An attempt to discriminate between the Books of Plenary Inspiration, contained in the Bible, and those written by the Inspiration generally assigned to the whole.*"

The prophets are divided into anterior and posterior. The *anterior prophets* comprising the books of Joshua, Judges, the two books of Samuel, and the two books of Kings, and were so called because they wrote by inspiration concerning those things which had happened *anterior* to their time. The *posterior* prophets, comprising the four greater, and twelve lesser prophets, were so called, because they wrote by inspiration concerning those things which were to happen *posterior* to their time.

The various arrangements of the canon by the Jews were most probably made under the fanciful notion, that the higher degree of inspiration included as many books of the Old Testament as there are letters in the Hebrew alphabet,—like the alphabetical divisions of Ps. cxix. and others. It is a somewhat singular coincidence that the plenarily inspired Books, according to Swedenborg, reckoning the Pentateuch one book; the two Books of Samuel, and the two Books of the Kings, as only two, agreeably to ancient usage; and the Books of Jeremiah and Lamentations as one book, as Josephus did; they make, in all, twenty-two,—precisely the number required.

XI. THE FOUR DIFFERENT STYLES IN WHICH THE WORD OF GOD IS WRITTEN.

"There are four different styles in which the Word of God is written. The *first* was in use in the most ancient [or Adamic] church; whose method of expressing themselves was such, that when they mentioned earthly and worldly things, they thought of the spiritual and celestial things which they represented; so that they not only expressed themselves by representatives, but also, reduced their thoughts into a kind of series of historical particulars, in order to give them more light, and in this they found the greatest delight. This style is meant when Hannah prophesied, saying, 'Speak ye what is high; let what is ancient come forth from your mouth' (1 Sam. ii. 3). Such representatives are called by David 'Dark sayings of old' (Ps. lxxviii. 2-4). From the posterity of the most ancient church, Moses received what he wrote concerning the creation, the Garden of Eden, etc., till the time of Abram [Gen. xi. 27]. The *second* style is the historical, occurring in the books of Moses from the time of Abram, and afterwards in Joshua, Judges, Samuel, and the Kings, in which the historical facts actually occurred as they are related in the letter, although all and each of them contains things altogether different in the internal sense. The *third* style is prophetical, which took its rise from that which was esteemed as highly in the most ancient church;

this style, however, is not connected, and in appearance historical, like that of the most ancient church, but is broken and interrupted, being scarcely ever intelligible except in the internal sense. In this are contained the greatest arcana, succeeding each other in a beautiful and orderly connection, relating to the internal and external man, to the various states of the church, to heaven itself, and in their inmost sense to the Lord. The *fourth* style is that of the Psalms of David, which is intermediate between the prophetic style, and that of common speech; here, under the person of David, as a King, the Lord is treated of in the internal sense."—A. C. 66.

XII. THE ANCIENT WORD.

"That previous to the Word which was given by Moses and the prophets to the people of Israel, men were acquainted with sacrificial worship, and prophesied from the mouth of Jehovah, may appear from what is recorded in the books of Moses: Ex. xxxiv. 13; Deut. vii. 5; chap. xii. 3; Numb. xxv. 1, 2, 3; chap. xxii. 40; chap. xxiii. 1, 2, 14, 29, 30; Numb. xxiv. 17; chap. xxii. 13, 18; chap. xxiii. 3, 5, 8, 16, 26; chap. xxiv. 1, 13; Deut. xxxii. 7, 8; chap. xiv. 14–20; Psalm cx. 4. The Word among the ancients was written by mere correspondences. It was used by the natives of the land of Canaan, and its confines, as of Syria, Mesopotamia, Arabia, Chaldea, Assyria, Egypt, Zidon, Tyre, and Nineveh; the inhabitants of all which kingdoms were initiated into representative worship, and consequently were skilled in the science of correspondences. When in process of time that Word began to be generally falsified, it was removed by the divine Providence of the Lord, and at last was lost, and another Word, written by correspondences less remote, was given, which was the Word published by the prophets amongst the children of Israel.

"That the ancients had a Word, is evident from the writings of Moses, who mentions it, and also gives quotations from it, Numb. xxi. 14, 15, 27–30; and that the historical parts of that Word were called the Wars of Jehovah, and the prophetical parts, Enunciations. From the historical parts of that Word, Moses has given this quotation, 'Wherefore it is said in the book of the Wars of Jehovah, I marched into Suph, and the rivers of Arnon, and the channel of the rivers; that turned aside where Ar dwelleth, and stopped at the border of Moab,' Numb. xxi. 14, 15: by the wars of Jehovah mentioned in that Word, as in ours, the Lord's combats with the hells are meant and described, and his victories over them, when he should come into the world: the same combats are also meant and described in many passages in the historical part of our Word, as in the wars of Joshua with the inhabitants of the land of Canaan, and in the wars of the judges, and of the kings of Israel. From the prophetical parts of that Word, Moses has given this quotation: 'Wherefore say the Enunciators, Come into Heshbon; the city of Sihon shall be built and strengthened; for there is a fire gone out of Heshbon, a flame from the city of Sihon; it hath consumed Ar of Moab, and the possessors of the high places of Arnon. Woe to thee, Moab! thou art undone, O people of Chemosh! He hath sent his sons that escaped, and his daughters, into captivity unto Sihon king of the Amorites; we have shot them with darts. Heshbon is perished even unto Dibon, and we have laid waste even unto Nophah, which reacheth unto Medeba,' Numb. xxi. 27–30: the translators render it, They that speak in proverbs, but they are more properly called Enunciators, and their compositions, Prophetical Enunciations, as may appear from the signification of the word *Moshalim* in the Hebrew tongue, which not only means proverbs, but also prophetical Enunciations; as in Numb. xxiii. 7, 18; chap. xxiv. 3, 15: it is there said that Balaam uttered his Enunciation, which was also a prophecy concerning the Lord; his Enunciation is called *Moshal*, in the singular number: it may be further observed, that the passages thence quoted by Moses are not proverbs, but prophecies. That that Word, like ours, was divinely inspired, is plain from a passage in Jeremiah, where nearly the same expressions occur: 'A fire shall come forth out of Heshbon, and a flame from the midst of Sihon, and shall devour the corner of Moab, and the crown of the head of the sons of Shaon. Woe be unto thee, O Moab! the people of Chemosh perisheth; for thy sons are taken away captives, and thy daughters captives,' chap. xlviii. 45, 46. Beside these, mention is also made of a prophetical book, called, The Book of Jasher, or, the book of the Upright, by David and by Joshua; by David in the following passage: 'David lamented over Saul, and over Jonathan; also he bade them teach the children of Judah the bow; behold it is written in the book of Jasher,' 2 Sam. i. 17, 18; and by Joshua in this passage; 'Joshua said, Sun, stand thou still upon Gibeon, and thou moon, in the valley of Ajalon; is not this written in the book of Jasher,' or the Book of the Upright." Josh. x. 12, 13.—*S. S.*, n. 101, 102, 103. *T. C. R.* 265. *A. R.* 21.

"The prevalence of religious worship from the most early ages of the world, and the universal knowledge of a God amongst the inhabitants of the globe, with some notion of a life after death, are not to be ascribed to men, nor to their self-derived intelligence, but to the ancient Word, and in succeeding times to the Israelitish Word. From these two sources, religious knowledge was propagated through all parts of India, with its islands; through Egypt and Ethiopia into the kingdoms of Africa; from the maritime parts of Asia into Greece; and from thence into Italy. But as the Word could not be written otherwise than by representatives, which are such earthly existences as correspond with heavenly ones, and are consequently significative of them, therefore the religious notions of the gentiles were changed into idolatry, and in Greece were turned into fables: and the divine properties and attributes were considered as so many separate gods, governed by one supreme Deity, whom they called Jove, possibly from Jehovah. That they had a knowledge of Paradise, of the flood, of the sacred fire, of the four ages, beginning with that of gold, and ending with that of iron, by which in the Word are signified the four states of the church, as in Daniel, chap. ii. 31–35, is well known. That the Mahometan religion, which succeeded and destroyed the former religious persuasions of many nations, was taken from the Word of both Testaments, is also well known."—*S. S.*, n. 177. *T. C. R.*, n. 275.

"In the writings of Moses, chiefly in the beginning of Genesis, where occur documents of a much higher antiquity than Moses' own time."—*Dr. J. Hernigas' Notes to Dr. Seiler's Biblical Hermeneutics, trans. by Rev. Dr. W. Wright*, p. 93.

"That the book of Genesis was, in part, composed or compiled from previously existing documents, or from true traditionary accounts existing in the church at the time of its composition by Moses, is a point which is now very generally admitted among those who are conversant with Biblical criticism." This was also the opinion of Vitringa, Le Cane, Calmet, and Astruc. —See the *Introduction of Horne, Eichhorn*,

Jahn, and Berthollet; *Dr. Pye Smith's Cong. Lect.*, p. 207; and *Stuart on the O. T. Canon*, p. 54; *Dr. Henderson on Divine Inspiration*, p. 312, and note, p. 485.

"That there was a Bible before our Bible is indicated in the book before us [*Bunsen's Egypt's Place in Universal History*], rather than proved as it might be."—*Dr. R. Williams, Essays and Reviews*, 9th ed., p. 62.

XIII. WHY WAS NOT THE INTERNAL SENSE OF THE WORD REVEALED BEFORE?

Swedenborg says, that "the spiritual sense of the Word was not revealed before, because if it had been, the church would have profaned it, and thereby have profaned the sanctity of the Word itself: and the case would have been according to what the Lord says in Matthew: 'If thine eye be evil, thy whole body shall be full of darkness; if, therefore, the light that is in thee be darkness, how great is that darkness.' vi. 23. By eye, in the spiritual sense of the Word, is meant the understanding."—*D. P.*, n. 264.

And, again, on the same subject he says, another "reason why the science of correspondences, which is the key to the spiritual sense of the Word, was not [fully] disclosed to earlier ages, was, because the Christians of the primitive church were men of such great simplicity, that it was impossible to disclose it to them; for had it been disclosed, they would have found no use in it, nor would they have understood it. [That the wise among them, however, have had *some* perception of its *existence*, is plain from the numerous extracts we have made from their writings. They moreover considered that it was well to withhold their mysteries from men indiscriminately, and hence their doctrine and duty of reserve.]

After those first ages of Christianity, there arose thick clouds of darkness, and overspread the whole Christian world, in consequence of the establishment of the Papal dominion. But after the Reformation, inasmuch as men began to divide faith from charity, and to worship God under three persons, consequently three Gods, whom they conceive to be one, therefore at that time heavenly truths were concealed from them; for if they had been discovered they would have been falsified, and would have been abused to the confirmation of faith alone, without being at all applied to charity and love: thus also men would have closed heaven against themselves."—*S. S.*, n. 24.

XIV. THE AUTHORIZED ENGLISH VERSION OF THE BIBLE.

It must not be forgotten, what indeed might naturally be expected, and is now generally acknowledged among the learned, that in numerous instances the common English translation of the Holy Word, incorrectly or imperfectly conveys the meaning of the divine original. The translators were not plenarily inspired men. A literal and faithful translation of the Word is now a great desideratum in the New Church. For the want of it, the science of correspondences, when applied, frequently fails to educe a just, intelligible, and consecutive sense. It will afford some aid to the ordinary reader to know, 1st.—That in many instances the marginal readings are more faithful renderings than the text (exmp. Isa. i. 18; v. 1). 2d.—That in all those passages where the term LORD is printed in the Old Testament in capital letters, the original is Jehovah (exmp. Isa. xliii. 10, 11, 12; Ezek. xxxiii. 11). And 3d.—That the words printed in *italics* have no corresponding expressions in the original, and in many places ought to have been omitted (exmp. Psalm ii. 2; cxxxiii. 3).

Dr. A. Clarke affirms in his Preface to the Bible, that in the Common Version there are "*many thousand errors in the Italics, which make God to speak what he never did speak.*" Dr. Trapp writes as follows: "*Our English translation of the Bible, though in the main a good one, is in some places intolerably faulty.*" Blackwall asserts, that "*the former translation, though amended by the present in several places, is yet equal to it in very many, and superior in a considerable number;*" and that "*innumerable instances might be given of faulty translations of the divine original.*"—See *Classics* (1731), pref. Dr. Waterland says, "*our present translation is undoubtedly capable of very great improvement.*"—*Script. Vindic.*, part iii., p. 64. J. Wesley writes, "*I do not say that our common English version is incapable of being brought, in several places, nearer to the original.*" Bishop Lowth calls it "*a version of second-hand,*" and speaks of a new translation as "*a necessary work.*"—*Prelim. Dissert. to Isaiah*, p. 69. Professor Dr. Symonds says, "*Whoever examines our version in present use, will find that it is ambiguous and incorrect, even in matters of the highest importance.*" —Observations on the Expediency of Revising the Present Version, 1789.

Bishop Marsh says, "*We cannot possibly pretend that our authorized version does not require amendment.*" Durell affirms, that "*the version now in use in many places does not exhibit the sense of the text, and mistakes it, besides, in an infinite number of instances.*"—*Crit. on Job*, 1772, pref. Dr. Blayney remarks, that "*the common version is far from what it should be, and has mistaken the true sense of the Hebrew in not a few places.*"—*Prelim. Disc. to Jeremiah*, 1789. And Dr. Kennicott suggests, that "*great improvements might now be made, because the Hebrew and Greek languages have been much cultivated and far better understood, since the year 1600.*"—*Remarks*, etc., 1787, p. 6.

The Rev. J. Oxlee, in a letter to the Archbishop of Canterbury, in 1845, asserts that "*Many gross perversions, not to say mistranslations, of the sacred text, have been occasioned by dogmatical prejudices, and sectarian zeal.*" Pp. 137, 138.

A writer in the *Biblioth. Lit.* avows that "*the common English version has many considerable faults, and very much needs another review.*"—1723, p. 72. And Pilkington emphatically observes that "*Many of the inconsistencies, improprieties, and obscurities, are occasioned by the translators misunderstanding the true import of the Hebrew words and phrases, showing the benefit and expediency of a more correct and intelligent translation of the Bible.*"—*Remarks*, 1759, p. 77.

Professor Selwyn observes, that "the very fact of the Translators having often placed one interpretation in the text, and another in the margin, and their conscientious practice of distinguishing, by a different type, the words introduced by themselves, as required by a difference of idiom, sufficiently disclaims all assumption of infallibility, and invites the endeavors of succeeding times to the perfecting of this noble work. . . . The importance of this work of improvement is enhanced a hundredfold, by the circumstances of these latter times, by the wonderful extension of the English language over the world, and by the increasing efforts made to multiply translations of the Scriptures into the tongues of heathen nations and islands, for which our authorized version forms the general basis. . . . I will mention [among others] one good result to be hoped for, from the undertaking of an authorized revision. It is the quickening impulse that will be given to sacred studies, both in criticism and interpretation. Let us no longer be deterred from this good work, by vague fears of unknown difficulties. Neither let us give way to the ungrounded fear that the reverence and love of the people for the English Bible, as a whole, will be weakened by the correction of some defective renderings; their reverence and love rest on a far wider and deeper basis."

Professor Noyes observes, that "more may be done to make the Sacred Writings understood and respected, by a revised translation of them, than in any other single mode. . . . It would do more for the cause of revealed religion than many an elaborate argument in its defence."

"Respectable and excellent, as our common version is, considering the time and circumstances under which it was made," remarks Dr. J. Pye Smith, "no person will contend that it is incapable of important amendment. A temperate, impartial, and careful revision, would be an invaluable benefit to the cause of Christianity; and the very laudable exertions which are now made to circulate the Bible, render such a revision, at the present time, a matter of still more pressing necessity."

For additional opinions, etc., see *Newcome's Hist.*, *View of the Eng. Bib. Translations*; *An Essay for a New Translation of the Bible*, London, 1727, by H. R., etc., etc. Throughout his voluminous works, Swedenborg has adopted a new, more literal, and more accurate rendering into the Latin language, of those portions of the Word which he explains or quotes. He sometimes translated into the Latin from the original, and at others used the excellent, but literal version of Schmidius. The translation of his works into English, therefore, supplies a more correct rendering of numerous portions of the Word than our authorized English version.

XV. DEGREES.

A clear understanding of the subject of degrees, is of so much importance to a right comprehension of the Word of God, and the science of correspondences, and has been so amply unfolded and so clearly illustrated by Swedenborg, that I cannot refrain from presenting to the intelligent and earnest reader the following extracts:

"*That Degrees are of two kinds, Degrees of Altitude, and Degrees of Latitude.*— The knowledge of degrees is, as it were, the key to open the causes of things, and enter into them; without it scarcely anything of cause can be known, for without it, the objects and subjects of both worlds appear so general (*univoca*) as to seem to have nothing in them but what is seen with the eye; when nevertheless, this, respectively to the things which lie interiorly concealed, is as one to thousands, yea to myriads. The interior things which lie hid, can by no means be discovered, unless degrees be understood; for exterior things advance to interior things, and these to inmost, by degrees; not by continuous degrees, but by discrete degrees. Decrements or decreasings from grosser to finer, or from denser to rarer, or rather increments and increasings from finer to grosser, or from rarer to denser, like that of light to shade, or of heat to cold, are called continuous degrees. But discrete degrees are entirely different: they are in the relation of prior, posterior, and postreme, or of end, cause, and effect. They are called discrete degrees, because the prior is by itself, the posterior by itself, and the postreme by itself; but still, taken together, they make a one. The atmospheres which are called æther and air, from highest to lowest, or from the sun to the earth, are discriminated into such degrees; and are as simples, the congregates of these simples, and again the congregates of these congregates, which taken together, are called a composite. These last degrees are discrete, because they exist distinctly; and they are understood by degrees of altitude; but the former degrees are continuous, because they continually increase; and they are understood by degrees of latitude.

"All and singular the things which exist in the spiritual and natural worlds, coëxist at once from discrete and continuous degrees, or from degrees of altitude and degrees of latitude. That dimension which consists of discrete degrees is called altitude, and that which consists of continuous degrees is called latitude: their situation relatively to sight does not change their denomination.

"Without a knowledge of these degrees nothing can be known of the difference between the three heavens, or of the difference between the love and wisdom of the angels, or of the difference between the heat and light in which they are, or of the difference between the atmospheres which surround and contain them.

"Moreover, without a knowledge of these degrees, nothing can be known of the difference of the interior faculties of the mind in men: or, therefore, of their state as to reformation and regeneration; or of the difference of the exterior faculties, which are of the body, as well of angels as of men; and nothing at all of the difference between spiritual and natural, or therefore of correspondence; yea, of any difference of life between men and beasts, or of the difference between the more perfect and the imperfect beasts; or of the differences between the forms of the vegetable kingdom, and between the materials which compose the mineral kingdom. Whence it may appear, that those who are ignorant of these degrees, cannot from any judgment see causes; they only see effects, and judge of causes from them, which is done for the most part by an induction continuous with effects; when, nevertheless causes do not produce effects by continuity, but discretely, for a cause is one thing, and an effect another; there is a difference as between prior and posterior, or as between the thing forming and the thing formed."—*D. L. W.*, n. 184, 185.

"All things which exist in the world, of which trinal dimension is predicated, or which are called compound, consist of degrees of altitude or discrete degrees. But to illustrate this by example. It is well known by ocular experience that each muscle in the human body consists of very minute fibres, and that these fasciculated, constitute those larger ones, called moving fibres, and that bundles of these produce the compound which is called a muscle. It is the same with the nerves; very small nervous fibres are put together into larger ones, which appear like filaments, and by a collection of such filaments the nerve is produced. It is also the same in the other compaginations, confasciculations, and collections of which the organs and viscera consist; for these are compounds of fibres and vessels variously fashioned by similar degrees. The case is the same also with all and every thing of the vegetable kingdom, and with all and every thing of the mineral kingdom: in wood there is a compagination of filaments in threefold order; in metals and stones there is a conglobation of parts also in threefold order. These considerations show the nature of discrete degrees, namely, that one is formed from another, and by means of the second, a third, or composite; and that each degree is discrete from another."—*D. L. W.*, n. 190.

"That in successive order the first degree constitutes the highest, and the third the lowest; but that in simultaneous order, the first degree constitutes the inmost, and the third the outmost. There is successive order, and simultaneous order: the successive order of these degrees is from highest to lowest, or from top to bottom. The angelic heavens are in this order; the third heaven is the highest, the second is the middle, and the first is the lowest; such is their relative situations: in similar successive order are the states of love and wisdom there with the angels, as also of heat and light, and likewise of the spiritual atmospheres; in similar order are all the perfections of forms and powers there. When the degrees of altitude, or discrete degrees, are in successive order, they may be compared to columns divided into three degrees, by which there is an ascent and descent; in the superior mansion of which are the things the most perfect and most beautiful, in the middle the less perfect and less beautiful, and in the lowest the still less perfect and less beautiful. But simultaneous order, which consists of similar degrees, has another appearance: in this the highest things of successive order, which, as was said, are the most perfect and most beautiful, are in the inmost, inferior things in the middle, and the lowest things in the circumference. They are as in a solid substance consisting of those three degrees, in the middle or centre of which are the most subtle parts, about it are parts less subtle, and in the extremes, which constitute the circumference, there are parts composed of these, and consequently more gross: it is like that column, which was spoken of above, subsiding into a plane, whose highest part constitutes the inmost, whose middle part the middle, and its lowest the extreme.

"Since the highest of successive order is the inmost of simultaneous order, and the lowest is the outmost, therefore in the Word, superior signifies interior, and inferior signifies exterior; and upwards and downwards, and height and depth signify the same.

"In every ultimate there are discrete degrees in simultaneous order: the moving fibres in every muscle, the fibres in every nerve, and the fibres and vessels in every viscus and organ, are in such order; in their inmost are the most simple and perfect things, whereof their outmost is composed. A similar order of those degrees is in every seed, and in every fruit, and in every metal and stone; the parts of them, of which the whole consists, are such; in inmost, intermediate, and outmost principles of the parts, are in those degrees, for they are successive compositions, or confasciculations, and conglobations, from simples, which are their first substances or materials.

"In a word, there are such degrees in every ultimate, thus in every effect; for every ultimate consists of prior things, and these of their first; and every effect consists of a cause, and this of an end; and the end is the all of the cause, and the cause is the all of the effect, and the end constitutes the inmost, the cause the middle, and the effect the ultimate. That the case is the same with the degrees of love and wisdom, of heat and light, and with the organic forms of the affections and thoughts in man will be seen in what follows. The series of these degrees in successive order and simultaneous order, is also treated of in the *Doctrine of the New Jerusalem concerning the Sacred Scriptures*, n. 38, and elsewhere; where it is shown that there are similar degrees in all and every part of the Word."—*D. L. W.*, n. 205–208.

"That the ascending and descending degrees, which are called prior and posterior, and degrees of altitude or discrete degrees, are in their power in their ultimate, may be confirmed by all those things which were adduced by way of confirmation from sensible and perceptible things in the preceding pages; but here I choose to confirm them only by efforts, powers, and motions, in dead subjects and in living subjects. It is well known that endeavor of itself does nothing, but that it acts by powers corresponding to it, and by them produces motion; hence that endeavor is the all in the powers, and through the powers in the motion; and motion being the ultimate degree of endeavor, that by this it produces its efficacy. Endeavor, power, and motion, are not otherwise connected than according to degrees of altitude, conjunction by which is not by continuity, for they are discrete, but by correspondences; for endeavor is not power, nor power, motion; but power is produced by endeavor, being endeavor excited, and motion is produced by power; wherefore there is no potency in endeavor alone, or in power alone, but in motion, which is their product. That this is the case still appears doubtful, because it has not been illustrated by application to things sensible and perceptible in nature; but nevertheless such is their progression into potency.

"Let us apply these principles to living endeavor, living power, and living motion. The living endeavor in a man, who is a living subject, is his will united to his understanding; the living powers in him are what constitute the interiors of his body, in all of which there are moving fibres variously interwoven; and living motion in him is action, which is produced through those powers by the will united to the understanding. The interiors of the will and understanding constitute the first degree, the interiors of the body constitute the second, and the whole body, which is their complex, constitutes the third degree. That the interiors of the mind have no potency but by powers in the body, and that powers have no potency but by action of the body, is a well known fact. These three do not act by continuity, but discretely; and to act discretely is to act by correspondences. The interiors of the mind correspond to the interiors of the body, and the interiors of the body to its exteriors, by which actions exist; wherefore the two former are in potency by means of the exteriors of the body. It may seem as if endeavor and powers in a man are in some potency, although there is no action, as in dreams and states of rest; but in these cases the determination of endeavors and powers, fall on the common moving principles of the body, which are the heart and lungs; but when the action of these ceases, the powers also cease, and the endeavor with the powers."—*D. L. W.*, n. 218, 219.

"The ancient Egyptians believed in the unity of the Godhead, and expressed his attributes by Triads." It is remarkable that the ancient trinities of the Hindoos, as well as the Egyptians, emblematized *the male principle, the female principle, and the offspring*, and that this is identical with the early Chinese philosophy.

According to Pythagoras, the symbol of all things, or fulness, was, the Monad, or active principle, or Father; the Duad, or passive principle, or Mother; and the result, or operation of both united.

The philosopher Damascius asserts, that, "throughout the world a Triad shines forth, which resolves itself into a Monad." And also, that this doctrine was the fundamental principle of the Orphic philosophy. Voscius observes that this idea holds a principal place in the mythology of the ancients. —See *Pritchard's Analysis of Egyptian Mythology*, pp. 39–47.

Numberless pantheistic superstitions and absurd cosmogonies, etc., were founded on the corruptions of this philosophy, as it became more depraved and sensual.

The three degrees of initiation into the ancient mysteries of Egypt, Greece, etc., were, without doubt, derived from the above doctrine of discrete degrees. Among various nations the number three always conveys the idea of fulness and perfection.

I take the present opportunity of observing, that the signs, symbols, and three degrees of Free-Masonry, are a peculiar compound of a few correspondences, adopted from the ancient cavern mysteries, most probably from those of the Sun-worship of Heliopolis, and phrases and figures borrowed from the symbolic sculpture, painting, etc., of more modern times, and incorporated into ceremonies which, on mere assumption, without the slightest evidence, are said to have originated with the building of Solomon's temple. (See the works of Hutchinson, Preston, Capt. G. Smith, Dr. Ashe, Dr. Oliver, etc., on *Free-Masonry*.)

The Christian symbols of the middle ages, with the exception of some coincidences, most likely accidental, were not correspondences at all, but only enigmatical comparisons, often very obscure. A large proportion of them were derived from heathen mythologies and Jewish traditions. The remainder were founded upon some fanciful associations or resemblances, which particular objects and their habitudes, mystic words and signs, arbitrary marks and combinations, the forms and properties of the vestments, utensils, and instruments connected with religious worship, and the various professions and trades, etc., were supposed to bear to certain moral rules and sentiments, regarded as necessary for the right direction and government of the conduct. This symbolism was further used to designate the presumed or admitted qualities of persons; or was applied to distinguish them from each other. It was also employed as a tropical vehicle of doctrinal mysteries and monastic professions, vows, charms, etc., and for the purposes of secret association and recognition. (See *Glossary of Architecture*, and Pugin's *Glossary of Ecclesiastical Ornament and Costume*.)

Vitruvius informs us that the Ionic order of Grecian architecture was formed on the model of woman, and the Doric on that of man. Architecture is called by De Staël and Goethe "frozen music." "A Gothic church," said Coleridge, "is a petrified religion."

"All styles of architecture are hieroglyphics upon a large scale; exhibiting to the heedful eye, forms of worship widely differing from each other; and proving, that in almost every religion with which we are acquainted, the form of the temple was the *hierogram* of its god, or of the peculiar opinions of its votaries."—*Bardwell's Temples*, p. 55.

"In the most ancient monuments of India and Egypt, as in those of the middle ages, architecture, statuary, and painting, are the material expressions of religious thought."—*Portal's Des Coleurs Symboliques*.

The science of Correspondences being lost, the abstract ethics of Christianity were thus sought to be extensively imprinted on the memory and conscience. In correspondence there is nothing arbitrary or fanciful. The thing signified must be the proximate cause of that to which it corresponds, and be recognized in its form and use. The former must live, so to speak, within the latter, as the soul lives in the body, or as thought enshrines itself in speech, or as the intellect exists in the eye, or as the affections of the heart animate the countenance; all which act together as cause and effect.

"Even in the most remote periods of history, *three* was considered a mystic number, and regarded with reverence.

The Assyrians had their triads. In ancient Egypt every town and district had its own triad, which it worshipped, and which was a union of certain attributes, the third member proceeding from the other two. Sir Gardiner Wilkinson, in his *Ancient Egyptians*, vol. iv., ch. xii., p. 230, mentions a stone, with the words, 'one Bail, one Athor; one Akovi; hail Father of the World! hail triformous God!' Thoms, in his *Dissertation on Ancient Chinese Vases*, says, 'The Chinese have a remarkable preference for the number three; they say, One produced two, two produced three, and three produced all things.' The Buddhists, who are of Modern date in China, use the term 'The threefold precious One.' The Taow sect have also their 'three pure ones.' In the Hindoo religion combinations of three are equally frequent. They have several Trimasties or Tremastis, three principal deities,—Brahma, Vishnu, and Mahadeva; another triad is Brahma, Vishnu, and Siva, including a mystical union of three principal rivers, the Ganges, Yamuna, and Sarawati. Siva has three eyes; the sun is called three-bodied; the triangle with the Hindoos is a favorite type for the triune-coequality, hence the pentagram (a figure composed of two equilateral triangles, placed with the apex of one towards the base of the other, and so forming six triangles by the intersections of their sides), is in great favor with them; further, they use three mystic letters, to denote their deity (*seven* is also a mystic number with them and other ancient races), and many other combinations of three. The same preference for this number is observable in the Greek and Roman mythology, which mentions three theocracies, three graces, three fates, three harpies, three syrens, three heads of Cerberus, etc. And, taking three as a unit, 3×3 muses, 3×4 principal gods (Dii majores), and 3×4 labors of Hercules," etc.—*Larwood and Hotten's History of Sign Boards*, p. 269.

"According to the theology of the Chaldeans, Egyptians, and ancient Greeks, in every order of things [or degrees], a triad is the immediate progeny of a monad. . . . . And hence it is said in one of the Chaldean oracles, *In every world a triad shines forth, of which a monad is the ruling principle*."—See Taylor's *Iamblicus*, pref., p. viii.

"Parmenides, in Plato, distinguishes three divine unities subordinate; the *first*, of that which is perfectly and most properly *one* [perfect love or goodness]; the second, of that which is called by him *one-many* (a perfect intellect), [perfect wisdom or all truths]; the third, of that which is thus expressed one and many [or love and wisdom in union, operating all divine uses]."—See Cudworth's *Intel. Sys.*, vol. ii., p. 40.

Origen observes that the Holy Scriptures contain a *triple sense*, analogous to the triple constitution of man. The sentiments of the Holy Scriptures are to be impressed upon our minds in a threefold manner, in order that whosoever belongs to the simpler sort of persons, may receive edification from the flesh of the Scripture (this we call their obvious or literal meaning), but he who is somewhat more advanced, from its soul; but whosoever is perfect, and similar to those to whom the apostle alludes, where he says, 'we speak wisdom' . . . . from the spiritual law which contains a shadow of good things to come; for as man consists of *spirit, body, and soul*, so also the Holy Writ which God has planned to be granted for the salvation of mankind."—*De Princip.*, iv., 108; the passage is translated by Dr. Credner, article INTERPRETATION, *Kitto's Bib. Cyc*.

A faint and imperfect idea of this sublime doctrine is found in *Dr. H. More's Threefold Cabala*.

1 JOHN v. 7, 8.

The long, learned, and frequent disputations respecting the authenticity and genuineness of the seventh verse, in no way affect the present argument. I may here observe, that it is now generally allowed to have been spuriously introduced into an ancient copy of the 1st Ep. of John. It exists, however, with some verbal differences, in the Greek MS. known by the title of the "Codex Montfortianus," in Trinity College, Dublin—supposed to be the Codex Britannicus, of Erasmus, which Martin of Utrecht considered to be as old as the eleventh century, and Dr. A. Clarke regarded as a production of about the thirteenth, but which Porson, Griesbach, and Bishop Marsh considered as written so late as the fifteenth or sixteenth; it is also found in the Greek MS. entitled "Codex Ottobonianus," in the Vatican Library, a MS. of the fifteenth century (collated by Scholz; see also Dr. Wiseman). The first Greek writer who cited the passage, appears to have been the translator of the Latin acts of the Council of Lateran, which was held A. D. 1215. It is also quoted in the fourteenth century by Manuel Calecas, a Dominican monk. It is inserted in several of the MSS. of the Latin Vulgate, but not in the most ancient. It is cited by Vigilius, Bishop of Thrapsus, in Africa, and also by a contemporary African writer, Victor Vitensis, in his *History of the Vandal Persecution*, A. D. 484, when four hundred bishops of Africa were called upon to give an account of the Christian faith to an Arian king and persecutor. Some of the Latin writers, as Virgilius, Ambrose, etc., according to Dr. A. Clarke, insert the passage thus: "There are three that bare record in heaven, the Father, the Word, and the Holy Spirit, and these *three* are one in CHRIST JESUS;" or as translated by Scott Porter, a distinguished Unitarian: "There are three who utter testimony in heaven, the Father, the Word, and the Spirit, and in CHRIST JESUS they are one." See also *Biblioth. Sussex; Bishops Marsh and Horsley; Travis's Letter to Gibbon; Porson's Letters*, l. iv., and *Dr. H. Ware's Works*, p. 243; where the principal arguments and opinions in favor of, and against, the authenticity of these verses, etc., may be seen.

XVI. DRUIDISM.

Druidism was the religion of the Ancient Britons, and was considered by the Gauls as having originated with them. Julius Cæsar gives some account of the Druids in his De Bell. Gall: lib. vi., c. 1; but as his information was only, or chiefly, derived from hearsay evidence, it cannot be altogether implicitly received.

Druidism appears to have existed prior to the patriarchal history. In one form or other, it was the prevailing religion and philosophy of Europe, and possessed many close affinities with the religion which was, at the same period, common to Egypt, Phœnicia, Syria, Persia, Babylonia, Nineveh, and all the East. The term Druid is considered to be a compound of *Deru, an oak*, and *Gwyddon, wise men*.

The worship was conducted in circular temples, often comprising a trine of circles, and at altars in the open air, under trees, in groves, or on mountains, or hills, and in these respects it appears to have resembled the representative worship of the Ancient Church. They had three orders of priests or bards, who were also physicians. The chief ruling priest, or presiding bard, was clothed in a robe of cerulean blue, wore a garland of oak leaves, and a tiara of gold; the second, or oviate bard class, was clad in light green,—a color which appears to have designated science and philosophy; and the third was clad in white linen, or with a purple border, fastened by a girdle in which appeared the crystal stone set in gold, in reference to religion and morality, or the union of truth and charity, and their purifying results in the mind and life. They regarded the oak, from which the garlands of the chief priests were gathered, with peculiar veneration. The mistletoe, a parasite of the oak, was estimated, for its medicinal virtues, at the highest value, and designated "Healer of all." The three joys of the bards of the Isle of Britain, are declared to have been: "the increase of knowledges; the reformation of manners; and the triumph of peace." The original British harp was strung with hair, and consisted of twelve strings.

From ancient MSS. relating to British Druidism, and recently brought to light.*—Much of their ancient learning, hitherto deemed unintelligible, like much of the mythology of the Greeks and Romans, may be reduced to some degree of order and sense; and it then shows its original connection with the science of correspondences.

Though the worship of the Ancient Church had become idolatrous so early as the Patriarchal age (Josh. xxiv. 2; Ex. xxxiv. 13), yet it retained, for many generations, more or less of its original representative character. Druidism has been often misrepresented and misunderstood, in consequence of confounding its pure with its corrupt era.

They worshipped the Sun, as the most glorious representative image of God, and a remnant of these observances is still extant in Ireland, in the Beltein bonfires and fairs of the 1st of May. In the idolatrous observances of Moloch, another name for the sun, the priests and people leaped from the flames. In later and more degraded times, human sacrifices were doubtless offered, and children were cast into the fire, as propitiations for sin, as is evident from the frequent testimony of the Old Testament, and from ancient history.

The Hebrew and oriental nations called the name of the supreme God, Baal (lord, in the sense of master, or he that rules and subdues),—a name afterwards superstitiously and blasphemously attributed, in every variety of form, to the idols of those countries. The Druids denominated him Bel (Celtic).

The Hebrew word *Shaddai*, or *Saddai*, denoting the Almighty, succoring, aiding, and assisting, had also its counterpart in the West; for the word *Seadah* was one of the characteristic names of Bel. The Druids also addressed God, and spoke of Him under the expressive epithet of *Hu*, signifying the self-existent Being; *he that is*, and the near relation between this word and "*I am that I am*," must strike the most careless.

The British Druids, among a multitude of heterogeneous notions, superstitions, dogmas, absurd customs, and inhuman ceremonies, introduced in the lapse of ages, and which ultimately degenerated into a system of abominable cruelty and licentiousness, appear, notwithstanding, to have retained from ancient times, and preserved even to a late age, some ideas derived through the commercial intercourse of the Phœnicians. From these ancient sources their philosophy, which combine a system of ethics and theology, under the cover of symbolic types, the human mind had to pass through three *degrees, circles, regions,* or *spheres;* viz., 1. Inchoation; 2. Progression; and 3. Consummation. In the 1st degree man

---

* These MSS. have been printed under the title of *Myfyrian Archaiology;* they were carefully transcribed by the late Owen Jones, of London, a native of Denbighshire, and eventually published, in three volumes, at his sole expense. These volumes were published in London, in the year 1801, under the supervision of three editors, Owen Jones, Edward Williams, and William Owen.

collects knowledge, in order to be acquainted with his duty; in the 2d he acquires moral strength, to enable him to discharge it; and in the 3d he attains a state of perfection. They further taught that in passing through the prior degree, man, by negligence and misconduct, might retrograde, and fall into the lowest states of existence. The stages of degradation were described as threefold. The mediums of man's progress in states of exaltation were likewise described as threefold, viz., 1. Humility [or obedience of life]; 2. Truth [or illumination of the intellect]; and, 3. Mercy [or love influencing all the affections of the will]. If man fell into states of degradation, it was taught that he could only be renewed again by passing through principles; and mediating changes and gradations, and *knowledge, benevolence,* and *power,* were represented as the trinal weapons with which he was to obtain the victory in his conflict with his passions and propensities. Man's future state of existence was taught to be an eternal progression towards the perfections of Deity. With them, the animal life was wholly evil; the human life, a mixed condition of being, and the future life, a state of unmingled and ever-increasing happiness. The changes from one state to another they denominated "transmigration."

The ancient Druids appear to have believed originally in one supreme, invisible, omnipotent, and omnipresent Deity, whose body or form, as defined by Pythagoras, was as the glorious light, but whose soul or essence was the eternal truth. They held the doctrine of the true nature of the soul, and the metempsychosis as indicating changes of mental condition; thus it was symbolically and not literally understood, till their worship became idolatrous. They described principles "in the mind," according to correspondence, representing them under the forms of men, beasts, birds, trees, etc. They taught that *knowledge* and *virtue* are the *only* qualifications which can dignify and ennoble man, and that *ignorance* and *vice* inevitably overwhelm him with degradation and contempt, that right or wrong conduct depended on the influence of these principles in the mind, and prepared them, on the one hand, for eternal felicity; or, on the other, for never-ending misery. They described man's life in the world to come, as exactly corresponding with his state. Their ancient and uncorrupted Triads are most remarkable, and are often as true, and as philosophically just, as they are beautiful and interesting. Among many others are the following:

"The three consummate perfections of God are:—The one infinite life; infinite knowledge; and infinite plenitude of power.

"Three things [or principles], which are the causes productive of living beings:—The divine love, of which is the all-perfect wisdom: the divine wisdom, in the perception of all possible means; and the divine power, which is by the joint will [or union] of the divine love and wisdom.

"There are three things of which God necessarily consists:—The greatest life; the greatest knowledge; and the greatest power: and of what is greatest there can be no more than one of anything.

"The three grand powers of the soul [are]:—Affection; understanding; and will [or determination], or the conjunction of the understanding and the affection.

"The three grand operations of the mind or man [are]:—To think; to choose; and to perform.

"The three branches of wisdom [are]: The wisdom which relates to God; the wisdom which relates to mankind; and the wisdom which relates to oneself: the three knowledges which appertain to wisdom [are]: The knowledge of God; the knowledge of mankind; and the knowledge of one's own heart."

In the patriarchal history, we read that Jacob tarried all night at a place called Luz, which means in English a *bending*, and also *a separation or departure*. And he took the stone he had used as a pillow, and set it up for a pillar, and consecrated it by pouring oil upon the top of it; and called it Bethel, which means *the house of God*, and he took it as the witness of a solemn vow. (Gen. xxviii. 11-22.) The pillar and the heap were constituted witnesses of a covenant, and of a boundary, or separation: and the place is called Mizpeh, or Mizpah, *a watch-tower, sentinel*, etc.—See *Dr. A. Clarke; Cassel's Lexicon*.

From Bethel is derived Barthulia, Bethyllia, Baithylia, or *living stones* of the Phœnicians, which, consecrated by being anointed with oil, were the representative images of *living truth*, or *truth alive* in the natural degree. From this signification the apostle Peter calls the Lord Jesus Christ, who was THE ANOINTED, "*a living stone.*" And as the patriarch called the stone he set up and consecrated "God's house," so the apostle exhorts those that "have purified their souls in obeying the truth, through the Spirit, and unfeigned love of the brethren (1 Pet. i. 22), to lay aside all malice, and all guile, and hypocrisy, and envies and all evil speakings," and as new-born babes, "to desire the sincere milk of the Word, that they might grow thereby;" and "that coming unto the Lord Jesus Christ as unto *a living stone*, they also, as *lively stones*, are built up a spiritual house." (1 Pet. ii. 2-5.)

The Baetylia, Bethyllia, or living or anointed stones, so celebrated in antiquity, and to which divine honors were paid, especially by the Phœnicians, who had commercial intercourse with all nations, particularly the British Isles, where those monuments abound, were originally of a similar class. These became abused to idolatrous purposes; thence, they were strongly prohibited. See Lev. xxv. 1; Amos iii. 14. When consecrated they were supposed to be *instinct* with the power and energy of some divinity. "The practice," says Bishop Lowth, "was very common in different ages and places. Arnobius, lib. i., gives an account of his own practice in this respect: 'Si quando conspexiam lubricatum lapidem, et ex olivi unguine, sorditatum; tanquam inessit vis proesens, adulabar, affabar, et beneficia poscebam nihil sentiente de trunes' (Isa. lvii. 6). Which may be translated as follows: 'If at any time I beheld an anointed stone, as if there had been a power inherent in it, I made my obeisance to it. I addressed myself unto it, and requested benefits from it, not at all considering it a stock.' Such were the Baetylia, or living stones of the ancient Phœnicians. Hence the use of the image of the apostle Peter."

In accommodation to the prejudices of the mass of the people who idolatrously worshipped stone pillars, or obelisks, the earlier Christians substituted crosses of various kinds, or cut them upon the upper stones, or placed them upon the pillars or their bases, as the symbols of redemption, and to enforce the self-denying doctrine of the Christian religion. Hence the origin of boundary crosses, market crosses, sepulchral crosses, way-side crosses, and those erected as memorials of battles, murders, or fatal events, and in remembrance of the dead. They appear to have been first cut on the top of single upright stones (*Britton*), and afterwards ornamented by degrees, until finally they were most elaborately finished. "That, however, which began in pious consideration to the weakness of man, ended in confirming that weakness, and in substituting a superstition almost heathen for the spiritual doctrines of Christianity."—*Rev. H. H. Milman.*

Legends are connected with most of the druidical circles, implying that the stones were originally petrified men and women at a wedding, a festival, or a dance.

Stonehenge was called the giants' dance.

Stanton Drew is said to have been a wedding party petrified.

Dance Main implies the dance of stones, once young women, who danced there on the Sabbath day.

Rollrich, a band of marauding soldiers turned into stones.

Similar legends exist also in other countries. They are connected with fairies and demons.

"The prohibition to worship stones by the earlier Christian Ecclesiastical laws and ordinances, and which without doubt relate to these monuments, attest the antiquity, and greatly contributed to their destruction."—*Wright,* p. 63.

For many of the foregoing extracts I am greatly indebted to a series of able and excellent papers on Druidism, by T. W., in the 1st vol. of the *Anglo-American New Church Repository,* to which I refer the reader. See also *Toland's Hist. of the Druids; Williams's Druopœdia; Davies's Celtic Researches, and Mythology of the British Druids; Hulbert's Religion of Britain; Roberts's Hist. of the Isle of Man; Bowlaise's Hist. of Cornwall; Rose's Tech. Anglic.; Weaver's Mon. Ant.; Identity of the Religions called Druidical and Hebrew; and James's Manual of British Druidism.*

The pyramids of Egypt, India, and Mexico,—the Druidical remains of Stonehenge, and at a distance of twenty miles from them, those of Abury in Wiltshire, Stanton Drew, or the stone town of the Druids in Somersetshire,—Rollwright of Rollrich, in Oxfordshire, Arber-low in Derbyshire, and the Hurlers and Dance-Man in Cornwall: the sepulchral mounds known by the name of cairns, carnes, or carnedes (in Welsh carydd, and in French galgals), that is a heap of stones; also cromlehs, cromleichs, or cromlechs; Kist-vaens, or "stone-chests," called in the Channel Islands, Antels or altars (Gen. xii. 7, 8; xxvi. 25), and Pequilays (that is, "heaps of stones"), but which Wright supposes are "sepulchral chambers denuded of their mounds;" tolmen, or stones of passage, and in French dolmen, or stone tables, as Kits-Coty House, in Kent, Chun-Quoit, in Cornwall, etc.; and Druidical circles or orals of stone (Josh. iv. 5); the upright rude pillars, massive pyramidal blocks of stone, and obelisks, which are found scattered all over the habitable globe, and on most of which "no tool of man had been lifted" (Ex. xx. 25; Deut. xxvii. 4, 5), were raised as memorials of affection; as sepulchral monuments, both of honor and infamy (Gen. xxxv. 20; Josh. vii. 26); as records of victories and exploits; in remembrance of special mercies and events; as witnesses of contracts and covenants (Gen. xxxi. 51, 52); or as attestations of faithfulness; those known in North Wales by the name of "men pillars;" those set up for boundaries, land marks, or way marks (Jer. xxxi. 31); called in England hoar-stones, or by some dialectic name, such as hare-stones, war-stones, wor-stones, hoor-stones, her-stones, etc.; together with the March-stones, held sacred by the Romans; had all, without doubt, their real origin in the correspondence of stones, though so early used for idolatrous and impious purposes.—See *Grose's Antiq.,* vol. i., p. 135; *Pinkerton's Collect,* part x., p. 261; *Smith's Michaelis,* vol. iii., p. 374; *Hulbert's Religions of Britain,* p. 22; *Weaver's Mon.*

Ant.; Hamper's Observations on Pillars of Memorial; Dr. A. Clarke, in loc.; Camden's Britannia; Stukeley's Stonehenge; and *Wright's Celt. Rom. and Sax. Ant.*

Stonehenge, an Anglo-Saxon word meaning "hanging-stones," and built of hewn stones, arranged in triliths, the most stupendous remains of Druid worship, the grand national temple, was doubtless, at first, representative, in all its arrangements and particulars,— though that worship was soon afterwards greatly corrupted, and the knowledge of representatives became lost in superstition and idolatry. With the serpentine temple at Abury, it appears to have combined the adoration of the sun, moon, and stars, and the worship of the serpent. In all probability, their religious maxims, rites, and ceremonies, which also comprehended their laws and customs, were derived from the Phœnicians, and originated in Heliopolis, called in the Word, Ox (Gen. xli. 45; xlvi. 20). Stonehenge was called by the ancient Britons Choir Ghaur, that is *great church.* Others have considered it to mean "The circular plan of assembly." This and the other Druid circles or ovals were used not only as places for worship, sacrifices, and augury; for the celebration of festivals and other Druidical rites; but is also supposed that they were used for forums; for the re-inauguration of priests and kings; for the use of general assemblies; for the meeting of councils, local and national; for the promulgation of laws; and for elections and as seats of judgment. In Gaelic they are denominated clactans, which means "places of worship." Dr. Jamieson, in his *Historical account of the Culdees*, says, "that at this day, 'going to and from church,' and 'going to and from the stones,' are phrases used synonymously" (b. 25). Moses erected twelve pillars of stones at the foot of Mount Sinai; and, about forty years afterwards, Joshua pitched twelve stones in Gilgal, as a memorial of the passage of the Israelites through Jordan, which, in after ages, became a place of idolatrous worship. Gilgal means, in English, a circle. When the covenant was ratified between Laban and Jacob (Gen. xxxi. 44-49), Jacob set up a stone as a pillar of witness, and commanded his brethren to gather stones, and "make a heap," and they did eat thereon. Laban called it Jegar-sahadutha, which is a pure Chaldee word; but Jacob called it Galeed, which is a pure Hebrew word of the same meaning, translated by Calmet, "the circle of witness," and by Dr. Oliver and Dr. A. Clarke, "heap or round heap of witness." Camden informs us that it is the custom, "in several places, to cast heaps of stones on the graves of malefactors and self-murderers;" thence he supposes it was that "the worst of traitors were called Karn-hhadron," *a carn thief* (Josh. viii. 29; 2 Sam. xvii.).

The term cromleh has been derived from the Amoric word *crum*, crooked or bowing, and *leh*, stone, in supposed allusion to the reverence which persons paid to them by bowing. Toland says that cromleh means a bowing-stone; but Rowland derives the name from the Hebrew words signifying "a devoted or consecrated stone." "It was usual," remarks Bryant, "among the Egyptians, to place with much labor one vast stone upon another, for a religious memorial. The stones they thus placed, they sometimes poised so equally, that they were affected with the least external force; nay, a breath of wind would sometimes make them vibrate."—*Anal. Mythol.*, vol. iii., *in Moore*, p. 30. These rocking-stones and rock basins, as the Chese-Wring, in Cornwall, etc., which were formerly regarded as Druidical, are now concluded by geologists not to be artificial, but the result of natural causes;

they nevertheless received superstitious veneration.

The Druid religion is equally applicable to Gaul. It was unlawful to commit their maxims, doctrines, and mysteries, to writing. At the time of Julius Cæsar's invasion of Britain, he found the Druid religion most corrupt and idolatrous, and mixed with Pagan mythology. They offered human sacrifices; though modern discoveries have made it extremely likely that the custom was far from ancient. Many of their traditions, maxims, and doctrines, as recorded by various ancient writers, point to a much higher state of civilization and philosophy than we find recorded by the Roman emperor, and it is difficult to reconcile their existence, much less their origin, to so low and degraded a condition.

Enough has been said to show the true origin not only of their doctrines, but also of those records, which for ages to come will show that the science of correspondences was once widely diffused, and we can trace the operations of Divine Providence in preserving these memorials, which throw, when rightly viewed, so powerful a light on the Holy Word.

XVII. THE PYTHAGOREAN DOCTRINE OF METEMPSYCHOSIS.

"The doctrine of metempsychosis, or transmigration, is found almost everywhere. In Greece, and Rome, and Egypt, and the East, it is seen, and in forms more or less disguised, traces of it are discernible in nearly all the religions of which we know anything distinctly. Differing somewhat in detail, it was always substantially as follows. He who is not good, passes at death into the form of some kindred animal, and thence into another and another, until the circle of expiation being completed, he becomes again a man, and a redeemed and happy one. Now this doctrine was taught very earnestly by Pythagoras; a man whom we can sneer at only when we can forget the vast influence he exerted in his own day and through such men as Plato ever since, and the golden truths still discernible in the fragmentary remnants of his doctrines, and the fact that the system of the universe established by Copernicus was but a revival of his own, and the many other indications of the extent and accuracy of his knowledge. How, then, could he have taught such a folly? But are we sure that it was all folly, that it contains no certain, no valuable truth? Let us ask if the science of correspondence can explain it. Man, the microcosm, or little world, as Pythagoras and Plato and so many of the ancients called him, represents the universe. Thus, all animals that ever were or can exist, live by virtue of the fact that they severally represent some of the elements, faculties, or qualities of the human character. Goodness does not consist so much in the absence of any of these, as in the presence of all and their due subordination, and their harmonious performance of their several functions.

"[When] a man begins to reform [his character, he] is penetrated with a profound sense of evil. He becomes aware, perhaps, that he is lost and buried in foul and gross gluttony, and in his remorse he feels that he is not a man, that sin has transformed him, that he is no better than a hog! He says with the Psalmist, 'I am as a beast before thee!' And he repents and reforms and casts this sin away. Then he discovers that his ferocity makes him a tiger, and the same process again relieves him; and then it may be he sees in himself the cunning of the fox, or other and yet other faults which disfigure and conceal his human nature. So he goes on, until humility, self-acknowledgment, repentance, and reform, have cast out the devils and restored him to the power, the consciousness, and the happiness of manhood. Now, we know that Pythagoras had an inner and secret doctrine never published, and taught only in private to the initiated under the most solemn obligation of secresy. Is it too much to suppose that these two doctrines, the inner and the outer, had some relation to each other? What would he have gained by teaching the doctrine as we have stated it above, to the gross and grovelling world about him? What better thing could he do than to teach them *the same truth* in the lower form of the metempsychosis, as he gave it to the public? It is to be noticed that this doctrine, in its lower and grosser form, is adapted to do for the lower and grosser classes of minds, the very same good which the same doctrine in its higher form is able to confer upon minds in a condition to receive it and be subject to its influence. They who would not resist gluttony, or ferocity, or low cunning, because they disfigured their spiritual humanity, might do so, if they were persuaded that they must expiate these sins in the bestial forms and life of the hog, the tiger, and the fox. In this lower form, its influence upon minds to which it was then fitted, would elevate those which were capable of improvement into a capacity of hearing and profiting by the higher. This would be in exact conformity with the law which prevails over the relation between internal and external truth. On similar grounds, I account for the universal prevalence of the doctrine of metempsychosis, which Pythagoras himself derived from Egypt. Apply this law to the Bible, and we shall come to this result, that observance of the precepts of the literal sense is precisely the way in which we may be elevated into the purer atmosphere, where the voice of an inner law may be heard. So, too, there are applications of the science of correspondences to the ancient classical mythology, which often makes it significant. Sysiphus and Tantalus, and the like, are no longer the wild and meaningless creations of fantasy, and we can understand their permanence, and charm, and power, amid the beautiful cultivation of the Greek mind. Pegasus, the winged horse, again alights upon Helicon, and opens a new Hippocrene, and again Minerva tames his fire, and gives him to the warrior who is called to do battle with the monster Chimera."—*Parsons' Essays*, Am. ed., pp. 91–96.

"No doubt was ever entertained that the Pythagorean doctrine was purely Egyptian. Pythagoras was initiated in their mysteries, and is reported to have been the disciple of Souchedes, an Egyptian chief, prophet, or high-priest."—Clem. Stromata., lib. i., *cited by Pritchard*.

"In the ancient dialect of Astronomy, the earth was said to enter successively into the constellations of the ram, the bull, the goat, etc., and thus to pass from one animal into another, until she had gone through all the signs of the zodiac. Now, as deceased souls remain for some time in the sphere of the earth, thus travelling the constellations, they were said, in a language that has been completely misunderstood, *to transmigrate into animals*, particularly into such as predominated at the time of their decease."—See *Abbe Pluche's Hist. of the Heav.*, vol. i., p. 242.

Plato asserted, like the Brahmins of the present day, not only the transmigration of men and beasts, but even vegetables; and the fire-philosophers of the sixteenth century gave credit to the same doctrine. "Both Ficinus and Darwin ascribe materialism to Plato, asserting that his doctrine of conscious spiritual existence, after a change of matter, was merely allegorical, and that the degradation of men into brutes, alluded to the brutalization of the passions."—*Maid of Penmore*, note, p. 161.

"The Druids were believers in the metempsychosis, or transmigration of souls, as Cæsar says: 'In primis hoc volunt permudere, non interire animas, sed ab aliis post mortem transire ad alios.' The Druids, like other priests, had two doctrines,—a sacred and a vulgar. No doubt Cæsar's account of the metempsychosis belonged to the vulgar religion, while the true meaning involved some mystic knowledge of the natural [and mental] history of man. Serranus, the French translator of Plato, supposes the doctrine of the metempsychosis to be mythic, and to have some allusion to future resurrection. Ficinus asserts that it is allegorical, and must be understood of the manners, affections, and tempers of men. That it was allegorical there can be very little doubt. Pythagoras learnt this doctrine in Egypt; and all the world is witness how the Egyptians concealed the most imposing doctrines under the cloak of fables [or allegories]."—*Identity of the Religions called Druidical and Hebrew*, p. 56.

"Apullius was not truly turned into an ass; or Ulysses' fellows into swine; or Lycon into a wolf; or Nebuchadnezzar into an ox,—but only in their minds into beastly qualities; they degenerated from the use of reason, not having all that while either lost the shape of human bodies, or the essence of reasonable souls."—*Rose's Mystagogus Poeticus, or Muse's Interpreter*, 1675, p. 245.

"Though there are not in men's bodies the souls of beasts, yet there are too many qualities of beasts, and bestial dispositions."—*Ib.*, p. 157.

XVIII. THE HIEROGLYPHICS, HIEROGLYPHS, OR SACRED WRITINGS AND ENGRAVINGS, AND THE REPRESENTATIVE IMAGES OF THE EGYPTIANS.

I shall preface this section with a brief account of the remarkable circumstances which led to an acquaintance with some of the principles of alphabetical hieroglyphics, always mixed up, however, with ideographical or symbolic signs. Of the *most ancient and sacred hieroglyphics*, it will be shown that the science of correspondences will alone furnish an explanation,—of which, indeed, they were remains.

While the French troops were carrying on the war in Egypt, and a commission of learned men, associated with the expedition, were exploring this ancient country, with a view to advance the arts and sciences, one division of the army occupied the village of Raschid, or Reschid, which we call Rosetta, and the engineers were employed, in August, 1798, upon some military works. As they were digging the foundations of Fort St. Julian, on the eastern mouth of the Nile, near Rosetta, M. Boussard discovered a large, mutilated, oblong block of black granite, which was covered with a considerable portion of a trigrammatical inscription, in different characters, and which, according to the late researches of Harris, was originally placed in a temple of Tum, or Tomos, the setting sun, erected to that god by Pharaoh Necho (see *Birch's Hieroglyphs*). It was subsequently surrendered to General Hutchinson, who presented it to George III.; it is now in the British Museum.

"The upper portion of this block is inscribed with fourteen lines of hieroglyphics, all mutilated by the fracture of the stone. Immediately below them are thirty-two lines in the demotic, or euchorial character, but little injured by fracture or defacement. Unfortunately, this portion is at once the most perfect, and the least important, of the three. The lowest portion of the block contains fifty-four lines of Greek, of which the first twenty-seven are perfect and uninjured; the remainder are all, more or less, mutilated at the end of the lines, by an oblique fracture inclining inwards, so that the extent of mutilation regularly increases, as the inscription approaches its termination, and the last line is the most imperfect of all."—*Osburn's Monumental Hist. of Egypt*, p. 14.

The Greek portion of the inscription* was in a great measure perfected by the conjectural emendations, and translated by the critical skill of the celebrated Professor Porson, and, some years after his decease, was published in vol. xvi., *Trans. of the Soc. Ant.* A fac-simile copy of the original was circulated among all the learned men in Europe. Dr. Heyne, also, and others, contributed to its completion and interpretation. This inscription is a statute of the Egyptian priests, setting forth the services rendered to his country by Ptolemy V., or Ptolemy Epiphanes,† and decreeing, in the name of the priests assembled at Memphis, his apotheosis, and the various honors to be paid to him. Ptolemy Epiphanes was the fifth successor of Sagus, or Sotor, the Macedonian general, to whom Egypt was assigned, in the partition of the empire of Alexander the Great. The only other instance which appears to be known of a king of Egypt being made a God in his lifetime, is in the case of his remote predecessor. Horus, the last Pharaoh of the XVIII. dynasty.

* "The Greek translation is a loose paraphrase, aiming at nothing more than the general scope and import of the original."—*Osburn, Mem. Hist. of Egypt*, pp. 50, 51.

† Epiphanes means *thing forth*, as a deity;—a God *confessed*.

The Greek inscription suggested the idea which was soon confirmed, that the same decree was the subject of the two other inscriptions, which were written in two distinct kinds of Egyptian characters,—the sacred or hieroglyphic, and the enchorial, Coptic, or native character of the country.

The Egyptian writing has been divided into various kinds, as, the pure, or picture; the linear, or emblematic; the phonetic, or writing by sound; and the demotic, or epistolary. Clement of Alexandria informs us that the Egyptians made use of three sorts of characters. But among these they had also many secret systems of communication. Bin Washih affirms, that there existed a great number of hieroglyphic alphabets. In the ancient Book of Job, written in great part according to the science of correspondences (not in a connected series like the inspired Word of God), somewhat similar to the Egyptian hieroglyphics, mention is expressly made of the primitive species of idolatry prevalent in the East, viz., the adoration of the sun and moon (xxxi. 26, 27), and also of the most ancient mode of writing by sculpture (xix. 23, 24). "The writing in use, among the ancient Egyptians, was called by the Greeks *hieroglyphics*, that is sacred engravings or reliefs, because they saw the temples of Egypt covered with inscriptions in that writing, and because the scribes of it belonged to an order of the priesthood." *Osbur. Mon. Hist. Eg.*, vol. i., p. 22.

The antiquity of Egypt is proverbial among all nations. *Lucian in lib. De Syria Dea*, writes, "that the Egyptians are said to be the first among men that had a conception of God, and a knowledge of sacred concerns. They were also the first that had a knowledge of sacred names." Conformably to this, also, an oracle of Apollo, quoted by Eusebius, asserts, that "the Egyptians were the first that disclosed, by infinite actions, the path that leads to the Gods."—*Jamblicus on the Mysteries of the Egyptians, etc.*, by Taylor, note, p. 295. "The Egyptians have always been acknowledged as the most ancient people; from whom laws, arts, sciences, and ceremonies, were first derived to other countries."—*Muret's Rites of Funeral, Ancient and Modern*, trans. by Lorrain, 1683, p. 1. Egypt is also called by Bunsen "the oldest monumental nation in the world."—*Egypt's Place in Univ. Hist.*, pref., p. xxiv. He adds: "We have no hesitation in asserting at once, that there exist Egyptian monuments, the date of which can be accurately fixed, of a higher antiquity than those of any other nation known in history, viz., above five thousand years."—*Ib.*, p. xxviii.

It was, doubtless, in that early age, that hieroglyphics had their origin for correspondences, of a still more remote date, which were succeeded by the phonetic, hieratic, and demotic alphabets, the oldest of which does not carry us back further than about 1500 years B.C. From this period hieroglyphics and correspondences became corrupted, and their true significance was finally lost, or perverted to idolatrous superstitions, and fanciful cosmogonies and worship. Bryant, therefore, in his *Anal. of Ancient Mythol.*, truly says, that "We must make a material distinction between the hieroglyphics of old, when Egypt was under her own kings, and those of later date, when that country was under the government of the Greeks; at which time their learning was greatly impaired, and their ancient mythology ruined."—i., 332.

Egyptian writing has been arranged as follows: 1. Hieroglyphic (*Herod*), or hierographic (the writing of the gods, *Manetho*, the learned priest), sculptured characters, expressed alphabetically, figuratively, or symbolically. The largest proportion by far is what Champollion le Jeune calls phonetic. 2. Hieratic, a cursive way of writing, called also sacerdotal, from being in general use by the priests or sacred scribes, and which is identical with that of the hieroglyphics from which it has descended (Clem. Alex.). All the MSS. in this character exhibit a tachygraphy, or short-hand of the hieroglyphical writing, and it appears to have been chiefly employed in the transcription of texts and inscriptions, connected with sacred subjects. 3. Euchorial (Rosetta Stone), called by the Greek authors, *demotic* (demode), or popular (Diod.). because it was the common writing of the country; this was also denominated *epistolographic*, or epistolary (Clem. Alex.), and was derived from the hieratic, as the hieratic was derived from the hieroglyphic, and has been divided into the mimic, the tropic, and the enigmatic (Goulianol). It admits of symbolic, figurative, and alphabetic characters. The alphabetic occurs most frequently, the figurative is the least used, and the symbolic is chiefly confined to express ideas connected with Egyptian theology. (See *Pettigrew's Hist. Egyp. Mummies*, p. 144; *Osburn's Mon. Hist. of Eg.*, vol. i., p. 22; *Champollion, de l'Ecriture Hie. d'Anc. Egypt; Birch's Hieroglyphics*, p. 1.)

Though this entire subject is at present involved in considerable obscurity, yet it is certain that the true hieroglyphics, or sacred writings, the signification of which was for ages confined to the priesthood, appear to be those, and those only, the arcana of which the science of correspondences is destined to unfold. Zoëga, a learned Dane, was the first person who suggested that the elliptic ovals, now termed *cartouches*, contain *proper names;* and he first employed the word phonetic, from the Greek, expressive of sound. See his book *On Obelisks*, 1797; and also *Gliddon's Ancient Egypt*, pp. 3, 5. But the group of proper names in the demotic text of the Rosetta Stone, was discovered by De Lacy. The inscription on the stone we have stated is trilinguar, or rather trigrammatic: the first or upper portion containing one of the numerous hieroglyphic alphabets; the second, or middle one, is that known as the enchorial, or the popular character, which it is asserted was the Coptic, as yet free from the admixture of Greek words (see Bunsen's *Egypt's Place in History*, p. 314); and the third is Greek, but, as we have remarked, a mere loose paraphrase. The event recorded of this stone took place at Memphis, and the stone appears to have been engraved in the ninth year of the reign of the beforementioned Ptolemy, or 196 years before the Christian era, and belongs, says Bunsen, in the work just cited, "to the time of the *lowest decline*, as regards *language*, character, and hieroglyphic structure." "The language," says Osburn, "was rapidly undergoing changes; the hieroglyphic art had become degraded; the arrangement is vile, and the arrangement clumsy." So that, after all, it affords but little information on the subject of the *true ancient hieroglyphics*. The most learned and profound classic, Coptic, and Arabic scholars, and the most eminent archæologists and Egyptologists, have employed the most extensive learning, the most acute penetration, and persevering industry, in the investigation of these inscriptions, and have ascertained the meaning of so many of the letters, syllables, and words, "which the signs represented," as to give the greatest interest and importance to many other historical documents of Egypt, and the papyri MSS., containing biographical records, legal contracts, funeral ceremonies, and various customs. But, "though the stone has now been familiar to the scholars of Europe for half a century, a *complete translation* of its symbols still remains a desideratum." — *Chambers' Inf. for the People*, art. ARCHÆOL.

While the labors of learned men have thus thrown considerable light on the *hieroglyphic* and *phonetic alphabets*, and have thence illustrated the *later* antiquities, and the comparatively modern history of Egypt, when symbolic signs had become phonetic, they have effected, as yet, but little in deciphering the most ancient and pure hieroglyphics. "Everywhere, I conceive," says Salt, "the real hieroglyphics and phonetic characters will be found to be mingled together; and this, of course, will require a double study."—*Salt's Phonetic System of Hiero*. Even the sacred symbols were used, not as the representatives of *things*, but also of sounds (see the marvellous discoveries of Dr. Young and Champollion, and the critical researches of Lepsius), so that even the phonetics bear a double meaning. "The ideographic signs," adds Gliddon, "abound in Egyptian legends." "Hieroglyphic characters," according to Bunsen, "were adopted in phonetic writing at a very early period. The *new empire*, that is the 18th dynasty of the Egyptians, commenced a little before Moses, and on the monuments of that age, the Egyptian writing continued phonetic, with figurative signs."—See *Eg. pl. in Hist.*, pp. 4, 8. "All the Greek annalists," says he, "belong to the *latest times* of Egypt; most of them to an age when the old myths were multiplied and adulterated."—*Ib.*, p. 414. It must also be remembered that only a very small proportion of the existing monuments and inscriptions of Egypt have, as yet, been examined. What has been done, however, with any degree of certainty, only serves to confirm what Swedenborg has advanced on this perplexing, yet deeply interesting subject, and which is as follows:—

"It is commonly known, that in

Egypt there were hieroglyphics, and that they were inscribed on the columns and walls of the temples and other buildings; it is acknowledged, however, that at this day, no one is able to determine their signification. Those hieroglyphics were no other than the correspondences between the spiritual and the natural, to which science the Egyptians, more than any people of Asia, applied themselves, and according to which the very early nations of Greece formed their fables; for this, and this only, was the most ancient style of composition."—*App. W. H.*, n. 4.

"The science of correspondences, which is likewise the science of representatives, was accounted by the ancients the science of sciences, and was particularly cultivated by the Egyptians, being the origin of their hieroglyphics."

"It was the peculiar science of their wise men, by which they knew what was signified by animals of all kinds, what by trees of all kinds, and what by mountains, hills, rivers, and fountains; what also of the sun, moon, and stars." "By the same science they attained besides to the knowledge of spiritual subjects, for the things represented being such as belong to spiritual wisdom among the angels in heaven, were themselves the origin of the representatives." "Now as all their divine worship was representative, consisting of mere correspondences, therefore they celebrated it upon mountains and hills, also in groves and gardens; for the same reason they consecrated fountains, turned their faces toward the east in their adoration of God; and also made themselves carved images of horses, oxen, calves, lambs, nay, even of birds, fishes, and serpents, and placed them in their houses and other places, arranged in a certain order, according to the spiritual principles of the church to which they corresponded, or which they represented, and thence signified." "They placed similar things in the vicinity, and at the entrance, and within their temples, that they might recall to their memories the holy things which they signified. In process of time, when the science of correspondences was lost, their posterity began to worship the images themselves as sacred, not knowing that their ancestors saw nothing sacred in them, and that they were only so according to the correspondences they represented, and thence signified. Thus arose the idolatries which filled the whole earth, as well Asia, with its adjacent islands, as Africa and Europe."—*T. C. R.*, n. 833; *D. P.*, n. 255.

"The Egyptians carved pieces of wood and stone into representative configurations of various moral virtues and of spiritual truths; and whereas every man, beast, bird, and fish, corresponds to some quality; therefore each particular thing carved represents partially somewhat of virtue, or truth, and several together represent virtue itself, or truth itself, in a common extended form."—*C. S. L.*, n. 76.

"The Egyptians from ancient time knew Jehovah, by reason that even in Egypt there had been an ancient church, as may manifestly appear from this consideration, that they had amongst them the representatives and significatives of that church; the Egyptian hieroglyphics are nothing else [but such representatives and significatives], for by them were signified things spiritual, they knew also that they actually corresponded; and inasmuch as they began to apply such things in their sacred worship, and to worship them, and at length also to turn them into things magical, and thereby to be associated to the diabolical even in hell, therefore they altogether destroyed the ancient church amongst themselves."—*A. C.* 7097.

"The Egyptians made an evil use of [these correspondences], therefore to them they were not scientific truths, but scientific falsities: yet the same things in the ancient church were scientific truths, inasmuch as they applied them rightly to divine worship."—*A. C.* 6917.

In the *British Magazine*, for Dec. 1841, vol. xx., p. 639, the following question was considered:—"Are the facts announced by Swedenborg, on the subject of hieroglyphics, in perfect harmony with, or in opposition to, the modern discoveries of Science?" A writer under the signature of H. endeavored to prove the latter. An admirable and learned reply, from the pen of M. Frederic Portal, Member of the Asiatic Society of Paris, was inserted in the same periodical for May, 1842, vol. xxi., p. 520. From this paper I make the following conclusive extracts:—

"According to Swedenborg, as cited above, the hieroglyphics of the Egyptians, and the fabulous fictions of antiquity, were founded on the same science. (*T. C. R.*, n. 201; *S. S.*, n. 20; *A. C.*, n. 6692, 6917, 7097, 7926, 9011.) When he speaks of hieroglyphics, he particularly applies this word to the representations of statuary or sculpture, and to the paintings of anaglyphs. In all the passages in which he speaks of hieroglyphics, he refers to their origin; for he says that at the epoch of the Pharaohs and of Moses, this system, in a religious point of view, was already corrupted, and he adds, that the Israelitish nation was elected in order to restore and preserve these representative symbols of the church. (*A. C.*, n. 6692.)

"Swedenborg, then, establishes a complete conformity between hieroglyphics, as they existed in their origin, and the correspondences of the Bible. Let us examine what hieroglyphics at their origin were, and what they became at a later period.

"Hieroglyphics were, at first, a series of pure symbols. That is the opinion of Swedenborg, you will say. But it is equally the opinion of Champollion and of the learned Lepsius. Champollion says, 'According to all appearance, the Egyptians at first made use of figurative and symbolic characters.' (*Précis. du Système Hieroglyphique*, 2d edit., p. 358.) 'I am of opinion,' says M. Lepsius, ' that the Egyptians had originally a system of writing entirely ideographic. If we cannot arrive at a time when phonetic signs were not yet introduced among the Egyptians, we at least find, at a later period, entire formulæ and phrases still in use, composed solely of symbolic characters.' (*Annali dele' Instituto di Corrispondenza Archeologica*, vol. ix., prim. fas. p. 24: Roma, 1837.) Even at the time when the Egyptian method of writing became, in part, syllabic or phonetic, the symbolic system did not cease to prevail. So says M. Lepsius:—'We find, at first,' he observes, 'a multitude of words, which, having formerly been expressed by ideographic signs alone, and transcribed at a later period into phonetic letters, have nevertheless preserved for the first phonetic letter, the ideographic sign itself.' (*Annali dele' Instituto*, ibid., p. 48.) Let us turn to the dissertation of M. Lepsius, and consider this sentence of the learned Egyptologue:—'We have already,' says he, 'spoken repeatedly of this primitive and continual tendency not to forego the use of symbolic signs. In effect, this symbolic system of writing, propagated from one generation to another from so many ages back, had too much identified itself with the religion, the mythic traditions, and the customs of the Egyptians, ever to be capable of being displaced by the uniform system, destitute of attractions either for the eye or the fancy, of a purely phonetic method of writing.' (*Annali dele' Instituto*, ibid., p. 58.) In effect, the symbolic system of writing was so inherent in the Egyptian religion and the royal power that flowed from it, that, according to the remark of Champollion, in inscriptions, the abstract ideas which belonged to the religious and royal departments, were specially represented by symbolic characters; as is the case on the Rosetta stone with the ideas *God, immortality, divine life, power, good, benefit, law or decree, superior region, inferior region, panegyric, temple,* etc. (*Champollion; Precis.,* p. 403.)

"Finally, the phonetic system of writing itself still preserved the symbolic character. The letters pronounced by the mouth were still, to the eye and the understanding, true symbols. Such is the opinion of Champollion; and he explains by it that great number of signs which represent the same letter, and which they name *homophones.* (*Champ.,* ibid., 370.) Thus the phonetic system of writing was, at its origin, symbolic, and always preserved this character. We are not, however, ignorant, that homophones were employed, at a later period, for the artist-like arrangement of inscriptions; that symbolism was neglected, to please the eye; and that at the decline of the system under the domination of the Greeks and Romans, the hierogrammatists delighted to make a parade of empty skill in varying the orthography of words without end. Symbolism was continually materializing itself, as Swedenborg announces and science evinces; but it is not the less true, that the phonetic words consecrated by religion, and which thence were no longer liable to variation, preserved their primitive character by being always written with symbolic signs. The names of the gods prove this in the most irrefragable manner.

"From the preceding facts, we conclude, that Swedenborg was justified in affirming that the hieroglyphics were symbols. But did our author really mean to say, that all the hieroglyphics, without exception, were symbolic? On this subject he has said nothing; and the rules of induction alone may serve as our guides in this inquiry. Swedenborg formally lays it down, that the Bible, from one end to the other, is symbolic—not only in every phrase, but in every word, and in every letter, even to the least *iota*. Nevertheless, on turning to his explications, whether of Genesis, of Exodus, or of the Apocalypse, we perceive, from the first verses, that Swedenborg ranges the words under three perfectly distinct categories; 1st, that of symbolic words; 2d, that of figurative words; 3d, that of words taken in their proper and natural sense, as adverbs, prepositions, pronouns, conjunctions, etc. The Egyptian system of writing, according to the discoveries of Champollion, literally traces its outlines on this system of *symbolic, figurative,* and *phonetic* words."—*British Mag.,* vol. xxi., p. 520.

M. Portal then produces numerous perfect coincidences between the signification which Swedenborg gives to various terms and things, and the signification supposed by modern writers to have been anciently assigned by the Egyptians to the same terms and things. From among others I cite the following:—

Correspondences from Swedenborg.
To *create* signifies to regenerate.— A. C., n. 472.

Recent Discoveries in the Egyptian Hieroglyphics.
To *create* signifies to save. The sign of the hieroglyphic for Saviour upon the monuments being the same as that for Creator.—*Salvolini, Campagne de Rhamses,* p. 101.

The *earth* signifies the external man.—*A. C.*, n. 90.

The *face* signifies the interiors of the mind, or the spiritual and celestial things existing interiorly with man. *A. C.*, n. 2219, 5571.

Clay, or red earth, is a symbol of the life of love of the external man, or the lowest natural good.—*A. C.*, n. 95, 1300, 1301, 3104; *A. E.*, n. 487.

The number eight signifies the commencement of a new period of temptation, of reformation, of regeneration, and corresponds to purification.—*A. C.*, n. 2044, 2633.

Stones signify natural truths, and precious stones the truths of intelligence, or spiritual truths.—*A. R.*, n. 90; *C. L. L.*, n. 76.

The scarabæus represents *the earth and the external man.*—*Horopollon et les Symboles des Egyptiens*, p. 98.

In the Egyptian Grammar of Champollion, *the face* is the symbolic sign of that which is *interior*—within.—*Les Symboles des Egyptiens comparéss a ceux des Hebreux*, p. 55.

Vessel of *clay* in the balance of judgment symbolized the actions of the deceased,—his moral life, his love, and his piety.—*Inscription of the Manuscript of* TENTAMOUN.

The month *Thoth* was the first of the Egyptian year, and eight was one of the symbols of the god Thoth, the reformer and regenerator, who pours the waters of purification on the head of the initiated.—*Les Symboles*, etc., p. 93.

It may be added, as a further illustration, that in the Christian symbolism of the middle ages, the octagonal form of fonts, pillars, etc., appears to have been regarded as emblematical of regeneration, or entrance on a new state.—See also *Hand-Book of English Ecclesiology*, p. 130 *et seq.*

The monuments of Egypt call precious stones hard stones of truth.—*Champ. Gram. Egypt.*, p. 100.

In addition to the above, I will add a few more examples:

Swedenborg says that by the *mice*, with which the land of Philistia was overrun, when the Philistines took the ark of God (1 Sam. v., vi.), were signified the devastation of the church; and that the five images of golden mice or rats which were made, represented that, by means of good, signified by gold, the devastation of the church is removed.—*T. C. R.*, n. 203.

A breastplate signifies divine truth shining forth from divine good in ultimates; for it was filled with twelve precious stones, and worn, by the representative high-priest among the Jews, over the region of the heart. It was called a breastplate of Judgment; and Urim and Thummim which are plurals, meaning a shining fire and brilliancy, or perfections and splendors,

According to Horopollen (lib. i., cap. 47), total destruction was represented in Egyptian hieroglyphics, by the symbol of a mouse or rat, from its constant gnawing.—*Hist. of the Jews*, Family Library, vol. i., note, p. 313.

"The Egyptian judges wore a breastplate, on which were cut symbolic figures *on a blue ground*. The blue was typical of the sapphire, a precious stone of a blue color, and both signified truth;" and, consequently, that the judges would preside in the love of truth.—*Gliddon*.

and denoting integrity and justice in ultimates (Ex. xxviii.). The precious stones signify all heavenly principles in their order,—thus, the love of truth, charity, mercy, judgment, and justice; and, in a spiritual sense, instruction and responses from the literal sense of the Word: for by the breastplate divine responses were given by a tacit perception, or inaudible voice, and judgment was executed accordingly (Num. xxvii. 18–21). Blue was a color admitted into the breastplate, and, being derived from the deep azure of the oriental sky, signified the celestial love of truth, or the good of charity.—*A. C.*, n. 3862, 9823–73; *A. E.*, n. 1063: *T. C. R.*, n. 218.

The Lion signifies, in a good sense, divine truth in *power;* and in a contrary sense, the false principle destroying truth.—*A. R.*, n. 241, 471, 573, 574. To denote his omnipotence, the Lord is called by the expressive appellation of "the Lion of the tribe of Judah." (Rev. v. 5.)

A *lion* was the principal hieroglyphic, and always denoted *strength.*—*Nuttall's Arch. Dict.*

A fox in the word signifies one who is principled in self-derived prudence, thus, craftiness.—*D. P.* 311. See Luke xiii. 32; Ps. iii. 10; Sam. v. 18

A fox or jackal (for it is uncertain which animal is meant in Hebrew, probably both), says Champollion, was always used to express *knowledge*, hierogrammateus, or sacred scribe, or a wise and cunning man, because that class of animals are crafty.—See *Birch's Hieroglyphs*, p. 220.

Swedenborg writes as follows:—*Good* hath *life* in itself, because it is from the Lord, who is *life* itself.—*A. C.*, n. 5070. Good is actually spiritual fire, from which spiritual heat, which makes *alive*, is derived.—*A. C.*, n. 4906.

The same hieroglyphic character, which, according to Birch and Osburn, stands, when alone, as a symbol for *life*, also represents the idea of goodness.—See *Mon. Hist. Eg.*, p. 30.

Swedenborg says, the Nile, in a bad sense, represents sensual things as to what is false, or false scientifics, which pervert the word.—*A. C.*, 5196, 6693, 5113. And in the same sense fishes denote those who think sensually, and then confide in scientifics only, and thence conceive falses.—*A. C.*, n. 991. "The adulteration of the good of the word, and the falsification of its truth, is defilement or uncleanness, and impurity itself."—*A. R.*, n. 924. "Men of learning and erudition, who have

A fish, with a sharp muzzle, common in the Nile, symbolized, in the earliest and best periods of the monarchy, *uncleanness.*—*Osburn's Mon. Hist. Eg.*, p. 37.

confirmed themselves deeply in false principles, are more sensual than others."—*A. R.*, n. 424; *A. C.*, n. 6316.

The *serpent* signifies the sensual principle of man's mind and life. Hence the Lord says he would give his disciples power "*to tread upon serpents*," and to "*take up serpents*," denoting power to subdue or depress the sensual principle, and elevate it from a defiled, grovelling condition to a state of purity and blessedness, and these changes take place by progressive steps, and by threefold degrees.—*A. C.*, n. 258; *A. R.*, n. 455. Treading the serpent under foot, denotes the complete subjugation of the sensual principle; grasping the serpent in the right hand, denotes its elevation as the purified instrument of spiritual and moral power; and lifting up the serpent on the shoulder, has the same meaning, but in a higher sense. The *right* hand of man denotes the power of wisdom from Divine Truth; and the right shoulder denotes all power. (*Isa.* ix. 6.)

Belzoni found a vast tomb in Egypt, cut in the rocks, where, 3000 years ago, a king of Egypt was entombed. Among a great variety of paintings, of which he took copies, and exhibited them in a model of the tomb, in London, was a representation of *three* companies of men, in single file, in succession; the *first* company standing erect with the right foot extended on a long *serpent*, the neck of it under the first man's foot, and the tail under the last; the *second* company followed standing on the ground, and grasping a long *serpent*, which passed horizontally through the right hand of each man in succession, as it hung down by his side; and the *third*, lifting up a long *serpent* on their right shoulders, and holding it there with their right hands, through which it passed horizontally from one man to the other, so that with the two latter companies, the first man of each grasped the neck of the serpent close to the head, and the last man grasped the tail.—*For this illustration I was indebted to the Rev. W. Mason, of Melbourne, who saw the model.*

The Rev. S. Noble, in his *Plenary Inspiration of the Scriptures Asserted*, refers to this very remarkable tomb, and to other Egyptian symbols, thus:— "Could all written and traditionary learning be extirpated from the earth, Egypt would still present her imperishable monuments, silently but irrefutably proclaiming, that there, indeed, the relation of analogy between the various kingdoms of nature, with their individual objects, and each other; and between all of these, again, and things moral, spiritual, and divine; was once—yea, for ages,—well understood; that there it stamped a character upon all elevated science, and that it regulated there even the first elements of knowledge. What can be more evident, than that her celebrated hieroglyphics, which have so long confounded the skill of the learned, are built on this analogy, and are expressions of it, and that if ever they are deciphered, it must be by its means? Who could inspect that extraordinary exhibition, a year or two since open in London, representing the tomb of an Egyptian king, explored by Mr. Belzoni, and behold the multitude of representations of natural objects, evidently designed to convey a mystical meaning, without feeling satisfied that the arrangement of them must be governed by some rule, and that it assumed for its basis a known analogy? Who can escape the same impressions on viewing the Egyptian antiquities in the British Museum? To particularize only one palpable emblem, the meaning of which requires no discussion to establish it: Who can behold those monstrous fists, carved out of the *hardest of rocks*, without being convinced that they are designed to symbolize that irresistible *power* that would crush opposers into annihilation? that their meaning is similar to that *stone* mentioned in the Gospel, of which it is said, that 'on whomsoever it shall fall, it will grind him to powder'? (Matt. xxi. 44.) So it is evident, that in the wonderful scheme of symbolic writing contrived by this singular people, the natural objects depicted were put to convey ideas quite distinct from anything belonging to the objects themselves: they delineated one thing to express another; they evidently were guided by some analogy which they saw between the two: and it is much more reasonable to conclude that they followed a principle known by them to exist in the nature of things, than that the whole of so complicated a system was merely founded on arbitrary assumption."—Pp. 216-218.

Dr. Conyers Middleton, in a letter to Dr. Waterland, writes as follows on the hieroglyphic of the serpent:—"Moses, we read, *was learned in all the wisdom of the Egyptians* (Acts vii. 22), and their learning, especially in things *sacred and divine*, was wholly *mystical and symbolical:* proposed always under the figures of men, beasts, and birds, which were called hieroglyphics, or sacred characters, invented and used by them, as Kircher has shown (*Obelis. Pamph.*, 1, 2; de Institu et Fabrica Hierogl., c. 2, p. 102), before Moses's time. Among these the serpent, as all authors inform us, was of more common use with them than any other animal, whose nature they imagined to have something very excellent and divine in it.* So that it supplied the place of two letters in their symbolic alphabet, and served them as a hieroglyphic of various significations; more particularly as *an emblem of subtlety and cunning*, as well as of *lust and sensual pleasure.†* Dr. Spencer, explaining the customs of the Egyptians, of delivering all the sublime parts of knowledge under the cover of *symbols, types*, and *emblems*, observes, that "*when God called out Moses to his prophetical office, he considered him as one who had been trained in that kind of learning, and it is consonant therefore to the character and history of Moses, to imagine that God designed that he should write and treat of all the sublimer things committed to him, in that mystical and hieroglyphical way of literature, in which he had been educated.*"‡

An endeavor to explain a sacred inscription according to the science of correspondences, will be read with interest. "On a temple of Minerva, at Sais, are inscribed the following hieroglyphics: an infant, an old man, a hawk, a fish, and a river horse, which, by a writer on the subject, have been translated to mean, 'All ye who come into and go out of the world, know that the gods hate impudence.' Now this translation may possibly be correct, so far as regards their hieroglyphic [or external] meaning [designed to meet the public eye], a hawk always bearing reference to the attributes or persons of the gods; but viewing these characters also as a sacred inscription, having been put there by the priests, who were

---

* Kircher, ib. l. iv; Ideœ. Hierogl., p. 347. So also Tacitus: "Primi, etc." "The Egyptians were the first, who, by the forms of animals, figured the senses of the mind."—*Annal.* xi., 14.

† Ib., l. ii., c. 6, p. 131; *Item Pieni Valerian Hierogl.*, l. xiv.

‡ De Legg. Heb. etc., l. i., c. 15, p. 211: see also text of this work.

acquainted with the 'wisdom of the Egyptians,' will they not also bear the following signification? '*Those who worship God, shall receive* innocence, natural truth, [*viz*] intelligence, science, and divine understanding.' The inscription bearing reference to what is to be found by those who enter into the temple, and entering in signifying conjunction by worship, admits of the words printed in italics being introduced. Or as the Egyptians generally wrote from left to right, '*Those who worship the Lord, shall receive* divine understanding, then all scientifics, all elevated intelligence, rational truth, and then perfect innocence.' It must be borne in mind, that the Minerva of the Egyptians was different from that of the Greeks, the former people not only investing that deity with wisdom, but with all good attributes. . . . Although in later periods the Egyptians worshiped numberless deities, with the Jews they originally worshiped but one. According to Plutarch, they held only two *principles*, one good, the other evil. Osiris, the good genius, was, strictly speaking, synonymous with REASON; and Syphon, or the passions, WITHOUT REASON. A closer analogy with the New Church doctrines than this, I think, can scarcely be found, and similar instances are very numerous."—*J. D.* in *N. J. Mag.*, vol. iv., p. 235.

For many centuries before the Christian era, the science of correspondences was rapidly on the decline, and we may affirm that from the period of the Persian conquest, about 525 B. C., nearly all idea of the spirituality which originally pervaded the Egyptian hieroglyphics, appears to have been lost. In the eighth chapter of Ezekiel, 7–10, we have a literal description of the prevalent idolatry of Egypt, about this very period. "Dark and mysterious recesses," says Maurice, "ornamented with every form of creeping things and abominable beasts; were called mystic cells, and in them were represented, by the animals, etc., the secret mysteries sacred to, or hieroglyphical of, Isis and Osiris."

Causes were no longer investigated; effects only were regarded. Even the priests gave to their mythology a merely physical explanation, and the people became infatuated and ignorant idolaters. The pretended secrets of the priesthood were of the grossest description, and seem to have been connected with the science of Astronomy, as far as was then known. They acknowledged no other deities than the sun, moon, and planets. From their apparent and real motions and positions, together with the asterisms of the Zodiac, "borrowed from the Greeks," they drew horoscopes, and prognosticated events; they foretold their genial or baneful influences on the labors of agriculture, and in the cure of diseases, and attributed to them the meteorological changes of the atmosphere, and the flowings and recessions of the river Nile; thus binding all things in the indissoluble chain of necessity or fate. (See *Epist. Porphyrii præmis. Jamblich. De Myster, Ægypt*, etc., cited in *Prichard's Anal. of Egypt. Mythol.*, pp. 30–35. *Euseb. Evan. Præp.*, lib. iii., cap. iv. ix.)

Dr. Cudworth, in his *Intellectual System*, vol. i. (new ed.), insists, but without sufficient data, that the recondite and esoteric sense of the Egyptian mythology was maintained to a much later age: and cites and translates the following remarkable passage from *Porphyrius' Epistle concerning Chæremon:* "But Chæremon, and those others who pretend to write of the first causes of the world, declare only the last and lowest principles, as likewise they who treat of the planets, the zodiac, the dreams, the horoscopes, and the robust princes. And these things that are in the Egyptian almanac (or ephemerides), contain the least part of Hermionical institutions, namely, the phases and occultations of the stars, the increase and decrease of the moon, and the like astrological matters; which things have *the lowest* place in the Egyptian œtiology."—*Ib.*, vol. i., p. 539.

In reference to a corrupt system of religion, M. Portal justly observes, that "the older it becomes, the more it materializes itself: it becomes gradually worse, until it arrives at fetichism; the religion of the negroes is the last expression of the dogmas of Ethiopia and Egypt. Already in the times of Moses the Egyptian religion showed all the elements of decay and dissolution; the symbol had become God; the truth, forgotten by the people, was banished into the sanctuaries, and soon the priests themselves were to lose the signification of the sacred language. These principles may be applied to India and its degenerate Brahmins, to China and its disgraceful priests, to all the various kinds of perverted worship, and to those Jews who sacrificed to the idols of strange gods."

The Rev. G. Oliver, in his Twelve Lectures on the Signs and Symbols of Free-Masonry, cites from Aben Washih's Hieroglyphics, the following description of a perfect, or regenerated man. The representation has descended from a very remote age; and is full of interest, as elucidating the fact that sculptured forms and pictured images were employed by the Egyptians in their hieroglyphics, to represent abstract qualities and spiritual states of the mind, but of which Oliver offers no explanation.

"A man of perfect wisdom and understanding, accomplished in all his ways, and without the least blame, was painted with a beautiful face; with wings like an angel; holding in his hands a book, in which he looked; a sword, and a balance; and behind him two vases, one of them full of water and the other of blazing fire: under his right foot a ball, with a crab painted on it; and under his left a deep pot full of serpents, scorpions, and different reptiles, the covering of which had the shape of an eagle's head."

According to the science of correspondences, this hieroglyphic would appear to have been composed by one who was well acquainted with the nature and process of regeneration, and its correspondent images; as illustrations I have added a few passages from the H. W. "A man perfect in wisdom and understanding, accomplished in all his ways, and without the least blame," can only be a description of one who is regenerated, of which the ceremonies of initiation were representative (John i. 47; Luke i. 6). "He was painted with a beautiful face," to represent the inward states of a good life, made visibly manifest in the outward countenance (Acts vi. 15; Judges xiii. 6). "He was represented with wings like an angel," to denote the powers or ability of elevating his perceptions and thoughts into an angelic sphere: "holding a book in his hands, in which he was looking," to denote that this power was from the reception of divine wisdom, and his steady application thereto, that he might become intelligent, and "*wise unto salvation*" (Rev. x. 2). The sword was a symbol of active warfare against all that opposed his progress (Luke xxii. 36; Ps. cxlix. 6): and the balance was significative of the estimation in which he held all that was good and true, and the just judgment he conscientiously passed upon all the activities of his mind and life: the vessels behind him, one filled with water, and the other with blazing fire,*

---

* "*Behold I, saith the Lord Jesus, give unto you power to tread on serpents and scorpions, and over all the power of the enemy, and* (Luke x. 19) *nothing shall by any means hurt you.*"

represent his understanding and his will, their purification from falsity and evil passions, and their reception of wisdom and goodness, or truth and love; under his right foot was placed a ball with a crab painted upon it, to denote the natural mind, and its constant inclination to revert to its original state; under the left foot was placed a deep pot full of serpents, scorpions, and various reptiles, to denote that carnal passions and propensities were all held in due subjection; and the power to accomplish this final work, was indicated by the covering, which bore the shape of an eagle's head, to signify the omnipotence of wisdom.*

One of the leading modes of framing these ancient signs appears to merologists to be this, that the *effect* is put for the supposed *cause*. " This is precisely the principle of all the correspondences of Swedenborg. He says that the reason why a given physical object is said to *correspond* to a certain idea, is, because it has flowed from that idea as its efficient cause."—*Hayden.*

" The black and white ibis or crane was, from the very earliest period, of which we have any record, accounted a symbol of speech, and of reason, whereof speech is the natural vehicle. The Coptic words *hop*, 'judgment,' and *hop*, ' to hide,' ' to conceal '(all wisdom in early times being occult), are palpably derived from the name of the ibis."

The name of this beautiful bird is *hippep*, the cry of the black and white ibis consists of the syllables *ep-ep*. Thoth or Tat, the god of letters and intelligence, had an ibis for his sacred animal, and was represented with the head of that bird. That Thoth was worshipped in Egypt from a very remote period, we have the incontestible evidence of cotemporary monuments. (*Osburne*, pp. 203, 201, 341.)

He was regarded as having invented the ancient Hieroglyphic system in the city of Heliopolis. The great antiquity of worship at On—Heliopolis, the city of the sun, is attested by the monuments. (*Hengstenberg, Egypt and Moses*, § ii.)

In conclusion: though the pure hieroglyphics of Egypt were thus sculptured, engraved, or depicted, according to the science of correspondences, yet it must not be forgotten, that there is an infinite difference between them and the plenarily inspired Word of God. In the hieroglyphics, like as in the book of Job, is enshrined the human wisdom of successive ages, combined with traditionary remains of divine truth, derived from the most ancient dispensations of religion, which, veiled by corresponding symbols, was thus preserved for the use of ages; but in the Holy Word, the pure truths of heaven are revealed by the Lord Himself in one grand, dependent, and harmonious series. The hieroglyphics are, at best, but a checkered mosaic of human arrangement; while the Word of God exhibits the perfect order of Him who created the heavens and the earth. The former are, as it were, the dead and lifeless resemblances; the latter contains living and life-giving realities; " For by every word proceeding out of the mouth of God doth man live." The hieroglyphics of Egypt are, notwithstanding, a most important evidence to the existence and prevalence of the science of correspondences in the earliest period of which we have any authentic history.

" It is an observation of Maimonides, ' That he who would understand all that the prophets have said, must particularly apply himself to the study of the parabolic, metaphorical, and enigmatical parts of Scripture.' "

---

* " *They that wait upon the Lord shall mount up with wings as eagles; they shall run and not be weary, they shall walk and not faint,*" Isa. xl. 31.

"The Egyptians appear to have been the earliest cultivators of this species of composition, and in this the Jews were rather imitators than originals. That this was a part of the wisdom of Egypt, in which Moses excelled, is suggested by Philo, in his Life of Moses, by Clemens of Alexandria, in his Stromata, and by many others. That the Chaldeans also were addicted to the use of emblems and allegories, appears from some ancient writers, for whom, see Stanley's History of Philosophy. The Syrians and Phœnicians are affirmed to have prosecuted the same study, according to Jerome, Josephus, Eusebius," etc.—*Wemyss' Key to the Symbolical Language of Scripture*, p. 5.

Mr. S. Sharpe, whose eminence as an Egyptologist entitles him to speak with authority, has no doubt that the Egyptians, many centuries before Moses, were acquainted with the use of alphabetical characters.

Eichhorn maintains that convenient implements and materials for writing existed in the age of Moses (*Einleitung, A. T.*, 1823, § 405), while Ewald argues that a very ancient Semitic tribe had acquired the use of the art before the historical age, and not from the Egyptians.—*Gesch. des Volkes Isr.*, i., p. 66, seq.

"Plutarch, in his treatise of Isis and Osiris, tells us (*Plut. de Isid and Osir.*, p. 354), that the theology of the Egyptians had two meanings; the one holy and symbolical, the other vulgar and literal; and consequently that the figures of animals which they had in their temples, and which they seem to adore, were only so many hieroglyphics to represent the Divine attributes. Pursuant to this distinction, he says, that Osiris signifies the active Principle, or the most holy Being (*Ibid.*, pp. 373, 374, 375); Isis the Wisdom or Rule of his operation; Orus the first production of his Power, the model or plan by which he produced everything, or the archetype of the world. We shall see hereafter whether it be reasonable to think that the Pagans had ever any knowledge of a trinity of distinct persons in the indivisible Unity of the Divine Nature. Thus much at least is plain, that the Chaldeans and Egyptians believed all the attributes of the Deity might be reduced to three,—Power, Understanding, and Love. In reality, whenever we disengage ourselves from matter, impose silence on the senses and imagination, and raise our thoughts to the contemplation of the infinite Being, we find that the eternal Essence presents itself to our mind under the three forms of Power, Wisdom, and Goodness. These three attributes comprehend the totality of his nature, and whatever we can conceive of Him. Not to speak, therefore, of the primitive traditions which might possibly be the source of these three ideas concerning the divine Nature, it is nothing extraordinary if the Egyptians and Orientals, who had very refining metaphysical heads, should of themselves have discovered them. The Greeks and Romans were fonder of the sciences which depend on sense and imagination, and for this reason we find their Mythology seldom turns upon anything but the external operations of the Deity in the productions of nature; whereas that of the former chiefly regards his internal operations and attributes. By the help of these principles the theology of the Pagans may be reduced to three principal divinities, without doing violence to original authors, and without racking one's brains to digest their ideas. All these names, nevertheless, denote but one and the same power, but mankind have confounded the work with the artificer, the image with the original, the shadow with the substance; they have forgotten the ancient doctrine, they have lost the meaning of our allegories, and stop at the outward symbols without entering into the spirit of them: this is the source of those numberless errors which prevail at present throughout all Greece, degrade religion and render it contemptible. Moreover I find that it is a steadfast maxim in all nations, that men are not what they were in the golden age, that they are debased and degraded, and that religion is the only means to restore the soul to its original grandeur, to make her wings grow again, and to raise her to the ethereal regions from whence she is fallen. It is necessary first to become man by civil and social virtues, and then to resemble the gods by that love of the sovereign Beauty, Order, and Perfection which makes us love virtue for itself: this is the only worship worthy of the immortals, and this is all my doctrine." — *Ramsay's Travels of Cyrus*, pp. 18 to 22.

"In order to illustrate the symbolic language properly, a very extensive acquaintance with ancient literature is requisite. The subject involves in it mythology, hieroglyphics, oriental customs, in short, all the learning of Egypt and the East."—*Wemyss' Key to the Symbolical Language of Scripture*, p. 4.

"The lion, which in Egyptian or Coptic, was called labo, or labor, that is, *valde hirsutus*, stood for the letter L, in the Hieroglyphic alphabet; and though this letter was represented by several other signs, yet the Egyptians, in writing the name of Ptolemy, and indeed of all the Roman emperors, always employed the figure of the lion, in preference to any other, no doubt, as a mark of the strength and courage of these sovereigns, as the lion is, and has always been, the symbol of these qualities."

"For the same reason, no doubt, the eagle, which in Egyptian was called Akhôm, represented the letter A, and was always employed in preference to any other signs, in spelling the names and the titles of all the Roman emperors in which it occurred, because that bird [signified exalted and far seeing intelligence], and was taken as the symbol of the Roman empire itself."

"In these instances, and others of the same sort, which might be adduced, we perceive something like a rule, which directed the Egyptians in the selection of their hieroglyphical characters, choosing those objects the names of which began with the sound of that very letter."

"[And] This, in point of fact, is something like the rule followed by the Hebrew, Chaldee, and Syriac alphabets; in which languages each letter stands for a name, expressing a particular substance, or a particular object; and that the very first letter, be it a vowel, be it a consonant, with which this name began, had and preserved the very same sound which it had in its own respective alphabet. One great difference, however, exists between them. In the Hebrew, Syriac, and Chaldaic alphabets, we find only one sign for each letter, and this sign invariable; but in the Egyptian alphabet there are many hieroglyphics, or images, to represent and express the same letter, which images they used, now the one and now the other, always selecting the character which had some correspondence, some relation, some analogy, with the idea, with the object, or with the person, they wished to record, or to express."—*Spineto's Lectures on the Elements of Hieroglyphics*, Lect. iii., pp. 89, 90, 94.

"Clement, a priest of Alexandria, who lived about the end of the second century of our era, a man of great learning, and who had paid a great deal of attention to the study of antiquity, asserted that the Egyptians had three different modes of writing, or, in other words, three different sorts of characters. These were, the *epistolographic*, or common characters, used in all the common transactions of life; the *hieratic*, or sacerdotal, employed merely in the writing of books by the priesthood; and the *hieroglyphics*, destined to religious uses, and generally on public monuments. Of the former sets of characters, Clement does no more than mention the names, but he correctly divides all hieroglyphics into *curiologic*, which employ the first elements of letters; and *symbolical*, which he subdivides into *imitative, tropical,* and *enigmatical*."

"Something of the same sort, but not quite so clear, has also been recorded by Porphyry in the 'Life of Pythagoras,' in which he says, that the Egyptians had three different kinds of letters, *epistolographic, hieroglyphical,* and *symbolical*."—*Spineto's Elements of Hieroglyphics*, Lect. 7, pp. 231, 233.

"When Herodotus visited Memphis, he saw the Egyptians, so renowned for their wisdom and their knowledge, in the utmost dejection, their temples ruined, their cities destroyed; and the high idea which even then he conceived of Egypt, allows us to imagine what his impression would have been if he had been permitted to visit this celebrated country during the period of its highest splendor. From this time the Greeks never failed to go to Egypt for the sake of instruction, and it was in the schools of the Egyptian priests that the philosophers, the legislators, and the wise men of Greece acquired a great portion of their knowledge; and yet what a difference between the priests of this period and those who lived under the Pharaohs! The priests of the Pharaonic ages were well versed in astronomy, physics, geometry, mechanics, and chemistry, in short, in most of the sciences; while their successors, the teachers of Herodotus and Plato, were but the passive echoes of their predecessors, and scarcely could be said to have preserved the first rudiments and the general outlines of so much learning."—*Spineto's Elements of Hieroglyphics*, Lect. 10th, pp. 362, 363.

XIX. HOW WAS IT THAT THE SPIRITUAL METHOD OF INTERPRETATION PRACTICED BY THE EARLY CHRISTIAN FATHERS, CEASED IN THE CHURCH, OR WHAT WERE THE CAUSES OF ITS DECLINE?

[After perusing the interesting notes from the Fathers, especially from Origen, to be found in the text and notes of this volume, and bearing in mind the admission of Mosheim, himself an opponent of such system of interpretation that "the spiritual method of interpretation was the rule and not the exception in the early church," a question naturally arises, and may be fairly asked, How was it that this method of interpreting Holy Scripture ceased in the church, or what were the causes of its decline?

In attempting to answer this question, we would first observe that the primitive Christian church held a threefold relation to the world. In the first place to the Jewish church and dispensation; in the second, to the Gentile world; and thirdly, to the baptized but ill-instructed proselytes from both. To a great extent this relationship would enter into and modify all the teachings *ex cathedrâ*; and it would therefore necessarily interfere not only to control the style of teaching, but also to introduce other styles of reasoning of a class widely different from that which would be useful among those who were really believers in Christian doctrine. Even in the times of the apostles this was felt to be the case; hence Paul's writings, though so frequently misunderstood, had reference chiefly to the great controversy between *Jewish* converts and *Gentile* converts, the former insisting that the law of Moses should be united with the faith of Christ, and the latter claiming to be free from that law. But as a matter of fact three distinct styles of teaching would be necessary, and three distinct kinds of evidence would be required by these different classes of minds, and it is evident that that which would be most cogent with one class would, in consequence of a different standpoint, be almost useless with another. This, we think, will account for the various modes of reasoning, not only among the Fathers, but also even in the Epistles of the apostles themselves.

The Jews, having the word of the Old Testament among them, and being, therefore, supposed to be acquainted with its contents, and more especially its prophetical contents, as well as the mode of interpretation common among themselves, would at once be prepared to receive the spiritual expositions of the apostles and early teachers. Such teaching would be, to them, no new thing; all that would be new would be the authoritative exposition of certain passages, and their application to their own circumstances, to the doctrines taught by the apostles, and to the events in the life of our Lord Jesus Christ. We should expect to find, therefore, as in fact we do, an entire absence of any dogmatic statement as to the spiritual sense either of history or prophecy. Both parties stood on common ground. So far from regarding proofs thus deduced from the Old Testament with suspicion or distrust, the Jews would naturally accept them as being of the same character they would themselves use. The apostles therefore followed the plan adopted by our Lord himself. In no case does He even assume that his hearers are unacquainted with the *fact* of the existence of a spiritual sense, but simply expounds that sense by the assertion, "This is that which was written by the prophet." And this very absence of any dogmatic reference to a spiritual sense by our Lord, and subsequently by his apostles, affords a strong presumptive evidence of the character of the Jewish belief with regard to the Old Testament. Certain it is that so far as the New Testament is concerned, no protest against the spiritual method of interpretation is to be found.

And even with regard to the second class—the converts from the Gentile world, or those to whom Christianity was preached, they were as commonly aware that the mythological literature of the past had frequently attached to it something which, if not a spiritual sense, was at least allegorical in its nature,—a fact which would but place the Old Testament on the same ground as their myths, but with the addition of a divine authority, and the apostles and their followers on the same plane as their own philosophers, but with the addition of a divine commission. Accustomed as they must have been to the idea of a twofold signification—to an esoteric and exoteric doctrine—even if ignorant of what such interpretations were, there would still be a groundwork or base for the reception of a spiritual system of exposition both of the law and the prophets; an affirmative groundwork, because it would excite none of that opposition which would be likely to arise if the methods of interpretation were new, or if it violated the ordinary habits of thought and investigation. With this class, therefore, no apology for the introduction of a style of spiritual interpretation would be necessary, and it need excite no surprise that we find none in the apostolic writings.

But, further, the grand doctrine which the apostles had to bring before the world was the actual fulfilment of prophecy in the incarnation of our blessed Lord. This was in fact the central point of all their teachings, for upon this doctrine Christianity itself was founded; and all those teachings have a more or less direct bearing upon the doctrine, or upon those which describe the effects resulting from that divine work. It needs but a slight acquaintance with the Epistles to perceive that they are for the most part argumentative treatises rather than *expositions*, and that as a consequence, an extensive introduction of the spiritual sense of the Word and its teachings, even if the laws thereof were perfectly known, would be out of place; the most simple statements would be the most forcible; while the other or more recondite meanings would as naturally fall into the background—and this without in any way settling the question as to the importance attached by the writers to the one or the other system of interpretation.

Doubtless the Epistles of the Apostles were to some extent answers to questions propounded by the early Christians as to points of doctrine on which they desired some authoritative opinion. Indeed this is generally admitted. But they would thus assume a different character from the ordinary preaching of those early days, which must necessarily have been directed to the elucidation of the question how is the Law to be understood in Christianity, or to the rehearsal of that which the Apostles had heard from our Lord's own lips. They were plainly told that the law was a schoolmaster or type to lead them to Christ; but the principal efforts of those early teachers must have been directed to the method of the "how?" for with the early Christians, and especially the converts from Gentilism, the mere statement would assume an entirely different aspect from that which it has assumed in later ages, when it has become a foregone conclusion, from the very fact that it has been superseded by Christianity. A glance will show the different ground on which the church stood in primitive and later ages, and enable us to see that a widely different method of reasoning would be absolutely indispensable. This method, we take it, is to be found in the commentaries of the Christian Fathers rather than in their polemic works.

But the stage into which the church rapidly passed, when she was surrounded by foes both within and without, must have rendered a very different style of teaching and preaching necessary, from that which was prevalent in the first and purer times. And this soon became, in fact, essential to its very existence. This displayed itself in two directions: 1st, in a gradual narrowing down of the doctrines of Christianity within certain limits, and in the effort to define these by symbols or creeds; and, 2d, in the relation which the Word of God occupied on the one hand with reference to the church itself, and on the other with reference to its opponents. This evidently was not the result of real growth in the church, for such growth would have been in the direction of increased instead of diminished spirituality. It clearly sprang from the necessity of meeting false teaching, and of preserving something like uniformity of doctrine in the church; and as the attacks were varied, so would the front of the opposing church be altered to meet the attack. The very importance of the work would necessarily dwarf every other; and, to a great extent, such writings only would be preserved as bore upon the great controversies of the day. But this direction of the thought and reasoning of the church was forced upon it in her militant condition. Doctrinal statements must of very necessity be based upon and enforced by literal expressions in the Word. It would have been alike impolitic and foolish to attempt to uphold and defend the creeds by any arguments drawn from the figurative exposition of the Word *unless both parties had agreed to some common mode of interpretation*,—a thing which in that state of the church was impossible. For each expositor was left to himself to work out his convictions as best he might, keeing in view as a plan the method adopted by our Lord, and accepted in the canonical epistles.

The increased spread of semi-infidelity in the church led, however, to some other results. The heresies which became prevalent soon changed their character. At first they might have been, to a great extent, merely intellectual in their nature; but this distinctive character ceased, and error rapidly led on to its own legitimate conclusion—evil. Not evil *out of*, but evil *in* the church,—practices of the vilest kinds, brought from the idolatries of Gentilism, which were incorporated into a corrupted Christianity, and which were apparently confirmed by some of the teachings of that Christianity. It was made "all things to all men." It is true that the moral law would, by its teachings, have preserved the church from any serious evil,—but in the first place the very method of teaching and expounding the law led the way to the introduction of licentious doctrines,—which were based on a *supposed figurative teaching of the law*, which obtained all the more force in the church from the universal prevalence of that system of interpretation; and secondly in part from the doctrine then beginning to be taught that the moral law was included in the Mosaic law which was "abolished in Christ." The evil, however, was not, as is generally supposed, the result of the practice of spiritual exposition,—*it arose from the want of specific laws by which that interpretation could be governed and directed*. One interpretation, therefore, was, to the ignorant or licentious, as good as another,—while the debased will would naturally choose that one which was most in harmony with its own predilections. But other conditions arose, and when the more pious of the church revolted at the licentiousness introduced, it was necessary to get rid altogether of the restrictions which might be supposed to be exercised upon some minds by the moral law, and at the same time to counteract all those plain literal expressions of the Word, which taught the necessity of righteousness and truth. And this was speciously done by the Gnostics, who, while recognizing a spiritual sense, reversed the position of the two, and taught that the literal expressions of Scripture were to be expounded by the spiritual, and the simple and plain ones by those which were obscure,—a method of reasoning which would render even an approach to truth in any science impossible. It was like reasoning from the unknown to the known. But it sufficed for the purpose. In the hand of evil men we may readily understand how the Word of God might, by such a system, be made the minister of evil. No wonder that the church found herself compelled, under these fearful circumstances, to once more change her front, and abandon, at least in her polemic life, every trace of belief in a spiritual sense, seeing that the principle had been changed into the most fearful weapon she had ever had to encounter. Not that the *existence* of a spiritual sense was denied. On the other hand, it was fully admitted. But it was felt that an appeal to its teachings would at once be fatal to any argument in which it was introduced. And as a consequence the church began to feel more and more that it could be built and safely rest upon a literal foundation in the Word,—a position perfectly true in itself,—but which in the then condition of the church, was untenable on any other ground than the abandonment of the spiritual sense. She could exist only by confining all her attention to the letter of the Word, and by teaching that in that letter only Revelation existed in all its purity, and in all its power.—ED.]

XX. THE DOCUMENT THEORY, AND THE ASSYRIAN TABLETS.

[When speaking of the early chapters of Genesis, the author states that Swedenborg affirms that they are parts of a previous revelation. This statement of doctrine was derived from the spiritual world, and it does not appear that he was at all acquainted with the results of Biblical criticism, or followed the progress of modern thought in regard to the letter of the Word. Indeed it is only in comparatively very recent times that criticism can be said to have held a high position in Biblical studies. But so long ago as the middle of the last century a French writer, named Austruc, called attention to the fact that on examining the two accounts of the creation in Genesis, he found that in each account a different name is used for the Divine Being—one of which parts he styled *Jehovistic*, and the other *Elohistic*, from the name used. He also traced the same circumstance as occurring in other parts of the early chapters of Genesis, and came to the conclusion that those chapters were copies of two earlier documents, interwoven together by Moses. The leading features of modern thought upon this subject, may be thus generalized. Stabelin, DeWette, Ewald, and others, consider that the account in Genesis is founded on two principal documents. That of *Elohim* is considered as being closely counted in all its parts, and forming a complete history; while that of *Jehovah*, is regarded as a supplementary document supplying details where the *Elohistic* is either abrupt or deficient. Hengstenberg. Ranke, and others, however, consider the book as the work of one hand, and the use of the names as being intentional on his part, and depending upon the view of the subject presented. The former theory, however, appears to be far more generally received, and certainly appears to be based on a greater amount of probability than the latter—and especially from the statement made on this subject by Swedenborg, who not only points to a previously existing document or documents, but specifically states that those parts are portions of the most ancient Word, though we are left in doubt as to what was the form in which that Word was preserved to the time of Moses. This view in no way interferes with his statement that every part of the Word is divinely inspired—because in this case not only the dictation, but the selection also were the work of the Divine Mind.

So long as men were satisfied with this chronology of Usher, the chronology of Genesis was a matter of slight importance—because it was easy to affirm that the chronology of other nations, if inconsistent, was *necessarily* mythical. But the researches of modern days have made it impossible to accept Usher's statements, and have compelled the learned to admit that the long calendar of names in Gen. iv. and v. must have been names of kingdoms and dynasties, extending over long ranges of time, and not of necessity actually united together. This view has become necessary from the discoveries of recent times, which it is impossible now to ignore. The geological proofs of the antiquity of the earth, and of man, and of the impossibility of such a flood as is described in Gen. vii., led the way to a fresh examination of those accounts of the creation and deluge to be found in the mythic literature of ancient peoples. Side by side with the Biblical account of the creation and deluge, we have the Mexican, the Hindoo, the account of Berosses, that of Abydenus, cited by Eusebius, and many others. But the one which has caused the greatest sensation, was that on the Assyrian tablets discovered by the late Mr. Smith, of the British Museum, in Babylonia. Sir H. Rawlinson affirmed, at the meeting at which the tablets were first read, that the legend dated at least 5000 years before the Christian era, or 2500 years before the deluge. This astounding statement has very recently received a strange confirmation. At a meeting of the Biblical Archæological Society, held Nov., 1882, a paper was read on the Chaldean cylinders, discovered by Mr. Rassam, in his excavations in Babylonia. They date from the time of Nabonides, and record among other things, that this sovereign, digging under the foundations of the Sun-God temple at Sipara, forty-five years after the death of Nebuchadnezzar, came upon a cylinder of Naramsin, the son of Sargon, which no one had seen for 3200 years. This gives us the date of that ancient sovereign 3750 B. C., or within 50 years of the creation, according to Usher. Professor Oppert pointed out, that there was in those early days a "lively intercourse between Chaldea and Egypt." The *Jewish World* considers that these tablets prove the existence more than 5500 years ago of two highly civilized and highly cultured empires in Egypt and Chaldea: and that constant intercourse between them passed through Southern Palestine, the home of Abraham, but 1800 years before his birth; that Abraham was a native of one, and an honored visitor at the other; and that it was hardly likely he would have been unaffected by the culture in which he was born, or the rival civilization of those two empires. They consider that it must modify the view which regards Abram as a wandering Bedouin Sheikh. Certainly it proves not only a high antiquity of the race, but also that there existed in those days a method of writing, which would be as easily read now as in the days of Nabonides.

There may be said, then, to be four great accounts of the deluge extant, the Assyrian, the Bhagavat, that of Berosas, and that of the Bible, and there can be little doubt that the two former are more ancient than the Biblical account, evidencing the fact of a widely spread tradition, long before the time of Moses. If, however, as is now generally believed by Biblical philologists, the first eleven chapters of Genesis were merely reproductions by Moses of existing documents,—parts of a more ancient Word and revelation, it may still be, that the two older accounts are but inflections of that, and traditionary records of events, in which the real actors had passed from the historical to the unhistorical or mythical form of existence in the lapse of ages. It has been already shown by the author that the science of correspondences was widely known not only in the most ancient and ancient churches, but also as a knowledge or science, among the most ancient Egyptians, the Druids, etc.: and it needs but a small acquaintance with the subject to trace the existence of that science in all the ancient productions of India, Mexico, and Scandinavia,—and in all the myths spread over the nations of antiquity. It is only by means of this science that such accounts can be rationally understood; but read by it, they form the strongest evidences of the principle we have laid down,—that this science was widely known among the ancients, and point therefore to a time when it was common among different nations, who must, therefore, have had one common spiritual origin. We believe that that origin is to be looked for in the ancient and most ancient churches, whose wisdom has been transmitted to us in this mythical form—interesting indeed even for their antiquity—but far more interesting from the light which they may ultimately be made to throw on the early moral and religious history of our race.

The author intended to have treated the history of Creation, the Garden of Eden, Babel, and the subsequent events connected with the rainbow; but the materials were left, at the time of his death, in an unfinished and incomplete state.—ED.]

[XXI—THE THREE TERMS, CORRESPONDENCES, REPRESENTATIVES, AND SIGNIFICATIVES.

IN dealing with the spiritual sense of the Word of God, and in unfolding its splendors, it is obvious that we must use the ordinary language of our race; but, as the ideas to be conveyed are distinct from any which have before existed, it will also follow that many of the terms employed will have new and peculiar meanings attached to them, which, indeed, we find to be the case in the writings of the church. To obtain, *exactly*, the ideas intended to be conveyed, we must first obtain, exactly, the ideas contained in the mere words themselves. If we were to attempt to study Euclid before we had mastered the axioms and definitions, and before we had a clear notion of the forms described by the terms used, we should find that we should be led only into a state of absolute confusion. The problem is only clear when its terms are clearly understood. It is precisely so in the case before us, and with reference to the terms, correspondence, representative, significative. Each has a distinct meaning; and though, through carelessness, the words are sometimes used as though they were synonymous, we shall readily see the loss of spiritual ideas which results by such careless use of words.

The three words are no more synonymous in New-Church theology than they are in the language itself. Each conveys its own idea.

Correspondence is derived from three Latin words, *cor, re, spondeo*, and literally means to answer again from the heart. The word is employed in common language to imply that epistolary communications have passed between two or more persons; and this is only considered complete when the second person, the one addressed, has replied to the communication of the addressor, or, literally, *has spoken to him again from his heart*. It is used in New-Church phraseology to imply the relationship which exists between two things united, as cause and effect, when a discrete degree subsists between them—we say when a discrete degree subsists between them, because it is necessary to guard against supposing that correspondence exists wherever there is a relation of cause and effect between any two material subjects, or subjects on the same plane of existence. The material cause is, in all such instances, a merely secondary one, acting from another hidden within itself or operating through it.

We will endeavor to make this important word, so frequently used in the foregoing pages, more clearly understood, as, not only does much depend upon a clear appreciation of its meaning, but the very word will then, when used, open up to the inquiring mind fields of investigation, which will repay the student, yet will ever surpass the powers he can bring to bear on the work.

Every created object may be said to be composed of two parts—a life, power, or energy, and a form capable of bringing that life, power, or energy into effect. The more we study the Divine works in nature, the more we find this true, and the more exact the analogy we perceive between these two principles or parts. This, at once, opens to us a most important fact, that there must be here a union of two forms, one spiritual and the other natural; the spiritual form being the life, power, and energy, and the material, the one presented to the senses, being the form by which these are brought into act; and the relationship existing between the two will show that *they must necessarily be the same*, not necessarily as to *shape*, *but as to use*. Now that which is true of the part is true also of the whole; and, therefore, the entire universe must be a form capable of bringing into effect a life, energy, or power, with which it is replete, and which acts through it; and there must be the same relationship between these two. But what are these two?

We reply, all creation is first derived from the suns of the material universe, and the various worlds are but forms, capable of receiving and bringing forth their life, power, and energy. But material suns are themselves only effects, and behind or within them, as a grand cause, shines the Sun of heaven itself—the glorious effulgence of the life, power, and energy of the Lord himself; and these material suns are but forms capable of bringing these things into outward and material effects.

But the cause both precedes and enters into the effect. Let us trace this idea a little further. The Lord himself is the grand and glorious Cause of all things —the essential life, power, and energy of which we have spoken; and from himself He created the glorious world of heaven, with all its spiritual realities. But here let us digress a moment and take an illustration. No man, as a mediate cause, produces anything but a form of that which existed previously in his own mind. This is true of the artist, every stroke of whose pencil, every idea of whose form of beauty, existed and was made in his imagination before it was transferred to his canvass or marble. We can see that it is equally true of the poet, architect, or mechanic. The idea, as separate from the object, exists prior to the object itself, and the outward work is but the material form, as it is the effect, of the spiritual idea or spiritual form. But in a higher sense is this the case with the Lord. His love and his wisdom are the first and only *realities*, and as compared with these all other things are only appearances. But they were also the creating principles, and the first things created by them would necessarily have impressed upon them that same law to which we have already referred; these must and would be the most perfect forms, most perfectly adapted for the reception and use of the life, power, and energy of the Divine Creator. But they would also, as such forms, in accordance with the law laid down, be not only the embodiment but also the manifestation of those principles, bringing them forth to view, they being seen in the uses such forms are capable of accomplishing. In the highest sense, therefore, the things of heaven are as effects, embodiments, and shadowings forth of the divine principles which exist in them and which are their causes.

But, 2dly, the same law may be applied to man and to the world of nature by which he is surrounded. All these proceed from the same grand Cause, and exist under the same divine law we have been considering. Passing through the spiritual world and its spiritual forms, which are the forms of thought and affection, the forms of the principles of the human soul which belongs to that world, the same life, power, and energy, coming down with material forms through the suns of the spiritual and material universes, created and formed all things in perfect harmony with themselves, rendering nature a material form exactly imaging forth the spiritual form within and the inmost Divine form; for nature is but a form created most perfectly to receive and bring into ultimate effect the life, power, and energy of God. This truth was seen by the Apostle when he wrote "the invisible things of Him from the creation of the world are clearly seen, being understood by the things which are made, even his eternal power and Godhead" (Rom. i. 20).

But one of these is spiritual and the other material, yet one is the effect and the other the cause—one life, power, and energy, the other the form proceeding therefrom, most perfectly adapted to bring them into outward manifestation. There is, therefore, not only as regards mere *form*, but also as regards *use*, a perfect and complete analogy between the two—a perfect adaptation of one to the other; and this analogy, this adaptation, this relation of cause and effect, is what the New Church means by Correspondence. The material form, the external character, and the uses of all outward substances, being the outcome of the spiritual principles dwelling in them, become to the outward world of matter precisely what the inward causes are to the world of mind. They "answer thought to thought and heart to heart." Correspondence, then, is no arbitrary relationship, like metaphor or figure, but one founded alike on the inward and outward nature of the things by which we are surrounded; and a knowledge thereof leads us, indeed, "through Nature up to Nature's God." It enables us also to see the truth of that oldest maxim the world knows, old and associated with a mythical personage, even when Moses studied the secrets of Egyptian lore, "all things that exist in earth exist in heaven, but in a heavenly form; and all things which exist in heaven exist in earth, but in an earthly form." And, carrying this idea from the revelation of God's works to the revelation of God's will—his Holy Word—following out the relationship of cause and effect, we shall be enabled to read in that Word the glorious things of Him who is its inmost life, the possibilities of the human soul, the glorious states it was designed to reach, the wondrous conditions through which it passes, and the merciful means by which man's advancement to heaven is secured.

The second term used in the foregoing work is *representative*. This word, compounded of *re* and *presentio*, literally means to show or present again, or in another form. Correspondence, we have seen, is the relation of cause and effect, and depends on the nature and use of the things spoken of. Representation, while it recognizes and springs from correspondence, belongs not to the *nature* of things, but to their actions, or the things which spring from them. An illustration will best show what this difference is. The kingly government, apart from the king, is the correspondent form of the divine government, and springs from it as an effect from a cause. But *the person* of the king, with the government connected with it, and the actions of government, do not correspond to, but represent the divine government of the Lord. Into correspondence, cause and effect only enter; into representation apparent cause and effect may enter. This possible introduction of appearances and the laws which govern them will, therefore, show how wide a distinction obtains between the two words. One, indeed, is the result of the Divine life alone, the other of the admixture of the Divine and human. Thus, iron corresponds to the divine truth in a natural form and degree; but smelted and hammered and shaped and sharpened into the sword or spear, that is, with the results of human labor added to the Divine work, it becomes the representative, not the correspondent, of that degree of truth existing and used in the human soul. Again, the whole of the things used in the sacrificial service of the temple were correspondences; but their use, and the worship, of which they formed a part, were representatives.

The places mentioned in the Word are also representatives, derived in part from the correspondence of the position in reference to certain other places in the land of Canaan, or to the land itself;—in part from the surrounding scenery or some particular object, as a mountain, valley, river, and the like; in part from the tribe of the people occupying it; and in part from the meaning of the name of the place, hence frequently changed; the whole dependent, however, on the fixed laws of correspondence described.

The third word, *signify*, is derived from the Latin *signum*, a sign, and refers entirely to the actions spoken of or the words uttered, and is governed by the same laws of appearances which apply to representation, to which indeed it is more nearly allied than to correspondence, though of course the laws of correspondence enter so largely into it that in reality it becomes only a modification of those laws. The word is indeed frequently used in this very form in the prophetic portions of the Word, the actions of the prophets and kings being declared to be "a sign" to the people, a sign not only of good but of evil, because the true correspondence was bent and distorted by the miserable states of those whose sins of life hindered heavenly causes from producing heavenly effects in the world, and compelled them to flow into opposite and disorderly channels.

To summarize, then: Correspondence is the relation between spiritual and natural things; representation is the action of things which are correspondences in themselves; and significatives are the words and appearances resulting from the actions of either one or the other.

Each of these became necessary in the great work of Revelation. They became necessary because of the condition of man himself. The divine language must ever be infinitely above the comprehension of human thought, and infinitely above the capacity of human language. The one can no more receive it than the other can convey it. For the divine wisdom to reach and affect the human soul, it was necessary that a process should be gone through, imaged and represented to us by the actions and uses of the atmosphere surrounding the world in which we live. The rays of heat and light from the sun, were they received without any modification, would be destructive of all life in the objects upon which they fell. Yet they are the sources of all animal, vegetable, and mineral life to all things, but only so after being received into and modified by the motions inherent in the particles composing the atmosphere. Just in the same way the laws of correspondence form a spiritual atmosphere, enabling the divine light and love to flow into the soul and animate all its principles. It is true, indeed, that the Scriptures are the Word of God to us, whether we acknowledge the existence of correspondence or not; but our ignorance of its existence would no more interfere with this fact than would our ignorance of the laws, constitution, and uses of the atmosphere debar us from its beneficent effects. Enough may be seen by every reader to enable the divine life to act, even though the symbols known be few, and the light, like that of the sun seen through densest clouds; but still as infinitely above what man would be without revelation, as the cloudy day is above midnight darkness. But with this knowledge Nature and the Holy Word become one grand Revelation, making known to us our Father's will and purpose, and leading us on to the perfect and eternal day of his presence.—ED.]

[The following hymn, translated from the Greek by the Rev. I. M. Neale, D.D., and inserted in *Hymns, Ancient and Modern*"—the hymn-book most widely used by the Church of England—affords a specimen of the early method of treating the wars of Israel. It should have been appended as a note to Chapter IX.

"WHOM RESIST, STEADFAST TO THE FAITH.

"Christian, dost thou see them
　On the holy ground,
How the troops of Midian
　Prowl and prowl around?
Christian, up and smite them,
　Counting gain but loss;
Smite them by the merit
　Of the holy cross.

"Christian, dost thou feel them,
　How they work within,
Striving, tempting, luring,
　Goading into sin?
Christian, never tremble;
　Never be downcast;
Smite them by the virtue
　Of the Lenten fast.

"Christian, dost thou hear them,
　How they speak thee fair?
'Always fast and vigil?
　Always watch and prayer?'
Christian, answer boldly,
　'While I breathe I pray:'
Peace shall follow battle,
　Night shall end in day.

"Well I know thy trouble,
　O my servant true;
Thou art very weary,
　I was weary too;
But that toil shall make thee
　Some day all mine own,
And the end of sorrow
　Shall be near my throne!"—ED.]

INDEX.

Aaron, breastplate of, 174, 529; answer by, 542.
Ablutions, antiquity of, Townley, 98 n.; Lord, ib.
Accommodation of letter of Word, 118.
Adam, 247; sig. of name, Darwin, 217 n.; O'Brien, 248 n.; Baruel, ib.; Vitringa, ib.; Morell, ib.; Philo-Judæus, ib.; Von Behlen, ib.; sig of, 339.
Agate, 540.
Allegory, ancients spoke in, a universal language, Voltaire, 50 n.; Warburton, ib.; Hutchinson, ib.; Clemens Alexandrinus, ib.; Marsh, 66 n.; Horne, ib.; Origen, 70 n.; Augustine, ib.; More, 86 n.; Law, ib.; Jones, 108 n.
Alms, sig. of, 355.
Amalek, battle of Israel with, 127; battle with, Origen, 129 n.
Amethyst, 541.
Analogy between sexes, Grindon, Good, 130 n.; Cory, ib.; Davis, ib.; Milton, ib.; Croker, 135 n.; Townley, ib.
Ancient Word, the, 564; first chapters of Genesis taken from, 565.
Animal Kingdom, correspondence of, 149, 190; birds, fishes, and reptiles, 190; the lion, 192; the horse, 188, 193; horses of fire, 198; colored horses, 199; Pegasus, 202; mythological horses, 203.
Animals, symbolism of, 191 n.
Apostles, testimony of, to spiritual sense, 65.
Apparent and genuine truths, 112; harmonized by true doctrine, 121; false principles confirmed by apparent truths, how, 122.
Architecture, symbolic, 148 n.
Ark, 256; insufficiency of accommodation, ib.; Dr. Pye Smith on, ib.; traditions of, 258; difficulties in the literal sense, 259; a figure of the human mind, 261; resting on Ararat, 262.
Assyria, signification of, 168.
Assyria and Egypt, state of, 167; why spoken of (E. S.), 169 n.
Augustine, St., on want of rule of interpretation, 40 n.; on veil of Moses, 63 n.; on allegory, 76 n.; on origin of idolatry, 51 n.; on letter and spirit, 105 n.; spiritual truths easily seen, 113 n.; opposite meanings, 188 n.; on creation, 243 n.; on fall of man, 248 n.

Babel, a symbol, Vaughan, tower of, 263 n.
Bacon, Lord, on mythologies, 522.
Bald-head, 81 n.
Beryl, 542.
Bible, a record of earthly events, Duke of Argyll, 18 n.; Bishop Thirlwall, 19 n.; not the Word of God, 35 n.; admitted by Christians to be a divine revelation, 303.
Blindness, spiritual, 384; miracle of cure of, 359.
Body, cor. of, 78; illustrations of, symbol of, Howard, 80 n.; Serle, ib; Roberts, 81 n.; Moore, ib.; cor. of motions and parts of, 157; Bronze age (ED.), 246 n.; cor. of motions of, 368.
Bramble, cor. of. 219.
Brass, 253; serpent of, ib.
Bronze Age (ED.), 246 n.
Builders, wise and foolish, 234.
Bush, Prof., definition of Scripture, 33 n., 170
Butter and honey, cor. of, 595, 597.

Cana, in Galilee, miracle at, 285.
Canaan, land of, 69; sig. of, 363; journey from Egypt to, 366.
Canaanites, early idea of, sig. of, 68 n.
Carbuncle, 573.
Cardinal points, sig. of, 163.
Celestial sense of the Word, 144.
Cherubim, 296 n.
Chœnix, 494.
Christian *Examiner* on the letter of Scripture, 22 n.
Christian symbolism of middle ages, 148 n.
Chronologists, contradictory views of, as to date of creation, 307; Chrysophrasus, 538.
Circumcision, a rep. ceremonial, 66 n.
Clouds and darkness, cor. of, 327.
Colenso, the Bible a human book, 23.
Colors, cor. of. 170; Portal on, 170 n.; sig. of, ib.; writers of Light (*Temple Bar*), 172 n.; St. Pierre, 173 n.; Swedenborg, ib.
Conjunction with heaven effected by the Word, 572, 589; effects resulting from reading the Word, 573; with children, 576.
Continuous degrees, 146.

Copper, cor. of, 253.
Correspondence; illustrations of, from various authors, 40 note; definition of, 39, 71; cor. and metaphor, 71; Swedenborg's definitions of, 73; cor. of soul and body, why, 75; originates in the nature of angels and of the Lord, *ib.;* of the heart, 75, 81; the eye, 75; the face, 77; of the body and its motions, 78, 80, 157; of flesh, 81; of the veins or kidneys, 82; of the hand, *ib.;* of the foot, *ib.;* of the ear, 83; not a speculation, 85; the only forms by which spiritual truth from the Lord can be revealed, 85; cor. representatives and significatives defined, 87; the key of knowledge, *ib.;* cor. of mountains and hills, 90; of light and heat, 91; of treasures, *ib.;* of darkness, 92; of fire, 93; of water, 95; of baptism, 98; of water-floods, 100; of Ezekiel's vision, 102; between earth and heaven, 106 *n.;* of war, 124; of eating and drinking, 135; of the passover, 136; of the holy supper, 137; of the animal world, 149, 190; of the vegetable world, *ib.,* 206; of incense, 149; of perfumes, 160; of the cardinal points, 163; of colors, 170; of weights and measures, 176, 180; of musical instruments, 170, 182; of stringed instruments, 184; of the harp, 185; Swedenborg on, 186; of the horn, 188; of ancient instruments, *ib.;* of singing and dancing, 189; of birds, fishes, and reptiles, 192; of the lion, 192; of the horse, 188, 193; of serpents, 204; of flowers, 208; of medicinal plants, 209; of the oak, 210; of the olive, 211; of the vine, 213; of the fig-tree, 215; of fruit and leaves, *ib.;* of the bramble, 219; of the hyssop, 224; of the cedar, *ib.;* of the palm-tree, 225; of evergreens, 226; of leprosy, 230; of wood, *ib.;* of earths and minerals, 233; of stones, *ib.;* of sulphur and pitch, 237; of salt, *ib.;* of sun, moon, and stars, 239; of tree of life, 295; a universal language, 321; defined, *ib.;* anciently known, 322; origin of, 325; proofs of, *ib.;* descent of divine truth by, 326; bowing the heavens and coming down, *ib.;* opinions of writers on subject. (See OPINIONS.)
Creation, history of, 242; and first chapters of Genesis, Celsus, 242 *n.;* Lyell, *ib.;* Philo, 243 *n.;* Bodinus, 243 *n.;* Augustine, *ib.;* Middleton, Origen, *ib.; Westminster Review, ib.;* Nott and Glyddon, *ib.;* Bunsen, 244 *n.;* Honert, *ib.;* Kitto, *ib.;* Bloomfield, *ib.;* Jones, *ib.;* Sewell, *ib.;* St. Cyril, 245 *n.; Philosophical Dictionary, ib.;* Heringa, 246 *n.;* Horne, *ib.;* Ferguson, *ib.;* Eadie, *ib.;* Warburton, *ib.;* Rentish, *ib.*
Creation of the world, 305; God present in his works, *ib.;* no difficulty in attributing creation to God, 306; the account in Genesis not a literal history, 307; opinions of the Fathers on this subject, *ib.;* contradictory views of chronologists, *ib.;* harmony of geology with Scripture, 308; creation out of nothing not a doctrine of revelation, 310; creation according to divine order, *ib.;* the sun the instrumental cause of creation, 311; the Lord the first great cause, 312; the sun a concentration of the creative rays of the divine Sun, 313; Sir H. Davy's opinion of, *ib.;* connection between the Creator and his works, 314; an image of God, 315; the invisible things of God in creation, 316.
Cubit, 495, 497.
Cyanus, 540.

Dancing, cor. of, 189.
Darkness, cor. of, 92.
Darkness and clouds, cor. of, 327.
Day spring, *n.*
Day and night, 557.
Decalogue, two tables of, 515; writing on, *ib.;* epitome of whole duty of man, *ib.;* written on both sides, 516; how written, 517; first pair broken, why, 518; tables of the ancients respecting, 521; second pair of tables, 525; distinction between the tables and the writing of them, 526.
Degrees, discrete, 144; continuous, 146; discrete, nature of, 630.
Deluge, a parable, 260.
Diamond, 539.
Doctrine must be drawn from letter of Word, 113.
Drinking, cor. of 135.
Dual nature of all things, 132.

Ear, cor. of, 83.
Earths and minerals, cor. of, 233.
Eating, cor. of, 135.
Eden, 247; its position, etc., Sir W. Jones, 247 *n.;* Rabbi Bar Abraham, *ib.;* Dr. A. Clarke, *ib.;* Sherwin, *ib.;* Newman, *ib.;* Bohn, *ib.;* 339; its trees, *ib.;* its situation, 340.
Egypt, sig. of, 167; and Assyria, ancient state of, 167 *n.;* why spoken of, Swedenborg, 169 *n.;* idolatry of, 571 and *n.;* journey from to Canaan, 366.
Elisha, miracle of at Gilgal, 378; spiritual death, what it is, 379.
Ephah, 494, 495, 496.
Epistles, testimony of, to spiritual sense, 65; difference between and the Gospels, 585.
Error of reading the Word in the same spirit as other books, 331.
Essenes, their belief in outward letter and inward spirit, 28 *n.*
Evangelists, four, ancient use of in ordination, 18; oaths administered on, *ib.;* held over the head in ordination of bishops, *ib.;* use of in communion service of Church of England, *ib.;* Tatian's harmony of, 17 *n.*

INDEX.

Evergreens, 226.
Evidence required to prove divinity of Word, 14.
Eye, cor. of, 75.
Eyes, cor. of, 356.
Ezekiel's vision of holy waters, 369.

Face, cor of, 77.
Fall of Man, Tucker, 248 *n.*; Origen, *ib.*; Augustine, *ib.*; Heylin, *ib.*; Horne, 249 *n.*; More, *ib.*; Bridge, *ib.*; Diderot, *ib.*; Lamb, 254 *n.*; effects of, 563.
Fallacies of the senses, 114, 123.
Famine, sig. of, 379.
Feet, cor. of, 356; washing of, 357.
Fig-tree, cor. of, 215; the barren, Origen, 216 *n.*; French, *ib.*; Owen Feltham, *ib.*; Serle, *ib.*
Fire, cor. of, 93; perpetual fire, 93 *n.*; a symbol, Bloomfield, *ib.*; Lauretus, *ib.*; sin of kindling sacred, Zoroaster, 95 *n.*; Eusebius, *ib.*; Bray, *ib.*; Vaux, *ib.*; Morheim, *ib.*; Channing, *ib.*
First, middle, and end in all things, 143.
Flesh, cor. of, 81.
Flood, 255; not universal, 256; traditions referring to, 258; a parable, 260.
Flowers, cor. of, 208; language of, *ib. n.*
Foot, cor. of, 82.
Forty, sig. of, 82.
Foursquare, sig. of, 501.
Frankincense, cor. of, 616.
Freemasonry, symbols of, 148 *n.*
Furlong, sig. of, 495.

Gates of holy city, 164; cor. of, 555; the Lord, the true gate, 556.
Genesis, 242.
Genuine and apparent truths, 112.
Geology, harmony of with Scripture, 308.
Gerah, 493.
Giants, 245 *n.*
Glorification of the Lord's human, 154; represented by the sacrifices in the Israelitish worship, 274.
God, ancient opinions respecting, in Egypt, Serle, 141 *n.*; Plato, *ib.*; Heraclitus, *ib.*; Jones, 442 *n.*; names of, Hermes, 161 *n.*; Holloway, 162 *n.*; Jerome, *ib.*; St. Ignatius, *ib.*; Swedenborg, *ib.*; cor of, 554, 644.
God, speaking to man's will and intellect, 332.
Gold, color of, 170 *n.*; cor. of, 236, 554, 644.
Golden age, 235.
Gospels, position of at council of Ephesus, 18 *n.*; lights carried before them in Eastern churches, *ib.*; literally true, but representative in every particular, 279; parables and miracles of, 62, 279; Clowes on parables, 280; frequently in a series, *ib.*; miracles, 281; Origen's opinion of, 282 *n.*;
Rev. J. Williams on, 283; Swedenborg's definition of, 283; Hindmarsh on, 284.
Grand man, position of inhabitants of this earth in, 589.
Groves, sig. of, 511.

Hailstones, cor. of, 329.
Hand, cor. of, 75.
Hands, cor. of, 355.
Heat and light, cor. of, 91.
Heavens and earth, cor. of, 332.
"**He** that was, and is, and is to come."
Heraldry, symbolism of, Lord Lindsay, 170 *n.*
Hin, 494, 495.
Holloway (*letter and spirit*) Christ everywhere in Scripture, 27 *n.*; on origin of idolatry, 51 *n.*; on rituals of the law, 64 *n.*; on creation, 245 *n*
Holy supper, sig. of, 137.
Holy waters, Ezekiel's vision of, 369.
Homer, 494, 499.
Honey, the Word compared to, 333; cor. of, 595, 597.
Horne, on the spiritual sense of the Psalms, 37 *n.*; liable to abuse, 88 *n.*; on the Psalms and history of David, 264 *n.*
Human body, cor. of motions of, 368; cor. of, 635; physiology of, 636; the head and hair, *ib.*; Nazariteship, 638; Samson, his rep. character, 639.
Human race, mythological account of origin of, 150 *n.*
Human style of writers of the Word prepared by God, 109 *n.*
Hyssop, cor. of, 224.

Ideas flow into expressions, 34.
Idolatry, origin of, L'Abbé Bazin, 50 *n.*; Voltaire, 51 *n.*; Holloway, *ib.*; Grote, *ib.*; Taylor's *Iamblichus,* *ib.*; St. Austin, *ib.*; Warburton, *ib.*; Servius, *ib*; Cudworth, *ib.*, 52 *n.*; Ellis, 51 *n.*; Pemble, 52 *n.*; Orange, *ib.*, 239; origin of, 323.
Imagery, 72.
Influx defined, 78.
Inspiration of two kinds, plenary and secondary, 15; comparison of orthodox and true estimates of, 16; low estimate of, by Dr. Palfrey, 19; McLellan, *ib.*; Dr. Davidson, *ib.*; Bp. Thirlwall, *ib.* note; Dewey, 20; Prof. Andrews Norton, 24; Newman, 22 *n.*; Swains on, *ib.*; Colenso, 23.
Instruments of music, ancient, 184 *n.*
Internal and external of the Word constitute one series, 39.
Israelites, deliverance of, a spiritual narrative, 61, 64 *n.*; inconsistencies in numbers of, 175.

James, sig. of, 166, 286.
Jasher, 542.

Jehovah, on name of, Maimonides, 142 n.; Serle, ib.; Druidical triad, ib.; D. H. H. (Am. N. J. Mag.), ib.; Cudworth, ib.; Fontenelle, ib.; Pythagoras, ib.; Dr. A. Clarke, ib.; apostolic translation of, 268.
Jerome, on purity of the word, 25 n.
Jerusalem, a symbol of Christian Church, Sherlock, 68 n.; sig. of, 550; destruction of, 609.
John, sig. of, 166, 286.
Jones, Rev. V., on origin of idolatry, 523.
Jones (Rev. W., Nayland), on the hidden wisdom of Scripture, 25 n.; the world a parable, 41 n., 42 n.; on correspondence, 108 n.; on Father, Son, and Holy Ghost, 142 n.; on creation, 244 n.
Jude, reference to ancient mythology, 524.

Key of knowledge, 87, 593.
Keys of heaven and hell, 590.
Kidneys, or reins, 82.
Kings representative of the Lord's regal principle, 270.
Knowledge, three degrees of, 330; mutually strengthen each other, 331.
Knowledge, tree of, 248.

Lameness, cure of, 359.
Lead (a weight), 493.
Leprosy and its cure, 230.
Letter and spirit, ancient opinions on, Jennings, 104 n.; the Therapeutæ, ib.; Origen, 105 n.; St. Augustine, ib.; Neale, ib.; Berk, ib.; More, ib.; Hurwit, ib.; Wake, 274 n.; opinions of a Jewish sect in Poland, 104 n.
Letter of the Word, a dead body containing a living soul, 28 n.; truth in, 112; doctrine must be drawn from, 113; compared to skin of body, Noble, 113 n.; use of, 116.
Life flows from the soul to the body; three degrees of, 141.
Life, tree of, 225, 295.
Light and heat, cor. of, 91; trinity of, 172 n.
Light, a symbol of truth, 91 n.; Iamblichus, ib.; Roberts, ib.; tensity of (Temple Bar), 172 n.
Light of the world, 557.
Literal sense of Word indefensible and full of difficulties, 24; passages in reference to incarnation not explainable in, 28; compared to man, 32.
"**Living** oracles," 64 n.
Lord, birth and life of, 285; his temptations, 287; the chief prophet, 291.
Lord's prayer, development in (Ed.), 116 n.
Lots, casting, sig. of, 353.
Love, wisdom, and life, a trinity in God and man, 350.

Macrocosm and microcosm, 323, 330.
Magi and their gifts, 159; on the, Hutchinson, 159 n.; Cudworth, ib.; Polycarp, ib.; Origen, ib.; Borlase, ib.; Porphyry, ib.; Moore, ib.; Swedenborg, ib.; Herodotus, 160 n.; and their offerings, 642.
Mahometanism, 570; its truth for the Word, ib.
Man a microcosm, 332.
Man born blind, miraculous cure of, 383.
Marah, waters of, 231.
Marriage, origin of, 232; sig. of, 551.
Martineau, Miss H., rejection of gospels by, 23 n.
Measures and weights, 176, 180.
Measuring line, sig. of, 499.
"**Mene**, mene, tekel, upharsin," 500.
Metaphor and correspondence, Hindmarsh on, 72.
Microcosm, 41.
Mineral kingdom, cor. of, 149.
Mingled seed, fabrics, etc., 139.
Miracles, 279; Clowes on, 281; Swedenborg on, 283; nature and design of, 377.
Miracles of our Lord, on, Origen, 282 n., 288 n.; Hilary, 282 n.; John of Jerusalem, ib., 288 n., 291 n.; Irenæus, 282 n.; Hind, 283 n.; Williams, ib.; Heber, ib.; Tracts for Times, 289 n.
Miraculous evidences of the Lord's divinity, 357.
Mirror, seeing in, Clarke, 117 n.; Maimonides, ib.
Misery the consequence of sin, Brown, 119 n.; Wilson, ib.
Moon, cor. of, 239.
More, H., the law of Moses a living creature, 31 n.; the world a macrocosm, 41 n.; on history of David, 61 n.; on symbols, 86 n.; on Adam, 88 n.; mystical sense of names, 105 n.; on numbers, 176 n.; on the fall, 291 n.; on the serpent, 250 n.
Moses; the veil upon his face, 63; law of, sig. of, 268; prayer of, explained, 345.
Most ancient church, possessed no outward Word, 563; character of its people, 567; the origin of mythology, 568; had immediate revelation, 564.
Mountains and hills, cor. of, 90, 332.
Mount Zion, why mentioned, Jerome, 90 n.
Musical instruments, sig. of, 170; description of, 182; stringed, 184; ancient, list of, 184 n.; harp, 185; Swedenborg on, 186; horn, 188; ancient instruments, 188.
Myrrh, cor. of, 647.
Mythology, origin of, 552; Lord Bacon on, 522.

Names symbolical, More, 105 n.
Nativity of the Lord, 643; nature of, 644.
Natural forms outbirths from spiritual causes, 54, 72; from the Lord, 89.
Natural good, its relation to spiritual good, 645.

Nature, an effect from a higher cause, 304; three kingdoms of, 348; animal kingdom, *ib.*; vegetable kingdom, 349; fertile ground and barrenness, *ib.*

Nazariteship, its sig., 638.

New heavens and new earth, 549; cor. of, *ib.*

New Jerusalem, 550; the bride, the Lamb's wife, 551; having the glory of God, 552; measured with a golden reed, 553; city pure gold, 554; four-square, *ib.*; its foundations, walls, and gates, 555; its temple, 556; the Lamb its light, *ib.*; no night there, 557; sovereignty of its citizens, 559; qualities for citizenship, 560.

Newman (*Phases of Faith*) on Scripture and reason, 22 *n*.

Night, cor. of, 557, 611; flight in, 610.

Noah a rep. character, 260; saved by the same waters which destroyed the ungodly, 262.

Noble, Rev. S., on what constitutes the Word of God, 36.

Numbers, sig. of, 170, 176; simple numbers, *ib. n.*; seven, ill., 170 *n.*; on, Swedenborg, 176 *n.*; More, *ib.*; Colman, *ib.*; *Sabbath Leisure, ib.*; Dehon, *ib.*; Von Bohlen, *ib.*; Cahen, *ib.*; three, 178; forty, 179; relative numbers, 178; why changed in literal sense, 175; general sig. of, 399; multiplication of, 401; numbering, sig. of, *ib.*; one, 403; two, 411; three, 419; four, 426; five, 434; six, 445; seven, 451; eight, 459; nine, ten, 469; eleven, 475; twelve, 478; compound numbers, rules for ascertaining, sig. of, 487, 666, 391.

Oak, cor. of, 210.

Obedience the gate of admission into heaven and the Church, 560.

Old Testament, books in, not plenarily inspired, 486.

Olive, cor. of, 211.

Omer, 494, 495.

Onyx, 542.

Opinions of ancient and modern authors as to the Word, 337; Origen on the transfiguration, *ib.*; Parkhurst on Gen. ii. 8, *ib.*; Rabbi Simon Bar Abraham on the Garden of Eden, 338 *n.*; Parkhurst on the word "Testimony," 341; Lowth on Isa. xxvii. 1, 342; Horne on Ps. viii., *ib.*; Pascal, 343; S. P. C. K. tracts, *ib.*; Rev. W. Jones (Nayland) on correspondences, 344; Swains on, *ib.*; other writers in confirmation of correspondence, 345.

Opposites, law of, 81.

Origen on the moral sense of Scripture, 30 *n.*; on the spirit of the law, 68 *n.*; on allegory, 70 *n.*; on letter and spirit, 105 *n.*; on war with Amalek, 129 *n.*; on the barren fig-tree, 216 *n.*; on the fall, 248; on the gospels, 282; on the miracles of our Lord, *ib.*, 288 *n.*; on triple sense of Scripture and triple constitution of man, 347.

Ox and ass, why forbidden to plow with, 139.

Pagan mysteries derived from holy sources, 50 *n*.

Painted windows, 171 *n*.

Palm-tree, cor. of, 225.

Parables, why used, 62, 279; Clowes on, 280; frequently in series, *ib.*

Passover, sig. of, 136.

Patriarchs, the three, 161.

Paul, definition of inspiration, 33; a minister of the spirit of the law, 64 *n*.

Perfumes, 160.

Persons, why named in the word, 165.

Peter, sig. of, 165, 286.

Peter, St., reference to ancient mythology, 524; sig. of, 591; why keys of heaven were said to be given him, 592.

Plagues visited on them who fight against Jerusalem, 363.

Plants, symb. of, Potter, 206 *n.*; Ridley, *ib.*; Bulwer, *ib.*; *Dublin Review,* 208 *n.*; Courcelles, 209 *n.*; Owens, *ib.*; Carpenter, 211 *n.*; Harris, *ib.*, 253 *n.*; Hewlett, 221 *n.*; St. Basil, *ib.*; Montgomery Martin, 222 *n.*; Dr. Channing, *ib.*; Bryant, 227 *n.*; Serle. *ib.*

Precious stones, Aaron's breastplate, 529; different order of stones and tribes, 530; position of stones and names, 532; first row, 535; ruby, 536; sardius, *ib.*; topaz, 537; second row, 538; Chrysophrasus, *ib.*; sapphire, 539; diamond, *ib.*; third row, 540; Cyanus, *ib.*; agate, *ib.*; amethyst, 541; fourth row, *ib.*; tarshish, *ib.*; onyx, 542; beryl, 542; method of answer by, *ib.*; in walls of holy Jerusalem, 555.

Preservation, continual creation, 619.

Prophecy a miracle, Collins, 14 *n*.

Prophetic style of Word, Warburton, 104 *n*.

Prophets, state of, while speaking or writing, 15.

Psalms, spiritual sense of, 37 *n.*; Bp. Horne on, 265 *n*.

Rainbow, sig. of, 172.

Reed, cor. of, 553.

Regeneration of man a threefold work, 155.

Religion not intuitive, 570.

Rephidim, battle of, 127.

Representatives, correspondences, and significatives, 87; not originally derived from man, 58.

Responses from heaven, by literal sense of Word, how made, 547.

Revelation, book of, 292; predictions, use of, *ib.*; contents, *ib.*

Ruby, 536.

Sabbatarians, 104 *n*.

Sabbath day, flight on, 610, 614.
Sacrifices, not by divine precept, Outram, 271 *n.*
Sacrificial worship, 266; Origen on, 68 *n.;* origin of external worship, 266; clean beasts and fowls, sig. of, 267; institution of, *ib.;* burnt offerings, *ib.,* 275; sacrifices in Jewish church, 267; Mosaic ritual, 268; sin and trespass offerings not expiations of moral turpitude, 269; result of Jews falling into this error, 270; of Christians, 276; sacrifices, why selected, 273; opinions of Barnabas and Eusebius, 273 *n.;* called a "covenant," 274; also, "bread and meat of God," *ib.;* polluted or imperfect offerings, *ib.;* domesticated animals, 275; worship from love signified by Abel's offering, *ib.;* worship from faith sig. by Cain's offering, *ib.,* 275; the Lord's perfect sacrifice, 278.
Salt, cor. of, 237, 599; why offered with sacrifices, 238; pillar of, *ib.;* to be offered with all sacrifices, 600; its opposite, *ib.;* its preservative power, 601; its fructifying power, 602; Elisha's miracle at Jericho, 603; its conjoining principle, 604; use with food, 606.
Samson, his history, 80; rep. of, 639.
Sandals or shoes, on loosing of, 25 *n.*
Science and religion, connection between, 389.
Scriptural imagery not to be accounted for by ordinary criticism, 109 *n.*
Seasons of year, cor. of, 612.
Seeing and seeing not, 63 *n.*
Serpent, cor. of, 250; serpent worship, *ib. n.;* symbol of, More, 250 *n.;* Philo, *ib.;* Bellamy, *ib.,* 250, 251 *n.;* Middleton, 250 *n.;* Schlegel, 251; Gene, *ib.;* Teller, *ib.;* Roberts, *ib.;* Coleridge, 252 *n.;* Davidson, *ib.;* serpent of brass, 253; cor. of, 616; venomous and non-venomous, 618; in Eden, *ib.;* its subtilty, 620; Dan a serpent in the path, 622; rod of Moses changed to, *ib.;* serpent of brass, 623; its poison, 624; power given to tread on, 625; mythological use of, *ib.*
Sexual system in nature, 130 *n.*
Shekel, 493, 496.
Significatives, what they are, 87.
Siloam, pool of, 385.
Singing, sig. of, 189.
Sins, what is meant by the Lord bearing, 277.
Sound, resulting from affection, Sherlock, 182 *n.; Public Opinion, ib.*
Space and time, 632; their analogues, 633.
Spirit of the law, Locke, 64 *n.;* Jerome, *ib.;* Holloway, *ib.;* Fisk, *ib.;* Dr. Luntz, *ib.;* Serle, *ib.;* Middleton, *ib.;* Clement, *ib.;* St. Cyril, 67 *n.; Tracts for the Times,* ib.; Origen, 68 *n.,* 139 *n.,* 274 *n.;* Townley, 139 *n.;* Pascal, 268 *n.;* Greswell, 274 *n.;* Hutchinson, 276 *n.*
Spiritual and natural worlds, relation between, 627; spiritual and natural body of man, 628; spiritual substances, 629; spiritual forms, how in nature, 631.
Spiritual life, three degrees of, 158; sense, evidence of existence of, 60; truths easily seen, Augustine, 113 *n.;* Swedenborg, 114 *n.;* Pascal, *ib.;* Gregory, *ib.;* Addison, *ib.;* Gaussen, *ib.*
Spring, season of, rep. of regeneration, 222.
Stone (a weight), 494.
Stones, cor. of, 223; corner-stone, 234; precious and common, examples of uses of, 504; use of in altars, memorials, etc., 507; the decalogue, 515; breastplate of Aaron, 529; stones of Jerusalem, 608. (See also PRECIOUS STONES.)
Stringed instruments, 184.
Substances, spiritual and divine, 633.
Sulphur and pitch, cor. of, 237.
Sun, an image of the Lord, laws on, 202 *n.;* prismatic rays of, 239; worship of, Bunsen, 239 *n.; Nature Delineated, ib.*
Sun, moon, and stars, 239; worship of, *ib. n.;* cor. of, 360; called on to praise the Lord, 361; darkened, 362; woman clothed with, *ib.;* an instrumental cause of creation, 311; a concentration of the rays of the spiritual sun, 313; trinity in, 347.
Swedenborg, on the style of the Word, 23 *n.;* twofold sense of Word, like soul and body, 28 *n.;* on origin of idolatry, 50 *n.;* on the expressions of the Word, 104 *n.;* spiritual truths easily seen in the letter, 114 *n.;* on angelic esse and existere, 141 *n.;* on celestial sense of the Word, 144 *n.;* on cor. of animals, 149 *n.;* on the Magi, 159 *n.;* that the patriarchs represented states of the church, 162 *m.;* on Egypt and Assyria, 169 *n.;* on colors, 173; on numbers, 176 *n.;* on scientifics of the ancients, 202 *n.;* on the cedar, 226 *n.;* on worship in most ancient church, 266 *n.;* on the cherubim, 296 *n.;* versions of Word used by, 320; not inspired but illumined, 584.
Symbolism, Chippendale on, 61 *n.*
Symbols, often duplex, 86 *n.*

Talent, or pound, 493, 499.
Tatian's harmony of the gospels, 17 *n.*
Temple, the living, 556.
Theopneustos, 33.
Therapeutæ, 104 *n.*
Three, symbol of, Thornton, 143 *n.,* 151 *n.;* Davis, 143 *n.;* Conybeare, *ib.;* Levis, *ib.;* Pythagoras, 150 *n.;* Channing, *ib.;* Pinkerton, 151 *n.*
Threefold nature of God and man, 132; of all things, 150.
Tomline, Bp., definition of inspiration, 18.
Transfiguration of the Lord, 286, 332.
Treasure, 91; hid in field, 25 *n.*
Trees, cor. of, 206; tree of knowledge, 248;

tree of life, 225, 295; worship of, 206 n.; anatomy of, 207; going forth to choose a king, 218.
Tribute money, sig. of, 387.
Trinal distinctions in nature, 149; in mind, 150; in understanding, 167.
Trinity, divine, 141 and n.: in God and Nature Marcus, 150 n.
Triunity, or trinity, of God exhibited in creation, 347: in the sun, ib.
Two opposite meanings in Scripture, St. Augustine. 88 n.; More, ib.; Maclean, ib.

Understanding and will, cor. of, 131.
Urim and thummim. 174 n.; 529; answer by, 542. (See also PRECIOUS STONES.)
Uses in the animal and vegetable world, 232.

Vegetable kingdom, cor. of, 149, 206.
Veil on face of Moses, St. Augustine, 63 n.; Boyle, ib.
Vessel of clay, 180 n.
Virgins, parable of, 213.
Visible world a picture of heaven, Browne, 40 n.; Milton, ib.; Barrow, ib.; Leighton, ib.; Prescott. ib.; Jones, ib.; More, ib.; Kingsley. ib.; Serle, ib.; Clowes, ib.; Neale and Webb, ib.; Richer, ib.; Tertullian, 42 n.; Julian, ib.; Schlegel, ib.; Plato, ib.; Cudworth, ib.; Platinus, ib.; Empedocles, ib.; Van Mildert, ib.; Burgon, ib.; Tucker, ib.

War, sig. of, 124.
Wars of Jehovah, book of, 565.
Washing feet, sig. of, 357.
Water, cor. of, 95; symbol of, Trench, 98 n.; the Lord at Jacob's well, 99; baptism by, 98, 99; waterfloods, 100; defect of, ib.; Ezekiel's vision of holy waters, 102; the flood, 255;
Weights and measures, 176, 180: table of, 490; sig. of, 496.
Wicked men and nations, rep. of good, how, 263.
Wilderness and solitary place, sig. of, 330.
Will rep. by heart, 76.
Will and understanding, cor. of, 131.
Williams, Rev. I., on spiritual sense of Word, 30 n.; on the miracles of our Lord, 283 n.
Winter, flight in, 610.
Word of God, character of the letter, 24; effects of thinking only of the letter, ib.; necessity of inquiring what constitutes, 25; Swedenborg's definition of, 26; purpose for which given, 27; the letter and the spirit, ib. note; the spiritual sense pervades and fills the letter. 32; divinity of, consists in spiritual sense, ib.; meaning of term, 33; not designed to teach man such things as he can acquire by outward means, 35; but the things of genuine religion, ib.; without the Word man could know nothing of God or of eternal life, ib.; what constitutes the difference between the plenarily inspired and other books (Noble), 36; contains true histories and prophecies which have been fulfilled, ib.; these not sufficient to make it divine, ib.; from God, 38; the external and internal sense make one series, 39; style of, a divine style (Swedenborg), 39; man has life by and through (Swedenborg), ib.; in heaven, 61; not weakened by spiritual sense, Hilary, 102 n.; Cyril, ib.; *Christian Witness*, ib.; why written as we have it, 107; language and human style of writers of, specially prepared by God, 109 n.; why the literal sense was given, 110; truth in the letter of, 112; uses of the letter of, 116; twofold expressions in, reason for, 133; its celestial sense, 144; threefold character of, 152; its letter rep. by the burning bush, 295; its spirit by Jacob's vision of a ladder, ib.; its literal sense by a cloud, 296; plenary inspiration of, 317; produced in same order as creation, 318; Theopneustos, ib.; correspondence the sure rule of interpretation, 321; universal presence of the Lord in, 328; literal and spiritual senses compared, 353; the letter rep. by the Lord's garments on which lots were cast, ib.; the spiritual sense by his vest woven without seam, ib.; kept entire, ib.; Christ "the Rock," 354; organs of the body, why mentioned in, 355; conjunction with heaven effected by, 572, 589; in heaven, 577; character of, 578; how written, 579; direct inspiration, 580; its histories, 581; effects of reading, ib.; verbal and plenary inspiration, 583; uninspired parts in Bible, 586; why written on this earth, 588.
Words symbols of ideas, 34; words of men contain human thoughts, 35; words of God contain divine thoughts, ib.
Worship internal only in Adamic church, 266; see also SACRIFICIAL WORSHIP.
Written Word, why given, 107.

INDEX TO APPENDIX.

Ancient Word, account of, 686; where mentioned, *ib.*; Swedenborg on, *ib.*; Hernigas, 687; other authorities, *ib.*; that there was a previous word, Williams, 688.

Apocrypha, contents of, 666; position of, Burnett, *ib.*

Assyrian tablets, 724.

Authorized version (English), 688; the translators not inspired, *ib.*; its errors, Dr. A. Clarke, 689; Bishop Marsh, *ib.*; Oxlee, *ib.*; Pilkington, *ib.*; Noyes, 690; Dr. Pye Smith, *ib.*; Newcome, *ib.*

Books of Word not plenarily inspired, 656; sketch of those of Old Testament, 657; Philo-Judæus, *ib.*; Norton, *ib.*; Theodore, of Mopsuesta, *ib.*

Chronicles, books of, Gray and Percy, 657; Taylor, *ib.*; Ewald, *ib.*; Morey, *ib.*; Bunsen, 658; use and value of, *ib.*; Stuart, *ib.*; Newman, *ib.*

Correspondences, Representatives, and Significatives, 726.

Degrees, 690; discrete and continuous, *ib.*; Swedenborg on, *ib.*; necessity of knowledge of, 691; ascending and descending degrees, 692; ancient Egyptian triads, 693; Pritchard, *ib.*; Egyptian and Grecian mysteries, 694; freemasonry, *ib.*; Ionic and Grecian architecture, *ib.*; Indian do., *ib.*; Assyrian triads, Larwood and Hotten, 695; Taylor, *ib.*; Cudworth, *ib.*; Origen, *ib.*; More, *ib.*

Document theory, 724.

Druidism, 696; Cæsar's account of, not reliable, *ib.*; extent of, *ib.*; worship and rites of, *ib.*; the mistletoe, 697; a corruption of worship of ancient Church, *ib.*; Baal, *ib.*; Shaddai, *ib.*; doctrines of, *ib.*; monotheists, *ib.*; triads of, *ib.*; Dr. A. Clarke on, 699; Bethel, *ib.*; stone pillars, *ib.*; Milman on, *ib.*; legends respecting, 700; authorities, list of, 700; pyramids and other ancient remains, cairns, cromlechs, kist vaens, etc., *ib.*; Stonehenge, 701; druidism in Gaul, *ib.*

Ecclesiastes, attributed to Solomon, 662; not referred to in New Testament, 663; supposed date of, Zirkel, *ib.*; Maltby on, *ib.*; Dr. A. Clarke, *ib.*; Jahn, *ib.*; *Critical History and Defence of O. T. Canon*, *ib.*; said by some to be written in old age of Solomon, *ib.*

Egypt, triads, 693; mysteries of, 694; hieroglyphics, *see* HIEROGLYPHICS.

Epistles of Apostles, inspiration of, Dr. A. Clarke, 676; Dr. Whitby, *ib.*; illustrations of uninspired parts, 677; *Tracts for Times*, *ib.*; Swedenborg on, 678; Morell, *ib.*; Dewey, *ib.*; Powell, *ib.*; Maltby, 679; Warrington, 680; Stanley, *ib.*; Kitto on Epistle to Hebrews, *ib.*; Matthew Arnold, 681; Dr. Arnold, *ib.*; Kitto on the Pauline Epistles, *ib.*; Paley on the inscriptions to Paul's Epistles, *ib.*; Duke of Somerset, *ib.*; Jerome's opinion, *ib.*; Paul's quotations from heathen writers, 682; Williams on the Hebrews, *ib.*; Williams on the Epistles of Peter, *ib.*; doubts as to authorship, Eichhorn, *ib.*; Kitto, *ib.*

Esther, opinion as to origin of book of, 660; Greek and Romish versions contain more than A. V., *ib.*; Luther's opinion of, *ib.*; Gilfillan, *ib.*; divine Being not mentioned in it, *ib.*

Ezra and Nehemiah, opinions as to, Calmet, 659; anciently reckoned as one book, *ib.*; contents, *ib.*; not included in Ezra's canon, *ib.*

Freemasonry, degrees of, 694.

Gemara. (See RABBINICAL LITERATURE.)

Hieroglyphics, Egyptian, 701; the Rosetta stone, *ib.*; its inscription and style of writing, 705; antiquity of Egypt, Osborne, *ib.*; origin of hieroglyphics and different styles of writing, *ib.*; phonetic signs, *ib.*; Swedenborg, on, *ib.*; Portal's defence of Swedenborg, 709; correspondences and hieroglyphics compared, 710; examples, *ib.*; Belzoni's tomb, Mason, 713; Noble, on, *ib.*; hieroglyphic of the serpent, Middleton, 714; inscription on the Temple of Minerva, *ib.*; decline of hieroglyphics, 715; Cudworth on esoteric hieroglyphics, *ib.*; in time of Moses, Portal, 716; hieroglyphic description of a perfect man, Oliver, *ib.*; the effect put for the supposed cause, Hayden, *ib.*; difference between hieroglyphics and the Word of God, *ib.*; doctrines of Egypt and Assyria, Ramsay, 718; Wemyss, 719; the lion, *ib.*; the eagle, *ib.*; difference between Hebrew and the alphabets and Egyptian hieroglyphics, *ib.*; Clement, on, *ib.*; Spineto, *ib.*

Human race, high antiquity of, 725.

Jewish canon of Scripture, 683; Chetubim, *ib.*; hagiographa, *ib.*; Kitto on, 684; Jewish writers, *ib.*; Prideaux, *ib.*; Walton, *ib.*; Theodoret and Jerome on the position given to Lamentation and Daniel in, *ib.*; anterior and posterior prophets, 685; origin of various Jewish arrangements of, *ib.*

Job, book of, contents, 661; history of, Middleton, *ib.*; Noble, *ib.*; Gliddon, 662; Roberts, *ib.*; Heb. Rev., *ib.*

INDEX.

John, 1, v. 7, 8, authenticity of, 696.

Masorah. (See RABBINICAL LITERATURE.)
Metempsychosis, doctrine of, 702.
Midian, war with, ancient Greek hymn founded on, 730.
Mishna. (See RABBINICAL LITERATURE.)

Nehemiah, book of. (See EZRA.)

Plenarily inspired books, inquiry as to which are, 651; Swedenborg on, *ib.;* Prof. Bush, *ib.;* Philo, *ib.;* Tatian, *ib.;* Origen, *ib.; Rev. Text for Lond. Univ., ib.*
Proverbs, book of, contents, 662; many parts very ancient, and founded on correspondence, *ib.;* Nicholls, *ib.;* Von Bohlen, *ib.*
Pythagorean doctrine of metempsychosis, account of, 702; Parsons, *ib.;* Clement, *ib.;* ancient supposed motion of earth, Abbé Planche, *ib.;* Plato's doctrine, *ib.;* a belief of the Druids, 704; Rose, *ib.*

Rabbinical literature, 666; targums, *ib.;* oral and traditionary law, *ib.;* Mishna, *ib.;* Gemara, *ib.;* Masorah, *ib.;* Rabbinical rules, 675.
Ruth, contents of, 659.

Scripture, canon of, Stuart, 653; Milner, *ib.;* Wordsworth, *ib.;* Newman, *ib.;* want of, illustrated, *ib.; Eclectic Review, ib.;* Noble, 655; Hindmarsh, 656; Knight, *ib.*
Septuagint, history of, 667.
Song of Solomon, a supposed epithalamium, 663; contents of, 664; not cited in Scripture, *ib.; Crit. Bib., ib.;* Dr. A. Clarke, *ib.;* Wharton, *ib.;* Lowth, *ib.;* supposed not to be written by Solomon, Pye Smith, 665; Rosenmuller, *ib.;* Theodore of Mopsuesta, *ib.;* structure of, Davidson, *ib.; Eclectic Review, ib.;* Michaelis, *ib.;* Stuart, 666.
Spiritual sense of Word, why not earlier revealed, 688.

Targums. (See RABBINICAL LITERATURE.)

Versions used by Swedenborg, 668.

Word, integrity and miraculous preservation of, 670; Oldhausen, *ib.;* various readings in, *ib.;* Conybeare, *ib.;* its wonderful accuracy, Gaussen, 671; Eichhorn, *ib.;* Wiseman, *ib.;* copies in ancient libraries, 672; Horne, *ib.;* Michaelis, *ib.;* Van der Hooght's edition, 674; no doctrine affected by various readings, *ib.; Int. Rep., ib.;* Rabbinical rules for transcribing, 675; Chappelon, 676.
Word of God, its four different styles, 685.
Word, spiritual sense of, cause of decline of in Christian Church, 720; relation of Church to the world, *ib.;* the controversies in the Christian Church, *ib.;* Jewish preparation for Christian teaching, 721; preparation of heathens, *ib.;* the position of doctrine of incarnation, 722; origin of apostolic epistles, *ib.;* condition of warfare in Church, *ib.;* its results, *ib.;* doctrinal statements based on literal expressions, 723; the law abolished, *ib.;* early heresies, *ib.;* Gnosticism, *ib.;* fall of Church, *ib.;* used for evil purposes, *ib.*

INDEX OF PASSAGES OF SCRIPTURE
WHOLLY OR PARTLY EXPLAINED.

Genesis.

i. 242	viii. 1, 9, 20 266	xxv. 22 406
i. 15 619	viii. 21 158	xxvii. 7 471
i. 31 446	viii. 22 613	xxviii. 12, 13 293
ii. 2 452	ix. 13 172	xxviii. 18 235
ii. 8 337	ix. 33 295	xxxi. 7 471
ii. 9 209	xi. 2 263	xxxviii. 27 405
ii. 10 96	xiv. 4 479	xlii. 1-7 453
iii. 1 620	xiv. 8, 9 427	xlv. 22 435
iii. 24 295	xiv. 18-20 520	xlviii. 13 417
iv. 1 266	xiv. 20 470	xlix. 9 192
v. 1 339	xv. 13 180	xlix. 17 622
vi. 255	xv. 18 366	xlix. 28 480
vi. 7 122	xvii. 1 466	
vi. 16 153	xvii. 12 461	**Exodus.**
vii. 255	xvii. 20 480	iii. 3, 4 295
vii. 2 412	xviii. 6 420	iii. 18 425
viii. 255	xviii. 32 470	v. 2 367
	xix. 26 266	vii. 19 16

viii.	191	
x. 23.	92	
xiv. 16.	495	
xv. 20.	184	
xv. 23-25.	190	
xv. 25.	231	
xvi. 18.	296	
xvi. 21.	239	
xvi. 26.	446	
xvii. 1-6.	96	
xvii. 8, 13.	127	
xx. 5.	428	
xx. 9-11.	447	
xx. 12.	121	
xx. 24, 25.	509	
xx. 25.	269	
xxi. 1.	435	
xxi. 2.	447	
xxiii. 14.	420	
xxiii. 11, 17.	178	
xxiii. 30.	174	
xxiv. 1.	412	
xxiv. 12.	515	
xxv. 3.	253	
xxvi. 1.	174, 472	
xxvi. 7.	476	
xxvi. 25.	462	
xxvii. 1, etc.	428	
xxviii. 15-21.	529	
xxviii. 16.	429	
xxviii. 21.	480	
xxviii. 30.	295	
xxix. 40.	495	
xxx. 4, 5.	174	
xxx. 12, 13.	496	
xxx. 34.	158	
xxxii. 15.	516	
xxxiii. 18.	345	
xxxiv. 1.	296	
xxxiv. 1-4.	518	
xxxiv. 18.	454	
xxxv. 3.	94	
xxxvi. 14.	476	
xxxvi. 30.	462	
xxxix. 8-14.	529	

Leviticus.

ii. 13.	238, 600	
vi. 13.	94	
x. 1.	347	
x. 1, 2.	94	
xi. 3-9.	149	
xiv. 4.	230	
xix. 35, 36.	496	
xxi. 16.	359	
xxiii. 32.	467	
xxiii. 39.	462	
xxiv. 2-4.	212	
xxv.	179	
xxv. 3, 4.	448	
xxv. 22.	463-467	
xxvi. 8.	436	
xxvi. 26.	472	

Numbers.

vi. 8.	638	
vi. 10.	463	
xv. 30.	269	
xxi. 8.	512	
xxi. 8, 9.	253	
xxxv. 14, 15.	448	

Deut.

ii. 33.	124
iii. 6.	124
iv. 13.	472
iv. 24.	95

vi. 4.	407
viii. 4.	179
viii. 7-9.	227
ix. 9.	179
x. 10.	179
xv. 21.	275
xvi. 16.	420
xvii. 16.	194
xxii. 9-11.	139
xxiii. 44.	240
xxvii. 5, 6.	509
xxxii. 2.	227
xxxii. 17, 18.	232
xxxiii. 16.	295
xxxiii. 33.	252
xxxiii. 41.	240

Joshua.

vi.	179
viii. 30.	509
xv. 19.	295
xxiv. 26.	210

Judges.

vi. 20, 21.	510
ix. 15.	218
xiii. 19, 20.	510
xvi. 17.	81

1 Samuel.

xiv. 27.	597
xv. 22, 23.	271
xvi. 14.	186

2 Samuel.

xxiv. 1, 15.	402

1 Kings.

iv. 21.	366
vi. 7.	235
x. 2.	161
x. 20.	481
xviii. 31.	509
xix. 19.	481

2 Kings.

ii. 11, 12.	198
ii. 23.	81
ii. 23, 24.	412
iv.	221
iv. 38.	378
vi. 17.	93, 198
xiii. 14.	198
xviii. 3, 4.	512
xxiii. 11.	204
xxv. 1-3.	467
xxv. 2.	477

Job.

xxxix. 25.	193

Psalms.

i. 1.	157-161
i. 2-4.	223
iv.	184
iv. 5.	275
v.	184
vii. 16.	637
viii.	184
xi. 6.	237
xvi. 17.	82
xviii. 4.	100
xviii. 10.	328
xix. 1.	346
xx. 7, 8.	195
xxiii. 16.	188
xxiii. 21.	193
xxiv. 12.	98

xxvii. 4.	407
xxvii. 6.	187
xxxiii. 1-4.	187
xxxiii. 6.	346
xxxiii. 17.	195
xxxvi. 8.	101
xxxvii. 19.	399
xl. 6-8.	272
xlii. 5.	186
xlii. 7.	191
xliii. 3.	188
xliv. 3.	98
xlv.	156, 160
xlv. 6.	236
xlv. 9.	236
xlvi. 4.	101
l. 5.	271
l. 7-14.	270
l. 10, 11.	205
li. 7.	222
li. 8.	84
li. 15-17.	272
lii. 8.	212
liii. 4.	94
liv.	184
lviii. 4.	624
lxi. 9.	97
lxix. 2, 15.	101
lxxi. 22.	185, 187
lxxiii. 6.	295
lxxiii. 17.	296
lxxvi. 56.	196
lxxx. 8-11.	214
xcii. 12.	225
civ. 2.	257
civ. 15.	213
civ. 16.	225, 395
cvii. 22.	275
cvii. 31.	238
cx. 3.	612
cx. 10.	179
cxiv. 4.	332
cxviii. 22.	234
cxix. 3.	335
cxix. 16.	454
cxix. 164.	179
cxxi. 5, 6.	239
cxxiv. 1, 4, 5.	101
cxxxii. 13-16.	21
cxxxiii. 1, 2.	213
cxxxix. 21, 22.	121
cxlvii. 4.	401
cxlvii. 7.	187
cxlvii. 10.	195
cxlviii.	332
cxlviii. 9, 13.	225
cxlix. 3.	187
cl.	183
cl. 3-5.	188

Isaiah.

i. 5.	637
i. 11, etc.	271
i. 29, 30.	211
ii. 4.	125
iv. 3-6.	94
v. 1-7.	214
v. 9, 10.	496
v. 12.	185
v. 28.	196
vi. (Jehovah)	154
vi. 2.	449
vii. 18, 19.	100, 168
vii. 20.	640
vii. 21.	204
viii. 14, 15.	192
viii. 17.	120
ix. 18.	94

INDEX.

xi. 6-8 204	xxxix. 2 450	xiv. 12 363
xiii. 4 401	xxxix. 17-20 138	xiv. 20 199
xiii. 12 236	xl. 2, etc 497	
xvii. 6 413	xl. 9 463	**Malachi.**
xviii. 2 101	xl. 31 464	i. 7, 8 275
xix. 18 437	xl. 41 464	i. 11 160
xix. 23-25 167	xli. 22 274	iii. 3 391
xxvii. 1 342	xliii. 16 481	iv. 2 239
xxvii. 9 510	xlv. 13 450	
xxviii. 16 234	xlvii. 1-5 369	**Matthew.**
xxix. 10-12 25	xlvii. 3-9 102	i. 21 285
xxx. 26 454	xlvii. 12 225	ii. 11 159
xxx. 33 231	xlvii. 35 498	ii. 16 415
xxxi. 196		ii. 18 161
xxxii. 20 204	**Daniel.**	iii. 4 155
xxxiii. 14 94	iii 185	iii. 7 252
xxxiv. 8-10 237	v. 25-27 181	iii. 10 222
xxxiv. 13 217	v. 25-29 500	iv. 2 179
xxxv. 1, 2 217	vii. 2, 3 430	v. 22 161
xxxv. 9 193	vii. 7 472	v. 29 356
xxxviii. 20 184	ix. 25 455	v. 38, 39 269
xl. 12 497	xii. 12 488	vi. 3 355
xl. 12, 17 175		vi. 11 .... 116 n., 136
xl. 20 231	**Hosea.**	vi. 23 .... 92, 407
xl. 31 .... 158, 368	ii. 18 .... 323, 625	vi. 28-33 221
xli. 17, 18 101	ii. 18-20 205	vii. 8 156
xliii. 2 100	iii. 2 499	vii. 16-20 .... 208, 221
xliii. 7 155	iii. 5 264	vii. 24 592
xliv. 14-17 211	vi. 2 421	vii. 24-27 234
l. 11 94	vi. 6 272	viii. 16, 17 277
liii. 3 277	xiv. 2 275	viii. 20 290
lv. 1, 2 373	xiv. 3 195	ix. 13 272
lv. 10 97	xiv. 5-7 227	x. 9, 10 416
lviii. 11 97		x. 16 334
lix. 4-7 192	**Joel.**	x. 20-28 166
lx. 13 229	ii. 10 241	x. 35 121
lx. 17 .... 234, 243, 350	ii. 22 215	x. 36 124
lx. 20 240	ii. 23 295	xi. 5, 6 369
lx. 21 228	iii. 10 124	xii. 43-45 455
lxv. 25 204	iii. 18 91	xiii. 6 239
lxvi. 12 101		xiii. 9 83
	Amos.	xiii. 23 157
Jeremiah.	i. 3, etc 421	xiii. 28, 29 163
i. 16 231	ii. 9 207	xiii. 33 422
ii. 13 100	iv. 8 414	xiii. 58 167
ii. 17 101	v. 23 185	xiv. 20, 21 481
iv. 23, 25 334	vi. 1-5 185	xiv. 25 432
vi. 10 83	viii. 11 .... 100, 379	xv. 6 264
vii. 21-23 .... 269, 271	ix. 3 624	xv. 13 221
viii. 13 215		xv. 34-37 455
viii. 17 622	**Micah.**	xvi. 18, 19 590
x. 5 226	iii. 6 558	xvi. 19, 23 165
xvii. 5-8 224	iv. 4 227	xvi. 21 422
xvii. 7, 8 227	v. 5 464	xvi. 36 114
xxi. 12 97	vi. 6-8 271	xvii. 1 .... 165, 286
xxii. 33-40 269		xvii. 20 334
xxiv. 1, 3 215	**Habakkuk.**	xvii. 25-27 387
xxxiv. 18 518	ii. 11 231	xviii. 1, etc 332
li. 20-23 134	ii. 19 231	xviii. 8, 9 82
li. 25 334	iii. 18 198	xviii. 19, 20 417
	iii. 19 184	xviii. 21, 22 .... 197, 456
Lamentations.		xix. 5 408
ii. 1, 2 236	**Zechariah.**	xix. 17 408
	i. 8 201	xix. 28 482
Ezekiel.	i. 18 430	xx. 3, 5 468
i .... 290 n.	ii. 1, 2 .... 181, 499	xxi. 33 217
iv. 6 179	ii. 5 93	xxi. 42 234
vi. 3 333	iv. 2, etc 414	xxii. 37-39 517
ix. 2 449	iv. 3, 14 211	xxiii. 8, 9 408
xvii. 24 224	v. 5-8 499	xxiii. 17 188
xx. 46-49 229	vi. 1-5 431	xxiii. 27 615
xxii. 19, 20 233	vi. 1-8 201	xxiv. 20 608
xxvi. 10 196	viii. 23 473	xxiv. 29 362
xxxv. 26 81	xii. 4 196	xxv. 1, 2 437
xxxvi. 25 98	xiii. 1 98	xxv. 1-13 213
xxxvii. 9 430	xiii. 8, 9 421	xxv. 14, 15 .... 408, 438
xxxvii. 24 264	xiv. 9 407	xxv. 31-46 216

xxvi. 28............... 277
xxvi. 36............... 165
xxvi. 53............... 482
xxvii. 45............... 468
xxviii. 16............... 477

Mark.
iii. 17............... 167
iv. 28............... 154
vi. 5............... 167
vi. 7............... 356
vi. 38, etc............... 439
vii. 37............... 165
viii. 23............... 165
ix............... 286
ix. 44............... 94
ix. 49............... 236
x. 21............... 409
xii. 26............... 296
xii. 28–34............... 272
xiii. 33............... 157
xv. 33............... 450
xvi. 9............... 179
xvi. 18............... 204, 625

Luke.
ii. 7............... 290
ii. 19............... 280
ii. 42............... 482
iii. 16............... 93
iv. 8............... 165
viii. 7............... 222
viii. 35............... 359
viii. 43, 44............... 483
viii. 51............... 165
ix............... 286
ix. 28, 29............... 462
ix. 44............... 83
ix. 53, 54............... 166
ix. 58............... 290
x. 1............... 138
x. 19............... 204
x. 18............... 625
x. 35............... 417
x. 41, 42............... 409
xii. 6............... 440
xii. 52............... 440
xiii. 7............... 224, 422
xiii. 32............... 154
xiv. 16, 20............... 442
xv. 8............... 473
xvi. 22............... 163
xvi. 26............... 121
xvi. 27, 28............... 443
xvii. 32............... 238
xix. 13............... 474
xix. 14............... 274
xxi. 1–4............... 418
xxii. 15............... 290

John.
i. 11............... 290
i. 13............... 155
i. 14............... 296

ii. 1–12............... 283
ii. 6............... 451
ii. 21............... 153, 608
iii. 14, 15............... 254
iii. 15............... 628
iv. 6–15............... 280
iv. 32............... 137
iv. 35............... 433
v. 25............... 360
vi. 31............... 136
vi. 32............... 137
vi. 51............... 364
vii. 6–30............... 99
vii. 38............... 97
viii. 17, 18............... 409
viii. 43............... 279
ix. 6, 7............... 383
x. 18............... 278
x. 30............... 410
xii. 2............... 161
xii. 13............... 225
xii. 49............... 279
xiii. 8............... 96
xiii. 4–17............... 279
xiv. 12............... 285
xv. 1............... 214
xv. 1–5............... 229
xvii. 11, 21............... 411
xix. 15............... 290
xix. 23............... 296
xix. 24............... 477
xx. 4............... 368
xx. 9............... 484

Acts.
xiii. 22............... 264

1 Cor.
v. 7............... 136
xv. 36–42............... 223

2 Cor.
xi. 3............... 250

Ephesians.
v. 25–27............... 99
vi. 10–17............... 125

1 Tim.
i. 5............... 278

Phil.
ii. 12............... 278

Hebrews.
ii. 10............... 278
ii. 18............... 277
iii. 25............... 277
iv. 15............... 290
v. 8, 9............... 278
vii. 28............... 277
viii. 5............... 268
ix. 9............... 268

ix. 20............... 268, 269
x. 1............... 268
x. 1–9............... 273
x. 20............... 278

1 Pet.
ii. 4............... 234
ii. 21............... 278
iii. 21............... 287

2 Pet.
i. 18............... 287

1 John.
ii. 11–20............... 121

Revelation.
i. 3............... 293
i. 4............... 456
i. 7............... 293
i. 8............... 154, 288
i. 15............... 623
i. 20............... 456
ii. 7, etc............... 609
ii. 18............... 160, 236
iii. 21............... 155
iv. 3............... 172
iv. 6............... 433
v............... 199
v. 1............... 457
v. 5............... 159, 193
v. 8............... 159, 185, 188
vi............... 199
vii. 9............... 225
ix. 5............... 444
ix. 17............... 196
xi. 1............... 181, 500
xi. 3, 4............... 418
xi. 4............... 211
xi. 13............... 474
xii. 1............... 241, 362, 484
xii. 11............... 278
xii. 3............... 457
xii. 4............... 423
xiii. 18............... 399
xiv. 2............... 185, 188
xiv. 6............... 294
xiv. 14............... 163
xv. 2............... 188
xvi. 13............... 424
xvi. 13, 14............... 192
xvii. 3............... 458
xvii. 3, 4............... 200
xvii. 11............... 465
xix. 11............... 198
xix. 17, 18............... 138
xix. 20............... 237
xxi............... 549
xxi. 12–14............... 485
xxi. 13............... 424
xxi. 15–17............... 501
xxi. 16............... 433
xxii. 2............... 486

THE END.